REPULSE OF THE BRITISH BEFORE FORT STEPHENSON,

AUG. 2d. 1813.

"Col. Short, who commanded the regulars composing the forlorn hope, was ordering his men to leap the ditch — cut down the pickets, and give the Americans no quarters, when he fell mortally wounded into the ditch hoisted his handkerchief on the end of his sword and begged for that mercy, which he had a moment before ordered to be denied to his enemy."

HISTORICAL COLLECTIONS

OF

OHIO;

CONTAINING

A COLLECTION OF THE MOST INTERESTING FACTS, TRADITIONS, BIOGRAPHICAL SKETCHES, ANECDOTES, ETC.

RELATING TO ITS

GENERAL AND LOCAL HISTORY:

WITH

DESCRIPTIONS OF ITS COUNTIES, PRINCIPAL TOWNS AND VILLAGES.

ILLUSTRATED BY

180 ENGRAVINGS,

GIVING

VIEWS OF THE CHIEF TOWNS,—PUBLIC BUILDINGS,—RELICS OF ANTIQUITY,—HISTORIC LOCALITIES,—NATURAL SCENERY, ETC.

BY HENRY HOWE.

CINCINNATI:

PUBLISHED BY HENRY HOWE, AT E. MORGAN & CO'S.

Price Three Dollars.

1851.

CINCINNATI:
Morgan & Overend, Printers.

PREFACE.

Introductory to this work, we state some facts of private history.

In the year 1831, Mr. John W. Barber of New Haven, Ct., prepared a work upon that our native city, which combined history, biography and description, and was illustrated by engravings connected with its rise, progress and present condition. Its success suggested to him the preparation of one, on a similar plan, relative to the State. For this object he travelled through it, from town to town, collecting the materials and taking sketches. After two years of industrious application in this, and in writing the volume, the Historical Collections of Connecticut was issued, a work which, like its successors, was derived from a thousand different sources, oral and published.

As in the ordinary mode, the circulation of books through "the trade," is so slow in progress and limited in sale, that no merely local work, however meritorious, involving such an unusually heavy outlay of time and expense as that, will pay even the mechanical labor, it, as well as its successors, was circulated by travelling agents *solely*, who thoroughly canvassed the state, until it found its way into thousands of families in all ranks and conditions,—in the retired farm-house equally with the more accessible city mansion.

That book, so novel in its character, was received with great favor, and highly commended by the public press and the leading minds of the state. It is true, it did not aspire to high literary merit:—the dignified style,—the generalization of facts,—the philosophical deductions of regular history were not there. On the contrary, not the least of its merits was its simplicity of style, its fullness of detail, introducing minor, but interesting incidents, the other, in "its stately march," could not step aside to notice, and in avoiding that philosophy which only the scholastic can comprehend. It seemed, in its variety, to have something adapted to all ages, classes and tastes, and the unlearned reader, if he did not stop to peruse the volume, at least, in many instances could derive gratification from the pictorial representation of his native village,—of perhaps the very dwelling in which he first drew breath, and around which entwined early and cherished associations. The book, therefore, reached MORE MINDS, and has been more extensively read, than any regular state history ever issued; thus adding another to the many examples often seen, of the productions of industry and tact, proving of a more extended utility than those emanating from profound scholastic acquirements.

This publication became the *pioneer* of others: a complete list of all, with the dates of their issue, follows:

1836.	The Hist. Coll. of	Connecticut;	by	*John W. Barber.*
1839.	"	" Massachusetts;	"	*John W. Barber.*
1841.	"	" New York;	"	*J. W. Barber and H. Howe.*
1843.	"	" Pennsylvania;	"	*Sherman Day.*
1844.	"	" New Jersey;	"	*J. W. Barber and H. Howe.*
1845.	"	" Virginia;	"	*Henry Howe.*
1847.	"	" Ohio;	"	*Henry Howe.*

From this list it will be perceived that OHIO makes the SEVENTH state work published on the *original plan* of Mr. Barber, all of which thus far circulated, were alike favorably received in the states to which each respectively related.

Early in January, 1846, we, with some previous time spent in preparation, commenced our tour over Ohio, being the FOURTH state through which we have travelled for such an object. We thus passed more than a year, in the course of which we were in seventy-nine of its eighty-three counties, took sketches of objects of interest, and every where obtained information by conversation with early settlers and men of intelligence. Beside this, we have availed ourselves of all published sources of information, and have received about four hundred manuscript pages in communications from gentlemen in all parts of the state.

In this way, we are enabled to present a larger and more varied amount of materials respecting Ohio, than was ever before embodied; the whole giving a view of its present condition and prospects, with a history of its settlement, and incidents illustrating the customs, the fortitude, the bravery, and the privations of its early settlers. That such a work, depicting the rise and unexampled progress of a powerful state, destined to a controlling influence over the well-being of the whole nation, will be looked upon with interest, we believe: and furthermore expect, that it will be received in the generous spirit which is gratified with honest endeavors to please, rather than in the captious one, that is dissatisfied short of an unattainable perfection.

Whoever expects to find the volume entirely free from defects, has but little acquaintance with the difficulties ever attendant upon procuring such materials. In all of the many historical and descriptive works whose fidelity we have had occasion to test, some misstatements were found. Although we have taken the best available means to insure accuracy, yet from a variety of causes unnecessary here to specify, some errors may have occurred. If any thing materially wrong is discovered, any one will confer a favor by addressing a letter to the publishers, and it shall be corrected.

Our task has been a pleasant one. As we successively entered the various counties, we were greeted with the frank welcome, characteristic of the west. And an evidence of interest in the enterprize has been variously shown, not the least of which, has been by the reception of a mass of valuable communications, unprecedented by us in the course of the seven years we have been engaged in these pursuits. To all who have aided us,—to our correspondents especially, some of whom have spent much time and research, we feel under lasting obligations, and are enabled by their assistance to present to the public a far better work, than could otherwise have been produced.

H. H.

OHIO.

OUTLINE HISTORY *

The territory now comprised within the limits of Ohio was formerly a part of that vast region claimed by France, between the Alleghany and the Rocky Mountains, first known by the general name of Louisiana. In 1673, Marquette, a zealous French Missionary, accompanied with Monsieur Joliet, from Quebec, with five boatmen, set out on a mission from Mackinac to the unexplored regions lying south of that station. They passed down the lake to Green Bay, thence from Fox River crossed over to the Wisconsin, which they followed down to its junction with the Mississippi. They descended this mighty stream a thousand miles to its confluence with the Arkansas. On their return to Canada, they did not fail to urge, in strong terms, the immediate occupation of the vast and fertile regions watered by the Mississippi and its branches.

On the 7th of August, 1679, M. de la Salle, the French commandant of Fort Frontenac, on Lake Ontario, launched, upon Lake Erie, the *Griffin*, a bark of about 60 tons, with which he proceeded through the Lakes to the Straits of Michillimackinac. Leaving his bark at this place, he proceeded up Lake Michigan, and from thence to the south west, till he arrived at Peoria Lake, in Illinois. At this place he erected a fort, and after having sent Father Lewis Hennepin on an exploring expedition, La Salle returned to Canada. In 1683, La Salle went to France, and, by the representations which he made, induced the French Government to fit out an expedition for the purpose of planting a colony at the mouth of the Mississippi. This expedition failed, La Salle being murdered by his own men.

This disaster did not abate the ardor of the French in their great plan of obtaining possession of the vast region westward of the English colonies. A second expedition sailed from France, under the command of M. D'Iberville. This officer entered the mouth of the Mississippi, and explored the river for several hundred miles

* The principal sources from which this outline is derived, are the MSS. of Hon. Thomas Scott, of Chillicothe, Secretary of the Convention which framed the constitution of Ohio; the historical sketch prefixed to Chase's Statutes, and Perkins' Annals of the West.

Permanent establishments were made at different points; and from this time the French colony west of the Alleghanies steadily increased in numbers and strength. Previous to the year 1725, the colony had been divided into quarters, each having its local governor, or commandant, and judge, but all subject to the superior authority of the council general of Louisiana. One of these quarters was established north west of the Ohio.

At this period, the French had erected forts on the Mississippi, on the Illinois, on the Maumee, and on the lakes. Still, however, the communication with Canada was through Lake Michigan. Before 1750, a French post had been fortified at the mouth of the Wabash and a communication was established through that river and the Maumee with Canada. About the same time, and for the purpose of checking the progress of the French, the Ohio Company was formed, and made some attempts to establish trading houses among the Indians. The French, however, established a chain of fortifications back of the English settlements, and thus, in a measure, had the entire control of the great Mississippi valley. The English government became alarmed at the encroachments of the French, and attempted to settle boundaries by negotiations. These availed nothing, and both parties were determined to settle their differences by the force of arms.

The claims of the different European monarchs to large portions of the western continent were based upon the first discoveries made by their subjects. In 1609, the English monarch granted to the London Company, all the territories extending along the coast for two hundred miles north and south from Point Comfort, and "*up into the land, throughout, from sea to sea,* west and north-west." In 1662, Charles II. granted to certain settlers upon the Connecticut all the territory between the parallels of latitude which include the present State of Connecticut, from the Atlantic to the Pacific ocean. The claims which Massachusetts advanced, during the revolution, to an interest in the western lands, were founded upon a similar charter, granted thirty years afterwards.

When the king of France had dominions in North America, the whole of the late territory of the United States, north-west of the river Ohio, was included in the province of Louisiana, the north boundary of which, by the treaty of Utrecht, concluded between France and England in 1713, was fixed at the 49th parallel of latitude north of the Equator. After the conquest of the French possessions in North America by Great Britain, this tract was ceded by France to Great Britain, by the treaty of Paris, in 1763.

The principal ground whereon the English claimed dominion beyond the Alleghanies was, that the Six Nations owned the Ohio valley, and had placed it with their other lands under the protection of England. Some of the western lands were also claimed by the British as having been actually purchased, at Lancaster, Penn., in 1744, at a treaty between the colonists and the Six Nations at that place. In 1748, the "Ohio Company," for the purpose of securing the Indian trade, was formed. In 1749, it appears that the English built a trading house upon the Great Miami, at a spot since called Loramie's Store. In 1751, Christopher Gist, an agent of the Ohio Company, who was appointed to examine the western lands, made a visit to the Twigtwees, who lived upon the Miami river, about one hundred miles from its mouth.

Early in 1752, the French having heard of the trading house on the Miami, sent a party of soldiers to the Twigtwees and demanded the traders as intruders upon French lands. The Twigtwees refused to deliver up their friends. The French, assisted by the Ottawas and Chippewas, then attacked the trading house, which was probably a block house, and after a severe battle, in which fourteen of the natives were killed and others wounded, took and destroyed it, carrying away the traders to Canada. This fort, or trading house, was called, by the English, *Pickawillany*. Such was the first British settlement in the Ohio valley, of which we have any record.

After Braddock's defeat, in 1755, the Indians pushed their excursions as far east as the Blue Ridge. In order to repel them, Major Lewis, in Jan., 1756, was sent with a party of troops on an expedition against the Indian towns on the Ohio. The point apparently aimed at was the upper Shawanese town, situated on the Ohio, three miles above the mouth of the Great Kanawha. The attempt proved a failure, in consequence, it is said, of the swollen state of the streams, and the treachery of the guides. In 1764, Gen. Bradstreet, having dispersed the Indian forces besieging Detroit, passed into the Wyandot country by way of Sandusky Bay. He ascended the bay and river as far as it was navigable for boats, and there made a camp. A treaty of peace was signed by the Chiefs and head men. The Shawnees of the Scioto river, and the Delawares of the Muskingum, however, still continued hostile. Col. Boquet, in 1764, with a body of troops, marched from Fort Pitt into the heart of the Ohio country on the Muskingum river. This expedition was conducted with great prudence and skill, and without scarcely any loss of life, as treaty of peace was effected with the Indians, who restored the prisoners they had captured from the white settlements. The next war with the Indians was in 1774, generally known as Lord Dunmore's. In the summer of that year, an expedition, under Col. M'Donald, was assembled at Wheeling, marched into the Muskingum country and destroyed the Indian town of Wapatomica, a few miles above the site of Zanesville. In the fall, the Indians were defeated after a hard fought battle at Point Pleasant, on the Virginia side of the Ohio. Shortly after this event, Lord Dunmore made peace with the Indians at Camp Charlotte, in what is now Pickaway country.

During the revolutionary war, most of the western Indians were more or less united against the Americans. In the fall of 1778, an expedition against Detroit was projected. As a preliminary step, it was resolved that the forces in the west, under Gen. M'Intosh, should move up and attack the Sandusky Indians. Preliminary to this,

Fort Laurens, so called in honor of the President of Congress, was built upon the Tuscarawas, a short distance below the site of Bolivar, Tuscarawas county. The expedition to Detroit was abandoned and the garrison of Fort Laurens, after suffering much from the Indians and from famine, were recalled in August, 1779. A month or two previous to the evacuation of this fort, Col. Bowman headed an expedition against the Shawanees. Their village, Chillicothe, three miles north of the site of Xenia, on the Little Miami, was burnt. The warriors showed an undaunted front, and the whites were forced to retreat. In the summer of 1780, an expedition directed against the Indian towns, in the forks of the Muskingum, moved from Wheeling, under Gen. Broadhead. This expedition, known as "the Coshocton campaign," was unimportant in its results. In the same summer, Gen. Clark led a body of Kentuckians against the Shawnees. Chillicothe, on the Little Miami, was burnt on their approach, but at Piqua, their town on the Mad River, six miles below the site of Springfield, they gave battle to the whites and were defeated. In September, 1782, this officer led a second expedition against the Shawanese. Their towns, Upper and Lower Piqua, on the Miami, within what is now Miami county, were destroyed, together with the store of a trader.

There were other expeditions into the Indian country from Kentucky, which, although of later date, we mention in this connection. In 1786, Col. Logan conducted a successful expedition against the Mackachack towns, on the head waters of Mad River, in what is now Logan county. Edwards, in 1787, led an expedition to the head waters of the Big Miami, and, in 1788, Todd led one into the Scioto valley. There were also several minor expeditions, at various times, into the present limits of Ohio.

The Moravian missionaries, prior to the war of the revolution, had a number of missionary stations within the limits of Ohio. The missionaries, Heckewelder and Post, were on the Muskingum as early as 1762. In March, 1782, a party of Americans, under Col. Williamson, murdered, in cold blood, ninety-four of the defenceless Moravian Indians, within the present limits of Tuscarawas county. In the June following, Col. Crawford, at the head of about 500 men, was defeated by the Indians, three miles north of the site of Upper Sandusky, in Wyandot county. Col. Crawford was taken prisoner in the retreat, and burnt at the stake with horrible tortures.

By an act of the Parliament of Great Britain, passed in 1774, the whole of the late north-western Territory was annexed to, and made a part of, the province of Quebec, as created and established by the royal proclamation of the 7th of October, 1763. But nothing therein contained, relative to the boundary of the said province of Quebec, was in any wise to affect the boundaries of any other colony.

The colonies having, in 1776, renounced their allegiance to the British king, and assumed rank as free, sovereign and independent States, each State claimed the right of soil and jurisdiction over the district of country embraced within its charter. The charters of several of the States embraced large portions of western unappropriated lands. Those States which had no such charters, insisted that these lands ought to be appropriated for the benefit of all the States, according to their population, as the title to them, if secured at all, would be by the blood and treasure of all the States. Congress repeatedly urged upon those States owning western unappropriated lands, to make liberal cessions of them for the common benefit of all.

The claim of the English monarch to the late north-western Territory was ceded to the United States, by the treaty of peace, signed at Paris, September 3d, 1783. The provisional articles which formed the basis of that treaty, more especially as related to the boundary, were signed at Paris, November 30th, 1782. During the pendency of the negociation relative to these preliminary articles, Mr. Oswald, the British commissioner, proposed the river Ohio as the western boundary of the United States, and but for the indomitable perseverance of the revolutionary patriot, John Adams, one of the American commissioners, who opposed the proposition, and insisted upon the Mississippi as the boundary, the probability is, that the proposition of Mr. Oswald would have been acceded to by the United States commissioners.

The States who owned western unappropriated lands, with a single exception, redeemed their respective pledges by ceding them to the United States. The State of Virginia, in March, 1784, ceded the right of soil and jurisdiction to the district of country embraced in her charter, situated to the north-west of the river Ohio. In September, 1786, the State of Connecticut also ceded her claim of soil and jurisdiction to the district of country within the limits of her charter, situated west of a line beginning at the completion of the forty-first point degree of north latitude, one hundred and twenty miles west of the western boundary of Pennsylvania; and from thence by a line drawn north parallel to, and one hundred and twenty miles west of said line of Pennsylvania, and to continue north until it came to forty-two degrees and two minutes north latitude. The State of Connecticut, on the 30th of May, 1801, also ceded her jurisdictional claims to all that territory called the "Western Reserve of Connecticut." The States of New York and Massachusetts also ceded all their claims.

The above were not the only claims which had to be made prior to the commencement of settlements within the limits of Ohio. Numerous tribes of Indian savages, by virtue of prior possession, asserted their respective claims, which also had to be extinguished. A treaty for this purpose was accordingly made at Fort Stanwix, October 27th, 1784, with the Sachems and warriors of the Mohawks, Onondagas, Senecas, Cayugas, Oneidas, and Tuscaroras; by the third article of which treaty, the said Six Nations ceded to the United States all claims to the country west of a line extending along the west boundary of Pennsylvania, from the mouth of the Oyounayea to the river Ohio.

2

A treaty was also concluded at Fort McIntosh, January 21st, 1785, with the Wyandot, Delaware, Chippewa, and Ottawa nations, by which the boundary line between the United States and the Wyandot and Delaware nations was declared to begin "at the mouth of the river Cuyahoga, and to extend up said river to the Portage, between that and the Tuscaroras branch of the Muskingum, thence down that branch to the crossing place above Fort Laurens, then westerly to the Portage of the Big Miami, which runs into the Ohio, at the mouth of which branch the fort stood which was taken by the French, in 1752; then along said Portage to the Great Miami, or Omee river, and down the south side of the same to its mouth; then along the south shore of Lake Erie to the mouth of the Cuyahoga river, where it began." The United States allotted all the lands contained within said lines to the Wyandot and Delaware nations, to live and hunt on, and to such of the Ottawa nation as lived thereon; saving and reserving for the establishment of trading posts, six miles square at the mouth of the Miami, or Omee river, and the same at the Portage, on that branch of the Big Miami which runs into the Ohio, and the same on the Lake of Sandusky where the fort formerly stood, and also two miles square on each side of the Lower Rapids of Sandusky river.

The Indian title to a large part of the territory within the limits of Ohio having been extinguished, legislative action on the part of Congress became necessary before settlements were commenced; as in the treaties made with the Indians, and in the acts of Congress, all citizens of the United States were prohibited settling on the lands of the Indians, as well as on those of the United States. Ordinances were accordingly made by Congress for the government of the North-western Territory, and for the survey and sale of portions of lands to which the Indian title had been extinguished.

In May, 1785, Congress passed an ordinance for ascertaining the mode of disposing of these lands. Under that ordinance, the first seven ranges, bounded on the east by Pennsylvania, and on the south by the Ohio river, were surveyed. Sales of parts of these were made at New York, in 1787, the avails of which amounted to $72,974, and sales of other parts of said range were made at Pittsburg and Philadelphia, in 1796. The avails of sales made at the former place amounted to $43,446, and at the latter, $5,120. A portion of these lands were located under United States military land warrants. No further sales were made in that district until the Land Office was opened at Steubenville, July 1st, 1801.

On the 27th of October, 1787, a contract in writing was entered into between the Board of Treasury for the United States of America, of the one part, and Manassah Cutler and Winthrop Sargeant, as agents for the directors of the New England Ohio Company of associates, of the other part, for the purchase of the tract of land bounded by the Ohio, from the mouth of the Scioto to the intersection of the western boundary of the seventh range of townships then surveying; thence by said boundary to the northern boundary of the tenth township from the Ohio; thence by a due west line to Scioto; thence by the Scioto to the beginning. The bounds of that contract were afterwards altered in 1792. The settlement of this purchase commenced at Marietta, at the mouth of the Muskingum river, in the spring of 1788, and was the first settlement formed within the limits of Ohio. An attempt at settlement within the bounds of Ohio had been made in April, 1785, at the mouth of the Scioto, on the site of Portsmouth, by four families from Redstone, Pa.; but difficulties with the Indians compelled its abandonment.

The same year in which Marietta was first settled, Congress appointed Gen. Arthur St. Clair, an officer of the revolution, *Governor;* Winthrop Sargeant, *Secretary;* and the Hon. Samuel Holden Parsons, James Mitchell Varnum, and John Cleves Symmes, *Judges;* in, and over the Territory. The territorial government was organized, and sundry laws were made, or adopted, by the Governor and Judges Parsons and Varnum. The county of Washington, having its limits extended westward to the Scioto, and northward to Lake Erie, embracing about half the territory within the present limits of the State, was established by the proclamation of the Governor.

On the 15th of October, 1788, John Cleves Symmes, in behalf of himself and his associates, contracted with the Board of Treasury for the purchase of a large tract of land situated between the Great and Little Miami river, and the first settlement within the limits of that purchase, and second in Ohio, was commenced in November of that year, at Columbia, at the mouth of the Little Miami, five miles above the site of Cincinnati.

"A short time after the settlement at Marietta had commenced, an association was formed under the name of the "*Scioto Land Company.*" A contract was made for the purchase of a part of the lands included in the Ohio Company's purchases. Plats and descriptions of the land contracted for, were, however, made out, and Joel Barlow was sent as an agent to Europe to make sales of the lands for the benefit of the company; and sales were effected of parts thereof to companies and individuals in France. On February 19th, 1791, two hundred and eighteen of these purchasers left Havre de Grace, in France, and arrived in Alexandria, D. C., on the 3d of May following. During their passage, two were added to their number. On their arrival, they were told that the Scioto Company owned no land. The agent insisted that they did, and promised to secure to them good titles thereto, which he did, at Winchester, Brownsville, and Charleston (now Wellsburg). When they arrived at Marietta, about fifty of them landed. The rest of the company proceeded to Gallipolis, which was laid out about that time, and were assured by the agent that the place lay within their purchase. Every effort to secure titles to the lands they had purchased having failed, an application was made to Congress, and in June, 1798, a grant was made to them of a tract of land on the Ohio, above the mouth of the Scioto river, which is called the '*French Grant.*'"

The Legislature of Connecticut, in May, 1795, appointed a committee to receive proposals and make sale of the lands she had reserved in Ohio. This committee sold the lands to sundry citizens of Connecticut and other States, and, in September of the same year, executed to several purchasers deeds of conveyance therefor. The purchasers proceeded to survey into townships of five miles square the whole of said tract lying east of the Cuyahoga; they made divisions thereof according to their respective proportions, and commenced settlements in many of the townships, and there were actually settled therein, by the 21st of March, 1800, about one thousand inhabitants. A number of mills had been built, and roads cut in various directions to the extent of about 700 miles.

The location of the lands appropriate for satisfying military land bounty warrants in the district appropriated for that purpose, granted for services in the revolutionary war, commenced on March 13th, 1800; and the location of the lands granted to the Canadian and Nova Scotia refugees commenced February 13th, 1802. The lands east of the Scioto, south of the military bounty lands, and west of the fifteenth range of townships, were first brought into market, and offered for sale by the United States on the first Monday of May, 1801.

The State of Virginia, at an early period of the revolutionary war, raised two description of troops, *State* and *Continental*, to each of which bounties in land were promised. The lands within the limits of her charter, situate to the north-west of Ohio river, were withdrawn from appropriation on treasury warrants, and the lands on Cumberland river, and between the Green and Tennessee rivers on the south-easterly side of the Ohio, were appropriated for these military bounties. Upon the recommendation of Congress, Virginia ceded her lands north of the Ohio, upon certain conditions; one of which was, that in case the lands south of Ohio should be insufficient for their legal bounties to their troops, the deficiency should be made up from lands north of the Ohio, between the rivers Scioto and Little Miami.

In 1783, the Legislature of Virginia authorized the officers of their respective lines to appoint superintendants to regulate the survey of the bounty lands promised. Richard C. Anderson was appointed principal surveyor of the lands of the troops of the continental establishment. An office for the reception of locations and surveys was opened at Louisville, Kentucky, August 1st, 1784, and on the 1st of August, 1787, the said office was open for the reception of surveys and locations on the north side of the Ohio.

In the year 1789, January 9th, a treaty was made at Fort Harmer, between Gov. St. Clair and the Sachems and warriors of the Wyandot, Chippewa, Potawatomie, and Sac nations, in which the treaty at Fort McIntosh was renewed and confirmed. It did not, however, produce the favorable results anticipated. The Indians, the same year, assuming a hostile appearance, were seen hovering round the infant settlements near the mouth of the Muskingum and between the Miamies, and nine persons were killed within the bounds of Symmes' purchase. The new settlers became alarmed and erected block-houses in each of the new settlements. In June, 1789, Major Doughty, with 140 men, from Fort Harmar, commenced the building of Fort Washington, on a spot now within the present limits of Cincinnati. A few months afterwards, Gen. Harmar arrived, with 300 men, and took command of the fort.

Negociations with the Indians proving unavailing, Gen. Harmar was directed to attack their towns. In pursuance of his instructions, he marched from Cincinnati, in September, 1790, with 1,300 men, of whom less than one-fourth were regulars. When near the Indian villages, on the Miami of the lake in the vicinity of what is now Fort Wayne, an advanced detachment of 210, consisting chiefly of militia, fell into an ambush and was defeated with severe loss. Gen. Harmar, however, succeeded in burning the Indian villages, and in destroying their standing corn, and having effected this service, the army commenced its march homeward. They had not proceeded far when Harmar received intelligence that the Indians had returned to their ruined towns. He immediately detached about one-third of his remaining force, under the command of Col. Hardin, with orders to bring them to an engagement. He succeeded in this early the next morning; the Indians fought with great fury, and the militia and the regulars alike behaved with gallantry. More than one hundred of the militia, and all the regulars except nine, were killed, and the rest were driven back to the main body. Dispirited by this severe misfortune, Harmar immediately marched to Cincinnati, and the object of the expedition in intimidating the Indians was entirely unsuccessful.

As the Indians continued hostile, a new army, superior to the former, was assembled at Cincinnati, under the command of Gov. St. Clair. The regular force amounted to 2,300 men; the militia numbered about 600. With this army, St. Clair commenced his march towards the Indian towns on the Maumee. Two forts, Hamilton and Jefferson, were established and garrisoned on the route, about forty miles from each other. Misfortune attended the expedition almost from its commencement. Soon after leaving Fort Jefferson, a considerable party of the militia deserted in a body. The first regiment, under Major Hamtramck, was ordered to pursue them and to secure the advancing convoys of provisions, which it was feared they designed to plunder. Thus weakened by desertion and division, St. Clair approached the Indian villages. On the third of November, 1791, when at what is now the line of Darke and Mercer counties, he halted, intending to throw up some slight fortification for the protection of baggage, and to await the return of the absent regiment. On the following morning, however, about half an hour before sun rise, the American army was attacked with great fury, as there is good reason to believe, by the whole disposable force of the north-west tribes. The Americans were totally defeated. Gen. Butler and upwards of six hundred men were killed.

Indian outrages of every kind were now multiplied, and emigration was almost entirely suspended.

President Washington now urged forward the vigorous prosecution of the war for the protection of the North-west Territory; but various obstacles retarded the enlistment and organization of a new army. In the spring of 1794, the American army assembled at Greenville, in Darke county, under the command of Gen. Anthony Wayne, a bold, energetic and experienced officer of the revolution. His force consisted of about two thousand regular troops, and fifteen hundred mounted volunteers from Kentucky. The Indians had collected their whole force, amounting to about two thousand men, near a British fort, erected since the treaty of 1783, in violation of its obligations, at the foot of the rapids of the Maumee. On the 20th of August, 1794, Gen. Wayne encountered the enemy, and after a short and deadly conflict, the Indians fled in the greatest confusion, and were pursued under the guns of the British fort. After destroying all the houses and corn fields above and below the British fort, on the Maumee, the victorious army returned to the mouth of Au Glaize, where Wayne erected Fort Defiance. Previous to this action, various fruitless attempts had been made to bring the Indians to peace. Some of the messengers sent among the Indians for that object were murdered.

The victory of Wayne did not at first reduce the savages to submission. Their country was laid waste, and forts were erected in the heart of their territory before they could be entirely subdued. At length, however, they became thoroughly convinced of their inability to resist the American arms and sued for peace. A grand council was held at Greenville, where eleven of the most powerful north-western tribes were represented, to whom Gen. Wayne dictated the terms of pacification. The boundary established by the treaty at Fort McIntosh was confirmed and extended westward from Loramie's to Fort Recovery, and thence south-west to the mouth of Kentucky river. The Indians agreed to acknowledge the United States as their sole protector, and never to sell their lands to any other power. Upon these and other conditions, the United States received the Indian nations into their protection. A large quantity of goods was delivered to them on the spot, and perpetual annuities, payable in merchandise, &c., were promised to each tribe who became a party to the treaty.

While the war with the Indians continued, of course, but little progress was made in the settlement in the west. The next county that was established after that of Washington, in 1788, was Hamilton, erected in 1790. Its bounds included the country between the Miamies, extending northward from the Ohio river, to a line drawn due east from the standing stone forks of the Great Miami. The name of the settlement opposite the Licking was, at this time, called *Cincinnati.*

At this period, there was no fixed seat of government. The laws were passed whenever they seemed to be needed, and promulgated at any place where the territorial legislators happened to be assembled. In 1789, the first Congress passed an act recognizing the binding force of the ordinance of 1787, and adapting its provisions to the federal constitution. At this period, the judges appointed by the national executive constituted the supreme court of the territory. Inferior to this court, were the county court, courts of common pleas, and the general quarter sessions of the peace. Single judges of the common pleas, and single justices of the quarter sessions, were also clothed with certain civil and criminal powers to be exercised out of court.

In 1795, the governor and judges undertook to revise the territorial laws, and to establish a system of statutory jurisprudence, by adoptions from the laws of the original States, in conformity to the ordinance. For this purpose they assembled in Cincinnati, in June, and continued in session until the latter part of August. The general court was fixed at Cincinnati and Marietta; other courts were established, and laws and regulations were adopted for various purposes.

The population of the territory now continued to increase and extend. From Marietta, settlers spread into the adjoining country. The Virginia military reservation drew a considerable number of revolutionary veterans, and others, from that State. The region between the Miamies, from the Ohio far up toward the sources of Mad river, became chequered with farms, and abounded in indications of the presence of an active and prosperous population. The neighborhood of Detroit became populous, and Connecticut, by grants of land within the tract, reserved in her deed of cession, induced many of her hardy citizens to seek a home on the borders of Lake Erie. In 1796, Wayne county was established, including all the north-western part of Ohio, a large tract in the north-eastern part of Indiana, and the whole territory of Michigan. In July, 1797, Adams county was erected, comprehending a large tract lying on both sides of Scioto, and extending northward to Wayne. Other counties were afterwards formed out of those already established. Before the end of the year 1798, the North-west Territory contained a population of five thousand free male inhabitants, of full age, and eight organized counties.

The people were now entitled, under the ordinance of 1787, to a change in their form of government. That instrument provided that whenever there were five thousand free males, of full age, in the territory, the people should be authorized to elect representatives to a territorial legislature. These, when chosen, were to nominate ten freeholders of 500 acres, of whom the president was to appoint five, who were to constitute the legislative council. Representatives were to serve two, and councilmen five years. The first meeting of the territorial legislature was appointed on the 16th of September, 1799, but it was not till the 24th of the same month that the two houses were organized for business; at which time they were addressed by Gov. St. Clair. An act was passed to confirm and give force to those laws enacted by the governor and judges, whose validity had been doubted. This act, as well as every other which originated in the council, was prepared and brought forward by Jacob Burnet, afterwards a distinguished judge and senator, to whose labors, at this session, the territory was indebted for some of its most beneficial laws. The whole number of acts passed and approved by the governor was thirty-seven. William H. Harrison, then secretary of the territory, was elected as delegate to Congress, having eleven of twenty-one votes.

"Within a few months after the close of this session, Connecticut ceded to the United States her claim of jurisdiction over the north-eastern part of the territory; upon which the president conveyed, by patent, the fee of the soil to the governor of the State, for the use of grantees and purchasers claiming under her. This tract, in the summer of the same year, was erected into a new county by the name of Trumbull. The same congress which made a final arrangement with Connecticut, passed an act dividing the North-western Territory into two governments, by a line drawn from the mouth of the Kentucky to Fort Recovery, and thence northward to the territorial line. East of this line, the government, already established, was continued; while west of it another, substantially similar, was established. This act fixed the seat of the eastern government at Chillicothe; subject, however, to be removed at the pleasure of the legislature."

On the 30th of April, 1802, Congress passed an act authorizing the call of a convention to form a State constitution. This convention assembled at Chillicothe, November 1st, and, on the 29th of the same month, a constitution of State government was ratified and signed by the members of the convention. It was never referred to the people for their approbation, but became the fundamental law of the State by the act of the convention alone; and, by this act, Ohio became one of the States of the Federal Union.

"Besides framing the constitution, the convention had another duty to perform. The act of congress, providing for the admission of the new State into the Union, offered certain propositions to the people. These were, first, that section sixteen in each township, or, where that section had been disposed of, other contiguous and equivalent lands, should be granted to the inhabitants for the use of schools; second, that thirty-eight sections of land, where salt-springs had been found, of which one township was situated on the Scioto, one section on the Muskingum, and one section in the United States military tract, should be granted to the State, never, however, to be sold or leased for a longer term than ten years; and third, that one-twentieth of the proceeds of public lands sold within the State, should be applied to the construction of roads from the Atlantic, to and through the same. These propositions were offered on the condition that the convention should provide, by ordinance, that all lands sold by the United States after the thirtieth day of June, 1802, should be exempt from taxation, by the State, for five years after sale.

"The ordinance of 1785, had already provided for the appropriation of section sixteen to the support of schools in every township sold by the United States; and this appropriation thus became a condition of the sale and settlement of the western country. It was a consideration offered to induce purchases of public lands, at a time when the treasury was well-nigh empty, and this source of revenue was much relied upon. It extended to every township of land within the territory, except those in the Virginia military reservation and wherever the reserved section had been disposed of, after the passage of the ordinance, Congress was bound to make other equivalent provision for the same object. The reservation of section sixteen, therefore, could not, in 1802, be properly made the object of a new bargain between the United States and the State: and many thought that the salt reservations and the twentieth of the proceeds of the public lands were very inadequate equivalents for the proposed surrender of the right to tax. The convention, however, determined to accept the propositions of Congress, on their being so far enlarged and modified as to vest in the State, for the use of schools, section sixteen in each township sold by the United States, and three other tracts of land, equal in quantity, respectively, to one thirty-sixth of the Virginia reservation, of the United States military tract, and of the Connecticut reserve, and to give three per centum of the proceeds of the public lands sold within the State, to be applied under the direction of the legislature, to roads in Ohio. Congress assented to the proposed modifications, and thus completed the compact."

The first General Assembly under the State constitution met at Chilicothe, March 1st, 1803. The legislature enacted such laws as were deemed necessary for the new order of things, and created eight new counties, namely: Gallia, Scioto, Franklin, Columbiana, Butler, Warren, Green, and Montgomery. The first State officers elected by the assembly were as follows, viz.: *Michael Baldwin*, Speaker of the House of Representatives; *Nathaniel Massie*, Speaker of the Senate; *William Creighton, Jr.*, Secretary of State; *Col. Thomas Gibson*, Auditor; *William McFarland*, Treasurer; *Return J. Meigs, Jr.*, *Samuel Huntington*, and *William Sprigg*, Judges of the Supreme Court; *Francis Dunlavy*, *Wyllys Silliman*, and *Calvin Pease*, Judges of the District Courts.

The second General Assembly convened in December, 1803. At this session, the militia law was thoroughly revised and a law was passed to enable aliens to enjoy the same proprietary rights in Ohio as native citizens. At this session, also, the revenue system of the State was simplified and improved. Acts were passed providing for the incorporation of townships, and for the establishment of boards of commissioners of counties.

In 1805, by a treaty with the Indians at Fort Industry, the United States acquired, for the use of the grantees of Connecticut, all that part of the western reserve which lies west of the Cuyahoga. By subsequent treaties, all the country watered by the Maumee and the

Sandusky have been acquired, and the Indian title to lands in Ohio is now extinct.

In the course of the year 1805, the conspiracy of Aaron Burr began to agitate the western country. The precise scope of the conspiracy does not distinctly appear. "The immediate object, probably, was to seize on New Orleans and invade Mexico. The ulterior purpose may have been to detach the west from the American Union. In December, 1806, in consequence of a confidential message from the governor, founded on the representations of an agent of the general government deputed to watch the motions of Burr, the legislature passed an act authorizing the arrest of persons engaged in an unlawful enterprise, and the seizure of their goods. Under this act, ten boats, with a considerable quantity of arms, ammunition, and provisions, belonging to Burr's expedition, were seized. This was a fatal blow to the project."

The Indians, who since the treaty at Greenville had been at peace, about the year 1810, began to commit aggressions upon the inhabitants of the west. The celebrated *Tecumseh* was conspicuously active in his efforts to unite the native tribes against the Americans, and to arrest the farther extension of the settlements. His proceedings, and those of his brother, '*the Prophet*,' soon made it evident that the west was about to suffer the calamities of another Indian war, and it was resolved to anticipate their movements. In 1811, Gen. Harrison, then governor of Indiana Territory, marched against the town of the 'Prophet,' upon the Wabash. The battle of Tippecanoe ensued, in what is now Cass county, Indiana, in which the Indians were totally defeated. This year was also distinguished by an occurrence of immense importance to the whole west. This was the voyage, from Pittsburg to New Orleans, of the *first steamboat* ever launched upon the western waters.

"In June, 1812, the United States declared war against Great Britain. Of this war the west was a principal theatre. Defeat, disaster, and disgrace marked its opening scenes; but the latter events of the contest were a series of splendid achievements. Croghan's gallant defence of Fort Stephenson; Perry's victory upon Lake Erie; the total defeat, by Harrison, of the allied British and savages, under Proctor and Tecumseh, on the Thames; and the great closing triumph of Jackson at New Orleans, reflected the most brilliant lustre upon the American arms. In every vicissitude of this contest, the conduct of Ohio was eminently patriotic and honorable. When the necessities of the national government compelled congress to resort to a direct tax, Ohio, for successive years, cheerfully assumed, and promptly paid her quota out of her State treasury. Her sons volunteered with alacrity their services in the field; and no troops more patiently endured hardship or performed better service. Hardly a battle was fought in the north-west, in which some of these brave citizen soldiers did not seal their devotion to their country with their blood.

"In 1816, the seat of the State government was removed to Columbus, the proprietors of the town having, pursuant to an agreement entered into, in good faith, erected the State-house and other public buildings, for the accommodation of the legislature and the officers of state.

"In January, 1817, the first resolution relating to a canal, connecting the Ohio river with Lake Erie, was introduced into the legislature. In 1819, the subject was again agitated. In 1820, on the recommendation of Gov. Brown, an act was passed, providing for the appointment of three canal commissioners, who were to employ a competent engineer and assistants, for the purpose of surveying the route of the canal. The action of the commissioners, however, was made to depend on the acceptance by congress of a proposition on behalf of the State, for a donation and sale of the public lands, lying upon and near the route of the proposed canal. In consequence of this restriction, nothing was accomplished for two years. In 1822, the subject was referred to a committee of the house of representatives. This committee recommended the employment of an engineer, and submitted various estimates and observations to illustrate the importance and feasibility of the work. Under this act, James Geddes, of New York, an experienced and skillful engineer, was employed to make the necessary examinations and surveys. Finally, after all the routes had been surveyed, and estimates made of the expense had been laid before the legislature at several sessions, an act was passed in Feb., 1825, " To provide for the internal improvement of the State by navigable canals," and thereupon the State embarked in good earnest in the prosecution of the great works of internal improvement."

The construction of these and other works of internal improvement, has been of immense advantage in developing the resources of Ohio, which, in little more than half a century, has changed from a wilderness to one of the most powerfu States of the Union.

COUNTIES.

ADAMS.

Adams lies on the Ohio river, about fifty miles east of Cincinnati, and derives its name from John Adams, second President of the United States. It was formed, July 10th, 1797, by proclamation of Gov. St. Clair, and covered a large tract of country, being then one of the four counties into which the N. W. Territory was divided. The land is generally hilly and broken, and, in the eastern part, not fertile. The staples are wheat, corn, pork and oats. Many of the first settlers were from Virginia, Kentucky and Ireland. The following is a list of its townships in 1840, with their population:

Franklin,	1,358	Meigs,	1,071	Tiffin,	1,533
Green,	1,081	Monroe,	828	Wayne,	858
Jefferson,	938	Scott,	916	Winchester,	1,112
Liberty,	1,096	Sprigg,	1,984		

The population of Adams, in 1820, was 10,406; in 1830, 12,278 and in 1840, 13,271, or 24 persons to a square mile.

The first settlement within the Virginia military tract, and the only one between the Scioto and Little Miami until after the treaty of Greenville, in 1795, was made in this county, at Manchester, by the then Col., late Gen. Nathaniel Massie. McDonald, in his unpretending, but excellent little volume, says:

Massie, in the winter of the year, 1790, determined to make a settlement in it, that he might be in the midst of his surveying operations and secure his party from danger and exposure. In order to effect this, he gave general notice in Kentucky of his intention, and offered each of the first twenty-five families, as a donation, one in-lot, one out-lot, and one hundred acres of land, provided they would settle in a town he intended to lay off at his settlement. His proffered terms were soon closed in with, and upwards of thirty families joined him. After various consultations with his friends, the bottom on the Ohio river, opposite the lower of the Three Islands, was selected as the most eligible spot. Here, he fixed his station, and laid off into lots a town, now called Manchester; at this time a small place, about twelve miles above Maysville, (formerly Limestone,) Kentucky. This little confederacy, with Massie at the helm, (who was the soul of it,) went to work with spirit. Cabins were raised, and by the middle of March, 1791, the whole town was enclosed with strong pickets, firmly fixed in the ground, with block houses at each angle for defence.

Thus was the first settlement in the Virginia military district, and the fourth settlement in the bounds of the State of Ohio, effected. Although this settlement was commenced in the hottest Indian war, it suffered less from depredation, and even interruptions, from the Indians, than any settlement previously made on the Ohio river. This was no doubt owing to the watchful band of brave spirits who guarded the place—men who were reared in the midst of danger and inured to perils, and as watchful as hawks. Here were the Beasleys, the Stouts, the Washburns, the Ledoms, the Edgingtons, the Denings, the Ellisons, the Utts, the McKenzies, the Wades, and others, who were equal to the Indians in all the arts and stratagems of border war.

As soon as Massie had completely prepared his station for defence, the whole population went to work, and cleared the lower of the Three Islands, and planted it in corn. The island was very rich, and produced heavy crops. The woods, with a little industry, supplied a choice variety of game. Deer, elk, buffalo, bears, and turkeys, were abundant, while the river furnished a variety of excellent fish. The wants of the inhabitants, under these circumstances, were few and easily gratified.

When this station was made, the nearest neighbors north-west of the Ohio, were the inhabitants at Columbia, a settlement below the mouth of the Little Miami, five miles above Cincinnati, and at Gallipolis, a French settlement, near the mouth of the Great Kenhawa.

The station being established, Massie continued to make locations and surveys. Great precautions were necessary to avoid the Indians, and even these did not always avail, as is shown by the following incidents, the first of which is derived from the narrative of Israel Donalson, in the American Pioneer, and the others from McDonald's sketches.

I am not sure whether it was the last of March or first of April I came to the territory to reside; but on the night of the 21st of April, 1791, Mr. Massie and myself were sleeping together on our blankets, (for beds we had none,) on the loft of our cabin, to get out of the way of the fleas and gnats. Soon after lying down, I began dreaming of Indians, and continued to do so through the night. Sometime in the night, however, whether Mr. Massie waked of himself, or whether I wakened him, I cannot now say, but I observed to him I did not know what was to be the consequence, for I had dreamed more about Indians that night than in all the time I had been in the western country before. As is common, he made light of it, and we dropped again to sleep. He asked me next morning if I would go with him up the river, about four or five miles, to make a survey, and that William Lytle, who was then at the fort, was going along. We were both young surveyors, and were glad of the opportunity to practice. Accordingly we three, and a James Tittle, from Kentucky, who was about buying the land, got on board of a canoe, and was a long time going up, the river being very high at the time. We commenced at the mouth of a creek, which from that day has been called Donalson creek. We meandered up the river; Mr. Massie had the compass, Mr. Lytle and myself carried the chain. We had progressed perhaps one hundred and forty, or one hundred and fifty poles, when our chain broke or parted, but with the aid of the tomahawk we soon repaired it. We were then close to a large mound, and were standing in a triangle, and Lytle and myself were amusing ourselves pointing out to Tittle the great convenience he would have by building his house on that mound, when the one standing with his face up the river, spoke and said, boys, there are Indians; no, replied the other, they are Frenchmen. By this time I had caught a glimpse of them; I said they were Indians, I begged them to fire. I had no gun, and from the advantage we had, did not think of running until they started. The Indians were in two small bark canoes, and were close into shore and discovered us just at the instant we saw them; and before I started to run I saw one jump on shore. We took out through the bottom, and before getting to the hill, came to a spring branch. I was in the rear, and as I went to jump, something caught my foot, and I fell on the opposite side. They were then so close, I saw there was no chance of escape, and did not offer to rise. Three warriors first came up, presented their guns all ready to fire, but as I made no resistance they took them down, and one of them gave me his hand to help me up. At this time Mr. Lytle was about a chain's length before me, and threw away his hat; one of the Indians went forward and picked it up. They then took me back to the bank of the river, and set me down while they put up their stuff, and prepared for a march. While setting on the bank of the river, I could see the men walking about the block-house on the Kentucky shore, but they heard nothing of it. They went on rapidly that evening, and camped, I think, on the waters of Eagle creek, started next morning early, it raining hard, and one of them saw my hat was somewhat convenient to keep off the rain, came up and took it off my head, and put it on his own. By this time I had discovered some friendship in a very lusty Indian, I think the one that first came up to me; I made signs to him that one had taken my hat, he went and took it off the other Indian's head, and placed it again on mine, but had not gone far before they took it again. I complained as before, but my friend shook his head, took down and opened his budget, and took out a sort of blanket cap, and put it on my head. We went on; it still rained hard, and the waters were very much swollen, and when my friend discovered that I was timorous, he would lock his arm in mine, and lead me through, and frequently in open woods when I would get tired, I would do the same thing with him, and walk for miles. They did not make me carry any thing until Sunday or Monday. They got into a thicket of game, and killed, I think, two bears and some deer; they then halted and jerked their meat, eat a large portion, peeled some bark, made a kind of box, filled it, and put it on me to carry. I soon got tired of it and threw it down: they raised a great laugh, examined my back, applied some bear's oil to it, and then put on the box again. I went on some distance and threw it down again; my friend then took it up, threw it over his head, and carried it. It weighed, I thought, at least fifty pounds.

While resting one day, one of the Indians broke up little sticks and laid them up in the form of a fence, then took out a grain of corn, as carefully wrapped up as people used to wrap up guineas in olden times; this they planted and called out squaw, signifying to me that that would be my employment with the squaws. But, notwithstanding my situation at the time, I thought they would not eat much corn of my raising. On Tuesday, as we were traveling along, there came to us a white man and an Indian on horseback; they had a long talk, and when they rode off, the Indians I was with seemed considerably alarmed; they immediately formed in Indian file, placed me in the centre, and shook a war club over my head, and showed me by these gestures that if I attempted to run away they would kill me. We soon after arrived at the Shawanee camp, where we continued until late in the afternoon of the next day. During our stay there they trained my hair to their own fashion, put a jewel of tin in my nose, &c., &c. The Indians met with great formality when we came to the camp, which was very spacious. One side was entirely cleared out for our use, and the party I was with passed the camp to my great mortification, I thinking they were going on; but on getting to the further end they wheeled short round, came into the camp, sat down—not a whisper. In a few minutes two of the oldest got up, went round, shook hands, came and sat down again; then the Shawanees rising simultaneously, came and shook hands with them. A few of the first took me by the hand; but one refused, and I did not offer them my hand again, not considering it any great honor. Soon after a kettle of bear's oil and some craclins were set before us, and we began eating, they first chewing the meat, then dipping it into the bear's oil, which I tried to be excused from, but they compelled me to it, which tried my stomach, although by this time hunger had compelled me to eat many a dirty morsel. Early in the afternoon, an Indian came to the camp, and was met by his party just outside, when they formed a circle and he spoke, I thought, near an hour, and so profound was the silence, that had they been on a board floor, I thought the fall of a pin might have been heard. I rightly judged of the disaster, for the day before I was taken I was at Limestone, and was solicited to join a party that was going down to the mouth of Snag creek, where some Indian canoes were discovered hid in the willows. The party went and divided, some came over to the Indian shore, and some remained in Kentucky, and they succeeded in killing nearly the whole party.

There was at this camp two white men; one of them could swear in English, but very imperfectly, having I suppose been taken young; the other, who could speak good English, told me he was from South Carolina. He then told me different names which I have forgot, except that of Ward; asked if I knew the Wards that lived near Washington, Kentucky. I told him I did, and wanted him to leave the Indians and go to his brother's, and take me with him. He told me he preferred staying with the Indians, that he might nab the whites. He and I had a great deal of chat, and disagreed in almost every thing. He told me they had taken a prisoner by the name of Towns, that had lived near Washington, Kentucky, and that he had attempted to run away, and they killed him. But the truth was, they had taken Timothy Downing the day before I was taken, in the neighborhood of Blue Licks, and had got within four or five miles of that camp, and night coming on, and it being very rainy, they concluded to camp. There were but two Indians, an old chief and his son; Downing watched his opportunity, got hold of a squaw-axe and gave the fatal blow. His object was to bring the young Indian in a prisoner; he said he had been so kind to him he could not think of killing him. But the instant he struck his father, the young man sprung upon his back and confined him so that it was with difficulty he extricated himself from his grasp. Downing made then for his horse, and the Indian for the camp. The horse he caught and mounted; but not being a woodsman, struck the Ohio a little below Scioto, just as a boat was passing. They would not land for him until he rode several miles and convinced them that he was no decoy, and so close was the pursuit, that the boat had only gained the stream when the enemy appeared on the shore. He had severely wounded the young Indian in the scuffle, but did not know it until I told him. But to return to my own narrative: two of the party, viz., my friend and another Indian, turned back from this camp to do other mischief, and never before had I parted with a friend with the same regret. We left the Shawanee camp about the middle of the afternoon, they under great excitement. What detained them I know not, for they had a number of their horses up, and their packs on, from early in the morning. I think they had at least one hundred of the best horses that at that time Kentucky could afford. They calculated on being pursued, and they were right, for the next day, viz., the 28th of April, Major Kenton, with about ninety men, were at the camp before the fires were extinguished; and I have always viewed it as a providential circumstance that the enemy had departed, as a defeat on the part of the Kentuckians would have been inevitable. I never could get the Indians in a position to ascertain their precise number, but concluded there were sixty or upward, as sprightly looking men as I ever saw together, and well equipped as they could wish for. The Major himself agreed with me that it was a happy circumstance that they were gone.

We traveled that evening, I thought, seven miles, and encamped in the edge of a prairie, the water a short distance off. Our supper that night consisted of a raccoon roasted undressed. After this meal I became thirsty, and an old warrior, to whom my friend had given me in charge, directed another to go with me to the water, which made him angry; he struck me, and my nose bled. I had a great mind to return the stroke, but did not. I then determined, be the result what it might, that I would go no farther with them. They tied me and laid me down as usual, one of them lying on the rope on each side of me; they went to sleep, and I to work gnawing and picking the rope (made of bark) to pieces, but did not get loose until day was breaking. I crawled off on my hands and feet until I got into the edge of the prairie, and sat down on a trussuck to put on my moccasins, and had put on one and was preparing to put on the other, when they raised the yell and took the back track, and I believe they made as much noise as twenty white men could do. Had they been still they might have heard me, as I was not more than two chains' length from them at the time. But I started and ran, carrying one moccasin in my hand; and in order to evade them, chose the poorest ridges I could find; and when coming to tree-logs lying crosswise, would run along one and then along the other. I continued on that way until about ten o'clock, then ascending a very poor ridge, crept in between two logs, and being very weary soon dropped to sleep, and did not waken until the sun was almost down; I traveled on a short distance further and took lodging for the night in a hollow tree. I think it was on Saturday that I got to the Miami. I collected some logs, made a raft by peeling bark and tying them together; but I soon found that too tedious and abandoned it. I found a turkey's nest with two eggs in it, each one having a double yelk; they made two delicious meals for different days. I followed down the Miami, until I struck Harmar's trace, made the previous fall, and continued on it until I came to Fort Washington, now Cincinnati. I think it was on Sabbath, the first day of May; I caught a horse, tied a piece of bark around his under jaw, on which there was a large tumor like a wart. The bark rubbed that, and he became restless and threw me, not hurting me much, however; I caught him again, and he again threw me, hurting me badly. How long I lay insensible I don't know; but when I revived he was a considerable distance from me. I then traveled on very slow, my feet entirely bare and full of thorns and briars. On Wednesday, the day that I got in, I was so far gone that I thought it entirely useless to make any further exertion, not knowing what distance I was from the river; and I took my station at the root of a tree, but soon got into a state of sleeping, and either dreamt, or thought that I should not be loitering away my time, that I should get in that day; which, on reflection, I had not the most distant idea. However, the impression was so strong that I got up and walked on some distance. I then took my station again as before, and the same thoughts occupied my mind. I got up and walked on. I had not traveled far before I thought I could see an opening for the river; and getting a little further on, I heard the sound of a bell. I then started and ran, (at a slow speed undoubtedly;) a little further on, I began to perceive that I was coming to the river hill; and having got about half way down, I heard the sound of an axe, which was the sweetest music I had heard for many a day. It was in the extreme out-lot; when I got to the lot I crawled over the fence with difficulty, it being very high. I approached the person very cautiously till within about a chain's length, undiscovered, I then stopped and spoke; the person I spoke to was Mr. William Woodward, (the founder of the Woodward High School.) Mr. Woodward looked up, hastily cast his eyes round, and saw that I had no deadly weapon; he then spoke. "In the name of God," said he, "who are you?" I told him I had been a prisoner and had made my escape from the Indians. After a few more questions he told me to come to him. I did so. Seeing my situation, his fears soon subsided; he told me to sit down on a log and he would go and catch a horse he had in the lot, and take me in. He caught his horse, set me on him, but kept the bridle in his own hand. When we got into the road, people began to inquire of Mr. Woodward, "who is he—an Indian?" I was not surprised nor offended at the inquiries, for I was still in Indian uniform, bare headed, my hair cut off close, except the scalp and foretop, which they had put up in a piece of tin, with a bunch of turkey feathers, which I could not undo. They had also stripped off the feathers of about two turkeys and hung them to the hair of the scalp; these I had taken off the day I left them. Mr. Woodward took me to his house, where every kindness was shown me. They soon gave me other clothing; coming from different persons, they did not fit me very neatly; but there could not be a pair of shoes got in the place that I could get on, my feet were so much swollen.

In the spring of the year 1793, the settlers at Manchester commenced clearing the out-lots of the town; and while so engaged, an incident of much interest and excitement occurred. Mr. Andrew Ellison, one of the settlers, cleared a lot immediately adjoining the fort. He had completed the cutting of the timber, rolled the logs together and set them on fire. The next morning, a short time before daybreak, Mr. Ellison opened one of the gates of the fort, and went out to throw his logs together. By the time he had finished this job, a number of the heaps blazed up brightly, and as he was passing from one to the other, he observed, by the light of the fires, three men walking briskly towards him. This did not alarm him in the least, although, he said, they were dark skinned fellows; yet he concluded they were the Wades, whose complexions were very dark, going early to hunt. He continued to right his log-heaps, until one of the fellows seized him by the arms, and called out in broken English, "How do? how do?" He instantly looked in their faces, and to his surprise and horror, found himself in the clutches of three Indians. To resist was useless. He therefore submitted to his fate, without any resistance or an attempt to escape.

The Indians quickly moved off with him in the direction of Paint creek. When breakfast was ready, Mrs. Ellison sent one of her children to ask their father home; but he could not be found at the log-heaps. His absence created no immediate alarm, as it was thought he might have started to hunt after the completion of his work. Dinner time arrived, and Ellison not returning, the family became uneasy, and began to suspect some accident had happened to him. His gun-rack was examined, and there hung his rifle and his pouch in their usual place. Massie raised a party, and made a circuit around the place, and found, after some search, the trails of four men, one of whom had on shoes; and as Ellison had shoes on, the truth, that the Indians had made him a prisoner, was unfolded. As it was almost night at the time the trail was discovered, the party returned to their station. Next morning, early preparations were made by Massie and his party to pursue the Indians. In doing this they found great difficulty, as it was so early in the spring that the vegetation was not of sufficient growth to show plainly the trail of the Indians, who took the precaution to keep on hard and high land, where their feet could make little or no impression. Massie and his party, however, were as unerring as a pack of well-trained hounds, and followed the trail to Paint creek, when they found the Indians gained so fast on them, that pursuit was vain. They therefore abandoned it, and returned to the station.

The Indians took their prisoner to Upper Sandusky, and compelled him to run the gauntlet. As Ellison was a large man and not very active, he received a severe flogging as he passed along the line. From this place he was taken to Lower Sandusky, and was again compelled to run the gauntlet, and was then taken to Detroit, where he was generously ransomed by a British officer for one hundred dollars. He was shortly afterwards sent by his friend, the officer, to Montreal, from whence he returned home before the close of the summer of the same year.

Another incident connected with the station at Manchester occurred shortly after this time, which, although somewhat out of order as to time, I will take the liberty to relate in this place. John Edgington, Asahel Edgington, and another man, started out on a hunting expedition towards Brush creek. They camped out six miles in a north-east direction from where West Union now stands, and near where Treber's tavern is now situated, on the road from Chillicothe to Maysville. The Edgingtons had good success in hunting, having killed a number of deer and bears. Of the deer killed, they saved the skins and hams alone. The bears, they fleeced; that is, they cut off all the meat which adhered to the hide without skinning, and left the bones as a skeleton. They hung up the proceeds of their hunt on a scaffold, out of the reach of the wolves and other wild animals, and returned home for pack horses. No one returned to the camp with the two Edgingtons. As it was late in December, no one apprehended danger, as the winter season was usually a time of repose from Indian incursions. When the Edgingtons arrived at their old hunting camp, they alighted from their horses and were preparing to strike a fire, when a platoon of Indians fired upon them, at the distance of not more than twenty paces. Asahel Edgington fell to rise no more. John was more fortunate. The sharp crack of the rifles, and the horrid yells of the Indians, as they leaped from their place of ambush, frightened the horses, who took the track towards home at full speed. John Edgington was very active on foot, and now an occasion offered which required his utmost speed. The moment the Indians leaped from their hiding place, they threw down their guns and took after him. They pursued him screaming and yelling in the most horrid manner. Edgington did not run a booty race. For about a mile the Indians stepped in his tracks almost before the bending grass could rise. The uplifted tomahawk was frequently so near his head, that he thought he felt its edge. Every effort was made to save his life, and every exertion of the Indians was made to arrest him in his flight. Edgington, who had the greatest stake in the race, at length began to gain on his pursuers, and after a long race, he distanced them, made his escape, and safely reached home. This, truly, was a most fearful and well contested race. The big Shawnee chief, Captain John, who headed the Indians on this occasion, after peace was made and Chillicothe settled, frequently told the writer of this sketch of the race. Captain John said, that "the white man who ran away was a smart fellow, that the white man run and I run, he run and run, at last, the white man run clear off from me."

The first court in this county was held in Manchester. Winthrop Sargent, the secretary of the territory, acting in the absence of the governor, appointed commissioners, who located the county seat at an out of the way place, a few miles above the mouth of Brush creek, which they called Adamsville. The locality was soon named, in derision, *Scant*. At the next session of the court, its members became divided, and part sat in Manchester and part at Adamsville. The governor, on his return to the territory, finding the people in great confusion, and much bickering between them, removed the seat of justice to the mouth of Brush creek, where the first court was held in 1798. Here a town was laid out by Noble Grimes, under the name of Washington. A large log court house was built, with a jail in the lower story, and the governor appointed two more of the Scant party judges, which gave them a majority. In 1800, Charles Willing Byrd, secretary of the territory, in the absence of the governor, appointed two more of the Manchester party judges, which balanced the parties, and the contest was maintained until West Union became the county seat. Joseph Darlinton* and Israel Donalson, were among the first judges of the Common Pleas. These gentlemen, now living in this county, were also members of the convention for forming the constitution of the State, there being, in 1847, only three others of that body living.

West Union, the county seat, is on the Maysville and Zanesville turnpike, 8 miles from the Ohio at Manchester, and 106 southerly from Columbus. The name was given to it by Hon. Thomas Kirker, one of the commissioners who laid it out in 1804, and one of its earliest settlers. It stands on the summit of a high ridge, many hundred feet above the level of the Ohio. As early as 1815, a newspaper was established here by James Finlay, entitled the Political Censor. The annexed view shows, on the left, the jail and market, and in the centre, the court house and county offices. These last stand in a pleasant area, shaded by locusts. The court house is a substantial stone building, and bears good testimony to the

* In 1803, Gen. Darlinton was appointed Clerk of Common Pleas and Clerk of the Supreme Court. The first office he left a few months since, and the last he still retains.

skill of its builder, ex-Governor Metcalf, of Kentucky, who, commencing life as a mason, has acquired the *sobriquet* of "Stone Hammer." The first court house here was of logs. West Union contains 4 churches: 1 Associate Reformed, 1 Presbyterian, 1 Methodist and 1 Baptist; 2 newspapers, a classical school, and 9 mercantile stores. It had, in 1820, a population of 406; in 1840, 452.

Public Buildings, West Union.

In the eastern part of this county are considerable beds of iron ore, that have been in use many years; it is a mineral region, and large hills are composed of aluminous slate. Some years since, a singular phenomenon occurred in this section, described by Dr. Hildreth, in the 29th volume of Silliman's Journal:

A part of the summer of the year 1830 was excessively dry in the south-west portion o Ohio. During the drought, the water all disappeared from Brush creek, which heads among some slaty hills, leaving its bed entirely dry for several weeks. Towards the close of this period, loud and frequent explosions took place from the slate at the bottom of the creek, throwing up large fragments of rock and shaking the earth violently for some distance. The inhabitants living near its borders became much alarmed, thinking a volcano was breaking out. On examining the spot, large pieces of iron pyrites were found mixed with the slate-stone. The water, which had heretofore protected the pyrites from the atmosphere, being all evaporated, the oxygen found its way through the crevices of the slate to these beds, and acting chemically upon them, new combinations took place, forcing up the superincumbent strata with great violence and noise. When the water again covered he bed of the creek, the explosions ceased.

The barren hills in this part of the county, and of some of the other river counties, remain, in many cases, the property of the General Government. They afford, however, a fine range for the cattle and hogs of the scattered inhabitants, and no small quantity of lumber, such as staves, hoop poles and tanner's bark, which are unscrupulously taken from the public lands. Dr. John Locke, from whose Geological Report these facts are derived, says:

Indeed, there is a vagrant class who are supported by this kind of business. They erect a cabin towards the head of some ravine, collect the chestnut-oak bark from the neighboring hill tops, drag it on sleds to points accessible by wagons, where they sell it for perhaps $2 per cord to the wagoner. The last sells it at the river to the flat boat shipper, at $6 per cord, and he again to the consumer at Cincinnati, for $11. Besides this common trespass, the squatter helps himself out by hunting deer and coons, and, it is said, occasionally by taking a sheep or a hog, the loss of which may very reasonably be charged to the wolves. The poor families of *the bark cutters* often exhibit the very picture of improvidence. There begins to be a fear among the inhabitants that speculators may be tempted to purchase up these waste lands and deprive them of their present 'range' and lumber. The speculator must still be a non-resident, and could hardly protect his purchase. The inhabitants have a hard, rough region to deal with, and need all of the advantages which their mountain tract can afford.

Winchester, 12 miles NW. of the county seat, is a thriving town, with 7 stores and about 400 people; Manchester, 8 SW., has 4 stores and about 250 population; Jacksonville, 10 NE., has a population of about 200; Locust Grove, Rockville, Bentonville, Cherry Fork, Eckmansville and Rome, are small towns having post offices.

ALLEN.

Allen was formed April 1st, 1820, from Indian territory, and named in honor of a colonel of that name in the war of 1812: it was temporarily attached to Mercer county for judicial purposes. The surface is generally level; the soil varies from a sandy loam to clay, and is well adapted to grain and grass. The principal crops are wheat, corn, rye and oats, with timothy, clover and flaxseed. The county is well settled for a new one, which arises from the U. S., and State land offices having formerly been within it, and the land, therefore, was taken by actual settlers. The population is of a mixed character, and the southern part has many Germans. The following is a list of its townships in 1840, with their population:

Amanda,	282	Goshen,	236	Shawanee,	429
Auglaise,	732	Jackson,	570	Union,	669
Bath,	1,382	Marion,	315	Washington,	457
Clay,	435	Moulton,	263	Wayne,	404
Duchaquet,	692	Perry,	565		
German,	856	Pusheta,	768		

The population of Allen, in 1840, was 9,081, or 16 inhabitants to a square mile.

Lima, the county seat, is 95 miles WNW. from Columbus, and was laid off as the seat of justice for the county in the spring of 1831. It is several miles north of the centre of the county, the southern portion of which has been an Indian reservation. The annexed view was taken near the residence of Col. Jas. Cunningham, on the Wapakonetta road. The stream shown in the view is the Ottawa river, usually called Hog river—a name derived from the following circumstance: McKee, the British Indian agent, who resided at the Machachac towns, on Mad river, during the incursion of General Logan, in 1786, was obliged to flee with his effects. He had his swine driven on to the borders of this stream; the Indians thereafter called it *Koshko sepe*, which, in the Shawnee language, signifies Hog river. Lima contains 1 Presbyterian, 1

Methodist, and 1 Baptist church; 6 dry goods and 4 grocery stores, a foundery, 2 newspaper printing offices, and a population estimated at about 500. The town is progressing with the gradual increase of the country.

Lima.

Wapakonetta is 10 miles from St. Mary's, and 12 from Lima, on the Auglaize, and contains 1 Catholic and 1 Methodist church and 3 stores; it is settled principally by Germans, and in population is somewhat less than Lima. After the Shawnees were driven from Piqua by Gen. Clark, they settled a town here, which they called *Wapaghkonetta.** By the treaty at the Maumee rapids, in 1817, the Shawnees were given a reservation of ten miles square in this county, within which was their council house at Wapakonetta, and also a tract of twenty-five square miles, which included their settlement on Hog Creek; by the treaty of the succeeding year, made at St. Mary's, 12,800 acres adjoining the east line of the Wapakonetta Reserve were added.

At the village there is a fine orchard, at least sixty years of age, and from its being planted in regular order, it is supposed to have been done by Frenchmen settled among the Indians. The society of Friends, for a number of years, had a mission at Wapakonetta.

From the year 1796 till the formation of the state constitution, Judge Burnet, of Cincinnati, attended court regularly at that place, Marietta and Detroit, the last of which was then the seat of justice for Wayne county. The jaunts between these remote places, through a wilderness, were attended with exposure, fatigue and hazard, and were usually performed on horseback, in parties of two or three or

* John Johnston says "*Wapagh-ko-netta:* this is the true Indian orthography. It was named after an Indian chief long since dead, but who survived years after my intercourse commenced with the Shawanoese. The chief was somewhat *club-footed,* and the word has reference, I think, to that circumstance, although its full import I never could discover. For many years prior to 1829, I had my Indian head quarters at Wapagh-ko-netta. The business of the agency of the Shawanoese, Wyandotts, Senecas and Delawares, was transacted there."

more. On one of these occasions, while halting at Wapakonetta, he witnessed a game of ball among the people, of which he has given an interesting narration in his letters.

Blue Jacket, the war chief, who commanded the Shawanees in the battle of 1794, at Maumee, resided in the village, but was absent. We were, however, received with kindness, by the old village chief, Buckingelas. When we went to his lodge, he was giving audience to a deputation of chiefs from some western tribes. We took seats at his request, till the conference was finished, and the strings of wampum disposed of—he gave us no intimation of the subject matter of the conference, and, of course, we could not ask for it. In a little time he called in some of his young men, and requested them to get up a game of football for our amusement. A purse of trinkets was soon made up, and the whole village, male and female, were on the lawn. At these games the men played against the women, and it was a rule, that the former were not to touch the ball with their hands on penalty of forfeiting the purse; while the latter had the privilege of picking it up, running with, and throwing it as far as they could. When a squaw had the ball, the men were allowed to catch and shake her, and even throw her on the ground, if necessary, to extricate the ball from her hand, but they were not allowed to touch, or move it, except by their feet. At the opposite extremes of the lawn, which was a beautiful plain, thickly set with blue grass, stakes were erected, about six feet apart—the contending parties arrayed themselves in front of these stakes; the men on the one side, and the women on the other. The party which succeeded in driving the ball through the stakes, at the goal of their opponents, were proclaimed victors, and received the purse. All things being ready, the old chief went to the centre of the lawn, and threw up the ball, making an exclamation, in the Shawanee language, which we did not understand. He immediately retired, and the contest began. The parties seemed to be fairly matched, as to numbers, having about a hundred on a side. The game lasted more than an hour, with great animation, but was finally decided in favor of the *ladies*, by the power of an herculean squaw, who got the ball, and in spite of the men who seized her to shake it from her uplifted hand, held it firmly, dragging them along, till she was sufficiently near the goal to throw it through the stakes. The young squaws were the most active of their party, and, of course, most frequently caught the ball. When they did so, it was amusing to see the strife between them and the young Indians, who immediately seized them, and always succeeded in rescuing the ball, though sometimes they could not effect their object till their female competitors were thrown on the grass. When the contending parties had retired from the field of strife, it was pleasant to see the feelings of exultation depicted in the faces of the victors; whose joy was manifestly enhanced by the fact, that their victory was won in the presence of white men, whom they supposed to be highly distinguished, and of great power in their nation. This was a natural conclusion for them to draw, as they knew we were journeying to Detroit for the purpose of holding the general court; which, they supposed, controled and governed the nation. We spent the night very pleasantly among them, and in the morning resumed our journey.

In August, 1831, treaties were negotiated with the Senecas of Lewiston and the Shawnees of Wapakonetta, by James Gardiner, Esq., and Col. John M'Elvain, special commissioners appointed for this purpose. The terms offered were so liberal that the Indians consented to give up their land and remove beyond the Mississippi. The Shawnees had at this time about 66,000 acres in this county, and in conjunction with the Senecas about 40,300 acres at Lewiston. The Indians were removed to the Indian territory on Kanzas river, in the Far West, in September, 1832, D. M. Workman and David Robb being the agents for their removal. The latter, Mr. Robb, in a communication respecting the Indians, has given the following interesting facts.

Intemperance to a great extent prevailed among the Indians; there was, however, as wide a contrast in this respect as with the whites, and some of the more virtuous refused to associate with the others. This class also cultivated their little farms with a degree of taste and judgment: some of these could cook a comfortable meal, and I have eaten both butter and a kind of cheese made by them. Many of them were quite ingenious and natural mechanics, with a considerable knowledge of, and an inclination to use tools. One chief had an assortment of carpenters' tools which he kept in neat order. He made plows, harrows, wagons, bedsteads, tables, bureaus, &c. He was frank, liberal and conscientious. On my asking him who taught him the use of tools, he replied, no one; then pointing up to the sky, he said, "the Great Spirit taught me."

With all their foibles and vices, there is something fascinating in the Indian character, and one cannot long associate with them without having a perceptible growing attachment. The Indian is emphatically the natural man, and it is an easy thing to make an Indian out of a white person, but very difficult to civilize or christianize an Indian. I have known a number of whites who had been taken prisoners by the Indians when young, and without exception, they formed such attachments that, after being with them some time, they could not be induced to return to their own people. There was a woman among the Shawnees, supposed to be near an hundred years of age, who was taken prisoner, when young, in eastern Pennsylvania. Some years after, her friends, through the agency of traders, endeavored to induce her to return, but in vain. She became, if possible, more of a squaw in her habits and appearance than any female in the nation.

As a sample of their punctuality in performing their contracts, I would state that I have often loaned them money, which was always returned in due season, with a single exception. This was a loan to a young man who promised to pay me when they received their annuity. After the appointed time he shunned me, and the matter remained unsettled until just prior to our departure for their new homes. I then stated the circumstance to one of the chiefs, more from curiosity to see how he would receive the intelligence than with the expectation of its being the means of bringing the money. He, thereupon, talked with the lad upon the subject, but, being unsuccessful, he called a council of his brother chiefs, who formed a circle, with the young man in the centre. After talking to him a while in a low tone, they broke out and vociferously reprimanded him for his dishonest conduct; but all proved unavailing. Finally, the chiefs, in a most generous and noble spirit, made up the amount from their own purses, and pleasantly tendered it to me.

The Indians being firm believers in witchcraft, generally attributed sickness and other misfortunes to this cause, and were in the habit of murdering those whom they suspected of practising it. They have been known to travel all the way from the Mississippi to Wapakonetta, and shoot down a person in his cabin merely on suspicion of his being a wizzard, and return unmolested. When a person became so sick as to lead them to think he was in danger of death, it was usual for them to place him in the woods alone, with no one to attend except a nurse or doctor, who generally acted as an agent in hurrying on their dissolution. It was distressing to see one in this situation. I have been permitted to do this only through the courtesy of relatives, it being contrary to rule for any to visit them except such as had medical care of them. The whole nation are at liberty to attend the funerals, at which there is generally great lamentation. A chief, who died just previous to their removal, was buried in the following manner. They bored holes in the lid of his coffin—as is their custom—over his eyes and mouth, to let the Good Spirit pass in and out. Over the grave they laid presents, &c., with provisions, which they affirmed the Good Spirit would take him in the night. Sure enough!—these articles had all disappeared in the morning, by the hand of an *evil spirit clothed in a human body*. There were many funerals among the Indians, and their numbers rapidly decreased: intemperance, and pulmonary, and scrofulous diseases, made up a large share of their bills of mortality, and the number of deaths to the births were as one to three.

A few anecdotes will illustrate the wit and dishonesty of some, and the tragical encounters of others of the Indians. Col. M'Pherson, the former sub-agent, kept goods for sale, for which they often got in debt. Some were slow in making payments, and one in particular was so tardy that M'Pherson earnestly urged him to pay up. Knowing that he was in the habit of taking hides from the tanners, the Indian inquired if he would take hides for the debt. Being answered in the affirmative, he promised to bring them in about four days. The Indian, knowing that M'Pherson had at this time a flock of cattle ranging in the forest, went in pursuit, shot several, from which he took off the hides, and delivered them punctually according to promise.

While we were encamped, waiting for the Indians to finish their ceremonies prior to emigration, we were much annoyed by an unprincipled band of whites who came to trade, particularly in the article of whiskey, which they secreted from us in the woods. The Indians all knew of this depot, and were continually going, like bees from the hive, day and night, and it was difficult to tell whether some who lead in the worship passed most of the time in that employment or in drinking whiskey. While this state of things lasted, the officers could do nothing satisfactorily with them, nor were they sensible of the consequence of continuing in such a course The government was bound by treaty stipulations to maintain them one year only, which was passing away, and winter was fast approaching, when they could not well travel, and if they could not arrive until spring, they would be unable to raise a crop, and consequently would be out of bread. We finally assembled the chiefs and other influential men, and presenting these facts vividly before them, they became alarmed and promised to reform. We then authorized them to tomahawk every barrel, keg, jug, or bottle of whiskey that they could find, under the promise to pay for all and protect them from harm in so doing. They all agreed to this, and went to work that night to accomplish the task. Having lain down at a late hour to sleep, I was awakened by one who said he had found and brought me a jug of whiskey: I handed him a quarter of a dollar, set the whiskey down, and fell asleep again. The same fellow then came, stole jug and all, and sold the contents that night to the Indians at a shilling a dram—a pretty good speculation on a half gallon of "*whisk*," as the Indians call it. I suspected him of the trick, but he would not confess it until I was about to part with them at the end of the journey, when he came to me and related the circumstances, saying that it was too good a story to keep.

One of our interpreters, who was part Indian and had lived with them a long time, related the following tragical occurrence. A company of Shawnees met some time previous to my coming among them, had a drunken frolic and quarrelled. One vicious fellow who had an old grudge against several of the others, and stabbed two of the company successively until they fell dead, was making for the third, when his arm was arrested by a large athletic Indian, who, snatching the knife from him, plunged it into him until he fell. He attempted to rise and got on his knees, when the other straddled him, seized him by the hair, lifted up his head with one hand, while with the other he drew his knife across his throat, exclaiming—"lie there, my friend! I guess you not eat any more hommony."

After we had rendezvoused, preparatory to moving, we were detained several weeks waiting until they had got over their tedious round of religious ceremonies, some of which were public and others kept private from us. One of their first acts was to take away the fencing from the graves of their fathers, level them to the surrounding surface, and cover them so neatly with green sod, that not a trace of the graves could be seen. Subsequently, a few of the chiefs and others visited their friends at a distance, gave and received presents from chiefs of other nations, at their head quarters.

Among the ceremonies above alluded to was a dance, in which none participated but the warriors. They threw off all their clothing but their britchclouts, painted their faces and naked bodies in a fantastical manner, covering them with the pictures of snakes and disagreeable insects and animals, and then armed with war clubs, commenced dancing, yelling and frightfully distorting their countenances: the scene was truly terrific. This was followed by the dance they usually have on returning from a victorious battle, in which both sexes participated. It was a pleasing contrast to the other, and was performed in the night, in a ring, around a large fire. In this they sang and marched, males and females promiscuously, in single file, around the blaze. The leader of the band commenced singing, while all the rest were silent until he had sung a certain number of words, then the next in the row commenced with the same, and the leader began with a new set, and so on to the end of their chanting. All were singing at once, but no two the same words. I was told that part of the words they used were *hallelujah!* It was pleasing to witness the native modesty and graceful movements of those young females in this dance.

When their ceremonies were over, they informed us they were now ready to leave They then mounted their horses, and such as went in wagons seated themselves, and set out with their "high priest" in front, bearing on his shoulders "the ark of the covenant," which consisted of a large gourd and the bones of a deer's leg tied to its neck. Just previous to starting, the priest gave a blast of his trumpet, then moved slowly and solemnly while the others followed in like manner, until they were ordered to halt in the evening for encampment, when the priest gave another blast as a signal to stop, erect their tents and cook supper. The same course was observed through the whole of the journey. When they arrived near St. Louis, they lost some of their number by cholera. The Shawnees who emigrated numbered about 700 souls, and the Senecas about 350. Among them was also a detachment of Ottawas, who were conducted by Capt. Hollister from the Maumee country.

The principal speaker among the Shawnees at the period of their removal, was *Wiwelipea.* He was an eloquent orator—either grave or gay, humorous or severe, as the occasion required. At times his manner was so fascinating, his countenance so full of varied expression, and his voice so musical, that surveyors and other strangers passing through the country, listened to him with delight, although the words fell upon their ears in an unknown language. He removed out west with his tribe. The chief *Catahecassa*, or *Black Hoof*, died at Wapakonetta, shortly previous to their removal, at the age of 110 years. The sketches annexed of Black Hoof and Blue Jacket, are derived from Drake's Tecumseh.

Among the celebrated chiefs of the Shawanoes, Black Hoof is entitled to a high rank. He was born in Florida, and at the period of the removal of a portion of that tribe to Ohio and Pennsylvania, was old enough to recollect having bathed in the salt water. He was present, with others of his tribe, at the defeat of Braddock, near Pittsburg, in 1755, and was engaged in all the wars in Ohio from that time until the treaty of Greenville, in 1795. Such was the sagacity of Black Hoof in planning his military expeditions, and such the energy with which he executed them, that he won the confidence of his whole nation, and was never at a loss for *braves* to fight under his banner. "He was known far and wide as the great Shawanoe warrior, whose cunning, sagacity, and experience, were only equalled by the fierce and desperate bravery with which he carried into operation his military plans. Like the other Shawanoe chiefs, he was the inveterate foe of the white man, and held that no peace should be made, nor any negociation attempted, except on the condition that the whites should repass the mountains, and leave the great plains of the west to the sole occupancy of the native tribes.

"He was the orator of his tribe during the greater part of his long life, and was an excellent speaker. The venerable Colonel Johnston, of Piqua, to whom we are indebted for much valuable information, describes him as the most graceful Indian he had ever seen, and as possessing the most natural and happy faculty of expressing his ideas. He was well versed in the traditions of his people; no one understood better their peculiar relations to the whites, whose settlements were gradually encroaching on them, or could detail with more minuteness the wrongs with which his nation was afflicted. But although a stern and uncompromising opposition to the whites had marked his policy through a series of forty years, and nerved his arm in a hundred battles, he became at length convinced of the madness of an ineffectual struggle against a vastly superior and hourly increasing foe. No sooner had he satisfied himself of this truth, than he acted upon it with the decision which formed a prominent trait in his character. The temporary success of the Indians in several engagements previous to the campaign of General Wayne, had kept alive their expiring hopes; but their signal defeat by that gallant officer convinced the more reflecting of their leaders of the desperate character of the conflict. Black Hoof was among those who decided upon making terms with the victorious American commander; and having signed the treaty of 1795, at Greenville, he continued faithful to his stipulations during the remainder of his life. From that day, he ceased to be the enemy of the white man; and as he was not one who could act a negative part, he became the firm ally and friend of those against whom his tomahawk had been so long raised in vindictive animosity. He was their friend, not from sympathy or conviction, but in obedience to a necessity which left no middle course, and under a belief that submission alone could save his tribe from destruction; and having adopted this policy, his sagacity and sense of honor, alike forbade a recurrence either to open war or secret hostility. He was the principal chief of the Shawanoe nation, and possessed all the influence and authority which are usually attached to that office, at the period when Tecumseh and his brother the Prophet commenced their hostile operations against the United States."

When Tecumseh and the Prophet embarked in their scheme for the recovery of the lands as far south as the Ohio river, it became their interest as well as policy to enlist Black Hoof in the enterprise; and every effort which the genius of the one, and the cunning of the other, could devise, was brought to bear upon him. But Black Hoof continued faithful to the treaty which he had signed at Greenville, in 1795, and by prudence and influence kept the greater part of his tribe from joining the standard of Tecumseh or engaging on the side of the British in the late war with England. In that contest he became the ally of the United States, and although he took no active part in it, he exerted a very salutary influence over his tribe. In January, 1813, he visited Gen. Tupper's camp, at Fort McArthur, and while there, about ten o'clock one night, when sitting by the fire in company with the General and several other officers, some one fired a pistol through a hole in the wall of the nut, and shot Black Hoof in the face: the ball entered the cheek, glanced against the bone, and finally lodged in his neck: he fell, and for some time was supposed to be dead, but revived, and afterwards recovered from this severe wound. The most prompt and diligent inquiry as to the author of this cruel and dastardly act, failed to lead to his detection. No doubt was entertained that this attempt at assassination was made by a white man, stimulated perhaps by no better excuse than the memory of some actual or ideal wrong, inflicted on some of his own race by an unknown hand of kindred color with that of his intended victim.

Black Hoof was opposed to polygamy, and to the practice of burning prisoners. He is reported to have lived forty years with one wife, and to have reared a numerous family of children, who both loved and esteemed him. His disposition was cheerful, and his conversation sprightly and agreeable. In stature he was small, being not more than five feet eight inches in height. He was favored with good health, and unimpaired eye sight to the period of his death.

Blue Jacket, or Weyapiersenwah.—In the campaign of General Harmar, in the year 1790, Blue Jacket was associated with the Miami chief, Little Turtle, in the command of the Indians. In the battle of the 20th of August, 1794, when the combined army of the Indians was defeated by General Wayne, Blue Jacket had the chief control. The night previous to the battle, while the Indians were posted at Presque Isle, a council was held, composed of chiefs from the Miamis, Potawatimies, Delawares, Shawanoes, Chippewas, Ottawas and Senecas—the seven nations engaged in the action. They decided against the proposition to attack General Wayne that night in his encampment. The expediency of meeting him the next day then came up for consideration. Little Turtle was opposed to this measure, but being warmly supported by Blue Jacket, it was finally agreed upon. The former was strongly inclined to peace, and decidedly opposed to risking a battle under the circumstances in which the Indians were then placed. "We have beaten the enemy," said he, "twice, under separate commanders. We cannot expect the same good fortune always to attend us. The Americans are now led by a chief who never sleeps. The night and the day are alike to him; and, during all the time that he has been marching upon our villages, notwithstanding the watchfulness of our young men, we have never been able to surprise him. Think well of it. There is something whispers me, it would be prudent to listen to his offers of peace." The councils of Blue Jacket, however, prevailed over the better judgment of Little Turtle. The battle was fought and the Indians defeated.

In the month of October following this defeat, Blue Jacket concurred in the expediency of sueing for peace, and at the head of a deputation of chiefs, was about to bear a flag to General Wayne, then at Greenville, when the mission was arrested by foreign influence. Governor Simcoe, Colonel McKee and the Mohawk chief, Captain John Brant, having in charge one hundred and fifty Mohawks and Messasagoes, arrived at the rapids of the Maumee, and invited the chiefs of the combined army to meet them at the mouth of the Detroit river, on the 10th of October. To this Blue Jacket assented, for the purpose of hearing what the British officers had to propose. Governor Simcoe urged the Indians to retain their hostile attitude towards the United States. In referring to the encroachments of the people of this country on the Indian lands, he said, "Children: I am still of the opinion that the Ohio is your right and title. I have given orders to the commandant of Fort Miami to fire on the Americans whenever they make their appearance again. I will go down to Quebec, and lay your grievances before the great man. From thence they will be forwarded to the king your father. Next spring you will know the result of every thing what you and I will do." He urged the Indians to obtain a cessation of hostilities, until the following spring, when the English would be ready to attack the Americans, and by driving them back across the Ohio, restore their lands to the Indians. These councils delayed the conclusion of peace until the following summer. Blue Jacket was present at the treaty of Greenville, in 1795, and conducted himself with moderation and dignity.

Westminster, Lafayette, Allentown, Gallatin, St. Johns and Uniopolis are small places, the largest of which, Westminster, does not contain over 45 dwellings. Fort Amanda, a stockade in the last war, was on a commanding site on the west bank of the Big Anglaise, near the western line of the county, and on the site of an old Ottawa town. It was built by Kentucky troops, and named after some favorite lady of that state.

ASHLAND.

Ashland was formed February 26th, 1846. The surface on the south is hilly, the remainder of the county rolling. The soil of the upland is a sandy loam; of the valleys—which comprise a large part of the county—a rich sandy and gravelly loam, and very productive. The principal crop is wheat, of which probably no portion of the state, of equal extent, produces more. A great quantity of oats, corn, potatoes, &c., is raised, and grass and fruit in abundance. A majority of the population are of Pennsylvania origin. Its present territory originally comprised the townships of Vermillion, Montgomery, Orange, Green and Hanover, with parts of Monroe, Mifflin, Milton and Clear Creek, of Richland county; also the principal part of the townships of Jackson, Perry, Mohecan and Lake, of Wayne county; of Sullivan and Troy, Lorain county; and Ruggles, of Huron county. This tract, in 1840, contained a population of about 20,000, or 50 inhabitants to a square mile.

Public Buildings in Ashland.

Ashland, the county seat, was laid out in 1816, by William Montgomery, and bore, for many years, the name of Uniontown; it was changed to its present name in compliment to Henry Clay, whose seat near Lexington, Ky., bears that name. Daniel Carter, from Butler co., Pa., raised the first cabin in the county, about the year 1811, which stood where the store of Wm. Granger now is, in Ashland. Robert Newell, 3 miles east, and Mr. Fry, 1½ miles north of the village, raised cabins about the same time. In 1817, the first store was opened by Joseph Sheets, in a frame building now kept as a store by the widow Yonker. Joseph Sheets, David Markley, Samuel Ury, Nicholas Shæffer, Alanson Andrews, Elias Slocum and George W. Palmer were among the first settlers of the place. Ashland is a flourishing village, 89 miles NW. of Columbus, and 14 from Mansfield. It contains 5 churches, viz: 2 Presbyterian, 1 Episcopal Methodist, 1 Lutheran, and 1 Disciples, 9 dry goods, 4 grocery, 1 book, and 2 drug stores, 2 newspaper printing offices, a flourishing classical academy, numbering over 100 pupils of both sexes, and a population estimated at 1300. The above view was taken in front of the site selected for the erection of a court house, the Methodist church building—seen on the left—being now used for that purpose: the structures with steeples, commencing on the right, are the 1st Presbyterian church, the academy, and the 2d Presbyterian church.

At the organization of the first court of common pleas for this county, at Ashland, an old gentleman, by the name of David Burns, was one of the grand jurors, who, as a remarkable fact, it is said, was also a member of the first grand jury ever empaneled in Ohio. The court met near the mouth of Wegee creek, in Belmont county, in 1795: the country being sparsely settled, he was compelled to travel forty miles to the place of holding court.

Jeromeville, 8 miles SE. of Ashland, on Lake Fork of Mohiccan, contains 6 stores and about 500 people. In the late war, it was the only settlement within the present limits of the county, and consisted of a few families, who erected pickets for their safety. There was at that time a Frenchman, named Jerome, who resided there and gave name to the locality. He had been an Indian trader, and had taken a squaw for a wife. The people of that nation always became more easily domesticated among the Aborigines than the English. From very early times it was the policy of the French government not to allow their soldiers to take wives with them into the wilderness. Hence the soldiers and traders frequently married among the Indians, and were enabled to sustain themselves with far less difficulty.

The Delaware Indians had a settlement at or near Jeromeville, which they left at the beginning of the war. Their chief was old Captain Pipe, who resided near the road to Mansfield, one mile south of Jeromeville. When young he was a great warrior, and the implacable foe of the whites. He was in St. Clair's defeat, where, according to his own account, he distinguished himself and slaughtered white men until his arm was weary with the work. He had a daughter of great beauty. A young chief, of noble mien, became in love with her, and on his suit being rejected, mortally poisoned himself with the May apple. A Captain Pipe, whose Indian name was *Tauhangecaupouye*, removed to the small Delaware Reserve, in the upper part of Marion county, and when his tribe sold out, about 20 years since, accompanied them to the far west, where he has since died.

Loudonville 18 S., Rowsburg 9 E., Savannah 7 NW., Orange 4 E., and Haysville 8 S. of Ashland, are villages having each from 50 to 60 dwellings. At the last is the Haysville Literary Institute: the building is a substantial brick edifice. Sullivan 14 NE., and Perrysville 18 SW., have each but a few dwellings.

ASHTABULA.

Ashtabula was formed June 7, 1807, from Trumbull and Geauga and organized January 22, 1811. The name of the county was derived from Ashtabula river, which signifies, in the Indian language, *Fish* river. For a few miles parallel with the lake shore it is level, the remainder of the surface slightly undulating, and the soil generally clay. Butter and cheese are the principal articles of export. Generally, not sufficient wheat is raised for home consumption, but the soil is quite productive in corn and oats. The following is a list of its townships, in 1840, with their population.

Andover,	881	Kingsville,	1420	Richmond,	384
Ashtabula,	1711	Lenox,	550	Rome,	765
Austinburg,	1048	Milford,	173	Saybrook,	934
Cherry Valley,	689	Monroe,	1326	Sheffield,	683
Conneaut,	2650	Morgan,	643	Trumbull,	439
Denmark,	176	New Lyme,	527	Wayne,	767
Geneva,	1215	Orwell,	458	Williamsfield,	892
Harpersfield,	1399	Phelps,	530	Windsor,	875
Hartsgrove,	553	Pierpont,	639		
Jefferson,	710	Plymouth,	706		

The population of the county, in 1820, was 7,369; in 1830, 14,584; in 1840, 23,724, or 34 inhabitants to a square mile.

This county is memorable from being not only the first settled on the Western Reserve, but the earliest in the whole of northern Ohio. The incidents connected with its early history, although unmarked by scenes of military adventure, are of an interesting nature. They have been well collected and preserved by the Ashtabula Historical Society. This association, with a praiseworthy industry, have collected nearly a thousand folio pages of manuscript, relating principally to this county. Some of the articles are finely written, and as a whole, give a better idea of the toils, privations, customs and mode of pioneer life than any work that has ever met our notice. From this collection we have extracted nearly all the historical materials embodied under the head of this county.

On the 4th of July, 1796, the first surveying party of the Western Reserve landed at the mouth of Conneaut creek. Of this event, John Barr, Esq., in his sketch of the Western Reserve, in the National Magazine for December, 1845, has given a narration.

The sons of revolutionary sires, some of them sharers of themselves in the great baptism of the republic, they made the anniversary of their country's freedom a day of ceremonial and rejoicing. They felt that they had arrived at the place of their labors, the—to many of them—sites of home, as little alluring, almost as crowded with dangers, as were the levels of Jamestown, or the rocks of Plymouth to the ancestors who had preceded them in the conquest of the seacoast wilderness of this continent. From old homes and friendly and social associations, they were almost as completely exiled as were the cavaliers who debarked upon the shores of Virginia, or the Puritans who sought the strand of Massachusetts. Far away as they were from the villages of their birth and boyhood; before them the trackless forest, or the untraversed lake, yet did they resolve to cast fatigue and privation and peril from their thoughts for the time being, and give to the day its due, to patriotism its awards. Mustering their numbers, they sat them down on the eastward shore of the stream now known as Conneaut, and, dipping from the lake the liquor in which they pledged their country—their goblets some *tin cups* of no rare workmanship, yet every way answerable, with the ordnance accompaniment of two or three fowling pieces discharging the required national salute—the first settlers of the Reserve spent their landing-day as became the sons of the Pilgrim Fathers—as the advance pioneers of a population that has

Conneaut, the Plymouth of the Reserve, in July,* 1796.

since made the then wilderness of northern Ohio to "blossom as the rose," and prove the homes of a people as remarkable for integrity, industry, love of country, moral truth and enlightened legislation, as any to be found within the territorial limits of their ancestral New England.

The whole party numbered, on this occasion, fifty-two persons, of whom two were females, (Mrs. Stiles and Mrs. Gunn, and a child.) As these individuals were the advance of after millions of population, their names become worthy of record, and are therefore given, viz.: Moses Cleveland, agent of the company; Augustus Porter, principal surveyor; Seth Pease, Moses Warren, Amos Spafford, Milton Hawley, Richard M. Stoddard, surveyors; Joshua Stowe, commissary; Theodore Shepard, physician; Joseph Tinker, principal boatman; Joseph McIntyre, George Proudfoot, Francis Gay, Samuel Forbes, Elijah Gunn, wife and child, Amos Sawten, Stephen Benton, Amos Barber, Samuel Hungerford, William B. Hall, Samuel Davenport, Asa Mason, Amzi Atwater, Michael Coffin, Elisha Ayres, Thomas Harris, Norman Wilcox, Timothy Dunham, George Goodwin, Shadrach Benham, Samuel Agnew, Warham Shepard, David Beard, John Briant, Titus V. Munson, Joseph Landon, Job V. Stiles and wife, Charles Parker, Ezekiel Hawley, Nathaniel Doan, Luke Hanchet, James Hasket, James Hamilton, Olney F. Rice, John Lock, and four others whose names are not mentioned.

On the 5th of July, the workmen of the expedition were employed in the erection of a large, awkwardly constructed log building; locating it on the sandy beach on the east shore of the stream, and naming it "Stow Castle," after one of the party. This became the storehouse of the provisions, &c., and the dwelling-place of the families.

The spot where the above described scene took place, has much altered in the lapse of half a century. One of the party, Amzi Atwater, Esq., now living in Portage county, in a communication before us, says:

---

* The view was constructed from a sketch as the place is now, altered to represent its ancient appearance. The word Conneaut, in the Seneca language, signifies "*many fish*," and was applied originally to the river.

It was then a mere sand beach overgrown with timber, some of it of considerable size, which we cut to build the house and for other purposes. The mouth of the creek, like others of the lake streams in those days, was frequently choked up with a sand bar so that no visible harbor appeared for several days. This would only happen when the streams were low and after a high wind either down the lake or directly on shore for several days. I have passed over all the lake streams of this state east of the Cuyahoga and most of those in New York on hard, dry sand bars, and I have been told that the Cuyahoga has been so. They would not long continue, for as soon as the wind had subsided and the water in the streams had sufficiently risen, they would often cut their way through the bar in a different place and form new channels. Thus the mouths of the streams were continually shifting until the artificial harbors were built. Those blessed improvements have in a great measure remedied those evils and made the mouths of the streams far more healthy.

Judge James Kingsbury, who arrived at Conneaut shortly after the surveying party, wintered with his family at this place in a cabin which stood on a spot now covered by the waters of the lake. This was about the first family that wintered on the Reserve.

The story of the sufferings of this family has often been told, but in the midst of plenty, where want is unknown, can with difficulty be appreciated. The surveyors, in the prosecution of their labors westwardly, had principally removed their stores to Cleveland, while the family of Judge Kingsbury remained at Conneaut. Being compelled by business to leave in the fall for the state of New York, with the hope of a speedy return to his family, the Judge was attacked by a severe fit of sickness confining him to his bed until the setting in of winter. As soon as able he proceeded on his return as far as Buffalo, where he hired an Indian to guide him through the wilderness. At Presque Isle, anticipating the wants of his family, he purchased twenty pounds of flour. In crossing Elk Creek on the ice, he disabled his horse, left him in the snow, and mounting his flour on his own back, pursued his way filled with gloomy forebodings in relation to the fate of his family. On his arrival late one evening, his worst apprehensions were more than realized in a scene agonizing to the husband and father. Stretched on her cot lay the partner of his cares, who had followed him through all the dangers and hardships of the wilderness without repining, pale and emaciated, reduced by meagre famine to the last stages in which life can be supported, and near the mother, on a little pallet, were the remains of his youngest child, born in his absence, who had just expired for the want of that nourishment which the mother, deprived of sustenance, was unable to give. Shut up by a gloomy wilderness, she was far distant alike from the aid or sympathy of friends, filled with anxiety for an absent husband, suffering with want and destitute of necessary assistance, and her children expiring around her with hunger.

Such is the picture presented, by which the wives and daughters of the present day may form some estimate of the hardships endured by the pioneers of this beautiful country. It appears that Judge Kingsbury, in order to supply the wants of his family, was under the necessity of transporting his provisions from Cleveland on a hand sled, and that himself and hired man drew a barrel of beef the whole distance at a single load.

Mr. Kingsbury has since held several important judicial and legislative trusts, and is yet living in Newberg, about four miles distant from Cleveland. He was the first who thrust a sickle into the first wheat field planted on the soil of the Reserve. His wife was interred at Cleveland, about the year 1843. The fate of her child—the first white child born on the Reserve, starved to death for want of nourishment—will not soon be forgotten.

The harbor of Conneaut is now an important point of transhipment. It has a pier, with a lighthouse upon it, 2 forwarding houses, and 11 dwellings. Several vessels ply from here, and it is a frequent stopping place for steamers. Two miles south of the harbor, 22 from Jefferson, 28 from Erie, Pa., is the borough of Conneaut, ... on the west bank of Conneaut creek. It contains 1 Baptist, 1 Presbyterian, 1 Methodist, and 1 Christian church, 11 mercantile stores, 1 newspaper printing office, a fine classical academy, Mr. L. W. Savage and Miss Mary Booth, Principals, and about 1000 inhabitants. East and West Conneaut and South Ridge are small places in this, the township of Conneaut, which once bore the name of Salem.

The first permanent settlement in Conneaut was in 1799. Thomas Montgomery and Aron Wright settled here in the spring of 1798. Robert Montgomery and family, Levi and John Montgomery, Nathan and John King, and Samuel Bemus and family came the same season.

When the settlers arrived, some twenty or thirty Indian cabins were still standing, which were said to present an appearance of neatness and comfort not usual with this race. The Massauga tribe, which inhabited the spot, were obliged to leave in consequence of the murder of a white man named Williams.

Two young men taken at the defeat of St. Clair, were said to have been prisoners for a considerable time among the Indians of this village. On their arrival at Conneaut they were made to run the gauntlet, and received the orthodox number of blows and kicks usual on such occasions. In solemn council it was resolved that the life of Fitz Gibbon should be saved, but the other, whose name is not recollected, was condemned to be burned. He was bound to a tree, a large quantity of hickory barks tied into faggots and piled around him. But from the horrors of the most painful of deaths he was saved by the interposition of a young squaw belonging to the tribe. Touched by sympathy she interceded in his behalf, and by her expostulations, backed by several packages of fur and a small sum of money, succeeded in effecting his deliverance: an act in the lowly Indian maid which entitles her name to be honorably recorded with that of Pocahontas, among the good and virtuous of every age.

There were mounds situated in the eastern part of the village of Conneaut and an extensive burying ground near the Presbyterian church, which appear to have had no connection with the burying places of the Indians. Among the human bones found in the mounds were some belonging to men of gigantic structure. Some of the skulls* were of sufficient capacity to admit the head of an ordinary man, and jaw bones that might have been fitted on over the face with equal facility: the other bones were proportionably large. The burying ground referred to contained about four acres, and with the exception of a slight angle in conformity with the natural contour of the ground, was in the form of an oblong square. It appeared to have been accurately surveyed into lots running from north to south, and exhibited all the order and propriety of arrangement deemed necessary to constitute Christian burial. On the first examination of the ground by the settlers, they found it covered with the ordinary forest trees, with an opening near the centre containing a single butternut. The graves were distinguished by slight depressions disposed in straight rows, and were estimated to number from two to three thousand. On examination in 1800, they were found to contain human bones, invariably blackened by time, which on exposure to the air, soon crumbled to dust. Traces of ancient cultivation observed by the first settlers on the lands of the vicinity, although covered with forest, exhibited signs of having once been thrown up into squares and terraces, and laid out into gardens.

There is a fragment or chip of a tree in the possession of the Historical Society, which is a curiosity. The tree of which that was a chip, was chopped down and butted off for a saw log, about three feet from the ground, some thirty rods SE. of Fort Hill, in Conneaut, in 1829, by Silas A. Davis, on land owned by B. H. King. Some marks were found upon it near the heart of the tree. The Hon. Nehemiah King, with a magnifying glass, counted 350 annualer rings in that part of the stump, outside of these marks. Deducting

---

* In the spring of 1815, a mound on Harbor street, Conneaut, was cut through for a road. One morning succeeding a heavy rain, a Mr. Walker, who was up very early, picked up a jaw bone together with an artificial tooth which lay near. He brought them forthwith to Mr. P. R. Spencer, at present the Secretary of the Ashtabula Historical Society, who fitted the tooth in a cavity from which it had evidently fallen. The tooth was metallic, probably silver, but little was then thought of the circumstance.

350 from 1829, leaves 1479, which must have been the year when these cuts were made. This was 13 years before the discovery of America, by Columbus. It perhaps was done by the race of the mounds, with an axe of copper, as that people had the art of hardening that metal so as to cut like steel.

The adventure of Mr. Salmon Sweatland, of Conneaut, who crossed Lake Erie in an open canoe, in September, 1817, is one of unusual interest. He had been accustomed, with the aid of a neighbor, Mr. Cozzens, and a few hounds, to drive the deer into the lake, where, pursuing them in a canoe, he shot them with but little difficulty. The circumstances which took place at this time, are vividly given in the annexed extract from the records of the Historical Society.

It was a lovely morning in early autumn, and Sweatland, in anticipation of his favorite sport, had risen at the first dawn of light, and without putting on his coat or waistcoat left his cabin, listening in the mean time in expectation of the approach of the dogs. His patience was not put to a severe trial ere his ears were saluted by the deep baying of the hounds, and on arriving at the beach he perceived that the deer had already taken to the lake, and was moving at some distance from the shore. In the enthusiasm of the moment he threw his hat upon the beach, his canoe was put in requisition, and shoving from the shore he was soon engaged in a rapid and animated pursuit. The wind, which had been fresh from the south during the night and gradually increasing, was now blowing nearly a gale, but intent on securing his prize, Sweatland was not in a situation to yield to the dictates of prudence. The deer, which was a vigorous animal of its kind, hoisted its flag of defiance, and breasting the waves stoutly showed that in a race with a log canoe and a single paddle, he was not easily outdone.

Sweatland had attained a considerable distance from the shore and encountered a heavy sea before overtaking the animal, but was not apprized of the eminent peril of his situation until shooting past him the deer turned towards the shore. He was however brought to a full appreciation of his danger when, on tacking his frail vessel and heading towards the land, he found that with his utmost exertions he could make no progress in the desired direction, but was continually drifting farther to sea. He had been observed in his outward progress by Mr. Cousins, who had arrived immediately after the hounds, and by his own family, and as he disappeared from sight, considerable apprehensions were entertained for his safety.

The alarm was soon given in the neighborhood, and it was decided by those competent to judge that his return would be impossible, and that unless help could be afforded he was doomed to perish at sea. Actuated by those generous impulses that often induce men to peril their own lives to preserve those of others, Messrs. Gilbert, Cousins and Belden took a light boat at the mouth of the creek and proceeded in search of the wanderer, with the determination to make every effort for his relief. They met the deer returning towards the shore nearly exhausted, but the man who was the object of their solicitude was no where to be seen. They made stretches off shore within probable range of the fugitive for some hours, until they had gained a distance of five or six miles from land, when meeting with a sea, in which they judged it impossible for a canoe to live, they abandoned the search, returned with difficulty to the shore, and Sweatland was given up for lost.

The canoe in which he was embarked was dug from a large whitewood log, by Major James Brookes, for a fishing boat: it was about fourteen feet in length and rather wide in proportion, and was considered a superior one of the kind. Sweatland still continued to lie off, still heading towards the land, with the faint hope that the wind might abate, or that aid might reach him from the shore. One or two schooners were in sight in course of the day, and he made every signal in his power to attract their attention, but without success. The shore continued in sight, and in tracing its distant outline he could distinguish the spot where his cabin stood, within whose holy precincts were contained the cherished objects of his affections, now doubly endeared from the prospect of losing them forever. As these familiar objects receded from view, and the shores appeared to sink beneath the troubled waters, the last tie which united him in companionship to his fellow-men seemed dissolved, and the busy world, with all its interests, forever hidden from his sight.

Fortunately Sweatland possessed a cool head and a stout heart, which, united with a tolerable share of physical strength and power of endurance, eminently qualified him for the part he was to act in this emergency. He was a good sailor, and as such would not yield to despondency until the last expedient had been exhausted. One only expedient remained, that of putting before the wind and endeavoring to reach the Canada shore, a distance of about fifty miles. This he resolved to embrace as his forlorn hope.

It was now blowing a gale, and the sea was evidently increasing as he proceeded from the shore, and yet he was borne onwards over the dizzy waters by a power that no human agency could control. He was obliged to stand erect, moving cautiously from one extremity to the other, in order to trim his vessel to the waves, well aware that a single lost stroke of the paddle, or a tottering movement, would swamp his frail bark and bring his adventure to a final close. Much of his attention was likewise required in bailing his canoe from the water, an operation which he was obliged to perform by making use of his *shoes*, a substantial pair of *stoggies*, that happened fortunately to be upon his feet.

Hitherto he had been blessed with the cheerful light of heaven, and amidst all his perils could say, "The light is sweet, and it is a pleasant thing for the eyes to behold the sun," but to add to his distress, the shades of night were now gathering around him, and he was soon enveloped in darkness. The sky was overcast, and the light of a few stars that twinkled through the haze alone remained to guide his path over the dark and troubled waters. In this fearful condition, destitute of food and the necessary clothing, his log canoe was rocked upon the billows during that long and terrible night. When morning appeared he was in sight of land, and found he had made Long Point, on the Canada shore. Here he was met by an adverse wind and a cross sea, but the same providential aid which had guided him thus far still sustained and protected him; and after being buffeted by the winds and waves for nearly thirty hours, he succeeded in reaching the land in safety.

What were the emotions he experienced on treading once more "the green and solid earth," we shall not attempt to inquire, but his trials were not yet ended. He found himself faint with hunger and exhausted with fatigue, at the distance of forty miles from any human habitation, whilst the country that intervened was a desert filled with marshes and tangled thickets, from which nothing could be obtained to supply his wants. These difficulties, together with the reduced state of his strength, rendered his progress towards the settlements slow and toilsome. On his way he found a quantity of goods, supposed to have been driven on shore from the wreck of some vessel, which, although they afforded him no immediate relief, were afterwards of material service.

He ultimately arrived at the settlement, and was received and treated with great kindness and hospitality by the people. After his strength was sufficiently recruited, he returned with a boat, accompanied by some of the inhabitants, and brought off the goods. From this place he proceeded by land to Buffalo, where, with the avails of his treasure, he furnished himself in the garb of a gentleman, and finding the *Traveler*, Capt. Chas. Brown, from Conneaut, in the harbor, he shipped on board and was soon on his way to rejoin his family. When the packet arrived off his dwelling, they fired guns from the deck and the crew gave three loud cheers. On landing, he found his funeral sermon had been preached, and had the rare privilege of seeing his own *widow* clothed in the habiliments of mourning.

The first regular settlement made within the present limits of the county was at Harpersfield, on the 7th of March, 1798. Alexander Harper, Wm. M'Farland and Ezra Gregory, with their families, started from Harpersfield, Delaware county, New York, and after a long and fatiguing journey arrived on the last of June, at their new homes in the wilderness. This little colony of about twenty persons, endured much privation in the first few months of their residence. The whole population of the Reserve amounted to less than 150 souls, viz: ten families at Youngstown, three at Cleveland, and two at Mentor. In the same summer three families came to Burton, and Judge Hudson settled at Hudson.

Cut short of their expected supplies of provision for the winter, by the loss of a vessel they had chartered for that purpose, the little colony came near perishing by famine, having at one time been reduced to *six kernels* of parched corn to each person; but they were saved by the intrepidity of the sons of Col. Harper, James and William. These young men made frequent journies to Elk Creek, Pa., from which they packed on their backs bags of corn, which was about all the provision the settlers had to sustain life during a long and tedious winter. Some few of their journies were performed on the ice of Lake Erie, whenever it was sufficiently strong to bear them, which was seldom. On the first occasion of this kind they were progressing finely on the ice, when their sled broke through into the water. A third person who happened to be with them at this time exclaimed, "What shall we do?" "Let it go," James replied. "No!" exclaimed William, who was of a different temperament, "you go into the woods and strike a fire while I get the grain." He then with great difficulty secured the grain, by which operation he got completely wet through, and a cutting wind soon converted his clothing into a sheet of ice. He then went in search of his companions and was disappointed in finding they had not built a fire. The truth was, they had grown so sleeply with the intense cold as to be unable to strike fire. He soon had a cheerful blaze, and then converted himself into a nurse for the other two, who on getting warm were deadly sick. . . . . . .

County Buildings at Jefferson.

Jefferson, the county seat, is 56 miles from Cleveland and 204 NE. of Columbus. It is an incorporated borough, laid out regularly on a level plat of ground, and contains 3 stores, 1 Pres., 1 Bap., 1 Episcopal, and 1 Methodist Church, and 73 dwellings. The township of the same name in which it is situated, was originally owned by Gideon Granger of Conn. In the spring of 1804 he sent out Mr. Eldad Smith from Suffield in that state, who first opened a bridle path to Austinburg, and sowed and fenced ten acres of wheat. In the summer of the next year, Michael Webster, Jr., and family, and Jonathan Warner, made a permanent settlement. In the fall following, the family of James Wilson built a cabin on the site of the tavern shown in the view. The court house was finished in 1810 or '11, and the first court held in 1811; Timothy R. Hawley, Clerk, Quintus F. Atkins, Sheriff.

Ashtabula is on Ashtabula river, on the Buffalo and Cleveland road, 8 miles from Jefferson. It is a pleasant village, adorned with neat dwellings and shrubbery. The borough contains 1 Presbyterian, 1 Episcopal, 1 Methodist, and 1 Baptist church, 10 mercantile stores, and a population estimated at 1200.

The harbor of Ashtabula is 2½ miles from the village at the mouth of the river. It has several forwarding establishments, 20 or 30 houses, the lake steamers stop there, and considerable business is carried on; about a dozen vessels are owned at this port. The commercial business of this and Lake county has been much injured by the internal improvement system of the state, which has diverted the back country trade into other channels. When the Erie canal

North Public Square, Ashtabula.

was finished, Northern Ohio felt its invigorating effects, for from the depression of the times after the late war, until the opening of that canal and the commencement of steam navigation on the lake, business languished and made but little progress. The invigorating effects of that work prompted a spirit in Ohio for similar enterprises. The representatives of this vicinity in the legislature drank deeply of the general enthusiasm, although aware that in any event their constituents would receive but a general benefit.

The prosperity of Ashtabula received a severe shock in the loss of the steamer Washington, destroyed by fire on Lake Erie, off Silver Creek, in June, 1838, by which misfortune about 40 lives were lost. This boat was built at Ashtabula harbor, and most of her stock was owned by persons of moderate circumstances in this place. She was commanded by Capt. N. W. Brown. A passenger who was on board published, a few days after, the following account of this disastrous event.

The W. left Cleveland on her passage down from Detroit, June 14th, at 8 A. M., proceeded on her way until Saturday 2 o'clock, A. M., when she arrived in the vicinity of Silver Creek, about 33 miles from Buffalo. The boat was discovered to be on fire, which proceeded from beneath the boilers. The passengers were alarmed, and aroused from their slumbers; such a scene of confusion and distress ensued as those only of my readers can imagine who have been in similar circumstances. Despair did not however completely possess the mass, until it became evident that the progress of the flames could not be arrested. From that moment the scene beggars all description. Suffice it to say, that numbers precipitated themselves from the burning mass into the water; some of them with a shriek of despair, and others silently sunk beneath the waves; others momentarily more fortunate swam a short distance and drowned; others still, on pieces of boards and wood, arrived on the beach; yet some even of them, sank into a watery grave. The small boat had by this time put off loaded with about 25 souls for the shore. Those arrived safe, picking up one or two by the way.

The writer of this article was one of the number. Other small boats came to our assistance, which, together with the Washington's boat, saved perhaps a majority of the passengers on board. There is reason to believe that as many as 40 perished. It is impossible to compute the precise number. Many remained on the boat till it was wrapped in one sheet of flame. Of those there is reason to believe that numbers perished in the conflagration; while others, half burned, precipitated themselves into the watery element, thus suffering the double agency of death by fire and water. Most of the crew were saved, the Captain among the number, who, during the awful calamity, acted with the utmost decision and intrepidity. Indeed, no blame, so far as the writer has been informed, has been attached to any officer or hand on the boat. The utmost exertion was used to move her on the shore, until it became necessary to stop the engine in order to let down the small boat, which having been done, the fire had progressed so far as to render it impossible to again start the machinery. I give a few particulars of the losses of the passengers. Mr. Shudds is the only survivor of his family of seven. A lady passenger lost three children, a sister and mother. Mr. Michael Parker lost his wife and parents, sister and her child. But I will not further continue the cases of individual bereavement.

Kingsville, 14 miles NE. of Jefferson, contains 1 Baptist, 1 Presbyterian, and 1 Methodist church; 3 stores, a woolen factory, and about 400 people. It is a pleasant village and has a public square on which stand the churches. It is surrounded by a fine and intelligent agricultural community. At this place is the Kingsville Academy, a thriving institution, in good repute, with about 130 pupils, under the charge of Mr. Z. Graves, and supported by the public spirit of the vicinity. The water privileges are good at Kingsville: Conneaut creek runs near the village, on which are several mills and factories, and a branch runs through it, on which, within half a mile, are 5 improved water privileges.

Six miles westerly from Jefferson is Austinburg, a village similar in character to the above. It contains 1 Presbyterian, 1 Congregational, and 1 Free Will Baptist church, and about 300 people. West of the town, on a commanding site, is the Grand River Institute, Rev. Thomas Tenney, Principal. The buildings are spacious and comfortable and the institution flourishing, having a large fund for its support and about 150 pupils of both sexes.

The original proprietors of this township were Wm. Battell, of Torringford, Solomon Rockwell & Co., of Winchester, and Eliphalet Austin, of New Hartford, Ct. By the instrumentality of Judge Austin, from whom the town was named, two families moved to this place from Connecticut in 1799. The Judge preceded them a short time driving, in company with a hired man, some cattle 150 miles through the woods on an Indian trail, while the rest came in a boat across the lake. There was at this time a few families at Harpersfield; at Windsor, southwest, about 20 miles, a family or two; also at Elk creek, 40 miles northeast, and at Vernon, 40 miles southeast, were several families, all of whom were in a destitute condition for provisions. In the year 1800, another family moved from Norfolk, Conn. In the spring of 1801, there was an accession of ten families to the settlement, principally from Norfolk, Conn. Part of these came from Buffalo by water, and part by land through the wilderness. During that season wheat was carried to mill at Elk creek, a distance of 40 miles, and in some instances one half was given for carrying it to mill and returning it in flour.

On Wednesday, October 24th, 1801, a church was constituted at Austinburg with sixteen members. This was the first church on the Western Reserve, and was founded by the Rev. Joseph Badger, the first missionary on the Reserve, a sketch of whom is in another part of this volume. It is a fact worthy of note, that in 1802, Mr.

Badger moved his family from Buffalo to this town, in the first wagon that ever came from that place to the Reserve. In 1803, Austinburg, Morgan and Harpersfield experienced a revival of religion by which about 35 from those places united with the church at Austinburg. This revival was attended with the phenomena of "*bodily exercises*," then common in the west. They have been classified by a clerical writer as 1st, the *Falling* exercise; 2d, the *Jerking* exercise; 3d, the *Rolling* exercise; 4th, the *Running* exercise; 5th, the *Dancing* exercise; 6th, the *Barking* exercise; 7th, *Visions* and *Trances*. We make room for an extract from his account of the 2d of the series, which sufficiently characterises the remainder.

It was familiarly called The Jerks, and the first recorded instance of its occurrence was at a sacrament in East Tennessee, when several hundred of both sexes were seized with this strange and involuntary contortion. The subject was instantaneously seized with spasms or convulsions in every muscle, nerve and tendon. His head was thrown or jerked from side to side with such rapidity that it was impossible to distinguish his visage, and the most lively fears were awakened lest he should dislocate his neck or dash out his brains. His body partook of the same impulse and was hurried on by like jerks over every obstacle, fallen trunks of trees, or in a church, over pews and benches, apparently to the most imminent danger of being bruised and mangled. It was useless to attempt to hold or restrain him, and the paroxysm was permitted gradually to exhaust itself. An additional motive for leaving him to himself was the superstitious notion that all attempt at restraint was resisting the spirit of God.

The first form in which these spasmodic contortions made their appearance was that of a simple jerking of the arms from the elbows downwards. The jerk was very quick and sudden, and followed with short intervals. This was the simplest and most common form, but the convulsive motion was not confined to the arms; it extended in many instances to other parts of the body. When the joint of the neck was affected, the head was thrown backward and forward with a celerity frightful to behold, and which was impossible to be imitated by persons who were not under the same stimulus. The bosom heaved, the countenance was disgustingly distorted, and the spectators were alarmed lest the neck should be broken. When the hair was long, it was shaken with such quickness, backward and forward, as to crack and snap like the lash of a whip. Sometimes the muscles of the back were affected, and the patient was thrown down on the ground, when his contortions for some time resembled those of a live fish cast from its native element on the land.

The most graphic description we have is from one who was not only an eye witness, but an apologist. He says, "Nothing in nature could better represent this strange and unaccountable operation, than for one to goad another, alternately on every side, with a piece of red hot iron. The exercise commonly began in the head, which would fly backward and forward, and from side to side, with a quick jolt, which the person would naturally labor to suppress, but in vain; and the more any one labored to stay himself and be sober, the more he staggered, and the more his twitches increased. He must necessarily go as he was inclined, whether with a violent dash on the ground, and bounce from place to place like a foot-ball, or hop round, with head, limbs and trunk twitching, and jolting in every direction, as if they must inevitably fly asunder. And how such could escape without injury, was no small wonder among spectators. By this strange operation the human frame was commonly so transformed and disfigured, as to lose every trace of its natural appearance. Sometimes the head would be twitched right and left, to a half round, with such velocity, that not a feature could be discovered, but the face appeared as much behind as before; and in the quick progressive jerk, it would seem as if the person was transmuted into some other species of creature. Head dresses were of little account among the female jerkers. Even handkerchiefs bound tight round the head would be flirted off almost with the first twitch, and the hair put into the utmost confusion; this was a very great inconvenience, to redress which the generality were shorn, though directly contrary to their confession of faith. Such as were seized with the jerks, were wrested at once, not only from under their own government, but that of every one else, so that it was dangerous to attempt confining them or touching them in any manner, to whatever danger they were exposed, yet few were hurt, except it were such as rebelled against the operation, through wilful and deliberate enmity, and refused to comply with the injunctions which it came to enforce."

From the universal testimony of those who have described these spasms, they appear to have been wholly involuntary. This remark is applicable also to all the other bodily exercises. What demonstrates satisfactorily their involuntary nature is, not only that, as above stated, the twitches prevailed in spite of resistance, and even more for attempts to suppress them; but that wicked men would be seized with them while sedulously guarding against an attack, and cursing every jerk when made. Travellers on their journey, and laborers at their daily work, were also liable to them.

We conclude our sketch of the county with some amusing incidents, related in the MSS. of the Society; although trivial in themselves, they are important in illustration.

There is a stream in Geneva, called "*Morse's Slough*," and it took its cognomen in this wise. For a time after the Spencers, Austin, Hale, and Morse commenced operations on the lake shore, in the NE. corner of Geneva, they plied their labors there only a week at the time, or as long as a back load of provisions, that each carried, might happen to last. Whatever time of the week they went out, those having families returned on Saturday night to the settlements, and those without, returned whenever out of provisions. The main portion of provisions by them thus transported, consisted of Indian or corn bread: and whoever has been used to the labors of the woods, swinging the axe, for instance, from sun to sun, and limited to that kind of diet almost solely, will know that it requires a johnny-cake of no slight dimensions and weight to last an axeman a *whole week*. It must, in short, be a mammoth of its species! Such a loaf, baked in a huge Dutch oven, was snugly and firmly pinioned to the back of James M. Morse, as he, with others, wended his way to the lake shore, intent upon the labors of the week.

The stream was then nameless, but nevertheless had to be crossed, and Morse must cross it to reach the scene of his labors. Although a light man, he had become ponderous by the addition of this tremendous johnny-cake. The ice lay upon the streams, and men passed and re-passed unloaded without harm. Not so those borne down with such incumbrance as distinguished the back of Morse, who was foremost among the gang of pioneers, all marching in Indian file and similarly encumbered. They came to the stream. Morse rushed upon the ice—it trembled—cracked—*broke*—and in a moment he was initiated into the mysteries beneath, with the johnny-cake holding him firmly to the bottom.

The water and mud, though deep, were not over his head. The company, by aid of poles, approached him, removed the Gloucester hump of deformity from his shoulders, relieved him from his uncouth and unenvied attitude, and while he stood dripping and quivering on the margin of the turbid element—amid a shout of laughter they named this stream "*Morse's Slough*."

A young man by the name of Elijah Thompson, of Geneva, was out hunting in the forest with his favorite dog. While thus engaged, his dog left him as if he scented game, and soon was engaged with a pack of seven wolves. Young Thompson, more anxious for the dog than his own safety, rushed to the rescue, firing his rifle as he approached, and then clubbing it, made a fierce onset upon the enemy. His dog, being badly wounded and nearly exhausted, could give him no assistance, and the contest seemed doubtful. The wolves fought with desperation; but the young man laid about him with so much energy and agility, that his blows told well, and he soon had the satisfaction of seeing wolf after wolf skulk away under the blows which he dealt them, until he remained master of the field, when, with the remains of his rifle—the barrel—on his shoulder, and his bleeding and helpless dog under his arm, he left the scene panting and weary, though not materially injured in the conflict.

Mrs. John Austin, of the same township, hearing, on one occasion, a bear among her hogs, determined to defeat his purpose. First hurrying her little children up a ladder into her chamber, for safety, in case she was overcome by the animal, she seized a rifle, and rushing to the spot saw the bear only a few rods distant, carrying off a hog into the woods, while the prisoner sent forth deafening squeals, accompanied by the rest of the sty in full chorus. Nothing daunted, she rushed forward to the scene with her rifle ready cocked, on which the monster let go his prize, raised himself upon his haunches and faced her. Dropping upon her knees to obtain a steady aim, and resting her rifle on the fence, within six feet of the bear, the intrepid female pulled the trigger. Perhaps fortunately *for her*, the rifle missed fire. Again and again she snapped her piece, but with the same result. The bear, after keeping his position some time, dropped down on all fours, and leaving the hogs behind, retreated to the forest and resigned the field to the woman.

The early settlers experienced great difficulty in preserving their swine from the ravages of wild beasts. Messrs. Morgan and Murrain, who, with their wives, dwelt in the same cabin, had with difficulty procured a sow which, with her progeny, occupied a strong pen contiguous to the dwelling. During a dark night, their husbands being necessarily absent, the repose of the ladies was disturbed by a very shrill serenade from the pen: arousing from their slumbers, they discovered a large bear making an assault upon the swine. They attempted, by loud screams and throwing fire brands, to terrify the animal; but not succeeding, they took an unloaded rifle, and having heard their husbands say that it required just two fingers of powder, they poured liberally into the muzzle, one of them in the meanwhile measuring lengthwise of her fingers, until the full amount was obtained, then driving in a ball they sallied out to the attack. One lady held the light, while the other fired the gun. Such another report, from a tube of equal capacity, is seldom heard. The ladies both fell prostrate and insensible, and the gun flew into the bushes. The bear was doubtless alarmed, but not materially injured.

On the night of the 11th of August, 1812, the people of Conneaut were alarmed by a false report that the British were landing from some of their vessels. A sentinel, placed on the shore, descrying boats approaching, mistook them for the enemy. In his panic he threw away his musket, mounted his horse, and dashing through the settlement, cried with a stentorian voice, "turn out! *turn out!* save your lives, the British and Indians are landing, and will be on you in fifteen minutes!" The people, aroused from their beds, fled in the utmost terror to various places of covert in the forest. Those of East Conneaut had sheltered themselves in a dense grove, which being near the high road, it was deemed that the most perfect silence should be maintained. By that soothing attention mothers know how to bestow, the cries of the children were measurably stilled; but one little dog, from among his companions, kept up a continual unmitigated yelping. Various means having in vain been employed to still him, until the patience of the ladies was exhausted, it was unanimously resolved, that that *particular* dog should *die*, and he was therefore sentenced to be hanged, without benefit of clergy. With the *elastics* supplied by the ladies, for a halter, and a young sapling for a gallows, the young dog passed from the shores of time to yelp no more.

Rock Creek, 8 miles s. of Jefferson, contains 2 churches, 2 stores, 1 saw, 1 grist, 1 oil mill, 2 tanneries, and about 60 dwellings. It is on a creek of the same name, which furnishes considerable water. Eagleville is a somewhat smaller manufacturing village, 4 miles sw. of Jefferson, on Mill creek, a good mill stream. Windsor, 20 miles sw. of Jefferson, contains about 40 dwellings. There are other small villages in the county, generally bearing the names of the townships in which they are situated.

ATHENS.

Athens was formed from Washington, March 1, 1805, and derived its name from Athens, its seat of justice. The surface is broken and hilly, with intervals of rich bottom lands. The hilly lands are covered with a fertile soil, and a heavy growth of trees. The principal crops are wheat, corn, oats and tobacco. Excellent coal abounds, iron ore is found in many places, and quantities of salt are made. The Hocking canal commences at Carrol, on the Ohio canal, in Fairfield county, and follows the river valley to Athens, a distance of 56 miles. The business, now small, is rapidly increasing. The coal trade of this valley is destined to be very great, ere many years. Below are the names of its townships, in 1840, with their population at that time.

Alexander,	1450	Carthage,	737	Trimble,	762
Ames,	1431	Dover,	1297	Troy,	1056
Athens,	1593	Elk,	1261	Vinton,	227
Bern,	381	Lee,	848	Ward,	345
Brown,	257	Lodi,	754	Waterloo,	741
Canaan,	800	Rome,	866	York,	1601

Population of Athens county, in 1820, was 6,342; in 1830, 9,778, and in 1840, 19,108, or 30 inhabitants to a square mile.

In Evan's map of the middle British colonies, published in 1755, there is placed on the left bank of the Hocking, somewhere in this region, a town, station or fort, named "*French Margarets.*" Probably Margarets creek, in this county, was named from it. In the county above, (Hocking,) have been found the remains of an old press, for packing furs and peltries, which are yet visible, and attest that French cupidity and enterprise had introduced an extensive trade among the Indians.

Lord Dunmore, in his famous expedition against the Indian towns upon the Scioto, in the autumn of 1774—just prior to the commencement of the revolutionary war, descended the Ohio, and landed at the mouth of the Great Hockhocking, in this county. He was there during the bloody battle of Point Pleasant—on an air line 28 miles distant—between General Lewis and the Indians. At this place he established a depot and erected some defences, called Fort Gower, in honor of Earl Gower. From that point he marched up the valley of the river, encamping, tradition says, a night successively at Federal creek, Sunday creek, and at the falls of the Hocking. From the last, he proceeded to the Scioto, where the detachment under General Lewis joined him, and the war was brought to a close by a treaty or truce with the hostile tribes. Dunmore, on his return, stopped at Fort Gower, where the officers passed a series of resolutions, for which, see Pickaway county, with other details of this expedition.

Colonel Robert Paterson, one of the original proprietors of Cincinnati, with a party of Kentuckians, was attacked, near the mouth of the Hocking, by the Indians, two years after the erection of Fort Gower. The circumstances are given under the head of Montgomery county.

Athens, the county seat, is situated on a commanding site on the Hockhocking river, 72 miles SE. of Columbus. It contains 1 Presbyterian, 1 Cumberland Presbyterian, and a Methodist church, a classical academy, 11 mercantile stores, and by the census of 1840, had 710 inhabitants. It was made the county seat in March, 1805. The Ohio University, the oldest college in Ohio, is situated here, but has temporarily suspended its operations, for the purpose of recovering from pecuniary embarrassment. It was first chartered by the territorial government, and afterwards, in 1804, by the state legislature. It was early endowed by Congress with the two townships of Athens and Alexander, containing 46,000 acres of land, which, with the connecting resources, yield an annual income of about $5000. The buildings are substantial and neat, and stand in a pleasant green. This institution has exerted a most beneficial influence upon the morals and intelligence of this region. Among its graduates are many who do it honor, and it will, doubtless, when

Ohio University, at Athens.

again in successful operation—as it soon will be—continue its good work.

This county was settled shortly after Wayne's victory. The following named persons are recollected as settling in Athens and vicinity, two or three years subsequent to that event, viz: Solomon Tuttle, Christopher Stevens, Jonathan Watkins, Alvan and Silas Bingham, Henry and David Bartlett, John Chandler, and John and Moses Hewit. On Federal creek, also, were Nathan Woodbury, George Ewing—father of Hon. Thomas Ewing—Ephraim Cutler and Benjamin Brown. The first mill was erected about 1800, on Margarets creek, prior to which some of the settlers were accustomed to make tedious voyages, in canoes, down the Hocking, up the Ohio, and 4 miles up the Muskingum, above Marietta, to get their corn ground, while others, comprising a majority, depended upon hand mills and hommony blocks.

The annexed vivid sketch of the captivity and escape of Moses Hewit (one of the earliest settlers in this county) from the Indians, is from the history of the Bellville settlement, written by Dr. S. P. Hildreth, and published in the Hesperian, edited by William D. Gallagher.

Moses Hewit was a native of New England, the land of active and enterprising men, and born in Worcester, Massachusetts, in the year 1767. He removed to the waters of the Ohio, in 1790, in company with his uncle, Captain John Hewit, soon after the settlement of the Ohio Company; at the breaking out of the Indian war, he resided on the island now known by the name of "Blennerhasset," in the block house of Captain James, where he married a cousin, the daughter of Captain Hewit. After his marriage, he lived a short time at the mouth of the Little Kenawha, but as the Indians became dangerous, he joined the company of settlers at "Neil's station," a short distance above, on the same stream. At this period, all the settlements on both banks of the Ohio were broken up, and the inhabitants retired to their garrisons for mutual defence.

The garrison at the middle settlement, in Belprie, was called "Farmer's Castle," and was a strong stockaded defence, with comfortable dwelling houses erected along the margin of the stout palisades which surrounded it. It stood near the bank of the Ohio river, on the waters of which nearly all the intercourse between the stations was conducted in light canoes. At this garrison, Mr. Hewit was a frequent visitor, but not an inmate. Some of the more fearless inhabitants, on the left bank, still continued to live in their own dwellings, considering themselves in a manner protected by the Ohio river, and by the vigilance of the "spies," who daily scoured the adjacent forests. Mr. Hewit was, at this time, in the prime of life and manhood; possessed of a vigorous frame, nearly six feet high, with limbs of the finest mould, not surpassed by the Belvidere Apollo, for manly beauty. The hands and feet were small in proportion to the muscles of the arms and legs. Of their strength, some estimate may be formed, when it is stated that he could, with a single hand, lift with ease a large blacksmith's anvil, by grasping the tapering horn which projects from its side. To this great muscular strength was added a quickness of motion, which gave to the dash of his fist the rapidity of thought, as it was driven into the face or breast of his adversary. The eye was coal black, small and sunken, but when excited or enraged, flashed fire like that of the tiger. The face and head were well developed, with such powerful masseter and temporal muscles, that the fingers of the strongest man, when once confined between his teeth, could no more be withdrawn than from the jaws of a vice.

With such physical powers, united to an unrefined and rather irritable mind, who shall wonder at his propensity for, and delight in, personal combat; especially when placed in the midst of rude and unlettered companions, where courage and bodily strength were held in unlimited estimation. Accordingly, we find him engaged in numberless personal contests, in which he almost universally came off victorious. One instance of his activity and reckless daring took place at Marietta, about the year 1796. In some quarrel at a tavern, the vigor of his arm was laid so heavily upon one of his opponents, that serious apprehensions were felt for his life. Complaint was made to the magistrate, and a warrant issued for his apprehension. Of this he had timely notice, and not relishing the inside of a jail at that inclement season of the year, it being in February, he started for the river, intending to cross into Virginia, out of the jurisdiction of the constable. It so happened that the rains on the head waters had raised the river to half bank, and broken up the ice, which completely covered the stream with fragments of all dimensions, so closely arranged that no canoe could be forced through them. Although late in the night, there was yet the light of the moon, and rushing down the bank, with the constable and a numerous posse at his back, he leaped fearlessly on to the floating ice, and springing from fragment to fragment, with the activity of a fox, he reached the opposite shore in safety, about half a mile below the point where he commenced this perilous adventure. The constable, seeing the object of his pursuit afloat on the ice, came to a halt, concluding that, although he had escaped from the penalty of the law, he could not avoid the fate which awaited him, and that he would certainly be drowned before he could gain the shore. But, as fortune is said to favor the brave, he escaped without harm, and his life was preserved for wise and providential purposes.

Sometime in the month of May, 1792, while living at Neil's station, on the Little Kenawha, Mr. Hewit rose early in the morning and went out about a mile from the garrison in search of a stray horse, little expecting any Indians to be near, having heard of none in that vicinity for some time. He was sauntering along at his ease, in an obscure cattle path, thinking more of his stray animal than of danger, when all at once three Indians sprang from behind two large trees, that stood one on each side of the track, where they had been watching his approach. So sudden was the onset, and so completely was he in their grasp, that resistance was vain, and would probably have been the cause of his death. He therefore quietly surrendered, thinking that in a few days he should find some way of escape. For himself, he felt but little uneasiness; his great concern was for his wife and child, from whom, with the yearnings of a father's heart, he was thus forcibly separated, and whom he might never see again.

In their progress to the towns on the Sandusky plains, the Indians treated their prisoner, Hewit, with as little harshness as could be expected. He was always confined at night by fastening his wrists and ancles to saplings, as he lay extended upon his back upon the ground, with an Indian on each side. By day his limbs were free, but always marching with one Indian before, and two behind him. As they approached the prairies, frequent halts were made to search for honey, the wild bee being found in every hollow tree, and often in the ground beneath decayed roots, in astonishing numbers. This afforded them many luscious repasts, of which the prisoner was allowed to partake. The naturalization of the honey bee to the forests of North America, since its colonization by the whites, is, in fact, the only real addition to its comforts that the red man has ever received from the destroyer of his race; and this industrious insect, so fond of the society of man, seems also destined to destruction by the *bee-moth*, and like the buffalo and the deer, will soon vanish from the woods and prairies of the West.

While the Indians were occupied in these searches, Hewit closely watched an opportunity for escape, but his captors were equally vigilant. As they receded from the danger of pursuit, they became less hurried in their march, and often stopped to hunt and amuse themselves. The level prairie afforded fine ground for one of their favorite sports, the foot race. In this, Hewit was invited to join, and soon found that he could easily outrun two of them, but the other was more than his match, which discouraged him from trying to escape, until a more favorable opportunity. They treated him familiarly, and were much pleased with his lively, cheerful manners. After they had reached within one or two day's march of their village, they made a halt to hunt, and left their prisoner at their camp, although they had usually taken him with them, as he complained of being sick. To make all safe, they placed him on his back, confining his wrists with stout thongs of raw-hide to saplings, and his legs raised at a considerable elevation, to a small tree. After they had been gone a short time, he began to put in operation the plan he had been meditating for escape, trusting that the thickness of his wrists, in comparison with the smallness of his hands, would enable him to withdraw them from the ligatures. After long and violent exertions, he succeeded in liberating his hands, but not without severely lacerating the skin and covering them with blood. His legs were next freed by untying them, but not without a great effort, from their elevation.

Once fairly at liberty, the first object was to secure some food for the long journey which was before him. But as the Indian's larder is seldom well stocked, with all his search, he could only find two small pieces of jerked venison, not more than sufficient for a single meal. With this light stock of provision, his body nearly naked, and without even a knife or a tomahawk, to assist in procuring more, he started for the settlements on the Muskingum, as the nearest point where he could meet with friends. It seems that the Indians returned to the camp soon after his escape, for that night while cautiously traversing a wood, he heard the cracking of a breaking twig not far from him. Dropping silently on to the ground where he stood, he beheld his three enemies in pursuit. To say that he was not agitated, would not be true; his senses were wide awake, and his heart beat quick, but it was a heart that never knew fear. It so happened that they passed a few yards to one side of him, and he remained unseen. As soon as they were at a sufficient distance, he altered his course and saw no more of them.

Suffering every thing but death, from the exhausting effects of hunger and fatigue, he, after nine days, struck the waters of the Big Muskingum, and came in to the garrison, at Wolf creek mills. During this time he had no food but roots and the bark of the slippery-elm, after the two bits of venison were expended. When he came in sight of the station, he was so completely exhausted that he could not stand or halloo. His body was entirely naked, excepting a small strip of cloth round the loins, and so torn, bloody and disfigured, by the briers and brush, that he thought it imprudent to show himself, lest he should be taken for an Indian, and shot by the centries. It is a curious physiological fact, that famine and hunger will actually darken the skin in the manner mentioned by the prophet Jeremiah, when foretelling the fate of the Israelites; and may be accounted for by the absorption of the bile into the blood, when not used up in the process of digesting the food. In this forlorn state, Hewit remained until evening, when he crawled silently to the gateway, which was open, and crept in before any one was aware of his being near. As they all had heard of his capture, and some personally knew him, he was instantly recognized by a young man, as the light of the fire fell on his face, who exclaimed, "here is Hewit." They soon clothed and fed him, and his fine constitution directly restored his health.

The course pursued by Mr. Hewit was in the direction of a favorite and well known trail, or war path of the Indians, from Sandusky to the settlements on the Muskingum, and struck that river at a point called "Big Rock," from an enormous block of sandstone that had tumbled out of a cliff and lay on the shore. The line of the trail lay between the waters of the Muskingum and those of the Scioto, crossing some of the branches of both these rivers. The war paths of the Indians were generally known to the old hunters, as in times of peace there was considerable intercourse for trade and hunting between the borderers and the Indian tribes. After the war was closed, by the masterly campaign of Gen. Wayne, the sturdy settlers on the shores of the Ohio, sallied out from their garrisons, where they had been more or less closely confined for five years, and took possession of the various farms, which had fallen to their lots either as " donation lands," or as proprietors in the Ohio Company, some of which had been partially cleared and cultivated before the commencement of hostilities. During this period, they suffered from famine, sickness, and death, in addition to the depredations of the Indians. The small-pox and putrid sore throat, had both visited them in their garrisons, destroying, in some instances, whole families of children in a few days. The murderous savage without, with sickness and famine within, had made their castles wearisome dwelling places, although they protected them from the tomahawk, and saved the settlements from being entirely broken up.

In the year 1797, Mr. Hewit cast his lot in the valley of the Hockhocking river, near the town of Athens, and settled quietly down to clearing his farm. He was by nature endowed with a clear, discriminating, and vigorous mind; and, although his education was very limited, extending only to reading and writing, yet his judgment was acute, and his reasoning powers highly matured by intercourse with his fellow-men. For some years before his death, he was a member of the Methodist church, which has the praise of reclaiming more depraved men than perhaps any other sect, and became a valuable citizen and useful man in society. A short time previous to his decease, which took place in the year 1814, he was appointed a Trustee of the Ohio University, at Athens. At that early time, the duties of a Trustee mainly consisted in leasing out and managing the fiscal affairs of the college domain, embracing two townships of land. For this business he was well fitted, and his judgment and good sense, were of real value to the institution, however little he might be qualified to act in literary matters.

The life of Mr. Hewit affords an interesting subject of contemplation. Hundreds of others, who were among the western borderers in early days, afford similar examples of reckless daring, and outrageous acts, while surrounded with war, tumult and danger, who, when peace was restored and they returned to the quiet scenes of domestic and civil life, became some of the most useful, influential, and distinguished men. It shows how much man is the creature of habit; and that he is often governed more by the character, and the outward example of men around him, and the times in which he lives, than by any innate principle of good or evil, which may happen to predominate within him.

About four miles north of Athens, are mounds and ancient fortifications with gateways. One of the mounds which was composed of a kind of stone, differing from any in the vicinity, was taken for the construction of a dam across the Hocking; there were in it over a thousand perches, and some of the stones weighed two hundred pounds. In the mound were found copper rings and other relics. There are many mounds in some other parts of the county.

Dr. S. P. Hildreth, of Marietta, a gentleman of well-known scientific attainments, thus speaks in Silliman's Journal of the fossil remains in this region.

The sandstone rocks contain many relics of fossil trees, of that ancient and curious family, bearing those rare devices and figures on their bark, so artificial in their appearance as to induce a common belief among the ignorant, of their being the work of man before the flood, and buried by that catastrophe in huge heaps of sand, since consolidated into rock. The excavations in sandstone rocks have been, as yet, so few and partial, that but a small number have been brought to light, although the strata through this valley are one vast cemetery of the plants of a former creation. I have seen some specimens fonnd in quarrying stones for a cellar, or in grading a road, and have heard of many more, proving that there is an abundant supply laid up for future geologists, when the country becomes more cultivated, and extensive openings shall be made in the earth. On the heads of Shade river, a few miles sw. of Athens, there is a large deposit of fossil trees, the wood being replaced by a dark ferruginous silex.

The yellow pine is very abundant in the lower part of the Hocking valley, and was probably at no very remote period, the prevailing growth of this part of the country. On this point, Dr. Hildreth also gives the following interesting facts.

Extensive districts in which a pine is not now found, are thickly scattered with pitch pine knots, lying on the surface, the relics of former forests, which some disease, or probably the depredations of insects, had destroyed. In these situations large quantities of pitch and tar were formerly made. In numerous mounds, opened under my direction, the charcoal found about the human bones, which they almost universally contain, and which the aborigines first burned before casting up the mound of earth and stone, as a sacred monument for the dead, is most generally the charcoal of pine wood—leading also to the conclusion, that at their erection, yellow pine was the prevailing tree of the forest, for it is not probable they would take the trouble of bringing it from any distance.

By the United States Statistics it appears there were 92,800 bushels of salt produced in the county, and 47 men employed in the manufacture, in 1840. This has since increased. The principal salt wells now in the county, are those of Ewing, Vinton & Co., Fuller & Walker, and Samuel Denmans, at Chauncey ; Hydes, Perkins & Prudens, near Athens.

Nelsonville, on the Hocking canal, 13 miles above Athens, is a flourishing village, in the heart of the coal region and trade, and contains about 300 people : considerable tobacco is packed here. Chauncey, also on the canal 7 miles above Athens, is a village of about 200 inhabitants, where the manufacture of salt is extensively carried on, together with coal mining ; at one mine the coal is obtained by sinking a shaft 120 feet perpendicular. M'Arthurstown, 26 miles wsw. of Athens, has about 250 people, and is in a good country. Hockingport, at the mouth of the Hocking, Hocking City, Amesville, Hebardsville, Albany, Millfield, Chesterfield, Savannah and Trimble, are small places.

BELMONT.

Belmont was established, September 7th, 1801, by proclamation of Gov. St. Clair, being the ninth county formed in the N. W. Territory. The name is derived from two French words, signifying a fine mountain. It is a hilly and picturesque tract, and contains much excellent land. The principal crops are wheat, oats, Indian corn and tobacco, of which last, about two million pounds are annually raised. It has about 68,000 sheep, and coal abounds. The following are the names of its townships in 1840, with their population.

Colerain,	1389	Pultney,	[illegible]47	Warren,	2410
Flushing,	1683	Richland,	3735	Washington,	1388
Goshen,	1882	Smith,	1956	Wayne,	1734
Kirkwood,	2280	Somerset,	1932	Wheeling,	1389
Mead,	1496	Union,	2127	York,	1294
Pease,	2449				

Population of Belmont county in 1820, 20,329 ; in 1830, 28,543 ; in 1840, 30,902, or 51 inhabitants to a square mile.

Belmont county was one of the earliest settled within the State of Ohio, and the scene of several desperate encounters with the Indians. About 1790, or perhaps two or three years later, a fort called Dillie's fort was erected on the west side of the Ohio, opposite Grave creek.

About 250 yards below this fort, an old man named Tate was shot down by the Indians very early in the morning, as he was opening his door. His daughter-in-law and grandson pulled him in and barred the door. The Indians endeavoring to force it open, were kept out for some time by the exertions of the boy and woman. They at length fired through and wounded the boy. The woman was shot from the outside as she endeavored to escape up chimney, and fell into the fire. The boy, who had hid behind some barrels, ran and pulled her out, and returned again to his hiding place. The Indians now effected an entrance, killed a girl as they came in, and scalped the three they had shot. They then went out behind that side of the house from the fort. The boy, who had been wounded in the mouth, embraced the opportunity, and escaped to the fort. The Indians, twelve or thirteen in number, went off unmolested, although the men in the fort had witnessed the transaction and had sufficient force to engage with them.

Captina creek is a considerable stream entering the Ohio, near the southeast angle of Belmont. On its banks at an early day, a sanguinary contest took place known as "*the battle of Captina.*" Its incidents have often and variously been given. We here relate them as they fell from the lips of Martin Baker, of Monroe, who was at that time a lad of about 12 years of age in Baker's fort.

One mile below the mouth of Captina, on the Virginia shore, was Baker's fort, so named from my father. One morning, in May, 1794, four men were sent over according to the custom, to the Ohio side, to reconnoitre. They were Adam Miller, John Daniels, Isaac M'Cowan, and John Shoptaw. Miller and Daniels took up stream, the other two down. The upper scout were soon attacked by Indians, and Miller killed; Daniels ran up Captina about 3 miles, but being weak from the loss of blood issuing from a wound in his arm, was taken prisoner, carried into captivity, and subsequently released at the treaty of Greenville. The lower scout having discovered signs of the enemy, Shoptaw swam across the Ohio and escaped, but M'Gowan going up towards the canoe, was shot by Indians in ambush. Upon this, he ran down to the bank, and sprang into the water, pursued by the enemy, who overtook and scalped him. The firing being heard at the fort, they beat up for volunteers. There were about fifty men in the fort. There being much reluctance among them to volunteer, my sister exclaimed, "*She wouldn't be a coward.*" This aroused the pride of my brother, John Baker, who before had determined not to go. He joined the others, 14 in number, including Capt. Abram Enochs. They soon crossed the river, and went up Captina in single file, a distance of a mile and a half, following the Indian trail. The enemy had come back on their trails and were in ambush on the hill side awaiting their approach. When sufficiently near they fired upon our people, but being on an elevated position, their balls passed harmless over them. The whites then treed. Some of the Indians came behind and shot Capt. Enochs and Mr. Hoffman. Our people soon retreated, and the Indians pursued but a short distance. On their retreat my brother was shot in the hip. Determined to sell his life as dearly as possible, he drew off one side and secreted himself in a hollow with a rock at his back, offering no chance for the enemy to approach but in front. Shortly after, two guns were heard in quick succession; doubtless one of them was fired by my brother, and from the signs afterwards, it was supposed he had killed an Indian. The next day the men turned out and visited the spot. Enochs, Hoffman and John Baker, were found dead and scalped. Enoch's bowels were torn out, his eyes and those of Hoffman screwed out with a wiping stick. The dead were wrapped in white hickory bark, and brought over to the Virginia shore, and buried in their bark coffins. There were about thirty Indians engaged in this action, and seven skeletons of their slain were found long after secreted in the crevices of rocks.

M'Donald, in his biographical sketch of Gov. M'Arthur, who was in the action, says, that after the death of Capt. Enochs, that M'Arthur, although the youngest man in the company, was unanimously called upon to direct the retreat. The wounded who were able to walk were placed in front, while M'Arthur with his Spartan Band covered the retreat. The moment an Indian showed himself in pursuit, he was fired upon, and generally it is believed with effect. The Indians were so severely handled, that they gave up the pursuit. The Indians were commanded by the Shawnee Chief, *Charley Wilkey*. He told the author [M'Donald] of this narrative, that the battle of Captina was the most severe conflict he ever witnessed; that although he had the advantage of the ground and the first fire, he lost the most of his men, half of them having been either killed or wounded.

The celebrated Indian hunter, Lewis Wetzel, was often through this region. Belmont has been the scene of at least two of the daring adventures of this far-famed borderer.

While hunting, Wetzel fell in with a young hunter who lived on Dunkard's creek, and was persuaded to accompany him to his home. On their arrival they found the house in ruins and all the family murdered, except a young woman who had been bred with them, and to whom the young man was ardently attached. She was taken alive, as was found by examining the trail of the enemy, who were three Indians and a white renegado. Burning with revenge, they followed the trail until opposite the mouth of Captina, where the enemy had crossed. They swam the stream and discovered the Indians camp, around the fires of which lay the enemy in careless repose. The young woman was apparently unhurt, but was making much moaning and lamentation. The young man, hardly able to restrain his rage, was for firing and rushing instantly upon them. Wetzel, more cautious, told him to wait until day light when there was a better chance of success in killing the whole party. At dawn the Indians prepared to depart. The young man selecting the white renegado, and Wetzel the Indian, they both fired simultaneously with fatal effect. The young man rushed forward knife in hand to relieve the mistress of his affections, while Wetzel reloaded and pursued the two surviving Indians, who had taken to the woods until they could ascertain the number of their enemies. Wetzel, as soon as he was discovered, discharged his rifle at random in order to draw them from their covert. The ruse took effect, and taking to his heels he loaded as he ran, and suddenly wheeling about discharged his rifle through the body of his nearest and unsuspecting enemy. The remaining Indian seeing the fate of his companion, and that his enemy's rifle was unloaded, rushed forward with all energy, the prospect of prompt revenge being fairly before him. Wetzel led him on dodging from tree to tree, until his rifle was again ready, when suddenly turning he fired, and his remaining enemy fell dead at his feet. After taking their scalps, Wetzel and his friend, with their rescued captive, returned in safety to the settlement.

A short time after Crawford's defeat, in 1782, Wetzel accompanied Thomas Mills, a soldier in that action, to obtain his horse, which he had left near the site of St. Clairsville. They were met by a party of about forty Indians, at the Indian springs, two miles from St. Clairsville, on the road to Wheeling. Both parties discovered each other at the same moment, when Lewis instantly fired and killed an Indian, while the Indians wounded his companion in the heel, overtook and killed him. Four Indians pursued Wetzel. About half a mile beyond, one of the Indians having got, in the pursuit, within a few steps, Wetzel wheeled and shot him, and then continued the retreat. In less than a mile farther, a second one came so close to him that, as he turned to fire, he caught the muzzle of his gun, when, after a severe struggle, Wetzel brought it to his chest, and discharging it, his opponent fell dead. Wetzel still continued on his course, pursued by the two Indians. All three were pretty well fatigued, and often stopped and treed. After going something more than a mile, Wetzel took advantage of an open ground, over which the Indians were passing, stopped suddenly to shoot the foremost, who thereupon sprang behind a small sapling. Wetzel fired and wounded him mortally. The remaining Indian then gave a little yell, exclaiming, "No catch that man, gun always loaded." After the peace of 1795, Wetzel pushed for the frontier, on the Mississippi, where he could trap the beaver, hunt the buffalo and deer, and occasionally shoot an Indian, the object of his mortal hatred. He finally died, as he had lived, a free man of the forest.

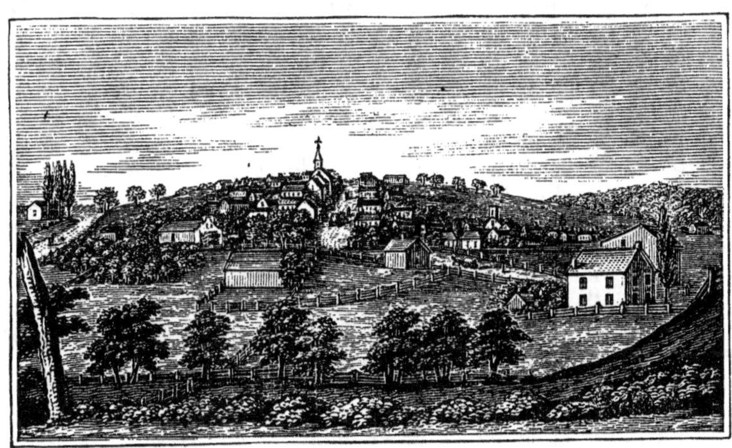

St. Clairsville.

St. Clairsville, the county seat, is situated on an elevated and romantic site, in a rich agricultural region, on the line of the National road, 11 miles west of Wheeling, and 116 east of Columbus. It contains 6 places for public worship: 2 Friends, 1 Presbyterian, 1 Episcopal, 1 Methodist, and 1 Union, 1 female seminary, 12 mercantile stores, 2 or 3 newspaper offices, H. Anderson's map engraving and publishing establishment, and, in 1840, had 829 inhabitants. Cuming's tour, published in 1810, states that this town "was laid out in the woods, by David Newell, in 1801. On the south side of Newell's plat, is an additional part, laid out by William Matthews, which was incorporated with Newell's plat, on the 23d January, 1807, by the name of St. Clairsville." By the act of incorporation, the following officers were appointed until the first stated meeting of the inhabitants should be held for an election, viz. John Patterson,

President; Sterling Johnston, Recorder; Samuel Sullivan, Marshall, Groves Wm. Brown, John Brown, and Josiah Dillon, Trustees; William Congliton, Collector; James Colwell, Treasurer, and Robert Griffeth, Town Marshall. The view given was taken from an elevation west of the town, near the National road, and Neiswanger's old tavern, shown on the extreme right. The building in the distance, on the left, shaded by poplars, is the Friend's meeting house; in the centre is shown the spire of the court house, and on the right, the tower of the Presbyterian church.

St. Clairsville derives its name from the unfortunate but meritorious Arthur St. Clair. He was born in Scotland, in 1734, and after receiving a classical education in one of the most celebrated universities of his native country, studied medicine; but having a taste for military pursuits, he sought and obtained a subaltern's appointment, and was with Wolfe in the storming of Quebec. After the peace of 1763, he was assigned the command of Fort Ligonier, in Pennsylvania, and received there a grant of one thousand acres. Prior to the revolutionary war, he held several civil offices. His military skill and experience, intelligence and integrity were such, that when the revolutionary war commenced, he was appointed Colonel of Continentals. In August, 1776, he was promoted to the rank of Brigadier, and bore an active part in the battles of Trenton and Princeton. He was subsequently created a Major General, and ordered to repair to Ticonderoga, where he commanded the garrison, and on the approach of Burgoyne's army, abandoned it. Charges of cowardice, incapacity and treachery were brought against him, in consequence. He was tried by a court martial, who, with all the facts before them, acquitted him, accompanying their report with the declaration, that "Major General St. Clair is acquitted, with the highest honor, of the charges against him." Congress subsequently, with an unanimous voice, confirmed this sentence. The facts were, that the works were incomplete and incapable of being defended against the whole British army, and although St. Clair might have gained great applause by a brave attempt at defence, yet it would have resulted in the death of many of his men, and probably the capture of the remainder; a loss which, it was afterwards believed in camp, and perhaps foreseen by St. Clair, would have prevented the taking of Burgoyne's army. In daring to do an unpopular act, for the public good, St. Clair exhibited a high degree of moral courage, and deserves more honor than he who wins a battle.

St. Clair served, with reputation, until the close of the war. In 1785, while residing on his farm, at Ligonier, he was appointed a delegate to the Continental Congress, and was soon after chosen President of that august body. After the passage of the ordinance for the government of the North-western territory, he was made governor, and continued in the office until within a few weeks of the termination of the territorial form of government, in the winter of 1802–3, when he was removed by President Jefferson.

The remainder of the sketch of Gov. St. Clair, we give in extracts from the Notes of Judge Burnet, who was personally acquainted with him. Beside being clearly and beautifully written, it contains important facts in the legislative history of Ohio.

During the continuance of the first grade of that imperfect government, he enjoyed the respect and confidence of every class of the people. He was plain and simple in his dress and equipage, open and frank in his manners, and accessible to persons of every rank. In these respects, he exhibited a striking contrast with the Secretary, Colonel Sargent; and that contrast, in some measure, increased his popularity, which he retained, unimpaired, till after the commencement of the first session of the legislature. During that session, he manifested a strong desire to enlarge his own powers, and restrict those of the Assembly; which was the more noticed, as he had opposed the usurpations of the legislative council, composed of himself, or in his absence, the Secretary, and the Judges of the General Court; and had taken an early opportunity of submitting his views on that subject to the General Assembly. . . . .

The effect of the construction he gave, of his own powers, may be seen in the fact, that of *the thirty bills*, passed by the two Houses, during the first session, and sent to him for his approval, he refused his assent to *eleven;* some of which were supposed to be of much importance, and all of them calculated, more or less, to advance the public interest. Some of them he rejected, because they related to the establishment of new counties; others, because he thought they were unnecessary or inexpedient. Thus more than a third of the fruits of the labor of that entire session was lost, by the exercise of the arbitrary discretion of one man. . . . .

This, and some other occurrences of a similar character, which were manifest deviations from his usual course, not easily accounted for, multiplied his opponents very rapidly, and rendered it more difficult for his friends to defend and sustain him. They also created a state of bad feeling between the legislative and executive branches, and eventually terminated in his removal from office, before the expiration of the territorial government.

The governor was unquestionably a man of superior talents, of extensive information, and of great uprightness of purpose, as well as suavity of manners. His general course, though in the main correct, was in some respects injurious to his own popularity; but it was the result of an honest exercise of his judgment. He not only believed that the power he claimed belonged legitimately to the executive, but was convinced that the manner in which he exercised it, was imposed on him as a duty, by the Ordinance; and was calculated to advance the best interests of the territory. . . . .

Soon after the governor was removed from office, he returned to the Legonier valley, poor, and destitute of the means of subsistence; and unfortunately, too much disabled, by age and infirmity, to embark in any kind of active business. During his administration of the territorial government, he was induced to make himself personally liable for the purchase of a number of pack-horses and other articles necessary to fit out an expedition against the Indians, to an amount of some two or three thousand dollars, which he was afterwards compelled to pay. Having no use for the money at the time, he did not present his claim to the government. After he was removed from office, he looked to that fund as his dependence for future subsistence; and, under a full expectation of receiving it, he repaired to Washington City, and presented his account to the proper officer of the treasury. To his utter surprise and disappointment, it was rejected, on the mortifying ground, that, admitting it to have been originally correct, it was barred by the statute; and that the time which had elapsed, afforded the highest presumption that it had been settled, although no voucher or memorandum to that effect could be found in the department. To counteract the alledged presumption of payment, the original vouchers, showing the purchase, the purpose to which the property was applied, and the payment of the money, were exhibited. It was, however, still insisted, that as the transaction was an old one, and had taken place before the burning of the war office, in Philadelphia, the lapse of time furnished satisfactory evidence that the claim must have been settled, and the vouchers destroyed in that conflagration.

The pride of the old veteran was deeply wounded, by the ground on which his claim was refused; and he was induced, from that consideration, as well as by the pressure of poverty and want, to persevere in his efforts to maintain the justice and equity of his demand; still hoping that presumption would give way to truth. For the purpose of getting rid of his solicitations, Congress passed an act, purporting to be an act for his relief; but which merely removed the technical objection, founded on lapse of time, by authorizing a settlement of his demands, regardless of the limitation, This step seemed necessary, to preserve their own character; but it left *the worn out veteran* still at the mercy of the accounting officers of the department, from whom he had nothing to expect, but disappointment. During the same session, a bill was introduced into the House of Representatives, granting him an annnuity, which was rejected, on the third reading, by a vote of 48 to 50.

After spending the principal part of two sessions, in useless efforts, subsisting, during the time, on the bounty of his friends, he abandoned the pursuit in despair, and returned to the Legonier valley, where he lived several years in the most abject poverty, in the family of a widowed daughter, as destitute as himself. At length, Pennsylvania, his adopted state, from considerations of personal respect, and gratitude for past services, as well as from a laudable feeling of state pride, settled on him an annuity of three hundred dollars, which was soon after raised to six hundred and fifty dollars. That act of beneficence gave to the gallant old soldier a comfortable subsis·ence for the little remnant of his days which then remained. The honor resulting to the state, from that step, was very much enhanced, by the fact, that the individual on whom their bounty was bestowed, was a foreigner, and was known to be a warm opponent, in politics, to the great majority of the legislature and their constituents.

He lived, however, but a short time to enjoy the bounty. On the 31st of August, 1818, that venerable officer of the Revolution, after a long, brilliant and useful life, died of an injury occasioned by the running away of his horse, near Greensburgh, in the eighty-fourth year of his age.

Bridgeport, on the west bank of the Ohio, opposite the city of Wheeling, and on the National road, is an important point for the forwarding goods to the West. It contains 1 church, 1 grist and 1 saw mill, 3 stores, 3 forwarding and commission houses, and had, in 1840, 329 inhabitants.

In the spring of 1791, the cabin of Captain Joseph Kirkwood, at this place, was attacked at night by a party of Indians, who, after a severe action, were repulsed. This Captain Kirkwood "was the gallant and unrewarded Captain Kirkwood, of the Delaware line, in the war of the revolution, to whom such frequent and honorable allusion is made in Lee's memoir of the Southern campaigns. The state of Delaware had but one continental regiment, which, at the defeat at Camden, was reduced to a single company. It was therefore impossible, under the rules, for Kirkwood to be promoted; and he was under the mortification of beholding inferior officers in the regiments of other states, promoted over him, while he, with all his merit, was compelled to remain a captain, solely in consequence of the small force Delaware was enabled to maintain in the service. He fought with distinguished gallantry through the war, and was in the bloody battles of Camden, Holkirks, Eutaw and Ninety Six."

Captain Kirkwood moved to this place in 1789, and built his cabin on the knoll, about thirty yards west of the present residence of Mr. M'Swords. At the time of the attack on the cabin, there was an unfinished block-house standing on the highest part of the knoll, only a few yards distant. On the night of the attack, a party of fourteen soldiers, under the command of Captain Joseph Biggs, together with Captain Kirkwood and family, were in the cabin. About two hours before day break, the captain's little son Joseph, had occasion to leave the cabin for a few moments, and requested Captain Biggs to accompany him. They were out but a few minutes, and although unknown to them, were surrounded by Indians. They had returned, and again retired to sleep in the upper loft.

when they soon discovered the roof in a blaze, which was the first intimation they had of the presence of an enemy. Captain K. was instantly awakened, when he and his men commenced pushing off the roof, the Indians at the same time firing upon them, from under cover of the block-house. Captain Biggs, on the first alarm, ran down the ladder into the room below, to get his rifle, when a ball entered a window and wounded him in the wrist. Soon the Indians had surrounded the house, and attempted to break in the door with their tomahawks. Those within braced it with puncheons from the floor. In the panic of the moment, several of the men wished to escape from the cabin, but Captain K. silenced them with the threat of taking the life of the first man who made the attempt, asserting that the Indians would tomahawk them as fast as they left. The people of Wheeling—one mile distant—hearing the noise of the attack, fired a swivel, to encourage the defenders, although fearful of coming to the rescue. This enraged the Indians the more; they sent forth terrific yells, and brought brush, piled it around the cabin, and set it on fire. Those within, in a measure smothered the flames, first with the water and milk in the house, and then with damp earth, from the floor of the cabin. The fight was kept up about two hours, until dawn, when the Indians retreated. Had they attacked earlier, success would have resulted. The loss of the Indians, or their number, was unknown—only one was seen. He was in the act of climbing up the corner of the cabin, when he was discovered, let go his hold and fell. Seven of those within were wounded, and one, a Mr. Walker, mortally. He was a brave man. As he lay, disabled and helpless, on his back, on the earth, he called out to the Indians, in a taunting manner. He died in a few hours, and was buried the next day, at Wheeling, with military honors. A party of men, under Gen. Benjamin Biggs, of West Liberty, went in pursuit of the Indians, but without success. A niece of Captain Kirkwood, during the attack, was on a visit about twenty miles distant, on Buffalo creek. In the night, she dreamed that the cabin was attacked, and heard the guns. So strong an impression did it make, that she arose and rode down with all her speed to Wheeling, where she arrived two hours after sunrise.

After this affair, Captain Kirkwood moved with his family to Newark, Delaware. On his route, he met with some of St. Clair's troops, then on their way to Cincinnati. Exasperated at the Indians, for their attack upon his house, he accepted the command of a company of Delaware troops, was with them at the defeat of St. Clair, in the November following, "where he fell, in a brave attempt to repel the enemy with the bayonet, and thus closed a career as honorable as it was unrewarded."

Elizabeth Zane, who acted with so much heroism at the siege of Wheeling, in 1782, lived many years since about two miles above Bridgeport, on the Ohio side of the river, near Martinsville. She was twice married, first to Mr. M'Laughlin, and secondly to Mr. Clark. The anecdote we derive from a published source.

When Lynn, the ranger, gave the alarm that an Indian army was approaching, the fort having been for some time unoccupied by a garrison, and Colonel Zane's house having been used for a magazine, those who retired into the fortress had to take with them a supply of ammunition for its defence. The supply of powder, deemed ample at the time, was now almost exhausted, by reason of the long continuance of the siege, and the repeated endeavors of the savages to take the fort by storm: a few rounds only remained. In this emergency, it became necessary to renew their stock from an abundant store which was deposited in Colonel Zane's house. Accordingly, it was proposed that one of the fleetest men should endeavor to reach the house, obtain a supply of powder, and return with it to the fort. It was an enterprise full of danger; but many of the heroic spirits shut up in the fort were willing to encounter the hazard. Among those who volunteered to go on this enterprise, was Elizabeth, the sister of Colonel E. Zane. She was young, active and athletic, with courage to dare the danger, and fortitude to sustain her through it. Disdaining to weigh the hazard of her own life against that of others, when told that a man would encounter less danger by reason of his greater fleetness, she replied, "and should he fall, his loss will be more severely felt; you have not one man to spare; a woman will not be missed in the defence of the fort." Her services were then accepted. Divesting herself of some of her garments, as tending to impede her progress, she stood prepared for the hazardous adventure; and when the gate was thrown open, bounded forth with the buoyancy of hope, and in the confidence of success. Wrapt in amazement, the Indians beheld her springing forward, and only exclaiming, "a squaw," "a squaw," no attempt was made to interrupt her progress: arrived at the door, she proclaimed her errand. Colonel Silas Zane fastened a table cloth around her waist, and emptying into it a keg of powder, again she ventured forth. The Indians were no longer passive. Ball after ball whizzed by, several of which passed through her clothes: she reached the gate, and entered the fort in safety; and thus was the garrison again saved by female intrepidity. This heroine had but recently returned from Philadelphia, where she had received her education, and was wholly unused to such scenes as were daily passing on the frontiers. The distance she had to run was about forty yards.

Among the best sketches of backwoods life, is that written by Mr. John S. Williams, editor of the American Pioneer, and published in it in October, 1843. In the spring of 1800, his father's family removed from Carolina and settled with others on Glenn's run, about six miles northeast of St. Clairsville. He was then a lad, as he relates, of seventy five pounds weight. From his sketch, "Our Cabin; or Life in the Woods," we make some extracts.

Emigrants poured in from different parts, cabins were put up in every direction, and women, children and goods tumbled into them. The tide of emigration flowed like water through a breach in a mill-dam. Every thing was bustle and confusion, and all at work that could work. In the midst of all this, the mumps, and perhaps one or two other diseases, prevailed and gave us a seasoning. Our cabin had been raised, covered, part of the cracks chinked, and part of the floor laid when we moved in, on Christmas day! There had not been a stick cut except in building the cabin. We had intended an inside chimney, for we thought the chimney ought to be in the house. We had a log put across the whole width of the cabin for a mantel, but when the floor was in we found it so low as not to answer, and removed it. Here was a great change for my mother and sister, as well as the rest, but particularly my mother. She was raised in the most delicate manner in and near London, and lived most of her time in affluence, and always comfortable. She was now in the wilderness, surrounded by wild beasts; in a cabin with about half a floor, no door, no ceiling over head, not even a tolerable sign for a fireplace, the light of day and the chilling winds of night passing between every two logs in the building, the cabin so high from the ground that a bear, wolf, panther, or any other animal less in size than a cow, could enter without even a squeeze. Such was our situation on Thursday and Thursday night, December 25th, 1800, and which was bettered but by very slow degrees. We got the rest of the floor laid in a very few days, the chinking of the cracks went on slowly, but the daubing could not proceed till weather more suitable, which happened in a few days; door-ways were sawed out and steps made of the logs, and the back of the chimney was raised up to the mantel, but the funnel of sticks and clay was delayed until spring. . .

Our family consisted of my mother, a sister, of twenty-two, my brother, near twenty-one and very weakly, and myself, in my eleventh year. Two years afterwards, Black Jenny followed us in company with my half-brother, Richard, and his family. She lived two years with us in Ohio, and died in the winter of 1803–4.

In building our cabin it was set to front the north and south, my brother using my father's pocket compass on the occasion. We had no idea of living in a house that did not stand

Our Cabin; or Life in the Woods.

square with the earth itself. This argued our ignorance of the comforts and conveniencies of a pioneer life. The position of the house, end to the hill, necessarily elevated the lower end, and the determination of having both a north and south door, added much to the airiness of the domicil, particularly after the green ash puncheons had shrunk so as to have cracks in the floor and doors from one to two inches wide. At both the doors we had high, unsteady, and sometimes icy steps, made by piling up the logs cut out of the wall. We had, as the reader will see, a window, if it could be called a *window*, when, perhaps, it was the largest spot in the top, bottom, or sides of the cabin at which the wind *could not* enter. It was made by sawing out a log, placing sticks across, and then, by pasting an old newspaper over the hole, and applying some hog's lard, we had a kind of glazing which shed a most beautiful and mellow light across the cabin when the sun shone on it. All other light entered at the doors, cracks and chimney.

Our cabin was twenty four by eighteen. The west end was occupied by two beds, the center of each side by a door, and here our symmetry had to stop, for on the opposite side of the window, made of clapboards, supported on pins driven into the logs, were our shelves. Upon these shelves my sister displayed in ample order, a host of pewter plates, basins, and dishes, and spoons, scoured and bright. It was none of your new-fangled pewter made of lead, but the best London pewter, which our father himself bought of Townsend, the manufacturer. These were the plates upon which you could hold your meat so as to cut it without slipping and without dulling your knife. But, alas! the days of pewter plates and sharp dinner knives have passed away never to return. To return to our internal arrangements. A ladder of five rounds occupied the corner near the window. By this, when we got a floor above, we could ascend. Our chimney occupied most of the east end; pots and kettles opposite the window under the shelves, a gun on hooks over the north door, four split-bottom chairs, three three-legged stools, and a small eight by ten looking-glass sloped from the wall over a large towel and combcase. These, with a clumsy shovel and a pair of tongs, made in Frederick, with one shank straight, as the best manufacture of pinches and blood-blisters, completed our furniture, except a spinning-wheel and such things as were necessary to work with. It was absolutely necessary to have *three-legged* stools, as four legs of any thing could not all touch the floor at the same time.

The completion of our cabin went on slowly. The season was inclement, we were weak-handed and weak-pocketed; in fact, laborers were not to be had. We got our chimney up breast high as soon as we could, and got our cabin daubed as high as the joists outside. It never was daubed on the inside, for my sister, who was very nice, could not consent to "live right next to the mud." My impression now is, that the window was not constructed till spring, for until the sticks and clay was put on the chimney we could possibly have no need of a window; for the flood of light which always poured into the cabin from the fireplace would have extinguished our paper window, and rendered it as useless as the moon at noonday. We got a floor laid over head as soon as possible, perhaps in a month; but when it *was* laid, the reader will readily conceive of its imperviousness to wind or weather, when we mention that it was laid of loose clapboards split from a red oak, the stump of which may be seen beyond the cabin. That tree grew in the night, and so twisting that each board laid on two diagonally opposite corners, and a cat might have shook every board on our ceiling.

It may be well to inform the unlearned reader that clapboards are such lumber as pioneers split with a frow, and resemble barrel staves before they are shaved, but are split longer, wider and thinner; of such our roof and ceiling were composed. Puncheons were planks made by splitting logs to about two and a half or three inches in thickness, and hewing them on one or both sides with the broad-axe. Of such our floor, doors, tables and stools were manufactured. The eave-bearers are those end logs which project over to receive the butting poles, against which the lower tier of clapboards rest in forming the roof. The trapping is the roof timbers, composing the gable end and the ribs, the ends of which appear in the drawing, being those logs upon which the clapboards lie. The trap logs are those of unequal length above the eave bearers, which form the gable ends, and upon which the ribs rest. The weight poles are those small logs laid on the roof, which weigh down the course of clapboards on which they lie, and against which the next course above is placed. The knees are pieces of heart timber placed above the butting poles, successively, to prevent the weight poles from rolling off. . . . . .

The evenings of the first winter did not pass off as pleasantly as evenings afterward. We had raised no tobacco to stem and twist, no corn to shell, no turnips to scrape; we had no tow to spin into rope-yarn, nor straw to plait for hats, and we had come so late we could get but few walnuts to crack. We had, however, the Bible, George Fox's Journal, Barkley's Apology, and a number of books, all better than much of the fashionable reading of the present day—from which, after reading, the reader finds he has gained nothing, while his understanding has been made the dupe of the writer's fancy—that while reading he had given himself up to be led in mazes of fictitious imagination, and losing his taste for solid reading, as frothy luxuries destroy the appetite for wholesome food. To our stock of books were soon after added a borrowed copy of the Pilgrim's Progress, which we read twice through without stopping. The first winter our living was truly scanty and hard; but even this winter had its felicities. We had part of a barrel of flour which we had brought from Fredericktown. Besides this, we had a part of a jar of hog's lard brought from old Carolina; not the tasteless stuff which now goes by that name, but pure leaf lard, taken from hogs raised on pine roots and fattened on sweet potatoes, and into which, while rendering, were immersed the boughs of the fragrant bay tree, that imparted to the lard a rich flavor. Of that flour, shortened with this lard, my sister every Sunday morning, and at *no other time*, made short biscuit for breakfast—not these greasy gum-elastic biscuit, we mostly meet with now, rolled out with a pin, or cut out with a cutter; or those that are, perhaps, speckled by or puffed up with refined lye called salæratus, but made out, one by one, in her fair hands, placed in neat juxtaposition in a skillet or spider, pricked with a fork to prevent blistering, and baked before an open fire—not half-baked and half-stewed in a cooking stove. . . . . .

In the ordering of a good Providence the winter was open, but windy. While the wind was of great use in driving the smoke and ashes out of our cabin, it shook terribly the timber standing almost over us. We were sometimes much and needlessly alarmed. We had never seen a dangerous looking tree near a dwelling, but here we were surrounded by the tall giants of the forest, waving their boughs and uniting their brows over us, as if in defiance of our disturbing their repose, and usurping their long and uncontested preëmption rights. The beech on the left often shook his bushy head over us as if in absolute disapprobation of our settling there, threatening to crush us if we did not pack up and start. The walnut over the spring branch stood high and straight; no one could tell which way it inclined, but all concluded that if it had a preference, it was in favor of quartering on our cabin. We got assistance to cut it down. The axeman doubted his ability to control its direction, by reason that he must necessarily cut it almost off before it would fall. He thought by felling the tree in the direction of the reader, along near the chimney, and thus favor the little lean it seemed to have, would be the means of saving the cabin. He was successful. Part of the stump still stands. These, and all other dangerous trees, were got down without other damage than many frights and frequent desertions of the premises, by the family while the trees were being cut. The ash beyond the house crossed the scarf and fell on the cabin, but without damage. . . . . . .

The monotony of the time for several of the first years was broken and enlivened by the howl of wild beasts. The wolves howling around us seemed to moan their inability to drive us from their long and undisputed domain. The bears, panthers and deers seemingly got miffed at our approach or the partiality of the hunters, and but seldom troubled us. One bag of meal would make a whole family rejoicingly happy and thankful then, when a loaded East Indiaman will fail to do it now, and is passed off as a common business transaction without ever once thinking of the Giver, so independent have we become in the short space of forty years! Having got out of the wilderness in less time than the children of Israel, we seem to be even more forgetful and unthankful than they. When spring was fully come and our little patch of corn, three acres, put in among the beech roots, which at every step contended with the shovel-plough for the right of soil, and held it too, we enlarged our stock of conveniences. As soon as bark would run, (peel off,) we could make ropes and bark boxes. These we stood in great need of, as such things as bureaus, stands, wardrobes, or even barrels, were not to be had. The manner of making ropes of linn bark, was to cut the bark in strips of convenient length, and water-rot it in the same manner as rotting flax or hemp. When this was done, the inside bark would peel off and split up so fine as to make a pretty considerably rough and good-for-but-little kind of a rope. Of this, however, we were very glad, and let no ship owner with his grass ropes laugh at us. We made two kinds of boxes for furniture. One kind was of hickory bark with the outside shaved off. This we would take off all around the tree, the size of which would determine the calibre of our box. Into one end we would place a flat piece of bark or puncheon cut round to fit in the bark, which stood on end the same as when on the tree. There was little need of hooping, as the strength of the bark would keep that all right enough. Its shrinkage would make the top unsightly in a parlor now-a-days, but then they were considered quite an addition to the furniture. A much finer article was made of slippery-elm bark, shaved smooth and with the inside out, bent round and sewed together where the ends of the hoop or main bark lapped over. The length of the bark was around the box, and inside out. A bottom was made of a piece of the same bark dried flat, and a lid like that of a common band box, made in the same way. This was the finest furniture in a lady's dressing room, and then, as now, with the finest furniture, the lapped or sewed side was turned to the wall and the prettiest part to the spectator. They were usually made oval, and while the bark was green were easily ornamented with drawings of birds, trees, &c., agreeably to the taste and skill of the fair manufacturer. As we belonged to the Society of Friends, it may be fairly presumed that our band boxes were not thus ornamented. . . . . . .

We settled on beech land, which took much labor to clear. We could do no better than clear out the smaller stuff and burn the brush, &c., around the beeches which, in spite of the girdling and burning we could do to them, would leaf out the first year, and often a little the second. The land, however, was very rich, and would bring better corn than might be expected. We had to tend it principally with the hoe, that is, to chop down the nettles, the water-weed, and the touch-me-not. Grass, careless, lambs-quarter, and Spanish needles were reserved to pester the better prepared farmer. We cleared a small turnip patch, which we got in about the 10th of August. We sowed in timothy seed, which took well, and next year we had a little hay besides. The tops and blades of the corn were also carefully saved for our horse, cow, and the two sheep. The turnips were sweet and good, and in the fall we took care to gather walnuts and hickory nuts, which were very abundant. These, with the turnips which we scraped, supplied the place of fruit. I have always been partial to scraped turnips, and could now beat any three dandies at scraping them. Johnny-cake, also, when we had meal to make it of, helped to make up our evening's repast. The Sunday morning biscuit had all evaporated, but the loss was partially supplied by the nuts and turnips. Our regular supper was mush and milk, and by the time we had shelled our corn, stemmed tobacco, and plaited straw to make hats, &c., &c., the mush and milk had seemingly decamped from the neighborhood of our ribs. To relieve this difficulty, my brother and I would bake a thin johnny-cake, part of which we would eat, and leave the rest till morning. At daylight we would eat the balance as we walked from the house to work.

The methods of eating mush and milk were various. Some would sit around the pot, and every one take therefrom for himself. Some would set a table and each have his tin cup of milk, and with a pewter spoon take just as much mush from the dish or the pot, if it was on the table, as he thought would fill his mouth or throat, then lowering it into the milk, would take some to wash it down. This method kept the milk cool, and by frequent repetitions the pioneer would contract a faculty of correctly estimating the proper amount of each. Others would mix mush and milk together. . . . . .

To get grinding done was often a great difficulty, by reason of the scarcity of mills, the freezes in winter, and droughts in summer. We had often to manufacture meal (*when we had corn*) in any way we could get the corn to pieces. We soaked and pounded it, we shaved it, we planed it, and, at the proper season, grated it. When one of our neighbors got a hand-mill, it was thought quite an acquisition to the neighborhood. In after years, when in time of freezing or drought, we could get grinding by waiting for our turn no more than one day and a night at a horse mill, we thought ourselves happy. To save meal we often made pumpkin bread, in which when meal was scarce, the pumpkin would so predominate as to render it next to impossible to tell our bread from that article, either by taste, looks, or the amount of nutriment it contained. Salt was five dollars per bushel, and we used none in our corn bread, which we soon liked as well without it. Often has sweat ran into my mouth, which tasted as fresh and flat as distilled water. What meat we had at first was fresh, and but little of that, for had we been hunters we had no time to practice it.

We had no candles, and cared but little about them except for summer use. In Carolina we had the real fat light-wood, not merely pine knots, but the fat straight pine. This, from the brilliancy of our parlor, of winter evenings, might be supposed to put, not only candles, lamps, camphine, Greenough's chemical oil, but even gas itself, to the blush. In the West we had not this, but my business was to ramble the woods every evening for seasoned sticks, or the bark of the shelly hickory, for light. 'Tis true that our light was not as good as even candles, but we got along without fretting, for we depended more upon the goodness of our eyes than we did upon the brilliancy of the light.

Barnesville, 18 miles wsw. of St. Clairsville, is a large and flourishing town, containing 2 churches, 1 male academy, 1 masonic hall, and a population of about 750. Martinsville, 2 miles NW. of Wheeling city, on the Ohio river, contains 3 churches, 3 stores, and a population of 400. Morristown, 10 miles W. of St. Clairsville, on the National road, has 5 stores, 2 churches, and 350 people. Flushing, 10 miles NW. of St. Clairsville, has 3 stores and 250 people. Bellaire, Belmont, Hendrysburg, Jacobsburg, Somerton, Uniontown, West Wheeling, Burlington, Centreville, Farmington, Loydsville, Shepperdstown, and Steinersvile, are also small villages.

BROWN.

Brown was formed from Adams and Clermont, March 1, 1817, and named from Gen. Jacob Brown, an officer of the war of 1812. Excepting the Ohio river hills, the surface is level or undulating, and the soil generally fertile: the northern part, more especially, is adapted to grazing, and the southern to grain. The staples are wheat, corn, rye, oats and pork. The following are the names of its townships in 1840, with their population.

Byrd,	2422	Huntington,	1957	Pleasant,	1485
Clark,	1290	Jackson,	1253	Scott,	1101
Eagle,	888	Lewis,	2044	Sterling,	608
Franklin,	1199	Perry,	1869	Union,	2071
Green,	358	Pike,	792	Washington,	848

Population of Brown county, in 1820, 13,367; in 1830, 17,866; in 1840, 22,715, or 44 inhabitants to a square mile.

A short time previous to the settlement of this county, a severe battle was fought at a locality, called "the salt lick," in Perry township, in the northern part of the county, between a party of Kentuckians and some Indians, under Tecumseh. The circumstances are here given from Drake's life of that celebrated Indian chief.

"In the month of March, 1792, some horses were stolen by the Indians, from the settlements in Mason county, Kentucky. A party of whites, to the number of thirty-six, was immediately raised for the purpose of pursuing them. It embraced Kenton, Whiteman, M'Intyre, Downing, Washburn, Calvin and several other experienced woodsmen. The first named, Simon Kenton, a distinguished Indian fighter, was placed in command. The trail of the Indians being taken, it was found they had crossed the Ohio, just below the mouth of Lee's creek, which was reached by the pursuing party towards evening. Having prepared rafts, they crossed the Ohio that night, and encamped. Early next morning the trail was again taken and pursued, on a north course, all day, the weather being bad and the ground wet. On the ensuing morning, twelve of the men were unable to continue the pursuit, and were permitted to return. The remainder followed the trail until eleven o'clock, A. M., when a bell was heard, which they supposed indicated their approach to the Indian camp. A halt was called, and all useless baggage and clothing laid aside. Whiteman and two others were sent ahead as spies, in different directions, each being followed by a detachment of the party. After moving forward some distance, it was found that the bell was approaching them. They halted, and soon perceived a solitary Indian riding towards them. When within one hundred and fifty yards, he was fired at and killed. Kenton directed the spies to proceed, being now satisfied that the camp of the Indians was near at hand. They pushed on rapidly, and after going about four miles, found the Indians encamped on the south-east side of the east fork of the Little Miami, a few miles above the place where the town of Williamsburg has since been built. The indications of a considerable body of Indians were so strong, that the expediency of an attack at that hour of the day was doubted by Kenton. A hurried council was held, in which it was determined to retire, if it could be done without discovery, and lie concealed until night, and then assault the camp. This plan was carried into execution. Two of the spies were left to watch the Indians, and ascertain whether the pursuing party had been discovered. The others retreated for some distance, and took a commanding position on a ridge. The spies watched until night, and then reported to their commander, that they had not been discovered by the enemy. The men being wet and cold, they were now marched down into a hollow, where they kindled fires, dried their clothes, and put their rifles in order. The party was then divided into three detachments,—Kenton commanding the right, M'Intyre the centre, and Downing the left. By agreement, the three divisions were to move towards the camp, simultaneously, and when they had approached as near as possible, without giving an alarm, were to be guided in the commencement of the attack, by the fire from Kenton's party. When Downing and his detachment had approached close to the camp, an Indian rose upon his feet, and began to stir up the fire, which was but dimly burning. Fearing a discovery, Downing's party instantly shot him down. This was followed by a general fire from the three detachments, upon the Indians who were sleeping under some marquees and bark tents, close upon the margin of the stream. But unfortunately, as it proved in the sequel, Kenton's party had taken "Boone," as their watch-word. This name happening to be as familiar to the enemy as themselves, led to some confusion in the course of the engagement. When fired upon, the Indians, instead of retreating across the stream, as had been anticipated, boldly stood to their arms, returned the fire of the assailants, and rushed upon them. They were reinforced, moreover, from a camp on the opposite side of the river, which, until then, had been unperceived by the whites. In a few minutes, the Indians and the Kentuckians were blended with each other, and the cry of "Boone," and "Che Boone," arose simultaneously from each party.

"It was after midnight when the attack was made, and there being no moon, it was very dark. Kenton, perceiving that his men were likely to be overpowered, ordered a retreat, after the attack had lasted for a few minutes; this was continued through the remainder of the night and part of the next day, the Indians pursuing them, but without killing more than one of the retreating party. The Kentuckians lost but two men, Alexander M'Intyre and John Barr. The loss of the Indians was much greater, according to the statements of some prisoners, who, after the peace of 1795, were released and returned to Kentucky. They related, that fourteen Indians were killed, and seventeen wounded. They stated further, that there were in the camp about one hundred warriors, among them several chiefs of note, including Tecumseh, Battise, Black Snake, Wolf and Chinskau; and that the party had been formed for the purpose of annoying the settlements in Kentucky, and attacking boats descending the Ohio river. Kenton and his party were three days in reaching Limestone, during two of which they were without food, and destitute of sufficient clothing to protect them from the cold winds and rains of March. The foregoing particulars of this expedition are taken from the manuscript narrative of Gen. Benjamin Whiteman, one of the early and gallant pioneers to Kentucky, now a resident of Green county, Ohio.

"The statements of Anthony Shane and of Stephen Ruddell, touching this action, vary in some particulars from that which has been given above, and also from the narrative in McDonald's Sketches. The principal difference relates to the number of Indians in the engagement, and the loss sustained by them. They report but two killed, and that the Indian force was less than that of the whites. Ruddell states, that at the commencement of the attack, Tecumseh was lying by the fire, outside of the tents. When the first gun was heard, he sprang to his feet, and calling upon Sinnamatha to follow his example, and charge, he rushed forward and killed one of the whites [John Barr] with his war-club. The other Indians, raising the war-whoop, seized their arms, and rushing upon Kenton and his party, compelled them, after a severe contest of a few minutes, to retreat. One of the Indians, in the midst of the engagement, fell into the river, and in the effort to get out of the water, made so much noise, that it created a belief on the minds of the whites, that a reinforcement was crossing the stream to aid Tecumseh. This is supposed to have hastened the order from Kenton, for his men to retreat. The afternoon prior to the battle, one of Kenton's men, by the name of M'Intyre, succeeded in catching an Indian horse, which he tied in the rear of the camp; and, when a retreat was ordered, he mounted and rode off. Early in the morning, Tecumseh and four of his men set off in pursuit of the retreating party. Having fallen upon the trail of M'Intyre, they pursued it for some distance, and at length overtook him. He had struck a fire, and was cooking some meat. When M'Intyre discovered his pursuers, he instantly fled at full speed. Tecumseh and two others followed, and were fast gaining on him, when he turned and raised his gun. Two of the Indians, who happened to be in advance of Tecumseh, sprung behind trees, but he rushed upon M'Intyre and made him prisoner. He was tied and taken back to the battle ground. Upon reaching it, Tecumseh deemed it prudent to draw off his men, lest the whites should rally and renew the attack. He requested some of the Indians to catch the horses, but they, hesitating, he undertook to do it himself, assisted by one of the party. When he returned to camp with the horses, he found that his men had killed M'Intyre. At this act of cruelty to a prisoner, he was exceedingly indignant; declaring that it was a cowardly act to kill a man when tied, and a prisoner. The conduct of Tecumseh, in this engagement, and in the events of the following morning, is creditable alike to his courage and humanity. Resolutely brave in battle, his arm was never uplifted against a prisoner, nor did he suffer violence to be inflicted upon a captive, without promptly rebuking it."

McDonald, in speaking of this action, says:

"The celebrated Tecumseh commanded the Indians. His cautious and fearless intrepidity made him a host wherever he went. In military tactics, night attacks are not allowable, except in cases like this, when the assailing party are far inferior in numbers. Sometimes, in night attacks, panics and confusion are created in the attacked party, which may render them a prey to inferior numbers. Kenton trusted to something like this on the present occasion, but was disappointed; for when Tecumseh was present, his influence over the minds of his followers infused that confidence in his tact and intrepidity, that they could only be defeated by force of numbers."

Georgetown, the county seat, is 107 miles from Columbus, 30 from Hillsboro, 46 from Wilmington, 21 from Batavia and West Union. It was laid off in the year 1819, and its original propietors were Allen Woods and Henry Newkirk. It is a smart business town, containing 1 Presbyterian, 1 Baptist, 1 Christian Disciples, and 1 Methodist church, a newspaper printing office, and about 800 inhabitants. The view shows the public square, with the old court

Public Square, Georgetown.

house on the left, and on the right, in the distance, a new and elegant Methodist church. It is contemplated to erect, shortly, a new court house, in good architectural taste. Georgetown was the residence of the late Gen. THOMAS L. HAMER, who died in Mexico.

He commenced the practice of the law in Georgetown, in the year 1820, which he continued until June, 1846, at which time he volunteered in the Mexican war. He was elected Major of the 1st Reg. Ohio Volunteers, and received the appointment of Brig. Gen. from the President, before his departure for the seat of war. In that station, he acquitted himself with great ability up to the period of his death. He was in the battle at Monterey, and on Maj. Gen. Butler's being wounded, succeeded him in the command. He distinguished himself on this occasion, by his coolness and courage.

Gen. Hamer was endowed with most extraordinary abilities as an orator, advocate and lawyer. He represented the district in which he resided, six years in congress, and distinguished himself as an able and sagacious statesman; and at the time of his death, was a member elect to congress.

The estimation in which he was held by his professional brethren, may be feebly gathered from the proceedings of the members of the bar of his county, the proceedings of which meeting were presented to the Supreme Court of Ohio, for Brown county, on the 23d of April, and the court requested to have the same entered upon their journals; whereupon, Judge Read expressed the views of the court, as follows:

"It is with pleasure that the court direct the proceedings of the bar to be entered of record, as the customary tribute to distinguished worth. It is proper to add, that the court sympathize deeply with the family of Gen. Hamer, and the bar, and the community, in the loss we have sustained. Gen. Hamer was an ornament to the bar, and had distinguished himself in the counsels of the nation, and won to himself renown upon her battle fields. It is proper that one should cherish his memory, and keep his virtues and example before us. We, therefore, direct the clerk to enter these proceedings of record, as a testimonial of the high estimation entertained for the deceased by the court and the bar, and as a slight expression of the deep regret felt for his loss."

In the county, there are two large settlements of colored persons, numbering about 500 each. One of these is 3 miles north of Georgetown; the other is in the NE. part of the county, about 16 miles distant. They emigrated from Virginia, in the year 1818, and were originally the slaves of Samuel Gist, who manumitted and settled them here, upon two large surveys of land. Their situation, unfortunately, is not prosperous.

Ripley, from the Kentucky side of the Ohio.

Ripley is upon the Ohio, 10 miles from Georgetown, 9 below Maysville, and 50 above Cincinnati. The town was laid out about the period of the war of 1812, by Col. James Poage, a native of Virginia, and first named Staunton, from Staunton, Va.; it was afterwards changed to Ripley, from Gen. Ripley, an officer of distinction in the war. When the county was first formed, the courts were directed to be held at the house of Alex. Campbell, in this town, until a permanent seat of justice should be established. For a time, it was supposed that this would be the county seat; a court house was begun, but before it was finished, the county seat was permanently established at Georgetown. The courts were, for a time, held in the 1st Presbyterian church, which was the first public house of worship erected. Ripley is the largest and most business place in the county, and one of the most flourishing villages on the Ohio river, within the limits of the state. The view shows the central part of the town only; it extends about a mile on the river. Ripley contains 2 Presbyterian, 1 Methodist, 1 Associate Reformed, 1 New Light, and 1 Catholic church, 20 stores, 1 newspaper printing office, 1 iron foundery, 1 carding machine, 3 flouring mills, and had, in 1840, 1245 inhabitants; since, it has considerably increased. The Ripley female seminary, under the charge of Wm. C. Bissell and lady, has about forty pupils. The "Ripley College" was chartered by the state, but not endowed: it is now a high school, under the care of the Rev. John Rankin, and an assistant, and has about forty pupils, of both sexes. This institution admits colored children within its walls; and there are quite a number of people, in this region, who hold to the doctrine of equal rights, politically and socially, to all, irrespective of color.

Aberdeen, opposite Maysville, Ky., was founded by Nathan Ellis, who was either from Scotland or of Scotch extraction. It contains several stores and churches, and had, in 1840, 405 inhabitants. Higginsport, on the river, 7 miles from Georgetown, is a considerable village, and has 3 churches, 4 stores, and, in 1840, had 393 inhabitants. Russelville is also a village of note, 7 miles E. of Georgetown, and is famous for its churches, of which it has seven, together with as many stores, and about 350 inhabitants. In the Perry township, in the extreme north part of the county, are many Catholics. They have a cathedral of much splendor, and a nunnery. Decatur, Hamersville, Arnheim, Sardinia, Fincastle, Carlisle, New Hope, Fayetteville and Greenbush are small villages in the county.

BUTLER.

Butler was formed in 1803, from Hamilton, and named in honor of Gen. Richard Butler, a distinguished officer of the revolution, who fell in St. Clair's defeat. The surface is level. It is all within the blue limestone formation, and is one of the richest agricultural tracts in Ohio. Its staples are corn, wheat, oats and pork. It produces more corn than any county of the state, the annual crop being over two millions of bushels! A large proportion of its population are of German descent. The following are the names of its townships, in 1840, with their population.

Fairfield,	3580	Milford,	1868	Ross,	1524
Hanover,	1680	Morgan,	1726	St. Clair,	2307
Lemon,	3065	Oxford,	3422	Union,	2118
Liberty,	1479	Reily,	1758	Wayne,	1562
Madison,	2208				

In 1820, its population was 21,755; in 1830, 27,143; in 1840 28,207, or 59 inhabitants to a square mile.

The large and flourishing town of Hamilton, the county seat, is 22 miles N. of Cincinnati, on the left bank of the Great Miami. It contains 1 Presbyterian, 1 Episcopal, 1 Methodist, 1 German Lutheran, 1 Associate Reformed, 1 Baptist, and 1 Catholic church, a

Public Square, Hamilton.

flourishing female academy, 2 newspaper printing offices, 3 flouring mills, 3 cotton factories, 3 saw mills, 2 foundries, 2 machine shops, and about 16 mercantile stores; in 1840, its population was 1409, since which it has considerably increased. Hamilton is destined to be an important manufacturing town. The hydraulic works, lately built here, rank among the best water powers west of the Alleghanies. This work is formed by a canal, commencing at the Big Miami, four miles above the town, and emptying into the river near the bridge, at Hamilton. By it a very great amount of never failing water power has been created, sufficient, with a small additional investment, to propel 200 runs of 4½ mill stones. It is durably constructed, and is adding much to the business of the community.

View of Rossville, from Hamilton.

Hamilton is neatly built, and has an elegant public square, on which stand the county buildings; it is enclosed by an iron fence, handsomely covered with green turf, and shaded by locusts and other ornamental trees. A noble bridge, erected at the expense of about $25,000, connects this town with its neighbor, Rossville, on the opposite bank of the Miami, which the engraving shows as it appears from the market, in Hamilton. Rossville is also a flourishing place, superior to Hamilton, as a mercantile town, as that is as a manufacturing one. This arises from the circumstance, that it is more convenient to the greater proportion of the farmers of the county, who reside on that side of the Miami. It contains 1 Presbyterian and 1 Baptist church, 1 flouring mill, about 18 mercantile stores, and had, in 1840, 1140 inhabitants; its population has since increased.

The route of St. Clair, in his disastrous campaign, in 1791, passed through this county. In September, of that year, Fort Hamilton was built at the crossing of the Great Miami, on the site of Hamilton. It was intended as a place of deposit for provisions, and to form the first link in the communication between Fort Washington and the object of the campaign. It was a stockade of fifty yards square, with four good bastions, and platforms for cannon in two of them, with barracks. In the summer succeeding, an addition was made to the fort, by order of Gen. Wilkinson, which consisted in enclosing, with pickets, an area of ground on the north part, so that it extended up the river to about the north line of the present Stable street. The southern point of the work extended to the site of the Associate Reformed church.

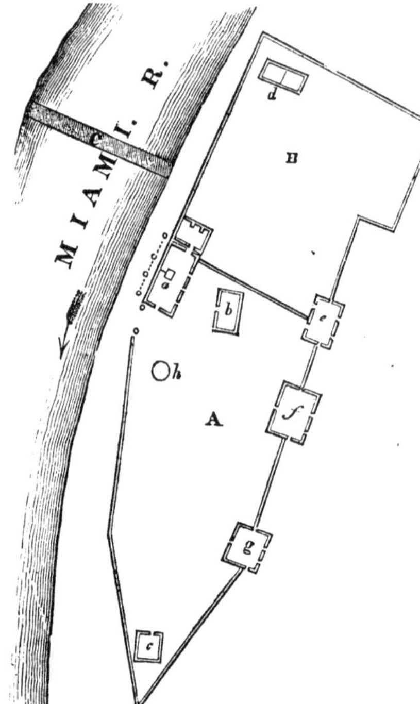

Fort Hamilton.

The plan given of the fort, is from the survey of Mr. Jas. M'Bride,* of Hamilton, made by him several years after.

References.—A. The old fort built by St. Clair. B. Addition. *a.* Officers quarters. *b.* Mess room. *c.* Magazine. *d.* Artificers shop. *e, f, g.* Block houses. C. Present bridge across the Miami, shown in the view of Rossville.

---

* This gentleman has written a large volume—as yet unpublished—filled with valuable facts and anecdotes connected with the history of the Miami valley. For the historical sketch of Hamilton, and several incidents in various parts of our work, we are indebted to these MSS.

Late in the fall of 1792, an advance corps of troops, under the command of Major Rudolph, arrived at Fort Hamilton, where they wintered. They consisted of three companies of light dragoons, one of rifle, and one of infantry. Rudolph was a Major of dragoons, from lower Virginia. His reputation was that of an arbitrary and tyrannical officer. Sometime in the spring, seven soldiers deserted to the Ohio river, where, procuring a canoe, they started for New Orleans. Ten or fifteen miles below the falls of the Ohio, they were met by Lieut. (since Gen.) Clark, and sent back to Fort Hamilton, where a court martial sentenced three of them to be hung, two to run the gauntlet, and the remaining two to lie in irons, in the guard house, for a stipulated period. John Brown, Seth Blin and —— Gallaher, were the three sentenced to be hung. The execution took place the next day, on a gallows erected below the fort, just south of the site of the present Associate Reformed church, and near the residence of James B. Thomas.

Five hundred soldiers were drawn up in arms around the fatal spot, to witness the exit of their unfortunate comrades. The appearance of the sufferers, at the gallows, is said to have been most prepossessing. They were all young men of spirit, and handsome appearance, in the opening bloom of life, with their long hair floating over their shoulders. John Brown was said to have been a young man, of very respectable connections, who lived near Albany, New York. Early in life, he had formed an attachment for a young woman in his neighborhood, of unimpeachable character, but whose social standing did not comport with the pride of his parents. He was forbidden to associate with her, and required to pay his addresses to another. Broken-hearted and desponding, he left his home, enlisted in a company of dragoons, and came to the west. His commanding officer treated him so unjustly, that he was led to desert. When under the gallows, the sergeant, acting as executioner, inquired why the sentence of the law should not be enforced upon him, he replied, with emphasis—pointing to Major Rudolph—" that he had rather die nine hundred deaths, than be subject to the command of such a man ;" and was swung off, without a murmur. Seth Blin was the son of a respectable widow, residing in the state of New York. The rope being awkwardly fastened around his neck, he struggled greatly. Three times he raised his feet, until they came in contact with the upper part of the gallows, when the exertion broke his neck.

Immediately after the sentence had been pronounced on these men, a friend hastened to Fort Washington, where he obtained a pardon from Gen. Wilkinson. But he was too late. The execution had been hastened by Major Rudolph, and he arrived at Hamilton fifteen minutes after the spirits of these unfortunate men had taken their flight to another world. Their bodies were immediately committed to the grave, under the gallows. There, in the dark and narrow house, in silence, lies the only son of a widowed mother, the last of his family. A vegetable garden is now cultivated over the spot, by those who think not nor know not of the once warm heart that lies cold below.

The two other deserters were sentenced to run the gauntlet sixteen times, between two ranks of soldiers, which was carried forthwith into execution. The lines were formed in the rising ground, east of the fort, where now lies Front street, and extended from Smithman's corner to the intersection of Ludlow street. One of them, named Roberts, having passed eight times through the ranks, fell, and was unable to proceed. The attendant physician stated that he could stand it no longer, as his life had already been endangered.

Sometime after Gen. Wayne arrived at the post, and although frequently represented as an arbitrary man, he was so much displeased with the cruelty of Major Rudolph, that he gave him his choice, to resign or be cashiered. He chose the former, returned to Virginia, and subsequently, in company with another gentleman, purchased a ship, and went on a trading voyage to Europe. They were captured (it is stated) by an Algerine cruiser, and Rudolph was hung at the yard arm of his own vessel. I have heard some of those who were under his command, in Wayne's army, express satisfaction at the fate of this unfortunate man.

In the summer of 1792, two wagoners were watching some oxen, which had been turned out to graze on the common below the fort; a shower of rain coming on, they retired for shelter under a tree, which stood near where the sycamore grove now is. Some Indians, who had been watching from under the covert of the adjoining underbrush, rushed suddenly upon them, killed one and took the other prisoner. The latter was Henry Shafor, who, after his return, lived, until a few years past, two or three miles below Rossville, on the river.

In September, 1793, the army of Wayne marched from Cincinnati to Fort Hamilton, and encamped in the upper part of the prairie, about half a mile south of the present town, nearly on the same ground on which Gen. St. Clair had encamped in 1791. Here they threw up a breastwork, the remains of which may yet be traced at the point where the present road strikes the Miami river, above Traber's mill. A few days after, they continued their march toward the Indian country.

Gen. Wayne detailed a strong guard of men for the defence of the fort, the command of which was given to Major Jonathan Cass, of the army of the revolution, and father of the Hon. Lewis Cass, of the U. S. Senate. Major Cass continued in command until the treaty of Greenville.

On the 17th of December, 1794, Israel Ludlow laid out, within Symmes's purchase, the original plot of the town of Hamilton, which he, at first, for a short time only, called Fairfield. Shortly after, a few settlers came in. The first settlers were Darius C. Orcut, John Green, Wm. M'Clennan, John Sutherland, John Torrence, Benj. F. Randolph, Benj. Davis, Isaac Wiles, Andrew Christy and Wm. Hubbert.

Previous to 1801, all the lands on the west side of the Great Miami were owned by the United States, consequently there were no improvements made on that side of the river, except by a few squatters. There was one log house built at an early period, near the west end of the bridge, now owned by the heirs of Lewis P. Sayre. On the first Monday in April, 1801,—at the first sale of the United States lands west of the Miami, held at Cincinnati,—a company purchased the site of Rossville, on which, March 14th, 1804, they laid out the town. Mr. John Reily was the agent of the proprietors.

The first settlers of Hamilton suffered much from the fever and ague, and being principally disbanded soldiers, without energy, and many of them dissipated, but little improvement was made for the first few years. In those early times, horse-racing was a favorite amusement, and an affair of all engrossing interest. On public days, indeed on almost every other Saturday, the streets and commons in the upper part of the town were converted into race paths. The race course comprehended the common from 2d to 4th street. At 2d street, a short distance north of the site of the Catholic church, was an elevated scaffold on which stood the judges of the race. On grand occasions, the plain within the course and near it, were occupied with booths, erected with forks and covered with boughs. Here every thing was said, done, eaten, sold and drank. Here was Black Jack with his fiddle, and his votaries making the dust fly, with a four-handed, or rather four-footed reel; and every fifteen or twenty minutes was a rush to some part to see a "*fisty cuff*." Among the bustling crowd of jockies were assembled all classes. Even Judges of the court mingled with the crowd, and sometimes presided at the contests of speed between the ponies of the neighborhood.

Soon after the formation of Butler county, Hamilton was made the county seat. The first sessions of the court were held in the tavern of Mr. Torrence, now the residence of Henry S. Earhart. The sessions of the court after this were held in the former mess room of the fort. It was a rough one story frame building, about 40 by 20 feet, weather-boarded, without either filling or plastering, and stood about where the market now is. It was elevated from the ground about three feet by wooden blocks affording a favorite shelter for the hogs and sheep of the village. The Judges seat was a rough platform of unplaned boards, and a long table in front, like a carpenter's work bench, was used by the bar. In 1810, the court was removed to a room over the stone jail, and in 1817, transferred to the present court house.

The court, at their July term, in 1803, selected the old magazine within the fort as a county jail. It was a heavy built log building, about 12 feet square, with a hipped roof coming to a common center and surmounted by a ball. The door had a hole in the center shaped like a half-moon, through which air, light and food were conveyed, while on the outside it was secured by a pad-lock and hasp. It was very insecure, and escapes were almost as frequent as committals. It was the only jail for Butler county, from 1803 to 1809. A small log house formerly a sutlers store, was used as a clerk's office. It has since been altered into a private dwelling, at present occupied by Dutch Jacob. The house erected by Gen. Wilkinson, in '92, for officer's quarters, (see a plan of fort,) was converted into a tavern kept by the county sheriff, Wm. M'Clellan, while the barracks and artificers shops were used as stables.

Jno. Cleves Symmes

J. C. Symmes's Signature.

JOHN CLEVES SYMMES, the author of the "Theory of Concentric Spheres, demonstrating that the Earth is hollow, habitable within, and widely open about the Poles," died at Hamilton, May 28th, 1829. He was born in New Jersey about the year 1780. His father,

Timothy Symmes, was the brother of John Cleves Symmes, well-known as the founder of the first settlements of the Miami valley. In the early part of his life he received a common school education, and in 1802 was commissioned an ensign in the army. In 1813, he was promoted to a captaincy, in which capacity he served until the close of the war with honor. He was in the hard-fought battle of Bridgewater, and at the sortie of Fort Erie, where with his command he captured a battery, and personally spiked the cannon. At the close of the war he retired from the army, and for about three years was engaged in furnishing supplies to the troops stationed on the Upper Mississippi. After this, he resided for a number of years at Newport, Ky., and devoted himself to philosophical researches connected with his favorite theory. In a short circular, dated at St. Louis, in 1818, Capt. Symmes first promulgated the fundamental principles of his theory to the world. From time to time, he published various articles in the public prints upon the subject. He also delivered lectures, first at Cincinnati in 1820, and afterwards in various places in Kentucky and Ohio.

"In the year 1822, Capt. Symmes petitioned the Congress of the United States, setting forth, in the first place, his belief of the existence of a habitable and accessible concave to this globe; his desire to embark on a voyage of discovery to one or other of the polar regions; his belief in the great profit and honor his country would derive from such a discovery; and prayed that Congress would equip and fit out for the expedition, two vessels of two hundred and fifty, or three hundred, tons burthen; and grant such other aid as government might deem necessary to promote the object. This petition was presented in the Senate by Col. Richard M. Johnson, a member from Kentucky, on the 7th day of March, 1822, when, (a motion to refer it to the committee of Foreign Relations having failed,) after a few remarks it was laid on the table.—*Ayes*, 25. In December, 1823, he forwarded similar petitions to both houses of Congress, which met with a similar fate. In January, 1824, he petitioned the General Assembly of the state of Ohio, praying that body to pass a resolution approbatory of his theory; and to recommend him to Congress for an outfit suitable to the enterprise. This memorial was presented by Micajah T. Williams; and, on motion, the further consideration thereof was indefinitely postponed."

His theory was met with ridicule, both in this country and Europe, and became a fruitful source of jest and levity, to the public prints of the day. Notwithstanding, he advanced many plausible and ingenious arguments, and won quite a number of converts among those who attended his lectures, one of whom, a gentleman now residing at Hamilton, wrote a work in its support, published in Cincinnati in 1826, in which he states his readiness to embark on a voyage of discovery, for the purpose of testing its truth. Captain Symmes met with the usual fate of projectors, in living and dying in great pecuniary embarrassment. In person, he was of the medium stature and simple in his manners. He bore the character of an honest, exemplary man, and was respected

J. C. Symmes' Monument.

by all his associates. He was buried at Hamilton. The monument represented by the cut, has been built, but is not yet placed over his remains. It is surmounted by a globe, "open at the poles."

Mr. John Reily, of this county, is one of the five members living of the convention which framed the Constitution of Ohio. His friend, Judge Burnet, in his late work, has given an eloquent tribute to his character and services.

Middletown is 12 miles ne. of Hamilton, and 20 below Dayton, in a rich and beautiful country. The Miami canal runs east of the central part of the town, and the Miami river bounds it on the west.

Lebanon Street, Middletown.

It is connected with Dayton and Cincinnati, and with West Alexandria, in Preble county, by turnpikes. The Warren county canal enters the main canal at this town. Two or three miles above, a dam is thrown across the Miami, from which a connecting feeder supplies the Miami canal. This work furnishes much water power, which, with a little expense, can be increased and used to great advantage. There are within three miles of Middletown, 8 flouring mills on the river and canal. Middletown was laid out in 1802, by Stephen Vail and James Sutton. Calvin Morrell, James Brady, Cyrus Osbourn, Daniel Doty, Elisha Wade and Richard Watts were among its early settlers. It contains 1 Presbyterian, 1 Baptist, and 1 Methodist church, a classical academy, 16 mercantile stores, 2 forwarding houses, 1 grist mill and 1 woolen factory, and in 1840, had 809 inhabitants. The view of Lebanon street, was taken at its intersection with Broadway. Liebee's block is shown on the right, Deardorf's mill and the bridge over the Miami partly appear in the distance.

In the northwest corner of the county, 12 miles from Hamilton, on a high and beautiful elevation, is the handsome town of Oxford, the seat of the Miami University. It contains 9 mercantile stores, 1 woolen factory, 2 Presbyterian, 1 Associate Reformed, and 1 Methodist church, and in 1840, had 1179 inhabitants. The Associate church have established a theological school here, under the care of the Rev. Dr. Claybaugh; it is yet in its infancy, promises well, and has a valuable collection of books.

The Miami University buildings are in the east part of the town, in a large enclosure of fifty acres, part of which is in the

Miami University at Oxford.

original forest, and the remainder covered with a green sward, and ornamented with scattering shade trees. Including the preparatory department, there are about 150 students in the institution, which is under the charge of a President—the Rev. E. D. MacMaster—and 4 professors, beside the principal of the preparatory department. "The course of studies are not less extensive than those of the best colleges in the Union, and its faculty are earnestly endeavoring to establish the institution on a solid foundation." It was chartered in 1809, by the legislature of Ohio, and a township of land given by Congress for its support. The University was not regularly opened for the reception of students, until Nov. 15th, 1824. From that period until 1841, it had 308 graduates.

Somerville, 14 miles NNW. from Hamilton, had in 1840, 318 inhabitants; Millville, 7 W. from Hamilton, Monroe, 12 NE., Chester, 10 SE., and Darrtown, 10 NW., had each about 200 inhabitants. Jacksonburg, Miltonville, Reily and Trenton are also small villages. In this county are numerous ancient works, mounds, fortifications, &c.

CARROL.

CARROL was formed in the session of 1832–3, from Columbiana, Stark, Tuscarawas, Harrison and Jefferson, and named from Chas. Carrol, of Carrolton, Md., the last survivor of the signers of the Declaration of American Independence. The surface is hilly, and the staples are wheat, oats and corn; coal and iron abound. The population mainly originated from Pennsylvania, Virginia and Maryland, with some Germans and Irish. The following is a list of its townships in 1840, with their population.

Augusta,	1234	Harrison,	1308	Perry,	1344
Brown,	2165	Lee,	1372	Ross,	1593
Centre,	1139	Loudon,	966	Union,	889
East,	995	Monroe,	1060	Washington,	1014
Fox,	1491	Orange,	1528		

The population of Carrol in 1840, was 18,108, or 45 inhabitants to a square mile.

View in Carrolton.

Carrolton, the county seat, is 125 miles ENE. from Columbus. It was originally called Centreton, but on the organization of the county, changed to its present name. It is rather compactly built, with a public square in the centre—shown in the above view—on which stand the county buildings. It contains 1 Presbyterian, 1 Lutheran, 1 Methodist Episcopal, and 1 Associate Reformed church, 6 mercantile stores, 2 printing offices, and 800 inhabitants.

Leesburg, 12 miles SW. of Carrolton, has 2 churches, 3 stores, and about 60 dwellings. It is on One Leg, a stream so named from a one legged Indian who anciently dwelt upon its margin. The Indian name of this water course is the "*Kannoten.*" The "Dining Fork of the Kannoten" derived its appellation, from the first explorers in this region dining upon its banks. Hagerstown, 1½ miles east of Leesburg, is a somewhat smaller village, having a church, 3 stores, and a classical academy. New Harrisburg, Malvern, Magnolia, Pekin, Augusta, Norristown, Lodi, Minerva, Mechanicstown and Harlem, are small places; at the last of which is a chalybeate spring, said to possess excellent medicinal qualities.

CHAMPAIGN.

CHAMPAIGN was formed from Greene and Franklin, March 1st, 1805, and the temporary seat of justice fixed in Springfield, at the house of George Fithian: it derived its name from the character of its surface. About half of it is level or slightly undulating, one quarter rolling, one fifth rather hilly, and about five per cent. wet prairie, and best adapted for grazing. The county is drained by Mad river and its tributaries. The stream flows through a beautiful country, and with its tributaries furnishes extensive mill privileges. The soil is generally rich, and the principal crops are wheat, corn, oats, barley and hay: wool and beef cattle are also important staples. The following is a list of its townships in 1840, with their population.

Adams,	970	Jackson,	1431	Salem,	1402
Concord,	935	Johnson,	1213	Union,	1249
Goshen,	1406	Mad River,	1894	Urbana,	2456
Harrison,	790	Rush,	1226	Wayne,	1300

The population of Champaign in 1820, was 8,479; in 1830, 12,137; and in 1840, 16,720, or 44 inhabitants to a square mile.

Urbana, the county seat, is 42 miles WNW. from Columbus. It was laid out in 1805, by Col. Wm. Ward, originally from Greenbriar, Va. He was proprietor of the soil, and gave a large number of the lots to the county, with the provision that their sales should be appropriated for public objects. He also named the place, from the word *urbanity*. The two first settlers were the clerk of the court, Joseph C. Vance, father of Ex-Gov. Vance, and George Fithian, who opened the first tavern in a cabin, now forming a part of the dwelling of Wm. Thomas, on South Main street. Samuel M'Cord opened the first store, in the same cabin, in March, 1806, and built, the same year, the first shingled house, now the store of Wm. & Duncan M'Donald. In 1807, a temporary court house was erected, now the residence of Duncan M'Donald. A brick court house was subsequently built on the public square, which stood many years, and then gave place to the present substantial and handsome building. In 1807, the Methodists—those religious pioneers—built the first church, a log structure, which stood in the northeast part of the town, on the lot on which Mr. Ganson resides. Some years later, this denomination erected a brick church, now devoted to the manufacture of carriages and wagons by Mr. Childs, in the central part of the town. The first settlers in the village were Joseph C. Vance, Thos. and Ed. W. Pearce, George Fithian, Samuel M'Cord, Zeph. Luse, Benj. Doolittle, Geo. and Andrew Ward, Wm. H. Fyffe, Wm. and John Glenn, Fred. Ambrose, John Reynolds and Samuel Gibbs. Of those living in the county at that time, our informant recollects the names of Jacob Minturn, Henry and Jacob Vanmetre, Nathaniel Cartmell, Justice Jones, Felix Rock, Thomas Anderson, Abner Barret, Thomas Pearce, Benj. and Wm. Cheney, Matthew and Chas. Stuart, Parker Sullivan, John Logan, John Thomas, John Runyon, John Lafferty, John Owens, John Taylor, John Guttridge, John Cartmell, John Dawson, John Pence, Jonathan Long, Bennet Taber, Nathan Fitch, Robt. Nowce, Jacob Pence and Arthur Thomas.

The last named, Capt. Arthur Thomas, lived on King's creek, three miles from Urbana. He was ordered, in the war of 1812, with his company, to guard the public stores at Fort Findlay. On his return,

Public Square, Urbana.

himself and son lost their horses, and separated from the rest of the company to hunt for them. They encamped at the Big Spring, near Solomonstown, about 5 miles north of Bellfontaine, and the next morning were found killed and scalped. Their bodies were brought into Urbana, by a deputation of citizens. On the 4th of July, two months previous to this event, "The Watch Tower," the first newspaper in the county was commenced at Urbana; its publishers were Corwin & Blackburn.

Urbana was a point where the main army of Hull concentrated, ere leaving for Detroit. They encamped in the eastern part of the town, on the home-lot of Judge Elisha C. Berry. In the last war it was a general rendezvous for troops, before starting for the north. They encamped in various parts of the town. Quite a number of sick and disabled soldiers were sent here, some of whom died: the old court house was used as a hospital.

The celebrated Simon Kenton was here at an early day. Judge Burnet in his letters, states, that when the troops were stationed at Urbana, a mutinous plan was formed by part of them to attack and destroy a settlement of friendly Indians, who had removed with their families within the settlement under assurance of protection. Kenton remonstrated against the measure, as being not only mutinous, but treacherous and cowardly. He contrasted his knowledge and experience of the Indian character with their ignorance of it. He vindicated them against the charge of treachery, which was alledged as a justification of the act they were about to perpetrate, and reminded them of the infamy they would incur by destroying a defenceless band of men, women and children, who had placed themselves in their power, relying on a solemn promise of protection. He appealed to their humanity, their honor and their duty as soldiers. Having exhausted all the means of persuasion in his power, and finding them resolved to execute their purpose, he took a rifle and declared with great firmness that he would accompany them to the Indian encampment, and shoot down the first man who dared to molest them; that if they entered his camp they should do it by passing over his corpse. Knowing that the *old veteran* would redeem his pledge, they abandoned their purpose, and the poor Indians were saved. Though he was as brave as Cesar, and reckless of danger when it was his duty to expose his person; yet he was mild, even tempered, and had a heart that could bleed at the distresses of others.

There were several Indian councils in Urbana, at an early day, which were usually held in a grove near the burying ground: distinguished Shawnee and Wyandot chiefs were generally present. Before the settlement of the town, in the spring of 1795, Tecumseh was established on Deer creek, near the site of Urbana, where he engaged in his favorite amusement of hunting, and remained until the succeeding spring. His biographer gives some anecdotes of him, which occurred within the present limits of the county.

While residing on Deer creek, an incident occurred, which greatly enhanced his reputation as a hunter. One of his brothers, and several other Shawanoes of his own age, proposed to bet with him, that they could each kill as many deer, in the space of three days, as he could. Tecumseh promptly accepted the overture. The parties took to the woods, and at the end of the stipulated time, returned with the evidences of their success. None of the party, except Tecumseh, had more than twelve deer skins; he brought in upwards of thirty—near three times as many as any of his competitors. From this time he was generally conceded to be the greatest hunter in the Shawanoe nation.

In 1799, there was a council held about six miles north of the place where Urbana now stands, between the Indians and some of the principal settlers on Mad river, for the adjustment of difficulties which had grown up between these parties. Tecumseh, with other Shawanoe chiefs, attended this council. He appears to have been the most conspicuous orator of the conference, and made a speech on the occasion, which was much admired for its force and eloquence. The interpreter, Dechouset, said that he found it very difficult to translate the lofty flights of Tecumseh, although he was as well acquainted with the Shawanoe language, as with the French, which was his mother tongue.

Some time during the year 1803, a stout Kentuckian came to Ohio, for the purpose of exploring the lands on Mad river, and lodged one night at the house of Capt. Abner Barrett, residing on the head waters of Buck creek. In the course of the evening, he learned, with apparent alarm, that there were some Indians encamped within a short distance of the house. Shortly after hearing this unwelcome intelligence, the door of Captain Barrett's dwelling was suddenly opened, and Tecumseh entered with his usual stately air: he paused in silence, and looked around, until at length his eye was fixed upon the stranger, who was manifesting symptoms of alarm, and did not venture to look the stern savage in the face. Tecumseh turned to his host, and pointing to the agitated Kentuckian, exclaimed, "a big baby! a big baby!" He then stepped up to him, and gently slapping him on the shoulder several times, repeated, with a contemptuous manner, the phrase, "*big baby! big baby!*" to the great alarm of the astonished man, and to the amusement of all present.

On the 22d of March, 1830, a severe tornado, proceeding from the SW. to the NE., passed over the northern part of Urbana. It demolished the Presbyterian church and several dwellings, and materially injured the Methodist church. Two or three children were carried high in air, and killed; boards, books and various fragments were conveyed many miles.

Urbana is a beautiful town, and has, in its outskirts, some elegant private residences. The engraving is a view in its central part, taken from near Reynold's store. The court house and Methodist church are seen in the distance. The building on the left, now occupied as a store by Wm. M'Donald, was, in the late war, Doo little's tavern, the head quarters of Governor Meigs. The one in front, with the date "1811," upon it, and now the store of D. & T. M'Gwynne, was then a commissaries office, and the building where Col. Richard M. Johnson was brought wounded from the battle of the Thames, and in which he remained several days, under a surgeon's care. Urbana contains 1 Associate Reformed, 1 Presbyterian,

1 Baptist, and 1 Methodist church, 2 newspaper printing offices, 1 woollen factory, 1 foundery, 2 machine shops and 20 mercantile stores. In 1840, Urbana had 1070 inhabitants, which is far below its present population.

Mechanicsburg, 10 miles E. of Urbana, on the Columbus road and head waters of Little Darby, is a flourishing village, containing 5 or 6 stores, 2 churches, 1 saw and 2 flour mills, a woollen factory, and had, in 1840, 258 inhabitants. Addison, 16 sw., St. Paris, 10 w., Westville, 4 w. of Urbana, and Woodstock and Lewisburg, in the NE. part of the county, are villages containing each from 36 to 60 dwellings. Middletown, Carysville, Millerstown, Middleburg and Texas are small places.

CLARK.

CLARK. was formed March 1, 1817, from Champaign, Madison and Greene, and named in honor of Gen. George Rogers Clarke. The first settlement in Clarke, was at Chribb's station, in the forks of Mad river, in the spring of 1796. The inhabitants of Moorefield, Pleasant, Madison, German and Pike are principally of Virginia extraction; Mad river, of New Jersey; Harmony, of New England and English; and Greene, of Pennsylvania origin. This county is very fertile and highly cultivated, and is well watered by Mad river, Buck and Beaver creeks, and their tributaries, which furnish a large amount of water power. Its principal products are wheat, corn and oats. The following is a list of its townships, in 1840, with their population.

Bethel,	2033	Madison,	1115	Pike,	1437
German,	1667	Mad river,	1339	Pleasant,	1092
Greene,	1059	Moorefield,	1073	Springfield,	4443
Harmony,	1645				

The population of the county, in 1820, was 9,553; in 1830, 13,074, and in 1840, 16,882, or 43 inhabitants to a square mile.

The old Indian town of Piqua, the ancient Piqua of the Shawnees, and the birth place of TECUMSEH, was situated on the north side of Mad river, about five miles west of Springfield, and occupied the site on which a small town, called West Boston, has since been built. Drake'e life of Tecumseh, says.

The principal part of Piqua stood upon a plain, rising fifteen or twenty feet above the river. On the south, between the village and head river, there was an extensive prairie—on the northeast, some bold cliffs, terminating near the river—on the west and northwest, level timbered land; while on the opposite side of the stream, another prairie, of varying width, stretched back to the high grounds. The river sweeping by in a graceful bend—the precipitous, rocky cliffs—the undulating hills, with their towering trees—the prairies, garnished with tall grass and brilliant flowers—combined to render the situation of Piqua both beautiful and picturesque. At the period of its destruction, Piqua was quite populous. There was a rude log hut within its limits, surrounded by pickets. It was, however, sacked and burnt on the 8th of August, by an army of one thousand men, from Kentucky, after a severe and well-conducted battle with the Indians who inhabited it. All the improvements of the Indians, including more than two hundred acres of corn and other vegetables then growing in their fields, were laid waste and destroyed. The town was never after re-built by the Shawnees. Its inhabitants removed to the Great Miami river, and erected another town, which they called Piqua, after the one that had just been destroyed; and in defence of which they had fought with the skill and valor characteristic of their nation.

The account appended of the destruction of Piqua by General George Rogers Clarke, was published twenty years since, in Bradford's notes on Kentucky.

On the 2d of August, 1780, Gen. Clarke took up the line of march from where Cincinnati now stands, for the Indian towns. The line of march was as follows:—the first division, commanded by Clarke, took the front position; the centre was occupied by artillery, military stores and baggage; the second, commanded by Col. Logan, was placed in the rear. The men were ordered to march in four lines, at about forty yards distant from each other, and a line of flankers on each side, about the same distance from the right and left line. There was also a front and a rear guard, who only kept in sight of the main army. In order to prevent confusion, in case of an attack of the enemy, on the march of the army, a general order was issued, that in the event of an attack in front, the front was to stand fast, and the two right lines to wheel to the right, and the two left hand lines to the left, and form a complete line, while the artillery was to advance forwards to the centre of the line. In case of an attack on either of the flanks or side lines, these lines were to stand fast, and likewise the artillery, while the opposite lines wheeled and formed on the two extremes of those lines. In the event of an attack being made on the rear, similar order was to be observed as in an attack in front.

In this manner, the army moved on without encountering any thing worthy of notice until they arrived at Chillicothe, (situated on the little Miami river, in Greene county,) about 2 o'clock in the afternoon, on the 6th day of August. They found the town not only abandoned, but most of the houses burnt down and burning, having been set on fire that morning. The army encamped on the ground that night, and on the following day cut down several hundred acres of corn; and about 4 o'clock in the evening, took up their line of march for the Piqua towns, which were about twelve miles from Chillicothe, [in Clarke county.] They had not marched more than a mile from Chillicothe, before there came on a very heavy rain, with thunder and lightning and considerable wind. Without tents or any other shelter from the rain, which fell in torrents, the men were as wet as if they had been plunged into the river, nor had they it in their power to keep their guns dry. It was nearly dark before the rain ceased, when they were ordered to encamp in a hollow square, with the baggage and horses in the centre—and as soon as fires could be made, to dry their clothes, &c. They were ordered to examine their guns, and be sure they were in good order, to discharge them in the following manner. One company was to fire, and time given to re-load, when a company at the most remote part of the camp from that which had fired, was to discharge theirs, and so on alternately, until all the guns were fired. On the morning of the 8th, the army marched by sunrise, and having a level, open way, arrived in sight of Piqua, situated on the west side of the Mad river, about 2 o'clock, P. M. The Indian road from Chillicothe to Piqua, which the army followed, crossed the Mad river about a quarter of a mile below the town, and as soon as the advanced guard crossed into a prairie of high weeds, they were attacked by the Indians, who had concealed themselves in the weeds. The ground on which this attack, as well as the manner in which it was done, left no doubt but that a general engagement was intended. Col. Logan was therefore ordered, with about four hundred men, to file off to the right, and march up the river on the east side, and to continue to the upper end of the town, so as to prevent the Indians from escaping in that direction, while the remainder of the men, under Cols. Lynn, Floyd and Harrod, were ordered to cross the river and encompass the town on the west side, while Gen. Clarke, with the troops under Col. Shaughter, and such as were attached to the artillery, marched directly towards the town. The prairie in which the Indians were concealed, who commenced the attack, was only about two hundred yards across to the timbered land, and the division of the army destined to encompass the town on the west side, found it necessary to cross the prairie, to avoid the fire of a concealed enemy. The Indians evinced great military skill and judgment, and to prevent the western division from executing the duties assigned them, they made a powerful effort to turn their left wing. This was discovered by Lloyd and Flynn, and to prevent being outflanked, extended the line of battle west, more than a mile from the town, and which continued warmly contested on both sides until about 5 o'clock, when the Indians disappeared every where unperceived, except a few in the town. The field piece, which had been entirely useless before, was now brought to bear upon the houses, when a few shot dislodged the Indians which were in them.

A nephew of Gen. Clarke, who had been many years a prisoner among the Indians, and who attempted to come to the whites just before the close of the action, was supposed to be an Indian, and received a mortal wound; but he lived several hours after he arrived among them.

The morning after the battle, a Frenchman, who had been taken by the Indians a short time before, on the Wabash, and who had stolen away from them during the action, was found in the loft of one of the Indian cabins. He gave the information, that the Indians did not expect that the Kentuckians would reach their town on that day, and if they did not, it was their intention to have attacked them in the night, in their camp, with the tomahawk and knife, and not to fire a gun. They had intended to have made an attack the night before, but were prevented by the rain, and also the vigilance evinced by the Kentuckians, in firing off their guns and re-loading them, the reasons for which they comprehended, when they heard the firing. Another circumstance showed that the Indians were disappointed in the time of their arriving; they had not dined. When the men got into the town, they found a considerable quantity of provisions ready cooked, in large kettles and other vessels, almost untouched. The loss on each side was about equal—each having about 20 killed.

The Piqua town was built in the manner of the French villages. It extended along the margin of the river for more than three miles; the houses, in many places, were more than twenty poles apart. Col. Logan, therefore, in order to surround the town on the east, as was his orders, marched fully three miles, while the Indians turned their whole force against those on the opposite side of the town; and Logan's party never saw an Indian during the whole action. The action was so severe a short time before the close, that Simon Girty, a white man, who had joined the Indians, and who was made a chief among the Mingoes, drew off three hundred of his men, declaring to them, it was folly in the extreme to continue the action against men who acted so much like madmen, as General Clarke's men, for they rushed in the extreme of danger, with a seeming disregard of the consequences. This opinion of Girty, and the withdrawal of the three hundred Mingoes, so disconcerted the rest, that the whole body soon after dispersed.

It is a maxim among the Indians, never to encounter a fool or a madman, (in which terms they include a desperate man,) for they say, with a man who has not sense enough to take a prudent care of his own life, the life of his antagonist is in much greater danger than with a prudent man.

It was estimated that at the two Indian towns, Chillicothe and Piqua, more than five hundred acres of corn was destroyed, as well as every species of eatable vegetables. In consequence of this, the Indians were obliged, for the support of their women and children, to employ their whole time in hunting, which gave quiet to Kentucky for a considerable time.

The day after the battle, the 9th, was occupied in cutting down the growing corn, and destroying the cabins and fort, &c., and collecting horses. On the 10th of August, the army began their march homeward, and encamped in Chillicothe that night, and on the 11th, cut a field of corn, which had been left for the benefit of the men and horses, on their return. At the mouth of the Licking, the army dispersed, and each individual made his best way home.

Thus ended a campaign, in which most of the men had no other provisions for twenty-five days, than six quarts of Indian corn each, except the green corn and vegetables found at the Indian towns, and one gill of salt; and yet not a single complaint was heard to escape the lips of a solitary individual. All appeared to be impressed with the belief, that if this army should be defeated, that few would be able to escape, and that the Indians then would fall on the defenceless women and children in Kentucky, and destroy the whole. From this view of the subject, every man was determined to conquer or die.

The late Abraham Thomas, of Miami county, was in this campaign against Piqua. His reminiscences, published in 1839, in the Troy Times, give some interesting facts omitted in the preceding. It also differs, in some respects, from the other, and is probably the most accurate.

In the summer of 1780, Gen. Clarke was getting up an expedition, with the object of destroying some Indian villages on Mad river. One division of the expedition, under Col. Logan, was to approach the Ohio by the way of Licking river; the other, to which I was attached, ascended the Ohio from the falls in boats, with provisions and a six-pound cannon. The plan of the expedition was for the two divisions to meet at a point in the Indian country, opposite the mouth of Licking, and thence march in a body to the interior. In ascending the Ohio, Daniel Boone and myself acted as spies on the Kentucky side of the river, and a large party, on the Indian side, was on the same duty; the latter were surprised by the Indians, and several killed and wounded. It was then a toilsome task to get the boats up the river, under constant expectation of attacks from the savages, and we were much rejoiced in making our destination. Before the boats crossed over to the Indian side, Boone and myself were taken into the foremost boat, and landed above a small cut in the bank, opposite the mouth of Licking. We were desired to spy through the woods for Indian signs. I was much younger than Boone, ran up the bank in great glee, and cut into a beech tree with my tomahawk, which I verily believe was the first tree cut into by a white man, on the present site of Cincinnati. We were soon joined by other rangers, and hunted over the other bottom: the forest every where was thick set with heavy beech and scattering underbrush of spice-wood and pawpaw. We started several deer, but seeing no sign of Indians, returned to the landing. By this time the men had all landed, and were busy in cutting timber for stockades and cabins. The division, under Col. Logan, shortly crossed over from the mouth of Licking, and after erecting a stockade, fort and cabin, for a small garrison and stores, the army started for Mad river. Our way lay over the uplands of an untracked, primitive forest, through which, with great labor, we cut and bridged a road for the accommodation of our pack horses and cannon. My duty, in the march, was to spy some two miles in advance of the main body. Our progress was slow, but the weather was pleasant, the country abounded in game; and we saw no Indians, that I recollect, until we approached the waters of Mad river. In the campaigns of these days, none but the officers thought of tents—each man had to provide for his own comfort. Our meat was cooked upon sticks set up before the fire; our beds were sought upon the ground, and he was the most fortunate man, that could gather small branches, leaves and bark to shield him from the ground, in moist places. After the lapse of so many years, it is difficult to recollect the details or dates, so as to mark the precise time or duration of our movements. But in gaining the open country of Mad river, we came in sight of the Indian villages. We had been kept all the night before on the march, and pushed rapidly towards the points of attack, and surprised three hundred Indian warriors, that had collected at the town, with the view of surprising and attacking us the next morning. At this place, a stockade fort had been reared near the village, on the side we were approaching it, but the Indians feared to enter it, and took post in their houses.

The village was situated on a low prairie bottom of Mad river, between these cond bank and a bushy swamp piece of ground, on the margin of the river: it could be approached only from three points. The one our troops occupied, and from up and down the river. Gen. Clarke detached two divisions to secure the two last named points, while he extended his line to cover the first. By this arrangement, the whole body of Indians would have been surrounded and captured, but Col. Logan, who had charge of the lower division, became entangled in the swamp, and did not reach his assigned position before the attack commenced. The party I had joined was about entering the town, with great impetuosity, when Gen. Clarke sent orders for us to stop, as the Indians were making port holes in their cabins, and we should be in great danger, but added, he would soon make port holes for us both; on that, he brought his six-pounder to bear on the village, and a discharge of grape shot scattered the materials of their frail dwellings in every direction. The Indians poured out of their cabins in great consternation, while our party, and those on the bank, rushed into the village, took possession of all the squaws and papooses, and killed a great many warriors, but most of them at the lower part of the bottom. In this skirmish, a nephew of Gen. Clarke, who had some time before run away from the Monongahela settlements, and joined the Indians, was severely wounded. He was a great reprobate, and, as said, was to have led the Indians in the next morning's attack; before he expired, he asked forgiveness of his uncle and countrymen. During the day, the village was burned, the growing corn cut down; and the next morning we took up the line of march for the Ohio. This was a bloodless victory to our expedition, and the return march was attended with no unpleasant occurrence, save a great scarcity of provisions. On reaching the fort, on the Ohio, a party of us immediately crossed the river for our homes, for which we felt an extreme anxiety. We depended chiefly on our rifles for sustenance; but game not being within reach, without giving to it more time than our anxiety and rapid progress permitted, we tried every expedient to hasten our journey without hunting, even to boiling green plums and nettles. These, at first, under sharp appetites, were quite palatable, but soon became bitter and offensive. At last, in traversing the head waters of Licking, we espied several buffalo, directly in our track. We killed one, which supplied us bountifully with meat until we reached our homes.

View at Piqua, the birth-place of Tecumseh.

The view given was taken near the residence of Mr. John Keifer. The hill, shown on the left in the engraving, was the one upon which stood the fort, previously mentioned. About twenty-five years since, when the hill was first cleared and cultivated by Mr. Keifer, charred stumps were found around its edge, indicating the line of the stockade, which included a space of about two acres; the plow of Mr. Keifer brought up various relics, as skeletons, beads, gun-barrels, tomahawks, camp kettles, &c. Other relics led to the supposition that there was a store of a French trader destroyed at the time of the action at the south-western base of the hill. When the country was first settled, there were two white oak trees in the village of Boston, which had been shot off some fifteen or twenty feet from the ground, by the cannon balls of Clarke; their tops showed plainly the curved lines of the balls, around which they had sprouted bush-like; these trees were felled many years since by the Bostonians for fuel. There is a tradition here, that during the action, the Indians secreted their squaws and children in "the cliffs" about a mile up the stream from the fort. The village of Boston, we will observe in digression, was once the competitor with Springfield for the county seat; it never had but a few houses, and now has three or four only: one of them is shown on the right of the view, beyond which, a few rods only, is Mad river.

We subjoin a sketch of the life of Tecumseh, derived from Drake's memoir of this celebrated chief:

Puckeshinwa, the father of Tecumseh, was a member of the Kiscopoke, and Methoataske, the mother, of the Turtle tribe of the Shawanoe nation; they removed from Florida to Ohio about the middle of the last century. The father rose to the rank of a chief, and fell at the battle of Point Pleasant, in 1774. After his death, his wife returned to the south, where she died, at an advanced age. Tecumseh was born at Piqua, about the year 1768, and like Napoleon, in his boyish pastimes, showed a passion for war; he was the acknowledged leader among his companions, by whom he was loved and respected, and over whom he exercised an unbounded influence; it is stated that the first battle in which he was, occurred on the site of Dayton, between a party of Kentuckians under Col.

Benjamin Logan, and some Shawanoes. When about 17 years of age, he manifested signal prowess, in an attack on some boats on the Ohio, near Limestone, Ky. The boats were all captured, and all in them killed, except one person, who was burnt alive. Tecumseh was a silent spectator, never having before witnessed the burning of a prisoner; after it was over, he expressed his strong abhorrence of the act, and by his eloquence persuaded his party never to burn any more prisoners.

From this time his reputation as a brave, and his influence over other minds, increased, and he rose rapidly in popularity among his tribe; he was in several actions with the whites prior to Wayne's treaty, among which was the attack on Fort Recovery, and the battle of the Fallen Timbers. In the summer of 1795, Tecumseh became a chief; from the spring of this year until that of 1796, he resided on Deer Creek, near the site of Urbana, and from whence he removed to the vicinity of Piqua, on the Great Miami. In 1798, he accepted the invitation of the Delawares, then residing in part on White river, Indiana, to remove to that neighborhood with his followers. He continued in that vicinity a number of years, and gradually extended his influence among the Indians.

In 1805, through the influence of Laulewasikaw, the brother of Tecumseh, a large number of Shawanoes established themselves at Greenville. Very soon after, Laulewasikaw assumed the office of a *prophet;* and forthwith commenced that career of cunning and pretended sorcery, which enabled him to sway the Indian mind in a wonderful degree.

Throughout the year 1806, the brothers remained at Greenville, and were visited by many Indians from different tribes, not a few of whom became their followers. The Prophet dreamed many wonderful dreams, and claimed to have had many supernatural revelations made to him; the great eclipse of the sun which occurred in the summer of this year, a knowledge of which he had by some means attained, enabled him to carry conviction to the minds of many of his ignorant followers, that he was really the earthly agent of the Great Spirit. He boldly announced to the unbelievers, that on a certain day, he would give them proof of his supernatural powers, by bringing darkness over the sun; when the day and hour of the eclipse arrived, and the earth, even at mid-day, was shrouded in the gloom of twilight, the Prophet, standing in the midst of his party, significantly pointed to the heavens, and cried out, "did I not prophecy truly? Behold! darkness has shrouded the sun!" It may readily be supposed that this striking phenomenon, thus adroitly used, produced a strong impression on the Indians, and greatly increased their belief in the sacred character of their Prophet.

The alarm caused by the assembling of the Indians still continuing, Gov. Harrison, in the autumn of 1807, sent to the head chiefs of the Shawanoe tribe, an address, in which he exhorted them to send away the people at Greenville, whose conduct was foreshadowing evil to the whites. To the appeal of the governor, the prophet made a cunning and evasive answer; it made no change in the measures of this artful man, nor did it arrest the spread of fanaticism among the Indians, which his incantations had produced.

In the spring of 1808, Tecumseh and the prophet removed to a tract of land on the Tippecanoe, a tributary of the Wabash, where the latter continued his efforts to induce the Indians to forsake their vicious habits, while Tecumseh was visiting the neighboring tribes and quietly strengthening his own and the prophet's influence over them. The events of the early part of the year 1810, were such as to leave but little doubt of the hostile intentions of the brothers the Prophet was apparently the most prominent actor, while Tecumseh was in reality the main spring of all the movements, backed, it is supposed, by the insidious influence of British agents, who supplied the Indians gratis with powder and ball, in anticipation, perhaps, of hostilities between the two countries, in which event an union of all the tribes against the Americans was desirable. By various acts the feelings of Tecumseh became more and more evident; in August, he having visited Vincennes to see the governor, a council was held, at which, and a subsequent interview, the real position of affairs was ascertained.

Governor Harrison had made arrangements for holding the council on the portico of his own house, which had been fitted up with seats for the occasion. Here, on the morning of the fifteenth, he awaited the arrival of the chief, being attended by the Judges of the Supreme Court, some officers of the army, a sergeant and twelve men, from Fort Knox, and a large number of citizens. At the appointed hour, Tecumseh, supported by forty of his principal warriors, made his appearance, the remainder of his followers being encamped in the village and its environs. When the chief had approached within thirty or forty yards of the house, he suddenly stopped, as if awaiting some advances from the governor; an interpreter was sent, requesting him and his followers to take seats on the portico. To this Tecumseh objected—he did not think the place a suitable one for holding the conference, but preferred that it should take place in a grove of trees—to which he pointed—standing a short distance from the house. The governor said he had no objection to the grove, except that there were no seats in it for their accommodation. Tecumseh replied, that constituted no objection to the grove, the earth being the most suitable place for the Indians, who loved to repose upon the bosom of their mother. The governor yielded the point, and the benches and chairs having been removed to the spot, the conference was begun, the Indians being seated on the grass.

Tecumseh opened the meeting by stating, at length, his objections to the treaty of Fort Wayne, made by Governor Harrison, in the previous year; and in the course of his speech boldly avowed the principle of his party to be that of resistance to every cession of land, unless made by all the tribes, who, he contended, formed but one nation. He admitted that he had threatened to kill the chiefs who signed the treaty of Fort Wayne, and that it was his fixed determination not to permit the *village* chiefs, in future, to manage their affairs, but to place the power with which they had been heretofore invested, in the hands of the war chiefs. The Americans, he said, had driven the Indians from the sea-coast, and would soon push them into the lakes; and, while he disclaimed all intention of making war upon the United States, he declared it to be his unalterable resolution to take a stand, and resolutely oppose the further intrusion of the whites upon the Indian lands. He concluded, by making a brief but impassioned recital of the various wrongs and aggressions inflicted by the white men upon the Indians, from the commencement of the revolutionary war down to the period of that council; all of which was calculated to arouse and inflame the minds of such of his followers as were present.

The governor rose in reply, and in examining the right of Tecumseh and his party to make objections to the treaty of Fort Wayne, took occasion to say that the Indians were not one nation, having a common property in the lands. The Miamis, he contended, were the real owners of the tract on the Wabash, ceded by the late treaty, and the Shawanoes had no right to interfere in the case; that upon the arrival of the whites on this continent, they had found the Miamis in possession of this land, the Shawanoes being then residents of Georgia, from which they had been driven by the Creeks, and that it was ridiculous to assert that the red men constituted but one nation; for, if such had been the intention of the Great Spirit, he would not have put different tongues in their heads, but have taught them all to speak the same language.

The governor having taken his seat, the interpreter commenced explaining the speech to Tecumseh, who, after listening to a portion of it, sprung to his feet and began to speak with great vehemence of manner.

The governor was surprised at his violent gestures, but as he did not understand him, thought he was making some explanation, and suffered his attention to be drawn towards Winnemac, a friendly Indian lying on the grass before him, who was renewing the priming of his pistol, which he had kept concealed from the other Indians, but in full view of the governor. His attention, however, was again directed towards Tecumseh, by hearing

General Gibson, who was intimately acquainted with the Shawanoe language, say to lieutenant Jennings, "those fellows intend mischief; you had better bring up the guard." At that moment, the followers of Tecumseh seized their tomahaws and war clubs, and sprung upon their feet, their eyes turned upon the governor. As soon as he could disengage himself from the armed chair in which he sat, he rose, drew a small sword which he had by his side, and stood on the defensive. Captain G. R. Floyd, of the army, who stood near him, drew a dirk, and the chief Winnemac cocked his pistol. The citizens present were more numerous than the Indians, but were unarmed; some of them procured clubs and brick-bats, and also stood on the defensive. The Rev. Mr. Winans, of the Methodist church, ran to the governor's house, got a gun, and posted himself at the door to defend the family. During this singular scene, no one spoke, until the guard came running up, and appearing to be in the act of firing, the governor ordered them not to do so. He then demanded of the interpreter an explanation of what had happened, who replied that Tecumseh had interrupted him, declaring that all the governor had said was *false*, and that he and the Seventeen Fires had cheated and imposed on the Indians. The governor then told Tecumseh that he was a bad man, and that he would hold no further communication with him; that as he had come to Vincennes under the protection of a council-fire, he might return in safety, but that he must immediately leave the village. Here the council terminated.

The undoubted purpose of the brothers now being known, Gov. Harrison proceeded to prepare for the contest he knew must ensue. In June of the year following, (1811,) he sent a message to the Shawanoes, bidding them beware of hostilities, to which Tecumseh gave a brief reply, promising to visit the governor. This visit he paid in July, accompanied by 300 followers, but as the Americans were prepared and determined, nothing resulted, and Tecumseh proceeded to the south, as it was supposed, to enlist the Creeks in the cause.

In the meanwhile, Harrison took measures to increase his regular force; his plan was to again warn the Indians to obey the treaty of Greenville, but at the same time to prepare to break up the prophet's establishment, if necessary. On the 5th of October, having received his reinforcements, he was on the Wabash, about 60 miles above Vincennes, where he built Fort Harrison. On the 7th of November following, he was attacked by the Indians at Tippecanoe, and defeated them. Peace on the frontiers was one of the happy results of this severe and brilliant action.

With the battle of Tippecanoe, the prophet lost his popularity and power among the Indians, he having, previously to the battle, promised them certain victory.

On the first commencement of the war of 1812, Tecumseh was in the field, prepared for the conflict. In July, there was an assemblage at Brownstown of those Indians who were inclined to neutrality. A deputation was sent to Malden to Tecumseh to attend this council. "No," said he indignantly, "I have taken sides with the king, my father, and I will suffer my bones to bleach upon this shore, before I will recross that stream to join in any council of neutrality." He participated in the battle of Brownstown, and commanded the Indians in the action near Maguaga. In the last he was wounded, and it is supposed that his bravery and good conduct led to his being shortly after appointed Brigadier General in the service of the British King. In the seige of Fort Meigs, Tecumseh behaved with great bravery and humanity. (See Wood co.)

Immediately after the signal defeat of Proctor, at Fort Stephenson, he returned with the British troops to Malden by water, while Tecumseh, with his followers, passed over by land, round the head of Lake Erie, and joined him at that point. Discouraged by the want of success, and having lost all confidence in Gen. Proctor, Tecumseh seriously meditated a withdrawal from the contest, but was induced to remain.

When Perry's battle was fought, it was witnessed by the Indians from the distant shore. On the day succeeding the engagement, Gen. Proctor said to Tecumseh, "my fleet has whipped the Americans, but the vessels being much injured, have gone into Put-in Bay to refit, and will be here in a few days." This deception, however, upon the Indians was not of long duration. The sagacious eye of Tecumseh soon perceived indications of a retreat from Malden, and he promptly inquired into the matter. Gen. Proctor informed him that he was only going to send their valuable property up the Thames, where it would meet a reinforcement, and be safe. Tecumseh, however, was not to be deceived by this shallow device; and remonstrated most urgently against a retreat. He finally demanded, in the name of all the Indians under his command, to be heard by the general, and, on the 18th of September, delivered to him, as the representative of their great father, the king, the following speech:—

"Father, listen to your children! you have them now all before you.

"The war before this, our British father gave the hatchet to his red children, when our old chiefs were alive. They are now dead. In that war our father was thrown upon his back by the Americans; and our father took them by the hand without our knowledge; and we are afraid that our father will do so again at this time.

"Summer before last, when I came forward with my red brethren and was ready to take up the hatchet in favor of our British father, we were told not to be in a hurry, that he had not yet determined to fight the Americans.

"Listen! when war was declared, our father stood up and gave us the tomahawk, and told us that he was then ready to strike the Americans; that he wanted our assistance, and that he would certainly get our lands back, which the Americans had taken from us.

"Listen! you told us at that time, to bring forward our families to this place, and we did so; and you promised to take care of them, and they should want for nothing, while the men would go and fight the enemy; that we need not trouble ourselves about the enemy's garrisons; that we knew nothing about them, and that our father would attend to that part of the business. You also told your red children that you would take good care of your garrison here, which made our hearts glad.

"Listen! when we were last at the Rapids, it is true we gave you little assistance. It is hard to fight people who live like ground-hogs.

"Father, listen! our fleet has gone out; we know they have fought; we have heard the great guns; but we know nothing of what has happened to our father with one arm. Our ships have gone one way, and we are much astonished to see our father tying up every thing and preparing to run away the other, without letting his red children know what his intentions are. You always told us to remain here and take care of our lands; it made our hearts glad to hear that was your wish. Our great father, the king, is the head, and you represent him. You always told us you would never draw your foot off British ground; but now, father, we see that you are drawing back, and we are sorry to see our father doing so without seeing the enemy. We must compare our father's conduct to a fat dog, that carries his tail on its back, and when affrighted, drops it between its legs and runs off.

"Father, listen! the Americans have not yet defeated us by land; neither are we sure that they have done so by water; *we, therefore, wish to remain here and fight our enemy, should they make their appearance*. If they defeat us, we will then retreat with our father.

"At the battle of the Rapids, last war, the Americans certainly defeated us; and when we returned to our father's fort at that place, the gates were shut against us. We were afraid that it would now be the case; but instead of that, we now see our British father preparing to march out of his garrison.

"Father, you have got the arms and ammunition which our great father sent for his red children. If you have an idea of going away, give them to us, and you may go and welcome, for us. Our lives are in the hands of the Great Spirit. We are determined to defend our lands, and if it be his will, we wish to leave our bones upon them."

Tecumseh entered the battle of the Thames with a strong conviction that he should not survive it. Further flight he deemed disgraceful, while the hope of victory in the impending action, was feeble and distant. He, however, heroically resolved to achieve the latter or die in the effort. With this determination he took his stand among his followers, raised the war-cry and boldly met the enemy. From the commencement of the attack on the Indian line, his voice was distinctly heard by his followers, animating them to deeds worthy of the race to which they belonged. When that well-known voice was heard no longer above the din of arms, the battle ceased. The British troops having already surrendered, and the gallant leader of the Indians having fallen, they gave up the contest and fled. A short distance from where Tecumseh fell, the body of his friend and brother-in-law, Wasegoboah, was found. They had often fought side by side, and now, in front of their men, bravely battling the enemy, they side by side closed their mortal career.

"Thus fell the Indian warrior Tecumseh, in the 44th year of his age. He was of the Shawanoe tribe, five feet ten inches high, and with more than the usual stoutness, possessed all the agility and perseverance of the Indian character. His carriage was dignified, his eye penetrating, his countenance, which even in death, betrayed the indications of a lofty spirit, rather of the sterner cast. Had he not possessed a certain austerity of manners, he could never have controlled the wayward passions of those who followed him to battle. He was of a silent habit; but when his eloquence became roused into action by the reiterated encroachments of the Americans, his strong intellect could supply him with a flow of oratory that enabled him, as he governed in the field, so to prescribe in the council. Those who consider that in all territorial questions, the ablest diplomatists of the United States are sent to negotiate with the Indians, will readily appreciate the loss sustained by the latter in the death of their champion. . . . . . Such a man was the unlettered savage, Tecumseh, and such a man have the Indians lost forever. He has left a son, who, when his father fell, was about seventeen years old, and fought by his side. The prince regent, in 1814, out of respect to the memory of the old, sent out as a present to the young Tecumseh, a handsome sword. Unfortunately, however, for the Indian cause and country, faint are the prospects that Tecumseh the son, will ever equal, in wisdom or prowess, Tecumseh the father."

It is stated by Mr. James, a British historian, that Tecumseh, after he fell, was not only scalped, but that his body was actually *flayed*, and the skin converted into razor-straps by the Kentuckians. Amid the great amount of conflicting testimony relating to the circumstances of Tecumseh's death, it is extremely difficult, if not impossible, to ascertain the precise facts. It is, however, generally believed that he fell by a pistol-shot, fired by Col. Richard M. Johnson of Kentucky, who acted a most prominent part in this battle.

Springfield, the county seat, is 43 miles w. of Columbus, on the National road, and on the line of the railroads connecting Cincinnati with Sandusky city. It was laid out in 1803, by James Demint. It is surrounded by a handsome and fertile country, is noted for the morality and intelligence of its inhabitants, and, by many, is considered the most beautiful village within the limits of Ohio. The eastern fork of Mad river washes it on the north, a stream described "as unequalled for fine mill seats, its current very rapid, and the water never so low in the driest season as to interfere with the mills now upon it." Through the place runs the *Lagonda*, or Buck creek, a swift and unfailing mill stream. Within a range of three miles of the town are upwards of twenty mill seats. Springfield suffered much during the era of speculation, but is now prospering, and from its natural advantages, is destined to hold a prominent place among the manufacturing towns of the state. The engraving shows its appearance as viewed from the National road, a quarter of a mile east; the main street appears in front, on the left the academy, and on the right the court house, and one of the churches. The view is from a familiar position, but the village, like many other beautiful towns, is so situated that no drawing from any one point can show it to advantage.

East View of Springfield.

Several of the first settlers of Springfield still remain in and around it; among them may be mentioned the names of John Humphreys, David Lowry and Griffeth Foos, the last of whom occupied the first house built in the town as a tavern.

The Ohio Conference of the Methodist Episcopal church has a flourishing high school at Springfield, for both sexes. A lyceum has been in successful operation about fourteen years, and the public libraries of the town comprise about 4000 volumes. Springfield contains 1 Presbyterian, 1 Methodist Episcopal, 1 Methodist Protestant, 1 Episcopal, 1 Associate Reformed Presbyterian, 1 Baptist, 1 Lutheran, 1 Universalist, and 1 African Methodist church; 2 or 3 printing offices; 3 drug, 1 book, 1 hardware, and 15 dry good stores; 1 paper, 1 oil, and 3 flouring mills; 1 cotton, 1 woolen, and 1 sash factory; 1 foundery and machine shop; and in 1830, had a population of 1080; in 1840, 2094; in 1846, 2952; and in 1847, about 3500.

Springfield was the scene of an interesting incident in the life of Tecumseh, which is given at length by his biographer.

In the autumn of this year, [1807,] a white man by the name of Myers, was killed a few miles west of where the town of Urbana now stands, by some straggling Indians. This murder, taken in connection with the assemblage of the Indians under Tecumseh and the prophet, created a great alarm on the frontier, and actually induced many families to remove back to Kentucky, from whence they had emigrated. A demand was made by the whites upon these two brothers for the Indians who had committed the murder. They denied that it was done by their party, or with their knowledge, and declared that they did not even know who the murderers were. The alarm continued, and some companies of militia were called out. It was finally agreed, that a council should be held on the subject in Springfield, for the purpose of quieting the settlements. Gen. Whiteman, Maj. Moore, Capt. Ward, and one or two others, acted as commissioners on the part of the whites. Two parties of Indians attended the council; one from the north, in charge of McPherson; the other, consisting of sixty or seventy, came from the neighborhood of Fort Wayne, under the charge of Tecumseh. Roundhead, Blackfish, and several other chiefs, were also present. There was no friendly feeling between these two parties, and each was willing that the blame of the murder should be fixed upon the other. The party under McPherson, in compliance with the wishes of the commissioners, left their arms a few miles from Springfield. Tecumseh and his party refused to attend the council, unless permitted to retain their arms. After the conference was opened, it being held in a maple grove, a little north of where Werden's hotel now stands, the commissioners, fearing some violence, made another effort to induce Tecumseh to lay aside his arms. This he again refused, saying, in reply, that his tomahawk was also his pipe, and that he might wish to use it in that capacity before their business was closed. At this moment, a tall, lank-sided Pennsylvanian, who was standing among the spectators, and who, perhaps, had no love for the shining tomahawk of the self-willed chief, cautiously approached, and handed him an old, long stemmed, dirty looking earthen pipe, intimating, that if Tecumseh would deliver up the fearful tomahawk, he might smoke the aforesaid pipe. The chief took it between his thumb and finger, held it up, looked at it for a moment, then at the owner, who was gradually receding from the point of danger, and immediately threw it, with an indignant sneer, over his head, into the bushes. The commissioners yielded the point, and proceeded to business.

After a full and patient inquiry into the facts of the case, it appeared that the murder of Myers was the act of an individual, and not justly chargeable upon either party of the Indians. Several speeches were made by the chiefs, but Tecumseh was the principal speaker. He gave a full explanation of the views of the prophet and himself, in calling around them a band of Indians—disavowed all hostile intentions towards the United States, and denied that he or those under his control had committed any aggressions upon the whites. His manner, when speaking, was animated, fluent and rapid, and made a strong impression upon those present. The council terminated. In the course of it, the two hostile parties became reconciled to each other, and quiet was restored to the frontier.

The Indians remained in Springfield for three days, and on several occasions amused themselves by engaging in various games and other athletic exercises, in which Tecumseh generally proved himself victorious. His strength, and power of muscular action were remarkably great, and in the opinion of those who attended the council, corresponded with the high order of his moral and intellectual character.

Wittemberg College.

"Wittemberg College is organized on a large, and liberal prospective scale, and on the same basis as Yale College, Ct., having both a collegiate and theological department, under the same Board and Faculty. It is under the auspices of the Lutheran church, and was chartered in 1845. Arrangements are made for six professorships. It is located about a third of a mile from Springfield, on beautiful forest grounds, containing 24 acres, surrounded with springs of the best water, and with the most charming scenery. The town, railroad, Buck creek, and Mad river are in view from the building. The institution is under the superintendence of Rev. Ezra Keller, D. D., assisted by competent instructors. It has now been in operation for one year, and has had 72 students connected with it. A freshman and sophomore class has been formed. An Athæneum, and two literary societies have also been established. A general library, philosophical apparatus, and cabinet of natural and artificial curiosities have been begun. The German is taught as a living language. Tuition and boarding are furnished on very moderate terms. The government of the institution is made as nearly as possible to that of a well-regulated family."

New Carlisle, 12 miles west of Springfield, is a flourishing village, in a beautiful and fertile country. It contains 2 Presbyterian, 1 Methodist, and 1 Free or Union church, 6 stores, an extensive coach factory, a fine brick school house, and by the census of 1840, has 452 inhabitants. South Charleston, 12 miles SE. from Springfield, on the Xenia and Jefferson turnpike, has 2 churches, several stores, and had in 1840, 240 inhabitants, since which it has much increased. Enon, on the Dayton turnpike, 7 miles from Springfield, has 2 churches, several stores, and about 60 dwellings: on the outskirts of this town is a beautiful mound, 30 or 40 feet in height. North Hampton, Tremont, Vienna, Donaldsville, Brighton, Harmony, Noblesville, Catawba, and Cortsville, are small villages. (*See Addenda.*)

CLERMONT.

Clermont, the 8th county, created in the North-west Territory, was formed Dec. 9th, 1800, by proclamation of Gov. St. Clair. The name was probably derived from Clermont, in France. The surface is generally rolling and quite broken near the Ohio: in the northeast, there is much "wet land." A large portion of the soil is rich. The geological formation is the blue fossiliferous limestone, interstratified with clay marl, and covered, in most places, with a rich vegetable mould. The principal crops are corn, wheat, oats, hay, potatoes, tobacco, barley, buckwheat and rye; the principal exports are beef, pork, flour, hay and whiskey. It is well watered, and the streams furnish considerable water power. The following is a list of its townships, in 1840, with their population.

Batavia,	2197	Monroe,	1617	Union,	1421
Franklin,	2219	Ohio,	2894	Washington,	2102
Goshen,	1445	Stonelick,	1478	Wayne,	976
Jackson,	883	Tate,	2292	Williamsburgh,	1459
Miami,	2061				

The population of Clermont, in 1820, was 15,820; in 1830, 20,466; and in 1840, 23,106, or 40 inhabitants to a square mile.

The communication below, from Mr. Benjamin Morris, gives some facts respecting the history of the county and its early settlers.

In June, 1804, and in the 19th year of my age, I came to Bethel, which, with Williamsburgh, were the only towns in the county. They were laid out about 1798 or '99, and were competitors for the county seat. When I came, Clermont was an almost unbroken wilderness, and the settlers few and far between. In the language of the day, there was

Denham's town, now Bethel; Lytlestown, now Williamsburgh; Witham's settlement, now Williamsville; Apples', Collins', and Buchanan's settlements. The following are names of part of the settlers in and about Williamsburgh, in 1804:—Wm. Lytle, R. W. Waring, David C. Bryan, James and Daniel Kain, Nicholas Sinks, Jasper Shotwell, and Peter Light. Wm. Lytle was the first clerk of the county, and was succeeded by R. W. Waring and David C. Bryan. Peter Light was a justice of the peace under the territorial and state governments, and county surveyor. Daniel Kain was sheriff, and later justice of the peace under the state government. David C. Bryan represented the county several years in the state legislature, before he was appointed clerk. I was at Williamsburgh at the sitting of the court of common pleas in June, 1804. Francis Dunleavy was the presiding judge, and Philip Gatch, Ambrose Ransom, and John Wood, associates, while the attendant lawyers were Jacob Burnet, Arthur St. Clair—son of Gov. St. Clair—Joshua Collet, Martin Marshall and Thomas Morris.

The following are part of the settlers in and about Bethel, in 1804: Obed Denham—proprietor of the town—James Denham, Houton Clark, John Baggess, Dr. Loofborough, John and Thomas Morris, Jeremiah Beck, Henry Willis and James South. John Baggess for many years was a representative in the legislature, justice of the peace and county surveyor. John Morris was appointed associate judge after the death of Judge Wood, in 1807; he was also justice of the peace, and one of the first settlers at Columbia. Houton Clark was one of the first, if not the very first, justice of the peace in Clermont. Thomas Morris practised law in the county about forty years, was a representative in the legislature, and once appointed a judge of the supreme court. In the winter of 1832–33, he was elected to the United States Senate, where he acted a conspicueus part in the anti-slavery movements of the day. The most prominent political act of his life, was his reply to a speech of Mr. Clay. He died suddenly, Dec. 7th, 1844: posterity only can judge of the correctness or incorrectness of his course. A neat marble monument marks his resting place, near Bethel. Jeremiah Beck and Henry Willis were farmers and justices of the peace. Ulrey's Run takes its name from Jacob Ulrey, who settled on its west side in 1798, and was the earliest settler upon it. The place is now known as "the Ulrey farm." Bred in the wilds of Pennsylvania, he was a genuine backwoodsman, and a terror to the horse thieves, who infested the county at an early day. Deer and bear were plenty around him, and a large portion of his time was passed in hunting them, for their skins. The early settlers around him received substantial tokens of his generosity, by his supplying them with meat.

The first newspaper in Clermont, "The Political Censor," was printed at Williamsburg, in 1813: it was edited by Thos. S. Foot, Esq.; the second, called "The Western American," was printed in the same town, in 1814: David Morris, Esq., editor.

A considerable number of the early settlers in Clermont, were from Kentucky. Of those before named, the following were from that state:—R. W. Waring, Jasper Shotwell, Peter Light, Obed and James Denham, Houton Clark, John Boggess, Jeremiah Beck, Henry Willis and James South. Nicholas Sinks was from Va.; David C. Bryan, from New Jersey, and John and Thomas Morris and the Kain family, (I believe,) from Pa. After 1804, the county increased rapidly by settlers from New Jersey, Kentucky and Pennsylvania, with some from Maryland, New England, and a few from North Carolina.

Neville was laid out in 1811, Gen. Neville, proprietor. Point Pleasant and New Richmond were laid out about 1814; Jacob Light, proprietor of the latter. George Ely laid out Batavia afterwards. The early settlers about that place, as well as I remember, were George Ely, Ezekiel Dimmit, Lewis Duckwall, Henry Miley, Robert and James Townsley, Titus Everhart and Wm. Patterson. Before Milford was laid out, Philip Gatch, Ambrose Ransom and John Pollock settled in its vicinity. Philip Gatch was a member from Clermont, of the convention which formed the state constitution, and for years after was associate judge. Ransom, as before stated, was associate judge; and John Pollock, for many years speaker of the house of representatives, and later, associate judge. Philip Gatch was a Virginian. He freed his slaves before emigrating, which circumstance led to his being selected as a member of the convention to form the state constitution.

The most prominent settlers in the south part of Clermont, were the Sargeant, Pigman, Prather, Buchanan and Fee families. The oldest members of the Sargeant family, were the brothers James, John and Elijah. They were from Maryland. James, who had freed his slaves there, was, in consequence, chosen a member of the convention which formed the state constitution. The Sargeants, who are now numerous in this part of the county, are uncompromising opponents of slavery. The Pigman family were Joshua, sen., Joshua, jr., and Levi. The Buchanan family were William, Alexander, Robert, Andrew, James, John, &c. James Buchanan, the son of John, was at one time speaker of the Ohio house of representatives. The Buchanans were from Pennsylvania, and the Pigmans from Maryland. There were several brothers of the Fee family, from Pennsylvania. William, the most prominent, was the proprietor of Felicity, and a member of the legislature. His brothers were Thomas, Elisha and Elijah; other early settlers were Samuel Walrioen, James Daughters and Elijah Larkin, who has been postmaster at Neville, for more than a quarter of a century. In the vicinity of Withamsville, the early settlers were Nathaniel and Gideon Witham, James Ward, Shadrach, Robert and Samuel Lane. The Methodists were the most numerous in early times, and next, the Baptists; there were but a few Presbyterians among the first settlers.

When I first came into the county, the "*wet land*," of which there is such a large proportion in the middle and northern part, was considered almost worthless; but a great change has taken place in public opinion in relation to its value. It is ascertained, that by judicious cultivation, it rapidly improves in fertility. At that time, these lands were covered by water more than half the summer, and we called them *slashes:* now the water leaves the surface in the woods, early in the spring. Forty years ago, the evenings were cool as soon as the sun went down. I have no recollection of warm nights, for many years after I came, and their coolness was a matter of general remark among the emigrants from the old states. I believe it was owing to the immense forests that covered the country, and shut out the rays and heat of the sun from the surface of the ground, for after sunset there was no warm earth to impart heat to the atmosphere.

Batavia, the county seat, is situated on the north bank of the east fork of the Little Miami river, 21 miles easterly from Cincinnati, and 103 sw. of Columbus. This town was laid out about the year

County Buildings, Batavia.

1820, by George Ely. About that time, the county seat was temporarily removed from Williamsburg to New Richmond, and Feb. 21st, 1824, permanently transferred to Batavia. It contains 1 Presbyterian and 1 Methodist church, 4 stores, 2 newspaper printing offices, and had, by the census of 1840, 537 inhabitants.

Williamsburg is on the east fork of the Miami, 7 miles east of Batavia, and had, in 1840, 385 inhabitants. As previously mentioned, it was laid out by Gen. William Lytle, one of the earliest settlers of Clermont. His life was one of much incident. We derive the annexed facts respecting him, from Cist's Advertiser.

GEN. WM. LYTLE was born in Cumberland, Pa.; and in 1779, his family emigrated to Kentucky. Previous to the settlement of Ohio, young Lytle was in several desperate engagements with the Indians, where his cool, heroic bravery won general admiration. Before the treaty of Greenville, while making surveys in the Virginia military district, in Ohio, he was exposed to incessant dangers, suffered great privations, and was frequently attacked by the Indians. This business he followed for the greater portion of his life. In the war of 1812, he was appointed Major General of Ohio militia, and, in 1829, surveyor general of the public lands of Ohio, Indiana and Michigan. In 1810, Gen. Lytle removed from Williamsburg to Cincinnati, where he died, in 1831. As a citizen, he was distinguished for public spirit and benevolence, and in his personal appearance and character, strikingly resembled President Jackson. Beside the facts given under the head of Logan county, we have space for but a single anecdote, exhibiting his Spartan-like conduct at Grant's defeat, in Indiana. In that desperate action, the Kentuckians, overpowered by nearly four times their number, performed feats of bravery scarcely equalled even in early border warfare.

In this struggle, Lytle, then hardly 17 years of age, had both his arms shattered, his face powder burnt, his hair singed to the roots, and nineteen bullets passed through his body and clothing. In this condition, a retreat being ordered, he succeeded in bringing off the field several of his friends, generously aiding the wounded and the exhausted, by placing them on horses, while he himself ran forward in advance of the last remnant of the retreating party, to stop the only boat on the Ohio at that time, which could take them over and save them from the overwhelming force of their savage adversaries.

On reaching the river, he found the boat in the act of putting off for the Kentucky shore. The men were reluctant to obey his demand for a delay, until those still in the rear should come up—one of them declaring that "it was better that a few should perish, than that all should be sacrificed." He threw the rifle, which he still carried on his shoulder, over the root of a fallen tree, and swore he would shoot the first man who pulled an oar until his friends were aboard. In this way the boat was detained until they came up, and were safely lodged from the pursuing foe. Disdaining personally to take advantage of this result, the boat being crowded almost to dipping, he ran up the river to where some horses stood panting under the willows, after their escape from the battle field, and mounting one of the strongest, forced him into the river, holding on to the mane by his teeth, until he was taken, in the middle of the stream, into the boat, bleeding, and almost fainting from his wounds, by the order of his gallant captain, the lamented Stucker, who had observed his conduct with admiration throughout, and was resolved that such a spirit should not perish; for by this time the balls of the enemy were rattling like hail about their ears.

There was living many years since, near Williamsburg, Cornelius Washburn, or, as he was commonly called, *Neil Washburn*, who, in the early difficulties with the Indians, was distinguished for his sagacity and courage. Of his ultimate fate, we are somewhat uncertain: it is said, however, that the progress of civilization was too rapid for him, and that he long since left for the wilds of the far west, to pass his time in the congenial employment of hunting the bear and trapping the beaver. We have derived some facts from the lips of one who knew him well, Mr. Thomas M'Donald, the brother of the author of the sketches and the first person who erected a cabin in Scioto county.

In the year '90, I first became acquainted with Neil Washburn, then a lad of sixteen, living on the Kentucky side of the Ohio, six miles below Maysville. From his early years, he showed a disposition to follow the woods. When only nine or ten, he passed his time in setting snares for pheasants and wild animals. Shortly after, his father purchased for him a shot gun, in the use of which he soon became unexcelled. In the summer of '90, his father being out of fresh provisions, crossed the Ohio with him in a canoe, to shoot deer, at a lick near the mouth of Eagle creek. On entering the creek, their attention was arrested by a singular hacking noise, some distance up the bank. Neil landed, and with gun in hand, cautiously crawling up the river bank, discovered an Indian, about twenty feet up a hickory tree, busily engaged in cutting around the bark, to make a canoe, in which he probably anticipated the gratification of crossing the river and committing depredations upon the Kentuckians. However this may have been, his meditations and work were soon brought to a close, for the intrepid boy no sooner saw the dusky form of the savage, than he brought his gun to a level with his eye, and fired: the Indian fell dead to the earth, with a heavy sound. He hastily retreated to the canoe, from fear of the presence of other Indians, and re-crossed the Ohio. Early the next morning, a party of men, guided by Neil, visited the spot, and found the body of the Indian at the foot of the tree. Neil secured the scalp, and the same day showed it, much elated, to myself and others, in the town of Washington, in Mason. Several persons in the village made him presents, as testimonials of their opinion of his bravery.

In the next year, he was employed as a spy between Maysville and the mouth of the Little Miami, to watch for Indians, who were accustomed to cross the Ohio into Kentucky, to steal and murder. While so engaged, he had some encounters with them, in which his unerring rifle dealt death to several of their number. One of these was at the mouth of Bullskin, on the Ohio side.

In '92, the Indians committed such great depredations upon the Ohio, between the Great Kanawha and Maysville, that Gen. Lee, the government agent, in employing spies, endeavored to get some of them to go up the Ohio, above the Kanawha, and warn all single boats not to descend the river. None were found sufficiently daring to go, but Neil. Furnished with an elegant horse, and well armed, he started on his perilous mission. He met with no adventures until after crossing the Big Sandy. This he swam on his horse, and had reached about half a mile beyond, when he was suddenly fired upon by a party of Indians, in ambush. His horse fell dead, and the Indians gave a yell of triumph; but Neil was unhurt. Springing to his feet, he bounded back like a deer, and swam across the Big Sandy, holding his rifle and ammunition above his head. Panting from exertion, he rested upon the opposite bank to regain his strength, when the Indians, whooping and yelling, appeared on the other side, in full pursuit. Neil drew up, shot one of their number, and then continued his retreat down the Ohio, but meeting and exchanging shots with others, he saw it was impossible to keep the river valley in safety, and striking his course more inland, to evade his enemies, arrived safely at Maysville.

In the fall of the same year, he was in the action with Kenton and others, against Tecumseh, in what is now Brown county, for the particulars of which, see page 67. Washburn continued as a spy throughout the war, adding "the sagacity of lion to the cunning of the fox." He was with Wayne in his campaign, and at the battle of the Fallen Timbers, manifested his usual prowess.

Neil Washburn was in person near six feet in height, with broad shoulders, small feet, and tapered beautifully from his chest down. He was both powerful and active. His eyes were blue, his hair light, and complexion fair. A prominent Roman nose alone marred the symmetry of his personal appearance.

In this county are several quite populous towns. New Richmond, which had, in 1840, a population of 772, Moscow, which had 228, Point Pleasant 150, Neville 228, and Chilo 102, are all upon the Ohio river. Near the first is a Fourierite association, but not in a thriving condition. Bethel, 12 miles SE. of Batavia, had, in 1840, 366 inhabitants; Felicity, 21 southerly, had 442, and Milford, 10 NW., had 460 inhabitants. Felicity and Milford have much improved within the last few years. The last named is on the east bank of the Little Miami river, over which is a bridge, connecting it with the Little Miami railroad, on the opposite bank. There are other small villages in the county, but none of much note.

CLINTON.

Clinton, was organized in 1810, and named in honor of Gov. Geo. Clinton, Vice Pres. of United States. The surface is generally level; on the west undulating, and the soil is fertile. It is particularly adapted to Indian corn and grass. It has some prairie land, and its streams furnish good water power. The principal staples are corn, wheat, oats, wool and pork. The following is a list of its townships in 1840, with their population.

Chester,	1784	Liberty,	1050	Vernon,	1434
Clarke,	1297	Marion,	643	Washington,	1170
Green,	1842	Richland,	1385	Wayne,	1366
Jefferson,	474	Union,	3284		

The population of Clinton in 1820, was 8,085 ; in 1830, 11,406 ; and in 1840, 15,729, or 39 inhabitants to a square mile.

This county was settled about the year 1803, principally by emigrants from Kentucky, Pennsylvania and North Carolina. The first settlement, however, was made in 1797, by Wm. Smally. Most of the first emigrants were backswoodmen, and well fitted to endure the privations incident upon settling a new country. They lived principally upon game, and gave little attention to agricultural pursuits As the country grew older, game became scarce, emigrants flocked from different parts of the Union, and the primitive manner of living gave place to that more conformable to the customs of older states.

The following are the names of some of the most noted of the early settlers: Thos. Hinkson, Aaron Burr and Jesse Hughes, the first associate judges ; Nathan Linton, the first land surveyor ; Abraham Ellis and Thomas Hardin, who had been soldiers of the revolution ; Joseph Doan, James Mills and Henry Babb, who served as commissioners ; Morgan Mendican, who erected the first mill in the county, on Todd's Fork ; and Capt. James Spencer, who was distinguished in various conflicts with the Indians.

The first house for divine worship was erected by Friends, at Center, in 1806. The first court was held in a barn, belonging to Judge Hughes, and for a number of years subsequent, in a small house belonging to John M'Gregor.

There are some of the ancient works so common throughout the west on Todd's Fork, near Springfield meeting house. The "Deserted Camp," situated about three miles northeast of Wilmington, is a point of notoriety with the surveyors of land. It was so called from the circumstance, that a body of Kentuckians, on their way to attack the Indian towns on the Little Miami, encamping over night lost one of their number, who *deserted* to the enemy, and giving warning of their approach, frustrated the object of the expedition.

Wilmington, the county seat, is in the township of Union, on Todd's Fork, 72 miles sw. from Columbus. It is regularly laid out on undulating ground, and contains 5 houses for divine worship, 1 newspaper printing office, 1 high school, 19 mercantile stores, and a population estimated at 1500. The engraving represents one of the principal streets of the village, as it appears from the store of Joseph Hale ; the building with a spire is the court house, a structure of considerable elegance. Wilmington was laid out in 1810, principally settled by emigrants from North Carolina, and named from Wilmington in that state. The first log house was built by Wm. Hobsin, and Warren Sabin's was the first tavern. The first church, a small brick edifice, was erected by the Baptists. In 1812, the first court was held. The earliest settlers were Warren Sabin, Samuel T. Londen, Wm. Hobsin, Larkin Reynolds, John Swane, Jas. Montgomery, John M'Gregor, sen., and Isaiah Morris. This

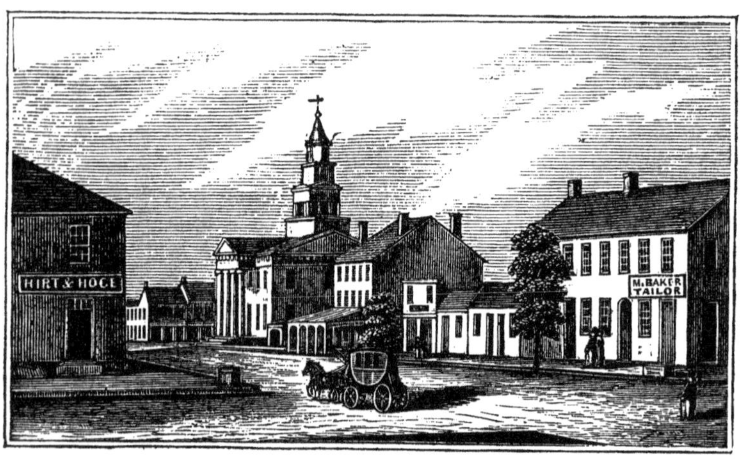

View in Wilmington.

last named gentleman, a native of Pennsylvania, descended the Ohio river with his uncle, in a flat-bottomed boat, in the spring of 1803, and landed first at Columbia, where his uncle opened a store, from a small stock of goods he had brought. After remaining at that place about three months, he removed his goods to Lebanon, and not long after died, leaving his nephew, then a lad of seventeen years of age, without any means of support. He however made friends, and eventually moved to Wilmington, where, on the 8th of July, 1811, he opened *the first store* in the town, in company with Wm. Ferguson. He was obliged, in moving from Lebanon, to make his way through the forest, cutting a wagon road part of the distance: the town having been laid out in the woods, it was with great difficulty that he could get through to the little one story frame house, erected in the midst of trees, logs and brush, on which he then settled and has since resided. Mr. Morris was the first postmaster in the town, the first representative from the county, to the legislature, and has since held various public offices.*

William Smally was born in western Pennsylvania, in 1764. At the age of six years he was stolen by the Indians, carried into the interior of Ohio, and remained with them until twenty years of age. While with them, he witnessed the burning of several white prisoners. On one occasion, he saw an infant snatched from its mother's arms and thrown into the flames. In 1784, he left the Indians, rejoined his parents near Pittsburg, and a few years after, moved with them to the vicinity of Cincinnati. He was in Harmar's campaign, and at St. Clair's defeat, in the last of which, he discharged his rifle thirty five times, twenty one of which, it is said, took effect. He likewise accompanied Wayne's army

* From the communication of Wm. H. Spencer, to whose researches we are mainly indebted for the historical and biographical materials embraced under the head of Clinton county.

Being on one occasion sent forward with others, on some mission to the Indians, they were fired upon on their approach to the camp, and his two companions killed. He evaded the danger by springing behind a tree, and calling to one of the chiefs, whom he knew, telling him that he had deserted the whites, and had come to join them. This not only saved his life, but caused him to be treated with great kindness. He, however, took an early opportunity, escaped to the army, and at the battle of the Fallen Timbers, showed his usual cool courage.

In 1797, he settled on Todd's Fork in this county, and resided there for a number of years, depending principally upon hunting for a subsistence. His personal appearance was good, but his address resembled that of a savage. A little anecdote illustrates his determined character. He purchased land on which he resided from a lawyer of Cincinnati, who refused to make him a deed. Smally armed himself, called upon him and demanded a bond for his land, with the threat that if not furnished in three days, he would take his scalp. This positive language soon brought the lawyer to a sense of his dangerous situation, and before the expiration of the time, he gave Smally the desired paper. Mr. Smally passed the latter part of his life in poverty. In 1836, he emigrated to Illinois, where he died in 1840.

Col. Thomas Hinkson was born in 1772, in Westmoreland county, Pa. His father had emigrated from Ireland in early life, had become an excellent woodsman, and visited Kentucky at a very early period. He established a station near the junction of Hinkson and Stoner, which form the south fork of Licking river. Here the subject of this notice was raised, until the age of eighteen years, when in the autumn of 1790, as a volunteer in the Kentucky militia, he accompanied the expedition of Gen. Harmar. He was in the battle near the Miami villages, under Col. Hardin's command in front of the town, and witnessed the total overthrow and massacre of the detachment of Maj. Wyllis. In this battle he received a slight wound in the left arm, and narrowly escaped with his life. He was afterwards in the disastrous defeat of Gen. St. Clair, but amidst the general slaughter, escaped unhurt. Hitherto he had served as a private, but was subsequently selected as a lieutenant in the mounted volunteers from Kentucky, who formed a part of the forces of Gen. Wayne against the same Indians in 1794. He was in the battle near the Rapids of the Maumee, but never pretended that he had done any thing worthy of distinction on that memorable day. During these several campaigns, however, he had formed the acquaintance of most of the leading men of Kentucky, and others of the N. W. Territory, which was highly advantageous to him in after life. Shortly after Wayne's battle, he returned to Kentucky, married and settled on a farm inherited from his father, situated in Harrison county, where he lived until the spring of 1806, when he emigrated to Ohio, and in 1807, settled on a farm about eight miles east of Wilmington, but then in the county of Highland. He was soon afterwards elected a justice of the peace for the latter county, and captain of the militia company to which he belonged, in which several capacities he served until the erection of Clinton county, in 1810, when, without his knowledge, he was elected by the legislature one of the associate judges for the new county. He made no pretentions to legal knowledge, nor will the writer claim anything for him in this respect, further than good common sense, which generally prevents a man from making a very foolish decision.

After this appointment, he remained quietly at home in the occupations common to farmers, until the declaration of war in 1812, nor did he manifest any disposition for actual service, until after Hull's surrender. That event cast a gloom over the west. All of Michigan, Northern Ohio, Indiana and Illinois were exposed to savage depredations. Some troops had been hastily assembled at Urbana and other points, to repel invasion. Captain Hinkson was then in the prime of life, possessing a robust and manly frame seldom equalled, even among pioneers. He was a man of few words, and they to the purpose intended. He briefly explained to his family that he believed the time had come to serve his country. He immediately set out for head-quarters, and tendered his services to Gov. Meigs, then at Urbana. The president having previously made a requisition on the governor of Ohio, for two companies of rangers, to scour the country between the settlements and the enemy, Capt. H. was appointed to command one of those companies, with liberty to choose his own followers. This was soon done, and a company presented to the governor ready for duty. By this time the Indians had actual possession of the exposed territory, and it was the duty of these companies to hold them in check, and keep the army advised of their numbers and position. In performing this duty, many incidents might be related in the life of Capt. Hinkson, but one or two must suffice. Having at one time ventured to the Miami of the Lake, to ascertain the condition of the enemy, they found them encamped near the foot of the rapids of that river, with a select company of rangers, commanded by Capt. Clark, from Canada, numbering in all from three to five hundred, and under the command of the celebrated Tecumseh. The ground on the hill was for miles covered with a thick undergrowth, which enabled Capt. Hinkson and company to approach nearly within gun-shot of the enemy, without being seen. It was late in the afternoon, and while waiting for the approach of night, to enable them to withdraw more successfully, the company was secretly drawn up near the brink of the hill, and directed in whispers to merely take aim at the enemy. This was rather a hazardous display of humor, but as many of his men had never been in battle, Capt. H. told the writer it was merely to try their nerves. While engaged in this sport, they discovered Capt. Clark in the adjacent cornfield below, in hot pursuit after a flock of wild turkeys, which were running toward the place of concealment. Here was a crisis. He must be slain in cold blood, or made a prisoner. The latter alternative was adopted. The company was disposed so as to flank the captain and his turkeys. They were alarmed and flew into the tree tops, and while the captain was gazing up for his prey, Capt. Hinkson approached and politely requested him to ground arms, upon pain of instant death, in case he gave the least alarm. He at first indicated signs of resistance, but soon found " discretion the better part of valor," and surrendered himself a prisoner of war. Being at least one hundred miles from the army, in sight of such a force, Capt. Hinkson and company were in a very delicate condition. No time was to be lost. A retreat was commenced in the most secret manner, in a southerly direction, at right angles from the river. By travelling all night they eluded pursuit, and brought their prize safely to camp.

Shortly afterwards, Gen. Tupper's brigade arrived near the rapids and encamped for the night, during which, Capt. H. and company acted as piquet guard, and in the morning a few were selected to accompany him on a secret reconnaisance down the river. Unluckily they were met at the summit of a hill, by a detachment of the same kind from the enemy. Shots were exchanged, and the alarm now fairly given to both parties. This brought on the skirmish which ensued between that brigade and the Indians. While fighting in the Indian mode, near Wm. Venard, Esq., (one of Capt. Hinkson's men, who had been severely wounded,) Capt. H. saw a dusky figure suddenly rise from the grass. He had a rifle never before known to miss fire. They both presented their pieces, which simultaneously snapped without effect. In preparing for a second trial, it is supposed the Indian was a little ahead of the captain, when a shot from Daniel Workman, (another ranger,) sent the Indian to his long home.

After this skirmish, the Indians withdrew to Frenchtown, and block houses were hastily thrown up near the spot where Fort Meigs was afterwards erected, and where the Ohio troops were encamped, when the fatal disaster befel Gen. Winchester, at Raisin, Jan. 22d, 1813. The news was carried by express, and the main body retreated, leaving Capt. H. and company to perform the sorrowful duty of picking up some poor stragglers from that bloody defeat, and burning the block houses and provisions within twenty four hours, which was done before it was known that the enemy had retired to Malden. The Ohio brigade, and others from Pennsylvania and Virginia, soon rallied again, and formed a junction at the rapids, where they commenced building the fort, so renowned for withstanding two sieges in the spring and summer of 1813. During its erection, Capt. Hinkson was attacked with a peculiar fever, then raging in the army, from which he did not recover fit for duty, until late in the spring. With a shattered constitution he returned to his home, and was immediately elected colonel of the 3d regiment of the 2d brigade and 1st division Ohio militia, which was then a post of honor, requiring much patience and discretion, in a region rather backward in supporting the war.

The reader will, in this narrative, see nothing beyond a simple memorial of facts, which is all that the unassuming character requires. He was a plain, gentlemanly individual, of a very mild and even temper; a good husband and kind father, but rather indifferent to his own interest in money matters, by which he became seriously involved, lost his property and removed to Indiana in 1821, where he died in 1824, aged 52 years.

Clarksville, 9 miles sw. of Wilmington, Martinsville, 9 s., Port William, 9 N, New Vienna, 11 SE. and Burlington, 11 NW., are all considerable villages, each having more or less stores and churches; and the last, which is said to be the largest, having a population, estimated at about 300. Sabina, Sligo, Blanchester, Cuba, Lewisville, Westboro', Centerville and Morrisville, are small places.

COLUMBIANA.

Columbiana was formed from Jefferson and Washington, March 25th, 1803. Kilbourn, in his Gazetteer, says: "Columbiana is a fancy name, taken from the names Columbus and Anna. An anecdote is told pending its adoption in the legislature, that a member jocularly moved that the name Maria should be added thereto, so as to have it read Columbiana-maria." The southern part is generally broken and hilly, and the northern level or undulating. This is an excellent agricultural tract: it is well watered, abounds in fine mineral coal, iron ore, lime and free stone. The water lime stone of this county, is of the best quality. Salt water abounds on Yellow and Beaver creeks, which also afford a great amount of water power. This is the greatest wool-growing county in Ohio, and is exceeded by but three or four in the Union. The principal products are wool, wheat, corn, oats and potatoes. About one third of the population are of German origin, and there are many of Irish extraction. The following is a list of its townships, in 1840, with their population.

Beaver,	1973	Hanover,	2963	Springfield,	1994
Butler,	1711	Knox,	2111	St. Clair,	1739
Center,	3472	Liverpool,	1096	Unity,	1984
Elkrun,	873	Madison,	1472	Washington,	814
Fairfield,	2108	Middletown,	1601	Wayne,	1086
Franklin,	893	Perry,	1630	West,	1915
Goshen,	1397	Salem,	1903	Yellow Creek,	2686
Greene,	3212	Smith,	2029		

The population of Columbiana, in 1820, was 22,033; in 1830, 35,508, and, in 1840, 40,394, which was greater than any other counties in Ohio, excepting Hamilton and Richland. The number of inhabitants to a square mile, was then 46. In 1846, the county was reduced by the formation of Mahoning, to which the townships of Beaver, Goshen, Greene, Smith and Springfield now belong.

This county was settled just before the commencement of the present century. In 1797, a few families moved across the Ohio and settled in its limits. One of them, named Carpenter, made a settlement near West Point. Shortly after, Captain Whiteyes, a noted Indian chief, stopped at the dwelling of Carpenter. Being intoxicated, he got into some difficulty with a son of Mr. C., a lad of about 17 years of age, and threatened to kill him. The young man upon this turned and ran, pursued by the Indian, with uplifted tomahawk, ready to bury it in his brains. Finding that the latter was fast gaining upon him, the young man turned and shot him, and shortly afterwards he expired. As this was in time of peace, Carpenter was apprehended and tried at Steubenville, under the territorial laws, the courts being then held by justices of the peace. He was cleared, it appearing that he acted in self-defence. The death of Whiteyes created great excitement, and fears were entertained that it would provoke hostilities from the Indians. Great exertions were made to reconcile them, and several presents were given to the friends of the late chief. The wife of Whiteyes received from three gentlemen, the sum of $300; one of these donors was the late Bezaleel Wells, of Steubenville. This was the last Indian blood shed by white men in this part of Ohio.

Adam Poe, who, with his brother Andrew, had the noted fight with the Indians, once resided in this county, in Wayne township, on the west fork of Little Beaver. The son of Andrew—Deacon Adam Poe—is now living in the vicinity of Ravenna, Portage county, and has the tomahawk with which the Indian struck his father. The locality where the struggle occurred, he informs us, was nearly opposite the mouth of Little Yellow creek. We annex the particulars of this affair, from "Doddridge's Notes," substituting, however, the name of Andrew for Adam, and *vice versa*, as they should be placed.

In the summer of 1782, a party of seven Wyandots, made an incursion into a settlement, some distance below Fort Pitt, and several miles from the Ohio river. Here, finding an old man alone, in a cabin, they killed him, packed up what plunder they could find, and commenced their retreat. Among their party was a celebrated Wyandot chief, who, in addition to his fame as a warrior and counsellor, was, as to his size and strength, a real giant.

The news of the visit of the Indians soon spread through the neighborhood, and a party of eight good riflemen was collected, in a few hours, for the purpose of pursuing the Indians. In this party were two brothers of the names of Adam and Andrew Poe. They were both famous for courage, size and activity.

This little party commenced the pursuit of the Indians, with a determination, if possible, not to suffer them to escape, as they usually did on such occasions, by making a speedy flight to the river, crossing it, and then dividing into small parties, to meet at a distant point, in a given time.

The pursuit was continued the greater part of the night after the Indians had done the mischief. In the morning, the party found themselves on the trail of the Indians, which led to the river. When arrived within a little distance of the river, Andrew Poe, fearing an ambuscade, left the party, who followed directly on the trail, to creep along the brink of the river bank, under cover of the weeds and bushes, to fall on the rear of the Indians, should he find them in ambuscade. He had not gone far, before he saw the Indian rafts at the water's edge. Not seeing any Indians, he stepped softly down the bank, with his rifle cocked. When about half way down, he discovered the large Wyandot chief and a small Indian, within a few steps of him. They were standing with their guns cocked, and looking in the direction of our party, who, by this time, had gone some distance lower down the bottom. Poe took aim at the large chief, but his rifle missed fire. The Indians, hearing the snap of the gun-lock, instantly turned round and discovered Poe, who being too near them to retreat, dropped his gun and instantly sprang from the bank upon them, and seizing the large Indian by the cloths on his breast, and at the same time embracing the neck of the small one, threw them both down on the ground, himself being upmost. The Indian soon extricated himself, ran to the raft, got his tomahawk, and attempted to dispatch Poe, the large Indian holding him fast in his arms with all his might, the better to enable his fellow to effect his purpose. Poe, however, so well watched the motions of the Indian, that when in the act of aiming his blow at his head, by a vigorous and well-directed kick with one of his feet, he staggered the savage, and knocked the tomahawk out of his hand. This failure, on the part of the small Indian, was reproved, by an exclamation of contempt, from the large one.

In a moment, the Indian caught up his tomahawk again, approached more cautiously, brandishing his tomahawk, and making a number of feigned blows, in defiance and derision. Poe, however, still on his guard, averted the real blow from his head, by throwing up his arm and receiving it on his wrist, in which he was severely wounded; but not so as to lose entirely the use of his hand.

In this perilous moment, Poe, by a violent effort, broke loose from the Indian, snatched up one of the Indian's guns, and shot the small Indian through the breast, as he ran up the third time to tomahawk him.

The large Indian was now on his feet, and grasping Poe by a shoulder and leg, threw him down on the bank. Poe instantly disengaged himself and got on his feet. The Indian then seized him again, and a new struggle ensued, which, owing to the slippery state of the bank, ended in the fall of both combatants into the water.

In this situation, it was the object of each to drown the other. Their efforts to effect their purpose were continued for some time with alternate success, sometimes one being under the water, and sometimes the other. Poe at length seized the tuft of hair on the scalp of the Indian, with which he held his head under the water, until he supposed him drowned.

Relaxing his hold too soon, Poe instantly found his gigantic antagonist on his feet again, and ready for another combat. In this, they were carried into the water beyond their depth. In this situation, they were compelled to loose their hold on each other, and swim for mutual safety. Both sought the shore to seize a gun, and end the contest with bullets. The Indian, being the best swimmer, reached the land first. Poe seeing this, immediately turned back into the water to escape, if possible, being shot, by diving. Fortunately, the Indian caught up the rifle with which Poe had killed the other warrior.

At this juncture, Adam Poe, missing his brother from the party, and supposing, from the report of the gun which he shot, that he was either killed or engaged in conflict with the Indians, hastened to the spot. On seeing him, Andrew called out to him to "kill the big Indian on shore." But Adam's gun, like that of the Indian's, was empty. The contest was now between the white man and the Indian, who should load and fire first. Very fortunately for Poe, the Indian, in loading, drew the ramrod from the thimbles of the stock of the gun with so much violence, that it slipped out of his hand and fell a little distance from him; he quickly caught it up, and rammed down his bullet. This little delay gave Poe the advantage. He shot the Indian as he was raising his gun, to take aim at him.

As soon as Adam had shot the Indian, he jumped into the river to assist his wounded brother to shore; but Andrew, thinking more of the honor of carrying the big Indian home, as a trophy of victory, than of his own safety, urged Adam to go back, and prevent the struggling savage from rolling himself into the river, and escaping. Adam's solicitude for the life of his brother, prevented him from complying with this request.

In the mean time, the Indian, jealous of the honor of his scalp, even in the agonies of death, succeeded in reaching the river and getting into the current, so that his body was never obtained.

An unfortunate occurrence took place during this conflict. Just as Adam arrived at the top of the bank, for the relief of his brother, one of the party, who had followed close behind him, seeing Andrew in the river, and mistaking him for a wounded Indian, shot at him and wounded him in the shoulder. He, however, recovered from his wounds.

During the contest between Andrew Poe and the Indians, the party had overtaken the remaining six of them. A desperate conflict ensued, in which five of the Indians were killed. Our loss was three men killed, and Adam Poe severely wounded.

Thus ended this Spartan conflict, with the loss of three valiant men on our part, and with that of the whole of the Indian party, with the exception of one warrior. Never, on any occasion, was there a greater display of desperate bravery, and seldom did a conflict take place, which, in the issue, proved fatal to so great a proportion of those engaged in it.

The fatal issue of this little campaign on the side of the Indians, occasioned an universal mourning among the Wyandot nation. The big Indian, with his four brothers, all of whom were killed at the same place, were among the most distinguished chiefs and warriors of their nation.

The big Indian was magnanimous, as well as brave. He, more than any other individual, contributed, by his example and influence, to the good character of the Wyandots, for lenity towards their prisoners. He would not suffer them to be killed or ill treated. This mercy to captives, was an honorable distinction in the character of the Wyandots, and was well understood by our first settlers, who, in case of captivity, thought it a fortunate circumstance to fall into their hands.

New Lisbon, the county seat, is in the township of Center, 155 miles NE. of Columbus, 35 from Steubenville, and 56 from Pittsburg. It is on the line of the Sandy and Beaver canal, on the middle fork of Little Beaver, and is surrounded by a populous and well cultivated country. The town is remarkably compact and substantially built; many of its streets are paved, and it has the appearance of a small city. The view was taken from the southeastern part of the public square; and shows, on the left, the county buildings, and on the right, the market. New Lisbon was laid out in 1802, by the

Public Square, New Lisbon.

Rev. Lewis Kinney, of the Baptist denomination, and proprietor of the soil; a year or two after, it was made the county seat. It contains 1 Friends meeting house, 1 Presbyterian, 1 Episcopal and 1 Reformed Methodist, 1 Disciples, 1 Dutch Reformed, and 1 Seceder church, 3 newspaper printing offices, 2 woolen manufactories, 2 founderies, 2 flouring mills, 14 mercantile stores, and about 1800 inhabitants. Carriage making and tanning are extensively carried on in this village.

The Cottage of a German Swiss Emigrant.

In travelling through the west, one often meets with scenes that remind him of another land. The foreigner who makes his home upon American soil, does not at once assimilate in language, modes of life, and current of thought with that congenial to his adopted country. The German emigrant is peculiar in this respect, and so much attached is he to his fatherland, that years often elapse ere there is any perceptible change. The annexed engraving illustrates these remarks. It shows the mud cottage of a German Swiss emigrant, now standing in the neighborhood of others of like character, in the northwestern part of this county. The frame work is of wood, with the interstices filled with light colored clay, and the whole surmounted by a ponderous shingled roof, of a picturesque form. Beside the tenement, hop vines are clustering around their slender supporters, while hard by stands the abandoned log dwelling of the emigrant—deserted for one more congenial with his early predilections.

Eastern entrance into Salem.

Salem is 10 miles north of New Lisbon, in the midst of a beautiful agricultural country, thickly settled by Friends, who are industrious and wealthy. This flourishing town was laid out about 1806, by Zadock Street, John Strong and Samuel Davis, members of the society of Friends, from Redstone, Pa. Until within a few years, it was an inconsiderable village. It now contains 2 Friends meeting houses, 2 Baptist, 1 Methodist and 1 Presbyterian church, a classical academy, in good repute, under the charge of Rev. Jacob Coon, 24 mercantile stores, 2 woolen factories, 3 founderies, 1 grist mill, 2 engine shops, ana about 1300 inhabitants. There are four newspapers published here, one of which is the American Water Cure Advocate, edited by Dr. John P. Cope, principal of a water cure establishment, in full operation, in this village. The engraving shows the principal street of the town, as it appears on entering it from the east: Street's woolen factory is seen on the left.

Wellsville is at the mouth of Yellow creek, on the great bend of the Ohio river, where it approximates nearest to Lake Erie, 50 miles below Pittsburg, and 14 from New Lisbon. It was laid out in the autumn of 1824, by William Wells, from whom it derived its name. Until 1828, it contained but a few buildings; it is now an important point for the shipment and transhipment of goods, and does a large

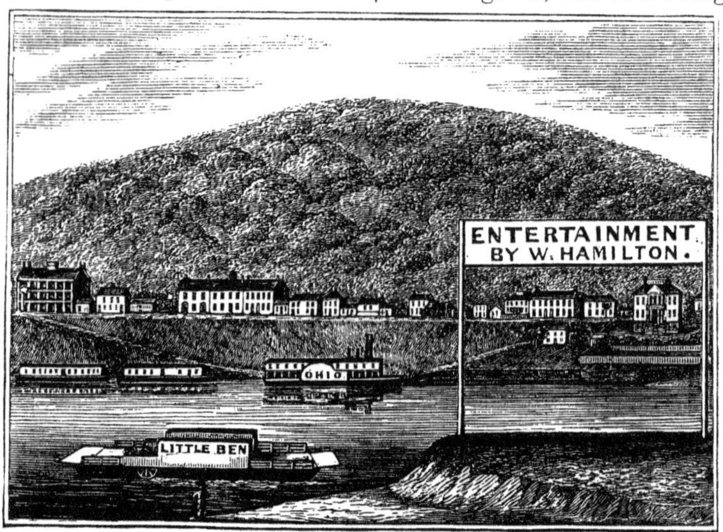

Wellsville, on the Ohio.

business with the surrounding country. The landing is one of the best, in all stages of water, on the river. This flourishing town has 1 Presbyterian, 1 Episcopal Methodist, 1 Reformed Methodist, and 1 Disciples church, 1 newspaper printing office, 1 linseed oil and 1 saw mill, 1 pottery, 1 raw carding machine, 1 foundery, 16 mercantile stores, and, in 1840, had a population of 759, and in 1846, 1066. The view, taken from the Virginia bank of the Ohio, shows but a small part of the town. About a mile below, on the river bank, in a natural grove, are several beautiful private dwellings. The "Cleveland and Pittsburg railroad," 97 miles in length, will commence at Cleveland and terminate at Wellsville, and whenever built, will tend to make Wellsville a place of great business and population. A survey for this work has been recently made, and there is a good prospect of its being constructed.

The first paper mill in Ohio, and the second west of the Alleghanies, was erected in 1805–6, on Little Beaver creek, near its mouth, in this county. It was called the Ohio paper mill: its proprietors were John Bever and John Coulter.

Liverpool, 4 miles above Wellsville, on the Ohio, has a population of about 600. The manufacture of earthen-ware is carried on there to a considerable extent. Hanover, 10 miles west of New Lisbon, on the Sandy and Beaver canal, is a thriving town, containing 3 churches, 8 stores, and about 600 inhabitants. The following are the names of other towns in the county, with their population in 1840, some of which are smart business places. Columbiana, 273; Gillford, 263; Unity, 204; Georgetown, 219; New Garden, 194; Fairfield, 181; Calcutta, 135; Franklin Square, 151; Washingtonville, 107: Benton, Clarkson, Chambersburg, Dugannon, Damascus, Elkton, Middle Beaver, Palestine, Rochester, Salinesville and Westville are small places.

COSHOCTON.

Coshocton was organized April 1st, 1811. The name is a Delaware word, and is derived from that of the Indian village *Goschachquenk*, which is represented on a map in Loskiel, as having stood north of the mouth of the Tuscarawas river, in the fork formed by its junction with the Walhonding. The surface is mostly rolling; in some parts hilly, with fine broad vallies along the Muskingum and its tributaries. The soil is varied, and abruptly so: here we see the rich alluvion almost overhung by a red-bush hill, while, perhaps, on the very next acclivity, is seen the poplar and sugar tree, indicative of a fertile soil. With regard to sand and clay, the changes are equally sudden. The hills abound in coal and iron ore, and several salt wells have been sunk, and salt manufactured. The principal products are wheat, corn, oats and wool. It was first settled by Virginians and Pennsylvanians. The following is a list of its townships, in 1840, with their population.

Adams,	838	Keene,	1043	Perry,	1339
Bedford,	1141	Lafayette,	848	Pike,	1115
Bethlehem,	827	Linton,	1196	Tiverton,	665
Clark,	703	Mill Creek,	907	Tuscarawas,	1144
Crawford,	1134	Monroe,	557	Virginia.	1005
Franklin,	670	New Castle,	905	Washington,	1029
Jackson,	1896	Oxford,	760	White Eyes,	997
Jefferson,	771				

The population of the county, in 1820, was 7086; in 1830, 11,162, and in 1840, 21590, or 38 inhabitants to a square mile.

Previous to the settlement of the country, there were several military expeditions into this region. The first in importance and in order of time, was that made by Col. Boquet, in October, 1764. The following is extracted from the lecture of Charles Whittlesey, Esq., delivered at Cleveland, Dec. 17th, 1846.

The Indians were very much displeased, when they saw the English taking possession of their country, for they preferred the Frenchmen, who had been their friends and traders more than one hundred years, and had married Indian women. A noted chief of the Ottawa tribe, known by the name of Pontiac, formed the resolution to destroy all the English frontier posts at one assault, in which he was encouraged by the French traders.

He succeeded in forming an alliance with the Ottawas, having 900 warriors; the Potowotomies, with 350; Miamies of the lake, 350; Chippewas, 5000; Wyandots, 300; Delawares, 600; Shawnees, 500; Kickapoos, 300; Ouatanons of the Wabash, 400, and the Pinankeshaws, 250; in all, able to muster 8950 warriors. This may be called the "First

Great Northwestern Confederacy" against the whites. The *second* took place under Brandt, or Thayandanegea, during the revolution, and was continued by Little Turtle; the third, under *Tecumseh*, in the last war. Pontiac's projects were brought to a focus in the fall of 1763, and the result was nearly equal to the design. The Indians collected at all the northwestern forts, under the pretence of trade and friendly intercourse; and having killed all the English traders who were scattered through their villages, they made a simultaneous attack upon the forts, and were in a great measure successful.

The inhabitants of Pennsylvania and Virginia were now subject to great alarm, and frequently robberies and murders were committed upon them by the Indians, and prisoners were captured. General Gage was at this time the commander-in-chief of the British forces in America, and his head-quarters were at Boston. He ordered an expedition of 3000 men for the relief of Detroit, to move early in the year 1764. It was directed to assemble at Fort Niagara, and proceeded up Lake Erie in boats, commanded by General Bradstreet. The other was the expedition I design principally to notice at this time. It was at first composed of the 42d and 77th regiments, who had been at the siege of Havana, in Cuba, under the command of Col. Henry Boquet. This force left Philadelphia, for the relief of Fort Pitt, in July, 1763, and after defeating the Indians at Bushy Run, in August, drove them across the Ohio. It wintered at Fort Pitt, where some of the houses, built by Col. Boquet, may still be seen, his name cut in stone upon the wall.

General Gage directed Col. Boquet to organize a corps of 1500 men, and to enter the country of the Delawares and the Shawnees, at the same time that General Bradstreet was engaged in chastising the Wyandots and Ottawas, of Lake Erie, who were still investing Detroit. As a part of Col. Boquet's force was composed of militia from Pennsylvania and Virginia, it was slow to assemble. On the 5th of August, the Pennsylvania quota rendezvoused at Carlisle, where 300 of them deserted. The Virginia quota arrived at Fort Pitt on the 17th of September, and uniting with the provincial militia, a part of the 42d and 60th regiments, the army moved from Fort Pitt on the 3d of October. General Bradstreet, having dispersed the Indian forces besieging Detroit, passed into the Wyandot country, by way of Sandusky bay. He ascended the bay and river, as far as it was navigable for boats, and there made a camp. A treaty of peace and friendship was signed by the chiefs and head men, who delivered but very few of their prisoners.

When Col. Boquet was at Fort Loudon, in Pennsylvania, between Carlisle and Fort Pitt, urging forward the militia levies, he received a despatch from General Bradstreet, notifying him of the peace effected at Sandusky. But the Ohio Indians, particularly the Shawnees of the Scioto river, and the Delawares of the Muskingum, still continued their robberies and murders along the frontier of Pennsylvania; and so Col. Boquet determined to proceed with his division, notwithstanding the peace of General Bradstreet, which did not include the Shawnees and Delawares. In the march from Philadelphia to Fort Pitt, Col. Boquet had shown himself to be a man of decision, courage and military genius. In the engagement at Bushy Run, he displayed that caution in preparing for emergencies, that high personal influence over his troops, and a facility in changing his plans as circumstances changed during the battle, which mark the good commander and the cool-headed officer. He had been with Forbes and Washington, when Fort Pitt was taken from the French. The Indians who were assembled at Fort Pitt, left the siege of that place and advanced to meet the force of Boquet, intending to execute a surprise and destroy the whole command. These savages remembered how easily they had entrapped General Braddock, a few years before, by the same movement, and had no doubt of success against Boquet. But he moved always in a hollow square, with his provision train and his cattle in the centre, impressing his men with the idea that a fire might open upon them at any moment. When the important hour arrived, and they were saluted with the discharge of a thousand rifles, accompanied by the terrific yells of so many savage warriors, arrayed in the livery of demons, the English and provincial troops behaved like veterans, whom nothing could shake. They achieved a complete victory, and drove the allied Indian force beyond the Ohio.

From Fort Pitt, Col. Boquet proceeded westward, on the north bank of the Ohio, with such caution, that the Indians were unable to draw him into an ambuscade. At the mouth of Big Beaver, the troops crossed by a ford, and on the 6th of October, reached the Little Beaver, passed up its east branch, and across the highlands to the waters of the Yellow creek, through an open and bushy country. Reaching Sandy creek, they passed down its banks, and crossing the stream by a ford, reached a beautiful plain—where the village of Bolivar now stands—on which they encamped. By the 16th of October, Col. Boquet erected a stockade, two miles and forty rods below the ford, at a ravine, and completed his arrangements against a surprise.

The Indians being convinced that they could not succeed in any attempt against him, made a treaty of peace, and engaged to restore all the prisoners taken from the whites.

On Monday, the 22d, the troops broke up camp, and proceeded down the west bank of the Muskingum towards the Wakatomaka towns, about the mouth of the Whitewoman. The deputations accompanied them as guides. They reached the highland, one mile north of the mouth of the Walhonding or Whitewoman, on Thursday, and made a camp. The distance of this point from the mouth of Big Beaver or Mahoning river, by the route of the army, is 101 miles and 83 rods. Col. Boquet caused a stockade to be built, with four redoubts, and erected cabins and store-houses, determined to wait for the arrival of the prisoners.

On the 9th of November, 206 prisoners, including women and children, had been delivered, of whom 32 men and 58 women and children were from Virginia, and 49 males and 67 females from Pennsylvania.

On the 18th of November, the army broke up its cantonement at the Whitewoman and returned to Fort Pitt, which they reached on the 28th of the same month. This expedition was conducted with so much skill and prudence, that none of those frightful disasters that often result from Indian wars occurred. The savages, although in great strength, found no opportunity to make an attack. No prisoners were taken, none died of sickness, and every man of the party returned except one, who was killed and scalped by an Indian, when separated from camp. The Pennsylvania troops were under Lieut. Col. Francis, and Lieut. Col. Clayton. Col. Reid was next in command to Col. Boquet.

The provincial troops were discharged, and the regulars sent to garrison Fort Loudon, Fort Bedford and Carlisle. Col. Boquet arrived at Philadelphia in January, and received a complimentary address from the legislature, and also from the house of Burgesses of Virginia. Before these resolutions reached England, the king promoted him to be a brigadier general. He was ordered to the command of the post of Mobile, and the next season died there.

The scene which took place when the captives were brought in by the Indians, as mentioned in the preceding account, is thus related by Mr. Hutchins.

Language indeed can but weakly describe the scene, one to which the poet or painter might have repaired to enrich the highest colorings of the variety of the human passions, the philosopher, to find ample subject for the most serious reflection, and the man to exercise all the tender and sympathetic feelings of the soul. There were to be seen fathers and mothers recognizing and clasping their once lost babes, husbands hanging round the necks of their newly recovered wives, sisters and brothers unexpectedly meeting together, after a long separation, scarcely able to speak the same language, or for some time to be sure that they were the children of the same parents. In all these interviews joy and rapture inexpressible were seen, while feelings of a very different nature were painted in the looks of others, flying from place to place, in eager inquiries after relatives not found; trembling to receive an answer to questions; distracted with doubts, hopes and fears on obtaining no account of those they sought for; or stiffened into living monuments of horror and woe, on learning their unhappy fate.

The Indians too, as if wholly forgetting their usual savageness, bore a capital part in heightening this most affecting scene. They delivered up their beloved captives with the utmost reluctance—shed torrents of tears over them—recommending them to the care and protection of the commanding officer. Their regard to them continued all the while they remained in camp. They visited them from day to day, brought them what corn, skins, horses, and other matters had been bestowed upon them while in their families, accompanied with other presents, and all the marks of the most sincere and tender affection. Nay, they didn't stop here, but when the army marched, some of the Indians solicited and obtained permission to accompany their former captives to Fort Pitt, and employed themselves in hunting and bringing provisions for them on the way. A young Mingo carried this still farther, and gave an instance of love which would make a figure even in romance.

A young woman of Virginia, was among the captives, to whom he had formed so strong an attachment as to call her his wife. Against all the remonstrances of the imminent danger to which he exposed himself by approaching the frontier, he persisted in following her, at the risk of being killed by the surviving relatives of many unfortunate persons, who had been taken captive or scalped by those of his nation.

Among the captives, a woman was brought into camp at Muskingum with a babe about three months old at the breast. One of the Virginia volunteers soon knew her to be his wife! She had been taken by the Indians about six months before. He flew with her to his tent and clothed her and his child with proper apparel. But their joy after the first transports, was soon dampened by the reflection that another dear child about two years old, taken with the mother had been separated from her, and was still missing, although many children had been brought in.

A few days afterwards, a number of other persons were brought in, among them was several children. The woman was sent for, and one supposed to be hers was produced to her. At first sight she was not certain, but viewing the child with great earnestness, she soon recollected its features, and was so overcome with joy, that forgetting her sucking child, she dropt it from her arms, and catching up the new found child, in ecstacy, pressed it to her breast, and bursting into tears, carried it off unable to speak for joy. The father rising up with the babe she had let fall, followed her in no less transport and affection.

But it must not be deemed that there were not some, even grown persons who showed an unwillingness to return. The Shawnees were obliged to bind some of their prisoners, and force them along to the camp, and some women who had been delivered up, afterwards found means to escape, and went back to the Indian tribes. Some who could not make their escape, clung to their savage acquaintances at parting, and continued many days in bitter lamentations, even refusing sustenance.

Another expedition was undertaken in the summer of 1780, and directed against the Indian villages at the forks of the Muskingum. The narrative of this, usually known as "*the Coshocton campaign*," we derive from Doddridge's Notes.

The place of rendezvous was Wheeling. The number of regulars and militia, about eight hundred. From Wheeling they made a rapid march, by the nearest route, to the place of their destination. When the army reached the river, a little below Salem, the lower Moravian town, Col. Broadhead sent an express to the missionary in that place, the Rev. John Heckewelder, informing him of his arrival in his neighborhood, with his army, requesting a small supply of provisions, and a visit from him in his camp. When the missionary arrived at the camp, the general informed him of the object of the expedition he was engaged in, and inquired of him, whether any of the christian Indians were hunting, or engaged in business in the direction of his march. On being answered in the negative, he stated that nothing would give him greater pain, than to hear that any of the Moravian Indians had been molested by the troops, as these Indians had always, from the commencement of the war, conducted themselves in a manner that did them honor.

A part of the militia had resolved on going up the river, to destroy the Moravian villages, but were prevented from executing their project by Gen. Broadhead, and Col. Shepherd, of Wheeling. At White Eyes' Plain, a few miles from Coshocton, an Indian prisoner was taken. Soon afterwards two more Indians were discovered, one of whom was wounded, but he, as well as the other, made their escape.

The commander, knowing that these two Indians would make the utmost dispatch in going to the town, to give notice of the approach of the army, ordered a rapid march, in the midst of a heavy fall of rain, to reach the town before them, and take it by surprise. The plan succeeded. The army reached the place in three divisions. The right and left wings approached the river a little above and below the town, while the center marched directly upon it. The whole number of the Indians in the village, on the east side of the river, together with ten or twelve from a little village, some distance above, were made prisoners, without firing a single shot. The river having risen to a great height, owing to the recent fall of rain, the army could not cross it. Owing to this, the villages with their inhabitants on the west side of the river, escaped destruction.

Among the prisoners, sixteen warriors were pointed out by Pekillon, a friendly Delaware chief, who was with the army of Broadhead. A little after dark, a council of war was held, to determine on the fate of the warriors in custody. They were doomed to death, and by order of the commander, they were bound, taken a little distance below the town and dispatched with tomahawks and spears, and scalped.

Early the next morning, an Indian presented himself on the opposite bank of the river and asked for the big captain. Broadhead presented himself, and asked the Indian what he wanted? To which he replied, "I want peace." "Send over some of your chiefs," said Broadhead. "May be you kill," said the Indian. He was answered, "They shall not be killed." One of the chiefs, a well-looking man, came over the river, and entered into conversation with the commander in the street; but while engaged in conversation, a man of the name of Wetzel came up behind him, with a tomahawk concealed in the bosom of his hunting shirt, and struck him on the back of his head. He fell and instantly expired. About 11 or 12 o'clock, the army commenced its retreat from Coshocton. Gen. Broadhead committed the care of the prisoners to the militia. They were about twenty in number. After marching about half a mile, the men commenced killing them. In a short time they were all despatched, except a few women and children, who were spared and taken to Fort Pitt, and after some time, exchanged for an equal number of their prisoners.

Public Square, Coshocton.

Coshocton, the county seat, is finely situated on the Muskingum, at the junction of the Tuscarawas, with the Walhonding river, 83 miles northeast from Columbus, and 30 from Zanesville. The ground on which it is built, for situation, could scarcely be improved, as it lies in four broad natural terraces, each elevated about nine feet above the other, the last of which, is about one thousand feet wide. The town is much scattered. About sixty rods back from the Muskingum, is the public square, containing four acres, neatly fenced, planted with young trees and covered with a green sward; on it stand the county buildings, represented in the engraving. Coshocton was laid out in April, 1802, by Ebenezer Buckingham and John Matthews, under the name of *Tuscarawa*, and changed to its present appellation in 1811. The county was first settled only a few years prior to the formation of the town: among the early settlers, were Col. Chas. Williams, Wm. Morrison, Isaac Hoglin, Geo. M'Culloch, Andrew Craig and Wm. Whitten. Coshocton contains 2 Presbyterian, 1 Methodist Episcopal, and 1 Protestant Methodist church, 6 mercantile stores, 2 newspaper printing offices, 1 woolen factory, 1 flouring mill, and had in 1840, 625 inhabitants. In times of high water, steamboats occasionally run up to Coshocton.

"A short distance below Coshocton," says Dr. Hildreth in Silliman's Journal, "on one of those elevated gravelly alluvions, so common on the rivers of the west, has been recently discovered a very singular ancient burying ground. From some remains of wood still [1835] apparent in the earth around the bones, the bodies seem all to have been deposited in coffins; and what is still more curious, is the fact, that the bodies buried here were generally not more than from three to four and a half feet in length. They are very numerous, and must have been tenants of a considerable city, or their numbers could not have been so great. A large number of graves have been opened, the inmates of which are all of this pigmy race. No metallic articles or utensils have yet been found, to throw any light on the period or nation to which they belonged. Similar burying grounds have been found in Tennessee, and near St. Louis, in Missouri."

We learn orally from another source, that this burying ground covered, in 1830, about 10 acres. The graves were arranged in regular rows, with avenues between, and the heads of all were placed to the west and the feet to the east.

In one of them was a skeleton with pieces of oak boards and iron wrought nails. The corpse had evidently been dismembered before burial, as the skull was found among the bones of the pelvis, and other bones were displaced. The skull itself was triangular in shape, much flattened at the sides and back, and in the posterior part having an orifice, evidently made by some weapon of war, or bullet. In 1830, dwarf oaks of many years' growth were over several of the graves. The grave yard has since been plowed over. Nothing was known of its origin by the early settlers. Below the grave yard is a beautiful mound.

On the west bank of the Muskingum, opposite to and connected with Coshocton by a bridge, is Roscoe. This town was laid off in 1816, by James Calder, under the name of Caldersburg. An addition was subsequently laid off by Ransom & Swane, which being united with it, the place was called Roscoe, from Wm. Roscoe, the English author. The Walhonding canal, which extends to the village of Rochester, a distance of 25 miles, unites with the Ohio canal at Roscoe. This town is at present a great wheat depot on the canal, and an important place of shipment and transhipment. Its capacities for a large manufacturing town are ample. "The canals bring together the whole water power of the Tuscarawas and Walhonding, the latter standing in the canal at this place, forty feet above the level of the Muskingum, and the canal being comparatively little used, the whole power of the stream, capable of performing almost any thing desired, could be used for manufacturing purposes; and sites for a whole manufacturing village, could be purchased comparatively for a trifle." Roscoe contains 1 Methodist Episcopal church, 5 dry goods and 2 grocery stores, 2 forwarding houses, 1 fulling, 2 saw and 2 flouring mills, and had in 1840, 468 inhabitants. From the hills back of town, a fine prospect is presented up the vallies of the Tuscarawas and Walhonding, and down that of the Muskingum.

The following are the names of small villages in the county, with their population, according to the census of 1840: since then some of them have much increased. East Union, 210; West Carlisle, 213; New Castle, 155; Rochester, 111; West Bedford, 103; and Keene, 100; New Bedford, Evansburg, Birmingham, Chili, Jacobsport, Lewisville, Plainfield, Van Buren and Warsaw, each less than 100.

CRAWFORD.

Crawford was formed from old Indian Territory, April 1st, 1820. The surface is generally level, and in part slightly rolling: the south and west part is beautiful prairie land. The plains are usually covered with a rich vegetable loam of from 6 to 15 inches deep: the subsoil in most parts of the county is clay, mixed with lime; in many places—particularly the plains—a mixture of marl. Several rich beds of shell marl have already been discovered. The whole county is well adapted to grazing. The principal products are wheat, corn, oats, clover and timothy seeds, grass, wool and horned cattle. There are some fine limestone quarries. The following is a list of the townships in 1840, with their population:

Antrim,	261	Holmes,	744	Pitt,	423
Bucyrus,	1654	Jackson,	636	Sandusky,	679
Center,	132	Liberty,	1469	Sycamore,	958
Chatfield,	878	Lykens,	742	Tymochtee,	1659
Cranberry,	680	Mifflin,	316	Whetsone,	1124
Crawford,	812				

The population of Crawford, in 1830, was 4,788, and in 1840, 13,167. In 1845, the county was much reduced by the formation of Wyandot.

This county derived its name from Col. William Crawford, who was born in Virginia, in 1732, the same year with Washington. In 1758, he was a captain in Forbes expedition, which took possession of Fort Duquesne, on the site of Pittsburg. Washington was the friend of Crawford, and often in his visits to the then west, was an inmate of his humble dwelling, in Fayette county. He was a brave and energetic man, and, at the commencement of the revolution, raised a regiment by his own exertions, and received the commission of colonel of continentals. He often led parties against the Indians across the Ohio. In 1782, he reluctantly accepted the command of an expedition against the Ohio Indians. On this occasion he was taken prisoner, and burnt to death amid the most excruciating tortures, on the Tyemochtee, in the former limits of this, but now within the new county of Wyandot.

Bucyrus, the county seat, is on the Sandusky river—here a small stream—62 miles N. of Columbus, and 46 from Sandusky city. The view shows, on the right, the Lutheran church, and on the left, the county buildings and the academy. It contains 1 Presbyterian, 1 Lutheran, 1 Baptist, 1 Methodist and 1 Protestant Methodist church; 14 stores, 1 grist, 1 saw and 2 fulling mills, 1 newspaper printing office and a population of about 1,000: in 1840, it had 704 inhabitants. On the land of R. W. Musgrave, in the southeastern part of the town, a gas well has recently been dug. On first reaching the water—a distance of about 18 feet—it flew up about 6 feet with a loud, roaring noise; a pump has been placed over it, and the gas is conducted to the surface by a pipe, which, when a torch is applied, burns with a brilliant flame.

Bucyrus was laid out Feb. 11th, 1822, by Samuel Norton and James Kilbourne, proprietors of the soil. The first settler on the site of the town was Samuel Norton, who moved in from Pa. in 1819. He wintered in a small cabin made of poles, which stood just north of his present residence on the bank of the Sandusky. This region of country was not thrown into market until August, 1820, at which time it abounded in bears, wolves, catamounts, foxes and other wild animals. When he came, there were but a few settlers in the county, principally squatters on the Whetstone, the nearest of whom was on that stream eight miles distant. North and west of Mr. N. there was not a single settler in the county. Others of the early settlers in the town, whose names are recollected, were David and Michael Beedle, Daniel M'Michael, John Kent, Wm. Young, Jacob Shaeffer, Thomas and James Scott, James Steward, David Stein, George Black, John Blowers and Nehemiah Squires. The first frame house was built by Samuel Bailey, and is the small frame building standing next to, and north of F. Margraf's residence. The first brick dwelling is the one now owned by Wm. Timanus, on the public square. The Methodists built the first church.

View in Bucyrus.

On the 13th of August, 1838, part of the skeleton of a mastodon was discovered in wet, marshy land belonging to Abraham Hahn, on the Sandusky plains, near Bucyrus. "This skeleton was particularly interesting and important to science, as the head and skull bones were perfect in all their parts, and furnished the only known specimen from which a correct idea could be obtained respecting the massive and singularly-shaped head of this animal." The horizontal length of the skull was 3 feet 3 inches; perpendicular height, 3 ft. 2½ inches; weight of skull and upper jaw, 160 pounds, to which added the weight of the lower jaw, 77 pounds, made 237 pounds. The length of the back molar tooth was 7½ inches.

Kniseley's or Crawford sulphur spring is 7 miles NE. of Bucyrus, in Sandusky township. The water is highly impregnated with sulphuretted hydrogen, tarnishes silver and deposites a sulphurous precipitate a short distance from the spring. One of its most remarkable features is a deposit of a reddish or purple sediment at the bottom, giving to the water a color resembling a tincture of iodine. The water is a gentle cathartic, and is diuretic and diaphoretic in its effects. The place is now improved, a boarding house being there, and it proves a valuable resort for invalids. A few rods from it is a burning spring. The Annapolis sulphur is a beautiful, clear and copious spring, owned by Mr. Sliffer, who has neatly enclosed it with an iron railing. It possesses medicinal virtues.

Opposite Bucyrus, near the river, is a chalybeate spring of tonic qualities. There are various beds of peat in the county, the most extensive of which is in a wet prairie, called Cranberry marsh, in Cranberry township, which, as shown on the map, contains nearly 2,000 acres. This marsh formerly annually produced thousands of bushels of cranberries. The peat upon this marsh is estimated at two millions and five hundred thousand cords, by Dr. C. Briggs in the State Geographical report, from which we have derived the principal facts in this paragraph.

Galeon, 11 miles SE. of Bucyrus, has 3 stores, 2 or 3 churches and about 375 inhabitants. Leesville, about 10 E. of Bucyrus, has 2 stores, 2 churches and about 250 inhabitants. Near this place is a locality called "the battle ground," where, it is said, Crawford, when on his way to Upper Sandusky, had a skirmish with some Indians. De Kalb, West Liberty, Middletown, New Washington, Annapolis, Benton, Oletangy and Osceola, are small places; at the last named, the Broken Sword creek has a fall of 32 feet within a space of two miles.

CUYAHOGA.

CUYAHOGA was formed from Geauga county, June 7th, 1807, and organized in May, 1810. The name was derived from the river, and is said to signify, in the Indian language, "*crooked*," a term significant of the river, which is very winding, and has its sources farther north than its mouth. The surface is level or gently undulating. Near the lake the soil is sandy, elsewhere generally a clayey loam. The vallies of the streams are highly productive in corn and oats; in other parts, the principal crops are wheat, barley and hay. The county produces a great variety and amount of excellent fruit; also, cheese, butter, beef cattle and wool. Bog iron ore is found in the west part, and furnaces are in operation. Excellent grindstone quarries are worked, and grindstones largely exported. The sandstone from these quarries, is beginning to be a prominent article of commerce, being in some cases shipped for building purposes, as far west as Chicago. The following is a list of its townships, in 1840, with their population.

Bedford,	2021	Independence,	754	Rockport,	1235
Brecksville,	1124	Mayfield,	852	Royalton,	1051
Brooklyn,	1409	Middleburg,	339	Solon,	774
Cleveland,	7037	Newburg,	1342	Strongville,	1151
Dover,	966	Olmstead,	659	Warrensville,	1085
Euclid,	1774	Parma,	965	Orange,	1114

The population of Cuyahoga, in 1810, was 1495; in 1820, 6328; in 1830, 10,362, and in 1840, 26,512, or 43 inhabitants to a square mile.

As early as 1755, there was a French station within the present limits of Cuyahoga. On Lewis Evans' map of the middle British colonies, published that year, there is marked upon the west bank of the Cuyahoga, the words, "*French house,*" which was doubtless the station of a French trader. The ruins of a house, supposed to be those of the one alluded to, have been discovered on Foot's farm, in Brooklyn township, about five miles from the mouth of the Cuyahoga. The small engraving annexed, is from the map of Evans, and delineates the geography as in the original.

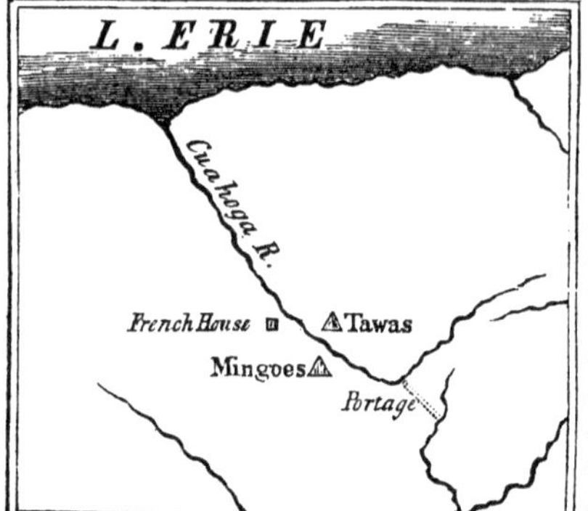

In 1786, the Moravian missionary Zeisberger, with his Indian converts, left Detroit, and arrived at the mouth of the Cuyahoga, in a vessel called the Mackinaw. From thence, they proceeded up the river about ten miles from the site of Cleveland, and settled in an abandoned village of the Ottawas, within the present limits of Independence, which they called *Pilgerruh*, i. e. *Pilgrim's rest*. Their stay was brief, for in the April following, they left for Huron river, and settled near the site of Milan, Erie county, at a locality they named *New Salem*.

The British, who, after the revolutionary war, refused to yield possession of the lake country west of the Cuyahoga, occupied to its shores until 1790. Their traders had a house in Ohio city, north of the Detroit road, on the point of the hill, near the river, when the surveyors first arrived here in 1796. From an early day, Washington, Jefferson and other leading Virginia statesmen regarded the mouth of the Cuyahoga, as an important commercial position.

The first permanent settlement within the limits of Cuyahoga, was made at CLEVELAND, in the autumn of 1796. On the 4th of July previous, the first surveying party of the Reserve, landed at Conneaut. In September and October, the corps laid out the city, which was named in honor of the land company's agent, Gen. Moses Cleveland.* By the 18th of October, the surveyors quitted the place, leaving Mr. Job V. Stiles and family, and Mr. Edward Paine, who were the only persons that passed the winter of 1796 and '7, within the limits of the town. Their lonely residence was a log cabin, which stood near the site of the Commercial bank. The nearest white settlement west, was at the mouth of the Raisin; south or east at Fort M'Intosh, at the mouth of Big Beaver; and northeast, at Conneaut. Those families that wintered at Conneaut, suffered severely for want of food.

The surveying party, on reaching the Reserve the succeeding season, again made Cleveland their head quarters. Early this season, Elijah Gunn and Judge Kingsbury removed here from Conneaut, with their families, and in the fall, the latter removed to Newburg, where he still resides, at an advanced age. The little colony was increased also by the arrival of Major Lorenzo Carter and Ezekiel Hawley, with their families.

In 1798, Rodolphus Edwards and Nathaniel Doane, with their families, settled in Cleveland. To faintly show the difficulty of travelling at that time, it is stated that Mr. Doane was ninety-two days on his journey from Chatham, Conn. In the latter part of the summer and in the fall, every person in the town was sick, either with the billious fever or the fever and ague. Mr. Doane's family consisted of nine persons: the only one of them having sufficient strength to take care of them and bring a pail of water, was Seth Doane, then a lad of thirteen years of age, and even he had daily attacks of the fever and ague. Such was the severity of the billious fever at that time, that a person having only daily attacks of fever and ague, was deemed lucky. There was much suffering for the want of food, particularly that proper for the sick. The only way this family was supplied, for two

* GEN. MOSES CLEVELAND was born in Canterbury, Conn., about the year 1755, and graduated at Yale College, in 1777. He was bred a lawyer, and practised his profession in his native town. He married a sister of Gen. Henry Champion, of Colchester, and died at Canterbury, in 1806, leaving a large fortune. He was a man of note among his townsmen, and often represented them in the legislature of Connecticut. In person, he was of medium stature, thick set and portly, and of a very dark complexion.

months or more, was through the exertions of this boy, who daily, after having an attack of the ague, went to Judge Kingsbury's, in Newburg—five miles distant—got a peck of corn, mashed it in a hand-mill, waited until a second attack of the ague was over, and then started on his return. There was at one time a space of several days when he was too ill to make the trip, during which, turnips comprised about all the vegetables the family had. Fortunately, Major Carter having only the fever and ague, was enabled, through the aid of his hounds and trusty rifle, to procure abundance of venison and other wild game. His family being somewhat acclimated, suffered less than that of Mr. Doane. Their situation can scarcely be conceived of at the present day. Destitute of a physician, and with a few medicines, necessity taught them to use such means as nature had placed within their reach. For calomel, they substituted pills from the extract of the bark of the butternut, and in lieu of quinine, used dog wood and cherry bark.

In November, four men, who had so far recovered as to have ague attacks no oftener than once in two or three days, started in the only boat for Walnut creek, Pa., to obtain a winter's supply of flour for the colony. When below Euclid creek, a storm arose, drove them ashore, stove their boat in pieces, and it was with difficulty they saved their lives and regained the city. During the winter and summer following, the colony had no flour, except that ground in hand and coffee mills, which, for want of proper means to separate from the bran, was made into a bread similar to that of Graham's. In this summer, the Conn. land company opened the first road on the Reserve, which commenced about ten miles from the lake on the Pennsylvania line, and extended to Cleveland. In January, '99, Mr. Doane moved to Doane's corners, and from that time until April, 1800—a space of fifteen months—Major Carter's was the only white family in Cleveland. During the spring of '99, Wheeler W. Williams, from Norwich, Conn., and Major Wyatt, erected a small grist and a saw mill at the falls, on the site of Newburg, which being the first mill on the Reserve, spread joy among the pioneers. A short time prior to this, each house in Cleveland had its own hand grist mill, in the chimney corner, which is thus described by one of the early settlers. "The stones were of the common grindstone grit, and about four inches thick and twenty in diameter. The runner was turned by hand, with a pole set in the top of it, near the verge. The upper end of the pole went into another hole inserted into a board, and nailed on the under side of the joist, immediately over the hole in the verge of the runner. One person turned the stone, and another fed the corn into the eye with his hands. It was very hard work to grind, and the operators alternately changed places."

In 1800, several settlers came, among whom were David Clark and Major Amos Spafford, and from this time the town slowly progressed. The first ball in Cleveland, was on the 4th of July, 1801, and was held at Major Carter's log cabin, on the side hill; John and Benjamin Wood and R. H. Blinn, managers, and Major Samuel Jones, musician and master of ceremonies. The company consisted of about thirty, of both sexes. Mr. Jones' proficiency on the violin, won him great favor. Notwithstanding the dancers had a rough puncheon floor, and no better beverage to enliven their spirits than whiskey, sweetened with maple sugar, yet it is doubtful if the anniversary of American independence was ever celebrated in Cleveland by a more joyful and harmonious company, than those who danced the scamper-down, double-shuffle, western-swing and half-moon, forty-six years ago in the log cabin of Major Carter.

The Indians were accustomed, at this period, to meet every autumn at Cleveland, in great numbers, and pile up their canoes at the mouth of the Cuyahoga. From thence they scattered into the interior, and passed the winter in hunting. In the spring, they returned, disposed their furs to traders, and launching their bark canoes upon the lake, returned to their towns, in the region of the Sandusky and Maumee, where they remained until the succeeding autumn, to raise their crops of corn and potatoes. In this connection, we give an incident, showing the fearlessness and intrepidity of Major Lorenzo Carter, a native of Rutland, Vt., and a thorough pioneer, whose rough exterior covered a warm heart. Some time in the spring of '99, the Chippewas and Ottawas, to the number of several hundred, having disposed of their furs, determined to have one of their drinking frolics at their camp, on the west bank of the Cuyahoga. As a precautionary measure, they gave up their tomahawks and other deadly weapons to their squaws to secrete, so that, in the height of their frenzy, they need not harm each other. They then sent to the Major for whiskey, from time to time, as they wanted it; and in proportion as they became intoxicated, he weakened it with water. After a while, it resulted in the Indians becoming partially sober, from drinking freely of diluted liquor: perceiving the trick, they became much enraged. Nine of them came on to the Major's, swearing vengeance on him and family. Carter being apprised of their design, and knowing they were partially intoxicated, felt himself to be fully their match, although possessing but poor weapons of defence. Stationing himself beind his cabin door with a fire poker, he successively knocked down three or four, as they attempted to enter, and then leaping over their prostrate bodies, furiously attacked those on the outside, and drove them to their canoes. Soon after, a deputation of squaws came over to make peace with the Major, when, arming himself, he fearlessly repaired to their camp alone, and settled the difficulty. Such eventually became his influence over the Indians, that they regarded him as a magician, and many of them were made to believe that he could shoot them with a rifle, and not break their skins.

The first militia muster in Cuyahoga county, was held on the 16th of June, 1806, at Doane's Corners. Nathaniel Doane was captain; Sylvanus Burke, lieutenant; and Samuel Jones, ensign, with about fifty privates. The surveying party being at Cleveland, and many strangers, this event attracted much attention. Never had so many whites been collected together in this vicinity, as on this occasion. The military marched and countermarched to the lively roll of the drum of Joseph Burke, who had been drum major in the revolution, and the soul-stirring strains of the fife of Lewis Dill. "Yankee Doodle," "Hail Columbia," and "Who's Afeard," were among the tunes that aroused the martial spirit of many a gallant heart, as he wielded, perhaps, some ancient relic of the revolution upon his shoulder.

Early in the spring previous, a small boat, containing a Mr. Hunter, wife and child, a colored man named Ben, and a small colored boy, who were moving to Cleveland, were overtaken on the lake by a squall of wind, and driven ashore east of Rocky river. The bluff being perpendicular, they were unable to ascend. They, however, climbed up the rocks as far as possible—the surge constantly beating over them—with the vain hope that the storm would subside; but on Saturday it increased, and during Sunday, Mrs. Hunter expired, the children having died previously. On Monday, Mr. Hunter expired. Black Ben held out until Tuesday, when, the storm subsiding, some French traders, going in a vessel from Cleveland to Detroit, discovered him, took him aboard, and returned with him to Cleveland. Thus, for three days and four nights, had he been without sleep or food, and with little clothing, exposed to the continued surge, and holding on for life to some small bushes in the crevices of the rocks. Ben was treated with great kindness by Major Carter, in whose family he remained an invalid over a year.

Early the second spring succeeding, a similar incident occurred near the same place. Stephen Gilbert, Joseph Plumb, Adolphus Spafford and Mr. Gilmore started on a fishing expedition, for Maumee river, in a Canadian batteaux. They had aboard some goods and provisions, sent by Major Perry to his son Nathan, at Black river, and a hired woman, named Mary, as a passenger to that plaee. A Mr. White, of Newburg, and two sons of Mr. Plumb, not arriving in time, started by land for the mouth of Black river, intending to overtake the boat at that point. Pursuing the Indian trail, on the bank of the lake, they discovered, when about half way, the wreck of the boat on the beach, by the rocky shore, about sixty feet below them, in what is now Dover, and near it, Mr. Plumb, seriously injured, and suffering with cold. From him, they learned that a squall of wind had upset their boat, when about a mile from shore, and that all but him had drowned.

They were all good swimmers but Plumb, who luckily got astraddle of the boat after it had upset, and floated ashore. The others made for the shore, Gilbert telling his companions to divest themselves of their clothing as much as possible: but all their efforts failed, the coldness of the water chilled them, so that they could not swim. Having learned the circumstances from Mr. Plumb, they made every effort to reach him, but were prevented by the steepness of the rocks. Mr. White and one of Mr. Plumb's sons hastened to Black river, to procure means of relief, leaving the other son to comfort his father. After they left, he climbed up an iron-wood sapling, which bent with his weight, and dropping about thirty feet perpendicular, joined his parent. In the night, Quintus F. Atkins and Nathan Perry returned with White, and recovered Mr. Plumb, by hauling him up the bank with a rope, by the light of a torch. This was no easy task for men worn down by fatigue, Mr. Plumb's weight being 220 pounds. The corpses of Gilmer and Spafford were afterwards found and buried at Cleveland; that of the colored woman was discovered and interred at Black river. This was a melancholy event to the colony. Of the eighteen deaths that had taken place among the inhabitants of Cleveland, from the first settlement in 1796, a period of twelve years, eleven had been by drowning. During this time, the nearest settled physicians were at Hudson, 24, and Austinburg, 50 miles.*

On the 26th of June, 1812, an Indian, named O'Mic, was hung for murder, at Cleveland, on the public square. Fearing an attempt at rescue on the part of the Indians, a

* The preceding part of this historical sketch, is mainly from the MSS. of John Barr, Esq., of Cleveland, who is collecting materials for a history of the Western Reserve.

large number of armed citizens from this and the adjoining counties assembled. At the hour of execution, he objected to going upon the scaffold; this difficulty was removed by the promise of a pint of whiskey, which he swallowed, and then took his departure for the land of spirits. In 1813, Cleveland became a depot of supplies and rendezvous for troops engaged in the war. A small stockade was erected at the foot of Ontario street, on the lake bank, and a permanent garrison stationed here, under Major (now General) Jessup, of the U. S. army. The return of peace was celebrated by libations of whiskey and the roar of artillery. One worthy, known as "Uncle Abram," was much elevated on the occasion. He carried the powder in an open tin pail, upon his arm, while another, to touch off the gun, carried a stick with fire at the end, kept alive by swinging it through the air. Amid the general excitement, a spark found its way to Uncle Abram's powder, about the time the gun was discharged; and his body was seen to rise twenty feet in the air, and return by its own gravity to the earth, blackened and destitute of clothing. He was dead, if his own vociferations were to be believed; but they were not, and he soon recovered from his wounds.

Cleveland is at the northern termination of the Ohio canal, 139 miles NE. from Columbus, 255 from Cincinnati, 130 from Pittsburg, 190 from Buffalo, 455 from New York, and 130 from Detroit. It was incorporated as a village in 1814, and as a city in 1836. Excepting a small portion of it on the river, it is situated on a gravelly plain, elevated about 100 feet above the lake, of which it has a most commanding prospect. Some of the common streets are 100 feet wide, and the principal business one, Main street, has the extraordinary width of 132 feet. It is one of the most beautiful towns in the Union, and much taste is displayed in the private dwellings and disposition of shrubbery. "The location is dry and healthy, and the view of the meanderings of the Cuyahoga river, and of the steamboats and shipping in the port, and leaving or entering it, and of the numerous vessels on the lake under sail, presents a prospect exceedingly interesting, from the high shore of the lake.

"Near the center of the place is a public square of ten acres, divided into four parts, by intersecting streets, neatly enclosed, and shaded with trees. The court house and one or two churches front on this square.

"The harbor of Cleveland is one of the best on Lake Erie. It is formed by the mouth of the Cuyahoga river, and improved by a pier on each side, extending 425 yards into the lake, 200 feet apart, and faced with substantial stone masonry. Cleveland is the great mart of the greatest grain-growing state in the Union, and it is the Ohio and Erie canals that have made it such, though it exports much by the way of the Welland canal to Canada. It has a ready connection with Pittsburg, through the Pennsylvania and Ohio canal, which extends from the Ohio canal at Akron to Beaver creek, which enters the Ohio below Pittsburg. The natural advantages of this place are unsurpassed in the west, to which it has a large access by the lakes and the Ohio canal. But the Erie canal constitutes the principal source of its vast advantages; without that great work, it would have remained in its former insignificance." The construction of two contemplated railroads, the first connecting Cleveland with Wellsville, on the Ohio; and the last, with Columbus, will add much to the business facilities of the place.

The government of the city is vested in a mayor and council, which consists of three members from each of the three wards into which the city is divided, and also an alderman from each ward. The following is a list of the mayors of the city since its organization, with the time of their election: John W. Willey, 1836 and 1837; Joshua Mills, 1838 and 1839; Nicholas Dockstader, 1840; John W. Allen, 1841; Joshua Mills, 1842; Nelson Hayward, 1843; Saml. Starkweather, 1844 and 1845; George Hoadley, 1846, and J. A. Harris, 1847.

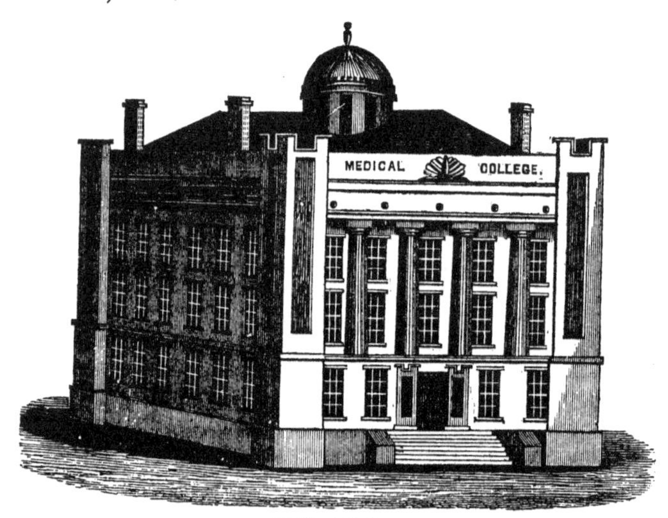

Medical College.

The Cleveland medical college, although established but four or five years, is in a very flourishing condition, and has gained so much in public estimation, as to be equalled in patronage by only one or two similar institutions in the west. It has seven professors, and all the necessary apparatus and facilities for instruction.

In 1837, the government purchased nine acres on the height overlooking the lake, for the purpose of erecting a marine hospital; up to the present time, but little more than the foundation has been laid. It is to be of Ionic architecture, of hewn stone, and will combine convenience and beauty.

There are in Cleveland a large number of mercantile and mechanical establishments, 4 banks, 3 daily, 6 weekly, and 1 semi-monthly newspapers, and 21 religious societies, viz: 3 Episcopal, 2 Presbyterian, 1 Methodist Episcopal, 1 Baptist, 1 Catholic, 1 Bethel, 1 Wesleyan Methodist, 1 German Evangelical Protestant, 1 German Mission Society of the Protestant Episcopal Church, 1 German Evangelical Lutheran, 1 Evangelical Association of North America, 1 Associate Presbyterian, 1 Seceder, 1 Disciples, 1 Jewish, 1 Universalist and 2 Second Advent. The business of the port of Cleveland, both by canal and lake, is very heavy, and constantly increasing. The number of arrivals by lake, in 1845, was 2136; of these, 927 were steamers. The tonnage then owned at this port, amounted to 13,493, and number of vessels, of all kinds, 85. The total value of the imports and exports by the lake, was over $9,000,000.

The population of Cleveland, on the east side of the Cuyahoga, was, in the year 1796, 3; 1798, 16; 1825, 500; 1831, 1100; 1835, 5080; 1840, 6071, and 1846, 10,135. Of the last, 6780 were natives of the United States; 1472 of Germany; 808 of England; 632 of Ireland; 144 of Canada; 97 of the Isle of Man, and 96 of Scotland.

Ohio city is beautifully situated on a commanding eminence on the west side of the Cuyahoga, opposite Cleveland. It was incorporated as a city, March 3d, 1836, and its government vested in a mayor and council. The city is divided into three wards, and is well laid out and built. There are three churches, viz.: 1 Presbyterian, 1 Methodist Episcopal and 1 Episcopalian—the last of which is a Gothic structure of great beauty. The population of Ohio city, in 1840, was 1,577, and in 1845, 2,462.

Chagrin Falls.

The village of Chagrin Falls is in the new township of the same name, on Chagrin river, 17 miles SE. from Cleveland.

The name *Chagrin*, originally applied to the river, then to the present village of Willoughby, in Lake county, and later to this town, "is supposed to have been derived from the sore disappointment of some surveyors who mistook it for the Cuyahoga river, and followed their respective lines to the lake. It had, however, long been previously known by that name, in consequence, it is said, of the wreck and sufferings of a French crew near its mouth, the particulars of which have not been preserved." In Evans' map, published in 1755, the river is called "Elk." Prior to the war of 1812, the Indians were numerous in this vicinity. In July, 1817, a person now living in the village, in company with another, visited the spot and killed a variety of wild game, such as bears, deer, turkeys, &c., and a short distance east, alarmed a drove of from 40 to 50 elk. There were then several ancient mounds and burial places on the village site. On the 1st of April, 1833, two families commenced the foundation of the settlement, and on that day the first blow was struck with an axe upon the village site, and shortly after a log house and saw mill built where the furnace now stands. In the succeeding fall, the town was laid out by Noah Graves and Dr. S. S. Handerson. It was commenced without cash capital, and has been built up by the indefatigable enterprise of its inhabitants, many of whom are of Connecticut origin. For want of money, bartering and exchange of labor has been extensively practised. Notwithstanding these disadvantages, the village has scarcely an equal in Ohio in its rapid progress from a wilderness to a flourishing town. All that it requires to make it a large place, is a canal or railroad, to furnish transportation facilities to Lake Erie.

Chagrin Falls contains 1 Congregational, 1 Methodist Episcopal, 1 Wesleyan Methodist and 1 Free Will Baptist church; 1 academy, 9 mercantile stores, 1 axe and edge tool, 1 sash, 1 wheel and wheel head, 1 wooden bowl and three woolen factories; 1 paper, 2 flouring and 3 saw mills; 1 printing office and bindery; 1 furnace and machine establishment, 1 carriage, 2 tin, 3 harness and 3 cabinet shops, and about 1,200 inhabitants. The Cleveland and Pittsburg stages pass through the town, and a carriage daily runs to the former place. Near the village is an inexhaustible grindstone quarry, which is extensively worked. The township of Chagrin Falls was organized in June, 1844, within which, including the village, there is a fall of 225 feet in the river, about one third of which is improved. The view shows the village as it appears from an elevation below, called either the side or slide bank. It was drawn and engraved by Mr. Jehu Brainerd of Cleveland. In the distance represented, the river has about one hundred feet descent.

We introduce an incident in the life of an early settler, a lady, who was recently living but a few miles distant from Chagrin Falls.

Joel Thorp, with his wife Sarah, moved with an ox team, in May, '99, from North Haven, Connecticut, to Millsford, in Ashtabula county, and were the first settlers in that region. They soon had a small clearing on and about an old beaver dam, which was very rich and mellow. Towards the first of June, the family being short of provisions, Mr. Thorp started off alone to procure some through the wilderness, with no guide but a pocket compass, to the nearest settlement, about 20 miles distant, in Pennsylvania. His family, consisting of Mrs. Thorp and three children, the oldest child, Basil, being but eight years of age, were before his return reduced to extremities for the want of food. They were compelled, in a measure, to dig for and subsist on roots, which yielded but little nourishment. The children in vain asked food, promising to be satisfied with the least possible portion. The boy Basil remembered to have seen some kernels of corn in a crack of one of the logs of the cabin, and passed hours in an unsuccessful search for them. Mrs. Thorp emptied the straw out of her bed and picked it over to obtain the little wheat it contained, which she boiled and gave to her children. Her husband, it seems, had taught her to shoot at a mark, in which she acquired great skill. When all her means for procuring food were exhausted, she saw, as she stood in her cabin door, a wild turkey flying near. She took down her husband's rifle, and, on looking for ammunition, was surprised to find only sufficient for a small charge. Carefully cleaning the barrel, so as not to lose any by its sticking to the sides as it went down, she set some apart for priming and loaded the piece with the remainder, and started in pursuit of the turkey, reflecting that on her success depended the lives of herself and children. Under the excitement of her feelings she came near defeating her object, by frightening the turkey, which flew a short distance and again alighted in a potato patch. Upon this, she returned to the house and waited until the fowl had begun to wallow in the loose earth. On her second approach, she acted with great caution and coolness, creeping slyly on her hands and knees from log to log until she had gained the last obstruction between herself and the desired object. It was now a trying moment, and a crowd of emotions passed through her mind as she lifted the rifle to a level with her eye. She fired; the result was fortunate: the turkey was killed and herself and family preserved from death by her skill. Mrs. Thorp married three times. Her first husband was killed, in Canada, in the war of 1812; her second was supposed to have been murdered. Her last husband's name was Gordiner. She died in Orange, in this county, Nov. 1st, 1846.

Bedford, on the Pittsburg road, 12 miles from Cleveland, has 1

Baptist, 1 Methodist and 1 Disciples church ; 3 stores, 1 flouring and 3 saw mills, 1 woolen factory and about 80 dwellings. Newberg, 6 miles from Cleveland, on the same road with the above, has 1 Presbyterian and 1 Methodist church and a few dwellings. Euclid, a beautiful village, 8 miles east of Cleveland, has 1 Presbyterian, 1 Disciples church, 1 academy, 4 stores and 42 dwellings. Two miles east of it is the smaller village of East Euclid, which has 1 Baptist and 1 Methodist church. The Presbyterian church at Euclid, built in 1817, was the first frame meeting-house, with a spire, erected on the Reserve.

The township of Euclid (says the Barr MSS.) was purchased of the Western Reserve Land Company under peculiar circumstances. While the surveyors of the Reserve were about to commence operations, they found some disposition among their men in camp to strike for higher wages. To settle this difficulty, Gen. Cleveland, the agent, agreed that a township should be surveyed and set apart, so that each individual of the party who should desire might have the privilege of purchasing a lot on long credit and at a stipulated price. This settled the difficulty, and this township was the one selected. In 1798, Joseph Burke and family, and in 1801, Timothy Doane and family, settled in Euclid.

Albion and Strongville are two connecting villages, scattered along on the Cleveland and Columbus road, about 14 miles from the former, and contain 1 Presbyterian, 1 Methodist, 1 Baptist and 1 Episcopal church; 3 stores, 1 woolen factory and about 80 dwellings. On the same road, about 4 miles from Cleveland, and separated by a creek, are the small villages of Brooklyn Centre and Brighton, jointly containing 1 Presbyterian and 2 Methodist churches. In the western part of the county, on branches of Rocky river, are the small but thriving manufacturing villages of Norris Falls and Berea. Rockport, Doan's Corners and Warrensville, are small places. At or near the latter, is a settlement of *Manks*—a term applied to natives of the Isle of Man.

DARKE.

DARKE was formed, Jan. 3d, 1809, from Miami county, and organized in March, 1817. The surface is generally level, and has some prairie land. It is well timbered with poplar, walnut, blue ash, sugar maple, hickory and beech. Much of it is well adapted to grazing, and it produces superior wheat. The following is a list of its townships in 1840, with their population.

Adams,	698	Gibson,	276	Richland,	589
Allen,	194	Greenville,	1851	Twin,	1047
Brown,	293	Harrison,	1666	Van Buren,	421
Butler,	1116	Jackson,	304	Washington,	898
Franklin,	291	Mississinewa,	124	Wayne,	727
German,	1173	Neave,	635	York,	371

Population of Darke, in 1820, was 3717; in 1830, 6204; and in 1840, 13,145, or 20 inhabitants to a square mile.

Gen. Wm. Darke, from whom this county derived its name, was born in Pennsylvania, in 1736, and removed at the age of five years, with his parents to near Shepherdstown, Va. He was with the Virginia provincials at Braddock's defeat, taken prisoner in the revolutionary war, at Germantown, commanded as colonel, two Virginia regiments at the siege of York, was a member of the Virginia Convention, of '88, and was repeatedly a member of the legislature of that ancient commonwealth. He distinguished himself at St. Clair's defeat, and died, Nov. 20th, 1801. Gen. Darke was by profession a farmer. He possessed an herculean frame, rough manners, a strong but uncultivated mind, and a frank and fearless disposition.

This county has been the theatre of two important events in the early history of the west,—St. Clair's defeat and the treaty of Greenville. The first in order of time, was the defeat of St. Clair, which took place on the northern boundary of the county, within two or three miles of the Indiana line.

The great object of St. Clair's campaign was to establish a military post at the Miami village, at the junction of the St. Mary and St. Joseph, at what is now Fort Wayne, Ia., with intermediate posts of communication between it and Fort Washington, to awe and curb the Indians in that quarter, as the only preventive of future hostilities.

Acting under his instructions, St. Clair proceeded to organize his army. At the close of April, (1791,) he was at Pittsburg, to which point troops and munitions of war were being forwarded. On the 15th of May, he reached Fort Washington, but owing to various hindrances, among which was the mismanagement of the quartermaster's department, the troops instead of being in readiness to start upon the expedition, by the 1st of August, as was anticipated, were not prepared until many weeks later. From Fort Washington, the troops were advanced to Ludlow's station, six miles distant. Here the army continued until Sept. 17th, when being 2300 strong, exclusive of militia, they moved forward to a point upon the Great Miami, where they built Fort Hamilton. From thence, they moved forty four miles farther, and built Fort Jefferson, which they left on the 24th of October, and began their toilsome march through the wilderness. We copy below from the Notes of Judge Burnet.

During this time, a body of the militia, amounting to three hundred, deserted, and returned to their homes. The supplies for the army being still in the rear, and the general entertaining fears that the deserters might meet and sieze them for their own use, determined, very reluctantly, to send back the first regiment, for the double purpose of bringing up the provisions, and, if possible, of overtaking and arresting some of the deserters.

Having made that arrangement, the army resumed its march, and on the 3d of November, arrived at a creek running to the southwest, which was supposed to be the St. Mary's, one of the principal branches of the Maumee, but was afterwards ascertained to be a branch of the Wabash. It being then late in the afternoon, and the army much fatigued by a laborious march, they were encamped on a commanding piece of ground, having the creek in front.

It was the intention of the general to occupy that position till the first regiment, with the provisions, should come up. He proposed on the next day, to commence a work of defence, agreeably to a plan concerted between himself and Maj. Ferguson, but he was not permitted to do either; for on the next morning, November 4th, half an hour before sunrise, the men having been just dismissed from parade, an attack was made on the militia posted in front, who gave way and rushed back into the camp, throwing the army into a state of disorder, from which it could not be recovered, as the Indians followed close at their heels. They were, however, checked a short time by the fire of the first line, but immedi-

SUPERIOR STREET, CLEVELAND.

ately a very heavy fire was commenced on that line, and in a few minutes it was extended to the second.

In each case, the great weight of the fire was directed to the center, where the artillery was placed ; from which the men were frequently driven with great slaughter. In that emergency resort was had to the bayonet. Col. Darke was ordered to make the charge with a part of the second line, which order was executed with great spirit. The Indians instantly gave way, and were driven back several hundred yards, but for want of a sufficient number of riflemen to preserve the advantage gained, the enemy soon renewed their attack, and the American troops, in turn, were forced to give away.

At that instant, the Indians entered the American camp on the left, having forced back the troops stationed at that point. Another charge was then ordered and made by the battalions of Majors Butler and Clark, with great success. Several other charges were afterwards made, and always with equal effect. These attacks, however, were attended with a very heavy loss of men, and particularly of officers. In the charge made by the second regiment, Maj. Butler was dangerously wounded ; and every officer of that regiment fell, except three, one of whom was shot through the body. The artillery being silenced, and all the officers belonging to it killed, but Capt. Ford, who was dangerously wounded, and half the army having fallen, it became necessary to gain the road, if possible, and make a retreat.

For that purpose, a successful charge was made on the enemy, as if to turn their right flank, but in reality, to gain the road, which was effected. The militia then commenced a retreat, followed by the United States' troops, Maj. Clark, with his battalion, covering the rear. The retreat, as might be expected, soon became a flight. The camp was abandoned, and so was the artillery, for the want of horses to remove it. The men threw away their arms and accoutrements, even after the pursuit had ceased, which was not continued more than four miles. The road was almost covered with those articles, for a great distance.

All the horses of the general were killed, and he was mounted on a broken down packhorse, that could scarcely be forced out of a walk. It was therefore impossible for him to get forward in person, to command a halt, till regularity could be restored, and the orders which he dispatched by others, for that purpose, were wholly unattended to. The rout continued to Fort Jefferson, where they arrived about dark, twenty seven miles from the battle-ground. The retreat began at half past nine in the morning, and as the battle commenced half an hour before sunrise, it must have lasted three hours, during which time, with only one exception, the troops behaved with great bravery. This fact accounts for the immense slaughter which took place.

Among the killed, were Maj. Gen. Butler, Col. Oldham, Major Ferguson, Maj. Hart, and Maj. Clark. Among the wounded, were Col. Sargeant, the Adjutant General, Col. Darke, Col. Gibson, Maj. Butler, and Viscount Malartie, who served in the character of an aid. In addition to these, the list of officers killed contains the names of Captains Bradford, Phelon, Kirkwood, Price, Van Swearingen, Tipton, Purdy, Smith, Piatt, Gaither, Crebbs, and Newman : Lieutenants Spear, Warren, Boyd, McMath, Burgess, Kelso, Read, Little, Hopper, and Lickins; also, Ensigns Cobb, Balch, Chase, Turner, Wilson, Brooks, Beatty, and Purdy ; also, Quartermasters Reynolds and Ward, Audj. Anderson and Doc. Grasson. And in addition to the wounded officers whose names are mentioned above, the official list contains the names of Captains Doyle, Trueman, Ford, Buchanan, Darke, and Hough ; also, of Lieutenants Greaton, Davidson, DeButts, Price, Morgan, McCrea, Lysle, and Thompson ; also, Adjutants Whistler and Crawford, and Ensign Bines.

The melancholy result of that disastrous day was felt and lamented by all, who had sympathy for private distress, or public misfortune.

The only charge alledged by the general against his army, was want of discipline, which they could not have acquired, during the short time they had been in the service. That defect rendered it impossible, when they were thrown into confusion, to restore them again to order, and is the chief reason why the loss fell so heavily on the officers. They were compelled to expose themselves in an unusual degree in their efforts to rally the men, and remedy the want of discipline. In that duty, the general set the example, though worn down by sickness, and suffering under a painful disease. It was alledged by the officers, that the Indians far outnumbered the American troops. That conclusion was drawn, in part, from the fact, that they outflanked and attacked the American lines with great force, at the same time, on every side.

When the fugitives arrived at Fort Jefferson, they found the first regiment, which was just returning from the service on which it had been sent, without either overtaking the deserters, or meeting the convoy of provisions. The absence of that regiment, at the time of the battle, was believed by some, to be the cause of the defeat. They supposed, that had it been present, the Indians would have been defeated, or would not have ventured an attack at the time they made it; but Gen. St. Clair expressed great doubt on that subject. He seemed to think it uncertain, judging from the superior number of the enemy, whether he ought to consider the absence of that corps from the field of action, as fortunate or otherwise. On the whole, he seemed to think it fortunate, as he very much doubted, whether, if it had been in the action, the fortune of the day would have been changed; and if it had not, the triumph of the enemy would have been more complete, and the country would have been left destitue of the means of defence.

As soon as the troops reached Fort Jefferson, it became a question whether they ought to continue at that place, or return to Fort Washington. For the purpose of determining that question, the general called on the surviving field officers, to wit: Col. Darke, Major Hamtramck, Maj. Zeigler, and Maj. Gaither, and also the Adjutant General, Col. Sargeant, for their advice, as to what would be the proper course to be pursued, under existing circumstances. After discussing the subject, they reported it to be their unanimous opinion, that the troops could not be accommodated in the fort; that they could not be supplied with provisions, at that place; and as it was known there were provisions on the road, at the distance of one or two marches, it would be proper, without loss of time, to proceed and meet them. That advice was adopted, and the army put in motion at 10 o'clock, and marched all night. On the succeeding day, they met a quantity of flour, and on the day after, a drove of cattle, which having been disposed of, as the wants of the troops required, the march was continued to Fort Washington.

The loss sustained by the country, from the fall of so many gallant officers and men, was most seriously regretted. Gen. Butler and Maj. Ferguson, were spoken of with peculiar interest. The public feeling was, however, in some measure alleviated, by the fact, that those brave men, officers and privates, fell covered with honor, in defending the cause of their country.

The principal complaint made by the commander-in-chief was, that some of his orders, of great consequence, given to Col. Oldham, over night, were not executed; and that some very material intelligence, communicated by Capt. Hough, to Gen. Butler, in the course of the night, before the action, was not imparted to him; and that he did not hear of it, till his arrival at Fort Washington.

It is important to the fame of the commanding general, that in consequence of the almost treasonable negligence of the agents of government, whose duty it was to furnish supplies, the army had been for many days on short allowance, and were so at the time of the battle. That fact had made it indispensably necessary, either to retreat, or send back the first regiment, which was the flower of the army, to bring up the provisions and military stores. The latter alternative was chosen, and in the absence of that corps, the attack was made.

In regard to the negligence charged on the War Department, it is a well-authenticated fact, that boxes and packages were so carelessly put up and marked, that during the action a box was opened marked "flints," which was found to contain gun-locks. Several mistakes of the same character were discovered, as for example, a keg of powder marked "for the infantry," was found to be damaged cannon-powder, that could scarcely be ignited.

Under all these disadvantages, it was generally believed by candid intelligent men, that the commanding general was not justly liable to much censure, if any. With one exception, at the commencement of the action, the troops behaved with great bravery. They maintained their ground for three tedious hours, in one uninterrupted conflict with a superior force; nor did they attempt to leave the field, till it was covered with the bodies of their companions, nor until further efforts were unavailing, and a retreat was ordered.

The general, less anxious for himself than for others, was the last to leave the ground, after the retreat had been ordered. For sometime after the disaster, he was universally censured; but when a thorough investigation had been made by a committee of Congress, of which Mr. Giles, of Virginia, was the chairman, it was found that the campaign had been conducted with skill and personal bravery; and that the defeat was chiefly owing to the want of discipline in the militia, and to the negligence of those whose duty it was to procure and forward the provisions and military stores, necessary for the expedition.

After the publication of that report, the Secretary of War, believing himself to be injured, addressed a letter to Congress, complaining that injustice had been done him by the committee; in consequence of which the report was recommitted to the same committee, who, after hearing the statements and explanations of the Secretary, and reconsidering the whole matter, re-affirmed their first report.

This defeat of St. Clair drew upon his head, from one part of the country to the other, "one loud and merciless outcry of abuse and even detestation." Many a general, with far less bravery and military skill, has, when successful, been applauded by the unthinking multitude with vehement acclamations. The following, derived from the narrative of his campaign, shows that he deserved a better fate.

During the engagement, Gen. St. Clair and Gen. Butler were continually going up and down the lines; as one went up one, the other went down the opposite. St. Clair was so severely afflicted with the gout as to be unable to mount or dismount a horse without assistance. He had four horses for his use; they had been turned out to feed over night and were brought in before the action. The first he attempted to mount was a young horse, and the firing alarmed him so much that he was unable to accomplish it, although there were three or four people assisting him. He had just moved him to a place where he could have some advantage of the ground, when the horse was shot through the head, and the boy that was holding him through the arm. A second horse was brought, and the furniture of the first disengaged and put on him; but at the moment it was done, the horse and servant who held him were killed. The general then ordered the third horse to be got ready and follow him to the left of the front line, which by that time was warmly engaged, and set off on foot to the point designated. However, the man and horse were never heard of afterward, and were supposed to have both been killed. Gen. St. Clair's fourth horse was killed under the Count de Malartie, one of his aids, whose horse had died on the march.

On the day of the battle, St. Clair was not in his uniform; he wore a coarse cappo coat and a three-cornered hat. He had a long que and large locks, very gray, flowing beneath his beaver. Early in the action, when near the artillery, a ball grazed the side of his face and cut off a portion of one of his locks. It is said, that, during the action, eight balls passed through his clothes and hat. After his horses were killed, he exerted himself on foot, for a considerable time during the action, with a degree of alertness that surprised every body who saw him. After being on foot some time, and when nearly exhausted, a pack horse was brought to him. This he rode during the remainder of the day, although he could scarcely prick him out of a walk. Had he not been furnished with a horse, although unhurt, he must have remained on the field.

During the action, Gen. St. Clair exerted himself with a courage and presence of mind worthy of the best fortune. He was personally present at the first charge made upon the enemy with the bayonet, and gave the order to Col. Darke. When the enemy first entered the camp by the left flank, he led the troops that drove them back; and when a retreat became indispensable, he put himself at the head of the troops which broke through the enemy and opened the way for the rest, and then remained in the rear, making every exertion in his power to obtain a party to cover the retreat; but the panic was so great that his exertions were of but little avail. In the height of the action, a few of the men crowded around the fires in the center of the camp. St. Clair was seen drawing his pistols and threatening some of them, and ordering them to turn out and repel the enemy.

In commenting upon his honorable acquittal of all blame by the committee of Congress, appointed to inquire into the causes of the failure of the expedition, Judge Marshall, in his Life of Washington, remarks, with his usual felicity of manner, "More satisfactory testimony in favor of St. Clair is furnished by the circumstance, that he still retained the undiminished esteem and good opinion of President Washington."

To the foregoing description of the battle, we extract from the narrative of Major Jacob Fowler, now living in Covington, Ky., his own personal experience in the events of that fatal day. Mr. Cist, in his Advertiser, in which it was published, says: "There was hardly a battle fought, in the early struggles with the Indians, in which Mr. Fowler did not participate. He is now (July, 1844) at the age of eighty—his eye has not waxed dim, nor his natural force abated. He can still pick off a squirrel with his rifle at 100 yards distance. He can walk as firmly and as fast as most men at fifty, and I cannot perceive a gray hair in his head. His mind and memory are as vigorous as his physical functions."

Excepting in a single instance, St. Clair kept out no scouting parties during his march, and we should have been completely surprised by the attack when it was made, if it had not been that volunteer scouting parties from the militia were out the evening before, and the constant discharge of rifles throughout the night warned us to prepare for the event. The militia were encamped about a quarter of a mile in front of the residue of the army, so as to receive, as they did, the first shock of the attack, which was made a little after daybreak. The camp was on the bank of a small creek, one of the heads of the Wabash river, the ground nearly level and covered with a heavy growth of timber. As surveyor, I drew the pay and rations of a subaltern, but, as an old hunter, was not disposed to trust myself among the Indians without my rifle. Indeed I found it very serviceable during the march, the army being upon not more than half rations the whole campaign.

My stock of bullets becoming pretty low, from hunting, as soon as it was daylight that morning, I started for the militia camp to get a ladle for running some more, when I found that the battle had begun, and met the militia running in to the main body of the troops. I hailed one of the Kentuckians, who I found had been disabled in the right wrist by a bullet, asking him if he had balls to spare. He told me to take out his pouch and divide with him. I poured out a double handful and put back what I supposed was the half, and was about to leave him, when he said, "stop, you had better count them." It was no time for laughing, but I could hardly resist the impulse to laugh, the idea was so ludicrous of counting a handfull of bullets when they were about to be so plenty as to be had for the picking up, by those who should be lucky enough to escape with their lives. "If we get through this day's scrape, my dear fellow," said I, "I will return you twice as many." But I never saw him again, and suppose he shared the fate that befel many a gallant spirit on that day. I owe the bullets, at any rate, at this moment.

On returning to the lines, I found the engagement begun. One of Capt. Pratt's men lay near the spot I had left, shot through the belly. I saw an Indian behind a small tree, not twenty steps off, just outside the regular lines. He was loading his piece, squatting down as much as possible to screen himself. I drew sight at his butt and shot him through; he dropped, and as soon as I had fired I retreated into our lines to reload my rifle. Finding the fire had really ceased at this point, I ran to the rear line, where I met Col. Darke, leading his men to a charge. These were of the six months' levies. I followed with my rifle. The Indians were driven by this movement clear out of sight, and the colonel called a halt and rallied his men, who were about 300 in number. As an experienced woodsman and hunter, I claimed the privilege of suggesting to the colonel that where we then stood—there being a pile of trees blown out of root—would form an excellent breastwork, being of length sufficient to protect the whole force, and that we might yet need it; I judged by the shouting and firing that the Indians behind us had closed up the gap we had made in charging, and told the colonel so. Now, if we return and charge on these Indians on our rear, we shall have them with their backs on us, and will no doubt be able to give a good account of them. "Lead the way, then," said he, and rode to the rear to march the whole body forward. We then charged on the Indians, but they were so thick we could do nothing with them. In a few minutes they were around us, and we found ourselves along side of the army-baggage and the artillery, which they had been taking possession of. I then took a tree, and after firing twelve or fourteen times, two or three rods being my farthest shot, I discovered that many of those I had struck were not brought down, as I had not sufficient experience to know I must shoot them in the hip to bring them down. As to the regulars, with their muskets, and in their unprotected state, it was little better than firing at random.

By this time, there were but about 30 men of Col. Darke's command left standing, the rest being all shot down and lying around us, either killed or wounded. I ran to the colonel, who was in the thickest of it, waving his sword to encourage his men, and told him we should all be down in five minutes more if we did not charge on them. "Charge, then!" said he, to the little line that remained, and they did so. Fortunately, the army had charged on the other side at the same time, which put the Indians, for the moment, to the flight. I had been partially sheltered by a small tree; but a couple of Indians, who had taken a larger one, both fired at me at once, and, feeling the steam of their guns at my belly, I supposed myself cut to pieces. But no harm had been done, and I brought my piece to my side and fired, without aiming at the one that stood his ground, the fellow being so close to me that I could hardly miss him. I shot him through the hips, and while he was crawling away on all fours, Col. Darke, who had been dismounted, and stood close by me, made at him with his sword and struck his head off. By this time, the cock of my rifle lock had worn loose and gave me much trouble ; meeting with an acquaintance from Cincinnati, named M'Clure, who had no gun of his own, but picked up one from a militia man, I told him my difficulty. "There is a first-rate rifle," said he, pointing to one at a distance. I ran and got it, having ascertained that my bullets would fit it.

Here I met Capt. J. S. Gano, who was unarmed, and handing to him the rifle I went into battle with, I observed to him that we were defeated, and would have to make our own escape as speedily as possible ; that if we got off, we should need the rifles for subsistence in the woods. The battle still raged, and at one spot might be seen a party of soldiers gathered together, having nothing to do but to present mere marks for the enemy. They

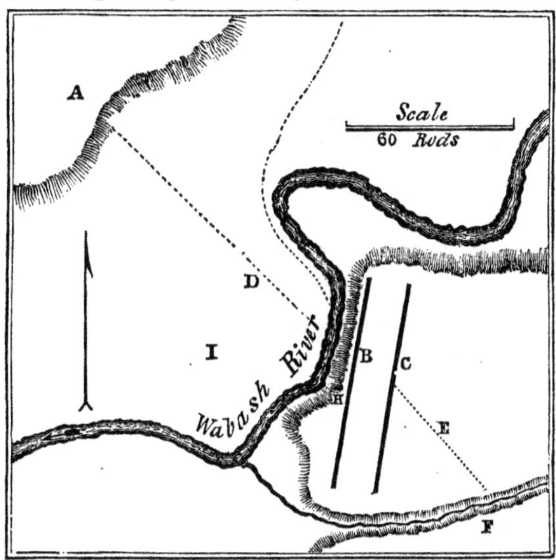

Plan of St. Clair's Battle Field.

appeared stupified and bewildered with the danger. At another spot, the soldiers had broken into the marquees of the officers, eating the breakfast from which those had been called into the battle. It must be remembered, that neither officers nor men had eaten anything the whole morning. Some of the men were shot down in the very act of eating. Just where I stood, there were no Indians visible, although their rifle balls were striking all around. At last, I saw an Indian break for a tree about 40 yards off, behind which he loaded and fired four times, bringing down his man at every fire, and with such quickness as to give me no chance to take sight in the intervals of his firing. At length, I got a range of two inches inside his back bone and blazed away ; down he fell, and I saw no more of him.

A short time after, I heard the cry given by St. Clair and his adjutant sergeant to charge to the road, which was accordingly done. I ran across the army to where I had left my relative, Capt. Piatt, and told him that the army was broken up and in full retreat. "Don't say so," he replied ; "you will discourage my men, and I can't believe it." I persisted a short time, when, finding him obstinate, I said, "If you will rush on your fate, in God's name do it." I then ran off towards the rear of the army, which was making off rapidly.

Piatt called after me, saying, "Wait for me." It was no use to stop, for by this time the savages were in full chase and hardly twenty yards behind me. Being uncommonly active in those days, I soon got from the rear to front of the troops, although I had great trouble to avoid the bayonets which the men had thrown off in the retreat, with the sharp points towards their pursuers.

It has been stated that the Indians followed us 30 miles, but this is not true, and my duty as surveyor having led me to mark the miles every day as we proceeded on our march out, it was easy to ascertain how far we were pursued. The Indians, after every other fire, fell back to load their rifles, and gained lost time by running on afresh......Even during the last charge of Col. Darke, the bodies of the dead and the dying were around us, and the freshly scalped heads were reeking with smoke, and, in the heavy morning frost, looked like so many pumpkins through a cornfield in December. It was on the 4th November, and the day severely cold for the season; my fingers became so benumbed at times, that I had to take the bullets in my mouth and load from it, while I had the wiping stick in my hand to force them down.

References.—A. High ground, on which the militia were encamped at the commencement of the action. B. C. Encampment of the main army. D. Retreat of the militia at the beginning of the battle. E. St. Clair's trace, on which the defeated army retreated. F. Place where Gen. Butler and other officers were buried. G. Trail to Girty's Town, on the river St. Marys, at what is now the village of St. Marys. H. Site of Fort Recovery, built by Wayne; the line of Darke and Mercer runs within a few rods of the site of the fort. I. Place where a brass cannon was found buried, in 1830: it is on the bottom where the Indians were three times driven to the high land with the bayonet.

The map of the battle-ground is from the survey of Mr. John S. Houston, of Celina. The localities* were pointed out to him by Mr. M'Dowl, who was in the action, and is now living near Recovery. In a letter, dated Celina, March 20th, 1847, Mr. Houston gives some notes of a conversation with Mr. M'Dowl.

Mr. M'Dowl states, that on the morning of the battle, he and several others had just gone out to look after and guard their horses, when suddenly they heard the most hideous yells from the opposite side of the river, with discharges of musketry. He instantly rushed to camp, found his regiment repairing for action, joined them, and was with the party who so gallantly charged the enemy in the bottom. On the retreat, he was among those who defended the rear, and kept the enemy in check for several miles. The ground was covered with a slushy snow, which much retarded their progress; and after a while, many of them were so dispirited and hungry—having eaten no breakfast—that they threw down their arms and made the best of their way pell-mell among the retreating crowd. About this time, M'Dowl saw a female carrying her infant, a year old. She was so tired that she was about to fall by the way-side, when he took the child and carried it some distance. Afterwards, to save her own life, the woman threw away the child in the snow. The Indians took it up, carried it to the Sandusky towns, and raised it.† Soon after this, M'Dowl overtook a youth, some eighteen years old, wounded in the leg, hobbling along, and dispirited. He gave him a drink of spirits and a little bread, he himself had not had time to eat, which refreshed and encouraged him. Soon after, a poney came dashing by. This, M'Dowl caught, and mounting the youth upon it, he safely reached the fort.

At Stillwater creek, twelve miles from the battle-ground, the Indians, who were no longer numerous, left them, and returned to share their booty. "Oh!" said an old squaw, who died many years ago, on the St. Mary's, "my arm that night was weary scalping white man."

Some years ago—said the old man to me—and here his cheeks were moistened with tears—I was travelling in Kentucky, to visit a sister I had not seen in many years, when I arrived at Georgetown, and entered my name on the ledger, with the place of my residence—"*Recovery, Ohio.*" After I had been sitting some time at ease, before a comfortable fire, a gentleman, who had noticed the entry of my name and residence, opened a friendly conversation about the place and country. He soon remarked that he was at the defeat of St. Clair, and that if it had not been for the assistance of a young man of Butler's regiment, he would have been there yet.

After a few more questions and replies, both parties recognized each other. The gentleman was the youth who had been shot, on the retreat, and whose life—as previously stated

* The references A and D were not on the map; neither was the high ground on the east side of the river, which we have placed on it from personal recollection.—*H. H.*

† It is stated in some accounts that about fifty, and in others, that near two hundred women were killed in the action and flight.—*H. H.*

—was saved by the interposition of M'Dowl. At this discovery, their surprise and consequent mutual attachment may be imagined. The gentleman insisted upon taking him to his house, and introducing him to his wife and daughters. He had become wealthy by merchandizing, and on parting with M'Dowl, gave him a new suit of clothes and other presents, which he has carefully preserved to this day.

M'Clung, in his Sketches of Western Adventure, relates some anecdotes, showing the heroism and activity of a young man who was in this action.

The late William Kennan, of Fleming county, at that time a young man of eighteen, was attached to the corps of rangers who accompanied the regular force. He had long been remarkable for strength and activity. In the course of the march from Fort Washington, he had repeated opportunities of testing his astonishing powers in that respect, and was universally admitted to be the swiftest runner of the light corps. On the evening preceding the action, his corps had been advanced, as already observed, a few hundred yards in front of the first line of infantry, in order to give seasonable notice of the enemy's approach. Just as day was dawning, he observed about thirty Indians within one hundred yards of the guard fire, advancing cautiously towards the spot where he stood, together with about twenty rangers, the rest being considerably in the rear.

Supposing it to be a mere scouting party, as usual, and not superior in number to the rangers, he sprung forward a few paces in order to shelter himself in a spot of peculiarly rank grass, and firing with a quick aim upon the foremost Indian, he instantly fell flat upon his face, and proceeded with all possible rapidity to reload his gun, not doubting, for a moment, but that the rangers would maintain their position, and support him. The Indians, however, rushed forward in such overwhelming masses, that the rangers were compelled to fly with precipitation, leaving young Kennan in total ignorance of his danger. Fortunately the captain of his company had observed him when he threw himself in the grass, and suddenly shouted aloud, "Run Kennan! or you are a dead man!" He instantly sprung to his feet, and beheld Indians within ten feet of him, while his company was already more than one hundred yards in front.

Not a moment was to be lost. He darted off with every muscle strained to its utmost, and was pursued by a dozen of the enemy with loud yells. He at first pressed straight forward to the usual fording place in the creek, which ran between the rangers and the main army, but several Indians who had passed him before he arose from the grass, threw themselves in the way, and completely cut him off from the rest. By the most powerful exertions, he had thrown the whole body of pursuers behind him, with the exception of one young chief, (probably Messhawa,) who displayed a swiftness and perseverance equal to his own. In the circuit which Kennan was obliged to take, the race continued for more than four hundred yards. The distance between them was about eighteen feet, which Kennan could not increase, nor his adversary diminish. Each, for the time, put his whole soul into the race.

Kennan, as far as he was able, kept his eye upon the motions of his pursuer, lest he should throw the tomahawk, which he held aloft in a menacing attitude, and at length, finding that no other Indian was immediately at hand, he determined to try the mettle of his pursuer in a different manner, and felt for his tomahawk in order to turn at bay. It had escaped from its sheath, however, while he lay in the grass, and his hair had almost lifted the cap from his head, when he saw himself totally disarmed. As he had slackened his pace for a moment, the Indian was almost in reach of him, when he recommenced the race; but the idea of being without arms, lent wings to his flight, and, for the first time, he saw himself gaining ground. He had watched the motions of his pursuer too closely, however, to pay proper attention to the nature of the ground before him, and he suddenly found himself in front of a large tree which had been blown down, and upon which brush and other impediments lay to the height of eight or nine feet.

The Indian (who heretofore had not uttered the slightest sound) now gave a short quick yell, as if secure of his victim. Kennan had not a moment to deliberate. He must clear the impediment at a leap, or perish. Putting his whole soul into the effort, he bounded into the air with a power which astonished himself, and clearing limbs, brush, and every thing else, alighted in perfect safety upon the other side. A loud yell of astonishment burst from the band of pursuers, not one of whom had the hardihood to attempt the same feat. Kennan, as may be readily imagined, had no leisure to enjoy his triumph, but dashing into the bed of the creek (upon the banks of which his feat had been performed) where the high banks would shield him from the fire of the enemy, he ran up the stream until a convenient place offered for crossing, and rejoined the rangers in the rear of the encampment.

panting from the fatigue of exertions which have seldom been surpassed. No breathing time was allowed him, however. The attack instantly commenced, and as we have already observed, was maintained for three hours, with unabated fury.

When the retreat commenced, Kennan was attached to Maj. Clarke's battalion, and had the dangerous service of protecting the rear. This corps quickly lost its commander, and was completely disorganized. Kennan was among the hindmost when the flight commenced, but exerting those same powers which had saved him in the morning, he quickly gained the front, passing several horsemen in the flight. Here he beheld a private in his own company, an intimate acquaintance, lying upon the ground, with his thigh broken, and in tones of the most piercing distress, implored each horseman who hurried by to take him up behind him. As soon as he beheld Kennan coming up on foot, he stretched out his arms and called aloud upon him to save him. Notwithstanding the imminent peril of the moment, his friend could not reject so passionate an appeal, but seizing him in his arms, he placed him upon his back, and ran in that manner for several hundred yards. Horseman after horseman passed them, all of whom refused to relieve him of his burden.

At length the enemy was gaining upon him so fast, that Kennan saw their death certain, unless he relinquished his burden. He accordingly told his friend, that he had used every possible exertion to save his life, but in vain; that he must relax his hold around his neck or they would both perish. The unhappy wretch, heedless of every remonstrance, still clung convulsively to his back, and impeded his exertions until the foremost of the enemy (armed with tomahawks alone) were within twenty yards of them. Kennan then drew his knife from its sheath and cut the fingers of his companion, thus compelling him to relinquish his hold. The unhappy man rolled upon the ground in utter helplessness, and Kennan beheld him tomahawked before he had gone thirty yards. Relieved from his burden, he darted forward with an activity which once more brought him to the van. Here again he was compelled to neglect his own safety in order to attend to that of others.

The late Governor Madison, of Kentucky, who afterwards commanded the corps which defended themselves so honorably at Raisin, a man who united the most amiable temper to the most unconquerable courage, was at that time a subaltern in St. Clair's army, and being a man of infirm constitution, was totally exhausted by the exertions of the morning, and was now sitting down calmly upon a log, awaiting the approach of his enemies. Kennan hastily accosted him, and inquired the cause of his delay. Madison, pointing to a wound which had bled profusely, replied that he was unable to walk further, and had no horse. Kennan instantly ran back to a spot where he had seen an exhausted horse grazing, caught him without difficulty, and having assisted Madison to mount, walked by his side until they were out of danger. Fortunately, the pursuit soon ceased, as the plunder of the camp presented irresistible attractions to the enemy. The friendship thus formed between these two young men, endured without interruption through life. Mr. Kennan never entirely recovered from the immense exertions which he was compelled to make during this unfortunate expedition. He settled in Fleming county, and continued for many years a leading member of the Baptist church. He died in 1827.

The number of Indians engaged in this action can never be ascertained with any degree of certainty. They have been variously estimated from 1000 to 3000.

Col. John Johnston, long an Indian agent in this region, and whose opportunities for forming a correct opinion on this subject are worthy of consideration, in a communication to us, says: "The number of Indians at the defeat of St. Clair, must have been large. At that time game was plenty, and any number could be conveniently subsisted. Wells, one of our interpreters was there, with, and fought for the enemy. To use his own language, he tomahawked and scalped the wounded, dying and dead, until he was unable to raise his arm. The principal tribes in the battle were the Delawares, Shawanoese, Wyandots, Miamies and Ottawas, with some Chippewas and Putawatimes. The precise number of the whole I had no accurate means of knowing; it could not be less than 2000."

The following song is not the best of poetry, but it has been frequently sung with sad emotion, and is worthy of preservation as a relic of olden time.

SAINCLAIRE'S DEFEAT.

'Twas November the fourth, in the year of ninety-one,
We had a sore engagement near to Fort Jefferson;
Sinclaire was our commander, which may remembered be,
For there we left nine hundred men in t' West'n Ter'tory.

At Bunker's Hill and Quebeck, where many a hero fell,
Likewise at Long Island, (it is I the truth can tell,)
But such a dreadful carnage may I never see again
As hap'ned near St. Mary's, upon the river plain.

Our army was attacked just as the day did dawn,
And soon were overpowered and driven from the lawn.
They killed Major *Ouldham*, *Levin* and *Briggs* likewise,
And horrid yells of sav'ges resounded through the skies.

Major *Butler* was wounded the very second fire ;
His manly bosom swell'd with rage when forc'd to retire;
And as he lay in anguish, nor scarcely could he see,
Exclaim'd, " Ye hounds of hell, O ! revenged I will be."

We had not been long broken when General *Butler* found
Himself so badly wounded, was forced to quit the ground.
" My God !" says he, " what shall we do ; we're wounded every man;
Go charge them, valiant heroes, and beat them if you can."

He leaned his back against a tree, and there resigned his breath,
And like a valiant soldier sunk in the arms of death;
When blessed angels did await, his spirit to convey ;
And unto the celestial fields he quickly bent his way.

We charg'd again with courage firm, but soon again gave ground,
The war-whoop then redoubled, as did the foes around.
They killed Major *Ferguson*, which caused his men to cry,
" Our only safety is in flight ; or fighting here to die."

" Stand to your guns," says valiant *Ford*, " let's die upon them here
Before we let the sav'ges know we ever harbored fear."
Our cannon-balls exhausted, and artill'ry-men all slain,
Obliged were our musketmen the en'my to sustain.

Yet three hours more we fought them, and then were forc'd to yield,
When three hundred bloody warriors lay stretch'd upon the field.
Says Colonel *Gibson* to his men, " My boys be not dismay'd ;
I'm sure that true Virginians were never yet afraid.

Ten thousand deaths I'd rather die, than they should gain the field ;"
With that he got a fatal shot, which caused him to yield.
Says Major *Clark*, " My heroes, I can here no longer stand,
We'll strive to form in order, and retreat the best we can."

The word, Retreat, being past around, there was a dismal cry,
Then helter skelter through the woods, like wolves and sheep they fly.
This well-appointed army, who but a day before,
Defied and braved all danger, had like a cloud pass'd o'er.

Alas! the dying and wounded, how dreadful was the thought,
To the tomahawk and scalping-knife, in mis'ry are brought.
Some had a thigh and some an arm broke on the field that day,
Who writhed in torments at the stake, to close the dire affray.

To mention our brave officers, is what I wish to do ;
No sons of Mars e'er fought more brave, or with more courage true.
To Captain *Bradford* I belonged, in his artillery,
He fell that day amongst the slain, a valiant man was he.

Sometime after the defeat of St. Clair, Wilkinson, who had succeeded him in the command of Fort Washington, ordered an expedition to visit the battle-ground. Capt. Buntin, who was with the party, afterwards addressed a letter to St. Clair, from which we make an extract.

In my opinion, those unfortunate men who fell into the enemy's hands, with life, were used with the greatest torture, having their limbs torn off; and the women have been treated with the most indecent cruelty, having stakes as thick as a person's arm drove through their bodies. The first, I observed when burying the dead; and the latter was discovered by Col. Sargent and Dr. Brown. We found three whole carriages; the other five were so much damaged that they were rendered useless. By the general's orders, pits were dug in different places, and all the dead bodies that were exposed to view, or could be conveniently found (the snow being very deep) were buried. During this time, there was sundry parties detached, some for our safety, and others in examining the course of the creek; and some distance in advance of the ground occupied by the militia, they found a large camp, not less than three quarters of a mile long, which was supposed to be that of the Indians the night before the action. We remained on the field that night, and next morning fixed geared horses to the carriages, and moved for Fort Jefferson. . . . As there is little reason to believe that the enemy have carried off the cannon, it is the received opinion that they were either buried or thrown into the creek, and I think the latter the most probable; but as it was frozen over with thick ice, and that covered with a deep snow, it was impossible to make a search with any prospect of success. In a former part of this letter I have mentioned the camp occupied by the enemy the night before the action: had Col. Oldham been able to have complied with your orders on that evening things at this day might have worn a different aspect.

Mr. M'Dowl, previously mentioned, was one of those who visited the battle-ground.

He states that although the bodies were much abused and stripped of all of value, that they recognized and interred them in four large graves. Gen. Butler was found in the shattered remains of his tent. After he was wounded, he was borne to the tent, and while two surgeons were dressing his wounds, a ball struck one of them in the hip. At this instant, an Indian, who was determined to have the scalp of Butler, rushed in, and while attempting to scalp him, was shot by the dying surgeon.

In December, 1793, Gen. Wayne having arrived with his army at Greenville, sent forward a detachment to the spot of St. Clair's defeat.

They arrived on the ground, on Christmas day, and pitched their tents on the battle-ground. When the men went to lie down in their tents at night, they had to scrape the bones together and carry them out to make their beds. The next day holes were dug, and the bones remaining above ground were buried; six hundred skulls being found among them. The flesh was entirely off the bones, and in many cases, the sinews yet held them together. After this melancholy duty was performed, a fortification was built, and named Fort Recovery, in commemoration of its being recovered from the Indians, who had possession of the ground in 1791. On the completion of the fort, one company of artillery and one of riflemen were left, while the rest returned to Greenville.

The site of St. Clair's battle became the scene of a sanguinary affair in the summer of 1794, while Wayne's army was encamped at Greenville, of which Burnet's Notes give the best description we have seen.

On the 30th of June, a very severe and bloody battle was fought under the walls of Fort Recovery, between a detachment of American troops, consisting of ninety riflemen and fifty dragoons, commanded by Maj. McMahon, and a very numerous body of Indians and British, who at the same instant, rushed on the detachment, and assailed the fort on every side, with great fury. They were repulsed, with a heavy loss, but again rallied and renewed the attack, keeping up a heavy and constant fire during the whole day, which was returned with spirit and effect, by the garrison.

The succeeding night was foggy and dark, and gave the Indians an opportunity of carrying off their dead, by torch-light, which occasionally drew a fire from the garrison. They, however, succeeded so well, that there were but eight or ten bodies left on the ground, which were too near the garrison to be approached. On the next morning, McMahon's detachment having entered the fort, the enemy renewed the attack, and continued it with great desperation during the day, but were ultimately compelled to retreat from the same field, on which they had been proudly victorious on the 4th of November, 1791.

The expectation of the assailants must have been to surprise the post, and carry it by storm, for they could not possibly have received intelligence of the movement of the escort, under Maj. McMahon, which only marched from Greenville, on the morning preceding, and on the same evening, deposited in Fort Recovery, the supplies it had convoyed. That occurrence could not, therefore, have led to the movement of the savages.

Judging from the extent of their encampment, and their line of march, in seventeen columns, forming a wide and extended front, and from other circumstances, it was believed their numbers could not have been less than from fifteen hundred to two thousand warriors. It was also believed, that they were in want of provisions, as they had killed and eaten a number of pack-horses in their encampment, the evening after the assault, and also, at their encampment on their return, seven miles from Recovery, where they remained two nights, having been much encumbered with their dead and wounded.

From the official return of Maj. Mills, adjutant general of the army, it appears that twenty two officers and non-commissioned officers were killed, and thirty wounded. Among the former, were Maj. McMahon, Capt. Hartshorn, and Lieut. Craig; and among the wounded, Capt. Taylor of the dragoons, and Lieut. Darke of the legion. Capt. Gibson, who commanded the fort, behaved with great gallantry, and received the thanks of the commander-in-chief, as did every officer and soldier of the garrison, and the escort, who were engaged in that most gallant and successful defence.

Immediately after the enemy had retreated, it was ascertained, that their loss had been very heavy, but the full extent of it was not known till it was disclosed at the treaty of Greenville. References were made to that battle, by several of the chiefs in council, from which it was manifest, that they had not, even then, ceased to mourn the distressing losses sustained on that occasion. Having made the attack with a determination to carry the fort, or perish in the attempt, they exposed their persons in an unusual degree, and of course, a large number of the bravest of their chiefs and warriors, perished before they abandoned the enterprise.

From the facts afterwards communicated to the general, it was satisfactorily ascertained that there were a considerable number of British soldiers and Detroit militia engaged with the savages, on that occasion. A few days previous to that affair, the general had sent out three small parties of Chickasaw and Choctaw Indians, to take prisoners, for the purpose of obtaining information. One of those parties returned to Greenville on the 28th, and reported that they had fallen in with a large body of Indians, at Girty's town, (crossing of the St. Mary's,) on the evening of the 27th of June, apparently bending their course towards Chillicothe, on the Miami; and that there were a great many white men with them. The other two parties followed the trail of the hostile Indians, and were in sight when the assault on the post commenced. They affirm, one and all, that there were a large number of armed white men, with painted faces, whom they frequently heard conversing in English, and encouraging the Indians to persevere; and that there were also three British officers, dressed in scarlet, who appeared to be men of distinction, from the great attention and respect which was paid to them. These persons kept at a distance, in the rear of the assailants. Another strong corroborating proof that there were British soldiers and militia in the assault, is, that a number of ounce-balls and buck-shot were found lodged in the block-houses and stockades of the fort; and that others were picked up on the ground, fired at such a distance as not to have momentum sufficient to enter the logs.

It was supposed that the British engaged in the attack, expected to find the artillery that was lost on the fatal 4th of November, which had been hid in the ground and covered with logs, by the Indians, in the vicinity of the battle-field. This inference was supported by the fact, that during the conflict, they were seen turning over logs, and examining different places, in the neighborhood, as if searching for something. There were many reasons for believing, that they depended on that artillery, to aid in the reduction of the fort; but fortunately, most of it had been previously found by its legitimate owners, and was then employed in its defence.

James Neill, a pack-horse-man in the American service, who was taken prisoner by the Indians, during the attack, and tied to a stump, about half a mile from the fort, after his return, stated to the general, that the enemy lost a great number in killed and wounded; that while he was at the stump, he saw about twenty of their dead, and a great many wounded, carried off. He understood there were fifteen hundred Indians and white men in the attack; and on their return to the Miami, the Indians stated, that no men ever fought better than they did at Recovery; and that their party lost twice as many men in that attack, as they did at St. Clair's defeat.

Jonathan Alder, who was then living with the Indians, gives in his MSS. auto-biography, an account of the attack on the fort. He states that Simon Girty was in the action, and that one of the American officers was killed by Thomas M'Kee, a son of the British agent, Col. Alex. M'Kee. We have room but for a single extract, showing the risk the Indians encountered, to bring off their wounded.

In the morning, when we arose, an old Indian addressed us, saying, "We last night went out to take the fort by surprise, and lost several of our men, killed and wounded. There is one wounded man lying near the fort, who must be brought away, for it would be an eternal shame and scandal to the tribe to allow him to fall into the hands of the whites to be massacred. I wish to know who will volunteer to go and bring him away." Big Turtle, who knew where he lay, answered, that he would go; but as no one else volunteered, the old Indian pointed out several of us successively, myself among the number, saying that we must accompany Big Turtle. Upon this, we rose up without a word, and started. As soon as we came into the edge of the cleared ground, those in the fort began shooting at us. We then ran crooked, from one tree to another, the bullets in the meanwhile flying about us like hail. At length, while standing behind a big tree, Big Turtle ordered us not to stop any more, but run in a straight line, as we were only giving them time to load,—that those foremost in going should have the liberty of first returning. He then pointed out the wounded man, and we started in a straight line, through a shower of bullets. When we reached him, we were within sixty yards of the fort. We all seized him and retreated for our lives, first dodging from one side and then to the other, until out of danger. None of us were wounded but Big Turtle; a ball grazed his thigh, and a number of bullets passed through his hunting shirt, that hung loose. When we picked up the wounded man, his shirt flew up, and I saw that he was shot in the belly. It was green all around the bullet holes, and I concluded that we were risking our lives for a dead man.

A small village, now containing a few houses only, was laid off on the site of St. Clair's defeat, in 1836, by Larkin & M'Daniels: it is 23 miles north of Greenville. Many relics of the battle have been discovered; muskets, swords, tomahawks, scalping knives, cannon balls, grape and musket shot, &c. Among the bones found, is that of a skull, now in possession of Mr. Wm. M'Daniels, showing the marks of a bullet, a tomahawk and a scalping knife. St. Clair lost several cannon, all of which but *one* were subsequently recovered by Wayne. This was long known to be missing, and about a dozen years since was discovered, buried in the mud near the mouth of the creek: it is now in possession of an artillery company in Cincinnati. When the low ground in the valley of the river was cleared, several years since, a large quantity of bullets and grape shot were found in the bodies of trees, from twenty to thirty feet above the ground, from which it seems, that the troops and artillery, having been stationed on high ground, fired over the enemy. On burning the trees, the lead melting run down their trunks, discoloring them so much, as to be perceived at a considerable distance.

The remains of Maj. McMahon and his companions, who fell at the time of the attack on the fort, were buried within its walls. Some years since, their bones were disinterred and reburied with the honors of war, in one coffin, in the village grave-yard. McMahon was known from the size of his bones, having been about 6 feet 6 inches in height: a bullet hole was in his skull, the ball having entered his temple and come out at the back of his head. He was originally from near the Mingo bottom, just below Steubenville. He was a famous Indian fighter and captain, and classed by the borderers on the Upper Ohio with Brady and the Wetzels.

Fort Jefferson, 5 miles south of Greenville, was built by St. Clair. In the summer of 1792, a large body of Indians surrounded this fort.

Before they were discovered, a party of them secreted themselves in some underbrush and behind some bogs, near the fort. Knowing that Capt. Shaylor, the commandant, was passionately fond of hunting, they imitated the noise of turkeys. The captain, not dreaming of a decoy, hastened out with his son, fully expecting to return loaded with game. As they approached near the place, the savages rose, fired, and his son, a promising lad, fell. The captain turning, fled to the garrison. The Indians pursued closely, calculating either to take him prisoner or enter the sally gate with him, in case it were opened for his admission. They were, however, disappointed, though at his heels; he entered and the gate was closed, the instant he reached it. In his retreat, he was badly wounded by an arrow in his back.

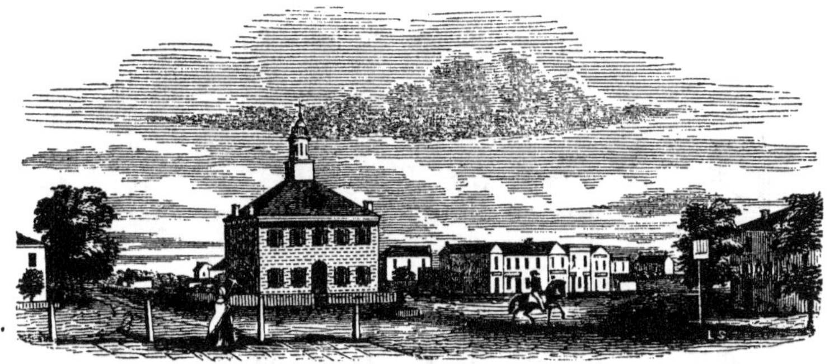

View in Greenville.

Greenville, the county seat, is in the township of Greenville, 92 miles west of Columbus, and 10 from the Indiana line. It was laid off, Aug. 10th, 1808, by Robert Gray and John Devor, and contains 1 Baptist, 1 Episcopal, 1 Methodist, and 1 Christian church, 16 mercantile stores, 1 flouring mill, 1 newspaper printing office, and about 800 inhabitants.

Greenville is a point of much historical note. In December, '93, Wayne built a fort at this place, which he called Fort Greenville. He remained until the 28th of July, '94, when he left for the Maumee rapids, where he defeated the Indians on the 20th of the month succeeding. His army returned to Greenville on the 2d of November, after an absence of three months and six days. Fort Greenville was an extensive work, and covered the greater part of the site of the town. The annexed plan is from the survey of Mr. James M'Bride, of Hamilton. The blocks represent the squares of the town, within the lines of the fort. Traces of the embankment are plainly discernable, and various localities within the fort are pointed out by the citizens of the town. The quarters of Wayne, were on the site of the residence of Stephen Perrine, on Main street. Henry House, now of this county, who was in Wayne's campaign, says, that the soldiers built log huts, arranged in rows, each regiment occupying one row, and each hut—of which there were many hundred—occupied by six soldiers. He also affirms that Wayne drilled his men to load while running; and every night when on the march, had good breast-works erected, at which the men had been so wel practiced, as to be able to accomplish in a few minutes.

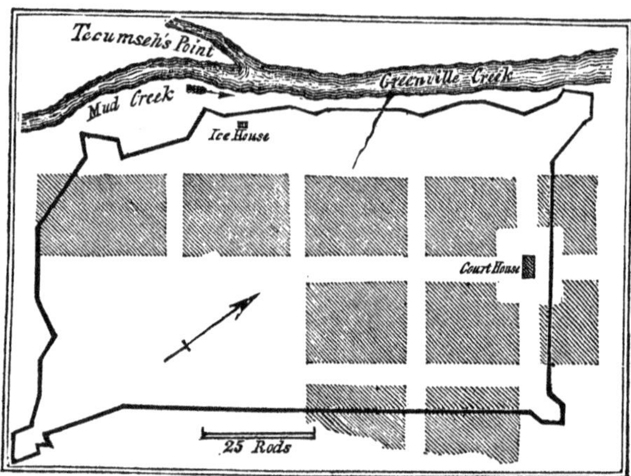

Fort Greenville.

On the 3d of August, 1795, Wayne concluded a treaty of peace with the Indians, at Greenville. The number of Indians present was 1,130, viz: 180 Wyandots, 381 Delawares, 143 Shawnees, 45 Ottawas, 46 Chippewas, 240 Pottawatamies, 73 Miamies and Eel river, 12 Weas and Piankeshaws, and 10 Kickapoos and Kaskaskias. The principal chiefs were Tarhe, Buckongehelas, Black Hoof, Blue Jacket, and Little Turtle. Most of the chiefs had been tampered with by M'Kee and other British agents; but their people, having been reduced to great extremities by the generalship of Wayne, had, notwithstanding, determined to make a permanent peace with the "*Thirteen Fires*," as they called the federal states. The basis of the treaty of Greenville was, that hostilities were to cease, and all prisoners restored. Article 3d, defined the Indian boundary as follows:

The general boundary line between the lands of the United States, and the lands of the said Indian tribes, shall begin at the mouth of the Cuyahoga river, and run thence up the same to the Portage between that and the Tuscarawas branch of the Muskingum, thence down that branch to the crossing place above Fort Laurens, thence westerly, to a fork of that branch of the Great Miami river, running into the Ohio, at or near which fork stood Loromie's store, and where commenced the portage between the Miami of the Ohio, and St. Mary's river, which is a branch of the Miami, which runs into Lake Erie: thence, a westerly course to Fort Recovery, which stands on the branch of the Wabash; thence, southerly in a direct line to the Ohio, so as to intersect that river opposite the mouth of Kentucke or Cuttawa river.

The following are the reservations within the limits of Ohio, granted to the Indians by this treaty.

1st. One piece of land 6 miles square, at or near Loramie's store, before mentioned. 2d. One piece 2 miles square, at the head of the navigable water or landing on the St. Mary's river, near Girty's town. 3d. One piece, six miles square, at the head of the navigable water of the Auglaise river. 4th. One piece, six miles square, at the confluence of the Auglaise and Miami rivers, where Fort Defiance now stands. 8th. One piece, twelve miles square, at the British fort on the Miami of the lake, at the foot of the rapids. 9th. One piece, six miles square, at the mouth of the said river where it empties into the lake. 10th. One piece, six miles square, upon Sandusky lake, where a fort formerly stood. 11th. One piece, two miles square, at the lower rapids of the Sandusky river.

These with the other tracts were given, "for the same considerations, and as an evidence of the returning friendship of the said Indian tribes, of their confidence in the United States, and desire to provide for their accommodation, and for that convenient intercourse which will be beneficial to both parties."

A second treaty was concluded at Greenville, July 22d, 1814, with the Wyandots, Delawares, Shawnees, Senecas and Miamies.

The commissioners on the part of the United States, were Gen. Wm. Henry Harrison and Gov. Lewis Cass. By it, these tribes engaged to aid the United States in the war with Great Britain and her savage allies. The prominent chiefs were Tarhe, Capt. Pipe and Black Hoof. Both of the treaties were held on the same spot, within the present garden of Abraham Scribner, in Greenville. On the 22d of July, 1840, just 26 years after the last treaty, there was a great celebration at this place, called "the Greenville Treaty Celebration," at which the many thousands present were addressed at length by Gen. Harrison.

From the year 1805 to 1808, the celebrated Tecumseh, with his brother the prophet, resided at Greenville. It was the point where they formed their plans of hostility to the whites. During their residence at this place, they were visited by many Indians, who were wrought into the highest excitement by the eloquence of Tecumseh and the cunning of the prophet.

On the plan of Fort Greenville, is laid down "*Tecumseh Point*," at the junction of the rivulet with Greenville creek, about a quarter of a mile from the court house. At this place are some Indian graves,—here Tecumseh had a cabin, and formerly near it was a spring, called "Tecumseh's Spring." In 1832, the remnant of the Shawnees, then moving to their new homes in the far west, from their reservation on the Auglaize, took this place on their route, instead of Cincinnati, as desired by the United States agents. They encamped on Tecumseh's point, to the number of several hundred, and remained a day or two, to take a final farewell of a place so dear to their memories.

New Madison, 10 miles southwest of Greenville, near the site of old Fort Black, is a new and thriving village, containing about 50 houses. Fort Jefferson, Fort Recovery, New Castine, Ithaca, New Harrison, Gettysburg, Versailles, Beamsville and Palestine are small towns.

DEFIANCE.

Defiance was erected March 4th, 1845, from Williams, Henry and Paulding, and named from Fort Defiance. It is watered by the Auglaize, the Tiffin and the Maumee: this last named stream was anciently called "*Miami of the Lake*," and sometimes "*Omee*." The Maumee is navigable by steamers, in high water, to Fort Wayne, and in ordinary stages to that place for keel boats carrying 60 tons. The Auglaize is navigable for keel boats to Wapakoneta, and the Tiffin, which is a narrow, deep stream, is navigable, for pirogues of a few tons, about 50 miles. Much grain comes down those various streams. Prior to the building of the Wabash canal, Northern Indiana received a large part of its supplies by the Maumee. Much of this county is covered by the Black Swamp, and the surface, where cleared and drained, is very fertile. The county is divided into the following townships.

Adams,	Delaware,	Highland,	Tiffin,
Crane,	Farmer,	Hicksford,	Washington.
Defiance,	Hicksville,	Richland,	

Defiance having been formed since the last census, its population is unknown.

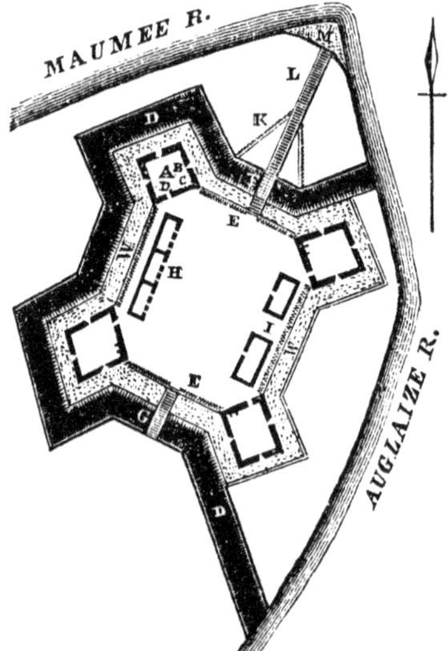

Fort Defiance.

The annexed plan and description of Fort Defiance, is found in the memoranda of Benj. Van Cleve, communicated by his son, John W. Van Cleve, of Dayton, to the American Pioneer.

At each angle of the fort was a block-house. The one next the Maumee is marked A, having port-holes B, on the three exterior sides, and door D and chimney C on the side facing to the interior. There was a line of pickets on each side of the fort, connecting the block-houses by their nearest angles. Outside of the pickets and around the block-houses was a glacis, a wall of earth eight feet thick, sloping upwards and outwards from the feet of the pickets, supported by a log wall on the side of the ditch and by facines, a wall of faggots, on the side next the Auglaize. The ditch, fifteen feet wide and eight feet deep, surrounded the whole work except on the side toward the Auglaize; and diagonal pickets, eleven feet long and one foot apart, were secured to the log wall and projected over the ditch. E and E were gateways. F was a bank of earth, four feet wide, left for a passage across the ditch. G was a falling gate or drawbridge, which was raised and lowered by pullies, across the ditch, covering it or leaving it uncovered at pleasure. The officers' quarters were at H, and the storehouses at I. At K, two lines of pickets converged towards L, which was a ditch eight feet deep, by which water was procured from the river without exposing the carrier to the enemy. M was a small sand-bar at the point.

Defiance, the county seat, is on the south bank of the Maumee, at its junction with the Auglaize, on the line of the canal, 152 miles NW. of Columbus, 58 from Toledo and 50 from Fort Wayne. It was laid out in 1822, by Benj. Level and Horatio G. Philips, and contains 1 Methodist and 1 Catholic church, 5 mercantile stores and a population of about 700. It is destined, from its natural position, to be, when the country is fully settled, a large and flourishing place; it already has an extensive trade with a large district of country.

Defiance is on the site of a large Indian settlement, which extended for miles up and down the river. Gen. Wayne, on his advance march, arrived at this place, Aug. 8th, 1794. His army found it surrounded by a highly cultivated country, there being vegetables of every kind in abundance, and not less than one thousand acres of corn around the Indian town, beside immense apple and peach orchards. It had been a great trading point between the Canadian French and the Indians. On the 9th of August, Wayne commenced the erection of a fort, which he called Fort Defiance. The army remained here several days and then moved northward, and on the 20th, routed the Indians at the Maumee rapids. On their return, they completed the fortress. Fort Defiance was built at the confluence of the Auglaize and Maumee, traces of which work are now plainly discernable. The situation is beautiful and commanding: it

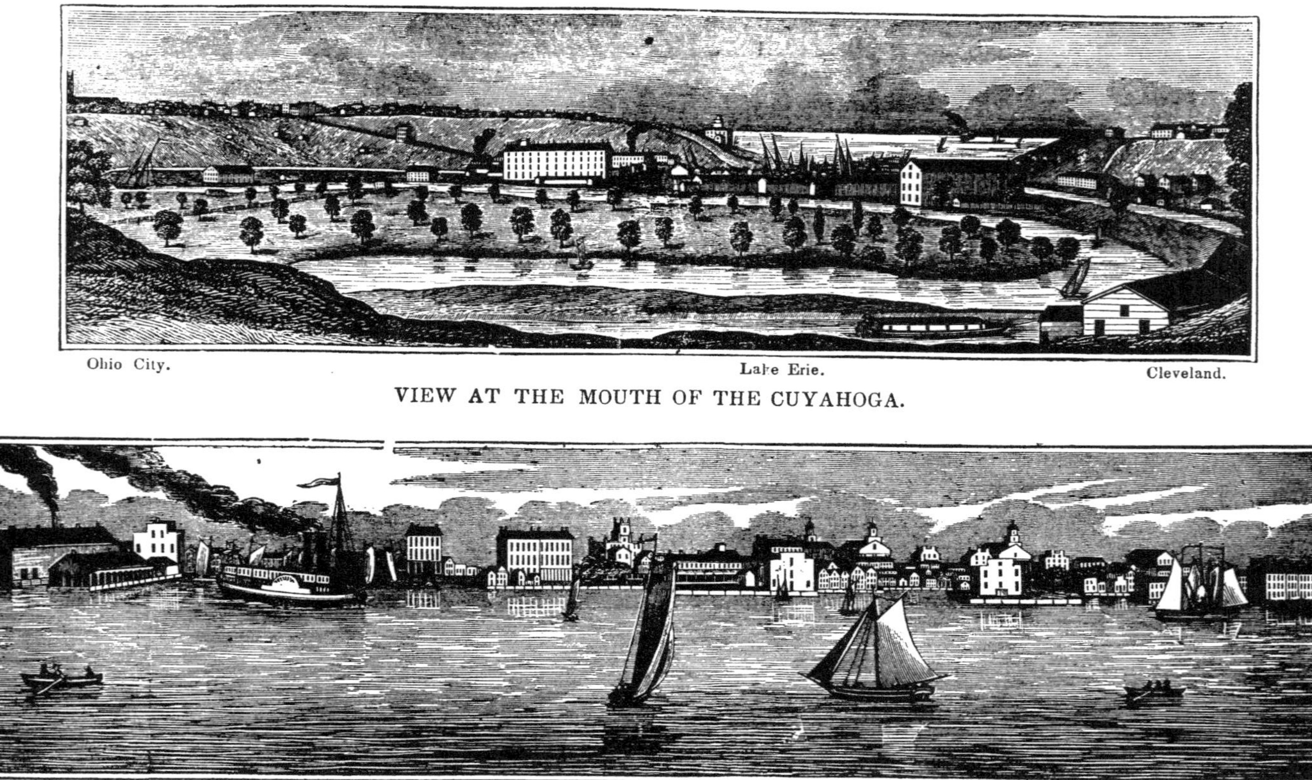

VIEW AT THE MOUTH OF THE CUYAHOGA.

is indicated in the view of Defiance by the flag shown on the left, Gen. Winchester, previous to his defeat at the river Raisin, in the war

Defiance from the North bank of the Maumee.

of 1812, encamped in a picketed fort, which he built on the Auglaize, about 100 yards south of the other, and named Fort Winchester.

Brunersburg, Independence, Clarksville, Evansport, Delaware and Hicksville, are small places. (*See Addenda.*)

DELAWARE.

Delaware was formed from Franklin county, Feb. 10th, 1808. The surface is generally level and the soil clay, except the river bottoms. About one third of the surface is adapted to meadow and pasture and the remainder to the plough. The principal products are wheat, corn, oats, pork and wool. The following is a list of its 21 townships, with their population in 1840.

Bennington,	1051	Harlem,	963	Peru,	737
Berkshire,	1407	Harmony,	676	Porter,	678
Berlin,	827	Kingston,	657	Radnor,	1174
Brown,	908	Liberty,	811	Scioto,	877
Concord,	1185	Lincoln,	549	Thompson,	660
Delaware,	1019	Oxford,	774	Trenton,	1188
Genoa,	1193	Orange,	789	Troy,	838

The population of Delaware county, in 1820, was 7,639; in 1830, 11,522, and in 1840, 22,060 or 36 inhabitants to a square mile.

The name of this county originated from the Delaware tribe, some of whom once dwelt within its limits, and had extensive cornfields adjacent to its seat of justice. John Johnston says:

"The true name of this once powerful tribe is *Wa,be,nugh,ka,* that is, 'the people from the east,' or 'the sun rising.' The tradition among themselves is, that they originally, at some very remote period, emigrated from the west, crossed the Mississippi, ascending the Ohio, fighting their way, until they reached the Delaware river, [so named from Lord Delaware,] near where Philadelphia now stands, in which region of county they became fixed.

"About this time, they were so numerous that no enumeration could be made of the nation. They welcomed to the shores of the new world that great law-giver, Wm. Penn, and his peaceful followers, and ever since this people have entertained a kind and grateful recollection of them; and to this day, speaking of good men, they would say, '*wa,she,a, E,le,ne*'—such a man is a Quaker, *i. e.* all good men are Quakers. In 1823, I removed to the west of the Mississippi persons of this tribe, who were born and raised within 30 miles of Philadelphia. These were the most squalid, wretched and degraded of their race, and often furnished chiefs with a subject of reproach against the whites, pointing to these of their people and saying to us, 'see how you have spoiled them'—meaning, they had acquired all the bad habits of the white people, and were ignorant of hunting and incapable of making a livelihood as other Indians.

"In 1819, there were belonging to my agency in Ohio, 80 Delawares, who were stationed near Upper Sandusky, and in Indiana, 2,300 of the same tribe.

"Bockinghelas was the principal chief of the Delawares for many years after my going into the Indian country: he was a distinguished warrior in his day, and an old man when I knew him. Killbuck, another Delaware chief, had received a liberal education at Prince ton College, and retained until his death the great outlines of the morality of the Gospel."

Delaware, the county seat, is pleasantly situated, on rolling ground, upon the western bank of the Olentangy river, 24 miles N. from Columbus. It was laid out in the spring of 1808, by Moses Byxbe, Esq. The engraving shows the public buildings on one of the principal streets of this neat and thriving town. The churches shown are respectively, commencing on the right, the 1st Presbyterian, the Episcopal and the 2d Presbyterian: between the two first, the Methodist church, a substantial stone structure, partially appears in the distance. The large building seen beyond the 2d Presbyterian church, is the "Hinton House," one of the largest and best constructed hotels in Ohio.

The Delaware Springs are situated in the southern part of the village, and large numbers of persons come here for the benefit of its waters. "Tradition states that the Indians resorted to these springs, to use the waters and kill the deer and buffalo, which came here in great numbers. Before the grounds were enclosed, in the early settlement of the country, the domestic animals for miles around made this a favorite resort in the heats of summer, and appeared satisfied with no other water.

"The principal spring is a fine fountain of water, issuing forth into an artificial stone basin at the rate of 12 or 15 gallons per minute. The spring is of that class termed white sulphur, or cold hydro-sulphurous water. The water is said to be similar to that of the

View in Winter Street, Delaware.

celebrated white sulphur springs of Virginia, and equal in their mineral and medicinal qualities. The water is cooler, being as low as 53°, contains more gas and is therefore lighter and more pleasant than that of the Virginia water. Many cures have been effected of persons afflicted with scrofulous diseases, dyspepsia, bilious derangements of the liver and stomach, want of appetite and digestion, cases of erysipelas, when all the usual remedies had failed, and injuries inflicted by the excessive use of calomel.

Prof. H. Michell, in giving his analysis of the waters, says; "Of gaseous products, I find that one wine pint of the water, taken immediately from the spring, contains of sulphurated hydrogen gas, 12 cubic inches; of carbonic acid gas, 3 do. One hundred grains of the deposit, which resulted from evaporating several gallons of the water, yielded, on analysis, of muriate of soda, 48 grains; do. of lime, 20 do.; sulphate of magnesia, 16 do.; do. of lime, 8 do.; carbonate of soda, 5 do.; total of the above, 97 grains. The above results show that these waters approach as nearly to the well-known waters of Aix la Chappelle and Harrowgate as those do respectively to each other......They are decidedly deobstruent, and calculated to remove glandular enlargements, as well of the liver as of the other viscera. In cases of slow fever, disturbed state of the functions of digestion, or more confirmed dyspepsia—morbid secretions from the kidneys or bladder, gravel and chronic eruptions on the skin, I can strongly recommend their use; and, though last, not least, their power of subduing general constitutional irritation, and quieting and restoring tone to the system, when it has been necessary to have recourse to the frequent and long-continued action of calomel or other mercurial preparations, is, I am persuaded, of the greatest efficacy."

Ohio Wesleyan University.

The Ohio Wesleyan University has been recently established at Delaware, with fine prospects of success—the Rev. Edward Thomson, D. D., President. The college edifice stands on a pleasant elevation, in the southern part of the village, and embraces within its grounds ten acres of land, including the sulphur spring, the position of which is indicated in the engraving by the figures seen in the distance among the trees on the left. The population of Delaware, in 1840, was 898—since which, it has probably doubled its number of inhabitants.

The White Sulphur Fountain.

The White Sulphur Fountain is beautifully situated on the rapids of the Scioto, 18 miles above Columbus and 10 sw. of Delaware, and is surrounded for miles by a fine undulating and healthy country.

The buildings are neat, entirely new and, for the first time, opened this season (1847) to visitors. The fountain is a most remarkable curiosity, and rises from the bed of the Scioto through solid rock. It was first discovered in 1820, while boring for salt water, a hole of about 2½ inches in diameter. The operators had pierced through about 90 feet of solid rock, when the auger suddenly fell two feet and up gushed with great force a stream of strong white sulphur water, which has continued to rise with its original force and violence to the present time. Experiments have shown some curious results; among which was that of placing an air-tight tube in an upright position, one end being inserted into the hole, when the water shot out of its top with as much force as when issuing from the rock beneath. The water, which is pure, is supposed to be driven by its own gas: its temperature is 50°, and it deposits on the ground around a very heavy white deposit.

On the grounds of the establishment is a beautiful chalybeate spring, having a temperature of 47°. "This place has every natural advantage that can be desired for making it one of the greatest places of resort for health and recreation, west of the mountains. From present indications, it is evidently destined to become so, as soon as preparations can be made to accommodate the public to a sufficient extent, which will soon be done, as improvements here are making rapid progress."

There are several small towns in the county: the most important of these are Sunbury and Berkshire—the first of which is 12 miles E. of Delaware, and is a neat village, containing 4 stores, 3 churches and about 300 inhabitants. (*See Addenda.*)

ERIE.

Erie was formed in 1838, from Huron and Sandusky counties. The surface is level, with some prairie land. Inexhaustible quarries of limestone and freestone abound. The freestone from Margaretta township resembles the famous Portland stone: when taken from the quarry it is soft and is frequently sawed with the hand-saw, and hardens on exposure to the atmosphere. The limestone is of the species called marine-shell marble. It is of the best quality, full of organic remains, and susceptible of an exquisite polish. Quantities of bog iron ore are found. The soil is generally alluvial and very fertile. The principal crops are wheat, corn, oats and potatoes. The following is a list of its townships in 1840, with their population.

Berlin,	1628	Margaretta,	1104	Perkins,	839
Florence,	1655	Milan,	1531	Portland,	1434
Groton,	854	Oxford,	736	Vermillion,	1334
Huron,	1488				

The population of Erie in 1840, was 12,457, or about 48 inhabitants to a square mile.

The name of this county was originally applied to the Erie tribe of Indians. This nation is said to have had their residence at the east end of the lake, near where Buffalo now stands. They are represented to have been the most powerful and warlike of all the

Indian tribes, and to have been extirpated by the Five Nations or Iroquois, two or three centuries since.*

Father Lewis Hennepin, in his work published about 1684, in speaking of certain Catholic priests, thus alludes to the Eries: " These good fathers were great friends of the Hurons, who told them that the Iroquois went to war beyond Virginia, or New Sweden, near a lake which they called '*Erige*,' or '*Erie*,' which signifies, '*the cat*,' or '*nation of the cat*;' and because these savages brought captives from the nation of the cat in returning to their cantons along this lake, the Hurons named it, in their language, '*Erige*,' or '*Ericke*,' '*the lake of the cat*,' and which our Canadians, in softening the word, have called 'Lake Erie.' "

Charlevoix, writing in 1721, says respecting Lake Erie: " The name it bears is that of an Indian nation of the Huron [Wyandot] language, which was formerly seated on its banks, and who have been entirely destroyed by the Iroquois. *Erie*, in that language, signifies *cat*, and in some accounts, this nation is called the *cat nation*. This name probably comes from the large number of that animal formerly found in this country."

The French established a small trading post at the mouth of Huron river, and another on the shore of the bay on or near the site of Sandusky city, which were abandoned before the war of the revolution. The small map annexed is copied from part of Evans's map of the Middle British Colonies, published in 1755. The reader will perceive upon the east bank of Sandusky river, near the bay, a French fort there described as "*Fort Junandat, built in* 1754." The words Wandots are doubtlesss meant for Wyandot towns.

In 1764, while Pontiac was besieging Detroit, Gen. Bradstreet collected a force of 3,000 men, which embarked at Niagara in boats and proceeded up the lake to the relief of that post. Having burned the Indian corn-fields and villages at Sandusky and along the rich bottoms of the Maumee, and dispersed the Indians whom they there then found, he reached Detroit without opposition.† Having dispersed the Indians besieging Detroit, he passed into the Wyandot country by way of Sandusky bay. He ascended the bay and river as far as it was navigable for boats and there made a camp. A treaty of peace and friendship was signed by the chiefs and head men.‡

Erie, Huron, and a small part of Ottawa counties comprise that portion of the Western Reserve known as "the fire-lands," being a tract of about 500,000 acres, granted by the State of Connecticut to the sufferers by fire from the British in their incursions into that State.§ The history which follows of the fire-lands and the settle-

* These facts are derived from the beautiful " tradition of the Eries," published in the Buffalo Commercial, in the summer of 1845. That tradition (says the editor) " may be implicitly relied upon, every detail having been taken from the lips of Blacksnake and other venerable chiefs of the Senecas and Tonawandas, who still cherish the traditions of their fathers."

† Lanman's Michigan.

‡ Whittlesey's address on Boquet's expedition.

§ For some facts connected with the history of the fire-lands, see sketch of the Western Reserve, to be found elsewhere in this volume.

ment of this county, is from the MSS. history of the fire-lands, by the late C. B. Squier, Esq., of Sandusky City.

The largest sufferers, and, consequently, those who held the largest interest in the fire-lands, purchased the rights of many who held smaller interests. The proprietors of the fire-lands, anxious that their new territory should be settled, offered strong inducements for persons to settle in this then unknown region. But, aside from the ordinary difficulties attending a new settlement, the Indian title to the western part of the reserve was not then extinguished; but by a treaty held at Fort Industry, on the Maumee, in July, 1805, this object was accomplished, and the east line of the Indian territory was established on the west line of the reserve.

The proprietors of the fire-lands were deeply interested in this treaty, upon the result of which depended their ability to possess and settle their lands. Consequently, the Hon. Isaac Mills, secretary of the company, with others interested, left Connecticut to be present at these negotiations. Cleveland was the point first designated for holding the treaty. But upon their arrival, it was ascertained that the influence of the British agents among the Indians was so great as to occasion them to refuse to treat with the agents of the United States, unless they would come into their own territory, on the Miami of the Lakes, as the Maumee was then termed. Having arrived at the Maumee, they found several agents of the British government among the Indians, using every possible effort to prevent any negotiation whatever, and it was fifteen or twenty days before they could bring them to any reasonable terms. Soon after the conclusion of the treaty, the settlements commenced upon the fire-lands.

It is quite difficult to ascertain who the first settlers were upon the fire-lands. As early, if not prior to the organization of the state, several persons had squatted upon the lands, at the mouth of the streams and near the shore of the lake, led a hunter's life and trafficked with the Indians. But they were a race of wanderers and gradually disappeared before the regular progress of the settlements. Those devoted missionaries, the Moravians, made a settlement, which they called New Salem, as early as 1790, on Huron river, about two miles below Milan, on the Hathaway farm. They afterwards settled at Milan.

The first regular settlers upon the fire-lands were Col. Jerard Ward, who came in the spring of 1808, and Almon Ruggles and Jabez Wright, in the autumn succeeding. Ere the close of the next year, quite a number of families had settled in the townships of Huron, Florence, Berlin, Oxford, Margaretta, Portland and Vermillion. These early settlers generally erected the ordinary log cabin, but others of a wandering character built bark huts, which were made by driving a post at each of the four corners and one higher between each of the two end corners, in the middle, to support the roof, which were connected together by a ridge pole. Layers of bark were wound around the side of the posts, each upper layer lapping the one beneath to shed rain. The roof was barked over, strips being bent across from one eave over the ridge pole to the other and secured by poles on them. The occupants of these bark huts were squatters, and lived principally by hunting. They were the semi-civilized race that usually precedes the more substantial pioneer in the western wilderness.

For two or three years previous to the late war, the inhabitants were so isolated from other settlements that no supplies could be had, and there was much suffering for want of food and clothing; at times, whole families subsisted for weeks together on nothing but parched and pounded corn, with a very scanty supply of wild meat. Indeed, there was not a family in the fire-lands, between 1809 and '15, who did not keenly feel the want of both food and clothing. Wild meat, it is true, could usually be procured; but living on this alone would much enfeeble and disease any one but an Indian or a hunter accustomed to it for years.

For even several years after the war, raccoon caps, with the fur outside, and deerskin jackets and pantaloons, were almost universally worn. The deerskin pantaloons could not be very well tanned, and when dried, after being wet, were hard and inflexible: when thrown upon the floor they bounded and rattled like tin kettles. A man, in a cold winter's morning, drawing on a pair, was in about as comfortable a position as if thrusting his limbs into a couple of frosty stove pipes.

To add to the trials and hardships of the early settlers, it soon became very sickly, and remained so for several years. The following is but one of the many touching scenes of privation and distress that might be related:

A young man with his family settled not far from the Huron river, building his cabin in the thick woods, distant from any other settlement. During the summer, he cleared a small patch, and in the fall, became sick and died. Soon after, a hunter on his way home, passing by the clearing, saw every thing still about the cabin, mistrusted all was not right, and knocked at the door to inquire. A feeble voice bade him enter. Opening the door he was startled by the appearance of the woman, sitting by the fire, pale, emaciated, and holding a puny, sickly babe! He immediately inquired their health. She burst into tears and was unable to answer. The hunter stood for a moment aghast at the scene. The woman, recovering from her gush of sorrow, at length raised her head and pointed towards the bed, saying, "there is my little Edward—I expect he is dying—and here is my babe, so sick I cannot lay it down; I am so feeble I can scarcely remain in my chair, and my poor husband lies buried beside the cabin!" and then, as if frantic by the fearful recital, she exclaimed in a tone of the deepest anguish, "Oh! that I was back to my own country, where I could fall into the arms of my mother!" Tears of sympathy rolled down the weather-beaten cheeks of the iron-framed hunter as he rapidly walked away for assistance. It was a touching scene.

A majority of the inhabitants of this period were of upright characters; bold, daring and somewhat restless, but generous-minded. Although enduring great privations, much happiness fell to the kind of life they were leading. One of them says: "When I look back upon the first few years of our residence here, I am led to exclaim, O! happy days of primitive simplicity! What little aristocratic feeling any one might have brought with him was soon quelled, for we soon found ourselves equally dependent on one another; and we enjoyed our winter evenings around our blazing hearths in our log huts cracking nuts full as well, aye! much better than has fallen to our lots since the distinctions and animosities consequent upon the acquisition of wealth have crept in among us."

Another pioneer says: "In illustration of that old saw,

'A man wants but little here below,
Nor wants that little long,'

I relate the following. A year or two after we arrived, a visit was got up by the ladies, in order to call on a neighboring family who lived a little out of the common way. The hostess was very much pleased to see them, and immediately commenced preparing the usual treat on such occasions—a cup of tea and its accompaniments. As she had but one fire-proof vessel in the house, an old broken bake kettle, it, of course, must take some time. In the first place, some pork was tried up in the kettle to get lard—*secondly*, some cakes were made and fried in it—*thirdly*, some shortcakes were made in it—*fourthly*, it was used as a bucket to draw water—*fifthly*, the water was heated in it, and *sixthly* and lastly, the tea was put in and a very sociable dish of tea they had. In those good old times, perfectly fresh to my recollection, the young men asked nothing better than buckskin pantaloons to go a courting in, and the young ladies were not too proud to go to meeting barefoot."

The following little anecdote illustrates the intrepidity of a lady in indulging her social feelings. A gentleman settled with his family about two miles west of the Vermillion river without a neighbor near him. Soon after, a man and wife settled on the opposite side of the river, three miles distant; the lady on the west side was very anxious to visit her stranger neighbor on the east, and sent her a message setting a day when she should make her visit, and at the time appointed went down to cross the river with her husband, but found it so swollen with recent rains as to render it impossible to cross on foot. There was no canoe or horse in that part of the country. The obstacle was apparently insurmountable. Fortunately the man on the other side was fertile in expedients; he yoked up his oxen, anticipating the event, and arrived at the river just as the others were about to leave. Springing upon the back of one of the oxen he rode him across the river, and when he had reached the west bank, the lady, Europa-like, as fearlessly sprang on the back of the other ox, and they were both borne across the raging waters, and safely landed upon the opposite bank; and when she had concluded her visit, she returned in the same manner. The lady still lives on the same spot, and is noted for her goodness of heart, and cultivated manners.

Early in the settlement of the fire-lands the landholders injudiciously raised the price of land to $5 per acre. The lands belonging to the general government on the west were opened for sale at $2 per acre; immigration ceased, and as most of the settlers had bought their land on a credit, the hard times which followed the last war pressed severely upon them, and the settlements languished. Money was so scarce in 1820 and 1822, that even those who had their farms paid for, were in the practice of laying up sixpences and shillings for many months to meet their taxes. All kinds of trade was carried on by barter. Many settlers left their improvements and removed further west, finding themselves unable to pay for their lands.

The first exports of produce of any consequence commenced in 1817; in 1818 the article of salt was $8 per barrel; flour was then $10, and a poor article at that.

There was no market for several years beyond the wants of the settlers, which was sufficient to swallow up all the surplus products of the farmer; but when such an outlet was wanted, it was found at Detroit, Monroe, and the other settlements in the upper regions of Lake Erie. As to the commercial advantages, there was a sufficient number of vessels on the lake to do the business of the country, which was done at the price of $2,50 per barrel bulk, from Buffalo to this place, a distance of 250 miles. Now goods are transported from New York to Sandusky City as low as forty-seven cents per hundred, or $9 per ton. Most kinds of merchandize sold at a sale corresponding to the prices of freight. Domestic shirtings from fifty to sixty-two cents per yard; satinets $2,50 to $3,50 do.; green teas $1,50 to $2,50 per lb.; brown sugar from twenty-five to thirty cents per lb.; loaf do. from forty to fifty per do., etc., etc. Butter was worth twenty-five cents, and corn $1,00 per bushel. As to wheat there was scarcely a price known for some of the first years, the inhabitants mostly depended on buying flour by the barrel on account of the want of mills.

The Indians murdered several of the inhabitants in the fire-lands. One of the most barbarous murders was committed in the spring of 1812, upon Michael Gibbs and one Buel, who lived together in a cabin about a mile southeast of the present town of Sandusky. The murderers were two Indians named Semo and Omic. The whites went in pursuit of them; Omic was taken to Cleveland, tried, found guilty and executed. Semo was afterwards demanded of his tribe, and they were about to give him up, when, anticipating his fate, he gave the war-whoop, and shot himself through the heart.

In the late war, previous to Perry's victory, the inhabitants were in much dread of the Indians. Some people upon Huron river were captured by them; and also at the head of Cold creek, where a Mrs. Putnam and a whole family by the name of Snow (the man excepted) were attacked. Mrs. Snow and one little child was cruelly butchered, and the rest taken captive, together with a Mrs. Butler and a girl named Page, and carried to Canada. They were, however, released or purchased by the whites a few months after. Other depredations and murders were committed by the savages.

Sandusky City, the county seat, is situated on Sandusky bay, 105 miles north of Columbus, and 60 from Cleveland and Detroit. Its situation is pleasant, rising gradually from the lake, and commanding a fine view of it. The town is based upon an inexhaustible quarry of the finest limestone, which is not only used in building elegant and substantial edifices in the town, but is an extensive article of export. A few hundred yards back from the lake is a large and handsome public square, on which, fronting the lake, are the principal churches and public buildings.

The first permanent settlement at Sandusky City was made in June, 1817, at which time the locality was called *Ogontz* place, from an Indian chief who resided here previous to the war of 1812. The town was laid out under the name of *Portland* in 1817, by its proprietors, Hon. Zalmon Wildman of Danbury, Ct., and Hon. Isaac Mills of New Haven, in the same state. On the first of July of that year, a small store of goods was opened by Moores Farwell, in the employment of Mr. Wildman. The same building is now standing on the bay shore, and is occupied by Mr. West. There were at this time but two log huts in the place besides the store, which was a frame, and had been erected the year previous. One of the huts stood on the site of the Verandah hotel, and the other some sixty rods east. The first frame dwelling was erected by Wm. B. Smith in the fall of 1817, the second soon after by Cyrus W. Marsh, and a third in the succeeding spring by Moores Farwell. The Methodist Episcopal church, a small frame building, and the first built, was erected in 1830; the Episcopal and Presbyterian churches in 1835; the Wesleyan chapel in 1836, and the rest since.

Sandusky City contains 1 Episcopal, 1 Methodist, 1 Congregational,

1 Reformed Methodist, 1 Catholic and 1 German Lutheran church, 1 high school, a large number of dry goods and grocery stores, several forwarding and commission houses, 2 furnaces, 1 oil mill, 2 extensive machine shops for the manufacture of the iron for railroad cars, 2 printing offices, 2 banks, and a population estimated at

Milan from near the Sandusky City Road.

3000. This town is now very thriving, and promises to be, ere many years, a large city. A great impetus has been given to its prosperity by the construction of two railroads which terminate here; the first the Mad River and Little Miami railroad connect it with Cincinnati; the other connects it with Mansfield, from which place it is constructing through Mount Vernon and Newark to Columbus: a branch will diverge from Newark to Zanesville. This last is one of the best built railroads in the country, and is doing a very heavy transportation business. The commerce of Sandusky City is heavy, and constantly increasing. The arrivals at this port in 1846 were 447, clearances 441; and 843,746 bushels of wheat were among the articles exported.

On the farm of Isaac A. Mills, west of the town, are some ancient works and mounds. In the late Canadian "patriot war," this city was a rendezvous for "patriots;" they had an action on the ice near Point-au-Pelee island with British cavalry in the winter of 1838. They were under Captain Bradley of this city, who has since commanded a company of volunteers in the war with Mexico. In this action the "patriots" behaved with cool bravery, and although attacked by a superior force, delivered their fire with steadiness, and repelled their enemy with considerable loss.

Twelve miles from Sandusky City, and eight from Lake Erie is the flourishing town of Milan, in the township of the same name. It stands upon a commanding bluff on the right bank of Huron river. The above engraving shows its appearance from a hill west of the road to Sandusky City, and a few rods back of Kneeland Townsend's old distillery building, which appears n front. In the middle ground is shown the Huron river and the canal; on the right the bridge across the river; on the hill, part of the town appears, with the tower of the Methodist, and spire of the Presbyterian church.

Below we give in a communication from the Rev. E. Judson, of Milan, a historical and descriptive sketch of the village and township:

On the spot where the town of Milan now stands, there was, at the time of the survey of the fire-lands, in 1807, an Indian village, containing within it a Christian community, under the superintendance of Rev. Christian Frederic Dencké, a Moravian missionary. The Indian name of the town was Petquotting. The mission was established here in 1804. Mr. Dencké brought with him several families of Christian Indians, from the vicinity of the Thames river, in Upper Canada. They had a chapel and a mission house, and were making good progress in the cultivation of Christian principles, when the commencement of the white settlements, induced them, in 1809, to emigrate with their missionary to Canada. There was a Moravian mission attempted as early as 1787. A considerable party of Christian Indians had been driven from their settlement at Gnadenhutten, on the Tuscarawas river, by the inhuman butchery of a large number of the inhabitants by the white settlers. After years of wandering, with Zeisberger for their spiritual guide, they at length formed a home on the banks of the Cuyahoga river, near Cleveland, which they named Pilgerruh, ("Pilgrim's rest.") They were soon driven from this post, whence they came to the Huron, and commenced a settlement on its east bank, and near the north line of the township. To this village they gave the name of New Salem. Here the labors of their indefatigable missionary, were crowned with very considerable success. They were soon compelled to leave, however, by the persecutions of the pagan Indians. It seems to have been a portion of these exiles who returned, in 1804, to commence the new mission.

The ground on both sides of the Huron river, through the entire length of the township, is distinctly marked at short intervals, by the remains of a former race. Mounds and enclosures, both circular and angular, some of which have strongly marked features, occur at different points along the river.

The land in the township of Milan, was brought into market in 1808. In the summer of the following year, David Abbott purchased 1800 acres, in the northeast section of the township, and lying on both sides of the Huron, for the purpose of commencing a settlement. He removed here, with his family, in 1810. Jared Ward purchased a part of Mr. Abbott's tract, and removed here, in 1809. He was the first "actual white settler," who had an interest in the soil. The progress of the settlement was at first rapid. When hostilities with Great Britain commenced, in 1812, there were within the township twenty three families, and about forty persons capable of bearing arms. The progress of the settlement was interrupted by the war, and few or no emigrants arrived between 1812 and 1816. This interruption was not the only evil experienced by the inhabitants. The British, in the early part of the war, commanded Lake Erie, and could at any moment make a descent upon the place. Many of the Indians were hostile, and were supposed to be instigated to acts of cruelty, by the willingness of the British commander at Fort Malden, to purchase the scalps of American citizens. Occasional outrages were perpetrated; houses were burned, and in a few instances individuals were murdered in cold blood, while others were taken prisoners. Near the southwestern corner of the township, at a place known as the Parker farm,—from its having been first purchased and occupied by Charles Parker,—there was a block-house, used as a place of resort during the war. A military guard was kept here. Two young men, apprehensive of no immediate danger, on a pleasant morning, in the fall of 1812, left the block-house and wandered to the distance of a mile, for the purpose of collecting honey from a "bee tree." While in the act of, cutting down the tree, they were surprised by the Indians, who, it seems, had been for sometime watching for their prey; one of them named Seymour, was killed on the spot; the other was recognized by one of the Indians, made a captive and treated kindly. The Indian who captured him, had been a frequent guest in the family where the young man had resided.

Sometime previous two men, Buell and Gibbs, had been murdered by the Indians, near Sandusky. Thirteen persons, women and children, had been captured near the present village of Castalia, some six miles to the westward of Sandusky. Of these, five, most of whom belonged to the family of D. P. Snow, were massacred. All the men belonging to the settlement were absent at the time of the massacre. These repeated butcheries, supposed at the time to be instigated by the British commander at Fort Malden, whither the scalps of all who were murdered were carried, kept the people of Milan in a constant state of alarm. In August, Gen. Hull surrendered Detroit to the British, and from this time to the achievement of Perry's victory, in September of the following year, the inhabitants were in constant apprehension for their personal safety. The sighing of the breeze, and the discharge of the hunter's rifle, alike startled the wife and the mother, as she trembled for her absent husband, or her still more defenceless "little one." During this interval, General Simon Perkins, of Warren, with a regiment of militia, had been stationed at "Fort Avery," a fortification hastily thrown up on the east bank of the Huron river, about a mile and a half north of the present town of Milan; but the inexperience of the militia, and the constant presence in the neighborhood of scouting parties of Indians, whom no vigilance could detect, and no valor defeat, rendered the feeling of insecurity scarcely less than before. Some left the settlements, not to return till peace was restored. Those who remained were compelled, at frequent intervals, to collect in the fort for safety, or made sudden flights to the interior of the state, or to the more populous districts in the vicinity of Cleveland, where a few days of quiet would so far quell their fears as to lead them to return to their homes, to be driven off again by fresh alarms. With the return of peace, in 1815, prosperity was restored to the settlements, and the emigration was very considerable. The emigrants were almost exclusively of the New England stock, and the establishment of common schools and the organization of Christian churches, were among the earliest fruits of their enterprising spirit. The town of Milan was "laid out" in 1816, by Ebenezer Merry, who had two years previously removed to its township. Mr. Merry was a native of West Hartford, in Connecticut, and by his example contributed much, as the proprietor of the town, to promote good morals among the early inhabitants. He took measures immediately for the erection of a flouring mill and saw mill, which contributed materially to the improvement of the town, and were of great service to the infant settlements in the vicinity. In the first settlement of the place, grain was carried more than fifty miles down the lake in open boats, to be ground; and sometimes from points more in the interior, on the shoulders of a father, whose power of endurance was greatly heightened by the anticipated smiles of a group of little ones, whose subsistence for weeks together had been venison and hommony.

Mr. Merry was a man of acute observation, practical benevolence and unbounded hospitality. He repeatedly represented the county in the legislature of the state, was twice elected to a seat on the bench of the common pleas; an honor in both instances declined. He died, Jan. 1, 1846, at the age of 73, greatly beloved.

David Abbott, as the first purchaser of land in the township, with a view to its occupancy as a permanent "settler," deserves some notice in this brief sketch. Mr. Abbott was a native of Brookfield, Mass. He was educated at Yale College. His health failed, and he was obliged to forego a diploma, by leaving college in the early part of his senior year. He soon after entered upon the study of the law, and located himself at Rome, Oneida co., N. Y., whence he came to Ohio, in 1798, and spent a few years at Willoughby, whence he removed to Milan, in 1809. He was sheriff of Trumbull county, when the whole Western Reserve was embraced within its limits; was a member of the convention for the formation of the Constitution of the State, previous to its admission to the Union, in 1802; was one of the electors of President and Vice President, in 1812; clerk of the supreme court for the county, and repeatedly a member of both houses of the state legislature. He was a man of eccentric habits, and his life was filled up with the stirring incidents, peculiar to a pioneer in the new settlements of the west. He several times traversed the entire length of Lake Erie, in an open boat, of which he was both helmsman and commander, and in one instance was driven before a tempest, diagonally across the lake, a distance of more than a hundred miles, and thrown upon the Canada shore. There was but one person with him in the boat, and he was employed most of the time in bailing out the water with his hat, the only thing on board capable of being appropriated to such use. When the storm had subsided and the wind veered about, they retraced their course in the frail craft that had endured the tempest unscathed; and after a weeks absence were hailed by their friends with great satisfaction, having been given up as lost. Mr. Abbott died in 1822, at the age of 57. Of the other citizens who have deceased, and whose names deserve honorable mention as having contributed in various ways to the prosperity of the town, are Ralph Lockwood, Dr. A. B. Harris and Hon. G. W. Choate.

The religious societies of the place, are a Presbyterian, Methodist and Protestant Episcopal church, each of which enjoys the stated preaching of the gospel, and is in a flourishing state. The two former have substantial and valuable church edifices, the latter society have one in process of erection.

In 1832, a substantial and commodious brick edifice was erected as an academy, furnishing, beside two public school rooms and suitable apartments for a library, and apparatus, ten rooms for the accommodation of students. The annual catalogue for the last ten years, has exhibited an average number of about 150 pupils.

In 1833, a company of citizens, who had been previously incorporated for the purpose, entered vigorously upon the work of extending the navigation of Lake Erie, to this place by improving the navigation of the river some five miles from its mouth, and excavating a ship canal for the remaining distance of three miles. After much delay, occasioned by want of funds, and an outlay of about $75,000, the work was completed, and the first vessel, a schooner of 100 tons, floated in the basin, July 4th, 1839. The canal is capable of being navigated by vessels, of from 200 to 250 tons burden. The chief exports of the place, are wheat, flour, pork, staves, ashes, wool and grass seeds. The surrounding country is rapidly undergoing the improvements incident to the removal of the primitive forests, and with the increased productiveness, the business of the town has rapidly increased.

The value of exports for the year 1844, was $825,098 ; of this, more than three fourths consisted of wheat and flour. The importation of merchandize, salt, plaster, etc., for the same period, was in value $634,711. The almost entire loss of the wheat crop for 1845, very essentially diminished the amount of business from the harvest of 1845, to that of the following year. The last half of 1846, shows a decided increase over any previous season.

In the foregoing sketch, our correspondent does not give the population of the town. We should judge it to be not far from 2000.

Castalia, a neat village, 5 miles southwest of Sandusky City, at the head of Coal creek, and bordering on a beautiful prairie of about 3000 acres, was laid out in 1836, by Marshall Burton, and named from the Grecian fount. It contains 2 churches, 5 stores, and about 400 inhabitants.

The source of Coal creek, is a beautiful and curious flooding spring, rising from a level prairie at the village. This spring is about 200 feet in diameter, and 60 feet deep. The water is so pure, that the smallest particle can be seen at the bottom, and when the sun is in the meridian, all the objects at the bottom, logs, stumps, &c., reflect the hues of the rainbow, forming a view of great beauty. The constituents of the water are lime, soda, magnesia and iron, and it petrifies all objects, such as grass, stumps, bushes, moss, &c., which come in contact with it. The stream courses about three miles through the prairie, and empties into Lake Erie. The water is very cold, but never freezes, and at its point of entrance into the lake, prevents the formation of ice. The stream at present furnishes power for twenty two runs of stone. Upon it, are the well-known Castalia and Coal creek mills, the water wheels of which are imperishable from decay, in consequence of their being incrusted by petrifaction. About two miles north of Castalia, is a cave, lately discovered and not as yet fully explored. Seven apartments have been entered, which abound in beautiful stalactites and stalagmites. A dog running into an aperture at the mouth of the cave, in pursuit of a rabbit, led to its discovery. The fountain and cave attract many visiters.

Huron, at the mouth of Huron river, 10 miles east of Sandusky City, is an older town than the county seat, and was formerly the greatest business place in the county. It is as yet an important point for the shipment of wheat, and contains 3 churches, 4 forwarding houses, 4 stores and about 400 inhabitants. Vermillion, at the mouth of Vermillion river, is a thriving village, containing from 50 to 70 dwellings. Birmingham, a few miles above, on the same stream, is a somewhat smaller village. Berlinville, Berlin Center and Venice are small places in the county.

FAIRFIELD.

Fairfield was formed, December 9th, 1800, by proclamation of Gov. St. Clair, and so named from the beauty of its *fair fields*. It contains every variety of soil, from the richest to the most sterile.

The western and northern parts are mostly level, the soil of which is very fertile, consisting of a rich loam, with a subsoil of clay. The remainder of the northern and western parts, together with the middle and a part of the eastern portion, is undulating; the soil good, consisting of a clayey loam, mixed with vegetable mould, and in many parts, interspersed with gravel. The southern part is hilly and broken, the soil of which is thin and barren, composed in many places of sand and gravel. The staples are wheat, rye, oats, buckwheat, corn, barley, potatoes and tobacco. The following is a list of its townships, in 1840, with their population.

Amanda,	1937	Hocking,	2120	Pleasant,	2025
Bern,	2431	Lancaster,	3278	Richland,	1960
Bloom,	2288	Liberty,	2778	Rush Creek,	2426
Clear Creek,	1716	Madison,	1085	Violet,	2400
Greenfield,	2148	Perry,	1171	Walnut,	2098

The population of the county, in 1820, was 16,508; in 1830, 24,753; and in 1840, 31,858, or 59 inhabitants to a square mile.

View in Main Street, Lancaster.

Lancaster, the county seat, is situated on the Hockhocking river and canal, on the Zanesville and Chillicothe turnpike, 28 miles southeast of Columbus, 37 from Zanesville, 18 from Somerset, 19 from Logan, 35 from Chillicothe, 20 from Circleville, and 27 from Newark. It stands in a beautiful and fertile valley, and is a flourishing, well-built town. It contains 1 Presbyterian, 1 Methodist, 1 Catholic, 1 Lutheran, 1 Protestant Methodist, 1 Baptist and 1 German Reformed church, about 20 mercantile stores, 2 newspaper offices, and had, in 1840, 2,120 inhabitants: it has since much increased. The engraving shows the appearance of the principal street in the town. It was taken near the court house, and represents the western part of the street; the court house is shown on the right, and the market on the left, of the view.

From the lecture delivered before the Lancaster Literary Institute, in March, 1844, by George Sanderson, Esq., we derive the following sketch of the history of the town and county.

The lands watered by the sources of the Hockhocking river, and now comprehende within the limits of Fairfield county, when first discovered by the early settlers at Marietta, were owned and occupied by the Wyandot tribe of Indians. The principal town of the nation stood along the margin of the prairie, between the south end of Broad street and T. Ewing's canal basin, and the present town of Lancaster, and extending back to the base of the hill, south of the Methodist Episcopal church. It is said, that the town contained in 1790, about one hundred wigwams, and a population of 500 souls. It was called TARHE, or in English the *Crane-town,* and derived its name from that of the principal chief of the tribe. Another portion of the tribe then lived at *Tobey-town,* nine miles west of Tarhetown, (now Royalton,) and was governed by an inferior chief called *Tobey.* The chief's wigwam, in Tarhe, stood upon the bank of the prairie, near where the fourth lock is built on the Hocking canal, and near where a beautiful spring of water flowed into the Hockhocking river. The wigwams were built of the bark of trees, set on poles, in the form of a sugar camp, with one square open, fronting a fire, and about the height of a man. The Wyandot tribe numbered at that day about 500 warriors. . . . . By the treaty of Greenville, in 1795, the Wyandots ceded all their territory on the Hockhocking river to the United States.

The Crane chief, soon after the treaty, with many of the tribe, removed and settled at Upper Sandusky; others remained behind for four or five years after the settlement of the country, as if unable or unwilling to tear themselves away from the graves of their forefathers and their hunting grounds. They were, however, so peaceably disposed towards the settlers, that no one felt willing to drive them away. In process of time, the game and fur became scarce, and the lingering Indian, unwilling to labor for a living, was forced, by stern necessity, to quit the country, and take up his abode with those of his tribe, who had preceded him at Upper Sandusky.

In 1797, Ebenezer Zane opened the road, known as "Zane's Trace," from Wheeling to Limestone, (now Maysville.) It passed through the site of Lancaster, at a fording about 300 yards below the present turnpike bridge, west of the town, and then called the "crossings of the Hockhocking." He located one of his three tracts of land, given by congress for the performance of this task, on the Hockhocking, at Lancaster.

In 1797, Zane's trace having opened a communication between the eastern states and Kentucky, many individuals in both directions, wishing to better their condition in life, by emigrating and settling in the "backwoods," so called, visited the Hockhocking valley for that purpose. Finding the country surpassingly fertile, abounding in fine springs of the purest water, they determined to make it their new homes.

In April, 1798, Capt. Joseph Hunter, a bold and enterprising man, with his family, emigrated from Kentucky, and settled on Zane's trace, upon the bank of the prairie, west of the crossings, and about one hundred and fifty yards northwest of the present turnpike road, and which place was called "Hunter's settlement." Here he cleared off the underbrush, felled the forest trees and erected a cabin, at a time when he had not a neighbor nearer than the Muskingum or Scioto rivers. This was the commencement of the first settlement in the Upper Hockhocking valley, and Capt. Hunter is regarded as the founder of the flourishing and populous county of Fairfield. He lived to see the county densely settled and in a high state of improvement, and died about the year 1829. His wife was the first white woman that settled in the valley, and shared with her husband all the toils, sufferings, hardships and privations incident to the formation of the new settlement. During the spring of the same year, (1798,) Nathaniel Wilson, the elder, John and Allen Green, John and Joseph M'Mullen, Robert Cooper, Isaac Shaeffer and a few others, reached the valley, erected cabins and put out a crop of corn.

In 1799, the tide of emigration set in with great force. In the spring of this year, two settlements were made in the present township of Greenfield. Each settlement contained twenty or thirty families. One was called the *Forks of the Hockhocking,* and the other *Yankeetown.* Settlements were also made along the river below Hunter's, on Rush creek, Raccoon and Indian creeks, Pleasant run, Fetter's run, at Tobeytown, Muddy Prairie, and on Clear creek. In the fall of 1799, Joseph Loveland and Hezekiah Smith, erected a log grist mill at the upper falls of the Hockhocking, now called the Rock mill. This was the first grist mill built on the Hockhocking.

In April, 1799, Samuel Coates, sen., and Samuel Coates, jr., from England, built a cabin in the prairie at the "Crossings of the Hockhocking," kept bachelors hall and raised a crop of corn. In the latter part of the year, a mail route was established along Zane's trace, from Wheeling to Limestone. The mail was carried through on horseback, and at first, only once a week. Samuel Coates, sen., was the postmaster, and kept his office at the Crossings. This was the first established mail route through the interior of the territory, and Samuel Coates was the first postmaster at the new settlements.

The settlers subsisted principally on corn bread, potatoes, milk and butter, and wild meats. Flour, tea and coffee were scarcely to be had; and when brought to the country, such prices were asked, as to put it out of the reach of many to purchase. Salt was an indispensable article, and cost at the Scioto salt works, $5 per 50 pounds. Flour brought $16 per barrel; tea, $2,50; coffee, $1,50; spice and pepper, $1 per pound.

In the fall of 1800, Ebenezer Zane laid out Lancaster, and by way of compliment to a number of emigrants from Lancaster co., Pa., called it New Lancaster. It retained that name until 1805, when, by an act of the legislature, the word "New" was dropped. A sale of lots took place soon after the town was laid off, and sold to purchasers at prices ranging from five to fifty dollars each. The greater portion of the purchasers were mechanics, and they immediately set about putting up log buildings. Much of the material needed for that purpose, was found upon their lots and in the streets, and so rapidly did the work of improvement progress, during the fall of 1800 and following winter, that in the spring of 1801, the principal streets and alleys assumed their present shapes, and gave assurance that New Lancaster would, at no distant day, become a town of some importance.

About this time, merchants and professional men made their appearance. The Rev. John Wright, of the Presbyterian church, settled in Lancaster, in 1801, and the Rev. Asa Shinn and Rev. James Quinn, of the Methodist church, travelled on the Fairfield circuit.

Shortly after the settlement, and while the stumps yet remained in the streets, a small portion of the settlers occasionally indulged in drinking frolics, ending frequently in fights. In the absence of law, the better disposed part of the population, determined to stop the growing evil. They accordingly met and resolved, that any person of the town found intoxicated, should, for every such offence, *dig a stump* out of the streets, or suffer personal chastisement. The result was, that after several offenders had expiated their crimes, dram drinking ceased, and for a time all became a sober, temperate and happy people.

On the 9th day of December, 1800, the Governor and Council of the N. W. Territory, organized the county of Fairfield, and designated New Lancaster as the seat of justice. The county then contained within its limits, all, or nearly all, of the present counties of Licking and Knox; a large portion of Perry, and small parts of Pickaway and Hocking counties.

The first white male child born in Fairfield, was the son of Mrs. Ruhama Greene. This lady emigrated to this region in 1798, and settled three miles west of Lancaster, where her child was born. The sketch appended of her, is from Col. John M'Donald, of Ross county.

Mrs. Ruhama Greene was born and raised in Jefferson county, Virginia. In 1785, she married a Mr. Charles Builderback, and with him crossed the mountains and settled at the mouth of Short creek, on the east bank of the Ohio, a few miles above Wheeling. Her husband, a brave man, had on many occasions distinguished himself in repelling the Indians, who had often felt the sure aim of his unerring rifle. They therefore determined at all hazards to kill him.

On a beautiful summer morning in June, 1789, at a time when it was thought the enemy had abandoned the western shores of the Ohio, Capt. Charles Builderback, his wife and brother, Jacob Builderback, crossed the Ohio to look after some cattle. On reaching the shore, a party of fifteen or twenty Indians rushed out from an ambush, and firing upon them, wounded Jacob in the shoulder. Charles was taken while he was running to escape. Jacob returned to the canoe and got away. In the mean time, Mrs. Builderback secreted herself in some drift-wood, near the bank of the river. As soon as the Indians had secured and tied her husband, and not being enabled to discover her hiding-place, they compelled him, with threats of immediate death, to call her to him. With a hope of appeasing their fury, he did so. She heard him, but made no answer. "Here," to use her words, "a struggle took place in my breast, which I cannot describe. Shall I go to him and become a prisoner, or shall I remain, return to our cabin and provide for and take care of our two children." He shouted to her a second time to come to him, saying, "that if she obeyed, perhaps it would be the means of saving his life." She no longer hesitated, left her place of safety, and surrendered herself to his savage captors. All this took place in full view of their cabin, on the opposite shore, and where they had left their two children, one a son about three years of age, and an infant daughter. The Indians, knowing that they would be pursued as soon as the news of their visit reached the stockade, at Wheeling, commenced their retreat. Mrs. Builderback and her husband travelled together that day and the following night. The next morning, the Indians separated into two bands, one taking Builderback, and the other his wife, and continued a westward course by different routes.

In a few days, the band having Mrs. Builderback in custody, reached the Tuscarawas river, where they encamped, and were soon rejoined by the band that had had her husband in charge. Here the murderers exhibited his scalp on the top of a pole, and to convince her that they had killed him, pulled it down and threw it into her lap. She recognized it at once by the redness of his hair. She said nothing, and uttered no complaint. It was evening; her ears pained with the terrific yells of the savages, and wearied by constant travelling, she reclined against a tree and fell into a profound sleep, and forgot all her sufferings, until morning.* When she awoke, the scalp of her murdered husband was gone, and she never learned what became of it.

As soon as the capture of Builderback was known at Wheeling, a party of scouts set off in pursuit, and taking the trail of one of the bands, followed it until they found the body of Builderback. He had been tomahawked and scalped, and apparently suffered a lingering death.

The Indians, on reaching their towns on the Big Miami, adopted Mrs. Builderback into a family, with whom she resided until released from captivity. She remained a prisoner about nine months, performing the labor and drudgery of squaws, such as carrying in meat from the hunting grounds, preparing and drying it, making moccasins, leggings and other clothing for the family in which she was raised. After her adoption, she suffered much from the rough and filthy manner of Indian living, but had no cause to complain of ill-treatment otherwise.

In a few months after her capture, some friendly Indians informed the commandant at Fort Washington, that there was a white woman in captivity at the Miami towns. She was ransomed and brought into the fort, and in a few weeks was sent up the river to her lonely cabin, and to the embrace of her two orphan children. She then re-crossed the mountains, and settled in her native county.

In 1791, Mrs. Builderback married Mr. John Green, and in 1798, they emigrated to the Hockhocking valley, and settled about three miles west of Lancaster, where she continued to reside until the time of her death, about the year 1842. She survived her last husband about ten years.

Near the town of Lancaster, stands a bold and romantic eminence, about two hundred feet high, known as Mt. Pleasant, which was called by the Indians, "the Standing Stone." A writer on geology says, in reference to this rock: "What is properly called the sandstone formation, terminates near Lancaster, in immense detached mural precipices, like the remains of ancient islands; one of these, called Mt. Pleasant, seated on the borders of a large plain,

* Her husband commanded a company at Crawford's defeat. He was a large, noble looking man, and a bold and intrepid warrior. He was in the bloody Moravian campaign, and took his share in the tragedy, by shedding the first blood on that occasion, when he shot, tomahawked and scalped Shebosh, a Moravian chief. But retributive justice was meted to him. After being taken prisoner, the Indians inquired his name. "Charles Builderback," replied he, after some little pause. At this revelation, the Indians stared at each other with a malignant triumph. "Ha!" said they, "you kill many Indians—you big captain—you kill Moravians." From that moment, probably, his death was decreed.

21

affords from its top a fine view of the adjacent country. The base is a mile and a half in circumference, while the apex is only about thirty by one hundred yards, resembling, at a distance, a huge pyramid. These lofty towers of sandstone are like so many monuments,

Mount Pleasant.

to point out the boundaries of that ancient western Mediterranean, which once covered the present rich prairies of Ohio."

It is a place much resorted to by parties of pleasure. The Duke of Saxe Weimar, when in this country some twenty years since, visited this mount and carved his name upon the rocks. The lecture delivered before the Literary Institute, gives a thrilling narrative of the visit of two gallant scouts to this spot, at an early day—their successful fight with the Indians—the re-capture of a female prisoner, and their perilous escape from the enemy.

There are several small villages in the county, some of which are thriving business places. They are Amanda, Baltimore, Bazil, Bremen, Carroll, Greencastle, Havenport, Lockville, Monticello, Millersport, New Geneva, New Strasburg, New Salem, Pickerington, Pleasantville, Royalton, Rushville, (East and West,) Waterloo and Winchester.

FAYETTE.

Fayette was formed in March, 1810, from Ross and Highland, and named from the Marquis De La Fayette. The surface is generally level; about half of the soil is a dark, vegetable loam, on a clayey sub-soil, mixed with a limestone gravel; the rest is a yellow, clayey loam. The principal productions are wheat and corn, cattle, hogs, sheep and wool. In the northeastern part is a small tract, called "*the barrens*," so termed from the land being divested of undergrowth and tall timber; it is covered with a grass well adapted to pasturage. The growth of the county, in former years, was retarded by much of the land being owned by non-residents and not in market, and also from the wet lands, which, contrary to the original opinion, have, when drained, proved very productive. The following is a list of its townships in 1840, with their population.

Concord,	1074	Madison,	765	Union,	1945
Green,	1616	Marion,	879	Wayne,	1540
Jefferson,	1948	Paint,	1212		

The population of Fayette, in 1820, was 6,336; in 1830, 8,183, and in 1840, 10,979; or 26 inhabitants to a square mile.

View in Washington.

Washington, the county seat, is on a fork of Paint creek, 43 miles ssw. of Columbus. It contains 1 Presbyterian, 1 Methodist church, 1 academy, 8 mercantile stores, 2 newspaper printing offices, 2 woollen factories, 1 saw and 2 grist mills and 97 dwellings. It was laid out in 1810 as the county seat, on land given for that purpose by Benj. Temple, of Kentucky, out of his survey.

The following are the names of some of the first settlers of this county, viz.: Colonel James Stewart, Jesse Milliken, Wade Loofborough, Thos. M'Donald, Doctor Thomas M'Gara, John Popejoy, Gen. B. Harrison, Jesse Rowe, John Dewitt, Hamilton and Benjamin Rogers, William Harper, James Hays, Michael Carr, Peter Eyeman, William Snider, Judge Jacob Jamison, Samuel Waddle, James Sanderson, and Smith and William Rankin.

Colonel Stewart, at an early date, settled near the site of Bloomingburg, about 5 miles northerly from Washington. His untiring industry in improving the country in his vicinity, and the moral influence which he had in the community, will be long remembered. Jesse Milliken was one of the first settlers of Washington, was the first post-master and the first clerk of both the Supreme and Common Pleas Courts of the county, in all of which offices he continued until his death, in Aug., 1835. He was also an excellent surveyor, performed much of the first surveying done in the county, and erected some of the first houses built in the town. Wade Loofborough, Esq., was one of the first citizens and lawyers in the county. Thomas M'Donald was one of the first settlers in this part of Ohio, built the first cabin in Scioto county, was engaged with Gen. Massie and others in laying off the county into surveys. He rendered valuable services in Wayne's campaign, in which he acted as a spy, and was also in the war of 1812.

Dr. Thos. M'Gara, now residing in Greenfield, Highland county, was one of the first settlers and first physician of the town of Washington, where he practiced his profession for a number of years. He represented the county in the legislature, and was associate judge. John Popejoy, Esq., was one of the first justices in the county; he built the one story house on Court street, on the lot No. 5. It is said that he kept his docket on detached scraps of paper in the most convenient cracks of his cabin, and that his ink was made of walnut bark. Although many amusing anecdotes are related of him, yet he was a good man, sincerely desirous of promoting peace and good will in the community. When a lawsuit was brought before him, his universal practice was, if possible, to prevail upon the parties to settle the dispute amicably. He always either charged no costs, or took it in beer, cider, or some other innocent beverage, of which the witnesses, parties and spectators partook, at his request, and the parties generally left his court in better humor and better satisfied than when they entered.

The first Court of Common Pleas in the county was held by Judge Thompson, at the cabin of John Devault, a little north of where Bloomingburg now stands. The judge received a severe lecture from old Mrs. Devault, for sitting upon and rumpling her bed. The grand jury held their deliberations in the stable and in the hazel brush. Judge Thompson was a man of strict and Puritan-like morality, and distinguished for the long (and in some instances tedious) moral lectures, given in open court, to the culprits brought before him.

The pioneers of Fayette county were principally from Virginia and Kentucky, and were generally hale and robust, brave and generous. Among the Kentuckians was a family of great notoriety, by the name of Funk. The men, from old Adam down to Absalom, were of uncommonly large size, and distinguished for their boldness, activity and fighting propensities. Jake Funk, the most notorious, having been arrested in Kentucky for passing counterfeit money, or some other crime, was bailed by a friend, a Kentuckian by the name of Trumbo. Having failed to appear at court, Trumbo, with about a dozen of his friends, well armed, proceeded to the house of the Funks for the purpose of taking Jake, running him off to Kentucky and delivering him up to the proper authorities, to free himself from paying bail.

The Funks, having notice of the contemplated attack, prepared themselves for the conflict. Old Adam, the father, took his seat in the middle of the floor to give command to his sons, who were armed with pistols, knives, &c. When Trumbo and his party appeared, they were warned to desist; instead of which, they made a rush at

Jake, who was on the porch. A Mr. Wilson, of the attacking party grappled with Jake, at which the firing commenced on both sides. Wilson was shot dead. Ab. Funk was also shot down. Trumbo having clinched Jake, the latter drew him to the door, and was about to cut his throat with a large knife, when old Adam cried out, "Spare him!—don't kill him!—his father once saved me from being murdered by the Indians!"—at which he was let off, after being severely wounded, and his companions were glad to escape with their lives. The old house at which this fight occurred is still standing, on the east fork, about 8 miles N. of Washington, with the bullet-holes in the logs as a memento of the conflict.

The Funk family were no enemies to whiskey. Old Adam, with some of his comrades, being one day at Roebuck's grocery—the first opened in the county, about a mile below Funk's house—became merry by drinking. Old Adam, wishing to carry a gallon of whiskey home, in vain endeavored even to procure a wash-tub for the purpose. Observing one of Roebuck's pigs running about the yard, he purchased it for a dollar and skinned it whole, taking out the bone about two inches from the root of the tail, which served as a neck for the bottle. Tying up the other holes that would, of necessity, be in the skin, he poured in the liquor and started for home with his companions, where they all got drunk from the contents of the hog-skin.*

Captain John was a Shawanee chief, well known to the early settlers of the Scioto valley. He was over six feet in height, strong and active, full of spirit and fond of frolic. In the late war, he joined the American army, and was with Logan at the time the latter received his death wound. We extract two anecdotes respecting him from the notice by Col. John M'Donald. The scene of the first was in Pickaway, and the last, in this county.

When Chillicothe was first settled by the whites, an Indian named John Cushen, a half blood, made his principal home with the M'Coy family, and said it was his intention to live with the white people. He would sometimes engage in chopping wood, and making rails and working in the corn-fields. He was a large, muscular man, good humored and pleasant in his interviews with the whites. In the fall season, he would leave the white settlement to take a hunt in the lonely forest. In the autumn of 1779, he went up Darby creek to make his annual hunt. There was an Indian trader by the name of Fallenash, who traversed the country from one Indian camp to another with pack-horses, laden with whiskey and other articles. Captain John's hunting camp was near Darby creek, and John Cushen arrived at his camp while Fallenash, the Indian trader, was there with his goods and whiskey. The Indians set to for a real drunken frolic. During the night, Capt. John and John Cushen had a quarrel, which ended in a fight: they were separated by Fallenash and the other Indians, but both were enraged to the highest pitch of fury. They made an arrangement to fight the next morning, with tomahawks and knives. They stuck a post on the south side of a log, made a notch in the log, and agreed that when the shadow of the post came into the notch the fight should commence. When the shadow of the post drew near the spot, they deliberately, and in gloomy silence, took their stations on the log. At length the shadow of the post came into the notch, and these two desperadoes, thirsting for each other's blood, simultaneously sprang to their feet, with each a tomahawk in his right hand and a scalping-knife in the left, and flew at each other with the fury of tigers,

* The preceding items of history respecting Fayette, are derived from a communication from a gentleman residing in Washington.

swinging their tomahawks around their heads and yelling in the most terrific manner. Language fails to describe the horrible scene. After several passes and some wounds, Captain John's tomahawk fell on Cushen's head and left him lifeless on the ground. Thus ended this affair of *honor*, and the guilty one escaped.

About the year 1800, Captain John, with a party of Indians, went to hunt on the waters of what is called the Rattlesnake fork of Paint creek, a branch of the Scioto river. After they had been some time at camp, Captain John and his wife had a quarrel and mutually agreed to separate, which of them was to leave the camp is not now recollected. After they had divided their property, the wife insisted upon keeping the child; they had but one, a little boy of two or three years of age. The wife laid hold of the child, and John attempted to wrest it from her; at length John's passion was roused to a fury, he drew his fist, knocked down his wife, seized the child and carrying it to a log cut it into two parts, and then, throwing one half to his wife, bade her take it, but never again show her face, or he would treat her in the same manner. Thus ended this cruel and brutal scene of savage tragedy.

Bloomingburg, on the east fork of Paint, 5 miles easterly from Washington, has 4 stores, 3 churches and about 300 inhabitants. Jeffersonville, 10 NW. from Washington, has one church, 2 stores and about 200 inhabitants. Waterloo, Martinsburg, Staunton and Mount Vernon are small places.

FRANKLIN.

Franklin was formed from Ross, April 30th, 1803, and named from Benj. Franklin. The prevailing character of the soil is clay, and the surface is generally level. It contains much low and wet land, and is better adapted to grazing than grain, but along the numerous water courses are many fertile and well-cultivated farms. The principal products are corn, wheat, oats, hay, potatoes, pork and wool. The following is a list of its townships in 1840, with their population.

Blendon,	972	Jefferson,	1040	Plain,	1263
Brown,	425	Madison,	1815	Pleasant,	811
Clinton,	965	Mifflin,	832	Prairie,	603
Franklin,	1345	Montgomery,	7497	Sharon,	1168
Hamilton,	1238	Norwich,	740	Truro,	1418
Jackson,	787	Perry,	1039	Washington,	842

The population of Franklin, in 1820, was 10,300; in 1830, 14,756, and in 1840, 24,880, or 49 inhabitants to a square mile.

The tract comprised within the limits of the county, was once the residence of the Wyandot Indians. They had a large town on the site of the city of Columbus, and cultivated extensive fields of corn on the river bottoms opposite their town. Mr. Jeremiah Armstrong, who now or recently kept a hotel at Columbus, was taken prisoner when a boy from the frontier of Pennsylvania, and brought captive to this place: after residing with them a number of years, he was ransomed and returned to his friends. Mr. Robert Armstrong, also a native of Pennsylvania, being an orphan boy, was bound to a trader, and while trapping and trading on the Alleghany, himself and employer were surprised by some Wyandots and Senecas. The master was killed and Armstrong brought to their town at Franklinton. He was raised by the Indians, became a great favorite, lived, married and died among them. He was occasionally an interpreter for the United States. He left two sons, now with the Wyandots in the far west; both of them were educated, and one of them admitted to the Ohio bar.*

In the year 1780, a party of whites followed a band of Indians from the mouth of the Kanawha, overtook them on or near the site of Columbus and gave them battle and defeated them. During the fight, one of the whites saw two squaws secrete themselves in a large hollow tree, and when the action was over they drew them out and carried them captive to Virginia. This tree was alive and standing, on the west bank of the Scioto, as late as 1845.†

In June, 1810, there was an old Wyandot chief, named Leatherlips, executed in this county on the charge of withcraft. We take the account of this event from Drake's life of Tecumseh, where it is abridged from an article by Otway Curry, in the Hesperian.

General Harrison entertained the opinion that his death was the result of the prophet's command, and that the party who acted as executioners went directly from Tippecanoe to the banks of the Scioto, where the tragedy was enacted. Leatherlips was found encamped upon that stream, twelve miles above Columbus. The six Wyandots who put him to death, were headed, it is supposed, by the chief Roundhead. An effort was made by some white men, who were present, to save the life of the accused, but without success. A council of two or three hours took place: the accusing party spoke with warmth and bitterness of feeling: Leatherlips was calm and dispassionate in his replies. The sentence of death, which had been previously passed upon him, was reaffirmed. "The prisoner then walked slowly to his camp, partook of a dinner of jerked venison, washed and arrayed himself in his best apparel, and afterwards painted his face. His dress was very rich—his hair gray, and his whole appearance graceful and commanding." When the hour for the execution had arrived, Leatherlips shook hands in silence with the spectators. "He then turned from his wigwam, and with a voice of surpassing strength and melody commenced the chant of the death song. He was followed closely by the Wyandot warriors, all timing with their slow and measured march the music of his wild and melancholy dirge. The white men were likewise all silent followers in that strange procession. At the distance of seventy or eighty yards from the camp, they came to a shallow grave, which, unknown to the white men, had been previously prepared by the Indians. Here the old man knelt down, and in an elevated but solemn tone of voice, addressed his prayer to the Great Spirit. As soon as he had finished, the captain of the Indians knelt beside him and prayed in a similar manner. Their prayers, of course, were spoken in the Wyandot tongue. . . . . "After a few moments delay, the prisoner again sank down upon his knees and prayed, as he had done before. When he had ceased, he still continued in a kneeling position. All the rifles belonging to the party had been left at the wigwam. There was not a weapon of any kind to be seen at the place of execution, and the spectators were consequently unable to form any conjecture as to the mode of procedure which the executioners had determined on for the fulfilment of their purpose. Suddenly one of the warriors drew from beneath the skirts of his capote, a keen, bright tomahawk—walked rapidly up behind the chieftain—brandished the weapon on high for a single moment, and then struck with his whole strength. The blow descended directly upon the crown of the head, and the victim immediately fell prostrate. After he had lain awhile in the agonies of death, the Indian captain directed the attention of the white men to the drops of sweat which were gathering upon his neck and face; remarked with much apparent exultation, that it was conclusive proof of the sufferer's guilt. Again the executioner advanced, and with the same weapon inflicted two or three additional and heavy blows. As soon as life was entirely extinct, the body was hastily buried, with all its apparel and decorations, and the assemblage dispersed."

One of Mr. Heckewelder's correspondents, as quoted in his historical account of the Indian nations, makes Tarhe, better known by the name of Crane, the leader of this party.

---

* Col. John Johnston. † Jonathan Alder, of Madison county.

This has been denied; and the letter of Gen. Harrison on the subject, proves quite conclusively that this celebrated chief had nothing to do with the execution of Leatherlips. Mr. Heckewelder's correspondent concurs in the opinion that the original order for the death of this old man, was issued from the head-quarters of the prophet and his brother Tecumseh.

The annexed anecdote, derived from J. W. Van Cleve, of Dayton, shows a more pleasing feature in the character of the Indian.

A party, surveying on the Scioto, above the site of Columbus, in '97, had been reduced to three scanty meals for four days. They came to the camp of a Wyandot Indian with his family, and he gave them all the provisions he had, which comprised only two rabbits and a small piece of venison. This Wyandot's father had been murdered by the whites in time of peace: the father of one of the surveyors had been killed by the Indians in time of war. He concluded that the Indian had more reason to cherish hostility towards the white man than he toward the Indian.

The first settlement of this county was commenced in 1797. Some of the early settlers were Robert Armstrong, George Skidmore, Lucas Sullivant, Wm. Domigan, the Deardorfs, the M'Elvains, the Sellses, James Marshall, John Dill, Jacob Grubb, Jacob Overdier, Arthur O'Harra, Colonel Culbertson and John Brickell. This last named gentleman was taken prisoner when a boy, in Pennsylvania, brought into Ohio and held captive four and a half years among the Delawares. He was liberated at Fort Defiance, shortly after the treaty of Greenville. We cannot but digress here and extract from his narrative, published in the Pioneer, an affecting account of his separation from his Indian father, who bore the singular name of Whingwy Pooshies.

On the breaking up of spring we all went up to Fort Defiance, and on arriving on the shore opposite, we saluted the fort with a round of rifles, and they shot a cannon thirteen times. We then encamped on the spot. On the same day Whingwy Pooshies told me I must go over to the fort. The children hung round me crying, and asked me if I was going to leave them? I told them I did not know. When we got over to the fort, and were seated with the officers, Whingwy Pooshies told me to stand up, which I did; he then rose and addressed me in about these words: "My son, there are men the same color with yourself. There may be some of your kin there, or your kin may be a great way off from you. You have lived a long time with us. I call on you to say if I have not been a father to you?—if I have not used you as a father would use a son?" I said, "You have used me as well as a father could use a son." He said, "I am glad you say so. You have lived long with me; you have hunted for me; but our treaty says you must be free. If you choose to go with the people of your own color, I have no right to say a word, but if you choose to stay with me, your people have no right to speak. Now reflect on it and take your choice, and tell us as soon as you make up your mind."

I was silent a few minutes, in which time it seemed as if I thought of almost every thing. I thought of the children I had just left crying; I thought of the Indians I was attached to, and I thought of my people which I remembered; and this latter thought predominated, and I said, "I will go with my kin." The old man then said, "I have raised you—I have learned you to hunt. You are a good hunter—you have been better to me than my own sons. I am now getting old and I cannot hunt. I thought you would be a support to my age. I leaned on you as on a staff. Now it is broken—you are going to leave me, and I have no right to say a word, but I am ruined." He then sank back in tears to his seat. I heartily joined him in his tears—parted with him, and have never seen nor heard of him since.

In the month of August, 1797, Franklinton was laid out by Lucas Sullivant. The settlement at that place was the first in the county. Mr. Sullivant was a self-made man and noted as a surveyor. He had often encountered great peril from the attacks of Indians while making his surveys.

Next after the settlement of Franklinton, a Mr. Springer and his son-in-law, Osborn, settled on Darby; then next was a scattering settlement along Alum creek, which last was probably about the summer of 1798. Among the first settlers here were Messrs. White, Nelson, Shaw, Agler and Reed. About the same time, some improvements were made near the mouth of Gahannah, (formerly called Big belly,) and the settlements thus gradually extended along the principal water courses. In the mean time, Franklinton was the point to which emigrants first repaired, to spend some months, or probably years, prior to their permanent location. For several years, there was no mill nor considerable settlement nearer than the vicinity of Chillicothe. In Franklinton, the neighbors constructed a kind of hand-mill, upon which they generally ground their corn. Some pounded it, and occasionally a trip was made with a canoe or periogue, by way of the river, to the Chillicothe mill. About the year 1799, a Mr. John D. Rush erected an inferior mill on the Scioto, a short distance above Franklinton; it was, however, a poor concern, and soon fell to ruin. A horse-mill was then resorted to, and kept up for some time; but the first mill of any considerable advantage to the country was erected by Col. Kilbourne, near Worthington, about the year 1805. About the same time, Carpenter's mill, near Delaware, and Dyer's, on Darby, were erected. About one year, probably, after the first settlement of Franklinton, a Mr. James Scott opened the first small store in the place, which added much to the convenience of the settlers. For probably seven or eight years, there was no post-office nearer than Chillicothe, and when other opportunities did not offer, the men would occasionally raise by contribution the means, and employ a man to go the moderate distance of forty-five miles to the post-office to inquire for letters and newspapers. During the first years of the settlement, it was extremely sickly—perhaps as much so as any part of the state. Although sickness was so general in the fall season as to almost entirely discourage the inhabitants, yet, on the return of health, the prospective advantages of the country, the luxuriant crops, and abundance of game of all kinds, together with the gradual improvement in the health of the country generally, induced them to remain. The principal disease of the country being fever and ague, deaths were comparatively seldom.*

Franklinton lies on the west side of the Scioto, opposite Columbus. It was the first town laid off in the Scioto valley N. of Chillicothe. From the formation of the county, in 1803, it remained its seat of justice until 1824, when it was removed to Columbus. During the late war, it was a place of general rendezvous for the N. W. army, and sometimes from one to three thousand troops were stationed there. In those days, it was a place of considerable note: it is now a small village, containing, by the census of 1840, 394 inhabitants.

Worthington is a neat town, 9 miles N. of Columbus, containing 3 churches, and by the census of 1840, 440 inhabitants. At this place is a classical academy, in the old botanic college building, in fine repute, under the charge of the Rev. R. K. Nash; also a flourishing female seminary, under the patronage of the Ohio Methodist Conference, of which the Rev. Alex. Nelson is the principal. The building is of brick, and stands in a pleasant green.

Worthington Female Seminary.

The township of Sharon, in which Worthington is, was very early settled by "the Scioto Company," formed in Granby, Connecticut, in the winter of 1801–2, and consisting at first of eight associates. They drew up articles of association, among which was one limiting their number to forty, each of whom must be unanimously chosen by ballot, a single negative being sufficient to prevent an election. Col. James Kilbourne was sent out the succeeding spring to explore

* From "A Brief History and Description of Franklin County, to accompany Wheeler's map."

the country, select and purchase a township for settlement. He returned in the fall without making a purchase, through fear that the state constitution, then about to be formed, should tolerate SLAVERY, in which case the project would have been abandoned.

It is here worthy of notice, that Col. Kilbourne, on this visit, constructed the FIRST MAP OF OHIO, which he compiled from maps of its different sections in the office of Col., afterwards Gov. Worthington, then register of the United States land office at Chillicothe. The part delineating the Indian territory was from a map made by John Fitch, of steamboat memory, who had been a prisoner among the Indians, which, although in a measure conjectural, was the most accurate of that part of the N. W. territory.

Immediately upon receiving the information that the constitution of Ohio prohibited slavery, Col. Kilbourne purchased this township, lying within the United States military land district, and in the spring of 1803, returned to Ohio and commenced improvements. By the succeeding December, one hundred settlers, mainly from Hartford county, Connecticut, and Hampshire county, Massachusetts, arrived at their new home. Obeying to the letter the articles of association, the first cabin erected was used for a school-house and church of the Protestant Episcopal denomination: the first Sabbath after the arrival of the third family, divine worship was held therein, and on the arrival of the eleventh family, a school was commenced. This early attention to religion and education has left its favorable impress upon the character of the people to the present day. The succeeding 4th of July was appropriately celebrated. Seventeen gigantic trees, emblematical of the seventeen states forming the Federal Union, were cut so that a few blows of the axe, at sunrise on the 4th, prostrated each successively with a tremendous crash, forming a national salute novel in the world's history.

COLUMBUS, the capital of Ohio and seat of justice for Franklin county, "is 106 miles southerly from Sandusky City, 139 miles southwest from Cleveland, 148 southwestwardly from Steubenville, 184 in the same direction from Pittsburg, Pa., 126 miles west from Wheeling, Va., about 100 northwest from Marietta, 105 northwest from Gallipolis, 45 north from Chillicothe, 90 in the same direction from Portsmouth, at the mouth of the Scioto river, 118 northwardly from Maysville, Ky., 110 northeast from Cincinnati, 68 easterly from Dayton, 104 southwardly from Lower Sandusky, and 175 due south from Detroit, Michigan. North lat. 39 deg. 57 min., west long. 6 deg. from Washington city, or 83 deg. from London. It is situated exactly on the same parallel of latitude with Zanesville and Philadelphia, from which latter place, it is 450 miles distant; and on the same meridian with Detroit, Michigan; and Milledgeville, Georgia. The National road passed through it east and west, and the Columbus and Sandusky turnpike extends from this point north to Lake Erie. In all other directions roads are laid out, and many of them in good repair. By the Columbus feeder, water communication is opened with the Ohio canal, and thence to Lake Erie and the Ohio river."

From the first organization of the state government until 1816, there was no permanent state capital. The sessions of the legislature were held at Chillicothe until 1810; the sessions of 1810–11 and 1811–12, were held at Zanesville; after that, until December, 1816, they were again held at Chillicothe, at which time the legislature was first convened at Columbus.

Among the various proposals to the legislature, while in session at Zanesville, for the establishment of a permanent seat of government, were those of Lyne Starling, Jas. Johnston, Alex. M'Laughlin and John Kerr, the after proprietors of Columbus, for establishing it on the "high bank of the Scioto river, opposite Franklinton," which site was then a native forest. On the 14th Feb., 1812, the legislature passed a law accepting their proposals, and in one of its sections, selected Chillicothe as a temporary seat of government merely. By an act amendatory of the other, passed Feb. 17th, 1816, it was enacted, "that from and after the second Tuesday of October next, the seat of government of this state shall be established at the town of Columbus."

On the 19th of Feb., 1812, the proprietors signed and acknowledged their articles at Zanesville, as partners, under the law for laying out, &c., of the town of Columbus. The contract having been closed between the proprietors and the state, the town was laid out in the spring of 1812, under the direction of Moses Wright. On the 18th of June, the same day war was declared with Great Britain, the first public sale of lots, by auction, was held. Among the first settlers, or as early as 1813, were George M'Cormick, Geo. B. Harvey, Jno. Shields, Michael Patton, Alex. Patton, Wm. Altman, John Collett, Wm. M'Elvain, Daniel Kooser, Peter Putnam, Jacob Hare, Christian Heyl, Jarvis, George and Benj. Pike, Wm. Long and Dr. John M. Edmiston. The first building erected for public worship was a cabin, on Spring street, in the spring of 1814, on a lot of Dr. Hoge's, which was used by the Presbyterians. It was not long occupied for that purpose: that denomination then worshipped in the Franklinton meeting-house until 1818, when the 1st Presbyterian church was organized in Columbus, and a frame meeting-house erected on Front street, where Dr. Hoge preached until the erection of "the 1st Presbyterian church," about 1825. In 1814, the Methodist church of Columbus was organized; and the same year they erected, on the lot where the present Methodist church stands, a small hewed log-house, which served the double purpose of school-house and church until about 1824, when a permanent building was erected.

The first penitentiary was erected in 1813. The state house was erected in 1814; the brick of this edifice were partly made from a beautiful mound near by, which has given the name to a street. On the 10th of Feb., 1816, the town was incorporated as "the borough of Columbus." The first board of councilmen elected were Henry Brown, Michael Patton, Jarvis Pike, Robt. and Jeremiah Armstrong, John Kerr, John Cutler, Caleb Houston and Robt. M'Coy. About the year 1819, the United States or old court-house was erected. In 1824, the county seat was removed from Franklinton to Columbus. The present city charter was granted March 3d, 1834. The first newspaper in Columbus was commenced about the beginning of 1814, and was called "the Western Intelligencer and Columbus Gazette:" it was the foundation, the original of "the Ohio State Journal."

For the first few years Columbus improved rapidly. Emigrants flowed in, apparently, from all quarters, and the improvements and general business of the place kept pace with the increase of population. Columbus, however, was a rough spot in the woods, off from any public road of much consequence. The east and west travel passed through Zanesville, Lancaster and Chillicothe, and the mails came in cross-line on horseback. The first successful attempt to carry a mail to or from Columbus, otherwise than on horseback, was by Philip Zinn, about the year 1816, once a week between Chillicothe and Columbus. The years from 1819 to '26, were the dullest years of Columbus; but soon after it began to improve. The location of the national road and of the Columbus feeder to the Ohio canal, gave an impetus to improvements.*

Columbus is beautifully situated on the east bank of the Scioto about half a mile below its junction with the Olentangy. The streets are spacious, the site level, and it has many elegant private dwellings. Columbus has a few manufactories only; it does, however, a heavy mercantile business, there being many stores of various kinds. It contains 17 churches, viz.: 2 Methodist Episcopal, 1 German Metho-

* From the brief history in the Columbus Directory, for 1843.

dist, 2 Presbyterian, 1 Baptist, 1 German Lutheran, 1 do. Evangelical Protestant, 1 do. Reformed, 2 Episcopal, 1 Catholic, 1 Welch Presbyterian, 1 United Brethren, 1 Universalist and 1 Bethel, and 1 Baptist for colored persons. The principal literary institutions in this city, are the Columbus institute, a flourishing classical institution for males, Mr. and Mrs. Schencks' female seminary, and the German theological Lutheran seminary, which last has been established about 17 years, Rev. Wm. Lehmann, professor of theology. There are in Columbus 6 weekly, 2 tri-weekly and 1 semi-monthly newspapers and several banks. Its population, in 1815, was about 700; in 1820, about 1,400; in 1830, 2,437; in 1840, 6,048, and in 1846, 10,016.

Ohio Lunatic Asylum.

The great state institutions located at Columbus, do honor to Ohio, give great interest to the city, and present strong attractions to strangers.

Ohio Lunatic Asylum.—This noble structure occupies a commanding position in an open space of ground, about one mile east of the state house. There are thirty acres of land attached to it, with an extensive plat in front of the building, handsomely ornamented by shrubbery. The institution is under the direction of Dr. William M'Awl, with whom are several assistants. The buildings present a continuous front of 376 feet: the main building is 296 feet in length and 46 feet in depth. The wings project beyond it 11 feet and extend back 218 feet, thus forming a large court in its rear. The wings are 39 feet wide.

"The buildings were commenced in the year 1836. They contain upwards of five millions of brick, and have cost (including the labor of convicts, which was a large item,) upwards of $150,000. They cover an acre of ground, and contain 440 rooms. They are capable of accommodating (besides the officers, assistants, attendants, &c.,) 350 patients. The style of the buildings is in good taste, and does credit to the architect, (N. B. Kelley, Esq.,) by whom the designs were prepared, and who presided over their execution.

"The institution went into operation in the month of November, 1838. Since that time, there have been in it 866 patients: 461 males and 405 females; 247 pay patients, 649 supported by the state; 358 have been discharged cured—92 have died; 420 were "*recent cases*," (of less than a year's duration when the patient was received,) 446 were old cases, (of more than a year's duration.) Of the recent cases discharged, 90.59-100 per cent. (or 289) were cured—of the old cases, 27 per cent. (or 69.) In addition to this, a great number of those incurable have been much improved in their condition.

"During the past year, [1846,] 175 patients have been admitted: 88 males and 87 females. Of these, 101 were "recent cases," 74 were old cases; 71 have been discharged "cured," 18 have died. In the recent cases discharged, 95.38-100 per cent. were cured—in the old cases, 20.93-100 per cent. A number are still improving, with fair prospects of recovery. These results compare favorably with those in the best institutions, both in this country and abroad. The number of patients in the institution at the close of the fiscal year, was 291."

Ohio Blind Institution.

The Ohio Institution for the Education of the Blind, is situated about three quarters of a mile easterly from the state house, on the national road, and is under the superintendence of W. Chapin, Esq. The building is a large and handsome structure of brick, in front of which the ground is pleasantly laid out into graveled walks, with flowers and shade trees. The institution was established in 1837, is now flourishing and has about 100 pupils. They are taught in a liberal course of instruction in the several English branches, with lectures on moral and natural science. They are also instructed in vocal and instrumental music, and have among them an excellent band of music. In the afternoon, they are engaged in several mechanical branches and fancy and ornamental work. The institution is flourishing, and the pupils contented and cheerful.

THE OHIO ASYLUM FOR THE INSTRUCTION OF THE DEAF AND DUMB, is situated one third of a mile east of the state house. The buildings, which are of brick, cost about $25,000, including the grounds, which are handsomely laid out and adorned with shrubbery. The number of pupils is about 130. The institution is under the superintendence of H. N. Hubbell, Esq., and is in a thriving condition. Its site was selected in 1829, and it soon after went into operation

Ohio Deaf and Dumb Asylum.

The pupils are daily instructed in the branches usually taught at other seminaries. The girls spend a portion of their time in domestic, and the boys in mechanical operations.

These noble institutions are sustained by the state, with a liberality that pure benevolence must delight to witness. Their several superintendents feel vividly the importance of their responsibilities, and discharge them in a happy and judicious manner.

THE OHIO PENITENTIARY, the most imposing edifice in Columbus, is situated on the east bank of the Scioto, about half a mile north of the state house. The main building, shown in the annexed view, is built of Ohio marble. It contains the warden's house, the office and guard rooms, and in each of its wings are 350 cells for prisoners, arranged in five tiers. With the penitentiary walls, this building forms a hollow square of six acres: about one third of this area is shown in the large view. A railroad, about two miles long, extends from the prison to a stone quarry, at which a portion of the prisoners work in getting out stone.

The prisoners are all employed in several useful manufactures, and such is the efficiency of discipline, that the industry of the convicts equals any association of voluntary or paid laborers. The discipline of the prison is conducted by rules, printed copies of which are given to the prisoners. At the sound of a bell, at noon, they leave work and arrange themselves in thirteen different companies, in front of their workshops. One of these companies is composed entirely of blacks. When the bell strikes a second time, they march to their dinner, with their heads to the left, so as to bring their faces in view of the attendant, and prevent conversation.

Ohio Penitentiary.

They move in close order, with the lock-step, and make a shuffling noise, that echoes loudly upon the walls of the area. Arrived at the table, they arrange themselves before their seats. At the sound of a small bell, they take off their caps, and when it again sounds, commence eating. They eat from wooden dishes made in the prison, and drink from tin cups; in the morning, their beverage is rye coffee, at noon, water. Their knives and forks are coarse, with wooden handles. A late visitor describes, in a public print, the discipline of the prison and treatment of its convicts.

The present warden has gathered around him assistants who have in their hearts much of the milk of human kindness. The new directory approves and seconds his labors, and as the result of these labors of love, the subordination is more perfect than ever before, the lash is very rarely used, the convicts are rarely reported, an air of cheerful alacrity characterizes the operations of the various shops, and all the movements of those who are compelled to pay the penalties of their crimes within the walls of the Ohio Penitentiary.

There are, at this time, about five hundred convicts in the penitentiary. Their labor yields to the state a surplus of $16,000 or $18,000 annually. They receive an abundance of substantial food, and enjoy good health. On the Sabbath, they all attend religious services in the chapel. Their religious instruction is under the charge of Rev. Mr. Finley, one of the pioneer missionaries of the Methodist church, in the west—an old veteran of more than sixty winters, who is robust and vigorous, and whose heart overflows with love for poor, weak humanity. His tearful appeals have had *their* effect, too, and many of his charge do right from religious principle. There is a choir connected with the congregation, that meets regularly for practice before service on Sabbath. During service, the effect is almost electric when those five hundred voices peal forth their sacred songs. With tears streaming from their eyes, have I heard these unfortunate men confessing their gratitude for the blessed lessons they had been taught in the penitentiary.

There is connected, also, with the penitentiary, a Sabbath school. Nearly one fifth of the convicts are permitted to avail themselves of its benefits. The instructions there given by Christians of the city, who attend for the purpose, exert an important, all-powerful influence for good upon the minds of the convicts. Superadded to all this, there is an excellent library of several hundred volumes, secured mainly through the labors of the present warden and chaplain. The former chaplain, (Rev. Mr. Mills,) laid the foundation. The convicts rejoice in the benefits of this library, and speak of it with grateful emotions. They all have Bibles in their cells, also. They are permitted to write, within stated periods, to their friends and relatives, and receive as many letters as are sent to them, when containing nothing improper. At a meeting held a few Sabbaths since, in the chapel, and in reply to a question propounded, about *fifty* of them acknowledged that they had learned to *read* since they entered the prison.

Temperance addresses are occasionally delivered in the chapel of the penitentiary. Messrs. T. and G. recently addressed the inmates. The question was put, "How many committed the crimes of which they stand convicted, owing to the use and while under the influence of intoxicating drinks." More than *four hundred* arose on their feet. *Seventy* or *eighty* admitted that they had been engaged in vending or making liquor. *Nearly every one* declared, by rising, his purpose to abstain entirely from the use of intoxicating drink the rest of his days.

We here insert a curiosity, from the Columbus Gazette, of Aug. 29th, 1822. At an early day, there was a law passed offering a bounty for the scalps of squirrels. Whether it was in force at this time, we do not know; if so, it must have made quite a draft on the treasury.

Grand Squirrel Hunt!—The squirrels are becoming so numerous in the county, as to threaten serious injury, if not destruction, to the hopes of the farmer during the ensuing fall. Much good might be done by *a general turn out* of all citizens whose convenience will permit, for two or three days, in order to prevent the alarming ravages of those mischievous neighbors. It is therefore respectfully submitted to the different townships, each to meet and choose two or three of their citizens to meet in a *hunting caucus*, at the house of Christian Heyl, on Saturday, the 31st inst., at 2 o'clock P. M. Should the time above stated prove too short for the townships to hold meetings, as above recommended, the following persons are respectfully nominated and invited to attend the meeting at Columbus.

Montgomery—Jeremiah M'Lene and Edward Livingston. *Hamilton*—George W. Williams and Andrew Dill. *Madison*—Nicholas Goetschius and W. H. Richardson. *Truro*—Abiather V. Taylor and John Hanson. *Jefferson*—John Edgar and Elias Ogden. *Plain*—Thomas B. Patterson and Jonathan Whitehead. *Harrison*—F. C. Olmsted and Capt. Bishop. *Sharon*—Matthew Matthews and Bulkley Comstock. *Perry*—Griffith Thomas and William Mickey. *Washington*—Peter Sells and Uriah Clark. *Norwich*—Robert Elliott and Alanson Perry. *Clinton*—Col. Cook and Samuel Henderson. *Franklin*—John M'Elvain and Lewis Williams. *Prairie*—John Hunter and Jacob Neff. *Pleasant*—James Gardiner and Reuben Golliday. *Jackson*—Woollery Coonrod and Nicholas Hoover. *Mifflin*—Adam Reed and William Dalzell.

In case any township should be unrepresented in the meeting, those present will take the liberty of nominating suitable persons for said absent township.

Ralph Osborn,	Lucas Sullivant,
Gustavus Swan,	Samuel G. Flenniken,
Christian Heyl,	John A. M'Dowell.

A subsequent paper says: "the hunt was conducted agreeably to the instructions in our last paper. On counting the scalps, it appeared that *nineteen thousand six hundred and sixty scalps* were produced. It is impossible to say what number in all were killed, as a great many of the hunters did not come in. We think we may safely challenge any other county in the state to kill squirrels with us."

The following is a list of villages in this county, not previously mentioned, with their population in 1840. Dublin, 166; Harrisburg, 81; Lockbourne, 139, and Reynoldsburg, 309. Central college is a new and flourishing institution, in Blendon township, of which the Rev. Mr. Covert is president.

HIGH STREET, COLUMBUS.

GALLIA.

Gallia was formed from Washington, April 30th, 1803. The word Gallia is the ancient name of France, from whence it was originally settled. The surface is generally broken, excepting in the eastern part and on the Ohio river and Kiger creek, where it is more level, and the soil fertile. Much of the county is well adapted to wheat, and a great part covered with a sandy loam. The principal crops are corn, wheat, oats and beans. The following is a list of its townships, in 1840, with their population.

Addison,	692	Guyan,	342	Perry,	973
Cheshire,	791	Harrison,	688	Raccoon,	1610
Clay,	745	Huntington,	972	Springfield,	991
Gallipolis,	1413	Morgan,	744	Walnut,	424
Green,	1047	Ohio,	626	Wilkesville,	738
Greenfield,	639				

The population of the county was, in 1820, 7098; in 1830, 9733, and in 1840, 13,445, or 25 inhabitants to a square mile.

The first settlement in the county was at Gallipolis. It was settled in 1791, by a French colony, sent out under the auspices of "*the Scioto company.*" This company was in some way connected with the Ohio company. What that connection was, does not fully appear.* Col. Duer, of New York, "secretary to the board of treasury," a Mr. Flint and a Mr. Craig seem to have been the most prominent members of the company.

In May or June, 1788, Joel Barlow, the agent of the company, left this country for Europe. He distributed proposals† at Paris, from which the annexed is an extract.

A climate wholesome and delightful, frost even in winter almost entirely unknown, and a river called, by way of eminence, the *beautiful,* and abounding in excellent fish of a vast size. Noble forests, consisting of trees that spontaneously produce sugar, (*the sugar maple,*) and a plant that yields ready-made candles, (*myrica cerifera.*) Vension in plenty, the pursuit of which is uninterrupted by wolves, foxes, lions or tigers. A couple of swine will multiply themselves a hundred fold in two or three years, without taking any care of them. No taxes to pay, no military services to be performed.

Volney, who came to America in 1795, in his "View," where we find the above, says:

---

* Volney speaks of the Ohio company as being the original proprietors, and the Scioto as purchasers from them. Judge Hall, in his Statistics of the West, says the Scioto company, which was formed from or by the Ohio company, as a subordinate. Barlow, he says, was sent to Europe by the Ohio company—which fact the biographical sketch of Barlow also states—and by them the lands in question were conveyed to the Scioto company. Kilbourn's gazetteer says: "the Scioto company, which intended to buy of congress all the tract between the western boundary of the Ohio company's purchase and the Scioto, directed the French settlers to Gallipolis, supposing it to be west of the Ohio company's purchase, though it proved not to be." The company, he adds, failing to make their payments, the whole of the proposed purchase remained with government.—*Annals of the West.*

† Volney states that these proposals were distributed in 1790.

These munificent promisers forgot to say, that these forests must be cut down before corn could be raised; that for a year, at least, they must bring their daily bread from a great distance; that hunting and fishing are agreeable amusements, when pursued for the sake of amusement, but are widely different when followed for the sake of subsistence: and they quite forgot to mention, that though there be no bears or tigers in the neighborhood, there are wild beasts infinitely more cunning and ferocious, in the shape of men, who were at that time at open and cruel war with the whites.

In truth, the market value of these lands at that time, in America, was no more than six or seven cents an acre. In France, in Paris, the imagination was too heated to admit of doubt or suspicion, and people were too ignorant and uninformed to perceive where the picture was defective, and its colors too glaring. The example, too, of the wealthy and reputedly wise confirmed the popular delusion. Nothing was talked of, in every social circle, but the paradise that was opened for Frenchmen in the western wilderness; the free and happy life to be led on the blissful banks of the Scioto. At length, Brissot published his travels,* and completed the flattering delusion: buyers became numerous and importunate, chiefly among the better sort of the middle class: single persons and whole families disposed of their all, flattering themselves with having made excellent bargains.

With the proposals, a map was shown at Paris by the agents of the Scioto company, Joel Barlow, from the United States, an Englishman by the name of Playfair, and a Frenchman, named De Saisson. An impression of this map is in the possession of Mons. J. P. R. Bureau, of Gallipolis, one of the original settlers. From it the annexed engraving was taken, omitting some non-essentials. The original is sixteen inches long and twelve wide.

It is in French, handsomely engraved and colored, with the lands of the two companies and the tract east of them, all divided into townships of six miles square. It represents the Scioto company's tract as extending about one hundred miles north of the mouth of the Kanawha, and including more or less of the present counties of Meigs, Athens, Muskingum, Licking, Franklin, Pickaway, Ross, Pike, Scioto, Gallia, Lawrence, Perry, Jackson, Hocking, and Fairfield. This tract, on the map, is divided into 142 townships and 32 fractions. The north line of the Ohio land company's tract is 18 miles south of the other, and included the present county of Morgan, and parts of Washington, Meigs, Athens, Muskingum, Guernsey and Monroe, there divided into 91 townships and 16 fractions. The tract east of that of the Ohio company, extends 48 miles farther north. Upon the original, are the words "Sept rangs de municipalite acquis par des individues et occupes depuis, 1786;"

---

* Volney here refers to the travels of Brissot de Warville. Brissot published several volumes relating to America, as we infer from his preface to his "New Travels in America," a work issued in the spring of 1791, and consisting in part of a series of letters written from this country, in 1788. In his preface to the last, he says: "the third volume was published in 1787, by Mr. Claviere and me." In the last, he refers to the charges against the Scioto company, in this wise. "This company has been much calumniated. It has been accused of selling lands which it does not possess, of giving exaggerated accounts of its fertility, of deceiving the emigrants, of robbing France of her inhabitants, and of sending them to be butchered by the savages. But the title of this association is incontestable; the proprietors are reputable men; the description which they have given of the lands is taken from the public and authentic reports of Mr. Hutchins, geographer of congress. No person can dispute their prodigious fertility." He elsewhere speaks, in this volume, in high terms of the company.

i. e. Seven ranges of townships acquired by individuals, and occupied since 1786.

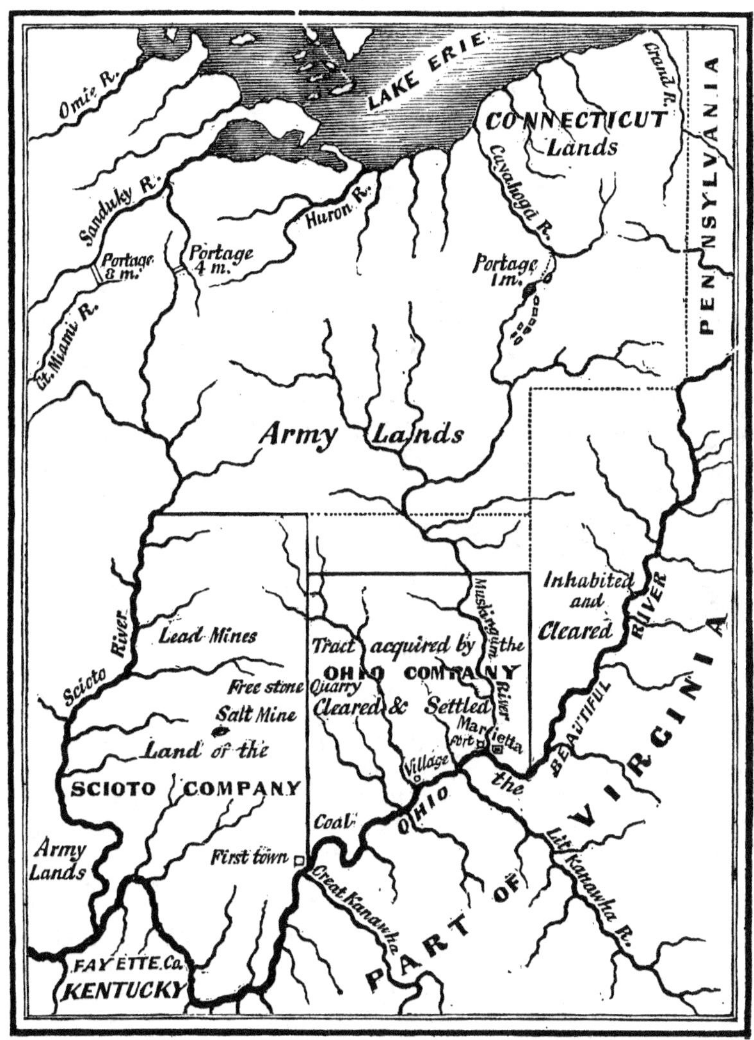

"Plan of the Purchase of the Ohio and Scioto Land Companies."

The map is inaccurate in its geography, and *fraudulent* in its statements. It represents the country as "cleared and inhabited," when it was a wilderness, the only settlement being at Marietta, with perhaps some offshoots from it on the Ohio and Muskingum.

The glowing representations made by the agents of the company, were well-timed for their enterprise. It was about the beginning of the French revolution, and the "flattering delusion" took strong hold The terms to induce emigration, were as follows: the company proposed to take the emigrant to their lands and pay the cost, and the latter bound himself to work three years for the company, for which he was to receive fifty acres, a house and a cow.* Printed deeds, executed at Paris, with all due formality, were given to some of the purchasers, by Playfair and De Saisson. About five hundred Frenchmen left their native country, landed mostly at Alexandria, and made their way to the promised land. They were persons ill-

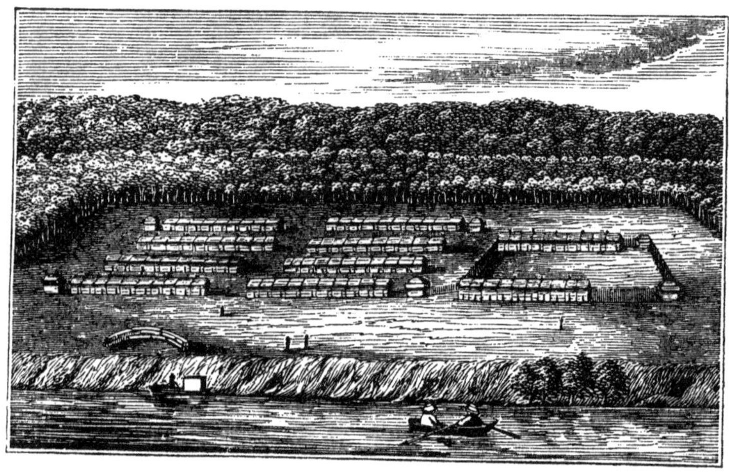

Gallipolis in 1791.

fitted for such an enterprise. Among them were not a few carvers and gilders to his majesty, coach and peruke makers, friseurs and other *artistès*, about equally well fitted for a backwoods life, with only ten or twelve farmers and laborers.

On the map is shown the "first town," *i. e.* "*Premiere Ville,*" lying opposite the mouth of the Kanawha. It was laid out by the Ohio company, under the name of Fair Haven; but as the ground there is low and liable to overflow, Gallipolis was located four miles below, upon a high bank, ten feet above the flood of 1832.†

This location was made just before the arrival of the French. Col. Rufus Putnam sent Major Burnham, with about forty men, for that purpose, who made the clearing and erected block-houses and cabins. Col. Robert Safford, now living near Gallipolis, was of this party, and cut the first tree. From his description, we give the view of the place at that time, the greater part of which stood on the site of the public square.

On the public square stood 80 log cabins, 20 in each row. At each of the corners were block-houses, two stories in height. In front of the cabins, close by the river bank, was a small log breastwork, erected for a defence while building the cabins. Above the

* J. P. R. Bureau. † Ibid.

cabins, on the square, were two other parallel rows of cabins, which, with a high stockade fence and block-houses at each of the upper corners, formed a sufficient fortification in times of danger. These upper cabins were a story and a half in height, built of hewed logs, and finished in better style than those below, being intended for the richer class. In the upper cabins was a room used for a council chamber and a ball room.

The Scioto company contracted with Putnam to erect these build ings and furnish the settlers with provisions; but failed of payment, by which he lost a large amount.

We continue the history of Gallipolis, in the annexed extract from a communication in the Pioneer, by Waldeurard Meulette, one of the colonists.

At an early meeting of the colonists, the town was named Gallipolis, (town of the French.) I did not arrive till nearly all the colonists were there. I descended the river in 1791, in flat boats, loaded with troops, commanded by Gen. St. Clair, destined for an expedition against the Indians. Some of my countrymen joined that expedition; among others was *Count Malartie*, a captain in the French guard of Louis XVI. General St. Clair made him one of his aid-de-camps in the battle, in which he was severely wounded. He went back to Philadelphia, from whence he returned to France. The Indians were encouraged to greater depredations and murders, by their success in this expedition, but most especially against the American settlements. From their intercourse with the French in Canada, or some other cause, they seemed less disposed to trouble us. Immediately after St. Clair's defeat, Col. *Sproat*, commandant at Marietta, appointed four spies for Gallipolis—two Americans and two French, of which I was one, and it was not until after the treaty at Greenville, in 1795, that we were released.

Notwithstanding the great difficulties, the difference of tempers, education and professions, the inhabitants lived in harmony, and having little or nothing to do, made themselves agreeable and useful to each other. The Americans and hunters, employed by the company, performed the first labors of clearing the township, which was divided into lots.

Although the French were willing to work, yet the clearing of an American wilderness and its heavy timber, was far more than they could perform. To migrate from the eastern states to the "far west," is painful enough now-a-days, but how much more so it must be for a citizen of a large European town! even a farmer of the old countries would find it very hard, if not impossible, to clear land in the wilderness. Those hunters were paid by the colonists to prepare their garden ground, which was to receive the seeds brought from France; few of the colonists knew how to make a garden, but they were guided by a few books on that subject, which they had brought likewise from France. The colony then began to improve in its appearance and comfort. The fresh provisions were supplied by the company's hunters, the others came from their magazines. When, of the expeditions of General St. Clair and Wayne, many of the troops stopped at Gallipolis to take provisions, which had been deposited there for that purpose by government; the Indians, who, no doubt, often came there in the night, at last saw the regulars going morning and evening round the town in order to ascertain if there were any Indian traces, and attacked them, killing and wounding several—a soldier, besides other wounds, was tomahawked, but recovered. A French colonist, who had tried to raise corn at some distance from the town, seeing an Indian rising from behind some brushwood against a tree, shot him in the shoulder; the Indian hearing an American patrole, must have thought that the Frenchman made a part of it; and sometime afterward a Frenchman was killed, and a man and woman made prisoners, as they were going to collect ashes to make soap, at some distance from town.

After this, although the Indians committed depredations on the Americans on both sides of the river, the French had suffered only by the loss of some cattle carried away, until the murder of the man above related. The Scioto company, in the mean time, had nearly fulfilled all their engagements during six months, after which time they ceased their supply of provisions to the colonists, and one of their agents gave as a reason for it, that the company had been *cheated* by one or two of their agents in France, who, having received the *funds* in France for the purchased lands, had kept the money for themselves and run off with it to England, without having purchased or possessing any of the tract which the had sold to the deceived colonists. This intelligence exasperated them, and was the more sensibly felt, as a scarcity of provisions added to their disappointment. The winter was uncommonly severe; the creek and the Ohio were frozen; the hunters had no longer any meat to sell; flat boats could not come down with flour to furnish as they had done before. This produced almost a famine in the settlement, and a family of eight persons, father, mother and children, was obliged to subsist for eight or ten days on dry beans, boiled in water, without either salt, grease or bread, and those had never known, before that time, what it was to want for any thing. On the other hand, the dangers from the Indians seemed to augment every day.

The colonists were by this time weary of being confined to a few acres of land; their industry and their labor was lost; the money and clothes which they had brought were nearly gone. They knew not to whom they were to apply to get their lands; they hoped that if Wayne's campaign forced the Indians to make a lasting peace, the Scioto company would send immediately, either to recover or to purchase those promised lands; but they soon found out their mistake. After the treaty of Greenville, many Indians passing through Gallipolis, on their way to the seat of government, and several travellers, revealed the whole transaction, from which it was ascertained that the pretended Scioto company was composed of New Englanders, the names of very few only being known to the French, who, being themselves ignorant of the English language, and at such a distance from the place of residence of their defrauders, and without means for prosecuting them, could get no redress. Far in a distant land, separated forever from their friends and relations—with exhausted means, was it surprising that they were disheartened, and that every social tie should have been loosened, nearly broken, and a great portion of the deceived colonists should have become reckless? May the happy of this day, never feel as *they* did, when all hope was blasted, and they were left so destitute! Many of the colonists went off and settled elsewhere with the means that remained to them, and resumed their trades in more populous parts of the country; others led a half-savage life, as hunters for skins: the greater part, however, resolved, in a general assembly, to make a memorial of their grievances, and send it to congress. The memorial claimed no rights from that body, but it was a detail of their wrongs and sufferings, together with an appeal to the generosity and feelings of congress; and they did not appeal in vain. One of the colonists proposed to carry the petition; he only stipulated that his expenses should be paid by a contribution of the colonists, whether he succeeded or not in their object; but, he added, that if he obtained for himself the quantity of land which he had paid for, and the rest had none, he should be repaid by their gratitude for his efforts.* At Philadelphia, he met with a French lawyer, M. Duponceau, and through his means he obtained from congress a grant of 24,000 acres of land, known by the name of the French grant, opposite to Little Sandy, for the French, who were still resident at Gallipolis. The act annexed the condition of settling on the lands three years before reviewing the deed of gift. The bearer of the petition had his 4000 acres; the rest was divided among the remaining French, amounting to ninety-two persons, married and single.

Each inhabitant had thus a lot of 217½ acres of land; but before the surveys and other arrangements could be made, some time was necessary, during which, those who had reclaimed the wilderness and improved Gallipolis being reluctant to lose all their labor, and finding that a company, owning the lands of Marietta, and where there was a settlement previous to that of the French colony, had met to divide lands which they had purchased in a common stock, the colonists sent a deputation for the purpose of proposing to the company to sell them the spot where Gallipolis was and is situated, and to be paid in proportion to what was improved, which was accepted. When at last the distribution of the lots of the French grant was achieved, some sold their share, others went to settle on it, or put tenants, and either remained at Gallipolis, or went elsewhere; but how few entered again heartily into a new kind of life, after having lost many of their lives and much of their health, amid hardships, excess of labor, or the indolence which follows discouragement and hopeless efforts! Few of the original settlers remain at Gallipolis: not many at the French grant.

Breckenridge, in his Recollections, gives some reminiscences of Gallipolis, related in a style of charming simplicity and humor. He

* Our contributor is not clear here; we presume he meant to say: "But he added, that if he obtained as much, he would expect for himself the quantity of land he had paid for, viz: 4000 acres; and if the rest who had no land got some, he would be repaid by their gratitude for his efforts."—*Ed.*

was at Gallipolis in 1795, at which time he was a boy of nine year of age.

Behold me once more in port, and domicilated at the house, or the inn, of Monsieur, or rather, Dr. Saugrain, a cheerful, sprightly little Frenchman, four feet six, English measure and a chemist, natural philosopher, and physician, both in the English and French signi fication of the word. . . . . This singular village was settled by people from Paris and Lyons, chiefly artisans and artists, peculiarly unfitted to sit down in the wilderness and clear away forests. I have seen half a dozen at work in taking down a tree, some pulling ropes fastened to the branches, while others were cutting around it like beavers. Sometimes serious accidents occurred in consequence of their awkwardness. Their former employment had been only calculated to administer to the luxury of highly polished and wealthy societies. There were carvers and gilders to the king, coach makers, freizurs and peruke makers, and a variety of others who might have found some employment in our larger towns, but who were entirely out of their place in the wilds of Ohio. Their means by this time had been exhausted, and they were beginning to suffer from the want of the comforts, and even the necessaries of life. The country back from the river was still a wilderness, and the Gallipotians did not pretend to cultivate any thing more than small garden spots, depending for their supply of provisions, on the boats which now began to descend the river; but they had to pay in cash and that was become scarce. They still assembled at the ball-room twice a week; it was evident, however, that they felt disappointment, and were no longer happy. The predilections of the best among them, being on the side of the Bourbons, the honors of the French revolution, even in their remote situation, mingled with their private misfortunes, which had at this time nearly reached their acme, in consequence of the discovery that they had no title to their lands, having been cruelly deceived by those from whom they had purchased. It is well known that congress generously made them a grant of twenty thousand acres, from which, however, but few of them ever derived any advantage.

As the Ohio was now more frequented, the house was occasionally resorted to, and especially by persons looking out for land to purchase. The doctor had a small apartment which contained his chemical apparatus, and I used to sit by him, as often as I could watching the curious operation of his blow-pipe and crucible. I loved the cheerful little man, and he became very fond of me in return. Many of my countrymen used to come and stare at his doings, which they were half inclined to think, had a too near resemblance to the black art. The doctors little phosphoric matches, igniting spontaneously when the glass tube was broken, and from which he derived some emolument, were thought by some, to be rather beyond mere human power. His barometer and thermometer, with the scale neatly painted with the pen, and the frames richly carved, were objects of wonder, and probably some of them are yet extant in the west. But what most astonished some of our visitors, was a large peach in a glass bottle, the neck of which would only admit a common cork; this was accomplished by tying the bottle to the limb of a tree, with the peach when young inserted into it. His swans which swam around basins of water amused me more than any wonders exhibited by the wonderful man.

The doctor was a great favorite with the Americans, as well for his vivacity and sweetness of temper, which nothing could sour, as on account of a circumstance which gave him high claim to the esteem of the backwoodsmen. He had shown himself, notwithstanding his small stature and great good nature, a very hero in combat with the Indians. He had descended the Ohio in company with two French philosophers, who were believers in the primitive innocence and goodness of the children of the forest. They could not be persuaded, that any danger was to be apprehended from the Indians; as they had no intentions to injure that people, they supposed no harm could be meditated on their part. Dr. Saugrain was not altogether so well convinced of their good intentions, and accordingly kept his pistols loaded. Near the mouth of the Sandy, a canoe with a party of warriors approached the boat; the philosophers invited them on board by signs, when they came rather too willingly. The first thing they did on coming on board of the boat, was to salute the two philosophers with the tomahawk; and they would have treated the doctor in the same way but that he used his pistols with good effect—killed two of the savages, and then leaped into the water, diving like a dipper at the flash of the guns of the others, and succeeded in swimming to the shore with several severe wounds whose scars were conspicuous.

The doctor was married to an amiable young woman, but not possessing as much vivacity as himself. As Madam Saugrain had no maid to assist her, her brother, a boy of my age, and myself, were her principal helps in the kitchen. We brought water and wood, and washed the dishes. I used to go in the morning about two miles for a little milk, sometimes on the frozen ground, barefooted. I tried a pair of savots, or wooden shoes, but was unable to make any use of them, although they had been made by the carver to the king. Little perquisites, too, sometimes fell to our share from blacking boots and shoes; my companion generally saved his, while mine would have burned a hole in my pocket, if it had remained there. In the spring and summer, a good deal of my time was passed in the garden, weeding the beds. While thus engaged, I formed an acquaintance with a young lady, of eighteen or twenty, on the other side of the palings, who was often similarly occupied. Our friendship, which was purely Platonic, commenced with the story of Blue Beard, recounted by her, and with the novelty and pathos of which I was much interested. This incident may perhaps remind the reader of the story of Pyramus and Thisbe, or perhaps of the hortical ecologue of Dean Swift, "Dermot and Shela"

Connected with this lady, is an incident which I feel a pleasure in relating. One day while standing alone on the bank of the river, I saw a man who had gone in to bathe, and who had got beyond his depth, without being able to swim. He had began to struggle for life, and in a few seconds would have sunk to rise no more. I shot down the bank like an arrow, leaped into a canoe, which fortunately happened to be close by, pushed the end to him, and as he rose, perhaps for the last time, he seized it with a deadly convulsive grasp, and held so firmly that the skin afterward came off the parts of his arms which pressed against the wood. I screamed for help; several persons came and took him out, perfectly insensible. He afterwards married the young lady, and raised a numerous and respectable family. One of his daughters married a young lawyer, who now represents that district in congress. . . . . .

Toward the latter part of summer, the inhabitants suffered severely from sickness and want of provisions. Their situation was truly wretched. The swamp in the rear, now exposed by the clearing between it and the river, became the cause of a frightful epidemic, from which few escaped, and many became its victims. I had recovered from the ague, and was among the few exempted from the disease: but our family, as well as the rest, suffered much from absolute hunger, a most painful sensation, as I had before experienced. To show the extremity of our distress, on one occasion the brother of Madam Saugrain and myself pushed a light canoe to an island above town, where we pulled some corn, took it to mill, and excepting some of the raw grains, had nothing to eat from the day before, until we carried home the flour and made some bread, but had neither milk nor meat. I have learned to be thankful when I had a sufficiency of wholesome food, however plain, and was blessed with health; and I could put up with humble fare, without a murmur, although accustomed to luxuries, when I have seen those who have never experienced absolute starvation, turn up their noses at that, which was a very little worse than the best they had ever known. . . . . . .

I had been nearly a year at Gallipolis, when Capt. Smith, of the United States army came along in advance of the barge of Gen. Wilkinson, and according to the request of my father, took me into his custody, for the purpose of bringing me once more to my native place. He remained two or three days waiting for the general, and in the meanwhile procured me hat, shoes and clothes befitting a gentleman's son, and then took me on board his boat. Shortly after the general overtook us, I was transferred on board his barge, as a playmate for his son Biddle, a boy of my own age. The general's lady, and several ladies and gentlemen, were on board his boat, which was fitted up in a style of convenience, and even magnificence, scarcely surpassed even by the present steamboats. It was propelled against the stream by twenty five or thirty men, sometimes by the pole, the cordelle, and often by the oar. There was also a band of musicians on board, and the whole had the appearance of a mere party of pleasure. My senses were overpowered—it seemed an Elysium! The splendor of the furniture—the elegance of the dresses—and then, the luxuries of the table, to a half-starved creature like me, produced an effect which can scarce be easily described. Every repast was a royal banquet, and such delicacies were placed before me, as I had never seen before, and in sufficient abundance to satiate my insatiable appetite. I was no more like what I had been, than the cast-off skin of the black snake resembles the new dress in which he glistens in the sunbeam. The general's countenance was continually lighted up with smiles, and he seemed *faire le bonheur*, of all around him,—it seemed his business to make every one happy about him. His countenance and manners were such as I have rarely seen, and now that I can form a more just estimate of them, were such as better fitted him for a court than a republic. His lady was truly an estimable person, of the mildest and softest manners. She gave her son and myself a reproof one day, which I never forgot. She saw us catching minnows with pin-hooks, made us desist, and then explained in the sweetest manner, the cruelty of taking away life wantonly from the humblest thing in creation.

In 1807, Breckenridge again saw Gallipolis.

As we passed Point Pleasant and the island below it, Gallipolis, which I looked for with anxious feelings, hove in sight. I thought of the French inhabitants—I thought of my friend Saugrain; and I recalled, in the liveliest colors, the incidents of that portion of my life which was passed here. A year is a long time at that period—every day is crowded with new and great and striking events. When the boat landed, I ran up the bank and looked around; but alas! how changed! The Americans had taken the town in hand, and no trace of *antiquity*, that is, of twelve years ago, remained. I hastened to the spot where I expected to find the abode, the little log house, tavern and labratory of the doctor, but they had vanished like the palace of Aladdin. After some inquiry, I found a little Frenchman, who, like the old woman of Goldsmith's village, was "the sad historian of the deserted plain,"—that is, deserted by one race, to be peopled by another. He led me to where a few logs might be seen, as the only remains of the once happy tenement which had sheltered me—but all around it was a common; the town had taken a different direction. My heart sickened; the picture which my imagination had drawn—the scenes which my memory loved to cherish, were blotted out and obliterated. A volume of reminiscences seemed to be annihilated in an instant! I took a hasty glance at the new town, as I returned to the boat. I saw brick houses, painted frames, fanciful enclosures, ornamental trees! Even the pond, which had carried off a third of the French population by its *malaria*, had disappeared, and a pretty green had usurped its place, with a neat brick court house in the midst of it. This was too much; I hastened my pace, and with sorrow, once more pushed into the stream.

Public Square, Gallipolis.

Gallipolis, the county seat, is pleasantly situated on the Ohio river, 102 miles southeasterly from Columbus. It contains 1 Presbyterian, 1 Episcopal and 1 Methodist church, 12 or 14 stores, 2 newspaper printing offices, and by the census of 1840, had 1,221 inhabitants, and now has about 1700. A part of the population is of French descent, but they have in a great measure lost their national characteristics. Some few of the original French settlers are yet living. The engraving of the public square, shows the market and court house near the center of the view, with a glimpse of the Ohio river on the left.

The failure of the Gallipolis bank, at this place, a few years since, excited a strong sensation throughout the state. The history of the institution we derive from the communication of one familiar with it.

The charter of the bank of Gallipolis, was passed in the year 1818, but the commissioners named in it, never judged it advisable to open books for subscription, until the spring of 1839, when they were opened at the solicitation of M. B. Sherwood, of Buffalo, he proposing, on behalf of the Erie County bank in that city, to subscribe to a large amount. Mr. Sherwood brought such strong testimonials of integrity of character, and ability to accomplish what he proposed, as to satisfy the commissioners, and he was permitted to subscribe for $200,000 of the stock, paying thereon $20,000, by a certificate of stock deposit in the Erie County bank ; this certificate was paid at the time, to show that Mr. Sherwood was in earnest, in organizing the bank in good faith. He stated at the time, that those for whom he acted, were men of wealth—had established two banks in New York, the Staten Island and the Erie County banks, and were anxious to connect their business with a western bank, as it would much facilitate the transaction of their business, and prove of mutua advantage and profits to both institutions.

When the time came for putting the bank into operation, Mr. Sherwood was presen with about $40,000 in specie and the paper of specie-paying banks ; the bank was examined by a commissioner, Geo. House, appointed by the governor, Wilson Shannon, and authorized to do business as a bank, by the governor's proclamation. The president, Mr. Smith, the cashier, Mr. Scovill, and Whiting, chief clerk, were also from Buffalo. The other directors were among the most respectable men of Gallipolis. The bank failed in January, 1841, when it became apparent, that a most stupendous system of fraud had been carried on by means of this bank and others, all under the management of the same band cf swindlers, Sherwood, Cole and others.

The manner seems to have been this. The directors of the Gallipolis bank had procured bills to be struck by Rawdon, Wright & Hatch, of New York, engravers, to the amount of $175,000, and this was the entire amount of bills as was supposed by the resident directors ; but it turns out that the president and cashier, under the direction of Sherwood, had in some way procured bills to be struck to the amount of some $1,200,000, without the knowledge of the other directors, and while the books and accounts were kept, and the circulation predicated upon bills to the amount of $175,000, Sherwood was scattering broad-cast over the land, this vast fraudulent circulation, unknown to the resident directors, until it was brought to light by the vast over-issue, coming in after the failure.

There were other banks with which the same company was connected, to wit, the Manhatten bank, in Lucas county, Ohio, the Circleville bank, at Circleville, Ohio, the West Union bank, at West Union, Ohio, and the Mineral Point bank, in Wisconsin. Sherwood seems to have operated largely in state stocks, paying for them in the paper of these fraudulent banks. When the explosion came, he and these banks were indebted to Illinois, near $100,000 ; to Indiana, about $600,000, besides an unredeemed circulation of these banks, of not less than from $300,000 to $400,000.

Before the failure of the bank in January, 1841, a Mr. Farrington appeared in Gallipolis, in October of 1840, where he remained until January following, when he presented a transfer of the stock belonging to Kinney & Smith, in whose names it stood for the use of the Erie County bank, as was stated, and became himself president of the bank, under representations, on his part, of his great wealth. During the months of October, November and December, 1840, several strangers, of the names of Hill, Weed and others, appeared in Gallipolis, talked largely of their wealth, proposed entering into business, but never went beyond talking ; what their business was, no one knew. After the failure of the bank, it became apparent that these men were the associates of Farrington, and that their business at Gallipolis, had been to fill their pockets with the Gallipolis bank paper, and then to go off and pay it out for whatever they could obtain. They bought up property of every description at exorbitant prices, in order to swindle the community.

Farrington, Hill, Weed and some others, the men who had engaged in swindling in the fraudulent bank of Millington, in Maryland, seem to have purchased of Sherwood & Co., the chance of what could be made by means of the Gallipolis bank, before the explosion should take place. Hill, in a letter to Farrington, received after his arrest, states that Sherwood had cheated them, as he, Hill, was satisfied that there was a greater over-issue than had been represented.

At the time of the failure of the bank, Farrington was arrested, and, with Scovill, Whiting and some others, indicted, tried, convicted, and sent to the penitentiary for six years. Whiting was arrested at Lowell, in Massachusetts, brought to Gallipolis, and confined to await his trial ; but with the aid of certain persons, he escaped, and has never since been retaken. Sherwood was compelled to run for Texas, to protect himself from justice

The assets of the bank, at the time of the failure, were applied by the resident directors, to the redemption of its liabilities, as far as they would go, having been handed over to those presenting claims against the bank, as fast as the claims were presented. The circulation redeemed was very large, but no one can tell the amount. The whole affair was as stupendous a scheme of swindling, as has ever been carried on in the country, and the whole resting upon the credit of two banks in New York, organized under the free banking law of that state, with stocks, which were probably borrowed of the states of Indiana and Illinois.

Gen. Edward W. Tupper, in July, 1812, raised for a six months' duty, a force of 1000 men, principally from this, Lawrence and Jackson counties. Daniel Womeldorf, of this county, commanded a company of cavalry. They marched to the northwest, and had a skirmish with the enemy at the foot of the Maumee rapids, with unimportant results. Gen. Tupper resided in Gallipolis, and died many years since. Capt. Womeldorf, is living in the county.

The following are the names of small villages in this county, with their population, in 1840. Patriot 119, Wilkesville 119, Centerville 84, Porter 75, and Vinton 82. (*See Addenda.*)

GEAUGA.

Geauga was formed from Trumbull, in 1805, since which its original limits have been much reduced. In March, 1840, the county of Lake was mainly formed from its northern part. The name Geauga, or Sheauga, signifies, in the Indian language, raccoon: it was originally applied to Grand river; thus, "Sheauga sepe," *i. e. Raccoon river.* The surface is rolling and heavily timbered, and the soil generally clay. The principal exports are sheep, cattle, butter and cheese. The following is a list of its townships, in 1840, with their population.

Auburn,	1198	Claridon,	879	Newburgh,	1209
Bainbridge,	988	Hampden,	840	Parkman,	1181
Batavia,	771	Hurtsburgh,	911	Russell,	742
Burton,	1022	Montville,	567	Thompson,	1038
Chardon,	1910	Munson,	1263	Troy,	1208
Chester,	962				

The population of Geauga, in 1820, was 7791; in 1830, 15,813, and in 1840, 16,299, or 42 inhabitants to a square mile.

This county being at the head waters of Chagrin, Cuyahoga and part of Grand rivers, is high ground, and more subject to deep snows than any other part of the Reserve. It was formerly much subject to very high sweeping winds or tornadoes. In August, 1804, John Miner was killed at Chester. He had lately moved from Burton, with part of his family, into a log house which he had built at that place. A furious storm suddenly arose, and the timber commenced falling on all sides, when he directed his two children to go under the floor, and stepped to the door to see the falling timber: at that instant, three trees fell across the house and killed him instantly. The children remained in the house until the next morning, when the oldest made her way to a neighbor, about two miles distant, and related the sad tidings.*

The first settlement in Geauga, was at Burton, in the year 1798, when three families settled there from Connecticut. This settlement was in the interior of the country, at a considerable distance from any other. The hardships and privations of the early settlers of the Reserve, are well described in the annexed article from the pen of one who was familiar with them.

The settlement of the Reserve commenced in a manner somewhat peculiar. Instead of beginning on one side of a county, and progressing gradually into the interior, as had usually been done in similar cases, the proprietors of the Reserve, being governed by different and separate views, began their improvements wherever their individual interests led them. Hence we find many of the first settlers immured in a dense forest, 15 or 20 miles or more from the abode of any white inhabitants. In consequence of their scattered situation, journeys were some times to be performed of 20 or 50 miles, for the sole purpose of having the staple of an ox-yoke mended, or some other mechanical job, in itself trifling, but absolutely essential for the successful prosecution of business. These journeys had to be performed through the wilderness, at a great expense of time, and, in many cases, the only safe guide to direct their course, were the township lines made by the surveyors.

The want of mills to grind the first harvests, was in itself a great evil. Prior to the year 1800, many families used a small hand-mill, properly called a *sweat-mill*, which took the hard labor of two hours to supply flour enough for one person a single day. About the year 1800, one or two grist-mills, operating by water power, were erected. One of these was at Newburg, now in Cuyahoga county. But the distance of many of the settlements from the mills, and the want of roads, often rendered the expense of grinding a single bushel, equal the value of two or three.

The difficulties of procuring subsistence for a family, in such circumstances, must be obvious. Few, however, can now fully realize circumstances then very common. Often would a man leave his family in the wilderness with a stinted supply of food, and with his team or pack horse go perhaps some 20 or 30 miles for provision. The necessary appendages of his journey would be an axe, a pocket compass, fire works, and blanket and bells. He cut and beat his way through the woods with his axe, and forded almost impassable streams. When the day was spent, he stopped where he was, fastened his bells to his beasts, and set them at liberty to provide for themselves. Then he would strike a fire, not only to dissipate, in some degree, the gloom and damps of night, but to annoy the gnats and musketoes, and prevent the approach of wolves, bears and panthers. Thus the night passed, with the trees for his shelter. At early dawn, or perhaps long before, he is listening to catch the sound of bells, to him sweet music, for often many hours of tedious wanderings were consumed, ere he could find his team and resume his journey. If prospered, on reaching his place of destination, in obtaining his expected supply, he follows his lonely way back to his anxious and secluded family, and perhaps has scarce time to refresh and rest himself, ere the same journey and errand had to be repeated.

CHARDON is 170 miles NE. of Columbus, and 28 from Cleveland. It was laid out about the year 1808, for the county seat, and named from Peter *Chardon* Brookes, of Boston, then proprietor of the soil. There are but few villages in Ohio, that stand upon such an elevated, commanding ridge as this, and it can be seen in some directions for several miles: although but about 14 miles from Lake Erie, it is computed to be 600 feet above it. The village is scattered and small. In the center is a handsome green, of about eleven acres, on which stands the public buildings, two of which, the court house and Methodist church, are shown in the engraving. The Baptist church and a classical academy, which are on or face the public

* Judge Amzi Atwater.

square, are not shown in this view. Chardon has 6 stores, a newspaper printing office, and in 1840, had 446 inhabitants.

Geauga suffered much from the "*great drouth*," in northern Ohio,

View in Chardon.

in the summer of 1845, the following brief description of which was communicated to Dr. S. P. Hildreth, by Seabury Ford, Esq., of Geauga, and published in Silliman's Journal.

The district of country which suffered the most, was about one hundred miles in length, and fifty or sixty in width; extending nearly east and west parallel with the lake, and in some places directly bordering on the shore of this great inland sea. There was no rain from the last of March, or the 1st of April, until the 10th of June, when there fell a little rain for one day, but no more until the 2d of July, when there probably fell half an inch, as it made the roads a little muddy. From this time, no more rain fell until early in September. This long-continued drouth reduced the streams of water to mere rills, and many springs and wells heretofore unfailing became dry, or nearly so. The grass crop entirely failed, and through several counties the pasture grounds in places were so dry, that in walking across them the dust would rise under the feet, as in highways. So dry was the grass in meadows, that fires, when accidentally kindled, would run over them as over a stubble-field, and great caution was required to prevent damage from them. The crop of oats and corn was nearly destroyed. Many fields of wheat so perished that no attempt was made to harvest them. Scions set in the nursery, dried up for lack of sap in the stocks, and many of the forest trees withered, and all shed their leaves much earlier than usual. The health of the inhabitants was not materially affected, although much sickness was anticipated. Grasshoppers were multiplied exceedingly in many places, and destroyed every green thing that the drouth had spared, even to the thistles and elder tops by the road side.

The late frosts and cold drying winds of the spring months, cut off nearly all the fruit, and what few apples remained, were defective at the core, and decayed soon after being gathered in the fall. Many of the farmers sowed fields of turnips in August and September, hoping to raise winter food for their cattle, but the seed generally failed to vegetate for lack of moisture. So great was the scarcity of food for the domestic animals, that early in the autumn large droves of cattle were sent into the valley of the Scioto, where the crops were more abundant, to pass the winter, while others were sent eastward into the borders of Pennsylvania. This region of country abounds in grasses, and one of the staple commodities is the produce of the dairy. Many stocks of dairy cows were broken up and dispersed, selling for only four or five dollars a head, as the cost of wintering would be more than their worth in the spring. Such great losses and suffering from the effects of drouth, has not been experienced in Ohio for many years, if at all since the settlement of the country. As the lands become more completely cleared of the forest trees, dry summers will doubtless be more frequent. In a region so near a large body of water, we should expect more rain than in one at a distance. The sky in that district is, nevertheless, much oftener covered with clouds than in the southern portion of the state, where rains are more abundant; but the dividing ridge, or height of land between Lake Erie and the waters of the Ohio, lacks a range of high hills to attract the moisture from the clouds and cause it to descend in showers of rain.

Burton, a pleasant village, 8 miles SE. of Chardon, contains 1 Presbyterian, 1 Methodist and 1 Disciples church, an academy, and about 175 inhabitants. Parkman, on a branch of Grand river, and named from Robert B. Parkman, is 16 miles SE. of Chardon, and contains an academy, 1 Methodist and 1 Universalist church, 1 flouring, 1 saw and 1 fulling mill, and about 30 dwellings. Three dams are thrown across the river at this place, having unitedly about 60 feet fall, and furnishing much power. There are other small places in the county, at which are post-offices: they are Auburn, Bundysburg, East Claridon, Fowler's Mill, Hamden, Huntsburg, Newburg, Thompson, Welshfield and Chester Cross Roads. At Chester, is the Geauga seminary, under the patronage of the Western Reserve Free-Will Baptist society. This flourishing institution has about 200 pupils, Elder Daniel Branch, A. M., principal.

GREENE.

Greene was formed from Hamilton and Ross, May 1st, 1803, and named from Gen. Nathaniel Greene, of the revolution. The soil is generally clayey; the surface on the east is flat and well adapted to grazing, the rest of the county is rolling and productive in wheat and corn. Considerable water power is furnished by the streams. There are some fine limestone quarries, and near Xenia, on Cæsar's creek, is a quarry of beautifully variegated marble. The principal productions are wheat, corn, rye, grass, grass seed, oats, barley, sheep and swine. The following is a list of the townships, in 1840, with their population.

Bath,	1717	Miami,	1230	Sugar Creek,	2379
Beaver Creek,	1762	Ross,	1310	Xenia,	5190
Cæsar's Creek,	1730	Silver Creek,	2435		

The population of Greene, in 1820, was 10,509: in 1830, 15,122; and in 1840, 17,753, or 43 inhabitants to a square mile.

The Shawnee town, "*Old Chillicothe*," was on the Little Miami, in this county, about 3 miles north of the site of Xenia: it was a place of note, and is frequently mentioned in the annals of the early explorations and settlements of the west.

In the year 1773, Capt. Thomas Bullit, of Virginia, one of the first settlers of Kentucky, was proceeding down the Ohio river, with a party, to make surveys and a settlement there, when he stopped and left his companions on the river, and passed through the wilderness to Old Chillicothe, to obtain the consent of the Indians to his intended settlement. He entered the town alone, with a flag of truce, before he was discovered. The Indians, astonished at his boldness flocked around him, when the following dialogue ensued between him and a principal chief.

Indian Chief. What news do you bring? are you from the Long Knife? If you are an ambassador, why did you not send a runner?

Bullit. I have no bad news. The Long Knife and the Red men are at peace, and I have come among my brothers to have a friendly talk with them about settling on the other side of the Ohio.

Indian Chief. Why did you not send a runner?

Bullit. I had no runner swifter than myself, and as I was in haste, I could not wait the return of a runner. If you were hungry and had killed a deer, would you send your squaw to town to tell the news, and wait her return before you would eat?

This reply of Bullit put the bystanders in high humor; they relaxed from their native gravity and laughed heartily. The Indians conducted Bullit into the principal wigwam of the town, and regaled him with venison, after which, he addressed the chief as follows:

Brothers:—I am sent with my people, whom I left on the Ohio, to settle the country on the other side of that river, as low down as the falls. We came from Virginia. I only want the country to settle and to cultivate the soil. There will be no objection to your hunting and trapping in it, as heretofore. I hope you will live with us in friendship.

To this address, the principal chief made the following reply.

Brother:—You have come a hard journey through the woods and the grass. We are pleased to find that your people in settling our country, are not to disturb us in our hunting; for we must hunt to kill meat for our women and children, and to have something to buy powder and lead, and procure blankets and other necessaries. We desire you will be strong in discharging your promises towards us, as we are determined to be strong in advising our young men to be kind, friendly and peaceable towards you. Having finished his mission, Capt. Bullit returned to his men, and with them descended the river to the falls.*

Some of this party of Bullit's shortly after laid out the town of Louisville, Kentucky.

The celebrated Daniel Boone was taken prisoner, with 27 others, in Kentucky, in February, 1778, in the war of the revolution, and brought to Old Chillicothe. Through the influence of the British Governor, Hamilton, Boone, with 10 others, was taken from thence to Detroit.

The governor took an especial fancy to Boone, and offered considerable sums for his release, but to no purpose, for the Indians also had taken their fancy, and so great was it that they took him back to Old Chillicothe, adopted him into a family, and fondly caressed him. He mingled with their sports, shot, fished, hunted and swam with them, and had become deeply ingratiated in their favor, when on the 1st of June, they took him to assist them in making salt in the Scioto valley, at the old salt wells, near, or at, we believe, the present town of Jackson, Jackson county. They remained a few days, and when returned to Old Chillicothe, his heart was agonized by the sight of 450 warriors, armed, painted and equipped in all the paraphanalia of savage splendor, ready to start on an expedition against Boonesborough. To avert the cruel blow that was about to fall upon his friends, he alone, on the morning of the 16th of June, escaped from his Indian companions, and arrived in time to foil the plans of the enemy, and not only saved the borough, which he himself had founded, but probably all the frontier parts of Kentucky, from devastation.

Boone told an aged pioneer, yet living,* that when taken prisoner on this occasion, the Indians got out of food, and after having killed and eaten their dogs, were ten days without any other sustenance than that of a decoction made from the oozings of the inner-bark of the white oak, which after drinking, Boone could travel with the best of them. At length, the Indians shot a deer, and boiled its entrails to a jelly, of which they all drank, and it soon acted freely on their bowels. They gave some to Boone, but his stomach refused it. After repeated efforts, they forced him to swallow about half a pint, which he did with wry faces and disagreeable retchings, much to the amusement of the simple savages who laughed heartily. After this medicine had well operated, the Indians told Boone that he might eat; but that if he had done so before, it would have killed him. They then all fell to, and soon made amends for their long fast. At Detroit, he astonished the governor by making gun-powder, he having been shut up in a room with all the materials.

---

* Notes on Kentucky. † Joseph Wood, Esq., of Marietta.

Another early pioneer,* who knew Boone well, says in a communication to us:

It is now (1847) 54 years since I first saw Daniel Boone. He was then about 60 years old, of a medium size, say 5 feet 10 inches, not given to corpulency, retired, unobtrusive, and a man of few words. My acquaintance was made with him in the winter season, and well remember his dress was of tow cloth, and not a woollen garment on his body, unless his stockings were of that material. Home-made was the common wear of the people of Kentucky, at that time: sheep were not yet introduced into the country. I slept four nights in the house of one West, with Boone: there were a number of strangers, and he was constantly occupied in answering questions. He had nothing remarkable in his personal appearance. His son, Capt. N. Boone, now an old man, is serving in the 1st regiment United States Dragoons.

In July, 1779, the year after Boone escaped from Old Chillicothe, Colonel John Bowman, with 160 Kentuckians, marched against the town. The narrative of this expedition is derived from the "Notes on Kentucky."

The party rendezvoused at the mouth of the Licking, and at the end of the second night got in sight of the town undiscovered. It was determined to await until daylight in the morning before they would make the attack; but by the imprudence of some of the men, whose curiosity exceeded their judgment, the party was discovered by the Indians before the officers and men had arrived at the several positions assigned them. As soon as the alarm was given, a fire commenced on both sides, and was kept up, while the women and children were seen running from cabin to cabin, in the greatest confusion, and collecting in the most central and strongest. At clear day-light, it was discovered that Bowman's men were from seventy to one hundred yards from the cabins, in which the Indians had collected, and which they appeared determined to defend. Having no other arms than tomahawks and rifles, it was thought imprudent to attempt to storm strong cabins, well defended by expert warriors. In consequence of the warriors collecting in a few cabins contiguous to each other, the remainder of the town was left unprotected, therefore, while a fire was kept up at the port holes, which engaged the attention of those within, fire was set to 30 or 40 cabins, which were consumed, and a considerable quantity of property, consisting of kettles and blankets, were taken from those cabins. In searching the woods near the town, 133 horses were collected.

About 10 o'clock, Bowman and his party commenced their march homeward, after having nine men killed. What loss the Indians sustained, was never known, except Blackfish, their principal chief, who was wounded through the knee and died of the wound.† After receiving the wound, Blackfish proposed to surrender, being confident that his wound was dangerous, and believing that there were among the white people surgeons that could cure him, but that none among his own people could do it.

The party had not marched more than eight or ten miles on their return home, before the Indians appeared in considerable force on their rear, and began to press hard upon that quarter. Bowman selected his ground, and formed his men in a square; but the Indians declined a close engagement, only keeping up a scattering fire, it was soon discovered that their object was to retard their march until they could procure reinforcements from the neighboring villages.

As soon as a strong position was taken by Col. Bowman, the Indians retired, and he resumed the line of march, when he was again attacked in the rear. He again formed for battle, and again the Indians retired, and the scene was acted over several times. At length, John Bulger, James Harrod and George Michael Bedinger, with about 100 more mounted on horseback, rushed on the Indian ranks and dispersed them in every direction. After which the Indians abandoned the pursuit. Bowman crossed the Ohio at the mouth of the Little Miami, and after crosssing, the men dispersed to their several homes.

In the summer after this expedition, Gen. Clark invaded the In-

* Col. John Johnston.

† This is an error. A late publication gives evidence that he was killed in an excursion into Kentucky, by a white woman.—H. H.

SCENE AT THE OHIO PENITENTIARY, COLUMBUS.

The view was taken within the inner inclosure of the Penitentiary, and shows the manner in which the prisoners march to and from their work. Their shops appear on three sides of the area, while the Prison building bounds it on the fourth.

dian country. On his approach, the Indians reduced Old Chillicothe to ashes. See page 85.

The article relating to early times in Greene county, is slightly abridged from a communication by Thomas C. Wright, Esq., the county auditor.

First Court House in Greene.

After Abdolonymus had been taken from his humble station in life, and made king of Sidonea, it is said he kept a pair of wooden shoes near his throne, to remind him of his former obscurity, and check the pride which power is so apt to engender in the heart of man. The above drawing is deemed worthy of preservation, not only as a memento of early times, and serving as a contrast to the present advanced state of improvement, but on account of the historical associations it raises in the memory of the first judicial proceedings and organization of Greene county.

The house, of which the engraving is a correct representation, is yet standing, 5½ miles west of Xenia, near the Dayton road. It was built by Gen. Benj. Whiteman, a short distance south of the log cabin mill of Owen Davis, on Beaver creek. This mill, the first erected in Greene, was finished in 1798. A short distance east, were erected two block-houses, and it was intended, should danger render it necessary, to connect them by a line of pickets, and include the mill within the stockade. This mill was used by the settlers of "the Dutch Station," some 30 miles distant, in the center of Miami county.

On the 10th of May, 1803, the first court for organizing Greene county, was held in this house, then the residence of Peter Borders. Wm. Maxwell, Benj. Whiteman and James Barret were the associate judges, and John Paul, clerk. The first business of the court was to lay off the county into townships, and after transacting some other business, they adjourned "until court in course," having been in session one day.

The first court for the trial of causes, was held in the same house, on Tuesday, Aug. 2d, 1803, with the same associate judges, and Francis Dunlavy, presiding judge, and Daniel Simms, prosecuting attorney. "And there came a grand jury, to wit: Wm. J. Stewart, foreman, John Willson, Wm. Buckles, Abrm. Van Eaton, James Snodgrass, John Judy, Evan Morgan, Robt. Marshall, Alex. C. Armstrong, Joseph C. Vance, Joseph Willson, John Buckhannon, Martin Mendenhall and Harry Martin, who were sworn a grand jury of inquest, for the body of Greene county." After receiving the charge, "they retired out of court;" a circumstance not to be wondered at, as there was but one room in the house. Their place of retirement, or jury room, was a little squat-shaped pole hut, shown on the right of the view.

And now, while their honors, with becoming gravity, are sitting behind a table ready for business, and the grand jury making solemn inquest of crimes committed, the contrast between the state of the county then and at present, naturally presents itself to the mind. Since then, forty-four years ago—a period within the recollection of many of our citizens—

and what a change! Then it was almost an entire wilderness—a primeval forest, planted by the hand of nature. The first house in Greene county was built by Daniel Willson, who is now living near Centerville, Montgomery county. It was raised on the 7th day of April, 1796, about 4 miles from where Bellbrook has long since been laid out, in Sugarcreek township. In 1798, Thomas Tounsley settled near the falls of Massie's creek, some 8 miles from Xenia. The same year, James Galloway, sen., settled on the Little Miami, 2 miles north of Oldtown. Isaiah and Wm. Garner Sutton erected the first house in Cæsar's creek township, in 1799, about 5 miles south of Xenia, near where the Bullskin road crosses Cæsar's creek. Cæsarsville was laid out by T. Carneal, in 1800, and the first house in it was built the year following. It was expected to become the county seat, but was finally rejected in favor of Xenia. Cæsarsville, at the time of this court, contained a few log cabins, and so scattered about, miles apart, the traveller might find one of these primitive dwellings sending up its smoke from a mud and stick chimney among the giants of the forest, each cabin with a little patch of a corn-field, thickly dotted over with girdled trees. A bridle-path, or blazed trees, led the traveller from one to the other. But they were the abodes of contentment, simplicity of manners, whole-hearted hospitality and generosity of soul, which does honor to human nature and gives a charm to existence. We glance at the county as it now appears, teeming with population, in an advanced state of improvement and cultivation—farm contiguous to farm, with large barns—the hewed log-houses which succeeded log-cabins are mostly gone, and in their stead are commodious brick, stone and frame dwellings—flourishing orchards, numerous excellent mills—the whole county intersected with roads in every direction—a railroad running through it, connecting it with the Queen city, and the same connection will soon be with Lake Erie, affording a speedy transportation to market of the immense quantities of produce raised by the farmers. The change is so great that it brings to mind the wonder-working wand of Prospero, which being waved over a wilderness, had transformed it into a blooming garden. But the magical wand, in this case, was free, white labor, persevering industry and good management.

But to return to the court. From a careful examination of the records and other sources of information, I cannot learn there was any business for the grand jury when they retired. But they were not permitted to remain idle long: the spectators in attendance promptly took the matter into consideration. They, doubtless, thought it a great pity to have a learned court and nothing for it to do: so they set to and cut out employment for their honors by engaging in divers hard fights at fisty-cuffs, right on the ground. So it seems our pioneers fought for the benefit of the court. At all events, while their honors were waiting to settle differences according to law, they were making up issues and settling them by trial "*by combat*"—a process by which they avoided the much complained of "laws delay," and incurred no other damages than black eyes and bloody noses, which were regarded as mere trifles, of course. Among the incidents of the day, characteristic of the times, was this: A Mr. ——, from Warren county, was in attendance. Owen Davis, the owner of the mill, who, by the way, was a brave Indian fighter, as well as a kind-hearted, obliging man, charged this Warren county man with speculating in pork, alias stealing his neighbor's hogs. The insult was resented—a combat took place forthwith, in which Davis proved victorious. He then went into court, and planting himself in front of the judges, he observed, addressing himself particularly to one of them, "Well, Ben, I've whipped that d—d hog-thief—what's the damage—what's to pay? and thereupon, suiting the action to the word, he drew out his buckskin purse, containing 8 or 10 dollars, and slammed it down on the table—then shaking his fist at the judge, whom he addressed, he continued, "Yes, Ben, and if you'd steal a hog, d—n you, I'd whip you too." He had, doubtless, come to the conclusion, that, as there was a court, the luxury of fighting could not be indulged in gratis, and he was for paying up as he went. Seventeen witnesses were sworn and sent before the grand jury, and nine bills of indictment were found the same day—all for affrays and assaults and batteries committed after the court was organized. To these indictments the parties all pleaded guilty, and were fined—Davis among the rest, who was fined eight dollars for his share in the transactions of the day.

The following is the first entry made on the record after the grand jury retired: "The court then proceeded to examine the several candidates for the surveyor's office, and James Galloway, jun., being well qualified, was appointed surveyor of said county." On the 2d day of the term, Joseph C. Vance (father of ex-Gov. Vance, of Champaign county,) was appointed to make the necessary arrangements for establishing the seat of justice, who, with David Huston and Joseph Willson, his securities, entered into a bond, with a penalty of 1500 dollars, for the faithful performance of his duties. He surveyed and laid out the town of Xenia (which, by the way, is an old French word, signifying a new-year's gift,) the same season, for at the next December term, he was allowed "$49.25 for laying off the town of

Xenia, finding chainmen, making plots and selling lots." On the 3d day of the term, Daniel Symmes was allowed twenty dollars for prosecuting in behalf of the state. The presiding judge then left the court, but it was continued by the associate judges for the transaction of county business. In addition to the duties now pertaining to associate judges, they discharged the duties now performed by the board of county commissioners. Archibald Lowry and Griffith Foos, were each licensed to keep a tavern in the town of Springfield, on the payment of eight dollars for each license. A license was also granted to Peter Borders to keep a tavern at his house, on the payment of four dollars, "together with all legal fees." So our old log-house has the honor of having the first learned court held within its rough walls; and, in addition to that, it was, in fact, the first *hotel* ever licensed in the county in which hog and hommony, and new corn whiskey could be had in abundance. Perhaps the court was a little interested in granting the license. Like old Jack Fallstaff, they might like "to take their own ease in their own inn." James Galloway, sen., was appointed county treasurer. The court then adjourned, having been in session three days.

Napoleon said, it was "but one step from the sublime to the ridiculous." Old Faneuil Hall has the proud boast of being the cradle of liberty; and it may be claimed for our old cabin, that it is the cradle of Greene county—in which it was organized—in which was had the first judicial proceedings—whose walls first resounded with the eloquence of those long-robed gentlemen, of whom Martial has satirically said, "*Iras et verba locant.*"

On the 19th day of the same month, (August,) the associate judges held another court for the transaction of county business. They continued to meet and adjourn from day to day, waiting for the lister of taxable property to return his book, until the 22d, when they made an order, that 50 cents should be paid for each wolf killed within the bounds of the county, and "that the largest block-house should be appropriated to the use of a jail;" and Benjamin Whiteman, Esq., was appointed, in behalf of the county, to contract for repairing it—a decisive mark of civilization—and that the rights of *meum* and *tuum* were hereafter to be observed and enforced. Among the allowances, at this term, there was one of 6 dollars to Joseph C. Vance, for carrying the election returns of Sugar creek township to Cincinnati; and a like sum to David Huston, for returning the poll-book of Beaver creek. He afterwards held the office of associate judge 21 years, and twice represented Greene county in the state legislature. He lived the life of an honest man—was beloved and respected by all who knew him. He died in 1843. The clerk and sheriff were allowed 20 dollars each for ex-officio fees, and Jacob Shingledecker, 9 dollars and 50 cents, for preparing the block-house to serve as a jail—a great perversion from the original design of the building, as it was intended, at first, to keep unwelcome visitors out, and ended in keeping unwilling visitors *in*. It was ordered by the court, that the inhabitants of Mad River township should be exempted from the payment of taxes, or rather, their taxes were reduced two cents on each horse and one cent on each cow. The reason assigned for this favor, was "*for erecting public buildings.*" As we have seen no public buildings yet but the two block-houses, and the one which figures at the head of this communication, the reader would, doubtless, be much surprised that the erection of these should be deemed sufficiently meritorious as, in part, to exempt the inhabitants from the payment of taxes. But these public buildings were situated in Cincinnati. We apprehend that but few of our citizens are aware of the fact, that the first settlers in this county contributed to the erection of public buildings in Cincinnati—the old stone court-house, we suppose, which was burnt down while used as barracks in time of the last war, and the hewed log jail which stood on the north side of the public square.

The first supreme court was held in the same house, on the 25th day of October, 1803, by their honors Samuel Huntingdon and Wm. Spriggs, judges; William Maxwell, sheriff, John Paul, clerk, and Arthur St. Clair, Esq., of Cincinnati, prosecuting attorney. Richard Thomas was admitted an attorney and counsellor at law. Nothing more was done, and the court adjourned the same day.

At the November term of the court of common pleas, the first thing was to arraign Thomas Davis, a justice of the peace, for misconduct in office. He pleaded guilty, was fined one dollar, and ordered, in the language of the record, "*to stand committed until performance.*" But what the misconduct was for which he was fined, the record sayeth not; neither is it known whether he raised the dollar, or was made familiar with the inside of the block-house. On the first day of this term, the Rev. Robert Armstrong received a license to solemnize the rites of matrimony. He and the Rev. Andrew Fulton were sent, by the general associate synod of Scotland, as missionaries to Kentucky, and arrived at Maysville in 1798; but, not liking the institution of slavery, Mr. Fulton went to the neighborhood where South Hanover now is, Indiana, and Mr. Armstrong came to Greene county, Ohio. This was the commencement of the Seceder denomination in this county. From this small beginning, it has become the most numerous, perhaps, of any other in the county. They form a large portion of an orderly, law-abiding and industrious population—strict in observing the Sabbath and in the discharge of their religious duties, and correct in moral conduct. They are mostly farmers, in independent circumstances. Mr. Armstrong was a small man, of vast learning, with the simplicity, in some things, of a child. An anecdote is told of his being at a log-rolling, assisting to carry a log, and having but a few inches of handspike, the weight of it rested mostly on him. The person with whom he was lifting, seeing his situation, said, "stop, Mr. Armstrong—let me give you more handspike." "No," said the rev. gentleman, "no more stick for me; I have already as much as I can carry." He was universally esteemed and respected. He died in 1818. He brought a very large library of books with him, and was very liberal in lending them. To this circumstance, perhaps, may be attributed the fact, that more books have been sold and read in this county than in any other of the same population in the state.

At this term, in the case of Wm. Orr vs. Peter Borders, leave was given to amend the declaration, on payment of costs—an indication that some attention began to be paid to special pleading. The first civil case that was tried by a jury, was that of Wallingsford vs. Vandolah. A verdict was rendered for the plaintiff of 24 cents, upon which "he paid the jury and constables fees."

At the December term of the common pleas, four cases of assault and battery were tried by jury, which took up the first day. The day following, this entry was made: William Chipman vs. Henry Storm, "judgment confessed for *one cent* damages and costs." But such is the imperfect manner in which the records were kept, that it is impossible to ascertain what the subject matter of the controversy was in which such heavy damages were admitted. The court decided, that the fee paid to the states' attorney, at the August term, was illegal, and should be refunded. This was the result of "the sober second thoughts" of the court about that twenty dollar fee, for which the attorney came from Cincinnati, more than 50 miles, through the woods, and drew nine bills of indictment and attended to the cases. At this term, Andrew Read, an early settler near where the beautiful village of Fairfield now is, took his seat on the bench as associate judge, to fill the vacancy occasioned by the election of William Maxwell to the office of sheriff. The first view and survey of a new road route was granted at this term. It was to commence at Springfield, pass the Yellow spring and intersect the Pinkney road near Isaac Morgan's. Wm. Maxwell, Lewis Davis, and Thomas Tounsley were appointed viewers, and James Galloway, jun., surveyor. So our fellow-citizen, Maj. Galloway, was the first county surveyor, surveyed the first road by order of the court, and afterwards made a map of the county, in its present metes and bounds, showing all the surveys and sections of the land, with their divisions and subdivisions into tracts. Tavern licenses were granted to Thomas Fream, William Moore, and James M'Pherson, to keep taverns in their houses for one year, and so ended the term.

The June term of 1804, was the last court ever held in the old log house. It was composed of the same judges, clerk and sheriff, with Arthur St. Clair, Esq., of Cincinnati, prosecuting attorney. The writer of this has been informed, he wore a cocked hat and a sword. William M'Farland was foreman of the grand jury. A singular incident took place at the opening of this court. There was a shelf in one corner, consisting of a board on two pins inserted in the wall, containing a few books, among which counsellor St. Clair searched for a bible, on which to swear the jury. At length he took down a volume, and observed, with his peculiar lisp, "Well, gentlemen, here is a book which looks *thist* like a testament." The foreman of the grand jury was accordingly sworn upon it—but the book, which so much resembled a testament in external appearance, turned out, in fact, to be an odd volume of The Arabian Nights Entertainment!! From this mistake, or some unknown cause, the practice of swearing on the Evangelists, has gone entirely out of use in this county, being substituted by swearing with the uplifted hand, or affirming. The grand jury found several bills of indictment, and were discharged the same day.

In proportion as cases of assault and battery begin to decrease, a sprinkling of civil suits make their appearance on the docket. Fourteen cases were called the first day, and all continued, except one, in which judgment was confessed, and stay of execution granted until next term. The entry of continuance was in this form: A. B. *vs.* C. D. E. F. and G. H. pledges for the defendant in the sum $——. This form was observed in all cases, the amount being more or less, according to the subject matter in controversy. On Wednesday of this term, Joseph Tatman produced his commission as associate judge, and took the oath of office. He afterwards, in 1816, in company with Samuel and William Casad, laid out the town of Fairfield, not far from the site of an old Indian town, named Piqua, at which Gen. George R. Clark defeated the Indians, in 1780. On this day, 22 cases were called: 11 continued, 2 settled, 1 judgment, 5 ruled for plea in 40 days, one in

10 days, 1 discontinued and 1 abated by death. This was certainly a pretty fair beginning, and quite encouraging to the learned profession.

The total amount of taxable property returned by the "listers," was $393.04, and this levy included houses and mills, if any. As to houses, there was but one returned, and that was valued for taxation at *one dollar!* Considering the sparseness of population, and small amount of property in the county, the proportion of litigation was greater then, than at this time, 1847, when the total amount of taxable property is $6,583,673. So much of a change in 43 years. They fought less and lawed more. In newly settled counties, there appears to be a peculiar fondness among the people for lawsuits. After a court has been organized in a new county, they still continue to settle their difficulties by combat, until fines become troublesome. The court then becomes the arena in which their contentions and quarrels are carried and finally disposed of. If one cannot afford the fine or imprisonment which would be incurred, by taking personal satisfaction, he can bring a suit, if any cause of action can be found, and no matter how small the amount claimed, or frivolous the matter, if he can only cast his adversary and throw him in the costs, he is as much gratified as if he had made him halloa "enough—take him off." It is this spirit which gives rise to so many trifling and vexatious law suits.

And now we take leave of our primitive dwelling house, court house and tavern. It is still standing, and occupied as a residence. While our drawing was being taken, an old-fashioned long-handled frying-pan was over the fire—its spacious bottom well paved with rashers of ham, sending forth a savory odor, enough to make a hungry persons' mouth water. What scenes it has witnessed—what memories it recalls. It has witnessed the organization of the county—the first administration of law and justice—the first exercise of the right of suffrage through the ballot-box, and the first legal punishment of criminals. Near it the first corn was ground into meal for the use of the settlers, and here they rallied to build block-houses to protect them from the hostile attacks of the Indians. As a tavern many a weary traveller, through the tall and lonely forest, has been sheltered and refreshed beneath its humble roof. How many buckeye lads and lasses have been reared within its walls—for

"Buirdly chiels and clever hizzies
Are bred in sic a way as this is!"

How many jovial dances have been had on its puncheon floor. While we may suppose some lame or lazy fellow seated on a stool in a corner, prepared with an awl or Barlow knife, to extract splinters from the heels of the dancers, as fast as the sets were over. How many courtships have been carried on during the long winter nights—the old folks asleep, and the young lovers comfortably toasting their shins over the decaying embers—happy in present love, and indulging in bright anticipations of housekeeping in a cabin.

Long mayest thou stand, old relic, as a memento of pioneer life, primitive simplicity and good old-fashioned honesty, to remind the rising generation of the hardships and privations our pioneer fathers encountered, in first settling the county, and to show by this humble beginning, compared with the present state of improvement, how much honest labor, pains-taking industry and thrifty management can accomplish.

Xenia, the county seat, is on the Little Miami railroad, 64 miles north of Cincinnati, and 61 from Columbus. It is a handsome, flourishing and well-built town, with broad streets, and some fine stores and elegant dwellings. The engraving represents a part of the principal street: the court house, shown on the left, is the most elegant, as yet built, in Ohio.

Xenia was laid off in the forest, in the autumn of 1803, by Joseph C. Vance, on the land of John Paul, who gave the ground bounded by Main, Market, Detroit and Greene streets, for the public buildings. The first cabin was erected in April, 1804, by John Marshall, in the southwest corner of the town. The first good hewed log house was erected for the Rev. James Fowler, of the Methodist persuasion, from Petersburg, Va.: it is still standing, and is now the hatter's shop, a short distance west of the old bank. David A.

Sanders built the first frame house, on the spot occupied by the new bank: it is yet standing, on Main street, in Gowdy's addition.

View in Xenia.

The first supreme court was held Oct. 3d, 1804. The grand jury held their deliberations under a sugar tree, in the rear of the present residence of James Gowdy.

The first court of common pleas in Xenia, was on the 15th of November, 1804, and was held by the associate judges. A license was granted to "William A. Beatty, to keep a tavern in the town of Xenia for one year, on the payment of $8.00!" This was the first tavern ever licensed in the place. It was a double hewed log house, two stories high, and was in progress of erection at the same time with Fowler's house. It stood on the south side of Main street, opposite the public square, on the spot where there now is a two story brick house, occupied as a drug store. In the west room, above stairs, the court was held. The first election in the place was held in this house. It continued to be a tavern until after the last war with Great Britain, and, until Mr. James Collier built his brick tavern on Detroit street, was the *grand hotel* of the place. In a corner of the west room, there was an old-fashioned bar—the upper part enclosed with upright slats of wood, with a little wicket, through which the grog was handed out in half pint glass cruets. In time of the war, the recruiting officers put up at this house; and here might be seen the recruiting sergeant rattling dollars on a drum's head, and calling for half pints, appealing to the patriotism of the bystanders, tempting them with gingling dollars, and adding thereto the potency of whiskey, to enlist recruits for the army. Court continued to be held in this house for the years 1804 and 1805, and until a new court house was built.

In 1804, the building of the first jail was let to Amos Darough; it was received from the contractor in October. It stood on ground now covered by the new court house, and was constructed of hewed logs. It was burnt down the year following; and in April, 1806, a new jail was accepted from William A. Beatty. It stood on the site of the present market house—was a rough log building; two stories high, with a cabin roof, and was burnt down in time of the war with England. The building of the first court house was let on the 8th day of April, 1806, to William Kendall, who was allowed six dollars for clearing the timber from the public square. The house was built of brick, 40 feet square and 28 feet high, with a cupola in the center of the roof, 10 feet in diameter and 15 feet high. It was finished, and on the 14th day of August, 1809, accepted.

On the 6th of April. 1806, "a license was granted to James Gowdy, for retailing merchandise, on his complying with the law!" He opened his goods in a log house, with a mud and stick chimney, which stood on Greene street, at the north end of where Mr. John Ewing's store now is. He was the first merchant in the place.

The first punishment for crime was in 1806. The person was convicted for stealing leather, to half-sole a pair of shoes. There was a sugar tree on the public square, which served as a whipping-post. He was tied up to the tree, and underwent the sentence of the court, which was to receive ***one stripe*** on his bare back, which was inflicted by James Collier. The sugar tree served as a whipping-post for the last time on the 8th of October, 1808. A man was convicted for stealing a shovel-plow and clevis, and the sentence was that he should receive eight lashes on his bare back, "and stand committed until performance." He drank a pint of whiskey just before hugging the tree, though it did not prevent him from halloaing lustily, while receiving the eight stripes.*

Xenia contains 1 German Lutheran, 1 Methodist Episcopal, 1 Methodist Protestant, 1 Seceder, 1 Associate Reformed and 1 Baptist church, beside 2 churches for colored persons—two church edifices are erecting, one by the Presbyterian and the other by the Associate Reformed denomination—17 mercantile stores, 1 foundery, 2 newspaper printing offices, 1 bank, a classical academy in fine repute, and in 1840, had 1414 inhabitants, and in 1847, about 2800.

JOSIAH HUNT resided in this county in the time of the last war with Great Britain. He was a stout, well-formed, heavy-set man, capable of enduring great hardships and privations, and was then a member of the Methodist Episcopal church. There was a tone of candor and sincerity, as well as modesty, in his manner of relating the thrilling scenes in which he had been an actor, which left no doubt of their truth in the minds of those who heard him. He was one of Wayne's legion, and was in the battle of the Fallen Timber, on the 20th of August, 1794.

At the commencement of the onset, just after entering the fallen timber, Hunt was rushing on, and about to spring over a fallen tree, when he was fired at by an Indian, concealed behind it. The latter was compelled to fire in such haste that he missed his aim. It was, however, a close shave, for the bullet whizzed through the lock of his right temple, causing that ear to ring for an hour after. The Indian's body was entirely naked from the waist up, with a red stripe painted up and down his back. As soon as he fired, he took to his heels. Hunt aimed at the center of the red stripe, the Indian running zig-zag "like the worm of a fence." When he fired the Indian bounded up and fell forward. He had fought his last battle.

He was an excellent hunter. In the winter of 1793, while the army lay at Greenville, he was employed to supply the officers with game, and in consequence was exempted from garrison duty. The sentinels had orders to permit him to leave and enter the fort whenever he chose. The Indians made a practice of climbing trees in the vicinity of the fort, the better to watch the garrison. If a person was seen to go out, notice was taken of the direction he went, his path ambushed and his scalp secured. To avoid this danger, Hunt always left the fort in the darkness of night, for said he, "when once I had got into the woods without their knowledge, I had as good a chance as they." He was accustomed, on leaving the fort, to proceed some distance in the direction he intended to hunt the next day, and bivauck for the night. To keep from freezing to death, it was necessary to have a fire; but to show a light in the enemy's country, was to invite certain destruction. To avoid this danger he dug a hole in the ground with his tomahawk, about the size and depth of a hat crown. Having prepared it properly, he procured some "*roth*," meaning thick white oak bark, from a dead tree, which will retain a strong heat when covered with its ashes. Kindling a fire from flint and steel at the bottom of his "coal pit," as he termed it, the bark was severed into strips and placed in layers crosswise, until the pit was full. After it was sufficiently ignited, it was covered over with dirt, with the exception of two air holes in the margin, which could be opened or closed at pleasure. Spreading down a layer of bark or brush to keep him off the cold ground, he set down with the "coal pit" between his legs, enveloped himself in his blanket, and slept cat-dozes in an upright position. If his fire became too much smothered, he would freshen it up by blowing into one of the air holes. He declared he could make himself sweat whenever he chose. The snapping of a dry twig was sufficient to awaken him, when uncovering his head, he keenly scrutinized in the darkness and gloom around—his right hand on his trusty rifle "ready for the mischance of the hour." A person now, in full security from danger, enjoying the comforts and refinements of civilized life, can scarcely bring his mind to realize his situation, or do justice to the powers of bodily endurance, firmness of nerve, self-reliance and

* From Thomas Coke Wright.

courage, manifested by him that winter. A lone man in a dreary interminable forest, swarming with enemies, blood-thirsty, crafty and of horrid barbarity, without a friend or human being to afford him the least aid, in the depth of winter, the freezing winds moaning through the bare and leafless branches of the tall trees, while the dismal howling of a pack of wolves—

> "Cruel as death, and hungry as the grave;
> Burning for blood, bony, gaunt and grim,"

might be heard in the distance, mingled with the howlings of the wintry winds, were well calculated to create a lonely sensation about the heart and appal any common spirit. There would he sit, nodding in his blanket, undistinguishable in the darkness from an old stump, enduring the rigor of winter, keeping himself from freezing, yet showing no fire,—calm, ready and prompt to engage in mortal combat, with whatever enemy might assail, whether Indian, bear or panther. At day-light he commenced hunting, proceeding slowly and with extreme caution, looking for game and watching for Indians at the same time. When he found a deer, previously to shooting it, he put a bullet in his mouth, ready for reloading his gun with all possible dispatch, which he did before moving from the spot, casting searching glances in every direction for Indians. Cautiously approaching the deer, after he had shot it, he dragged it to a tree and commenced the process of skinning with his back towards the tree, and his rifle leaning against it, in reach of his right hand. And so with his rear protected by the tree, he would skin a short time, then straighten up and scan in every direction, to see if the report of his rifle had brought an Indian in his vicinity, then apply himself to skinning again. If he heard a stick break, or any—the slightest noise indicating the proximity of animal life, he clutched his rifle instantly, and was on the alert prepared for any emergency. Having skinned and cut up the animal, the four-quarters were packed in the hide, which was so arranged as to be slung to his back like a knapsack, with which he wended his way to the fort. If the deer was killed far from the garrison, he only brought in the fore-quarters. One day he got within gun-shot of three Indians unperceived by them. He was on a ridge and they in a hollow. He took aim at the foremost one, and waited some time for a chance for two to range against each other, intending, if they got in that position, to shoot two and take his chance with the other in single combat. But they continued marching in Indian file, and though he could have killed either of them, the other two would have made the odds againts him too great, so he let them pass unmolested. Amidst all the danger to which he was constantly exposed, he passed unharmed.

Owing to the constant and powerful exercise of the faculties, his ability to hear and discriminate sounds was wonderfully increased, and the perceptive faculties much enlarged. He made $70 that winter by hunting, over and above his pay as a soldier.

At the treaty at Greenville, in 1795, the Indians seemed to consider Hunt as the next greatest man to Wayne himself. They inquired for him, got round him, and were loud and earnest in their praises and compliments: "Great man, Capt. Hunt—great warrior—good hunting man; Indian no can kill!" They informed him that some of their bravest and most cunning warriors, had often set out expressly to kill him. They knew how he made his secret camp-fires, the ingenuity of which excited their admiration. The parties in quest of him had often seen him—could describe the dress he wore, and his cap, which was made of a raccoon's skin with the tail hanging down behind, the front turned up and ornamented with three brass rings. The scalp of such a great hunter and warrior they considered to be an invaluable trophy. Yet they never could catch him off his guard—never get within shooting distance, without being discovered and exposed to his death-dealing rifle.

Many years ago he went to Indiana, nor has the writer* of this ever heard from him since, nor is it known among his old friends here, whether he is living.

Nine miles north of Xenia, on the Little Miami river and railroad, are the Yellow Springs. It has been fitted up as a place of fashionable resort. The improvements, consisting of a hotel and numerous cottages, are in a picturesque situation. "The springs are strongly impregnated with sulphur and possess medicinal qualities, deemed equal in utility to any in the United States." The Duke of Saxe Weimer says in his Travels:

The spring originates in a limestone rock, the water has a little taste of iron, and de-

---

* Thomas Coke Wright.

posites a great quantity of ochre, from which it takes its name. The spring is said to give 110 gallons of water per minute, which is received in a basin surrounded with cedar trees. The yellow stream which comes from the basin, runs a short distance over a bed of limestone and is afterwards precipitated into the valley. These limestone rocks form very singular figures on the edge of this valley; the detached pieces resemble the Devil's Wall of the Hartz.

Clifton is a flourishing manufacturing village, 10 miles north of Xenia, on the Little Miami, and contains 2 churches, 3 stores, 1 cotton and woollen factory, 1 paper, 1 grist and 1 saw mill, and over 300 inhabitants. The name originated from the cliffs which bound the river at this place. The stream commences running through a deep ravine at the eastern extremity of the village, and after circling around the town, leaves it on the southwest. For more than two miles it runs through a deep and narrow gorge, bounded by perpendicular and impending rocks, overhung by evergreens, and presenting scenery of a wild and picturesque character. In this distance the stream is estimated, in an ordinary stage of water, to afford sufficient power for one hundred and five pair of burr stones. The mills and factories above mentioned are upon it, and the woollen and cotton factory is built in the ravine and extends completely across it. The view given, was taken a short distance below this building, and shows a little water-fall on the northern wall of the bounding cliffs, at that point about 50 feet high.

Cascade at Clifton.

Fairfield, 12 miles northwest of Xenia, on the Dayton and Springfield turnpike, is a smart business place, in a rich country. It contains 4 churches, 5 stores and about 400 inhabitants. Bellbrook, 9 southwest of Xenia, has 3 stores, 4 churches and about 350 inhabitants. Jamestown, 11 east of Xenia, on the Dayton, Xenia and Washington turnpike, has 8 stores, 3 churches and 50 dwellings. Spring Valley, 7 southwest of Xenia, is a small manufacturing village, at which is a woollen factory, 1 oil, 1 grist and 1 carding mill.

Cedarville, on Massie's creek, 8 miles from Xenia, has 3 stores and churches, and about 300 inhabitants. Burlington and Paintersville are small places. On Massie's creek, 7 miles northeast of Xenia, is an ancient stone fort and a mound.

GUERNSEY.

Guernsey was organized in March, 1810. The upland is hilly and of various qualities, and the soil clay or clayey loam. There is much excellent land in the bottom of Wills' creek and its branches, which cover about one third of the county. The principal crops are wheat, corn and tobacco. Wool is a staple product of the county, together with beef cattle, horses and swine. The following is a list of its townships in 1840, with their population.

Adams,	866	Knox,	538	Richland,	1772
Beaver,	1686	Liberty,	835	Seneca,	1356
Buffalo,	1025	Londonderry,	1629	Spencer,	1669
Cambridge,	2033	Madison,	1569	Washington,	1008
Center,	976	Millwood,	1722	Westland,	1077
Jackson,	1155	Monroe,	1098	Wheeling,	769
Jefferson,	755	Oxford,	2133	Wills,	1887

The population of Guernsey in 1820, was 9,292; in 1830, 18,036; and in 1840, 27,729, or 45 inhabitants to the square mile.

Previous to the first settlement of the county, there was a party of whites attacked by Indians on Wills' creek, near the site of Cambridge. The particulars which follow are from the pen of Col. John M'Donald, author of the Biographical Sketches.

In the year 1791 or '92, the Indians having made frequent incursions into the settlements, along the Ohio river, between Wheeling and the Mingo bottom, sometimes killing or capturing whole families; at other times stealing all the horses belonging to a station or fort, a company consisting of seven men, rendezvoused at a place called the Beech bottom, on the Ohio river, a few miles below where Wellsburg has been erected. This company were John Whetzel, William M'Collough, John Hough, Thomas Biggs, Joseph Hedges, Kinzie Dickerson, and a Mr. Linn. Their avowed object was to go to the Indian towns to steal horses. This was then considered a legal, honorable business, as we were then at open war with the Indians. It would only be retaliating upon them in their own way. These seven men were all trained to Indian warfare, and a life in the woods from their youth. Perhaps the western frontier, at no time, could furnish seven men whose souls were better fitted, and whose nerves and sinews were better strung to perform any enterprise which required resolution and firmness. They crossed the Ohio, and proceeded with cautious steps, and vigilant glances on their way through the cheerless, dark, and almost impervious forest, in the Indian country, till they came to an Indian town, near where the head waters of the Sandusky and Muskingum rivers interlock. Here they made a fine haul, and set off homeward with fifteen horses. They travelled rapidly, only making short halts, to let their horses graze, and breathe a short time to recruit their strength and activity. In the evening of the second day of their rapid retreat, they arrived at Wills creek, not far from where the town of Cambridge has been since erected. Here Mr. Linn was taken violently sick, and they must stop their march, or leave him alone, to perish in the dark and lonely woods. Our frontier men, notwithstanding their rough and unpolished manners, had too much of my Uncle Toby's "sympathy for suffering humanity," to forsake a comrade in distress. They halted, and placed sentinels on their back trail, who remained there till late in the night, without seeing any signs of being pursued. The sentinels on the back trail returned to the camp, Mr. Linn still lying in excruciating pain. All the simple remedies in their power were administered to the sick man, without producing any effect. Being late in the night, they all lay down to rest, except one who was placed as guard. Their camp was on the bank of a small branch. Just before day-break the guard took a small bucket, and dipped some water out of the stream ; on carrying it to the fire he discovered the water to be muddy. The muddy water waked his suspicion that the enemy might be approaching them, and were walking down in the stream, as their footsteps would be noiseless in the water. He waked his companions, and communicated his suspicion. They arose, examined the branch a little distance, and listened attentively for some time ; but neither saw nor heard any thing, and then concluded it must have been raccoons, or some other animals, puddling in the stream. After this conclusion the company all lay down to rest, except the sentinel, who was stationed just outside of the light. Happily for them the fire had burned down, and only a few coals afforded a dim light to point out where they lay. The enemy had come silently down the creek, as the sentinel suspected, to within ten or twelve feet of the place where they lay, and fired several guns over the bank. Mr. Linn, the sick man, was lying with his side towards the bank, and received nearly all the balls which were at first fired. The Indians then, with tremendous yells, mounted the bank with loaded rifles, war-clubs and tomahawks, rushed upon our men, who fled barefooted and without arms. Mr. Linn, Thomas Biggs and Joseph Hedges were killed in and near the camp. William M'Collough had run but a short distance when he was fired at by the enemy. At the instant the fire was given, he jumped into a quagmire and fell ; the Indians supposing that they killed him, ran past in pursuit of others. He soon extricated himself out of the mire, and so made his escape. He fell in with John Hough, and came into Wheeling. John Whetzel and Kinzie Dickerson met in their retreat, and returned together. Those who made their escape were without arms, without clothing or provision. Their sufferings were great ; but this they bore with stoical indifference, as it was the fortune of war. Whether the Indians who defeated our heroes followed in pursuit from their towns, or were a party of warriors, who accidentally happened to fall in with them, has never been ascertained. From the place they had stolen the horses, they had travelled two nights and almost two entire days, without halting, except just a few minutes at a time, to let the horses graze. From the circumstance of their rapid retreat with the horses, it was supposed that no pursuit could possibly have overtaken them, but that fate had decreed that this party of Indians should meet and defeat them. As soon as the stragglers arrived at Wheeling, Capt. John M'Collough collected a party of men, and went to Wills creek, and buried the unfortunate men who fell in and near the camp. The Indians had mangled the dead bodies at a most barbarous rate. Thus was closed the horse stealing tragedy.

Of the four who survived this tragedy, none are now living to tell the story of their suffering. They continued to hunt and to fight as long as the war lasted. John Whetzel and Dickerson died in the country near Wheeling.* John Hough died a few years since, near Columbia, Hamilton county, Ohio. The brave Capt. William M'Collough, fell in 1812, in the battle of Brownstown, in the campaign with Gen. Hull.

Cambridge, the county seat, is on the national road, 77 miles east of Columbus and 24 east of Zanesville. It is a flourishing village and contains 1 Presbyterian, 1 Seceder, 1 Methodist Episcopal and 1 Reformed Methodist church, an academy, 9 mercantile stores, 2 carding machines, 1 flouring and 2 fulling mills, 1 newspaper printing office and about 1000 inhabitants. The view represents the town as it appears from a hill on the west, about 300 yards north of the national road : the bridge across Wills creek is shown on the right, and the town on the hill in the distance.

In 1798, soon after "Zane's trace" was cut through the county, a Mr. Graham made the first settlement on the site of Cambridge. At this time, the only dwelling between Lancaster and Wheeling was at Zanesville. He remained about two years, and was succeeded by George Beymer, from Somerset, Pennsylvania. Both of these persons kept a house of entertainment, and a ferry for travellers on their way to Kentucky and other parts of the west. Mr. Beymer, in April, 1803, gave up his tavern to Mr John Beatty, who moved in from Loudon county, Virginia. Mr. Wyatt Hutchinson, who, until recently, kept a tavern in this town, was a member of Beatty's family, which consisted of eleven persons. The Indians then hunted in this

Cambridge, from the hill west.

vicinity, and often encamped on the creek. In June, 1806, Cambridge was laid out; and on the day the lots were first offered for sale, several families from the British isle of Guernsey, near the coast of France, stopped here and purchased lands. These were followed by other families, amounting in all to some fifteen or twenty, from the same island; all of whom settling in the county, gave origin to its present name. Among the heads of these families, are recollected the names of Wm. Ogier, Thos. Naftel, Thos. Lanphesty, James Bishard, Chas. and John Marquand, John Robbins, Daniel Ferbroch, Peter, Thomas and John Sarchet, and Daniel Hubert.

Washington is 8 miles east of Cambridge, on the national road. It is a very thriving village, and does an extensive business with the surrounding country, which is very fertile. It has 1 Lutheran, 1 Presbyterian, 1 Methodist, 1 Union and 1 Catholic church—the last of which is an elegant and costly gothic edifice; 6 mercantile stores, 1 woollen factory, and a population nearly equal to Cambridge. It was laid out about the year 1805, by Simon Beymer, proprietor of the soil, and a native of Cumberland county, Pennsylvania. There were two companies raised in this county, and which entered into service, in the war with Great Britain—one of which was commanded by Simon Beymer, and the other by Cyrus P. Beatty. The first cannel coal found in this country was discovered several years since, five miles west of Cambridge, near Wills creek. This bituminous coal does not materially differ from the common slaty coal of the country; it contains rather more bituminous and less carbonaceous matter.*

* See communication of Hon. Benj. Tappan, in the 28th, and that of Dr. S. P. Hildreth, in the 29th volume of Silliman's Journal.

Middletown, 14 miles east of Cambridge, on the national road, has 4 stores, two or three churches and about 250 inhabitants. On and about the Salt fork in this vicinity, there were twelve or fifteen families settled about the year 1803: the names recollected are Hite, Burns, Cary, Smith, Masters, Hall, Wilson and Warren. Fairview, 6 miles east of the above, on the national road, is a larger town, containing several churches and stores and about 425 inhabitants. Senecaville, 10 miles southeast of Cambridge, is a flourishing town, containing several churches and stores, and about 300 inhabitants. Cumberland, Claysville, Williamsburg, Mount Ephraim, Liberty, Winchester, Londonderry, Birmingham and Antrim, are villages, the largest of which may contain 70 dwellings. At Antrim is Madison College, which has 40 pupils: at Cambridge is a high school, a female seminary and a printing office.

HAMILTON.

HAMILTON was the second county established in the N. W. territory. It was formed Jan. 2d, 1790, by proclamation of Governor St. Clair, and named from Gen. Alex. Hamilton. Its original boundaries were thus defined: "Beginning on the Ohio river, at the confluence of the Little Miami, and down the said Ohio to the mouth of the Big Miami; and up said Miami to the standing stone forks or branch of said river, and thence with a line to be drawn due east to the Little Miami, and down said Little Miami river to the place of beginning." The surface is generally rolling, soil on the uplands, clay, and in the river and creek vallies, deep alluvion, with a sub-stratum of sand. The agricultural productions are more varied than any other county in the state; beside the ordinary farm products of wheat, corn, rye, barley, oats and grass, there is produced a great variety of fruits and vegetables for the Cincinnati market. Much attention has been given of late to the cultivation of vineyards upon the Ohio river hills, for the manufacture of wine, and it promises to be a business of great extent in the course of a few years. The following is a list of its townships in 1840, with their population.

Anderson,	2311	Fulton,	1505	Storrs,	740
Colerain,	2272	Green,	2939	Sycamore,	3207
Columbia,	3022	Miami,	2189	Symmes,	1033
Crosby,	1875	Mill Creek,	6249	Whitewater,	1883
Delphi,	1466	Springfield,	3092	CINCINNATI, (CITY,)	46382

The population of Hamilton, in 1820, was 31,764, in 1830, 52,380, and in 1840, 80,165, or, omitting the city of Cincinnati, 79 persons to the square mile.

This county was the second settled in Ohio, and the first within Symmes' purchase. The history of its settlement we append from Burnet's Notes.

Soon after the settlement was commenced at Marietta, three parties were formed to occupy and improve separate portions of Judge Symmes' purchase, between the Miami rivers. The first, led by Major Benjamin Stites, consisted of eighteen or twenty, who landed in November, 1788, at the mouth of the Little Miami river, within the limits of a tract of ten thousand acres, purchased by Major Stites from Judge Symmes. They constructed a log fort, and laid out the town of Columbia, which soon became a promising village. Among them were Colonel Spencer, Major Gano, Judge Goforth, Francis Dunlavy, Major Kibbey, Rev. John Smith, Judge Foster, Colonel Brown, Mr. Hubbell, Captain Flinn, Jacob White and John Riley.

They were all men of energy and enterprise, and were more numerous than either of the parties who commenced their settlements below them on the Ohio. Their village was also more flourishing, and for two or three years contained a larger number of inhabitants than any other in the Miami purchase. This superiority, however, did not continue, as will appear from the sequel.

The second party destined for the Miami, was formed at Limestone, under Matthias Denman and Robert Patterson, amounting to twelve or fifteen in number. After much difficulty and danger, caused by floating ice in the river, they landed on the north bank of the Ohio, opposite the mouth of Licking, on the 24th of December, 1788. Their purpose was to establish a station, and lay out a town according to a plan agreed on, before they left Limestone. The name adopted for the proposed town was Losanteville, which had been manufactured by a pedantic foreigner, whose name, fortunately, has been forgotten. It was formed, as he said, from the words *Le os ante ville*, which he rendered "the village opposite the mouth." Logicians may decide whether the words might not be rendered more correctly, the mouth before the village. Be that as it may, the settlement then formed was immediately designated by the name adopted for the projected town—though the town itself never was laid out, for reasons which will be explained hereafter. Yet, from the facts stated, a very general belief has prevailed that the original name of the town of Cincinnati was Losanteville, and that through the influence of Gov. St. Clair and others, that name was abandoned, and the name of Cincinnati substituted. This impression, though a natural one, under the circumstances of the case, was nevertheless incorrect.

It is impossible to say what influence operated on the minds of the proprietors, to induce them to adopt the name of Cincinnati, in preference to the one previously proposed. Judge Symmes, being on the spot, might have advised it; but it is not probable that Gov. St. Clair had agency in it, as he was at the time negotiating a treaty with the north-western Indians, at Marietta, between which place and Cincinnati, there was then but very little intercourse. The truth may be gathered from the facts of the case, which are these.

Matthias Denman, of Springfield, New Jersey, had purchased the fraction of land on the bank of the Ohio, and the entire section adjoining it on the north, which, on the survey of Symmes' grant should be found to lie opposite the mouth of Licking river. In the summer of 1788, he came out to the west to see the lands he had purchased, and to examine the country. On his return to Limestone, he met among others, Col. Patterson, of Lexington, and a surveyor by the name of Filson. Denman communicated to them his intention of laying out a town on his land, opposite Licking; and, after some conversation, agreed to take them in as partners, each paying a third of the purchase-money; and, on the further condition, that Col. Patterson should exert his influence to obtain settlers, and that Filson, in the ensuing spring, should survey the town, stake off the lots, and superintend the sale. They also agreed on the plan of the town, and to call it Losanteville. This being done, Patterson and Filson, with a party of settlers, proceeded to the ground, where they arrived late in December. In the course of the winter, before any attempt had been made to lay out the town, Filson went on an exploring expedition with Judge Symmes and others, who had in contemplation to become purchasers and settle in the country. After the party had proceeded some thirty or forty miles into the wilderness, Filson, for some cause not now known, left them, for the purpose of returning to the settlements on the Ohio; and in that attempt was murdered by the Indians. This terminated his contract with Denman, as no part of the consideration had been paid, and his personal services, in surveying the town and superintending the sale of the lots, had become impracticable.

Mr. Denman, being yet at Limestone, entered into another contract with Col. Patterson and Israel Ludlow, by which Ludlow was to perform the same services as were to have been rendered by the unfortunate Filson, had he lived to execute his contract. A new plan of a town was then made, differing, in many important respects, from the former,—particularly as to the public square, the commons, and the names of the streets. The whimsical name which had been adopted for the town to be laid out under the first contract, was repudiated, and Cincinnati selected, as the name of the town, to be laid out under the new contract. Late in the succeeding fall, Col. Ludlow commenced a survey of the town which has since become the Queen City of the West. He first laid off the lots, which, by previous agreement, were to be disposed of as donations to volunteer settlers, and completed the survey at his leisure.

A misapprehension has prevailed, as appears from some recent publications, in regard to the price paid by the proprietors for the land on which the city stands. The original purchase by Mr. Denman, included a section and a fractional section, containing about eight hundred acres; for which he paid five shillings per acre, in continental certificates, which were then worth, in specie, five shillings on the pound—so that the specie price per acre was fifteen pence. That sum multiplied by the number of acres, will give the original cost of the plat of Cincinnati.

The third party of adventurers to the Miami purchase, were under the immediate care and direction of Judge Symmes. They left Limestone on the 29th of January, 1789, and on their passage down the river, were obstructed, delayed, and exposed to imminent danger from floating ice, which covered the river. They, however, reached the Bend, the place of their destination, in safety, early in February. The first object of the Judge was to found a city at that place, which had received the name of North Bend, from the fact that it was the most northern bend in the Ohio river below the mouth of the Great Kanawha.

The water-craft used in descending the Ohio, in those primitive times, were flat-boats made of green oak plank, fastened by wooden pins to a frame of timber, and caulked with tow, or any other pliant substance that could be procured. Boats similarly constructed on the northern waters, were then called *arks*, but on the western rivers, they were denominated *Kentucky boats*. The materials of which they were composed, were found to be of great utility in the construction of temporary buildings for safety, and for protection from the inclemency of the weather, after they had arrived at their destination.

At the earnest solicitation of the Judge, General Harmar sent Captain Kearsey with forty-eight rank and file, to protect the improvements just commencing in the Miami country. This detachment reached Limestone in December, 1788, and in a few days after, Captain Kearsey sent a part of his command in advance, as a guard to protect the pioneers under Major Stites, at the Little Miami, where they arrived soon after. Mr. Symmes and his party, accompanied by Captain Kearsey, landed at Columbia, on their passage down the river, and the detachment previously sent to that place joined their company. They then proceeded to the Bend, and landed about the first or second of February. When they left Limestone, it was the purpose of Captain Kearsey to occupy the fort built at the mouth of the Miami, by a detachment of United States troops, who afterwards descended the river to the falls.

That purpose was defeated by the flood in the river, which had spread over the low grounds and rendered it difficult to reach the fort. Captain Kearsey, however, was anxious to make the attempt, but the Judge would not consent to it; he was of course much disappointed, and greatly displeased. When he set out on the expedition, expecting to find a fort ready built to receive him, he did not provide the implements necessary to construct one. Thus disappointed and displeased, he resolved that he would not attempt to construct a new work, but would leave the Bend and join the garrison at Louisville.

In pursuance of that resolution, he embarked early in March, and descended the river with his command. The Judge immediately wrote to Major Willis, commandant of the garrison at the Falls, complaining of the conduct of Captain Kearsey, representing the exposed situation of the Miami settlement, stating the indications of hostility manifested by the Indians, and requesting a guard to be sent to the Bend. This request was promptly granted, and before the close of the month, Ensign Luce arrived with seventeen or eighteen soldiers, which, for the time, removed the apprehensions of the pioneers at that place. It was not long, however, before the Indians made an attack on them, in which they killed one soldier, and wounded four or five other persons, including Major J. R. Mills, an emigrant from Elizabethtown, New Jersey, who was a surveyor, and an intelligent and highly respected citizen. Although he recovered from his wounds, he felt their disabling effects to the day of his death.

The surface of the ground where the Judge and his party had landed, was above the reach of the water, and sufficiently level to admit of a convenient settlement. He therefore determined, for the immediate accommodation of his party, to lay out a village at that place, and to suspend, for the present, the execution of his purpose, as to the city, of which he had given notice, until satisfactory information could be obtained in regard to the comparative advantages of different places in the vicinity. The determination, however, of laying out such a city, was not abandoned, but was executed in the succeeding year on a magnificent scale. It included the village, and extended from the Ohio across the peninsular to the Miami river. This city, which was certainly a beautiful one, on paper, was called Symmes, and for a time was a subject of conversation and of criticism; but it soon ceased to be remembered—even its name was forgotten, and the settlement continued to be called North Bend. Since then, that village has been distinguished as the residence and the home of the soldier and statesman, William Henry Harrison, whose remains now repose in a humble vault on one of its beautiful hills.

In conformity with a stipulation made at Limestone, every individual belonging to the party received a donation lot, which he was required to improve, as the condition of obtaining a title. As the number of these adventurers increased in consequence of the protection afforded by the military, the Judge was induced to lay out another village, six or seven miles higher up the river, which he called South Bend, where he disposed of some donation lots; but that project failed, and in a few years the village was deserted and converted into a farm.

During these transactions, the Judge was visited by a number of Indians from a camp in the neighborhood of Stites' settlement. One of them, a Shawnee chief, had many complaints to make of frauds practised on them by white traders, who fortunately had no connection with the pioneers. After several conversations, and some small presents, he professed to be satisfied with the explanation he had received, and gave assurances that the Indians would trade with the white men as friends.

In one of their interviews, the Judge told him he had been commissioned and sent out to their country, by the thirteen fires, in the spirit of friendship and kindness; and that he was instructed to treat them as friends and brothers. In proof of this he showed them the flag of the Union, with its stars and stripes, and also his commission, having the great seal of the United States attached to it; exhibiting the American eagle, with the olive branch in one claw, emblematical of peace, and the instrument of war and death in the other. He explained the meaning of those symbols to their satisfaction, though at first the chief seemed to think they were not very striking emblems either of peace or friendship; but before he departed from the Bend, he gave assurances of the most friendly character. Yet, when they left their camp to return to their towns, they carried off a number of horses belonging to the Columbia settlement, to compensate for the injuries done them by wandering traders, who had no part or lot with the pioneers. These depredations having been repeated, a party was sent out in pursuit, who followed the trail of the Indians a considerable distance, when they discovered fresh signs, and sent Captain Flinn, one of their party, in advance, to reconnoitre. He had not proceeded far before he was surprised, taken prisoner, and carried to the Indian camp. Not liking the movements he saw going on, which seemed to indicate personal violence, in regard to himself, and having great confidence in his activity and strength, at a favorable moment he sprang from the camp, made his escape, and joined his party. The Indians, fearing an ambuscade, did not pursue. The party possessed themselves of some horses belonging to the Indians, and returned to Columbia. In a few days, the Indians brought in Captain Flinn's rifle, and begged Major Stites to restore their horses—alledging that they were innocent of the depredations laid to their charge. After some further explanations, the matter was amicably settled, and the horses were given up.

The three principal settlements of the Miami country were commenced in the manner above described; and although they had one general object, and were threatened by one common danger, yet there existed a strong spirit of rivalry between them—each feeling a pride in the prosperity of the little colony to which he belonged. That spirit produced a strong influence on the feelings of the pioneers of the different villages, and produced an *esprit du corps*, scarcely to be expected under circumstances so critical and dangerous as those which threatened them. For some time it was a matter of doubt which of the rivals, Columbia, Cincinnati, or North Bend, would eventually become the chief seat of business.

In the beginning, Columbia, the eldest of the three, took the lead, both in the number of its inhabitants, and the convenience and appearance of its dwellings. It was a flourishing village, and many believed it would become the great business town of the Miami country. That delusion, however, lasted but a short time. The garrison having been established at Cincinnati, made it the head-quarters, and the depot of the army. In addition to this, as soon as the county courts of the territory were organized, it was made the seat of justice of Hamilton county. These advantages convinced every body that it was destined to become the emporium of the Miami country.

At first, North Bend had a decided advantage over it; as the troops detailed by General Harmar for the protection of the Miami pioneers were landed there, through the influence of Judge Symmes. That consideration induced many of the first adventurers to plant themselves at the Bend, believing it to be the place of the greatest safety. But, as has been stated, that detachment soon took its departure for Louisville. It appears also that Ensign

Luce, the commandant of the party which succeeded it, did not feel bound to erect his fort at any particular place, but was at liberty to select the spot best calculated to afford the most extensive protection to the Miami settlers. Viewing his duty in that light, he put up a small temporary work, sufficient for the security of his troops, regardless of the earnest entreaty of the Judge, to proceed at once to erect a substantial, spacious block-house, sufficient for the protection of the inhabitants of the village.

The remonstrances and entreaties of the Judge had but little influence on the mind of this obstinate officer; for, in despite of them all, he left the Bend, and proceeded to Cincinnati with his command, where he immediately commenced the construction of a military work. That important move was followed by very decided results—it terminated the strife for supremacy, by removing the only motive which had induced former emigrants to pass the settlements above, and proceed to the Bend. As soon as the troops removed from that place to Cincinnati, the settlers of the Bend, who were then the most numerous, feeling the loss of the protection on which they had relied, became uneasy, and began to follow; and ere long the place was almost entirely deserted, and the hope of making it even a respectable town, was abandoned.

In the course of the ensuing summer, Major Doughty arrived at Cincinnati, with troops from Fort Harmar, and commenced the construction of Fort Washington, which was the most extensive and important military work in the territory belonging to the United States.

About that time there was a rumor prevailing in the settlement, said to have been endorsed by the Judge himself, which goes far to unravel the mystery, in which the removal of the troops from the Bend was involved. It was said and believed, that while the officer in command at that place was looking out very leisurely for a suitable site, on which to build the block-house, he formed an acquaintance with a beautiful black-eyed female, who called forth his most assiduous and tender attentions. She was the wife of one of the settlers at the Bend. Her husband saw the danger to which he would be exposed, if he remained where he was. He therefore resolved at once to remove to Cincinnati, and very promptly executed his resolution.

As soon as the gallant commandant discovered that the object of his admiration had changed her residence, he began to think that the Bend was not an advantageous situation for a military work, and communicated that opinion to Judge Symmes, who strenuously opposed it. His reasoning, however, was not as persuasive as the sparkling eyes of the fair dulcinea then at Cincinnati. The result was a determination to visit Cincinnati, and examine its advantages for a military post, which he communicated to the Judge, with an assurance that if, on examination, it did not prove to be the most eligible place, he would return and erect the fort at the Bend.

The visit was quickly made, and resulted in a conviction that the Bend could not be compared with Cincinnati as a military position. The troops were accordingly removed to that place, and the building of a block-house commenced. Whether this structure was on the ground on which Fort Washington was erected by Major Doughty, cannot now be decided.

That movement, produced by a cause whimsical, and apparently trivial in itself, was attended with results of incalculable importance. It settled the question whether North Bend or Cincinnati was to be the great commercial town of the Miami country. Thus we see what unexpected results are sometimes produced by circumstances apparently trivial. The incomparable beauty of a Spartan dame, produced a ten years' war, which terminated in the destruction of Troy; and the irresistible charms of another female, transferred the commercial emporium of Ohio from the place where it had been commenced, to the place where it now is. If this captivating American Helen had continued at the Bend, the garrision would have been erected there—population, capital and business would have centered there, and there would have been the Queen City of the West.

* * * * * *

A large number of the original adventurers to the Miami purchase, had exhausted their means by paying for their land, and removing their families to the country. Others were wholly destitute of property, and came out as volunteers, under the expectation of obtaining, gratuitously, such small tracts of land as might be forfeited by the purchasers, under Judge Symmes, for not making the improvements required by the conditions stipulated in the terms of sale and settlement of Miami lands, published by the Judge, in 1787; which will be more fully explained in a subsequent chapter. The class of adventurers first named was comparatively numerous, and had come out under an expectation of taking immediate possession of their lands, and of commencing the cultivation of them for subsistence. Their situation, therefore, was distressing. To go out into the wilderness to till the soil, appeared to be certain death; to remain in the settlements threatened them with starvation. The best provided of the pioneers found it difficult to obtain subsistence; and, of course, the class now spoken of were not far from total destitution. They depended on game, fish, and such products of the earth as could be raised on small patches of ground in the immediate vicinity of the settlements.

Occasionally, small lots of provision were brought down the river by emigrants, and sometimes were transported on pack-horses, from Lexington, at a heavy expense, and not without danger. But supplies, thus procured, were beyond the reach of those destitute persons now referred to.

Having endured these privations as long as they could be borne, the more resolute of them determined to brave the consequences of moving on to their lands. To accomplish the object with the least exposure, those whose lands were in the same neighborhood, united as one family; and on that principle, a number of associations were formed, amounting to a dozen or more, who went out resolved to maintain their positions.

Each party erected a strong block-house, near to which their cabins were put up, and the whole was enclosed by strong log pickets. This being done, they commenced clearing their lands, and preparing for planting their crops. During the day, while they were at work, one person was placed as a sentinel, to warn them of approaching danger. At sunset they retired to the block-house and their cabins, taking every thing of value within the pickets. In this manner they proceeded from day to day, and week to week, till their improvements were sufficiently extensive to support their families. During this time, they depended for subsistence on wild game, obtained at some hazard, more than on the scanty supplies they were able to procure from the settlements on the river.

In a short time these stations gave protection and food to a large number of destitute families. After they were established, the Indians became less annoying to the settlements on the Ohio, as part of their time was employed in watching the stations. The former, however, did not escape, but endured their share of the fruits of savage hostility. In fact, no place or situation was exempt from danger. The safety of the pioneer depended on his means of defence, and on perpetual vigilance.

The Indians viewed those stations with great jealousy, as they had the appearance of permanent military establishments, intended to retain possession of their country. In that view they were correct; and it was fortunate for the settlers, that the Indians wanted either the skill or the means of demolishing them. . . . .

The truth of the matter is, their great error consisted in permitting those works to be constructed at all. They might have prevented it with great ease, but they appeared not to be aware of the serious consequences which were to result, until it was too late to act with effect. Several attacks were, however, made at different times, with an apparent determination to destroy them; but they failed in every instance. The assault made on the station erected by Captain Jacob White, a pioneer of much energy and enterprise, at the third crossing of Mill creek from Cincinnati, on the old Hamilton road, was resolute and daring; but it was gallantly met and successfully repelled. During the attack, which was in the night, Captain White shot and killed a warrior, who fell so near the block-house, that his companions could not remove his body. The next morning it was brought in, and judging from his stature, as reported by the inmates, he might have claimed descent from a race of giants. On examining the ground in the vicinity of the block-house, the appearances of blood indicated that the assailants had suffered severely.

In the winter of 1790–1, an attack was made, with a strong party, amounting, probably, to four or five hundred, on Dunlap's station, at Colerain. The block-house at that place was occupied by a small number of United States' troops, commanded by Col. Kingsbury, then a subaltern in the army. The fort was furnished with a piece of artillery, which was an object of terror to the Indians; yet that did not deter them from an attempt to effect their purpose. The attack was violent, and for some time the station was in imminent danger.

The savages were led by the notorious Simon Girty, and outnumbered the garrison, at least, ten to one. The works were entirely of wood, and the only obstacle between the assailants and the assailed, was a picket of logs, that might have been demolished, with a loss not exceeding, probably, twenty or thirty lives. The garrison displayed unusual gallantry—they frequently exposed their persons above the pickets, to insult and provoke the assailants; and judging from the facts reported, they conducted with as much folly as bravery.

Col. John Wallace, of Cincinnati, one of the earliest and bravest of the pioneers, and as amiable as he was brave, was in the fort when the attack was made. Although the works were completely surrounded by the enemy, the colonel volunteered his services to go to Cincinnati for a reinforcement. The fort stood on the east bank of the Big Miami.

Late in the night, he was conveyed across the river, in a canoe, and landed on the opposite shore. Having passed down some miles below the fort, he swam the river, and directed his course for Cincinnati. On his way down, the next day, he met a body of men from that place and from Columbia, proceeding to Colerain. They had been informed of the attack, by persons hunting in the neighborhood, who were sufficiently near the fort to hear the firing when it began.

He joined the party, and led them to the station by the same route he had travelled from it; but before they arrived, the Indians had taken their departure. It was afterwards ascertained that Mr. Abner Hunt, a respectable citizen of New Jersey, who was on a surveying tour in the nighborhood of Colerain, at the time of the attack, was killed before he could reach the fort. His body was afterwards found, shockingly mangled.

O. M. Spencer, in his "Indian Captivity," says:

The Indians tied Hunt to a sapling, within sight of the garrison, who distinctly heard his screams, and built a large fire so near as to scorch him, inflicting the most acute pain; then, as his flesh, from the action of the fire and the frequent application of live coals, became less sensible, making deep incisions in his limbs, as if to renew his sensibility of pain; answering his cries for water, to allay the extreme thirst caused by burning, by fresh tortures; and, finally, when, exhausted and fainting, death seemed approaching to release the wretched prisoner, terminating his sufferings by applying flaming brands to his naked bowels.

Soon as the settlers of Cincinnati landed they commenced erecting three or four cabins, the first of which was built on Front, east of and near Main street. The lower table of land was then covered with sycamore and maple trees, and the upper with beech and oak. Through this dense forest the streets were laid out, their corners being marked upon the trees. This survey extended from Eastern row, now Broadway, to Western row, and from the river as far north as to Northern row, now Seventh street.

In January, 1790, Gen. Arthur St. Clair, then governor of the N. W. territory, arrived at Cincinnati to organize the county of Hamilton. In the succeeding fall, Gen. Harmar marched from Fort Washington on his expedition against the Indians of the northwest. In the following year, (1791,) the unfortunate army of St. Clair marched from the same place. On his return, St. Clair gave Major Zeigler the command of Fort Washington and repaired to Philadelphia. Soon after, the latter was succeeded by Col. Wilkinson. This year, Cincinnati had little increase in its population. About one half of the inhabitants were attached to the army of St. Clair, and many killed in the defeat.

In 1792, about 50 persons were added by emigration to the population of Cincinnati, and a house of worship erected. In the spring following, the troops which had been recruited for Wayne's army landed at Cincinnati and encamped on the bank of the river, between the village of Cincinnati and Mill creek. To that encampment Wayne gave the name of "Hobson's choice," it being the only suitable place for that object. Here he remained several months, constantly drilling his troops, and then moved on to a spot now in Darke county, where he erected Fort Greenville. In the fall, after the army had left, the small-pox broke out in the garrison at Fort Washington, and spread with so much malignity that nearly one third of the soldiers and citizens fell victims. In July, 1794, the army left Fort Greenville, and on the 20th of August, defeated the enemy at the battle of "the Fallen Timbers," in what is now Lucas county, a few miles above Toledo. Judge Burnet thus describes Cincinnati, at about this period.

"Prior to the treaty of Greenville, which established a permanent peace between the United States and the Indians, but few improvements had been made, of any description, and scarcely one of a permanent character. In Cincinnati, Fort Washington was the most remarkable object. That rude, but highly interesting structure, stood between Third and Fourth streets produced, east of Eastern Row, now Broadway, which was then a two-pole alley, and was the eastern boundary of the town, as originally laid out. It was composed of a number of strongly built, hewed-log cabins, a story and a half high, calculated for soldier's barracks. Some of them, more conveniently arranged, and better finished, were intended for officers' quarters. They were so placed as to form a hollow square of about an acre of ground, with a strong block-house at each angle. It was built of large logs, cut from the ground on which it stood, which was a tract of fifteen acres, reserved by Congress in the law of 1792, for the accommodation of the garrison.

"The artificers' yard was an appendage to the fort, and stood on the bank of the river, immediately in front. It contained about two acres of ground, enclosed by small contiguous buildings, occupied as work-shops and quarters for laborers. Within the enclosure, there was a large two story frame house, familiarly called the 'yellow house,' built for the accommodation of the Quartermaster General, which was the most commodious and best finished edifice in Cincinnati.

"On the north side of Fourth street, immediately behind the fort, Colonel Sargent, secretary of the territory, had a convenient frame house, and a spacious garden, cultivated with care and taste. On the east side of the fort, Dr. Allison, the surgeon general of the army, had a plain frame dwelling, in the center of a large lot, cultivated as a garden and fruitery, which was called Peach Grove.

"The Presbyterian church, an interesting edifice, stood on Main street, in front of the spacious brick building now occupied by the first Presbyterian congregation. It was a substantial frame building, about 40 feet by 30, enclosed with clapboards, but neither lathed, plastered nor ceiled. The floor was of boat plank, resting on wooden blocks. In that humble edifice, the pioneers and their families assembled, statedly, for public worship; and, during the continuance of the war, they always attended with loaded rifles by their sides. That building was afterwards neatly finished, and some years subsequently, [1814,] was sold and removed to Vine street, where it now remains, the property of Judge Burke.

"On the north side of Fourth street, opposite where St. Paul's church now stands, there stood a frame school house, enclosed, but unfinished, in which the children of the village were instructed. On the north side of the public square, there was a strong log building, erected and occupied as a jail. A room in the tavern of George

Avery, near the frog-pond, at the corner of Main and Fifth streets, had been rented for the accommodation of the courts; and as the penitentiary system had not been adopted, and Cincinnati was a

The First Church in Cincinnati.

[The engraving represents the first Presbyterian church, as it appeared in February, 1847. In the following spring, it was taken down, and the materials used for the construction of several dwellings in the part of Cincinnati called *Texas*. The greater proportion of the timber was found to be perfectly sound. In 1791, a number of the inhabitants formed themselves into a company, to escort the Rev. James Kemper from beyond the Kentucky river to Cincinnati; and after his arrival, a subscription was set on foot to build this church, which was erected in 1792. This subscription paper is still in existence, and bears date January 16th, 1792. Among its signers, were Gen. Wilkinson, Captains Ford, Peters and Shaylor, of the regular service, Dr. Allison, surgeon to St. Clair and Wayne, Winthrop Sargeant, Capt. Robert Elliot and others, principally citizens, to the number of 106, not one of whom survive.]

seat of justice, it was ornamented with a pillory, stocks and whipping-post, and occasionally with a gallows. These were all the structures of a public character then in the place. Add to these, the cabins and other temporary buildings for the shelter of the inhabitants, and it will complete the schedule of the improvements of Cincinnati, at the time of the treaty of Greenville. The only vestige of them, now remaining, is the church of the pioneers. With that exception, and probably two or three frame buildings which have been repaired, improved and preserved, every edifice in the city has been erected since the ratification of that treaty. The stations of defence scattered through the Miami valley, were all temporary, and have long since gone to decay, or been demolished.

"It may assist the reader in forming something like a correct idea of the appearance of Cincinnati, and of what it actually was at that time, to know, that the intersection of Main and Fifth streets, now the center of business and tasteful improvement, there was a pond of water, full of alder bushes, from which the frogs serenaded the neighborhood during the summer and fall, and which rendered it necessary to construct a causeway of logs, to pass it. That morass remained in its natural state, with its alders and its frogs, several years after Mr. B. became a resident of the place, the population of which, including the garrison and followers of the army, was about six hundred. The fort was then commanded by William H. Harrison, a captain in the army, but afterwards president of the United States. In 1797, General Wilkinson, the commander-in-chief of the army, made it his head-quarters for a few months, but did not, apparently, interfere with the command of Captain Harrison, which continued till his resignation in 1798.

"During the period now spoken of, the settlements of the territory, including Cincinnati, contained but few individuals, and still fewer families, who had been accustomed to mingle in the circles of polished society. That fact put it in the power of the military to give character to the manners and customs of the people. Such a school, it must be admitted, was by no means calculated to make the most favorable impression on the morals and sobriety of any community, as was abundantly proved by the result.

"Idleness, drinking and gambling prevailed in the army to a greater extent than it has done to any subsequent period. This may be attributed to the fact, that they had been several years in the wilderness, cut off from all society but their own, with but few comforts or conveniences at hand, and no amusements but such as their own ingenuity could invent. Libraries were not to be found—men of literary minds, or polished manners, were rarely met with; and they had long been deprived of the advantage of modest, accomplished female society, which always produces a salutary influence on the feelings and moral habits of men. Thus situated, the officers were urged, by an irresistible impulse, to tax their wits for expedients to fill up the chasms of leisure which were left on their hands, after a full discharge of their military duties; and, as is too frequently the case, in such circumstances, the bottle, the dice-box and the card-table were among the expedients resorted to, because they were the nearest at hand, and the most easily procured.

"It is a distressing fact, that a very large proportion of the officers under General Wayne, and subsequently under General Wilkinson, were hard drinkers. Harrison, Clark, Shomberg, Ford, Strong and a few others, were the only exceptions. Such were the habits of the army when they began to associate with the inhabitants of Cincinnati, and of the western settlements generally, and to give tone to public sentiment.

"As a natural consequence, the citizens indulged in the same practices, and formed the same habits. As a proof of this, it may be stated, that when Mr. Burnet came to the bar, there were nine resident lawyers engaged in the practice, of whom he is, and has been for many years, the only survivor. They all became confirmed sots, and descended to premature graves, excepting his brother, who was a young man of high promise, but whose life was terminated by a rapid consumption, in the summer of 1801. He expired under the shade of a tree, by the side of the road, on the banks of Paint creek, a few miles from Chillicothe."

On the 9th of November, 1793, Wm. Maxwell established, at Cincinnati, "the Centinel of the North-Western Territory," with the motto, "open to all parties—influenced by none." It was on a half sheet, royal quarto size, and was the first newspaper printed north of the Ohio river. In 1796, Edward Freeman became the owner of the paper, which he changed to "Freeman's Journal," which he continued until the beginning of 1800, when he removed to Chillicothe. On the 28th of May, 1799, Joseph Carpenter issued the first number of a weekly paper, entitled the "Western Spy and Hamilton Gazette." On the 11th of January, 1794, two keel boats sailed from Cincinnati to Pittsburg, each making a trip once in four weeks. Each boat was so covered as to be protected against rifle and musket balls, and had port-holes to fire out at, and was provided with six pieces, carrying pound balls, a number of muskets and ammunition, as a protection against the Indians on the banks of the Ohio. In 1801, the first sea vessel equipped for sea, of 100 tons, built at Marietta, passed down the Ohio, carrying produce; and the banks of the river at Cincinnati were crowded with spectators to witness this novel event. Dec. 19th, 1801, the territorial legislature passed a bill, removing the seat of government from Chillicothe to Cincinnati.

January 2d, 1802, the territorial legislature incorporated the town of Cincinnati, and the following officers were appointed: David Zeigler, president; Jacob Burnet, recorder; Wm. Ramsay, David E. Wade, Chas. Avery, John Reily, Wm. Stanley, Samuel Dick and Wm. Ruffner, trustees; Jo. Prince, assessor; Abram Cary, collector, and James Smith, town marshal. In 1795, the town contained 94 cabins, 10 frame houses, and about 500 inhabitants. In 1800, the population was estimated at 750, and in 1810, it was 2,540.

We give, on an adjoining page, a view of Cincinnati, taken by J. Cutler, as it appeared about the year 1810. It is from an engraving in "the Topographical Description of Ohio, Indiana Territory, and Louisiana, by a late officer of the army," and published at Boston, in 1812.

That work states, that Cincinnati contains about 400 dwellings, an elegant court-house, jail, 3 market-houses, a land office for the sale of congress lands, 2 printing offices, issuing weekly gazettes, 30 mercantile stores, and the various branches of mechanism are carried on with spirit. Industry of every kind being duly encouraged by the citizens, it is likely to become a considerable manufacturing place. It has a bank, issuing notes under the authority of the state, called the Miami Exporting Company. . . . . A considerable trade is carried on between Cincinnati and New Orleans in keel boats, which return laden with foreign goods. The passage of a boat, of forty tons, down to New Orleans, is computed at about 25, and its return at about 65 days.

In 1819, a charter was obtained from the state legislature, by which Cincinnati was incorporated as a city. This, since repeatedly amended and altered, forms the basis of its present municipal authority.

Cincinnati is 116 miles southwest Columbus; 120 southeast Indianapolis, Ia.; 90 north northwest Lexington, Ky.; 270 north northeast Nashville, Tenn.; 455 below Pittsburg, Pa., by the course of the river; 132 above Louisville, Ky.; 494 above the mouth of the

Ohio river, and 1447 miles above New Orleans by the Mississippi and Ohio rivers; 518 by post route west of Baltimore; 617 miles west by south of Philadelphia; 950 from New York by Lake Erie, Erie canal and Hudson river, and 492 from Washington City. It is in 39 deg. 6 minutes 30 seconds north lat., and 7 deg. 24 minutes 25 seconds west long. It is the largest city of the west, north of New Orleans, and the fifth in population in the United States. It is situated on the north bank of the Ohio river, opposite the mouth of Licking river, which enters the Ohio between Newport and Covington, Ky. The Ohio here has a gradual bend towards the south.

This city is near the eastern extremity of a valley, about twelve miles in circumference, surrounded by beautiful hills, which rise to the height of 300 feet by gentle and varying slopes, and mostly covered with native forest trees. The summit of these hills presents a beautiful and picturesque view of the city and valley. The city is built on two table lands, the one elevated from 40 to 60 feet above the other. Low water mark in the river, which is 108 below the upper part of the city, is 432 feet above tide water at Albany, and 133 feet below the level of Lake Erie. The population in 1800, was 750 ; in 1810, 2540 ; in 1820, 9602 ; in 1830, 24,831 ; in 1840, 46,338, and in 1847, over 90,000. Employed in commerce in 1840, 2,226 ; in manufactures and trades, 10,866: navigating rivers and canals, 1748 ; in the learned professions, 377. Covington and Newport opposite, in Ky., and Fulton and the adjacent parts of Mill creek township on the north, are in fact, suburbs of Cincinnati, and if added to the above population would extend it to 105,000. The shores of the Ohio at the landing, is substantially paved to low water mark and is supplied with floating wharves, adapted to the great rise and fall of river, which renders the landing and shipping of goods at all times convenient.

Cincinnati seems to have been originally laid out on the model ot Philadelphia, with great regularity. North of Main street, between the north side of Front street and the bank of the river, is the landing, an open area of 10 acres, with about 1000 feet front. This area is of great importance to the business of the city, and generally presents a scene of much activity. The corporate limits include about four square miles. The central part is compactly and finely built, with spacious warehouses, large stores and handsome dwellings; but in its outer parts, it is but partially built up and the houses irregularly scattered. Many of them are of stone or brick, but an equal or greater number are of wood, and are generally from two to four stories high. The city contains over 11,000 edifices public and private; and of those recently erected, the number of brick exceeds those of wood, and the style of architecture is constantly improving. Many of the streets are well paved, extensively shaded with trees and the houses ornamented with shrubbery. The climate is more variable than on the Atlantic coast, in the same latitude. Snow rarely falls sufficiently deep, or lies long enough, to furnish sleighing. Few places are more healthy, the average annual mor-

CINCINNATI IN 1810.

tality being 1 in 40. The inhabitants are from every state in the Union and from various countries in Europe. Besides natives of Ohio, Pennsylvania and New Jersey have furnished the greatest number; but many are from New York, Virginia, Maryland and New England. Nearly one fifth of the adult population are Germans. But England, Ireland, Scotland, France and Wales, have furnished considerable numbers.

The Ohio river at Cincinnati, is 1800 feet, or about one third of a mile wide, and its mean annual range from low to high water, is about 50 feet; the extreme range may be about 10 feet more. The greatest depressions are generally in August, September and October; and the greatest rise in December, March, May and June. The upward navigation is generally suspended by floating ice for eight or ten weeks in the winter. Its current at its mean height, is about 3 miles an hour; when higher and rising, it is more; and when very low, it does not exceed 2 miles. The quantity of rain and snow which falls annually at Cincinnati, is near 3 feet 9 inches. The wettest month is May, and the driest January. The average number of clear and fair days in a year, is 146; of variable, 114; of cloudy, 105. There have been, since 1840, from thirty to thirty eight steamboats annually built with an average aggregate tonnage of 6500 tons.

Among the public buildings of Cincinnati, is the court house on Main street; it is a spacious building. The edifice of the Franklin and Lafayette bank of Cincinnati, on Third street, has a splendid portico of Grecian Doric columns, 4 feet 6 inches in diameter, extending through the entire front, was built after the model of the Parthenon, and is truly classical and beautiful. The first and second Presbyterian churches are beautiful edifices, and the Unitarian church is singularly neat. There are several churches built within the last three years, which possess great beauty, either internally or externally. But the most impressive building is the Catholic Cathedral, which at far less cost, surpasses in beauty and picturesque effect, the metropolitan edifice at Baltimore. There are many fine blocks of stores, on Front, Walnut, Pearl, Main and Fourth streets, and the eye is arrested by many beautiful private habitations. The most showy quarters are Main street, Broadway, Pearl and Fourth street, west of its intersection with Main.

There are 76 churches in Cincinnati, viz.: 7 Presbyterian, (4 old and 3 new school;) 2 Congregational; 12 Episcopal Methodist; 2 Methodist Protestant; 2 Wesleyan Methodist; 1 Methodist Episcopal south; 1 Bethel; 1 Associate Reformed; 1 Reformed Presbyterian; 6 Baptist; 5 Disciples; 1 Universalist; 1 Restorationist; 1 Christian; 8 German Lutheran and Reformed; English Lutheran and Reformed 1 each; 1 United Brethren; 1 Welch Calvinistic; 1 Welch Congregational; 1 Unitarian; 2 Friends; 1 New Jerusalem; 8 Catholic, 6 of which are for Germans; 2 Jews Synagogues; 5 Episcopal and 1 Second Advent.

There are 5 market houses and 3 theatres, of which 1 is German.

Cincinnati contains many literary and charitable institutions. The Cincinnati college was founded in 1819. The building is in the center of the city, and 's the most beautiful edifice of the kind

St. Xavier's College.

in the state. It is of the Grecian Doric order, with pilaster fronts and facade of Dayton marble, and cost about $35,000. It has 7 professors or other instructors, about 160 pupils, one quarter of whom are in the collegiate department. Woodward college, named from its founder, who gave a valuable block of ground in the north

Lane Seminary.

part of the city, has a president and five professors, or other instructors, and including its preparatory department, near 200 students. The Catholics have a college called St. Xavier's, which has about 100 students and near 5000 volumes in its libraries. Lane seminary, a theological institution, is at Walnut Hills, 2 miles from the centre of the city. It went into operation in 1833, has near 100 students, and over 10,000 volumes in its libraries. There is no charge for tuition. Rooms are provided and furnished at $5 per annum, and the students boarded at 90 and 62½ cents per week. The Medical college was chartered and placed under trustees, in 1825. It has a large and commodious building, a library of over 2000 volumes, 7 professors and about 150 students. The Cincinnati law school is connected with Cincinnati college, has 3 professors and about 30 students. The mechanics' institute, chartered in 1828, has a valuable philosophical and chemical apparatus, a library and a reading room. The common free schools of the city are of a high order, with fine buildings, teachers and apparatus. In the high schools, there are not less than 1500 pupils; in the common and private 5000, and including the students in the collegiate institutions, there are 7000 persons in the various departments of education. In 1831, a college of teachers was established, having for its object the elevation of the profession, and the advancement of the interest of schools in the Mississippi valley, which holds an annual meeting in Cincinnati, in October. The young men's mercantile library association has a fine library and reading rooms. The library contains over 3800 volumes, and the institution promises to be an honor and a blessing to the commercial community. The apprentices' library, founded in 1821, contains 2200 volumes.

The charitable institutions of the city are highly respectable. The Cincinnati orphan asylum is in a building, which cost $18,000. Attached is a library and well-organized school, with a provision even for infants; and it is surrounded by ample grounds. It has trained up over 300 children for usefulness. The Catholics have one male and female orphan asylum. The commercial hospital and lunatic asylum of Ohio, was incorporated in 1821. The edifice, in the northwest part of the city, will accommodate 250 persons; 1100 have been admitted within a year. A part of the building is used for a poor house; and there are separate apartments for the insane.

The city is supplied by water raised from the Ohio river, by a steam engine, of 40 horse power, and forced into two reservoirs, on a hill, 700 feet distant; from whence it is carried in pipes to the intersection of Broadway and Third streets, and thence distributed through the principal streets in pipes. These works are now owned by the city.

Cincinnati is an extensive manufacturing place. Its natural destitution of water power is extensively compensated at present by steam engines, and by the surplus water of the Miami canal, which affords 3000 cubic feet per minute. But the Cincinnati and White Water canal, which extends 25 miles and connects with the White Water canal of Indiana, half a mile south of Harrison, on the state line, will furnish a great increase of water power, equal to 90 runs of millstones. The manufactures of the city, already large, may be expected to greatly increase. By a late enumeration, it appears that the manufactures of Cincinnati of all kinds, employs 10,647 persons, a capital of $14,541,842, and produces articles of over seventeen millions of dollars value.

The trade of Cincinnati embraces the country from the Ohio to the lakes, north and south; and from the Scioto to the Wabash, east and west. The Ohio river line, in Kentucky, for 50 miles down, and as far up as the Virginia line, make their purchases here. Its manufactures are sent into the upper and lower Mississippi country.

There are six incorporated banks, with aggregate capital of $5,800,000, beside two unincorporated banks. Cincinnati is the greatest pork market in the world. Not far from three millions of dollars worth of pork are annually exported.

Cincinnati enjoys great facilities for communication with the surrounding country. The total length of canals, railroads and turnpikes which center here, completed and constructing, is 1125 miles. Those who have made it a matter of investigation predict, that Cincinnati will eventually be a city of a very great population. A writer* in Cist's "Cincinnati in 1841," in a long article on this subject, commences with the startling announcement: "Not having before my eyes the fear of men, 'who—in the language of Governeur Morris—with too much pride to study and too much wit to think, undervalue what they do not understand, and condemn what they do not comprehend,' I venture the prediction, that within one hundred years from this time, Cincinnati will be the greatest city in America; and by the year of our Lord, 2000, the greatest city in the world." We have not space here to recapitulate the arguments on which this prediction is based. The prediction itself we place on record for future reference.†

The few following pages are devoted to incidents which have transpired within the city or county. They are derived mainly from published sources.

A Legend of Jacob Wetzel.—The road along the Ohio river, leading to *Storrs* and *Delhi*, some four hundred yards below the junction of Front and Fifth streets, crosses what, in early days, was the outlet of a water-course, and notwithstanding the changes made by the lapse of years, and the building improvements adjacent, the spot still possesses many features of its original surface, although now divested of its forest character. At the period of this adventure—Oct. 7th, 1790—besides the dense forest of maple and beech, its heavy undergrowth of spice-wood and grape-vine made it an admirable lurking place for the savage beasts, and more savage still, the red men of the woods.

Wetzel had been out on his accustomed pursuit—hunting—and was returning to town, at that time a few cabins and huts collected in the space fronting the river, and extending from Main street to Broadway. He had been very successful, and was returning to procure a horse to bear a load too heavy for his own shoulders, and, at the spot alluded to, had sat down on a decaying tree-trunk to rest himself, and wipe the sweat from his brow, which his forcing his way through the brush had started, cool as was the weather, when he heard the rustling of leaves and branches, which betokened that an animal or an enemy was approaching. Silencing the growl of his dog, who sat at his feet, and appeared equally con-

* J. W. Scott, editor of the Toledo Blade.

† The preceding descriptive sketch of Cincinnati is abridged from that in M'Culloch's Gazetteer, by Charles Cist, editor of the Advertiser, with the statistics brought down to 1847.

scious of danger, he sprang behind a tree and discovered the dark form of an Indian, half hidden by the body of a large oak, who had his rifle in his hands, ready for any emergency that might require the use of it—as he, too, appeared to be on his guard, having heard the low growling of the dog. At this instant, the dog also spied the Indian and barked aloud, which told the Indian of the proximity of his enemy. To raise his rifle was but the work of a moment, and the distinct cracks of two weapons were heard almost at the same time. The Indian's fell from his hands, as the ball of the hunter's had penetrated and broken the elbow of his left arm, while the hunter escaped unhurt. Before the Indian could possibly reload his rifle in his wounded condition, Wetzel had rushed swiftly upon him with his knife, but not before the Indian had drawn his. The first thrust was parried off by the Indian with the greatest skill, and the shock was so great in the effort that the hunter's weapon was thrown some thirty feet from him. Nothing daunted, he threw himself upon the Indian with all his force and seized him around the body; at the same time encircling the right arm, in which the Indian still grasped his knife. The Indian, however, was a very muscular fellow, and the conflict now seemed doubtful indeed. The savage was striving with all his might to release his arm, in order to use his knife. In their struggle, their feet became interlocked, and they both fell to the ground, the Indian uppermost, which extricated the Indian's arm from the iron grasp of the hunter. He was making his greatest endeavors to use his knife, but could not, from the position in which they were lying, as Wetzel soon forced him over on his right side, and, consequently, he could have no use of his arm.

Just at this point of the deadly conflict, the Indian gave an appalling yell, and, with renewed strength, placed his enemy underneath him again, and with a most exulting cry of victory, as he sat upon his body, raised his arm for that fatal plunge. Wetzel saw death before his eyes, and gave himself up for lost, when, just at this most critical juncture, his faithful dog, who had not been an uninterested observer of the scene, sprang forward and seized the Indian with such force by the throat, as caused the weapon to fall harmless from his hand. Wetzel, seeing such a sudden change in his fate, made one last and desperate effort for his life, and threw the Indian from him. Before the prostrate savage had time to recover himself, the hunter had seized his knife, and with redoubled energy rushed upon him, and with his foot firmly planted on the Indian's breast, plunged the weapon up to the hilt in his heart. The savage gave one convulsive shudder, and was no more.

As soon as Wetzel had possessed himself of his rifle, together with the Indian's weapons, he started immediately on his way. He had gone but a short distance when his ears were assailed by the startling whoop of a number of Indians. He ran eagerly for the river, and, fortunately, finding a canoe on the beach near the water, was soon out of reach, and made his way, without further danger, to the cove at the foot of Sycamore street.

The Indians came up to the place of the recent renconter, and discovered the body of a fallen comrade. They gave a most hideous yell when, upon examination, they recognized in the dead Indian the features of one of their bravest chiefs.

O. M. Spencer taken Captive.—In July, 1792, two men, together with Mrs. Colemar and Oliver M. Spencer, then a lad, were returning in a canoe from Cincinnati to Columbia. They were fired upon by two Indians, in ambush on the river bank; one of the men was killed, and the other, a Mr. Light, wounded. Mrs. Coleman jumped from the canoe into the river, and without making any exertions to swim, floated down nearly two miles It is supposed she was borne up by her dress, which, according to the fashion of that time, consisted of a stuffed quilt and other buoyant robes. Spencer was taken and carried captive to the Maumee, where he remained about eight months and was ransomed. A narrative of his captivity, written by himself, has been published by the Methodists.

Death of Col. Robt. Elliott.—In 1794, Col. Robert Elliott, contractor for supplying the United States army, while travelling with his servant from Fort Washington to Fort Hamilton, was waylaid and killed by the Indians, at the big hill, south of where Thos. Fleming lived, and near the line of Hamilton and Butler counties. When shot, he fell from his horse. The servant made his escape by putting his horse at full speed, followed by that of Elliott's, into Fort Hamilton. The savage who shot the colonel, in haste to take his scalp, drew his knife, and seized him by the wig which he wore. To his astonishment, the scalp came off at the first touch, when he exclaimed, "*dam lie!*" In a few minutes, the surprise of the party was over, and they made themselves merry at the expense of their comrade. The next day, a party from the fort, under the guidance of the servant, visited the spot, placed the body in a coffin and proceeded on their way to Fort Washington. About a mile south of Springdale, they were fired upon by Indians, and the servant, who was on the horse of his late master, was shot at the first fire. The party retreated, leaving the body of Elliott with the savages, who had broken open the coffin, when the former rallied, re-took the body and carried it, with that of the servant, to Cincinnati, and buried them side by side in the Presbyterian cemetery, on Twelfth street. Several years after, a neat monument was erected, with the following inscription.

In memory of
ROBERT ELLIOTT,
SLAIN BY A PARTY OF INDIANS,
Near this point,
While in the service of his country.
Placed by his son,
Com. J. D. ELLIOTT, U. S. Navy.
1835.

DAMON AND FIDELITY.

A Witch Story.—About the year 1814, one of our most wealthy and respectable farmers on Mill creek, who had taken great pains and expended much money in procuring and propagating a fine breed of horses, was unfortunate in losing a number of them, by a distemper which appeared to be of a novel character. As the disease baffled all his skill, he soon became satisfied that it was the result of witchcraft. Under that impression, he consulted such persons as were reputed to have a knowledge of sorcery, or who pretended to be fortune-tellers. These persons instructed him how to proceed to discover and destroy the witch. One of the experiments he was directed to make, was to boil certain ingredients, herbs, et cetera, over a hot fire, with pins and needles in the cauldron, which, he was told, would produce great mental and bodily distress in the witch or wizzard. He tried that experiment, and while the pot was boiling furiously, placed himself in his door, which overlooked the principal part of his farm, including the field in which his horses were kept. It so happened, that, while standing in the door, he saw his daughter-in-law, who lived in a cabin about 80 rods from his own house, hastening to the spring for a bucket of water. His imagination connected that hurried movement with his incantation so strongly, that he immediately ordered his son to move his family from the farm.

From some cause, he had formed an opinion that a Mrs. Garrison, an aged woman, in feeble health, fast sinking to the grave, living some eight or ten miles from his farm, was the principal agent in the destruction of his horses. He had frequently expressed that opinion in the neighborhood. Mrs. Garrison had heard of it, and, as might be expected, her feelings were injured and her spirits much depressed by the slanderous report. One of the charms he had been directed to try, was to shoot a silver bullet at a horse while the witch was evidently in him. This he was told would kill the witch and cure the animal. He accordingly prepared a silver ball, and shot it at a very fine brood mare which was affected by the distemper. The mare, of course, was killed; and as it so happened, that, in a very short time after, poor Mrs. Garrison died, the experiment was declared to be successful, and the experimenter believes to this day that his silver bullet killed the poor old woman. However that may be, his slanderous report had a great effect on her health, and no doubt hastened her death.

Explosion of the Moselle.—The new and elegant steamboat, Moselle, Capt. Perkin, left the wharf in Cincinnati, April 26th, 1838, (full of passengers,) for Louisville and St. Louis; and, with the view of taking a family on board at Fulton, about a mile and a half above the quay, proceeded up the river and made fast to a lumber raft for that purpose. Here the family was taken on board; and, during the whole time of their detention, the captain had madly held on to all the steam that he could create, with the intention, not only of showing off to the best advantage the great speed of his boat, as it passed down the river the entire length of the city, but that he might overtake and pass another boat which had left the wharf for Louisville, but a short time previous. As the Moselle was a *new brag* boat, and had recently made several exceedingly quick trips to and from Cincinnati, it would not do to risk her popularity for speed, by giving to another boat (even though that boat had the advantage of time and distance) the most remote chance of being the first to arrive at the destined port. This insane policy,—this poor ambition of proprietors and captains, has almost always inevitably tended to the same melancholy results. The Moselle had but just parted from the lumber raft to which she had been fast,—her wheels had scarcely made their first revolution,—when her boilers burst with an awful and astounding noise, equal to the most violent clap of thunder. The explosion was destructive and heart-rending in the extreme; heads, limbs and bodies, were seen flying through the air in every direction, attended with the most horrible shrieks and groans from the wounded and dying. The boat, at the time of the accident, was about thirty feet from the shore, and was rendered a perfect wreck. It seemed to be entirely shattered as far back as the gentlemen's cabin; and her hurricane deck, the whole length, was entirely swept away. The boat immediately began to sink, and float with a strong current down the river, at the same time receding farther from the shore,—while the passengers, who yet remained unhurt in the gentlemen's and ladies' cabins, became panic-struck, and most of them, with a fatuity which seems unaccountable, jumped into the river. Being above the ordinary business parts of the city, there was no boats at hand, except a few large and unmanageable wood-floats, which were carried to the relief of the sufferers, as soon as possible, by the few persons on the shore. Many were drowned, however, before they could be rescued, and many sunk, who were never seen afterwards. There was one little boy on the shore who was seen wringing his hands in agony, imploring those present to save his father, mother and three sisters,—all of whom were struggling in the water to gain the shore,—but whom the little fellow had the awful misfortune to see perish, one by one, almost within his reach; an infant child, belonging to the family, was picked up alive, floating down the river on one of the frag-ments of the hurricane deck.

The boat sunk about fifteen minutes after the explosion, leaving nothing to be seen but her chimneys, and a small portion of her upper works.

The Moselle was crowded with passengers from stem to stern, principally Germans, bound to St. Louis. Nearly all on board (with the exception of those in the ladies' cabin) were killed or wounded. Most of the sufferers were among the hands of the boat and the steerage passengers. The captain was thrown by the explosion into the street, and was picked up dead and dreadfully mangled. Another man was forced through the roof of one of the neighboring houses; the pilot was thrown about a hundred feet into the air, whence he fell and found his grave in the river,—and many were the limbs and other fragments of human bodies, which were found scattered about upon the river, and far along the shore. The number destroyed by the explosion, was estimated at over two hundred persons.

The Asiatic Cholera.—The cholera made its appearance in Cincinnati, in October, 1832. The reports of the board of health, as published in the city papers, commenced on the 10th of that month, and terminated on the 3d of November. The whole number of deaths, as then published, was 351, which was probably much less than the real number. The greatest number of deaths in any one day, was on Oct. 21st, when 42 persons died.

The following articles are derived from the newspapers of Cincinnati, and relate to events of the few past years.

The Great Freshet of February, 1832.—The Ohio river commenced rising at this place about the 9th inst. On the 12th, it began to swell over the banks, and on the 14th, many merchants and others near the river, were compelled to remove their goods to the second story of their houses. It continued to rise rapidly till Saturday morning, Feb. 18th, when it came to a stand, having risen *sixty three feet* above low water mark. Differences of opinion exists as to its comparative height, with the rises of 1792 and 1815. It is supposed to have been about 5 feet higher than in 1792 or 1815. About noon, on the 18th, it commenced falling very slowly, and yet continues to fall. In the course of two or three days it probably will be confined within its banks.

The rise was of the most distressing character. It carried desolation into all the lower part of the city. Hundreds of families were turned houseless upon the community. During the early part of the rise, many in the lower part of the city were awakened at night by the water pouring in upon them, and were obliged to fly; others betook themselves to the upper stories, and were brought away in boats the next morning. Many families continue to reside in the upper part of their dwellings, making use of boats in going from and returning to their stores and houses.

We have heard of the death of but two individuals, Mr. John Harding and Mr. William Aulsbrook; the former, a man of family, the latter, a single man. They were in the employ of Mr. William Tift, of this city, and lost their lives in endeavoring to keep the water out of his cellar. While at work the back wall of the building gave way—the cellar filled in an instant, and they were unable to get out. They both were very worthy men.

The water extended over about thirty-five squares of the thickly settled part of the city, from John street on the west, to Deer creek on the east, and north to Lower Market and Pearl streets. The distance of about a mile west of John street was likewise submerged This part of the city, however, is but thinly settled.

The amount of damage sustained by merchants, owners of improved real estate and others cannot be correctly ascertained. Many houses have floated away, a great num ber have moved from their foundations and turned over; many walls have settled so as to injure the houses materially; and a great quantity of lumber and other property has floated off. The large bridge over the mouth of Mill creek floated away, and that over Deer creek is much injured. Thousands and tens of thousands of dollars worth of dry goods groceries, &c., have been destroyed or materially injured. Business of almost every description was stopped; money became scarce, and wood and flour enormously high.

Active measures were taken by the citizens for the relief of the sufferers. A town meeting was held at the council chamber, on the 15th inst. G. W. Jones was appointed chairman, and Samuel H. Goodin, secretary. On motion, a committee of 15 (3 from a ward) was appointed to take up collections for the relief of the sufferers, consisting of the following persons: E. Hulse, N. G. Pendleton, E. C. Smith, J. W. Gazlay, Jno. Wood, G. W. Jones, W. G. Orr, W. Holmes, A. Owen, P. Britt, J. Resor, O. Lovell and G. C. Miller.

A committee of vigilance was also appointed, whose duty it was to remove persons and goods surrounded with water. The following persons composed that committee: J. Pierce, Wm. Phillips, Saml. Fosdick, Wm. Stephenson, Chas. Fox, Henry Tatem, I. A. Butterfield, Jas. M'Intire, N. M. Whittemore, M. Coffin, Jas. M'Lean, J. Aumack, J. D. Garrard, A. G. Dodd and Fullom Perry.

T. D. Carneal, J. M. Mason, J. C. Avery, Chas. Fox and R. Buchanan were appointed a committee to procure shelter for those whose houses were rendered untenable. On motion, it was resolved that persons who may need assistance, be requested to make application to the council chamber, where members of the committee of vigilance shall rendezvous, and where one or more shall at all times remain for the purpose of affording relief. At a subsequent meeting, 20 were added to the committee of vigilance.

It gives us pleasure to state, that the members of the foregoing committees most faithfully discharged their respective duties. A provision house was opened by the committee of vigilance, on Fourth street, where meats, bread, wood, clothes, &c., were liberally given to all who applied. The ladies supported their well-known character for benevolence, by contributing clothing and food to the sufferers. The committee appointed to collect funds, found the citizens liberal in their donations. All who had vacant houses and rooms, cheerfully appropriated them to the use of those made houseless. Public buildings, school houses, and basement stories of churches, were appropriated to this purpose. Mr. Brown of the ampitheatre, Mr. Franks, proprietor of the gallery of paintings, Mr. R. Letton, proprietor of the Museum, appropriated the entire proceeds of their houses, the first, on the night of 17th; the second, on the 18th, and the third, on that of the 20th, for the relief of the sufferers. The Beethoven society of sacred music also gave a concert for the same purpose, in the second Presbyterian church, on Fourth street, on the night of the 24th.

Destruction of the Philanthropist newspaper printing office by a mob, July 30th, 1836.—The paper had then been published in Cincinnati about three months, and was edited by James G. Birney. As early as the 14th of July, the press room was broken open and the press and materials defaced and destroyed. July 23d, a meeting of citizens was convened at the Lower Market house "to decide whether they will permit the publication or distribution of abolition papers in this city." This meeting appointed a committee, who opened a correspondence with the conductors of that print—the executive committee of the Ohio anti-slavery society—requesting them to discontinue its publication. This effort being unsuccessful, the committee of citizens published the correspondence, to which they appended a resolution, in one clause of which they stated, "That in discharging their duties, they have used all the measures of persuasion and conciliation in their power. That their exertions have not been successful, the above correspondence will show. It only remains, then, in pursuance of their instructors, to publish their proceedings and adjourn without day. But ere they do this, they owe it themselves, and those whom they represent, to express their utmost abhorrence of every thing like violence; and earnestly to implore their fellow citizens to abstain therefrom." The sequel is thus given by a city print.

On Saturday night, July 30th, very soon after dark a, concourse of citizens assembled at the corner of Main and Seventh streets, in this city, and upon a short consultation, broke open the printing office of the Philanthropist, the abolition paper, scattered the type into the streets, tore down the presses and completely dismantled the office. It was owned by A. Pugh, a peaceable and orderly printer, who printed the Philanthropist for the anti-slavery society of Ohio. From the printing office, the crowd went to the house of A. Pugh, where they supposed there were other printing materials, but found none, nor offered any violence. Then to the Messrs. Donaldson's, where only ladies were at home. The residence of Mr. Birney, the editor, was then visited; no person was at home, but a youth, upon whose explanations the house was left undisturbed. A shout was raised for Dr. Colby's; and the concourse returned to Main street, proposed to pile up the contents of the office in the street and make a bonfire of them. A gentleman mounted the pile, and advised against burning it, lest the houses near might take fire. A portion of the press was then dragged down Main street, broken up and thrown into the river. The Exchange was then visited and refreshments taken. After which, the concourse again went up Main street, to about opposite the Gazette office. Some suggestions were hinted that it should be demolished, but the hint was overruled. An attack was then made upon the residence of some blacks, in Church alley; two guns were fired upon the assailants and they recoiled. It was supposed that one man was wounded, but that was not the case. It was some time before a rally could again be made, several voices declaring they did not wish to endanger themselves. A second attack was made, the houses found empty and their interior contents destroyed. . . . On the afternoon of Aug. 2d, pursuant to a call, a very large and respectable meeting of citizens met at the court house, and passed a series of resolutions, the first of which was "that this meeting deeply regret the cause of the recent occurrences, and entirely disapprove of mobs, or other unlawful assemblages." The concluding resolution was approbatory of the course of the colonization society, and expressed an opinion that it was "the only method of getting clear of slavery."

Riot of September, 1841.—This city has been in a most alarming condition for several days; and from until 8 o'clock on Friday evening, until 3 o'clock yesterday [Sunday] morning, almost entirely at the mercy of a lawless mob, ranging in number from 200 to 1500.

On Tuesday evening last, as we are informed, a quarrel took place on the corner of Sixth street and Broadway, between a party of Irishmen and some negroes: some two or three of each party were wounded. On Wednesday night, the quarrel was renewed in some way, and sometime after midnight a party of excited men, armed with clubs, &c., attacked a house occupied as a negro boarding-house on Macalister street, demanding the surrender of a negro, whom they said was secreted in the house, and uttering the most violent threats against the house and the negroes in general. Several of the adjoining houses were occupied by negro families. The violence increased and was resisted by those in or about the houses—an engagement took place, in which several were wounded on each side. On Thursday night, another rencontre took place in the neighborhood of the Lower Market, between some young men and boys and some negroes, in which one or two boys were badly wounded, as was supposed, with knives. On Friday evening, before 8 o'clock, a mob, the principal organization of which, we understand, took place in Kentucky, openly assembled in Fifth street market, unmolested by the police or citizens. They marched from their rendezvous towards Broadway and Sixth street, armed with clubs, stones, &c. Reaching the scene of operations with shouts and blasphemous imprecations, they attacked a negro confectionary in Broadway, next to the synagogue, and demolished the doors and windows. This attracted an immense crowd. About this time, before 9 o'clock, they were addressed by J. W. Piatt, who exorted them to peace and obedience to the law; but his voice was drowned by shouts and throwing of stones. The Mayor also attempted to address them. The savage yell was instantly raised: "down with him! run him off!" were shouted and intermixed with horrid imprecations and exhortations to the mob to move onward. A large portion of the leading disturbers appeared to be strangers—some connected with river navigation and backed by boat hands of the lowest order. They advanced to the attack with stones, &c., and were repeatedly fired upon by the negroes. The mob scattered, but immediately rallied again, and again were in like manner repulsed. Men were wounded on both sides and carried off—and many reported dead. The negroes rallied several times, advanced upon the crowd, and most unjustifiably fired down the street into it, causing a great rush down the street. These things were repeated until past 1 o'clock, when a party procured an iron six pounder from near the river, loaded with boiler punchings, &c., and hauled it to the ground, against the exhortations of the mayor and others. It was posted on Broadway and pointed down Sixth street. The yells continued, but there was a partial cessation of firing. Many of the negroes had fled to the hills. The attack upon the houses was recommenced with the firing of guns upon both sides, which continued during most of the night; and exaggerated rumors of the killed and wounded filled the streets. The cannon was discharged several times. About 2 o'clock, a portion of the military, upon the call of the mayor, proceeded to the scene of disorder and succeeded in keeping the mob at bay. In the morning, and throughout the day, several blocks, including the battle-ground, were surrounded with sentinels and kept under martial law,—keeping within the negroes there, and adding to them such as were brought in during the day for protection.

A meeting of citizens was held at the court house on Saturday morning, at which the mayor presided. This meeting was addressed by the mayor and others, and a series of resolutions passed discountenancing mobs—invoking the aid of the civil authorities to stay the violence, repudiating the doctrines of the abolitionists, etc., etc. The city council also held a special session, to concert measures to vindicate the majesty of the law and restore peace to the city. Intense excitement continued during the day, the mob and their leaders boldly occupying the streets without arrest. The negroes held a meeting in a church, and respectfully assured the mayor and citizens, that they would use every effort to conduct as orderly citizens, to suppress imprudent conduct among their own people, etc., etc. They expressed their readiness to conform to the law of 1807, and give bond, or to leave within a specified time—and tendered their thanks to the mayor, watch, officers and gentlemen of the city, for the efforts made to save their property, their lives, their wives and children.

At 3 P. M., the mayor, sheriff, marshall and a portion of the police, proceeded to the battle-ground, and there, under the protection of the military, though in the presence of the mob, and so far controlled by them, as to prevent the taking away of any negroes upon their complying with the law. Several of the negroes gave bond and obtained permission to go away with their sureties, who were some of our most respectable citizens, but were headed even within the military sentinels, and compelled to return within the ground. It was resolved then to embody the male negroes, and march them to jail for security, under the protection of the civil and military authority. From 250 to 300 were accordingly escorted to that place with difficulty, surrounded by the military and officers, and a dense mass of men, women and boys, confounding all distinction between the orderly and disorderly, accompanied with deafening yells. They were safely lodged, and still remain in prison, separated from their families. The crowd was in that way dispersed.

The succeeding night, the military were ordered out, the firemen were out, clothed with authority as a police band. About eighty citizens enrolled themselves as assistants of the marshall. A troop of horse, and several companies of volunteer infantry continued on duty, until near midnight. Some were then permitted to sleep upon their arms; others remained on duty until morning, guarding the jail, &c.

As was anticipated, the mob efficientlv organized, early commenced operations, dividing their force and making their attacks at different points, thus distracting the attention of the police. The first successful onset was made upon the printing office of the Philanthropist. They succeeded in entering the establishment, breaking up the press, and running with it amid savage yells, down through Main street to the river into which it was thrown. The military appeared in the alley near the office, interrupting the mob for a short time. They escaped through the bye-ways, and when the military retired, returned to their work of destruction in the office, which they completed. Several houses were broken open in different parts of the city, occupied by negroes, and the windows, doors and furniture completely destroyed. Among these was the negro church on Sixth street. One of their last efforts was to fire or otherwise destroy the book establishment of Messrs. Truman & Smith, on Main street. From this they were driven by the police, and soon after, before daylight, dispersed from mere exhaustion.

It is impossible to learn either the number of killed and wounded on either side, probably several were killed and twenty or thirty variously wounded, though but few dangerously. Several of the citizen-police were hurt with stones, &c.; the authorities succeeded in arresting about forty of the mob, who are now in prison. The mob was in many cases encouraged and led on by persons from Kentucky. About 11 o'clock on Saturday night, a bonfire was lighted on that side of the river, and loud shouts sent up, as if a great triumph had been achieved. In some cases the motions of the mob were directed and managed by mere boys, who suggested the points of attack, put the vote, declared the result and led the way! After all the negro men had been disarmed and committeed to prison for safe keeping, under a solemn pledge that their wives and children should be protected, a band of white men were permitted to renew their brutal attacks upon these females and children. The excitement continued yesterday. The governor, who had arrived in town, issued his proclamation. The citizens rallied with spirit to aid the city authorities. Strong patroles of military and citizens, last night, prevented any further outbreak.

Bank Mob, Jan. 11, 1842.—Monday evening, the Miami Exporting Company Bank assigned its effects, and on Tuesday morning, (Jan. 11,) the bank of Cincinnati closed doors. Early in the morning, the crowd, in consequence of their failures, began to collect around the doors of these institutions, and by 11 o'clock, had broken into them, destroying all the movable property and whatever of books or papers could be laid hold of. About this time, ten of the city guards, headed by their brave captain, Mitchell, appeared, drove the rioters away, and, for a time, gallantly maintained their position; but they were called off. On retiring, they were assailed—they fired, and wounded some one or two persons. The mob had, with this exception, undisputed possession of the city, and commenced, first an attack upon Babes' Exchange Bank, and after that, upon Lougee's exchange office, both of which they destroyed, making havock of every thing which was at all destructible.

Distressing Fire, Feb. 28th, 1843.—On Saturday morning, about 5 o'clock, a fire broke out in the smoke-house of Messrs. Pugh & Alvord, at the corner of Walnut street and the canal, which, in its consequences, has been one of the most distressing that ever occurred in this city. The smoke-house was in the rear, and somewhat detached from the main building, being connected with it only by a wooden door and narrow passage-way, through which the meat was usually wheeled. It was thought the fire could be confined to the former, and for that purpose the pork-house was closed as tight as possible, by shutting all the doors and windows, to exclude a rush of air to feed the flames. In the course of half an hour, the main building was filled with smoke, rarified air and inflammable gas from the smoke-house; and when the flames burst through the wooden door connecting the two buildings, an instantaneous roar of flame was perceived, and in the twinkling of an eye, the whole of this spacious, substantial building was a mass of ruins. The whole roof was lifted in the air and thrown into the streets in large fragments—the second story walls, on the north and south sides, were thrown down, and the whole eastern end of both stories fronting on Walnut street, blown into the streets from its foundation up. The appearance of the explosion was awfully terrific, and its consequences fatal to several of our most estimable citizens. We annex the names of the killed and severely wounded, as far as we can now ascertain them. *Killed*—Joseph Bonsall, Caleb W. Taylor, H. S. Edmands, J. S. Chamberlain, H. O. Merrill, John Ohe, a German laborer, with two or three other German laborers. *Wounded severely*—George Shillito, H. Thorpe, T. S. Shaeffer, Mr. Alvord, (of the firm of Pugh & Alvord,) Samuel Schooley, Warren G. Finch, John Blakemore, Lewis Wisby, John M. Vansickle, Joseph Trefts, A. Oppenhermer, Jas. Tryatt, Robt. Rice, William H. Goodloe.

A few minutes before the explosion, the smoke settled to the ground around the corner of the building, on the canal and Walnut street fronts, which caused the removal of the masses of people which filled those spaces, unconscious of danger. But for this, the force of the explosion being in that direction, the destruction of life would have been frightfully extensive.

On Sunday morning, a special meeting of the city council was called, and in obedience to one of the resolutions passed, the mayor issued a proclamation, requesting the citizens to suspend their business on Monday, the 27th inst., and attend the funerals of the deceased. On Monday, the court of common pleas adjourned for this purpose, shops were closed, and the business of the day was set aside. The bells were tolled, and little was done save to aid in performing the last sad rites of the dead. They had fallen in the public service, and the public mind was anxious to testify to their virtues and bespeak the sorrow felt for the common loss. Never, indeed, did we ever observe a deeper solemnity than pervaded the immense masses who attended the funeral services of Chamberlain and Edmands. Close around their biers, pressed the brave firemen who had stood by their side whenever their common services were required; and as the men of God lifted up their voices in prayer, and spoke of the virtues of the dead, their emotion was too strong to be suppressed; and as they stood at the altar and the grave, they gave strong utterance to their own and the public sorrow. And thus were these useful citizens and worthy men borne to their long home.

Old Baptist Church at Columbia.

The engraving shows the old Baptist church, at Columbia, as it appeared in 1830, even to the loose weather-boarding. It was taken down in 1835, but we have not the date of its erection. The engraving is copied from one in the American Pioneer, where it is stated that this was the first house of worship built in Ohio, which, from some evidence produced below, we think is an error. The society which worshipped in it, was constituted in 1790, by Dr. Stephen Gano.

We have previously slightly noticed the history of the settlement at Columbia, the second in Ohio, and now present, in addition, some reminiscences from the narrative of the late O. M. Spencer, who was there as early as December, 1790.

It is, perhaps, unknown to many, that the broad and extensive plain stretching along the Ohio from the Crawfish to the mouth, and for three miles up the Little Miami, and now divided into farms, highly cultivated, was the ancient site of Columbia, a town laid out by Major Benjamin Stites, its original proprietor; and by him and others once expected to become a large city, the great capital of the west. From Crawfish, the small creek forming its northwestern boundary, more than one mile up the Ohio, and extending back about three-fourths of a mile, and half way up the high hill which formed a part of its eastern and northern limits, the ground was laid off into blocks, containing each eight lots of half an acre, bounded by streets intersected at right angles. The residue of the plain was divided into lots of four and five acres, for the accommodation of the town. Over this plain, on our arrival, we found scattered about fifty cabins, flanked by a small stockade nearly half a mile below the mouth of the Miami, together with a few block-houses for the protection of the inhabitants, at suitable distances along the bank of the Ohio.

Fresh in my remembrance is the rude log-house, the first humble sanctuary of the first settlers of Columbia, standing amidst the tall forest trees, on the beautiful knoll, where now [1834] is a grave-yard, and the ruins of a Baptist meeting-house of later years. There, on the holy Sabbath, we were wont to assemble to hear the word of life; but our fathers met, with their muskets and rifles, prepared for action, and ready to repel any attack of the enemy. And while the watchman on the walls of Zion was uttering his faithful and pathetic warning, the sentinels without, at a few rods distance, with measured step, were now pacing their walks, and now standing and with strained eyes endeavoring to pierce through the distance, carefully scanning every object that seemed to have life or motion.

The first clergyman I there heard preach was Mr. Gano, father of the late Gen. Gano, of this city, then a captain, and one of the earliest settlers of Columbia. Never shall I forget that holy and venerable man, with locks white with years, as with a voice tremulous with age, he ably expounded the word of truth.

I well recollect, that in 1791, so scarce and dear was flour, that the little that could be afforded in families, was laid by to be used only in sickness, or for the entertainment of friends; and although corn was then abundant, there was but one mill, (Wickerham's,) a floating mill, on the Little Miami, near where Turpin's now [1834] stands: it was built in a small flat boat tied to the bank, its wheel turning slowly with the natural current running between the flat and a small pirogue anchored in the stream, and on which one end of its shaft rested; and having only one pair of small stones, it was at best barely sufficient to supply meal for the inhabitants of Columbia and the neighboring families; and sometimes, from low water and other unfavorable circumstances, it was of little use, so that we were obliged to supply the deficiency from hand-mills, a most laborious mode of grinding.

The winter of 1791–2, was followed by an early and delightful spring; indeed, I have often thought that our first western winters were much milder, our springs earlier, and our autumns longer than they now are. On the last of February, some of the trees were putting forth their foliage; in March, the red bud, the hawthorn and the dog-wood, in full bloom, checkered the hills, displaying their beautiful colors of rose and lily; and in April, the ground was covered with May apple, bloodroot, ginseng, violets, and a great variety of herbs and flowers. Flocks of parroquets were seen, decked in their rich plumage of green and gold. Birds of various species, and of every hue, were flitting from tree to tree, and the beautiful redbird, and the untaught songster of the west, made the woods vocal with their melody. Now might be heard the plaintive wail of the dove, and now the rumbling drum of the partridge, or the loud gobble of the turkey. Here might be seen the clumsy bear, doggedly moving off, or urged by pursuit into a laboring gallop, retreating to his citadel in the top of some lofty tree; or approached suddenly, raising himself erect in the attitude of defence, facing his enemy and waiting his approach; there the timid deer, watchfully resting, or cautiously feeding, or aroused from his thicket, gracefully bounding off, then stopping, erecting his stately head and for a moment gazing around, or snuffing the air to ascertain his enemy, instantly springing off, clearing logs and bushes at a bound, and soon distancing his pursuers. It seemed an earthly paradise; and but for apprehension of the wily copperhead, who lay silently coiled among the leaves, or beneath the plants, waiting to strike his victim; the horrid rattle-snake, who more chivalrous, however, with head erect amidst its ample folds, prepared to dart upon his foe, generously with the loud noise of his rattle, apprised him of danger; and the still more fearful and insidious savage, who, crawling upon the ground, or noiselessly approaching behind trees and thickets, sped the deadly shaft or fatal bullet, you might have fancied you were in the confines of Eden or the borders of Elysium.

At this delightful season, the inhabitants of our village went forth to their labor, inclosing their fields, which the spring flood had opened, tilling their ground, and planting their corn for their next year's sustenance. I said, went forth, for their principal corn-field was distant from Columbus about one and a half miles east, and adjoining the extensive plain on which the town stood. That large tract of alluvial ground, still known by the name of Turkey Bottom, and which, lying about fifteen feet below the adjoining plain, and annually overflowed, is yet very fertile, was laid off into lots of five acres each, and owned by the inhabitants of Columbia; some possessing one, and others two or more lots; and to save labor, was enclosed with one fence. Here the men generally worked in companies exchanging labor, or in adjoining fields, with their fire-arms near them, that in case of an attack they might be ready to unite for their common defence. Here, their usual annual crop of corn from ground very ordinarily cultivated, was eighty bushels per acre; and some lots, well tilled, produced a hundred, and in very favorable seasons, a hundred and ten bushels to the acre. An inhabitant of New England, New Jersey, or some portions of Maryland, would scarcely think it credible, that in hills four feet apart, were four or five stalks, one and a half inches in diameter, and fifteen feet in height, bearing each two or three ears of corn, of which some were so far from the ground, that to pull them an ordinary man was obliged to stand on tiptoe.

North Bend is situated 16 miles below Cincinnati, and 4 from the Indiana line, at the northernmost point of a bend in the Ohio river. This place, which was of note in the early settlement of the country, has in later years derived its interest from having been the residence of Gen. Wm. H. Harrison, and the spot where rest his mortal remains. The family mansion stands on a level plat, about 300 yards back from the Ohio, amid scenery of a pleasing and retired character. The eastern half of the mansion, that is, all that part on the reader's right, from the door in the main building, is built of logs; but the whole of the building being clapboarded and painted white, has the same external appearance. The wings were alike: a part of the southern one was destroyed by fire since the decease of its illustrious occupant, a memento of which disaster is shown by the naked

Residence of the late President Harrison, at North Bend.

chimney, that rises like a monument over the ruins. The dwelling is respectably, though plainly furnished, and is at present occupied by the widow of the lamented Harrison, long distinguished for the virtues which adorn the female character.

About a quarter of a mile south of the family mansion, and perhaps half that distance from the river, is the tomb of Harrison. It

Tomb of President Harrison.

stands upon the summit of a small oval-shaped hill, rising about 100 feet from the plain, ornamented by a few scattering trees, and commanding a view of great beauty. The tomb is of brick, and is entered by a plain, unpainted door, on its western end. There is no inscription upon it, nor is any required to mark the restıng place of Harrison.

The annexed sketch of General Harrison, is mainly derived from that published in the National Portrait Gallery, in 1836.

WILLIAM HENRY HARRISON was born at Berkley, the family seat of his father, on James river, 25 miles from Richmond, Virginia, in 1773. He was the youngest of three sons of Benjamin Harrison, a descendant of the celebrated leader of the same name in the wars of Cromwell. Benjamin Harrison occupied a conspicuous part in our own revolutionary struggle, and was one of the most active of that daring band who set the ball in motion. He represented Virginia in congress, in 1774, '75, and '76. He was chairman of the committee of the whole house, when the declaration of independence was agreed to, and was one of its signers. He was elected governor of Virginia, and was one of the most popular officers that ever filled the executive chair. He died in 1791.

Fac-simile of Harrison's signature.

Wm. Henry Harrison was early placed at Hampden Sydney College, which he left at 17 years of age, his mind well imbued with classical literature, and deeply impressed with admiration of the principles of republican Greece and Rome. In obedience to the wishes of his father, whose hospitable and liberal conduct through life prevented him from promising wealth to his son, he entered on the study of medicine; and after a short preparatory course, he repaired, in the spring of 1791, to Philadelphia, to prosecute his studies with greater advantage. The death of his father immediately after his arrival, checked his professional aspirations; and the "note of preparation" which was sounding through the country, for a campaign against the Indians of the west, decided his destiny. He resolved to enter into the service of his government, and to create a name for himself worthy of his father. His guardian, the celebrated Robert Morris, opposed his wishes with all the eloquence of his great mind; but it was in vain that he placed the enterprise before the enthusiastic youth in all its hardships and privations. In order to deter him from his project, he painted an Indian war in a remote and untried wilderness in the darkest colors; he spoke of victory, against such foes, as not involving glory; but of defeat, as insuring disgrace. The remonstrançes of his friend and guardian were fruitless, and General Washington at length yielded to the importunities of the youth; he presented him with an ensign's commission. With characteristic ardor he departed for Fort Washington, now Cincinnati; where, however, he arrived too late to participate in the unfortunate campaign. The fatal 4th of November had passed, and he was only in time to learn the earliest intelligence of the death of Butler, and of Oldham, and of the unparalleled massacre of the army of St. Clair.

The return of the broken troops had no effect in damping the zeal of young Harrison. He devoted himself ardently to the study of the theory of the higher tactics; his education gave him advantages possessed by few young soldiers of that day; and when, in the succeeding year, the gallant Wayne assumed the command, Ensign Harrison was immediately noticed by this experienced commander, and selected by him for one of his aids. The judicious movements of the new army, and the success which crowned the campaign under Wayne, are a brilliant portion of our history. Harrison distinguished himself handsomely in Wayne's victory, and his chief did him the justice to name him specially in the official report of the engagement.

After the treaty of Greenville, 1795, Captain Harrison was left in command of Fort Washington; and shortly after the departure of General Wayne for the Atlantic states, he married the daughter of Judge Symmes, the proprietor of the Miami purchase. The writer of this brief sketch cannot let the opportunity slip, without offering a passing tribute to the virtues of this estimable woman. She is distinguished for her benevolence and her piety; all who know her, view her with esteem and affection; and her whole course through life, in all its relations, has been characterized by those qualifications that complete the character of an accomplished matron.

The idleness and dissipation of a garrison life comported neither with the taste nor active temper of Captain Harrison. He resigned his commission, and commenced his civil career, at the age of twenty-four years, as secretary of the north-western territory. His capacity was soon noticed by the leaders in the new territory, and he was elected, in 1799, the first delegate in congress for that extensive region, now comprising the states of Ohio, Indiana,

Illinois, and the territory of Michigan. The first and general object of his attention as a representative, was an alteration of the land system of the territory. The law, as it then existed, ordained that not less than four thousand acres (except in particular cases of fractions on the banks of rivers) could be sold at once. The operation of such an ordinance must have been fatal to that class of population, whose industry and labor have since caused the country to advance with such rapid strides to wealth and greatness; it was alone calculated to benefit the speculator and rich monopolist. He was appointed chairman of the committee on lands, (the only instance, it is believed, in the history of our legislation, in which a delegate was so distinguished,) and with the aid of the able men who cooperated with him, he presented the celebrated land report, based on his own previous motion. A bill was framed, and after undergoing some amendments in the senate, was passed into a law, by which one half of the public lands were divided into sections of six hundred and forty acres, and the other into half sections of three hundred and twenty acres. The old system of forfeiture for non-payment was abolished, and payment ordered to be made, one fourth in hand, and the balance at the end of two, three, and four years, allowing still one year, after the expiration of the fourth year, to enable the purchaser to extricate himself, if necessary. This was a point gained, although it was not all the delegate contended for. To this measure is to be imputed the rapid settlement of the country; and if Mr. Harrison had then been called from this world, without rendering any other service to his country, he would richly have merited the title of benefactor of the territory northwest of the Ohio.

The reputation acquired by the young delegate from his legislative success, created a party in his favor, who intimated a desire that he should supersede the venerable governor of the territory. But Mr. Harrison checked the development of this feeling as soon as it was made known to him. He cherished too high a veneration for the pure and patriotic St. Clair; he had too just an estimate of the splendid talents of the governor, and too much sympathy for the war-worn, though sometimes unfortunate hero, to sanction an attempt, which, whether successful or not, would have inflicted one more pang in the bosom of the veteran. A soldier can best feel for a soldier; he declined the interference of his friends, and the subject was dropped. But when, shortly after, Indiana was erected into a separate territory, he was appointed by Mr. Adams the first governor. Previously, however, to quitting congress, he was present at the discussion of the bill for the settlement of Judge Symmes' purchase; and although this gentleman was his father-in-law, he took an active part in favor of those individuals who had purchased from him before he had obtained his patent. It was viewed as a matter of doubt, whether those who had sued the judge in the courts of common law, would be entitled to the remedy in equity against him. He went before the committee in person, and urged them to insert a provision in their favor. Nor did he desist until assured by the attorney general and Mr. Harper, that these persons came fully under the provisions of the act as it then stood. This was the impulse of stern duty; for at the moment he was thus engaged, he considered himself as jeoparding a large pecuniary interest of his father-in-law.

In 1801, Governor Harrison entered upon the duties of his new office, at the old military post of Vincennes. The powers with which he was vested by law have never, since the organization of our government, been conferred upon any other officer,* civil or military; and the arduous character of the duties he had to perform, can only be appreciated by those who are acquainted with the savage and cunning temper of the northwestern Indians; with the genius of the early pioneers, and the nature of a frontier settlement. The dangers of such actions as the battle of Tippecanoe, the defence of Fort Meigs, and the battle of the Thames, are appreciated and felt by all; and the victories which were consequent upon them have crowned the victors with a never fading wreath: but these acts, brilliant as they were, fade when put in comparison with the unremitting labor and exposure to which, for many years after the organization of the first grade of territorial government, the new executive was exposed. The whole territory consisted of three settlements, so widely separated that it was impossible for them to contribute to their mutual defence or encouragement. The first was Clarke's grant at the falls of Ohio; the second, the old French establishment at Vincennes; and the third extended from Kaskaskia to Kahokia, on the Mississippi; the whole comprising a population of about five thousand souls. The territory thus defenceless, presented a frontier, assailable almost at every point, on the northeast, north, and northwest boundaries. Numerous tribes of warlike Indians were thickly scattered throughout the northern portion of the territory, and far beyond its limits,

* Among his duties was that of commissioner to treat with the Indians. In this capacity, he concluded fifteen treaties, and purchased their title to upwards of seventy millions of acres of land.

whose hostile feelings were constantly inflamed by the intrigues of British agents and traders, if not by the immediate influence of the English government itself, and not unfrequently by the uncontrollable outrages of the American hunters themselves; a circumstance which it always has been found impossible to prevent, in the early settlement of the west. Governor Harrison applied himself with characteristic energy and skill. It seems truly miraculous to us, when we retrospect into the early history of his government, that he should have been able to keep down Indian invasion in the infant state of the territory, seeing the great capacity the savages displayed for harassing him at a period when his resources and means had so much increased. The fact proclaims loudly the talents of the chief. Justice tempered by mildness; conciliation and firmness, accompanied by a never slumbering watchfulness; were the means he used. These enabled him to surmount difficulties, under which an ordinary capacity must have been prostrated. The voluminous correspondence of Governor Harrison with Mr. Jefferson, from 1802 till 1809, is a recorded testimony of the ability and success of his administration.

During the year 1811, however, the intrigues of British agents operating on the passions of the Indians, brought affairs to a crisis which rendered hostilities unavoidable. Tecumseh, and his prophet brother, had been laboring unceasingly, since 1805, to bring about this result. Harrison called upon Colonel Boyd, of the 4th United States regiment, then at Pittsburg, (who immediately joined him,) and embodied a militia force as strong as the emergency would permit. To these were added a small but gallant band of chivalrous volunteers from Kentucky, consisting of about sixty-five individuals. With these he commenced his march towards the prophet's town at Tippecanoe. On the 6th of November he arrived in sight of the Indian village, and in obedience to his orders, made several fruitless attempts to negotiate with the savages. Finding it impossible to bring them to any discussion, he resolved to encamp for the night, under a promise from the chiefs to hold a conference next day. He sent forward Brigade Major Clarke and Major Waller Taylor, to select a proper position for the encampment. These officers shortly after returned, and reported that they had found a situation well calculated for the purpose, and on examination, the commander approved of it. Subsequent examination has proved that the ground was admirably adapted to baffle the success of a sudden attack, the only kind which the great experience of Harrison assured him would be attempted. The men reposed upon the spot which each, individually, should occupy, in case of attack. The event justified the anticipations of the chief. On the morning of the 7th, before daylight, the onset was made with the usual yells and impetuosity. But the army was ready; Harrison had risen some time before, and had roused the officers near him. Our limits do not permit us to enter into a detail of the action; the arrangement of the troops was masterly, and spoke the well educated and experienced soldier. The Indians fought with their usual desperation, and maintained their ground for some time with extraordinary courage. Victory declared in favor of discipline, at the expense, however, of some of the most gallant spirits of the age. Among the slain were Colonels Daveis and Owen, of Kentucky, and Captain Spencer, of Indiana. Governor Harrison received a bullet through his stock, without touching his neck. The legislature of Kentucky, at its next session, while in mourning for her gallant dead, passed the following resolution, viz:

"*Resolved*, That Governor William H. Harrison has behaved like a hero, a patriot and general; and that for his cool, deliberate, skillful and gallant conduct, in the battle of Tippecanoe, he well deserves the thanks of the nation."

From this period, until after the declaration of war against England, Governor Harrison was unremittingly engaged in negotiating with the Indians, and preparing to resist a more extended attack from them. In August, 1812, he received the brevet of major general in the Kentucky militia, to enable him to command the forces marching to relieve Detroit. He immediately applied himself to the proper organization of his army on the northwestern frontier. The surrender of Hull changed the face of affairs; he was appointed a major general in the army of the United States, and his duties embraced a larger sphere. Every thing was in confusion, and every thing was to be done; money, arms and men were to be raised. It is under circumstances like these that the talents of a great general are developed more powerfully than in conducting a battle. To do justice to this part of the biography of Harrison, requires a volume of itself. Becoming stronger from reverses, collecting munitions of war, and defending Fort Meigs, were the prominent features of his operations, until we find him in pursuit of Proctor, on the Canadian shore. On the 5th of October, 1813, he brought the British army and their Indian allies, under Proctor and Tecumseh, to action, near the river Thames. The victory achieved by militia over the disciplined troops of England, on this brilliant day, was decisive; and like the battle of the Cowpens, in the war of the revolution, spread joy and animation over the whole union.

For this important action, congress presented General Harrison with a gold medal. The success of the day is mainly attributable to the novel expedient of charging through the British lines with mounted infantry. The glory of originating this manœuvre belongs exclusively to General Harrison.

The northwestern frontier being relieved, and important aid given to that of Niagara, General Harrison left his troops at Sacket's Harbor, under the command of Colonel Smith, and departed for Washington by the way of New York, Philadelphia and Baltimore. On the whole route he was received with enthusiasm, and honored with the highest marks of distinction that can be offered to a citizen bv a republican people.

Owing to a misunderstanding between Mr. Secretary Armstrong and himself, General Harrison resigned his commission in the spring of 1814. Mr. Madison sincerely deplored this step, and assured Governor Shelby, in a letter written immediately after the resignation, "that it would not have been accepted had he been in Washington." It was received and accepted by Secretary Armstrong, while the president was absent at the springs.

General Harrison retired to his farm at North Bend, in Ohio, from which he was successively called by the people, to represent them in the congress of the United States, and in the legislature of the state. In 1824–5, he was elected to the senate of the United States; and in 1828, he was appointed minister to Columbia, which station he held until he was recalled by President Jackson, not for any alledged fault, but in consequence of some difference of views on the Panama question. General Harrison again returned to the pursuits of agriculture at North Bend. In 1834, on the almost unanimous petition of the citizens of the county, he was appointed prothonotary of the court of Hamilton county.

In 1840, General Harrison was called by the people of the United States to preside over the country as its chief magistrate. His election was a triumphant one; of 294 votes for president, he received 234. From the time when he was first nominated for the office until his death, he had been rising in public esteem and confidence; he entered upon the duties of his office with an uncommon degree of popularity, and a high expectation was cherished that his administration would be honorable to himself and advantageous to the country. His death, which took place April 4th, 1841, just a month after his inauguration, caused a deep sensation throughout the country. He was the first president of the United States that had died in office. The members of his cabinet, in their official notification of the event, said: "The people of the United States, overwhelmed like ourselves by an event so unexpected and so melancholy. will derive consolation from knowing that his death was calm and resigned, as his life had been patriotic, useful and distinguished; and that the last utterance of his lips expressed a fervent desire for the perpetuity of the constitution and the preservation of its true principles. In death, as in life, the happiness of his country was uppermost in his thoughts."

President Harrison was distinguished by a generosity and liberality of feeling which was exercised beyond what strict justice to himself and family should have permitted. With ample opportuity for amassing immense wealth, he ever disdained to profit by his public situation for private emolument. His theory was too rigidly honest to permit him to engage in speculation, and his chivalry was too sensitive to permit him to use the time belonging to his country, for private benefit. After nearly fifty years devotion to his duties in the highest stations, he left at his death but little more to his family than the inheritance of an unsullied reputation.

About 30 rods in a westerly direction from the tomb of Harrison, on an adjacent hill, in a family cemetery, is the grave of Judge Symmes. It is covered by a tablet, laid horizontally upon brick work, slightly raised from the ground. On it is the following inscription:—

> Here rest the remains of John Cleves Symmes, who, at the foot of these hills, made the first settlement between the Miami rivers. Born on Long Island, state of New York, July 21st, A. D. 1742. Died at Cincinnati, February 26, A. D. 1814.

Mr. Symmes was born at Riverhead, on Long Island, and early in life was employed in land surveying, and in teaching school. He served in the war of the revolution, though in what capacity is not known, and was in the battle of Saratoga. Having removed to

New Jersey, he became chief justice of the state, and at one time represented it in congress. As early as 1787, and at the same time with the agents of the Ohio company, he made application to congress, in the name of himself and associates, for the purchase of a large tract of land lying between the two Miamies. "The price was 66 cents per acre, to be paid in United States military land

Block House, near North Bend.

warrants, and certificates of debt due from the United States to individuals. The payments were divided into six annual instalments. His associates were principally composed of the officers of the New Jersey line who had served in the war of the revolution. Among them were General Dayton and Elias Boudinot, D. D. His first contract was for one million of acres, made in October, 1788, but owing to the difficulty of making the payments, and the embarrassments growing out of the Indian war, the first contract was not fulfilled, and a new one was made for two hundred and forty-eight thousand acres, in May, 1794, and a patent issued to him and his associates in September following."* Meanwhile, in the spring of 1789, Judge Symmes had located himself at North Bend, where he laid out "Symmes' city," the fate of which has already been stated. The residence of Judge Symmes stood about a mile northwest of his grave. It was destroyed by fire in March, 1811, and all his valuable papers consumed. It was supposed to have been the act of an individual, out of revenge for his refusal to vote for him as a justice of the peace. At the treaty of Greenville, the Indians told him and others, that in the war, they had frequently brought up their rifles to shoot him, and then recognizing him, refrained from pulling the trigger. This was in consequence of his previous kindness to them, and speaks volumes in praise of his benevolence.

On the farm of the late Wm. Henry Harrison, jr., three miles

---

* Dr. S. P. Hildreth, in the American Pioneer.

below North Bend, and two from the Indiana line, was a settlement made at the same time with North Bend. It was called the Sugar Camp settlement, and was composed of about thirty houses. The settlers there erected a block house, near the Ohio river, as a protection against the Indians. It is now standing, though in a more dilapidated condition than represented in the engraving. It is built of logs, in the ordinary manner of block houses, the distinguishing feature of which is, that from the height of a man's shoulder, the building, the rest of the way up, projects a foot or two from the lower part, leaving, at the point of junction between the two parts, a cavity, through which to thrust rifles, on the approach of enemies.

There are several villages in the county, each containing from 200 to 700 inhabitants. They are Harrison, 20 miles from Cincinnati, on the Indiana line; Mt. Pleasant, on the west turnpike to Hamilton, 10 miles from C.; Springfield, on the east turnpike to Hamilton, 15 from C.; Montgomery, 13 miles from C., on the Lebanon road; Miami, 14 miles from C., on the road to Brookville, Indiana; Reading 10, and Sharon, 13 from C., each on the Lebanon turnpike; and Newtown, 10 from C., on the Batavia road. Elizabethtown, Cheviot, Cleve, Warsaw, Sharpsburg, Madisonville, Cummingsville, Burlington and Columbia are small places. About six miles north of Cincinnati, in a beautiful situation among the hills, has lately been built the Farmer's Academy, a chartered institution.

HANCOCK.

Hancock was formed, April 1st, 1820, and named from John Hancock, first president of the revolutionary congress. The surface is level; the soil is black loam, mixed with sand, and based on limestone and very fertile. Its settlers are generally of Pennsylvania origin. The principal products are pork, wheat, corn, oats and maple sugar. The following is a list of its townships in 1840, with their population.

Amanda,	490	Findlay,	1024	Portage,	675
Big Lick,	431	Jackson,	631	Richland,	332
Blanchard,	629	Liberty,	592	Ridge,	479
Cass,	588	Marion,	707	Union,	637
Delaware,	532	Orange,	314	Van Buren,	432
Eagle,	524	Pleasant,	252	Washington,	830

The population of Hancock in 1830, was 813; and in 1840, 10,099, or 17 inhabitants to a square mile.

The central and southern part of this county is watered by Blanchard's fork of the Auglaize and its branches. The Shawnee name of this stream was *Sho-po-qua-te-sepe*, or *Tailor's river.* It seems that Blanchard, from whom this stream was named, was a tailor, or one that sewed garments. He was a native of France, and a man of intelligence; but no part of his history could be obtained from him. He doubtless fled his country for some offense against its laws, intermarried with a Shawnee woman, and after living here thirty years, died in 1802, at or near the site of Fort Findlay. When the Shawnese emigrated to the west, seven of his children were living, one of whom was a chief.* In the war of 1812, a road was cut through this county, over which the troops for the northwest passed. Among these was the army of Hull, which was piloted by Isaac Zane, M'Pherson and Robert Armstrong.

View in Findlay.

Findlay, the county seat, is on Blanchard's fork, 90 miles northeast of Columbus. It contains 1 Presbyterian and 1 Methodist church, 1 academy, 2 newspaper printing offices, 13 mercantile stores, 1 foundery, 1 clothing, 1 flouring and 1 grist mill, and 112 families. A branch railroad has been surveyed from Cary, on the Mad river railroad, to this place, a distance of 16 miles, which will probably ere long be constructed. Findlay derives its name from Fort Findlay, built in the late war by James Findlay, who was a citizen of Cincinnati, a colonel in the late war, and afterwards a member of congress. This fort stood on the south bank of Blanchard's fork, just west of the present bridge. It was a stockade of about fifty yards square, with block houses at its corners, and a ditch in front. It was used as a depot for military stores and provisions.

About 9 o'clock one dark and windy night in the late war, Capt. Wm. Oliver, (now of Cincinnati,) in company with a Kentuckian, left Fort Meigs for Fort Findlay, on an errand of importance, the distance being about 33 miles. They had scarcely started on their dreary and perilous journey, when they unexpectedly came upon an Indian camp, around the fires of which, the Indians were busy cooking their suppers. Disturbed by the noise of their approach, the savages sprang up and ran towards them. At this they reined their horses into the branches of a fallen tree. Fortunately the horses, as if conscious of the danger, stood perfectly still, and the Indians passed around the tree, without making any discovery in the thick darkness. At this juncture, Oliver and his companion put spurs to their horses and dashed forwards into the woods, through which they passed all the way to their point of destination. They arrived safely, but with their clothes completely torn off by the brambles and bushes, and their bodies bruised all over by contusions against the trees. They had scarcely arrived in the fort, when the Indians in pursuit made their appearance, but too late, for their prey had escaped.

* Col. John Johnston.

The town of Findlay was first laid out by Ex-Gov. Joseph Vance and Elnathan Corry, in 1821, and in 1829 relaid out, lots sold and a settlement systematically commenced. In the fall of 1821, however, Wilson Vance (brother of the above) moved into Findlay with his family. There were then some ten or fifteen Wyandot families in the place, who had made improvements. They were a temperate, fine-looking people, and friendly to the first settlers. There were at this time but six other white families in the county, besides that of Mr. Vance. Mr. V. is now the oldest settler in the county. For the first two or three years, all the grain which he used, he brought in teams from his brothers' mills in Champaign county, about forty miles distant. To this should be excepted some little corn which he bought of the Indians, for which he occasionally paid as high as $1 per bushel, and ground it in a hand-mill.

There are some curiosities in the town and county, worthy of note. At the south end of Findlay are two gas wells. From one of them, the gas has been conducted by a pipe into a neighboring dwelling, and used for light. A short distance west of the bridge, on the north bank of Blanchard's fork at Findlay, is a chalybeate spring of excellent medicinal qualities, and from which issues inflammable gas. In the eastern part of the town, is a mineral spring possessing similar qualities. Three miles south of Findlay, is a sycamore of great height, and 34 feet in circumference at its base. Ten miles below Findlay, on the west bank of Blanchard's fork, on the road to Defiance, are two sugar maple trees, 30 feet distant at their base, which, about 60 feet up, unite and form one trunk, and thus continue from thence up, the body of one actually growing into the other, so that each loose their identity and form one entire tree.

Mount Blanchard, Williamstown, Canonsburg, Benton, Van Buren and Risdon are small places, the largest of which may contain 30 dwellings.

HARDIN.

HARDIN was formed from old Indian territory, April 1st, 1820. About half of the county is level, and the remainder undulating: the soil is part gravely loam and part clayey, and based on limestone. The principal productions are wheat, corn and swine. The following is a list of the townships in 1840, with their population.

Blanchard,	241	Jackson,	260	Pleasant,	569
Cissna,	259	Liberty,	170	Round Head,	564
Dudley,	349	Marion,	177	Taylor Creek,	400
Goshen,	549	M'Donald,	285	Washington,	203
Hale,	267				

The population of Hardin, in 1840, was 4583, or 9 inhabitants to a square mile.

Col. John Hardin, from whom this county was named, was an officer of distinction in the early settlement of the west. He was born of humble parentage, in Fauquier county, Virginia, in 1753. From his very youth, he was initiated into the life of a woodsman, and acquired uncommon skill as a marksman and a hunter. In the spring of 1774, young Hardin, then not 21 years of age, was appointed an ensign in a militia company, and shortly after, in an action with the Indians, was wounded in the knee. Before he had fully recovered from his wound, he joined the noted expedition of Dunmore. In the war of the revolution, he was a lieutenant in Morgan's celebrated rifle corps. He was high in the esteem of General Morgan, and was often selected for enterprises of peril, requiring discretion and intrepidity. On one of these occasions, while with the northern army, he was sent out on a reconnoitering expedition, with orders to take a prisoner, for the purpose of obtaining information. Marching silently in advance of his party, he ascended to the top of an abrupt hill, where he met two or three British soldiers and a Mohawk Indian. The moment was critical. Hardin felt no hesitation—his rifle was instantly presented, and they ordered to surrender. The soldiers immediately threw down their arms—the Indian clubbed his gun. They stood, while he continued to advance on them: but none of his men having come up, and thinking he might want some assistance, he turned his head a little and called to them to come on: at this moment, the Indian, observing his eye withdrawn from him, reversed his gun with a rapid motion, in order to shoot Hardin; when he, catching in his vision the gleam of light reflected from the polished barrel, with equal rapidity apprehended its meaning, and was prompt to prevent the dire effect. He brings his rifle to a level in his own hands, and fires without raising it to his face—he had not time, the attempt would have given the Indian the first fire, on that depended life and death—he gained it, and gave the Indian a mortal wound; who, also, firing in the succeeding moment, sent his ball through Hardin's hair. The rest of the party made no resistance, but were marched to camp. On this occasion, Hardin received the thanks of General Gates. In 1786, he settled in Washington county, Kentucky, and there was no expedition into the Indian country after he settled in Kentucky, except that of General St. Clair, which he was prevented from joining from an accidental lameness, in which he was not engaged. In these, he generally distinguished himself by his gallantry and success. In Harmar's expedition, however, he was unfortunate, being defeated by the Indians when on a detached command, near Fort Wayne. Colonel Hardin was killed in the 39th year of his age. He was—says Marshall, in his history of Kentucky, from which these facts are derived—a man of unassuming manners, and great gentleness of deportment; yet of singular firmness and inflexibility as to matters of truth and justice. Prior to the news of his death, such was his popularity in Kentucky, that he was appointed general of the first brigade.

Colonel Hardin was killed by the Indians, in 1792. He was sent by General Washington on a mission of peace to them—and was on his way to the Shawnees' town. He had reached within a few miles of his point of destination, and was within what is now Shelby county, in this state, when he was overtaken by a few Indians, who proposed encamping with him, and to accompany him the next day to the residence of their chiefs. In the night, they basely murdered him, as was alledged, for his horse and equipments, which were attractive and valuable. His companion, a white man, who spoke Indian, and acted as interpreter, was uninjured. When the chiefs heard of Hardin's death, they were sorry, for they desired to hear what the messenger of peace had to communicate. A town was laid out on the spot some years since, on the state road from Piqua through Wapakonetta, and named, at the suggestion of Col. John Johnston, *Hardin*, to perpetuate the memory and sufferings of this brave and patriotic man. A son of his was lately secretary to the commonwealth of Kentucky.

Fort M'Arthur was a fortification built in the late war, on the Scioto river, in this county, and on Hull's road. The site was a low, flat place, in the far woods, and with but little communication with the settlements, as no person could go from one to the other but at the peril of his life, the woods being infested with hostile Indians.

The fort was a weak stockade, enclosing about half an acre. There were two block houses; one in the northwest, and the other in the southeast angle. Seventy or eighty feet of the enclosure was composed of a row of log corn cribs, covered with a shed roof, sloping inside. A part of the pickets were of split timber, and lapped at the edges: others were round logs, set up endways, and touching each other. The rows of huts for the garrison were a few feet from the walls. It was a post of much danger, liable at any moment to be attacked.

It was at one time commanded by Captain Robert M'Clelland, who recently died in Greene county. He was brave, and when roused, brave to rashness. While he commanded at Fort M'Arthur, one of his men had gone a short distance from the walls for the purpose of peeling bark—while he was engaged at a tree, he was shot twice through the body, by a couple of Indians in ambush, whose rifles went off so near together that the reports were barely distinguishable. He uttered one piercing scream of agony, and ran with almost superhuman speed, but fell before he reached the fort. An instant alarm was spread through the garrison, as no doubt was entertained but that this was the commencement of a general attack, which had been long expected. Instead of shutting the gates to keep out danger, M'Clelland seized his rifle, and calling on some of his men to follow, of which but few obeyed, he hastened to the place of ambush and made diligent search for the enemy, who, by an instant and rapid retreat, had effected their escape; nor did he return until he had scoured the woods all around in the vicinity of the fort.*

Kenton.

Kenton, the county seat, is on the Scioto river and Mad river railroad, 71 miles northwest of Columbus, and 78 from Sandusky City. It was laid out only a few years since, and named from Gen. Simon Kenton, a sketch of whom is under the head of Logan county. The view shown was taken southwest of the town. The railroad is shown in front, with the depot on the left: the Presbyterian church appears near the center of the view. In the center of the town is a neat public square. From the facilities furnished by the railroad, Kenton promises to be an inland town of considerable business and population. It now contains 8 dry goods and 4 grocery stores, 1 newspaper printing office, 1 foundery, 1 grist and 1 saw mill, 1 Presbyterian and 1 Methodist church, and had in 1840, 300 inhabitants, since which it is estimated to have more than doubled its population. There is a house in this town, the rain flowing from its north ridge finds its way to Lake Erie, and that from its south ridge to the Gulf of Mexico. Patterson, 10 miles north, on the railroad, and Roundhead, 14 southwest of Kenton, are small villages. This

* Thomas C. Wright.

last was named from *Roundhead*, a Wyandot chief, who had a village there. Major Galloway, who visited it about the year 1800, says that there were then quite a number of apple trees in the village, and that the Indians raised many swine. Roundhead, whose Indian name was *Stiahta*, was a fine looking man. He had a brother named John Battise, of great size and personal strength. His nose, which was enormous, resembled, in hue, a blue potatoe, was full of indentations, and when he laughed, it shook like jelly. These Indians joined the British in the late war, and Battise was killed at Fort Meigs.

HARRISON.

Harrison was formed Jan. 1st, 1814, from Jefferson and Tuscarawas, and named from Gen. Wm. H. Harrison. It is generally very hilly: these hills are usually beautifully curving and highly cultivated. The soil is clayey, in which coal and limestone abound. It is one of the greatest wool-growing counties in Ohio, having, in 1847, 102,971 sheep. Large quantities of wheat, corn, oats and hay are produced, and a considerable number of horses, cattle and swine exported. The following is a list of its townships in 1840, with their population.

Archer,	1009	German,	1349	Nottingham,	1368
Athens,	1435	Green,	1465	Rumley,	1027
Cadiz,	2386	Monroe,	896	Short Creek,	2023
Franklin,	941	Moorefield,	1344	Stock,	826
Freeport,	1294	North,	1090	Washington,	1004

The population, in 1820, was 14,345, in 1830, 20,920, and in 1840, 20,099; or 50 inhabitants to a square mile.

In April, 1799, Alex. Henderson and family, from Washington county, Pennsylvania, squatted on the southwest quarter of the section on which Cadiz stands: at this time, Daniel Peterson resided at the forks of Short Creek, with his family, the only one within the present limits of Harrison. In 1800, emigrants, principally from Western Pennsylvania, began to cross the Ohio river; and in the course of five or six years, there had settled within the county the following named persons, with their families, viz.:

John Craig, John Taggart, John Jamison, John M'Fadden, John Kernahan, John Huff, John Maholm, John Wallace, John Lyons, Rev. John Rea, Danl. Welch, William Moore, Jas. Black, Saml. Dunlap, James Arnold, Joseph and Samuel M'Fadden, Saml. Gilmore, James Finney, Thos. and Robt. Vincent, Robert Braden, Jas. Wilkin, Samuel and George Kernahan, Thos. Dickerson, Joseph Holmes, James Hanna, Joseph, Wm. and Eleazer Huff, Baldwin Parsons, James Haverfield, Robert Cochran, Samuel Maholm, Hugh Teas, Joseph Clark, Morris West, Jacob Sheplar, Martin Snider, Saml. Osborn, Saml. Smith, and perhaps others, besides those in Cadiz and on Short Creek; Thomas Taylor, John Ross, Thos. Hitchcock, Arthur and Thomas Barrett, Robert and Thos. Maxwell, Absalom Kent, John Pugh, Michael Waxler, Wm. M'Clary, Joseph, Joel and Wm. Johnson, George Layport, William Ingles, Thos. Wilson, and perhaps others on Stillwater; John M'Connell, George Brown, John Love. Wm. and Robt. M'Cullough, Brokaw and others, on Wheeling creek.

Robt. Maxwell, Wm. and Joseph Huff and Michael Maxler, were great hunters, and the three former had been Indian spies, and had many perilous adventures with the Indians. On one occasion, after peace, an Indian boasted, in the presence of Wm. Huff and others, that he had scalped so many whites. Towards evening, the Indian left for his wigwam, but never reached it. Being, shortly after, found killed, some inquiry was made as to the probable cause of his death, when Huff observed, that he had seen him the last time, sitting on a log, smoking his pipe; that he was looking at him and reflecting what he had said about scalping white people, when suddenly his pipe fell from his mouth, and he, Huff, turned away, and had not again seen him until found dead.

Beside frequent trouble with the Indians, the first settlers were much annoyed by wild animals. On one occasion, two sons of Geo. Layport having trapped a wolf, skinned it alive, turned it loose, and a few days after it was found dead.

County Buildings at Cadiz.

One mile west of the east boundary line of Harrison county, there was founded, in 1805, a Presbyterian church, called "Beach Spring," of which Rev. John Rea is at present, and for more than 40 years has been, the stated pastor. Their beginning was small; a log cabin, of not more than 20 feet square, was sufficient to contain all the members and all that attended with them. Their log cabin being burned down by accident, a large house, sufficient to contain a thousand worshippers, was raised in its room, and from 50 communing members, they increased in a short time to 3 and 400, and became the largest Presbyterian church in the state.

Cadiz, the county seat, is a remarkably well-built and city-like town, 4 miles southeasterly from the center of the county, 117 easterly from Columbus, 24 westerly from Steubenville, and 24 northerly from Wheeling. It contains 1 Presbyterian, 1 Methodist Episcopal, 1 Associate, (Seceder,) and 1 Associate Reformed church. It also contains 2 printing presses, 12 dry goods, 7 groceries and 2 drug stores, and had, in 1840, 1028 inhabitants, and is now estimated to contain 1200.

Cadiz was laid out in 1803 or '4, by Messrs. Biggs and Beatty. Its site was then like most of the surrounding country, a forest, and its location was induced by the junction there of the road from Pittsburgh, by Steubenville, with the road from Washington, Pa., by Wellsburgh, Va., from where the two united, passed by Cambridge to Zanesville; and previous to the construction of the national road through Ohio, was travelled more, perhaps, than any other road northwest of the Ohio river. In April, 1807, it contained the following named persons, with their families: Jacob Arnold, innkeeper; Andrew M'Neeley, hatter, and justice of the peace; Joseph Harris, merchant; John Jamison, tanner; John M'Crea, wheelwright, Robt. Wilkin, brickmaker; Connell Abdill, shoemaker; Jacob Myers, carpenter, John Pritchard, blacksmith; Nathan Adams, tailor; James Simpson, reed-maker; Wm. Tingley, school teacher, and old granny Young, midwife and baker, who was subsequently elected (by the citizens of the township, in a fit of hilarity) to the office of justice of the peace; but females not being eligible to office in Ohio, the old lady was obliged to forego the pleasure of serving her constituents.

The first celebration of independence in Cadiz was on the 4th of July, 1806, when the people generally, of the town and country, for miles around, attended and partook of a fine repast of venison, wild turkey, bear meat, and such vegetables as the country afforded; while for a drink, rye whiskey was used. There was much hilarity and good feeling, for at this time, men were supported for office from their fitness, rather than from their political sentiments.

About one and a half miles west of Cadiz, on the northern peak of a high sandy ridge, are the remains of what is called the "*standing stone*," from which a branch of Stillwater derived its name. The owner of the land has quarried off its top some eight feet. It is sandstone, and was originally from 16 to 18 feet high, about 50 feet around its base, and tapered from midway up to a cone-like top, being only about 20 feet around near its summit. It is said to have been a place of great resort by the Indians, and its origin has been a subject of speculation with many persons. It is, however, what geologists term a *boulder*, and was brought to its present position from, perhaps, a thousand miles north, embedded in a huge mass of ice, in some great convulsion of nature, ages since.

The following is a list of the most important villages in the county with their distance and direction from Cadiz, and population in 1840 Harrisville, 9 southeast, 262; New Jefferson, 11 northeast, 155; New Rumley, 11 north, 136; Deersville, 12 west, 202; Freeport, 17 south of west, 255; Moorfield, 12 southwest, 210; Athens, 6 south, 319. At this last, is Franklin college, a respectable institution, founded in 1825, which has at present 65 students and a library of near 2,000 volumes. Quite a number of students have graduated there, and its situation, in regard to retirement, economy and health, is auspicious to its success. At present, Rev. Alex. D. Clark is president, Rev. Andrew M. Black, prof. of languages, and Rev. Joseph Gorden, prof. of mathematics.*

HENRY.

Henry was formed, April 1st, 1820, from old Indian territory, and named from Patrick Henry, the celebrated Virginian orator in the revolutionary era. This county is well supplied with running streams, and the soil naturally rich and productive. The principal products are Indian corn, oats, potatoes and maple sugar. The following is a list of its townships in 1840, with their population.

Adams,	188	Fredonia,	105	Richfield,	83
Damascus,	489	Napoleon,	609	Richland,	542
Flatrock,	476				

The population of Henry, in 1840, was 2,492, or 5 inhabitants to a square mile.

A greater part of this county is covered by the famous "*Black Swamp*." This tract reaches over an extent of country of one hundred and twenty miles in length, with an average breadth of forty miles, about equalling in area the state of Connecticut. It is at present thinly settled, and has a population of about 50,000 ; but, probably, in less than a century, when it shall be cleared and drained, it will be the garden of Ohio, and support half a million of people. The surface is generally high and level, and "sustains a dense growth of forest-trees, among which beech, ash, elm, and oak, cotton wood and poplar, most abound. The branches and foliage of this magnificent forest are almost impenetrable to the rays of the sun, and its gloomy silence remained unbroken until disturbed by the restless emigrants of the west." It is an interesting country to travel through. The perfect uniformity of the soil, the level surface of the ground, alike retaining and alike absorbing water, has given to the forest a homogeneous character: the trees are all generally of the same height, so that when viewed at a distance through the haze, the forest appears like an immense blue wall, stretched across the horizon. It is yet the abode of wild animals: flocks of deer are occasionally seen bounding through its labyrinths, flowers and flowering shrubs bloom in its midst, and beautiful birds make it vocal with melody.

Throughout the swamp, a mile or two apart, are slight ridges of limestone, from 40 rods to a mile wide, running usually in a westerly direction, and covered with black walnut, butternut, red elm and maple. The top soil of the swamp is about a foot thick, and composed of a black, decayed vegetable matter, extremely fertile. Beneath this, and extending several feet, is a rich yellow clay, having large quantities of the fertilizing substances of lime and silex. Lower

---

* The facts embodied under the head of Harrison county, were mainly derived from the communication of a gentleman residing in Cadiz.

still is a stratum of black clay of great depth. The water of the swamp is unpleasant to the taste, from containing a large quantity of sulphur: it is, however, healthy and peculiarly beneficial to persons of a costive habit, or having diseases of the blood. The soil is excellent for grain and almost all productions: garden vegetables and fruit thrive wonderfully. We were shown an orchard of apple trees, some of which had attained the height of 20 feet, and measured at their base 20 inches, which, when first planted, five years since, were mere twigs, but a few feet in height, and no larger than one's finger.

The notorious *Simon Girty* once resided 5 miles above Napoleon, at a place still called "*Girty's Point.*" His cabin was on the bank of the Maumee, a few rods west of the residence of Mr. Elijah Gunn. All traces of his habitation have been obliterated by culture, and a fine farm now surrounds the spot.

Simon Girty was from Pennsylvania, to which his father had emigrated from Ireland. The old man was beastly intemperate, and nothing ranked higher in his estimation than a jug of whiskey "Grog was his song, and grog would he have." His sottishness turned his wife's affection. Ready for seduction, she yielded her heart to a neighboring rustic, who, to remove all obstacles to their wishes, knocked Girty on the head and bore off the trophy of his prowess. Four sons of this interesting couple were left, Thomas, Simon, George and James. The three latter were taken prisoners, in Braddock's war, by the Indians. George was adopted by the Delawares, became a ferocious savage, and died in a drunken fit. James was adopted by the Shawnees, and became as depraved as his other brothers. It is said, he often visited Kentucky, at the time of its first settlement, and inflicted most barbarous tortures upon all captive women who came within his reach. Traders, who were acquainted with him, say, so furious was he, that he would not have turned on his heel to save a prisoner from the flames. To this monster are to be attributed many of the cruelties charged upon his brother Simon; yet he was caressed by Proctor and Elliott. Simon was adopted by the Senecas, and became an expert hunter. In Kentucky and Ohio, he sustained the character of an unrelenting barbarian. Sixty years ago, with his name was associated every thing cruel and fiend-like. To the women and children, in particular, nothing was more terrifying than the name of Simon Girty. At that time, it was believed by many that he had fled from justice and sought refuge among the Indians, determined to do his countrymen all the harm in his power. This impression was an erroneous one. Being adopted by the Indians, he joined them in their wars, and conformed to their usages. This was the education he had received, and their foes were his. Although trained in all his pursuits as an Indian, it is said to be a fact susceptible of proof, that, through his importunities, many prisoners were saved from death. His influence was great, and when he chose to be merciful, it was generally in his power to protect the imploring captive. His reputation was that of an honest man, and he fulfilled his engagements to the last cent. It is said, he once sold his horse rather than to incur the odium of violating his promise. He was intemperate, and when intoxicated, ferocious and abusive alike of friends and foes. Although much disabled the last ten years of his life, by rheumatism, he rode to his hunting grounds in pursuit of game. Suffering the most excruciating pains, he often boasted of his warlike spirit. It was his constant wish, one that was gratified, that he might die in battle. He was at Proctor's defeat, and was cut to pieces by Col. Johnson's mounted men.

The above we derive from Campbell's sketches. We have, in addition, some anecdotes and facts, which throw doubt over the character of Simon Girty, as there given.

In September, 1777, Girty led the attack on Fort Henry, on the site of Wheeling, during which he appeared at the window of a cabin, with a white flag, and demanded the surrender of the fort in the name of his Britannic majesty. He read the proclamation of Gov. Hamilton, and promised the protection of the crown if they would lay down their arms and swear allegiance to the king. He warned them to submit peaceably, and admitted his inability to restrain his warriors, when excited in the strife of battle. Col. Shepherd, the commandant, promptly replied, that they would never surrender to *him*, and that he could only obtain possession of the fort when there remained no longer an American soldier to defend it. Girty renewed his proposition, but it was abruptly ended by a shot from a thoughtless youth, and Girty retired and opened the siege, which proved unsuccessful. Baker's station, in that vicinity, was also attacked, not far from this time, by Girty and his band, but without success.

In August, 1782, a powerful body of Indians, led by Girty, appeared before Bryan 's station, in Kentucky, about five miles from Lexington. The Kentuckians made such a gallant resistance, that the Indians became disheartened, and were about abandoning the siege; upon this, Girty thinking he might frighten the garrison into a surrender, mounted a stump, within speaking distance, and commenced a parley. He told them who he was, that he looked hourly for reinforcements with cannon, and that they had better surrender at once; if they did so, no one should be hurt; otherwise, he feared they would all fall victims. The garrison were intimidated; but one young man, named Reynolds, seeing the effect of this harangue, and believing his story, as it was, to be false, of his own accord, answered him in this wise: "You need not be so particular to tell us your name; we know your name and you too. I've had a *villainous untrustworthy cur dog* this long while, named *Simon Girty*, in compliment to you; he's so like you—just as ugly and just as wicked. As to the cannon, let them come on; the country's roused, and the scalps of your red cut-throats, and your own too, will be drying on our cabins in twenty-four hours; and if, by chance, you or your allies do get into the fort, we've a big store of rods laid in, on purpose to scourge you out again." This method of Reynolds was effectual; the Indians withdrew, and were pursued a few days after, the defenders of the fort being reinforced, to the Blue licks, where the Indians lay in ambush, and defeated the Kentuckians with great slaughter. Girty was also at St. Clair's defeat and led the attack on Colerain.

Dr. Knight, in his narrative of his captivity and burning of Col. Crawford, (see Wyandot co.,) speaks of the cruelty of Simon Girty to the colonel and himself. Col. John Johnston corroborates the account of Dr. Knight. In a communication before us he says. "He was notorious for his cruelty to the whites, who fell into the hands of the Indians. His cruelty to the unfortunate Col. Crawford, is well known to myself, and although I did not witness the tragedy, I can vouch for the facts of the case, having had them from eye witnesses. When that brave and unfortunate commander was suffering at the stake by a slow fire, in order to lengthen his misery to the longest possible time, he besought Girty to have him shot, to end his torments, when the monster mocked him by firing powder without ball at him. Crawford and Girty had been intimately acquainted in the early settlement of Pennsylvania; I knew a brother of the latter at Pittsburg, in 1793.

When Simon Kenton was taken prisoner, his life was saved through the interposition of Girty. (See a sketch of Kenton in Logan county.)

Mr. Daniel M. Workman, now living in Logan county, gave us orally the following respecting the last years of Girty. In 1813, said he, I went to Malden and put up at a hotel kept by a Frenchman. I noticed in the bar-room, a grey headed and blind old man. The landlady, who was his daughter, a woman of about thirty years of age, inquired of me, "Do you know who that is?" pointing to the old man. On my replying, "No!" she rejoined, it is *Simon Girty!* He had then been blind about four years. In 1815, I returned to Malden and ascertained that Girty had died a short time previous. Simon Kenton informed me that Girty left the whites, because he was not promoted to the command of a company or a battalion. I was also so informed by my father-in-law, who was taken prisoner by the Indians. Girty was a man of extraordinary strength, power of endurance, courage and sagacity. He was in height about 5 feet 10 inches and strongly made.

Oliver M. Spencer, who was taken prisoner by the Indians while a youth, in 1792, in his narrative of his captivity makes some mention of the Girtys. While at Defiance, the old Indian priestess, *Cooh-coo-cheeh*, with whom he lived, took him to a Shawnee village, a short distance below, on a visit. There he saw the celebrated chief, Blue Jacket, and Simon Girty, of whom he speaks as follows:

One of the visitors of Blue Jacket, (the Snake,) was a plain, grave chief of sage appearance; the other, Simon Girty, whether it was from prejudice, associating with his look the fact, that he was a renegado, the murderer of his own countrymen, racking his diabolic invention to inflict new and more excruciating tortures, or not, his dark shaggy hair, his low forehead, his brows contracted, and meeting above his short flat nose; his grey sunken eyes, averting the ingenious gaze; his lips thin and compressed, and the dark and sinister expression of his countenance, to me, seemed the very picture of a villain. He wore the Indian costume, but without any ornament; and his silk handkerchief, while it supplied the place of a hat, hid an unsightly wound in his forehead. On each side, in his belt, was stuck a silver-mounted pistol, and at his left, hung a short broad dirk, serving occasionally the uses of a knife. He made of me many inquiries; some about my family, and the particulars of my captivity; but more of the strength of the different garrisons; the number of American troops at Fort Washington, and whether the president intended soon to send another army against the Indians. He spoke of the wrongs he had received at the hands of his countrymen, and with fiendish exultation of the revenge he had taken. He boasted of his exploits, of the number of his victories, and of his personal prowess; then raising his handkerchief, and exhibiting the deep wound in his forehead, (which I was afterwards told was inflicted by the tomahawk of the celebrated Indian chief, Brandt, in a drunken frolic,) said it was a sabre cut, which he received in battle at St. Clair's defeat; adding with an oath, that he had "sent the d——d Yankee officer" that gave it, "to h—l." He ended by telling me that I would never see home; but if I should turn out to be a good hunter and a brave warrior, I might one day be a chief." His presence and conversation having rendered my situation painful, I was not a little relieved when, a few hours after, ending our visit, we returned to our quiet lodge on the bank of the Maumee.

Just before Spencer was liberated from captivity, he had an interview with Joseph Girty, and not a very pleasant one either, judging from his narration of it.

Elliot ordered Joseph to take me over to James Girty's, where he said our breakfast would be provided. Girty's wife soon furnished us with some coffee, wheat bread, and stewed pork and venison, of which (it being so much better than the food to which I had been lately accustomed) I ate with great *gout;* but I had not more than half breakfasted, when Girty came in, and seating himself opposite me, said, "So, my young Yankee, you're about to start for home." I answered, "Yes, sir, I hope so." That, he said, would depend on my master, in whose kitchen he had no doubt I should first serve a few years' apprenticeship as a scullion. Then taking his knife, said, (while sharpening it on a whetstone,) "I see your ears are whole yet, but I'm d—n—y mistaken if you leave this without the Indian ear mark, that we may know you when we catch you again." I did not wait to prove whether he was in jest, or in downright earnest; but leaving my breakfast half finished, I instantly sprang from the table, leaped out of the door, and in a few seconds took refuge in Mr. Ironside's house. On learning the cause of my flight, Elliot uttered a sardonic laugh, deriding my unfounded childish fears, as he was pleased to term them; but Ironside looked serious, shaking his head, as if he had no doubt that if I had remained, Girty would have executed his threat.

We finish this notice of the Girtys by a brief extract from the MSS. of Jonathan Alder, who knew Simon—showing that he was by no means wholly destitute of kind feelings.

I knew Simon Girty to purchase at his own expense, several boys who were prisoners, take them to the British and have them educated. He was certainly a friend to many prisoners.

Napoleon, the county seat, is on the Maumee river and Wabash and Erie canal, 17 miles below Defiance, 40 above Toledo and 154 NW. of Columbus. It is a small village containing about 300 inhabitants. Florida, 8 miles above, on the canal, is also a small town.

HIGHLAND.

HIGHLAND was formed in May, 1805, from Ross, Adams and Clermont, and so named because on the *high land* between the Scioto and Little Miami. The surface is part rolling and part level, and the soil various in its quality. As a whole, it is a wealthy and productive county, and the wheat raised here being of a superior quality, commands the highest market price. The principal productions are wheat, Indian corn, oats, maple sugar, wool, swine and cattle. The following is a list of its townships, in 1840, with their population.

Brush Creek,	1502	Jackson,	2352	Paint,	2560
Clay,	783	Liberty,	3521	Salem,	1004
Concord,	1014	Madison,	1916	Union,	1089
Dodson,	795	New Market,	1302	White Oak,	887
Fairfield,	3544				

The population of Highland in 1820, was 12,308; in 1830, 16,347; in 1840, 22,269, or 40 inhabitants to a square mile.

This county was first settled about the year 1801; the principal part of the early settlers were from Virginia and North Carolina, many of whom were Friends. The first settlement was made in the vicinity of New Market, by Oliver Ross, Robert Huston, Geo. W. Barrere and others. Among the settlers of the county, was Bernard Weyer, the discoverer of the noted cave in Virginia, known as "*Weyer's cave*," who is yet living on the rocky fork of Paint creek. The celebrated pioneer and hunter, Simon Kenton, made a trace through this county, which passed through or near the site of Hillsboro': it is designated in various land titles as "*Kenton's Trace.*" In the southeastern part of the county, near the village of Sinking Spring, is an eminence five hundred feet above Brush creek, which washes its base, called "Fort Hill;" on its summit, is an ancient work of over half a mile in length; a full description and drawing of which, by Dr. John Locke, is in the Geological Reports of Ohio

Gorge in Rocky Fork of Paint Creek.

About 13 miles east of Hillsborough, near the county line and road to Chillicothe, the Rocky fork of Paint creek passes for about two miles, previous to its junction with the main stream, through a deep gorge, in some places more than a hundred feet in depth, and forming a series of wild picturesque views, one of which, at a place called "the narrows," is here represented. In the ravine are numerous caves, which are much visited. One or two of them have been explored for a distance of several hundred yards.

Hillsborough, the county seat, is on the dividing ridge between the Miami and Scioto, in a remarkably healthy situation, 62 miles south-easterly from Columbus, and 36 westerly from Chillicothe. It was laid out as the seat of justice in 1807, on land of Benjamin Ellicott, of Baltimore, the site being selected by David Hays, the commissioner appointed for that purpose. Prior to this, the seat of justice was at New Market, although the greater part of the population of Highland, was north and east of Hillsborough. The original town plat comprised 200 acres, 100 of which Mr. Ellicott gave to the

View in Hillsborough.

county, and sold the remainder at $2 per acre. It contains 1 Presbyterian, 1 Methodist and 1 Baptist church, 2 newspaper printing offices, 14 stores, and had in 1840, 868 inhabitants. It is a neat village, the tone of society elevated, and its inhabitants disposed to foster the literary institutions situated here.

The Hillsborough academy was founded in 1827; its first teacher was the Rev. J. M'D. Mathews. A charter was obtained shortly after, and the funds of the institution augmented by two valuable tracts, comprising 2000 acres, given by Maj. Adam Hoops and the late Hon. John Brown, of Kentucky. A handsome brick building has been purchased by its trustees, on a beautiful eminence near the town, which is devoted to the purposes of the institution. It has the nucleus for a fine library, and ere long will possess an excellent philosophical and chemical apparatus. It is now very flourishing, and has a large number of pupils; "the classical and mathematical courses are as thorough and extensive, as at any college in the west;" instruction is also given in other branches usually taught in colleges. Especial attention is given to training young men as teachers. It is under the charge of Isaac Sarns, Esq. The Oakland female seminary, a chartered institution, was commenced in 1839, by the Rev. J. M'D. Mathews, who has still charge of it. It now has over 100 pupils, and is in excellent repute. Diplomas are conferred upon its graduates. The academy is beautifully located in the outskirts of the village, and is well furnished with maps, apparatus, &c., and has a small library.

The Hon. William A. Trimble was born in Woodford, Ky., April 4th, 1786. His father, Capt. James Trimble, had emigrated with his family from Augusta, Va., to Kentucky. In the year 1804, being deeply impressed with the evils of slavery, he was about to remove into Highland, when he was taken unwell and died. His son William graduated at Transylvania university, after which he returned to Ohio, spent some time in the office of his brother Allen, since Gov. Trimble, later studied law at Litchfield, Conn., and returned to Highland and commenced the practice of his profession.

At the breaking out of the war of 1812, he was chosen major in the Ohio volunteers, was at Hull's surrender and was liberated on his patrole. Some time in the following winter he was regularly exchanged, and in March was commissioned major in the 26th regiment. In the defence of and sortie from Fort Erie, he acted with signal bravery, and received a severe wound, which was the prominent cause of his death, years after. He continued in the army until 1819, with the rank of brevet lieutenant colonel, at which time he was elected to the national senate, to succeed Mr. Morrow, whose time of service had expired. In December, 1819, he took his seat, and soon gave promise of much future usefulness. He progressed for two sessions of congress in advancing the public interest, and storing his mind with useful knowledge, when nature yielded to the recurring shocks of disease, and he died, Dec. 13th, 1821, aged 35 years.

Greenfield, in the northeast corner of the county, 19 miles from Hillsborough and 21 west of Chillicothe, on Paint creek, in a beautiful and highly cultivated country, is a flourishing town, containing 4 churches, a printing office, an academy, a large number of stores which do an extensive business, and a population nearly equal to the county seat. Large quantities of corn are raised in that section, on the bottom lands of the various streams. Near the town are excellent limestone quarries, and one of a fine-grained sandstone.

The following is a list of towns in the county, with their distances and directions from Hillsborough and population, in 1840; Leesburgh, 11 north, 298; Lexington, 11 west of north, 151; Lynchburg, 10 west, 102; Marshall, 9 south of east, 126; New Market, 6 south, 212; Petersburg, 10 north of east, 278; Rainsborough, 10 east, 115, and Sinking Spring, 16 southeast, 223; Belfast, Buford, Danville, Monroe, Mourytown, Dodsonville, Allensburgh and New Boston, are small places.

HOCKING.

Hocking was formed March 1st, 1818, from Ross, Athens and Fairfield. The land is generally hilly and broken, but along the streams, level and fertile. The principal products are Indian corn, wheat, tobacco and maple sugar. The following is a list of its townships in 1840, with their population.

Benton,	448	Jackson,	472	Starr,	622
Falls,	1625	Laurel,	836	Swan,	759
Good Hope,	469	Marion,	1370	Washington,	1124
Greene,	1189	Salt Creek,	821		

The population of Hocking, in 1820, was 2080; in 1830, 4008, and in 1840, 9735, or 22 inhabitants to a square mile.

The name of this county is a contraction of that of the river Hockhocking, which flows through it. *Hock-hock-ing*, in the language of the Delaware Indians, signifies *a bottle:* the Shawnees have it, *Wea-tha-kagh-qua sepe, i. e. bottle river.* Jno. White, in the American Pioneer, says: "about six or seven miles northwest of Lancaster, there is a fall in the Hockhocking, of about twenty feet: above the fall, for a short distance, the creek is very narrow and straight, forming a neck, while at the falls it suddenly widens on each side and swells into the appearance of the body of a bottle. The whole, when seen from above, appears exactly in the shape of a bottle, and from this fact, the Indians called the creek Hock-hocking."

Dr. S. P. Hildreth, in a late publication, has incidentally given a description of the wild scenery of the southwestern part of Hocking.

One of the favorite descents of the Indians was down the waters of Queer creek, a tributary of Salt creek, and opened a direct course to their town of old Chillicothe. It is a wild, romantic ravine, in which the stream has cut a passage, for several miles in extent, through the solid rock, forming mural cliffs, now more than one hundred and twenty feet in height. They are also full of caverns and grottoes, clothed with dark evergreens of the hemlock and cedar. Near the outlet of this rocky and narrow valley, there stood, a few years since, a large beech tree, on which was engraven, in legible characters, "*This is the road to hell*, 1782." These words were probably traced by some unfortunate prisoner then on his way to the old Indian town of Chillicothe. This whole region is full of interesting scenery, and affords some of the most wild and picturesque views of any other of equal extent in the state of Ohio. It was one of the best hunting grounds for the bear; as its numerous grottoes and caverns afforded them the finest retreats for their winter quarters. These caverns were also valuable on another account, as furnishing vast beds of nitrous earth, from which the old hunters, in time of peace, extracted large quantities of saltpetre for the manufacture of gunpowder, at which art some of them were great proficients. One of these grottoes, well known to the inhabitants of the vicinity, by the name of the "Ash cave," contains a large heap of ashes piled up by the side of the rock which forms one of its boundaries. It has been estimated, by different persons, to contain several thousand bushels. The writer visited this grotto in 1837, and should say there was at that time not less than three or four hundred bushels of clean ashes, as dry and free from moisture as they were on the day they were burned. Whether they are the refuse of the old saltpetre makers, or were piled up there in the course of ages, by some of the aborigines who made these caverns their dwelling places, remains as yet a subject for conjecture.

These ravines and grottoes have all been formed in the out-cropping edges of the sandstone and conglomerate rocks, which underlie the coal fields of Ohio, by the wasting action of the weather, and attrition of running water. The process is yet going on in several streams on the southwest side of Hocking county, where the water has a descent of thirty, forty or even fifty feet at a single pitch, and a fall of eighty or a hundred in a few rods. The falls of the Cuyahoga and the Hockhocking, are cut in the same geological formation. The water, in some of these branches, is of sufficient volume to turn the machinery of a a grist or saw mill, and being lined and overhung with the graceful foliage of the evergreen hemlock, furnishes some of the wildest and most beautiful scenery. This is especially so at the "Cedar falls," and "the falls of Black Jack." The country is at present but partially settled, but when good roads are opened and convenient inns established, no portion of Ohio can afford a richer treat for the lovers of wild and picturesque views.

There is a tradition among the credulous settlers of this retired spot, that lead ore was found here and worked by the Indians; and many a weary day has been spent in its fruitless search among the cliffs and grottoes which line all the streams of this region. They often find ashes and heaps of cinders; and the "pot holes" in a bench of the sand rock in the "Ash cave," evidently worn by the water at a remote period, when the stream ran here, although it is now eighty or one hundred feet lower, and ten or twelve rods farther north, they imagine, were in some way used for smelting the lead.

This tract of country once belonged to the Wyandots, and a considerable town of that tribe, situated at the confluence of a small stream with the river, one mile below Logan, gives the name *Oldtown* to the creek. The abundance of bears, deer, elks, and occasionally buffaloes, with which the hills and vallies were stored, together with the river fishing, must have made this a desirable residence. About five miles southeast of Logan, are two mounds, of the usual conical form, about sixty feet in diameter at the base, erected entirely from stones, evidently brought from a great distance to their present location.

For the annexed historical sketch of the county, we are indebted to a resident.

Early in the spring of 1798, several families from different places, passing through the territory of the Ohio company, settled at various points on the river, some of whom remained, while others again started in pursuit of "the far west." The first actual settler in the county was Christian Westenhaver, from near Hagerstown, Md., of German extraction, a good practical farmer and an honest man, who died in 1829, full of years, and leaving a numerous race of descendants. In the same spring came the Brians, the Pences and the Francisco's, from western Virginia, men renowned for feats of daring prowess in hunting the bear, an animal at that time extremely numerous. As an example of the

View in Logan.

privations of pioneer life, when Mr. Westenhaver ascended the river with his family, a sack of corn-meal constituted no mean part of his treasures. By the accidental upsetting of his canoe, this unfortunately became wet, and consequently blue and mouldy. Nevertheless it was kept, and only on special occasions served out with their bountiful supply of bear's meat, venison and turkeys, until the approaching autumn yielded them potatoes and *roasting ears*, which they enjoyed with a gusto that epicures might well envy. And when fall gave the settlers a rich harvest of Indian corn, in order to reduce it to meal they had to choose between the hommony mortar, or a toilsome journey of near thirty miles over an Indian trace to the mill. Notwithstanding these drawbacks, there is but little doubt that for many years there was more enjoyment of real life than ordinarily falls to a more artificial state of society. True, though generally united, disputes would sometimes arise, and when other modes of settlement were unavailing, the *last resort*, a duel, decided all. But in this, no "Colt's revolver" was put in requisition, but the pugilistic ring was effectual. Here the victor's wounded honor was fully satisfied, and a treat of "old Monongahela" (rye whiskey) by the vanquished, restored perfect good feelings among all parties. As to deciding disputes by law, it was almost unthought of. It is true, there were some few men 'ycelped *justices of the peace*, generally selected for strong natural sense, who admirably answered all the purposes of their election. One, a very worthy old gentleman, being present at what he considered an unlawful demonstration, commanded the peace, which command not being heeded, he immediately threw off his "*warmus*,"* rolled up his

* The "*warmus*" is a working garment, similar in appearance to a "roundabout," but more full, and being usually made of *red* flannel, is elastic and easy to the wearer. It is an article generally unknown in New England, New York, and the extreme northern or southern part of our country, but is more peculiar to the Germans of Pennsylvania. If any traveller, in passing through Ohio, should chance to see a large number of "lobster back" people on the farms, or about the village taverns, he may at once know, without any inquiry, that he is among the descendants of the worthy settlers of the "key-stone state."

sleeves, and shouted, "Boys! I'll be ——— if you shan't keep the peace," which awful display of magisterial power instantly dispersed the terror-stricken multitude. This state of things continued with slow, but almost imperceptible alterations, until 1818, when the number of inhabitants, and their advance in *civilization,* obtained the organization of the county.

Logan, the county seat, is on the Hockhocking river and canal, one mile below the great fall of the Hockhocking river, 47 miles SE. of Columbus, 18 below Lancaster, and 38 miles E. of Chillicothe. It was laid out about the year 1816, and contains 4 stores, 1 Presbyterian and 1 Methodist church, and about 600 inhabitants. The view, taken near the American hotel, shows in the center the court house, an expensive and substantial structure, and on the extreme right, the printing office. There are no other villages in the county of any note.

HOLMES.

Holmes was formed January 20th, 1824, from Coshocton, Tuscarawas and Wayne, and organized the succeeding year. The southwestern part is broken and very hilly, and the soil thin; the remainder of the county is hilly and uneven, but produces excellent wheat. Along Killbuck's creek, coal of a superior quality abounds. The principal products are wheat, Indian corn, oats, potatoes, maple sugar, swine, sheep and neat cattle. The following is a list of its townships in 1840, with their population.

Berlin,	1151	Mechanic,	1400	Ripley,	1279
German,	1281	Monroe,	898	Salt Creeek.	1730
Hardy,	1985	Paint,	1361	Walnut Creek,	1000
Killbuck,	906	Prairie,	1347	Washington,	1457
Knox,	1178	Richland,	1088		

The population of Holmes, in 1830, was 9123, and in 1840, 18,061, or 45 inhabitants to a square mile.

This county was named from Major Holmes, a gallant young officer of the war of 1812, who was killed in the unsuccessful attack upon Mackinac, under Colonel Croghan, August 4th, 1814. Its settlers principally originated from Pennsylvania, Maryland and Virginia: among them are also some Swiss Germans. It was first settled about 1810, by Thomas Butler, who settled about 7 miles north of Millersburg, on the Wooster road, and Peter Casey, who built a cabin half a mile west of the county seat. About this time, William and Samuel Morrison and George Carpenter settled on Doughty's fork, 8 miles south of the court house. In the late war, there was a block house erected, called "Morgan's block house," just over the northern line of the county, on the road to Wooster. There were 24000 acres of choice land scattered about the county of the Connecticut Western Reserve school land, which, not being in market until 1831, operated disadvantageously to the dense settlement of the country. Since then, Holmes has more than doubled its population.

Nearly 2 miles south of Millersburg, on land belonging to the Rev. Alexander Campbell, of Bethany, is a strongly impregnated chalybeate spring. In the northwest corner of Holmes, is "Odell's lake," a beautiful sheet of water, about three miles long, half a mile broad, and abounding in fish of various kinds.

View in Millersburg.

Millersburg, the county seat, is situated on elevated ground, surrounded by lofty hills, on Killbuck creek, 87 miles northeast of Columbus, and about 70 south of Cleveland. It was laid out in 1824, by Charles Miller and Adam Johnson, and public lots sold on the 4th of June, of that year. There had been previously, a quarter of a mile north, a town of the same name, laid out about the year 1816. The names recollected of the first settlers in the village, are Seth Hunt, Colonel Wm. Painter, Samuel S. Henry, George Stout, Samuel C. M'Dowell, R. K. Enos, Jonathan Korn, John Smurr, John Glasgow, Thomas Hoskins, James Withrow, James M'Kennan—the first lawyer in Holmes—and James S. Irvine, the first physician in the same. A short time previous to the sale, three houses were erected: the first was a frame, on the NE. corner of Jackson and Washington streets; the second, a frame, on the NE. corner of Washington and Adams streets; and the last, a log, on the site of S. C. Bever's residence. The Seceder church, the first built, was erected in 1830, and the Methodist Episcopal, in 1833. The village was laid out in the forest, and in 1830, the population reached to 320. About fourteen years since, on a Sunday afternoon, a fire broke out in the frame house on the corner of Washington and Adams streets, and destroyed a large part of the village. Among the buildings burnt, was the court house and jail, which were of log, the first standing on the NE. corner of the public square, and the other a few rods south of it. Millersburg contains 1 Presbyterian, 1 Episcopal Methodist, 1 Lutheran and 1 Seceder church, 2 newspaper printing offices, 10 dry goods and 3 grocery stores, 1 foundery, 1 grist mill, and had, in 1846, 673 inhabitants.

MARKET STREET, STEUBENVILLE.

In the eastern part of Holmes, is an extensive settlement of Dunkards, who originated from eastern Pennsylvania, and speak the German language. They are excellent farmers, and live in a good substantial style. The men wear long beards and shad-bellied coats, and use hooks and eyes instead of buttons. The females are attired in petticoats and short gowns, caps without frills, and when doing out-door labor, instead of bonnets, wear broad-brimmed hats.

Berlin, 7 miles E. of Millersburg, on the Dover road, has 2 churches, 5 stores, 1 foundery, 1 machine shop, and is a thriving business place, with a population of near 400. Nashville, 11 w. of M., has 3 churches, 3 stores, and something less than 300 inhabitants. Benton, Middletown, Lafayette, Oxford, Napoleon, Farmersville and New Carlisle are small villages.

HURON.

Huron was formed, February 7th, 1809, and organized in 1815. It originally constituted the whole of "the fire-lands." The name, *Huron*, was given by the French to the Wyandot tribe: its signification is probably unknown. The surface is mostly level, some parts slightly undulating; soil mostly sandy mixed with clay, forming a loam. In the northwest part are some prairies, and in the northern part are the sand ridges which run on the southern side of Lake Erie, and vary in width from a few rods to more than a mile. Huron was much reduced in 1838, in population and area, by the formation of Erie county. Its principal productions are hay and grass, wheat, corn, oats, barley, buckwheat, flaxseed, potatoes, butter, cheese, wool and swine. The following is a list of its townships in 1840, with their population.

Bronson,	1291	Lyme,	1318	Ridgefield,	1599
Clarksfield,	1473	New Haven,	1270	Ripley,	804
Fairfield,	1067	New London,	1218	Ruggles,	1244
Fitchville,	1294	Norwich,	676	Sherman,	692
Greenfield,	1460	Norwalk,	2613	Townsend,	868
Greenwich,	1067	Peru,	1998	Wakeman,	702
Hartland,	925	Richmond,	306		

The population of Huron in 1820, was 6,677; in 1830, 13,340, and in 1840, 23,934, or 52 inhabitants to a square mile.

Norwalk, the county seat, named from Norwalk, Ct., is 110 miles N. of Columbus and 16 from Sandusky City. It lies principally on a single street, extending nearly 2 miles and beautifully shaded by maple trees. Much taste is evinced in the private dwellings and churches, and in adorning the grounds around them with shrubbery. As a whole, the town is one of the most neat and pleasant in Ohio. The view given represents a small portion of the principal street: on the right is shown the court-house and jail, with a part of the public square, and in the distance is seen the tower of the Norwalk

33

institute. Norwalk contains 1 Presbyterian, 1 Baptist, 1 Episcopal, 1 Methodist and 1 Catholic church, 9 dry goods, 1 book and 4 gro-

View in Norwalk.

cery stores, 1 bank, 2 newspaper printing offices, 1 flouring mill, 2 foundries, and about 1800 inhabitants. The Norwalk institute is an incorporated academy, under the patronage of the Baptists: a large and substantial brick building, three stories in height, is devoted to its purposes; the institution is flourishing and numbers over 100 pupils, including both sexes. A female seminary has recently been commenced under auspicious circumstances, and a handsome building erected in the form of a Grecian temple. About a mile west of the village are some ancient fortifications.

The site of Norwalk was first visited with a view to the founding of a town, by the Hon. Elisha Whittlesey, Platt Benedict, and one or two others, in October, 1815. The place was then in the wilderness, and there were but a few settlers in the county. The examination being satisfactory, the town plat was laid out in the spring following, by Almon Ruggles, and lots offered for sale at from $60 to $100 each. In the fall of 1817, Platt Benedict built a log house, with the intention of removing his family, but in his absence it was destroyed by fire. He reconstructed his dwelling shortly after, and thus commenced the foundation of the village. In the May after, Norwalk was made the county seat, and the public buildings subsequently erected. The year after, a census was taken, and the population had reached 109. In the first few years of the settlement, the different denominations appearing to have forgotten their peculiar doctrines, were accustomed to meet at the old court house for sacred worship, at the second blowing of the horn. In 1820, the Methodists organized a class, and in 1821, the Episcopal society was constituted. From that time to the present, the village has grown with the progressive increase of the country.

In 1819, two Indians were tried and executed at Norwalk, for murder. Their names were Ne-go-sheck and Ne-gon-a-ba, the last of which is said to signify "*one who walks far.*" The circumstances of their crime and execution we take from the MSS. history of the "fire-lands," by the late C. B. Squier, Esq.*

* For some facts respecting the history of the "fire-lands," see Erie county and the sketch of the Western Reserve in this volume.

In the spring of 1816, John Wood of Venice, and George Bishop of Danbury, were trapping for muskrats on the west side of Danbury, in the vicinity of the "two harbors," so called; and having collected a few skins, had lain down for the night in their temporary hut. Three straggling Ottawa Indians came, in the course of the night, upon their camp and discovered them sleeping. To obtain their little pittance of furs, &c., they were induced to plan their destruction. After completing their arrangements, the two eldest armed themselves with clubs, singled out their victims, and each, with a well-directed blow upon their heads, dispatched them in an instant. They then forced their youngest companion, Negasow, who had been until then merely a spectator, to beat the bodies with a club, that he might be made to feel that he was a participator in the murder, and so refrain from exposing their crime. After securing whatever was then in the camp that they desired, they took up their line of march for the Maumee, avoiding, as far as possible, the Indian settlements on their course.

Wood left a wife to mourn his untimely fate, but Bishop was a single man. Their bodies were found in a day or two by the whites, under such circumstances, that evinced that they had been murdered by Indians, and a pursuit was forthwith commenced. The Indians living about the mouth of Portage river, had seen these straggling Indians passing eastward, now suspected them of the crime, and joined the whites in the pursuit. They were overtaken in the neighborhood of the Maumee river, brought back and examined before a magistrate. They confessed their crime and were committed to jail. At the trial the two principals were sentenced to be hung in June, 1819: the younger one was discharged. The county of Huron had at this time no secure jail, and they were closely watched by an armed guard. They nevertheless escaped one dark night. The guard fired and wounded one of them severely in the body, but he continued to run for several miles, till tired and faint with the loss of blood, he laid down, telling his companion he should die, and urging him to continue on. The wounded man was found after the lapse of two or three days, somewhere in Penn township in a dangerous condition, but he soon recovered. The other was recaptured near the Maumee by the Indians, and brought to Norwalk, where they were both hanged according to sentence.

In this transaction, the various Indian tribes evinced a commendable willingness that the laws of the whites should be carried out. Many of them attended the execution, and only requested that the bodies of their comrades should not be disturbed in their graves.

There are several large and thriving villages in this county, containing each several churches and stores, and doing considerable business. Bellevue, 13 miles W. of Norwalk, on the county line and Mad river railroad, has a population of nearly 700. Paris, or Plymouth, is 20 miles SSW., on the county line, and the Sandusky City and Mansfield railroad, New Haven 17 SSW. of N., on the same railroad, and Monroeville, 5 W. of N., have each about 500 inhabitants. Maxville, or Peru, 6 SSW. of N., Steamburg, 10 S., and Fitchville, 12 SE., are of less note, though villages of importance.

JACKSON.

Jackson was organized in March, 1816, and named from President Jackson. The surface is hilly, but in many parts produces excellent wheat. The county is rich in minerals, and abounds in coal and iron ore: and mining will be extensively prosecuted whenever communication is had with navigable waters by railroads. The early settlers were many of them western Virginians; and a considerable portion of its present inhabitants are from Wales and Pennsylvania, who are developing its agricultural resources. The exports are cattle, horses, wool, swine, mill-stones, lumber, tobacco and iron. The following is a list of its townships in 1840, with their population.

Bloomfield,	721	Jackson,	410	Milton,	912
Clinton,	824	Jefferson,	752	Richland,	548
Franklin,	1055	Liberty,	474	Scioto,	931
Hamilton,	415	Lick,	822	Washington,	481
Harrison,	378	Madison,	724		

The population of Jackson, in 1820, was 3,842, in 1830, 5,941, and in 1840, 9,744; or 20 inhabitants to the square mile.

Mr. Samuel Davis, who is now residing in Franklin county, near Columbus, was taken prisoner by the Indians, and made his escape while within the present limits of this county. He was born in New England, moved to the west, and was employed by the governor of Kentucky as a spy against the Indians on the Ohio. The circumstances of his captivity and escape are from his biography, by Col. John M'Donald.

In the fall of 1792, when the spies were discharged, Davis concluded he would make a winter's hunt up the Big Sandy river. He and a Mr. William Campbell prepared themselves with a light canoe, with traps and ammunition, for a fall hunt. They set off from Massie's station, (Manchester,) up the Ohio; thence up Big Sandy some distance, hunting and trapping as they went along. Their success in hunting and trapping was equal to their expectation. Beaver and otter were plenty. Although they saw no Indian sign, they were very circumspect in concealing their canoe, either by sinking it in deep water, or concealing it in thick willow brush. They generally slept out in the hills, without fire. This constant vigilance and care was habitual to the frontier men of that day. They hunted and trapped till the winter began to set in. They now began to think of returning, before the rivers would freeze up. They accordingly commenced a retrograde move down the river, trapping as they leisurely went down. They had been several days going down the river—they landed on a small island covered with willows. Here they observed signs of beaver. They set their traps, dragged their canoe among the willows, and remained quiet till late in the night. They now concluded that any persons, white, red, or black, that might happen to be in the neighborhood, would be in their camp. They then made a small fire among the willows, cooked and eat their supper, and lay down to sleep without putting out their fire. They concluded that the light of their small fire could not penetrate through the thick willows. They therefore lay down in perfect self-security. Sometime before day, as they lay fast asleep, they were awakened by some fellows calling in broken English, "Come, come—get up, get up." Davis awoke from sleep, looked up, and, to his astonishment, found himself and companion surrounded by a number of Indians, and two standing over him with uplifted tomahawks. To resist, in such a case, would be to throw away their lives in hopeless struggle. They surrendered themselves prisoners.

The party of Indians, consisting of upwards of thirty warriors, had crossed the Ohio about the mouth of Guyandotte river, and passed through Virginia to a station near the head of Big Sandy. They attacked the station and were repulsed, after continuing their attack two days and nights. Several Indians were killed during the siege, and several wounded. They had taken one white man prisoner from the station, by the name of Daniels, and taken all the horses belonging to the station. The Indians had taken, or made, some canoes, in which they placed their wounded and baggage, and were descending the river in their canoes. As they were moving down in the night, they discovered a glimpse of Davis's fire through the willows. They cautiously landed on the island, found Davis and Campbell fast asleep, and awakened them in the manner above related.

Davis and Campbell were securely fastened with tugs, and placed in their own canoe. Their rifles, traps, and the proceeds of their successful hunt, all fell into the hands of the Indians. The Indians made no delay, but immediately set off down the river in their canoes with their prisoners, while their main force went by land, keeping along the river bottoms with the horses they had taken from the station—keeping near the canoes, so as to be able to support each other in case of pursuit or attack. Early the next day, they reached the Ohio. The wounded and prisoners were first taken across the Ohio, and placed under a guard. They returned with the canoes, (leaving their arms stacked against a tree,) to assist in getting the horses across the river. It was very cold, and as soon as the horses would find themselves swimming, they would turn round and land on the same shore. The Indians had a great deal of trouble before they got the horses across the Ohio. The guard who watched Davis and his companions, were anxious, impatient spectators of the restive disposition of the horses to take the water. Upon one occasion, the guard left the prisoners twenty or thirty yards, to have a better view of the difficulty with the horses. Davis and his fellow-prisoners were as near to where the arms were stacked as were the Indian guard. Davis, who possessed courage and presence of mind in an eminent degree, urged his fellow-prisoners to embrace the auspicious moment, seize the arms, and kill the guard. His companions faltered—they thought the attempt too perilous—should they fail of success, nothing but instant death would be the consequence. While the prisoners were hesitating to adopt the bold plan of Davis, their guard returned to their arms, to the chagrin of Davis. This opportunity of escape was permitted to pass by without being used. Davis ever after affirmed, that if the opportunity which then presented itself for their escape had been boldly seized, their escape was certain. He frequently averred to the writer of this narrative, that if Duncan M'Arthur, Nat Beasly, or Sam. M'Dowel, had been with him upon this occasion, similarly situated, that he had no doubt they would not only have made their escape, but killed the guard and the wounded Indians, and carried off or destroyed the Indians' arms. He said, if it had not been for the pusillanimity of his fellow-prisoners, they might have promptly and boldly snatched themselves from captivity, and done something worth talking about. The opportunity, once let slip, could not again be recalled. The Indians, after a great deal of exertion, at length got the horses across the Ohio, and hastily fixed litters to carry their wounded They destroyed their canoes, and went ahead for their own country. This body of Indians was commanded by a Shawnee chief, who called himself Captain Charles Wilkey. After Wayne's treaty, in 1795, when peace blessed our frontiers, the writer of this sketch became well acquainted with this Captain Wilky. He was a short, thick, strong, active man, with a very agreeable and intelligent countenance. He was communicative and social in his manners. The first three or four years after Chillicothe was settled, this Indian mixed freely with the whites, and upon no occasion did he show a disposition to be troublesome. He was admitted by the other Indians who spoke of him, to be a warrior of the first order—fertile in expedients, and bold to carry his plans into execution. Davis always spoke of him as being kind and humane to him.

The Indians left the Ohio, and pushed across the country in the direction of Sandusky; and as they were encumbered with several wounded, and a good deal of baggage, without road or path, they travelled very slow, not more than ten or twelve miles a day. As many of the prisoners, taken by the Indians, were burned with slow fires, or otherwise tortured to death, Davis brooded over his captivity in sullen silence, and determined to effect his escape the first opportunity that would offer, that would not look like madness to embrace. At all events, he determined to effect his escape or die a fighting. The Indians moved on till they came to Salt Creek, in what is now Jackson county, O., and there camped for the night. Their manner of securing their prisoners for the night, was as follows: They took a strong tug, made from the raw hide of the buffalo or elk. This tug they tied tight around the prisoner's waist. Each end of the tug was fastened around an Indian's waist. Thus, with the same tug fastened to two Indians, he could not turn to the one side or the other, without drawing an Indian with him. In this uncomfortable manner, the prisoner had to lay on his back till the Indians thought proper to rise. If the Indians discovered the prisoner making the least stir, they would quiet him with a few blows. In this painful situation, the prisoners must lay till light in the morning, when they would be unconfined. As the company of Indians was numerous, the prisoners were unconfined in daylight, but were told that instant death would be the consequence of any movement to leave the line of march, upon any occasion whatever, unless accompanied by an Indian.

One morning, just before day began to appear, as Davis lay in his uncomfortable situation, he hunched one of the Indians, to whom he was fastened, and requested to be untied. The Indian raised up his head and looked round, and found it was still dark, and no Indians up about the fires. He gave Davis a severe dig with his fist, and bid him lay still. Davis's mind was now in a state of desperation. Fire and faggot, sleeping or awake, were constantly floating before his mind's eye. This torturing suspense would chill his soul with horror. After sometime, a number of Indians rose up and made their fires. It was growing light, but not light enough to draw a bead. Davis again jogged one of the Indians to whom he was fastened, and said the tug hurt his middle, and again requested the Indian to untie him. The Indian raised up his head and looked round, and saw it was getting light, and a number of Indians about the fires, he untied him. Davis rose to his feet, and was determined, as soon as he could look round and see the most probable direction of making his escape, to make the attempt, at all hazards. He " screwed his courage to the sticking point." It was a most desperate undertaking. Should he fail to effect his escape, death, instant, cruel death, was his certain doom. As he rose up to his feet, with this determined intention, his heart fluttered with tremors—his sight grew dim at the thought of the perilous plunge he was about to make. He rose up to his feet—stood a minute between the two Indians to whom he had been fastened, and took a quick glance at the Indians who were standing around him. In the evening, the Indians had cut two forks, which were stuck into the ground; a pole was laid across these forks, and all their rifles were leaned against the pole. If he made his start back from the Indian camp, the rifles of the Indians, who were standing round the fires, and who, he knew, would pursue him, would be before them; and as they started after him, they would have nothing to do but pick up a rifle as they ran. On the contrary, if he made his plunge through the midst of them, they would have to run back for their guns, and by that time, as it was only twilight in the morning, he could be so far from them that their aim would be very uncertain. All this passed through his mind in a moment. As he determined to make his dash through the midst of the Indians who were standing around the fires, he prepared his mind and body for the dreadful attempt. The success of his daring enterprise depended on the swiftness of his heels. He knew his bottom was good. A large, active Indian was standing between Davis and the fire. He drew back his fist and struck that Indian with all his force, and dropped him into the fire; and with the agility of a buck, he sprang over his body, and took to the woods with all the speed that was in his power. The Indians pursued, yelling and screaming like demons; but, as Davis anticipated, not a gun was fired at him. Several Indians pursued him for some distance, and for some time it was a doubtful race. The foremost Indian was so close to him, that he sometimes fancied that he felt his clutch. However, at length Davis began to gain ground upon his pursuers—the breaking and rustling of brush was still farther and farther off. He took up a long, sloping ridge; when he reached the top, he, for the first time, looked back, and, to his infinite pleasure, saw no person in pursuit. He now slackened his pace, and went a mile or two further, when he began to find his feet gashed and bruised by the sharp stones over which he had run, without picking his way, in his rapid flight. He now stopped, pulled off his waistcoat, tore it in two pieces, and wrapped them around his feet, instead of moccasons. He now pushed his way for the Ohio. He crossed the Scioto river, not far from where Piketon, in Pike county, now stands. He then marched over the rugged hills of Sunfish, Camp creek, Scioto Brush creek, and Turkey creek, and struck the Ohio river eight or ten miles below the mouth of Scioto. It was about the first of January. He was nearly three days and two nights without food, fire, or covering, exposed to the winter storms. Hardy as he undoubtedly was, these exposures and privations were almost too severe for human nature to sustain. But as Davis was an unwavering believer in that All-seeing eye, whose providence prepares means to guard and protect those who put their trust in him, his confidence and courage never forsook him for a moment, during this trying and fatiguing march.

When he arrived at the Ohio, he began to look about for some dry logs to make a kind of raft, on which to float down the stream. Before he began to make his raft, he looked up the Ohio, and to his infinite gratification, he saw a Kentucky boat come floating down the stream. He now thought his deliverance sure. Our fondest hopes are frequently blasted in disappointment. As soon as the boat floated opposite to him, he called to the people in the boat—told them of his lamentable captivity, and fortunate escape. The boatmen heard his tale of distress with suspicion. Many boats, about this time, had been decoyed to shore by similar tales of woe; and as soon as landed, their inmates cruelly massacred. The boatmen heard his story, but refused to land. They said they had heard too much about such prisoners, and escapes, to be deceived in his case. As the Ohio was low, he kept pace with the boat as it slowly glided along. The more pitiably he described his forlorn situation, the more determined were the boat crew not to land for him. He at length requested them to row the boat a little nearer the shore, and he would swim to them. To this proposition the boatmen consented. They commenced rowing the boat towards the shore, when Davis plunged into the freezing water and swam for the boat. The boatmen, seeing him swimming towards them, their suspicions gave way, and they rowed the boat with all their force to meet him. He was at length lifted into the boat, almost exhausted. (Our old boatmen, though they had rough exteriors, had Samaritan hearts.) The boatmen were not to blame for their suspicion. They now administered to his relief and comfort every thing that was in their power. That night, or the next morning, he was landed at Massie's station, (Manchester,) among his former friends and associates, where he soon recovered his usual health and activity.

Jackson, the county seat, was laid out in 1817, and is 73 miles SE. of Columbus, and 28 from Chillicothe. It contains 1 Presbyterian, 1 Baptist, 1 Episcopal Methodist and 1 Protestant Methodist church, 6 or 8 stores, 1 newspaper printing office, and, in 1840, had 297 inhabitants; since which, the town has rapidly improved, and is now judged to contain a population of 500. In this vicinity are several valuable mineral springs, and also remains of ancient fortifications.

The famous "old Scioto salt-works" are in this region, on the banks of Salt creek, a tributary of the Scioto. The wells were sunk to the depth of about 30 feet, but the water was very weak, requiring ten or fifteen gallons to make a pound of salt. It was first made by the whites about the year 1798, and transferred from the kettles to pack-horses of the salt purchasers, who carried it to the various settlements, and sold it to the inhabitants for three or four dollars per bushel, as late as 1808. This saline was thought to be so important to the country, that, when Ohio was formed into a state, a tract of six miles square was set apart by Congress, for the use of the state, embracing this saline. In 1804, an act was passed by the legislature, regulating its management, and appointing an agent to rent out small lots on the borders of the creek, where the salt water was most abundant to the manufacturers.* As better and more accessible saline springs have been discovered, these are now abandoned.

The expression, very common in this region, "*shooting one with a pack-saddle,*" is said to have originated, in early days, in this way. A person, who had come on horseback, from some distance, to the salt-works to purchase salt, had his pack-saddle stolen by the boilers, who were a rough, coarse set, thrown into the salt furnace, and destroyed. He made little or no complaint, but determined to have revenge for the trick played upon him. On the next errand of this nature, he partly filled his pack-saddle with gunpowder, and gave the boilers another opportunity to steal and burn it, which they embraced—when, lo! much to their consternation, a terrific explosion ensued, and they narrowly escaped serious injury.

These old salt-works were among the first worked by the whites in Ohio. They had long been known, and have been indicated on maps, published as early as 1755. The Indians, prior to the settlement of the country, used to come from long distances to make salt at this place; and it was not uncommon for them to be accompanied by whites, whom they had taken captive and adopted. Daniel Boone, when a prisoner, spent some time at these works. Jonathan Alder, a sketch of whom is under the head of Madison county, was taken prisoner, when a boy, by the Indians, in 1782, in Virginia, and adopted into one of their families, near the head waters of Mad river. He had been with them about a year, when they took him with them to the salt-works, where he met a Mrs. Martin, likewise a prisoner. The meeting between them was affecting. We give the particulars in his own simple and artless language.

It was now better than a year after I was taken prisoner, when the Indians started off to the Scioto salt-springs, near Chillicothe, to make salt, and took me along with them. Here I got to see Mrs. Martin, that was taken prisoner at the same time I was, and this was the first time that I had seen her since we were separated, at the council-house. When she

* Dr. Hildreth on the "Saliferous Rock formation in the valley of the Ohio;" Silliman's Journal, Vol. XXIV, No. 1, pp. 48, 49.

saw me, she came smiling and asked me if it was me. I told her it was. She asked me how I had been. I told her I had been very unwell, for I had had the fever and ague for a long time. So she took me off to a log, and there we sat down; and she combed my head, and asked me a great many questions about how I lived, and if I didn't want to see my mother and little brothers. I told her that I should be glad to see them, but never expected to again. She then pulled out some pieces of her daughter's scalp, that she said were some trimmings they had trimmed off the night after she was killed, and that she meant to keep them as long as she lived. She then talked and cried about her family, that was all destroyed and gone, except the remaining bits of her daughter's scalp. We staid here a considerable time, and, meanwhile, took many a cry together; and when we parted again, took our last and final farewell, for I never saw her again.

There was found in this county, about ten years since, the remains of a mastodon, described in the public prints of the time. Near the southern line of the county, is the iron furnace of Ellison, Tewksbury & Co., called "the Jackson Furnace." Allensville, Middleton, Oak Hill and Charleston, arė small post villages.

JEFFERSON.

Jefferson, named from President Jefferson, was the fifth county established in Ohio: it was created by proclamation of Gov. St. Clair, July 29th, 1797: its original limits included the country west of Pennsylvania and Ohio; and east and north of a line from the mouth of the Cuyahoga; southwardly to the Muskingum, and east to the Ohio: within those boundaries is Cleveland, Canton, Steubenville, Warren and many other large towns and populous counties. The surface is hilly and the soil fertile. It is one of the greatest manufacturing counties in the state, and abounds in excellent coal. The principal crops are wheat, Indian corn and oats. The following is a list of its townships in 1840, with their population.

Brush Creek,	757	Ross,	927	Steubenville,	5203
Cross Creek,	1702	Salem,	2044	Warren,	1945
Island Creek,	1867	Saline,	963	Wayne,	1746
Knox,	1529	Smithfield,	2095	Wells,	1492
Mount Pleasant,	1676	Springfield,	1077		

The population of Jefferson, in 1820, was 18,531; in 1830, 22,489, and in 1840, 25,031, or 62 inhabitants to a square mile.

The old Mingo town, three miles below Steubenville, now the site of the farms of Jeremiah H. Hallock, Esq. and Mr. Daniel Potter, was a place of note prior to the settlement of the country. It was the point where the troops of Col. Williamson rendezvoused in the infamous Moravian campaign, and those of Col. Crawford, in his unfortunate expedition against the Sandusky Indians. It was also, at one time, the residence of Logan, the celebrated Mingo chief, whose form was striking and manly, and whose magnanimity and eloquence has seldom been equalled. He was a son of the Cayuga chief Skikellimus, who dwelt at Shamokin, Pa., in 1742, and was converted to Christianity, under the preaching of the Moravian missionaries. Skikellimus highly esteemed James Logan, the secretary of the province, named his son from him, and probably had him baptized by the missionaries.

In early life, Logan for a while dwelt in Pennsylvania: and in Day's Historical Collections of that state, is a view in Mifflin county, of Logan's spring, which will long remain a memorial of this distinguished chief. The letter below, gives an incident which occurred there, that speaks in praise of Logan. It was written by the Hon. R. P. Maclay, a member of the state senate, and son of the gentleman alluded to in the anecdote, and published in the Pittsburg Daily American.

Senate Chamber, March 21, 1842.

To George Darsie, Esq., of the Senate of Pennsylvania.

Dear Sir—Allow me to correct a few inaccuracies as to place and names, in the anecdote of Logan, the celebrated Mingo chief, as published in the Pittsburg Daily American of March 17th, 1842, to which you called my attention. The person surprised at the spring now called the Big spring, and about six [four] miles west of Logan's spring, was William Brown—the first actual settler in a Kishacoquillas valley, and one of the associate judges in Mifflin county, from its organization till his death, at the age of ninety-one or two—and not Samuel Maclay, as stated by Dr. Hildreth. I will give you the anecdote as I heard it related by Judge Brown himself, while on a visit to my brother, who then owned and occupied the Big Spring farm.*

"The first time I ever saw that spring," said the old gentleman, "my brother, James Reed and myself, had wandered out of the valley in search of land, and finding it very good, we were looking about for springs. About a mile from this we started a bear, and separated to get a shot at him. I was travelling along, looking about on the rising ground for the bear, when I came suddenly upon the spring; and being dry, and more rejoiced to find so fine a spring than to have killed a dozen bears, I set my rifle against a bush and rushed down the bank and laid down to drink. Upon putting my head down, I saw reflected in the water, on the opposite side, the shadow of a tall Indian. I sprang to my rifle, when the Indian gave a yell, whether for peace or war I was not just then sufficiently master of my faculties to determine; but upon my seizing my rifle, and facing him, he knocked up the pan of his gun, threw out the priming, and extended his open palm toward me in token of friendship. After putting down our guns, we again met at the spring, and shook hands. This was Logan—the best specimen of humanity I ever met with, either *white* or *red*. He could speak a little English, and told me there was another white hunter a little way down the stream, and offered to guide me to his camp. There I first met your father. We remained together in the valley a week, looking for springs and selecting lands, and laid the foundation of a friendship which never has had the slightest interruption.

We visited Logan at his camp, at Logan's spring, and your father and he shot at a mark for a dollar a shot. Logan lost four or five rounds, and acknowledged himself beaten. When we were about to leave him, he went into his hut, and brought out as many deerskins as he had lost dollars, and handed them to Mr. Maclay—who refused to take them, alledging that we had been his guests, and did not come to rob him—that the shooting had been only a trial of skill, and the bet merely nominal. Logan drew himself up with great dignity, and said, 'Me bet to make you shoot your best—me gentleman, and me take your dollar if me beat.' So he was obliged to take the skins, or affront our friend, whose nice sense of honor would not permit him to receive even a horn of powder in return.

"The next year," said the old gentleman, "I brought my wife up and camped under a big walnut tree, on the bank of Tea creek, until I had built a cabin near where the mill now stands, and have lived in the valley ever since. Poor Logan" (and the big tears coursed each other down his cheeks) "soon after went into the Alleghany, and I never saw him again."

Yours, R. P. MACLAY.

Mrs. Norris, who lives near the site of Logan's spring, is a daughter of Judge Brown: she confirmed the above, and gave Mr. Day

* This spring is a few rods south of the Huntington road, in the rear of a blacksmith's shop, four miles west of Reedville.

the following additional incidents, highly characteristic of the benevolent chief, which we take from that gentleman's work.

Logan supported his family by killing deer, dressing the skins, and selling them to the whites. He had sold quite a parcel to one De Yong, a tailor, who lived in Ferguson's valley, below the gap. Tailors in those days dealt extensively in buckskin breeches. Logan received his pay, according to stipulation, in wheat. The wheat, on being taken to the mill, was found so worthless that the miller refused to grind it. Logan was much chagrined, and attempted in vain to obtain redress from the tailor. He then took the matter before his friend Brown, then a magistrate; and on the judge's questioning him as to the character of the wheat, and what was in it, Logan sought in vain to find words to express the precise nature of the article with which the wheat was adulterated, but said that it resembled in appearance the wheat itself, "It must have been *cheat*," said the judge. "Yoh!" said Logan, "that very good name for him." A decision was awarded in Logan's favor, and a writ given to Logan to hand to the constable, which, he was told, would bring him the money for his skins. But the untutored Indian—too uncivilized to be dishonest—could not comprehend by what magic this little paper would force the tailor, against his will, to pay for the skins. The judge took down his own commission, with the arms of the king upon it, and explained to him the first principles and operations of civil law. "Law good," said Logan; "make rogues pay." But how much more simple and efficient was the law which the Great Spirit had impressed upon his heart—*to do as he would be done by!*

When a sister of Mrs. Norris (afterwards Mrs. Gen. Potter) was just beginning to learn to walk, her mother happened to express her regret that she could not get a pair of shoes to give more firmness to her little step. Logan stood by, but said nothing. He soon after asked Mrs. Brown to let the little girl go up and spend the day at his cabin. The cautious heart of the mother was alarmed at such a proposition; but she knew the delicacy of an Indian's feelings—and she knew Logan, too—and with secret reluctance, but apparent cheerfulness, she complied with his request. The hours of the day wore very slowly away, and it was nearly night, when her little one had not returned. But just as the sun was going down, the trusty chief was seen coming down the path with his charge; and in a moment more the little one trotted into her mother's arms, proudly exhibiting a beautiful pair of moccasons on her little feet—the product of Logan's skill.

Logan took no part in the old French war, which ended in 1760, except that of a peace maker, and was always the friend of the white people until the base murder of his family, to which has been attributed the origin of Dunmore's war. This event took place near the mouth of Yellow creek, in this county, about 17 miles above Steubenville. The circumstances have been variously related. We annex them as given by Henry Jolly, Esq., who was for a number of years an associate judge on the bench of Washington county, in this state. The facts are very valuable, as coming from the pen of one who saw the party the day after the murder; was personally acquainted with some of the individuals, and familiar with that spot and the surrounding region.* He says:

I was about sixteen years of age, but I very well recollect what I then saw, and the information that I have since obtained, was derived from (I believe) good authority. In the spring of the year 1774, a party of Indians encamped on the northwest of the Ohio near the mouth of the Yellow creek. A party of whites, called "Greathouse's party," lay on the opposite side of the river. The Indians came over to the white party, consisting, I think, of five men and one woman, with an infant. The whites gave them rum, which three of them drank, and in a short time they became very drunk The other two men and the woman refused to drink. The sober Indians were challenged to shoot at a mark, to which they agreed; and as soon as they had emptied their guns, the whites shot them down. The woman attempted to escape by flight, but was also shot down; she lived long enough, however, to beg mercy for her babe, telling them that it was a kin to themselves. The whites had a man in the cabin, pre-

* This statement was written for Dr. S. P. Hildreth, by Mr. Jolly, and published in Silliman's Journal, for 1836.

pared with a tomahawk for the purpose of killing the three drunken Indians, which was immediately done. The party of men then moved off for the interior settlements, and came to "Catfish camp" on the evening of the next day, where they tarried until the day following. I very well recollect my mother feeding and dressing the babe; chirruping to the little innocent, and its smiling. However, they took it away, and talked of sending it to its supposed father, Col. George Gibson, of Carlisle, Pa., "who was then, and had been for many years a trader among the Indians." The remainder of the party at the mouth of Yellow creek, finding that their friends on the opposite side of the river were massacred, attempted to escape by descending the Ohio; and in order to prevent being discovered by the whites, passed on the west side of Wheeling island, and landed at Pipe creek, a small stream that empties into the Ohio a few miles below Grave creek, where they were overtaken by Cresap, with a party of men from Wheeling.* They took one Indian scalp, and had one white man (Big Tarrener) badly wounded. They, I believe, carried him in a litter from Wheeling to Redstone. I saw the party on their return from their victorious campaign. The Indians had for some time before these events, thought themselves intruded upon by the "Long Knife," as they at that time called the Virginians, and many of them were for war. However, they called a council, in which Logan acted a conspicuous part. He admitted their grounds of complaint, but at the same time reminded them of some aggressions on the part of the Indians, and that by a war they could but harrass and distress the frontier settlements for a short time; that "the Long Knife" would come like the trees in the woods, and that ultimately they should be driven from the good lands which they now possessed. He therefore strongly recommended peace. To him they all agreed; grounded the hatchet, and every thing wore a tranquil appearance; when behold, the fugitives arrived from Yellow creek; and reported that Logan's father, brother and sister, were murdered! Three of the nearest and dearest relations of Logan, had been massacred by white men. The consequence was, that this same Logan, who a few days before was so pacific, raised the hatchet, with a declaration that he would not ground it until he had taken *ten* for *one;* which I believe he completely fulfilled, by taking *thirty* scalps and prisoners in the summer of 1774. The above has often been related to me by several persons who were at the Indian towns at the time of the council alluded to, and also when the remains of the party came in from Yellow creek. Thomas Nicholson in particular, has told me the above and much more. Another person (whose name I cannot recollect) informed me that he was at the towns when the Yellow creek Indians came in, and that there was great lamentation by all the Indians of that place. Some friendly Indian advised him to leave the Indian settlements, which he did. Could any rational person believe for a moment, that the Indians came to Yellow creek with hostile intentions, or that they had any suspicion of similar intentions on the part of the whites, against them? Would five men have crossed the river, three of them become in a short time dead drunk, while the other two discharged their guns, and thus put themselves entirely at the mercy of the whites; or would they have brought over a squaw with an infant pappoos, if they had not reposed the utmost confidence in the friendship of the whites? Every person who is at all acquainted with Indians knows better; and it was the belief of the inhabitants who were capable of reasoning on the subject, that all the depredations committed on the frontiers, by Logan and his party, in 1774, were as a retaliation for the murder of Logan's friends at Yellow creek. *It was well known that Michael Cresap had no hand in the massacre at Yellow creek.*†

During the war which followed, Logan frequently showed his magnanimity towards prisoners who fell into his hands. Among them was Maj. Wm. Robinson, of Clarksburg, Va., from whose declaration, given in Jefferson's Notes, and information orally commu-

---

* Cresap did not live at Wheeling, but happened to be there at that time with a party of men, who had, with himself, just returned from an exploring expedition down the Ohio, for the purpose of selecting and appropriating lands (called in the west, locating lands) along the river in choice situations; a practice at that early day very common, when Virginia claimed both sides of the stream, including what is now the state of Ohio.—*S. P. H.*

† A brother of Capt. Daniel Greathouse, said to have been present at the massacre, was killed by the Indians the 24th March, 1791, between the mouth of the Scioto and Limestone, while emigrating to Kentucky in a flat boat, with his family. He seems to have made little or no resistance to the Indians, who attacked him in canoes. They probably knew who he was, and remembered the slaughter of Logan's family, as he was taken on shore, tied to a tree, and whipped to death with rods.—*S. P. H.*

nicated by his son, Col. James Robinson, now living near Coshocton, these facts are derived.

On the 12th of July, 1774, Major Robinson, then a resident on the west fork of Monongahela river, was in the field with Mr. Colburn Brown and Mr. Helen, pulling flax, when they were surprised and fired upon by a party of eight Indians, led by Logan. Mr. Brown was killed and the other two made prisoners. On the first alarm, Mr. Robinson started and ran. When he had got about 50 yards, Logan called out in English, "Stop, I won't hurt you!" "Yes, you will," replied Robinson, in tones of fear. "No, I won't," rejoined Logan, "but if you don't stop, by — I'll shoot you." Robinson still continued his race, but stumbling over a log, fell and was made captive by a fleet savage in pursuit. Logan immediately made himself known to Mr. Robinson and manifested a friendly disposition to him, told him that he must be of good heart and go with him to his town, where he would probably be adopted in some of their families. When near the Indian village, on the site of Dresden, Muskingum county, Logan informed him that he must run the gauntlet, and gave him such directions, that he reached the council-house without the slightest harm. He was then tied to a stake for the purpose of being burnt, when Logan arose and addressed the assembled council of chiefs, in his behalf. He spoke long and with great energy, until the saliva foamed from the sides of his mouth. This was followed by other chiefs in opposition, and rejoinders from Logan. Three separate times was he tied to the stake to be burnt, the councils of the hostile chiefs prevailing, and as often untied by Logan and a belt of wampum placed around him as a mark of adoption. His life appeared to hang on a balance; but the eloquence of Logan prevailed, and when the belt of wampum was at last put on him by Logan, he introduced a young Indian to him, saying, "this is your cousin, you are to go home with him and he will take care of you."

From this place, Mr. Robinson accompanied the Indians up the Muskingum, through two or three Indian villages, until they arrived at one of their towns on the site of New Comerstown, in Tuscarawas county. About the 21st of July, Logan came to Robinson and brought a piece of paper, saying that he must write a letter for him, which he meant to carry and leave in some house, which he should attack. Mr. Robinson wrote a note with ink, which he manufactured from gun-powder. He made three separate attempts before he could get the language, which Logan dictated, sufficiently strong to satisfy that chief. This note was addressed to Col. Cresap, whom Logan supposed was the murderer of his family. It was afterwards found, tied to a war club, in the cabin of a settler who lived on or near the north fork of Holston river.* It was doubtless left by Logan after murdering the family. A copy of it is given below, which on comparison with his celebrated speech, shows a striking similarity of style.

---

* See letter of Judge Innes, in the Pioneer, Vol. I, p. 14.

CAPTAIN CRESAP:

What did you kill my people on Yellow creek for? The white people killed my kin, at Conestoga, a great while ago; and I thought nothing of that. But you killed my kin again on Yellow creek and took my cousin prisoner. Then I thought I must kill too; and I have been three times to war since; but the Indians are not angry; only myself.

July 21st, 1774. CAPTAIN JOHN LOGAN.

Major Robinson, after remaining with the Indians about four months, returned to his home in Virginia. In 1801, he removed to Coshocton county, and settled on a section of military land, on the Muskingum, a few miles below Coshocton, where he died in 1815, aged 72 years. His son resides on the same farm.

Dunmore's war was of short duration. It was terminated in November of the same year, within the present limits of Pickaway county, in this state, under which head will be found a copy of the speech which has rendered immortal the name of Logan.

The heroic adventure of the two Johnson boys, who killed two Indians in this county, has often and erroneously been published. One of these, Henry, the youngest is yet living in Monroe county, in this state, where we made his acquaintance in the spring of 1846. He is a fine specimen of the fast vanishing race of Indian hunters, tall and erect, with the bearing of a genuine backwoodsman. His narrative, recently published in a Woodsfield paper, here follows:

I was born in Westmoreland county, Pa., on the 4th day of February, 1777. When I was about eight years old, my father having a large family to provide for, sold his farm with the expectation of acquiring larger possessions farther west. Thus he was stimulated to encounter the perils of a pioneer life. He crossed the Ohio river and bought some improvements on what was called Beach Bottom flats, two and a half miles from the river, and three or four miles above the mouth of Short creek. Soon after he came there, the Indians became troublesome. They stole horses and various other things, and killed a number of persons in our neighborhood.

When I was between eleven and twelve years old, I think it was the fall of 1788, I was taken prisoner with my brother John, who was about eighteen months older than I. The circumstances are as follows: On Saturday evening we were out with an older brother, and came home late in the evening; one of us had lost a hat, and John and I went back the next day to look for it. We found the hat, and sat down on a log and were cracking nuts. After a short time, we saw two men coming down from the direction of the house; from their dress we took them to be two of our neighbors, James Perdue and J. Russell. We paid but little attention to them till they came quite near us. To escape by flight was now impossible, had we been disposed to try it. We sat still until they came up to us. One of them said, "*how do brodder;*" my brother then asked them if they were Indians, and they answered in the affirmative, and said we must go with them. One of them had a blue buckskin, which he gave my brother to carry, and without further ceremony, we took up the line of march for the wilderness; not knowing whether we should ever return to the cheerful home we had left; and not having much love for our commanding officers, of course we obeyed martial orders rather tardily. One of the Indians walked about ten steps before, and the other about the same distance behind us. After travelling some distance we halted in a deep hollow and sat down. They took out their knives and whet them, and talked some time in the Indian tongue, which we could not understand. I told my brother that I thought they were going to kill us, and I believe he thought so too; for he began to talk to them, and told them that his father was cross to him and made him work hard, and that he did not like hard work, that he would rather be a hunter and live in the woods. This seemed to please them, for they put up their knives and talked more lively and pleasantly to us. We returned the same familiarity, and many questions passed between us; all parties were very inquisitive. They asked my brother which way home was, and he told them the contrary way every time they would ask him, although he knew the way very well: this would make them laugh; they thought we were lost and that we knew no better.

They conducted us over Short creek hills in search of horses, but found none; so we continued on foot. Night came on, and we halted in a low hollow, about 3 miles from Carpenter's fort, and about 4 from the place where they first took us. Our route being somewhat circuitous and full of zigzags, we made headway but slowly. As night began to close in around us, I became fretful; my brother encouraged me, by whispering to me that we would kill the Indians that night. After they had selected the place of encampment, one of them scouted round the camp, while the other struck fire, which was done by stopping the touch-hole of the gun and flashing powder in the pan. After the Indian got the fire kindled, he re-primed the gun and went to an old stump to get some dry tinder wood for fire; and while he was thus employed, my brother John took the gun, cocked it, and was about to shoot the Indian; but I was alarmed fearing the other might be close by, and be able to overpower us; so I remonstrated against his shooting and took hold of the gun and prevented the shot. I, at the same time, begged him to wait till night and I would help him to kill them both. The Indian that had taken the scout came back about dark. We took our suppers, talked some time and went to bed on the naked ground to try to rest, and study out the best mode of attack. They put us between them, that they might be the better able to guard us. After a while one of the Indians, supposing we were asleep, got up and stretched himself down on the other side of the fire, and soon began to snore. John, who had been watching every motion, found they were sound asleep, and whispered to me to get up. We got up as carefully as possible. John took the gun which the Indian struck fire with, cocked it and placed it in the direction of the head of one the Indians; he then took a tomahawk and drew it over the head of the other; I pulled the trigger and he struck at the same instant; the blow, falling too far back on the neck, only stunned the Indian; he attempted to spring to his feet, uttering most hideous yells. Although my brother repeated the blows with some effect, the conflict became terrible and somewhat doubtful. The Indian, however, was forced to yield to the blows he received upon his head, and, in a short time, he lay quiet and still at our feet. After we were satisfied that they were both dead, and fearing there were others close by, we hurried off, and took nothing with us but the gun I shot with. We took our course towards the river, and in about three quarters of a mile we found a path which led to Carpenter's fort. My brother here hung up his hat, that we might know on our return where to turn off to find our camp. We got to the fort a little before daybreak. We related our adventure, and a small party went back with my brother and found the Indian that was tomahawked; the other had crawled away a short distance with the gun. A skeleton and a gun were found, some time after, near the place where we had encamped.

The last blood shed in battle between the whites and Indians in this part of the Ohio country, was in Jefferson county, in August, 1793. This action, known as "Buskirk's battle," took place on the farm of Mr. John Adams, on what was then known as Indian Cross creek now as Battle-Ground run. The incidents given below were published in a Steubenville paper, a few years since.

A party of twenty eight Indians having committed depredations on this side of the river, a force of thirty eight Virginians, all of them veteran Indian fighters, under Capt. Buskirk, crossed the river to give them battle. And although they knew they were in the vicinity of the enemy, they marched into an ambuscade, and but for a most singular circumstance, would have been mowed down like pigeons. The whites marched in Indian file with their captain, Buskirk, at their head. The ambush quartered on their flank, and they were totally unsuspicious of it. The plan of the Indians was to permit the whites to advance in numbers along the line before firing upon them. This was done, but instead of each selecting his man, every gun was directed at the captain, who fell with *thirteen* bullet holes in his body. The whites and Indians instantly treed, and the contest lasted more than an hour. The Indians, however, were defeated, and retreated towards the Muskingum with the loss of several killed, while the Virginians, with the exception of their captain, had none killed and but three wounded.

STEUBENVILLE is on the Ohio river, 22 miles above Wheeling, 35 below Pittsburg and 147 E. by N. from Columbus. It derives its name from a fort, called Fort Steuben, erected on its site as early as 1789. It stood on High street, near the site of the female seminary. It was built of block-houses connected by palisade fences, and was dismantled at the time of Wayne's victory, previous to which it had been garrisoned by U. S. infantry, under the command of Col. Beatty, father of the Rev. Dr. Beatty, of Steubenville. On the opposite side of the river then stood a block-house.

Steubenville Female Seminary.

The town was laid out in 1798, by Bezaleel Wells and the Hon. James Ross of Pennsylvania, from whom Ross county, in this state, derived its name. Mr. Ross, who has attained high honor, is yet living; but Mr. Wells died poor, after having been at one time considered the most wealthy person in eastern Ohio. On the 14th of February, 1805, the town was incorporated and the following officers appointed: David Hull, president; John Ward, recorder; David Hog, Zacheus A. Beatty, Benj. Hough, Thos. Vincents, John England, Martin Andrews and Abm. Cazier, trustees; Samuel Hunter, treasurer; Matthew Adams, assessor; Charles Maxwell, collector, and Anthony Beck, town marshall.

Steubenville is situated upon a handsome and elevated plain, in the midst of beautiful scenery. The country adjacent is rich and highly cultivated, affording the finest soil for wheat and sheep. Messrs. Bezaleel Wells and Dickerson introduced the merino sheep at an early day, and established in the town, in 1814, a woolen manufactory, which laid the foundation for the extensive manufactures of the place. Steubenville contains about 30 mercantile stores, 2 printing offices, (1 daily newspaper,) 1 Episcopal, 2 Presbyterian, 3 Methodist, 1 Catholic, 1 Baptist, 1 Associate Reformed, 1 New Jerusalem and 1 church for persons of color, 1 bank, 5 woolen, 1 paper, 1 cotton and 2 glass manufactories, 1 iron foundery and numerous other manufacturing and mechanical establishments. In the vicinity are 7 copperas manufactories. From 800 to 1000 hands are employed in these various establishments, and over a million bushels of coal annually consumed, which is obtained from inexhaustible coal beds in the vicinity, at 3 cents per bushel. The town is very thriving and rapidly increasing. Its population in 1810, was 800; in 1820, 2,479; in 1830, 2,964; in 1840, 4,247, and in 1847, about 7,000.

Much attention is given to the cause of education in Steubenville. There are 5 public and 4 select schools, a male academy and a female seminary. The male institution, called "Grove academy," is flourishing. It is under the charge of the Rev. John W. Scott, has 3 teachers and 80 scholars. The female seminary is pleasantly situated on the bank of the Ohio, commanding an extensive view of the river and the surrounding hills. It is under the charge of the Rev. Charles C. Beatty, D. D., superintendent, and Mrs. Hetty E. Beatty, principal. It was first established in the spring of 1829, and now receives only scholars over twelve years of age. It is in a very high degree flourishing, having a widely extended reputation. The establishment cost nearly $40,000, employs from 10 to 12 teachers and usually has 150 pupils, the full number which it can accommodate.

Mount Pleasant, 21 miles sw. of Steubenville, is a large and flourishing village, containing 4 churches, beside 2 Friends meeting houses, 8 or 10 stores, a female seminary, and by the census of 1840, had 666 inhabitants; and now has about 1000. Richmond, 11 nw. of S., has 5 stores, a classical academy for males, 2 churches, 1 Friends meeting house and about 500 inhabitants. Smithfield, 14 sw. of S., has about the same number of stores, churches and inhabitants, as Richmond. The following are names of villages in Jefferson, with their population in 1840: Warren 209, Knoxville 166, Springfield 138, Tiltonville 137, Portland 113, Wintersville 107, New Trenton 103, New Somerset 98, New Amsterdam 85, Newburgh 75, York 54 and Monroesville 49.

KNOX.

Knox was named from General Henry Knox, a native of Boston, general in the war of the revolution, and secretary of war in Washington's administration. It was formed from Fairfield, March 1st, 1808. The north and east part is hilly—the central west and south part, undulating or level. The bottom lands of the streams are very

CINCINNATI, FROM THE OHIO.

rich, particularly those of Vernon river, which stream affords abundance of water power. The principal productions are wheat, Indian corn, oats, tobacco, maple sugar, potatoes and wool. The following is a list of its townships in 1840, with their population.

Berlin,	1100	Harrison,	833	Miller,	977
Bloomfield,	1252	Hillier,	1012	Monroe,	1258
Brown,	1204	Howard,	999	Morgan,	912
Butler,	647	Jackson,	994	Morris,	1077
Chester,	1297	Jefferson,	994	Pike,	1216
Clay,	1304	Liberty,	1205	Pleasant,	888
Clinton,	920	Middlebury,	1002	Union,	1098
Franklin,	1343	Milford,	1157		

The population of Knox, in 1820, was 8,326, in 1830, 17,125, and in 1840, 29,584; or 48 inhabitants to a square mile.

The early settlers of the county were mainly from the middle states, with some of New England origin. In 1805, Mount Vernon was laid out, and named by the proprietors of the soil, who were Joseph Walker, Thos. B. Paterson and Benj. Butler, from the seat of Washington. At this time, the county was thinly settled. Two years after, the principal settlers were, as far as their names are recollected, the Rileys, Darlings, Shriplins, Butlers, Kritchfields, Welkers, Dials, Logues, and De Witts, on Vernon river. In other parts of the county, the Hurds, Beams, Hunts and Dimick, Kerr, Ayres, Dalrymple, Houck, Hilliard, the Youngs, Mitchells, Bryants, Knights and Walkers. In the spring of 1807, there were only three families living on the plat of Mount Vernon, viz.: Benjamin Butler, tavern-keeper, from Penn., Peter Coyle, and James Craig. The early settlers of the village were, beside those named, Joseph and James Walker, Michael Click, David and Wm. Petigrue, Samuel Kratzer, Gilman Bryant, and Rev. James Smith, who came in 1808, and was the first Methodist clergyman.

When the settlers first came, there were two wells, only a few rods apart, on the south bank of Vernon river, on the edge of the town, the origin of which remains unknown. They were built of neatly hammered stone, laid in regular masonry, and had the appearance of being overgrown with moss. Near by, was a salt lick, at which the Indians had been accustomed to encamp. Almost immediately after the first settlement, all traces of the wells were obliterated, as was supposed, by the Indians. A similar well was later brought to light, a mile and a half distant, by the plow of Philip Cosner, while plowing in a newly cleared piece of forest land. It was covered with poles and earth, and was about 30 feet deep.

In the spring of 1807, Gilman Bryant opened the first store in Mt. Vernon, in a small sycamore cabin, in the western part of the town. A hewed log and shingle-roofed building stood on the northeast corner of Wood and Main streets: it was the first tavern, and was kept by Benj. Butler. The first frame building was put up in 1809, and is now standing on lot 138 Main street. The old court-house, erected about 1810, opposite the present court-house, on the public square, was the first brick building: it was two stories high, and thirty-six feet square. The first brick building was erected in the spring of 1815, by Gilman Bryant, now standing next to and south of his present residence. The first church, the old school Presbyterian, (now down,) was built about 1817. It was of brick, 40 feet square, and one story high: the first pastor was the Rev. James Scott. The first licensed preacher in the county was the Rev. Wm. Thrift, a Baptist, from Loudon county, Va., who came in 1807, and travelled about from house to house. The first crops raised in the county were corn and potatoes. They were grown on the bottom lands, which were the first cleared: those lands were too rich for wheat, making "*sick wheat*," so termed, because when made into bread, it had the effect of an emetic, and produced feelings similar to sea-sickness.

At an early day, the Indians, in great numbers, came to Mount Vernon to trade. They encamped on the river bank, and brought large quantities of furs and cranberries to dispose of for goods. The whites of the present day might take some beneficial hints from their method of trading at the store in this place. They walked in deliberately and seated themselves, upon which the merchant presented each with a small piece of tobacco. Having lighted their pipes, they returned the residue to their pouches. These were made of a whole mink skin, dressed with the hair on, with a slit cut in the throat, as an opening. In it, they kept, also, some *kinnickinnick* bark, or *sumach*, which they always smoked with their tobacco, in the proportion of about three of the former to one of the latter. After smoking and talking awhile together, one only at a time arose, went to the counter, and, taking up a yard stick, pointed to the first article he desired, and inquired the price. The questions were in this manner: "how many buckskins for a shirt pattern?" or "cloth for leggings?" &c. According to their *skin currency*,

A muskrat skin was equal to a quarter of a dollar; a raccoon skin, a third of a dollar; a doe skin, half a dollar, and a buck skin, "the almighty dollar." The Indian, learning the price of an article, payed for it by picking out and handing over the skins, before proceeding to purchase the second, when he repeated the process, and so on through the whole, paying for every thing as he went on, and never waiting for that purpose until he had finished. While the first Indian was trading, the others looked uninterruptedly on, and when he was through, another took his place, and so on, in rotation, until all had traded. No one desired to trade before his turn, and all observed a proper decorum, and never attempted to "beat down," but, if dissatisfied with the price, passed on to the next article. They were cautious not to trade while intoxicated; but usually preserved some of their skins to buy liquor, and end their visit with a frolic.

The early settlers in the town all felt as one family. If one got a piece of fresh meat, he shared it with his neighbors, and when a person was sick, all sympathized. At night, they met in each other's cabins, to talk, dance, and take a social glass. There was no distinction of party, for it was a social democracy. At their weddings, a puncheon table, formed like a bench, without a cloth, was covered with refreshments. These were plain and simple: wild turkeys, that had been gobbling about in the woods, were stewed and eaten with a relish; corn, that had grown on the river flats, made into "*pone*," served as wedding cake; while metheglin and whiskey, the only articles probably not indigenous, were the beverages that washed them down. Their plates were either of wood or pewter, perhaps both, and no two alike; their knives, frequently butcher knives, and their forks often of wood. A dance was the finale of their festivities. They made merry on the puncheon floor to the music of the fiddle. Cotillions were unknown, while jigs, four-handed reels, the double shuffle and break down "were all the rage."

After Mount Vernon was laid out, the settlers from the region round about were accustomed to come into town on Saturdays, to clear the stumps out of the streets. Early in the afternoon they quitted work, and grew jolly over a large kettle of "*stew*." This was made as follows: First, a huge kettle, of gallons' capacity, was placed upon the ground, resting upon three stones, and a fire kindled under it. In it was put two or three buckets of water, a few pounds of maple sugar, a few ounces of allspice, which had been pounded in a rag, a pound of butter, and, finally, two or three gallons of whiskey. When boiled, the stew was taken off, a circle was formed around, and the men helped themselves liberally, with tin cups, to the liquor, told hunting stories, wrestled, ran, hopped and jumped, engaged in foot races, shot at mark for goods or tobacco purchased at the store, and occasionally enlivened the scene by a fight.

Upon the organization of the county, there was a spirit of rivalry as to which should be the county seat, Mount Vernon or Clinton, a town laid out a mile and a half north, by Samuel Smith—then a place of the most population, now among the "things that were." The commissioners appointed to locate the seat of justice, first entered Mount Vernon, and were received with the best cheer, at the log tavern of Mr. Butler. To impress them with an idea of the public spirit of the place, the people were very busy at the moment of their entrance and during their stay, at work, all with their coats off, grubbing the streets. As they left for Clinton, all quitted their labor, not "of love;" and some rowdies, who dwelt in cabins scattered round about in the woods, away from the town, left "the crowd," and stealing ahead of the commissioners, arrived at Clinton first. On the arrival of the others at that place, these fellows pretended to be in a state not comformable to temperance principles, ran against the commissioners, and by their rude and boisterous conduct, so disgusted the worthy officials as to the apparent morals of the inhabitants of Clinton, that they returned and made known their determination that Mount Vernon should be the favored spot. That night, there were great rejoicings in town. Bonfires were kindled, stew made and drank, and live trees split with gunpowder.

The first settler north of Mount Vernon, was Nathaniel M. Young, from Pa., who, in 1803, built a cabin on the south fork of Vernon river, three miles west of Fredericktown. Mr. Young and his neighbors being much troubled with wolves, got together and made a written agreement to give nine bushels of corn for every wolf's scalp. In the winter of 1805–6, Mr. Young, John Lewis and James Bryant caught forty-one wolves, in steel traps and pens. Wolf pens were about 6 feet long, 4 wide and 3 high, formed like a huge square box, of small logs, and floored with puncheons. The lid, also of puncheons, was very heavy, and moved by an axle at one end, made of a small, round stick. The trap was set by a figure four, with any kind of meat except that of wolf's, the animals being fonder of any other than their own. On gnawing the meat, the lid fell and enclosed the unamiable native. Often, to have sport for the dogs, they pulled out the legs of a wolf through the crevices of the logs, hamstrung, and then let him loose, upon which the dogs sprang upon him, while he, crippled by the operation, made but an ineffectual resistance. In the adjoining county of Delaware, a man, somewhat advanced in years, went into a wolf-trap to render the adjustment of the spring more delicate, when the trap sprung upon him, and, knocking him flat on his face, securely caught him as was ever any of the wolf species. He was unable to lift up the lid, and several miles from any house. There he lay all one day and night, and would have perished had not a passing hunter heard his groans and relieved him from his peril.

Mount Vernon, the county seat, is 45 miles NE. of Columbus. It is beautifully situated on ground slightly ascending from Vernon river. The town is compactly and substantially built, and some of the dwellings elegant. Main, the principal business street, is about a mile in length, on which are many brick blocks, three stories in neight. The view was taken in this street, at the southern extremity of the public square, looking north: on the left is shown the market and court-house, on the right, the Episcopal church, an elegant stone edifice, and in the centre, the tower of the old school Presbyterian church and the jail. This flourishing town contains 2 Presbyterian, 2 Methodist, 1 Baptist, 1 Lutheran, 1 Catholic and 1 Episcopal church, 20 dry goods, 6 grocery, 2 hardware, 3 apothecary and 2 book stores; 1 fulling, 4 grist and 5 saw mills, 3 newspaper printing offices, and had, in 1840, 2,363 inhabitants, and has now over 3,000. The railroad, constructing from Sandusky City to Columbus, will connect this place with those.

Public Square, Mount Vernon.

Five miles east of Mount Vernon, on a beautiful, healthy and elevated ridge, encompassed on three sides by the Vernon river, is the village of Gambier, so named from lord Gambier, and widely known as the seat of Kenyon college. This town, exclusive of the college, contains about 200 inhabitants. It was laid out under the auspices of the venerable Bishop Chase, in July, 1826, in the center of a 4,000 acre tract, belonging to Kenyon college. This institution was then founded, with funds obtained by Bishop Chase in England, and named after lord Kenyon, one of its principal benefactors. It was first chartered as a theological seminary. It is richly endowed, having 8,000 acres of land, and its property is valued at $100,000. The college proper has about 50 students; the theological seminary about 20; the senior grammar school about 20, and Milnor Hall, an institute for boys, about 25. In the various libraries are near 10,000 volumes.

The main college building is romantically situated. You enter a gate into a large area: in the foreground is a large grassy, cleared plat of several acres, on the right of which stands Rosse chapel, an elegant Grecian structure; on the left and below, is the beautiful Vernon valley, bounded by forest-clad hills, over which the eye passes in the perspective for miles and miles, until the blue of distant hills and sky meet and blend in one. Through the centre of the grassy plat passes a footpath, which, at the distance of 200 yards, continues its straight line in a narrow opening through a forest, and terminates at the college, about one third of a mile distant, the spire of which rises darkly above the green foliage, like that of an ancient abbey, while the main building is mostly concealed. The whole scene, the graceful, cheerful architecture of the chapel, on the right, the valley on the left, the pleasant, grassy green in front, the forest beyond, with the sombre, half-concealed building in the distance, give an ever-enduring impression. Standing at the gate, with

Kenyon College.

the back to the college, the scene changes: a broad avenue terminates at the distance of half a mile, at the head of which, in a commanding position, faces Bexley Hall, a building appropriated to the theological seminary. It is a large, elegant, and highly ornamented Gothic structure, of a light color, with battlements and turrets, standing boldly relieved against the blue sky, except its lower portion, where it is concealed by the shrubbery of a spacious yard in front. To the left, and near the Hall, an imposing residence, late occupied by Bishop M'Ilvaine, faces the avenue. Away off to the right, among the trees, is Milnor Hall, and scattered about in various directions, near and far, private dwellings, offices and various structures, some plain and others adorned, some in full view and others partly hid by the undulations of the ground, trees and shrubbery.

Fredericktown is a flourishing and well-built village, 7 miles NW. of Mount Vernon, which was laid out in 1807, by John Kerr. Vernon river, on which it is situated, furnishes considerable water power: on the middle branch of that stream, near the village, are some ancient fortifications and mounds. The town contains 2 Presbyterian, 2 Methodist and 1 Universalist church; 8 dry goods and 1 grocery store, 2 grist, 2 saw, 2 carding and 2 fulling mills, and had, in 1840, 444 inhabitants—since which, it has increased. Chesterville, 12 miles NW. from Mount Vernon, on Vernon river, has 2 churches, 5 stores, 2 flouring mills, and about 400 inhabitants. Martinsburgh, 12 SE. of the county seat, on the Zanesville road, has 4 stores, 2 churches, an excellent academy, and about 400 inhabitants. Millwood, Bladensburgh, Amity, Danville, Centerburg, Mt. Liberty, Sparta, Palmyra and Mount Holly, are villages, the largest of which may contain 300 inhabitants.

LAKE.

LAKE was formed March 6th, 1840, from Geauga and Cuyahoga, and so named from its bordering on Lake Erie. The surface is more rolling than level; the soil is good, and generally clayey loam, interspersed with ridges of sand and gravel. The principal crops are wheat, corn, oats, barley, buckwheat, hay and potatoes. Dairy products, beef cattle and wool are also among the staples. This county is peculiar for the quality and quantity of its fruit, as apples, pears, peaches, plums, grapes, &c. Many thousand dollars' worth are annually exported, and many of its inhabitants leave every spring, to engage in the business of grafting at the south and west. The situation of this county is very favorable to the preservation of the fruit from the early frosts, the warm lake winds often preventing its destruction, while that some twenty miles inland, is cut off. Bog iron ore is found in large quantities in Perry and Madison, and there are several furnaces in the county. The following is a list of its townships in 1840, with their population:

Concord,	1136	Madison,	2801	Perry,	1337
Kirtland,	1777	Mentor,	1245	Willoughby,	1943
Leroy,	898	Painesville,	2580		

Population of Lake, in 1840, 13,717, or 65 inhabitants to the square mile.

Mentor was the first place settled in this county. In the summer of 1799, two families were there.* Among the earliest settlers of Lake, was the Hon. John Walworth, who was born at New London, Ct., in 1765.

When a young man, he spent five years at sea and in Demarara, South America. About the year 1792, he removed, with his family, to the then new country east of Cayuga lake, New York. In 1799, he visited Cleveland, and after his return, in the fall of that year, journeyed to Connecticut, purchased over two thousand acres of land in the present township of Painesville, with the design of making a settlement. On the 20th of February, 1800, he commenced the removal of his family and effects. They were brought on as far as Buffalo, in sleighs. At that place, after some little detention, the party being enlarged by the addition of some others, drove in two sleighs on to the ice of the lake, and proceeded until abreast of Cattaraugus creek, at which point they were about ten miles from land. At dusk, leaving their sleighs and horses some 50 or 60 rods from shore, they made their camp under some hemlock trees, where all, men, women and children passed an agreeable night, its earlier hours being enlivened by good cheer and social converse. The next afternoon, they arrived at Presque isle, (now Erie, Pa.,) where, leaving his family, Mr. Walworth went back to Buffalo, for his goods. On his return to Erie, he, with his hired man and two horses and a yoke of oxen, followed the lake shore, and arrived in safety at his new purchase. His nearest neighbors east, were at Harpersfield, 15 miles distant. On the west, a few miles distant, within or near the present limits of Mentor, was what was then called the Marsh settlement, where was then living Judge Jesse Phelps, Jared Wood, Ebenezer Merry, Charles Parker and Moses Parks. Mr. Walworth soon returned to Erie, on foot, and brought out his family and effects in a flat boat, all arriving safe at the new home on the 7th of April. The first fortnight they lived in a tent, during which period the sun was not seen. About the expiration of this time, Gen. Edward Paine—the first delegate to the legislature from the Lake county, in the winter of 1801–2—arrived with seven or eight hired men, and settled about a mile distant. Mutually assisting each other, cabins were soon erected for shelter, and gradually the conveniences of civilization clustered around them.

* Mrs. Tappan, in the MSS. of the Ashtabula Historical Society.

Shortly after the formation of the state government, Mr. Walworth, Solomon Griswold, of Windsor, and Calvin Austin, of Warren, were appointed associate judges of Trumbull county. In 1805, Judge Walworth was appointed collector of customs for the district of Erie. In August, he opened the collector's office at Cleveland, and in the March ensuing, removed his family thither. He held various offices until his decease, Sept. 10th, 1812, and was an extensive land agent. Judge Walworth was small in stature, and of weakly constitution. Prior to his removal to the west, it was supposed he had the consumption; but to the hardships and fatigue he endured, and change of climate, his physicians attributed the prolongation of his life many years. He was a fearless man, and possessed of that indomitable perseverance and strength of will, especially important in overcoming the obstacles in the path of the pioneer.*

View in Painesville.

Painesville, the county seat, and the largest village between Cleveland and Erie, Pa., is 31 miles E. of Cleveland, and 170 NE. of Columbus. The Grand river skirts the village on the east, in a deep and picturesque valley. Painesville is one of the most beautiful villages in the west: it is somewhat scattered, leaving ample room for the cultivation of gardens, ornamental trees and shrubbery. A handsome public square of several acres, adorned with young trees, is laid out near the center of the town, on which face some public buildings and private mansions. The view represents the principal public buildings in the place. The first on the left, is the Methodist church; the building next, without a spire, tower or cupola, is the Disciple church; the one beyond, the Presbyterian church, and that most distant, the court house: these two last front the west side of the public square. Painesville is a flourishing town, containing 1 Episcopal, 1 Presbyterian, 1 Disciples and 1 Methodist church, 14 mercantile stores, 1 flouring mill, 1 bank, 1 newspaper printing office, and has increased since 1840, when it had 1014 inhabitants. The Painesville academy is a classical institution for both sexes, and in fine repute: a large brick building is appropriated for its uses. Near the town is the Geauga furnace, which employs a heavy capital.

* From the Barr MSS.

Painesville was laid out about the year 1805, by Henry Champion, and originally named Champion: it was afterwards changed to that of the township which derived its name from Gen. Ed. Paine, a native of Connecticut, an officer of the revolution, and an early settler: he died only a few years since, at an advanced age, leaving the reputation of a warm hearted and excellent man.

Among the aborigines familiarly known to the early settlers at Painesville, was a fine specimen of manhood, called by the whites, Seneca; by the Indians, *Stigwanish*, which, being rendered in English, signifies the Standing Stone. Says an old pioneer, in the Barr MSS :

Whoever once saw him, and could not at once perceive the dignity of a Roman senator, the honesty of Aristides and the philanthropy of William Penn, must be unacquainted with physiognomy. He was never known to ask a donation, but would accept one exactly as he ought, when offered. But it was not suffered to rest there; an appropriate return was sure to be made, and he would frequently be in advance. He drank cider or Malaga wine moderately, but was so much of a teetotaller, as to have abjured ardent spirits since the time when, in a drunken frenzy, he aimed a blow with his tomahawk at his wife, which split the head of the papoose on her back. He seldom wanted credit in his trading transactions, and when he did, there was no difficulty in obtaining it, as he was sure to make punctual payment in specie. Once, when himself and wife dined with us at Painesville, he took much trouble to instruct her in the use of the knife and fork. Vain attempt! his usual politeness forsook him, and bursts of immoderate laughter succeeded, in which we were all compelled to join. The last time I saw Seneca—the fine old fellow—was at Judge Walworth's, in Cleveland, a short time before hostilities commenced with Great Britain. He expressed to me a fear that war was inevitable, and that the Indians, instigated by the British, would overwhelm our weak settlements; but gave the strongest assurances that if it should be possible, he would give us seasonable notice. If he was not prevented by age or infirmities from redeeming his pledge, he was probably killed by his own people, while endeavoring to leave their lines, or by some of ours, through a mistake of his character.

The Hon. Samuel Huntington, who was governor of the state from 1808 to 1810, resided at Painesville, in the latter part of his life, and died there in 1817. Prior to his removal to Painesville, he resided at Cleveland. One evening, while travelling towards Cleveland from the east, he was attacked, about two miles from the town, by a pack of wolves, and such was their ferocity, that he broke his umbrella to pieces in keeping them off, to which, and the fleetness of his horse, he owed the preservation of his life.

Three miles below Painesville, at the mouth of Grand river, is Fairport, laid out in 1812, by Samuel Huntington, Abraham Skinner, Seymour and Calvin Austin, and Simon Perkins. The first warehouse in this region, and perhaps on the lake, was built about 1803, on the river, two miles above, by Abraham Skinner, near which, in the dwelling of Mr. Skinner, the first court in the old county of Geauga, was held. Fairport has one of the best harbors on the lake, and so well defended from winds, and easy of access, that vessels run in when they cannot easily make other ports. The water is deep enough for any lake craft, and about $60,000 has been expended in improving the harbor, by the general government. Lake steamers stop here, and considerable commerce is carried on. Fairport contains 8 forwarding houses, several groceries, from 20 to 40 dwellings, and a light house, and a beacon to guide the mariner on the fresh water sea.

Richmond, one mile above Fairport, on the opposite and west side of the river, was laid out about ten years ago, in the era of speculation. A large village was built, a steamboat was owned there, and great things promised. Not having the natural elements of prosperity, it soon waned, some of its dwellings were removed to Painesville, while many others, deserted and decaying, are left to mark the spot.

Medical University, etc., Willoughby.

The neat and pleasant village of Willoughby, is on Chagrin river, 2½ miles from its mouth, 19 miles from Cleveland, and 11 s. w. of Painesville. The village and township were originally called Chagrin, and changed, in 1834, to the present name, in honor of Prof. Willoughby, of Herkimer county, N. Y. It was settled about the year 1799, by David Abbot, (see page 156,) Peter French, Jacob West, Ebenezer Smith, Elisha Graham and others. Abbot built the first grist mill on the site of the Willoughby mills: Smith was the first man who received a regular deed of his land from the Connecticut land company. In 1796, Charles Parker, one of the surveyors, built a house at the mouth of the river, and a number of huts for the use of the land company: the house was the first erected in the township, and probably the first in the county. Parker became a settler in 1802; in 1803 and 1804, John Miller, Christopher Colson, James Lewis and Jacob West settled in Willoughby. Dr. Henderson, the first regular physician, came in 1813, and the first organized town meeting was held April 3d, 1815. A bloody battle, says tradition, was fought at an early day between the Indians, on the spot where the medical college stands: human bones have been discovered, supposed to be of those who fell in that action.

The village of Willoughby contains 4 stores, 2 churches, 18 mechanic shops, 1 fulling mill, and in 1840, had 390 inhabitants. The engraving shows, on the right, the Presbyterian church, on the left, the Methodist church, and in the centre, on a pleasant green, the Medical University, a spacious brick edifice. This flourishing and well conducted institution, was founded in 1834: its number of pupils has been gradually increasing, and in 1846, its annual circular showed 174 students in attendance. The moderate expenses of the institute, the low price of board—from $1.25 to $1.50 per week—give it advantages to those of moderate means. Its president is Amasa Trowbridge, who, with seven other professors, and an anatomical demonstrator, form an ample corps of instructors.*

Kirtland is 9 miles southwest from Painesville, in a fine country, on an elevation on the southern side of a branch of Chagrin river, which here runs in a deep and romantic valley, interspersed with dwellings, cultivated farms and woodland. The village, at this time, contains about 250 inhabitants. The Western Reserve Teacher's Seminary, situated here, has 216 pupils of both sexes, is under the charge of Asa D. Lord, with several assistants, and is exerting a beneficial influence upon the cause of education in this region.

This village is widely known, from having formerly been the head quarters of the Mormons. While here, in the height of their prosperity, they numbered nearly 3000 persons. On their abandoning it, most of the dwellings went to decay, and it now has somewhat the appearance of a depopulated and broken down place. The view taken, shows the most prominent buildings in the village. In the center, is seen the Mormon Temple; on the right, the Teacher's Seminary, and on the left, on a line with the front of the temple, the old banking house of the Mormons. The temple, the main point of attraction, is 60 by 80 feet, and measures from its base to the top of the spire, 142 feet. It is of rough stone, plastered over, colored blue, and marked to imitate regular courses of masonry. It cost about $40,000. In front, over the large window, is a tablet, bearing the inscription: "House of the Lord, built by the church of the Latter Day Saints, A. D. 1834." The first and second stories are divided into two "grand rooms" for public worship. The attic is partitioned off into about a dozen small apartments. The lower grand room is fitted up with seats as an ordinary church, with canvas curtains hanging from the ceiling, which, on the occasion of prayer meetings, are let down to the tops of the slips, dividing the room into several different apartments, for the use of the separate collections of worshipers. At each end of the room is a set of pulpits, four in number, rising behind each other. Each pulpit is calculated for three persons, so that when they are full, twelve persons occupy each set, or twenty-four persons the two sets. These pulpits were for the officers of the priesthood. The set at the farther end of the room, are for the Melchisedek priesthood, or those who minister in spiritual concerns. The set opposite, near the entrance to the room, are for the Aaronic priesthood, whose duty it is to simply attend to the temporal affairs of the society. These pulpits all bear initials, signifying the rank of their occupants.

On the Melchisedek side, are the initials P. E., *i. e.* President of the Elders; M. P. H., President of the High Priests; P. M. H., Pres. of the High Council, and M. P. C., Pres. of the Full Church. On the Aaronic pulpits, are the initials P. D., *i. e.* President of Dea-

* Removed to Columbus.

cons; P. T. A., President of the Teachers; P. A. P., Pres. of the Aaronic Priesthood, and B. P. A., Bishop of the Aaronic Priesthood. The Aaronic priesthood were rarely allowed to preach, that being the especial duty of the higher order, the Melchisedek.

Mormon Temple, at Kirtland.

We have received a communication from a resident of Kirtland, dated in the autumn of 1846. It contains some facts of value, and is of interest as coming from an honest man, who has been a subject of the Mormon delusion, but whose faith, we are of opinion, is of late somewhat shaken.

The Mormons derive their name from their belief in the book of Mormon, which is said to have been translated from gold plates found in a hill, in Palmyra, N. Y. They came to this place in 1832, and commenced building their temple, which they finished in 1835. When they commenced building the temple, they were few in number, but before they had finished it, they had increased to two thousand.

There are in the church two Priesthoods—the Melchisedek and the Aaronic, including the Levitical, from which they derive their officers. This place, which they hold to be a *stake of Zion,* was laid off in half acres for a space of one square mile. When it was mostly sold, they bought a number of farms in this vicinity, at a very high price, and were deeply in debt for goods in New York, which were the causes of their eventually leaving for Missouri. They established a bank at Kirtland, from which they issued a number of thousand more dollars than they had specie, which gave their enemies power over them, and those bills became useless.

They adhered to their prophet, Smith, in all things, and left here in 1837, seven hundred in one day. They still hold this place to be a stake of Zion, to be eventually a place of gathering. There is a president with his two counsellors, to preside over this stake. The president is the highest officer; next is the high priest, below whom are the elders,—all of the Melchisedek priesthood. The lesser priesthood are composed of priests, teachers and deacons. They have twelve apostles, whose duty it is to travel and preach the gospel. There are seventy elders or seventies, a number of whom are travelling preachers: seven of the seventies preside over them. There were two seventies organized in Kirtland. They ordain most of the male members to some office. They have a bishop with two counsellors, to conduct the affairs of the church in temporal things, and set in judgment upon difficulties which may arise between members; but there is a higher court to which they can appeal, called the high council, which consists of twelve high priests. The president and his council set as judges over either of these courts. There are, however, three presidents who preside over the whole in all the world—so termed.

The method of conducting worship among the Mormons is similar to other denominations. The first ordinance is baptism for the remission of sins; they lay on hands for the gift of the Holy Ghost, and to heal the sick; anoint with oil; administer the sacrament; take little children and bless them; they hold to all the gifts of the Apostolic church, believing there is no true church without them, and have the gift of speaking in different tongues; they sometimes interpret for themselves, but commonly there is some one to interpret for them.

A prophet has lately risen among the Mormons, viz.: James J. Strang, of Wisconsin, who claims to be the successor of Joseph Smith. He has been with them only about two years, and was a young lawyer of western New York. He claims to have received communications from Heaven, at the very hour of Smith's death, commissioning him to lead the people. He has established a stake in Walworth county, Wisconsin, called the city of Voree, by interpretation, signifying "Garden of Peace," to which they are gathering, from Nauvoo and other places. He has lately visited Kirtland and re-established it as a *stake* of Zion, and organized the church with all its officers. There are now here about 100 members, who are daily increasing, and it is thought the place will be built up.

Strang is said to have found plates of brass or some other metal. He was directed by an angel, who gave him a stone to look through, by which he made the discovery. They were found three feet under ground, beneath an oak of a foot in diameter. These he has translated: they give an account of a race who once inhabited that land, and became a fallen people. Strang preaches pure bible doctrine, and receives only those who walk humbly before their God.

The Mormons still use the temple at Kirtland. This sect is now divided into three factions, viz.: the Rigdonites, the Twelveites, and the Strangites. The Rigdonites are the followers of Sidney Rigdon, and are but a few in number. The Twelveites—so named after their twelve apostles—are very fanatical, and hold to the spiritual wife system and the plurality of Gods. The Strangites maintain the original doctrines of Mormonism, and are located at this place and Voree.

We derive, from a published source, a brief historical sketch of Mormonism.

Joseph Smith, the founder of Mormonism, was born in Sharon, Vermont, Dec. 23d, 1805, and removed to Manchester, Ontario county, N. Y., about the year 1815, at an early age, with his parents, who were in quite humble circumstances. He was occasionally employed in Palmyra as a laborer, and bore the reputation of a lazy and ignorant young man. According to the testimony of respectable individuals in that place, Smith and his father were persons of doubtful moral character, addicted to disreputable habits, and moreover, extremely superstitious, believing in the existence of witchcraft. They at one time procured a mineral rod, and dug in various places for money. Smith testified that when digging he had seen the pot or chest containing the treasure, but never was fortunate enough to get it into his hands. He placed a singular looking stone in his hat, and pretended by the light of it to make many wonderful discoveries of gold, silver and other treasures, deposited in the earth. He commenced his career as the founder of the new sect, when about the age of 18 or 19, and appointed a number of meetings in Palmyra, for the purpose of declaring the divine revelations which he said were made to him. He was, however, unable to produce any excitement in the village; but very few had curiosity sufficient to listen to him. Not having means to print his revelations he applied to Mr. Crane, of the society of Friends, declaring that he was moved by the Spirit to call upon him for assistance. This gentleman bid him go to work, or the state-prison would end his career. Smith had better success with Martin Harris, an industrious and thrifty farmer of Palmyra, who was worth about $10,000, and who became one of his leading disciples. By his assistance, 5,000 copies of the Mormon bible (so called) were published, at an expense of about $3,000. It is possible that Harris might have made the advances with the expectation of a profitable speculation, as a great sale was anticipated. This work is a duodecimo volume containing 590 pages, and is, perhaps, one of the weakest productions ever attempted to be palmed off as a divine revelation. It is mostly a blind mass of words, interwoven with scriptural language and quotations, without much of a leading plan or design.

Soon after the publication of the Mormon bible, one Parley B. Pratt, a resident of Lorrain county, Ohio, happening to pass through Palmyra, on the canal, and hearing of the new religion, called on the prophet, and was soon converted. Pratt was intimate with Sidney Rigdon, a very popular preacher of the denomination called "Reformers," or "Disciples." About the time of the arrival of Pratt at Manchester, the Smiths were fitting out an expedition for the western country, under the command of Cowdery, in order to convert the Indians, or Lamanites, as they termed them. In October, 1830, this mission, consisting of Cowdery, Pratt, Peterson and Whitmer, arrived at Mentor, Ohio, the residence of Rigdon, well supplied with the new bibles. Near this place, in Kirtland, there were a few families belonging to Rigdon's congregation, who, having become extremely fanatical, were daily looking for some wonderful event to take place in the world: 17 of these persons readily believed in Mormonism, and were all re-immersed in one night by Cowdery. By the conversion of Rigdon soon after, Mormonism received a powerful impetus, and more than 100 converts were speedily added. Rigdon visited Smith at Palmyra, where he tarried about two months, receiving revelations, preaching, &c. He then returned to Kirtland, Ohio, and was followed a few days after by the prophet, Smith, and his connexions. Thus, from a state of almost beggary, the family of Smith were furnished with the "fat of the land" by their disciples, many of whom were wealthy.

A Mormon temple was erected at Kirtland, at an expense of about $40,000. In this building there was a sacred apartment, a kind of holy of holies, in which none but the priests were allowed to enter. An unsuccessful application was made to the legislature for the charter of a bank. Upon the refusal, they established an unchartered institution, commenced their banking operations, issued their notes, and made extensive loans. The society now rapidly increased in wealth and numbers, of whom many were doubtless drawn thither by mercenary motives. But the bubble at last burst. The bank being an unchartered institution, the debts due were not legally collectable. With the failure of this institution, the society rapidly declined, and Smith was obliged to leave the state to avoid the sheriff. Most of the sect, with their leader, removed to Missouri, where many outrages were perpetrated against them. The Mormons raised an armed force to "drive off the infidels," but were finally obliged to leave the state.

The last stand taken by the Mormons was at Nauvoo, Ill., a beautiful location on the Mississippi river. Here they erected a splendid temple, 120 feet in length by 80 in width, around which they built their city, which at one time contained about 10,000 inhabitants. Being determined to have their own laws and regulations, the difficulties which attended their sojourn in other places followed them here, and there was constant collision between them and the surrounding inhabitants. By some process of law, Joseph Smith (the prophet) and his brother Hyram were confined in the debtor's apartment in the jail at Carthage, in the vicinity of Nauvoo, and a guard of 8 or 10 men were stationed at the jail for their protection. While here, it appears a mob of about 60 men, in disguise, broke through the guard, and firing into the prison, killed both Joseph Smith and brother, Hyram, June 27th, 1844. Their difficulties still continued, and they determined to remove once more.

In 1840, a work was published at Painesville, by E. D. Howe, called a "History of Mormonism," which gives almost conclusive evidence that the historical part of the book of Mormons was written by one Solomon Spalding. From this work we derive the following facts.

Mr. Spalding was born in Connecticut, in 1761, graduated at Dartmouth, and having failed in mercantile business, removed in 1809 to Conneaut, in the adjoining county of Ashtabula. About the year

1812, his brother, John, visited him at that place. He gives the following testimony:

He then told me he had been writing a book, which he intended to have printed, the avails of which he thought would enable him to pay all his debts. The book was entitled the "Manuscript Found," of which he read to me many passages. It was an historical romance of the first settlers of America, endeavoring to show that the American Indians are the descendants of the Jews, or the lost tribes. It gave a detailed account of their journey from Jerusalem, by land and sea, till they arrived in America, under the command of NEPHI and LEHI. They afterwards had quarrels and contentions, and separated into two distinct nations, one of which he denominated Nephites, and the other Lamanites. Cruel and bloody wars ensued, in which great multitudes were slain. They buried their dead in large heaps, which caused the mounds so common in this country. Their arts, sciences and civilization were brought into view, in order to account for all the curious antiquities found in various parts of North and South America. I have recently read the Book of Mormon, and to my great surprise, I find nearly the same historical matter, names, &c., as they were in my brother's writings. I well remember that he wrote in the old style, and commenced about every sentence with "and it came to pass," or "now it came to pass," the same as in the Book of Mormon, and according to the best of my recollection and belief, it is the same as my brother Solomon wrote, with the exception of the religious matter. By what means it has fallen into the hands of Joseph Smith, jr., I am unable to determine. JOHN SPALDING.

Mr. Henry Lake, of Conneaut, also states:

I left the state of New York, late in the year, 1810, and arrived at this place the 1st of January following. Soon after my arrival, I formed a co-partnership with Solomon Spalding, for the purpose of rebuilding a forge which he had commenced a year or two before. He very frequently read to me from a manuscript which he was writing, which he entitled the "Manuscript Found," and which he represented as being found in this town. I spent many hours in hearing him read said writings, and became well acquainted with its contents. He wished me to assist him in getting his production printed, alledging that a book of that kind would meet with a rapid sale. I designed doing so, but the forge not meeting our anticipations, we failed in business, when I declined having any thing to do with the publication of the book. This book represented the American Indians as the descendants of the lost tribes, gave an account of their leaving Jerusalem, their contentions and wars, which were many and great. One time, when he was reading to me the tragic account of Laban, I pointed out to him what I considered an inconsistency, which he promised to correct; but by referring to the Book of Mormon, I find to my surprise that it stands there just as he read it to me then. Some months ago I borrowed the Golden Bible, put it into my pocket, carried it home, and thought no more of it. About a week after, my wife found the book in my coat pocket, as it hung up, and commenced reading it aloud as I lay upon the bed. She had not read twenty minutes till I was astonished to find the same passages in it that Spalding had read to me more than twenty years before, from his "Manuscript Found." Since that, I have more fully examined the said Golden Bible, and have no hesitation in saying that the historical part of it is principally, if not wholly taken from the "Manuscript Found." I well recollect telling Mr. Spalding, that the so frequent use of the words "And it came to pass," "Now it came to pass," rendered it ridiculous. Spalding left here in 1812, and I furnished him means to carry him to Pittsburgh, where he said he would get the book printed, and pay me. But I never heard any more from him or his writings, till I saw them in the Book of Mormon. HENRY LAKE.

The testimony of six other witnesses is produced in the work of Mr. Howe, all confirming the main facts as above given. As Mr. Spalding was vain of his writings, and was constantly showing them to his neighbors, reliable testimony to the same general facts might have been greatly multiplied.

The disposition Spalding made of his manuscripts is not known. From Conneaut, Spalding removed to Pittsburgh, about the year 1813, remained there a year or two, and from thence went to Amity, in the same state, where he died in 1816. His widow stated that while they resided at Pittsburgh; she thinks that the "Manuscript

Found" was once taken to the printing office of Patterson & Lambdin, but did not know whether it was ever returned. We again quote verbatim from the work of Mr. Howe.

Having established the fact, therefore, that most of the names and leading incidents contained in the Mormon bible, originated with Solomon Spalding, it is not very material, as we conceive, to show the way and manner by which they fell into the hands of the Smith family. To do this, however, we have made some inquiries.

It was inferred at once that some light might be shed upon the subject, and the mystery revealed, by applying to Patterson & Lambdin, in Pittsburgh. But here again death had interposed a barrier. That establishment was dissolved and broken up many years since, and Lambdin died about eight years ago. Mr. Patterson says he has no recollection of any such manuscript being brought there for publication, neither would he have been likely to have seen it, as the business of printing was conducted wholly by Lambdin at that time. He says, however, that many MS. books and pamphlets were brought to the office about that time, which remained upon their shelves for years, without being printed or even examined. Now, as Spalding's book can no where be found, or any thing heard of it after being carried to this establishment, there is the strongest presumption that it remained there in seclusion, till about the year 1823 or '24, at which time *Sidney Rigdon* located himself in that city. We have been credibly informed that he was on terms of intimacy with Lambdin, being seen frequently in his shop. Rigdon resided in Pittsburgh about three years, and during the whole of that time, as he has since frequently asserted, abandoned preaching and all other employment, for the purpose of *studying the bible*. He left there, and came into the county where he now resides, about the time Lambdin died, and commenced preaching some new points of doctrine, which were afterwards found to be inculcated in the Mormon bible. He resided in this vicinity about four years previous to the appearance of the book, during which time he made several long visits to Pittsburgh, and perhaps to the Susquehannah, where Smith was then digging for money, or pretending to be translating plates. It may be observed, also, that about the time Rigdon left Pittsburgh, the Smith family began to tell about finding a book that would contain a history of the first inhabitants of America, and that two years elapsed before they finally got possession of it.

We are, then, irresistibly led to this conclusion:—that Lambdin, after having failed in business, had recourse to the old manuscripts then in his possession, in order to *raise the wind*, by a book speculation, and placed the "Manuscript Found," of Solomon Spalding, in the hands of Rigdon, to be embellished, altered, and added to, as he might think expedient; and three years' study of the bible we should deem little time enough to garble it, as it is transferred to the Mormon book. The former dying, left the latter the sole proprietor, who was obliged to resort to his wits, and in a miraculous way to bring it before the world; for in no other manner could such a book be published without great sacrifice. And where could a more suitable character be found than Jo Smith, whose necromantic fame of arts and of deception, had already extended to a considerable distance? That Lambdin was a person every way qualified and fitted for such an enterprise, we have the testimony of his partner in business, and others of his acquaintance. Add to all these circumstances, the facts, that Rigdon had prepared the minds in a great measure, of nearly a hundred of those who had attended his ministration, to be in readiness to embrace the first mysterious *ism* that should be presented—the appearance of Cowdery at his residence as soon as the book was printed—his sudden conversion, after many pretensions to disbelieve it—his immediately repairing to the residence of Smith, 300 miles distant, where he was forthwith appointed an elder, high priest, and a scribe to the prophet—the pretended vision that his residence in Ohio was the "promised land,"—the immediate removal of the whole Smith family thither, where they were soon raised from a state of poverty to comparative affluence. We, therefore, must hold out Sidney Rigdon to the world, as being the original "author and proprietor" of the whole Mormon conspiracy, until further light is elicited upon the lost writings of Solomon Spalding.

Seven miles southerly from Painesville, is a small and abrupt eminence, of about 200 feet in height, called "*Little Mountain.*" A hotel is kept on the summit, and it commands a beautiful prospect of the adjacent country and Lake Erie, distant 10 miles. It is much visited, and is a favorite resort from the heats of summer. A cool breeze generally blows from the lake, to brace the nerves of the visitor, while around and below, the earth is clothed in beauty. Centerville, 12 miles east of the county seat, has 3 stores, 2 churches, and about 80 dwellings, scattered along the road for about a mile. Two and a half miles E. of the above, on the line of Ashtabula, is Unionville, which contains 4 stores, 2 churches, and about 100 dwellings, scattered along the road.

LAWRENCE.

Lawrence was organized March 1st, 1816, and named from Capt. James Lawrence, a native of Burlington, N. J., and a gallant naval officer of the war of 1812. Most of the county consists of high, abrupt hills, in which large quantities of sand or free stone exist: soil mostly clay. It is thinly settled, only about half the county having been, as yet, purchased of the general government. There is some rich land on the creek bottoms, and on that of the Ohio river, on which, and at the iron furnaces, are the principal settlements. This county is rich in minerals, and is the greatest iron manufacturing county in Ohio. Coal abounds in the western part, while clay, suitable for stone ware, is found under the ore, in the whole of the iron region. The agricultural products, which are small in quantity, are wheat, corn, oats, potatoes, hay and apples. The following is a list of the townships in 1840, with their population:

Aid,	610	Lawrence,	425	Symmes,	472
Decatur,	594	Mason,	695	Union,	1036
Elizabeth,	1534	Perry,	663	Upper,	1181
Fayette,	841	Rome,	879	Windsor,	815

The population of Lawrence, in 1820, was 3,499; in 1830, 6,366; and in 1840, 9,745, or 23 inhabitants to the square mile.

In the Indian war, prior to the treaty of Greenville, many boats, descending the Ohio, were attacked by the Indians, and the whites in them cruelly massacred. After the war had closed, wrecks of boats were frequently seen on the shore, to remind the traveller of the unhappy fate of those who had fallen a prey to the rifle, tomahawk and scalping-knife. Among the unpublished incidents of this nature, is one that belongs to the history of this county, obtained orally from one acquainted with the circumstances.

Among the early settlers of Mason County, Ky., was Mr. James Kelly, who emigrated from Westmoreland, Pa. Shortly after his arrival, the Indians carried on their murderous incursions with so much energy, as to seriously threaten the annihilation of the infant settlements. His father, alarmed for his safety, sent another son, William, to Kentucky, to bring his brother and family back to Pennsylvania. They embarked at Maysville, in a large canoe, with two men as passengers, who were to assist in navigating the boat. When about a mile below the mouth of the Big Guyandotte, and near the Virginia shore, they were suddenly fired upon by a party of Indians, secreted behind the trees on that bank of the river. William, who had risen up in the boat, was shot through the body, when James sprang up to save him from falling into the river, and receiving a death wound, fell forwards in the boat. The two men, as yet unharmed, steered for the Ohio shore. The instant the boat touched land, one of them, panic-stricken, sprang ashore, and running into the recesses of the forest, was never heard of more. The other passenger, however, was a man of undaunted courage. He determined to protect Mrs. Kelly and her little children, consisting of James, a boy of about 5 years of age, and an infant named Jane. They landed, and turned their course for Gallipolis, about 30 miles distant. In their haste, they had forgotten to get any provisions from the boat, and the prospect of reaching there, through a wilderness swarming with Indians, was gloomy. To add to the horrors of their situation, they had gone but a few miles, when Mrs. Kelly was bitten in the foot by a copper-head, and was unable to make farther progress. As the only resort, her companion told her that he must leave her alone in the woods, and travel to Gallipolis, procure a boat and a party, and come for her. Having secreted them among some pawpaws, he started on his solitary and perilous journey. The Indians were soon on his track, in hot pursuit; and taking inland to avoid them, three or four days elapsed ere he arrived at the point of destination. He there obtained a keel boat, and a party of thirty men, and started down the Ohio, with but a faint hope of finding Mrs. Kelly and her little ones alive.

During his absence, Mrs. Kelly had been accustomed, daily, to send her little son to the river's edge, to hail any boats that might pass. Fearing a decoy from the Indians, several went by without paying any attention to his cries. An hour or two before the arrival of the aid from Gallipolis, another boat, from farther up the river, passed down. At first, but little attention was given to the hailing of little James; but feelings of humanity prevailed over their fears, and reflecting also upon the improbability of the Indians sending such a mere child as a decoy, they took courage, turned to the shore, and took the sufferers aboard. They were then in a starving and deplorable condition; but food was soon given them by the kind-hearted boatmen, and their perils were over. Soon the Gallipolis boat hove in sight, and they were taken on board, and eventually to Pennsylvania.

Mrs. Kelly, in the course of a few years, married again. The infant Jane grew up to womanhood, and was remarkable for her beauty. The little boy James finally emigrated to the Muskingum country. From him and his mother our informant derived these facts.

Lawrence was settled about 1797, by people from Pennsylvania and Virginia, who were principally of Dutch and Irish descent. When the iron works were first established, only about one eighth of the land was entered, since which, the workmen have accumulated means to purchase more. At that day, the inhabitants were principally hunters, and for months together, our informant says, he did not see one wear a coat or shoes; hunting shirts and moccasons being the substitutes.

The iron region is about eight miles wide. It extends through the east part of Scioto, and the west part of this county, and enters Jackson county on the north, and Greenup county, Ky., on the south. Most of the iron in Lawrence is made into pig metal, which stands high for castings, and is equal to Scotch pig for foundery furnaces: it is also excellent for bar iron. The principal markets are Pittsburgh and Cincinnati. The four counties of Jackson, Lawrence, Scioto, and Greenup, Ky., make about 37,450 tons annually, which, at $30 per ton, the current market price, amounts to $1,123,500. There are 21 furnaces in the iron region, of which the following are in Lawrence, viz., Union, Pine Grove, Lawrence, Center, Mount Vernon, Buckhorn, Etna, Vesuvius, La Grange, Hecla, and Olive. The oldest of these, in this county, is Union, a view of which is given, showing on the left, the furnace, in the middle ground, the log huts of the workmen, with the store of the proprietors, while around is wild, hilly scenery, amid which these furnaces are usually embosomed. Each of the 21 furnaces employs, on an average, 70 yoke of oxen, "100 hands, sustain 500 persons, consume 560 barrels of flour, 1000 bushels of corn meal, 10,000 bushels of corn, 50,000 pounds of bacon, 20,000 pounds of beef, 1500 bushels of potatoes, beside other provisions, and tea, sugar and coffee in proportion." From this it will be seen, that their existence is highly important to the agriculturist. In the winter season, about 500 men come from abroad, to cut wood for the furnaces in Lawrence; some of whom walk distances of hundreds of miles from their cabin homes among the mountains of Virginia and Kentucky.

Union Furnace.

Burlington, the county seat, is on the southernmost point of the Ohio river in the state, 133 miles southeasterly from Columbus. It is a small village, containing 4 stores, an academy, 1 or 2 churches, a newspaper printing office, and from 40 to 60 dwellings.

When Lawrence was first organized, the commissioners neglected to lay a tax, and the expenses of the county were carried on by orders, which so depreciated that the clerk had to pay $6, in orders, for a quire of paper. The county was finally sued on an order, and judgment obtained for the plaintiff, but as the public property could not be levied upon, not any thing was then recovered. Eventually, the legislature passed laws compelling the commissioners to lay a tax, by which the orders were paid in full, with interest.

The annexed report of a case, that came before the court of common pleas in this county, is from the pen of a legal gentleman of high standing. It shows that in our day, the belief in *witchcraft* has not entirely vanished.

——— ——— *vs.* ENOCH H. FLEECE. } *Lawrence Common Pleas. Term* 1828. *Action on the case, for a false warranty in the sale of a horse. Plea, general issue.*

The plaintiff having proved the sale and warranty, called a witness to prove the defendant's knowledge of the unsoundness of the horse at the time of sale. This witness testified, that both he and defendant lived at Union Furnace, in Lawrence county, and that the latter was by trade a tanner; that he, witness, knew the horse previous to the sale to the plaintiff, and before he was owned by defendant, and was then, and at the time defendant purchased him, in bad health. He saw him daily employed in defendant's bark mill, and was fast declining, and when unemployed, *drooping* in his appearance, and so continued until sold to the plaintiff. Having been present at the sale, and hearing the warranty, the witness afterwards inquired of the defendant why he had done so, knowing the horse to be unsound. He answered by insisting that the horse was in no way ***diseased***, or in unsound ***health***, but that the drooping appearance arose from his being ***bewitch-***

ed, which he did not call *unsoundness*, and so soon as they could be got out of the horse, he would then be as well as ever. The defendant further stated, that the same witches which were in that horse, had been in one or two persons, and some cows, in the same settlement, and could only be driven out by a witch doctor, living on the head waters of the Little Scioto, in Pike county, or by burning the animal in which they were found; that this doctor had some time before been sent for to see a young woman who was in a *bad way*, and on examination found her bewitched. He soon expelled them, and also succeeded in ascertaining that an old woman not far off was the witch going about in that way, and she could be got rid of only by killing her. At some subsequent time, when defendant was from home, his wife sent for witness and others, to see and find out what was the matter with her cow, in a lot near the house. They found it frantic, running, and pitching at every thing which came near. It was their opinion, after observing it considerably, that it had the *canine madness*. The defendant, however, returned before the witness and others left the lot; he inspected the cow with much attention, and gave it as his opinion that they were mistaken as to the true cause of her conduct,—she was not mad, but bewitched; the same which had been in the horse, had transferred itself to the cow. By this time the animal, from exhaustion or other cause, had lain down. The defendant then went into the lot, and requested the persons present to assist in putting a rope about her horns, and then make the other end fast to a tree, where he could burn her. They laughed at the man's notion, but finally assisted him, seeing she remained quiet—still having no belief that he really intended burning her. This being done, the defendant piled up logs, brush and other things around, and finally over the poor cow, and then set fire to them. The defendant continued to add fuel, until she was entirely consumed, and afterwards told the witness he had never seen any creature so *hard to die;* that she continued to moan after most of the flesh had fallen from her bones, and he felt a pity for her, but die she must; that nothing but the witches in her kept her alive so long, and it was his belief they would be so burnt before getting out, that they never would come back. Night having set in before the burning was finished, the defendant and his family set up to ascertain if the witches could be seen about the pile of embers. Late at night, some one of the family called the defendant to the window—the house being near the place—and pointed to two witches, hopping around, over and across the pile of embers, and now and then seizing a brand and throwing it into the air, and in a short while disappeared. The next morning, on examination, the defendant saw their tracks through the embers in all directions. At a subsequent time, he told the same witness and others, that from that time the witches had wholly disappeared from the neighborhood, and would never return—and to burn the animal alive, in which they were found, was the only way to get clear of them: he *had been* very fearful they would torment his family.

The writer found, after the above trial, from a conversation with the defendant, that he had a settled belief in such things, and in the truth of the above statement.

Hanging Rock, 17 miles below the county seat, on the Ohio river, contains 1 church, 4 stores, a forge, a rolling mill, and a foundery—where excellent bar iron is made—and about 150 inhabitants. It is the great iron emporium of the county, and nearly all the iron is shipped there. It is contemplated to build a railroad from this place, of about 15 miles in length, to the iron region, connecting it with the various furnaces. The village is named from a noted cliff of sandstone, about 400 feet in height, called the "Hanging Rock," the upper portion of which projects over, like the cornice of a house.

Some years since, a wealthy iron master was buried at Hanging Rock, in compliance with his request, above ground, in an iron coffin. It was raised about two feet from the ground, supported by iron pillars, resting on a flat stone. Over all, was placed an octagonal building of wood, about 12 feet diameter and 15 high, painted white, with a cupola-like roof, surmounted by a ball. It was in fact a tomb, but of so novel a description as to attract crowds of strangers, to the no small annoyance of the friends of the deceased, who, in consequence, removed the building, and sunk the coffin into a grave near the spot.

LICKING.

Licking was erected from Fairfield, March 1st, 1808, and named from its principal stream, called by the whites Licking—by the Indians, *Pataskala*. The surface is slightly hilly on the east, the western part is level, and the soil generally yellow clay: the vallies are rich alluvion, inclining many of them to gravel. Coal is in the eastern part, and iron ore of a good quality. The soil is generally very fertile, and it is a wealthy agricultural county. The principal crops are wheat, corn, oats and grass. Wool and dairy productions are also important staples. The following is a list of the townships in 1840, with their population.

Bennington,	1244	Harrison,	1049	Mary Anne,	866
Bowling Green,	1464	Hartford,	1355	M'Keane,	1424
Burlington,	1423	Hopewell,	1150	Newark,	4138
Eden,	853	Jersey,	932	Newton,	1247
Etna,	1076	Liberty,	1115	Perry,	994
Fallsbury,	910	Licking,	1215	St. Albans,	1515
Franklin,	1131	Lima,	739	Union,	2219
Granville,	2255	Madison,	1119	Washington,	1348
Hanover,	943				

The population of Licking, in 1820, was 11,861, in 1830, 20,864, and in 1840, 35,096; or 53 inhabitants to the square mile.

This county contains a mixed population: its inhabitants originated from Pennsylvania, Virginia, New Jersey, New England, Wales and Germany. Among the early settlers were John Channel, Isaac Stadden, John Van Buskirk, Benjamin Green, Samuel Parr, Samuel Elliott, John and Washington Evans, Geo. Archer, John Jones, and many Welsh. It was first settled, shortly after Wayne's treaty of 1795, by John Ratliff and Ellis Hughes, in some old Indian cornfields, about five miles below Newark, on the Licking. These men were from western Virginia. They lived mainly by hunting, raising, however, a little corn, the cultivation of which was left, in a great measure, to their wives.

Hughes had been bred in the hot-bed of Indian warfare. The Indians having, at an early day, murdered a young woman to whom he was attached, and subsequently his father, the return of peace did not mitigate his hatred of the race. One night, in April, 1800, two Indians stole the horses of Hughes and Ratliff from a little enclosure near their cabins. Missing them in the morning, they started off, well-armed, in pursuit, accompanied by a man named Bland. They followed their trail in a northern direction all day, and at night camped in the woods. At the grey of the morning, they came upon the Indians, who were asleep and unconscious of danger. Concealing themselves behind the trees, they waited until the Indians had awakened, and were commencing preparations for their journey. They drew up their rifles to shoot, and just at that moment one of the Indians discovered them, and instinctively clapping his hand on his breast, as if to ward off the fatal ball, exclaimed in tones of affright, "me bad Indian!—me no do so more!" The appeal was in vain, the smoke curled from the glistening barrels, the report rang in the morning air, and the poor Indians fell dead. They returned to their cabins with the horses and "plunder" taken from the Indians, and swore mutual secrecy for this violation of law.

One evening, some time after, Hughes was quietly sitting in his cabin, when he was startled by the entrance of two powerful and well-armed savages. Concealing his emotions, he gave them a welcome and offered them seats. His wife, a muscular, squaw-like looking female, stepped aside and privately sent for Ratliff, whose cabin was near. Presently, Ratliff, who had made a detour, entered, with his rifle, from an opposite direction, as if he had been out hunting. He found Hughes talking with the Indians about the murder. Hughes had his tomahawk and scalping-knife, as was his custom, in a belt around his person, but his rifle hung from the cabin wall, which he deemed it imprudent to attempt to obtain. There all the long night sat the parties, mutually fearing each other, and neither summoning sufficient courage to stir. When morning dawned, the Indians left, shaking hands and bidding farewell, but, in their retreat, were very cautious not to be shot in ambush by the hardy borderers.

Hughes died near Utica, in this county, in March, 1845, at an advanced age, in the hope of a happy future. His early life had been one of much adventure: he was, it is supposed, the last survivor of the bloody battle of Point Pleasant. He was buried with military honors and other demonstrations of respect.

Newark, the county seat, is 37 miles, by the mail route, easterly from Columbus, at the confluence of the three principal branches of the Licking. It is on the line of the Ohio canal, and of the railroad now constructing from Sandusky City to Columbus, a branch from which, of about 24 miles in length, will probably diverge from this place to Zanesville. Newark is a beautiful and well-built town, on a level site, and has the most spacious and elegant public square in the state. It was laid out, with broad streets, in 1801, on the plan of Newark, N. J., by Gen. Wm. C. Schenk, Geo. W. Burnet, Esq., and John M. Cummings, who owned this military section, comprising 4,000 acres. The first hewed log-houses were built in 1802, on the public square, by Samuel Elliott and Samuel Parr. The first tavern, a hewed log structure, with a stone chimney, was opened on the site of the Franklin house, by James Black. In 1804, there were about 15 or 20 families, mostly young married people. Among the early settlers were Morris A. Newman, Adam Hatfield, Jas. Black, John Johnson, Patrick Cunningham, William Claypole, Abraham Miller, Samuel H. Smith, Annaniah Pugh, Jas. Petticord, John and Aquila Belt, Dr. John J. Brice, and widow Pegg. About the year 1808, a log building was erected on or near the site of the court-house, which was used as a court-house and a church, common for all denominations. The Presbyterians built the first regular church, about 1817, just west of the court-house, on the public square. The first sermon delivered in Newark, by a Presbyterian, and probably the first by any denomination in the county, was preached under peculiar circumstances.

In 1803, Rev. John Wright, missionary of the Western Missionary Society at Pittsburg, arrived on a Saturday afternoon at Newark, which then contained five or six log-cabins and Black's log tavern, at which he put up. On inquiring of the landlady, he found there was but one Presbyterian in the place, and as he was very poor, he concluded to remain at the tavern rather than intrude upon his hospitality. The town was filled with people attending a horse-race, which, not proving satisfactory, they determined to try over the next day. Mr. Wright retired to rest at an early hour, but was intruded upon by the horse racers, who swore that he must either join and drink with them, or be ducked under a pump, which last operation was coolly performed upon one of the company in his presence. About midnight, he sought and obtained admittance in the house of the Presbyterian, where he rested on the floor, not without strenuous urging from the worthy couple to occupy their bed. The next morning, which was Sunday, when the guests ascertained he was a clergyman, they sent an apology for their conduct, and requested him to postpone preaching until afternoon, when the race was over. The apology was accepted, but he preached in the morning to a few persons, and in the afternoon to a large congregation. The sermon, which was upon the sanctification of the Sabbath, was practical and pungent. When he concluded, a person arose and addressed the congregation, telling them that the preacher had told the truth; and although he was at the horse-race, it was wrong, and that they must take up a contribution for Mr. Wright. Over seven dollars were collected. In 1804, Mr. Wright settled in Lancaster, and after great difficulty, as the population was much addicted to vice, succeeded, in about 1807, through the aid of Mr. David Moore, in organizing the first Presbyterian church in Newark.

Newark contains 2 Prebyterian, 1 Baptist, 1 Episcopal, 1 Methodist, 1 Welsh Methodist, 1 German Lutheran, 1 Welsh Presbyterian and 1 Catholic church; 3 newspaper printing offices, 2 grist mills 1 foundery, 1 woolen factory, 6 forwarding houses, 10 groceries, 1 book, 2 hardware and 18 dry goods stores: in 1830, it had 999 inhabitants, and in 1840, 2,705, in 1847, 3,406.

Southwest of Newark, in the forks formed by a branch of Licking river and Raccoon creek, are numerous ancient works, which extend over a space of several miles in length and breadth.

On the 18th of May, 1825, occurred one of the most violent tornadoes ever known in Ohio. It has been commonly designated as "*the Burlington storm*," because in Burlington township, in this county, its effects were more severely felt than in any other part of its track. This event is told in the language of a correspondent.

It commenced between the hours of one and two, P. M., in the southeast part of Delaware county. After passing for a few miles upon the surface of the ground, in an easterly direction, it appeared to rise so high from the earth that the tallest trees were not affected by it, and then again descended to the surface, and with greatly increased violence and force proceeded through the townships of Bennington and Burlington, in Licking county, and then passed into Knox county, and thence to Coshocton county. Its general course was a little north of east. For force and violence of wind, this storm has rarely been surpassed in any country in the same latitude. Forests and orchards were completely uprooted and levelled, buildings blown down, and their parts scattered in every direction and carried by the force of the wind many miles distant. Cattle were taken from the ground and carried one hundred rods or more. The creek, which had been swollen by recent rains, had but little water in its bed after the storm had passed. The roads and fields recently plowed, were quite muddy from previous rains; but after the storm had passed by, both roads and fields were clean and dry. Its track through Licking county was from one-third to three-fifths of a mile wide, but became wider as it advanced farther to the eastward. Those who were so fortunate as to be witnesses of its progress, without being victims of its fury, represent the appearance of the fragments of trees, buildings, &c., high in the air, to resemble large numbers of birds, such as buzzards, or ravens. The ground, also, seemed to tremble, as it is asserted by many credible persons, who were, at the time, a mile from the tornado itself. The roar of the wind, the trembling of the ground, and the crash of the falling timber and buildings, is represented by all who were witnesses as being peculiarly dreadful.

Colonel Wright and others, who witnessed its progress, think it advanced at the rate of a mile per minute, and did not last more than a minute and a half or two minutes. The cloud was exceedingly black, and sometimes bore hard upon the ground, and at others, seemed to rise a little above the surface. One peculiarity was, that the fallen timber lay in every direction, so that the course of the storm could not be determined from the position of the fallen trees.

Many incidents are related by the inhabitants, calculated to illustrate the power, as well as the terror, of the storm, among which are the following. A chain from three to four feet long, and of the size of a common plow-chain, was taken from the ground near the house of John M'Clintock, and carried about half a mile, and lodged in the top of a sugar-tree stub, about 25 feet from the ground. An ox, belonging to Col. Wait Wright, was carried about 80 rods and left unhurt, although surrounded by the fallen timber, so that it required several hours chopping to release him. A cow, also, was taken from the same field and carried about 40 rods, and lodged in the top of a tree, which was blown down, and when found was dead, and about 8 feet from the ground. Whether the cow was blown against the tree-top before it was blown down, or was lodged in it after it fell, cannot be determined. A heavy ox cart was taken from the yard of Col. Wright, and carried about 40 rods, and struck the ground with such force as to break the axle and entirely to demolish one wheel. A son of Col. Wright, upwards of fourteen years of age, was standing in the house holding the door. The house, which was built of logs, was torn in pieces, and the lad was thrown with such violence across the room as to kill him instantly. A coat, which was hanging in the same room, was found, in the following November, in Coshocton county, more than forty miles distant, and was afterwards brought to Burlington, and was identified by Col. Wright's family. Other articles, such as shingles, pieces of timber and of furniture, were carried twenty, and even thirty miles. Miss Sarah Robb, about twelve years of age, was taken from her father's house and carried some distance, she could not tell how far; but when consciousness returned, found herself about forty rods from the house, and walking towards it. She was much bruised, but not essentially injured. The family of a Mr. Vance, on seeing the storm approach, fled from the house to the orchard adjoining. The upper part of the house was blown off and through the orchard; the lower part of the house remained. Two sons of Mr. Vance were killed—one immediately, and the other died in a day or two from his wounds. These, and the son of Col. Wright, above mentioned, were all the lives known to be lost by the storm. A house, built of large logs, in which was a family, and which a number of workmen had entered for shelter from the storm, was raised up on one side and rolled off the place on which it stood, without injuring any one. A yoke of oxen, belonging to Wm. H. Cooley, were standing in the yoke in the field, and after the storm, were found completely enclosed and covered with fallen timber, so that they were not released till the next day, but were not essentially injured. A black walnut tree, two and half feet in diameter, which had lain on the ground for many years, and had become embedded in the earth to nearly one half its size, was taken from its bed and carried across the creek, and left as many as 30 rods from its former location. A crockery crate, in which several fowls were confined, was carried by the wind several miles, and, with its contents, set down without injury.

Presbyterian Female Seminary. *Episcopal Female Seminary.*

Granville (Baptist) College. *Male Academy.*

Literary Institutions at Granville.

The village of Granville is six miles west of Newark, and is connected with the Ohio canal by a side cut of six miles in length. It is a neat, well-built town, noted for the morality and intelligence of its inhabitants and its flourishing and well-conducted literary institutions. It contains 6 churches, 6 stores, 3 academies—(beside a large brick building, which accommodates in each of its stories a distinct school,—and had in 1840, 727 inhabitants. The Granville college belongs to the Baptists, and was chartered in 1832. It is on a commanding site, one mile southwest of the village: its faculty consist of a president, two professors and two tutors. The four institutions at Granville, have, unitedly, from 15 to 20 instructors, and enjoy a generous patronage from all parts of the state. When all the schools and institutions are in operation, there are, within a mile, usually from 400 to 600 scholars.

The annexed historical sketch of Granville township, is from the published sketches of the Rev. Jacob Little.

In 1804, a company was formed at Granville, Mass., with the intention of making a settlement in Ohio. This, called "*the Scioto company*," was the third of that name which effected settlements in Ohio. (See pp. 169, 178.) The project met with great favor, and much enthusiasm was elicited; in illustration of which, a song was composed and sung to the tune of "Pleasant Ohio," by the young people in the house and at labor in the field. We annex two stanzas, which are more curious than poetical.

When rambling o'er these mountains
  And rocks, where ivies grow
Thick as the hairs upon your head,
  'Mongst which you cannot go;
Great storms of snow, cold winds that blow,
  We scarce can undergo;
Says I, my boys, we'll leave this place
  For the pleasant Ohio.

Our precious friends that stay behind,
  We're sorry now to leave;
But if they'll stay and break their shins,
  For them we'll never grieve;
Adieu, my friends! come on my dears,
  This journey we'll forego,
And settle Licking creek,
  In yonder Ohio.

The Scioto company consisted of 114 proprietors, who made a purchase of 28,000 acres. In the autumn of 1805, 234 persons, mostly from East Granville, Mass., came on to the purchase. Although they had been forty-two days on the road, their first business, on their arrival, having organized a church before they left the east, was to hear a sermon. The first tree cut was that by which public worship was held, which stood just front of the site of the Presbyterian church. On the first Sabbath, November 16th, although only about a dozen trees had been cut, they held divine worship, both forenoon and afternoon, at that spot. The novelty of worshiping in the woods, the forest extending hundreds of miles every way, the hardships of the journey, the winter setting in, the fresh thoughts of home, with all the friends and privileges left behind, and the impression that such must be the accommodations of a new country, all rushed on their nerves and made this a day of varied interest. When they began to sing, the echo of their voices among the trees was so different from what it was in the beautiful meeting house they had left, that they could no longer restrain their tears. *They wept when they remembered Zion.* The voices of part of the choir were for a season suppressed with emotion.

An incident occurred, which some Mrs. Sigourney should put into a poetical dress. Deacon Theophilus Reese, a Welsh Baptist, had two or three years before built a cabin a mile and a half north, and lived all this time without public worship. He had lost his cows, and hearing a lowing of the oxen belonging to the company, set out towards them. As he ascended the hills overlooking the town-plot, he heard the singing of the choir. The reverberation of the sound from hill-tops and trees, threw the good man into a serious dilemma. The music at first seemed to be behind, then in the tops of the trees or the clouds. He stopped, till by accurate listening, he caught the direction of the sound, and went on, till passing the brow of the hill, when he saw the audience sitting on the level below. He went home and told his wife that "the promise of God is a bond;" a Welsh phrase, signifying that we have security, equal to a bond that religion will prevail every where. He said "these must be good people. I am not afraid to go among them." Though he could not understand English, he constantly attended the reading meeting. Hearing the music on that occasion, made such an impression on his mind, that when he became old and met the first settlers, he would always tell over this story. The first cabin built, was that in which they worshiped succeeding Sabbaths, and before the close of winter they had a school and school house. That church, in forty years, has been favored with ten revivals, and received about one thousand persons.

The first Baptist sermon was preached in the log church by Elder Jones, in 1806. The

Welsh Baptist church was organized in the cabin of David Thomas, September 4, 1808. "The Baptist church in Christ and St. Albans," was organized June 6th, 1819. On the 21st of April, 1827, the Granville members were organized into "the Granville church," and the corner-stone of their church was laid September 21, 1829. In the fall, the first Methodist sermon was preached under a black walnut; the first class organized in 1810, and first church erected in 1824. An Episcopal church was organized May 9th, 1827, and a church consecrated in 1838. More recently, the Welsh Congregationalists and Calvinistic Methodists have built houses of worship, making seven congregations, of whom three worship in the Welsh language. There are, in the township, 405 families, of which 214 sustain family worship; 1431 persons over 14 years of age, of whom nearly 800 belong to these several churches. The town has 150 families, of which 80 have family worship. Twenty years ago, the township furnished 40 school teachers, and in 1846, 70, of whom 62 prayed in school. In 1846, the township took 621 periodical papers, beside three small monthlies. The first temperance society west of the mountains, was organized July 15th, 1828, and in 1831, the Congregational church adopted a by-law, to accept no member who trafficked in or used ardent spirits.

There are but six men now living who came on with families the first fall, viz: Hugh Kelley, Roswell Graves, Elias Gillman, William Gavit, Levi and Hiram Rose. Other males, who arrived in 1805, then mostly children, and still surviving, are Elkannah Linnel, Spencer, Thomas and Timothy Spelman, Dennis Kelley, William Jones, Franklin and Ezekiel Gavit, Cotton, Alexander and William Thrall, Augustine Munson, Amos Carpenter, Timothy, Samuel, Heland, Lemuel, C. C. and Hiram P. Rose, Justin and Truman Hillyer, Silvanus, Gideon, Isaac and Archibald Cornel, Simeon and Alfred Avery, Frederick More, Worthy Pratt, Ezekiel, Samuel and Truman Wells, Albert, Mitchell, Joshua, Knowles and Benjamin Linnel, Lester and Hiram Case, Harry and Lewis Clemens, Leverett, Harry and Charles Butler, and Titus Knox: which, added to the others, make forty-one persons.

When Granville was first settled, it was supposed that Worthington would be the capital of Ohio, between which and Zanesville, this would make a great half-way town. At this time, snakes, wolves and Indians abounded in this region. On the pleasant spring mornings, large numbers of snakes were found running on the flat stones. Upon prying up the stones, there was found a singular fact respecting the social nature of serpents. Dens were found containing very discordant materials, twenty or thirty rattle-snakes, black-snakes and copper-heads, all coiled up together. Their liberal terms of admission only seemed to require evidence of snakeship. Besides various turnouts to kill them, the inhabitants had one general hunt. Elias Gillman and Justin Hillyer were the captains, who chose sides, and the party beaten were to pay three gallons of whiskey. Tradition is divided as to the number killed that day. Some say 300. They killed that year between 700 and 800 rattle-snakes and copper-heads, keeping no account of the black and other harmless serpents. The young men would seize them by the neck and thrash them against the trees, before they had time to bite or curl round their arms. The copper-head, though smaller, was much more feared. The rattle-snake was larger, sooner seen, and a true southerner, always living up to the laws of honor. He would not bite without provocation, and by his rattles gave the challenge in an honorable way. Instead of this well-bred warfare, the copper-head is a wrathy little felon, whose ire is always up, and he will make at the hand or the foot in the leaves or grass, before he is seen, and his bite is as poisonous as that of his brother of the larger fang. The young men tested his temper, and found that in his wrath he would bite a red hot coal. Very few were bitten by the rattle-snake, and all speak well of his good disposition and gentlemanly manners; but so many were bitten in consequence of the fractious temper of the copper-head, that he has left no one behind him to sound a note in his praise.

The limb bitten became immediately swollen, turned the color of the snake, and the patient was soon unable to walk. In some cases the poison broke out annually, and in others, the limb for years was exposed to frequent swellings. After all that was suffered from poisonous reptiles, it was proved to a demonstration, that no animal is so poisonous as man. Carrying more poison in his mouth than any other creature, he can poison a venomous serpent to death, quicker than the serpent can him. Martin Root and two other young men, chopping together, saw a rattle-snake, set a fork over his neck, and put in his mouth a new quid from one of their mouths. They raised the fork, and the poor creature did not crawl more than his length before he convulsed, swelled up and died, poisoned to death by virus from the mouth of one of the lords of creation. Deacon Hayes and Worthy Pratt tried the same experiment upon copper-heads, with the same results. Many others killed venomous reptiles in the same way, and one man pretended that by the moderate use, he had taught a copper-head to take tobacco without injury.

About three miles northwest of the ancient works in the vicinity of Newark, and near the road between that place and Granville, are numerous mounds and other ancient works. The most curious object is the figure, shaped like and called "the Alligator," on the top of a high hill. Its dimensions are as follows, in feet: length of the head and neck, 32; do. of the body, 73; do. tail, 105; width from the ends of the fore feet over the shoulders, 100; do. hind feet over the hips, 92; do. between the legs across the body, 32; do. tail close to the body, 18; height at the highest point, 7; whole length, 210; do. head, neck and body, 105. It appears to be mainly composed of clay, and is overgrown with grass. Visitors have made a path from the nose along the back to where the tail begins to curl, at which point stands a large black walnut.

The noted "*Narrows of Licking*," are in the eastern part of the county. "This is a very picturesque spot; cliffs of sandstone rock, 50 feet in height, line the sides of the canal, especially on the left bank of the stream. In some places, they hang over in a semi-circular form, the upper portion projecting and defending the lower from the rains and weather. In one of these spots, the aborigines chose to display their ingenuity at pictorial writing, by figuring on the smooth face of the cliff, at an elevation of eight or ten feet above the water, the outlines of wild animals, and among the rest, the figure of a huge black human hand. From this circumstance, the spot is known to all the old hunters and inhabitants of this vicinity, by the name of 'the *black hand* narrows.' It is the scene of many an ancient legend and wild hunting story."

The following are names of villages in this county, with their population in 1840: some of them have much increased since, and are smart business places, containing several stores, churches, mills, &c. The six first named are on the national road. Brownsville 313, Hebron 473, Jacksontown 215, Kirkersville 179, Luray 109, Gratiot 147, Alexandria 200, Chatham 173, Etna 219, Fredonia 107, Hartford 106, Havana 54, Homer 201, Linnville 101, Lockport 125, and Utica 355. Johnstown, omitted in the census of 1840, is a village of note, in the northwest part of the county.

LOGAN.

Logan derived its name from Gen. Benj. Logan: it was formed March 1st, 1817, and the courts ordered "to be holden at the house of Edwin Matthews, or some other convenient place in the town of Bellville, until a permanent seat of justice should be established." The soil, which is various, is generally good: the surface broken around the head waters of Mad river, elsewhere rolling or level; in the western part are eight small lakes, covering each from two to seventy acres of land. The principal productions are wheat, corn, rye, oats and clover, flax and timothy seed. The following is a list of the townships in 1840, with their population:

Bloomfield,	565	Liberty,	807	Rush Creek,	1077
Rakes Creek,	222	M'Arthur,	1673	Stokes,	299
Harrison,	658	Miami,	1423	Union,	832
Jefferson,	1527	Monroe,	1203	Washington,	517
Lake,	1175	Perry,	1014	Zane,	1021

The population of Logan in 1820, was 3181; in 1830, 6432, and in 1840, 14,013, or 33 inhabitants to the square mile.

The territory comprised within the limits of this county, was a favorite abode of the Shawanoe Indians, who had several villages on Mad river, called the *Mack-a-chack* towns, the names and position of three of which are given to us by an old settler. The first, called Mack-a-chack, stood near West Liberty, on the farm of Judge Benj. Piatt; the second, Pigeon Town, was about three miles northwest, on the farm of George F. Dunn, and the third, Wappatomica, was just below Zanesfield.

The Mack-a-chack towns were destroyed in 1786, by a body of Kentuckians, under Gen. Benj. Logan. The narrative of this expedition is from the pen of Gen. William Lytle, (see page 98,) who was an actor in the scenes he describes.

It was in the autumn of this year, that Gen. Clarke raised the forces of the Wabash expedition. They constituted a numerous corps. Col. Logan was detached from the army at the falls of the Ohio, to raise a considerable force, with which to proceed against the Indian villages on the head waters of Mad river and the Great Miami. I was then aged 16, and too young to come within the legal requisition; but I offered myself as a volunteer. Col. Logan went on to his destination, and would have surprised the Indian towns against which he had marched, had not one of his men deserted to the enemy, not long before they reached the town, who gave notice of their approach. As it was, he burned eight large towns, and destroyed many fields of corn. He took 70 or 80 prisoners, and killed 20 warriors, and among them the head chief of the nation. This last act caused deep regret, humiliation and shame to the commander in chief and his troops.

We came in view of the two first towns, one of which stood on the west bank of Mad river, and the other on the northeast of it. They were separated by a prairie, half a mile in extent. The town on the northeast was situated on a high, commanding point of land, that projected a small distance into the prairie, at the foot of which eminence broke out several fine springs, This was the residence of the famous chief of the nation. His flag was flying at the time, from the top of a pole 60 feet high. We had advanced in three lines, the commander with some of the horsemen marching at the head of the center line, and the footmen in their rear. Col. Robert Patterson commanded the left, and I think Col. Thomas Kennedy the right. When we came in sight of the towns, the spies of the front guard made a halt, and sent a man back to inform the commander of the situation of the two towns. He ordered Col. Patterson to attack the towns on the left bank of Mad river. Col. Kennedy was also charged to incline a little to the right of the town on the east side of the prairie. He determined himself to charge, with the center division, immediately on the upper town. I heard the commander give his orders, and caution the colonels against allowing their men to kill any among the enemy, that they might suppose to be prisoners. He then ordered them to advance, and as soon as they should discover the enemy, to charge upon them. I had my doubts touching the propriety of some of the arrangements. I was willing, however, to view the affair with the diffidence of youth and inexperience. At any rate, I was determined to be at hand, to see all that was going on, and to be as near the head of the line as my colonel would permit. I was extremely solicitous to try myself in battle. The commander of the center line waved his sword over his head, as a signal for the troops to advance. Col. Daniel Boone, and Major, since Gen. Kenton, commanded the advance, and Col. Trotter the rear. As we approached within half a mile of the town on the left, and about three fourths from that on the right, we saw the savages retreating in all directions, making for the thickets, swamps, and high prairie grass, to secure them from their enemy. I was animated with the energy with which the commander conducted the head of his line. He waved his sword, and in a voice of thunder exclaimed, "Charge from right to left!"

The horses appeared as impatient for the onset as their riders. As we came up with the flying savages, I was disappointed, discovering that we should have little to do. I heard but one savage, with the exception of the chief, cry for quarter. They fought with desperation, as long as they could raise knife, gun or tomahawk, after they found they could not screen themselves. We dispatched all the warriors that we overtook, and sent the women and children prisoners to the rear. We pushed ahead, still hoping to overtake a larger body, where we might have something like a general engagement. I was mounted on a very fleet grey horse. Fifty of my companions followed me. I had not advanced more than a mile, before I discovered some of the enemy, running along the edge of a thicket of hazle and plum bushes. I made signs to the men in my rear, to come on. At the same time, pointing to the flying enemy, I obliqued across the plain, so as to get in advance of them. When I arrived within 50 yards of them, I dismounted and raised my gun. I discovered, at this moment, some men of the right wing coming up on the left. The warrior I was about to shoot, held up his hand in token of surrender, and I heard him order the other Indians to stop. By this time, the men behind had arrived, and were in the act of firing upon the Indians. I called to them not to fire, for the enemy had surrendered. The warrior that had surrendered to me, came walking towards me, calling his women and children to follow him. I advanced to meet him, with my right hand extended; but before I could reach him, the men of the right wing of our force had surrounded him. I rushed in among their horses. While he was giving me his hand, several of our men wished to tomahawk him. I informed them that they would have to tomahawk me first. We led him back to the place where his flag had been. We had taken thirteen prisoners. Among them were the chief, his three wives—one of them a young and handsome woman, another of them the famous grenadier squaw, upwards of six feet high—and two or three fine young lads. The rest were children. One of these lads was a remarkably interesting youth, about my own age and size. He clung closely to me, and appeared keenly to notice every thing that was going on.

When we arrived at the town, a crowd of our men pressed around to see the chief. I stepped aside to fasten my horse, and my prisoner lad clung close to my side. A young man by the name of Curner had been to one of the springs to drink. He discovered the young savage by my side, and came running towards me. The young Indian supposed he was advancing to kill him. As I turned around, in the twinkling of an eye, he let fly an arrow at Curner, for he was armed with a bow. I had just time to catch his arm, as he discharged the arrow. It passed through Curner's dress, and grazed his side. The jerk I gave his arm undoubtedly prevented his killing Curner on the spot. I took away his arrows, and sternly reprimanded him. I then led him back to the crowd which surrounded the prisoners. At the same moment, Col. M'Gary, the same man who had caused the disaster at the Blue Licks, some years before, coming up, Gen. Logan's eye caught that of M'Gary. "Col. M'Gary," said he, "you must not molest these prisoners." "I will see to that," said M'Gary in reply. I forced my way through the crowd to the chief, with my young charge by the hand. M'Gary ordered the crowd to open and let him in. He came up to the chief, and the first salutation was in the question, "Were you at the defeat of the Blue Licks?" The Indian, not knowing the meaning of the words, or not understanding the purport of the question, answered, "Yes." M'Gary instantly seized an axe from the hands of the grenadier squaw, and raised it to make a blow at the chief. I threw up my arm, to ward off the blow. The handle of the axe struck me across the left wrist, and came near breaking it. The axe sank in the head of the chief to the eyes, and he fell dead at my feet. Provoked beyond measure at this wanton barbarity, I drew my knife, for the purpose of avenging his cruelty by dispatching him. My arm was arrested by one of our men, which prevented me inflicting the thrust. M'Gary escaped from the crowd.

A detachment was then ordered off to two other towns, distant six or eight miles. The men and prisoners were ordered to march down to the lower town and encamp. As we marched out of the upper town, we fired it, collecting a large pile of corn for our horses, and beans, pumpkins, &c., for our own use. I told Capt. Stucker, who messed with me, that I had seen several hogs running about the town, which appeared to be in good order, and I thought that a piece of fresh pork would relish well with our stock of vegetables. He readily assenting to it, we went in pursuit of them; but as orders had been given not to shoot unless at an enemy, after finding the hogs we had to run them down on foot, until we got near enough to tomahawk them. Being engaged at this for some time before we killed one, while Capt. S. was in the act of striking the hog, I cast my eye along the edge of the woods that skirted the prairie, and saw an Indian coming along with a deer on his back. The fellow happened to raise his head at that moment, and looking across the prairie to the upper town, saw it all in flames. At the same moment, I spake to Stucker in a low voice, that here was an Indian coming. In the act of turning my head round to speak to Stucker, I discovered Hugh Ross, brother-in-law to Col. Kennedy, at the distance of about 60 or 70 yards, approaching us. I made a motion with my hand to Ross to squat down; then taking a tree between me and the Indian, I slipped somewhat nearer, to get a fairer shot, when at the instant I raised my gun past the tree, the Indian being about 100 yards distant, Ross's ball whistled by me, so close that I felt the wind of it, and struck the Indian on the calf of one of his legs. The Indian that moment dropped his deer, and sprang into the high grass of the prairie. All this occurred so quickly, that I had not time to draw a sight on him, before he was hid by the grass. I was provoked at Ross for shooting when I was near enough to have killed him, and now the consequence would be, that probably some of our men would lose their lives, as a wounded Indian only would give up with his life. Capt. Irwin rode up that moment, with his troop of horse, and asked me where the Indian was. I pointed as nearly as I could to the spot where I last saw him in the grass, cautioning the captain, if he missed him the first charge, to pass on out of his reach before he wheeled to re-charge, or the Indian would kill some of his men in the act of wheeling. Whether the captain heard me, I cannot say; at any rate, the warning was not attended to, for after passing the Indian a few steps, Captain Irwin ordered his men to wheel and re-charge across the woods, and in the act of executing the movement, the Indian raised up and shot the captain dead on the spot—still keeping below the level of the grass, to deprive us of any opportunity of putting a bullet through him. The troop charged again; but the Indian was so active, that he had darted into the grass, some rods from where he had fired at Irwin, and they again missed him. By this time several footmen had got up. Capt. Stucker and myself had each of us taken a tree that stood out in the edge of the prairie, among the grass, when a Mr. Stafford came up, and put his head first past one side and then the other of the tree I was behind. I told him not to expose himself that way, or he would get shot in a moment. I had hardly expressed the last word, when the Indian again raised up out of the grass. His gun, Stucker's, and my own, with four or five behind us, all cracked at the same instant. Stafford fell at my side, while we rushed on the wounded Indian with our tomahawks. Before we had got him dispatched, he had made ready the powder in his gun, and a ball in his mouth, preparing for a third fire, with bullet holes in his breast that might all have been covered with a man's open hand. We found with him Capt. Beasley's rifle—the captain having been killed at the Lower Blue Licks, a few days before the army passed through that place on their way to the towns.

Next morning, Gen. Logan ordered another detachment to attack a town that lay seven or eight miles to the north or northwest of where we then were. This town was also burnt, together with a large blockhouse that the English had built there, of a huge size and thickness; and the detachment returned that evening to the main body. Mr. Isaac Zane was at that time living at this last village, he being married to a squaw, and having at the place his wife and several children at the time.

The name of the Indian chief killed by M'Gary, was *Moluntha*, the great sachem of the Shawnees. The grenadier squaw was the sister to Cornstalk, who fell [basely murdered] at Point Pleasant.

Jonathan Alder (see Madison county) was at this time living with the Indians.

From his narrative, it appears that the news of the approach of the Kentuckians was communicated to the Indians by a Frenchman, a deserter from the former. Nevertheless, as the whites arrived sooner than they expected, the surprise was complete. Most of the Indians were at the time absent hunting, and the towns became an easy conquest to the whites. Early one morning, an Indian runner came into the village in which Alder lived, and gave the information that Mack-a-chack had been destroyed, and that the whites were approaching. Alder, with the people of the village, who were principally squaws and children, retreated for two days, until they arrived somewhere near the head waters of the Scioto, where they suffered much for want of food. There was not a man among them capable of hunting, and they were compelled to subsist on paw-paws, muscles and craw-fish. In about eight days, they returned to Zane's town, tarried a short time, and from thence removed to Hog creek, where they wintered: their principal living, at that place, was "raccoons, and that with little or no salt, without a single bite of bread, hommony, or sweet corn." In the spring they moved back to the site of their village, where nothing remained but the ashes of the dwellings and their corn burnt to charcoal. They remained during the sugar season, and then removed to Blanchard's fork, where, being obliged to clear the land, they were enabled to raise but a scanty crop of corn. While this was growing, they fared hard, and managed to eke out a bare subsistence by eating a "kind of wild potato" and poor raccoons, that had been suckled down so poor that dogs would hardly eat them: "for fear of losing a little, they threw them on the fire, singed the hair off, and ate skin and all."

The Indian lad to whom General Lytle alludes, was taken, with others of the prisoners, into Kentucky. The commander of the expedition was so much pleased with him, that he made him a member of his own family, in which he resided some years, and was at length permitted to return. He was ever afterwards known by the name of Logan, to which the prefix of captain was eventually attached. His Indian name was *Spemica Lawba*, i. e. "the High Horn." He subsequently rose to the rank of a civil chief, on account of his many estimable intellectual and moral qualities. His personal appearance was commanding, being six feet in height, and weighing near two hundred pounds. He from that time continued the unwavering friend of the Americans, and fought on their side with great constancy. He lost his life in the fall of 1812, under melancholy circumstances, which evinced that he was a man of the keenest sense of honor. The facts follow, from Drake's Tecumseh.

In November of 1812, General Harrison directed Logan to take a small party of his tribe, and reconnoitre the country in the direction of the rapids of the Maumee. When near this point, they were met by a body of the enemy, superior to their own in number, and compelled to retreat. Logan, captain Johnny [see p. 165] and Bright-horn, who composed the party, effected their escape to the left wing of the army, then under the command of Gen. Winchester, who was duly informed of the circumstances of their adventure. An officer of the Kentucky troops, General P., the second in command, without the slightest ground for such a charge, accused Logan of infidelity to our cause, and of giving intelligence to the enemy. Indignant at this foul accusation, the noble chief at once resolved to meet it in a manner that would leave no doubt as to his faithfulness to the United States. He called on his friend Oliver, [now Major Wm. Oliver, of Cincinnati,] and having told him of the imputation that had been cast upon his reputation, said that he would start from the camp next morning, and either leave his body bleaching in the woods, or return with such trophies from the enemy, as would relieve his character from the suspicion that had been wantonly cast upon it by an American officer.

Accordingly, on the morning of the 22d, he started down the Maumee, attended by his two faithful companions, captain Johnny and Bright-horn. About noon, having stopped for the purpose of taking rest, they were suddenly surprised by a party of seven of the enemy, among whom were young Elliott, a half-breed, holding a commission in the British service, and the celebrated Potawatamie chief, Winnemac. Logan made no resistance, but, with great presence of mind, extending his hand to Winnemac, who was an old acquaintance, proceeded to inform him, that he and his two companions, tired of the American service, were just leaving Gen. Winchester's army, for the purpose of joining the British. Winnemac, being familiar with Indian strategy, was not satisfied with this declaration, but proceeded to disarm Logan and his comrades, and placing his party around them, so as prevent their escape, started for the British camp at the foot of the rapids. In the course of the afternoon, Logan's address was such as to inspire confidence in his sincerity, and induce Winnemac to restore to him and his companions their arms. Logan now formed the plan of attacking his captors on the first favorable opportunity; and while marching along, succeeded in communicating the substance of it to captain Johnny and Bright-horn. Their guns being already loaded, they had little further preparation to make than to put bullets into their mouths, to facilitate the re-loading of their arms. In carrying on this process, captain Johnny, as he afterwards related, fearing that the man marching by his side had observed the operation, adroitly did away the impression by remarking, " me chaw heap tobac."

The evening being now at hand, the British Indians determined to encamp on the bank of Turkeyfoot creek, about twenty miles from Fort Winchester. Confiding in the idea that Logan had really deserted the American service, a part of his captors rambled around the place of their encampment in search of blackhaws. They were no sooner out of sight than Logan gave the signal of attack upon those who remained behind; they fired, and two of the enemy fell dead—the third, being only wounded, required a second shot to dispatch him; and in the mean time, the remainder of the party, who were near by, returned the fire, and all of them " treed." There being four of the enemy, and only three of Logan's party, the latter could not watch all the movements of their antagonists. Thus circumstanced, and during an active fight, the fourth man of the enemy passed round until Logan was uncovered by his tree, and shot him through the body. By this time, Logan's party had wounded two of the surviving four, which caused them to fall back. Taking advantage of this state of things, captain Johnny mounted Logan, now suffering the pain of a mortal wound, and Bright-horn, also wounded, on two of the enemy's horses, and started them for Winchester's camp, which they reached about midnight. Captain Johnny, having already secured the scalp of Winnemac, followed immediately on foot, and gained the same point early on the following morning. It was subsequently ascertained that the two Indians of the British party, who were last wounded, died of their wounds, making in all five out of the seven who were slain by Logan and his companions.

When the news of this gallant affair had spread through the camp, and, especially, after it was known that Logan was mortally wounded, it created a deep and mournful sensation. No one, it is believed, more deeply regretted the fatal catastrophe than the author of the charge upon Logan's integrity, which had led to this unhappy result.

Logan's popularity was very great; indeed, he was almost universally esteemed in the army for his fidelity to our cause, his unquestioned bravery, and the nobleness of his nature. He lived two or three days after reaching the camp, but in extreme bodily agony; he was buried by the officers of the army at Fort Winchester, with the honors of war. Previous to his death, he related the particulars of this fatal enterprize to his friend Oliver, declaring to him that he prized his honor more than life; and having now vindicated his reputation from the imputation cast upon it, he died satisfied. In the course of this interview, and while writhing with pain, he was observed to smile; upon being questioned as to the cause, he replied, that when he recalled to his mind the manner in which captain Johnny took off the scalp of Winnemac, while at the same time dexterously watching the movements of the enemy, he could not refrain from laughing—an incident in savage life, which shows the " ruling passion strong in death." It would, perhaps, be difficult, in the history of savage warfare, to point out an enterprize, the execution of which reflects higher credit upon the address and daring conduct of its authors, than this does upon Logan and his two companions. Indeed, a spirit even less indomitable, a sense of honor less acute, and a patriotic devotion to a good cause less active, than were manifested by this gallant chieftain of the woods, might, under other circumstances, have well conferred immortality upon his name.

Col. John Johnston, in speaking of Logan, in a communication to us, says:

Logan left a dying request to myself, that his two sons should be sent to Kentucky, and there educated and brought up under the care of Major Hardin. As soon as peace and tranquility was restored among the Indians, I made application to the chiefs to fulfill the wish of their dead friend to deliver up the boys, that I might have them conveyed to Frankford, the residence of Major Hardin. The chiefs were embarrassed, and manifested an unwillingness to comply, and in this they were warmly supported by the mother of the children. On no account would they consent to send them so far away as Kentucky, but agreed that I should take and have them schooled at Piqua; it being the best that I could do, in compliance with the dying words of Logan, they were brought in. I had them put to school, and boarded in a religious, respectable family. The mother of the boys, who was a bad woman, thwarted all my plans for their improvement, frequently taking them off for weeks, giving them bad advice, and even, on one or two occasions, brought whiskey to the school-house and made them drunk. In this way she continued to annoy me, and finally took them altogether to raise with herself among the Shawanoese, at Wapaghkonetta. I made several other attempts, during my connection with the Indians, to educate and train up to civilized life many of their youth, without any encouraging results—all of them proved failures. The children of Logan, with their mother, emigrated to the west twenty years ago, and have there became some of the wildest of their race.

Logan county continued to be a favorite place of residence with the Indians for years after the destruction of these towns. Major Galloway, who was here about the year 1800, gives the following, from memory, respecting the localities and names of their towns at that time. Zane's town, now Zanesfield, was a Wyandot village; Wapatomica, three miles below, on Mad river, was then deserted; M'Kee's town, on M'Kee's creek, about 4 miles south of Bellefontaine, so named from the infamous M'Kee, and was at that time a trading station; Read's town, in the vicinity of Bellefontaine, which then had a few cabins; Lewis town, on the Great Miami, and Soloman's town, at which then lived the Wyandot chief, *Tarhe*, "the Crane." From an old settler we learn, also, that on the site of Bellefontaine, was Blue Jacket's town, and 3 miles north, the town of Buckongehelas. Blue Jacket, or *Weyapiersensaw*, and Buckongehelas were noted chiefs, and were at the treaty of Greenville: the first was a Shawnee, and the last a Delaware. At Wayne's victory, Blue Jacket had the chief control, and, in opposition to Little Turtle, advocated giving the whites battle with so much force as to overpower the better councils of the other.

By the treaty of Sept. 29th, 1817, at the foot of the Maumee rapids, the Seneca and Shawnees had a reservation around Lewistown, in this county; by a treaty, ratified April 6th, 1832, the Indians vacated their lands and removed to the far west. On this last occasion, Jas. B. Gardiner was commissioner, John M'Elvain, agent, and David Robb, sub-agent.

The village of Lewistown derived its name from Captain John Lewis, a noted Shawnee chief. When the county was first settled, there was living with him, to do his drudgery, an aged white woman, named Polly Keyser. She was taken prisoner in early life, near Lexington, Ky., and adopted by the Indians. She had an Indian husband and two half-breed daughters. There were several other whites living in the county, who had been adopted by the Indians. We give below sketches of two of them: the first is from N. Z. M'Culloch, Esq., a grandson of Isaac Zane—the last from Col. John Johnston.

Isaac Zane was born about the year 1753, on the south branch of the Potomac, in Virginia, and at the age of about nine years, was taken prisoner by the Wyandots and carried to Detroit. He remained with his captors until the age of manhood, when, like most prisoners taken in youth, he refused to return to his home and friends. He married a Wyandot woman, from Canada, of half French blood, and took no part in the war of the revolution. After the treaty of Greenville, in 1795, he bought a tract of 1800 acres, on the site of Zanesfield, where he lived until his death, in 1816.

James M'Pherson, or *Squa-la-ka-ke*, "the red-faced man," was a native of Carlisle,

Cumberland county, Pa. He was taken prisoner by the Indians on the Ohio, at or near the mouth of the Big Miami, in Loughry's defeat; was for many years engaged in the British Indian department, under Elliott and M'Kee, married a fellow-prisoner, came into our service after Wayne's treaty of 1795, and continued in charge of the Shawanoese and Senecas of Lewistown until his removal from office, in 1830, since which he has died.

Logan county was first settled about the year 1806: the names of the early settlers recollected, are Robt. and Wm. Moore, Benj. and John Schuyler, Philip and Andrew Mathews, John Makimsom, John and Levi Garwood, Abisha Warner, Joshua Sharp and brother, Samuel, David and Robert Marmon, Samuel and Thomas Newell, and Benjamin Joseph Cox. In the late war, the settlements in this

Public Square, Bellefontaine.

county were on the verge of civilization, and the troops destined for the northwest passed through here. There were several block-house stations in the county: namely, Manary's, M'Pherson's, Vance's, and Zane's. Manary's, built by Capt. Jas. Manary, of Ross county, was three miles north of Bellefontaine, on the farm of John Laney; M'Pherson's stood three-fourths of a mile NW., and was built by Capt. Maltby, of Green county; Vance's, built by ex-Gov. Vance, then captain of a rifle company, stood on a high bluff on the margin of a prairie about a mile east of Logansville; Zane's block-house was at Zanesfield. At the breaking out of the war, many hundred of friendly Indians were collected and stationed at Zane's and M'Pherson's block-houses, under the protection of the government, who for a short time kept a guard of soldiers over them. It was at first feared that they would take up arms against the Americans, but subsequent events dissipating these apprehensions, they were allowed to disperse.

Bellefontaine, the county seat, is on the line of the Cincinnati and Sandusky City railroad, 50 miles NW. of Columbus. It was laid out March 18th, 1820, on the land of John Tulles and Wm. Powell, and named from the fine springs abounding in the vicinity. The first of the above lived at the time in a cabin on the town plot, yet standing in the south part of Bellefontaine. After the town was laid out, Joseph Gordon built a cabin, now standing, on the corner opposite Slicer's hotel. Anthony Ballard erected the first frame dwelling;

Wm. Scott kept the first tavern, where J. C. Scarff's drug store now is. Slicer's tavern was built for a temporary court-house. Joseph Gordon, Nathaniel Dodge, Anthony Ballard, Wm. Gutridge, Thos. Haynes and John Rhodes were among the first settlers of the town, the last of whom was the first merchant. The Methodists built the first church, a brick structure, destroyed by fire, which stood on the site of their present church. Bellefontaine contains 2 Presbyterian, 1 Episcopal Methodist and 1 Lutheran church; 1 newspaper printing office, 11 dry goods stores, and had, in October, 1846, 610 inhabitants.

Grave of Simon Kenton.

About 5 miles NE. of Bellefontaine, on the head waters of Mad river, is the grave of Gen. Simon Kenton. He resided for the last few years of his life in the small log-house shown on the right of the engraving, where he breathed his last. He was buried on a small grassy knoll, beside the grave of a Mr. Solomon Praetor, shown on the left. Around his grave is a rude and now dilapidated picketing, and over it, a small slab bearing the following inscription.

> In memory of Gen. SIMON KENTON, who was born April 3d, 1755, in Culpepper county, Va., and died April 29th, 1836, aged 81 years and 26 days. His fellow-citizens of the West will long remember him as the skillful pioneer of early times, the brave soldier and the honest man.

Simon Kenton first came out to Kentucky in the year 1771, at which time he was a youth of sixteen. He was almost constantly engaged in conflicts with the Indians from that time until the treaty of Greenville. He was probably in more expeditions against the Indians, encountered greater peril, and had more narrow escapes from death, than any man of his time. The many incidents of his romantic and eventful life are well detailed by his friend and biographer, Colonel John M'Donald, from whose work we extract the thrilling narrative of his captivity and hair-breadth escapes from a cruel and lingering death.

Kenton lay about Boon's and Logan's stations till ease became irksome to him. About the first of September of this same year, 1778, we find him preparing for another Indian expedition. Alexander Montgomery and George Clark joined him, and they set off from Boon's station, for the avowed purpose of obtaining horses from the Indians. They crossed the Ohio, and proceeded cautiously to Chillicothe, (now Oldtown, Ross county.) They arrived at the town without meeting any adventure. In the night they fell in with a drove of horses that were feeding in the rich prairies. They were prepared with salt and halters. They had much difficulty to catch the horses; however, at length they succeeded, and as soon as the horses were haltered, they dashed off with seven—a pretty good haul. They travelled with all the speed they could to the Ohio. They came to the Ohio near the mouth of Eagle creek, now in Brown county. When they came to the river, the wind blew almost a hurricane. The waves ran so high that the horses were frightened, and could not be induced to take the water. It was late in the evening. They then rode back into the hills some distance from the river, hobbled and turned their horses loose to graze; while they turned back some distance, and watched the trail they had come, to discover whether or no they were pursued. Here they remained till the following day, when the wind subsided. As soon as the wind fell they caught their horses, and went again to the river; but their horses were so frightened with the waves the day before, that all their efforts could not induce them to take the water. This was a sore disappointment to our adventurers. They were satisfied that they were pursued by the enemy; they therefore determined to lose no more time in useless efforts to cross the Ohio; they concluded to select three of the best horses, and make their way to the falls of the Ohio, where Gen. Clark had left some men stationed. Each made choice of a horse, and the other horses were turned loose to shift for themselves. After the spare horses had been loosed, and permitted to ramble off, avarice whispered to them, and why not take all the horses. The loose horses had by this time scattered and straggled out of sight. Our party now separated to hunt up the horses they had turned loose. Kenton went towards the river, and had not gone far before he heard a whoop in the direction of where they had heen trying to force the horses into the water. He got off his horse and tied him, and then crept with the stealthy tread of a cat, to make observations in the direction he heard the whoop. Just as he reached the high bank of the river, he met the Indians on horseback. Being unperceived by them, but so nigh that it was impossible for him to retreat without being discovered, he concluded the boldest course to be the safest, and very deliberately took aim at the foremost Indian. His gun flashed in the pan. He then retreated. The Indians pursued on horseback. In his retreat, he passed through a piece of land where a storm had torn up a great part of the timber. The fallen trees afforded him some advantage of the Indians in the race, as they were on horseback and he on foot. The Indian force divided; some rode on one side of the fallen timber, and some on the other. Just as he emerged from the fallen timber, at the foot of the hill, one of the Indians met him on horseback, and boldly rode up to him, jumped off his horse and rushed at him with his tomahawk. Kenton concluding a gun-barrel as good a weapon of defence as a tomahawk, drew back his gun to strike the Indian before him. At that instant another Indian, who unperceived by Kenton had slipped up behind him, clasped him in his arms. Being now overpowered by numbers, further resistance was useless—he surrendered. While the Indians were binding Kenton with tugs, Montgomery came in view, and fired at the Indians, but missed his mark. Montgomery fled on foot. Some of the Indians pursued, shot at, and missed him; a second fire was made, and Montgomery fell. The Indians soon returned to Kenton, shaking at him Montgomery's bloody scalp. George Clark, Kenton's other companion, made his escape, crossed the Ohio, and arrived safe at Logan's station.

The Indians encamped that night on the bank of the Ohio. The next morning they prepared their horses for a return to their towns, with the unfortunate and unhappy prisoner. Nothing but death in the most appalling form presented itself to his view. When they were ready to set off, they caught the wildest horse in the company, and placed Kenton on his back. The horse being very restif it took several of them to hold him, while the others lashed the prisoner on the horse. They first took a tug, or rope, and fastened his legs and feet together under the horse. They took another and fastened his arms. They took another and tied around his neck, and fastened one end of it around the horse's neck; the other end of the same rope was fastened to the horse's tail, to answer in place of a crupper. They had a great deal of amusement to themselves, as they were preparing Kenton and his horse for fun and frolic. They would yelp and scream around him, and ask him if he wished to steal more horses. Another rope was fastened around his thighs, and lashed around the body of his horse; a pair of moccasons was drawn over his hands, to prevent him from defending his face from the brush. Thus accoutered and fastened, the horse was turned loose to the woods. He reared and plunged, ran through the woods for some time, to the infinite amusement of the Indians. After the horse had run about, plunging, rearing, and kicking for some time, and found that he could not shake off, nor kick off his rider, he very quietly submitted himself to his situation, and followed the cavalcade as quiet and peaceable as his rider. The Indians moved towards Chillicothe, and in three days reached the town. At night they confined their prisoner in the following manner: He was laid on his back, his legs extended, drawn apart, and fastened to two saplings or stakes driven in the ground. His arms were extended, a pole laid across his breast, and his arms lashed to the pole with cords. A rope was tied around his neck, and stretched back just tight enough not to choke him, and fastened to a tree or stake near his head. In this painful and uncomfortable situation, he spent three miserable nights, exposed to gnats, and musketoes, and weather. O, poor human nature, what miserable wretches we are, thus to punish and harrass each other. (The frontier whites of that day, were but little behind the Indians, in wiles, in cruelty, and revenge.) When the Indians came within about a mile of the Chillicothe town, they halted and camped for the night, and fastened the poor unfortunate prisoner in the usual uncomfortable manner. The Indians, young and old, came from the town to welcome the return of their successful warriors, and to visit their prisoner. The Indian party, young and old, consisting of about 150, commenced dancing, singing and yelling around Kenton, stopping occasionally and kicking and beating him for amusement. In this manner they tormented him for about three hours, when the cavalcade returned to town, and he was left for the rest of the night, exhausted and forlorn, to the tender mercies of the gnats and musketoes. As soon as it was light in the morning, the Indians began to collect from the town, and preparations were made for fun and frolic at the expense of Kenton, as he was now doomed to run the gauntlet. The Indians were formed in two lines, about six feet apart, with each a hickory in his hands, and Kenton placed between the two lines, so that each Indian could beat him as much as he thought proper, as he ran through the lines. He had not ran far before he discovered an Indian with his knife drawn to plunge it into him; as soon as Kenton reached that part of the line where the Indian stood who had the knife drawn, he broke through the lines, and made with all speed for the town. Kenton had been previously informed by a negro named Cæsar, who lived with the Indians and knew their customs, that if he could break through the Indians' lines, and arrive at the council-house in the town before he was overtaken, that they would not force him a second time to run the gauntlet. When he broke through their lines, he ran at the top of his speed for the council-house, pursued by two or three hundred Indians, screaming like infernal furies. Just as he had entered the town, he was met by an Indian leisurely walking towards the scene of amusement, wrapped in a blanket. The Indian threw off his blanket; and as he was fresh, and Kenton nearly exhuasted, the Indian soon caught him, threw him down. In a moment the whole party who were in pursuit came up, and fell to cuffing and kicking him at a most fearful rate. They tore off his clothes, and left him naked and exhausted. After he had laid till he had in some degree recovered from his exhausted state, they brought him some water and something to eat. As soon as his strength was sufficiently recovered, they took him to the council-house, to determine upon his fate. Their manner of deciding his fate was as follows: Their warriors were placed in a circle in the council house; an old chief was placed in the center of the circle, with a knife and a piece of wood in his hands. A number of speeches were made. Kenton, although he did not understand their language, soon discovered by their animated gestures, and fierce looks at him, that a majority of their speakers were contending for his destruction. He could perceive that those who plead for mercy, were received coolly; but few grunts of approbation were uttered when the orators closed their speeches. After the orators ceased speaking, the old chief who sat in the midst of the circle, raised up and handed a war-club to the man who sat next the door. They proceeded to take the decision of their court. All who were for the death of the prisoner, struck the war-club with violence against the ground; those who voted to save the prisoner's life, passed the club to his next neighbor without striking the ground. Kenton, from their expressive gestures, could easily distinguish the object of their vote. The old chief who stood to witness and record the number that voted for death or mercy, as one struck the ground with a war-club he made a mark on one side of his piece of wood; and when the club was passed without striking, he made a mark on the other. Kenton discovered that a large majority were for death.

Sentence of death being now passed upon the prisoner, they made the welkin ring with shouts of joy. The sentence of death being passed, there was another question of considerable difficulty now presented itself to the consideration of the council; that was, the time and place, when and where, he should be burnt. The orators again made speeches on the subject, less animated indeed than on the trial; but some appeared to be quite vehement for instant execution, while others appeared to wish to make his death a solemn national sacrifice. After a long debate, the vote was taken, when it was resolved that the place of his execution should be Wapatomika, (now Zanesfield, Logan county.) The next morning he was hurried away to the place destined for his execution. From Chillicothe to Wapatomika, they had to pass through two other Indian towns, to wit: Pickaway and Machecheek. At both towns he was compelled to run the gauntlet; and severely was he whipped through the course. While he lay at Machecheek, being carelessly guarded, he made an attempt to escape. Nothing worse than death could follow, and here he made a bold push for life and freedom. Being unconfined, he broke and run, and soon cleared himself out of sight of his pursuers. While he distanced his pursuers, and got about two miles from the town, he accidentally met some Indians on horseback. They instantly pursued and soon came up with him, and drove him back again to town. He now, for the first time, gave up his case as hopeless. Nothing but death stared him in the face. Fate, it appeared to him, had sealed his doom; and in sullen despair, he determined to await that doom, that it was impossible for him to shun. How inscrutable are the ways of Providence, and how little can man control his destiny! When the Indians returned with Kenton to the town, there was a general rejoicing. He was pinioned, and given over to the young Indians, who dragged him into the creek, tumbled him in the water, and rolled him in the mud, till he was nearly suffocated with mud and water. In this way they amused themselves with him till he was nearly drowned. He now thought himself forsaken by God. Shortly after this his tormenters moved with him to Wapatomika. As soon as he arrived at this place, the Indians, young and old, male and female, crowded around the prisoner. Among others who came to see him, was the celebrated and notorious Simon Girty. It will be recollected that Kenton and Girty were bosom companions at Fort Pitt, and on the campaign with Lord Dunmore. As it was the custom of the Indians to black such prisoners as were intended to be put to death, Girty did not immediately recognize Kenton in his black disguise. Girty came forward and inquired of Kenton where he had lived. Was answered Kentucky. He next inquired how many men there were in Kentucky. He answered, he did not know; but would give him the names and rank of the officers, and he, Girty, could judge of the probable number of men. Kenton then named a great many officers, and their rank, many of whom had honorary titles, without any command. At length Girty asked the prisoner his name. When he was answered, Simon Butler. (It will be recollected, that he changed his name when he fled from his parents and home.) Girty eyed him for a moment, and immediately recognized the active and bold youth, who had been his companion in arms about Fort Pitt, and on the campaign with Lord Dunmore. Girty threw himself into Kenton's arms, embraced and wept aloud over him—calling him his dear and esteemed friend. This hardened wretch, who had been the cause of the death of hundreds, had some of the sparks of humanity remaining in him, and wept like a child at the tragical fate which hung over his friend. "Well," said he to Kenton, "you are condemned to die, but I will use every means in my power to save your life.

Girty immediately had a council convened, and made a long speech to the Indians, to save the life of the prisoner. As Girty was proceeding through his speech, he became very animated; and under his powerful eloquence, Kenton could plainly discover the grim visages of his savage judges relent. When Girty concluded his powerful and animated speech, the Indians rose with one simultaneous grunt of approbation, saved the prisoner's life, and placed him under the care and protection of his old companion, Girty.

The British had a trading establishment then at Wapatomika. Girty took Kenton with him to the store, and dressed him from head to foot, as well as he could wish: he was also provided with a horse and saddle. Kenton was now free, and roamed about through the country, from Indian town to town, in company with his benefactor. How uncertain is the fate of nations as well as that of individuals! How sudden the changes from adversity to prosperity, and from prosperity to adversity! Kenton being a strong, robust man, with an iron frame, with a resolution that never winced at danger, and fortitude to bear pain with the composure of a stoic, he soon recovered from his scourges and bruises, and the other severe treatment he had received. It is thought probable, that if the Indians had continued to treat him with kindness and respect, he would eventually have become one of them. He had but few inducements to return again to the whites. He was then a fugitive from justice, had changed his name, and he thought it his interest to keep as far from his former acquaintances as possible. After Kenton and his benefactor had been roaming about for some time, a war party of Indians, who had been on an expedition to the neighborhood of Wheeling, returned; they had been defeated by the whites, some of their men were killed, and others wounded. When this defeated party returned they were sullen, chagrined, and full of revenge, and determined to kill any of the whites who came within their grasp. Kenton was the only white man upon whom they could satiate their revenge. Kenton and Girty were then at Solomon's town, a small distance from Wapatomika. A message was immediately sent to Girty to return, and bring Kenton with him. The two friends met the messenger on their way. The messenger shook hands with Girty, but refused the hand of Kenton. Girty, after talking aside with the messenger some time, said to Kenton, they have sent for us to attend a grand council at Wapatomika. They hurried to the town; and when they arrived there the council-house was crowded. When Girty went into the house, the Indians all rose up and shook hands with him; but when Kenton offered his hand, it was refused with a scowl of contempt. This alarmed him; he began to admit the idea that this sudden convention of the council, and their refusing his hand, boded him some evil. After the members of the council were seated in their usual manner, the war chief of the defeated party rose up and made a most vehement speech, frequently turning his fiery and revengeful eyes on Kenton during his speech. Girty was the next to rise and address the council. He told them that he had lived with them several years; that he had risked his life in that time more frequently than any of them; that they all knew that he had never spared the life of one of the hated Americans; that they well knew that he had never asked for a division of the spoils; that he fought alone for the destruction of their enemies; and he now requested them to spare the life of this young man on his account. The young man, he said, was his early friend, for whom he felt the tenderness of a parent for a son, and he hoped, after the many evidences that he had given of his attachment to the Indian cause, they would not hesitate to grant his request. If they would indulge him in granting his request to spare the life of this young man, he would pledge himself never to ask them again to spare the life of a hated American.

Several chiefs spoke in succession on this important subject; and with the most apparent deliberation, the council decided, by an overwhelming majority, for death. After the decision of this grand court was announced, Girty went to Kenton, and embracing him very tenderly, said that he very sincerely sympathized with him in his forlorn and unfortunate situation; that he had used all the efforts he was master of to save his life, but it was now decreed that he must die—that he could do no more for him. Awful doom!

It will be recollected, that this was in 1778, in the midst of the American revolution. Upper Sandusky was then the place where the British paid their western Indian allies their annuities; and as time might effect what his eloquence could not, Girty, as a last resort, persuaded the Indians to convey their prisoner to Sandusky, as there would meet vast numbers to receive their presents; that the assembled tribes could there witness the solemn scene of the death of the prisoner. To this proposition the council agreed; and the prisoner was placed in the care of five Indians, who forthwith set off for Upper Sandusky. What windings, and twistings, and turnings, were seen in the fate of our hero.

As the Indians passed from Wapatomika to Upper Sandusky, they went through a small village on the river Scioto, where then resided the celebrated chief, Logan, of Jefferson memory. Logan, unlike the rest of his tribe, was humane as he was brave. At his wigwam the party who had the care of the prisoner, staid over night. During the evening, Logan entered into conversation with the prisoner. The next morning he told Kenton that he would detain the party that day—that he had sent two of his young men off the night before to Upper Sandusky, to speak a good word for him. Logan was great and good—the friend of all men. In the course of the following evening his young men returned, and early the next morning the guard set off with the prisoner for Upper Sandusky. When Kenton's party set off from Logan's, Logan shook hands with the prisoner, but gave no intimation of what might probably be his fate. The party went on with Kenton till they came in view of the Upper Sandusky town. The Indians, young and old, came out to meet and welcome the warriors, and view the prisoner. Here he was not compelled to run the gauntlet. A grand council was immediately convened to determine upon the fate of Kenton. This was the fourth council which was held to dispose of the life of the prisoner. As soon as this grand court was organized and ready to proceed to business, a Canadian Frenchman, by the name of Peter Druyer, who was a captain in the British service, and dressed in the gaudy appendages of the British uniform, made his appearance in the council. This Druyer was born and raised in Detroit—he was connected with the British Indian agent department—was their principal interpreter in settling Indian affairs; this made him a man of great consequence among the Indians. It was to this influential man, that the good chief Logan, the friend of all the human family, sent his young men to intercede for the life of Kenton. His judgment and address were only equalled by his humanity.

His foresight in selecting the agent who it was most probable could save the life of the prisoner, proves his judgment and his knowledge of the human heart. As soon as the grand council was organized, Capt. Druyer requested permission to address the council. This permission was instantly granted. He began his speech by stating, "that it was well-known that it was the wish and interest of the English that not an American should be left alive. That the Americans were the cause of the present bloody and distressing war—that neither peace nor safety could be expected, so long as these intruders were permitted to live upon the earth." This part of his speech received repeated grunts of approbation. He then explained to the Indians, "that the war to be carried on successfully, required cunning as well as bravery—that the intelligence which might be extorted from a prisoner, would be of more advantage, in conducting the future operations of the war, than would be the life of twenty prisoners. That he had no doubt but the commanding officer at Detroit could procure information from the prisoner now before them, that would be of incalculable advantage to them in the progress of the present war. Under these circumstances, he hoped they would defer the death of the prisoner till he was taken to Detroit, and examined by the commanding general. After which he could be brought back, and if thought advisable, upon further consideration, he might be put to death in any manner they thought proper." He next noticed, "that they had already a great deal of trouble and fatigue with the prisoner without being revenged upon him ; but that they had got back all the horses the prisoner had stolen from them, and killed one of his comrades ; and to insure them something for their fatigue and trouble, he himself would give $100 in rum and tobacco, or any other articles they would choose, if they would let him take the prisoner to Detroit, to be examined by the British general." The Indians, without hesitation, agreed to Captain Druyer's proposition, and he paid down the ransom. As soon as these arrangements were concluded, Druyer and a principal chief set off with the prisoner for Lower Sandusky. From this place they proceeded by water to Detroit, where they arrived in a few days. Here the prisoner was handed over to the commanding officer, and lodged in the fort as a prisoner of war. He was now out of danger from the Indians, and was treated with the usual attention of prisoners of war in civilized countries. The British commander gave the Indians some additional remuneration for the life of the prisoner, and they returned satisfied to join their countrymen at Wapatomika.

As soon as Kenton's mind was out of suspense, his robust constitution and iron frame in a few days recovered from the severe treatment they had undergone. Kenton remained at Detroit until the June following, when he, with other prisoners, escaped, and after enduring great privations, rejoined their friends.

About the year 1802, he settled in Urbana, where he remained some years, and was elected brigadier-general of militia. In the war of 1812, he joined the army of Gen. Harrison, and was at the battle of the Moravian town, where he displayed his usual intrepidity. About the year 1820, he moved to the head of Mad river. A few years after, through the exertions of Judge Burnet and General Vance, a pension of $20 per month was granted to him, which secured his declining age from want. He died in 1836, at which time he had been a member of the Methodist church about 18 years. The frosts of more than eighty winters had fallen on his head without entirely whitening his locks. His biographer thus describes his personal appearance and character.

General Kenton was of fair complexion, six feet one inch in height. He stood and walked very erect ; and, in the prime of life, weighed about one hundred and ninety pounds. He never was inclined to be corpulent, although of sufficient fullness to form a graceful person. He had a soft, tremulous voice, very pleasing to the hearer. He had laughing, grey eyes, which appeared to fascinate the beholder. He was a pleasant, good-humored and obliging companion. When excited, or provoked to anger, (which was seldom the case,) the fiery glance of his eye would almost curdle the blood of those with whom he came in contact. His rage, when roused, was a tornado. In his dealing, he was perfectly honest ; his confidence in man, and his credulity, were such, that the same man might cheat him twenty times ; and if he professed friendship, he might cheat him still.

West Liberty is 8 miles south of Bellefontaine, on the Cincinnati and Sandusky City railroad. This is a thriving, compact, business-like town, and in a beautiful country. It lies upon Mad river, one of the best mill streams in the state, the valley of which is here two or three miles wide. The Miami feeder, which enters the main trunk at Lockport, and now extends as far as Port Jefferson, in Shelby county, will probably be continued to the Mad river at this place, an act of the legislature having been passed to that effect. West Liberty contains 1 Presbyterian, 1 Methodist and 1 Christian church, 9 stores, 1 flouring, 1 saw, 1 carding and fulling mill, and a population but little less than the county seat.

Zanesfield, 4½ miles east of Bellefontaine, on Mad river, has 5 stores, 1 grist and 3 saw mills; 1 Methodist church, 1 Friends' meeting-house, and about 230 inhabitants. Cherokee, 6 miles north of Bellefontaine, Logansville, 10 west, Middleburgh, 11 southeast, and Quincy, 13 southwest, are places about the size and importance of Zanesfield. East Liberty, Rushsylvania and Richland are also small villages.

LORAIN.

Lorain was formed December 26th, 1822, from Huron, Cuyahoga and Medina. The surface is level, and the soil fertile and generally clayey. Parallel with the lake shore, are three sand ridges, which vary from 40 to 150 rods in width: they are respectively about 3, 7 and 9 miles from the lake, and are fertile. The agriculture of Lorain is rapidly improving. The principal crops are grass, wheat, corn, oats, rye and potatoes. Dairy products, wool and beef cattle are also staple products, and madder and oil of peppermint are also produced. Bog iron ore is found in quantities. The following is a list of the townships in 1840, with their population:

Amherst,	1186	Eaton,	764	Ridgeville,	818
Avon,	1211	Elyria,	1636	Rochester,	487
Blackriver,	668	Grafton,	713	Russia,	1302
Brighton,	999	Henrietta,	743	Sheffield,	521
Brownhelm,	934	Huntington,	743	Sullivan,	782
Camden,	504	Lagrange,	991	Troy	289
Carlisle,	1094	Pennfield,	405	Wellington,	781
Columbia,	876	Pittsfield,	704		

The population of Lorain, in 1830, was 5,696, and in 1840, 18,451, or 33 inhabitants to the square mile.

There was found in this county, a few years since, a curious ancient relic, which is thus described in the Lorain Republican, of June 7, 1843.

"In connection with our friend Mr. L. M. Parsons, we have procured two views or sketches of the engravings upon a stone column or idol, found upon the farm of Mr. Alfred Lamb, in Brighton, in this county, in 1838. The following is a side view of the pillar or column.

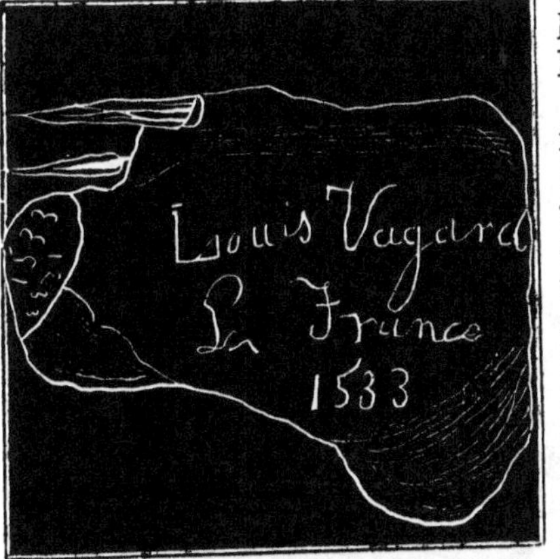

"It was found about three fourths of a mile from Mr. Lamb's house, covered with a thick coat of moss. Upon three different places are engraved the figures 1533. The horns represented are now broken off, but their place is easily defined. A flat stone, 8 inches in diameter and 1½ inches thick, was found beneath this column, on removing it from its erect position, upon which the figures 1533 were discovered, also engraved. Another stone was found about 10 feet distant, of like quality. It was about 6 inches long and 3 in diameter, (6 sided,) supported by 3 pillars about 3 inches long, of pyramidal form. No marks of tools were upon it. Upon the top part of the first mentioned pillars, above shown, was an engraving of a vessel under full sail, in form, as near as now can be ascertained, as follows. The engraving was most unfortunately nearly obliterated by the boys cracking hickory nuts upon it. These are about all the facts connected with these curious relics, which have come to our knowledge."

In connection with the above editorial, Mr. Parsons, in his communication, says:

"I believe there can be a good deal of evidence collected in this section of country, which will go to prove that it was once inhabited by a race who emigrated either from South America or the southern portion of North America, or at least had commercial relations with that country. I will refer to one circumstance, which, doubtless, antiquarians will regard as worthy of record. In the township of Perry, Lake county, about the year 1820, in digging into an Indian burying field, a club of nicaragua was found in connection with the bones of a man. The club was sound, but the bones were considerably decayed, and bore the same evidence of the effect of time as those usually found in our ancient burying grounds. The women are more utilitarians than antiquarians, for on calling for the club a few days after, I found they had cut it up to color with, and they said it was as good as any they ever got at stores."

Elyria, the county seat, is 7 miles from Lake Erie, 24 west of Cleveland, and 130 northeast of Columbus. The first settler in the town and township, was Mr. Heman Ely, from West Springfield,

Public Square, Elyria.

Mass., who came out here in March, 1817, and built a cabin about 12 rods southeast of his present residence. He brought with him some hired men, to make improvements on his land, a large tract of which he had purchased at this place and vicinity. The village was soon laid out, and some time in the succeeding year, Mr. Ely moved into his present residence, the first frame house erected in the township. The name Elyria, was formed from the surname of Mr. Ely and the last syllable of the given name of his wife, Ma-*ria*. Upon the organization of the county, the old court house was built, which was used as a church by the Presbyterians, until they built a house of worship, the first erected in the village. Elyria is a beautiful and thriving village; in its center is a handsome public square, shown in the engraving: the large building in front is the court house, beyond, on the right, is the public square, on which are seen, facing "Beebe's block," "the Mansion House" and "the brick block." The Gothic structure on the left, is the Presbyterian church, designed by R. A. Sheldon, of New York, and erected in 1846–7, by H. J. & S. C. Brooks, of Elyria; it is one of the most elegant churches in Ohio, built of sandstone, and finished throughout in a tasteful and substantial manner, at an expense of about $8000.

The village stands on a peninsula, formed by the forks of Black river, on which, near the town, are two beautiful falls, of 40 feet perpendicular descent, highly valuable for manufacturing purposes. At the falls on the west fork, the scenery is wild and picturesque; the rocks are lofty, and overhang the valley for perhaps some 30 feet. At that point is a large cavern, of a semi-circular form, about 75 feet deep, 100 broad at the entrance, with a level floor, and wall from 5 to 9 feet high, forming a cool and romantic retreat from the heats of summer. The sandstone bounding the valley, is of an excellent quality, and is much used for building purposes. Elyria contains 1 Episcopal, 1 Methodist, 1 Baptist, 1 Disciples and 1 or 2 Congregational churches, 1 classical academy, 6 dry goods, 3 grocery and 3 drug stores, 1 newspaper printing office, 1 woollen, 1 axe, and sash and blind factory, 1 furnace, 1 machine shop, 3 flouring mills and about 1500 inhabitants.

Collegiate Buildings, Oberlin.

Eight miles southwest of Elyria, is the village of Oberlin, so named from Rev. John Frederic Oberlin, pastor of Waldbach, Switzerland, who was remarkable for his great benevolence of character: he was born in Strasbourg, in 1740, and died at Waldbach, in 1826. The town is situated on a beautiful and level plain, girted around by the original forest in its primitive majesty. The dwellings at Oberlin are usually two stories in height, built of wood, and painted white, after the manner of the villages of New England, to which this has a striking resemblance. Oberlin contains 3 dry goods and 1 book store, a Presbyterian church, the collegiate buildings, and about 150 dwellings. The Oberlin Evangelist, which has a circulation of 5000, and the Oberlin Quarterly Review, are published here. The engraving shows, on the right, the Presbyterian church, a substantial brick building, neatly finished externally and internally, and capable of holding a congregation of 3000 persons; beyond it, on a green of about 12 acres, stands Tappan Hall; and facing the green, commencing on the left, are seen Oberlin Hall, Ladies' Hall and Colonial Hall, all of which buildings belong to the Institute. By the annual catalogue of 1846–7, there were at Oberlin 492 pupils, viz: in the theological department, 25; college, 106; teachers department, 16; shorter course, 4; male preparatory, 174; young ladies' course, 140; and ladies' preparatory, 28. Of these, there were males 314, and females 178. The annexed sketch of Oberlin was written by J. A. Harris, editor of the Cleveland Herald, and published in that print, in 1845.

The Oberlin Collegiate Institute is emphatically the people's college, and although some of its leading characteristics are peculiar to the institution, and are at variance with the general public opinion and prejudices, the college exerts a wide and healthful influence. It places a useful and thoroughly practical education within the reach of indigent and industrious young men and women, as well as those in affluent circumstances; and many in all ranks of life avail themselves of the rare advantages enjoyed at Oberlin. The average number of students the last five years is 528, and this, too, be it remembered, in an institution that has sprung up in what was a dense wilderness but a dozen years ago! To remove all incredulity, we will give a concise history of its origin and progress.

The Rev. John J. Shipherd was a prominent founder of Oberlin. His enterprising spirit led in the devising and incipient steps. Without any fund in the start, in August, 1832, he rode over the ground, for inspection, where the village of Oberlin now stands. It was then a dense, heavy, unbroken forest, the land level and wet, almost inaccessible by roads, and the prospects for a settlement forbidding in the extreme. In November, 1832, Mr. Shipherd, in company with a few others, selected the site. Five hundred acres of land were conditionally pledged by Messrs. Street and Hughes, of New Haven, Conn., on which the college buildings now stand. A voluntary board of trustees held their first meeting in the winter of 1832, in a small Indian opening on the site. The legislature of 1833–4, granted a charter with university privileges. Improvements were commenced, a log house or two were erected, people began to locate in the colony, and in 1834, the board of trustees resolved to open the school for the reception of colored persons of both sexes, to be regarded as on an equality with others. In January, 1835, Messrs. Mahan, Finney and Morgan were appointed as teachers, and in May of that year, Mr. Mahan commenced house-keeping in a small log dwelling. Such was the beginning—and the present result is a striking exemplification of what obstacles can be overcome, and what good can be accomplished under our free institutions, by the indomitable energy, earnest zeal, and unfaltering perseverance of a few men, when they engage heart and soul in a great philanthropic enterprise.

Oberlin is now a pleasant, thriving village, of about two thousand souls, with necessary stores and mechanics' shops, the largest church in the state, and a good temperance hotel. It is a community of tetotallers, from the highest to the lowest, the sale of ardent spirits never having been permitted within its borders. The college buildings number seven commodious edifices. Rev. A. Mahan, is president of the Collegiate Institute, assisted by fifteen able professors and teachers. Endowments—eight professorships are supported in part by pledges; 500 acres of land at Oberlin, and 10,000 acres in western Virginia.

OBJECTS OF THE INSTITUTION.

1. To educate youths of both sexes, so as to secure the development of a strong mind in a sound body, connected with a permanent, vigorous, progressive piety—all to be aided by a judicious system of manual labor.

2. To beget and to confirm in the process of education the habit of self-denial, patient endurance, a chastened moral courage, and a devout consecration of the whole being to God, in seeking the best good of man.

3. To establish universal liberty by the abolition of every form of sin.

4. To avoid the debasing association of the heathen classics, and make the bible a text-book in all the departments of education.

5. To raise up a church and ministers who shall be known and read of all men in deep sympathy with Christ, in holy living, and in efficient action against all which God forbids.

6. To furnish a seminary, affording thorough instruction in all the branches of an education for both sexes, and in which colored persons, of both sexes, shall be freely admitted, and on the terms of equality and brotherhood.

We confess that much of our prejudice against the Oberlin College has been removed by a visit to the institution. The course of training and studies pursued there, appear admirably calculated to rear up a class of healthy, useful, self-educated and self-relying men and women—a class which the poor man's son and daughter may enter on equal terms with others, with an opportunity to outstrip in the race, as they often do. It is the only college in the United States where females enjoy the privileges of males in acquiring an education, and where degrees are conferred on ladies; and this peculiar feature of the instruction has proved highly useful. By combining manual labor with study, the physical system keeps pace with the mind in strength and development, and the result in most cases is "sound minds in healthy bodies." Labor and attention to household duties are made familiar and honorable, and pleased as we were to note the intelligent and healthful countenances of the young ladies seated at the boarding ho ıse dinner table, the gratification was heightened shortly after by observing the same graceful fcrms clad in tidy long aprons, and busily engaged in putting the dining hall in order. And the literary exercises of the same ladies, proved that the labor of the hands in the institution had been no hindrance in the acquisition of knowledge.

Young in years as is Oberlin, the institution has sent abroad many well qualified and diligent laborers in the great moral field of the world. Her graduates may be found in nearly every missionary clime, and her scholars are active co-workers in many of the philanthropic movements that distinguish the age. It is the people's college, and long may i prove an increasing blessing to the people.

Black River, at the mouth of Black River, 8 miles from Elyria has a good harbor, capable of much improvement. It is the principal port of the county: it has a beacon, several forwarding houses and stores, and about 50 dwellings. La Porte, 3 miles SE. of E., on the Wooster and Akron road, has 1 Presbyterian, 1 Methodist and 1 Universalist church, 2 stores and about 50 dwellings. There are other small villages, among which may be named Corwinville, Fien Creek, Wellington Center and Grafton Center.

LUCAS.

Lucas, named from the Hon. Robert Lucas, governor of Ohio from 1832 to 1836, has been created within a few years. The surface is level, a portion of it covered by the black swamp, and the northern part a sandy soil. The principal productions are Indian corn, wheat, potatoes and oats. The following is a list of the townships in 1840, with their population:

Amboy,	452	Port Lawrence,	2335	Sylvania,	426
Chesterfield,	301	Providence,	160	Waterville,	755
Clinton,	353	Richfield,	204	Waynesfield,	1290
German,	452	Royalton,	401	Wing,	145
Gorham,	352	Springfield,	443	York,	435
Oregon,	264	Swan Creek,	494		

The population of Lucas, in 1840, was 9392, or about 5 inhabitants to the square mile.

This region of country—the Maumee valley—has been the theater of important historical incidents. The greatest event, Wayne's victory, or "the battle of Fallen Timbers," was fought August 20th, 1794, within the limits of this county.

On the 28th of July, Wayne having been joined by General Scott, with 1600 mounted Kentuckians, moved forward to the Maumee. By the 8th of August, the army had arrived near the junction of the Auglaize with that stream, and commenced the erection of Fort Defiance, at that point. The Indians, having learned from a deserter of the approach of Wayne's army, hastily abandoned their head quarters at Auglaize, and thus defeated the plan of Wayne to surprise them, for which object he had cut two roads, intending to march by neither. At Fort Defiance, Wayne received full information of the Indians, and the assistance they were to derive from the volunteers at Detroit and vicinity. On the 13th of August, true to the spirit of peace advised by Washington, he sent Christian Miller, who had been naturalized among the Shawanese, as a special messenger to offer terms of friendship. Impatient of delay, he moved forward, and on the 16th, met Miller on his return with the message, that if the Americans would wait ten days at Grand Glaize, [Fort Defiance,] they—the Indians—would decide for peace or war. On the 18th, the army arrived at *Roche de Bœuf*, just south of the site of Waterville, where they erected some light works as a place of deposite for their heavy baggage, which was named Fort Deposite. During the 19th, the army labored at their works, and about 8 o'clock on the morning of the 20th, moved forward to attack the Indians, who were encamped on the bank of the Maumee, at and around a hill called "Presque Isle," about two miles south of the site of Maumee City, and four south of the British Fort Miami. From Wayne's report of the battle, we make the following extract:

The legion was on the right, its flank covered by the Maumee: one brigade of mounted volunteers on the left, under Brig. Gen. Todd, and the other in the rear, under Brig. Gen. Barbee. A select battalion of mounted volunteers moved in front of the legion, commanded by Major Price, who was directed to keep sufficiently advanced, so as to give timely notice for the troops to form in case of action, it being yet undetermined whether the Indians would decide for peace or war.

After advancing about five miles, Major Price's corps received so severe a fire from the enemy, who were secreted in the woods and high grass, as to compel them to retreat. The legion was immediately formed in two lines, principally in a close thick wood, which extended for miles on our left, and for a very considerable distance in front; the ground being covered with old fallen timber, probably occasioned by a tornado, which rendered it impracticable for the cavalry to act with effect, and afforded the enemy the most favorable covert for their mode of warfare. The savages were formed in three lines, within supporting distance of each other, and extending for near two miles at right angles with the river. I soon discovered, from the weight of the fire and extent of their lines, that the enemy were in full force in front, in possession of their favorite ground, and endeavoring to turn our left flank. I therefore gave orders for the second line to advance and support the first; and directed Major General Scott to gain and turn the right flank of the savages, with the whole force of the mounted volunteers, by a circuitous route; at the same time I ordered the front line to advance and charge with trailed arms, and rouse the Indians from their coverts at the point of the bayonet, and when up, to deliver a close and well-directed fire on their backs, followed by a brisk charge, so as not to give them time to load again.

I also ordered Captain Mis Campbell, who commanded the legionary cavalry, to turn the left flank of the enemy next the river, and which afforded a favorable field for that corps to act in. All these orders were obeyed with spirit and promptitude; but such was the impetuosity of the charge by the first line of infantry, that the Indians and Canadian militia and volunteers were drove from all their coverts in so short a time, that although every possible exertion was used by the officers of the second line of the legion, and by Generals Scott, Todd and Barbee, of the mounted volunteers, to gain their proper positions, but part of each could get up in season to participate in the action; the enemy being drove, in the course of one hour, more than two miles through the thick woods already mentioned, by less than one half their numbers. From every account the enemy amounted to two thousand combatants. The troops actually engaged against them were short of nine hundred. This horde of savages, with their allies, abandoned themselves to flight, and dispersed with terror and dismay, leaving our victorious army in full and quiet possession of the field of battle, which terminated under the influence of the guns of the British garrison. * * * * *

The bravery and conduct of every officer belonging to the army, from the generals down to the ensigns, merit my highest approbation. There were, however, some whose rank and situation placed their conduct in a very conspicuous point of view, and which I observed with pleasure, and the most lively gratitude. Among whom, I must beg leave to

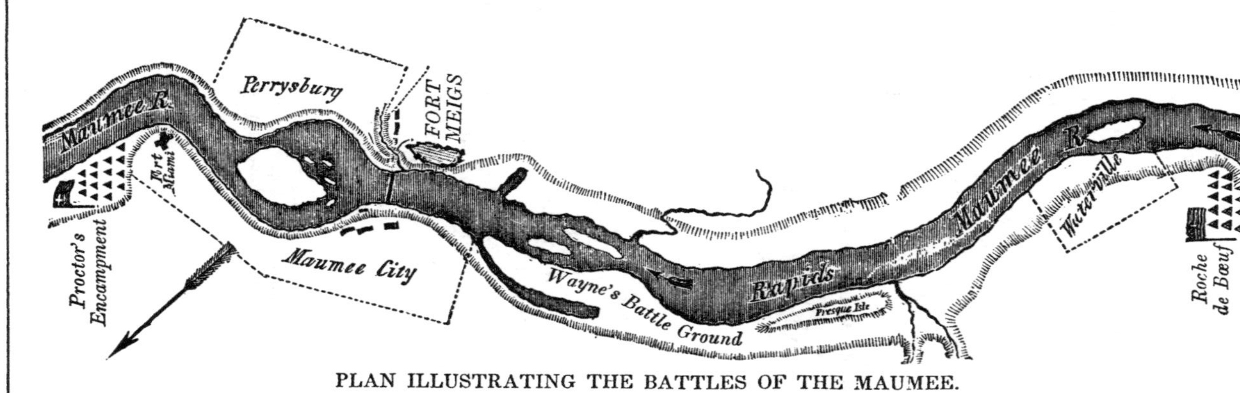

PLAN ILLUSTRATING THE BATTLES OF THE MAUMEE.

Explanations.—The map shows about 8 miles of the country along each side of the Maumee, including the towns of Perrysburgh, Maumee City and Waterville.

Just previous to the battle of the Fallen Timbers, in August, 1794, Wayne's army was encamped at a locality called *Roche de Bœuf*, a short distance above the present site of Waterville. The battle commenced at the *Presque Isle* hill. The routed Indians were pursued to even under the guns of the British *Fort Miami.*

Fort Meigs, memorable from having sustained two sieges in the year 1813, is shown on the east side of the Maumee, with the *British batteries* on both sides of the river, and above the British fort, the position of *Proctor's encampment.* For a more full delineation of this last, see Wood county.

mention Brigadier General Wilkinson and Colonel Hamtramck, the commandants of the right and left wings of the legion, whose brave example inspired the troops. To those I must add the names of my faithful and gallant aids-de-camp, Captains De Butt and T. Lewis, and Lieutenant Harrison, who, with the Adjutant General, Major Mills, rendered the most essential service by communicating my orders in every direction, and by their conduct and bravery exciting the troops to press for victory. * * *

The loss of the enemy was more than that of the federal army. The woods were strewed for a considerable distance with the dead bodies of Indians and their white auxiliaries, the latter armed with British muskets and bayonets.

We remained three days and nights on the banks of the Maumee, in front of the field of battle, during which time all the houses and corn-fields were consumed and destroyed for a considerable distance, both above and below Fort Miami, as well as within pistol-shot of the garrison, who were compelled to remain tacit spectators to this general devastation and conflagration, among which were the houses, stores and property of Colonel M'Kee, the British Indian agent and principal stimulator of the war now existing between the United States and the savages.

The loss of the Americans in this battle, was 33 killed and 100 wounded, including 5 officers among the killed, and 19 wounded.

One of the Canadians taken in the action, estimated the force of the Indians at about 1400. He also stated that about 70 Canadians were with them, and that Col. M'Kee, Capt. Elliott and Simon Girty were in the field, but at a respectful distance, and near the river. When the broken remains of the Indian army were pursued under the British fort, the soldiers could scarce be restrained from storming it. This, independent of its results in bringing on a war with Great Britain, would have been a desperate measure, as the fort mounted 10 pieces of artillery, and was garrisoned by 450 men, while Wayne had no armament proper to attack such a strongly fortified place. While the troops remained in the vicinity, there did not appear to be any communication between the garrison and the savages. The gates were shut against them, and their rout and slaughter witnessed with apparent unconcern by the British. That the Indians were astonished at the lukewarmness of their real allies, and regarded the fort, in case of defeat, as a place of refuge, is evident from various circumstances, not the least of which was the well known reproach of Tecumseh, in his celebrated speech to Proctor, after Perry's victory. The near approach of the troops drew forth a letter of remonstrance from Major Campbell, the British commandant, to General Wayne. A sharp correspondence ensued, but without any especial results. The morning before the army left, General Wayne, after arranging his force in such a manner as to show that they were all on the alert, advanced with his numerous staff and a small body of cavalry, to the glacis of the British fort, reconnoitering it with great deliberation, while the garrison were seen with lighted matches, prepared for any emergency. It is said that Wayne's party overheard one of the British subordinate officers appeal to Major Campbell, for permission to fire upon the cavalcade, and avenge such an insulting parade under his majesty's guns; but that officer chided him with the abrupt exclamation, "*be a gentleman! be a gentleman!*" On the 27th, Wayne's army returned to Fort Defiance, by easy marches, laying waste the villages and corn fields of the Indians, for about 50 miles on each side of the Mau mee: this was done with the hope that the fear of famine would prove a powerful auxiliary in producing peace.

Jonathan Alder, who was at this time living with the Indians, has given, in his MSS. autobiography, the Indian account of the battle of Fallen Timbers. He says, after describing the attack on Fort Recovery and the retreat to Defiance:

We remained here [Defiance] about two weeks, until we heard of the approach of Wayne, when we packed up our goods and started for the old English fort at the Maumee rapids. Here we prepared ourselves for battle, and sent the women and children down about three miles below the fort; and as I did not wish to fight, they sent me to Sandusky, to inform some Wyandots there of the great battle that was about to take place. I remained at Sandusky until the battle was over. The Indians did not wait more than three or four days, before Wayne made his appearance at the head of a long prairie on the river, where he halted, and waited for an opportunity to suit himself. Now the Indians are very curious about fighting; for when they know they are going into a battle, they will not eat any thing just previous. They say that if a man is shot in the body when he is entirely empty, there is not half as much danger of the ball passing through his bowels, as when they are full. So they started the first morning without eating any thing, and moving up to the end of the prairie, ranged themselves in order of battle at the edge of the timber There they waited all day without any food, and at night returned and partook of their suppers. The second morning they again placed themselves in the same position, and again returned at night and supped. By this time they had begun to get weak from eating only once a day, and concluded they would eat breakfast before they again started. So the next morning they began to cook and eat. Some were eating, and others, who had finished, had moved forward to their stations, when Wayne's army was seen approaching. Soon as they were within gunshot, the Indians began firing upon them; but Wayne, making no halt, rushed on upon them. Only a small part of the Indians being on the ground, they were obliged to give back, and finding Wayne too strong for them, attempted to retreat. Those who were on the way heard the noise, and sprang to their assistance. So some were running from, and others to the battle, which created great confusion. In the mean time, the light-horse had gone entirely around, and came in upon their rear, blowing their horns and closing in upon them. The Indians now found that they were completely surrounded, and all that could, made their escape, and *the balance* were all killed, which was no small number. Among these last, with one or two exceptions, were all the Wyandots that lived at Sandusky at the time I went to inform them of the expected battle. The main body of the Indians were back nearly two miles from the battle-ground, and Wayne had taken them by surprise, and made such a slaughter among them that they were entirely discouraged, and made the best of their way to their respective homes.

We insert below some anecdotes of the battle, the first three of which are derived from a published source, and the last, second-hand from Gen. Harrison.

At the time Capt. Campbell was endeavoring to turn the left flank of the enemy, three Indians, being hemmed in by the cavalry and infantry, plunged into the river, and endeavored to swim to the opposite side. Two negroes of the army, on the opposite bank, concealed themselves behind a log to intercept them. When within shooting distance, one of them shot the foremost through the head. The other two took hold of him to drag him to shore, when the second negro fired and killed another. The remaining Indian being now in shoal water, endeavored to tow the dead bodies to the bank. In the mean time the first negro had re-loaded, and firing upon the survivor, mortally wounded him. On approaching them, the negroes judged from their striking resemblance and devotion, that they were brothers. After scalping them, they let their bodies float down stream.

Another circumstance goes to show with what obstinacy the conflict was maintained, by individuals in both armies. A soldier who had got detached a short distance from the army, met a single Indian in the woods, when they attacked each other—the soldier with his bayonet, the Indian with his tomahawk. Two days after, they were found dead; the soldier with his bayonet in the body of the Indian—the Indian with his tomahawk in the head of the soldier.

Several months after the battle of Fallen Timbers, a number of Potawatamie Indians arrived at Fort Wayne, where they expressed a desire to see "*The Wind*," as they called Gen. Wayne. On being asked for an explanation of the name, they replied, that at the battle of the 20th of August, he was exactly like a hurricane, which drives and tears every thing before it.

Gen. Wayne was a man of most ardent impulses, and in the heat of action apt to forget that he was the general—not the soldier. When the attack on the Indians who were concealed behind the fallen timbers, was commencing by ordering the regulars up, the late Gen. Harrison, then aid to Wayne, being lieutenant with the title of major, addressed his superior—" Gen. Wayne, I am afraid you will get into the fight yourself, and forget to give me the necessary field orders." " Perhaps I may," replied Wayne, " and if I do, recollect the standing order for the day is, charge the d——d rascals with the bayonets."

That this Indian war was in a great measure sustained by British influence, admits of ample proof. That they lent their aid in this campaign and battle, is fully confirmed in the extract given from a letter from Gen. Harrison to Hon. Thomas Chilton, dated North Bend, Feb. 17th, 1834.

That the northwestern and Indian war was a continuation of the revolutionary contest, is susceptible of proof. The Indians in that quarter had been engaged in the first seven years of the war, as the allies of Great Britain, and they had no inclination to continue it after the peace of 1783. It is to British influence that their subsequent hostilities are to be attributed. The agents of that government never ceased to stimulate their enmity against the government of the United States, and to represent the peace which had been made as a temporary truce, at the expiration of which, " their great fathers would unite with them in the war, and drive the *long knives* from the land which they had so unjustly usurped from his red children." This was the cause of the detention of the posts of Detroit, Mackinaw, and Niagara, so long after the treaty of 1783. The reasons assigned for so doing, deceived nobody, after the failure of the negotiation attempted by Gen. Lincoln, Gov. Randolph and Col. Pickering, under British mediation voluntarily tendered.

The bare suggestion of a wish by the British authorities, would have been sufficient to induce the Indians to accept the terms proposed by the American commissioners. But at any rate, the withholding the supplies with which the Indians had been previously furnished, would have left no other alternative but to make peace. From that period, however, the war was no longer carried on " in disguise." Acts of open hostility were committed. In June, 1794, the Indians assembled at the Miami of the Lake, and were completely equipped out of the King's store, from the fort (a large and regularly fortified work) which had been built there in the preceding spring, for the purpose of supporting the operations of the Indians against the army of Gen. Wayne. Nor was the assistance limited to the supply of provisions and munitions of war. On the advance of the Indians, they were attended by a captain of the British army, a serjeant, and six *matrosses*, provided with fixed ammunition, suited to the caliber of two field pieces, which had been taken from Gen. St. Clair, and deposited in a creek near the scene of his defeat in 1791. Thus attended, they appeared before Fort Recovery, (the advanced post of our army,) on the 4th of July, 1794, and having defeated a large detachment of our troops, encamped under its walls, would probably have succeeded in taking the fort, if the guns which they expected to find had not been previously discovered and removed. In this action, Capt. Hartshorn, of the 1st sub-legion, was wounded by the Indians, and afterwards killed in a struggle with Capt. M'Kee of the British army.*

Upon the advance of the American army in the following month, the British fort at the Rapids was again the point of rendezvous for the Indians. There the deficiencies in arms, ammunition and equipments, were again supplied; and there they were fed with regular rations from the King's stores, consisting of flour and Irish beef, until the arrival of Gen. Wayne with his army, on the 20th of August. In the general action of that day, there were two militia companies from Amherstburg and Detroit. The captain of the cutter (who was also the clerk of the court at that place) was found among the killed, and one of his privates taken prisoner. These unequivocal acts of hostility on the part of Great Britain, did not pass unnoticed by our government, and although anxious to avoid a general war, the President determined that the aggression on our territory, by the erection of a fortress so far within our acknowledged limits, required some decisive measure.

---

* It is proper to state, that Capt. M'Kee asserted that he interfered to save Hartshorn, but that he refused quarter and attempted to kill him, (M'Kee,) and would have succeeded, if he had not been anticipated by his (M'Kee's) servant.

Authority was therefore given to Gen. Wayne, to dispossess the intruders, if, in his opinion, it was necessary to the success of his operations against the Indians.

Although the qualification of this order, in its literal sense, might be opposed to its execution after the entire defeat of the Indians—the daring violation of neutrality which was professed, by the supply of food, arms and ammunition to the enemy on the very morning of the action, afforded, in the opinion of Gen. Wayne, a sufficient justification for its being carried into effect. An accurate examination, however, of the defenses of the fort, made by the general at great personal hazard, showed but too clearly that our small howitzers, which had been transported on the backs of horses, our only artillery, could make no impression upon its massive earthen parapet, while the deep fosse and frasing by which it was surrounded, afforded no prospect of the success of an escalade, but at an expense of valuable lives, which the occasion did not seem to call for.

From my situation as aid-de-camp to the general in chief, I mention these things from personal knowledge. If, then, the relation I have given is correct, *it must be admitted that the war of the revolution continued in the western country until the peace of Greenville, in* 1795.

There were some individuals on both sides, who took an active part, either in the battle or its connecting events, who demand more than a passing notice. Among these, were the faithful spies of Wayne, whose exploits M'Donald in his sketches thus describes.

Gen. Wayne, having a bold, vigilant and dexterous enemy to contend with, found it indispensably necessary to use the utmost caution in his movements to guard against surprise. To secure his army against the possibility of being ambuscaded, he employed a number of the best woodsmen the frontier afforded to act as spies. Capt. Ephraim Kibby, one of the first settlers at Columbia, who had distinguished himself as a bold and intrepid soldier, commanded the principal part of this corps.

A very effective division of the spies was commanded by Capt. William Wells.* At-

---

* Wm. Wells, while a child, was captured by the Indians, and became the adopted son of Little Turtle, the most eminent forest-warrior and statesman of his time. In the defeats of Harmar and St. Clair, he took a distinguished part, commanding in the latter action 300 young Indian warriors, who were posted immediately in front of the artillery, and caused such carnage among those who served it. He arranged his party behind logs and trees, immediately under the knoll on which the guns were, and thence, almost uninjured, picked off the artillerists, until, it is said, their bodies were heaped up almost to the height of their pieces. After this sanguinary affair, his forecast enabled him to anticipate the final ascendancy of the whites, who would be aroused by their reverses to such exertions as must be successful with their preponderance of power, and he resolved to abandon the savages. His mode of announcing this determination, was in accordance with the simple and sententious habits of a forest life. He was traversing the woods in the morning, with his adopted father, the Little Turtle, when pointing to the heavens, he said, "when the sun reaches the meridian, I leave you for the whites; and whenever you meet me in battle, you must kill me as I shall endeavor to do by you." The bonds of affection and respect which had bound these two singular and highly gifted men together, were not severed or weakened by this abrupt dereliction. Capt. Wells soon after joined Wayne's army, and by his intimacy with the wilderness, and his perfect knowledge of the Indian haunts, habits and modes of Indian warfare, became an invaluable auxiliary to the Americans. He served faithfully and fought bravely through the campaign, and at the close, when peace had restored amity between the Indians and the whites, rejoined his foster-father, the Little Turtle; and their friendship and connexion was broken only by the death of the latter. When his body was found among the slain at Chicago, in August, 1812, the Indians are said to have drank his blood, from a superstitious belief that they should thus imbibe his warlike endowments, which had been considered by them as pre-eminent.

The above paragraph respecting Wells, is copied from the discourse of Henry Whiting, Esq., before the Historical Society of Michigan; that below, relating to his death, is from the mss. of Col. John Johnston.

William Wells, interpreter for the Miamies, and whose wife was of that nation, himself uncle to Mrs. Heald, the lady of the commandant at Fort Dearborn, Chicago, went from Fort Wayne with a party of 12 or 15 Miamies to that place, with a view of favoring the escape of the garrison to Fort Wayne. Nothing could have been more unfortunate than this, for Wells was peculiarly obnoxious to the Putawatimies, and especially to the chief,

tached to Wells's command were the following men. Robert M'Clellan, one of the most active men on foot that ever lived. Next to him was Henry Miller, who deserves here a passing notice. He and a younger brother, named Christopher, had been made captives by the Indians while quite young, and adopted into an Indian family. He lived with them until about 24 years of age, when, although he had adopted all their customs, he began to think of returning to his relatives among the whites. His resolution continually gaining strength by reflection, he determined to make the attempt, and endeavored to induce his brother to accompany him in his flight, but to no purpose. Christopher was young when captured, he was now a good hunter, an expert woodsman and a free and independent Indian. Henry Miller, however, escaped through the woods, and arrived safe among his friends in Kentucky. Capt. Wells was familiar with Miller during his captivity, and knew that he possessed that firm intrepidity which would render him a valuable companion in time of need. To these were added, Hickman, May and Thorp, all men of tried worth in Indian warfare.

Capt. Wells and his four companions were confidential and privileged gentleman in camp, who were only called upon to do duty upon very particular and interesting occasions. They were permitted a *carte blanche* among the horses of the dragoons, and when on duty always went well mounted; while the spies, commanded by Capt. Kibby, went on foot, and were kept constantly on the alert, scouring the country in every direction.

In June, 1794, while the head quarters of the army was at Greenville, Wayne dispatched Wells, with his corps, with orders to bring an Indian into the camp as prisoner. Accordingly he proceeded cautiously with his party through the Indian country. They crossed the St. Mary's and thence to the Auglaize, without meeting with any straggling party of Indians. In passing up the latter, they discovered a smoke, dismounted, tied their horses and cautiously reconnoitered. They found three Indians encamped on a high, open piece of ground, clear of brush or any undergrowth, rendering it difficult to approach them without being discovered. While reconnoitering, they saw not very distant from the camp, a fallen tree. They returned and went round, so as to get it between them and the Indians. The tree top being full of leaves would serve to screen them from observation. They crept forward on their hands and knees with the caution of the cat, until they reached it, when they were within 70 or 80 yards of the camp. The Indians were sitting or standing about the fire, roasting their venison, laughing and making merry antics, little dreaming that death was about stealing a march upon them. Arrived at the fallen tree, their plans were settled. M'Clellan, who was almost as swift of foot as a deer, was to catch the center Indian, while Wells and Miller were to kill the other two, one shooting to the right and the other to the left. Resting the muzzles of their rifles on a log of the fallen tree, they aimed for the Indians hearts. Whiz went the balls, and both Indians fell. Before the smoke had risen two feet, M'Clellan was running with uplifted tomahawk for the remaining Indian, who bounded down the river, but finding himself likely to be headed if he continued in that direction, he turned and made for the river, which at that place had a bluff bank about 20 feet high. On reaching it, he sprang off into the stream and sunk to

---

"the Black Bird," who was the leading warrior on the occasion. The Putawatimies were alone in arms against us, at the time, in that part of the country. The presence of Wells was fatal to the safety of the troops; the chief Blackbird had often spoken to myself in very bitter terms against him. On the 14th of August, 1812, a council was held between the officers and the chiefs, at which it was agreed, that the whole garrison with their arms, ammunition sufficient for the journey and clothing, should retire unmolested to Fort Wayne, and that the garrison, with all that it contained, should be delivered up to the Indians. In the night preceding the evacuation, all the powder and whiskey in the fort was thrown into a canal, communicating from the garrison to the Chicago river. The powder floated out and discovered the deception to the Indians; this greatly exasperated them and no doubt brought matters to a crisis. On the morning of the 15th of August, the troops marched out to commence their journey, and had proceeded but a short distance, when they were attacked by the Indians. Wells seeing that all was lost, and not wishing to fall into their hands, as he well knew that in that case, a cruel and lingering death awaited him, wetted powder and blacked his face, as a token of defiance, mounted his horse and commenced addressing the Indians with all the approbrious and insulting language he could think of. His purpose evidently was to induce them to dispatch him forthwith. His object was accomplished. They beeame so enraged at last with his taunts and jeers, that one of them shot him off his horse, and immediately pouncing upon him, cut his body open, took out his heart and eat it. The troops were massacred, the commanding officer and wife were saved. . . . Chicago means in Putawatimie, "the place of *the pole cat.*"

his middle in the soft mud at its bottom. M'Clellan came after and instantly sprang upon him, as he was wallowing and endeavoring to extricate himself from the mire. The Indian drew his knife: the other raised his tomahawk and bade him throw down his knife or he would kill him instantly. He did so, and surrendered without farther opposition.

By this time, Wells and his companion came to the bank, and discovered the two quietly sticking in the mud. Their prisoner being secure, they selected a place where the bank was less precipitous, went down, dragged the captive out and tied him. He was sulky and refused to speak either Indian or English. Some of the party went back for their horses, while the others washed the mud and paint from the prisoner. When cleaned, he turned out to be a white man, but still refused to speak, or give any account of himself. The party scalped the two Indians whom they had shot, and then set off for head quarters. Henry Miller having some suspicions that their prisoner might possibly be his brother Christopher, whom he had left with the Indians, years previous, rode up along side of him, and called him by his Indian name. At the sound, he started, stared around, and eagerly inquired how he came to know his name? The mystery was soon explained. Their prisoner was indeed Christopher Miller! A mysterious providence appeared to have placed him in a situation in the camp, by which his life was preserved. Had he been standing either to the right or to the left, he would inevitably have been killed, and an even chance too, if not by his own brother. But that fate which appears to have doomed the Indian race to extinction, permitted the white man to live.

When they arrived at Greenville, their prisoner was placed in the guard house. Wayne often interrogated him as to what he knew of the future intentions of the Indians. Capt. Wells and his brother Henry, were almost constantly with him, urging him to abandon the idea of ever again joining the Indians, and to unite with the whites. For some time he was reserved and sulky, but at length became more cheerful, and agreed that if they would release him from his confinement, he would remain among them. Capt. Wells and Henry Miller urged Wayne to release him, who did so, with the observation, that should he deceive them and return to the enemy, they would be one the stronger. He appeared pleased with his change of situation, and was mounted on a fine horse, and otherwise equipped for war. He joined the company of Wells, and continued through the war a brave and intrepid soldier.

As soon as Wells and his company had rested themselves, they were anxious for another *bout* with the red men. Time without action was irksome to such stirring spirits. Accordingly in July, they left Greenville, their number strengthened by the addition of Christopher Miller, with orders to bring in prisoners. When on these excursions, they were always mounted on elegant horses and dressed and painted in Indian style. They arrived in the country near the Auglaize, when they met a single Indian, and called upon him to surrender. Notwithstanding there were six against him, he refused, levelled his rifle, and as they approached him on horseback, fired, missed his mark and then ran. The thick underbrush enabling him to gain upon them, Christopher Miller and M'Clellan dismounted and pursued, and the latter soon overtook him. Upon this he turned and made a blow at M'Clellan with his rifle, which was parried. As it was M'Clellan's intention not to kill, he kept him at bay until Christopher came up, when they closed in, and made him prisoner without receiving injury. They then turned about and arrived with him at Greenville. He was reported to be a Pottawatamie chief of scarcely equalled courage and prowess. As Christopher Miller had performed his part on this occasion, to the entire satisfaction of the brave spirits with whom he acted, he had, as he merited, their entire confidence.

On one of Captain Wells's peregrinations through the Indian country, as he came to the bank of the St. Mary's, he discovered a family of Indians coming up the river in a canoe. He dismounted from his horse and concealed his men, while he went to the bank of the river, in open view, and called to the Indians to come over. As he was dressed in Indian costume and spoke in that language, they crossed to him, unsuspicious of danger. The moment the canoe struck the shore, Wells heard the nicking of the cocks of his comrades' rifles, as they prepared to shoot the Indians; but who should be in the canoe but his Indian father and mother, with their children! The others were now coming forward with their rifles cocked and ready to pour in a deadly fire upon this family. Wells shouted to them to desist, informing them who the Indians were, solemnly declaring that the first man who attempted to injure one of them should receive a ball in his head. "That family," said he to his men, "had fed him when hungry, clothed him when naked, and nursed him when sick, and had treated him as affectionately as their own children." This short speech moved the sympathetic hearts of his leather-hunting-shirt comrades, who entered at once into his feelings and approved of his lenity. Dropping their tomahawks and rifles, they went to the canoe and shook hands with the trembling Indians in the most friendly manner.

Wells assured them they had nothing to fear; and after talking with them some time, to dispel their anxiety, he told them "that Gen. Wayne was approaching with an overwhelming force; that the best thing the Indians could do was to make peace, and that the whites did not wish to continue the war. He urged his Indian father to keep for the future out of danger:" he then bade them farewell. They appeared grateful for his clemency, pushed off their canoe, and paddled with their utmost rapidity down stream. Capt. Wells and his comrades, though perfect desperadoes in fight, upon this occasion proved that they largely possessed that gratitude and benevolence which does honor to human kind.

While Wayne's army lay at the Indian village at the confluence of the Auglaize and Maumee, building Fort Defiance, the general, wishing to be informed of the intentions of the enemy, dispatched Capt. Wells's party to bring in another prisoner. They consisted of Wells, M'Clellan, the Millers, May and Mahaffy. They proceeded cautiously down the Maumee until opposite the site of Fort Meigs, where was an Indian village. This was on the 11th of August, nine days before the battle. Wells and his party boldly rode into this town, as if they had come from the British fort, and occasionally stopped and talked with the Indians in their language. The savages believed them to be Indians from a distance, who had come to take a part in the expected battle. After passing through the village, they met, some distance from it, an Indian man and woman on horseback, who were returning to town from hunting. They made them captives without resistance, and set off for Defiance.

A little after dark, they came near a large encampment of Indians, merrily amusing themselves around their camp fires. Ordering their prisoners to be silent, under pain of instant death, they went around the camp until they got about half a mile above it. They then held a consultation, tied and gagged their prisoners, and rode into the Indian camp with their rifles lying across the pummels of their saddles. They inquired when they had heard last of Gen. Wayne and the movements of his army, and how soon and where the expected battle would be fought? The Indians standing about Wells and his party were very communicative, and answered the questions without any suspicions of deceit in their visitors. At length an Indian, who was sitting at some distance, said in an under-tone, in another tongue, to some who were near him, that he suspected these strangers had some mischief in their heads. Wells overheard it, gave the preconcerted signal, and each fired his rifle into the body of an Indian, at not more than six feet distance. The moment the Indian had made the remark, he and his companions rose up with their rifles in hand, but not before each of the others had shot their man. The moment after Wells and party had fired, they put spurs to their horses, lying with their breasts on their animals' necks, so as to lessen the mark to fire at, and before they had got out of the light of the camp fires, the Indians had fired upon them. As M'Clellan lay in this position, a ball entered beneath his shoulder blade and came out at the top of his shoulder; Wells's arm was broken by a ball, and his rifle dropped to the ground; May was chased to the smooth rock in the Maumee, where, his horse falling, he was taken prisoner.

The rest of the party escaped without injury and rode full speed to where their prisoners were confined, and mounting them upon horses continued their route. Wells and M'Clellan being severely wounded, and their march slow and painful to Defiance, a distance of about 30 miles, ere they could receive surgical aid, a messenger was dispatched to hasten to that post for a surgeon and a guard. As soon as he arrived with the tidings of the wounds and perilous situation of these heroic and faithful spies, very great sympathy was manifested. Wayne's feeling for the suffering soldier was at all times quick and sensitive. We can, then, imagine the intensity of his solicitude when informed of the sufferings and perils of his confidential and chosen band. He instantly dispatched a surgeon and a company of the swiftest dragoons to meet, assist and guard these brave fellows to head-quarters, where they arrived safe, and the wounded in due time recovered.

May, who was taken prisoner, having formerly lived and ran away from the Indians, was recognized. They told him, the second day before the battle, "We know you—you speak Indian language—you not content to live with us: to-morrow we take you to that tree—pointing to a very large burr oak at the edge of the clearing near the British fort—we will tie you up and make a mark on your breast, and we will try what Indian can shoot nearest it." Accordingly, the next day he was tied to that tree, a mark made on his breast, and his body riddled with at least fifty bullets. Thus ended poor May!

This little band of spies, during the campaign, performed more real service than any other corps of equal number belonging to the army. They brought in, at different times, not less than 20 prisoners, and killed more than an equal number. As they had no rivals in the army, they aimed in each excursion to outdo their former exploits. What confidence! what self-possession was displayed by these men in their terrific encounters! To ride boldly into the enemy's camp, in full view of their blazing camp-fires, and enter into conversation with them without betraying the least appearance of trepidation or confusion, and openly commence the work of death, proves how well their souls were steeled against fear. They had come off unscathed in so many desperate conflicts, that they became callous to danger.

In the battle, Wayne's army took a white man prisoner, by the name of Lasselle. Col. John Johnston says respecting him:

ANTOINE LASSELLE I well knew: this man, a Canadian, was taken prisoner at Wayne's battle, painted, dressed and disguised as an Indian. He was tried by court-martial, at Roche de Bœuf, and sentenced to be hung. A gallows was erected and the execution ordered, when Col. John F. Hamtranck—a native of Canada, who joined the American standard under Montgomery, in the revolutionary war, and was, in 1794, colonel of the 1st regiment of infantry, under Wayne—interposed and begged the life of the prisoner. Gen. Wayne afterwards granted to Lasselle license to trade at Fort Wayne, and he was there as such many years during my agency at the post. He was a man of wit and drollery. and would often clasp his neck with both hands, to show how near he had been to hanging by order of mad Anthony.

Col. Johnston also says, respecting Col. M'Kee and Capt. Elliott, who were both alledged to have been in the action, and were notorious enemies of the Americans in the wars in the northwest:

M'KEE and ELLIOTT were Pennsylvanians, and the latter, I think, of Irish birth. They resided at the commencement of the revolutionary war in Path valley, Pa. A brother and a brother-in-law of mine lived in the same neighborhood; I therefore have undoubted authority for the facts. A number of tories resided in the township, M'Kee and Elliot being leaders. A large proportion of the inhabitants being whigs, the place became too warm to hold them. They fled to the enemy, and leagued with the Shawanese Indians in committing depredations on the frontier settlers. Both of these incendiaries had Indian wives and children, and finally their influence became so great among the savages, that they were appointed agents for Indian affairs by the British government, and continued as such until their death. Matthew Elliott was an uncle, by his father's side, to the late Commodore Elliott, and had a son killed in the late war, by the Indians under Logan. [See p. 302.] On the death of M'Kee, his son, a half-breed, was a deputy agent in Upper Canada. He was a splendid looking man, and married an accomplished white lady. He had too much of the Indian nature, and the marriage turned out somewhat unhappily.

In August, 1814, several letters were published in the National Intelligencer, from Col. M'Kee to Col. England, the British commandant at Detroit during the campaign of Wayne, the originals of which, the editor stated, were then in his possession. M'Kee was at this time superintendent of the Indians under his majesty. Some brief extracts below pile up the evidence already adduced of his hostility, and that of the English to the Americans.

Rapids, July 5th, 1794. SIR,—I send this by a party of Saginas, who returned yesterday from Fort Recovery, where the whole body of the Indians, except the Delawares, who had gone another route, *imprudently* attacked the fort on Monday, the 30th of last month. ....Every thing had been settled prior to their leaving the fallen timber, and it had been agreed upon to confine themselves to taking convoys and attacking at a distance from the forts, if they should have the address to entice the *enemy* out........

Rapids, Aug. 13th, 1794. SIR,—I was honored last night with your letter of the 11th, ***and am extremely glad to find you making such exertions to supply the Indians with provisions***......Scouts are sent up to view the situation of the army, [Wayne's,] and WE now muster 1000 Indians. All the lake Indians, from Sagina downwards, should not ***lose one moment in joining their brethren, as every accession of strength is an addition to their spirits.***

Maumee city, the county seat, is 124 miles NW. of Columbus, and 6 S. of Toledo. It was laid out under the name of *Maumee* in 1817, by Maj. Wm. Oliver and others, within what had been the reservation of 12 miles square, at the foot of the rapids of the Maumee, granted to the Indians at the treaty of Greenville, in 1795. The town is situated at the head of navigation on the Maumee, and on the Wabash and Erie canal, opposite Perrysburg and Fort Meigs.

Maumee City, from Fort Meigs.

The river banks upon which Maumee city and its neighbor, Perrysburg stand, are elevated near 100 feet above the water level. Both banks, at this point, curve gracefully inward, while the river above and below is somewhat contracted, thus forming a vast amphitheatre of about two miles in length and nearly one in breadth, while a beautiful cultivated island of 200 acres, and several small islets embosomed in its centre, enhance a scene rich in picturesque effect.

From a very early day, this was a favorite point with the Indians. As early as 1680, the French had a trading station just below the town, where, later in the spring of 1794, was built the British fort Miami, the ruins of which are still conspicuous. Part of Wayne's battle was within the limits of the town—the action commenced two or three miles south. At that point, by the road side, is a noted rock, of several tons weight, near the foot of Presque Isle hill, where it is said an Indian chief, named Turkey Foot, rallied a few of his men and stood upon it fighting until his strength becoming exhausted from loss of blood, he fell and breathed his last. Upon it have been carved by the Indians, representations of turkey's feet, now plainly to be seen, and it is said "the early settlers of and travellers through the Maumee valley, usually found many small pieces of tobacco deposited on this rock, which had been placed there by the Indians as devotional acts, by way of sacrifice, to appease the indignant spirit of the departed hero." During the siege of Fort Meigs, in the late war, the British encamped below the town, and erected several batteries within it, which played upon the American fort. These having been stormed and taken by Col. Dudley, on the 5th of May, 1813, that officer pushed his victory too far, and was, in turn, attacked by the enemy, who had been reinforced from below, and defeated with great slaughter on the site of the town. (See Wood county.)

The view of Maumee city, taken from the site of Fort Meigs, shows, in front, Maumee river and the bridge; beyond, on the left, the canal, and on the summit of the hill, a small portion of the town, which is much scattered. On the right is seen the Presbyterian church, on the left, the Methodist, and between, the Catholic; the Episcopal church does not appear in this view. Maumee city is a thriving town, and has an extensive water power, which, if fully improved, would be sufficient for 250 runs of stone: it now contains 16 dry goods, 8 grocery and 3 drug stores; 1 or 2 newspaper printing offices, 4 flouring, 1 oil and 2 saw mills; 1 pail factory, 1 tannery, a wool-carding and cloth-dressing establishment, and had in 1840, 840 inhabitants, since which it has much increased. A number of vessels, steamboats, propellers and canal boats have been built here. A spirit of rivalry exists between the towns at the foot of the rapids, Maumee city and Perrysburg, with Toledo. While the latter has outstripped them in prosperity, there is, perhaps, but little question that if the navigation of the river was improved, Maumee city and Perrysburg would draw to themselves a vast accession of business, and be important points for the shipment and transhipment of freight. The Maumee is navigable, in its present condition, for steamboats and schooners drawing seven feet of water; but, since the construction of boats of a heavier draught, it is necessary that an improvement, by excavating the channel along what is called "*the rock bar*," should be made. This bar, which is of blue limestone, commences about a mile and a half below Perrysburg. At a common stage, the water upon it is about six and half feet deep. To open a clear and unobstructed channel upon it for the largest lake boats, it has been estimated, would cost about $30,000. Government has frequently, but ineffectually, been petitioned to make this improvement.

Toledo is on the left bank of the Maumee river, and on the Wabash and Erie canal, 134 miles NW. of Columbus, 246 by canal N. of Cincinnati, about 50 S. of Detroit, about 100 W. of Cleveland, and 33 miles from Adrian, Michigan, where a railroad from Toledo intersects with the southern Michigan railroad. Toledo stretches along the river bank for more than a mile, and has two points at which business concentrates, called respectively the upper and lower landing. It was originally two distinct settlements—the upper, Port Lawrence, the lower, Vistula. Between these two points Toledo is thinly settled; but at them, and particularly at the upper, the stores, warehouses and dwellings are densely packed together. The view of the harbor from the upper landing is very fine: the eye takes in a distance of several miles of the river, bounded by well-defined projecting headlands, and often showing a large number of sails, presenting not only a scene of beauty, but evidence of the extensive commerce, of which this place is the center.

42

Toledo covers the site of a stockade fort, called Fort Industry erected about the year 1800, near what is now Summit street. A treaty was held in this fort with the Indians July 4th, 1805, by which the Indian title to the "fire-lands" was extinguished. Chas. Jouett was United States commissioner, and the Ottawa, Chippewa, Pottawatimie, Wyandot, Shawanee, Munsee and Delaware tribes, represented by their respective chiefs. The insignificant settlements of Port Lawrence and Vistula were later formed, and have now lost their identity in Toledo, the history, present condition and prospects of which we annex, in a communication from a gentleman of the place.

In the summer of 1832, Vistula, under the impetus given it by Captain Samuel Allen, from Lockport, N. Y., and Major Stickney, made quite a noise as a promising place for a town. People from various quarters were met by the writer, in June of that year, at the residence of Major Stickney. All seemed sanguine of a sudden and large growth for the new town, and many made purchases in and about it. At the same time, arrangements were being made by Major Oliver and Micajah T. Williams, of Cincinnati, with Daniel O. Comstock and Stephen B. Comstock, brothers, from Lockport, for the resuscitation of Port Lawrence, at the mouth of Swan creek. The Comstocks took an interest, and became the agents for the Port Lawrence property, now known as Upper Toledo. No sales of any importance were made before 1833. In Vistula, the first store was started by Mr. E. Briggs; W. J. Daniels, now a leading man, was his clerk. Soon after, Flagg & Bissell opened a more extensive store of goods—probably the first good assortment for the use of white people. In 1833, not much progress was made towards building a town in Vistula or Port Lawrence. In the latter, the first Toledo steamer was built, and called the Detroit. She was of 120 tons, and commanded by Captain Baldwin, son of a sea captain of that name, who was one of the earliest settlers of Port Lawrence. The best lots in Port Lawrence, 60 feet front by 120 deep, were offered by Stephen B. Comstock, for $50, coupled with a condition to make some little improvements. Four of these lots, if they were now not built upon, would sell for $5,000 each. Three of them are nearly covered by 3 story brick buildings, and form the center of business of Toledo. They are corners, on Monroe and Summit streets.

In 1834, speculation in lots began, and with slight intermission continued until the spring of 1837. Mr. Edward Bissell, from Lockport, a man of enterprise and activity, became a part owner, and gave a great impetus to the growth of Vistula. Through him and the Port Lawrence owners, many men of influence became interested in the new towns. Among these, Judge Mason, from Livingston county, N. Y., deserves mention, as he became agent of Bissell and the other chief owners, and made Vistula his residence.

In 1836, the Wabash and Erie canal was located, having three terminations, one at Maumee, one at Toledo, and one at Manhattan. Great exertions were made to induce the commissioners to terminate it at the foot of the Rapids; and also to have it continued below, on the high bank. All the points were accommodated, and the state has had a heavy bill to foot as the consequence. In 1837, the canal was let, and the contractors entered vigorously on its construction. The commissioners held out the opinion, that it would be completed in two years. Under the expectation of its early completion, many of the inhabitants of Toledo, who had been brought there by the speculations of 1835 and 1836, and the business it gave, held on in order to participate in the business it was expected to furnish. The seasons of 1838 and 1839 were uncommonly sickly, not only at Toledo, but along the entire line of the canal. This kept back the work on the canal, and it was not completed, so as to make its business sensiby felt, before the season of 1845. The Miami and Erie canal was opened through, from river to lake, the same season, and for a time had a great rush of business through it. But it was so imperfect, that great prejudice was excited against it as a channel of commerce. During the season of 1846, it was kept in good order, and recovered a portion of its lost popularity.

The productions of the south and southwest, that reached Toledo by these two canals, during the season of 1846, exceeded three millions of dollars in value, and more than doubled the receipts of the preceding year. The value sent up from Toledo can scarcely have been less than five million dollars. The aggregate of breadstuffs exported, exceeded three millions of bushels, being greater than any other port around the lakes, except Cleveland, that shipped by lake. It is expected that the business of these canals this year, will nearly double that of the season of 1846. The Wabash and Erie canal will then be extended 49 miles further down the Wabash; and the country on the lines of both canals being new, is being opened to cultivation, and having the roads that bring trade to the canals every year extended farther from their borders, and made better. By position and the aid of these canals, Toledo is evidently destined to be one of the greatest of the gathering points of agricultural productions in the country. Its situation is equally favorable for the distribution, over the lakes, of southern productions—sugar, tobacco, &c. The Miami and Erie canal is the best channel for the goods destined from the eastern cities to the great river valley below Cincinnati.

The Wabash and Erie canal, when completed to Evansville, on the Ohio, will be 460 miles in length, and control most of the external trade of Indiana and eastern Illinois. The Miami and Erie canal, connecting Toledo and Cincinnati, is 247 miles long. This, it is believed, will one day become one of the most important canals in the world.

Within the last two years, Toledo has expended near one hundred thousand dollars in grading and other permanent improvements that tend to give facility to commercial operations. Like all the other towns on Lake Erie, it has suffered, during the early years of its life, from sickness; and perhaps it has suffered still more, in its growth and prospects, from the exaggerations which public rumor has spread over the country, respecting its insalubrity. And yet it would be difficult to find a healthier looking or a more vigorous set of men, than are the first settlers of Toledo and other places on the harbor. Toledo has had sickness, but not more than Cleveland and Sandusky and Monroe, at the same period of their growth. The excavations for the canal and the grades, have undoubtedly contributed to the prevalence of intermittents, which is the chief cause of complaint. Every year will witness an improvement in this respect, until, like Cleveland, it will be forgotten as a place especially fruitful of malaria, and be spoken of chiefly for the activity and extent of its commerce, and the rapidity of its progress towards the high destiny which reflecting men have long anticipated for it.

Toledo was incorporated as a city in 1836, and has 1 Presbyterian, 1 Catholic, 1 Methodist, 1 Episcopal and 1 Lutheran church, 37 mercantile establishments—including 3 drug and 2 book stores —9 forwarding and commission houses, 2 banks, and its population is estimated at 2400; in 1840, it had 1322 inhabitants. A daily steamboat line connects Toledo with Buffalo, and another with Detroit. A railroad has been chartered and surveyed between Toledo and the west line of Indiana, in the direction of the falls of Illinois, or towards Chicago.

Toledo was the center of the military operations in "the Ohio and Michigan war," so called, which at the time threatened serious results, but was accompanied with so much of the ludicrous, as to be usually adverted to with emotions of merriment. In the language of "an actor in the scenes which he depicts," the narration below is given.

The dispute of Ohio and Michigan, about the line of division between them, originated in this wise. The ordinance of 1787, provided for the division of the North Western territory into not less than three nor more than five states; and if into five, then the three southern were to be divided from the two northern, by a line drawn east and west through the southern point of Lake Michigan, extending eastward to the territorial line in Lake Erie. The constitution of Ohio contained a provision, that if the said line should not go so far north as the north cape of the Maumee bay, then the northern boundary of Ohio should be a line drawn from the southerly part of Lake Michigan to the north cape of the Maumee bay. With this constitution, Ohio was admitted into the union. The line of the ordinance was an impossible line, inasmuch as it would never touch the territorial line by extending it eastward, but would, on the contrary, leave north of it a considerable portion of that part of Ohio known as the Western Reserve.

When Michigan became a territory, the people living between the two lines—that claimed by Michigan, known as the *Fulton* line, and that claimed by Ohio, as the *Harris* line—found it more convenient to be attached to Michigan, and agreeably to their wish, the territorial laws were extended over the disputed territory. In 1833, it appeared important that the boundary should be settled, and at the suggestion of J. W. Scott, Esq., of Toledo, Senator Tilden, of Norwalk, Ohio, brought the matter before the legislature, which passed a resolution asking congress to act upon the subject, for the purpose of quieting the claim of Ohio.

In 1835, the matter came before congress, and J. Q. Adams made an elaborate report against the claim of Ohio. Through the exertions of A. Palmer, S. B. Comstock, W. P. Daniels and others, the former was immediately dispatched to Columbus, with a petition from most of the inhabitants, to the legislature of Ohio, then in session, asking the extension of the laws of Ohio over the disputed territory. An act was soon after passed for that purpose, and the disputed territory was attached to the counties of Wood, Henry and Williams. This occasioned a counteraction on the part of Michigan. A double set of officers were created at the spring election, and war became inevitable. The inhabitants were mostly for the Ohio claim, but enough sided with Michigan to fill all the offices. These soon needed the aid of their neighbors of Monroe county, who were organized, and made some inroads under the sheriff's posse, and carried off to Monroe, some of the would-be citizens of Ohio.

Thereupon, Ohio levied troops, and Governor Lucas came on at their head, early in the spring of 1835. In the mean time, Governor Mason mustered troops from Michigan; and while Governor Lucas was encamped at old Fort Miami, 8 miles above Toledo and 4 miles above the disputed territory, Mason marched into Toledo, overrun all the water-melon patches, made fowls very scarce, and demolished utterly the ice house of Major Stickney, burst in the front door of his residence, and triumphantly carried him off a prisoner of war to Monroe.*

About this time appeared from the court of Washington, two ambassadors, with full powers to negotiate with the belligerants, for an amicable settlement of difficulties. These were Richard Rush, of Pennsylvania, and Colonel Howard, of Maryland. They were successful in their mission, chiefly because Michigan was satisfied with the laurels won, and Ohio was willing to stand on her dignity—8 miles from the ground in dispute. At the court next holden in Wood county, the prosecuting attorney presented bills of indictment against Governor Mason and divers others, in like manner offending; but the bills were thrown out by the grand jury. Thus was Ohio defeated in her resort to law, as she had before been in her passage at arms. At the next session of congress, the matter was taken up, and able arguments in favor of Ohio were made in the house, by Samuel F. Vinton, and in the senate, by Thomas Ewing. Here Ohio carried the day. Michigan, instead of the narrow strip, averaging about 8 miles wide, on her southern border, received as an equivalent the large peninsula between Lakes Huron, Michigan and Superior, now so well known for its rich deposit of copper and other minerals. The chief value to Ohio, of the territory in dispute, was the harbor at Toledo, formed by the mouth of the Maumee, essential, as her public men believed, to enable her to reap the benefit of the commerce made by her canals to Cincinnati and Indiana. The result has shown that they judged correctly. Toledo has proved to be the true point for the meeting of lake and canal commerce.

Manhattan, 3 miles below Toledo, was laid out a few years since, and much enterprise exhibited on the part of its founders: it is, however, a small place, containing in 1840, 282 inhabitants. Waterville, about 5 miles above Maumee City, is a neat village, containing about 300 inhabitants. Providence, near the line of Henry county, on the river, had in 1840, 130 inhabitants; in 1846, it was seriously injured by fire. There are other small towns in the county, but none of note.

---

* Many amusing incidents are related of the actors in this war. Dr. Russ, of New York, was with the forces of Mason, on their march from Monroe to Toledo, and gave to the writer a vivid description of the mixture of frolic and fear among the new soldiers. Reports were constantly being circulated of the great number of sharp-shooting Buckeyes who were ready, with poised rifles, to greet their arrival at Toledo; and so terror-stricken were the warriors by these stories of the wags, that nearly half of those who marched boldly from Monroe, availed themselves of the bushes, by the road-side, to with draw from the dangerous enterprise.

MADISON.

MADISON was organized in March, 1810, and named from James Madison, the fourth President of the U. States. The soil is clayey, and the surface level. Almost one-third of the surface is prairie land. Wool-growing has become an object of considerable business. It is principally a stock-raising county. The productions are grass, corn and oats, and beef cattle. Wool and pork are the principal staples. The following is a list of the townships in 1840, with their population.

Canaan,	607	Monroe,	385	Range,	820
Darby,	466	Pike,	529	Somerford,	761
Deer Creek,	545	Pleasant,	936	Stokes,	770
Fairfield,	505			Union,	1350

The population of Madison, in 1820, was 4799; in 1830, 6191; and in 1840, 9025, or 20 inhabitants to the square mile.

In the course of this work, we have made several extracts from the MSS. of Jonathan Alder, who was taken captive when a boy, and passed many years among the Indians. These MSS. contain about a hundred pages, and comprise a sketch of his life while with the Indians, together with a relation of many of their customs, and incidents that came under his observation. Mr. Alder is now living on Darby creek, in this county. We give a sketch of him, derived from the above-mentioned source.

JONATHAN ALDER was born in New Jersey, about 8 miles from Philadelphia, Sept. 17th, 1773. When at about the age of seven years, his parents removed to Wythe county, Va., and his father soon after died.

In the succeeding March, (1782,) while out with his brother David, hunting for a mare and her colt, he was taken prisoner by a small party of Indians. His brother, on the first alarm, ran, and was pursued by some of the party. "At length," says Alder, "I saw them returning, leading my brother, while one was holding the handle of a spear, that he had thrown at him and run into his body. As they approached, one of them stepped up and grasped him around the body, while another pulled out the spear. I observed some flesh on the end of it, which looked white, which I supposed came from his entrails. I moved to him, and inquired if he was hurt, and he replied that he was. These were the last words that passed between us. At that moment he turned pale and began to sink, and I was hurried on, and shortly after saw one of the barbarous wretches coming up with the scalp of my brother in his hand, shaking off the blood."

The Indians having also taken prisoner a Mrs. Martin, a neighbor to the Alders, with her young child, aged about four or five years, retreated towards their towns. Their route lay through the woods to the Big Sandy, down that stream to the Ohio, which they crossed, and from thence went overland to the Scioto, near Chillicothe, and so on to a Mingo village on Mad river.

Finding the child of Mrs. Martin burdensome, they soon killed and scalped it. The last member of her family was now destroyed, and she screamed in agony of grief. Upon this, one of the Indians caught her by her hair, and drawing the edge of his knife across her forehead, cried "sculp! sculp!" with the hope of stilling her cries. But, indifferent to life, she continued her screams, when they procured some switches, and whipped her until she was silent. The next day, young Alder having not risen, through fatigue, from eating, at the moment the word was given, saw, as his face was to the north, the shadow of a man's arm with an uplifted tomahawk. He turned, and there stood an Indian, ready for the fatal blow. Upon this he let down his arm, and commenced feeling of his head. He afterwards told Alder it had been his intention to have killed him; but as he turned he looked so smiling and pleasant, that he could not strike, and on feeling of his head and noticing that his hair was very black, the thought struck him, that if he could only get him to his tribe he would make a good Indian ; but that all that saved his life was the color of his hair.

After they crossed the Ohio, they killed a bear, and remained four days to dry the meat for packing, and to fry out the oil, which last they put in the intestines, having first turned and cleaned them.

The village to which Alder was taken, belonged to the Mingo tribe, and was on the north side of Mad river, which we should judge was somewhere within or near the limits of what is now Logan county. As he entered, he was obliged to run the gauntlet, formed by young children armed with switches. He passed through this ordeal with little or no injury, and was adopted into an Indian family. His Indian mother thoroughly washed him with soap and warm water with herbs in it, previous to dressing him in the Indian costume, consisting of a calico shirt, breech clout, leggins and moccasons. The family having thus converted him into an Indian, were much pleased with their new member. But Jonathan was at first very homesick, thinking of his mother and brothers. Every thing was strange about him ; he was unable to speak a word of their language ; their food disagreed with him ; and, child-like, he used to go out daily for more than a month, and sit under a large walnut tree near the village, and cry for hours at a time over his deplorable situation. His Indian father was a chief of the Mingo tribe, named Succohanos ; his Indian mother was named Whinecheoh, and their daughters respectively answered to the good old English names of Mary, Hannah and Sally. Succohanos and Whinecheoh were old people, and had lost a son, in whose place they had adopted Jonathan. They took pity on the little fellow, and did their best to comfort him, telling him that he would one day be restored to his mother and brothers. He says of them, " they could not have used their own son better, for which they shall always be held in most grateful remembrance by me." His Indian sister Sally, however, treated him " like a slave," and when out of humor, applied to him, in the Indian tongue, the un-lady-like epithet of " onorary, [mean,] lousy prisoner !" Jonathan for a time lived with Mary, who had become the wife of the chief, Col. Lewis, (see p. 304.) " In the fall of the year," says he, " the Indians would generally collect at our camp, evenings, to talk over their hunting expeditions. I would sit up to listen to their stories, and frequently fell asleep just where I was sitting. After they left, Mary would fix my bed, and with Col. Lewis, would carefully take me up and carry me to it. On these occasions they would often say—supposing me to be asleep—' poor fellow ! we have sat up too long for him, and he has fallen asleep on the cold ground ;' and then how softly would they lay me down and cover me up. Oh ! never have I, nor can I, express the affection I had for these two persons."

Jonathan, with other boys, went into Mad river to bathe, and on one occasion came near drowning. He was taken out senseless, and some time elapsed ere he recovered. He says, " I remember, after I got over my strangle, I became very sleepy, and thought I could draw my breath as well as ever. Being overcome with drowsiness, I laid down to sleep, which was the last I remember. The act of drowning is nothing, but the coming to life is distressing. The boys, after they had brought me too, gave me a silver buckle, as an inducement not to tell the old folks of the occurrence, for fear they would not let me come with them again ; and so the affair was kept secret."

When Alder had learned to speak the Indian language, he became more contented. He says, " I would have lived very happy, if I could have had health ; but for three or four years I was subject to very severe attacks of fever and ague. Their diet went very hard with me for a long time. Their chief living was meat and hommony ; but we rarely had bread, and very little salt, which was extremely scarce and dear, as well as milk and butter. Honey and sugar were plentiful, and used a great deal in their cooking, as well as on their food."

When he was old enough, he was given an old English musket, and told that he must go out and learn to hunt. So he used to follow along the water courses, where mud turtles were plenty, and commenced his first essay upon them. He generally aimed under them, as they lay basking on the rocks ; and when he struck the stone, they flew sometimes several feet in the air, which afforded great sport for the youthful marksman. Occasionally he killed a wild turkey, or a raccoon ; and when he returned to the village with his game, generally received high praise for his skill—the Indians telling him he would make " a great hunter one of these days."

We cannot, within our assigned limits, give many of the incidents and anecdotes related by Alder, or any thing like a connected history of his life among the Indians. In the June after he was taken, occurred Crawford's defeat. He describes the anxiety of the squaws while the men were gone to the battle, and their joy on their returning with scalps and other trophies of the victory. He defends Simon Girty from the charge of being the instigator of the burning of Crawford, and states that he could not have saved his life, because he had no influence in the Delaware tribe, whose prisoner Crawford was. Alder was dwelling at the Mackachack towns (see p. 299) when they were destroyed by Logan, in 1786; was in the attack on Fort Recovery, in 1794, (see p. 140,) and went on an expedition into "Kaintucky to steal horses" from the settlers.

Alder remained with the Indians until after Wayne's treaty, in 1795. He was urged by them to be present on the occasion, to obtain a reservation of land, which was to be given to each of the priscners; but, ignorant of its importance, he neglected going, and lost the land. Peace having been restored, Alder says, "I could now lie down without fear, and rise up and shake hands with both the Indian and the white man."

The summer after the treaty, while living on Big Darby, Lucas Sullivant (see p. 168) made his appearance in that region, surveying land, and soon became on terms of intimacy with Alder, who related to him a history of his life, and generously gave him the piece of land on which he dwelt; but there being some little difficulty about the title, Alder did not contest, and so lost it.

When the settlers first made their appearance on Darby, Alder could scarcely speak a word of English. He was then about 24 years of age, 15 of which had been passed with the Indians. Two of the settlers kindly taught him to converse in English. He had taken up with a squaw for a wife some time previous, and now began to farm like the whites. He kept hogs, cows and horses, sold milk and butter to the Indians, horses and pork to the whites, and accumulated property. He soon was able to hire white laborers, and being dissatisfied with his squaw—a cross, peevish woman—wished to put her aside, get a wife from among the settlers, and live like them. Thoughts too, of his mother and brothers, began to obtrude, and the more he reflected, his desire strengthened to know if they were living, and to see them once more. He made inquiries for them, but was at a loss to know how to begin, being ignorant of the name of even the state in which they were. When talking one day with John Moore, a companion of his, the latter questioned him where he was from. Alder replied that he was taken prisoner somewhere near a place called Greenbriar, and that his people lived by a lead mine, to which he used frequently to go to see the hands dig ore. Moore then asked him if he could recollect the names of any of his neighbors. After a little reflection, he replied, "Yes! a family of Gulions that lived close by us." Upon this, Moore dropped his head, as if lost in thought, and muttered to himself, "Gulion! Gulion!" and then raising up, replied, "My father and myself were out in that country, and we stopped at their house over one night, and if your people are living, I can find them."

Mr. Moore after this went to Wythe county, and inquired for the family of Alder; but without success, as they had removed from their former residence. He put up advertisements in various places, stating the facts, and where Alder was to be found, and then returned. Alder now abandoned all hopes of finding his family, supposing them to be dead. Some time after, he and Moore were at Franklinton, when he was informed there was a letter for him in the post office. It was from his brother Paul, stating that one of the advertisements was put up within six miles of him, and that he got it the next day. It contained the joyful news, that his mother and brothers were alive.

Alder, in making preparations to start for Virginia, agreed to separate from his Indian wife, divide the property equally, and take and leave her with her own people at Sandusky. But some difficulty occurred in satisfying her. He gave her all the cows, 14 in number, worth $20 each, 7 horses, and much other property, reserving to himself only 2 horses and the swine. Besides these, was a small box, about 6 inches long, 4 wide and 4 deep, filled with silver, amounting probably to about $200, which he intended to take, to make an equal division. But to this she objected, saying the box was hers before marriage, and she would not only have it, but all it contained. Alder says, "I saw I could not get it without making a fuss, and probably having a fight, and told her that if she would promise never to trouble nor come back to me, she might have it; to which she agreed."

Moore accompanied him to his brother's house, as he was unaccustomed to travel among the whites. They arrived there on horseback, at noon, the Sunday after new years. They walked up to the house and requested to have their horses fed, and pretending they were entire strangers, inquired who lived there. "I had concluded," says Alder, "not to make myself known for some time, and eyed my brother very close, but did not recollect his features. I had always thought I should have recognized my mother, by a mole on her face. In the corner sat an old lady, who I supposed was her, although I could not tell, for when I was taken by the Indians her head was as black as a crow, and now it was almost perfectly white. Two young women were present, who eyed me very close, and I heard one of them whisper to the other, "he looks very much like Mark," (my brother.) I saw they were about to discover me, and accordingly turned my chair around to my brother, and said, "You say your name is Alder?" "Yes," he replied, "my name is Paul Alder." "Well," I rejoined, "my name is Alder too." Now it is hardly necessary to describe our feelings at that time; but they were very different from those I had when I was taken prisoner, and saw the Indian coming with my brother's scalp in his hand, shaking off the blood.

"When I told my brother that my name was Alder, he rose to shake hands with me, so overjoyed that he could scarcely utter a word, and my old mother ran, threw her arms around me, while tears rolled down her cheeks. The first words she spoke, after she grasped me in her arms, were, "How you have grown!" and then she told me of a dream she had. Says she, "I dreamed that you had come to see me, and that you was a little *onorary* [mean] looking fellow, and I would not own you for my son; but now I find I was mistaken, that it is entirely the reverse, and I am proud to own you for my son." I told her I could remind her of a few circumstances that she would recollect, that took place before I was made captive. I then related various things, among which was that the negroes, on passing our house on Saturday evenings, to spend Sundays with their wives, would beg pumpkins of her, and get her to roast them for them against their return on Monday morning. She recollected these circumstances, and said she had now no doubt of my being her son. We passed the balance of the day in agreeable conversation, and I related to them the history of my captivity, my fears and doubts, of my grief and misery the first year after I was taken. My brothers at this time were all married, and Mark and John had moved from there. They were sent for, and came to see me; but my half brother John had moved so far, that I never got to see him at all."

This county was first settled by the whites in 1796. In the fall of 1795, Benjamin Springer came from Kentucky, selected some land about a mile north of Amity, on the west bank of Big Darby, which stream was named by the Indians, from a Wyandot chief named Darby, who for a long time resided upon it, near the line of this and Union counties. Springer having made a clearing and built a cabin, moved his family to the place in the spring of 1796. The next year, William Lapin, Joshua and James Ewing settled in the same neighborhood. The last named is now living.

Springer settled near Alder, and taught him the English language, which much endeared the latter to him. He reciprocated this benefit, by not only supplying him with meat, but others of the early settlers, who, had it not been for him, would have been in danger of starvation. He also, on different occasions, saved some of the settlers from being killed by the Indians.

In 1800, Mr. Joshua Ewing brought four sheep to his place, which were strange animals to the Indians. One day an Indian was passing by, when the dog of the latter caught one of the sheep, and Ewing shot him. The Indian would have shot Ewing in retaliation, had not Alder, who was present, with much difficulty prevailed upon him to refrain.

On the outbreak of hostilities, in 1812, the Indian chiefs held a council, and sent a deputation to Alder, to learn which side to espouse, saying that the British wished them to go and fight for them, holding out the promise that in such case they would support their families. He advised them to remain at first neutral, and told them they need not be afraid of the Americans harming their women and children. They followed the advice, for a while remained neutral, and eventually became warm friends of the Americans.

Deer Creek, in this county, was so called by the Indians, because of the many deer that used to frequent it to eat the moss that grew plentifully upon its banks. It was considered by the Indians the best hunting ground for deer in this whole region of country.

The first court in this county was held in a cabin, Judge Thompson, of Chillicothe, presiding. The grand jury retired to deliberate to an oak and hazle thicket that stood near. The principal business, for the first year or two, was to try men for fighting.

View in London.

London, the county seat, is 25 miles westerly from Columbus. It was laid off in 1810 or '11, as seat of justice, by Patrick M'Lene, by order of the commissioners; and by the autumn of 1812 had six or eight families. The view shows on the left the court house, and in the distance the academy. London contains 1 Presbyterian and 1 Methodist church, a classical academy, 1 newspaper printing office, 8 stores, and about 400 inhabitants. By the census of 1840, its population was 297.

West Jefferson, on the national road, 14 miles w. of Columbus, and 10 from London, has a Baptist church, an academy, 3 stores, and about 45 dwellings. At an early day, a fort or block house was built on the east bank of the Little Darby, about 20 rods south of where the national road crosses the creek, near the village.

Lafayette, 7 miles w. of Jefferson, on the national road, has about 30 dwellings. Mount Sterling, Midway, Solon and Summerford, are small places.

MAHONING.

Mahoning was formed from Trumbull and Columbiana, March 1st, 1846. It derived its name from Mahoning river. The name Mahoning is, according to Heckwelder, derived from either the Indian word *Mahoni*, signifying "a lick," or *Mahonink*, "at the lick."

The surface is rolling and the soil finely adapted to wheat and corn. Large quantities of the finer qualities of wool are raised. The valley of the Mahoning abounds in excellent bituminous coal, which is well adapted to the smelting of iron ore. Excellent iron ore is obtained in the Mahoning valley, and it is believed to be abundant. There are fifteen townships in the county ; the five southernmost, viz : Smith, Goshen, Greene, Beaver and Springfield, originally formed part of Columbiana, and the others, the southern part of Trumbull, the last of which are within the Western Reserve. The following is a list of the townships, with their population, in 1840.

Austintown,	1245	Coitsville,	1016	Milton,	1277
Beaver,	1973	Ellsworth,	988	Poland,	1561
Berlin,	1284	Goshen,	1397	Smith,	2029
Boardman,	933	Green,	3212	Springfield,	1994
Canfield,	1280	Jackson,	1124	Youngstown,	999

Total population in 1840, within the present limits of Mahoning, 21,712, or 51 inhabitants to the square mile.

The following sketch from a resident of the county, not only describes interesting incidents in the life of one of the first settlers on the Reserve, but gives facts of importance connected with the history of this region.

Col. James Hillman, of Youngstown, was one of the pioneers of the west, and rendered essential service to the early settlers of the Western Reserve. He is still living, and at the age of 84 enjoys good health and spirits, and walks with as much elasticity of step as most men 30 years younger. He was born in Northampton, Pa., and in 1784, was a soldier under Gen. Harmar, and was discharged at Fort M'Intosh, at Beaver town, on the Ohio, in August, 1785, after the treaty with the Indians.

His acquaintance with the country, now known as the Western Reserve, commenced in the spring of 1786, at which time he entered into the service of Duncan & Wilson, of Pittsburgh. They were engaged in forwarding goods and provisions, upon pack-horses, across the country to the mouth of the Cuyahoga, (now Cleveland,) thence to be shipped on the schooner Mackinaw, to Detroit. During the summer of 1786, he made six trips,—the caravan consisting of ten men and ninety horses. They usually crossed the Big Beaver, 4 miles below the mouth of the Shenango, thence up the left bank of the Mahoning, crossing it about three miles above the village of Youngstown, thence by way of the Salt Springs, in the township of Weathersfield, through Milton and Ravenna, crossing the Cuyahoga at the mouth of Breakneck, and again at the mouth of Tinker's creek, in Bedford, and thence down the river to its mouth, where they erected a log hut for the safe keeping of their goods, which was the first house built in Cleveland. At the mouth of Tinker's creek were a few houses built by the Moravian missionaries. They were then vacant, the Indians having occupied them one year only, previous to their removal to the Tuscarawas river. These, and three or four cabins at the Salt Springs, were the only buildings erected by the whites between the Ohio river and Lake Erie. Those at the Salt Springs were erected for the accommodation of persons sent there to make salt, and the tenants were dispossessed during the summer of 1785, by order of Gen. Harmar. During this year, 1786, Kribs, who was left in one of the cabins to take care of goods belonging to Duncan & Wilson, was murdered by the Indians, and his body was found by Hillman's party, shockingly mangled by the wolves. During the same season, James Morrow and Sam Simerson, returning from Sandusky, were killed by the Indians, at Eagle creek, west of Cleveland. Mr. Hillman was married in 1786—and in 1788, settled at Beaver town, where Duncan & Wilson had a store for the purpose of trading with the Indians.

From 1788 to 1796, Mr. Hillman resided in Pittsburgh, and traded with the Indians in Ohio, principally on the Reserve, bringing his goods in canoes up the Mahoning. His intercourse with the Indians during these eight years and before, afforded him the opportunity of acquiring a knowledge of their language, and gaining their confidence, both of which he obtained, and by means of which, he was enabled afterwards to be of great service to the early settlers of the Reserve.

In 1796, when returning from one of his trading expeditions, alone in his canoe, down the Mahoning river, he discovered a smoke on the bank, near the present site of the village of Youngstown, and on proceeding to the spot, he found Mr. Young, (the proprietor of the township,) who, with Mr. Wolcott, had just arrived to make a survey of his lands. The cargo of Mr. Hillman was not entirely disposed of, there remaining among other things some whiskey, the price of which was to the Indians, $1,00 a quart, in the currency of the country, a deer skin being a legal tender for one dollar, and a doe skin half a dollar. Mr. Young proposed purchasing a quart, and having a frolic on its contents during the evening, and insisted upon paying Hillman his customary price for it. Hillman urged that inasmuch as they were strangers in the country, and just arrived upon his territory, civility required him to furnish the means of the entertainment. He however yielded to Mr. Young, who immediately took the deer skin he had spread for his bed, (the only one he had,) and paid for his quart of whiskey. His descendants in the state of New York, in relating the hardships of their ancestors, have not forgotten that Judge Young exchanged his *bed* for a quart of whiskey.

Mr. Hillman remained with them a few days, when they accompanied him to Beaver town, to celebrate the 4th of July, and Mr. H. was induced to return and commence the settlement of the town, by building a house. This was about the first settlement made on the Western Reserve. In the fall of 1797, Mr. Brown and another person came on. It was during this season that Uriah Holmes, of Litchfield county, Ct., and Titus Hayes, arrived in Youngstown the same day, both having started from Connecticut on the same day, the one taking the route through the state of New York, via Buffalo, and the other through Pennsylvania.

The settlement of the country proceeded prosperously until the murder of the two Indians, Capt. George and Spotted John, at the Salt Springs, by M'Mahon and Story. This affair had nearly proved fatal to the settlements, and probably would but for the efforts of Mr. Hillman. The next day after the murder, for such it undoubtedly was, Col. Hillman, with Mr. Young and the late Judge Pease, of Warren, who had just arrived, went to the Salt Springs, with a view of pacifying the Indians; but they had gone, not however without having buried the bodies of their murdered companions. Col. Hillman and others expected trouble, and in order to show the Indians that the whites did not sanction the act, judged it advisable to take M'Mahon and Story prisoners; which they accordingly did the same day, at Warren. Col. H. had M'Mahon in custody, but Story, who was guarded by John Lane, escaped during the night. On the next day, M'Mahon was brought to Youngstown, the settlers resolving to send him to Pittsburgh, to be kept in confinement until he could be tried. The affairs of the settlement, were at that time in a critical and alarming state, so much so, that all of the inhabitants, both of Youngstown and Warren, packed up their goods, and were upon the point of removing from the country, as they had every reason to apprehend that the Indians would take speedy vengeance. It was at this juncture, that the firmness and good sense of Col. Hillman was the means of saving the infant settlement from destruction. He advised sending a deputation to the Indians then encamped on the Mahoning, near where Judge Price's mills now stand, and endeavor to avert the threatened danger. It was an undertaking imminently hazardous. Few men would have dared to go, and it is quite certain no other man in the settlement would have had any chance of success. He was acquainted with their language, and knew their principal men, and was aware that in his trading intercourse with them, he had acquired their confidence, and therefore felt no fear. Although urged to do so, he would not take any weapon of defence, but accompanied with one Randall, started very early the next morning, on his hazardous enterprize, and came in sight of the Indians before sunrise. The Indians, seventeen in number, were asleep, each with his gun and powder horn resting upon a forked stick at his head. Being in advance of Randall, he came within three rods of them before he was discovered. A squaw was the only one awake; she immediately gave the alarm, which started every warrior to his feet with gun in hand. But seeing Col. H. and his companion riding into their encampment without arms, and unsuspicious of treachery or harm, they dropped their guns and immediately gathered around their visitors.

Onondaga George, the principal man or chief, knew Hillman, and the late murder became the subject of a very earnest conversation; the chief exhibiting much feeling while talking about it. Hillman told him frankly the object of his visit, and talked freely of the affair, condemning M'Mahon, and assured him that M'Mahon was then on his way to Pittsburg, and should stand a trial for the murder he had committed. Nothing could be done, however, until Capt. Peters should arrive with his braves. They were then encamped farther up the river, near the present site of Deerfield, and were expected to arrive that day, a message having been sent for that purpose.

In the course of the day they came, the countenance of Capt. Peters, as soon as he saw a white man present, scowled with hatred, revenge and defiance. Hillman endeavored to pacify him, but with little effect. During the interview, a conversation was had between Captains George and Peters, in the Seneca language, in which Capt. George endeavored to persuade the other, that they ought to kill Hillman and Randall, and before the whites could unite in defence, dispatch them in detail. But Capt. George would not agree to it, unwilling that Hillman, to whom he had conceived a liking, should be killed. It was not known to either that Hillman was acquainted with the Seneca language, in which this conversation was held ; he was, however—and it may be conceived with what interest he listened to it. Hillman succeeded, after several attempts, in drawing Capt. Peters aside, and offered him a considerable sum, if he would go to Cuyahoga on some business for the whites. This *bribe*, it seems, had its desired effect. The Indians retired a short distance and held a consultation, during which Randall became so much alarmed, that he proposed that each should take his horse and endeavor to make his escape. Hillman would not go, but observing that the Indians had left their guns leaning upon two trees near by, told Randall to station himself, and if on their return, one of their number should be painted black, (which Hillman knew was their custom when one was to be killed,) then each should seize upon the guns, and sell his life as dearly as possible.

After a long time, however, they returned, Capt. Peters holding up a wampum belt with three strings, and saying that they had agreed to hold a council with the whites, on condition that *three* things should be done, as their wampum indicated. 1st. That George Foulk should act as interpreter ; 2d, that the council should be held within six days ; and 3d, that M'Mahon should be kept until the council. These things being agreed to, Hillman and Randall returned the same day to Youngstown, where they found all the inhabitants assembled, waiting in anxious suspense to learn the result of the expedition, and every preparation made for a sudden flight, in case it should have proved unsuccessful. Great was their joy on seeing Hillman and his companion arrive in safety, and telling what had been done.

The inhabitants immediately set themselves about making the necessary preparations for the council. On the day appointed, two Indians made their appearance, and were conducted by Mr. Hillman to the place prepared to hold their council. After the ceremony of smoking, commenced the speeches, and it was generally conceded that Captain Peters had the best of the argument, and throughout the whole of the consultation, showed a decided superiority over the whites opposed to him, in adroitness and force of argument, although our people had appointed three of their best men for that purpose, (the late Judge Pease, of Warren, and Gov. Huntington being of the number,) all of whom had prepared themselves for this encounter with Indian shrewdness. The result of the council was satisfactory to both parties ; that M'Mahon should be tried by a jury of his own color, according to the laws of his own country. There were about three hundred people present at the council, among whom was Mr. Hudson, of Portage county, and Mr. Ely, of Deerfield. Thus was tranquillity restored mainly through the instrumentality of Mr. Hillman, a service which was so highly appreciated by Ephraim Root, the agent of the Connecticut Land Company, that he agreed on the part of the company, that he would give him 100 acres of land ; the promise however was never redeemed.

Soon after, M'Mahon was sent out by order of Gov. St. Clair, under a strong guard, to abide his trial at a special court ordered for that purpose, to be held in Youngstown by the Judges, Return J. Meigs and Benjamin Ives. Gilman, Backus & Tod were attornies for the people ; and Mr. Simple, John S. Edwards and Benjamin Tappan for the prisoner. The court was attended by persons from a great distance, and it was generally believed, that many had come with a determination to rescue M'Mahon, in case he should be found guilty. He was, however, acquitted, principally upon the testimony of one Knox, who swore that M'Mahon *retreated* a step or two before he fired, which probably was not true, and was not believed by those who visited the spot on the day after the affair. Capt. Peters was upon the bench during the whole trial, and was satisfied that he had received a fair trial, and should, according to the laws of the whites, have been acquitted. As soon as Knox swore that M'Mahon *retreated* before he fired, Capt. Peters gave a characteristic " ugh," and whispered to Judge Meigs that the jury would acquit the prisoner.

Thus terminated this critical affair, after which the settlement increased with great rapidity, and Col. Hillman from that time has enjoyed the confidence and respect of his fellow citizens, twice expressed in electing him sheriff, under the territorial government, and in various other ways, and still lives respected and beloved by all.

Canfield, the county seat, is 166 miles NE. of Columbus and 16 S.

of Warren. It is on the main stage road from Cleveland to Pittsburgh, on a gentle elevation. It is a neat, pleasant village, embowered in trees and shrubbery, among which the Lombardy poplar stands conspicuous. It contained in 1846, 3 stores, a newspaper printing office, 1 Presbyterian, 1 Epis. 1 Met. 1 Congregational and 1 Lutheran church, and about 300 people. Since then the county buildings have been erected, and from being made the county seat, it will probably, by the time this reaches the eye of the reader, have nearly doubled in population and business importance.

Youngstown.

Youngstown is the largest and most flourishing town in Mahoning county, beautifully situated on the north bank of the Mahoning river, 65 miles from Pittsburgh, Penn., 9 miles from Canfield, the seat of justice, for the county of Mahoning, 14 from Warren, the county seat of Trumbull county, 30 from Ravenna, Portage county, and 27 from New Lisbon, Columbiana county. It contains about 1200 inhabitants, has 12 mercantile stores, 3 warehouses for receiving and forwarding goods and produce on the canal, 4 churches, 1 Presbyterian, 1 Episcopal Methodist, 1 Protestant Methodist and 1 Disciples. The Pennsylvania and Ohio canal passes through the village, and the products of the surrounding country are sent here for shipment. Few places in Ohio are more beautifully situated; few have greater facilities for manufacturing, or bid fairer to become places of wealth and importance. Bituminous coal and iron ore abound in the immediate vicinity of the village, and along the line of the canal, adequate, it is believed, to the wants of a large manufacturing place. Several of the coal banks are already opened and successfully and profitably worked. The mines of the Hon. David Tod, furnish about one hundred tons of coal per day, and those of Crawford, Camp & Co., about sixty; all of which have hitherto found a ready market at Cleveland for steamboat fuel. It has recently been ascertained that the coal in the valley of the

Mahoning, is well adapted, in its raw state, to the smelting of iron ore, and three furnaces similar to the English and Scotch furnaces, each capable of producing from sixty to one hundred tons of pig metal per week, have been erected in the township, and near to the village. A large rolling mill has been erected in the village, at which is made the various sizes of bar, rod and hoop iron, also sheet iron, nails and spikes. The "Youngstown Iron Company," and the "Eagle Iron and Steel Company," contemplate the erection of machinery for the purpose of making the T and H rails; and it is more than probable that the various rail roads now projected in Ohio and the adjoining states, will be supplied with rails from this point. In addition to the above, there is quite a number of small manufacturing establishments for making tin-ware, cloth, axes, wagons, buggies, &c., &c. The amount of capital invested in the manufacturing of iron, is probably $200,000.

The view given was taken from the southeast, a few hundred yards to the left of the road leading to Pittsburgh, and near the residence of Mr. Homer Hine, shown on the right. In front appears the canal and Mahoning river: on the left the rolling mill of the Youngstown iron company. In the distance a part of the town is shown: the spires seen are respectively, commencing on the right, those of the Presbyterian, Disciples and Episcopal Methodist churches; near, on the left of the last named, appears the Protestant Methodist church.

Poland is 8 miles from Canfield, on Yellow creek, a branch of the Mahoning. It is one of the neatest villages in the state. The dwellings are usually painted white, and have an air of comfort. Considerable business centers here from the surrounding country, which is fertile. In the vicinity is coal and iron ore of an excellent quality. Limestone of a superior kind abounds in the township: it is burnt and largely exported for building purposes and manure. Poland contains 5 stores, 1 Presbyterian and 1 Methodist church, an academy, an iron foundery, 1 grist, 1 saw, 1 oil and 1 clothing mill, and about 100 dwellings.

In a tamarack and cranberry swamp in this vicinity, "are found large numbers of a small black, or very dark brown, rattle-snake, about 12 or 14 inches in length, and of a proportionate thickness. They have usually three or four rattles. This species seem to be confined to the tamarack swamps, and are found no where else but in their vicinities, wandering in the summer months a short distance only from their borders. When lying basking in the sun, they resemble a short, dirty, broken stick or twig, being generally discolored with mud, over which they are frequently moving. Their bite is not very venomous, yet they are much dreaded by the neighboring people. Their habitations are retired and unfrequented, so that few persons are ever bitten. The Indian name for this snake is *Massasauga*."

At Lowell, 4 miles E. from Poland, on the canal and Mahoning river, is the extensive furnace of Wilkinson, Wilkes & Co.; 2 miles northerly, on the same stream, is a furnace of the Great Western Iron Company. Ellsworth, 5 miles W. of Canfield, has 2 stores, 2 churches, about 35 dwellings and an excellent academy, under the supervision of the Methodists. Austintown and Fredericksburg are small places in the northern part of the county. The following are villages formerly within Columbiana county. To some of them is attached their population, as in the census of 1840: Petersburg 187, Lima 129, N. Middletown 118, Green Village 351, Lewistown 79, N. Springfield 89, New Albany 52, Birmingham and Princeton.

MARION.

Marion was organized March 1st, 1824, and named from General Francis Marion, of South Carolina, a partisan officer of the revolution. The surface is level, except on the extreme east. The Sandusky plains, which is prairie land, covers that part of the county north of Marion and west of the Whetstone, and is well adapted to grazing: the remaining part, comprising about two-thirds of the surface, is best adapted to wheat. The soil is fertile. The principal farm-crops are corn, wheat and grass, a large proportion of the prairie land being appropriated to grazing: much live stock and wool is produced in the county: some of the flocks of sheep contain about 5000 head. The following is a list of the townships in 1840, with their population.

Big Island,	554	Grand Prairie,	716	Richland,	1138
Bowling Green,	324	Green Camp,	361	Salt Creek.	607
Canaan,	1027	Marion,	1638	Scott,	854
Claridon,	1084	Montgomery,	552	Tully,	870
Gilead,	1150	Morven,	976	Washington,	880
Grand,	605	Pleasant,	1414		

The population of Marion, in 1830, was 6558, and in 1840, 18,352, or 35 inhabitants to the square mile.

By the treaty concluded at the foot of the Maumee rapids, Sept. 29th, 1817, Lewis Cass and Duncan M'Arthur being commissioners on the part of the United States, there was granted to the Delaware Indians a reservation of three miles square, on or near the northern boundary of this county, and adjoining the Wyandot reservation of twelve miles square. This reservation was to be equally divided among the following persons: Captain Pipe, Zeshauau or James Armstrong, Mahautoo or John Armstrong, Sanoudoyeasquaw or Silas Armstrong, Teorow or Black Raccoon, Hawdorouwatistie or Billy Montour, Buck Wheat, William Dondee, Thomas Lyons, Johnny Cake, Captain Wolf, Isaac and John Hill, Tishatahoones or widow Armstrong, Ayenucere, Hoomaurou or John Ming, and Youdorast. Some of these Indians had lived at Jeromeville, in Ashland, and Greentown, in Richland county, which last village was burnt by the whites early in the late war. By the treaty concluded at Little Sandusky, August 3d, 1829, John M'Elvain being United States commissioner, the Delawares ceded this reservation to the United States for $3000, and removed west of the Mississippi.

Marion, the county seat, is 44 miles north of Columbus. It was laid out in 1821, by Eber Baker and Alexander Holmes, who were proprietors of the soil. It is compactly built; the view, taken in front of the Marion hotel, shows one of the principal streets: the court-house appears on the left, the Mirror office on the right, and

View in Marion.

Berry's hill in the distance. General Harrison passed through this region in the late war, and encamped with his troops just south of the site of the village, on the edge of the prairie, at a place known as "Jacob's well." The town is improving steadily, and has some fine brick buildings: it contains 1 Presbyterian, 1 Methodist and 1 German church, an academy, 2 newspaper printing offices, 15 dry goods, 1 drug and 5 grocery stores, 1 saw, 1 fulling, oil and carding mill, and about 800 inhabitants: in 1840 it had a population of 570.

Mount Gilead, 18 miles SE. of Marion, is a flourishing village, containing 2 churches, several stores, 2 or 3 mills, and about 400 inhabitants. Iberia, Caledonia, Cardington, Le Timbreville, Denmark, Big Island, Claridon and Holmesville, are small villages.

MEDINA.

Medina was formed February 18th, 1812, "from that part of the Reserve west of the 11th range, south of the numbers 5, and east of the 20th range, and attached to Portage county, until organized." It was organized in April, 1818. The county was settled principally from Connecticut, though within the last few years there has been a considerable accession of Germans. The surface is generally rolling, with much bottom land of easy tillage: the soil is principally clay and gravelly loam—the clayey portion scantily watered, the gravelly abundantly. The soil is better adapted to grass than grain. The principal productions are wheat, hay, wool, corn, oats, barley, butter and cheese. The following is a list of the townships in 1840, with their population.

Brunswick,	1110	Homer,	660	Sharon,	1314
Chatham,	555	Lafayette,	938	Spencer,	551
Granger,	954	Litchfield,	787	Wadsworth,	148[illegible]
Guilford,	1402	Liverpool,	1502	Westfield,	1031
Harrisville,	1256	Medina,	1435	York,	782
Hinckley,	1287	Montville,	915		

The population of Medina, in 1820, was 3090; in 1830, 7560, and in 1840, 18,360, or 43 inhabitants to the square mile.

The first regular settlement in the county, was made at Harrisville, on the 14th of February, 1811, by Joseph Harris, Esq., who removed from Randolph, Portage county, with his family, consisting of his wife and one child. The nearest white people were at Wooster, 17 miles distant.

The first trail made through the county north, toward the lake, was from Wooster, a short time after the declaration of war with Great Britain. The party consisted of George Poe, (son of Adam, see page 106,) Joseph H. Larwill and Roswell M. Mason. They carried their provision in packs, and laid out the first night on their blankets, in the open air, on the south side of "the big swamp." It was amusing, as they lay, to listen to the howling of the wolves, and hear the raccoons catch frogs and devour them, making, in their mastication, a peculiar and inimitable noise, which sounded loud in the stillness of the night. In the course of the evening, they heard bells of cattle north of them, and in the morning, discovered the settlement of Mr. Harris. From thence they proceeded down to the falls of Black river, at what is now Elyria, and at the mouth of the stream found a settler, named Read, whose habitation, excepting that of Mr. Harris, was the only one between there and Wooster.

In the June following Mr. Harris's arrival, he was joined by Russel Burr and George Burr and family, direct from Litchfield, Conn. In the summer after, on the breaking out of the war, Messrs. Harris and Burr removed their families, for a few months, to Portage county, from fear of the Indians, and returned themselves in October, to Harrisville. The following winter, provision was carried from the Middlebury mills, by the residence of Judge Harris, to Fort Stephenson, his cabin being the last on the route. The season is adverted to by the old settlers as "the cold winter." Snow lay to the depth of 18 inches, from the 1st of January to the 27th of February, during which the air was so cold that it did not diminish an inch in depth, during the whole time.

An Indian trail from Sandusky to the Tuscarawas, passed by the residence of Mr. Harris. It was a narrow, hard-trodden bridle-path. In the fall, the Indians came upon it from the west, to this region, remained through the winter to hunt, and returned in the spring, their horses laden with furs, jerked venison and bear's oil, the last an extensive article of trade. The horses were loose, and followed each other in single file. It was not uncommon to see a single hunter returning with as many as twenty horses laden with his winter's work, and usually accompanied by his squaw and pappooses, all mounted. The Indians often built their wigwams in this vicinity, near water, frequently a dozen within a few rods. They were usually made of split logs or poles, covered with bark. Some of the chiefs had theirs made of flags, which they rolled up and carried with them. The Indians were generally very friendly with the settlers, and it was rare to find one deficient in mental acuteness.

In the fall of the same year that Mr. Harris settled at Harrisville, William Litey, a native of Ireland, with his family, settled in Bath township, on or near the border of Portage county. In the winter of 1815, after the close of the war, the settlements began to increase. Among the early settlers, are recollected the names of Esquire Van Heinen, Zenas Hamilton, Rufus Ferris, James Moore, the Ingersoll's, Jones's, Sibley's, Frieze's, Root's, Deming's, Warner, Hoyt, Dean and Durham.

It was not uncommon for the early settlers on the Reserve, to collect from several townships, in numbers from two to five hundred, and engage in "*a grand hunt.*" But so many accidents happened —one man being killed and others wounded, by shooting across the corners—arising from the want of discipline, and the difficulty of restraining the men in their eagerness—that the custom fell into disrepute. We annex a description of the method of conducting these hunts, from a sketch of Tallmadge, by Charles Whittlesey, Esq.

A large tract of wild land, the half or fourth of a township, was surrounded by lines of men, with such intervals that each person could see or hear those next him, right and left. The whole acted under the command of a captain, and at least four subordinates, who were generally mounted. At a signal of tin horns or trumpets, every man advanced in line towards the center, preserving an equal distance from those on either hand, and making as much noise as practicable. From the middle of each side of the exterior line, a blazed line of trees was previously marked to the center as a guide, and one of the sub-officers proceeded along each as the march progressed. About a half or three-fourths of a mile from the central point, a ring of blazed trees was made, and a similar one at the ground of meeting, with a diameter at least equal to the greatest rifle range. On arriving at the first ring, the advancing lines halted till the commandant made a circuit, and saw the men equally distributed and all gaps closed. By this time, a herd of deer might be occasionally seen driving in affright from one line to another. At the signal, the ranks move forward to the second ring, which is drawn around the foot of an eminence, or the margin of an open swamp or lake. Here, if the drive has been a successful one, great numbers of turkeys may be seen flying among the trees away from the spot. Deer, in flocks, sweeping around the ring, under an incessant fire, panting and exhausted. When thus pressed, it is difficult to detain them long in the ring. They become desperate, and make for the line at full speed. If the men are too numerous and resolute to give way, they leap over their heads, and all the sticks, pitch-forks and guns raised to oppose them. By a concert of the regular hunters, gaps are sometimes made purposely to allow them to escape. The wolf is now seen skulking through the bushes, hoping to escape observation by concealment. If bears are driven in, they dash through the brush in a rage from one part of the field to another, regardless of the shower of bullets playing upon them. After the game appears to be mostly killed, a few good marksmen and dogs scour the ground within the circle, to stir up what may be concealed or wounded. This over, they advance again to the center with a shout, dragging along the carcasses which have fallen, for the purpose of making a count. It was at the hunt in Portage, that the bears were either exterminated or driven away from this vicinity. It embraced the "Perkins' Swamp" and several smaller ones, rendered passable by ice. At the close of this "*drive,*" *twenty-six* were brought to the center ground, and others reported.

Medina, the county seat, is on the stage road from Cleveland to Columbus, 28 miles from the first and 117 from the latter. It was originally called Mecca—and is so marked on the early maps of Ohio—from the Arabian city famous as the birth-place of Mahomet.

The Public Square, Medina.

It was afterwards changed to its present name, being the seventh place on the globe of that name. The others are *Medina*, a town of Arabia Deserta, celebrated as the burial-place of Mahomet; *Medina*, the capital of the kingdom of Woolly, West Africa; *Medina*, a town and fort on the island of Bahrein, near the Arabian shore of the Persian gulf; *Medina*, a town in Estremadura, Spain; *Medina*, Orleans county, N. Y., and *Medina*, Lenawee county, Michigan.

On the organization of the county, in 1818, the first court was held in a barn, now standing half a mile north of the court house. The village was laid out that year, and the next season a few settlers moved in. The township had been previously partially settled. In 1813, Zenas Hamilton moved into the central part, with his family, from Danbury, Conn. His nearest neighbor was some eight or ten miles distant. Shortly after came the families of Rufus Ferris, Timothy Doane, Lathrop Seymour, James Moore, Isaac Barnes, Joseph Northrop, Friend Ives, Abijah Mann, James Palmer, William Painter, Frederick Appleton, etc. etc.

Rev. Roger Searle, an Episcopalian, was the first clergyman, and the first church was in the eastern part of the township, where was then the most population. It was a log structure, erected in 1817. One morning all the materials were standing, forming a part of the forest, and in the afternoon, Rev. Mr. Searle preached a sermon in the finished church. From an early day, religious worship in some form was held in the township on the Sabbath. The men brought their families to "meeting" in ox-teams, in which they generally had an axe and an augur, to mend their carts in case of accidents, the roads being very bad. The first wedding was in March, 1818, at which the whole settlement were present. When the ceremony and rejoicings were over, each man lighted his flambeau of hickory bark, and made his way home through the forest. The early settlers got their meal ground at a log mill at Middlebury; although but about 20 miles distant, the journey there and back occupied five days. They had only ox-teams, and the rough roads they cut through the woods, after being passed over a few times, became impassable from mud, compelling them to continually open new ones.

Owing to the want of a market, the products of agriculture were very low. Thousands of bushels of wheat could at one time be bought for less than 25 cents per bushel, and cases occurred where 10 bushels were offered for a single pound of tea, and refused. As an example: Mr. Joel Blakeslee, of Medina, about the year 1822, sowed 55 acres in wheat, which he only could sell by bartering with his neighbors. He fed out most of it in bundles to his cattle and swine. All that he managed to dispose of for cash, was a smal quantity sold to a traveller, at 12½ cents per bushel, as feed for his horse. Other products were in proportion. One man brought an ox-wagon filled with corn from Granger, eight miles distant, which he gladly exchanged for three yards of satinet for a pair of pantaloons. It was not until the opening of the Erie canal, that the settlers had a market. From that time, the course of prosperity has been onward. The early settlers, after wearing out their woollen pantaloons, were obliged to have them seated and kneed with buckskin, in which attire they attended church. It was almost impossible to raise wool, in consequence of the abundance of wolves, who destroyed the sheep.

The view given on the annexed page of the public square in Medina, was taken from the steps of the new court house: the old court house and the Bap. ch. are seen on the right. The village contains 1 Presbyterian, 1 Episcopal, 1 Baptist, 1 Free Will Baptist, 1 Methodist and 1 Universalist church, 7 dry goods, 5 grocery, 1 book and 2 apothecary stores, 1 newspaper printing office, 1 woollen and 1 axe factory, 1 flouring mill, 1 furnace, and had in 1840, 655 inhabitants, since which it has increased.

Seville, 9 miles s. of Medina, has 4 stores, 1 woollen factory, 3 churches, and about 300 inhabitants. There are other small villages in the county, containing more or less stores and churches, and from 30 to 50 dwellings each: they are, Harrisville, Brunswick, Litchfield and Wadsworth, at the last of which is a fine academy for both sexes.

MEIGS.

Meigs, named from Return J. Meigs, elected governor of Ohio in 1810, was formed from Gallia and Athens, April 1st, 1819, and the courts were directed "to be temporarily held at the meeting-house in Salisbury township." The surface is broken and hilly. In the west, a portion of the soil is a dark, sandy loam, but the general character of the soil is clayey. Considerable quantities of corn, oats, wheat, hay and potatoes are raised and exported. Excepting Morgan and Athens, more salt is made in this than in any other county in Ohio: in 1840, 47,000 bushels were produced. The following is a list of the townships in 1840, with their population.

Bedford,	566	Letart,	640	Salem,	940
Chester,	1479	Olive,	746	Salisbury,	1507
Columbia	674	Orange,	836	Scipio,	941
Lebanon,	621	Rutland,	1412	Sutton,	1099

The population of Meigs, in 1820, was 4,480, in 1830, 6,159, and in 1840, 11,455; or 25 inhabitants to a square mile.

The mouth of Shade river, which empties into the Ohio, in the upper part of the county, is a gloomy, rocky place, formerly called "the Devil's hole." The Indians, returning from their murderous incursions into western Virginia, were accustomed to cross the Ohio at that point with their prisoners and plunder, follow up the valley of Shade river on their way to their towns on the Scioto.

The first settlers of the county were principally of New England origin, and emigrated from Washington county, which lies above. From one of these, now residing in the county, we have received a communication illustrating pioneer life.

People who have spent their lives in an old settled country, can form but a faint idea of the privations and hardships endured by the pioneers of our now flourishing and prosperous state. When I look on Ohio as it is, and think what it was in 1802, when I first settled here, I am struck with astonishment, and can hardly credit my own senses. When I emigrated, I was a young man, without any property, trade or profession, entirely dependent on my own industry for a living. I purchased 60 acres of new land on credit, 2½ miles from any house or road, and built a camp of poles 7 by 4 feet, and 5 high, with three sides, and a fire in front. I furnished myself with a loaf of bread, a piece of pickled pork, some potatoes, borrowed a frying-pan and commenced housekeeping. I was not hindered from my work by company; for the first week, I did not see a living soul, but, to make amends for the want of it, I had every night a most glorious concert of wolves and owls. I soon (like Adam) saw the necessity of a help-mate, and persuaded a young woman to tie her destiny to mine. I built a log-house, 20 feet square—quite aristocratic in those days—and moved into it. I was fortunate enough to possess a jack-knife; with that I made a wooden knife and two wooden forks, which answered admirably for us to eat with. A bedstead was wanted; I took two round poles for the posts, inserted a pole in them for a side rail, two other poles were inserted for the end pieces, the ends of which were put in the logs of the house—some puncheons were then split and laid from the side rail to the crevice between the logs of the house, which formed a substantial bed-cord, on which we laid our straw bed—the only bed we had—on which we slept as soundly and woke as happy as Albert and Victoria.

In process of time, a yard and a half of calico was wanted; I started on foot through the woods ten miles, to Marietta, to procure it; but, alas! when I arrived there I found that, in the absence of both money and credit, the calico was not to be obtained. The dilemma was a serious one, and how to escape I could not devise; but I had no sooner informed my wife of my failure, than she suggested that I had a pair of thin pantaloons, which I could very well spare, that would make quite a decent frock: the pants were cut up, the frock made, and in due time the child was dressed.

The long winter evenings were rather tedious, and in order to make them pass more smoothly, by great exertion, I purchased a share in the Belpre library, 6 miles distant. From this I promised myself much entertainment, but another obstacle presented itself—I had no candles; however, the woods afforded plenty of pine knots—with these I made torches, by which I could read, though I nearly spoiled my eyes. Many a night have I passed in this manner till 12 or 1 o'clock reading to my wife, while she was hatchelling, carding or spinning. Time rolled on, the payments for my land became due, and money, at that time, in Ohio, was a *cash article:* however, I did not despair. I bought a few steers: some I bartered for, and others I got on credit—my credit having somewhat improved since the calico expedition—slung a knapsack on my back, and started alone with my cattle for Romney, on the Potomac, where I sold them, then travelled on to Litchfield, Connecticut, paid for my land, and had just $1 left to bear my expenses home, 600 miles distant. Before I returned, I worked and procured 50 cents in cash; with this and my dollar I commenced my journey homeward. I laid out my dollar for cheap haircombs, and these, with a little Yankee pleasantry, kept me very comfortably at the private houses where I stopped till I got to Owego, on the Susquehanna, where I had a power of attorney to collect some money for a neighbor in Ohio.

I might proceed and enumerate scenes without number similar to the above, which have passed under my own observation, or have been related to me by those whose veracity I have no reason to doubt; but from what I have written, you will be able to perceive that the path of the pioneer is not strewed with roses, and that the comforts which many of our inhabitants now enjoy have not been obtained without persevering exertions, industry and economy. What, let me ask, would the young people of the present day think of their future prospects, were they now to be placed in a similar situation to mine in 1803? How would the young miss, taken from the fashionable, modern parlor, covered with Brussels carpets, and ornamented with pianos, mirrors, &c., &c., manage her spinning wheel, in a log-cabin, on a puncheon floor, with no furniture except, perhaps, a bake-oven and a splint broom?

Pomeroy, the county seat, is on the Ohio river, 76 miles in a direct line SE. of Columbus, 80 below Marietta, and 234 above Cincinnati. It is situated on a narrow strip of ground from 20 to 30 rods wide, under a lofty and steep hill, in the midst of wild and romantic scenery. It contains 1 Episcopal, 1 Methodist, 1 German Lutheran and 1 Presbyterian church; a newspaper printing office, 1 flouring and 2 saw mills, 2 founderies, 2 carding machines, 1 machine shop, 10 mercantile stores, and about 1600 inhabitants. It is a very flourishing town, deriving its importance principally from the coal mines situated here. We give below, in the language of a correspondent, an historical sketch of the village, with some notice of the coal mines.

The first settler within the limits of Pomeroy was Mr. Nathaniel Clark, who came about the year 1816. The first coal bank opened in Pomeroy was in 1819, by David Bradshaw. Bentley took 1200 bushels of coal to Louisville, and sold it for 25 cents a bushel, which was the first coal exported from Pomeroy. As early as 1805 or 6, there had been an attempt at exporting coal from Coalport, by Hoover and Cashell, but it proved unprofitable, and was abandoned after sending off one small load. About 1820, John Knight rented a large quantity of coal land from Gen. Putnam, at $20 a year, and commenced working the mines. On the 15th of July, 1825, Samuel Grant entered 80 acres, and Josiah Dill, 160 acres of Congress land, which lies in the upper part of Pomeroy. Subsequently, Mr. Dill laid out a few town lots on his land, but it did not improve to any extent until the Pomeroy improvement commenced, in 1833. In 1827, a post office was established here, called Nyesville, and Nial Nye appointed postmaster. In 1840, the town was incorporated, and in June, 1841, made the county seat.

In the spring of 1804, Samuel W. Pomeroy, an enterprizing merchant of Boston, Massachusetts, purchased of Elbridge Gerry, one of the original proprietors in the Ohio company, a full share of land in said company's purchase, the fraction of said share (262 acres) lying in the now town of Pomeroy. In 1832, Mr. Pomeroy put 1000 bushels of coal into boxes and shipped them on a flat boat for New Orleans, to be sent round to Boston; but the boat foundered before it left Coalport, and the expedition failed. In 1833, Mr. Pomeroy having purchased most of the coal land on the river for four miles, formed a company, consisting of himself, his two sons, Samuel W. Pomeroy, jr., and C. R. Pomeroy, and his sons-in-law, N. B. Horton and C. W. Dabney, under the firm of Pomeroy, Sons & Co., and began mining on a large scale. They built a steam saw-mill, and commenced building houses for themselves and their workmen. In 1834, they moved on, at which time there were 12 families in the town. In 1835, they built the steam tow-boat Condor, which could tow from four to six loaded boats or barges, and will tow back from 8 to 12 empty boats at a trip. It takes a week to perform a trip to Cincinnati and back, and she consumes 2000 bushels of coal each trip. The company employ about 25 boats or barges, that carry from 2000 to 11000 bushels of coal, each averaging, perhaps, 4000 bushels. The number of hands employed is about 200, and the number of bushels dug yearly about two millions; in addition to this, several individuals are engaged in the coal business, on a small scale. Five steamboats have been built in this place by the Pomeroy company.

The mining of coal is mostly done at Coalport, one mile below the corporation line. Here the company have laid out a town, and been at great expense to prepare every thing necessary for mining and exporting coal; the railways are so constructed, that the loaded car descending to the river draws up the empty one.

Immediately below Coalport is the town of Middleport, lately laid out by Philip Jones, which already contains several stores, and is building up fast. Adjoining Middleport is Sheffield, a pleasant town, which bids fair to become a place of business. In all probability, the time is not distant when the towns of Pomeroy, Coalport, Middleport and Sheffield will be one continuous village.

About the year 1791 or 2, Capt. Hamilton Carr, a noted spy in the service of the United States, in his excursions through these parts, discovered an enormous sycamore tree below the mouth of Carr's run, near where Murdock & Nyes's mill now stands, which was subsequently occupied as a dwelling house. Capt. Whitlock, of Coalport, informs me, that he himself measured that tree, and found the hollow to be 18 feet in diameter. Capt. Whitlock further states, that as late as 1821, he took dinner from the top of a sugar-tree stump, in a log-house near where the court-house now stands, the only table the people had in the house.

The view shown in the engraving was taken at the mines at Coalport, nearly two miles below the main village of Pomeroy. Here horizontal shafts are run into the hill, at an elevation of more than 100 feet above the river bed. The coal is carried out in cars on railways, and successively emptied from the cars on one grade to that below, and so on until the last cars in turn empty into the boats on the river, by which it is carried to market. The mining is conducted in a systematic manner, and most of those employed are natives of Wales, familiar with mining from youth.

"The coal strata dips to the north two or three feet in a hundred yards, requiring drains to free them from the water when opened on the south side of the hill. Above the coal is a deposit of shale and ash-colored marly clay, of eight or ten feet in thickness, which forms the roof of the mines—superincumbent on which is a deposit of stratified sand rock, rather coarse-grained, of nearly 100 feet in thickness. The shale abounds in fine fossil plants. In mining the coal, gunpowder is extensively used; a small charge throwing out large masses of coal. This coal, being of the black slaty structure, abounds in bituminous matter and burns very freely; its specific gravity is 1·27. Twenty grains of the coarse powder decompose 100 grains of nitrate of potash, which will give to this coal nearly 60 per cent. of charcoal. It must, therefore, be valuable for the manufacture of coke, an article that must ultimately be brought into use in the numerous furnaces along the great iron deposit, a few miles south and west of this place. It is a curious fact, that the coal deposits are very thin and rare near the Ohio river, from Pipe's creek, 15 miles below Wheeling, to Carr's run, in this county. As the main coal dips under the Ohio at both these places, the inference is, that the coal lies below the surface, and could readily be reached by a shaft, first ascertaining its distance from the surface by the operation of boring."*

Pomeroy Coal Mines.

Chester, 8 miles NE. of Pomeroy, on Shade river, was formerly the county seat: in 1840, it had 273 inhabitants. Rutland, 6 miles W. of Pomeroy, on Leading creek, is also a small village.

MERCER.

MERCER, named from Gen. Hugh Mercer, a Virginia officer who fell at Princeton, Jan. 3d, 1777, was formed from old Indian territory, April 1st, 1820. The land is flat, and much of it, while in the

* Dr. S. P. Hildreth, in the 29th volume of Silliman's Journal.

VIEW IN DAYTON.

On the left is shown the Montgomery County Court House—now being erected—the most costly and elegant in Ohio; the bridge across the Great Miami appears in the distance.

forest state, wet, but when cleared, very fertile, and well adapted to grass, small grain and Indian corn, which last is the principal production. The following is a list of the townships in 1840, with their population.

Black Creek,	340	Granville,	339	St. Mary's,	1515
Butter,	178	Jefferson,	368	Union,	566
Center,	1059	Marion,	1141	Washington,	214
Dublin,	705	Recovery,	298	Wayne,	377
German,	1499	Salem,	579		

The population of Mercer, in 1830, was 1737, and in 1840, 8277; or 16 inhabitants to the square mile.

Celina, the county seat, is in the heart of the county, on Wabash river. It is a new place, and does not contain at present over 100 dwellings. St. Mary's, formerly the county seat, is 10 miles E. and 105 NW. of Columbus. It lies on St. Mary's river and on the Miami extension canal, 67 miles N. of Dayton, and had, in 1840, 570 inhabitants. Each of these, with the improvement of the country, will probably be towns of importance.

St. Clair's battle was fought on the line of this and Darke county. The trace of Wayne is yet discernable through the county leading from Fort Recovery to Fort Adams, which last stood on the south bank of the St. Mary's, in the north part of the county, and about 12 miles east of the Indiana line.

In September, 1818, Hon. Lewis Cass and Hon. Duncan M'Arthur, commissioners on the part of the United States, made a treaty at St. Mary's with the Wyandots, Shawnees and Ottawas. In the following month, Messrs. Jennings, Cass and Parke, acting for the United States, made treaties at the same place with the Weas, Potawatomies, Delawares and Miamis.

The notorious Simon Girty at one time lived on the right bank of the St. Mary's, within the limits of the town of that name, between the river and canal. The spot on which his cabin is said to have stood, is marked by a depression. The old fort, St. Mary's, built by Wayne, stood in the village of St. Mary's, on the west bank of the river, on the lot now owned by Christian Benner, about 80 rods SE. of Rickley's tavern.

The last commander of Fort St. Mary's was Captain John Whistler. He was a soldier from his youth, came to America in Burgoyne's army, and was taken prisoner at Saratoga. He remained afterwards in the United States, entered the western army under St. Clair, and survived the disastrous defeat of Nov. 1791, at which time he acted as serjeant. In 1793, an order came from the war office, purporting that any non-commissioned officer who should raise 25 recruits, would receive the commission of an ensign. He succeeded in this way in obtaining the office, from which he rose to a captaincy, and commanded in succession Forts St. Mary's, Wayne and Dearborn, at Chicago. He built the latter without the aid of a horse or ox: the timber and materials were all hauled by the labor of the soldiers, their commander always at their head assisting. He could recruit more men and perform more labor than any other officer in the army. Age and hard service at length broke him down. He retired from the line of the army and received the appointment of military storekeeper at St. Louis, where he died about 20 years since.*

* Col. John Johnston.

The largest artificial lake, it is said, on the globe, is formed by the reservoir supplying the St. Mary's feeder of the Miami extension canal, from which it is situated three miles west. The reservoir is about nine miles long and from two to four broad. It is on the summit, between the Ohio and the lakes. About one half, in its natural

Artificial Lake.

state, was a prairie, and the remainder a forest. It was formed by raising two walls of earth, from ten to twenty-five feet high, called respectively the east and west embankment, the first of which is about two miles, and the last near four in length. These walls, with the elevation of the ground to the north and south, form a huge basin to retain the water. The reservoir was commenced in 1837, and completed in 1845, at an expense of several hundred thousand dollars. The west embankment was completed in 1843. The water filled in at the upper end to the depth of several feet, but as the ground rose gradually to the east, it overflowed for several miles to the depth of a few inches only. This vast body of water, thus exposed to the powerful rays of the sun, would, if allowed to have remained, have bred pestilence through the adjacent country. Moreover, whole farms that belonged to individuals, yet unpaid for by the state, were completely submerged. Under these circumstances, about 150 residents of the county turned out with spades and shovels, and by two days of industry, tore a passage for the water through the embankment. It cost several thousand dollars to repair the damage. Among those concerned in this affair were persons high in official station and respectability, some of whom here, for the first time, blistered their hands at manual labor. They were all liable to the state law making the despoiling of public works a penitentiary offence; but a grand jury could not be found in Mercer to find a bill of indictment.

The legislature, by a joint resolution, passed in 1837, resolved that no reservoir should be made for the public canals without the timber being first cleared: it was unheeded by officers in charge of this work. The trees were only girdled, and thus thousands of acres of most valuable timber, that would have been of great value to the commonwealth in building of bridges and other constructions on the public works, wantonly wasted.

The view of the reservoir was taken from the east embankment, and presents a singular scene. In front are dead trees and stumps scattered about, and the roofs of deserted cabins rising from the

Emlen Institute.

water. Beyond, a cluster of green prairie grass waves in the rippling waters, while to the right and left, thousands of acres of dead forest trees, with no sign of life but a few scattered willows bending in the water, combine to give an air of wintry desolation to the scene. The reservoir abounds in fish and wild fowl, while innumerable frogs make the air vocal with their bellowings. The water is only a few feet deep, and, in storms, the waves dash up 6 or 8 feet, and foam like an ocean in miniature. A few years since, a steamer, 25 feet in length, called "the Seventy-six," with a boiler of seventy gallons capacity, a pipe 4 feet in height, and commanded by Captain Gustavus Darnold, plied on its waters.

In the southern part of this county is a colony of colored people, amounting to several hundred persons. They live principally by agriculture, and own extensive tracts of land in the townships of Granville, Franklin and Mercer. They bear a good reputation for morality, and manifest a laudable desire for mental improvement. This settlement was founded by the exertions of Mr. Augustus Wattles, a native of Connecticut, who, instead of merely theorizing upon the evils which prevent the moral and mental advancement of the colored race, has acted in their behalf with a philanthropic, Christian-like zeal, that evinces he has their real good at heart. The history of this settlement is given in the annexed extract of a letter from him.

My early education, as you well know, would naturally lead me to look upon learning and good morals as of infinite importance in a land of liberty. In the winter of 1833–4, I providentially became acquainted with the colored population of Cincinnati, and found about 4,000 totally ignorant of every thing calculated to make good citizens. Most of them had been slaves, shut out from every avenue of moral and mental improvement. I started a school for them, and kept it up with 200 pupils for two years. I then proposed to the colored people to move into the country and purchase land, and remove from those contaminating influences which had so long crushed them in our cities and villages. They promised to do so, provided I would accompany them and teach school. I travelled through Canada, Michigan and Indiana, looking for a suitable location, and finally settled here, thinking this place contained more natural advantages than any other unoccupied country within my knowledge. In 1835, I made the first purchase for colored people in this county. In about three years, they owned not far from 30,000 acres. I had travelled into almost every neighborhood of colored people in the state, and laid before them the benefits of a permanent home for themselves and of education for their children. In my first journey through the state, I established, by the assistance and co-operation of abolitionists, 25 schools for colored children. I collected of the colored people such money as they had to spare, and entered land for them. Many, who had no money, afterwards succeeded in raising some, and brought it to me. With this I bought land for them.

I purchased for myself 190 acres of land, to establish a manual labor school for colored boys. I had sustained a school on it, at my own expense, till the 11th of November, 1842. Being in Philadelphia the winter before, I became acquainted with the trustees of the late Samuel Emlen, of New Jersey, a Friend. He left by his will $20,000, for the "support and education in school learning and the mechanic arts and agriculture, such colored boys, of African and Indian descent, whose parents would give them up to the institute." We united our means and they purchased my farm, and appointed me the superintendent of the establishment, which they call the Emlen Institute.

In 1846, Judge Leigh, of Virginia, purchased 3,200 acres of land in this settlement, for the freed slaves of John Randolph, of Roanoke. These arrived in the summer of 1846, to the number of about 400, but were forcibly prevented from making a settlement by a portion of the inhabitants of the county. Since then, acts of hostility have been commenced against the people of this settlement, and threats of greater held out, if they do not abandon their lands and homes.

MIAMI.

Miami was formed from Montgomery, January 16th, 1807, and Staunton made the temporary seat of justice. The word Miami, in the Ottawa language, is said to signify *mother*. The name *Miami*, was originally the designation of the tribe who anciently bore the name of "*Tewightewee*." This tribe were the original inhabitants of the Miami valley, and affirmed they were created in it. East of the Miami, the surface is gently rolling, and a large proportion of it a rich alluvial soil: west of the Miami, the surface is generally level, the soil a clay loam, and better adapted to small grain and grass than corn. The county abounds in excellent limestone, and has a large amount of water power. In agricultural resources, this is one of the richest counties in the state. The principal productions are wheat, corn, oats, hay, pork and flax-seed. The following is a list of the townships in 1840, with their population.

Bethel,	1586	Lost Creek,	1304	Spring Creek,	1501
Brown,	1230	Monroe,	1409	Staunton,	1231
Concord,	2408	Newburg,	1632	Union,	2221
Elizabeth,	1398	Newton,	1242	Washington,	2642

The population of Miami, in 1820, was 8851; in 1830, 12,807; and in 1840, 19,804, or 44 inhabitants to the square mile.

Prior to the settlement of Ohio, Gen. George Rogers Clarke led an expedition from Kentucky, against the Indians in this region, an account of which follows, from the reminiscences of Abraham Thomas, originally published in the Troy Times. This Mr. Thomas, it is said, cut the first sapling on the site of Cincinnati: he died only a few years since.

In the year 1782, after corn planting, I again volunteered in an expedition under General Clarke, with the object of destroying some Indian villages about Piqua, on the Great Miami river. On this occasion, nearly 1000 men marched out of Kentucky, by the route of Licking river. We crossed the Ohio at the present site of Cincinnati, where our last year's stockade had been kept up, and a few people then resided in log cabins. We proceeded immediately onward through the woods, without regard to our former trail, and crossed Mad river, not far from the present site of Dayton; we kept up the east side of the Miami, and crossed it about four miles below the Piqua towns. Shortly after gaining the bottom, on the west side of the river, a party of Indians on horseback, with their squaws, came out of a trace that led to some Indian villages near the present site of Granville. They were going on a frolic, or pow-wow, to be held at Piqua, and had with them a Mrs. M'Fall, who was some time before taken prisoner from Kentucky; the Indians escaped into the woods, leaving their women, with Mrs. M'Fall, to the mercy of our company. We took those along with us to Piqua, and Mrs. M'Fall returned to Kentucky. On arriving at Piqua, we found that the Indians had fled from the villages, leaving most of their effects behind. During the following night, I joined a party to break up an encampment of Indians, said to be lying about what was called the French store. We soon caught a Frenchman, tied him on horseback, for our guide, and arrived at the place in the night. The Indians had taken alarm and cleared out; we, however, broke up and burned the Frenchman's store, [Lorime's store, see Shelby county,] which had for a long time been a place of outfit for Indian marauders, and returned to the main body early in the morning, many of our men well stocked with plunder. After burning and otherwise destroying every thing about upper and lower Piqua towns, we commenced our return march.

In this attack, five Indians were killed during the night the expedition lay at Piqua; the Indians lurked around the camp, firing random shots from the hazel thickets, without doing us any injury; but two men, who were in search of their stray horses, were fired upon and severely wounded: one of these died shortly after, and was buried at what is now called "Coe's Ford," where we re-crossed the Miami, on our return. The other, Capt. M'Cracken, lived until we reached the site of Cincinnati, where he was buried. On this expedition, we had with us Capt. Barbee, afterwards Judge Barbee, one of my primitive neighbors in Miami county, Ohio, a most worthy and brave man, with whom I have hunted, marched and watched through many a long day, and finally removed with him to Ohio.

From the "Miami County Traditions," also published in the Troy Times, a few years since, we annex some reminiscences of the settlement of the county and its early settlers.

Among the first settlers who established themselves in Miami county, was John Knoop. He removed from Cumberland county, Penn., in 1797. In the spring of that year, he came down the Ohio to Cincinnati, and cropped the first season on Zeigler's stone house farm, four miles above Cincinnati, then belonging to John Smith. During the summer, he made two excursions into the Indian country, with surveying parties, and at that time selected the land he now owns and occupies. The forest was then full of Indians, principally Shawnees, but there were small bands of Mingoes, Delawares, Miamis and Potawatomies, peacefully hunting through the country. Early the next spring, in 1798, Mr. Knoop removed to near the present site of Staunton village, and in connection with Benjamin Knoop, Henry Garard, Benjamin Hamlet and John Tildus, established there a station for the security of their families. Mrs. Knoop, now living, there planted the first apple tree introduced into Miami county, and one is now standing in the yard of their house, raised from seed then planted, that measures little short of nine feet around it. * *

The inmates of a station in the county, called the Dutch station, remained within it for two years, during which time they were occupied in clearing and building on their respective farms. Here was born, in 1798, Jacob Knoop, the son of John Knoop, the first civilized native of Miami county. At this time, there were three young single men living at the mouth of Stoney creek, and cropping on what was afterwards called Freeman's prairie; one of these was D. H. Morris, a present resident of Bethel township; at the same time there resided at Piqua, Samuel Hilliard, Job Garard, Shadrac Hudson, Jonah Rollins, Daniel Cox, Thomas Rich and —— Hunter; these last named had removed to Piqua in 1797, and together with our company at the Dutch station, comprised all the inhabitants of Miami county, from 1797 to 1799. In the latter year, John, afterwards Judge Garard, Nathaniel and Abner Garard, and the year following, Uriah Blue, Joseph Coe and Abraham Hathaway joined us with their families. From that time, all parts of the county began to receive numerous immigrants. For many years, the citizens lived together on footings of the most social and harmonious intercourse—we were all neighbors to each other, in the Samaritan sense of the term—there were some speculators and property-hunters among us, to be sure, but not enough to disturb our tranquillity and general confidence. For many miles around we knew who was sick, and what ailed them, for we took a humane interest in the welfare of all. Many times were we called from six to eight miles to assist at a rolling or raising, and cheerfully lent our assistance to the task. For our accommodation, we sought the mill of Owen Davis, afterwards Smith's mill, on Beaver creek, a tributary of the Little Miami, some 27 miles distant. Our track lay through the woods, and two days were consumed in the trip, when we usually took two horse-loads. Owen was a kind man, considerate of his distant customers, and would set up all night to oblige them, and his conduct materially abridged our mill duties.

With the Indians, we lived on peaceable terms; sometimes, however, panics would spread among the women, which disturbed us a little, and occasionally we would have a horse or so stolen. But one man only was killed out of the settlement, from 1797 to 1811. This person was one Boyier, who was shot by a straggling party of Indians, supposed through mistake. No one, however, liked to trade with the Indians, or have any thing to do with them, beyond the offices of charity.

The country all around the settlement presented the most lovely appearance, the earth was like an ash-heap, and nothing could exceed the luxuriance of primitive vegetation; indeed, our cattle often died from excess of feeding, and it was somewhat difficult to rear them on that account. The white-weed or bee-harvest, as it is called, so profusely spread over our bottom and wood lands, was not then seen among us; the sweet annis, nettles, wild rye and pea-vine, now so scarce, every where abounded: they were almost the entire herbage of our bottoms; the two last gave subsistence to our cattle, and the first, with our nutritious roots, were eaten by our swine with the greatest avidity. In the spring and summer months, a drove of hogs could be scented at a considerable distance, from their flavor of the annis root. Our winters were as cold, but more steady than at present. Snow generally covered the ground, and drove our stock to the barn-yard, for three months, and this was all the trouble we had with them. Buffalo signs were frequently met with; but the animals had entirely disappeared before the first white inhabitant came into the country; but other game was abundant. As many as thirty deer have been counted at one time, around the bayous and ponds near Staunton. The hunter had his full measures of sport, when he chose to indulge in the chase; but ours was essentially an agricultural settlement. From the coon to the buck-skin embraced our circulating medium. Our imported commodities were first purchased at Cincinnati, then at Dayton, and finally, Peter Felix established an Indian merchandizing store at Staunton, and this was our first attempt in that way of traffick. For many years we had no exports but skins; yet wheat was steady at 50 cents, and corn at 25 cents per bushel; the latter, however, has since fallen as low as 12½ cents, and a dull market.

For some time, the most popular milling was at Patterson's, below Dayton, and with Owen Davis, on Beaver; but the first mill in Miami county is thought to have been erected by John Manning, on Piqua bend. Nearly the same time, Henry Garard erected on Spring creek, a corn and saw mill, on land now included within the farm of Col. Winans. It is narrated by the Colonel, and is a fact worthy of notice, that on the first establishment of these mills, they would run ten months in a year, and sometimes longer, by heads. The creek would not now turn one pair of stones two months in a year, and then only on the recurrence of freshets. It is thought this remark is applicable to all streams of the upper Miami valley, showing there is less spring drainage from the country, since it has become cleared of its timber, and consolidated by cultivation. * * * *

View in Troy.

Troy, the county seat, is a beautiful and flourishing village, in a highly cultivated and fertile country, upon the west bank of the Great Miami, 70 miles north of Cincinnati and 68 west of Columbus. It was laid out about the year 1808, as the county seat, which was first at Staunton, a mile east, and now containing but a few houses. Troy is regularly laid off into broad and straight streets, crossing each other at right angles, and contains about 550 dwellings. The view was taken in the principal street of the town, and shows, on the right, the court house and town hall, between which, in the distance, appear the spires of the New School Presbyterian and Episcopal churches. It contains 2 Presbyterian, 1 Episcopal Methodist, 1 Wesleyan do., 1 Episcopal and 1 Baptist church, a market, a branch of the state bank, 2 newspaper printing offices, 1 town and 1 masonic hall, 1 academy, 3 flouring and 5 saw mills, 1 foundery, 1 machine shop, 1 shingle and 1 plow factory, and a large number of stores and mechanic shops. Its population in 1840, was 1351; it has since more than doubled, and is constantly increasing. It is connected with Cincinnati, Urbana and Greenville, by turnpikes.

The line of the Miami canal, from Cincinnati, passes through the town from south to north; on it are six large and commodious warehouses, for receiving and forwarding produce and merchandize, and three more, still larger, are in progress of erection, and four smaller, for supplying boats with provisions and other necessaries. The business done during the current year, ending June 1st, 1847, in thirty of the principal business houses, in the purchase of goods.

produce and manufactures, amounts to $523,238, and the sales to $674,307. The articles bought and sold, are as follows: 174,000 bushels of wheat, 290,000 bushels of corn, 100,000 bushels of rye, barley and oats, 17,000 bbls. whiskey, 17,000 bbls. flour, 1,300 bbls. pork, 5,000 hogs, 31,000 lbs. butter, 2,000 bushels clover seed, 600 bbls. fish, 3,000 bbls. salt, 30,000 bushels flax seed, 304,000 lbs. bulk pork, 136,000 lbs. lard, 1,440 thousand feet of sawed lumber, &c. The shipments to and from the place, are about 20,000 tons.

There is an extensive hydraulic power here, not yet brought into use, which has recently been purchased by one of the most wealthy and enterprising citizens of the place, who is now maturing arrangements to bring it into immediate and extensive use, for manufacturing purposes.

View of Piqua.

Piqua is another beautiful and thriving town, 8 miles above Troy, and also on the river and canal. It was laid out in 1809, by Messrs. Brandon and Manning, under the name of Washington, which it bore for many years. The town plot contains an area of more than a mile square, laid out in uniform blocks, with broad and regular streets. On the north and east, and opposite the town, are the villages of Rossville and Huntersville, connected with it by bridges across the Miami.

It contains 1 New and 1 Old School Presbyterian, 1 Methodist Episcopal, 1 Methodist Wesleyan, 1 Episcopal, 1 Baptist, 1 Associate Reformed, 1 Lutheran, 1 Catholic and 1 Disciples church; 1 high school, a town hall, and a branch of the state bank. The manufacturing facilities in it and vicinity are extensive. The Miami furnishes power for 1 wool carding and fulling factory, 3 saw-mills, 1 grist mill adjacent to the town, and a saw and grist mill, with an oil mill, below the town. The water of the canal propels a saw mill, a clothing and fulling factory, with a grist mill. A steam saw mill, steam grist mill and tannery, with 2 steam iron turning and machine establishments, constitute, with the rest, the amount of steam and hydraulic power used. With these, are over 100 mechanical and manufacturing establishments in the town, among which are 25 coopers' shops—that business being very extensively carried on. There are also 15 grocery and variety stores, 12 dry goods, 3 leather, 1 book and 3 hardware stores, a printing office, 4 forwarding and 3 pork houses; and the exports and imports, by the canal, are very heavy. South of the town are seven valuable quarries of blue limestone, at which are employed a large number of hands, and adjacent to the town is a large boat yard.

In the town are 600 dwellings, many of which are of brick, and have fine gardens attached. Along the canal, has lately been erected a number of 3 story brick buildings for business purposes, and the number of business houses is 98. During the year 1846, eighty buildings were erected, and the value of real estate at that time was $476,000.

The population of Piqua, in 1830, was less than 500; in 1840, 1480; and in 1847, 3100.

The Miami river curves beautifully around the town, leaving between it and the village a broad and level plateau, while the opposite bank rises abruptly into a hill, called "Cedar Bluff," affording fine walks, and a commanding view of the surrounding country. In its vicinity are some ancient works. From near its base, on the east bank of the river, the view was taken. The church spires shown, commencing on the right, are respectively, the Episcopal, Catholic, New School Presbyterian, Wesleyan Methodist, Old School Presbyterian and Baptist; the town hall is seen on the left. From the Miami county traditions, we annex some facts respecting the history of Piqua.

Jonathan Rollins was among the first white inhabitants of Miami county. In connection with nine others, he contracted with Judge Symmes, for a certain compensation in lots and land, to become a pioneer in laying out a proposed town in the Indian country, at the lower Piqua village, where is situated the pleasant and flourishing town under that name. The party left Ludlow station, on Mill Creek, in the spring of 1797, and proceeded without difficulty to the proposed site. They there erected cabins, and enclosed grounds for fields and gardens. But the judge failing in some of his calculations, was unable to fulfill his part of the contract; and the other parties to it gradually withdrew from the association, and squatted around on public land, as best pleased themselves. It was some years after this, when land could be regularly entered in the public offices; surveying parties had been running out the county, but time was required to organize the newly introduced section system, which has since proved so highly beneficial to the western states, and so fatal to professional cupidity.

Some of these hardy adventurers settled in and about Piqua, where they have left many worthy descendants. Mr. Rollins finally took up land on Spring Creek, where he laid out the farm he now occupies. While this party resided at Piqua, and for years after, the Indians were constant visitors and sojourners among them. This place appears to have been, to that unfortunate race, a most favorite residence, around which their attachments and regrets lingered to the last. They would come here to visit the graves of their kindred, and weep over the sod that entombed the bones of their fathers. They would sit in melancholy groups, surveying the surrounding objects of their earliest attachments and childhood sports—the winding river, which witnessed their first feeble essays with the gig and the paddle—the trees where first they triumphed with their tiny bow, in their boastful craft of the hunter—the coppice of their nut gatherings—the lawns of their boyhood sports, and haunts of their early loves, would call forth bitter sighs and reproaches on that civilization, which, in its rudest features, was uprooting them from their happy home.

The Indians at Piqua soon found, in the few whites among them, stern and inflexible masters, rather than associates and equals. Upon the slightest provocation, the discipline of the fist and club, so humbling to the spirits of an Indian, was freely used upon them. One day, an exceedingly large Indian had been made drunk, and for some past offense took it in his head to kill one of his wives. He was following her with a knife and tomahawk, around their cabin, with a posse of clamorous squaws and pappooses at his heels, who were striving to check his violence. They had succeeded in wresting from him his arms, and he was standing against the cabin, when several of the white men, attracted by the outcry, approached the group. One of them, small in stature, but big in resolution, made through the Indian crowd to the offender, struck him in the face, and felled him to the ground, while the surrounding Indians looked on in fixed amazement.

"The word *Piqua* is the name of one of the Shawanoese tribes, and signifies, "*a man formed out of the ashes.*" The tradition is, that the whole Shawanoese tribe, a long time ago, were assembled at their annual feast and thanksgiving. They were all seated around a large

View at Upper Piqua.

fire, which having burnt down, a great puffing was observed in the ashes, when behold! a full formed man came up out of the coals and ashes; and this was the first man of the Piqua tribe. After the peace of 1763, the Miamis having removed from the Big Miami river a body of Shawanoes established themselves at lower and upper Piqua, which became their great head quarters in Ohio. Here they remained, until driven off by the Kentuckians, when they crossed over to St. Mary's and to Wapaghkonetta. The Upper Piqua is said to have contained, at one period, near 4000 Shawanoese. The Shawanoese were formerly a numerous people, and very warlike. We can trace their history to the time of their residence on the tide waters of Florida, and as well as the Delawares, they aver that they originally came from west of the Mississippi. Black Hoof, who died at Wapaghkonetta, at the advanced age of 105 years, told me that he remembered, when a boy, bathing in the salt waters of Florida: that his people firmly believed white or civilized people had been in the country before them—having found, in many instances, the marks of iron tools, axes upon trees and stumps, over which the sand had blown. Shawanoese means "*the south*," or "people from the south."*

Upper Piqua, three miles N. of Piqua, on the canal and Miami river, is a locality of much historic interest. It is, at present, the residence of Col. John Johnston—shown in the view—and was once a favorite dwelling place of the Piqua tribe of the Shawanoese. Col. Johnston, now at an advanced age, has for the greater part of his life resided at the west, as an agent of the U. S. government over the Indians. His mild and parental care of their interests, gave him great influence over them, winning their strongest affections, and causing them to regard him in the light of a father. To him we are indebted for many valuable facts, scattered through this volume, as well as those which follow respecting this place.

In the French war, which ended with the peace of 1763, a bloody battle was fought on the present farm of Col. Johnston, at Upper Piqua. At that time, the Miamis had their towns here, which are marked on ancient maps, "Tewightewee towns." The Miamis, Wyandots, Ottowas, and other northern tribes, adhered to the French, made a stand here, and fortified—the Canadian traders and French assisting. The Delawares, Shawanoes, Munseys, part of the Senecas residing in Pennsylvania, Cherokees, Catawbas, &c., adhering to the English interest, with the English traders, attacked the French and Indians. The siege continued for more than a week; the fort stood out, and could not be taken. Many were slain, the assailants suffering most severely. The besieged lost a number, and all their exposed property was burnt and destroyed. The Shawanoese chief, Blackhoof, one of the besiegers, informed Col. Johnston that the ground around was strewed with bullets, so that baskets full could have been gathered.

Soon after this contest, the Miamis and their allies left this part of the country, and retired to the Miami of the Lake, at and near Fort Wayne, and never returned. The Shawanoese took their place, and gave names to towns in this vicinity. Col. Johnston's place, "and the now large and flourishing town of Piqua, was called Chillicothe, after the tribe of that name; the site of his farm, after the Piqua tribe."

Fort Piqua, erected prior to the settlement of the country, stood at Upper Piqua, on the west bank of the river, near where the figure is seen in the distance, on the right of the engraving. It was designed as a place of deposit for stores for the army of Wayne. The portage from here to Fort Loramie, 14 miles, thence to St. Mary's, 12 miles, was all the land carriage from the Ohio to Lake Erie. Loaded boats frequently ascended to Fort Loramie, the loading taken out and hauled to St. Mary's, the boats also moved across on wheels, again loaded, and launched for Fort Wayne, Defiance and the lake. Sometimes, in very high water, loaded boats from the Ohio approached within six miles of St. Mary's. Before the settlement of the country, a large proportion of the army supplies were conveyed up this river. When mill dams were erected, the navigation was destroyed, and boating ceased.

In 1794, Capt. J. N. Vischer, the last commandant of Fort Piqua, was stationed here. During that year, two freighted boats, guarded by an officer and 23 men, were attacked by the Indians near the fort, and the men all massacred. Capt. Vischer heard the firing, but from the weakness of his command, could render no assistance. The plan of the Indians doubtless was, to make the attack in hearing of the fort, and thereby induce them to sally out in aid of their countrymen, defeat all, and take the fort. The commander was a discreet officer, and aware of the subtleness of the enemy, had the firmness to save the fort.

The family of Col. Johnston settled at Upper Piqua in 1811, the previous 11 years having been spent at Fort Wayne. Years after the destruction of the boats and party on the river, fragments of muskets, bayonets, and other remains of that disaster, were found at low water, imbedded in the sand. The track of the pickets, the form of the river bastion, the foundation of chimneys in the block-houses, still mark the site of Fort Piqua. The plow has levelled the graves of the brave men—for many sleep here—who fell in the service. At this place, Fort Loramie, St. Mary's, and Fort Wayne, large numbers of the regulars and militia volunteers were buried, in the wars of Wayne, as well as in the last war.

* Col. John Johnston.

In the late war, the far greater number of Indians who remained friendly, and claimed and received protection from the United States, were placed under the care of Col. Johnston, at Piqua. These were the Shawanoes, Delawares, Wyandots in part, Ottowas in part, part of the Senecas, all the Munseys, and Mohicans; a small number remained at Zanesfield, and some at Upper Sandusky, under Maj. B. F. Stickney, now of Toledo. The number here amounted, at one period, to six thousand, and were doubtless the best protection to the frontier. With a view of detaching the Indians here from the American interest, and taking them off to the enemy, and knowing that so long as Col. Johnston lived this could not be accomplished, several plots were contrived to assassinate him. His life was in the utmost danger. He arose many mornings, with but little hope of living until night, and the friendly chiefs often warned him of his danger; but he was planted at the post; duty, honor, and the safety of the frontier, forbade his abandoning it. His faithful wife staid by him; the rest of his family, papers and valuable effects, were removed to a place of greater security. On one occasion, his escape seemed miraculous.

Near the house, at the road side, by which he daily several times passed in visiting the Indian camp, was a cluster of wild plum bushes. No one would have suspected hostile Indians to secrete themselves there; yet there the intended assassins waited to murder him, which they must have soon accomplished, had they not been discovered by some Delaware women, who gave the alarm. The Indians—three in number—fled; a party pursued, but lost the trail. It afterwards appeared that they went up the river some distance, crossed to the east side, and passing down nearly opposite his residence, determined, in being foiled of their chief prize, not to return empty handed. They killed Mr. Dilbone and his wife, who were in a field, pulling flax: their children, who were with them, escaped by secreting themselves in the weeds. From thence, the Indians went lower down, three miles, to Loss Creek, where they killed David Garrard, who was at work a short distance from his house. The leader of the party, Pash-e-towa, was noted for his cold-blooded cruelty, and a short time previous, was the chief actor in destroying upwards of 20 persons—mostly women and children—at a place called Pigeon Roost, Indiana. He was killed, after the war, by one of his own people, in satisfaction for the numerous cruelties he had committed on unoffending persons.*

In the war of 1812, nothing was more embarrassing to the public agents, than the management of the Indians on the frontier. President Madison, from a noble principle, which does his memory high honor, positively refused to employ them in the war, and this was a cause of all the losses in the country adjacent to the upper lakes. Having their families in possession, the agents could have placed implicit confidence in the fidelity of the warriors. As it was, they had to manage them as they best could. Col. Johnston frequently furnished them with white flags, with suitable mottoes, to enable them to pass out-posts and scouts in safety. On one occasion, the militia basely fired on one of these parties, bearing a flag hoisted in full view. They killed two Indians, wounded a third, took the survivors prisoners, and after robbing them of all they possessed, conveyed them to the garrison at Greenville, to which post the party belonged. On reflection, they were convinced they had committed an unjustifiable act, and became alarmed for the consequences. They brought the prisoners to Upper Piqua, and delivered them to Col. Johnston. He took them, wishing to do the best in his power for the Indians, and on deliberation, decided to conduct them back to Greenville, and restore them, with their property, to their people. Application was made by Col. Johnston, to the officer commanding at Piqua, for a guard on the journey. These were Ohio militia, of whom not a man or officer dared to go. He then told the commander, if he would accompany him, he would go at all hazards, the distance being 25 miles, the road entirely uninhabited, and known to be infested with Indians, who had recently killed two girls near Greenville. But he alike refused. All his appeals to the pride and patriotism of officers and men proving unavailing, he decided to go alone, it being a case that required the promptest action, to prevent evil impressions spreading among the Indians. He got his

* Although Col. Johnston escaped death by the calamities of war, his immediate relations have been sufferers. His brother was killed by the Indians, and his scalp sold to M'Kee, Girty, or some other of the American renegadoes, who allied with the British and Indians against their own country. By a newspaper received this day, we also learn that his son, Capt. Abm. R. Johnston, of the 1st regiment U. S. dragoons, and aid to Gen. Kearney, was killed at the recent battle of San Pasqual, in California, while gallantly leading a furious charge against the enemy. This gentleman was born at Piqua, May 23d, 1815, graduated first at Miami University, and afterwards at West Point; entered the army, and was promoted to a captaincy, June 30, 1846, and was killed on the 6th of December following. He was a ripe scholar, and possessed noble qualities of character.

horse ready, bade farewell to his wife, scarcely ever expecting to see her again, and reached Greenville in safety; procured nearly all the articles taken from the Indians, and delivered them back, made them a speech, dismissed them, and then springing on his horse, started back alone, and reached his home in safety, to the surprise of all, particularly the militia, who, dastardly fellows, scarce expected to see him alive, and made many apologies for their cowardice.

During the war, Col. Johnston had many proofs of the fidelity of some of the friendly Indians. After the surrender of Detroit, the frontier of Ohio was thrown into the greatest terror and confusion. A large body of Indians still resided within its limits, accessible to the British. In the garrison of Fort Wayne, which was threatened, were many women and children, who, in case of attack, would have been detrimental to its defence, and it therefore became necessary to have them speedily removed. Col. Johnston assembled the Shawanee chiefs, and stating the case, requested volunteers to bring the women and children at Fort Wayne to Piqua. Logan (see p. 303) immediately arose and offered his services, and soon started with a party of mounted Indians, all volunteers. They reached the post, received their interesting and helpless charge, and safely brought them to the settlements, through a country infested with marauding bands of hostile savages. The women spoke in the highest terms of the vigilance, care and delicacy of their faithful conductors.

Covington, 6 miles westerly from Piqua, is a flourishing town, on Stillwater creek, which winds through a beautiful and fertile country. It contains 2 churches, 6 stores, and had, in 1840, 331 inhabitants. Milton, a flourishing village, 10 miles sw. of Troy, on Stillwater creek, at which point there is much hydraulic power, contains 1 or 2 churches, 4 stores, several mills and factories, and had, in 1840, 232 inhabitants. Fletcher, West Charleston, Cass, Hyattsville, and Tippecanoe, are small villages.

MONROE.

Monroe was named from James Monroe, president of the United States from 1817 to 1825; was formed, January 29th, 1813, from Belmont, Washington and Gurnsey. The south and east part is very hilly and rough; the north and west moderately hilly. Some of the western portion and the valleys are fertile. Coal of an excellent quality abounds in the western part, and iron ore is found. The staples are wheat, corn, pork and tobacco; of which last there is, with two exceptions, more raised than in any other county in Ohio. The following is a list of the townships, in 1840, with their population.

Adams,	897	Jackson,	806	Sunbury,	1358
Bethel,	545	Malaga,	1443	Switzerland,	983
Elk,	535	Ohio,	907	Union,	1351
Enoch,	1135	Perry,	980	Washington,	533
Franklin,	1144	Salem,	910	Wayne,	684
Green,	938	Seneca,	1349		

The population of Monroe in 1820, was 4645; in 1830, 8770, and in 1840, 18,544, or 33 inhabitants to a square mile.

The principal portion of the population originated from western Pennsylvania, with some western Virginians and a few New Englanders; one township is settled by Swiss, among whom are some highly educated men. The inhabitants are moral and industrious, and, to the honor of the county, a capital crime has never been committed within it.

The valleys of the streams are narrow and are bounded by lofty and rough hills. In many of the little ravines putting into the valleys, the scenery is in all the wildness of untamed nature. In places, they are precipitous and scarcely accessible to the footsteps of man, and often for many hundred yards the rocks bounding these gorges hang over some 30 or 40 feet, forming natural grottoes, of sufficient capacity to shelter many hundreds of persons, and enhancing the gloomy, forbidding character of the scenery.

The annexed historical sketch of the county, is from Daniel H. Wire, Esq., of Woodsfield.

The first settlement in the county was near the mouth of Sunfish, about the year 1799. This settlement consisted of a few families whose chief aim was to locate on the best hunting ground. A few years after, three other small settlements were made. The first was near where the town of Beallsville now stands; the second on the Clear fork of Little Muskingum, consisting of Martin Crow, Fred. Crow, and two or three other families; and the third was on the east fork of Duck creek, where some three or four families of the name of Archer settled. Not long after this, the settlements began to spread, and the pioneers were forced to see the bear and the wolf leave, and make way for at least more friendly neighbors, though perhaps less welcome. The approach of new comers was always looked upon with suspicion, as this was the signal for the game to leave. A neighbor at the distance of ten miles was considered near enough for all social purposes. The first object of a new comer after selecting a location, and putting the "hoppers" on the horse,—if he had any,—was to cut some poles or logs, and build a cabin of suitable dimensions for the *size* of his family; for as yet, rank and condition had not disturbed the simple order of society.

The windows of the cabin were made by sawing out about three feet of one of the logs, and putting in a few upright pieces; and in the place of glass, they took paper and oiled it with bear's oil, or hog's fat, and pasted it on the upright pieces. This would give considerable light and resist the rain tolerably well. After the cabin was completed, the next thing in order was to clear out a piece of ground for a corn patch. They plowed their ground generally with a shovel plow, as this was most convenient among the roots. Their harness consisted mostly of leather-wood bark, except the collar, which was made of husks of corn platted and sewed together. They ground their corn in a hand-mill or pounded it in a mortar, or hommony block, as it was called, which was made by burning a hole into the end of a block of wood. They pounded the corn in these mortars with a pestle, which they made by driving an iron wedge into a stick of suitable size. After the corn was sufficiently pounded, they sieved it, and took the finer portion for meal to make bread and mush of, and the coarser they boiled for hommony. Their meat was bear, venison and wild-turkey, as it was very difficult to raise hogs or sheep on account of the wolves and bear; and hence pork and woollen clothes were very scarce.

The mischievous depredations of the wolves, rendered their scalps a matter of some importance. They were worth from four to six dollars a piece. This made wolf-hunting rather of a lucrative business, and of course called into action the best inventive talent in the country; consequently many expedients and inventions were adopted, one of which I will give. The hunter took the ovary of a slut—at a particular time—and rubbed it on the soles of his shoes, then circling through the forest where the wolves were most plenty, the male wolves would follow his track; as they approached he would secrete himself in a suitable place, and as soon as the wolf came in reach of the rifle, he received its contents. This plan was positively practiced, and was one of the most effectual modes of hunting the wolf. A Mr. Terrel, formerly of this place, was hunting wolves in this way, not far from where Woodsfield stands. He found himself closely pursued by a number of wolves, and soon discovered from their angry manner, that they intended to attack him. He got up into the top of a leaning tree, and shot four of them before they would leave him. This is the only instance of the wolves attacking any person in this section of country. Hunters, the better to elude, especially the ever-watchful eye of the deer and turkey, had their hunting shirts colored to suit the season. In the fall of the year, they wore the color most resembling the fallen leaves; in the winter they used a brown, as near as possible the color of the bark of trees. If there was snow on the ground, they frequently drew a white shirt over their other clothes. In the summer they colored their clothes green.

In addition to what has already been said, it may not be improper to give a few things in relation to the social intercourse of the early settlers. And first, I would remark on good authority, that a more generous, warm-hearted and benevolent people, seldom have existed in any country. Although they were unwilling to see the game driven off by the rapid influx of emigrants; still the stranger, when he arrived among the hardy pioneers, found among them a cordiality, and a generous friendship, that is not found among those who compose, what is erroneously called, the better class of society, or the higher circle. There was no distinction in society, no aristocratic lines drawn between the upper and lower classes. Their social amusements proceeded from matters of necessity. A log rolling, or the raising of a log cabin, was generally accompanied with a quilting, or something of the sort, and this brought together a whole neighborhood of both sexes, and after the labors of the day were ended, they spent the larger portion of the night in dancing and other innocent amusements. If they had no fiddler, (which was not very uncommon,) some one of the company would supply the deficiency by singing. A wedding frequently called together all the young folks for fifteen or twenty miles around. These occasions were truly convivial; the parties assembled on the wedding day at the house of the bride, and after the nuptials were celebrated, they enjoyed all manner of rural hilarity, and most generally dancing formed a part, unless the old folks had religious scruples as to its propriety. About 10 o'clock the bride was allowed to retire by her attendants; and if the groom could steal off from his attendants and retire also, without their knowledge, they became the objects of sport for all the company, and were not a little quizzed. The next day the party repaired to the house of the groom to enjoy the *infair*. When arrived within a mile or two of the house, a part of the company would run for the bottle, and whoever had the fleetest horse, succeeded in getting the bottle, which was alway ready at the house of the groom. The successful racer carried back the liquor, and met the rest of the company and treated them, always taking good care to treat the bride and groom first; he then became the hero of that occasion, at least.

There are but few incidents relative to the Indian war which took place in this county, worthy of notice. When Martin Whetzel was a prisoner among the Indians, they brought him about twenty miles (as he supposed) up Sunfish creek. This would be some place near Woodsfield. Whetzel says they stopped under a large ledge of rocks, and left a guard with him, and went off; and after having been gone about an hour, they returned with a large quantity of lead, and moulded a great number of bullets. They fused the lead in a large wooden ladle, which they had hid in the rocks. They put the metal in the ladle, and by burning live coals on it, succeeded in fusing it. After Whetzel escaped from the Indians and returned home, he visited the place in search of the lead, but could never find it. In fact, he was not certain that he had found the right rock.

At the battle of Captina, (see page 55,) John Baker was killed. He had borrowed Jack Bean's gun, which the Indians had taken. This gun was recaptured on the waters of Wills creek, about sixteen or eighteen miles west of Woodsfield, and still remains in the posses ion of some of the friends of the notorious Bean and the lamented Baker, in this county, as a memorial of those brave Indian fighters. Henry Johnson, (see page 269,) who had the fight with the Indians, when a boy, is now living in the county.

In the latter part of the last century, the celebrated French traveller, Volney, travelled through Virginia, and crossed the Ohio into this county from Sistersville. He was under the guidance of two Virginia bear hunters through the wilderness. The weather was very cold and severe. In crossing the dry ridge, on the Virginia side, the learned infidel became weak with cold and fatigue. He was in the midst of an almost boundless wilderness, deep snows were under his feet, and both rain and snow falling upon his head; he frequently insisted on giving over the enterprize and dying where he was, but his comrades, more accustomed to backwoods fare, urged him on, until he at length gave out, exclaiming, "Oh, wretched and foolish man that I am, to leave my comfortable home and fireside, and come to this unfrequented place, where the lion and tiger refuse to dwell, and the rain hurries off! Go on my friends! better that one man should perish than three." They then stopped, struck a fire, built a camp of bark and limbs, shot a buck, broiled the ham, which, with the salt, bread and other necessaries they had, made a very good supper, and every thing being soon comfortable and cheery, the learned Frenchman was dilating largely and eloquently upon the ingenuity of man.

View in Woodsfield.

Woodsfield, the county seat, 118 miles easterly from Columbus, and 18 from the Ohio river, was founded in 1815, by Archibald Woods, of Wheeling, George Paul, Benj. Ruggles and Levi Barber. It contains 1 Episcopal Methodist and 1 Protestant Methodist church, a classical academy, 1 newspaper printing office, 6 stores, and had in 1830, 157 inhabitants, and in 1840, 262; estimated population in 1847, 450. The view was taken in the principal street of the village, on the left of which is seen the court house. At the foot of the street, on the left, but not shown in the view, is a natural mound, circular at the base and rising to the height of 60 feet.

Beallsville, 9 miles NE. of Woodsfield, contains 1 Methodist, 1 Presbyterian and 1 Disciples church. It had in 1840, 194 inhabitants; estimated population in 1847, 350. Mr. Beall and John Lynn, were the original proprietors. Clarington, at the mouth of Sunfish, was laid out by Daniel Person, and contains 1 Disciples church, and about 300 inhabitants. Malaga, Milton, Calais, Summerfield, Carlisle, Graysville and Antioch, are smaller places.

MONTGOMERY.

Montgomery was named from Gen. Richard Montgomery, of the American revolutionary army; he was born in Ireland, in 1737, and was killed in the assault upon Quebec, Dec. 31st, 1775. This county was created, May 1st, 1803, from Hamilton and Ross, and the temporary seat of justice appointed at the house of George Newcom, in Dayton. About one-half of the county is rolling and the rest level:

HARBOR OF TOLEDO.

PUBLIC SQUARE, NEWARK.

the soil of an excellent quality, clay predominating. East of the Miami, are many excellent limestone quarries, of a greyish white hue. Large quantities are exported to Cincinnati, where it is used in constructing the most elegant edifices; nearly all the canal locks from Cincinnati to Toledo are built with it. This, excepting Hamilton, is the greatest manufacturing county in Ohio, and abundance of water power is furnished by its various streams. Montgomery has more turnpike macadamized roads, than any other county in the state, and is one of the wealthiest and most densely populated. The principal products are corn, wheat, rye, oats, barley, flaxseed, potatoes, pork, wool and tobacco. The following is a list of the townships in 1840, with their population.

Butler,	1897	Jackson,	1688	Perry,	1883
Clay,	1633	Jefferson,	1895	Randolph,	1774
Dayton,	10334	Madison,	1594	Washington,	2259
German,	2629	Miami,	3249	Wayne,	1045

The population of Montgomery in 1820, was 16,061; in 1830, 24,374, and in 1840, 31,879, or 79 inhabitants to a square mile.

The thriving city of Dayton is in this county. This is a beautiful town. It is regularly laid out, the streets are of an unusual width, and much taste is displayed in the private residences: many of them are large and are ornamented by fine gardens and shrubbery. The following sketch is from a resident.*

Dayton, the county seat, is situated on the east side of the Great Miami, at the mouth of Mad river, and 1 mile below the southwest branch. It is 67 miles westerly from Columbus, 52 from Cincinnati and 110 from Indianapolis. The point at which Dayton stands was selected, in 1788, by some gentlemen, who designed laying out a town by the name of Venice. They agreed with John Cleves Symmes, whose contract with congress then covered the site of the place, for the purchase of the lands. But the Indian wars which ensued, prevented the extension of settlements from the immediate neighborhood of Cincinnati, for some years: and the project was abandoned by the purchasers. Soon after Wayne's treaty, in 1795, a new company, composed of Generals Jonathan Dayton, Arthur St. Clair, James Wilkinson and Col. Israel Ludlow, purchased the lands between the Miamis, around the mouth of Mad river, of Judge Symmes, and on the 4th of November, laid out the town. Arrangements were made for its settlement in the ensuing spring, and donations of lots were offered, with other privileges, to actual settlers. Forty-six persons entered into engagements to remove from Cincinnati to Dayton, but during the winter most of them scattered in different directions, and only 19 fulfilled their engagements. The first families who made a permanent residence in the place, arrived on the 1st day of April, 1796. The first 19 settlers of Dayton, were Wm. Gahagan, Samuel Thomson, Benj. Van Cleve, Wm. Van Cleve, Solomon Goss, Thomas Davis, John Davis, James M'Clure,

* J. W. Van Cleve, Esq.

John M'Clure, Daniel Ferrell, William Hamer, Solomon Hamer, Thomas Hamer, Abraham Glassmire, John Dorough, William Chenoweth, James Morris, William Newcom and George Newcom, the last of whom is still a resident of the place, and the only survivor of the whole number.

View in Dayton.

[The above view was taken near the corner of First and Ludlow streets. In front is shown the elegant residence of J. D. Phillips, Esq., and the First Presbyterian church; on the left, the cupola of the new court house and the spires of the German Reformed and Second Presbyterian churches appear.]

Judge Symmes was unable to complete his payments for all the lands he had agreed to purchase of the government, and those lying about Dayton reverted to the United States, by which the settlers were left without titles to their lots. Congress, however, passed a pre-emption law, under which those who had contracted for lands with Symmes and his associates, had a right to enter the same lots or lands at government price. Some of the settlers entered their lots, and obtained titles directly from the United States; and others made an arrangement with Daniel C. Cooper, to receive their deeds from him, and he entered the residue of the town lands. He had been a surveyor and agent for the first company of proprietors, and they assigned him certain of their rights of pre-emption, by which he became the titular proprietor of the town. He died in 1818, leaving two sons, who have both since died without children.

In 1803, on the organization of the state government, Montgomery county was established. Dayton was made the seat of justice, at which time only five families resided in the town, the other settlers having gone on to farms in the vicinity, or removed to other parts of the country. The increase of the town was gradual, until the war of 1812, which made a thoroughfare for the troops and stores on their way to the frontier. Its progress was then more rapid until 1820, when the depression of business put an almost total check to its increase. The commencement of the Miami canal, in 1827, renewed its prosperity, and its increase has been steady and rapid ever since. By the assessment of 1846, it is the second city in the state in the amount of taxable property, as the county also stands second.

The Cooper Female Academy.

[The Cooper Female Academy in Dayton, is a highly flourishing institution in excellent repute. Mr. E. E. Barney is the principal, under whom are 7 assistants and 174 pupils.]

The first canal boat from Cincinnati arrived at Dayton on the 25th of January, 1829, and the first one from Lake Erie on the 24th of June, 1845. In 1825, a weekly line of mail stages was established through Dayton from Cincinnati to Columbus. Two days were occupied in coming from Cincinnati to this place. There are now three daily lines between the two places, and the trip only takes an afternoon.

The first newspaper printed in Dayton, was the Dayton Repertory, issued by William M'Clure and George Smith, on the 18th of September, 1808, on a foolscap sheet. The newspapers now published here are the "Dayton Journal," daily and weekly; the "Dayton Transcript," twice a week; and the "Western Empire," weekly.

The population of Dayton was 383 in 1810; 1139 in 1820; 2954 in 1830; 6067 in 1840, and 9792 in 1845. There are 15 churches, of which the Presbyterians, Methodists and Lutherans each have two, and the Episcopalians, Catholics, Baptists, Disciples, New-lights, German Reformed, Albrights, Dunkers and African Baptists, have each one. There is a large water power within the bounds of the city, besides a great deal more in the immediate vicinity. A portion of that introduced in the city by a new hydraulic canal, is not yet in use; but there are now in operation within the corporate limits, 2 flouring mills, 4 saw mills, 2 oil mills, 3 cotton mills, 2 woollen factories, 2 paper mills, 5 machine shops, 1 scythe factory, 2 flooring machines, 1 last and peg factory, 1 gun-barrel factory and 3 iron founderies. The public buildings are 2 market houses, one of which has a city hall over it, an academy, a female academy, 3 common-school houses and a jail of stone. There are 2 banks. A court house is now building of cut stone, the estimated cost of which is $63,000. The architect, by whom it was designed, is Mr. Henry Daniels, now of Cincinnati, and the one superintending its construction, is Mr. Daniel Waymire. There are nine turnpike roads leading out of Dayton, and connecting it with the country around, in every direction. The Miami canal, from Cincinnati to Lake Erie, runs through it.

Among the early settlers of Montgomery county was Col. Robert Patterson. He was born in Pennsylvania in 1753, and emigrated to Kentucky in 1775. In 1804, he removed from Kentucky and settled about a mile below Dayton. He was the original proprietor of Lexington, Ky., and one-third owner of Cincinnati, when it was laid out. He was with Col. George Rogers Clarke in 1778, in his celebrated Illinois campaign; in the following year he was in Bowman's expedition against old Chillicothe;* in August, 1780, he was a captain under Clarke, in his expedition against the Shawnees, on the Little Miami and Mad river; was second in command to Col. Boone, August 19th, 1782, at the battle of the Lower Blue Licks; was colonel on the second expedition of Gen. Clarke, in the following September, into the Miami country; held the same office in 1786, under Col. Logan, in his expedition against the Shawnees. He died, August 5th, 1827. His early life was full of incidents, one of the most remarkable of which we give in his own language, as originally published in the Ohio National Journal.

In the fall of 1776, I started from M'Clellan's station, (now Georgetown, Ky.,) in company with Jos. M'Nutt, David Perry, James Wernock, James Templeton, Edward Mitchell and Isaac Greer, to go to Pittsburgh. We procured provision for our journey at the Blue Licks, from the well-known stone house, the Buffalo. At Limestone, we procured a canoe, and started up the Ohio river by water. Nothing material transpired during several of the first days of our journey. We landed at Point Pleasant, where was a fort commanded by Capt. Arbuckle. After remaining there a short time, and receiving dispatches from Capt. Arbuckle to the commandant at Wheeling, we again proceeded. Aware that Indians were lurking along the bank of the river, we travelled with the utmost caution. We usually landed an hour before sunset, cooked and eat our supper, and went on until after dark. At night we lay without fire, as convenient to our canoe as possible, and started again in the morning at day break. We had all agreed that if any disaster should befall us by day or by night, that we would stand by each other, as long as any help could be afforded. At length the memorable 12th of October arrived. During the day we passed several new improvements, which occasioned us to be less watchful and careful than we had been before. Late in the evening we landed opposite the island, [on the Ohio side of the river, in what is now Athens county,] then called the Hockhocking, and were beginning to flatter ourselves that we should reach some inhabitants the next day. Having eaten nothing that day, contrary to our usual practice, we kindled a fire and cooked supper. After we had eaten and made the last of our flour into a loaf of bread, and put it into an old brass kettle to bake, so that we might be ready to start again in the morning at day-break, we lay down to rest, keeping the same clothes on at night that we wore during the

* The Notes on Kentucky gives the number of men under Bowman, on this occasion, as 160; but the memoranda of Col. Patterson puts it at 400.—*J. W. Van Cleve, in the Am. Pioneer.*

day. For the want of a better, I had on a hunting shirt and britch clout, (so called,) and flannel leggins. I had my powder horn and shot pouch on my side, and placed the butt of my gun under my head. Five of our company lay on the east side of the fire, and James Templeton and myself on the west; we were lying on our left sides, myself in front, with my right hand hold of my gun. Templeton was lying close behind me. This was our position, and asleep, when we were fired upon by a party of Indians. Immediatey aftet the fire they rushed upon us with tomahawks, as if determined to finish the work of death they had begun. It appeared that one Indian had shot on my side of the fire. I saw the flash of the gun and felt the ball pass through me, but where I could not tell, nor was it at first painful. I sprang to take up gun, but my right shoulder came to the ground. I made another effort, and was half bent in getting up, when an Indian sprang past the fire with savage fierceness, and struck me with his tomahawk. From the position I was in, it went between two ribs, just behind the back bone a little below the kidney, and penetrated the cavity of the body. He then immediately turned to Templeton, (who by this time had got to his feet with his gun in hand,) and seized his gun. A desperate scuffle ensued, but Templeton held on, and finally bore off the gun. In the meantime, I made from the light, and in my attempt to get out of sight, I was delayed for a moment by getting my right arm fast between a tree and a sapling, but having got clear and away from the light of the fire, and finding that I had lost the use of my right arm, I made a shift to keep it up by drawing it through the straps of my shot pouch. I could see the crowd about the fire, but the firing had ceased and the strife seemed to be over. I had reason to believe that the others were all shot and tomahawked. Hearing no one coming towards me, I resolved to go to the river, and if possible to get into the canoe and float down, thinking by that means I might possibly reach Point Pleasant, supposed to be about 100 miles distant. Just as I got on the beach a little below the canoe, an Indian in the canoe gave a whoop, which gave me to understand that it was best to withdraw. I did so; and with much difficulty got to an old log, and being very thirsty, faint and exhausted, I was glad to sit down. I felt the blood running and heard it dropping on the leaves all around me. Presently I heard the Indians board the canoe and float past. All was now silent, and I felt myself in a most forlorn condition. I could not see the fire, but determined to find it and see if any of my comrades were alive. I steered the course which I supposed the fire to be, and having reached it, I found Templeton alive, but wounded in nearly the same manner that I was. Jas. Wernock was also dangerously wounded, two balls having passed through his body; Jos. M'Nutt was dead and scalped. D. Perry was wounded, but not badly, and Isaac Greer was missing. The miseries of that hour cannot well be described.

When daylight appeared we held a council, and concluded that inasmuch as one gun and some ammunition was saved, Perry would furnish us with meat, and we would proceed up the river by slow marches to the nearest settlements, supposed to be one hundred miles. A small quantity of provisions which was found scattered around the fire, was picked up and distributed among us, and a piece of blanket which was saved from the fire, was given to me to cover a wound on my back. On examination, it was found that two balls had passed through my right arm, and that the bone was broken; to dress this, splinters were taken from a tree near the fire, that had been shivered by lightning, and placed on the outside of my hunting shirt and bound with a string. And now being in readiness to move, Perry took the gun and ammunition, and we all got to our feet except Wernock, who, on attempting to get up fell back to the ground. He refused to try again, said that he could not live, and at the same time desired us to do the best we could for ourselves. Perry then took hold of his arm and told him if he would get up he would carry him; upon this he made another effort to get up, but falling back as before, he begged us in the most solemn manner to leave him. At his request, the old kettle was filled with water and placed at his side, which he said was the last and only favor required of us, and then conjured us to leave him and try to save ourselves, assuring us that should he live to see us again, he would cast no reflections of unkindness upon us. Thus we left him. When we had got a little distance I looked back, and distressed and hopeless as Wernock's condition really was, I felt to envy it. After going about 100 poles, we were obliged to stop and rest, and found ourselves too sick and weak to proceed. Another consultation being held, it was agreed that Templeton and myself should remain there with Edward Mitchell, and Perry should take the gun and go to the nearest settlement and seek relief. Perry promised that if he could not procure assistance, he would be back in four days. He then returned to the camp and found Wernock in the same state of mind as when we left, perfectly rational and sensible of his condition, replenished his kettle with water, brought us some fire, and started for the settlement.

Alike unable to go back or forward, and being very thirsty we set about getting water from a small stream that happened to be near us, our only drinking vessel an old wool hat, which was so broken that it was with great difficulty made to hold water; but by stuffing leaves in it, we made it hold so that each one could drink from once filling it. Nothing could have been a greater luxury to us, than a drink of water from the old hat. Just at night, Mitchell returned to see if Wernock was still living, intending if he was dead, to get the kettle for us. He arrived just in time to see him expire; but not choosing to leave him until he should be certain that he was dead, he stayed with him until darkness came on, and when he attempted to return to us, he got lost and lay from us all night. We suffered much that night for the want of fire, and through fear that he was either killed or that he had ran off; but happily for us, our fears were groundless, for next morning at sunrise, he found his way to our camp. That day we moved about 200 yards farther up a deep ravine, and farther from the river. The weather, which had been cold and frosty, now became a little warmer, and commenced raining. Those that were with me could set up, but I had no alternative but to lie on my back on the ground, with my right arm over my body. The rain continuing next day, Mitchell took an excursion to examine the hills, and not far distant, he found a rock projecting from the cliff sufficient to shelter us from the rain, to which place we very gladly removed. He also gathered pawpaws for us, which were our only food, except perhaps a few grapes.

Time moved slowly on until Saturday. In the meantime, we talked over the danger to which Perry was exposed, the distance he had to go and the improbability of his returning. When the time had expired which he had allowed himself, we concluded that we would, if alive, wait for him until Monday, and if he did not come then, and no relief should be afforded, we would attempt to travel to Point Pleasant. The third day after our defeat, my arm became very painful. The splinters and leaves of my shirt were cemented together with blood, and stuck so fast to my arm that it required the application of warm water for nearly a whole day to loosen them so that they could be taken off; when this was done, I had my arm dressed with white oak leaves, which had a very good effect. On Saturday, about 12 o'clock, Mitchell came with his bosom full of pawpaws, and placed them convenient to us, and returned to his station on the river. He had been gone about an hour, when to our great joy we beheld him coming with a company of men. When they approached us, we found that our trusty friend and companion, David Perry, had returned to our assistance with Capt. John Walls, his officers and most of his company. Our feelings of gratitude may possibly be conceived, but words can never describe them. Suffice to say that these eyes flowed down plenteously with tears, and I was so completely overwhelmed with joy, that I fell to the ground. On my recovery, we were taken to the river and refreshed plentifully with provisions, which the captain had brought, and had our wounds dressed by an experienced man, who came for that purpose. We were afterwards described by the captain to be in a most forlorn and pitiable condition, more like corpses beginning to putrify than living beings.

While we were at the cliff which sheltered us from the rain, the howling of the wolves in the direction of the fatal spot whence we had so narrowly escaped with our lives, left no doubt that they were feasting on the bodies of our much lamented friends, M'Nutt and Wernock. While we were refreshing ourselves at the river, and having our wounds dressed, Capt. Walls went with some of his men to the place of our defeat, and collected the bones of our late companions and buried them with the utmost expedition and care. We were then conducted by water to Capt. Wall's station, at Grave creek.

Miamisburg is 10 miles southerly from Dayton, on the Miami canal and river, and the state road from Dayton to Cincinnati. This locality was originally called "*Hole's Station*," and a few families settled here about the time Dayton was commenced. The town was laid out in 1818; Emanuel Gebhart, Jacob Kercher, Dr. John and Peter Treon, being the original proprietors. The early settlers were of Dutch origin, most of whom emigrated from Berks county, Pa. The German is yet much spoken, and two of the churches worship in that language. The river and canal supply considerable water power. The town is compactly built. The view was taken near J. Zimmer's hotel—shown on the right—and gives the appearance of the principal street, looking from that point in the direction of Dayton. A neat covered bridge crosses the Miami river at this place. Miamisburg contains 1 Dutch Reformed, 1 Lutheran and 1 Methodist church, 1 high school, 12 mercantile stores, 1 woollen and

View in Miamisburg.

1 cotton factory, 1 grist mill, 1 iron foundery, and had in 1840, 834, and in 1846, 1055 inhabitants.

In the lower part of Miamisburg, are the remains of an ancient work; and this region abounds in the works and fortifications so common in the west. About a mile and a quarter southeast of the village, on an elevation more than 100 feet above the Miami, is the largest mound in the northern states, excepting the mammoth mound at Grave creek, on the Ohio below Wheeling, which it about equals in dimensions. It measures about 800 feet around the base, and rises to the height of 67 feet. When first known, it was covered with forest trees, from the top of one of which,—a maple tree growing

Great Mound.

from its apex,—it is said, Dayton could be plainly seen. The mound has not been thoroughly examined, like that at Grave creek; but probably is similar in character. Many years since, a shaft was sunk from the top; at first, some human bones were exhumed, and at the depth of about 11 feet, the ground sounding hollow, the workmen were afraid to progress farther. Probably two vaults are in it, like those of Grave creek; one at the base in the center, the other over it, near the summit; it was, we suppose, this upper vault which gave forth the hollow sound. The mound is the steepest on the north and east sides, and is ascended with some little difficulty. It now sustains an orchard of about 40 apple, and a few peach and forest trees. The view from the summit is beautiful. At one's feet lays the village of Miamisburg, while the fertile valley of the river is seen stretching away for miles.

Center Street, Germantown.

Germantown, named from Germantown, Pa., is 13 miles sw. of Dayton, in a beautiful valley, surrounded by one of the most fertile sections of land in the west. It is steadily improving, and is noted for the substantial industry and wealth of its citizens. This thriving town was laid out in 1814, by Philip Gunckel, proprietor, who previously built a saw and grist mill on Twin creek, and opened a store at the same place. Most of its early settlers were of German descent, and emigrated from Berks, Lebanon and Center counties, Pa. Among these, were the Gunckels, the Emericks, the Schæffers, &c., whose descendents now comprise a large proportion of the inhabitants. The village is handsomely laid out in squares, the houses are of a substantial character and the streets ornamented by locusts. It contains 2 German Reformed, 1 Lutheran, 1 Episcopal Methodist and 1 United Brethren church, a flourishing academy for both sexes, 1 book, 2 grocery and 5 dry goods stores, 1 newspaper printing office, 1 brewery, 1 woollen factory, and about 1200 inhabitants.

Carrolton, Alexandersville, Centerville, Harrisburg, Union, Arlington, Phillipsburg, Salem, Pyrmont, New Lebanon, Johnsville, Farmersville, Sunbury, Liberty, Vandalia, Little York, Chambersburg, Texas, Mexico, M'Pherson, Lewisburg, North and West Dayton, are all small places, the largest of which may contain 60 dwellings.

MORGAN.

Morgan, named from Gen. Daniel Morgan, of the revolution, was organized March 1st, 1818. The Muskingum flows through the heart of the county, which, with its branches, furnishes considerable water power. The surface is very hilly; the soil limestone clay, strong and fertile. The principal products are salt, wheat, corn, oats, pork and tobacco. The following is a list of the townships in 1840, with their population.

Bloom,	1388	Malta,	1404	Olive,	1650
Bristol,	1647	Manchester,	1266	Penn,	1119
Brookfield,	1433	Meigsville,	1159	Union,	1334
Center,	1171	Morgan,	1518	Windsor,	1279
Deerfield,	1224	Noble,	1315	York,	1030
Jackson,	920				

The population of Morgan, in 1820, was 5299, in 1830, 11,800, and in 1840, 20,857; or 41 inhabitants to the square mile.

The first settlement in this county, made at Big Bottom, on the Muskingum, near the south line of the county, was broken up by the Indians. In the autumn of 1790, a company of 36 men went from Marietta and commenced the settlement. They erected a block-house on the first bottom on the east bank of the river, four miles above the mouth of Meigs creek. They were chiefly young, single men, but little acquainted with Indian warfare or military rules.

"Those best acquainted with the Indians, and those most capable of judging from appearances, had little doubt that they were preparing for hostilities, and strongly opposed the settlers going out that fall, and advised their remaining until spring; by which time, probably, the question of war or peace would be settled. Even Gen. Putnam, and the directors of the Ohio company, who gave away the land to have it settled, thought it risky and imprudent, and strongly remonstrated against venturing out at that time."

"But the young men were impatient, confident in their own prudence and ability to protect themselves. They went, put up a block-house which might accommodate the whole of them on an emergency, covered it, and laid puncheon floors, stairs, &c. It was laid up of large beech logs, and rather open, as it was not chinked between the logs; this job was left for a rainy day, or some more convenient season. Here was their first great error, as they ceased to complete the work, and the general interest was lost in that of the convenience of each individual; with this all was lost. The second error was, they kept no sentry, and had neglected to stockade or set pickets around the block-house." "No system of defence and discipline had been introduced. Their guns were lying in different places, without order, about the house. Twenty men usually encamped in the house, a part of whom were now absent, and each individual and mess cooked for themselves. One end of the building was appropriated for a fire-place, and when the day closed in, all came in, built a large fire, and commenced cooking and eating their suppers."

"The weather, for some time previous to the attack, as we learn from the diary of Hon. Paul Fearing, who lived at Fort Harmer, had been quite cold. In the midst of winter, and with such weather as this, it was not customary for the Indians to venture out on war parties, and the early borderers had formerly thought themselves in a manner safe from their depredations during the winter months.

"About twenty rods above the block-house, and a little back from the bank of the river, two men, Francis and Isaac Choate, members of the company, had erected a cabin and commenced clearing their lots. Thomas Shaw, a hired laborer in the employ of the Choates, and James Patten, another of the associates, lived with them. About the same distance below the garrison, was an old "tomahawk improvement" and a small cabin, which two men, Asa and Eleazer Bullard, had fitted up and now occupied. The Indian war path, from Sandusky to the mouth of the Muskingum, passed along on the opposite shore, in sight of the river.

"The Indians, who, during the summer, had been hunting and loitering about the settlements at Wolf creek mills and Plainfield, holding frequent and friendly intercourse with the settlers, selling them venison and bear meat in exchange for green corn and vegetables, had withdrawn early in the autumn, and gone high up the river into the vicinity of their towns, preparatory to winter quarters. Being well acquainted with all the approaches to these settlements, and the manner in which the inhabitants lived, each family in their own cabin, not apprehensive of danger, they planned and fitted out a war party for their destruction. It is said, they were not aware of there being a settlement at Big Bottom until they came in sight of it, on the opposite shore of the river, in the afternoon. From a high hill opposite the garrison, they had a view of all that part of the bottom, and could see how the men were occupied, and what was doing about the block-house. Having reconnoitered the station in this manner, just at twilight they crossed the river on the ice a little above, and divided their men into two parties; the larger one to attack the block-house, and the smaller one to make prisoners of the few men living in Choate's cabin, without alarming those below. The plan was skillfully arranged and promptly executed. As the party cautiously approached the cabin, they found the inmates at supper; a party of the Indians entered, while others stood without by the door, and addressed the men in a friendly manner. Suspecting no harm, they offered them a part of their food, of which they partook. Looking about the room, the Indians espied some leather thongs and pieces of cord that had been used in packing venison, and taking the white men by their arms told them they were prisoners. Finding it useless to resist, the Indians being more numerous, they submitted to their fate in silence.

"While this was transacting, the other party had reached the block-house unobserved; even the dogs gave no notice of their approach, as they usually do, by barking; the reason probably was, that they were also within by the fire, instead of being on the alert for their masters' safety. The door was thrown open by a stout Mohawk, who stepped in and stood by the door to keep it open, while his companions without shot down those around the fire. A man by the name of Zebulon Throop, from Massachusetts, was frying meat, and fell dead in the fire; several others fell at this discharge. The Indians then rushed in and killed all who were left with the tomahawk. No resistance seems to have been offered, so sudden and unexpected was the attack, by any of the men; but a stout, backwoods, Virginia woman, the wife of Isaac Meeks, who was employed as their hunter, seized an axe and made a blow at the head of the Indian who opened the door; a slight turn of the head saved his skull, and the axe passed down through his cheek into the shoulder, leaving a huge gash that severed nearly half his face; she was instantly killed by the tomahawk of one of his companions before she could repeat the stroke. This was all the injury received by the Indians, as the men were all killed before they had time to seize their arms, which stood in the corner of the room. While the slaughter was going on, John Stacy, a young man in the prime of life, and the son of Col. William Stacy, sprung up the stair-way and out on to the roof; while his brother Philip, a lad of sixteen years, secreted himself under some bedding in the corner of the room. The Indians on the outside soon discovered the former, and shot him while he was in the act of "begging them, for God's sake, to spare his life, as he was the only one left!"

"This was heard by the Bullards, who, alarmed by the firing at the block-house, had run out of their cabin to see what was the matter. Discovering the Indians round the house, they sprung back into their hut, seized their rifles and ammunition, and, closing the door after them, put out into the woods in a direction to be hid by the cabin from the view of the Indians. They had barely escaped when they heard their door, which was made of thin clapboards, burst open by the Indians. They did not pursue them, although they knew they had just fled, as there was a good fire burning, and their food for supper smoking hot on the table. After the slaughter was over and the scalps secured, one of the most important acts in the warfare of the American savages, they proceeded to collect the plunder. In removing the bedding, the lad, Philip Stacy, was discovered; their tomahawks were instantly raised to dispatch him, when he threw himself at the feet of one of their leading warriors, begging him to protect him. The savage either took compassion on his youth, or else his revenge being satisfied with the slaughter already made, interposed his authority and saved his life. After removing every thing they thought valuable, they tore up the floor, piled it on the dead bodies, and set it on fire, thinking to destroy the block-house with the carcases of their enemies. The building being made of green beech logs, the fires only consumed the floors and roof, leaving the walls still standing when visited the day after by the whites.

"There were twelve persons killed in this attack, viz., John Stacy, Ezra Putnam, son of Major Putnam, of Marietta; John Camp and Zebulon Throop—these men were from Massachusetts; Jonathan Farewell and James Couch, from New Hampshire; William James, from Connecticut; Joseph Clark, Rhode Island; Isaac Meeks, his wife and two children, from Virginia. They were well provided with arms, and no doubt could have defended themselves had they taken proper precautions; but they had no old revolutionary officers with them to plan and direct their operations, as they had at all the other garrisons. If they had picketed their house and kept a regular sentry, the Indians would probably never have attacked them. They had no horses or cattle for them to seize upon as plunder, and Indians are not very fond of hard fighting where nothing is to be gained; but seeing the naked block-house, without any defences, they were encouraged to attempt its capture. Colonel Stacy, who had been an old soldier, well acquainted with Indian warfare in Cherry valley, and had two sons there, visited the post only the Saturday before, and seeing its weak state, had given them a strict charge to keep a regular watch, and prepare immediately strong bars to the door, to be shut every night at sunset. They, however, fearing no danger, did not profit by his advice.

View in M'Connelsville.

"The party of Indians, after this, bent their steps towards the Wolf creek mills; but finding the people here awake and on the look-out, prepared for an attack, they did nothing more than reconnoitre the place, and made their retreat at early dawn, to the great relief of the inhabitants. The number of Indians who came over from Big Bottom was never known.

"The next day, Captain Rogers led a party of men over to Big Bottom. It was a melancholy sight to the poor borderers, as they knew not how soon the same fate might befall themselves. The action of the fire, although it did not consume, had so blackened and disfigured the dead, that few of them could be distinguished. That of Ezra Putnam was known by a pewter plate that lay under him, and which his body had prevented from entirely melting. His mother's name was on the bottom of the plate, and a part of the cake he was baking at the fire still adhered to it. William James was recognized by his great size, being six feet four inches in height, and stoutly built. He had a piece of bread clenched in his right hand, probably in the act of eating, with his back to the door, when the fatal rifle shot took effect. As the ground was frozen outside, a hole was dug within the walls of the house, and the bodies consigned to one grave. No further attempt was made at a settlement here till after the peace, in 1795."

M'Connelsville, the county seat, named from its original proprietor, Robert M'Connel, is situated upon the east bank of the Muskingum, 75 miles southeasterly from Columbus, 36 above Marietta, and 27 below Zanesville. The view was taken in the center of the town: on the left is seen the court house, the jail and county clerks' office, and in the distance, down the street, appears the Baptist church.

This thriving town contains 1 Presbyterian, 1 Congregational, 1 Baptist, 1 Protestant Methodist, and 1 Episcopal Methodist church; 15 mercantile stores, 2 newspaper printing offices, 1 foundery, 1 woollen factory, 2 flouring mills, and had in 1840, 957 inhabitants.

According to the United States statistics for 1840, more salt is manufactured in Morgan than in any other county in Ohio. It is procured by sinking wells, which, in some instances, are nearly 1000 feet in depth. The salt manufactured on the Muskingum finds its principal market in Cincinnati, where it is called "Zanesville salt," although the far greater part of it is made in this county. The sketch of the salt region on the Muskingum, we take from an article, by Dr. S. P. Hildreth, in the 24th volume of Silliman's Journal.

The first attempt at procuring salt on this river was made by Mr. Ayers, in the year 1817, a few miles below, and at the foot of the rapids at Zanesville, in the year 1819, by S. Fairlamb. He being a man of considerable mechanical ingenuity, constructed some simple machinery, connected with a water mill, which performed the operation of boring without much expense. Salt had been made for many years at the works on Salt creek, nine miles SE. of Ranesville, and some slight indications of salt on the rocks, at low water, led to this trial. Water was found, impregnated with muriate of soda, at about three hundred and fifty feet. It afforded salt of a good quality, but was not abundant, nor sufficiently saturated to make its manufacture profitable. Within the period of a few years after, several other wells were bored in this vicinity, but generally lower down the river. It was soon discovered that the water was stronger as they descended, and that the salt deposit was at a greater depth. At Duncan's falls, nine miles below, at the mouth of Salt creek, the rock had descended to four hundred and fifty feet, and with a proportionate increase in the strength of the water. At the latter place, the owner of a well not finding a sufficient supply of water for his furnace, although it was of the desired strength, pushed his well to the depth of four hundred feet below the salt rock. His praise-worthy perseverance, however, met not with its proper reward. No additional salt water was found, although it is highly probable that other salt strata are deposited below those already discovered, but at such a depth as to render it very difficult to reach them by the present mode of boring. As we descend the river, wells are found, at short distances, for thirty miles below Zanesville, gradually deepening until the salt rock is reached, at eight hundred and fifty feet below the surface. The water is also so much augmented in strength as to afford fifty pounds of salt to every fifty gallons. Twenty-two miles below the rapids, a stratum of flint rock, from nine to twelve feet in thickness, comes to the surface and crosses the river, making a slight ripple at low water. This rock has a regular dip to the south, and at M'Connelsville, five miles below, it is found at one hundred and fourteen feet; and two and a half miles further down, it is struck at one hundred and sixty feet. Where wells have been sunk through this rock, it affords a sure guide to the saliferous deposit, as the intermediate strata are very uniform in quality and thickness, and the practical operator can tell within a foot or two the actual distance to be passed between the two rocks, although the interval is six hundred and fifty feet. Above the point where the flint rock crops out, the rock strata appear to have been worn away, so that as you ascend the river the salt rock comes nearer to the surface, until at the forks of the Muskingum, it is only two hundred feet below. This flint rock is so very hard and sharp-grained, that it cuts away the best cast steel from the augers, nearly or quite as rapidly as the steel cuts away the rock, and requires three weeks of steady labor, night and day, to penetrate ten feet. With a few exceptions, the other strata are readily passed.

The lower salt rock often occasions much difficulty to the workmen, from the auger's becoming fixed in the hole. The sand of this rock, when beaten fine and allowed to settle compactly about the auger in the bottom of the well, becomes so hard and firm as to require the greatest exertions to break it loose, frequently fracturing the stout ash poles in the attempt. From the sand and small particles of the rock brought up by the pump, the salt stratum appears to be of a pure pearly whiteness; and the more porous and cellular its structure, the greater is the quantity of water afforded; as more freedom is given to the discharge of gas, which appears to be a very active agent in the rise of water, forcing it, in nearly all the wells, above the bed of the river, and in some to twenty-five or thirty feet above the top of the well.

Malta, on the west bank of the Muskingum, opposite M'Connelsville, is a thriving little place, containing 1 Episcopal Methodist, 1 Protestant Methodist church, 6 stores, a woollen factory, a flouring mill, and had, in 1840, 247 inhabitants. The following are the names of other villages in the county, with their population in 1840: Pennsville 198, Deavertown 182, Windsor 118, Sharon 109, Eagleport 63, Big Rock 61, Sarahsville 55, Morganville 36, Hiramsburgh 35, Airington 34, and Rosseau 33.

MUSKINGUM.

Muskingum was formed March 1, 1804, from Washington and Fairfield. The word Muskingum, says Kilbourn's Gazetteer, "is said to signify, in the old Indian language, *an elk's eye*, or the *glare of an elk's eye*." Col. John Johnston, of Upper Piqua, Miami county, says that "Muskingum is a Delaware word, and *means a town on the river side*. The Shawanoese call it *Wa-ka-tamo sepe*, which has the same signification.". The surface is rolling or hilly, and clay the predominating soil. It abounds with bituminous coal, and has pipe clay and burr-stone or cellular quartz, suitable for mill stones. There are numerous salt works. The brine is obtained by boring into a stratum of whitish sandstone—called salt rock—at a depth of several hundred feet. The ancient works are numerous, and iron ore is found. It is a rich and thickly settled county. The principal agricultural productions are corn, wheat, oats, potatoes, tobacco, wool and pork. The following is a list of the townships in 1840, with their population.

Adams,	988	Jefferson,	2128	Rich Hill,	1426
Blue Rock,	1074	Licking,	1322	Salem,	1002
Brush Creek,	1765	Madison,	1070	Salt Creek,	1252
Falls,	2002	Meigs,	1333	Springfield,	2334
Harrison,	1426	Monroe,	918	Union,	1625
Highland,	884	Muskingum,	1252	Washington,	1486
Hopewell,	1807	Newton,	2707	Wayne,	1276
Jackson,	1123	Perry,	1061	Zanesville,	5141

The population of Muskingum, in 1820, was 17,824; in 1830, 29,335; and in 1840, 38,746, or 52 inhabitants to a square mile.

The Muskingum country was principally occupied by the Wyandots, Delawares, and a few Senecas and Shawanoese. An Indian town once stood, years before the settlement of the country, in the vicinity of Duncan falls, from which circumstance the place is often called "Old Town." Near Dresden, was a large Shawanoese town, called Wakatomaca. The grave-yard was extensive, and when the whites first settled there, the remains of cabins were still visible. It was in this vicinity that the venerable Major Cass, the father of Hon. Lewis Cass, lived and died. He drew 4000 acres for his military services, and the location embraced within its limits the ancient town plot of the natives.

The annexed narrative of an expedition against Wakatomaca, is from Doddridge's Notes.

Under the command of Col. Angus M'Donald, 400 men were collected from the western part of Virginia, by the order of the Earl of Dunmore, the then governor of Virginia. The place of rendezvous was Wheeling, some time in the month of June, 1774. They went down the river in boats and canoes, to the mouth of Captina, from thence by the shortest route to the Wappatomica town, about sixteen miles below the present Coshocton. The pilots were Jonathan Zane, Thomas Nicholson and Tady Kelly. About six miles from the town, the army were met by a party of Indians, to the number of 40 or 50, who gave a skirmish, by the way of ambuscade, in which two of our men were killed and eight or nine wounded. One Indian was killed and several wounded. It was supposed that several more of them were killed, but they were carried off. When the army came to the town, it was found evacuated, the Indians had retreated to the opposite shore of the river, where they had formed an ambuscade, supposing the party would cross the river from the town. This was immediately discovered. The commanding officer then sent sentinels up and down the river, to give notice, in case the Indians should attempt to cross above or below the town. A private in the company of Captain Cressap, of the name of John Hargus, one of the sentinels below the town, displayed the skill of a backwoods sharpshooter. Seeing an Indian behind a blind across the river, raising up his head, at times, to look over the river, Hargus charged his rifle with a second ball, and taking deliberate aim, passed both balls through the neck of the Indian. The Indians dragged off the body and buried it with the honors of war. It was found the next morning, and scalped by Hargus.

Soon after the town was taken, the Indians from the opposite shore sued for peace. The commander offered them peace on condition of their sending over their chiefs as hostages. Five of them came over the river, and were put under guard as hostages. In the morning, they were marched in front of the army over the river. When the party had reached the western bank of the Muskingum, the Indians represented that they could not make peace without the presence of the chiefs of the other towns. On which, one of the chiefs was released to bring in the others. He did not return in the appointed time. Another chief was permitted to go on the same errand, who in like manner did not return. The party then moved up the river to the next town, which was about a mile above the first, and on the opposite shore. Here we had a slight skirmish with the Indians, in which one of them was killed and one of our men wounded. It was then discovered, that during all the time spent in the negotiation, the Indians were employed in removing their women and children, old people and effects, from the upper towns. The towns were burned and the corn cut up. The party then returned to the place from which they set out, bringing with them the three remaining chiefs, who were sent to Williamsburgh. They were released at the peace, the succeeding fall.

The army were out of provisions before they left the towns, and had to subsist on weeds, one ear of corn each day, with a very scanty supply of game. The corn was obtained at one of the Indian towns.

Additional to the above, we give the reminiscences of Abraham Thomas, originally published in the Troy Times. He was on this expedition, and later, among the early settlers of Miami county.

The collected force consisted of 400 men. I was often at their encampment; and against the positive injunctions of my parents, could not resist my inclination to join them. At this time, I was 18 years of age, owned my own rifle and accoutrements, and had been long familiar with the use of them. Escaping, I made the best possible provision I could from my own resources, and hastened to enter as a volunteer under old Mike, then Captain Cressap. The plan of the expedition was for every man to cross the Ohio, with seven days' provision in his pack. The object was to attack the Indians in their villages at Wapatomica. Some were on the waters of the Muskingum. On the first or second day's march, after crossing the Ohio, we were overtaken by a Colonel M'Donald, a British officer, who highly incensed the troops by ordering a halt for three days, during which we were consuming our provisions. While laying here, a violent storm through the night had wet our arms, and M'Donald ordered the men to discharge them in a hollow log, to deaden the report. My rifle would not go off, and I took the barrel out to unbreech it. In doing this, I made some noise in beating it with my tomahawk, on which M'Donald came towards me swearing, with an uplifted cane, threatening to strike. I instantly arose on my feet, with the rifle barrel in my hand, and stood in an attitude of defence. We looked each other in the eye for some time; at last he dropped his cane and walked off, while the whole troop set up a laugh, crying, the boy has scared the colonel. Cressap heard what was going on, and approached to defend me, but seeing how well I could defend myself, stood by, smiling at the fracas. The colonel having no reputation as an Indian fighter, was very naturally disliked as a leader, by Cressap and the men.

From this encampment we proceeded towards the Indian villages with the intention of surprising them; but late in the afternoon before we reached them, we encountered the Indians laying in ambush on the top of a second bottom. We had just crossed a branch, and was marching along its first bottom with a view of finding some place to cross a swamp that lay between us and the upper bottom. The men were marching in three parallel, Indian file columns, some distance apart. On espying a trace across the swamp, the heads of the columns, in passing it, were thrown together, and as soon as they had gained the bank, unexpectedly received the fire of the enemy. The troops immediately displayed to the right and left, under the bank, and commenced ascending it, when the skirmish became general and noisy for about thirty minutes. The Indians then gave way in every direction. In this fight, we had four or five killed and many wounded; it was supposed the Indians suffered much more.

During the engagement, while I was ascending the point of a bank, formed by a ravine from the second bottom, in company with two men, Martin and Fox, all aiming to gain the cover of some large oak trees on the top, they both fell. The first was killed, the last wounded in the breast, the ball having entered the bone, but was drawn out with the clothes. Those men were walking in a line with each other, and an Indian chief, concealed behind the tree for which I was aiming, shot them both with one ball. I took no notice whence the ball came, and hastened to the tree; just as I had gained it, the chief fell dead from the other side, and rolled at my feet. It seems a neighbor, who had seen him fire at Martin and Fox, and dodge behind the tree, stood ready to give him a shot whenever he should again make his appearance. The Indian had got his ball half down, and peeped out to look at me, when Wilson shot him in the head. The Indians retreated towards Wapatomica, flanked by two companies in hot pursuit; we followed in the rear, and as the last Indian was stepping out of the water, Captain Teabaugh, a great soldier and good marksman, brought him to the ground. I was at the time standing near Teabaugh, and shall never forget the thrilling emotion produced by this incident. During this battle, one of the men, Jacob Newbold, saw the colonel laying snug behind a fallen tree, sufficiently remote from danger, had there been no defence. It was immediately noised among the men, who were in high glee at the joke; one would cry out, "who got behind the log?" when an hundred voices would reply, "the colonel! the colonel!" At this, M'Donald became outrageous; I heard him inquire for the man who had raised the report, and threatened to punish him I went round and told Newbold what the colonel had said; "that's your sort," said he. Raising on his feet and going towards the colonel, declared he did see him slink behind the log during the battle. He gave his rifle to a man standing by, cut some hickories, and stood on the defence, at which the whole company roared with laughter, and the colonel took himself off to another part of the line. Night was now at hand, and the division was ordered, by the colonel, to encamp in an oak woods, in sight of the Indian villages, Cressap's party laying by themselves. This evening, Jack Hayes was spying down the creek, saw an Indian looking at us through the forks of a low tree; he levelled his rifle and shot him directly between the eyes, and brought him into camp. Just after night-fall, Col. M'Donald was hailed from over the creek by an Indian, who implored peace in behalf of his tribe. He was invited over by the colonel, who held a parley with him, but declined entering into terms until more Indians were present. It was then proposed, if two white men would go the Indians, they would send two more of their number to us; but none being willing to undertake the visit, two came over and stayed all night in the colonel's tent; but their only object was to watch the troops, and gain time to remove their families and effects from the town. Captain Cressap was up the whole night among his men, going the rounds, and cautioning them to keep their arms in condition for a morning attack, which he confidently expected. About two hours before day-break, he silently formed his men, examined each rifle, and let them across the creek into the villages, leaving M'Donald, with the other troops, in the encampment. At this time, the Indians who had passed the night in the camp, escaped. The village was directly surrounded, and the savages fled from it into the adjoining thicket in the utmost consternation. In this attack, none were killed on either side, but one Indian by Captain Cressap.

By this time, the camp was nearly out of provisions, with a three days' march before them. A small quantity of old corn and one cow was the entire spoils of the villages. Those were distributed among the men, the villages burned, and the troops immediately commenced their march for the Ohio river, where they expected to meet provisions sent down from Redstone. The men became exceedingly famished on this march, and myself being young, was so weak that I could no longer carry any thing on my person. An older brother and one or two others kept encouraging me; one of them had a good stock of tobacco. I saw him take it, and with an earnestness bordering on delirium, insisted on having some. As I had never used it before, they refused, thinking it would entirely disable me; but as I was so importunate, they at last gave me a small piece. I directly felt myself relieved. They gave me more, and in a short time my strength and spirits returned. I took my arms and baggage, and was able to travel with the rest of them, and was actually the first to reach the Ohio. Here we met the boats, but nothing in them but corn in the ear. Every man was soon at work with his tomahawk, crushing it on the stones, and mixing it with water in gourds or leaves fashioned in the shape of cups, while some provident ones enjoyed the aristocratic luxury of tin cups; but all seemed alike to relish the repast. A party of us crossed the Ohio that day for the settlement, when we came up with a drove of hogs, in tolerable order. We shot one and eat him on the spot, without criticizing with much nicety the mode or manner of preparation. Indeed, the meat of itself was so savoury and delicious, we thought of little else. In a few days, I returned to my parents, and after a little domestic storming and much juvenile vaunting of our exploits, settled down to clearing.

Zanesville, the county seat, is beautifully situated 54 miles east of Columbus, at the point where the national road crosses the Muskingum, and opposite the mouth of the Licking.

In May, 1796, congress passed a law authorizing Ebenezer Zane to open a road from Wheeling, in Virginia, to Limestone, now Maysville, Ky. In the following year, Mr. Zane, accompanied by his brother, Jonathan Zane, and his son-in-law, John M'Intire, both experienced woodsmen, proceeded to mark out the new road, which was afterwards cut out by the two latter. The cutting out, however, was a very hasty business, in which nothing more was attempted than to make the road passable for horsemen. As a compensation for opening this road, congress granted to Ebenezer Zane the privilege of locating military warrants upon three sections of land, not to exceed one mile square each; the first of these to be at the crossing of the Muskingum, the second at the Hockhocking, and the third at the Scioto. It has been generally said that these were free grants to Mr. Zane, for opening the road: but an examination of the law will show that it was only a permission for Mr. Zane to locate his warrant on land which had not been appropriated to that purpose. Mr. Zane first proposed to cross the Muskingum at Duncan's falls, but foreseeing the value of the hydraulic power created by the falls where Zanesville now stands, he crossed the river at that point, and thus became entitled to a section of land embracing the falls. Regarding the fertility of the soil and the beauty of the vicinity, his next choice was selected where Lancaster has since been built, rather than at the crossing of what now bears the name of Rush creek, which is really the main branch of the Hockhocking. At the Scioto, he was obliged to locate his warrant on the eastern side of the river, as the western shore lay within the Virginia military district. His location was made nearly opposite to Chillicothe. These choice tracts would no doubt have all been taken up before that time, but they had not been surveyed and brought into market. The country east of the Muskingum, and for some distance west, also, being hilly and comparatively poor, this was thought to be the least valuable section of the three, and E. Zane gave it to his brother Jonathan, and J. M'Intire, for assisting him and opening the road.

One of the conditions annexed to the grant of Mr. Zane, was that he should keep ferries across these rivers during the pleasure of congress. Messrs. Zane and M'Intire gave the Muskingum ferry for five years to William M'Culloch and Henry Crooks, on condition that they should move to the place and keep the ferry, which they did. The ferry was kept about where the upper bridge is situated, and the ford was near the site of the present dam. The ferry-boat was composed of two canoes, with a stick lashed across. The first flat-boat used for the ferry, was one in which Mr. M'Intire removed from Wheeling, in 1799. Mr. Zane resided at Wheeling. The first mail ever carried in Ohio, was brought from Marietta to M'Culloch's cabin, by Daniel Convers, in 1798, where, by the arrangement of the postmaster general, it met a mail from Wheeling and one from Limestone. M'Culloch, who could barely read, was authorized to assort the mails, and send each package in its proper direction, for which he received $30 per annum; but the service often fell to

MAIN STREET, ZANESVILLE.

the lot of Mr. Convers, as he was more expert. At that time, the aforesaid mails met here weekly. Four years after, a number of families having settled here, a regular post-office was opened, and Thomas Dowden appointed postmaster, who kept his office in a wooden building near the river, on Front street.

In 1799, Messrs. Zane and M'Intire laid out the town, which they called *Westbourn*, a name which it continued to bear until a post-office was established by the postmaster general, under the name of ZANESVILLE, and the village soon took the same name. A few

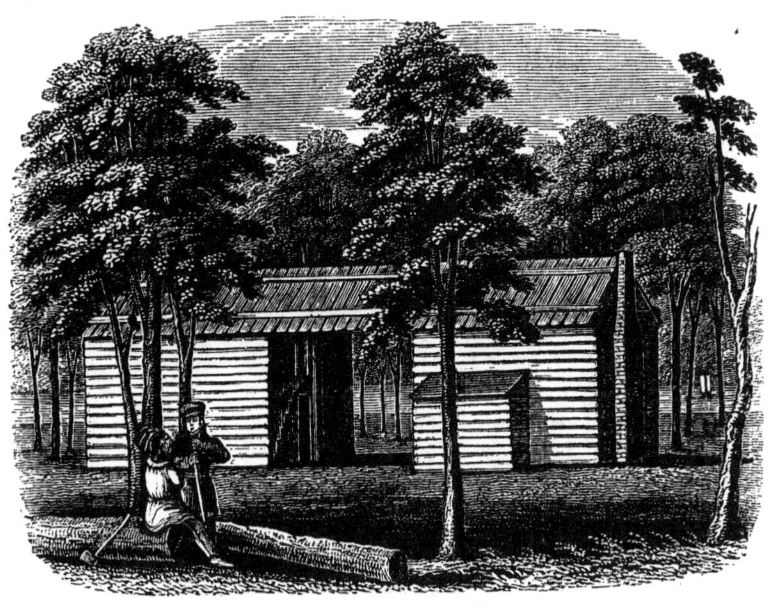

First Hotel at Zanesville.

families from the Kanawha, settled on the west side of the river soon after M'Culloch arrived, and the settlement received pretty numerous accessions until it became a *point* of importance. It contained one store and no tavern. The latter inconvenience however, was remedied by Mr. M'Intire, who, for public accommodation, rather than for private emolument, opened a house of entertainment. It is due to Mr. M'Intire and his lady, to say that their accommodations, though in a log cabin, were such as to render their house the traveller's home. Prior to that time, there were several grog shops where travellers might stop, and after partaking of a rude supper, they could spread their blankets and bearskins on the floor, and sleep with their feet to the fire. But the opening of Mr. M'Intire's house introduced the luxury of comfortable beds, and although his board was covered with the fruits of the soil and the chase, rather than the luxuries of foreign climes, the fare was various and abundant.

This, the first hotel at Zanesville, stood at what is now the corner of Market and Second streets, a few rods from the river, in an open maple grove, without any underbrush: it was a pleasant spot, well shaded with trees, and in full view of the falls. The engraving was made from the description of one who knew it well. Louis Phillipe, the present king of France, was once a guest of Mr. M'Intire. The Hon. Lewis Cass, in his "Camp and Court of Louis Phillipe," thus alludes to the circumstance. "At Zanesville, the party found the comfortable cabin of Mr. M'Intire, whose name has been preserved in the king's memory, and whose house was a favorite place of rest and refreshment for all the travellers who, at this early period, were compelled to traverse that part of the country. And if these pages should chance to meet the eyes of any of those who, like the writer, have passed many a pleasant hour under the roof of this uneducated, but truly worthy and respectable man, he trusts they will unite in this tribute to his memory."

At that time, all the iron, nail, castings, flour, fruit, with many other articles now produced here in abundance, were brought from Pittsburgh and Wheeling, either upon pack-horses across the country, or by the river in canoes. Oats and corn were usually brought about fifty miles up the river, in canoes, and were worth from 75 cents to $1 per bushel. Flour, $6 to $8 per barrel. In 1802, David Harvey opened a tavern at the intersection of Third and Main streets, which was about the first shingled roofed house in the town. Mr. M'Intire having only kept entertainment for public accommodation, discontinued, after the opening of Mr. Harvey's tavern.

In 1804, when the legislature passed an act establishing the county of Muskingum, the commissioners appointed to select a site for the county seat, reported in favor of Zanesville. The buildings were yet few in number, and the streets and lots were principally covered with the native growth; but the citizens, in order to put on the best appearance possible, turned out, while Zanesville was yet a candidate (if we may so speak) for the county seat, and cut out the bushes from some of the principal streets, and especially from the public square, that the situation might appear to the best possible advantage in the eyes of the commissioners. Some were anxious that the county seat should be at Coshocton, and others preferred the Cass section above Dresden, but Zanesville was finally selected, but in part because it was so near Marietta, as to render any county between the two places forever unnecessary. Muskingum included within its original limits the present counties of Muskingum and Coshocton, besides the greater part of what now constitutes the counties of Holmes, Tuscarawas and Guernsey, and a part of Perry, Morgan, Monroe and Carrol.

The county seat having been established, the town improved more rapidly, and as the unappropriated United States military lands had been brought into market during the preceding year, (1803,) and a land office established at Zanesville, many purchases and settlements were made in the county. The first court in Zanesville, sat in Harvey's tavern. In a short time afterwards, a wooden jail was erected, and also a wooden building, the lower part of which served as a residence for the sheriff and his family, and the upper room was used as a court room and as a place for all public meetings, political or religious. These buildings stood between the site of the present court house and jail, and were afterwards burnt down by a negro, who was confined on a charge of larceny.

An anecdote may serve to convey some idea of the difficulties of frontier life. It may also show that vice and crime were not less scorned then, than in later days. After the organization of the county, but before the erection of any public buildings, two men were apprehended on a charge of counterfeiting silver dollars. It was impracticable to send them to the jail at Marietta, a distance of sixty miles through the woods, until the next term of court, to which they were bound over. To turn them loose or permit them to escape, would encourage others to depredate in like manner; it was necessary, therefore, that they should be punished. Under these circumstances, Mr. M'Intire called on Daniel Convers, and in strong language stated his views, adding, "we must take them in charge and keep them until court." This was contrary to law, but as necessity knows no law, the justice was persuaded to surrender them to M'Intire and Convers, as they pledged themselves that if the prisoners were not forthcoming at the hour of trial, they would take their places and abide the penalty. After conducting them to a cabin selected for the purpose, and putting hand-cuffs on them, they were addressed by M'Intire, who, axe in hand, stood by the door: "Now, boys," said he, pointing to the blankets provided for their bed, "there is your bed; with your guilt or innocence we have nothing to do,—you shall have plenty to eat and to drink, but," added he, raising his right arm in a threatening manner, "*if you attempt to escape, d——n you, I'll kill you.*" The firm, resolute manner of the address, deterred them from making the attempt. M'Intire, with his axe by his side, took his seat by the door; and here, day after day and night after night, did he and his associates watch the prisoners until the term of court arrived, when they were tried and convicted. One confessed his crime, and told where their tools were secreted, about 18 miles off, on the Rocky fork of the Licking, where they were found and brought into court. Agreeably to the law then in force, he was sentenced to receive twenty-five lashes, well laid on, and to stand committed until all costs were paid. The other was to receive thirty-nine lashes, and also to be recommitted. Their sentence was immediately carried into effect, as to the stripes, which were well applied by Mr. Beymer, the sheriff. After having been re-committed to their prison, they were left on parole of honor, and their guards once more retired to their beds, free from care. Next morning, to the great gratification of all, it was found, notwithstanding their promise to the contrary, they were among the missing; their hand-cuffs having been carefully laid away for the use of their successors.

Mr. M'Intire, the founder and patron of Zanesville, was indefatigable in his attention to the interests of the town; no personal or pecuniary sacrifice being considered too great, in his anxiety to promote its prosperity.

The seat of government had been fixed temporarily at Chillicothe, but for several reasons, many members of the legislature were dissatisfied, and it was known that a change of location was desired by them. Muskingum possessed natural advantages favorable to agricultural and manufacturing purposes, which gave Zanesville a fair prospect of becoming an extensive town; while its nearly central situation rendered it a desirable site for the state metropolis. It was believed, therefore, by many, that if once the legislature could be induced to fix the temporary seat here, it would not be removed, but made permanent. The citizens of the town and county were alive to the importance of obtaining the change, and a committee, consisting of John M'Intire and others, was appointed to visit Chillicothe during the session of the legislature, and make whatever pledge might be necessary on the part of the county, as well as to aid the Muskingum delegate in obtaining the passage of the desired law. At the session of 1808 and 1809, the Muskingum delegation received assurances from their friends in the legislature, that if the county, at its own expense, would furnish suitable buildings for the use of the legislature, a law would no doubt be passed for making Zanesville the place of meeting. Encouraged by the cheering prospect, the county commissioners determined to erect a brick building in front of the old court house, which would make a respectable state house, if the law of removal should be passed, and should they fail in that, it would make an excellent court house. The county was without funds, but a few public spirited individuals stepped forward and offered to loan the money, and the buildings were accordingly erected in the summer of 1809, but not finished.

In February, 1810, the desired law was passed, fixing the seat of government at Zanesville, until otherwise provided. The county then went on to finish the buildings in such a manner as would best accommodate the legislature. A smaller building was also erected for the secretary of state and the treasurer. This building was used as a jail after the removal of the legislature, and the destruction of the old jail, until a new jail was erected in 1824, and afterwards, as offices for the clerk and county auditor. The county incurred a heavy debt in the erection of these buildings, and the county orders were long under par, but were ultimately redeemed. The legislature sat here during the sessions of '10,-'11 and '11-'12, when the present site of Columbus having been fixed upon for the permanent seat, the Chillicothe interest prevailed, and the temporary seat was once more fixed at that place, until suitable buildings could be erected at Columbus.

The project of removing the seat of government was agitated as early as 1807 or '8, and the anticipation entertained that Zanesville would be selected, gave increased activity to the progress of improvement. Much land was entered in the county, and many settlements made, although as late as 1813, land was entered within three miles of Zanesville. In 1809, parts of the town plat were covered with the natural growth of timber. It was feared by some, that re-action would succeed the defeat of the favorite project of making Zanesville the state capital; but this was not so. The natural resources of the country, and the numerous local advantages, amply supplied the necessary objects of pursuit, and saved the country from the lethargy which frequently follows disappointed effort.*

The annexed sketch of Zanesville, giving its condition, resources and prospects, is communicated by a citizen.

Zanesville has long been regarded as one of the principal towns in the state, and once bid fair to yield the palm only to Cincinnati. But the extensive internal improvements of the state have built up her rivals, while they have cut off, to some extent, her trade, and checked the rapidity of her growth. Zanesville, however, has advantages and resources which, when fully developed, must again give her a prominent place among the cities of the state.

Zanesville is situated on the east bank, in a bend of the Muskingum river, about 80 miles above its mouth, by water, and 65 miles by land. The river seems once to have run nearly in a right line, from which, however, it has gradually diverged to the westward, forming a horse-shoe curve, and depositing, through successive centuries, an alluvion of gravel, sand, &c., of great depth, on which Zanesville now stands. In sweeping around this curve, through the

---

* The preceding historical sketch of Zanesville, is from a series of editorial articles in the Zanesville Gazette, of 1835.

space of about $1\frac{3}{4}$ miles, the river falls 8 or 10 feet, and by the aid of a dam, a fall of between 16 and 17 feet is obtained, thus furnishing very extensive water power, which is used for hydraulic purposes. Near the toe of the shoe, Licking creek, or river, discharges her waters from the west, and while above the mouth of Licking, West Zanesville, containing some three hundred inhabitants, is located, South Zanesville, with nearly the same population, is situated immediately below. Further down the curve, and separated from South Zanesville by a bluff, is the beautiful village of Putnam, containing about 10 or 1200 inhabitants. A substantial and handsome bridge connects Zanesville with Putnam, while less than half a mile above, another similar bridge is thrown from Zanesville Main street, to a point in the stream, where the bridge forks, and one branch connects, on the route of the national or Cumberland road, with South Zanesville, while the other connects with West Zanesville, and the roads leading off in that direction. The "Cumberland road," constructed by the national government, and originally designed to run from the town of Cumberland, in Maryland, at the eastern foot of the Alleghany mountains, indefinitely westward, as the country becomes settled, crosses the Muskingum river, at Zanesville, bearing upon it a constant and immense travel; while the Muskingum, made navigable for steamboats, by dams, locks and short canals, opens a trade southward to the Ohio, and northward to the Ohio canal, near Dresden, which is 16 miles above, by water. The low level of the Ohio canal, between Licking and Portage summits, passes within 2 miles of Dresden, and a navigable side-cut of $2\frac{1}{2}$ miles, connects the canal with the river, at that place, which is the head of steamboat navigation. The trade of Zanesville having, through the river and side-cut, reached the canal, is conveyed southward through the interior of the state, or northward to the lake, and thence through the New York canal, &c.: or leaving the Ohio canal, through the Sandy and Beaver, it may branch off towards Pittsburgh and Philadelphia, before reaching Cleveland. The freight, however, designed for Pittsburgh and other points on the Ohio, and for the south, is usually shipped down the river upon steamboats, and on entering the Ohio, it may ascend or descend. One or more steamboats run regularly, during the business season, from Zanesville to Dresden, for the purpose of towing canal boats, carrying passengers, &c.; while others, of larger size, ply between Zanesville and Pittsburgh, Cincinnati, New Orleans, &c.

In addition to the hydraulic power furnished by the Muskingum and Licking, the hills which surround Zanesville abound in veins of bituminous coal, which lead to the free employment of steam power, and is almost exclusively used for fuel, except for cooking, and a good deal for that. But though Zanesville seems thus favored by nature with all the facilities for manufacturing, and art has constructed avenues of communication in every direction favorable to the procurement of the raw material and the transmission of manufactured goods, her citizens have not turned their attention heretofore, so much as they might have done, in that direction. Their former great advantages in the salt and wheat trade, seem, with other circumstances not necessary to specify, to have shaped their course differently; but the silent workings of causes growing out of public improvements, have satisfied business men that Zanesville must be made a manufacturing—a *producing* place—or diminish in importance; and a company is now, with praiseworthy spirit and enterprize, erecting a cotton mill, which, it is believed, will be the forerunner of many others. Zanesville should be the Lowell of the west; but this will never be brought about by old capitalists whose fortunes have been differently made, and whose thoughts have always run in other channels. A new population rising up and mingling with emigrants of skill and enterprize, may do it; but it must be in despite of such, as having amassed wealth, would play the part of the dog in the manger.

At present, there are in the above mentioned cluster of towns, 5 extensive flouring mills, 2 oil mills, 4 saw mills, 1 paper mill, on the most recent and approved plan of machinery, 5 iron founderies in active operation, and 2 others not doing business at present, 2 manufactories of yellow-ware, of beautiful finish, and much used for culinary purposes, 2 manufactories of glass, 2 of woollen goods, 2 machine shops, 1 last manufactory, with numerous other establishments of less note. There are 5 printing offices, 4 being in Zanesville, and 1 in Putnam. At these are published the Gazette, weekly; the Courier, weekly and tri-weekly; the Aurora, weekly; the Western Recorder, weekly; and Lord's Counterfeit Detector, monthly.

There are in Zanesville, 2 Catholic churches, 2 Baptist, 2 Episcopal Methodist, 1 Protestant Methodist, 3 Lutheran, 1 Presbyterian, 1 Episcopalian, 1 Universalist and 1 African. Some of these are extensive and beautiful buildings. In Putnam, there is a handsome Presbyterian church, of the new school order, and a spacious Episcopal Methodist church. For educational purposes, there is an extensive female seminary in Putnam, designed as a boarding school, and male and female district schools. South Zanesville and West Zanesville have district school buildings; and in Zanesville, much attention has been bestowed upon that subject for a few years past. The founder of the town, John M'Intire, left his immense estate, now worth probably $200,000, to found and sustain a school for the benefit of the poor of Zanesville, and a handsome brick edifice has been erected for their accommodation. The town owns two large buildings, one for males, the other for females, in which schools are kept that acknowledge no superiors. Each building is capable of accommodating 350 scholars; and the scholars, under one general head, are classified and placed in charge of assistants, but may, on any extraordinary occasion, be all brought into one room. The price of tuition for the wealthy, is from 50 to 75 cents per quarter; the public money pays the rest. But the beauty of the system is, that such as are not able to pay, are admitted to all the advantages enjoyed by the most wealthy, even to the learned languages, without money and without price. Every child, then, in Zanesville, is provided with the means of education.

There are in Zanesville upwards of thirty stores for the wholesaling and retailing of dry goods, besides hardware stores, wholesale and retail groceries, drug stores, confectionary establishments, shoe stores, hat stores, &c.

The court house, with a western wing for public offices, and a similar one on the east for an atheneum, has a handsome enclosure, with shade trees and fountain in front, making altogether an object of interest to the passing traveller, and a place of pleasant resort for citizens. The atheneum was commenced as a library company, by a few individuals, nearly twenty years ago, and soon becoming incorporated, put up a handsome two story brick building, as a wing to the court house. The lower rooms are rented for offices, while the upper are occupied by the company for their reading room, library, &c. Strangers have, by the charter, a right of admission, and during their stay in Zanesville, can always find there access to many of the leading journals of the United States, and to a library of between 3 and 4000 volumes, embracing very many choice and rare books, in literature and science; while additions are annually made with the funds arising from rents and $5 per annum paid by each stockholder. There is a commencement for a cabinet of minerals and curiosities; but that department has never flourished as its importance demands.

The water works of Zanesville are very great. The water is thrown, by a powerful forcing pump, from the river, to a reservoir upon a hill half a mile distant, 160 feet above the level of the pump, and thence let down and distributed by larger and smaller pipes into every part of the town, furnishing an ample supply for public and private purposes, as well as providing a valuable safeguard against fire. By attaching hose at once to the fire plugs, the water may be thrown without the intervention of an engine, by the pressure of the head, far above the roofs of the houses. The public pipes are all of iron, and at present there are between six and seven miles of pipe owned by the town, besides that owned by individuals, and used in conveying water from the streets and alleys to their own hydrants. Much of this, however, is of lead. The cost to the town has been about $42,000. The reservoir is calculated to contain about 750,000 gallons. The present population of Zanesville, is probably something under 8,000, excluding Putnam, West Zanesville and South Zanesville.

Putnam is less dense in its construction than Zanesville, and contains many beautiful gardens. It being principally settled by New Englanders, is in appearance a New England village. The town plat was owned, and the town laid out by Increase Matthews, Levi Whipple and Edwin Putnam. The latter two are dead; Dr. Matthews still resides in Putnam.

The town was originally called Springfield, but there being a Springfield in Clarke county, the name of the former was changed to Putnam. The view represents Putnam as it appears from the east bank of the Muskingum, about a mile below the steamboat

Putnam.

landing, at Zanesville. The bridge connecting Putnam with Zanesville, is seen on the right. On the left is shown a church, and the top of the seminary a little to the right of it.

The Putnam Female Seminary is an incorporated institution, and has been in operation about 10 years. The principal edifice stands in an area of 3 acres, and cost, with its furniture, about $20,000 Pupils under 14 years of age are received into the preparatory department. Those over 14 enter the upper department, in which

The Putnam Female Seminary.

the regular course of study requires 3 years, and excepting the languages, is essentially like a college course. It is proposed soon to extend the time to 4 years, and make the course the same as in colleges, substituting the German for Greek. The average number of pupils has been about 100. "By reason of the endowments, the term bills are very much less than at any similar school in the country. Exclusive of extra studies, the cost per year will not exceed $100 per scholar." There are 5 teachers in this flourishing institution, of which Miss Mary Cone is the principal. It is under the general direction of a board of trustees.

Dresden is situated on the Muskingum side cut of the Ohio canal, at the head of steamboat navigation on the Muskingum, 15 miles above Zanesville. It is the market of a large and fertile country by which it is surrounded, and does a heavy business. It possesses superior manufacturing advantages, there being a fall of twenty-nine feet from the main canal to low water mark on the river. The adjacent hills abound with coal and iron ore. It contains 1 Presbyterian and 1 Methodist church, about 15 stores, a market house, and 1000 or 1200 inhabitants.

Taylorsville, laid out in 1832 by James Taylor, is on the Muskingum, 9 miles below Zanesville, at what are called Duncan's Falls, and has about 500 inhabitants. On the opposite side of the river is a village called Duncan's Falls. In the two villages united, are 6 stores, 1 Catholic, 1 Lutheran and 1 Methodist church, 1 fulling mill, 1 carding machine, and two merchant mills. An Indian town existed in the neighborhood when the whites first made their settlement.

Chandlersville, 10 miles SE. of Zanesville, has 2 churches, 3 stores, and about 300 people. In boring for salt in that neighborhood, in January, 1820, some pieces of silver were dropped into the hole by some evil disposed person, and being brought up among the borings, reduced to a fine state, quite a sensation was produced. The parts were submitted to chemical analysis, and decided by a competent chemist to be very rich. A company was immediately formed to work the mine, under the name of "the Muskingum Mining Company," which was incorporated by the legislature. This company purchased of Mr. Samuel Chandler, the privilege of sinking a shaft near his well, from which the silver had been extracted. As this shaft was sunk near the well, it did so much injury, that Mr. Chandler afterwards recovered heavy damages of the company. The company expended about $10,000 in search of the expected treasure, ere they abandoned their ill-fated project.

Norwich, 12 miles E. of Zanesville, on the national road, has 4 stores, 2 churches, and about 500 inhabitants. The country in this region is well adapted to wheat, and the population embraces many substantial and independent farmers.

New Concord, 3 miles east of Norwich, on the same road, has in the place or immediate vicinity, several churches, 3 stores, and about 400 inhabitants. Pleasantly located, on an eminence north of the central part of the village, is Muskingum College. In March, 1837, the Trustees of New Concord Academy—an institution which had been in operation several years—were vested with college powers by the legislature of Ohio, to be known by the name of Muskingum College. It is a strictly literary institution, and the first

Muskingum College.

class graduated in 1839. Although pecuniary embarrassments have impeded its progress, it has continued uninterruptedly its operations as a college. These difficulties having been recently removed, its prospects are brightening.

Gratiot, on the national road, on the line of Licking county, contains 3 churches, 1 grist and 1 saw mill, a carding machine, and about 300 inhabitants.

The following are small villages in the county. The largest contains several stores and churches; but none have over 300 inhabitants. Uniontown, or Fultonham, Roseville, Adamsville, Mount Sterling, Frazeyburg, Otsego, Irville, Meigsville, Nashport, Hopewell, Newtonville, Jackson and Bridgeville.

OTTAWA.

Ottawa was formed March 6th, 1840, from Sandusky, Erie and Lucas counties. Ottawa, says Bancroft, is an Indian word, signifying "*trader.*" It was applied to a tribe, whose last home, in Ohio, was on the banks of the Maumee. The surface is level, and most of the county is within the Black Swamp, and contains much prairie and marshy land. A great part of the soil is owned by land companies in New York. A very small portion of the eastern part is within the "*fire-lands.*" There were but a few settlers previous to 1830, since which many have emigrated to it, from the central part of the state. On the peninsula which puts out into Lake Erie, are extensive plaster beds, from which large quantities of plaster are taken. Upon it are large limestone quarries, extensively worked. The principal crops are corn, potatoes, wheat and oats. The following is a list of the townships in 1840, with their population.

Bay,	231	Erie,	196	Portage,	357
Carroll,	262	Harris,	318	Salem,	108
Clay,	176	Kelley's Island,	68	Van Rensselaer,	27
Danbury,	515				

The population of Ottawa, in 1840, was 2258, or about 6 inhabitants to a square mile.

The first trial of arms in the war of 1812, upon the soil of Ohio, occurred in two skirmishes on the peninsula in this county, on the 29th of September, 1812, between a party of soldiers, principally

50

from Trumbull and Ashtabula counties, under the command of Capt. Joshua T. Cotton, and a superior body of Indians. Our men behaved with coolness and courage. The results were unimportant, and but a few were killed on either side.*

That noted event in the late war, in the northwest—*Perry's victory*—took place on Lake Erie, only a few miles distant from the line of Ottawa. A description of this action, we annex, from Perkins's Late War.

At Erie, Commodore Perry was directed to repair, and superintend a naval establishment, the object of which was to create a superior force on the lake. The difficulties of building a navy in the wilderness can only be conceived by those who have experienced them. There was nothing at this spot out of which it could be built, but the timber of the forest. Ship builders, sailors, naval stores, guns and ammunition, were to be transported by land, over bad roads, a distance of 400 miles, either from Albany by the way of Buffalo, or from Philadelphia by the way of Pittsburgh. Under all these embarrassments, by the first of August, 1813, Commodore Perry had provided a flotilla, consisting of the ships Lawrence and Niagara of twenty guns each, and seven smaller vessels, to wit, one of four guns, one of three, two of two, and three of one; in the whole fifty-four guns. While the ships were building, the enemy frequently appeared off the harbor and threatened their destruction; but the shallowness of the water on the bar—there being but five feet—prevented their approach. The same cause, which insured the safety of the ships while building, seemed to prevent their being of any service. The two largest drew several feet more water than there was on the bar. The inventive genius of Commodore Perry, however, soon surmounted this difficulty. He placed large scows on each side of the two largest ships, filled them so as to sink to the water edge, then attached them to the ships by strong pieces of timber, and pumped out the water. The scows then buoyed up the ships so as to pass the bar in safety. This operation was performed on both the large ships, in the presence of a superior enemy. Having gotten his fleet in readiness, Commodore Perry proceeded to the head of the lake, and anchored in Put-in-Bay, opposite to, and distant thirty miles from Malden, where the British fleet lay under the guns of the fort. He lay at anchor here several days, watching the motions of the enemy, determined to give him battle the first favorable opportunity. On the 10th of September, at sunrise, the British fleet, consisting of one ship of nineteen guns, one of seventeen, one of thirteen, one of ten, one of three, and one of one, amounting to sixty-four, and exceeding the Americans by ten guns, under the command of Commodore Barclay, appeared off Put-in-Bay, distant about ten miles. Commodore Perry immediately got under weigh, with a light breeze at southwest. At 10 o'clock, the wind hauled to the southeast, which brought the American squadron to the windward, and gave them the weathergage. Commodore Perry, on board the Lawrence, then hoisted his union jack, having for a motto the dying words of Captain Lawrence, "*Dont give up the ship,*" which was received with repeated cheers by the crew.

He then formed the line of battle, and bore up for the enemy, who at the same time hauled his courses and prepared for action. The lightness of the wind occasioned the hostile squadrons to approach each other but slowly, and prolonged for two hours, the solemn interval of suspense and anxiety which precedes a battle. The order and regularity of naval discipline heightened the dreadful quiet of the moment. No noise, no bustle, prevailed to distract the mind, except at intervals, the shrill pipings of the boatswain's whistle, or a murmuring whisper among the men, who stood around their guns, with lighted matches, narrowly watching the movements of the foe, and sometimes stealing a glance at the countenances of their commanders. In this manner, the hostile fleets gradually neared each other in awful silence. At fifteen minutes after eleven, a bugle was sounded on board the enemy's headmost ship, Detroit, loud cheers burst from all their crews, and a tremendous fire opened upon the Lawrence, from the British long guns, which, from the shortness of the Lawrence's, she was obliged to sustain for forty minutes without being able to return a shot.

Commodore Perry, without waiting for the other ships, kept on his course in such gallant and determined style, that the enemy supposed he meant immediately to board. At five minutes before twelve, having gained a nearer position, the Lawrence opened her fire, but

* Hon. Joshua R. Giddings, then a lad of 16, was present on the occasion. In the Ladies' Repository was published two or three years since a lengthy account of these skirmishes from his pen.

the long guns of the British sti l gave them greatly the advantage, and the Lawrence was exceedingly cut up without being able to do but very little damage in return. Their shot pierced her side in all directions, killing the men in the birth-deck and steerage, where they had been carried to be dressed. One shot had nearly produced a fatal explosion; passing through the light room, it knocked the snuff of the candle into the magazine; fortunately, the gunner saw it, and had the presence of mind immediately to extinguish it. It appeared to be the enemy's plan, at all events to destroy the commodore's ship; their heaviest fire was directed against the Lawrence, and blazed incessantly from all their largest vessels. Commodore Perry, finding the hazard of his situation, made all sail, and directed the other vessels to follow, for the purpose of closing with the enemy. The tremendous fire, however, to which he was exposed, soon cut away every brace and bowline of the Lawrence, and she became unmanageable. The other vessels were unable to get up; and in this disastrous situation, she sustained the main force of the enemy's fire for upwards of two hours, within cannister distance, though a considerable part of the time not more than two or three of her guns could be brought to bear on her antagonist. The utmost order and regularity prevailed during this scene of horror; as fast as the men at the guns were wounded, they were carried below, and others stepped into their places; the dead remained where they fell, until after the action. At this juncture, the enemy believed the battle to be won. The Lawrence was reduced to a mere wreck; her deck was streaming with blood, and covered with the mangled limbs and bodies of the slain; nearly the whole of her crew were either killed or wounded; her guns were dismounted, and the commodore and his officers helped to work the last that was capable of service. At two, Capt. Elliott was enabled, by the aid of a fresh breeze, to bring his ship into close action in gallant style; and the commodore immediately determined to shift his flag on board that ship; and giving his own in charge to Lieut. Yarnell, he hauled down his union jack, and taking it under his arm, ordered a boat to put him on board the Niagara. Broadsides were levelled at his boat, and a shower of musketry from three of the enemy's ships. He arrived safe and hoisted his union jack, with its animating motto, on board the Niagara. Capt. Elliott, by direction of the commodore, immediately put off in a boat, to bring up the schooners, which had been kept back by the lightness of the wind. At this moment, the flag of the Lawrence was hauled down. She had sustained the principal force of the enemy's fire for two hours, and was rendered incapable of defence. Any further show of resistance would have been a useless sacrifice of the relics of her brave and mangled crew. The enemy were at the same time so crippled, that they were unable to take possession of her, and circumstances soon enabled her crew again to hoist her flag. Commodore Perry now gave the signal to all the vessels for close action. The small vessels, under the direction of Captain Elliott, got out their sweeps, and made all sail. Finding the Niagara but little injured, the commander determined upon the bold and desperate expedient of breaking the enemy's line; he accordingly bore up and passed the head of the two ships and brig, giving them a raking fire from his starboard guns, and also a raking fire upon a large schooner and sloop, from his larboard quarter, at half pistol shot. Having gotten the whole squadron into action, he luffed and laid his ship alongside of the British commodore. The small vessels having now got up within good grape and canister distance on the other quarter, enclosed their enemy between them and the Niagara, and in this position kept up a most destructive fire on both quarters of the British, until every ship struck her colors.

The engagement lasted about three hours, and never was victory more decisive and complete. More prisoners were taken than there were men on board the American squadron at the close of the action. The principal loss in killed and wounded was on board the Lawrence, before the other vessels were brought into action. Of her crew, twenty-two were killed, and sixty wounded. When her flag was struck, but twenty men remained on deck fit for duty. The loss on board of all the other vessels, was only five killed, and thirty-six wounded. The British loss must have been much more considerable. Commodore Barclay was dangerously wounded. He had lost one arm in the battle of Trafalgar. The other was now rendered useless, by the loss of a part of his shoulder-blade; he received also a severe wound in the hip.

Commodore Perry, in his official dispatch, speaks in the highest terms of respect and commisseration for his wounded antagonist, and asks leave to grant him an immediate parole. Of Capt. Elliott, his second in command, he says, "that he is already so well known to the government, that it would be almost superfluous to speak. In this action, he evinced his characteristic bravery and judgment, and since the close of it, has given me the most able and essential assistance." The bold and desperate measure of pressing forward into action with the Lawrence alone, and exposing her to the whole fire of the enemy's fleet for two hours, before the other ships could be got up, has been censured as rash, and not warranted by the rules of naval war; but there are seasons when the commander must rely more on the daring promptness of his measures, than on nice calculations of comparative strength. Neither Bonaparte nor Nelson ever stopped to measure accurately the strength of the respective combatants. The result is the acknowledged and generally the best criterion of merit; and it should not detract from the eclat of the successful commander, that his measures were bold and decisive.

Two days after the battle, two Indian chiefs, who had been selected for their skill as marksmen, and stationed in the tops of the Detroit, for the purpose of picking off the American officers, were found snugly stowed away in the hold of the Detroit. These savages, who had been accustomed to ships of no greater magnitude than what they could sling on their backs, when the action became warm, were so panic-struck at the terrors of the scene, and the strange perils that surrounded them, that, looking at each other with amazement, they vociferated their significant "*quonh*," and precipitately descended to the hold. In their British uniforms hanging in bags upon their famished bodies, they were brought before Commodore Perry, fed, and discharged; no further parole being necessary, to prevent their afterwards engaging in the contest The slain of the crews of both squadrons were committed to the lake immediately after the action. The next day, the funeral obsequies of the American and British officers who had fallen, were performed at an opening on the margin of the bay, in an appropriate and affecting manner. The crews of both fleets united in the ceremony. The stillness of the weather—the procession of boats—the music—the slow and regular motion of the oars, striking in exact time with the notes of the solemn dirge—the mournful waving of the flags—the sound of the minute-guns from all the ships—the wild and solitary aspect of the place, gave to these funeral rites a most impressive influence, and formed an affecting contrast with the terrible conflict of the preceding day. Then the people of the two squadrons were engaged in the deadly strife of arms; now they were associated as brothers, to pay the last tribute of respect to the slain of both nations. Two American officers, Lieutenant Brooks and Midshipman Laub, of the Lawrence; and three British, Captain Finnis and Lieutenant Stoke of the Charlotte, and Lieutenant Garland of the Detroit, lie interred by the side of each other, in this lonely place, on the margin of the lake, a few paces from the beach.

This interesting battle was fought midway of the lake, between the two hostile armies, who lay on the opposite shores, waiting in anxious expectation, its result. The allied British and Indian forces, to the amount of four thousand five hundred, under Proctor and Tecumseh, were at Malden, ready, in case of a successful issue, to renew their ravages on the American borders.

Port Clinton, the county seat, laid out in 1827, is 120 miles north of Columbus. It is situated on a beautiful bay, on the right bank of Portage river. It has a good harbor—in which is a light-house—and about 60 dwellings. It is about the only village in the county, and may ultimately be a place of considerable trade.

Most of the islands in Lake Erie are off this county. Their exact situation and size was not known, until the recent survey by the United States government, and all the maps heretofore published are erroneous respecting them.

Kelly's Island, recently formed into a township of the same name, has 18 families, and 2800 acres. It is resorted to by steamers, for wood and water, and harborage in storms. Its harbor is good, and large quantities of excellent limestone are quarried, for building and other purposes: some of the most elegant structures in Detroit are built with it. The Put-in-Bay islands are North, South and Middle Bass, Sugar, Gibraltar, Strontian—so called from the quantity of strontian found there—with numerous small islets, containing half an acre and less. South Bass is the largest, and contains about 1300 acres. Upon it are several caves, which are much visited. Some of the officers slain at Perry's victory were hastily buried here, in the sand near the shore, and many of the bones have been washed away by the invading waters. Middle and North Bass have each about 700 acres. On Middle Bass is one family, and on South Bass two or three. This cluster is about 8 miles NW. of Kelly's Island, which, with that, are within the legal jurisdiction of this county.

Point-au-Pele—so called from lying off a locality of that name in Canada—is the largest island in the lake, being about 8 miles in length. It was on the ice near this island, that "the patriots"—so called, under Capt. Bradley, of Sandusky City, had the skirmish with the British cavalry a few years since, and repulsed them. The three Sisters—East, Middle and West Sister—are uninhabited. The last is the largest, and has not over 50 or 60 acres. Middle island has about the same area, and the Hen and Chickens are quite small.

PAULDING.

PAULDING was formed from old Indian territory, April 1st, 1820. It was named from John Paulding, a native of Peekskill, N. Y., and one of the three militia men who captured Major Andre, in the war of the revolution: he died in 1818. The surface is level, and the county covered by the Black Swamp. The principal crops are corn, wheat and oats. The following is a list of the townships in 1840, with their population.

Auglaize,	298	Carroll,	345
Brown,	181	Crain,	211

The population of Paulding, in 1840, was 1035, or about 2 inhabitants to a square mile.

Charloe, the county seat, is on the Auglaize river and Miami Extension canal, 137 miles NW. of Columbus, and 12 south of Defiance. It was laid out about the year 1840, and contains a few families only. Ockenoxy's town stood on the site of Charloe—so called from a chief who resided there, and who was reputed an obstinate, cruel man. The village, later, was called Charloe, from an Ottawa chief, distinguished for his eloquence and sprightliness in debate.

Five miles north, at the junction of the Wabash and Erie and Miami Extension canals, is a small village, called Junction. Eleven miles west from the junction, on the Wabash and Erie canal, is Antwerp, also a small town.

PERRY.

PERRY was formed March 1st, 1817, from Washington, Muskingum and Fairfield, and named from Commodore Oliver H. Perry. The surface is mostly rolling, and in the south hilly, the soil is clayey, and in the middle and northern part fertile. Much excellent tobacco is raised in the southern part, and wheat in the centre and north. The principal productions are wheat, corn, oats, hay, tobacco, beef cattle, pork and wool. The following is a list of the townships in 1840, with their population.

Bearfield,	1455	Jackson,	1700	Reading,	3936
Clayton,	1602	Madison,	1167	Salt Lick,	1243
Harrison,	1034	Monday Creek,	986	Thorn,	2006
Hopewell,	1544	Monroe,	999		

The population of Perry, in 1820, was 8429, in 1830, 14,063, and in 1840, 19,340; or 48 inhabitants to a square mile.

This county was first settled by Pennsylvania Germans, about the years 1802 and 1803. Of the early settlers the names of the following are recollected: John Hammond, David Pugh, Robt. M'Clung, Isaac Brown, John and Anthony Clayton, Isaac Reynolds, Daniel Shearer, Peter Overmyer, Adam Binckley, Wm. and Jacob Dusenbury, John Poorman, John Finck, Daniel Parkinson and John Lashley. The first church erected in the county was at New Reading: it was a Lutheran church, of which the Rev. Mr. Foster was the pastor: shortly after, a Baptist church was built about three miles east of Somerset.

The road through this county was, "from 1800 to 1815, the great thoroughfare between Kentucky, Indiana, Ohio and the eastern states, or until steamboat navigation created a new era in the history of travellers—a perpetual stream of emigrants rolled westward along its course, giving constant occupation to hundreds of tavern keepers, seated at short distances along its borders, and consuming all the spare grain raised by the inhabitants for many miles north and south of its line. Groups of merchants on horseback, with led horses, laden with Spanish dollars, travelled by easy stages every spring and autumn along its route, congregated in parties of ten or twenty individuals, for mutual protection, and armed with dirks, pocket pistols, and pistols in holsters, as robberies sometimes took place in the more wilderness parts of the road. The goods, when purchased, were wagoned to Pittsburgh, and sent in large flat boats, or keel boats, to their destination below, while the merchant returned on horseback to his home, occupying eight or ten weeks in the whole tour."

Somerset, the county seat, is 43 miles easterly from Columbus, on the Macadamized road leading from Zanesville to Lancaster, from each of which it is 18 miles, or midway, which circumstance gave it, when originally laid out, the name of *Middletown.*

In 1807, John Finck erected the first log-cabin in the vicinity of the place. Having purchased a half section of land, he laid out, in 1810, the eastern part of the town: the western part was laid out by Jacob Miller. They became the first settlers: the first died about 11, and the last about 20 years since. The present name, Somerset, was derived from Somerset, Penn., from which place and vicinity most of the early settlers came. The board of directors of the Lutheran seminary at Columbus have voted to remove it to this place. The town contains 1 Lutheran, 2 Catholic and 1 Methodist church; 1 iron foundery, 1 tobacco warehouse, 3 newspaper printing offices, 16 mercantile stores, and about 1400 inhabitants. A very large proportion of the population of the county are Catholics. They

View in Somerset.

have in the town a nunnery, to which is attached St. Mary's seminary, a school for young females. It is well conducted, and many Protestant families send their daughters here to be educated. The Catholics are also about building a college for the reception of all disposed to patronize it.

About two miles south of Somerset are the buildings shown in the annexed view. The elegant building in the centre is St. Joseph's church, recently erected; on the right is seen the convent building;

Convent of Dominican Friars, &c.

the structure partly shown beyond St. Joseph's church, is the oldest Catholic church in the state. The history, of which we give an extract from an article in the United States Catholic Magazine for January, 1847, entitled "the Catholic Church in Ohio."

The first chapel, of which we have any authentic record, that was ever consecrated to Almighty God within our borders, was St. Joseph's, in Perry county, which was solemnly blessed on the 6th of December, 1818, by Rev. Edward Fenwick and his nephew, Rev. N. D. Young, of the order of St. Dominic, both natives of Maryland, and deriving their jurisdiction from the venerable Dr. Flaget, who was then the only bishop between the Alleghenies and the Mississippi. This chapel was first built of logs, to which an addition of stone was subsequently made, so that it was, for a considerable time, "partly logs and partly stone." When the congregation, which consisted of only ten families when the chapel was first opened, had increased in number, the logs disappeared, and a new addition, or, to speak more correctly, a separate church of brick marked the progress of improvement, and afforded new facilities for the accommodation of the faithful. An humble convent, whose reverend inmates, one American, N. D. Young, one Irishman, Thomas Martin, and one Belgian, Vincent de Rymacher, cheerfully shared in all the hardships and privations incident to the new colony, was erected near the church, and, from its peaceful precincts, the saving truths of faith were conveyed, and its divine sacraments administered to many a weary emigrant who had almost despaired of enjoying those blessings in the solitude which he had selected for his home. The benedictions of the poor, and the refreshing dews of heaven, descended on the spiritual seed thus sown. It increased and multiplied the hundred fold. New congregations were formed in Somerset, Lancaster, Zanesville, St. Barnabas, Morgan county, Rehoboth and St. Patrick's, seven miles from St. Joseph's, and in Sapp's settlement, and various other stations still more distant, was the white habit of St. Dominic hailed by the lonely Catholic as the harbinger of glad tidings, and the symbol of the joy, the purity, and the triumphs which attest the presence of the Holy Spirit, and the fulfilment of the promises made by her divine founder to the church.

At this place, a number of young men are being educated for the priesthood of the Dominican order. A large library is connected with the institution, which affords facilities to the students in becoming acquainted with church history and literature. Among them are the writings of many of the fathers and rare books, some of which were printed before the discovery of America.

In this county are many ancient mounds, of various dimensions, and four or five miles in a NW. direction from Somerset, is an ancient stone fort. Although irregular in shape, it approaches a triangle. Near the center is a stone mound, about 12 feet high, and in the wall a smaller one. The fort encloses about forty acres. Just south of it is a square work, containing about half an acre.

Thornville, 9 miles N. of Somerset, near the reservoir of the feeder of the Ohio canal, is a thriving town, containing 2 churches, several forwarding houses, 3 stores, and about 500 inhabitants.

"This portion of country was settled about 1810; land was then so cheap in the neighborhood that one Beesacker purchased 20 acres for an old black mare; luckily, in laying out the country, two important roads intersected his purchase. He immediately had it surveyed into town lots: naming it New Lebanon, an embryo town sprung into existence. This took place about 1815. It was afterwards changed to Thornville, from being in the township of Thorn."

New Lexington, 9 miles S. of Somerset, contains 4 stores, 3 churches, and about 300 inhabitants. Rehoboth, 7 miles SE. of Somerset, has 2 churches, 3 stores, 2 tobacco warehouses, and about 300 people. New Reading, Crossinville, Oakfield and Straitsville are also small places, the first of which, by the census of 1840, had 193 inhabitants.

SCENE ON THE AUGLAIZE:—A HOME IN THE WILDERNESS.

PICKAWAY.

PICKAWAY was formed Jan. 12th, 1810, from Ross, Fairfield and Franklin: the name is a mis-spelling of *Piqua*, the name of a tribe of the Shawanoese, for the significatien of which see page 362. The name was immediately derived from the plains in the county. The surface is level, and the soil generally very fertile and productive in grain. In many places the eye will take in at a single glance 500 acres of corn at one view. The country has the four varieties of woodland, barren, plain and prairie. The barrens were originally covered with shrub oak, and were at first supposed to be valueless, but proved to be excellent for grass and oats. The original settlers were mainly from Pennsylvania and Virginia. The principal productions are corn, wheat, oats, grass, pork, wool and neat cattle. The following is a list of the townships in 1840, with their population.

Circleville,	2973	Madison,	851	Scioto,	920
Darby,	1052	Muhlenburgh,	653	Walnut,	1798
Deer Creek,	1376	Monroe,	1352	Washington,	1194
Harrison,	1149	Pickaway,	1574	Wayne,	779
Jackson,	993	Salt Creek,	1815		

The population of Pickaway in 1820, was 18,143, in 1830, 15,935, and in 1840, 20,169; or 40 inhabitants to the square mile.

Much of the land on the west side of the Scioto is farmed by tenants, who receive either a certain proportion of the profits, or pay stated rents. The farther removed the ownership of land from those who cultivate it, the worse is it for the development of the resources of a country. Slavery is worse than the tenant system, and actual ownership the best of all. Hence it is that the Virginia military district, much of which is held in large tracts by wealthy men, with tenants under them, does not thrive as well as some other parts of the state having a poorer soil, but cultivated by those who both hold the plow and own the land.

Within the county, on the west side of the river, is a territory of about 290 square miles, containing a population of 8,376, averaging a fraction less than 30 to the square mile; while the territory on the east side of the river, within the county, embracing only 209 square miles, sustains a population of 11,349—averaging almost 55 to the square mile. This disparity in the density of population of the territory on the east and west sides of the river, arises principally from four causes: 1st, the large surveys in which the land on the west side of the river was originally located. This prevented persons of small means from seeking farms there; 2d, the difficulty of finding the real owner of these surveys, who generally resided in some of the southern Atlantic states, or Kentucky, and who frequently had no agent here to sub-divide, show, or sell the lands; 3d, the frequent interference of different entries and surveys there with each other, which rendered the titles insecure. Though only a small portion of the lands were subject to this last difficulty, yet many persons were thereby deterred from purchasing and settling upon them; 4th, the greater disposition in the inhabitants there to engross large tracts of land, instead of purchasing smaller tracts, and expending more upon their improvements. This last continues to be the great obstacle in the way of increase of population *now* on those lands.

To an observing traveller, passing directly through the county from east to west, the contrast is very striking. While on the one side he finds the lands well improved, with fields of moderate size, well fenced, with a good barn and neat dwelling house to each adjacent farm; on the other, he finds occasionally baronial mansions, "like angel's visits, few and far between," with rarely a barn, and each field large enough for two or three good farms. Between these mansions he will find the old pioneer log dwellings, and the slovenly cultivation of the first settlers. The prices of the same quality of land on the east side are generally about double those on the west side. A part of this difference in the artificial appearance and cultivation of the country upon the opposite sides of the river, results, no doubt, from the different origin of the inhabitants. Those on the east side originated mostly from Pennsylvania; while those on the west side had their origin generally in the more northern slave states. Habits brought with the first emigrants cannot be changed at once, though time and the operation of our laws will gradually modify them. Already, in several neighborhoods west of the river, the plan of smaller farms and better improvements has commenced; and a few years of prosperous industry will produce the neat farm cottage and the well-stored barn, with the productive fields of variegated crops and delicious fruits, which render the pursuits of agriculture so desirable. These are the blessings designed by a bountiful Benefactor to compensate for the toils, exposures and hardships incident to the pursuit of farming. Without these comforts, it would be the barren drudgery of the toil-worn slave.*

Three and a half miles south of Circleville are the celebrated *Pickaway Plains*, said to contain the richest body of land in Ohio. "They are divided into two parts, the greater or upper plains, and

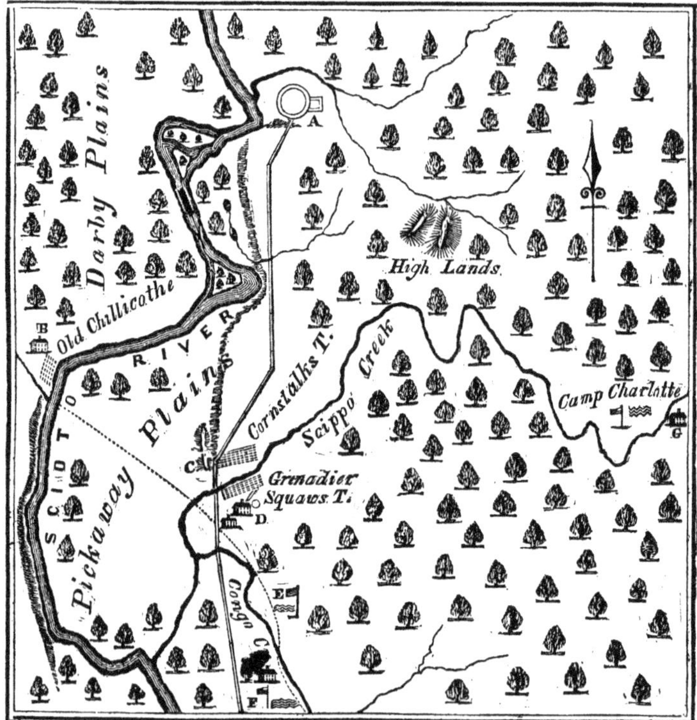

Map of the Ancient Shawanoese Towns, on the Pickaway Plain.

[*Explanations.*—A. Ancient works, on which Circleville now stands. B. Logan's cabin at Old Chillicothe, now Westfall, four miles below Circleville: from this place a trail led through Grenadier Squaw town, and from thence up the Congo valley, and crossed to the opposite side of the creek, about 1½ miles from its mouth. C. Black mountain, a short dis-

* Historical sketch of Pickaway county.

tance west of the old Barr mansion. D. Council house, a short distance NE. of the residence of Wm. Renick, jr. The two parallel lines at this point represent the gauntlet through which prisoners were forced to run, and O. the stake at which they were burnt, which last is on a commanding elevation. F. The camp of Col. Lewis, just south of the residence ol Geo. Wolf. E. The point where Lord Dunmore met with and stopped the army of Lewis when on their way to attack the Indians: it is opposite the mansion of Major John Boggs. G. The residence of Judge Gills, near which is shown the position of Camp Charlotte.]

the lesser or lower one. The soil was very black when first cultivated: the result of vegetable decomposition through a long succession of ages. These plains are based on water-worn gravel and pebbles. The upper plain is at least 150 feet above the bed of the river, which passes about a mile west of them. Their form is elliptical, with the longest diameter from northeast to southwest, being about seven miles by three and a half or four miles. They were destitute of trees when first visited by the whites. The fertility was such as to produce one hundred bushels of corn, or fifty of wheat, to the acre, for many years, but they are now less productive." These plains have but few trees or shrubs within reach of the eye, except along the distant borders. The early settlers in the vicinity procured all their fodder, a coarse, natural grass, from the plains, which grew several feet above a man's head. It was extremely difficult to break up, requiring the strongest teams. The cultivation of corn, which grew to the height of 12 or 15 feet, weakened their natural fertility. Originally, the plains were adorned with a great variety of beautiful flowers.

The annexed map is reduced from one 20½ inches by 17½, made from the survey of P. N. White, for Felix Renick, of Ross. The country represented is about 7 miles square. Of all places in the west, this pre-eminently deserves the name of "classic ground." Here, in olden time, burned the council-fires of the red man; here the affairs of the nation in general council were discussed, and the important questions of peace and war decided. On these plains the allied tribes marched forth and met General Lewis, and fought the sanguinary battle at Point Pleasant. Here it was that Logan made his memorable speech, and here, too, that the noted campaign of Dunmore was brought to a close by a treaty, or rather a truce, at Camp Charlotte.

From the "Remarks" appended to this map, by Mr. Renick, we extract the following.

Among the circumstances which invest this region with extraordinary interest, is the fact, that to those towns were brought so many of the truly unfortunate prisoners who were abducted from the neighboring states. Here they were immolated on the altar of the red man's vengeance, and made to suffer, to the death, all the tortures savage ingenuity could invent, as a sort of expiation for the aggressions of their race. Strange does it seem that human beings, on whom nature had bestowed such riches of intellect, could be brought, by force of habit, not only to commit, but to delight in committing, such enormous cruelties as they often practised on many of their helpless victims—acts which had the direct effect of bringing down retaliation, in some form or other, on their own heads. But that they should contend to the last extremity for so delightful a spot, will not be wondered at by the most common observer on a view of the premises. For picturesqueness, fertility of soil, and every other concomitant to make it desirable for human habitation, it is not surpassed by any other locality in the western country, or perhaps in the world. The towns were well supplied with good spring water; some of the adjacent bottom lands were susceptible of being made to produce, as nature has left them, one hundred bushels of Indian corn to the acre, and all other grains and vegetables in proportion.

The Black Mountain, represented on the map by C, (so called by the natives, but why so named tradition hath not informed us,) is a ridge somewhat in the shape of an inverted boat, elevated from 130 to 150 feet above the bottom prairie immediately in its vicinity, and commands from its summit a full view of the high plains and the country around it to a great extent. This facility the natives enjoyed, for they were in the practice yearly of burning over the country, which kept down the undergrowth, while the larger growth was so sparse as not materially to intercept the view. This elevated ridge answered the Indian some valuable purposes. No enemy could approach, in day time, who could not, from its summit, be descried at a great distance; and by repairing thither, the red man could often have a choice of the game in view, and his sagacity seldom failed him in the endeavor to approach it with success. The burning-ground, in the suburbs of Grenadier Squawtown, represented in the map, was also situated on an elevated spot, which commands a full view of all the other towns within the drawing, so that when a victim was at the stake, and the flames ascending, all of the inhabitants of the other towns, who could not be present, might, in a great measure, enjoy the scene by sight and imagination. The burning-ground at Old Chillicothe was somewhat similar, being in full view of the burning-ground at Squawtown, the Black Mountain, and two or three other small towns in other parts of the plains.

The Grenadier squaw, whose name the above town bore, was a sister to Cornstalk. She was represented as being a woman of great muscular strength; and, like her brother, possessed of a superior intellect.

From accounts most to be relied on, it was to Grenadier Squawtown that Slover, who was taken prisoner at Crawford's defeat, in 1782, was brought to suffer a similar death to that which Crawford, his commander, had undergone a few days before, but from which, through Providential aid, he was relieved and enabled to make his escape. The circumstances of his escape have been previously published; but as they seem to be inseparably connected with the history of this spot, I hope to be excused for repeating them here. After his capture, on his way thither, he had been very much abused at the different towns he passed through, beaten with clubs, &c. On his arrival here he had a similar punishment to undergo. A council was held over him, and he was doomed to die the death that Crawford had suffered. The day was appointed for the consummation of the horrid deed, and its morning dawned without any unpropitious appearances to mar the anticipated enjoyments of the natives collected from the neighboring towns to witness the scene. At the appointed time, Slover was led forth, stripped naked, tied to the fatal stake, and the fire kindled around him. Just as his tormentors were about to commence the torture, it seemed that the Great Spirit looked down, and said, "No! this horrid deed shall not be done!" Immediately the heavens were overcast; the forked lightnings in all directions flew; in mighty peals the thunder rolled, and seemed to shake the earth to its centre; the rain in copious torrents fell, and quenched the threatening flames before they had done the victim much injury—continuing to a late hour. The natives stood dumb-founded—somewhat fearing that the Great Spirit was not pleased with what they were about to do. But had they been never so much inclined, there was not time left that evening to carry out their usual savage observances. Slover was therefore taken from the stake, and conducted to an empty house, to an upper log of which he was fastened by a buffalo-tug tied around his neck, and his arms were pinioned behind him by a cord. Two warriors were set over him as a guard, to prevent his escape in the night. Here again Providence seemed to interfere in favor of Slover, by causing a restless sleep to come over his guard. Until a late hour the Indians sat up, smoking their pipes and talking to Slover—using all their ingenuity to tantalize him, asking "how he would like to eat fire," &c. At length one of them lay down, and soon fell asleep. The other continued smoking and talking with Slover some time. After midnight, a deep sleep came upon him. He also lay down, and soon thought of nothing save in dreams of the anticipated pleasure to be enjoyed in torturing their prisoner next day. Slover then resolved to make an effort to get loose, and soon extricated one of his hands from the cords. He then tried to unloose the tug around his neck, but without effect. He had not long been thus engaged before one of the Indians got up and smoked his pipe. While he was thus engaged, Slover kept very still for fear of a discovery; but the Indian being again overcome with sleep, again lay down. Slover then renewed his exertions, but for some time without effect, and he resigned himself to his fate. After resting awhile, however, he resolved to make another and a last effort. He put his hand again to the tug, and, as he related, he slipped it over his head without difficulty. He then got out of the house as quietly as possible, sprang over a fence into a cornfield. While passing through the field he came near running over a squaw and her children, who were sleeping under a tree. To avoid discovery, he deviated from a straight tract, and rapidly hurried to the upper plain, where, as he had expected, he found a number of Indian horses grazing. Day was then fairly breaking. He untied the cord from the other arm, which by this time was very much swelled. Selecting, as he thought, the best horse he could see, he made a bridle of the cord, mounted him, and rode off at full speed. About 10 o'clock, the horse gave out. Slover then had to travel on foot with all possible speed; and between musquitoes, nettles, brush, briars, thorns, &c., by the time he got home, he had more the appearance of a mass of raw flesh than an animate being.

The history of the expedition of Lord Dunmore against these towns on the Scioto, in 1774, we derive from the discourse upon this subject delivered by Chas. Whittlesey, Esq., before the historical and philosophical society of Ohio, at Columbus, in 1840.

In August, 1774, Lord Dunmore collected a force of 3,000 men, destined for the reduction of their towns on the Scioto, situated within the present limits of Pickaway county. One half of the corps was raised in Botetourt, Fincastle, and the adjoining counties, by Col. Andrew Lewis, and of these, 1,100 were in rendezvous at the levels of Green Briar on the 5th of September. It advanced in two divisions; the left wing, commanded by Lewis, struck the great Kenhawa, and followed that stream to the Ohio. The right wing, attended by Dunmore in person, passed the mountains at the Potomac gap, and came to the Ohio somewhere above Wheeling. About the 6th of October, a talk was had with the chiefs of the Six Nations and the Delawares, some of whom had been to the Shawanese towns on a mission of peace. They reported unfavorably. The plan of the campaign was to form a junction before reaching the Indian villages, and Lewis accordingly halted at the mouth of the Kenhawa on the 6th of October for communication and orders from the commander-in-chief. While there he encamped on the ground now occupied by the village of Point Pleasant, without entrenchments or other defences. On the morning of the 10th of October, he was attacked by 1,000 chosen warriors of the western confederacy, who had abandoned their towns on the Pickaway plains to meet the Virginia troops, and give them battle before the two corps could be united. The Virginia riflemen occupied a triangular point of land, between the right bank of the Kenhawa and the left bank of the Ohio, accessible only from the rear. The assault was therefore in this quarter. Within an hour after the scouts had reported the presence of the Indians, a general engagement took place, extending from one bank of one river to the other, half a mile from the point.

Colonel Andrew Lewis, who seems to have been possessed of military talent, acted with steadiness and decision in this emergency. He arrayed his forces promptly, and advanced to meet the enemy, with force equal to his own. Col. Charles Lewis, with 300 men, forming the right of the line, met the Indians at sunrise and sustained the first attack. Here he was mortally wounded in the onset, and his troops receiving almost the entire weight of the charge, were broken and gave way. Col. Fleming with a portion of the command, had advanced along the shore of the Ohio, and in a few moments fell in with the right of the Indian line, which rested on the river.

The effect of the first shock was to stagger the left wing, as it had done the right, and its commander, also, was severely wounded at an early stage of the conflict; but his men succeeded in reaching a piece of timber land, and maintained their position until the reserve under Col. Field reached the ground. It will be seen by examining Lewis's plan of the engagement, and the ground on which it was fought, that an advance on his part, and a retreat of his opponent, necessarily weakened their line by constantly increasing its length, if it extended from river to river, and would eventually force him to break it or leave his flanks unprotected. Those acquainted with Indian tactics inform us, that it is the great point of his generalship to preserve his flanks and overreach those of his enemy. They continued, therefore, contrary to their usual practice, to dispute the ground with the pertinacity of veterans along the whole line—retreating slowly from tree to tree, till one o'clock, P. M., when they reached a strong position. Here both parties rested, within rifle range of each other, and continued a desultory fire along a front of a mile and a quarter, until after sunset.

The desperate nature of this fight may be inferred from the deep-seated animosity of both parties towards each other, the high courage which both possessed, and the consequences which hung upon the issue. The Virginians lost one half their commissioned officers and 52 men killed. Of the Indians, 21 were left on the field, and the loss in killed and wounded is stated at 233. During the night, the Indians retreated and were not pursued.

Having failed in this contest with the troops while they were still divided in two parties, they changed their plan and determined at once to save their towns from destruction by offers of peace.

Soon after the battle was over, a reinforcement of 300 Fincastle troops, and also an express from Lord Dunmore, arrived, with an order directing this division to advance towards the Shawanese villages without delay. Notwithstanding the order was given in ignorance of the engagement, and commanded them to enter the enemy's country unsupported, Col. Lewis and his men were glad to comply with it, and thus complete the overthrow of the allied Indians.

The Virginians, made eager with success, and maddened by the loss of so many brave officers, dashed across the Ohio in pursuit of more victims, leaving a garrison at Point Pleasant. Our next information of them is, that a march of eighty miles, through an untrodden wilderness, has been performed, and on the 24th of Oct., they are encamped on the banks of Congo creek, in Pickaway township, Pickaway county, within striking distance of the Indian towns. Their principal village was occupied by Shawnees, and stood upon the ground where the village of Westfall is now situated, on the west bank of the Scioto, and on the Ohio canal, near the south line of the same county. This was the head-quarters of the confederate tribes, and was called Chillicothe; and because there were other towns, either at that time or soon after, of the same name, it was known as *Old* Chillicothe. One of them was located at the present village of Frankfort, in Ross county, on the north fork of Paint creek, and others on the waters of the Great Miami. In the mean time, Lord Dunmore and his men had descended the Ohio to the mouth of the Great Hockhocking, established a depot, and erected some defences called Fort Gower. From this point he probably started the express directed to Lewis, at the mouth of Kenhawa, about fifty miles below, and immediately commenced his march up the Hockhocking into the Indian country. For the next that is known of him, he is in the vicinity of Camp Charlotte, on the left bank of Sippo creek, about seven miles southeast of Circleville, where he arrived before Lewis reached the station on Congo, as above stated. Camp Charlotte was situated about four and one-half miles northeast of Camp Lewis, on the farm now [1840] owned by Thos. J. Winship, Esq., and was consequently farther from the Chillicothe villages than the position occupied by the left wing. There has been much diversity of opinion and statement respecting the location of the true Old Chillicothe town, and also in regard to the positions of Camp Charlotte and Camp Lewis. The associations connected with those places have given them an interest which will never decline. This is probably a sufficient excuse for presenting here, in detail, the evidence upon which the positions of these several points are established.

It was at the Chillicothe towns that Logan delivered his famous speech. It was not made in council, for he refused to attend at Camp Charlotte where the talk was held, and Dunmore sent a trader by the name of John Gibson to inquire the cause of his absence. The Indians, as before intimated, had made propositions to the governor for peace, and probably before he was aware of the result of the action at Kenhawa. When Gibson arrived at the village, Logan came to him, and by his (Logan's) request, they went into an adjoining wood and sat down. Here, after shedding abundance of tears, the honored chief told his pathetic story.* Gibson repeated it to the officers, who caused it to be published in the Virginia Gazette of that year. Mr. Jefferson was charged with making improvements and alterations when he published it in his notes on Virginia; but from the concurrent testimony of Gibson, Lord Dunmore, and several others, it appears to be as close a representation of the original as could be obtained under the circumstances. The only versions of the speech that I have seen are here contrasted, in order to show that the substance and sentiments correspond, and that it must be the production of Logan, or of John Gibson, the only white man who heard the original.

Williamsburg, Va., Feb. 4, 1775.	New York, Feb. 16, 1775.
The following is said to be a message from Captain Logan, an Indian warrior, to Gov. Dunmore, after the battle in which Colonel Charles Lewis was slain, delivered at the treaty:	Extract of a letter from Va.— "I make no doubt the following specimen of Indian eloquence and mistaken valor will please you, but you must make allowances for the unskillfulness of the interpreter."
"I appeal to any white man to say that he ever entered Logan's cabin but I gave him meat; that he ever came naked but I clothed him.	"I appeal to any white man to say, if ever he entered Logan's cabin hungry and I gave him not meat; if ever he came cold or naked and I gave him not clothing. "During the course of the last long and

* Affidavit of John Gibson, Jefferson's Notes, appendix, p. 16.

"In the course of the last war, Logan remained in his cabin an advocate for peace. I had such an affection for the white people, that I was pointed at by the rest of my nation. I should have ever lived with them had it not been for Col. Cresap, who, last year, cut off, in cold blood, all the relations of Logan, not sparing my women and children. There runs not a drop of my blood in the veins of any human creature. This called upon me for revenge. I have sought it. I have killed many, and fully glutted my revenge. I am glad there is a prospect of peace on account of the nation; but I beg you will not entertain a thought that any thing I have said proceeds from fear. Logan disdains the thought. He will not turn on his heel to save his life. Who is there to mourn for Logan? No one."

bloody war, Logan remained in his tent an advocate for peace. Nay, such was my love for the whites, that those of my own country pointed at me as they passed by and said, 'Logan is the friend of white men.' I had even thought to live with you, but for the injuries of one man. Colonel Cresap, the last spring, in cool blood, and unprovoked, cut off all the relatives of Logan; not sparing even my women and children. There runs not a drop of my blood in the veins of any human creature. This called on me for revenge. I have sought it. I have killed many. I have fully glutted my vengeance. For my country, I rejoice at the beams of peace. Yet, do not harbor the thought that mine is the joy of fear. Logan never felt fear. He will not turn on his heel to save his life. Who is there to mourn for Logan? Not one."

The right hand translation is literally the same as the copy given in Jefferson's Notes, page 124, and is doubtless the version given out by himself at the time.

It was repeated throughout the North American colonies as a lesson of eloquence in the schools, and copied upon the pages of literary journals in Great Britain and the Continent. This brief effusion of mingled pride, courage and sorrow, elevated the character of the native American throughout the intelligent world; and the place where it was delivered can never be forgotten so long as touching eloquence is admired by men.

Camp Charlotte was situated on the southwest quarter of section 12, town 10, range 21, upon a pleasant piece of ground in view of the Pickaway plains. It was without permanent defences, or, at least, there are no remains of intrenchments, and is accessible on all sides. The creek in front formed no impediment to an approach from that quarter, and the country is level in the rear. Camp Lewis is said to be upon more defensible ground on the northeast quarter of section 30, same township and range. The two encampments have often been confounded with each other........

Before Lord Dunmore reached the vicinity of the Indian towns, he was met by a flag of truce, borne by a white man named Elliott, desiring a halt on the part of the troops, and requesting for the chiefs an interpreter with whom they could communicate. To this his lordship, who, according to the Virginians, had an aversion to fighting, readily assented. They furthermore charged him with the design of forming an alliance with the confederacy, to assist Great Britain against the colonies in the crisis of the revolution, which every one foresaw. He, however, moved forward to Camp Charlotte, which was established rather as a convenient council ground, than as a place of security or defence. The Virginia militia came here for the purpose of fighting, and their dissatisfaction and disappointment at the result amounted almost to mutiny. Lewis refused to obey the order for a halt, considering the enemy as already within his grasp, and of inferior numbers to his own. Dunmore, as we have seen, went in person to enforce his orders, and it is said drew his sword upon Colonel Lewis, threatening him with instant death if he persisted in farther disobedience.

The troops were concentrated at Camp Charlotte, numbering about 2,500 men. The principal chiefs of the Scioto tribes had been assembled, and some days were spent in negotiations. A compact or treaty was at length concluded, and *four* hostages put in possession of the governor to be taken to Virginia. We know very little of the precise terms of this treaty, nor even of the tribes who gave it their assent. It is said the Indians agreed to make the Ohio their boundary, and the whites stipulated not to pass beyond that river. An agreement was entered into for a talk at Pittsburgh in the following spring, where a more full treaty was to be made; but the revolutionary movements prevented.

When the army returned, they took the route by Fort Gower, (see p. 49,) where, on the 5th of November, and 10 days after the arrival of Lewis at Camp Charlotte, the officers held a meeting "for the purpose of considering the grievances of *British America*: an officer present addressed the meeting in the following words:"

Gentlemen,—Having now concluded the campaign, by the assistance of Providence, with honor and advantage to the colony and ourselves, it only remains that we should give our country the stronger assurance that we are ready at all times, to the utmost of our power, to maintain and defend her just rights and privileges. We have lived about three months in the woods, without any intelligence from Boston, or from the delegates at Philadelphia. It is possible, from the groundless reports of designing men, that our countrymen may be jealous of the use such a body would make of arms in their hands at this critical juncture. That we are a respectable body is certain, when it is considered that we can live weeks without bread or salt; that we can sleep in the open air without any covering but that of the canopy of heaven; and that we can march and shoot with any in the known world. Blessed with these talents, let us solemnly engage to one another, and our country in particular, that we will use them for no purpose but for the honor and advantage of America, and of Virginia in particular. It behooves us, then, for the satisfaction of our country, that we should give them our real sentiments by way of resolves, at this very alarming crisis.

Whereupon the meeting made choice of a committee to draw up and prepare resolves for their consideration; who immediately withdrew, and after some time spent therein, reported that they had agreed to and prepared the following resolves, which were read, maturely considered, and agreed to nem. con. by the meeting, and ordered to be published in the Virginia Gazette:

Resolved, That we will bear the most faithful allegiance to his majesty King George the Third, while his majesty delights to reign over a brave and a free people; that we will, at the expense of life and every thing dear and valuable, exert ourselves in the support of the honor of his crown and the dignity of the British empire. But as the love of liberty and attachment to the real interests and just rights of America outweigh every other consideration, we resolve, that we will exert every power within us for the defence of American liberty, and for the support of her just rights and privileges, not in any precipitous, riotous, or tumultuous manner, but when regularly called forth by the unanimous voice of our countrymen.

Resolved, That we entertain the greatest respect for his excellency the Rt. Hon. Lord Dunmore, who commanded the expedition against the *Shawanese*, and who, we are confident, underwent the great fatigue of this singular campaign from no other motive than the true interests of the country.

Signed by order and in behalf of the whole corps.

Benjamin Ashby, Clerk.

Notwithstanding the evidence above produced, derived from the American Archives, it is said that the troops, who had wished to give an efficient blow, reached Virginia highly dissatisfied with the governor and the treaty: the conduct of the governor could not be well explained by them, "except by supposing him to act with reference to the expected contest with England and her colonies—a motive which the colonists regarded as little less than treasonable."*

Of the feeling in camp towards Dunmore at the time of the treaty, we have some evidence in the statement of the late venerable Abrm. Thomas, one of the early settlers of Miami county, published in the Troy Times, in 1839.

We (Dunmore's army) lay at the mouth of the Hocking for some time. One day, as I was going down to the boats, I met Dunmore just leaving them. He expressed his fears that Gen. Lewis was attacked by the Indians. The men had noticed Dunmore for several days with his ear close to the water, but did not then suspect the reason. He told me he thought he heard the roaring of guns upon the water, and requested me to put my ear to it, and although it was ten or twelve [28] miles distant, I distinctly heard the roar of musketry. The next day we took up the line of march for Chillicothe, up the Hockhocking. On the second or third day, some Indians came running into the camp, beseeching Dunmore to stop Lewis's division, which had crossed the Ohio and was in full pursuit of the Indians; to use their own words, "like so many devils, that would kill them all." This was the first certain information our men had of that battle. On the solicitation of the savages, Dunmore twice sent orders to check the progress of Lewis, but he refused to obey them,

* Annals of the West.

until Dunmore himself took command of the division and led them back to the Ohio. The troops were indignant at the conduct of Dunmore, and believed his object was to give up both divisions of the army to the Indians. It was thought he knew the attack would be made at Point Pleasant about the time it took place, calculated on the defeat of Lewis, and led our army into the defiles of the Hocking, that they might the more easily become the prey of infuriated savages, flushed with recent victory. An incident occurred here, showing the state of feeling among the men. At the time the Indians who came into the camp were sitting with Dunmore in his tent, a backwoodsman passing, observed them and stepped around the tent. When he thought he had them in range, he discharged his rifle through the canvass, with the intention of killing the three at once. It was a close cut—it missed: the man escaped through the crowd and no one knew who did it. From this time until he left the camp, Dunmore tried to conciliate what he could by indulgence and talking; but this would not have availed him had he not taken other precautions, for many in the camp believed him the enemy of their country and the betrayer of the army.

The chief, Cornstalk, whose town is shown on the map, was a man of true nobility of soul, and a brave warrior.

At the battle of Point Pleasant he commanded the Indians with consummate skill, and if at any time his warriors were believed to waver, his voice could be heard above the din of battle, exclaiming in his native tongue, "Be strong!—be strong!" When he returned to the Pickaway towns, after the battle, he called a council of the nation to consult what should be done, and upbraided them in not suffering him to make peace, as he desired, on the evening before the battle. "What," said he, "will you do now? The Big Knife is coming on us, and we shall all be killed. Now you must fight or we are undone." But no one answering, he said, "then let us kill all our women and children, and go and fight until we die." But no anwer was made, when, rising, he struck his tomahawk in a post of the council house and exclaimed, "I'll go and make peace," to which all the warriors grunted "ough! ough!" and runners were instantly dispatched to Dunmore to solicit peace.

In the summer of 1777, he was atrociously murdered at Point Pleasant. As his murderers were approaching, his son Elinipsico trembled violently. "His father encouraged him not to be afraid, for that the *Great Man above* had sent him there to be killed and die with him. As the men advanced to the door, the Cornstalk rose up and met them: they fired, and seven or eight bullets went through him. So fell the great Cornstalk warrior—whose name was bestowed upon him by the consent of the nation, as their great strength and support." Had he lived, it is believed that he would have been friendly with the Americans, as he had come over to visit the garrison at Point Pleasant to communicate the design of the Indians of uniting with the British. His grave is to be seen at Point Pleasant to the present day.

The last years of Logan were truly melancholy. He wandered about from tribe to tribe, a solitary and lonely man; dejected and broken-hearted by the loss of his friends and the decay of his tribe, he resorted to the stimulus of strong drink to drown his sorrow. He was at last murdered, in Michigan, near Detroit. He was, at the time, sitting with his blanket over his head before a camp fire, his elbows resting on his knees, and his head upon his hands, buried in profound reflection, when an Indian, who had taken some offence, stole behind him and buried his tomahawk in his brains. Thus perished the immortal Logan, the last of his race.*

CIRCLEVILLE, the county seat, is on the Ohio canal and Scioto river, 26 miles S. of Columbus, and 19 N. of Chillicothe. It was laid out in 1810 as the seat of justice, by Daniel Dresbach, on land originally belonging to Zeiger and Watt, and the first lot sold on the 10th of September. The town is on the site of ancient fortifications, one of which having been circular, originated the name of the place. The

* From Henry C. Brish, Esq., of Tiffin, Seneca county, who derived the circumstances from Good Hunter, an aged Mingo chief, and a familiar acquaintance of Logan.

52

old court-house, built in the form of an octagon, and destroyed in 1841, stood in the centre of the circle. Few, if any, vestiges remain of these forts, but we find them described at length in the Archælogia Americana, published in 1820. The description and accompanying cut are appended.

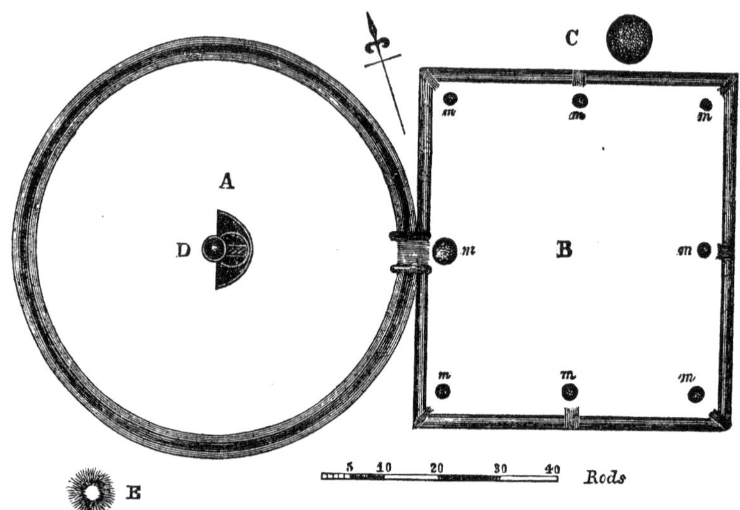

Ancient Fortifications at Circleville.

There are two forts, one being an exact circle, the other an exact square. The former is surrounded by two walls, with a deep ditch between them; the latter is encompassed by one wall, without any ditch. The former was 69 feet in diameter, measuring from outside to outside of the circular outer wall; the latter is exactly 55 rods square, measuring the same way. The walls of the circular fort were at least 20 feet in height, measuring from the bottom of the ditch, before the town of Circleville was built. The inner wall was of clay, taken up probably in the northern part of the fort, where was a low place, and is still considerably lower than any other part of the work. The outside wall was taken from the ditch which is between these walls, and is alluvial, consisting of pebbles, worn smooth in water, and sand, to a very considerable depth, more than 50 feet at least. The outside of the walls is about five or six feet in height now; on the inside, the ditch is at present generally not more than 15 feet. They are disappearing before us daily, and will soon be gone. The walls of the square fort are at this time, where left standing, about 10 feet in height. There were eight gateways, or openings, leading into the square fort, and only one into the circular fort. Before each of these openings was a mound of earth, perhaps four feet high, 40 feet perhaps in diameter at the base, and 20 or upwards at the summit. These mounds, for two rods or more, are exactly in front of the gateways, and were intended for the defence of these openings.

As this work is a perfect square, so the gateways and their watch-towers were equidistant from each other. These mounds were in a perfectly straight line, and exactly parallel with the wall. Those small mounds were at *m, m, m, m, m, m, m*. The black line at *d* represents the ditch, and *w, w*, represent the two circular walls.

D [the reader is referred to the plate] shows the site of a once very remarkable ancient mound of earth, with a semi-circular pavement on its eastern side, nearly fronting, as the plate represents, the only gateway leading into this fort. This mound is entirely removed; but the outline of the semi-circular pavement may still be seen in many places, notwithstanding the dilapidations of time and those occasioned by the hand of man.

The earth in these walls was as nearly perpendicular as it could be made to lie. This fort had originally but one gateway leading into it on its eastern side, and that was defended by a mound of earth several feet in height, at *m, i*. Near the centre of this work was a mound, with a semi-circular pavement on its eastern side, some of the remains of which may still be seen by an intelligent observer. The mound at *m, i,* has been entirely removed, so as to make the street level, from where it once stood.

B is a square fort, adjoining the circular one, as represented by the plate, the area of which has been stated already. The wall which surrounds this work is generally now about 10 feet in height, where it has not been manufactured into brick. There are seven gateways leading into this fort, besides the one which communicates with the square fortification—that is, one at each angle, and another in the wall, just half way between the angular ones. Before each of these gateways was a mound of earth of four or five feet in height, intended for the defence of these openings.

The extreme care of the authors of these works to protect and defend every part of the circle, is no where visible about this square fort. The former is defended by two high walls—the latter by one. The former has a deep ditch encircling it—this has none. The former could be entered at one place only—this at eight, and those about 20 feet broad. The present town of Circleville covers all the round and the western half of the square fort. These fortifications, where the town stands, will entirely disappear in a few years; and I have used the only means within my power to perpetuate their memory, by the annexed drawing and this brief description.

West Main Street, Circleville.

Another writer gives some aditional facts. Writing in 1834, he says:

On the sw. side of the circle stands a conical hill, crowned with an artificial mound. Indeed so much does the whole elevation resemble the work of man, that many have mistaken it for a large mound. A street has lately been opened across the little mound which crowned the hill, and in removing the earth, many skeletons were found in good preservation. A cranium of one of them was in my possession, and is a noble specimen of the race which once occupied these ancient walls. It has a high forehead and large and bold features, with all the phrenological marks of daring and bravery. Poor fellow, he died overwhelmed by numbers; as the fracture of the right parietal bone by the battle axe, and five large stone arrows sticking in and about his bones, still bear silent, but sure testimony. The elevated ground a little north of the town, across Hargus creek, which washes the base of the plain of Circleville, appears to have been the common burying-ground. Human bones in great quantities are found in digging away the gravel for repairing the streets, and for constructing the banks of the canal which runs near the base of the highlands. They were buried in the common earth, without any attempt at tumuli; and occupy so large a space, that only a dense population and a long period of time could have furnished such numbers.

Circleville is a thriving, business town, surrounded by a beautiful, level country. Opposite the town, the bottom land on the Scioto is banked up for several miles, to prevent being overflowed by the river. Circleville has 2 Presbyterian, 1 Lutheran, 1 Episcopal, 1 Methodist and 1 United Brethren church; an elegant court house, recently erected; 1 or 2 academies, 3 printing offices, about 20 mercantile stores, 1 bank, 9 warehouses on the canal, and had in 1830, 1136, and in 1840, 2330 inhabitants: it now has over 3000. The business by the canal is heavy. Of the clearances made from this port in 1846, there were of corn, 106,465 bushels; wheat, 24,918 bushels; broom corn, 426,374 pounds; bacon and pork, 1277,212 pounds, and lard, 1458,259 pounds.

Tarleton, 9 miles easterly from Circleville, is a thriving town, containing 6 or 8 stores, 3 churches, and had in 1840, 437 inhabitants. The following is a list of smaller places, with their distances and direction from Circleville, and population in 1840. Bloomfield, 9 N., 182; Darbyville, 12 NW., 164; New Holland, 18 W., 161; Williamsport, 9 W., 159; Jefferson 85; Palestine 63, and Millport 98. The last is a new place, on the canal, and has several mills, and much water power derived from the canal. At Williamsport is a chalybeate spring of some local celebrity.

PIKE.

PIKE was organized in February, 1815, and named from General Zebulon Montgomery Pike, who was born at Lamberton, Mercer county, N. J., January 5th, 1779, and was killed at the storming of York, Upper Canada, April 25th, 1813. Excepting the rich bottom lands of the Scioto and its tributaries, the surface is generally hilly. The river hills abound with excellent free-stone, extensively exported for building purposes. The principal productions are Indian corn, oats and wheat. The following is a list of the townships in 1840, with their population.

Beaver,	1075	Newton,	337	Perry,	565
Camp Creek,	299	Pee Pee,	813	Seal,	1875
Jackson,	1096	Pebble,	504	Sunfish,	325
Mifflin,	645				

The population of Pike in 1820, was 4253; in 1830, 6024, and in 1840, 7536, or 18 inhabitants to a square mile.

The first permanent settlers in the county were Pennsylvanians and Virginians. Within the last few years many Germans have settled in the eastern part. The first settlement in the vicinity of Piketon, was made on the Pee Pee prairie, by John Noland from Pennsylvania, Abraham, Arthur and John Chenoweth, three brothers from Virginia, who settled there about the same time Chillicothe was laid out, in 1796.

Piketon, the county seat, was laid out about the year 1814. It is on the Scioto, on the Columbus and Portsmouth turnpike, 64 miles from the first, 26 from the last, and 2 east of the Ohio canal. Piketon contains 1 Presbyterian, 1 Methodist and 1 German Lutheran church, an academy, a newspaper printing office, 4 mercantile stores, and had in 1840, 507 inhabitants. Piketon was originally called

View in Piketon.

Jefferson, and was laid off on what was called "Miller's Bank." The origin of this last name is thus given in the American Pioneer.

About the year 1795, two parties set off from Mason county, Ky., to locate land by making improvements, as it was believed the tract ceded to the United States, east of the Scioto, would be held by pre-emption. One of these parties was conducted by a Mr. Miller, and the other by a Mr. Kenton. In Kenton's company was a man by the name of Owens, between whom and Miller there arose a quarrel about the right of settling this beautiful spot. In the fray Owens shot Miller, whose bones may be found interred near the lower end of the high bank. His death and burial there, gave name to the high bank, which was then in Washington county, the Scioto being then the line between Washington and Adams counties. Owens was taken to Marietta, where he was tried and acquitted.

A short distance below the town are some ancient works. There the turnpike passes for several hundred feet between two parallel and artificial walls of earth, about 15 feet in elevation, and near six rods apart. On Lewis Evans' map of the middle British colonies, published in 1755, is laid down, on the right bank of the river, a short distance below the site of Piketon, a place called "Hurricane Toms:" it might have been the abode of an Indian chief or a French trader's station.

Waverly, 4 miles above Piketon on the Scioto river and Ohio canal, was laid out about the year 1829, by M. Downing. It contains 1 Presbyterian and 1 Methodist church, 4 stores, and had in 1840, 306 inhabitants. Cynthiana had in 1840, 71, Jasper 69, and Sharonville 61 inhabitants.

PORTAGE.

PORTAGE was formed from Trumbull, June 7th, 1807; all that part of the Reserve west of the Cuyahoga and south of the townships numbered five, was also annexed as part of the county, and the temporary seat of justice appointed at the house of Benj. Tappan. The name was derived from the old Indian *portage* path of about 7 miles in length, between the Cuyahoga and Tuscarawas, which was within its limits. The surface is slightly rolling; the upland is generally sandy or gravelly, and the flat land to a considerable extent clay. The county is wealthy and thriving. The dairy business is largely carried on, and nearly 1000 tons of cheese annually produced. The principal productions are wheat, corn, oats, barley, rye, buckwheat, butter, cheese and wool; of the last, the annual exports amount to about 240,000 pounds. The following is a list of the townships in 1840, with their population.

Atwater,	756	Freedom,	888	Ravenna,	1542
Aurora,	906	Hiram,	1080	Rootstown,	1112
Brimfield,	1154	Mantua,	1187	Shalersville,	1281
Charlestown,	851	Nelson,	1398	Streetsborough,	1136
Deerfield,	1184	Palmyra,	1359	Suffield,	1200
Edinburgh,	1085	Paris,	931	Windham,	907
Franklin,	1497	Randolph,	1649		

The population of Portage in 1820, was 10,093; in 1830, 18,792, and in 1840, 23,107, or 46 inhabitants to a square mile.

Ravenna, the county seat, so named from an Italian city, is 34 miles SE. of Cleveland and 140 NW. of Columbus. It is situated on the Cleveland and Pittsburgh road, on the crest of land dividing the waters flowing into the lakes from those emptying into the Gulf of Mexico: the Ohio and Pennsylvania canal runs a short distance south of the town.

This place was originally settled by the Hon. Benj. Tappan in June, 1799, at which time there was but one white person, a Mr. Honey, residing in the county. A solitary log-cabin in each place, marked the sites of the flourishing cities of Buffalo and Cleveland. On his journey out from New England, Mr. Tappan fell in with the late David Hudson, the founder of Hudson, Summit county, at Gerondaquet, New York, and "assisted him on the journey for the sake of his company. After some days of tedious navigation up the Cuyahoga river, he landed at a prairie, where is now the town of Boston, in the county of Summit. There he left all his goods under a tent with one K***** and his family to take care of them, and with another hired man proceeded to make out a road to Ravenna. There they built a dray, and with a yoke of oxen which had been driven from Connecticut river, and were found on his arrival, he conveyed a load of farming utensils to his settlement. Returning for a second load, the tent was found abandoned and partly plundered by the Indians. He soon after learned that Hudson had persuaded K***** to join his own settlement."*

On Mr. Tappan's "removing his second load of goods, one of his oxen was overheated and died, leaving him in a vast forest, distant from any habitation, without a team, and what was still worse, with but a single dollar in money. He was not depressed for an instant by these untoward circumstances. He sent one of his men through the woods, with a compass, to Erie, in Pa., a distance of about 100 miles, requesting from Capt. Lyman, the commandant at the fort, a loan of money. At the same time, he followed himself the township lines to Youngstown, where he became acquainted with Col. James Hillman, (see p. 338,) who did not hesitate to sell him an ox, on credit, at a fair price,—an act of generosity which proved of great value, as the want of a team must have broken up his settlement. The unexpected delays upon the journey and other hindrances, prevented them from raising a crop at this season, and they had, after the provisions brought with him were exhausted, to depend for meat upon their skill in hunting and purchases from the Indians, and for meal upon the scanty supplies procured from western Pennsylvania. Having set out with the determination to spend the winter, he erected a log cabin, into which himself and one Bixby, whom he had agreed to give 100 acres of land on condition of settlement, moved on the first day of January, 1800, before which, they had lived under a bark camp and their tent."*

View in Ravenna.

The engraving represents the public buildings in the central part of the village: in the centre is seen the court house and jail; on the right in the distance the Congregational, and on the left the Universalist church. Ravenna contains 1 Congregational, 1 Disciples, 1 Methodist and 1 Universalist church, 10 mercantile stores, an academy, 2 newspaper printing offices, and about 1200 inhabitants. It is a thriving, pleasant village and is noted for the manufacture of carriages.

About the time of Mr. Tappan's settlement at Ravenna, others were commenced in several of the townships of the county. The sketches of Deerfield and Palmyra we annex from the Barr MSS.

Deerfield received its name from Deerfield, Mass., the native place of the mother of Lewis Day, Esq. Early in May, 1799, Lewis Day and his son, Horatio, of Granby, Ct., and Moses Tibbals and Green Frost, of Granville, Mass., left their homes in a one horse wagon, and arrived in Deerfield on the 29th of the same month. This was the first wagon

* From the sketch of Hon. Benj. Tappan, in the Democratic Review, for June, 1840.

that had ever penetrated farther westward in this region than Canfield. The country west of that place had been an unbroken wilderness, until within a few days. Capt. Caleb Atwater, of Wallingford, Ct., had hired some men to open a road to township No. 1, in the 7th range, of which he was the owner. This road passed through Deerfield, and was completed to that place when the party arrived at the point of their destination. These emigrants selected sites for their future dwellings, and commenced clearing up the land. In July, Lewis Ely and family arrived from Granville and wintered here, while the first named, having spent the summer in making improvements, returned east. On the 4th of March, 1800, Alva Day, (son of Lewis,) John Campbell and Joel Thrall, all arrived in company. In April, George and Robert Taylor and James Laughlin, from Pennsylvania, with their families, made permanent settlements. Mr. Laughlin built a grist mill, which, on the succeeding year, was a great convenience to the settlers. On the 29th of June, Lewis Day returned from Connecticut, accompanied by his family, and his brother-in-law, Major Rogers, who the next year also brought out his family.

Much suffering was experienced on account of the scarcity of provisions. They were supplied from settlements on the opposite side of the Ohio, the nearest of which was Georgetown, 40 miles distant. These were conveyed on pack-horses through the wilderness. On the 22d of August, Mrs. Alva Day gave birth to the first child—a female—born in the township, and on the 7th of November, the first wedding took place. John Campbell and Sarah Ely—daughter of Lewis—were joined in wedlock by Calvin Austin, Esq., of Warren. He was accompanied from Warren, a distance of 27 miles, by the late Judge Pease, then a young lawyer of that place. They came on foot—there not being any road—and as they threaded their way through the woods, young Pease taught the justice the marriage ceremony, by oft repetition.

The first civil organization was effected in 1802, under the name of Franklin township, embracing all of the present Portage and parts of Trumbull and Summit counties. About this time, the settlement received accessions from New England, New York, New Jersey, Pennsylvania and Virginia. The Rev. Mr. Badger, the missionary of the Presbyterians, preached here as early as February 16, 1801. In 1803, Dr. Shadrac Bostwick organized an Episcopal Methodist society. The Presbyterian society was organized, Oct. 8th, 1818, and that of the Disciples in 1828.

In 1806, there was an encampment of seven Mohawk Indians in Deerfield, with whom a serious difficulty occurred. John Diver, it is thought, in a horse trade over-reached one of these Indians, named John Nicksaw. There was much dissatisfaction expressed by these Indians at the bargain, and Nicksaw vainly endeavored to effect a re-exchange of horses.

On stating his grievances to Squire Lewis Day, that gentleman advised him to see Diver again and persuade him to do justice. Nicksaw replied, "No! you speak him! me no speak him again!" and immediately left. On this very evening—Jan. 20th, 1806—there was a sleighing party at the house of John Diver. Early in the evening while amusing themselves, they were interrupted by the rude entrance of five Indians, John Nicksaw, John Mohawk, Bigson and his two sons, from the encampment.

They were excited with whiskey, and endeavered to decoy John Diver to their camp, on some frivolous pretence. Failing in this stratagem, they became more and more boisterous, but were quieted by the mildness of Daniel Diver. They changed their tone, reciprocated his courteousness, and vainly urged him to drink whiskey with them. They now again resumed their impudent manner, and charging Daniel with stealing their guns, declared they would not leave until he returned them. With much loss of time and altercation, he at last got them out of the house. Shortly after, John Diver opened the door and was on the point of stepping out, when he espied Mohawk standing in front of him, with uplifted tomahawk, in the attitude of striking. Diver shrunk back unobserved by the company, and not wishing to alarm them, said nothing at the time about the circumstance.

About 10 o'clock, the moon shining with unusual brightness, the night being cold and clear, with snow about two feet deep, Daniel observed the Indians, standing in a ravine several rods from the house. He ran up and accosted them in a friendly manner. They treacherously returned his salutation, said they had found their guns, and before returning to camp, wished to apologize for their conduct and part good friends. Passing along the line he took each and all by the hand, until he came to Mohawk, who was the only one that had a gun in his hands. He refused to shake hands, and at the moment Diver turned for the house, he received a ball through his temples destroying both of his eyes. He im mediately fell. On the report of the gun, John Diver ran to the spot, by which time Daniel had regained his feet and was staggering about. Mohawk was standing a few paces off, looking on in silence, but his companions had fled. John eagerly inquired of his brother what was the matter? "I am shot by Mohawk," was the reply. John instantly darted at Mohawk, intending to make him atone in a frightful manner for the injury done his brother. The savage fled towards the camp, and as Diver gained rapidly upon him, Mohawk threw himself from the road into the woods, uttering a horrid yell. Diver now perceiving the other Indians returning toward him, fled in turn to his brother, and took him into the house. The wound, although dangerous, was not mortal, and he was living as late as 1847.

The Indians hurried to their encampment, and from thence fled in a northwest direction • The alarm spread throughout the settlement, and in a few hours there were twenty-five men on the spot, ready for the pursuit. Before daylight this party—among which was Alva Day, Major H. Rogers, Jas. Laughlin, Alex. K. Hubbard, and Ira Mansfield—were in hot pursuit upon their trail. The weather being intensely cold, and the settlements far apart, they suffered exceedingly. Twenty of them had their feet frozen, and many of them were compelled to stop; but their number was kept good by additions from the settlements through which they passed.

On the succeeding night the party came up with the fugitives, encamped on the west side of the Cuyahoga, in the present town of Boston. The whites surrounded them; but Nicksaw and Mohawk escaped. They were overtaken and commanded to surrender, or be shot. Continuing their flight, Williams, of Hudson, fired, and Nicksaw fell dead; but Mohawk escaped. The whites returned to Deerfield with Bigson and his two sons. A squaw belonging to them was allowed to escape, and, it is said, perished in the snow. On arriving at the centre of Deerfield, where the tragedy had been acted, Bigson appeared to be overpowered with grief, and giving vent to a flood of tears, took an affectionate leave of his sons, expecting here to lose his life according to a custom of the Indians. They were taken before Lewis Day, Esq., who, after examination, committed them to prison at Warren.

Mr. Cornelius Feather, in the papers of the Ashtabula Historical Society, says:

It was heart-rending to visit this group of human misery, at Warren, and hear their lamentations. The poor Indians were not confined, for they could not run away. The narrator has seen this old frost-crippled chief Bigson, who had been almost frozen to death, sitting with the others on the bank of the Mahoning, and heard him, in the Indian tongue, with deep touching emotions, in the highest strain of his native oratory, addressing his companions in misery—speaking the language of his heart; pointing towards the rising, then towards the setting sun, to the north, to the south, till sobs choked his utterance, and tears followed tears down his sorrow-worn cheeks.

We now return to the Barr MSS. for another incident of early times, exhibiting something of Indian gratitude and customs

John Hendricks, an Indian, for some time lived in a camp on the bank of the Mahoning, with his family—a wife and two sons—and was much respected by the settlers. Early in 1802, one of his sons, a child about 4 years of age, was taken sick, and during his illness was treated with great kindness by Mr. Jas. Laughlin and lady, who lived near. He died on the 4th of March, and his father having expressed a desire to have him interred in the place where the whites intended to bury their dead, a spot was selected near the residence of Lewis Day, which is to this time used as a grave-yard. A coffin was prepared by Mr. Laughlin and Alva Day, and he was buried according to the custom of the whites. Observing the earth to fall upon the board and not upon the body of his deceased son, Hendricks exclaimed in a fit of ecstacy, "Body no broken!"

Some days after, Mr. Day observed these Indians near the grave, apparently washing some clothing, and then digging at the grave. After they had retired, prompted by curiosity, Mr. Day examined the grave and found the child's clothes just washed and carefully deposited with the body. Shortly after, he inquired of Hendricks why he had not buried them at the funeral. "Because they were not clean," replied he. These Indians soon left the neighborhood, and did not return for one or two years. Meeting with Mr. Laughlin, Hendricks ran towards him, and throwing himself into his arms, embraced and kissed him with the deepest affection, exclaiming, "body no broke! body no broke!"

The first improvements in Palmyra were made in 1799, by David Daniels, from Salisbury, Ct. The succeeding year he brought out his family. E., N. and W. Bacon, E. Cutler, A. Thurber, A. Preston, N. Bois, J. T. Baldwin, T. and C. Gilbert, D., A. and S. Waller, N. Smith, Joseph Fisher, J. Tuttle, and others came not long after.

On the first settlement of the township, there were several families of Onondaga and Oneida Indians who carried on a friendly intercourse with the people, until the difficulty at Deerfield, in 1806, in the shooting of Diver.

When this region was first settled, there was an Indian trail commencing at Fort M'Intosh, (where Beaver, Pa., now is,) and extending westward to Sandusky and Detroit. This trail followed the highest ground. It passed by the Salt Springs, in Howland, Trumbull county, and running through the northern part of Palmyra, crossed Silver creek in Edinburgh, 1½ miles north of the centre road. Along this trail, parties of Indians were frequently seen passing, for several years after the white settlers came. In fact, it seemed to be the great thoroughfare from Sandusky to Ohio river and Du Quesne. There are several large piles of stones by this trail in Palmyra, under which human skeletons have been discovered. These are supposed to be the remains of Indians slain in war, or murdered by their enemies; as tradition says, it is an Indian practice for each one to cast a stone upon the grave of an enemy, whenever he passes by. These stones appear to have been picked up along the trail, and cast upon the heaps at different times.

At the point where this trail crosses Silver creek, Frederick Daniels and others in 1814, discovered painted on several trees various devices, evidently the work of Indians. The bark was carefully shaved off two-thirds of the way around, and figures cut upon the wood. On one of these was delineated seven Indians, equipped in a particular manner, one of which was without a head. This was supposed to have been made by a party on their return westward, to give intelligence to their friends behind, of the loss of one of their party at this place; and on making search a human skeleton was discovered near by.

Franklin Mills is 6 miles west of Ravenna on the Cleveland road, Cuyahoga river and Mahoning canal. In the era of speculation a large town was laid out here, great prices paid for "city lots," and in the event large quantities of money exchanged hands. It however possesses natural resources that in time may make it an important manufacturing town, the Cuyahoga having here two falls, one of 17 and the other of 25 feet. The village is much scattered. It contains 1 Congregational, 1 Baptist, 1 Episcopal and 1 Methodist church, 4 mercantile stores, 2 flouring mills, 2 woollen factories, and about 400 inhabitants.

The noted Indian fighter, Brady, made his celebrated leap across the Cuyahoga about 200 yards above the bridge at this place. The appearance of the locality has been materially altered by blasting rocks for the canal. Brady's pond—so called from being the place where he secreted himself on the occasion related below, from a

Brady's Pond.

published source—is about $2\frac{1}{2}$ miles from the village, and a few hundred yards north of the road to Ravenna. It is a small but beautiful sheet of water, the shores of which are composed of a white sand, finely adapted to the manufacture of glass.

Capt. Samuel Brady seems to have been as much the Daniel Boone of the northeast part of the valley of the Ohio, as the other was of the southwest, and the country is equally full of traditionary legends of his hardy adventures and hair-breadth escapes. From undoubted authority, it seems the following incident actually transpired in this vicinity. Brady's residence was on Chartier's creek on the south side of the Ohio, and being a man of herculean strength, activity and courage, he was generally selected as the leader of the hardy borderers in all their incursions into the Indian territory north of the river. On this occasion, which was about the year 1780, a large party of warriors from the falls of the Cuyahoga and the adjacent country, had made an inroad on the south side of the Ohio river, in the lower part of what is now Washington county, on which was then known as the settlement of "Catfish Camp," after an old Indian of that name who lived there when the whites first came into the country on the Monongahela river. This party had murdered several families, and with the "plunder" had recrossed the Ohio before effectual pursuit could be made. By Brady a party was directly summoned, of his chosen followers, who hastened on after them, but the Indians having one or two days the start, he could not overtake them in time to arrest their return to their villages. Near the spot where the town of Ravenna now stands, the Indians separated into two parties, one of which went to the north, and the other west, to the falls of the Cuyahoga. Brady's men also divided; a part pursued the northern trail, and a part went with their commander to the Indian village, lying on the river in the present township of Northampton, in Summit county. Although Brady made his approaches with the utmost caution, the Indians, expecting a pursuit, were on the look-out, and ready to receive him, with numbers four-fold to those of Brady's, whose only safety was in hasty retreat, which, from the ardor of the pursuit, soon became a perfect flight. Brady directed his men to separate, and each one to take care of himself; but the Indians knowing Brady, and having a most inveterate hatred and dread of him, from the numerous chastisements which he had inflicted upon them, left all the others, and with united strength pursued him alone. The Cuyahoga here makes a wide bend to the south, including a large tract of several miles of surface, in the form of a peninsula: within this tract the pursuit was hotly contested. The Indians, by extending their line to the right and left, forced him on to the bank of the stream. Having, in peaceable times, often hunted over this ground with the Indians, and knowing every turn of the Cuyahoga as familiarly as the villager knows the streets of his own hamlet, Brady directed his course to the river, at a spot where the whole stream is compressed, by the rocky cliffs, into a narrow channel of only 22 feet across the top of the chasm, although it is considerably wider beneath, near the water, and in height more than twice that number of feet above the current. Through this pass the water rushes like a race-horse, chafing and roaring at the confinement of its current by the rocky channel, while, a short distance above, the stream is at least fifty yards wide. As he approached the chasm, Brady, knowing that life or death was in the effort, concentrated his mighty powers, and leaped the stream at a single bound. It so happened, that on the opposite cliff, the leap was favored by a low place, into which he dropped, and grasping the bushes, he thus helped himself to ascend to the top of the cliff. The Indians, for a few moments, were lost in wonder and admiration, and before they had recovered their recollection, he was half way up the side of the opposite hill, but still within reach of their rifles. They could easily have shot him at any moment before, but being bent on taking him alive, for torture, and to glut their long-delayed revenge, they forbore to use the rifle ; but now seeing him likely to escape, they all fired upon him ; one bullet severely wounded him in the hip, but not so badly as to prevent his progress. The Indians having to make a considerable circuit before they could cross the stream, Brady advanced a good distance ahead. His limb was growing stiff from the wound, and as the Indians gained on him, he made for the pond which now bears his name, and plunging in, swam under water a considerable distance, and came up under the trunk of a large oak, which had fallen into the pond. This, although leaving only a small breathing place to support life, still completely sheltered him from their sight. The Indians, tracing him by the blood to the water, made diligent search all round the pond, but finding no signs of his exit, finally came to the conclusion that he had sunk and was drowned. As they were at one time standing on the very tree, beneath which he was concealed,—Brady, understanding their language, was very glad to hear the result of their deliberations, and after they had gone, weary, lame and hungry, he made good his retreat to his own home. His followers also returned in safety. The chasm across which he leaped is in sight of the bridge where we crossed the Cuyahoga, and is known in all that region by the name of "*Brady's Leap.*"

Garrettsville, 12 miles NE. of Ravenna, on the Mahoning river, where there is considerable water power, has 4 churches, 4 stores, 1 woollen, 1 chair and 1 axe factory, 2 flouring mills, and about 400 inhabitants. Campbellsport, 3 miles SE. of Ravenna, has 1 linseed oil, 1 woollen factory and several warehouses, it being an important point of shipment on the canal. Mogadore, 14 or 15 miles SW. of R., on the line of Summit, has about 200 inhabitants, and is noted for its extensive stone-ware manufactories. Deerfield, 15 SE. of R., has a Methodist and Disciple's church, and about 200 inhabitants. Windham, 13 miles N. E. of R. has 1 academy, 3 churches, 3 stores, and about 400 inhabitants.

PREBLE.

PREBLE was formed from Montgomery and Butler, March 1st, 1808: it was named from Capt. Edward Preble, who was born at Portland, Maine, August 15th, 1761, and distinguished himself as a naval commander in the war of the revolution, and particularly in the Tripolitan war, and died on the 25th of August, 1806. The soil is various: the southern part is a light rich soil, and is interspersed by numerous streams: the remainder of the county is upland, in places wet, but fertile when brought under cultivation. There is an abundance of water power for milling purposes, and large quantities of flour are manufactured. The principal productions are corn, oats, wheat, swine, wool, flax-seed and beef cattle. The following is a list of the townships in 1840, with their population.

Dixon,	1281	Israel,	1538	Monroe,	1176
Gasper,	836	Jackson,	1257	Somers,	1823
Gratis,	1950	Jefferson,	2165	Twin,	1676
Harrison,	1696	Lanier,	1624	Washington,	2459

The population of Preble, in 1820, was 10,237; in 1830, 16,296; and in 1840, 19,481, or 47 inhabitants to a square mile.

Eaton, the county seat, is 24 miles west of Dayton, 94 west of Columbus, and 9 east of the state line. It was laid out in 1806, by

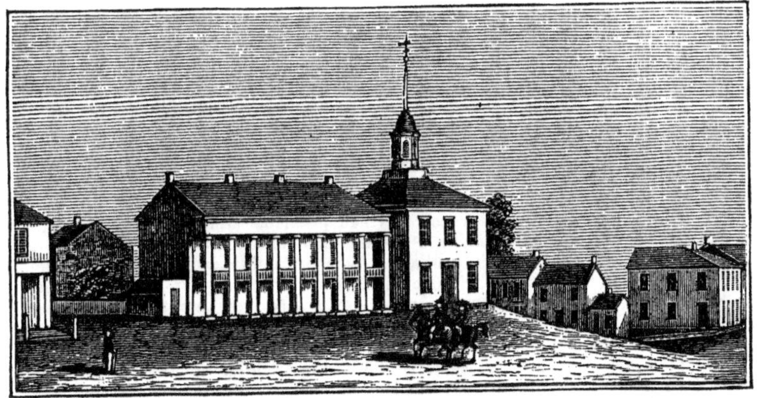

County Buildings at Eaton.

William Bruce, then proprietor of the soil. It was named from Gen. Wm. Eaton, who was born in Woodstock, Ct., in 1764, served in the war of the revolution, was graduated at Dartmouth in 1790, was appointed a captain under Wayne, in 1792, also consul at Tunis in 1798; in April, 1804, he was appointed navy agent of the United States, with the Barbary powers to co-operate with Hamet, bashaw, in the war against Tripoli, in which he evinced great energy of character: he died in 1811. He was brave, patriotic and generous.

The turnpike from Dayton west leads through Eaton, and one also connects the place with Hamilton. The village contains 1 Presbyterian, 1 Methodist and 1 Public church, 1 book, 2 grocery and 4 dry goods stores, 1 or 2 newspaper printing offices, 1 woollen factory, 1 saw mill, and about 1000 inhabitants. Near the town is an overflowing well of strong sulphur water, possessing medicinal properties. About two miles south is Halderman's quarry, from which is obtained a beautiful grey clouded stone: at the village is a limestone quarry, and the county abounds in fine building stone.

About a mile west of Eaton is the site of Fort St. Clair, erected in the severe winter of 1791–2. At this time, Fort Jefferson was the farthest advanced post, being forty-four miles from Fort Hamilton. This spot was chosen as a place of security, and to guard the communication between them. General Wilkinson sent Major John S. Gano, belonging to the militia of the territory, with a party to build the work. General Harrison, then an ensign, commanded a guard, every other night, for about three weeks, during the building of the fort. They had neither fire nor covering of any kind, and suffered much from the intense cold. It was a stockade, and had about 20 acres cleared around it. The outline can yet be distinctly traced.

On the 6th of November, 1792, a severe battle was fought almost under the cover of the guns of Fort St. Clair, between a corps of riflemen and a body of Indians. Judge Joel Collins of Oxford, who was in the action, gives the following facts respecting it, in a letter to James M'Bride, dated June 20th, 1843.

The parties engaged were a band of 250 Mingo and Wyandot warriors, under the command of the celebrated chief Little Turtle, and an escort of 100 mounted riflemen of the Kentucky militia, commanded by Capt. John Adair, subsequently governor of Kentucky. These men had been called out to escort a brigade of pack-horses, under an order from General Wilkinson. They could then make a trip from Fort Washington past Fort St. Clair, to Fort Jefferson, and return in six days, encamping each night under the walls of one of these military posts, for protection.

The Indians being elated by the check they had given our army the previous year, in defeating St. Clair, determined to make a descent upon the settlement then forming at Columbia, at the mouth of the Little Miami. Some time in September, 250 warriors *struck the war pole*, and took up their line of march. Fortunately for the infant settlement, in passing Fort Hamilton they discovered a fatigue party, with a small guard, chopping fire-wood, east of the fort. While the men were gone to dinner, the Indians formed an ambuscade, and on their return captured two of the men. The prisoners informed the Indians, that on the morning previous—which must have been on Friday—that a brigade of some 50 or 100 pack-horses, loaded with supplies for the two military posts in advance, had left Fort Hamilton, escorted by a company of riflemen, mounted on fine horses, and that if they made their trip in the usual time, they would be at Fort Hamilton, on their return, Monday night. Upon this information, Little Turtle abandoned his design of breaking up the settlement above Cincinnati, and fell back some 12 or 15 miles, with a view of intercepting the brigade on its return. He formed an ambuscade on the trace, at a well-selected position, which he occupied through the day that he expected the return of the escort. But as Captain Adair arrived at Fort Jefferson on Saturday night, he permitted his men and horses to rest themselves over Sunday, and thus escaped the ambuscade. On Monday night, when on their return, they encamped within a short distance of Fort St. Clair. The judge says: "The chief of the band of Indians being informed of our position, by his runners, concluded that by a night attack, he could drive us out of our encampment. Accordingly he left his ambush, and a short time before day-break, on Tuesday morning, the Indians, by a discharge of rifles and raising the hideous yells for which they are distinguished, made a simultaneous attack on three sides of the encampment, leaving that open next to the fort. The horses became frightened, and numbers of them broke from their fastenings. The camp, in consequence of this, being thrown into some confusion, Captain Adair retired with his men, and formed them in three divisions, just beyond the *shine of the fires*, on the side next the fort; and while the enemy were endeavoring to secure the horses and plunder the camp—which seemed to be their main object—they were in turn attacked by us, on their right, by the captain and his division; on the left, by Lieut. George Madison, and in their centre, by Lieut. Job Hale, with their respective divisions. The enemy, however, were sufficiently strong to detail a fighting party, double our numbers, to protect those plundering the camp and driving off the horses, and as we had left the side from the fort open to them, they soon began to move off, taking all with them.

"As soon as the day dawn afforded light sufficient to distinguish a white man from an Indian, there ensued some pretty sharp fighting, so close, in some instances, as to bring in use the war-club and tomahawk. Here Lieut. Hale was killed and Lieut. Madison wounded. As the Indians retreated, the white men hung on their rear, but when we pressed them too close, they would turn and drive us back. In this way a kind of running fight was kept up until after sun-rising, when we lost sight of the enemy and nearly all our horses, some where about where the town of Eaton now stands. On returning from the pursuit, our camp presented rather a discouraging appearance. Not more than six or eight horses were saved; some twenty or thirty lay dead on the ground The loss of the enemy remains unknown: the bodies of two Indians were found among the dead horses. We gathered up our wounded, six in number, took them to the fort, where a room was assigned them as a hospital, and their wounds dressed by Surgeon Boyd, of the regular army. The wound of one man, John James, consisted of little more than the loss of his scalp. It appeared from his statement, that in the heat of the action, he received a blow on the side of his head with a war-club, which stunned so as to barely knock him down, when two or three Indians fell to skinning his head, and in a very short time took from him an unusually large scalp, and in the hurry of the operation, a piece of one of his ears. He recovered, and I understood, some years afterwards, that he was then living. Another of the wounded, Luke Vores, was a few years since living in Preble county.

"By sunset on the day of the action, we had some kind of rough coffins prepared for the slain. For the satisfaction of surviving friends, I will name them, and state that in one grave, some fifty paces west of the site of Fort St. Clair, are the remains of Captain Joab Hale; next to him, on his left, we laid our orderly sergeant, Matthew English; then followed the four privates, Robert Bowling, Joseph Clinton, Isaac Jett and John Williams. Dejection and even sorrow hung on the countenances of every member of the escort, as we stood around or assisted in the interment of these, our fellow comrades. Hale was a noble and brave man, fascinating in his appearance and deportment as an officer. It was dusk in the evening before we completed the performance of this melancholy duty. What a change! The evening before, nothing within the encampment was to be seen or heard but life and animation. Of those not on duty, some were measuring their strength and dexterity at athletic exercises; some nursing, rubbing and feeding their horses; others cooking, &c. But look at us now, and behold the ways, chances and uncertainties of war. I saw and felt the contrast then, and feel it still, but am unable further to describe it here!"

Between the site of Fort St. Clair and Eaton is the village graveyard. This cemetery is adorned with several beautiful monuments. Among them is one to the memory of Fergus Holderman, who died in 1838. Upon it are some exquisitely beautiful devices, carved by "the lamented Clevenger," which are among his first attempts at sculpture. The principal object of attraction, however, is the monument to the memory of Lieut. Lowry and others, who fell with him in an engagement with a party of Indians commanded by Little Turtle, at Ludlow's spring, near the Forty Foot Pitch in this county, on the 17th of October, 1793. This monument has recently been constructed by La'Dow & Hamilton, of Dayton, at an expense of about $300, contributed by public-spirited individuals of this vicinity. It is composed of the elegant Rutland marble, is about 12 feet in height, and stands upon one of those small artificial mounds common in this region. The view was taken from the east, beyond which, in the extreme distance in the forest, on the left, is the site of Fort St. Clair. This Lieut. Lowry was a brave man. His last words were: "My brave boys, all you that can fight, now display your activity and let your balls fly!" The slain in the engagement were buried at the fort. On the 4th of July, 1822, the remains of Lowry were taken up and re-interred, with the honors of war, in this grave yard, twelve military officers acting as pall-bearers, followed by the orator, chaplain and physicians, under whose direction the removal was made, with a large concourse of citizens and two military companies. The remains of the slain commander and soldiers have been recently removed to the mound, which, with the monument, will "mark their resting place, and be a memento of their glory for ages to come."

Lowry's Monument.

We give a letter narrating an account of this action, written by Gen. Wayne to the secretary of war, and dated "Camp, southwest branch of the Miami, six miles advanced of Fort Jefferson, October 23d, 1793."

The greatest difficulty which at present presents, is that of furnishing a sufficient escort to secure our convoy of provisions and other supplies from insult and disaster; and at the same time retain a sufficient force in camp to sustain and repel the attacks of the enemy who appear desperate and determined. We have recently experienced a little check to our convoys, which may probably be exaggerated into something serious by the tongue of fame, before this reaches you. The following, however, is the fact, viz: Lieut. Lowry, of the 2d sub-legion, and Ensign Boyd, of the 1st, with a command consisting of 90 non-commissioned officers and privates, having in charge 20 wagons belonging to the quarter-master general's department, loaded with grain, and one of the contractor's, [wagons,] loaded with stores, were attacked early on the morning of the 17th inst., about 7 miles advanced of Fort St. Clair, by a party of Indians. Those gallant young gentlemen—who promised at a future day to be ornaments to their profession—together with 13 non-commissioned officers and privates, bravely fell, after an obstinate resistance against superior numbers, being abandoned by the greater part of the escort upon the first discharge. The savages killed or carried off about 70 horses, leaving the wagons and stores standing in the road, which have all been brought to this camp without any other loss or damage, except some trifling articles.

Little Turtle, whose name has been mentioned in the preceding pages, was a distinguished chief and counsellor of the Miamis, by whom he was called *Meshekenoghqua.* He commanded the Indians at St. Clair's defeat. We annex a sketch of him from Drake's Indian Biography.

It has been generally said, that had the advice of this chief been taken at the disastrous fight afterwards with General Wayne, there is but little doubt but he had met as ill-success as General St. Clair. He was not for fighting General Wayne at Presque Isle, and inclined rather to peace than fighting him at all. In a council held the night before the battle, he argued as follows: " We have beaten the enemy twice, under separate commanders. We cannot expect the same good fortune always to attend us. The Americans are now led by a chief who never sleeps; the night and the day are alike to him. And during all the time that he has been marching upon our villages, notwithstanding the watchfulness of our young men, we have never been able to surprise him. Think well of it. There is something whispers me, it would be prudent to listen to his offers of peace." For holding this language, he was reproached by another chief with cowardice, which put an end to all farther discourse. Nothing wounds the feelings of a warrior like the reproach of cowardice, but he stifled his resentment, did his duty in the battle, and its issue proved him a truer prophet than his accuser believed.

Little Turtle lived some years after the war, in great esteem among men of high standing. He was alike courageous and humane, possessing great wisdom. "And," says Schoolcraft, " there has been few individuals among aborigines who have done so much to abolish the rites of human sacrifice. The grave of this noted warrior is shown to visitors, near Fort Wayne. It is frequently visited by the Indians in that part of the country, by whom his memory is cherished with the greatest respect and veneration."

When the philosopher and famous traveller, Volney, was in America, in the winter of 1797, Little Turtle came to Philadelphia, where he then was, and who sought immediate acquaintance with the celebrated chief, for highly valuable purposes, which in some measure he effected. He made a vocabulary of his language, which he printed in the appendix to his travels. A copy in manuscript, more extensive than the printed one, is in the library of the Philosophical Society of Pennsylvania.

Having become convinced that all resistance to the whites was vain, he brought his nation to consent to peace, and to adopt agricultural pursuits. And it was with the view of soliciting congress and the benevolent society of Friends for assistance to effect this latter purpose, that he now visited Philadelphia. While here he was inoculated for the small pox, and was afflicted with the gout and rheumatism.

At the time of Mr. Volney's interview with him for information, he took no notice of the conversation while the interpreter was communicating with Mr. Volney, for he did not understand English, but walked about, plucking out his beard and eye-brows. He was dressed now in English clothes. His skin, where not exposed, Mr. Volney says, was as white as his; and on speaking upon the subject, Little Turtle said: " I have seen Spaniards in Louisiana, and found no difference of color between them and me. And why should there be any? In them, as in us, it is the work of the *father of colors*, the *sun* that burns us. You white people compare the color of your face with that of your bodies." Mr. Volney explained to him the notion of many, that his race was descended from the Tartars, and by a map showed him the supposed communication between Asia and America. To this, Little Turtle replied: " *Why should not these Tartars, who resemble us, have come from America? Are there any reasons to the contrary?* Or why should we not both have been in our own country?" It is a fact that the Indians give themselves a name which is equivalent to our word *indigine*, that is, *one sprung from the soil*, or natural to it.

When Mr. Volney asked Little Turtle what prevented him from living among the whites, and if he were not more comfortable in Philadelphia than upon the banks of the Wabash, he said: " Taking all things together you have the advantage over us; but here I am deaf and dumb. I do not talk your language; I can neither hear, nor make myself heard. When I walk through the streets, I see every person in his shop employed about something: one makes shoes, another hats, a third sells cloth, and every one lives by his labor. I say to myself, which of all these things can you do? Not one. I can make a bow or an arrow, catch fish, kill game, and go to war: but none of these is of any use here. To learn what is done here would require a long time." " Old age comes on." " I should be a piece of furniture useless to my nation, useless to the whites, and useless to myself." " I must return to my own country."

Col. John Johnston has given in his "Recollections," published in Cist's Advertiser, some anecdotes of Little Turtle.

Little Turtle was a man of great wit, humor and vivacity, fond of the company of gentlemen, and delighted in good eating. When I knew him, he had two wives living with him under the same roof in the greatest harmony; one, an old woman, about his own age—fifty—the choice of his youth, who performed the drudgery of the house; the other a young and beautiful creature of eighteen, who was his favorite; yet it never was discovered by any one that the least unkind feeling existed between them. This distinguished chief died at Fort Wayne about twenty-five years ago, of a confirmed case of the gout, brought on by high living, and was buried with military honors by the troops of the United States. The Little Turtle used to entertain us with many of his war adventures, and would laugh immoderately at the recital of the following:—A white man, a prisoner of many years in the tribe, had often solicited permission to go on a war party to Kentucky, and had been refused. It never was the practice with the Indians to ask or encourage white prisoners among them to go to war against their countrymen. This man, however, had so far acquired the confidence of the Indians, and being very importunate to go to war, the Turtle at length consented, and took him on an expedition into Kentucky. As was their practice, they had reconnoitered during the day, and had fixed on a house recently built and occupied, as the object to be attacked next morning a little before the dawn of day. The house was surrounded by a clearing, there being much brush and fallen timber on the ground. At the appointed time, the Indians, with the white man, began to move to the attack. At all such times no talking or noise is to be made. They crawl along the ground on hands and feet; all is done by signs from the leader. The white man all the time was striving to be foremost, the Indians beckoning him to keep back. In spite of all their efforts he would keep foremost, and having at length got within running distance of the house, he jumped to his feet and went with all his speed, shouting, at the top of his voice, Indians! Indians! The Turtle and his party had to make a precipitate retreat, losing forever their white companion, and disappointed in their fancied conquest of the unsuspecting victims of the log cabin. From that day forth this chief would never trust a white man to accompany him again to war.

During the presidency of Washington, the Little Turtle visited that great and just man at Philadelphia, and during his whole life after, often spoke of the pleasure which that visit afforded him. Kosciusko, the Polish chief, was at the time in Philadelphia, confined by sickness to his lodgings, and hearing of the Indians being in the city, he sent for them, and after an interview of some length, he had his favorite brace of pistols brought forth, and addressing the chief, Turtle, said—I have carried and used these in many a hard fought battle in defence of the oppressed, the weak and the wronged of my own race, and I now present them to you with this injunction, that with them you shoot dead the first man that ever comes to subjugate you or despoil you of your country. The pistols were of the best quality and finest manufacture, silver mounted, with gold touch-holes.

New Paris, about 11 miles NW. of Eaton, on the east fork of White Water river, is a flourishing town: it contains 2 or 3 churches, 4 stores, 1 woollen factory, 3 flouring and some saw mills, and about 600 inhabitants. In the neighborhood are limestone quarries, from which large quantities of excellent lime are made. Camden, a thriving town, 8 miles S. of Eaton, on the Hamilton turnpike, has 2 churches, 3 dry goods stores, 3 flouring and 2 or 3 saw mills, and about 450 inhabitants. West Alexandria, 5 miles E. of E., on the Dayton turnpike, Euphenia, on the national road, 11 NE., Lewisburg, 10 NE., and Winchester, 9 SE., are villages having each more or less churches and stores, and about 50 dwellings. Fair Haven, Westville, New Florence and Rising Sun are small places.

PUTNAM.

Putnam was formed from Old Indian territory, April 1st, 1820, and named from Gen. Israel Putnam, who was born at Salem, Mass., January 7th, 1718, and died at Brooklyn, Conn., May 29th, 1790. The surface is generally level, and much of the land being within the Black Swamp district, is wet, but when cleared and drained, very fertile. The principal productions are corn, wheat, potatoes, oats and pork. The following is a list of the townships in 1840, with their population.

Blanchard,	670	Monroe,	518	Richland,	387
Greensburgh,	275	Ottawa,	690	Riley,	621
Jennings,	350	Perry,	266	Sugar Creek,	505
Liberty,	125	Pleasant,	325	Union,	400

The population of Putnam, in 1830, was 230, and in 1840, 5132, or 9 inhabitants to a square mile.

A large proportion of the population is from eastern Ohio, and of Pennsylvania extraction. In Ottawa, Greensburgh, Riley and Jennings are many natives of Germany. The site of old Fort Jennings is in the southwest part. There were two Indian towns in the county of some note: the upper 'Tawa town was on Blanchard's fork; two miles below, on the site of the present Ottawa village, was the lower 'Tawa town.

Kalida, the county seat, is on Ottawa river, 114 miles northwest of Columbus. It was laid out in 1834, as the seat of justice, and named from a Greek word, signifying "*beautiful.*" It contains a Methodist church, 4 stores, a newspaper printing office, and 36 dwellings.

In Riley is a settlement of "Aymish or Omish," a sect of the "Memnonites or Harmless Christians." They derive their name from Aymen, their founder, and were originally known as Aymenites. This sect wear long beards, and reject all superfluities in dress, diet and property. They have ever been remarkable for industry, frugality, temperance and simplicity. At an early day many of the Omish emigrated from Germany to Pennsylvania. When they first came to the country they had neither churches nor grave yards. "A church," said they, "we do not require, for in the depth of the thicket, in the forest, on the water, in the field and in the dwelling, God is always present." Many of their descendants, deviating from the practice of their forefathers, have churches and burial grounds.

The view, "a home in the wilderness," represents a log tavern in the western part of the county, on the road to Charloe. It was built about 30 years since by two men, assisted by a female. It has long been a favorite stopping place for travellers, as many as twenty or thirty having, with their horses, frequently tarried here over night, when journeying through the wilderness. The situation is charming. It is on the banks of the Auglaize, which flows in a ravine some fifteen or twenty feet below. All around stand massive trees, with foliage luxuriantly developed by the virgin fertility of the soil, while numerous branches lave in the passing waters. We came suddenly upon the place on a pleasant day in June, 1846, and were so much pleased with its primitive simplicity and loveliness, as to stop and make a more familiar acquaintance. We alighted from our faithful "Pomp," turned him loose among the fresh grass, drew our portfolio from our saddle-bags, and while he was rolling amid the clover in full liberty, and the ladies of the house were seated sewing in the open space between the parts of the cabin, fanned by a gentle breeze, and perhaps listening to the warblings of the birds and murmurings of the waters,—we took a sketch, as a memorial of a scene we shall never forget, and to present to our readers a view of "a home in the wilderness."

Gilboa, Pendleton, Ottawa, Columbus, Grove, Madeira and Glandorff are all small places in this county, the largest of which, Gilboa, contains about 35 dwellings.

RICHLAND.

RICHLAND was organized March 1st, 1813, and named from the character of its soil. About one-half of the county is level, inclining to clay, and adapted to grass. The remainder is rolling, adapted to wheat, and some parts to corn, and well watered. The principal agricultural products are wheat, oats, corn, hay and potatoes; all of which are raised in great abundance—and rye, hemp, barley, flax-seed, &c. The following is a list of its townships in 1840, with their population: the county was much reduced in 1846, by the creation of Ashland.

Auburn,	1020	Madison,	3206	Sandusky,	1465
Bloomfield,	1294	Mifflin,	1800	Sharon,	1675
Blooming Grove,	1495	Milton,	1861	Springfield,	1685
Clear Creek,	1653	Monroe,	1627	Troy,	1939
Congress,	1248	Montgomery,	2445	Vermilion,	2402
Franklin,	1668	Orange,	1840	Vernon,	1040
Green,	2007	Perry,	1852	Washington,	1915
Hanover,	1485	Plymouth,	1934	Worthington,	1942
Jefferson,	2325				

The population of Richland, in 1820, was 9168; in 1830, 24,007; and in 1840, 44,823, or 49 inhabitants to the square mile.

A large proportion of the early settlers of Richland emigrated from Pennsylvania, many of whom were of German origin. It was first settled, about the year 1809, on branches of the Mohiccan. The names of the first settlers, as far as recollected, are, Henry M'Cart, Andrew Craig, James Cunningham, Abm. Baughman, Henry Nail, Samuel Lewis, Peter Kinney, Calvin Hill, John Murphy, Thomas Coulter, Melzer Tannehill, Isaac Martin, Stephen Van Schoick, Archibald Gardner and James M'Clure.

In September, 1812, shortly after the breaking-out of the late war with Great Britain, two block-houses were built in Mansfield. One stood about six rods west of the site of the court house, and the other a rod or two north. The first was built by a company commanded by Capt. Shaeffer, from Fairfield county, and the other by the company of Col. Chas. Williams, of Coshocton, A garrison was stationed at the place, until after the battle of the Thames.

At the commencement of hostilities, there was a settlement of friendly Indians, of the Delaware tribe, at a place called Greentown, about 12 miles southeast of Mansfield, within the present township of Green. It was a village consisting of some 60 cabins, with a council-house about 60 feet long, 25 wide, one story in height, and built of posts and clapboarded. The village contained several hundred persons. As a measure of safety, they were collected, in August, 1812, and sent to some place in the western part of the state, under protection of the government. They were first brought to Mansfield, and placed under guard, near where the tan-yard now is, on the run. While there, a young Indian and squaw came up to the block-house, with a request to the chaplain, Rev. James Smith of Mount Vernon, to marry them after the manner of the whites. In the absence of the guard, who had come up to witness the ceremony, an old Indian and his daughter, aged about 12 years, who were from Indiana, took advantage of the circumstance and escaped. Two spies from Coshocton, named Morrison and M'Culloch, met them near the run, about a mile northwest of Mansfield, on what is now the farm of E. P. Sturges. As the commanding officer, Col. Kratzer, had given orders to shoot all Indians found out of the bounds of the place, under an impression that all such must be hostile, Morrison, on discovering them, shot the father through the breast. He fell mortally wounded, then springing up, ran about 200 yards, and fell to rise no more. The girl escaped. The men returned and gave the information. A party of 12 men were ordered out, half of whom were under Serjeant John C. Gilkison, now of Mansfield. The men flanked on each side of the run. As Gilkison came up, he found the fallen Indian on the north side of the run, and at every breath he drew, blood flowed through the bullet hole in his chest. Morrison next came up, and called to M'Culloch to come and take revenge. Gilkison then asked the Indian who he was: he replied, "a friend." M'Culloch, who by this time had joined them, exclaimed as he drew his tomahawk, "d—n you! I'll make a friend of you!" and aimed a blow at his head; but it glanced, and was not mortal. At this he placed one foot on the neck of the prostrate Indian, and drawing out his tomahawk, with another blow buried it in his brains. The poor fellow gave one quiver, and then all was over.

Gilkison had in vain endeavored to prevent this inhuman deed, and now requested M'Culloch to bury the Indian. "D—n him! no!" was the answer; "they killed two or three brothers of mine, and never buried them." The second day following, the Indian was buried, but it was so slightly done that his ribs were seen projecting above ground for two or three years after.

This M'Culloch continued an Indian fighter until his death. He made it a rule to kill every Indian he met, whether friend or foe. Mr. Gilkison saw him some time after, on his way to Sandusky, dressed as an Indian. To his question, "where are you going?" he replied, "to get more revenge!"

There was living at this time, on the Black Fork of the Mohiccan, about half a mile west of where Petersburgh now is, a Mr. Martin Ruffner. Having removed his family for safety, no person was with him in his cabin, excepting a bound boy. About two miles southeast stood the cabin of the Seymours. This family consisted of the parents—both very old people—a maiden daughter Catharine, and her brother Philip, who was a bachelor.

One evening Mr. Ruffner sent out the lad to the creek bottom, to bring home the cows, when he discovered four Indians and ran. They called to him, saying that they would not harm him, but wished to speak to him. Having ascertained from him that the Seymours were at home, they left, and he hurried back and told Ruffner of the circumstance; upon which he took down his rifle and started for Seymour's. He arrived there, and was advising young Seymour to go to the cabin of a Mr. Copus, and get old Mr. Copus and his son to come up and help take the Indians prisoners, when the latter were seen approaching. Upon this young Seymour passed out of the back door and hurried to Copus's, while the Indians entered the front door, with their rifles in hand.

The Seymours received them with an apparent cordiality, and the daughter spread the table for them. The Indians, however, did not appear to be inclined to eat, but soon arose and commenced the attack. Ruffner, who was a powerful man, made a desperate resistance. He clubbed his rifle, and broke the stock to pieces; but he fell before superior numbers, and was afterwards found dead and scalped in the yard, with two rifle balls through him, and several fingers cut off by a tomahawk. The old people and daughter were found tomahawked and scalped in the house.

In an hour or so after dark, young Seymour returned with Mr. Copus and son, making their way through the woods by the light of a hickory bark torch. Approaching the cabin, they found all dark and silent within. Young Seymour attempted to open the door, when it flew back. Reaching forward, he touched the corpse of the old man, and exclaimed in tones of anguish, "here is the blood of my poor father!" Before they reached the place, they heard the Indians whistling on their powder chargers, upon which they put out the light and were not molested.*

These murders, supposed to have been committed by some of the Greentown Indians, spread terror among the settlers, who immediately fortified their cabins and erected several block-houses. Among the block-houses erected was Nail's on the Clear fork of the Mohiccan; Beems's on the Rocky fork; one on the site of Ganges, and a picketed house on the Black fork, owned by Thomas Coulter.

Shortly after this, a party of 12 or 14 militia from Guernsey county, who were out on a scout, without any authority burnt the Indian village of Greentown, at this time deserted.

---

* From Mr. Henry Nail.

At night they stopped at the cabin of Mr. Copus, on the Black fork, about 9 miles from Mansfield. The next morning, as four of them were at a spring washing, a few rods from the cabin, they were fired upon by a party of Indians in ambush. They all ran for the house, except Warnock, who retreated in another direction, and was afterwards found dead in the woods, about half a mile distant. His body was resting against a tree, with his handkerchief stuffed in the wound in his bowels. Two of the others, George Shipley and John Tedrick, were killed and scalped between the spring and the house. The fourth man, Robert Dye, in passing between the shed and cabin, suddenly met a warrior with his uplifted tomahawk. He dodged and escaped into the house, carrying with him a bullet in his thigh.

Mr. Copus at the first alarm had opened the door, and was mortally wounded by a rifle ball in his breast. He was laid on the bed, and the Indians shortly attacked the cabin. "Fight and save my family," exclaimed he, "for I am a dead man." The attack was fiercely made, and several balls came through the door, upon which they pulled up the puncheons from the floor and placed against it. Mrs. Copus and her daughter went up into the loft for safety, and the last was slightly wounded in the thigh, from a ball fired from a neighboring hill. One of the soldiers, George Launtz, was in the act of removing a chunk of wood to fire through, when a ball entered the hole and broke his arm. After this, he watched and saw an Indian put his head from behind a stump. He fired, and the fellow's brains were scattered over it. After about an hour, the Indians having suffered severe loss, retreated.* Had they first attacked the house, it is probable an easy victory would have been gained by them.

Mr. Levi Jones was shot by some Greentown Indians in the northern part of Mansfield, in the succeeding autumn, somewhere near the site of Riley's mill. He kept a store in Mansfield, and when the Greentown Indians left, refused to give up some rifles they had left as security for debt. He was waylaid, and shot and scalped. The report of the rifles being heard in town, a party went out and found his body much mutilated, and buried him in the old grave yard.

After the war, some of the Greentown Indians returned to the county to hunt, but their town having been destroyed, they had no fixed residence. Two of them, young men by the names of Seneca John and Quilipetoxe, came to Mansfield one noon, had a frolic in Williams's tavern, on the site of the North American Hotel, and quarreled with some whites. About 4 o'clock in the afternoon they left, partially intoxicated. The others, five in number, went in pursuit, vowing revenge. They overtook them about a mile east of town, shot them down, and buried them at the foot of a large maple on the edge of the swamp, by thrusting their bodies down deep in the mud. The skeletons remain to this day. The place is known as "Spook Hollow."

Mansfield, the county seat, is 68 miles northerly from Columbus, 25 from Mount Vernon, and about 45 from Sandusky City. Its situation is beautiful, upon a commanding elevation, overlooking a country handsomely disposed in hills and valleys. The streets are narrow, and the town is compactly built, giving it a city-like appearance. The completion of the railroad through here to Sandusky City has added much to its business facilities, and it is now thriving and increasing rapidly.

It was laid out in 1808, by James Hedges, Jacob Newman and Joseph H. Larwill. The last named gentleman pitched his tent on the rise of ground above the Big Spring, and opened the first sale of lots, on the 8th of October. The country all around was then a wilderness, with no roads through it. The first purchasers came in from the counties of Knox, Columbiana, Stark, &c. Among the first settlers were George Coffinberry, William Winship, Rollin Wel-

---

* We have three different accounts of this affair: one from Wyatt Hutchinson, of Guernsey, then a lieutenant in the Guernsey militia; one from Henry Nail, who was with some of the wounded men the night following; and the last from a gentleman living in Mansfield at the time. Each differs in some essential particulars. Much experience has taught us that it is almost impossible to get perfectly accurate verbal narrations of events that have taken place years since, and which live only in memory.

don, J. C. Gilkison, John Wallace and Joseph Middleton. In 1817, about 20 dwellings were in the place—all cabins, except the frame tavern of Samuel Williams, which stood on the site of the North American, and is now the private residence of Joseph Hildreth, Esq. The only store at that time was that of E. P. Sturges, a small frame which stood on the northwest corner of the public square, on the spot where the annexed view was taken. The Methodists erected the first church.

Public Square, Mansfield.

Mansfield contains 1 Baptist, 1 Union, 1 Seceder, 1 Disciples', 1 Methodist, 1 Presbyterian and 1 Congregational church—the last of which is one of the most substantial and elegant churches in Ohio—two newspaper printing offices, two hardware, 1 book and 20 dry goods stores, and had, in 1840, 1328 inhabitants, and in 1846, 2330, since which it has much increased.

Mansfield derived its name from Col. Jared Mansfield, who was born in New Haven Conn., about the year 1759. He graduated at Yale College in 1777, taught school first at New Haven, and afterwards at Philadelphia. Becoming known to Mr. Jefferson, he received the appointment of Professor of Natural Philosophy at the U. S. Military Academy at West Point. The publication of his Mathematical and Physical Essays about this time enhanced his reputation, and he took a high stand among the scientific men of the nation. About the year 1803, he was appointed by President Jefferson, Surveyor General of the United States for the Northwestern Territories, an office before held by Gen. Rufus Putnam. While in this office, he introduced many improvements in the mode of effecting surveys by rectangular co-ordinates, which have been since followed and received the sanction of law. Col. Mansfield subsequently resumed the Professorship of Natural Philosophy at the Military Academy, where he continued until a few years previous to his death, when he retired to Cincinnati, and subsequently died while on a visit to his native city, Feb. 3d, 1830, aged 71 years.

Col. Mansfield was distinguished for extraordinary mathematical genius and rare attainments. He was a man of unexceptionable moral character, generous and sincere.

At an early day, there was a very eccentric character who frequently was in this region, well remembered by the early settlers. His name was Jonathan Chapman, but he was usually known as

Johnny Appleseed. He was originally, it is supposed, from New England.

He had imbibed a remarkable passion for the rearing and cultivation of apple trees from the seed. He first made his appearance in western Pennsylvania, and from thence made his way into Ohio, keeping on the outskirts of the settlements, and following his favorite pursuit. He was accustomed to clear spots in the loamy lands on the banks of the streams, plant his seeds, enclose the ground, and then leave the place until the trees had in a measure grown. When the settlers began to flock in and open their "clearings," Johnny was ready for them with his young trees, which he either gave away or sold for some trifle, as an old coat, or any article of which he could make use. Thus he proceeded for many years, until the whole country was in a measure settled and supplied with apple trees, deriving self-satisfaction amounting to almost delight, in the indulgence of his engrossing passion. About 20 years since he removed to the far west, there to enact over again the same career of humble usefulness.

His personal appearance was as singular as his character. He was a small "chunked" man, quick and restless in his motions and conversation; his beard and hair were long and dark, and his eye black and sparkling. He lived the roughest life, and often slept in the woods. His clothing was mostly old, being generally given to him in exchange for apple trees. He went bare-footed, and often travelled miles through the snow in that way. In doctrine he was a follower of Swedenbourg, leading a moral, blameless life, likening himself to the primitive Christians, literally taking no thought for the morrow. Wherever he went he circulated Swedenborgian works, and if short of them, would tear a book in two and give each part to different persons. He was careful not to injure any animal, and thought hunting morally wrong. He was welcome every where among the settlers, and treated with great kindness even by the Indians. We give a few anecdotes, illustrative of his character and eccentricities.

On one cool autumnal night, while lying by his camp-fire in the woods, he observed that the musquitoes flew in the blaze and were burnt. Johnny, who wore on his head a tin utensil which answered both as a cap and a mush pot, filled it with water and quenched the fire, and afterwards remarked, "God forbid that I should build a fire for my comfort, that should be the means of destroying any of his creatures." Another time he made his camp-fire at the end of a hollow log in which he intended to pass the night, but finding it occupied by a bear and her cubs, he removed his fire to the other end, and slept on the snow in the open air, rather than to disturb the bear. He was one morning in a prairie, and was bitten by a rattlesnake. Some time after, a friend inquired of him about the matter. He drew a long sigh and replied, "Poor fellow! he only just touched me, when I in an ungodly passion, put the heel of my scythe on him and went home. Some time after I went there for my scythe, and there lay the poor fellow dead." He bought a coffee bag, made a hole in the bottom, through which he thrust his head and wore it as a cloak, saying it was as good as any thing. An itinerant preacher was holding forth on the public square in Mansfield, and exclaimed, "where is the bare-footed Christian, travelling to heaven?" Johnny, who was lying on his back on some timber, taking the question in its literal sense, raised his bare feet in the air, and vociferated "*here he is!*"

Shelby, 11 miles NW. of Mansfield, on the railroad, Lexington, 6 SW., Ganges, 11 N., Belleville, 9 S. on the Mount Vernon road, and Newville, 12 SE., are thriving villages, containing each from 40 to 80 dwellings. Olivesburg, Rome, Windsor, Lucas, Johnsville, Woodbury, Williamsport, Ontario, Bloominggrove, Newcastle, Millsborough, Shenandoah, London, Lafayette and Washington, are also small villages.

ROSS.

Ross was formed by proclamation of Gov. St. Clair, August 20th, 1798, being the sixth county formed in the North Western Territory. Its original limits were very extensive. It was named from the

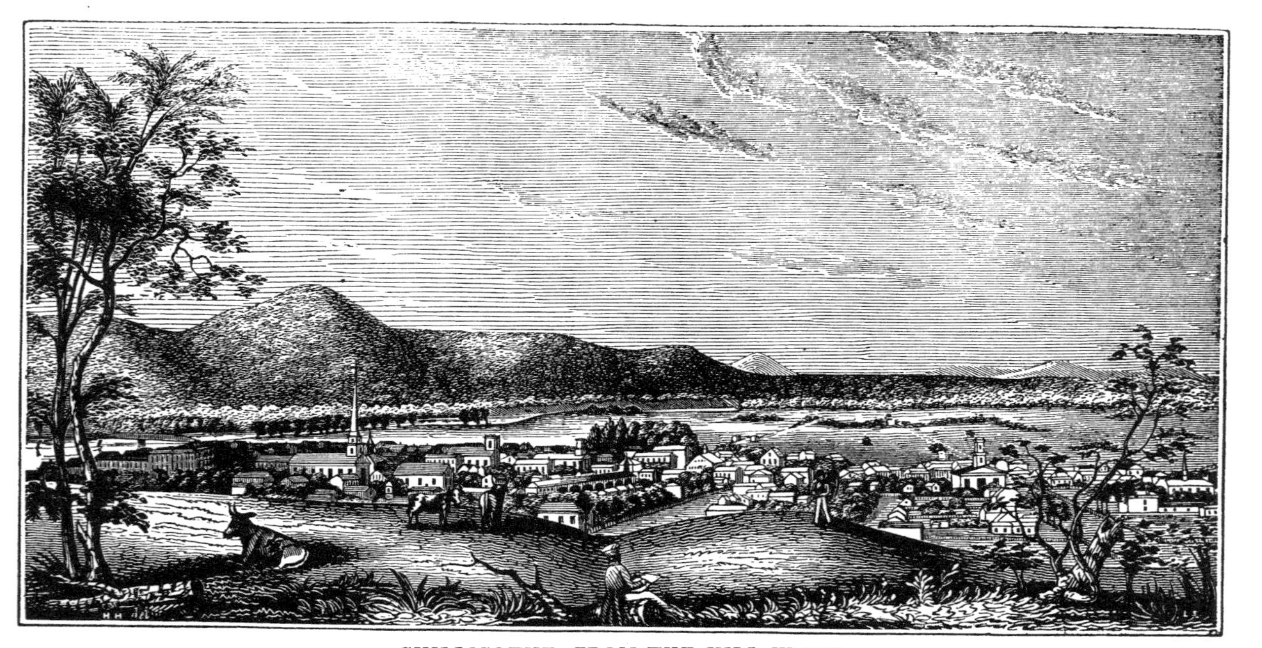

CHILLICOTHE, FROM THE HILL WEST.

Beneath is shown the principal part of the town; on the left, the Sciota river; beyond which, Mount Logan is seen rising to the hight of nearly six hundred feet.

Hon. James Ross, of Alleghany county, Pa., who at that time was the unsuccessful candidate of the Federalists for the office of governor of that state. Much of the surface off from the valleys is hilly; the land is generally good, and on the streams extremely fertile. The bottoms of the Scioto and Paint creek are famous for their abundant crops of corn. Much water power is furnished by the various streams. The principal crops are corn, wheat and oats. It is also famed for its fine breeds of cattle, and has many swine. The following is a list of its townships in 1840, with their population.

Buckskin,	1729	Green,	1820	Paxton,	1226
Colerain,	1281	Harrison,	631	Scioto,	5354
Concord,	2548	Huntington,	1159	Springfield,	1062
Deerfield,	1235	Jefferson,	871	Twin,	2195
Eagle,	411	Liberty,	1256	Union,	2631
Franklin,	582	Paint,	1380		

The population of Ross in 1820, was 20,610; in 1830, 25,150, and in 1840, 27,460, or 40 inhabitants to a square mile.

Such glowing descriptions of the beauty of the scenery and the fertility of the soil in the Scioto country, having been circulated through Kentucky, by Massie and others, who had explored it in 1792, that portions of the Presbyterian congregations of Caneridge and Concord, in Bourbon, under Rev. Robert W. Finley, determined to emigrate thither in a body. They were in a measure induced to this step by their dislike of slavery, and the uncertainty that existed in regard to the validity of the land titles in that state. The Rev. Mr. Finley, as a preliminary step, liberated his slaves, and addressed a letter of inquiry to Col. Nathaniel Massie, in December, 1794.

That letter induced Col. Massie, who was a large landholder, to visit Mr. Finley in the succeeding March. A large concourse of people who wished to engage in the enterprize, assembled on the occasion, and fixed on a day to meet at the Three Islands in Manchester, and proceed on an exploring expedition. Mr. Finley also wrote to his friends in western Pennsylvania informing them of the time and place of rendezvous.

About sixty men met according to appointment, who were divided into three companies, under Massie, Finley and Falenash. They proceeded on their route without interruption, until they struck the falls of Paint creek and proceeded a short distance down that stream, when they found themselves in the vicinity of some Indians who had encamped at Reeves' crossings, near Bainbridge. The Indians were of those who had refused to attend Wayne's treaty, and it was determined to give them battle, it being too late to retreat with safety. The Indians on being attacked soon fled with the loss of two killed and several wounded. One of the whites only, Joshua Robinson, was mortally wounded, and during the action a Mr. Armstrong, a prisoner with the Indians, escaped to his own people. The party gathered up all the plunder and retreated as far as Scioto Brush creek, where they were, according to expectation, attacked early the next morning. Only one man of the whites was wounded, Allen Gilfillan, and the party the next day reached Manchester and separated for their several homes.

After Wayne's treaty, Col. Massie and several of the old explorers again met at the house of Rev. Mr. Finley, formed a company and agreed to form a settlement in the ensuing spring, (1796,) and raise a crop of corn at the mouth of Paint creek. According to agreement, they met at Manchester about the first of April, to the number of forty and upwards, from Mason and Bourbon. Among them were Joseph M'Coy, Benj. and Wm. Rodgers, David Shelby, James Harrod, Henry, Bazil and Reuben Abrams, Wm. Jamison, Jas. Crawford, Samuel, Anthony and Robert Smith, Thos. Dick, Wm. and Jas. Kerr, Geo. and James Kilgore, John Brown, Samuel and Robt. Templeton, Ferguson Moore, Wm. Nicholson and J. B. Finley, now a Methodist clergyman. They divided into two companies, one of which struck across the country and the other came on in pirogues. The first arrived the earliest on the spot of their intended settlement, and had commenced erecting log huts above the mouth of Paint, at " the Prairie station," before the others had come on by water. About 300 acres of the prairie were cultivated in corn that season.

In August of this year, 1796, Chillicothe was laid out by Col. Nathaniel Massie, in a dense forest. He gave a lot gratis to each of the first settlers, and by the last of autumn about twenty cabins were erected. Not long after, a ferry was established across the Scioto at the north end of Walnut street. The opening of Zane's trace, very soon afterwards, produced a great change in the course of travel west, it having previously been along the Ohio in keel boats or canoes, or by land over the Cumberland mountains, through Crab Orchard in Kentucky.

The emigrants brought up some corn-meal in their pirogues, and after that was gone, their principal meal, until the next summer, was that pounded in hommony mortars, which when made into bread and anointed with bear's oil, was quite palatable.

When the settlers first came, whiskey was $4 50 per gallon ; but in the spring of 1797, when the keel boats began to run, the Monongahela whiskey makers having found a good market for their fire-water, rushed it in, in such quantities, that the cabins were crowded with it, and it soon fell to 50 cents. Men, women and children, with some exceptions, drank it freely, and many who had been respectable and temperate became inebriates. Many of Wayne's soldiers and camp-women settled in the town, so that it for a time became a town of drunkards and a sink of corruption. There was a little leaven, which in a few months began to develope itself.

In the spring of '97, one Brannon stole a great coat, handkerchief and shirt. He and his wife absconded, were pursued, brought back, and a formal trial had. Samuel Smith was appointed judge, a jury empannelled, one attorney appointed by the judge to manage the prosecution and another the defence, witnesses were examined, the cause argued and the evidence summed up by the judge. The jury having retired a few minutes, returned with a verdict of guilty, and that the culprit be sentenced according to the discretion of the judge ; who soon announced that he should have ten lashes on his naked back, or that he should sit on a bare pack-saddle on his poney, and that his wife—who was supposed to have had some agency in the theft—should lead the poney to every house in the village, and proclaim, " this is Brannon, who stole the great coat, handkerchief and shirt ;" and that James B. Finley—now the Rev. J. B. Finley, chaplain of the Ohio penitentiary—should see the sentence faithfully executed." Brannon chose the latter, and the ceremony, " this is Brannon who stole the great-coat, handkerchief and shirt," was at the door of every cabin in the village, in due form proclaimed by his wife, he sitting on a bare pack-saddle on his poney. It was performed in the presence of Mr. Finley, and when it was over, Brannon and his wife made off.

Dr. Edw. Tiffin and Mr. Thomas Worthington of Berkeley county, Va., were brothers-in-law, and being moved by abolition principles liberated their slaves, intending to remove into the Territory. For the purpose of making preparations for their removal in the spring, Mr. Worthington, in 1797, visited Chillicothe and purchased several of the in and out lots of the town, and on one of the former he erected a two story frame-house, the same in which Mr. Campbell now resides on Second street, which was the first frame-house erected in Chillicothe. On his return to Virginia, having purchased a part of the farm on which his widow now resides, and another at the north fork of Paint, he contracted with a Mr. Joseph Yates, a mill-wright, and a Mr. Geo. Haines, a blacksmith, to come out with him in the following winter or spring, and erect for him a grist and a saw-mill on his north fork tract. The summer, fall and following winter of that year, was marked with a rush of emigration, which spread over the high bank prairie, Pea-pea, Westfall, and a few miles up Paint and Deer creeks.

Nearly all the first settlers were either regular members, or had been raised in the Presbyterian church. Towards the fall of 1797, the leaven of piety retained by a portion of the first settlers began to diffuse itself through the mass, and a large log meeting-house was erected near the old grave-yard on this side of the bridge, and the Rev. Wm. Speer, a Presbyterian clergyman from Pennsylvania took charge. The sleepers served as seats for the hearers, and a split log table was used as a pulpit. Mr. Speer was a gentlemanly, moral man, tall and cadaverous in person, and wore the cocked hat of the revolutionary era.

Thomas James arrived in February, 1798, bringing with him the first load of bar-iron in the Scioto valley, and about the same time arrived Maj. Elias Langham, an officer of the revolution. Dr. Tiffin and his brother Joseph arrived the same month from Virginia, and opened a store not far from the log meeting-house. A store was also opened previously by John M'Dougal. On the 17th of April, the families of Col. Worthington and Dr. Tiffin arrived, at which time the first marriage in the Scioto valley was celebrating ; the parties were George Kilgore and Elizabeth Cochran. The ponies of the attendants of the wedding were hitched to the trees along the streets, which then were not cleared out, nearly the whole town being a wilderness. Mr. Joseph Yates, Mr. George Haines, and two or three others also arrived with the families of Tiffin and Worthington.

Col. Worthington was appointed by Gen. Rufus Putnan, surveyor general of the N. W. Territory, surveyor of a large district of congress lands, then to be surveyed on the east side of the Scioto, and Maj. Langham and a Mr. Matthews were appointed to survey the residue of the lands, which afterward composed the Chillicothe land district.

On their arrival, there were but four shingled-roof houses in town, on one of which the shingles were fastened with pegs. Col. Worthington's was then the only house in town with glass windows. The sash of the hotel was filled with greased paper.

The same season settlements were made about the Walnut Plains, by Samuel M'Culloch and others; Springer, Osbourn, Thomas and Elijah Chenowith and Dyer, settled on Darby creek: Lamberts and others on Sippo; on Foster's bottom, by Samuel Davis, the Fosters and others. The following families also settled in and about Chillicothe; John Crouse, Wm. Keys, Wm. Lamb, John Carlisle, John M'Lanberg, Wm. Candless, the Stocktons, the Gregg's, the Bates's and others.

Dr. Tiffin and his wife were the first Methodists that resided in the Scioto valley. He was a local preacher. In the fall, Worthington's grist and saw mills, on the north fork of the Paint were finished—the first mills worthy of the name in the valley.

Chillicothe was the point from which the settlements in the valley diverged. In May, 1799, a post-office was established at Chillicothe, and Joseph Tiffin appointed post-master. Mr. Tiffin and Thomas Gregg opened taverns; the first under the sign of "Gen. Anthony Wayne," was at the corner of Water and Walnut streets; and the last under the sign of "the Green Tree," was on the corner of Paint and Water streets. In 1801, Nathaniel Willis moved in and established "the Scioto Gazette."

In 1801, the settlers along the west side of the Scioto from Chillicothe to its mouth, were Joseph Kerr, Hugh Cochran, Joseph Campbell, the Johnsons, James Crawford, the Kirkpatricks, Chandlers, Beshongs, Montgomerys, Mountz's, Fosters, Pancakes, Davis's, Chenowiths, Sargents, Downings, Combess, Barnes's, Utts', Noels, Lucas's, Swaynes's, Williams and Collins, at Alexandria. On the east side of the Scioto, the Noels', Thompson, Marshall, M'Quart, the Miller's, Boylston, Talbot, Mustard, Clark, the Claypoles, Renicks, Harness's, Carnes's, and many others not recollected.*

CHILLICOTHE,† the seat of justice for Ross county, is situated on the west bank of the Scioto and on the line of the Ohio canal, 45 miles s. of Columbus, 93 from Cincinnati, 73 from Zanesville and 45 from the Ohio river at Portsmouth. The site is a level plain elevated about 30 feet above the river. The Scioto curves around it on the north, and Paint creek flows on the south. The plan and situation of Chillicothe, have been described as nearly resembling that of Philadelphia, the Scioto river and Paint creek representing in this case the Delaware and Schuylkill rivers, and both towns being level and regularly laid out into squares. But here the comparison terminates. The scenery around Philadelphia is dissimilar and far inferior, as the view shown in the annexed engraving testifies. In truth, there are but few places in the country where the scenery partakes so much of the beautiful and magnificent as in this vicinity.

---

* The preceding facts respecting the settlement of this county, are derived from the MSS. of Hon. Thomas Scott, of Chillicothe.

† Chillicothe appears to have been a favorite name with the Indians for their towns, there having been several of that name, viz: one on the site of Frankfort in this county; one on the site of Westfall in Pickaway; one three miles north of Xenia in Greene; one on the site or Piqua, Miami county, and one on the Maumee.

Col. John Johnston says, "Chillicothe is the name of one of the principal tribes of the Shawanoese. The Shawanoese would say, *Chillicothe otany, i. e.*, Chillicothe town. The Wyandots would say for Chillicothe town, *Tat,a,ra,ra-Do,tia*, or town at the leaning bank."

In 1800, the seat of government of the N. W. Territory was removed by law of congress from Cincinnati to Chillicothe. The sessions of the territorial legislature in that year and in 1801, were held in a small two story hewed log house, which stood on the corner of Second and Walnut streets, and was erected in 1798, by Mr. Bazil Abrams. To the main building, extending along Walnut street towards the Scioto, was attached a hewed log wing of two stories in height. In the lower room of the wing, Col. Thos. Gibson, then auditor for the territory kept his office, and in the upper lived a small family. In the upper room of the main building was a billiard table and a place of resort for gamblers; the lower room was used by the legislature, and as a court room, as a church, and a singing school. In the war of 1812, the building was a rendezvous and barracks for soldiers, and in 1840 was pulled down.

In 1800, the old state house was commenced, and finished the next year, for the accommodation of the legislature and courts. It is believed that it was the first public stone edifice erected in the territory. The mason work was done by Major Wm. Rutledge, a soldier of the revolution, and the carpentering by William Guthrie. The territorial legislature held their session in it for the first time in 1801. The convention that framed the constitution of Ohio was held in it, the session commencing on the first Monday in November, 1802. In April, 1803, the first state legislature met in the house, and held their sessions until 1810. The sessions of 1810–11, and 1811–12, were held at Zanesville, and from there removed back to Chillicothe and held in this house until 1816, when Columbus became the permanent capitol of the state. This time-honored edifice is yet standing in the central part of the town, and is used as a court house for the county.*

Old State House, Chillicothe.

Chillicothe was incorporated January 4th, 1802, and the following officers appointed: Samuel Finley, Ed. Tiffin, James Ferguson, Alexander M'Laughlin, Arthur Stewart, John Carlisle and Reuben Adams, members of the select council; Everard Harr, assessor; Isaac Brink, supervisor; Wm. Wallace, collector; Joseph Tiffin, town marshall.

In 1807, Chillicothe had 14 stores, 6 hotels, 2 newspaper printing

* American Pioneer.

offices, a Presbyterian and a Methodist church, both brick buildings, on Main street, and 202 dwelling houses.*

In the war of 1812, Chillicothe was a rendezvous for United States troops. They were stationed at Camp Bull, a stockade 1 mile N. of the town, on the west bank of the Scioto. A large number of British prisoners, amounting to several hundred, were at one time confined at the camp. On one occasion, a conspiracy was formed between the soldiers and their officers who were confined in jail. The plan was for the privates in camp to disarm their guard, proceed to the jail, release the officers, burn the town and escape to Canada. The conspiracy was disclosed by two senior British officers, upon which, as a measure of security, the officers were sent to the penitentiary in Frankfort, Ky.†

Four deserters were shot at camp at one time. The ceremony was impressive and horrible. The soldiers were all marched out under arms with music playing, to witness the death of their comrades, and arranged in one long extended line in front of the camp, facing the river. Close by the river bank at considerable distances apart, the deserters were placed, dressed in full uniform, with their coats buttoned up and caps drawn over their faces. They were confined to stakes in a kneeling position behind their coffins, painted black, which came up to their waists, exposing the upper part of their persons to the fire of their fellow-soldiers. Two sections of six men each were marched before each of the doomed. Signals were given by an officer instead of words of command, so that the unhappy men should not be apprised of the moment of their death. At the given signal, the first sections raised their muskets and poured the fatal volleys into the breasts of their comrades. Three of the four dropped dead in an instant; but the fourth sprang up with great force and gave a scream of agony. The reserve section stationed before him were ordered to their places, and another volley completely riddled his bosom. Even then the thread of life seemed hard to sunder.

On another occasion, an execution took place at the same spot, under most melancholy circumstances. It was that of a mere youth of nineteen, the son of a widow. In a frolic he had wandered several miles from camp, and was on his return when he stopped at an inn by the way-side. The landlord, a fiend in human shape, apprised of the reward of $50 offered for the apprehension of deserters, persuaded him to remain over night, with the offer of taking him into camp in the morning, at which he stated he had business. The youth unsuspicious of any thing wrong, accepted the offer made with so much apparent kindness, when lo! on his arrival the next day with the landlord, he surrendered him as a deserter, swore falsely as to the facts, claimed and obtained the reward. The court-martial, ignorant of the circumstances, condemned him to death, and it was not until he was no more, that his innocence was known.

The corpses of the deserters were placed in rough coffins made of poplar, and stained with lamp-black, and buried on the river margin. After a lapse of years, the freshets washing away the earth, exposed their remains, and they were subsequently re-interred in a mound in the vicinity.

Chillicothe contains 2 Presbyterian, 1 Associate Reformed Presbyterian, 2 Methodist, 1 Methodist Reformed, 1 Episcopal, 1 Catholic, 1 Baptist, 1 German Lutheran, 1 German Methodist, 1 colored Baptist and 1 colored Methodist church, 1 male academy and 1 female seminary, 38 retail and 2 wholesale dry goods, 4 wholesale grocery, 3 hardware, and 2 book stores, 8 forwarding houses, 5 weekly newspapers, 1 bank, 4 merchant mills, making 10,000 bbls. of flour annually, and 4 establishments which pack annually about 45,000 bbls. of pork. It is the centre of trade in the Scioto valley, and is connected with the river by the Ohio canal, which is rarely closed by ice. It has hydraulic works built at an expense of $75,000,

* Notes of a Traveller.

† Newspaper of the time.

which furnish water power in addition to that afforded by the canal. It lies on the route of the contemplated railroad from Cumberland to Cincinnati, and is at present progressing with a healthful and steady pace. On the hill west of the town is a mineral spring, said to possess fine medicinal properties. A beautiful cemetery, contain ing 14 acres, has recently been laid out, and it is contemplated tc supply the city with water from Paint creek, by hydraulic power, Its population in 1807, was about 1200; in 1820, 2416; in 1830, 2840; in 1840, 3977, and in 1847, about 6220.

Adena.

Two or three miles NW. of Chillicothe, on a beautiful elevation commanding a magnificent view of the fertile valley of the Scioto and its bounding hills, is Adena, the seat of the late Gov. Worthington. The mansion itself is of stone, is embosomed in shrubbery, and has attached a fine garden. It was erected in 1806, at which time it was the most elegant mansion in this part of the west, and crowds came to view it, in whose estimation the name of the place Adena, which signifies "Paradise," did not perhaps appear hyperbolical. The large panes of glass, and the novelty of papered walls appeared especially to attract attention. Its architect was the elder Latrobe, of Washington city, from which place the workmen also were. Nearly all the manufactured articles used in its construction, as the nails, door knobs, hinges, glass, &c., were from east of the mountains. The glass was made at the works of Albert Gallatin and Mr. Nicholson, at Geneva, Pa. The fire-place fronts were of Philadelphia marble, which cost $7 per hundred for transportation. The whole edifice probably cost double what it would have done if erected at the present day. It is now the residence of the widow of the late governor, of whom we annex a brief notice.

THOMAS WORTHINGTON, one of the earliest and most distinguished pioneers of Ohio, was born in Jefferson county, Virginia, about the year 1769, and settled in Ross county in 1798. He brought from Virginia a large number of slaves, whom he emancipated, and some of their descendants yet remain in Chillicothe. A man of ardent temperament, of energy of mind, and correct habits of life, he soon became distinguished both in business and in political stations. He was a member of the convention of 1803, to form a state constitution, in which he was both able and active. Soon after that, he became a senator in congress from the new state, and was a participant in the most important measures of the administrations of Jefferson and Madison. At the close of his career in congress, he was elected governor of the state, in which capacity he was the friend and aid of all the liberal and wise measures of policy which were the foundation of the great prosperity of Ohio. After his retirement from the gubernatorial chair, he was appointed a member of the first board of canal commissioners, in which capacity he served till his death. A large landholder, engaged in various and extensive business, and for thirty years in public stations, no man in Ohio did more to form its character and promote its prosperity. He died in 1827.

Near Adena, in a beautiful situation, is Fruit Hill, the seat of the late Gen. Duncan M'Arthur, and latterly the residence of his son-in-law, the Hon. Wm. Allen.

Duncan M'Arthur, who was of Scotch parentage, was born in Dutchess county, New York, in 1772, and when 8 years of age, his father removed to the frontiers of Pennsylvania. His father was in indigent circumstances, and Duncan, when of sufficient age, hired out as a laborer. At the age of 18 years, he was a volunteer in Harmar's campaign. In 1792, he was a private in the company of Capt. Wm. Enoch, and acted with so much intrepidity in the battle of Captina, (see p. 56,) as to render him very popular with the frontier men. After this, he was for a while a laborer at some salt-works near Maysville, Ky., and in the spring of 1793, engaged as a chain-bearer to Gen. Nathaniel Massie, and penetrated with him and others into the Scioto valley to make surveys, at a time when such an enterprize was full of danger from the Indians. He was afterwards employed as a spy against the Indians on the Ohio, and had some adventures with them, elsewhere detailed in this volume. He was again in the employment of Gen. Massie ; and after the treaty of Greenville, studied surveying, became an assistant surveyor to Gen. Massie, and aided him to lay out Chillicothe. He, in the course of this business, became engaged in the purchase and sale of lands, by which he acquired great landed wealth.

In 1805, he was a member of the legislature from Ross, in 1806, elected colonel, and in 1808, major-general of the state militia. In May, 1812, he was commissioned colonel in the Ohio volunteers, afterwards marched to Detroit, and himself and regiment were included in Hull's surrender. He was second in command on this unfortunate expedition ; but such was the energy he displayed, that, notwithstanding, after his return as a prisoner of war on parole, the democratic party, in the fall of 1812, elected him to congress by an overwhelming majority. In March, 1813, he was commissioned a brigadier-general in the army, and having been regularly exchanged as prisoner of war, soon after resigned his seat in congress to engage in active service.

About the time the enemy were preparing to attack Fort Stephenson, the frontiers were in great danger, and Harrison sent an express to M'Arthur to hurry on to the scene of action with all the force he could muster. Upon this, he ordered the second division to march in mass. " This march of the militia was named the '*general call*.' As soon as Governor Meigs was advised of the call made by General M'Arthur, he went forward and assumed in person the command of the militia now under arms. General M'Arthur went forward to the scene of action, and the militia followed in thousands. So promptly were his orders obeyed, that in a few days the Sandusky plains were covered with nearly eight thousand men, mostly from Scioto valley. This rush of militia to defend the exposed frontier of our country, bore honorable testimony that the patriotism of the citizens of the Scioto valley did not consist of noisy professions, but of practical service in defence of their country. This general turn-out of the militia proves that General Massie, and the few pioneers who followed him into the wilderness, and assisted him in making the first settlements in the fertile valley of the Scioto river, had infused their own daring and enterprizing spirit into the mass of the community. Among these eight thousand militia were found in the ranks, as private soldiers, judges, merchants, lawyers, preachers, doctors, mechanics, farmers, and laborers of every description ; all anxious to repulse the ruthless invaders of our soil. Indeed, the Scioto country was so stripped of its male population on this occasion, that the women, in their absence, were compelled to carry their grain to mill, or let their children suffer for want." These troops having arrived at Upper Sandusky, formed what was called the "grand camp of Ohio militia." Gen M'Arthur was detailed to the command of Fort Meigs. The victory of Perry, on the 10th of September, gave a fresh impetus to the army, and Harrison concentrated his troops at Portage river, where, on the 20th, the brigade of M'Arthur, from Fort Meigs, joined him. On the 27th, the army embarked in boats and crossed over to Malden, and a few days after, Gen. M'Arthur, with the greater part of the troops, was charged with the defence of Detroit.

After the resignation of Harrison, in the spring of 1814, M'Arthur, being the senior brigadier general, the command of the N. W. army devolved on him. As the enemy had retired discomfited from the upper end of Lake Erie, and most of the Indians were suing for peace, the greater part of the regular troops under his command were ordered to the Niagara frontier. M'Arthur had a number of small forts to garrison along the frontier, while he kept his main force at Detroit and Malden, to overawe the Canadians and the scattering Indians still in the British interest. The dull monotony of going from post to post was not the most agreeable service to his energetic mind. He projected an expedition into Canada, on which he was absent about a fortnight from Detroit, with 650 troops and 70 Indians. At or near Malcolm's mill, the detachment had an action with a force of about 500 Canadian militia, in which they defeated them with a loss of 27 killed and wounded, and made 111 prisoners; while the American loss was only 1 killed and 6 wounded. In this excursion, the valuable mills of the enemy, in the vicinity of Grand river, were destroyed, and their resources in that quarter essentially impaired. After returning from this successful expedition, the war languished in the northwest. General M'Arthur continued in service, and was at Detroit when peace was declared.

In the fall of 1815, he was again elected to the legislature. In 1816, he was appointed commissioner to negotiate a treaty with the Indians at Springwell, near Detroit; he acted in the same capacity at the treaty of Fort Meigs, in Sept., 1817, and also at the treaty at St. Mary's, in the succeeding year. In 1817, upon being elected to the legislature, he was a competitor with the late Charles Hammond, Esq., for the speaker's chair, and triumphed by a small majority. The next summer, the party strife on the United States' bank question, which had commenced the previous session, was violent. M'Arthur defended the right of that institution to place branches wherever it chose in the state, and on this issue was again a candidate for the legislature and was defeated. "A considerable majority of members elected this year were opposed to the United States bank. Mr. Hammond was again elected a member of the assembly, and by his talents, and readiness in wielding his pen, together with his strong and confident manner of speaking, was able to dictate law to this assembly. A law was passed at this session of the legislature, taxing each branch of the United States' bank, located in the state of Ohio, fifty thousand dollars. When the time arrived for collecting this tax, the branch banks refused to pay. Mr. Hammond had provided in the law for a case of this kind: the collector was authorized, in case the bank refused to pay the tax, to employ armed force, and enter the banking house and seize on the money, and this was actually done; the collector, with an armed force, entered the branch bank in the town of Chillicothe and took what money he thought proper.

"The bank brought suit in the United States' circuit court against all the state officers concerned in this forcible collection. Mr. Hammond, a distinguished lawyer, with other eminent counsel, were employed by the state of Ohio to defend this important cause. The district court decided the law of Ohio, levying the tax, unconstitutional, and, of course, null and void; and made a decree, directing the state to refund to the bank the money thus forcibly taken. The cause was appealed to the supreme court of the United States. Mr. Hammond defended the suit in all its stages. The supreme court decided this cause against the state of Ohio. Thus was settled this knotty and vexatious question, which, for a time, threatened the peace of the Union."

In 1819, M'Arthur was again elected to the legislature. In 1822, he was again chosen to congress, and became an undeviating supporter of what was then called the American system. "While General M'Arthur remained a member of congress, he had considerable influence in that body. His persevering industry, his energetic mind, his sound judgment, and practical business habits, rendered him a very efficient member. He would sometimes make short, pithy remarks on the business before the house, but made no attempts at those flourishes of eloquence which tickle the fancy and please the ear. After having served two sessions in congress, he declined a re-election, being determined to devote all his efforts to arrange his domestic concerns. He left the field of politics to others, and engaged with an unremitted attention to settle his land business."

In 1830, M'Arthur was elected governor of Ohio by the anti-Jackson party, and on the expiration of his term of office was a candidate for congress, and lost his election, which terminated his political career. By an unfortunate accident, in June, 1830, M'Arthur was horribly bruised and maimed. From this severe misfortune his bodily and mental powers constantly declined, until death, several years after, closed his career.

Duncan M'Arthur was a strong-minded, energetic man, and possessed an iron will. He was an hospitable man, close in business, and had many bitter and severe enemies. His life adds another to the many examples of the workings of our free institutions, of one rising from obscurity to the highest offices in the gift of a state.

The preceding biography, with that which follows of General Nathaniel Massie, is derived from M'Donald's sketches.

NATHANIEL MASSIE was born in Goochland county, Virginia, Dec. 28th, 1763. His father, a farmer in easy circumstances, and of plain good sense, educated his sons for the practical business of life. In 1780, Nathaniel, then being 17 years of age, was for a short time in the revolutionary army. After his return, he studied surveying, and in 1783 left to seek his fortunes in Kentucky. He first acted as a surveyor, but soon joined with it the locating of lands. " Young Massie soon became an expert surveyor, and it was a matter of astonishment (as he was raised in the dense population east of the mountains) how soon he acquired the science and habits of the backwoodsmen. Although he never practised the art of hunting, he was admitted by all who knew his qualifications as a woodsman, to be of the first order. He could steer his course truly in clear or cloudy weather, and compute distances more correctly than most of the old hunters. He could endure fatigue and hunger with more composure than the most of those persons who were inured to want on the frontier. He could live upon meat without bread, and bread without meat, and was perfectly cheerful and contented with his fare. In all the perilous situations in which he was placed, he was always conspicuous for his good feeling and the happy temperament of his mind. His courage was of a cool and dispassionate character, which, added to great circumspection in times of danger, gave him a complete ascendancy over his companions, who were always willing to follow when Massie led the way."

He also soon became interested with Gen. James Wilkinson in speculations in salt, then an article of great scarcity in the west—with what pecuniary success, however, is unknown. He was employed as a surveyor by Col. R. C. Anderson, principal surveyor of the Virginia military lands, and for a time was engaged in writing in the office of Col. Anderson, who had the control of the land warrants, placed in his hands by his brother officers and soldiers.

" A very large amount of these, so soon as the act of congress of August, 1790, removed all further obstruction, he placed in the hands of Massie, to enter and survey on such terms as he could obtain from the holders of them. As the risk of making entries was great, and as it was desirable to possess the best land, the owners of warrants, in most cases, made liberal contracts with the surveyors. One-fourth, one-third, and sometimes as much as one-half acquired by the entry of good lands, were given by the proprietors to the surveyors. If the owners preferred paying money, the usual terms were ten pounds, Virginia currency, for each thousand acres entered and surveyed, exclusive of chainmen's expenses. These terms cannot appear extravagant, when we consider that at that time the danger encountered was great, the exposure during the winter severe, and that the price of first-rate land in the west was low, and an immense quantity in market.

" The locations of land warrants in the Virginia military district between the Scioto and the Little Miami, prior to 1790, were made by stealth. Every creek which was explored, every line that was run, was at the risk of life from the savage Indians, whose courage and perseverance was only equalled by the perseverance of the whites to push forward their settlements."

In 1791, Massie made the first settlement within the Virginia military district at Manchester. (See p. 21.) During the winter of '92–'93, he continued to locate and survey the best land within a reasonable distance of the station of Manchester.

" In the fall of the year 1793, Massie determined to attempt a surveying tour on the Scioto river. This, at this time, was a very dangerous undertaking ; yet no danger, unless very imminent, could deter him from making the attempt. For that purpose, he employed about thirty men, of whom he chose three as assistant surveyors. These were John Beasley, Nathaniel Beasley, and Peter Lee. It was in this expedition Massie employed, for the first time, Duncan M'Arthur as a chainman or marker.

" In the month of October, some canoes were procured, and Massie and his party set off by water. They proceeded up the Ohio to the mouth of the Scioto, thence up the Scioto to the mouth of Paint creek. While meandering the Scioto, they made some surveys on the bottoms. After reaching the mouth of Paint creek, the surveyors went to work. Many surveys were made on the Scioto, as far up as Westfall. Some were made on Main, and others on the north fork of Paint creek, and the greatest parts of Ross and Pickaway counties in the district were well explored and partly surveyed. Massie finished his intended work without meeting with any disturbance from the Indians. But one Indian was seen during the excursion, and to him they gave a hard chase. He, however, escaped. The party returned home delighted with the rich country of the Scioto valley, which they had explored.

" During the winter of 1793–4, Massie, in the midst of the most appalling dangers, explored the different branches to their sources, which run into the Little Miami river, and thence passed in a northeastern direction to the heads of Paint and Clear creeks, and the branches that form those streams. By these expeditions he had formed, from personal observation, a correct knowledge of the geographical situation of the country composing the Virginia military district.

"During the winter of 1794–5, Massie prepared a party to enter largely into the surveying business. Nathaniel Beasley, John Beasley, and Peter Lee were again employed as the assistant surveyors. The party set off from Manchester, well equipped, to prosecute their business, or should occasion offer, give battle to the Indians. They took the route of Logan's trace, and proceeded to a place called the deserted camp, on Tod's fork of the Little Miami. At this point they commenced surveying, and surveyed large portions of land on Tod's fork, and up the Miami to the Chillicothe town, (now in Clark county,) thence up Massie's creek and Cæsar's creek nearly to their heads. By the time the party had progressed thus far, winter had set in. The ground was covered with a sheet of snow from six to ten inches deep. During the tour, which continued upwards of thirty days, the party had no bread. For the first two weeks a pint of flour was distributed to each mess once a day, to mix with the soup in which meat had been boiled. When night came, four fires were made for cooking—that is, one for each mess. Around these fires, till sleeping time arrived, the company spent their time in the most social glee, singing songs and telling stories. When danger was not apparent or immediate, they were as merry a set of men as ever assembled. Resting time arriving, Massie always gave the signal, and the whole party would then leave their comfortable fires, carrying with them their blankets, their firearms, and their little baggage, walking in perfect silence two or three hundred yards from their fires. They would then scrape away the snow and huddle down together for the night. Each mess formed one bed; they would spread down on the ground one half of the blankets, reserving the other half for covering. The covering blankets were fastened together by skewers, to prevent them from slipping apart. Thus prepared, the whole party crouched down together with their rifles in their arms, and their pouches under their heads for pillows; lying spoon-fashion, with three heads one way and four the other, their feet extending to about the middle of their bodies. When one turned the whole mass turned, or else the close range would be broken and the cold let in. In this way they lay till broad day light, no noise and scarce a whisper being uttered during the night. When it was perfectly light, Massie would call up two of the men in whom he had most confidence, and send them to reconnoiter and make a circuit around the fires, lest an ambuscade might be formed by the Indians to destroy the party as they returned to the fires. This was an invariable custom in every variety of weather. Self-preservation required this circumspection." Some time after this, while surveying on Cæsar's creek, his men attacked a party of Indians, and they broke and fled.

After the defeat of the Indians by Wayne, the surveyors were not interrupted by the Indians; but on one of their excursions, still remembered as "the starving tour," the whole party, consisting of 28 men, suffered extremely in a driving snow-storm for about four days. They were in a wilderness, exposed to this severe storm, without hut, tent, or covering, and what was still more appalling, without provision and without any road or even track to retreat on, and were nearly 100 miles from any place of shelter. On the third day of the storm, they luckily killed two wild turkeys, which were boiled and divided into 28 parts, and devoured with great avidity, heads, feet, entrails and all.

In 1796, Massie laid the foundation of the settlement of the Scioto valley, by laying out on his own land the now large and beautiful town of Chillicothe. The progress of the settlements brought large quantities of his land into market.

Massie was high in the confidence of St. Clair; and having received the appointment of colonel, it was through him that the militia of this region were first organized. Colonel Massie was an efficient member of the convention which formed the state constitution. He was afterwards elected senator from Ross, and at the first session of the state legislature, was chosen speaker. He was elected the first major general of the second division of the Ohio militia under the new constitution.

Gen. Massie was at this time one of the largest landholders in Ohio, and selected a residence at the falls of Paint creek, in this county, where he had a large body of excellent land. "In the year 1807, General Massie and Colonel Return J. Meigs were competitors for the office of governor of Ohio. They were the most popular men in the state. Col. Meigs received a small majority of votes. The election was contested by Massie on the ground that Col. Meigs was ineligible by the constitution, in consequence of his absence from the state, and had not since his return lived in the state a sufficient length of time to regain his citizenship. The contest was carried to the general assembly, who, after hearing the testimony, decided that 'Col. Meigs was ineligible to the office, and that Gen. Massie was duly elected governor of the state of Ohio.' Massie, however desirous he might have been to hold the office, was too magnanimous to accept it when his competitor had a majority of votes. After the decision in his favor he immediately resigned."

After this, he, as often as his leisure would permit, represented Ross county in the legislature. He died Nov. 3d, 1813, and was buried on his farm. "His character was well suited for the settlement of a new country; distinguished as it was by an uncommon degree of energy and activity in the business in which he was engaged. His disposition was ever marked with liberality and kindness."

Cave of the Scioto Hermit.

About eleven miles south of Chillicothe, on the road to Portsmouth, is the cave of the hermit of the Scioto. When built, many years ago, it was in the wilderness, the road having since been laid out by it. It is a rude structure, formed by successive layers of stone, under a shelving rock, which serves as a back and roof. Over it is a monument, bearing the following inscription:

> WILLIAM HEWIT,
>
> THE HERMIT,
>
> *occupied this cave* 14 *years, while all was wilderness around him.*
>
> *He died in* 1834, *aged* 70 *years.*

But little is known of the history of the hermit. He was, it is said, a Virginian, and married early in life into a family of respectability. Returning one night from a journey, he had occular proof of the infidelity of his wife, killed her paramour, and instantly fled tc the woods, never to return or associate with mankind.* He eventually settled in the Scioto valley and built this cave, where he passed a solitary life, his rifle furnishing him with provisions and clothing, which consisted of skins of animals. As the country gradually filled up, he became an object of curiosity to the settlers. He was mild and inoffensive in his address, avoided companionship with those around, and if any allusion was made to his history, evaded the subject. Occasionally he visited Chillicothe, to exchange the skins of his game for ammunition, when his singular appearance attracted observation. In person, he was large and muscular; the whole of his dress, from his cap to his moccasons, was of deerskin; his beard was long and unshaven, and his eye wild and piercing. In passing from place to place, he walked in the street to avoid encountering his fellow men. Many anecdotes are related of him.

He planted an orchard on government land, which afterwards became the property of a settler; but so sensitive was he in regard to the rights of others, that he would not pluck any of the fruit without first asking liberty of the legal owner. While sitting concealed in the recesses of the forest, he once observed a teamster deliberately cut down and carry off some fine venison he had placed to dry on a limb of a tree before his cave. Hewit followed, got before him, and as he came up, suddenly sprang from behind some bushes beside the road, and presenting his rifle to his bosom, with a fierce and determined manner bade him instantly return and replace the venison. The man tremblingly obeyed, receiving the admonition, "never again to rob the hermit." A physician riding by, stopped to gratify the curiosity of his companions. He found the hermit ill, administered medicine, visited him often gratuitously during his illness, and effected a cure. The hermit ever after evinced the warmest gratitude.

Bainbridge is on Paint creek and the Maysville and Chillicothe turnpike, 19 miles sw. from Chillicothe. It was laid out in 1805 by Nathaniel Massie, and will become the seat of justice for the projected county of Massie, in case it is established. It is surrounded by a beautiful country, and contains 2 churches, a forge, 1 newspaper printing office, 8 stores, and about 80 dwellings. About a mile NW. of the town is a small, natural tunnel, about 150 feet in length, through which courses a little sparkling rill. Frankfort, on the north fork of Paint creek, 11 miles NW. of Chillicothe, and Kingston, 10 NE. of Chillicothe, are also large and important villages. Bourneville, 11 miles sw. of Chillicothe, on the above named turnpike, South Salem, 16 sw., Richmond, 13 SE., and Aldelphi, 17 NE., have each from 30 to 60 dwellings. There are other small villages in Ross, but none of much note. In the county, in the valley of the Scioto and Paint creek, ancient works and mounds are very numerous.

* From Col. John M'Donald, to whose father this fact was communicated by Hewit.

SANDUSKY.

SANDUSKY was formed from old Indian territory, April 1st, 1820. The soil is fertile, and the surface is generally level. The Black Swamp covers the western part. Its first settlers were principally of New England origin, since which many have moved in from Pennsylvania and Germany. The principal productions are Indian corn, wheat, oats, potatoes and pork. The following is a list of its townships in 1840, with their population.

Ballville,	1007	Rice,	385	Townsend,	692
Green Creek,	1186	Riley,	426	Washington,	1074
Jackson,	929	Sandusky,	1696	Woodville,	486
Madison,	316	Scott,	684	York,	1301

The population of Sandusky, in 1830, was 2851, and in 1840, 10,182, or 24 inhabitants to a square mile.

The signification of the name of this county has frequently been a matter of dispute. John H. James, Esq., in the American Pioneer, truly says:

I have a note of a conversation with William Walker at Columbus, in 1835–6, at which time he was principal chief of the Wyandotts at Upper Sandusky, in which I asked the meaning of the word Sandusky. He said it meant "at the cold water," and should be sounded San-doos-tee. He said it "carried with it the force of a preposition." The Upper Cold Water and the Lower Cold Water, then, were descriptive Indian names, given long before the presence of the trader Sowdowsky. In the vocabulary of Wyandott words, given by John Johnston, Esq., formerly Indian agent in Ohio, as printed in Archæologia Americana, vol. i. p. 295, the word water is given *Sa, un-dus-tee*, and in page 297 he gives the name of Sandusky river as *Sa, undustee*, or *water within water pools*.

This region of country was once a favorite residence of the Indians. Hon. Lewis Cass, in his discourse before the Historical Society of Michigan, delivered Sept. 18th, 1829, gives some interesting statements respecting a tribe called "*the Neutral Nation.*"

Upon the Sandusky river, and near where the town of Lower Sandusky now stands, lived a band of the Wyandotts, called the Neutral Nation. They occupied two villages, which were cities of refuge, where those who sought safety never failed to find it. During the long and disastrous contests which preceded and followed the arrival of the Europeans, in which the Iroquois contended for victory, and their enemies for existence, this little band preserved the integrity of their territories and the sacred character of peace makers. All who met upon their threshold met as friends, for the ground on which they stood was holy. It was a beautiful institution, a calm and peaceful island looking out upon a world of waves and tempests.

The annexed is a note from the above.

This Neutral Nation, so called by Father Seguard, was still in existence two centuries ago, when the French missionaries first reached the upper lakes. The details of their history, and of their character and privileges, are meager and unsatisfactory; and this is the more to be regretted, as such a sanctuary among the barbarous tribes, is not only a singular institution, but altogether at variance with that reckless spirit of cruelty with which their wars are usually prosecuted. The Wyandott tradition represents them as having separated from the parent stock during the bloody wars between their own tribe and the Iroquois, and having fled to the Sandusky river for safety. That they here erected two forts, within a short distance of each other, and assigned one to the Iroquois and the other to the Wyandotts and their allies, where their war parties might find security and hospitality, whenever they entered their country. Why so unusual a proposition was made and acceded to, tradition does not tell. It is probable, however, that superstition lent its aid to the institution, and that it may have been indebted for its origin to the feasts and dreams and juggling ceremonies which constituted the religion of the aborigines. No other motive was sufficiently powerful to restrain the hand of violence and to counteract the threat of vengeance.

An intestine feud finally arose in this Neutral Nation, one party espousing the cause of the Iroquois and the other of their enemies; and like most civil wars, this was prosecuted with relentless fury. Our informant* says that since his recollection, the remains of a red cedar post were yet to be seen, where the prisoners were tied previously to being burned.

Lower Sandusky, the county seat, is 24 miles southwesterly from Sandusky City, and 105 west of north from Columbus. The annexed engraving shows the town as it appears from a hill northeast of it, on the opposite side of the river, near the residence of Mr. Jasper Smith, seen in front. On the left, the bridge across the Sandusky river partially appears; and a little to the right of it, Whyler's hotel. On the hill are shown the court house, and the Episcopal, Presbyterian and Catholic churches.

The town stands at the head of navigation on the Sandusky, at the lower rapids, where the Indians had a reservation of two miles square, granted to them by the treaty of Greenville. It is said that at an early day the French had a trading station at this point. Lower Sandusky contains 1 Episcopal, 1 Presbyterian, 1 Baptist, 1 Methodist and 1 Catholic church, 2 newspaper printing offices, 8 grocery and 11 dry goods stores, 1 woollen factory, 1 foundery, and had, in 1840, 1117 inhabitants, and now has near 2000. It is a thriving town, and considerable business is carried on. Its commerce is increasing. Small steamers and sail vessels constantly ply from here. The principal articles of export in 1846, were of wheat 90,000 bushels, pork 560 barrels, ashes 558 casks, flour 1010 barrels, corn 18,400 bushels, staves 1,100,000: imports, 1480 barrels of salt and 250 tons of merchandize.

Immediately opposite Lower Sandusky, on the east bank of the river, is the small village of Croghansville, laid out in 1817, which in a general description would be included in the former.

Fort Stephenson, or Sandusky, so gallantly defended by Colonel Croghan on the 2d of August, 1813, against an overwhelming force

---

* The informant above alluded to by Gov. Cass, we have reason to believe was Major B. F. Stickney, of Toledo, long an Indian agent in this region. That there may have been such a tradition among the Indians, we are unable to gainsay, but of its truth we have doubts. Major Stickney, in a lecture (as yet unpublished) delivered Feb. 28th, 1845, before the Young Men's Association of Toledo, says:

"The remains of extensive works of defence are now to be seen near Lower Sandusky. The Wyandotts have given me this account of them. At a period of two centuries and a half since, or more, all the Indians west of this point were at war with all the Indians east. Two walled towns were built near each other, and each was inhabited by those of Wyandott origin. They assumed a neutral character, and the Indians at war recognized that character. They might be called two neutral cities. All of the west might enter the western city, and all of the east the eastern. The inhabitants of one city might inform those of the other, that war parties were there or had been there; but who they were, or whence they came, or any thing more, must not be mentioned. The war parties might remain there in security, taking their own time for departure. At the western town they suffered the warriors to burn their prisoners near it; but the eastern would not. (An old Wyandott informed me, that he recollected seeing, when a boy, the remains of a cedar post or stake, at which they used to burn prisoners.) The French historians tell us that these neutral cities were inhabited, and their neutral character respected, when they first came here. At length a quarrel arose between the two cities, and one destroyed the inhabitants of the other. This put an end to all neutrality."

of British and Indians, was within the present limits of Lower Sandusky. Its site is indicated by the flag on the left in the engraving, which is about 30 rods southeast of the court house, on high ground,

Lower Sandusky.

much elevated above the river. The fort enclosed about an acre of ground, and the picketing was in good preservation as late as 1834. A private residence now stands within the area. We annex a narration of the assault on the fort, from a published source.

Having raised the siege of Camp Meigs, the British sailed round into Sandusky bay, while a competent number of their savage allies marched across through the swamps of Portage river, to co-operate in a combined attack on Lower Sandusky, expecting, no doubt, that General Harrison's attention would be chiefly directed to Forts Winchester and Meigs. The general, however, had calculated on their taking this course, and had been careful to keep patroles down the bay, opposite the mouth of Portage, where he supposed their forces would debark.

Several days before the British had invested Fort Meigs, General Harrison, with Major Croghan and some other officers, had examined the heights which surround Fort Stephenson; and as the hill on the opposite or southeast side of the river was found to be the most commanding eminence, the general had some thoughts of removing the fort to that place, and Major Croghan declared his readiness to undertake the work. But the general did not authorize him to do it, as he believed that if the enemy intended to invade our territory again, they would do it before the removal could be completed. It was then finally concluded that the fort, which was calculated for a garrison of only 200 men, could not be defended against the heavy artillery of the enemy; and that if the British should approach it by water, which would cause a presumption that they had brought their heavy artillery, the fort must be abandoned and burnt, provided a retreat could be effected with safety. In the orders left with Major Croghan, it was stated—"Should the British troops approach you in force with cannon, and you can discover them in time to effect a retreat, you will do so immediately, destroying all the public stores."

"You must be aware that the attempt to retreat in the face of an Indian force would be vain. Against such an enemy your garrison would be safe, however great the number."

On the evening of the 29th, General Harrison received intelligence, by express, from General Clay, that the enemy had abandoned the siege of Fort Meigs; and as the Indians on that day had swarmed in the woods round his camp, he entertained no doubt but that an immediate attack was intended either on Sandusky or Seneca. He therefore immediately called a council of war, consisting of M'Arthur, Cass, Ball, Paul, Wood, Hukill, Holmes and Graham, who were unanimously of the opinion that Fort Stephenson was untenable against heavy artillery, and that as the enemy could bring with facility any quantity of battering cannon against it, by which it must inevitably fall, and as it was an unimportant post, containing nothing the loss of which would be felt by us, that the garrison should therefore not be reinforced, but withdrawn, and the place destroyed. In pursuance of this decision, the general immediately dispatched the order to Major Croghan, directing him immediately to abandon Fort Stephenson, to set it on fire and repair with his

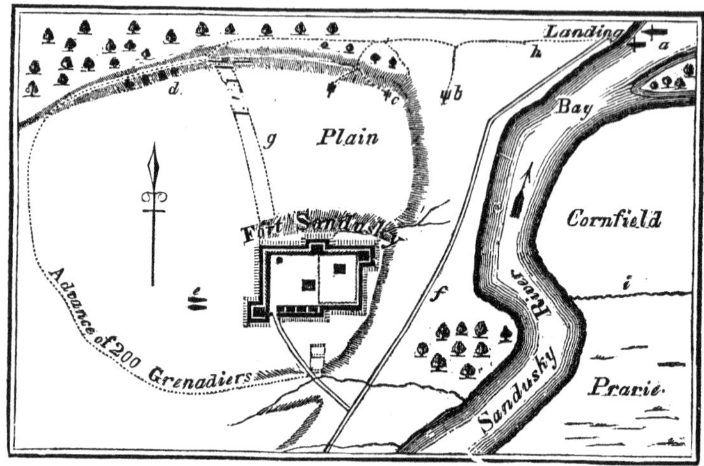

Fort Sandusky and Environs: scale, 200 *yards to the inch.*

[*References to the Environs.—a*—British gun-boats at their place of landing. *b*—Cannon, a six-pounder. *c*—Mortar. *d*—Batteries. *e*—Graves of Lieut. Col. Short and Lieut. Gordon, who fell in the ditch. *f*—Road to Upper Sandusky. *g*—Advance of the enemy to the fatal ditch. *i*—Head of navigation.

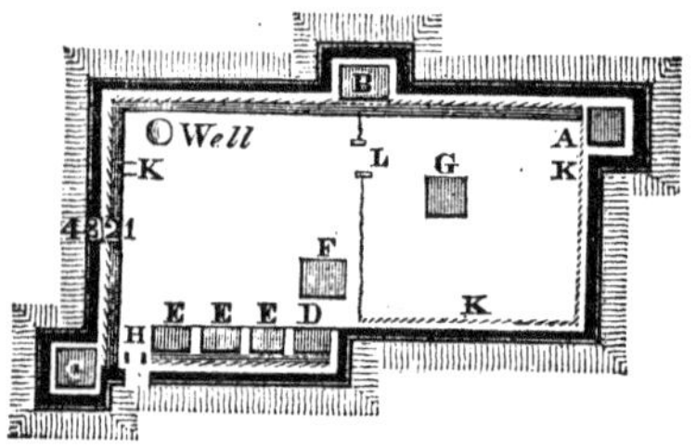

Fort Sandusky.

References to the Fort.—Line 1—Pickets. *Line* 2—Embankment from the ditch to and against the picket. *Line* 3—Dry ditch, nine feet wide by six deep. *Line* 4—Outward embankment or glacis. A—Block-house first attacked by cannon, *b*. B—Bastion from which the ditch was raked by Croghan's artillery. C—Guard block-house, in the lower left corner. D—Hospital during the attack. E E E—Military store-houses. F—Commissary's store-house. G—Magazine. H—Fort gate. K K K—Wicker gates. L—Partition gate.]

command to head quarters—cross the river and come up on the opposite side, and if he should find it impracticable to reach the general's quarters, to take the road to Huron, and pursue it with the utmost circumspection and dispatch. This order was sent by Mr. Conner and two Indians, who lost their way in the dark, and did not reach Fort Stephenson till 11 o'clock the next day. When Major Croghan received it, he was of opinion that he could not then retreat with safety, as the Indians were hovering round the fort in considerable force. He called a council of his officers, a majority of whom coincided with him in opinion that a retreat would be unsafe, and that the post could be maintained against the enemy, at least till further instructions could be received from head quarters. The major therefore immediately returned the following answer: "Sir, I have just received yours of yesterday, 10 o'clock, P. M., ordering me to destroy this place and make good my retreat, which was received too late to be carried into execution. We have determined to maintain this place, and by heavens we can." In writing this note, Major Croghan had a view to the probability of its falling into the hands of the enemy, and on that account made use of stronger language than would otherwise have been consistent with propriety. It reached the general on the same day, who did not fully understand the circumstances and motives under which it had been dictated. The following order was therefore immediately pre-

PORTSMOUTH, FROM THE KENTUCKY SHORE.

MARIETTA, FROM THE VIRGINIA SHORE.

pared, and sent with Colonel Wells in the morning, escorted by Colonel Ball, with his corps of dragoons.

"*July* 30, 1813.

"SIR—The general has just received your letter of this date, informing him that you had thought proper to disobey the order issued from this office, and delivered to you this morning. It appears that the information which dictated the order was incorrect; and as you did not receive it in the night, as was expected, it might have been proper that you should have reported the circumstance and your situation, before you proceeded to its execution. This might have been passed over; but I am directed to say to you, that an officer who presumes to aver that he has made his resolution, and that he will act in direct opposition to the orders of his general, can no longer be entrusted with a separate command. Colonel Wells is sent to relieve you. You will deliver the command to him, and repair with Colonel Ball's squadron to this place. By command, &c.

A. H. HOLMES, *Assistant Adjutant General.*"

Colonel Wells being left in the command of Fort Stephenson, Major Croghan returned with the squadron to head-quarters. He there explained his motives for writing such a note, which were deemed satisfactory; and having remained all night with the general, who treated him politely, he was permitted to return to his command in the morning, with written orders similar to those he had received before.

A reconnoitering party which had been sent from head-quarters to the shore of the lake, about 20 miles distant from Fort Stephenson, discovered the approach of the enemy, by water, on the evening of the 31st of July. They returned by the fort after 12 o'clock the next day, and had passed it but a few hours, when the enemy made their appearance before it. The Indians showed themselves first on the hill over the river, and were saluted by a six-pounder, the only piece of artillery in the fort, which soon caused them to retire. In half an hour the British gun-boats came in sight, and the Indian forces displayed themselves in every direction, with a view to intercept the garrison, should a retreat be attempted. The six-pounder was fired a few times at the gun-boats, which was returned by the artillery of the enemy. A landing of their troops with a five and a half inch howitzer was effected about a mile below the fort; and Major Chambers, accompanied by Dickson, was dispatched towards the fort with a flag, and was met on the part of Major Croghan by Ensign Shipp, of the 17th regiment. After the usual ceremonies, Major Chambers observed to Ensign Shipp, that he was instructed by General Proctor to demand the surrender of the fort, as he was anxious to spare the effusion of human blood, which he could not do, should he be under the necessity of reducing it, by the powerful force of artillery, regulars and Indians under his command. Shipp replied, that the commandant of the fort and its garrison were determined to defend it to the last extremity; that no force however great could induce them to surrender, as they were resolved to maintain their post, or to bury themselves in its ruins. Dickson then said that their immense body of Indians could not be restrained from murdering the whole garrison in case of success, of which we have no doubt, rejoined Chambers, as we are amply prepared. Dickson then proceeded to remark, that it was a great pity so fine a young man should fall into the hands of the savages—Sir, for God's sake, surrender, and prevent the dreadful massacre that will be caused by your resistance. Mr. Shipp replied, that when the fort was taken, there would be none to massacre. It will not be given up while a man is able to resist. An Indian at this moment came out of an adjoining ravine, and advancing to the ensign, took hold of his sword and attempted to wrest it from him. Dickson interfered, and having restrained the Indian, affected great anxiety to get him safe into the fort.

The enemy now opened their fire from their six-pounders in the gun-boats and the howitzer on shore, which they continued through the night with but little intermission and with very little effect. The forces of the enemy consisted of 500 regulars, and about 800 Indians commanded by Dickson, the whole being commanded by General Proctor in person. Tecumseh was stationed on the road to Fort Meigs with a body of 2000 Indians, expecting to intercept a reinforcement on that route.

Major Croghan through the evening occasionally fired his six-pounder, at the same time changing its place occasionally to induce a belief that he had more than one piece. As it produced very little execution on the enemy, and he was desirous of saving his ammunition, he soon discontinued his fire. The enemy had directed their fire against the northwestern angle of the fort, which induced the commander to believe that an attempt to storm his works would be made at that point. In the night, Captain Hunter was directed to remove the six-pounder to a block-house, from which it would rake that angle. By great industry and personal exertion, Captain Hunter soon accomplished this object in secrecy. The embrasure was masked, and the piece loaded with a half charge of powder, and double charge of slugs and grape-shot. Early in the morning of the 2d, the enemy opened their fire from their howitzer and three six-pounders, which they had landed in the night, and planted in a point of woods, about 250 yards from the fort. In the evening, about 4 o'clock, they concentrated the fire of all their guns on their northwest angle, which convinced Major Croghan that they would endeavor to make a breach and storm the works at that point; he therefore immediately had that place strengthened as much as possible with bags of flour and sand, which were so effectual that the picketing in that place sustained no material injury. Sergeant Weaver, with five or six gentlemen of the Petersburgh volunteers and Pittsburgh blues, who happened to be in the fort, was intrusted with the management of the six-pounder.

Late in the evening, when the smoke of the firing had completely enveloped the fort, the enemy proceeded to make the assault. Two feints were made towards the southern angle, where Captain Hunter's lines were formed; and at the same time a column of 350 men was discovered advancing through the smoke, within 20 paces of the northwestern angle. A heavy galling fire of musketry was now opened upon them from the fort, which threw them into some confusion. Colonel Short, who headed the principal column, soon rallied his men, and led them with great bravery to the brink of the ditch. After a momentary pause he leaped into the ditch, calling to his men to follow him, and in a few minutes it was full. The masked port-hole was now opened, and the six-pounder, at the distance of 30 feet, poured such destruction among them that but few who had entered the ditch were fortunate enough to escape. A precipitate and confused retreat was the immediate consequence, although some of the officers attempted to rally their men. The other column, which was led by Colonel Warburton and Major Chambers, was also routed in confusion by a destructive fire from the line commanded by Captain Hunter. The whole of them fled into the adjoining wood, beyond the reach of our fire-arms. During the assault, which lasted half an hour, the enemy kept up an incessant fire from their howitzer and five six-pounders. They left Colonel Short,* a lieutenant and twenty-five privates dead in the ditch; and the total number of prisoners taken was twenty-six, most of them badly wounded. Major Muir was knocked down in the ditch, and lay among the dead, till the darkness of the night enabled him to escape in safety. The loss of the garrison was one killed and seven slightly wounded. The total loss of the enemy could not be less than 150 killed and wounded.

When night came on, which was soon after the assault, the wounded in the ditch were in a desperate situation. Complete relief could not be brought to them by either side with any degree of safety. Major Croghan, however, relieved them as much as possible—he contrived to convey them water over the picketing in buckets, and a ditch was opened under the pickets, through which those who were able and willing, were encouraged to crawl into the fort. All who were able, preferred, of course, to follow their defeated comrades, and many others were carried from the vicinity of the fort by the Indians, particularly their own killed and wounded; and in the night, about 3 o'clock, the whole British and Indian force commenced a disorderly retreat. So great was their precipitation that they left a sail-boat containing some clothing and a considerable quantity of military stores: and on the next day, seventy stand of arms and some braces of pistols were picked up around the fort. Their hurry and confusion were caused by the apprehension of an attack from General Harrison, of whose position and force they had probably received an exaggerated account.

It was the intention of General Harrison, should the enemy succeed against Fort Stephenson, or should they endeavor to turn his left and fall on Upper Sandusky, to leave his camp at Seneca and fall back for the protection of that place. But he discovered by the firing on the evening of the 1st, that the enemy had nothing but light artillery, which could make no impression on the fort; and he knew that an attempt to storm it without making a breach, could be successfully repelled by the garrison; he therefore determined to wait for the arrival of 250 mounted volunteers under Colonel Rennick, being the advance of 700 who were approaching by the way of Upper Sandusky, and then to march against the enemy and raise the siege, if their force was not still too great for his. On the 2d, he sent several scouts to ascertain their situation and force; but the woods were so infested with Indians, that none of them could proceed sufficiently near the fort to make the necessary

* "Col. Short, who commanded the regulars composing the forlorn hope, was ordering his men to leap the ditch, cut down the pickets, and give the Americans no quarters, when he fell mortally wounded into the ditch, hoisted his white handkerchief on the end of his sword, and begged for that mercy which he had a moment before ordered to be denied to his enemy."

discoveries. In the night the messenger arrived at head-quarters with intelligence that the enemy were preparing to retreat. About 9 o'clock, Major Croghan had ascertained from their collecting about their boats, that they were preparing to embark, and had immediately sent an express to the commander-in-chief with this information. The general now determined to wait no longer for the reinforcements, and immediately set out with the dragoons, with which he reached the fort early in the morning, having ordered Generals M'Arthur and Cass, who had arrived at Seneca several days before, to follow him with all the disposable infantry at that place, and which at this time was about 700 men, after the numerous sick, and the force necessary to maintain the position, were left behind. Finding that the enemy had fled entirely from the fort, so as not to be reached by him, and learning that Tecumseh was somewhere in the direction of Fort Meigs, with 2000 warriors, he immediately ordered the infantry to fall back to Seneca, lest Tecumseh should make an attack on that place, or intercept the small reinforcements advancing from Ohio.

In his official report of this affair, General Harrison observes that—"It will not be among the least of General Proctor's mortifications, that he has been baffled by a youth, who has just passed his twenty-first year. He is, however, a hero worthy of his gallant uncle, Gen. George R. Clarke."

Captain Hunter, of the 17th regiment, the second in command, conducted himself with great propriety: and never was there a set of finer young fellows than the subalterns, viz.: Lieutenants Johnson and Baylor of the 17th, Meeks of the 7th, and Ensigns Shipp and Duncan of the 17th.

Lieutenant Anderson of the 24th, was also noticed for his good conduct. Being without a command, he solicited Major Croghan for a musket and a post to fight at, which he did with the greatest bravery.

"Too much praise," says Major Croghan, "cannot be bestowed on the officers, non-commissioned officers and privates under my command, for their gallantry and good conduct during the siege."

The brevet rank of lieutenant colonel was immediately conferred on Major Croghan, by the president of the United States, for his gallant conduct on this occasion. The ladies of Chillicothe also presented him an elegant sword, accompanied by a suitable address.

We take the above from Dawson's Life of Harrison, where it is quoted from some other source. In defending Gen. Harrison from the charges of cowardice and incompetency in not marching to the aid of the garrison previous to the attack, Dawson says:

The conduct of the gallant Croghan and his garrison received from every quarter the plaudits of their countrymen. This was what they most richly deserved. There was, however, some jealous spirits who took it into their heads to be dissatisfied with the course pursued by the commanding general. The order which was given to Colonel Croghan to evacuate and destroy the garrison previously to the attack, was loudly condemned, as well as the decision of the council of war, to fall back with the troops then at Seneca, to a position twelve miles in the rear. Both these measures, it has been said, were determined on by the unanimous advice of the council of war. It is not to be presumed that such men as composed that board, would have given advice which was in any way derogatory to the honor of the American arms. Every individual among them either had, before or afterwards, distinguished himself by acts of daring courage and intrepidity. We do not profess to be much acquainted with military matters, but the subject appears to us so plain as only to require a small portion of common sense perfectly to comprehend it. At the time that the determination was made to withdraw the garrison from Sandusky, it must be recollected that the general had only with him at Seneca about 400 infantry and 130 or 140 dragoons. The enemy, as he was informed by General Clay in the letter brought by Captain M'Cune, amounted to at least 5,000. With such a disparity of force, would it have been proper to have risked an action to preserve the post of Lower Sandusky, which of itself was of little or no importance, and which, the garrison being withdrawn, contained nothing of any value? The posts of Fort Meigs and Upper Sandusky were of the utmost importance; the former was amply provided with the means of defence, and was in no danger; but the latter, weak in its defences, and with a feeble garrison, containing many thousands of barrels of flour and other provisions, the sole resource of the army for the ensuing campaign, was to be preserved at any risk. The position at Seneca was not in the direct line from Fort Meigs to Upper Sandusky. The enemy, by taking the direct route, would certainly reach it before General Harrison, as several hours must have elapsed before he could have been informed of their movement, even if it had been discovered the moment it had been commenced, a circumstance not very likely to happen. It therefore became necessary for the security of Upper Sandusky, that a position better adapted to that purpose should be assumed. There was another and most important reason for this movement: twelve miles in the rear of Seneca, towards Upper Sandusky, the prairie or open country commences. The infantry which the commander-in-chief had with him were raw recruits; on the contrary, the squadron of dragoons were well disciplined, and had seen much service. In the country about Seneca, this important corps could have been of little service: in the open country to the rear, they would have defeated five times their number of Indians. It was for these reasons that it was determined by the council of war, to change the position of the troops at Seneca. If this movement did take place, the propriety of withdrawing the garrison of Lower Sandusky was obvious. The place was extremely weak, and in a bad position. It was not intended originally for a fort. Before the war it was used as the United States' Indian factory, and had a small stockade around it, merely for the purpose of keeping out drunken Indians. It was, moreover, commanded by a hill, within point blank shot, on the opposite side of the river. To those who suppose that General Harrison should have advanced upon the enemy, the moment he discovered that Sandusky was attacked, we must, in the language of the general and field officers who were present on the occasion, "leave them to correct their opinions in the school of experience." General Harrison had been reinforced a day or two before the siege of Sandusky, by the 28th regiment, raised in Kentucky. After having received this corps, he could not have marched more than 800 effective men without risking his stores, and, what was of still more consequence, 150 sick at Seneca, to be taken by the smallest party of Indians. The scouts of the army brought information that the Indians were very numerous in the direction of Fort Meigs. The general conjectured that a large portion of the Indians were then ready to fall on his flank or rear, or the defenceless camp at Seneca, should he advance. The information he received from the British prisoners confirmed this opinion; a body of 2000 being there under the command of Tecumseh. At the moment of which we are speaking, the volunteers of Ohio were rapidly approaching. Now, under these circumstances, does any reasonable man believe that General Harrison should have advanced with his 800 raw recruits, against a force in front which he knew to be so much superior in numbers, and with the probability of having one equally large hanging on his flank? What would have been thought of his abilities as a general, even if he had been successful against General Proctor, (of which, with his small force, there was little probability,) if in his absence Tecumseh, with his 2000 warriors, had rushed upon Camp Seneca, destroyed his stores, tomahawked his sick soldiers, and pursuing his route towards Upper Sandusky, defeated the Ohio volunteers, scattered as they were in small bodies, and finally ending his career with the destruction of the grand magazine of his army, upon the preservation of which all his hopes of future success depended? In all human probability this would have been the result, had General Harrison advanced to the relief of Fort Stephenson sooner than he did. It was certainly better to risk for a while the defence of that fort to the talents and valor of Croghan, and the gallant spirits who were with him, than to jeopardize the whole prospects of the campaign.

About 1½ miles above Lower Sandusky, at the falls of the river, is the manufacturing village of Ballsville, containing 1 cotton and 1 woollen factory, 2 flouring mills, and about 30 dwellings. It was about half a mile southwest of this village, that Col. Ball had a skirmish with the Indians, a day or two previous to the assault of Fort Stephenson. There is, or was a few years since, an oak tree on the site of the action, on the road to Columbus, with 17 hacks in it to indicate the number of Indians killed on the occasion. We have an account of this affair, derived from one of the dragoons present.

The squadron were moving towards the fort when they were suddenly fired upon by the Indians from the west side of the road, whereupon Colonel Ball ordered a charge, and he and suite and the right flank being in advance, first came into action. The colonel struck the first blow. He dashed in between two savages and cut down the one on the right; the other being slightly in the rear, made a blow with a tomahawk at his back, when, by a sudden spring of his horse, it fell short, and was buried deep in the cantel and pad of his saddle. Before the savage could repeat the blow, he was shot by Corporal Ryan. Lieut. Hedges (now General Hedges of Mansfield) following in the rear, mounted on a small horse, pursued a large Indian, and just as he had come up to him his stirrup broke, and he fell head first off the horse, knocking the Indian down. Both sprang to their feet, when

Hedges struck the Indian across his head, and as he was falling, buried his sword up to its hilt in his body. At this time, Captain Hopkins was seen on the left in pursuit of a powerful savage, when the latter turned and made a blow at the captain with a tomahawk, at which his horse sprang to one side. Cornet Hayes then came up and the Indian struck at him, his horse in like manner evading the blow. Serjeant Anderson now arriving, the Indian was soon dispatched. By this time the skirmish was over, the Indians, who were only about 20 in number, being nearly all cut down; and orders were given to retreat to the main squadron. Colonel Ball dressed his men ready for a charge, should the Indians appear in force, and moved down without further molestation to the fort, where they arrived at about 4 P. M.

Woodville is in the Black swamp, on the Portage river and the Western Reserve and Maumee turnpike, 15 w. of Lower Sandusky. It was laid out in 1838, by Hon. A. E. Wood, and contains 1 Lutheran, 1 Methodist church, 2 stores, 2 tanneries, and 30 dwellings. Hamer's Corners, 8 miles E. of the county seat, has 12 dwellings.

SCIOTO.

Scioto was formed May 1st, 1803. The name Scioto was originally applied by the Wyandots to the river; they however called it *Sci, on, to:* its signification is unknown.* The surface is generally hilly, and some of the hills are several hundred feet in height. The river bottoms are well adapted to corn, and on a great part of the hill land small grain and grass can be produced. Iron ore, coal, and excellent freestone are the principal mineral productions of value. The manufacture of iron is extensively carried on in the eastern part of the county, where there are six furnaces in operation, viz.: the Ohio, Junior, Franklin, Clinton, Scioto and Bloom. The principal agricultural products are corn, wheat and oats. The following is a list of the townships in 1840, with their population:

Bloom,	913	Jefferson,	578	Union,	570
Brush Creek,	401	Madison,	830	Vernon,	902
Clay,	696	Morgan,	265	Washington,	653
Green,	973	Nile,	860	Wayne,	1853
Harrison,	686	Porter,	1014		

The population of Scioto in 1820, was 5,750; in 1830, 8,730, and in 1840, 11,194, or 19 inhabitants to a square mile.

The mouth of the Scioto was a favorite point with the Indians from which to attack boats ascending or descending the Ohio. We have several incidents to relate, the first from Marshall's Kentucky, and the last two from M'Donald's Sketches.

A canoe ascending the Ohio about the last of March, 1790, was taken by the Indians near the mouth of Scioto, and three men killed. Within a few days after, a boat coming down was decoyed to shore by a white man who feigned distress, when fifty savages rose from concealment, ran into the boat, killed John May and a young woman, being the first persons they came to, and took the rest of the people on board prisoners. It is probable that they owed, according to their ideas of duty, or of honor, these sacrifices to the manes of so many of their slaughtered friends.

While the caprices of fortune, the progression of fate, or the mistaken credulity of Mr.

* Col. John Johnston.

May, and his imitator, is to be seen in the essay to ensure their safety, by advancing to meet these savages, with out-stretched hands as the expression of confidence and the pledge of friendship. Mr. May had been an early adventurer and constant visitor to Kentucky. He was no warrior; his object was the acquisition of land—which he had pursued, with equal avidity and success, to a very great extent. Insomuch, that had he lived to secure the titles, many of which have been doubtless lost by his death, he would probably have been the greatest land holder in the country.

Soon after this event, for the Indians still continued to infest the river, other boats were taken, and the people killed or carried away captive.

The 2d of April they attacked three boats on the Ohio, near the confluence of the Scioto; two being abandoned fell into the hands of the enemy, who plundered them: the other being manned with all the people, made its escape by hard rowing.

Such a series of aggression at length roused the people of the interior; and General Scott, with two hundred and thirty volunteers, crossed the Ohio at Limestone, and was joined by General Harmar with one hundred regulars of the United States—these march for the Scioto; the Indians had, however, abandoned their camp, and there was no general action. On the route a small Indian trail was crossed; thirteen men, with a subaltern, were detached upon it—they came upon four Indians in camp, the whole of whom were killed by the first fire.

This spring, 1792, four spies were employed to range from Limestone (now Maysville) to the mouth of Big Sandy river. These four were Samuel Davis, Duncan M'Arthur, (late governor of Ohio,) Nathaniel Beasley, (late canal commissioner, and major general of the militia,) and Samuel M'Dowel. These men, upon every occasion, proved themselves worthy of the confidence placed in them by their countrymen. Nothing which could reasonably be expected of men, but was done by them. Two and two went together. They made their tours once a week to the mouth of Big Sandy river. On Monday morning, two of them would leave Limestone, and reach Sandy by Wednesday evening. On Thursday morning, the other two would leave Limestone for the mouth of Sandy. Thus they would meet or pass each other about opposite the mouth of Scioto river; and by this constant vigilance, the two sets of spies would pass the mouth of Scioto, in going and returning, four times in each week. This incessant vigilance would be continued till late in November, or the first of December, when hostilities generally ceased, in the later years of the Indian wars. Sometimes the spies would go up and down the Ohio in canoes. In such cases one of them would push the canoe, and the other would go on foot, through the woods, keeping about a mile in advance of the canoe, the footman keeping a sharp look out for ambuscade, or other Indian sign. Upon one of those tours, when Davis and M'Arthur were together, going up the river with their canoe, they lay at night a short distance below the mouth of Scioto. Early the next morning they crossed the Ohio in their canoe—landed and went across the bottom to the foot of the hill, where they knew of a fine deer-lick. This lick is situated about two miles below Portsmouth, and near Judge John Collins' house. The morning was very calm, and a light fog hung over the bottom. When Davis and M'Arthur had proceeded near the lick, M'Arthur halted, and Davis proceeded, stooping low among the thick brush and weeds, to conceal himself. He moved on with the noiseless tread of the cat, till he got near the lick, when he straightened up to look if any deer were in it. At that instant he heard the sharp crack from an Indian's rifle, and the singing whistle of a bullet pass his ear. As the morning was calm and foggy, the smoke from the Indian's rifle settled around his head, so that the Indian could not see whether his shot had taken effect or not. Davis immediately raised his rifle to his face, and as the Indian stepped out of the smoke to see the effect of his shot, Davis, before the Indian had time to dodge out of the way, fired, and dropped him in his tracks. Davis immediately fell to loading his rifle, not thinking it safe or prudent to run up to an Indian with an empty gun. About the time Davis had his gun loaded, M'Arthur came running to him. Knowing that the shots he had heard were in too quick succession to be fired by the same gun, he made his best speed to the aid of his companion. Just as M'Arthur had stopped at the place where Davis stood, they heard a heavy rush going through the brush, when in an instant several Indians made their appearance in the open ground around the lick. Davis and M'Arthur were standing in thick brush, and high weeds; and being unperceived by the Indians, crept off as silently as they could, and put off at their best speed for their canoe—crossed the Ohio and were out of danger. All the time that Davis was loading his gun, the Indian he had shot did not move hand or foot, consequently he ever after believed he killed the Indian.

During the summer of 1794, as the packet-boat was on her way up, near the mouth of the Scioto, a party of Indians fired into the boat as it was passing near the shore, and one man, John Stout, was killed, and two brothers by the name of Colvin were severely wounded. The boat was hurried by the remainder of the crew into the middle of the stream, and then returned to Maysville. The four "spies" were at Maysville, drawing their pay and ammunition, when the packet-boat returned. Notwithstanding the recent and bloody defeat sustained in the packet-boat, a fresh crew was immediately procured, and the four spies were directed by Col. Henry Lee, (who had the superintendence and direction of them,) to guard the boat as far as the mouth of Big Sandy river. As the spies were on their way up the river with the packet-boat, they found concealed and sunk in the mouth of a small creek, a short distance below the mouth of the Scioto, a bark canoe, large enough to carry seven or eight men. In this canoe a party of Indians had crossed the Ohio, and were prowling about somewhere in the country. Samuel M'Dowel was sent back to give notice to the inhabitants, while the other three spies remained with the packet-boat till they saw it safe past the mouth of Big Sandy river.

At this place the spies parted from the boat, and commenced their return for Maysville. On their way up they had taken a light canoe. Two of them pushed the canoe, while the others advanced on foot to reconnoiter. On their return the spies floated down the Ohio in their canoe, till they came nearly opposite the mouth of the Scioto river, where they landed, and Duncan McArthur, [afterwards Governor of Ohio,] went out into the hills in pursuit of game. Treacle and Beasley went about a mile lower down the river and landed their canoe, intending also to hunt till McArthur should come up with them. McArthur went to a deer lick, with the situation of which he was well acquainted, made a blind, behind which he concealed himself, and waited for game. He lay about an hour, when he discovered two Indians coming to the lick. The Indians were so near him before he saw them that it was impossible for him to retreat without being discovered. As the boldest course appeared to him to be the safest, he determined to permit them to come as near to him as they would, shoot one of them, and try his strength with the other. Imagine his situation. Two Indians armed with rifles, tomahawks and scalping-knives, approaching in these circumstances, must have caused his heart to beat pit-a-pat. He permitted the Indians, who were walking towards him in a stooping posture, to approach undisturbed. When they came near the lick, they halted in an open piece of ground, and straightened up to look into the lick for game. This halt enabled McArthur to take deliberate aim from a rest, at only fourteen steps distance; he fired, and an Indian fell. McArthur remained still a moment, thinking it possible that the other Indian would take to flight. In this he was mistaken; the Indian did not even dodge out of his track when his companion sunk lifeless by his side.

As the Indian's gun was charged, McArthur concluded it would be rather a fearful job to rush upon him, he therefore determined upon a retreat. He broke from his place of concealment and ran with all his speed; he had run but a few steps when he found himself tangled in the top of a fallen tree: this caused a momentary halt. At that instant the Indian fired, and the ball whistled sharply by him. As the Indian's gun, as well as his own, was now empty, he thought of turning round and giving him a fight upon equal terms. At this instant several other Indians came in sight, rushing with savage screams through the brush. He fled with his utmost speed, the Indians pursuing and firing at him as he ran; one of their balls entered the bottom of his powder-horn and shivered the side of it next his body into pieces. The splinters of his shattered powder-horn were propelled with such force by the ball that his side was considerably injured and the blood flowed freely. The ball in passing through the horn had given him such a jar that he thought for some time it had passed through his side; but this did not slacken his pace. The Indians pursued him some distance. McArthur, though not very fleet, was capable of enduring great fatigue, and he now had an occasion which demanded the best exertion of his strength. He gained upon his pursuers, and by the time he had crossed two or three ridges he found himself free from pursuit, and turned his course to the river.

When he came to the bank of the Ohio, he discovered Beasley and Treacle in the canoe, paddling up the stream, in order to keep her hovering over the same spot, and to be more conspicuous should McArthur make his escape from the Indians. They had heard the firing, and the yelling in pursuit, and had no doubt about the cause, and had concluded it possible, from the length of time and the direction of the noise that McArthur might have effected his escape. Nathaniel Beasley and Thomas Treacle were not the kind of men to fly at the approach of danger and forsake a comrade. McArthur saw the canoe, and made a signal to them to come ashore. They did so, and McArthur was soon in the canoe, in the middle of the stream and out of danger. Thus ended this day's adventures of the spies and their packet-boat, and this was the last attack made by the Indians upon a boat in the Ohio river.

It is said that $1\frac{1}{2}$ miles below the old mouth of the Scioto, stood, about the year 1740, a French fort or trading station. Prior to the settlement at Marietta, an attempt at settlement was made at Portsmouth, the history of which is annexed from an article in the American Pioneer, by George Corwin, of Portsmouth.

In April, 1785, four families from the Redstone settlement in Pennsylvania, descended he Ohio to the mouth of the Scioto, and there moored their boat under the high bank where Portsmouth now stands. They commenced clearing the ground to plant seeds for a crop to support their families, hoping that the red men of the forest would suffer them to remain and improve the soil. They seemed to hope that white men would no longer provoke the Indians to savage warfare.

Soon after they landed, the four men, heads of the families, started up the Scioto to see the paradise of the West, of which they had heard from the mouths of white men who had traversed it during their captivity among the natives. Leaving the little colony, now consisting of four women and their children, to the protection of an over-ruling Providence, they traversed beautiful bottoms of the Scioto as far up as the prairies above, and opposite to where Piketon now stands. One of them, Peter Patrick by name, pleased with the country, cut the initials of his name on a beech, near the river, which being found in after times, gave the name of Pee Pee to the creek that flows through the prairie of the same name; and from that creek was derived the name of Pee Pee township in Pike county.

Encamping near the site of Piketon, they were surprised by a party of Indians, who killed two of them as they lay by their fires. The other two escaped over the hills to the Ohio river, which they struck at the mouth of the Little Scioto, just as some white men going down the river in a pirogue were passing. They were going to Port Vincennes, on the Wabash. The tale of woe which was told by these men, with entreaties to be taken on board, was at first insufficient for their relief. It was not uncommon for Indians to compel white prisoners to act in a similar manner to entice boats to the shore, for murderous and marauding purposes. After keeping them some time running down the shore, until they believed that if there were an ambuscade of Indians on shore they were out of its reach, they took them on board and brought them to the little settlement, the lamentations at which cannot be described, nor its feeling conceived, when their peace was broken and their hopes blasted by the intelligence of the disaster reaching them. My informant was one who came down in the pirogue.

There was, however, no time to be lost; their safety depended on instant flight—and gathering up all their movables, put off to Limestone, now Maysville, as a place of greater safety, where the men in the pirogue left them, and as my informant said, never heard of them more.

Thos. M'Donald built the first cabin in the county, but we are ignorant of its site or the date of its erection.* Early in the settlement of the country the village of Alexandria was founded at the mouth of the Scioto, on the west bank, opposite Portsmouth, which, at the formation of the county, was made "the temporary seat of justice and courts ordered to be held at the house of John Collins." Being situated upon low ground liable to inundations, the population of this place, once considerable, has now become so small that it does not exist as a town, though map-makers do not appear to have as yet learned the fact, and will not, perhaps, for years to come.

The "French Grant," a tract of 24,000 acres, is situated in the southeastern part of this county. "It was granted by Congress in March, 1795, to a number of French families who lost their lands at Gallipolis, by invalid titles. It extended from a point on the Ohio river $1\frac{1}{2}$ miles above, but opposite the mouth of Little Sandy creek in Kentucky, and extending eight miles in a direct line down the river, and from the two extremities of that line, reaching back at

* Col. John M'Donald, his brother, is our authority for this assertion.

right angles sufficiently far to include the quantity of land required, which somewhat exceeded four and a half miles." Twelve hundred acres additional were, in 1798, granted, adjoining it towards its lower end. Of this tract 4000 acres directly opposite Little Sandy creek were granted to Mons. J. G. Gervais, who laid out a town upon it which he called Burrsburg, which never had but a few inhabitants. Thirty years since there were but 8 or 10 French families residing on the French Grant, and we doubt if any are now left there.

Portsmouth, the county seat, is situated on the Ohio river just above the mouth of the Scioto, at the termination of the Ohio canal, 90 miles s. of Columbus, and 110 above Cincinnati by the river. It is a town of considerable business, and does a heavy trade with the iron works; three steamboats are continually plying between here and the iron region in the upper part of this and in Lawrence county, and two run regularly between here and Cincinnati. In the town is a well conducted free school, which has 9 teachers and 320 pupils. It is supported mainly by property bequeathed for this purpose, yielding about $2000 per annum. Portsmouth contains 1 Presbyterian, 1 Episcopal, 1 Methodist and 1 Catholic church, 2 printing offices, 1 rolling, 1 merchant and 1 oil mill, 1 carding machine, 1 forge, 2 founderies, 17 mercantile stores, and a population estimated at 2500. A company of eastern capitalists are constructing in the old channel of the Scioto, opposite Portsmouth, a commodious basin with dry docks attached for the building and repairing of steamboats.

In the vicinity of Portsmouth, on both sides of the Ohio, are some very extensive ancient works which have excited much curiosity.

Wheelersburg, 9 miles above Portsmouth, on the river, is a flourishing town with from 50 to 70 dwellings. Rockville, Lucasville, and Sciotoville, are small places.

SENECA.

Seneca was formed from old Indian territory, April 1st, 1820, organized, April 1st, 1824, and named from the tribe who had a reservation within its limits. The surface is level, and the streams run in deep channels. The county is well watered, has considerable water power, and the soil is mostly a rich loam. It was settled principally from Ohio, Pennsylvania, Maryland and New York, and by some few Germans. The principal farm products are wheat, corn, grass, oats, potatoes and pork. The following is a list of its townships in 1840, with their population.

Adams,	1250	Hopewell,	913	Reed,	1214
Big Spring,	926	Jackson,	596	Scipio,	1556
Bloom,	1168	Liberty,	1084	Seneca,	1393
Clinton,	2197	London,	763	Thompson,	1411
Eden,	1472	Pleasant,	974	Venice,	1222

The population of Seneca in 1830, was 5157, and in 1840, 18,139, or 35 inhabitants to the square mile.

Fort Seneca, a military post built in the late war, was 9 miles N. of the site of Tiffin. It was a stockade with a ditch, and occupied several acres on a plain, on the bank of the Sandusky. Some vestiges of the work yet remain. It was only a few miles above Fort Stephenson, and was occupied by Harrison's troops at the time of the attack on the latter. While here, and just prior to Perry's victory, Gen. Harrison narrowly escaped being murdered by an Indian, the particulars of which we derive from his memoirs.

The friendly Indians of the Delaware, Shawanese and Seneca tribes had been invited to join him. A number had accepted the invitation, and had reached Seneca before the arrival of the Kentucky troops. All the chiefs, and no doubt the greater part of the warriors were favorable to the American cause; but before their departure from their towns, a wretch had insinuated himself among them, with the intention of assassinating the commanding general. He belonged to the Shawanoese tribe, and bore the name of Blue Jacket; but was not the celebrated Blue Jacket, who signed the treaty of Greenville with Gen. Wayne. He had formerly resided at the town of Wapakoneta; he had, however, been absent for a considerable time, and had returned but a few days before the warriors of that town set out to join the American army. He informed the chiefs that he had been hunting on the Wabash, and at his request, he was suffered to join the party which were about to march to Seneca. Upon their arrival at M'Arthur's block-house, they halted and encamped for the purpose of receiving provisions from the deputy Indian agent, Col. M'Pherson, who resided there. Before their arrival at that place, Blue Jacket had communicated to a friend of his, (a Shawanese warrior,) his intention to kill the American general, and requested his assistance; this his friend declined, and endeavored to dissuade him from attempting it, assuring him that it could not be done without the certain sacrifice of his own life, as he had been at the American camp, and knew that there was always a guard round the general's quarters, who were on duty day and night. Blue Jacket replied, that he was determined to execute his intention at any risk, "that he would kill the general if he was sure that his guards would cut him in pieces not bigger than his thumb nail."

No people on earth are more faithful in keeping secrets than the Indians, but each warrior has a friend from whom he will conceal nothing; luckily for Gen. Harrison, the friend of the confidant of Blue Jacket's was a young Delaware chief named Beaver, who was also bound to the general by the ties of friendship. He was the son of a Delaware war chief of the same name, who had with others been put to death by his own tribe, on the charge of practicing sorcery. Gen. Harrison had been upon terms of friendship with the father, and had patronized his orphan boy, at that time ten or twelve years of age. He had now arrived to manhood, and was considered among the most promising warriors of his tribe: to this young chief the friend of Blue Jacket revealed the fatal secret. The Beaver was placed by this communication in an embarrassing situation, for should he disclose what he had heard, he betrayed his friend, than which nothing could be more repugnant to the feelings and principles of an Indian warrior. Should he not disclose it, consequences equally or even more to be deprecated were likely to ensue. The assassination of a friend, the friend of his father, whose life he was bound to defend, or whose death to revenge by the same principle of fidelity and honor which forbid the disclosure.

While he was yet hesitating, Blue Jacket came up to the Delaware camp, somewhat intoxicated, vociferating vengeance upon Col. M'Pherson, who had just turned him out of his house, and whom he declared he would put to death for the insult he had received. The sight of the traitor aroused the indignation and resentment of the Beaver to the highest pitch. He seized his tomahawk, and advancing toward the culprit, "You must be a great warrior," said he, "you will not only kill this white man for serving you as you deserve, but you will also murder our father, the American chief, and bring disgrace and mischief upon us all; but you shall do neither, I will serve you as I would a mad dog." A furious blow from the tomahawk of the Beaver stretched the unfortunate Blue Jacket at his feet, and a second terminated his existence; "There," said he to some Shawanoese who were present, "take him to the camp of his tribe, and tell them who has done the deed."

The Shawanoese were far from resenting it; they applauded the conduct of the Beaver, and rejoiced at their happy escape from the ignominy which the accomplishment of Blue Jacket's design would have brought upon them. At the great treaty which was held at Greenville in 1815, Gen. Cass, one of the commissioners, related the whole of the transaction to the assembled chiefs, and after thanking the Beaver, in the name of the United States, for having saved the life of their general, he caused a handsome present to be made him out of the goods which he had sent for the purpose of the treaty. It is impossible to say what was the motive of Blue Jacket to attempt the life of Gen. Harrison: he was not one of the Tippecanoe Shawanoese, and therefore could have no personal resentment against the general. There is little doubt that he came from Malden when he arrived at Wapakoneta, and that he came for the express purpose of attempting the life of the general; but whether he was instigated to it by any other person or persons, or had conceived the idea himself, has never been ascertained. Upon the arrival of the chiefs at Seneca, the principal war chief of the Shawanese requested permission to sleep at the door of the general's marquee, and this he did every night until the embarkation of the troops. This man, who had fought with great bravery on our side in the several sorties from Fort Meigs, was called *Capt. Tommy;* he was a great favorite of the officers, particularly the general and Commodore Perry, the latter of whom was accustomed to call him the general's Mamaluke.

The Senecas of Sandusky—so called—owned and occupied forty thousand acres of choice land, on the east side of Sandusky river, being mostly in this and partly in Sandusky county. Thirty thousand acres of this land was granted to them on the 29th of September, 1817, at the treaty held at the foot of Maumee Rapids, Hon. Lewis Cass and Hon. Duncan M'Arthur, being the commissioners of the United States. The remaining 10,000 acres, lying south of the other, was granted by the treaty at St. Mary's, concluded by the same commissioners on the 17th of September, in the following year. By the treaty concluded at Washington city, February 28th, 1831, James B. Gardiner being the commissioner of the general government, these Indians ceded their lands to the United States, and agreed to remove southwest of Missouri, on the Neosho river.

At this time, their principal chiefs were Coonstick, Small Cloud Spicer, Seneca Steel, Hard Hickory, Tall Chief and Good Hunter, the last two of whom were their principal orators. The old chief Good Hunter told Mr. Henry C. Brish, their sub-agent, that this band, which numbered about 400 souls, were in fact *the remnant of Logan's tribe,* (see p. 409,) and says Mr. Brish in a communication to us: "I cannot to this day surmise why they were called Senecas. I never found a Seneca among them. They were Cayugas,—who were Mingoes,—among whom were a few Oneidas, Mohawks, Onondagoes, Tuscarawas and Wyandots."

From Mr. Brish, we have received an interesting narrative of the execution for *witchcraft* of one these Indians, named Seneca John, who was one of the best men of his tribe.

About the year 1825, Coonstick, Steel and Crack'd Hoof, left the reservation for the double purpose of a three years hunting and trapping excursion, and to seek a location for a new home for the tribe in the far west.

At the time of their starting, Comstock, the brother of the two first, was the principal chief of the tribe. On their return in 1828, richly laden with furs and horses, they found Seneca John, their fourth brother, chief, in place of Comstock, who had died during their absence.

Comstock was the favorite brother of the two, and they at once charged Seneca John with producing his death by witchcraft. John denied the charge in a strain of eloquence rarely equalled. Said he, "I loved my brother Comstock more than I love the green earth I stand upon. I would give up myself, limb by limb, piecemeal by piecemeal,—I would shed my blood, drop by drop, to restore him to life." But all his protestation of innocence and affection for his brother Comstock, were of no avail. His two other brothers pronounced him guilty, and declared their determination to be his executioners.

John replied that he was willing to die, and only wished to live until the next morning, "to see the sun rise once more." This request being granted, John told them that he should sleep that night on Hard Hickory's porch, which fronted the east, where they would find him at sunrise. He chose that place because he did not wish to be killed in the presence of his wife, and desired that the chief, Hard Hickory, should witness that he died like a brave man.

Coonstick and Steel retired for the night to an old cabin near by. In the morning, in company with Shane, another Indian, they proceeded to the house of Hard Hickory, who was my informant of what there happened.

He said, a little after sunrise he heard their footsteps upon the porch, and opened the door just enough to peep out. He saw John *asleep* upon his blanket, and they standing around him. At length one of them awoke him. He arose upon his feet and took off a large handkerchief which was around his head, letting his unusually long hair fall upon his shoulders. This being done, he looked around upon the landscape, and at the rising sun, to take a farewell look of a scene that he was never again to behold, and then told them he was ready to die.

Shane and Coonstick each took him by the arm, and Steel walked behind. In this way they led him about ten steps from the porch, when Steel struck him with a tomahawk on the back of his head, and he fell to the ground, bleeding freely. Supposing this blow sufficient to kill him, they dragged him under a peach tree near by. In a short time, however, he revived; the blow having been broken by his great mass of hair. Knowing that it was Steel who struck the blow, John, as he lay, turned his head towards Coonstick and said, "now brother, do you take your revenge." This so operated upon the feelings of Coonstick, that he interposed to save him; but it enraged Steel to such a degree, that he drew his knife and cut John's throat from ear to ear, and the next day he was buried with the usual Indian ceremonies, not more than twenty feet from where he fell. Steel was arrested and tried for the murder in Sandusky county, and acquitted.

The grave of Seneca John was surrounded by a small picket enclosure. Three years after, when I was preparing to move them to the far west, I saw Coonstick and Steel remove the picket-fence and level the ground, so that no vestige of the grave remained.

A writer in the Sidney Aurora, a few years since, gave a narration of some of the religious rites of this tribe, just prior to their departure for their new homes. We extract his description of their sacrificing two dogs to the Great Spirit.

We rose early and proceeded directly to the council house, and though we supposed we were early, the Indians were already in advance of us.

The first object which arrested our attention, was a pair of the canine species, one of each gender suspended on a *cross!* one on either side thereof. These animals had been recently *strangled—not a bone was broken*, nor could a distorted hair be seen! They were of beautiful *cream* color, except a few dark spots on one, naturally, which same spots were put on the other, artificially, by the devotees. The Indians are very partial in the selection of dogs entirely *white*, for this occasion; and for which they will give almost any price.

Now for part of the decorations to which I have already alluded, and a description of one will suffice for both.

First—A scarlet ribbon was tastefully tied just above the nose; and near the eyes another; next round the neck was a white ribbon, to which was attached some bulbous, concealed in another white ribbon; this was placed directly under the right ear, and I suppose it was intended as an amulet, or charm. Then ribbons were bound round the forelegs, at the knees, and near the feet—these were red and white alternately. Round the body was a profuse decoration—then the hind legs were decorated as the fore ones. Thus were the victims prepared and thus ornamented for the burnt offering.

While minutely making this examination, I was almost unconscious of the collection of a large number of Indians who were there assembled to offer their sacrifices.

Adjacent to the cross, was a large fire built on a few logs; and though the snow was several inches deep, they had prepared a sufficient quantity of combustible material, removed the snow from the logs, and placed thereon their fire. I have often regretted that I did not see them light this pile. My own opinion is, they did not use the fire from their council-house; because I think they would have considered that as common, and as this was intended to be a holy service, they, no doubt, for this purpose struck fire from a flint, this being deemed sacred.*

* The Indians, we are informed, on these occasions, kindle their fire by the friction of two dry sticks.—*H. H.*

It was a clear, beautiful morning, and just as the first rays of the sun were seen in the tops of the towering forest, and its reflections from the snowy surface, the Indians simultaneously formed a semicircle enclosing the cross, each flank resting on the aforesaid pile of logs.

Good Hunter, who officiated as High Priest, now appeared, and approached the cross; arrayed in his pontifical robes, he looked quite respectable.

The Indians being all assembled—I say Indians, for there was not a squaw present during all this ceremony—at a private signal given by the High Priest, two young chiefs sprang upon the cross, and each taking off one of the victims, brought it down and presented it on his arms to the High Priest, who receiving it with great reverence, in like manner advanced to the fire, and with a very grave and solemn air, laid it thereon—and this he did with the other—but to which, whether male or female, he gave the preference, I did not learn. This done, he retired to the cross.

In a devout manner, he now commenced an oration. The tone of his voice was audible and somewhat chanting. At every pause in his discourse, he took from a white cloth he held in his left hand, a portion of dried, odoriferous herbs, which he threw on the fire; this was intended as incense. In the meanwhile his auditory, their eyes on the ground, with grave aspect, and in solemn silence, stood motionless, listening attentively to every word he uttered.

Thus he proceeded until the victims were entirely consumed, and the incense exhausted, when he concluded his service; the oblation now made, and the wrath of the Great Spirit, as they believed, appeased, they again assembled in the council-house, for the purpose of performing a part in their festival, different from any I yet had witnessed. Each Indian as he entered, seated himself on the floor, thus forming a large circle; when one of the old chiefs rose, and with that native dignity which some Indians possess in a great degree, recounted his exploits as a warrior; told in how many fights he had been the victor; the number of scalps he had taken from his enemies; and what, at the head of his braves, he yet intended to do at the "Rocky Mountains;" accompanying his narration with energy, warmth, and strong gesticulation; when he ended, he received the unanimous applause of the assembled tribe.

This meed of praise was awarded to the chief by "three times three," articulations, which were properly neither nasal, oral, nor guttural, but rather abdominal. Thus many others in the circle, old and young, rose in order, and *proforma*, delivered themselves of a speech. Among those was Good Hunter; but he

"Had laid his robes away
His mitre and his vest."

His remarks were not filled with such bombast as some others; but brief, modest, and appropriate; in fine, they were such as became a priest of one of the lost ten tribes of Israel.

After all had spoken who wished to speak, the floor was cleared, and the dance renewed, in which Indian and squaw united, with their wonted hilarity and zeal.

Just as this dance ended, an Indian boy ran to me, and with fear strongly depicted in his countenance, caught me by the arm, and drew me to the door, pointing with his other hand towards something he wished me to observe.

I looked in that direction, and saw the appearance of an Indian running at full speed to the council-house; in an instant he was in the house, and literally in the fire, which he took in his hands, and threw fire, coals and hot ashes in various directions, through the house, and apparently all over himself! At his entrance, the young Indians, much alarmed, had all fled to the further end of the house, where they remained crowded, in great dread of this personification of the Evil Spirit! After diverting himself with the fire a few moments, at the expense of the young ones, to their no small joy he disappeared. This was an Indian disguised with a hideous false face, having horns on his head, and his hands and feet protected from the effects of the fire. And though not a professed "Fire King," he certainly performed his part to admiration.

During the continuance of this festival, the hospitality of the Senecas was unbounded. In the council-house, and at the residence of Tall Chief, were a number of large fat bucks, and fat hogs hanging up, and neatly dressed. Bread also, of both corn and wheat, in great abundance.

Large kettles of soup ready prepared, in which maple sugar, profusely added, made a prominent ingredient, thus forming a very agreeable saccharine coalescence. All were invited, and all were made welcome; indeed, a refusal to partake of their bounty, was deemed disrespectful, if not unfriendly.

I left them in the afternoon enjoying themselves to the fullest extent; and so far as I could perceive, their pleasure was without alloy. They were eating and drinking; but on this occasion, no ardent spirits were permitted—dancing and rejoicing—caring, and, probably, thinking not of to-morrow.

View in Tiffin.

Tiffin, the county seat, is a compactly built village, on a level site, on the line of the railroad connecting Cincinnati with Sandusky City, and on the east bank of Sandusky river. It is 86 miles N. of Columbus and 34 from Sandusky City. It was laid out about the year 1821, by Josiah Hedges, and named from the Hon. Edward Tiffin, of Ross, president of the convention which formed the constitution of Ohio, and the first governor of the state of Ohio in 1803. The town is gradually increasing with the growth of the county. The view was taken in the principal street, and shows on the left the court house, and in the distance the spire of a Catholic church. It contains ? Lutheran, 2 Catholic, 1 Episcopal, 1 Methodist Episcopal, 1 Reformed Methodist and 1 German Reformed church, 5 grocery and 9 dry goods stores, 1 foundery, 2 newspaper printing offices, and had in 1840, 728 inhabitants: it now contains with the suburbs, about 1200.

Opposite Tiffin, on the west bank of the Sandusky, is the small village of Fort Ball, so named from a fort erected there in the late war, and probably so called from Lieut. Col. James V. Ball, the commander of a squadron of cavalry under Harrison, while at Fort Seneca in this county. The fort was a small stockade with a ditch, occupying perhaps one-third of an acre. It stood on the bank of the river, about fifty rods south of the present bridge, and was used principally as a military depot. Vestiges of this work yet remain.

On the old Indian reservation, in a limestone soil, are two white sulphur springs, respectively 10 and 12 miles from Tiffin, and about 2 apart. The water is clear, and petrifies all objects with which it comes in contact. The water furnishes power sufficient for two large merchant mills, flows in great quantities, and nearly alike in all seasons.

In the northeastern corner of the county, in the township of Thompson, is a subterranean streams, about 80 feet under ground. The water is pure and cold, runs uniformly, and in a northern direction. It is entered by a hole in the top, into which the curious can descend on foot, by the aid of a light.

The following is a list of villages and localities in the county with their population in 1840. Attica 118, Bascom 34, Bettsville 23, Bloomville 13, Caroline 27, Fort Ball 129, Fort Seneca 52, Green Spring 29, Lodi 30, Melmore 127, Risdon 39, Rome 80, Republic 161, Springville 35, Sulphur Spring 29.

Some of these have since much increased. The most important of them now is Republic. This thriving village is in the township of Scipio, on the line of the railroad, 9 miles E. of Tiffin. It was laid out about 13 years since, and contains 1 Presbyterian, 1 Methodist and 1 Universalist church, 1 book, 3 grocery and 9 dry goods stores, 1 machine shop for the making of steam engines, 1 clothing mill, and about 600 inhabitants. The houses are new and neat, and the inhabitants, many of whom are from western New York, have among them a flourishing academy, numbering about 100 pupils of both sexes.

SHELBY.

Shelby was formed from Miami in 1819, and named from Gov Shelby, of Kentucky. The southern half is undulating, rising in places along the Miami into hills. The northern portion is flat table land, forming part of Loramie's summit, 378 feet above Lake Erie, being the highest elevation in this part of the state. The soil is based on clay, with some fine bottom land along the streams. The southern part is best for grain, and the northern for grass. Proper drainage and tillage will render it an excellent county for grazing and small grain. Its principal crops are corn, grass, oats and wheat. The following is a list of the townships in the county in 1840, with their population.

Clinton,	1496	Jackson,	478	Salem,	1158
Cynthian,	1022	Loramie,	904	Turtle Creek,	746
Dinsmoor,	500	M'Lean,	513	Van Buren,	596
Franklin,	647	Orange,	783	Washington,	1688
Green,	762	Perry,	861		

The population of Shelby in 1820, was 2142, in 1830, 3671, and in 1840, 12,153; or 29 inhabitants to the square mile.

The mouth of Loramie's creek, in this county, 16 miles NW. of Sidney, is a place of historic interest. It was the first point of English settlement in Ohio. As early as 1752, there was a trading house at that place, called by the English *Pickawillany*, which was attacked and destroyed by the French and Indians that year; but little is known, however, of its history. (See page 7.)

At the time of the first settlement of Kentucky, a Canadian Frenchman, named Loramie, established there a store, or trading station, among the Indians. This man was a bitter enemy of the Americans, and it was for a long time the head-quarters of mischief towards the settlers.

The French had the faculty of endearing themselves to the Indians and no doubt Loramie was, in this respect, fully equal to any of his countrymen, and gained great influence over them. They formed with the natives attachments of the most tender and abiding kind. "I have," says Colonel Johnston, "seen the Indians burst into tears when speaking of the time when their French father had dominion over them; and their attachment to this day remains unabated."

So much influence had Loramie with the Indians, that when Gen. Clarke, from Kentucky, invaded the Miami valley in the autumn of 1782, his attention was attracted to the spot. He came on and burnt the Indian settlement here, and plundered and burnt the store of the Frenchman.

The store contained a large quantity of goods and peltry, which were sold by auction afterwards among the men by the general's orders. Among the soldiers was an Irishman named Burke, considered a half-witted fellow, and the general butt of the whole army. While searching the store, he found done up in a rag 25 half joes, worth about $200, which he secreted in a hole he cut in an old saddle. At the auction no one bid for the saddle, it being judged worthless, except Burke, to whom it was struck off for a trifling sum, amid roars of laughter for his folly. But a moment elapsed before Burke commenced a search, and found and drew forth the money as if by accident; then shaking it in the eyes of the men, exclaimed, "an' it's not so bad a bargain after all!"

Soon after this, Loramie, with a colony of the Shawanoese, emigrated to the Spanish territories, west of the Mississippi, and settled in a spot assigned them at the junction of the Kanzas and Missouri, where the remaining part of the nation from Ohio have at different times joined them.

In 1794, a fort was built at the place occupied by Loramie's store, by Wayne, and named *Fort Loramie*. The last officer who had command here was Capt. Butler, a nephew of Gen. Richard Butler, who fell at St. Clair's defeat. Says Colonel John Johnston:

His wife and children were with him during his command, A very interesting son of his, about eight years old, died at the post. The agonized father and mother were inconsolable. The grave was enclosed with a very handsome and painted railing, at the foot of which honeysuckles were planted, grew luxuriantly, entwined the paling, and finally enveloped the whole grave. Nothing could appear more beautiful than this arbor when in bloom.

The peace withdrew Capt. Butler and his troops to other scenes on the Mississippi. I never passed the fort without a melancholy thought about the lovely boy who rested there, and his parents far away never to behold that cherished spot again. Long after the posts had decayed in the ground the vines sustained the palings, and the whole remained perfect until the war of 1812, when all was destroyed, and now a barn stands over the spot.

The site of Loramie's store was a prominent point in the Greenville treaty boundary line. The farm of the heirs of the late James Furrow now covers the spot. Col. John Hardin was murdered in this county, in 1792, while on a mission of peace to the Indians. The town of Hardin has since been laid out on the spot. (See page 240.)

The first white family who settled in this county was that of James Thatcher, in 1804, who settled in the west part on Painter's run; Samuel Marshall, John Wilson and John Kennard—the last now living—came soon after. The first court was held in a cabin at Hardin, May 13th and 14th, 1819. Hon. Joseph H. Crane, of Dayton, was the president judge; Samuel Marshall, Robert Houston and Wm. Cecil, associates; Harvey B. Foot, clerk; Daniel V. Dingman, sheriff, and Harvey Brown, of Dayton, prosecutor. The first mill was a saw mill, erected in 1808 by Daniel M'Mullen and Bilderbach, on the site of Walker's mill.

Public Square, Sidney.

Sidney, the county seat, is 68 miles N. of W. from Columbus, 88 from Cincinnati, and named from Sir Philip Sydney, "the great light of chivalry." It was laid out as the county seat in the fall of 1819, on the farm of Charles Starrett, under the direction of the court.

The site is beautiful, being on an elevated table-ground on the west bank of the Miami. The only part of the plot then cleared was a corn-field, the first crop having been raised there in 1809, by Wm. Stewart. The court removed to Sidney in April, 1820, and held its meetings in the log-cabin of Abm. Cannon, on the south side of the field, on the site of Matthew Gillespie's store. During the same year, the first court house, a frame building, now Judge Walker's store, was built, and also the log jail. The first frame house was built in 1820, by John Blake, now forming the front of the National hotel. The first post-office in the county was established at Hardin in 1819, Col. James Wells, post-master; but was removed the next year to Sidney, where the colonel has continued since to hold the office, except during Tyler's administration. The first brick house was erected on the site of J. F. Frazer's drug store, by Dr. Wm. Fielding. The Methodists erected the first church on the ground now occupied by them. Mr. T. Truder had a little store when the town was laid out, on the east side of the river, near the lower crossing. The Herald, the first paper in the county, was established in 1836, and published by Thos. Smith. A block-house at one time stood near the spring.

In the centre of Sidney is a beautiful public square, on which stands the court house. A short distance in a westerly direction, passes the Sidney feeder, a navigable branch of the Miami canal. The town and suburbs contain 1 Methodist, 1 Presbyterian, 1 Associate Reformed, 1 Christian and 1 Catholic church; 1 drug, 2 iron, 5 hardware and 10 dry goods stores; 2 printing offices, 1 oil, 2 carding and fulling, 3 flouring and 4 saw mills, and in 1840, Sidney had 713 inhabitants, since which it has increased.

In Van Buren township is a settlement of COLORED people, numbering about 400. They constitute half the population of the township, and are as prosperous as their white neighbors. Neither are they behind them in religion, morals and intelligence, having churches and schools of their own. Their location, however, is not a good one, the land being too flat and wet. An attempt was made in July, 1846, to colonize with them 385 of the emancipated slaves of the celebrated John Randolph, of Va., after they were driven from Mercer county; but a considerable party of whites would not willingly permit it, and they were scattered by families among the people of Shelby and Miami who were willing to take them.

Port Jefferson, 5 miles NE. of Sidney, is at the head of the feeder, through which the waters of the Miami flow into the Miami canal, 13 miles distant. It contains 1 Methodist and 1 Baptist church, 3 stores, and about 50 dwellings. Hardin, 5 miles w. of Sidney; Newport, 12 w., Berlin, 16 WNW., Houston, 11 WSW., Lockport, 8 S., and Palestine, 9 E., are small, and some of them thriving villages.

STARK.

STARK was established Feb. 13th, 1808, and organized in January, 1809. It was named from Gen. John Stark, an officer of the revolution, who was born in Londonderry, New Hampshire, in 1728, and died in 1822. The surface is generally rolling; the central and northeast portions are slightly undulating. The soil is a sandy loam; in some parts of the north and east a clay soil predominates. It is a rich agricultural county, and produces more wheat, except Wayne, than any other in Ohio. It embraces within itself the requisite facilities for making it the seat of various manufactures—mineral coal, iron ore, flocks of the choicest sheep, and great water power. Limestone abounds, and inexhaustible beds of lime marl exist. The cultivation of the mulberry and manufacture of silk have been successfully commenced. It was settled mainly by Pennsylvania Germans, and from Germany and France. The principal agricultural products are wheat, corn, oats, potatoes, barley, grass, and flax and clover seed. The following is a list of its townships in 1840, with their population.

Bethlehem,	1019	Marlborough,	1670	Plain,	1838
Canton,	3298	Nimishillen,	1927	Sandy,	1265
Jackson,	1546	Osnaburgh,	2333	Sugar Creek,	1862
Lake,	2162	Paris,	2474	Tuscarawas,	1942
Lawrence,	2045	Perry,	2210	Washington,	1389
Lexington,	1640	Pike,	1409		

The population of Stark in 1820, was 12,406, in 1830, 26,552, and in 1840, 34,617; or 69 inhabitants to a square mile.

The first Moravian missionary in Ohio, Mr. Frederick Post, settled in 1761 in what is now Bethlehem township, on the north side of the Muskingum, at the junction of its two forks, the Sandy and Tuscarawas. The locality called Tuscararatown is on the south side of the river, just above Fort Laurens, and immediately contiguous to Bolivar. Just there was the Indian ford, on the line of the great Indian trail running west. The site of Post's dwelling, or missionary station, is indicated by a pile of stones, which had probably formed the back wall of the chimney. The site of the garden differs from the woods around it in the total want of heavy timber. The ruins of a trader's house, on the opposite side of the river, have been mistaken for those of the missionary station. The dwelling built by Post must have been the first house erected in Ohio by whites, excepting such as may have been built by traders or French Jesuits. The Indian and Moravian village of Schoenbrun was not commenced until 1772, eleven years later.

Loskiel's history of the missions says, in allusion to this mission—"On the Ohio river, where, since the last war, some Indians lived who had been baptized by the brethren, nothing could be done up to this time. However, brother Frederick Post lived, though of his own choice, about 100 English miles west of Pittsburgh, at Tuscararatown, with a view to commence a mission among those Indians. The brethren wished him the blessings of the Almighty to his undertaking; and when he asked for an assistant to help him in his outward concerns, and who might, during the same time, learn the language of the Delaware Indians, they (the brethren) made it known to the congregation of Bethlehem, whereupon the brother John Heckewelder concluded of his own choice to assist him."

"We know of Post that he was an active and zealous missionary, but had married an Indian squaw, contrary to the wishes and advice of the directory, who had the oversight of the Moravian missions, and by that act had forfeited so much of his standing that he would not be acknowledged as one of our missionaries in any other manner than under the direction and guidance of another missionary. Whenever he went farther, and acted on his own accord, he was not opposed, had the good will of the society of which he continued a member and its directory, and even their assistance, so far as to make known his wants to the congregation, and threw no obstacles in the way if any person felt inclined of his own choice to assist him; but he was not then acknowledged as *their* missionary, nor entitled to any farther or pecuniary assistance." This will explain the above passage in Loskiel.

"In Heckewelder's memoirs, written by himself, and printed in Germany, there is a short allusion to the same subject. He says, in substance, that he had in his early youth frequent opportunities of seeing Indians, and that gradually he became desirous of becoming useful to them; that already in his 19th year, his desire was in some measure gratified, as he was called upon by government to accompany the brother Frederick Post to the western Indians on the Ohio. He then mentions some of the fatigues and dangers of the journey, and that he returned in the latter half of the year 1762. In Heckewelder's narrative of the Indian missions of the United Brethren, he gives a more detailed account of this mission. He says, in effect, that Frederick Post, who had the preceding year [1761] visited the Indians on the Muskingum, thought he would be able to introduce christianity among them; that the writer of the narrative, by and with the consent of the directors of the society, went with him principally to teach the Indian children to read and write. They set out early in March, and came to where Post had the preceding year built a house on the bank of the river Muskingum, at the distance of about a mile from the Indian village, which lay to the south across the river. When they commenced clearing, the Indians ordered them to stop and appear before their council the next day, where Post appeared, and was charged with deceit, inasmuch as he had informed the Indians his intentions were to teach them the word of God, and now he took possession of their lands, &c. Post answered that he wanted no more land than sufficient to live from it, as he intended to be no burden to them, &c.; whereupon they concluded that he should have 50 steps in every direction, which was stepped off by the chief next day. He farther says, that an Indian treaty being to be held at Lancaster in the latter part of summer, Post was requested by the governor of Pennsylvania to bring some of the western Delawares to it, which he did, leaving Heckewelder, who returned the same fall, in October, from fear of a war, &c. Post probably never returned to this station."*

Canton, the county seat, is 120 miles NE. of Columbus. It is finely situated in the forks of the Nimishillen, a tributary of the Muskingum. It was laid out in 1806 by Bezaleel Wells, of Steubenville, and the first house erected the same year. Mr. Wells was the original pro-

---

* In Zeisberger's memoirs there is no allusion to this mission, though he and Post were frequently associates at an earlier date, and in 1745 were imprisoned together in New York as spies. The above article is abridged from papers in the Barr MSS., comprising a letter from Mr. Thomas Goodman, in which was copied one from Judge Blickensderfer, of Dover, who had carefully investigated the subject.

prietor of the town, and died in 1846. The view shows a part of the public square, with the court house on the left and the market in the centre. It is a very compact town, with many brick dwellings.

Public Square in Canton.

A large business is done here in the purchase of flour and wheat, and within the vicinity are many flouring mills. Canton contains 1 German Reformed, 1 Lutheran, 1 Presbyterian, 2 Catholic and 1 Methodist church; 10 dry goods, 2 book, 2 hardware and 7 grocery stores; 2 newspaper offices, 1 gun barrel and 2 woollen factories, 2 iron founderies, and about 2000 inhabitants. The Canton female institute is a flourishing institution, with near 100 pupils.

View in Main street, Massillon.

Massillon is on the Ohio canal and Tuscarawas river, 8 miles from Canton and 65 from Cleveland. It was laid out in March, 1826, by James Duncan, and named from John Baptiste Massillon, a celebrated French divine, who died in 1742, at the age of 79 The Ohio canal was located only a short time before the town was laid out, at which period, on its site was a grist mill, a distillery, and a few dwellings only.

The view was taken near the American hotel, shown on the right, and within a few rods of the canal, the bridge over which is seen in front. The town is compactly built, and is remarkable for its substantial appearance. It is very thriving, and is one of the greatest wheat markets in Ohio. At times, Main street is almost completely blocked by immense wagons of wheat, and the place has generally the bustling air of business. It lies in the centre of a very rich wheat region. The old town of Kendall, laid out about the year 1810 by Thomas Roach, joins on the east. Massillon contains 1 German Evangelical, 1 Presbyterian, 1 Episcopal, 1 Lutheran, 1 Disciples, 1 Episcopal Methodist and 1 Catholic church; 2 hardware, 2 wholesale grocery and 11 dry goods stores; 6 forwarding houses, 3 founderies, 3 machine shops, 1 newspaper office, 1 bank, 1 woollen factory, and had in 1840, 1420 inhabitants, and now has about 2000. "Just below the town commences a series of extensive plains, spreading over a space of 10 or 12 miles in length from east to west, and 5 or 6 in breadth. These were covered with a thin growth of oak timber, and were denominated *barrens*, but, on cultivation, they produce fine crops of wheat. The Tuscarawas has cut across these plains on their western end, and runs in a valley sunk about 30 feet below their general surface."

Waynesburgh, on the Sandy and Beaver canal, 12 miles SE. of Canton, is a flourishing place, with about 500 inhabitants. Canal Fulton, on the Ohio canal, 13 miles from Canton, contains not far from 60 dwellings, and is a smart business place, where much wheat is purchased. Bethlehem, Rochester and Navarre, are three villages nearly connected as one, about 10 miles SW. of Canton, on the Ohio canal and Tuscarawas river. The three places may contain not far from 1000 inhabitants, and have 10 forwarding houses, it being an important point for the shipment of wheat. Brookfield, Paris, Osnaburg, Harrisburgh, Freedom, Limaville, Minerva, Mapleton, Magnolia, Sparta, Berlin, Greentown, Uniontown, Milton and Louisville, are small villages. This last named village is almost entirely settled by French. It has been estimated that there are several thousand French in the county from the river Rhine. They form an excellent population, and readily assimilate to American customs. The French children enter the English schools, while the Germans show more attachment to those in their native language.

SUMMIT.

SUMMIT was erected from Portage, Medina and Stark, March 3d, 1840. It derived its name from having the highest land on the line of the Ohio canal, originally called "the Portage summit." Along the Cuyahoga it is uneven and hilly; elsewhere level or undulating. In Tallmadge and Springfield are immense beds of bituminous coal, from which large quantities are exported and used by the lake steamers. In Springfield, large quantities of stone-ware are made, at which place fine clay abounds. The soil is fertile and produces excellent fruit. The principal productions are wheat, corn, hay, oats, cheese, butter, and potatoes and fruit. The following is a list of the townships in 1840, with their population.

Bath,	1425	Green,	1536	Portage,	2382
Boston,	845	Hudson,	1220	Richfield,	1108
Copley,	1439	Northampton,	963	Stow,	1533
Coventry,	1308	Northfield,	1031	Tallmadge,	2134
Franklin,	1436	Norton,	1497	Twinsburgh,	1039

The population of Summit in 1840, was 22,469, or 45 inhabitants to the square mile.

The old Indian *Portage path*, between the Cuyahoga and the Tuscarawas branch of the Muskingum, lies within this county, and was part of the ancient boundary between the Six Nations and the western Indians.

It left the Cuyahoga at the village of Old Portage, about three miles north of Akron. It went up the hill westward about half a mile to the high ground, where it turned southerly and run about parallel with the canal to near the Summit lake; there took the low ground nearly south to the Tuscarawas, which it struck a mile or more above the New Portage. The whole length of the path was, by the survey of Moses Warren, in 1797, 8 miles, 4 chains and 55 links.

The first settlement made in this county was at Hudson, in the year 1800, by Mr. David Hudson, the history of which we derive from a series of articles written by Rev. J. Seward, and published some 10 or 15 years since in the Hudson Observer.

In the division of the Western Reserve among the proprietors, the townships of Chester and Hudson fell to the lot of Birdsey Norton and David Hudson.

In the year 1799, Mr. Hudson came out to explore his land, in company with a few others. On the way, he fell in with Benj. Tappan, since judge, then travelling to his town of Ravenna. They started in his boat from Gerondigut bay, on Lake Ontario, early in May, and soon overtook Elias Harmon, since judge, in a boat with his wife, bound to Mantua. On arriving at Niagara, they found the river full of ice. They had their boats conveyed around the falls, and proceeded on their dangerous way amidst vast bodies of floating ice, having some of the men on the shore pulling by ropes until out of danger from the current of the Niagara. Arrived at the mouth of the lake, they found it full of floating ice as far as the eye could reach, and were compelled to wait several days ere they could proceed, which they then did along near the shore. When off Ashtabula county, their boats were driven ashore in a storm, and that of Mr. Harmon's stove in pieces: he proceeded from thence by land to Mantua. Having purchased, and in a manner repaired Harmon's boat, Mr. Hudson shipped his effects in it, and they arrived at Cleveland on the 8th of June.

Morse's geography having given them about all the knowledge of the Cuyahoga that they possessed, they supposed it capable of sloop navigation to its forks. The season being dry, they had proceeded but a few miles when they found it in places only 8 or 10 inches deep, and were often obliged to get out, join hands and drag their boats over the shallow places, and made but slow progress. After a lapse of several days, they judged they were in the latitude of the town of which they were in search. Mr. Hudson went ashore and commenced hunting for a surveyor's line much too far north, and it was not until after six days laborious and painful search that he discovered, towards night, a line which led to the southwest corner of his township. The succeeding day being very rainy he lodged under an oak tree, without any covering except the clothes he wore, with the grateful pleasure of resting on his own land. In the morning, he returned highly elated to the boats and gave information of his success.

While in Ontario, New York, Tappan bought a yoke of oxen, and Hudson two yoke and two cows. These eight cattle they committed to the care of Meacham, a hired man in Tappan's service, who brought them safely on the Indian trail through Buffalo, until they found near the lake the west line of the seventh range on the Reserve. This line, it being the east line of the towns now named Painsville, Concord, Chardon, Monson, Newburg, Auburn, Mantua, Shalersville and Ravenna, they followed due south more than forty miles, crossing the Grand and Cuyahoga rivers and striking the Salt spring Indian trail near the southeastern corner of Ravenna. They followed this trail westwardly until they came to the new line recently made by Hudson and Tappan, which they followed to the spot where the boats were lying on the Cuyahoga, in Boston.

The difficulties encountered by these men in driving this small drove about three hundred miles on an obscure, crooked Indian path, and in following town lines through swamps, rivers and other obstacles fifty miles farther, almost through an uninhabited wilderness, were appalling; and what rendered their circumstances truly unpleasant, and in some cases hazardous, was that they were strangers to the country and without a guide. Their mode of travelling was to have several bags of flour and pork, together with two blankets and an axe, well secured on the backs of the oxen. They waded fordable streams and compelled their cattle to swim those that could not be forded, passing across those streams themselves with their provisions on rafts hastily made of sticks.

Mr. Hudson's company being thus collected, his first care, after making yokes for his oxen, was to open some road to his land. The gullies they crossed were numerous and frequent, and often abrupt to an angle of 45 degrees or more. On this road, bad as it was, they performed all their transportation in the year '99, while their oxen were tormented and rendered almost unmanageable by immense swarms of large flies, which displayed such skill in the science of phlebotomy, that, in a short time, they drew out a large share of the blood belonging to these animals: the flies actually killed one of Tappan's oxen this season.

After having conveyed their small stock of provisions on to the southwest corner of this town and erected a bark hut, Mr. Hudson's anxiety became very great lest he and his company should suffer for want of provisions, his stock being very much reduced in consequence of the Indians having robbed his boat. Not hearing from Lacey, a man he had left behind in western New York to bring on stores, and dreading the consequences of waiting for him any longer, Mr. Hudson started to meet him. Taking a boat at Cleveland, which was providentially going down the lake, on the 2d of July he found Lacey lying at his ease near Cattaraugus. With difficulty he there obtained some provisions, and having a prosperous voyage arrived in season, to the joy of those left in the wilderness, who must have been put upon short allowance had his arrival been delayed any longer.

The company being thus furnished with provisions, they built a large log house. Mr. Hudson also set his men to work in clearing a piece of land for wheat, and on the 25th of July he commenced surveying. The settlement now consisted of 13 persons. In August, every person except Mr. Hudson had a turn of being unwell. Several had the fever and ague, and in the progress of surveying the town into lots, the party frequently had to wait for some one of their number to go through with a paroxysm of ague and then resume their labors.

By the middle of September, they found to their surprise they had only nine days' provision on hand; and as Mr. Hudson had heard nothing from his agent, Norton, at Bloomfield, New York, he was once more alarmed lest they should suffer for want of food.

He immediately went to Cleveland and purchased of Lorenzo Carter a small field of corn for $50, designing to pound it in mortars and live thereon in case of necessity. He hastened back to his station, and having previously heard that Ebenezer Sheldon had made a road through the wilderness to Aurora, and that there was a bridle-path thence to Cleveland, he thought it probable that he might obtain pork for present necessity from that quarter. He accordingly set out on foot and alone, and regulated his course by the range of his shadow, making allowance for change in the time of day. He found the Cleveland path near the centre of Aurora, then a dense forest. Thence he proceeded about two and a half miles to squire Sheldon's cabin, and on inquiring found that he could obtain no provisions within a reasonable distance in that direction. The next morning, on his return, he found that the boat had arrived with an ample supply of provisions.

Having completed his surveying on the 11th of October, Mr. Hudson left on the next day for Connecticut, to bring out his family, in company with his little son and two men. Being disappointed in not finding a good boat at Cleveland, he took the wreck of one he had purchased of Harmon, and embarked upon the dangerous enterprize of crossing the lake in it. It was so leaky that it required one hand most of the time to bail out the water, and so weak that it bent considerably in crossing the waves. During their passage, the weather was generally cold and boisterous; three different times they narrowly escaped drowning by reason of the darkness of the night or violence of the wind. Being under the necessity of lying five days on Chatague point, they lived comfortably during that time on boiled chestnuts, in order to lengthen out their small stock of provisions. Arrived at Goshen, Conn., Mr. Hudson found his family in health, and by the 1st of January, 1800, was in readiness to leave his native state with all its tender associations. "Thus," says he "ends the eventful year 1799, filled with many troubles, out of all of which hath the Lord delivered me."

Having taken an affecting farewell of his friends and acquaintances whom he had left behind, Mr. Hudson set out from Goshen in January, with his family and others. They tarried at Bloomfield, Ontario county, New York, until spring, making preparations for their voyage through the lakes and up the Cuyahoga. They purchased four boats, from one to two tons burden, and repaired thoroughly the wreck of Harmon's boat. Lightly loading them with supplies to the value of about two thousand dollars, they completed every necessary preparation by the 29th of April.

"The next night," said Mr. Hudson, "while my dear wife and six children, with all my men, lay soundly sleeping around me, I could not close my eyes. The reflection that those men and women, with most all that I held dear in life, were now to embark in an expedition in which so many chances appeared against me; and should we survive the dangers in crossing the boisterous lakes, and the distressing sickness usually attendant on new settlements, it was highly probable that we must fall before the tomahawk and scalping-knife. As I knew at that time no considerable settlement had been made but what was established in *blood*, and as I was about to place all those who lay around me on the extreme frontier, and as they would look to me for safety and protection, I almost sunk under the immense weight of responsibility resting on me. Perhaps my feelings on this occasion were a little similar to those of the patriarch, when expecting to meet his hostile brother. But after presenting my case before Israel's God, and committing all to his care, I cheerfully launched out the next morning upon the great deep."

The crews of their boats consisted of Samuel Bishop and his four sons, David, Reuben, Luman and Joseph, Joel Gaylord, Heman Oviatt, Moses Thompson, Allen Gaylord, Stephen Perkins, Joseph and George Darrow, William M'Kinley, and three men from Vermont, by the names of Derrick, Williams and Shefford. The women in the company were the wives of Messrs. Hudson, Bishop and Nobles, with Miss Ruth Gaylord and Miss Ruth Bishop. The six children of Mr. Hudson completed the number.

They had little trouble until they reached the mouth of the Cuyahoga. The wind on that day being rather high, Mr. Hudson, in attempting to enter the river with his boat, missed the channel and struck on a sand-bar. In this very perilous situation, the boat shipped several barrels of water, and himself and all his family must have been drowned had not a mountain wave struck the boat with such violence as to float it over the bar. When up the river, within about two miles of their landing place, they stopped for the night a little north of Northfield, at a locality now known as the Pinery.

A tremendous rain in the night so raised the river by daybreak, that it overflowed the bank whereon they slept, and even their beds were on the point of floating. Every thing was completely drenched, and they were compelled to wait five days ere the subsiding waters would allow them to force their boats against the current. On the sixth day, May the 28th, they reached their landing place, from whence Mr. Hudson, leaving his wife and children, hurried to see the people whom he had left over winter, and whom he found well.

About the time they completed their landing, Elijah Noble arrived with the cattle and Mr. Hudson's horse, which had been driven from Ontario by nearly the same route that the cattle were the preceding year.

Being busy in arranging for them, Mr. Hudson did not take his horse to the river to bring up his family for several days. When he arrived, he found his wife, who had cheerfully submitted to all the inconveniences hitherto experienced, very much discouraged. She and the children suffered severely from the armies of gnats and musketoes which at this season of the year infest the woods. After all the persons belonging to the settlement had collected, thanksgiving was rendered to the God of mercy, who had protected them in perils, preserved their lives and brought them safely to their place of destination. Public worship on the Sabbath was resumed, it having been discontinued during the absence of Mr. Hudson. "I felt," said he, "in some measure the responsibility resting on first settlers, and their obligations to commence in that fear of God which is the beginning of wisdom, and to establish those moral and religious habits on which the temporal and eternal happiness of a people essentially depends."

Mr. David Hudson died March 17th, 1836, aged 75 years, leaving a memory revered, and an example of usefulness well worthy of imitation.

Hudson is 24 miles from Cleveland and 13 northeast of Akron, on the stage road from Cleveland to Pittsburgh. It contains 2 Con-

Western Reserve College.

gregational, 1 Episcopal and 1 Methodist church, 4 stores, 1 newspaper printing office, 2 female seminaries, and about 600 inhabitants. The village is handsomely situated and neatly built, and the tone of society elevated, which arises in a great measure from its being the seat of the Western Reserve College.

The college buildings are of brick, and situated upon a beautiful and spacious green, in an order similar to the edifices of Yale, on which institution this is also modeled, and of which several of its professors are graduates. The annexed view was taken near the observatory, a small structure shown on the extreme right. The other buildings are, commencing with that nearest—south college, middle college, chapel, divinity hall, president's house, athæneum, and a residence of one of the professors, near the road-side, nearly in front of the athenæum.

The Medical College at Cleveland is connected with this institution. By the catalogue of 1846–7, the whole number of professors and instructors in the college was 19; the whole number of students 320, viz.: 14 in the theological department; 216 in the medical do.; 71 undergraduates, and 19 preparatory.

The Rev. Charles B. Storrs, the first president of the Western Reserve College, was the son of the Rev. Richard S. Storrs, of Long Meadow, Mass., and was born in May, 1794. He pursued his literary studies at Princeton, and his theological at Andover, after which he journeyed at the south with the double object of restoring his health and preaching the gospel in its destitute regions. In 1822, he located himself as a preacher of the gospel at Ravenna. In this situation he remained, rapidly advancing in the confidence and esteem of the public, until March 2, 1828, when he was unanimously elected professor of Christian theology in the Western Reserve College, and was inducted into his office the 3d of Dec. following. The institution then was in its infancy. Some 15 or 20 students had been collected under the care and instruction of a tutor, but no permanent officers had been appointed. The government and much of the instruction of the college devolved on him. On the 25th of August, 1830, he was unanimously elected president, and inaugurated on the 9th of February, 1831. In this situation he showed himself worthy of the confidence reposed in him. Under his mild and paternal, yet firm and decisive administration of government, the most perfect discipline prevailed, while all the students loved and venerated him as a father. Under his auspices, together with the aid of competent and faithful professors, the institution arose in public estimation, and increased from a mere handful to nearly one hundred students. For many years he had been laboring under a bad state of health, and on the 26th of June, 1833, he left the institution to travel for a few months for his health. He died on the 15th of September ensuing, at his brother's house in Braintree, Mass. President Storrs was naturally modest and retiring. He possessed a strong and independent mind, and took an expansive view of every subject that occupied his attention. He was a thorough student, and in his method of communicating his thoughts to others, peculiarly happy. Though destitute in the pulpit of the tinsel of rhetoric, few men could chain an intelligent audience in breathless silence, by pure intellectual vigor and forcible illustration of truth, more perfectly than he. Some of his appeals were almost resistless. He exerted a powerful and salutary influence over the church and community in this part of the country, and his death was deeply felt.*

Akron, from the Medina road.

The large and flourishing town of Akron, the county seat, is on the Portage summit of the Ohio canal, at the junction of the Pennsylvania canal, 36 miles from Cleveland and 110 northeast of Columbus. The name of this town is derived from a Greek word signifying an elevation. Akron was laid out in 1825, where South Akron now is. In the fall of the same year, the Irish laborers on the Ohio canal put up about 100 cabins. South Akron grew rapidly for a few years; but in 1832, some buildings were put up half a mile farther north, and business in a short time centered here. In 1827, the Ohio canal was finished from Cleveland to this place. In 1841, Akron was made the county seat of the new county of Summit. The same year the canal connecting Akron with Beaver, Pa., was opened, and a new impetus given to the town by these advantages.

Akron contains 1 Episcopal, 1 Congregational, 1 Baptist, 1 Methodist, 1 Disciples, 1 Universalist, 1 German Lutheran, and 1 Catholic church, 20 mercantile stores, 10 grocery, 4 drug and 2 book stores, 4 woollen factories, 2 blast and 3 small furnaces, 1 carding machine manufactory, 5 flouring mills, 1 insurance company, 1 bank, 2 newspaper printing offices, and a great variety of mechanical establish-

* Abridged from the Hudson Observer of Sept. 28th, 1833.

ments. The mercantile business of this town is heavy and constantly increasing, and immense quantities of wheat are purchased. The water privileges here are good, and manufacturing will eventually be extensively carried on. In 1827, its population was about 600; in 1840, it was 1664, since which it is estimated to have doubled. Two miles south of Akron is Summit lake, a beautiful sheet of water on the summit of the Ohio canal. Part of its waters find their way to the St. Lawrence, and part to the Gulf of Mexico.

A resident of Akron has given us some facts respecting the settlement of the country, and one or two anecdotes, which we annex.

In 1811, Paul Williams, Amos and Minor Spicer came from New London, Conn., and settled in the vicinity of Akron, at which time there was no other white settlement between here and Sandusky. We give an anecdote of Minor Spicer, who is still living at Akron. In the late war, one night just before retiring, he heard some one call in front of his house, and went out and saw a large Indian with two rifles in his hand, and a deer quartered and hung across his horse. Spicer inquired what he wanted. The Indian replied in his own dialect, when the other told him he must speak English, or he would unhorse him. He finally gave them to understand that he wished to stay over night, a request that was reluctantly granted. His rifles were placed in a corner, his venison hung up, and his horse put into a large pig-stye, the only stable attached to the premises.

The Indian cut out a piece of venison for Mrs. Spicer to cook for him, which she did in the usual way, with a liberal quantity of pepper and salt. He drew up to the table and eat but a mouthful or two. The family being ready to retire, he placed his scalping-knife and tomahawk in the corner with his rifles, and stretched himself upon the hearth before the fire. When he supposed the family were asleep, he raised himself slowly from his reclining position and sat upright on the hearth, looking stealthily over his shoulder to see if all was still. He then got upon his feet and stepped lightly across the floor to his implements of death. At this juncture, the feelings of Spicer and his wife may be well imagined, for they were only feigning sleep and were intently watching. The Indian again stood for a moment, to see if he had awakened any one, then slowly drew from its scabbard the glittering scalping-knife. At this moment, Spicer was about putting his hand upon his rifle, which stood by his bed, to shoot the Indian, but concluded to wait further demonstration, which was an entirely different one from what he had anticipated, for the Indian took hold and cut a piece of his venison, weighing about two pounds, and laying it on the live coals until it was warmed through, devoured it and went to sleep. Mrs. Spicer's cooking had not pleased him, being seasoned too high. The day before, he and his father lost themselves in the woods, and after covering his parent, under a log, with his blanket, he had wandered until he saw Spicer's light.

James Brown, or as he was commonly called, "Jim Brown," was one of the early settlers in the north part of the county. He was known throughout the country as the head of a notorious band of counterfeiters. Few men have pursued the business so long without being convicted. Aside from this, he was to a certain extent respected, for he had the externals of a gentleman in his conversation and address, and had many friends. He was a fine looking man, over six feet in height, with a keen, penetrating eye. He even held the office of justice of the peace when last arrested. He had often been tried before, and as often escaped. Once he was sentenced to the penitentiary from Medina, and the sheriff had nearly reached Columbus, when he was overtaken with a writ of error and set at liberty. It is said that large numbers of young men have been drawn into his schemes, from time to time, and thereby found their way to the penitentiary. Many anecdotes are related of him.

He and a brother and one Taylor once supplied themselves with counterfeit paper, and proceeded to New Orleans, where they purchased a ship with it and set sail for China, intending to make large purchases there with counterfeit notes on the United States bank. A discovery, however, was made, and they were apprehended before they had got out of the river, and brought back for trial, but he escaped by turning states' evidence. He escaped so often, that it was said he could not be convicted. However, in 1846, he was taken the last time, tried at Columbus, and sentenced to the penitentiary for ten years. When first arrested, he said, "Well, boys! now the United States have taken hold of me, I may get floored; but I could have worried out a county."

Two miles east of Akron, and on both sides of the Little Cuyahoga, is the village of Middlebury. As early as 1807, a grist mill was built on the site of the town, by Aaron Norton and Joseph Hart, which was of great use to the early settlers for many miles around. The town was laid out in 1818, by Norton & Hart, and soon became the most thriving village in this whole region, until the

Middlebury, from the Tallmadge road.

canal was cut through to Cleveland, when Akron took away most of its trade. It is now improving, has a number of wealthy inhabitants, and the manufacturing capital is increasing. It contains 2 churches, 2 stores, 2 woollen, 3 comb and 1 fire engine factory, 1 machine, 1 carriage shop, and other mechanical establishments. The population is not far from 1000.

This village is in the township of Tallmadge. The first permanent settlement in Tallmadge was made in the fall of 1807, when the Rev. David Bacon, a missionary in the western settlements, assisted by Justin E. Frink, erected a log house on the south line, half a mile west of the centre north and south road. The first settlers in Tallmadge prior to 1812, were:

Dr. A. C. Wright, Joseph Hart, Adam Norton, Charles Chittenden, Jonathan Sprague, Nathaniel Chapman, Titus, his father, Titus and Porter, and others of his sons, William Niel, Joseph Bradford, Ephraim Clark, jr., George Kilbourne, Capt. John Wright, Alpha Wright, Eli Hill, Jotham Blakeley, Jotham Blakelee, Conrad Boosinger, Edmund Strong, John Wright, jr., Stephen Upson, Theron Bradley, Peter Norton, Elizur Wright, Justus Barnes, Shubel H. Lowrey, David, John, Samuel, David, jr., and Lot Preston, Drake Fellows, Samuel M'Coy, Luther Chamberlin, Rial M'Arthur, Justus Bradley, Deacon S., Norman, Hervey, Leander, Cassander, Eleazar and Salmon Sackett, Daniel Beach, John Carruthers, Reuben Upson and Aza Gillett.

The village of Cuyahoga Falls is 4 miles northeast of Akron, on the line of the Pennsylvania canal and on the Cuyahoga river. Manufacturing is already carried on here to a large extent, and the place is perhaps destined to be to the west what Lowell is to the east.

The Cuyahoga has a fall here of more than 200 feet in the distance of 2½ miles, across stratified rocks, which are worn away to nearly this depth in the course of this descent. In the ravine thus formed

Village of Cuyahoga Falls.

are a series of wild and picturesque views, one of which is represented in an engraving on an adjoining page.

The Indians called Cuyahoga Falls "Coppacaw," which signifies "*shedding tears.*" A Mr. O., an early settler in this region, was once so much cheated in a trade with them, that he shed tears, and the Indians ever afterwards called him *Coppacaw.*

The village was laid out in 1837, by Birdseye Booth, grew rapidly, and in 1840 was the rival of Akron for the county seat. It contains 1 Episcopal, 1 Wesleyan Methodist and 1 Presbyterian church, 1 academy, 7 mercantile stores, 1 bank, 1 insurance office, 4 paper, 2 flouring and 1 saw mill, 2 furnaces, 2 tanneries, 1 fork and scythe, and 1 starch factory, 4 warehouses, and about 1200 inhabitants.

The view was taken from near the Cleveland road, above the village, at Stow's quarry. On the right are seen the Methodist and Episcopal churches, in the centre the American House, and on the left the Cuyahoga river, the lyceum and Presbyterian church.

The township of Stow in this county, was named from Joshua Stow, Esq., of Middlesex county, Conn. He was a member of the first party of surveyors of the Western Reserve, who landed at Conneaut, July 4th, 1796. Augustus Porter, Esq., the principal surveyor, in his history of the survey, in the Barr manuscripts, gives the following anecdote of Mr. Stow.

In making the traverse of the lake shore, Mr. Stow acted as flag-man; he of course was always in advance of the party: rattlesnakes were plenty, and he coming first upon those in our track, killed them. I had mentioned to him a circumstance that happened to me in 1789: being with two or three other persons three days in the wood without food, we had killed a rattlesnake, dressed and cooked it, and whether from the savory quality of the flesh or the particular state of our stomachs, I could not say which, had eaten it with a high relish. Mr. Stow was a healthy, active man, fond of wood-life, and determined to adopt all its practices, even to the eating of snakes; and during almost any day while on the lake shore, he killed and swung over his shoulders and around his body from two to six or eight large rattlesnakes, and at night a part were dressed, cooked and eaten by the party with a good relish, probably increased by the circumstance of their being *fresh*, while all our other meat was salt.

Twinsburg, a pleasant village, 17 miles northerly from Akron, on the Cleveland road, contains 4 churches and about 40 dwellings. The literary institute situated here, under the charge of the Rev. Samuel Bissell, is a flourishing institution, having about 150 pupils. There are other small villages in the county, some of which are thriving places. Among them are Clinton, Tallmadge Centre, Mogadore, Richfield, Ellis Corners and Monroe Falls.

TRUMBULL.

Trumbull, named from two successive governors of Connecticut, was formed in 1800, and comprised within its original limits the whole of the Connecticut Western Reserve. This is a well cultivated and wealthy county. The surface is mostly level, and the soil loamy or sandy. In the northern part is excellent coal. The principal products are wheat, corn, oats, grass, wool, butter, cheese and potatoes. Mahoning has recently been formed from it and Columbiana. The following is a list of its townships in 1840, (excepting those now forming a part of Mahoning,) with their population at that time.

Bazetta,	1035	Gustavus,	1195	Mecca,	684
Bloomfield,	554	Hartford,	1121	Mesopotamia,	832
Braceville,	880	Howland,	1035	Newton,	1456
Bristol,	802	Hubbard,	1242	Southington,	857
Brookfield,	1301	Johnston,	889	Vernon,	788
Champion,	541	Kinsman,	954	Vienna,	969
Farmington,	1162	Liberty,	1225	Warren,	1996
Fowler,	931	Lordstown,	1167	Wethersfield,	1447
Greene,	647				

The population of these townships, including the whole of the present Trumbull county, in 1840, was 25,700, or 43 inhabitants to the square mile. The population of Trumbull in 1820, was 15,546; in 1830, 26,200, and in 1840, 38,070.

Previous to the settlement of this county, and indeed before the survey of the eastern part of the Western Reserve in 1796, salt was manufactured by the whites, at what is frequently spoken of as the "old salt works," which were situated, we are informed, in what is now the township of Wethersfield, on or near the Mahoning. They were known to the whites as early as 1755, and are indicated on Evans' map published that year. Augustus Porter, Esq., who had charge of the first surveying party of the Reserve, thus alludes to these works in the Barr mss., in connection with the history of his survey.

These works were said to have been established and occupied by Gen. Parsons, of Connecticut, by permission of the governor of that state. At this place we found a small piece of open ground, say 2 or 3 acres, and a plank vat of 16 or 18 feet square, and 4 or 5 feet deep, set in the ground, which was full of water, and kettles for boiling salt; the number we could not ascertain, but the vat seemed to be full of them. An Indian and a squaw were boiling water for salt, but from appearances, with poor success.

Amzi Atwater, Esq., now of Portage county, who was one of the first surveying party of the Reserve, in a communication to us, says:

It was understood that Gen. Parsons had some kind of a grant from the state of Connecticut, and came on there and commenced making salt, and was drowned on his return at Beaver Falls. On the first map made of the Reserve by Mr. Seth Pease, in 1798, a tract was marked off and designated as "the salt spring tract." I have understood that the heirs of Gen. Parsons advanced some claims to that tract, but I believe without success. At an early part of the settlement, considerable exertions were made by Reuben Harmon, Esq., to establish salt works at that place, but the water was too weak to make it profitable.

Public Square, Warren.

Warren, the county seat, is on the Mahoning river and Ohio and Penn. canal, 161 miles NE. of Columbus and 77 from Pittsburgh. It is a well-built and very pleasant town, through which beautifully winds the Mahoning. In the centre is a handsome public square, on which stands the court house. In June, 1846, this village was visited by a destructive fire, which destroyed a large number of buildings facing one side of the public square, since built up with beautiful stores. Warren was laid out in 1801, by Ephraim Quinby, Esq., and named from Moses Warren, of Lyme. The town plat is one mile square, with streets crossing at right angles. Warren contains 1 Presbyterian, 1 Episcopal, 1 Baptist, 1 Methodist and 1 Disciple's church, about 20 mercantile stores, 3 newspaper printing offices, 2 flour mills, 1 bank, 1 woollen factory and a variety of mechanical establishments; in 1840, its population was 1066; it is now estimated at 1600.

In a grave-yard on the river's bank lie the remains of the Hon. Zephaniah Swift, author of Swift's Digest, and once chief justice of the State of Connecticut. He died here September 27th, 1823, at the age of 64 years, while on a visit to a son and daughter.

We annex some facts connected with the settlement of this place and vicinity, from the narrative of Cornelius Feather, in the MSS. of the Ashtabula Historical Society.

The plat of Warren in September, 1800, contained but two log cabins, one of which was occupied by Capt. Ephraim Quinby, who was proprietor of the town and afterwards judge of the court. He built his cabin in 1799. The other was occupied by Wm. Fenton, who built his in 1798. On the 27th of this month, Cornelius Feather and Davison Fenton arrived from Washington county, Pa. At this time, Quinby's cabin consisted of three apartments, a kitchen, bed-room and jail, although but one prisoner was ever confined in it, viz: Perger Shehigh, for threatening the life of Judge Young, of Youngstown.

The whole settlements of whites within and about the settlement of Warren, consisted of 16 settlers, viz: Henry and John Lane, Benj. Davison, Esq., Meshach Case, Capt. John Adgate, Capt. John Leavitt, William Crooks and Phineas Leffingwell, Henry Lane, jr., Charles Daily, Edward Jones, George Loveless and Wm. Tucker, who had been a spy five years under Capt. Brady.

At this time, rattlesnakes abounded in some places. And there was one adventure with them worth recording, which took place in Braceville township.

A Mr. Oviatt was informed that a considerable number of huge rattlesnakes were scattered over a certain tract of wilderness. The old man asked whether there was a ledge of rocks in the vicinity, which way the declivity inclined, and if any spring issued out of the ledge. Being answered in the affirmative, the old man rejoined, "we will go about the last of May and have some sport." Accordingly they proceeded through the woods well armed with cudgels. Arrived at the battle-ground, they cautiously ascended the hill, step by step, in a solid column. Suddenly the enemy gave the alarm, and the men found themselves completely surrounded by hosts of rattlesnakes of enormous size, and a huge squadron of black snakes. No time was lost. At the signal of the rattling of the snakes, the action commenced, and hot and furious was the fight. In short, the snakes beat a retreat up the hill, our men cudgelling with all their might. When arrived at the top of the ledge, they found the ground and rocks in places almost covered with snakes retreating into their dens. Afterwards the slain were collected into heaps, and found to amount 486, a good portion of which were larger than a man's leg below the calf, and over 5 feet in length.

The news of this den of venomous serpents being spread, it was agreed that the narrator and two more young men in Warren, and three in Braceville, should make war upon it, until the snakes should be principally destroyed, which was actually accomplished.

One circumstance I should relate in regard to snake-hunting. Having procured an instrument like a very long chisel, with a handle 8 or 9 feet long, I proceeded to the ledge alone, placed myself on the body of a butternut tree, lying slanting over a broad crevice in the rocks, 7 or 8 feet deep, the bottom of which was literally covered with the yellow and black serpents. I held my weapon poised in my right hand, ready to give the deadly blow, my left hold of a small branch to keep my balance, when both my feet slipped, and I came within a hairs' breadth of plunging headlong into the den. Nothing but the small limb saved me from a most terrible death, as I could not have gotten out, had there been no snakes, the rocks on all sides being nearly perpendicular. It was a merciful and providential escape.

In August, 1800, a serious affair occurred with the Indians, which spread a gloom over the peaceful prospects of the new and scattered settlements of the whites, the history of which we derive from the above-mentioned source.

Joseph M'Mahon, who lived near the Indian settlement at the Salt Springs, and whose family had suffered considerable abuse at different times from the Indians in his absence, was at work with one Richard Story, on an old Indian plantation, near Warren. On Friday of this week, during his absence, the Indians coming down the creek to have a drunken frolic, called in at M'Mahon's and abused the family, and finally Capt. George, their chief, struck one of the children a severe blow with the tomahawk, and the Indians threatened to kill the whole family. Mrs. M'Mahon, although terribly alarmed, was unable to get word to her husband before noon the next day.

M'Mahon and Story at first resolved to go immediately to the Indian camp and kill the whole tribe, but on a little reflection, they desisted from this rash purpose, and concluded to go to Warren, and consult with Capt. Ephraim Quinby, as he was a mild, judicious man.

By the advice of Quinby, all the persons capable of bearing arms were mustered on Sunday morning, consisting of 14 men and 2 boys, under the command of Lieut. John Lane, who proceeded towards the Indian camp, determined to make war or peace as circumstances dictated.

When within half a mile of the camp, Quinby proposed a halt, and as he was well acquainted with most of the Indians, they having dealt frequently at his tavern, it was resolved that he should proceed alone to the camp, and inquire into the cause of their outrageous conduct, and ascertain whether they were for peace or war. Quinby started alone, leaving the rest behind, and giving direction to Lane that if he did not return in half an hour, he might expect that the savages had killed him, and that he should then march his company and engage in battle. Quinby not returning at the appointed time, they marched rapidly to the camp. On emerging from the woods they discovered Quinby in close conversation with Capt. George. He informed his party that they had threatened to kill M'Mahon and his family, and Story and his family, for it seems the latter had inflicted chastisement on the Indians for stealing his liquor, particularly on one ugly-looking, ill-tempered fellow, named Spotted John, from having his face spotted all over with hair moles. Capt. George had also declared, if the whites had come down the Indians were ready to fight them.

The whites marched directly up to the camp, M'Mahon first and Story next to him. The chief, Capt. George, snatched his tomahawk which was sticking in a tree, and flourishing it in the air, walked up to M'Mahon, saying, "*if you kill me, I will lie here—if I kill you, you shall lie there!*" and then ordered his men to *prime* and *tree!* Instantly as the tomahawk was about to give the deadly blow, M'Mahon sprang back, raised his gun already cocked, pulled the trigger, and Capt. George fell dead. Story took for his mark the ugly savage, Spotted John, who was at that moment placing his family behind a tree, and shot him dead, the same ball passing through his squaw's neck, and the shoulders of his oldest pappoos, a girl of about thirteen.

Hereupon the Indians fled with horrid yells; the whites hotly pursued for some distance, firing as fast as possible, yet without effect, while the women and children screamed and screeched piteously. The party then gave up the pursuit, returned and buried the dead Indians, and proceeded to Warren to consult for their safety.

It being ascertained that the Indians had taken the route to Sandusky, on Monday morning James Hillman was sent through the wilderness to overtake and treat with them. He came up with them on Wednesday, and cautiously advanced, they being at first suspicious of him. But making known his mission, he offered them first $100, then $200, and so on, to $500, if they would treat with him on just terms, return to their homes and bury the hatchet. But to all his overtures they answered, "No! No! No! we will go to Sandusky and hold a council with the chiefs there." Hillman replied, "you will hold a council there, light the war torch, rally all the warriors throughout the forests, and with savage barbarity, come and attempt a general massacre of all your friends, the whites, throughout the N. W. Territory." They rejoined, "that they would lay the case before the council, and within fourteen days, four or five of their number should return with instructions, on what terms peace could be restored."*

Hillman returned, and all the white settlers from Youngstown and the surrounding settlements, garrisoned at Quinby's house in Warren, constructed port-holes through the logs and kept guard night and day.

On the fourth or fifth day after the people garrisoned, a circumstance struck them with terror. John Lane went out into the woods a little distance, one cloudy day, and missing his way gave some alarm. In the evening, a man's voice known to be his, was heard several times, and in the same direction twelve or fourteen successive reports of a gun. It was judged that the Indians had returned, caught Lane, confined him and compelled him to halloo, with threats of death if he did not, under the hope of enticing the whites into an ambush, and massacreing them.

In the morning, as these noises continued, Wm. Crooks, a resolute man, went out cautiously to the spot whence they proceeded, and found that Lane had dislocated his ancle in making a misstep, and could not get into the fort without assistance.

The little party continued to keep guard until the fourteenth day, when exactly according to contract, four or five Indians returned with proposals of peace, which were, that M'Mahon and Story should be taken to Sandusky, tried by Indian laws, and if guilty, punished by them. This they were told could not be done, as M'Mahon was already a prisoner under the laws of the whites, in the jail at Pittsburgh, and Story had fled out of the country.

M'Mahon was brought to Youngstown and tried with prudence, General St. Clair chief judge. The only testimony that could be received of all those present at the tragedy,

---

* For a more full and perfectly reliable statement of Hillman's agency in this affair, see his memoir, p. 338.

was a boy who took no part in the affair, who stood close by Capt. George when he said, "If you kill me, I'll lie here; if I kill you, you will lie there." A young married woman who had been a prisoner among the Indians, was brought to testify as she understood the language. She affirmed that the words signified, that if M'Mahon should kill Captain George, the Indians should not seek restitution; nor should the whites if M'Mahon were killed. In regard to the death of Spotted John, the Indians finally claimed nothing, as he was an ugly fellow, belonging to no tribe whatever.

The Indians again took up their old abode, re-buried the bodies of their slain down the river two or three miles, drove down a stake at the head of each grave, hung a new pair of buckskin breeches on each stake, saying and expecting that "at the end of thirty days they would rise, go to the North Sea, and hunt and kill the *white bear*." An old pious Indian said, "No! they will not rise at the end of thirty days. When God comes at the last day, and calls all the world to rise and come to judgment, *then* they will rise."

The Indians nightly carried good supplies of cooked venison to the graves, which were evidently devoured. A white settler's old slut, with a litter of six or eight pups, nightly visited the savory meats, as they throve most wonderfully during the thirty days.

The Hon. Joshua R. Giddings in a note to the above, says:

M'Mahon served afterwards in the war of 1812, and in the northwestern army under Gen. Harrison. In the battle with the Indians on the Peninsula, north of Sandusky bay, on the 29th of September of that year, he was wounded in the side. After his recovery, he was discharged in November and started for home. He left Camp Avery, in Huron county, and took the path to the old Portage. Being alone and happening to meet a party of Indians, he fell a victim to their hostility.

The Rev. Joseph Badger, *the first missionary on the Reserve*, resided for eight years at Gustavus, in this county. He was born at Wilbraham, Mass., in 1757. He served as a soldier in the revolutionary war, graduated at Yale College in 1785, in 1787 was ordained as minister over a church in Blandford, Mass., where he remained for 14 years.

In 1800, such an opportunity for usefulness offered as he had long wished for. The missionary societies of the eastern states, had for many years been desirous of sending missionaries to the Indians which then dwelt in the northern portion of Ohio.

At their instance, Mr. Badger made a visit to this country during that year, and was so well satisfied with the opportunity of usefulness, which his residence among the Wyandots and other tribes would afford, that he returned after his family, and since that time his labors have been principally divided between the Western Reserve, and the country bordering on the Sandusky and Maumee rivers. Among his papers, the writer finds certificates of his appointment to the several missionary stations on the Reserve and at Lower Sandusky, as also commissions of the post-master's appointment, for the several places where he has from time to time resided. Mr. B's labors among the scattered inhabitants on the Reserve, and the Indians, were arduous and interesting. Many incidents common to frontier life are recorded in his journals. His duties as a missionary were all faithfully discharged, and he saw this portion of the west grow up under his own eye and teaching.

In 1812, he was appointed chaplain to the army by Gov. Meigs. He was at Fort Meigs during the seige of 1813—and through the war was attached to Gen. Harrison's command. He removed from Trumbull county in 1835, to Plain township, Wood county.

Mr. Badger was a man of energy, perseverance and fine intellectual endowments. His naturally strong and brilliant mind retained all its power, until within the last three years of his life. He was a faithful and devoted christain. He ardently loved his fellow men—his God he loved supremely. Few men have ever lived, who have given such an unequivocal proof of christian meekness and submission—few whose labors have more highly adorned the great and responsible profession of the ministry. Full of years, and of honors, and possessing the paternal affection of a people, who have been long accustomed to regard him as a father, he has at length gone to his final account.* He died in 1846, aged 89.

Newton Falls is 9 miles westerly from Warren, on the Ohio and Pennsylvania canal, in the forks of the east and west branches of the Mahoning, which unite just below the village. This flourishing

* From the Perrysburg Miami.

town has sprung into existence within the last 12 years; it was laid out by Thomas D. Webb, Esq., and Dr. H. A. Dubois. The water power is good; it is an important point of shipment on the canal, and its inhabitants are enterprising. It contains 1 Congregational, 1 Methodist, 1 Baptist and 1 Disciples church, 5 mercantile stores, 3 forwarding houses, 1 woollen factory, 1 paper mill, and about 900 inhabitants.

Niles, on the Mahoning river and on the canal, 5 miles southerly from Warren, contains 3 churches, 3 stores, 1 blast furnace, rolling mill and nail factory, 1 forge and grist mill, and about 300 inhabitants. There is some water power here. In the vicinity are large quantities of excellent iron ore and coal. In Braceville township is a Fourierite association, said to be in a properous condition.

TUSCARAWAS.

TUSCARAWAS was formed from Muskingum, Feb. 15th, 1808. The name is that of an Indian tribe, and in one of their dialects, signifies "*open mouth.*" This is a fertile, well-cultivated county, partly level and partly rolling and hilly. Iron ore and coal abound. It was first permanently settled about the year 1803, by emigrants from western Virginia and Pennsylvania, many of whom were of German origin. The principal productions are wheat, oats, corn and potatoes. The following is a list of its townships in 1840, with their population.

Bucks,	1547	Mill,	1225	Union,	945
Clay,	864	Oxford,	826	Warren,	1173
Dover,	2247	Perry,	1381	Warwick,	864
Fairfield,	866	Rush,	1293	Washington,	978
Goshen,	1885	Salem,	1121	Wayne,	2142
Jefferson,	992	Sandy,	1445	York,	865
Lawrence,	1523	Sugar Creek,	1450		

The population of Tuscarawas, in 1820, was 8328; in 1830, 14,298; and in 1840, 25,632, or 39 inhabitants to the square mile.

Several years previous to the settlement of Ohio, the Moravians had a missionary establishment in the present limits of this county, which was for a time broken up by the cruel massacre of ninety-six of the Indians at Gnadenhutten, March 8th, 1782. The history of the Moravian mission we annex in a communication from James Patrick, Esq., of New Philadelphia.

The first white inhabitants of Tuscarawas county, were the Moravian missionaries and their families. The Rev. Frederick Post and Rev. John Heckewelder had penetrated thus far into the wilderness previous to the commencement of the revolutionary war. Their first visits west of the Ohio date as early as the years 1761 and '62. Other missionary auxiliaries were sent out by that society, for the purpose of propagating the Christian religion among the Indians. Among these was the Rev. David Zeisberger, a man whose devotion to the cause was attested by the hardships he endured and the dangers he encountered.

Had the same pacific policy which governed the society of Friends in their first settlement of eastern Pennsylvania, been adopted by the white settlers of the west, the efforts of the Moravian missionaries in Ohio would have been more successful. But our western pioneers were not, either by profession or practice, friends of peace. They had an instinctive hatred to the aborigines, and were only deterred, by their inability, from exterminating the race. Perhaps the acts of cruelty practiced by certain Indian tribes on prisoners taken in previous contests with the whites, might have aided to produce this feeling on the part of the latter. Be that as it may, the effects of this deep-rooted prejudice greatly retarded the efforts of the missionaries.

They had three stations on the river Tuscarawas, or rather three Indian villages, viz.: Shoenbrun, Gnadenhutten and Salem. The site of the first is about two miles south of New Philadelphia; seven miles farther south was Gnadenhutten, in the immediate vicinity of the present village of that name; and about five miles below that was Salem, a short distance from the village of Port Washington. The first and last mentioned were on the west side of the Tuscarawas, now near the margin of the Ohio canal. Gnadenhutten is on the east side of the river. It was here that a massacre took place on the 8th of March, 1782, which, for cool barbarity, is perhaps unequalled in the history of the Indian wars.

The Moravian villages on the Tuscarawas were situated about mid-way between the white settlements near the Ohio, and some warlike tribes of Wyandots and Delawares on the Sandusky. These latter were chiefly in the service of England, or at least opposed to the colonists, with whom she was then at war. There was a British station at Detroit, and an American one at Fort Pitt, (Pittsburgh,) which were regarded as the nucleus of western operations by each of the contending parties. The Moravian villages of friendly Indians on the Tuscarawas were situated, as the saying is, between two fires. As Christian converts and friends of peace, both policy and inclination led them to adopt neutral grounds. With much difficulty they sustained this position, partially unmolested, until the autumn of 1781. In the month of August, in that year, an English officer named Elliott, from Detroit, attended by two Delaware chiefs, Pimoacan and Pipe, with three hundred warriors, visited Gnadenhutten. They urged the necessity of the speedy removal of the Christian Indians further west, as a measure of safety. Seeing the latter were not inclined to take their advice, they resorted to threats, and in some instances to violence. They at last succeeded in their object. The Christian Indians were forced to leave their crops of corn, potatoes and garden vegetables, and remove, with their unwelcome visitors, to the country bordering on the Sandusky. The missionaries were taken prisoners to Detroit. After suffering severely from hunger and cold during the winter, a portion of the Indians were permitted to return to their settlements on the Tuscarawas, for the purpose of gathering in the corn left on the stalk the preceding fall.

About one hundred and fifty Moravian Indians, including women and children, arrived on the Tuscarawas in the latter part of February, and divided into three parties, so as to work at the three towns in the corn-fields. Satisfied that they had escaped from the thraldom of their less civilized brethren west, they little expected that a storm was gathering among the white settlers east, which was to burst over their peaceful habitations with such direful consequences.

Several depredations had been committed by hostile Indians, about this time, on the frontier inhabitants of western Pennsylvania and Virginia, who determined to retaliate. A company of one hundred men was raised and placed under the command of Col. Williamson, as a corps of volunteer militia. They set out for the Moravian towns on the Tuscarawas, and arrived within a mile of Gnadenhutten on the night of the 5th of March. On the morning of the 6th, finding the Indians were employed in their corn-field, on the west side of the river, sixteen of Williamson's men crossed, two at a time, over in a large sap-trough, or vessel used for retaining sugar-water, taking their rifles with them. The remainder went into the village, where they found a man and a woman, both of whom they killed. The sixteen on the west side, on approaching the Indians in the field, found them more numerous than they expected. They had their arms with them, which were usual on such occasions, both for purposes of protection and for killing game. The whites accosted them kindly, told them they had come to take them to a place where they would be in future protected, and advised them to quit work, and return with them to the neighborhood of Fort Pitt. Some of the Indians had been taken to that place in the preceding year, had been well treated by the American governor of the fort, and been dismissed with tokens of warm friendship. Under these circumstances, it is not surprising that the unsuspecting Moravian Indians readily surrendered their arms, and at once consented to be controlled by the advice of Colonel Williamson and his men. An Indian messenger was dispatched to Salem, to apprize the brethren there of the new arrangement, and both companies then returned to Gnadenhutten. On reaching the village, a number of mounted militia started for the Salem settlement, but e'er they reached it, found that the Moravian

Indians at that place had already left their corn-fields, by the advice of the messenger, and were on the road to join their brethren at Gnadenhutten. Measures had been adopted by the militia to secure the Indians whom they had at first decoyed into their power. They were bound, confined in two houses, and well guarded. On the arrival of the Indians from Salem, (their arms having been previously secured without suspicion of any hostile intention,) they were also fettered, and divided between the two prison-houses, the males in one, the females in the other. The number thus confined in both, including men, women and children, have been estimated from ninety to ninety-six.

A council was then held to determine how the Moravian Indians should be disposed of. This self-constituted military court embraced both officers and privates. The late Dr. Dodridge, in his published notes on Indian wars, &c., says: "Colonel Williamson put the question, whether the Moravian Indians should be taken prisoners to Fort Pitt, or *put to death?*" requesting those who were in favor of saving their lives to step out and form a second rank. Only eighteen out of the whole number stepped forth as advocates of mercy. In these, the feelings of humanity were not extinct. In the majority, which was large, no sympathy was manifested. They resolved to *murder* (for no other word can express the act) the whole of the Christian Indians in their custody. Among these were several who had contributed to aid the missionaries in the work of conversion and civilization—two of whom emigrated from New Jersey after the death of their spiritual pastor, the Rev. David Brainard. One woman, who could speak good English, knelt before the commander and begged his protection. Her supplication was unavailing. They were ordered to prepare for death. But the warning had been anticipated. Their firm belief in their new creed was shown forth in the sad hour of their tribulation, by religious exercises of preparation. The orisons of these devoted people were already ascending the throne of the Most High! —the sound of the Christian's hymn and the Christian's prayer found an echo in the surrounding woods, but no responsive feeling in the bosoms of their executioners. With gun, and spear, and tomahawk, and scalping-knife, the work of death progressed in these slaughter-houses, till not a sigh or moan was heard to proclaim the existence of human life within—all, save two—two Indian boys escaped, as if by a miracle, to be witnesses in after times of the savage cruelty of the white man towards their unfortunate race.

Thus were upwards of ninety human beings hurried to an untimely grave by those who should have been their legitimate protectors. After committing the barbarous act, Williamson and his men set fire to the houses containing the dead, and then marched off for Shoenbrun, the upper Indian town. But here the news of their atrocious deeds had preceded them. The inhabitants had all fled, and with them fled for a time the hopes of the missionaries to establish a settlement of Christian Indians on the Tuscarawas. The fruits of ten years' labor in the cause of civilization, was apparently lost.

The hospitable and friendly character of the Moravian Indians, had extended beyond their white brethren on the Ohio. The American people looked upon the act of Williamson and his men as an outrage on humanity. The American Congress felt the influence of public sympathy for their fate, and on the 3d of September, 1788, passed an ordinance for the encouragement of the Moravian missionaries in the work of civilizing the Indians. A remnant of the scattered flock was brought back, and two friendly chiefs and their followers became the recipients of public favor. The names of these chiefs were Killbuck and White Eyes. Two sons of the former, after having assumed the name of Henry, out of respect to the celebrated Patrick Henry, of Virginia, were taken to Princeton College to be educated. White Eyes was shot by a lad, some years afterwards, on the waters of Yellow creek, Columbiana county.

Three tracts of land, containing four thousand acres each, was appropriated by congress to the Moravian society, or rather to the society for propagating the gospel among the heathen, which is nearly synonymous. These tracts embrace the three Indian towns already described, and by the provisions of the patent, which was issued 1798, the society was constituted trustees for the Christian Indians thereon settled. Extraordinary efforts were now made by the society in the good work of civilization. Considerable sums of money were expended in making roads, erecting temporary mills, and constructing houses. The Indians were collected near the site of the upper town, Shoenbrun, which had been burned at the time of the Williamson expedition, and a new village, called Goshen, erected for their habitations. It was here, while engaged in the laudable work of educating the Indian in the arts of civilized life, and inculcating the principles of Christian morality, that two of the missionaries, Edwards and Zeisberger, terminated their earthly pilgrimage. Their graves are yet to be seen, with plain tombstones, in the Goshen burying-ground, three miles south of New Philadelphia.

The habits and character of the Indians changed for the worse, in proportion as the whites settled in their neighborhood. If the extension of the white settlements west tended to improve the country, it had a disastrous effect upon the poor Indian. In addition to the contempt in which they were held by the whites, the war of 1812 revived former prejudices. An occasional intercourse with the Sandusky Indians had been kept up by some of those at Goshen. A portion of the former were supposed to be hostile to the Americans, and the murder of some whites on the Mohiccan, near Richland, by unknown Indians, tended to confirm the suspicion.

The Indian settlement remained under the care of Rev. Abram Luckenbach, until the year 1823. It was found impossible to preserve their morals free from contamination. Their intercourse with the white population in the neighborhood, was gradually sinking them into deeper degradation. Though the legislature of Ohio passed an act prohibiting the sale of spirituous liquors to Indians, under a heavy penalty, yet the law was either evaded or disregarded. Drunken Indians were occasionally seen at the county seat, or at their village at Goshen. Though a large portion of the lands appropriated for their benefit had been leased out, the society derived very little profit from the tenants. The entire expenses of the Moravian mission, and not unfrequently the support of sick, infirm or destitute Indians devolved on their spiritual guardians. Upon representation of these facts, congress was induced to adopt such measures as would tend to the removal of the Indians, and enable the society to divest itself of the trusteeship in the land.

On the 4th of August, 1823, an agreement or treaty was entered into at Gnadenhutten, between Lewis Cass, then governor of Michigan, on the part of the United States, and Lewis de Schweinitz, on the part of the society, as a preliminary step towards the retrocession of the land to the government. By this agreement, the members of the society relinquished their right as trustees, conditioned that the United States would pay $6,654, being but a moiety of the money they had expended. The agreement could not be legal without the written consent of the Indians, for whose benefit the land had been donated. These embraced the remainder of the Christian Indians formerly settled on the land, "including Killbuck and his descendants, and the nephews and descendants of the late Captain White Eyes, Delaware chiefs." The Goshen Indians, as they were now called, repaired to Detroit, for the purpose of completing the contract. On the 8th of November, they signed a treaty with Governor Cass, in which they relinquished their right to the twelve thousand acres of land in Tuscarawas county, for twenty-four thousand acres in one of the territories, to be designated by the United States, together with an annuity of $400. The latter stipulation was clogged with a proviso, which rendered its fulfilment uncertain. The Indians never returned. The principal part of them took up their residence at a Moravian missionary station on the river Thames, in Canada. By an act of congress, passed May 26, 1824, their former inheritance, comprising the Shoenbrun, Gnadenhutten and Salem tracts, were surveyed into farm lots and sold.* In the following year the Ohio canal was located, and now passes close to the site of the three ancient Indian villages. The population of the county rapidly increased, and their character and its aspect have consequently changed. A few years more, and the scenes and actors here described will be forgotten, unless preserved by that art which is preservative of the histories of nations and of men. Goshen, the last abiding place of the Christian Indians, on the Tuscarawas, is now occupied and cultivated by a German farmer. A high hill which overlooked their village, and which is yet covered with trees, under whose shade its semi-civilized inhabitants perhaps once "stretched their listless length," is now being worked in the centre as a coal mine. The twang of the bow-string, or the whoop of the young Indian, is succeeded by the dull, crashing sound of the coal-car, as it drops its burden into the canal boat. Yet there is one spot here still sacred to the memory of its former occupants. As you descend the south side of the hill, on the Zanesville road, a small brook runs at its base, bordered on the opposite side by a high bank. On ascending the bank, a few rods to the right, is a small enclosed graveyard, overgrown with low trees or brush-wood. Here lie the remains of several Indians, with two of their spiritual pastors, (Edwards and Zeisberger.) The grave of the latter is partly covered with a small marble slab, on which is the following inscription.

> DAVID ZEISBERGER,
> who was born 11th April, 1721, in Moravia, and departed this life 7th Nov., 1808, aged 87 years, 7 months and 6 days. This faithful servant of the Lord labored among the Moravian Indians, as a missionary, during the last sixty years of his life.

* The writer of this article was appointed agent of the United States for that purpose.

Some friendly hand, perhaps a relative, placed the stone on the grave, many years after the decease of him who rests beneath it.

Gnadenhutten is still a small village, containing 120 souls, chiefly Moravians, who have a neat church and parsonage-house. About a hundred yards east of the town is the site of the ancient Indian village, with the stone foundations of their huts, and marks of the conflagration that consumed the bodies of the slain in 1782. The notice which has been taken of this tragical affair in different publications, has given a mournful celebrity to the spot where it transpired. The intelligent traveller often stops on his journey to pay a visit to the graves of the Indian martyrs, who fell victims to that love of peace which is the genuine attribute of Christianity. From the appearance of the foundations, the village must have been formed of one street. Here and there, may be excavated, burnt corn and other relics of the fire. Apple trees, planted by the missionaries, are yet standing, surrounded by rough under-brush. A row of Lombardy poplars were planted for ornament, one of which yet towers aloft undecayed by time, a natural monument to the memory of those who are interred beneath its shade. But another monument, more suitable to the place and the event to be commemorated, will, it is hoped, be erected at no distant day. Some eight or ten individuals of the town and neighborhood, mostly farmers and mechanics, met on the 7th of October, 1843, and organized a society for the purpose of enclosing the area around the place where the bodies of the Christian Indians are buried, and erecting a suitable monument to their memory. The two prominent officers selected were Rev. Sylvester Walle, resident Moravian minister, president, and Lewis Peter, treasurer. The first and second articles of the constitution declare the intention of the "*Gnadenhutten Monument Society*" to be—"to make judicious and suitable improvements upon the plat of the old Indian village, and to erect on that spot an appropriate monument, commemorating the death of 96 Christian Indians, who were murdered there on the 8th day of March, A. D. 1782." It is further provided, that any person paying annually the sum of one dollar, shall be considered a member; if he pay the sum of ten dollars, or add to his one dollar payment a sum to make it equal to that amount, he is considered a member for life. Owing to the circumscribed means of the members, and the comparative obscurity of the village, the fund has yet only reached seventy dollars, whereas five hundred would be required to erect any thing like a suitable monument. Whether it will be ultimately completed, must depend on the liberality of the public. Sixty-five years have elapsed since the Moravian Indians paid the forfeit of their lives for adhering to the peaceable injunctions of their religion. Shall the disciples of Zeisberger, the philanthropist, the scholar, and the Christian—he who labored more than half a century to reclaim the wild man of the forest from barbarism, and shed on his path the light of civilization—shall no monument perpetuate the benevolent deeds of the missionary—no inscription proclaim the pious fidelity of his converts? If the reader feels a sympathy for the cause in which each became a sacrifice, he has now the power to contribute his mite in transmitting the memory of their virtues to posterity.

Miss Mary Heckewelder, who was living at Bethlehem, in Pennsylvania, as late as 1843, is generally said to have been the first white child born in Ohio. She was the daughter of the noted Moravian missionary of that name, and was born in Salem, one of the Moravian Indian towns on the Tuscarawas, in this county, April 16th, 1781.

Mr. Dinsmore, a planter of Boone county, Ky., orally informed us that in the year 1835, when residing in the parish of Terre Bonne, La., he became acquainted with a planter named Millehomme, who informed him that he was born in the forest, on the head waters of the Miami, on or near the Loramie Portage, about the year 1774. His parents were Canadian French, then on their route to Louisiana.

Half a mile below Bolivar are the remains of Fort Laurens, erected in the war of the revolution, and named from the president of the revolution congress. It was the scene of border warfare and bloodshed. The canal passes through its earthen walls. The parapet walls are now a few feet in height, and were once crowned with pickets made of the split trunks of trees. The walls enclose about an acre of land, and stand on the west bank of the Tuscarawas. Dr. S. P. Hildreth gives the annexed history of this work, in Silliman's Journal.

Fort Laurens was erected in the fall of the year 1778, by a detachment of 1000 men from Fort Pitt, under the command of General M'Intosh. After its completion, a garrison of 150 men was placed in it, and left in the charge of Col. John Gibson, while the rest of the army returned to Fort Pitt. It was established at this early day in the country of the Indians, seventy miles west of Fort M'Intosh, with an expectation that it would act as a salutary check on their incursions into the white settlements south of the Ohio river. The usual approach to it from Fort M'Intosh, the nearest military station, was from the mouth Yellow creek, and down the Sandy, which latter stream heads with the former, and puts of into the Tuscarawas just above the fort. So unexpected and rapid were the movements of General M'Intosh, that the Indians were not aware of his presence in their country, until the fort was completed. Early in January, 1779, the Indians mustered their warriors with such secrecy, that the fort was invested before the garrison had notice of their approach. From the manuscript notes of Henry Jolly, Esq., who was an actor in this, as well as in many other scenes on the frontier, I have copied the following historical facts.

"When the main army left the fort to return to Fort Pitt, Captain Clark remained behind with a small detachment of United States troops, for the purpose of marching in the invalids and artificers who had tarried to finish the fort, or were too unwell to march with the main army. He endeavored to take the advantage of very cold weather, and had marched three or four miles, (for I travelled over the ground three or four times soon after,) when he was fired upon by a small party of Indians very close at hand, I think twenty or thirty paces. This discharge wounded two of his men slighty. Knowing as he did that his men were unfit to fight Indians in their own fashion, he ordered them to reserve their fire, and to charge bayonet, which being promptly executed, put the Indians to flight, and after pursuing a short distance, he called off his men and retreated to the fort, bringing in the wounded." In other accounts I have read of this affair, it is stated that ten of Captain Clark's men were killed. "During the cold weather, while the Indians were lying about the fort, although none had been seen for a few days, a party of seventeen men went out for the purpose of carrying in fire-wood, which the army had cut before they left the place, about forty or fifty rods from the fort. Near the bank of the river was an ancient mound, behind which lay a quantity of wood. A party had been out for several preceding mornings and brought in wood, supposing the Indians would not be watching the fort in such very cold weather. But on that fatal morning, the Indians had concealed themselves behind the mound, and as the soldiers passed round on one side of the mound, a part of the Indians came round on the other, and enclosed the wood party, so that not one escaped. I was personally acquainted with some of the men who were killed."

The published statements of this affair say that the Indians enticed the men out in search of horses, by taking off their bells and tinkling them; but it is certain that no horses were left at the fort, as they must either starve or be stolen by the Indians; so that Mr. Jolly's version of the incident must be correct. During the siege, which continued until the last of February, the garrison were very short of provisions. The Indians suspected this to be the fact, but were also nearly starving themselves. In this predicament, they proposed to the garrison that if they would give them a barrel of flour and some meat, they would raise the siege, concluding if they had not this quantity they must surrender at discretion soon, and if they had they would not part with it. In this, however, they missed their object. The brave Colonel Gibson turned out the flour and meat promptly, and told them he could spare it very well, as he had plenty more. The Indians soon after raised the siege. A runner was sent to Fort M'Intosh with a statement of their distress, and requesting reinforcements and provisions immediately. The inhabitants south of the Ohio volunteered their aid, and General M'Intosh headed the escort of provisions, which reached the fort in safety, but was near being all lost from the dispersion of the pack-horses in the woods near the fort, from a fright occasioned by a *feu de joie* fired by the garrison, at the relief. The fort was finally evacuated in August, 1779, it being found untenable at such a distance from the frontiers; and Henry Jolly was one of the last men who left it, holding at that time in the continental service the commission of ensign.

New Philadelphia, the county seat, is 100 miles northeasterly from Columbus. It is on the east bank of the Tuscarawas, on a large level and beautiful plain. It was laid out in 1804, by John Knisely, and additions subsequently made. The town has improved much within the last few years, and is now flourishing. It contains 1 Presbyterian, 1 Methodist and 1 Disciples church, 5 mercantile

Central View in New Philadelphia.

stores, 2 printing offices, 1 oil and 1 grist mill, 1 woollen factory, and a population estimated at over 1000.

In the late war, some Indians, under confinement in jail in this town, were saved from being murdered by the intrepidity of two or three individuals. The circumstances are derived from two communications, one of which is from a gentleman then present.

About the time of Hull's surrender, several persons were murdered on the Mohiccan, near Mansfield, which created great alarm and excitement.

Shortly after this event, three Indians, said to be unfriendly, had arrived at Goshen. The knowledge of this circumstance created much alarm, and an independent company of cavalry, of whom Alexander M'Connel was captain, were solicited by the citizens to pursue and take them. Some half a dozen, with their captain, turned out for that purpose. Where daring courage was required to achieve any hostile movement, no man was more suitable than Alexander M'Connel. The Indians were traced to a small island near Goshen. M'Connel plunged his horse into the river and crossed, at the same time ordering his men to follow, but none chose to obey him. He dismounted, hitched his horse, and with a pistol in each hand commenced searching for them. He had gone but a few steps into the interior of the island when he discovered one of them, with his rifle, lying at full length behind a log. He presented his pistol—the Indian jumped to his feet, but M'Connel disarmed him. He also took the others, seized their arms, and drove them before him. On reaching his company, one of his men hinted that they should be put to death. "Not until they have had a trial according to law," said the captain; then ordering his company to wheel, they conducted the prisoners to the county jail.

The murder which had been perpetrated on the Mohiccan had aroused the feelings of the white settlers in that neighborhood almost to phrenzy. No sooner did the report reach them that some strange Indians had been arrested and confined in the New Philadelphia jail, than a company of about 40 men was organized at or near Wooster, armed with rifles, under the command of a Captain Mullen, and marched for New Philadelphia to dispatch these Indians. When within about a mile of the town, coming in from the west, John C. Wright, then a practicing lawyer at Steubenville, (later Judge,) rode into the place from the east on business. He was hailed by Henry Laffer, Esq., at that time sheriff of the county, told that the Indian prisoners were in his custody, the advancing company of men was pointed out to him, their object stated, and the inquiry made, "what is to be done?" "The prisoners must be saved, sir," replied Wright; "why don't you beat an alarm and call out the citizens?" To this he replied, "our people are much exasperated, and the fear is, that if they are called out they will side with the company, whose object is to take their lives." "Is there no one who will stand by you to prevent so dastardly a murder?" rejoined Wright. "None but M'Connel, who captured them." "Have you any arms?" "None but an old broadsword and a pistol." "Well," replied W., "go call M'Connel, get your weapons, and come up to the tavern; I'll put away my horse and make a third man to defend the prisoners; we must not have so digraceful a murder committed here."

Wright put up his horse, and was joined by Laffer and M'Connel. About this time the military company came up to the tavern door, and there halted for some refreshments. Mr. Wright knew the captain and many of the men, and went along the line, followed by the sheriff, inquiring their object and remonstrating, pointing out the disgrace of so cowardly an act as was contemplated, and assuring them, in case they carried out their brutal design, they would be prosecuted and punished for murder. Several left the line, declaring they would have nothing more to do with the matter. The captain became angry, ordered the ground to be cleared, formed his men and moved towards the jail. M'Connel was at the jail door, and the sheriff and Wright took a cross cut and joined him before the troops arrived. The prisoners had been laid on the floor against the front wall as a place of safety. The three arranged themselves before the jail door—M'Connel with the sword, sheriff Laffer had the pistol, and Wright was without weapon. The troops formed in front, a parley was had, and Wright again went along the line remonstrating, and detached two or three more men. He was ordered off, and took his position at the jail door with his companions. The men were formed, and commands, preparatory to a discharge of their arms, issued.

In this position the three were ordered off, but refused to obey, declaring that the prisoners should not be touched except they first dispatched *them*. Their firmness had its effect; the order to fire was given, and the men refused to obey. Wright again went along the line remonstrating, &c., while M'Connel and Laffer maintained their position at the door. One or two more were persuaded to leave the line. The captain became very angry and ordered him off. He again took his place with his two companions. The company was marched off some distance and treated with whiskey; and after some altercation, returned to the jail door, were arranged and prepared for a discharge of their rifles, and the three ordered off on pain of being shot. They maintained their ground without faltering, and the company gave way and abandoned their project. Some of them were afterwards permitted, one at a time, to go in and see the prisoners, care being taken that no harm was done. These three gentlemen received no aid from the citizens; the few that were about looked on merely. Their courage and firmness were truly admirable.

The Indians were retained in jail until Governor Meigs, who had been some time expected, arrived in New Philadelphia. He instructed Gen. A. Shane, then a lieutenant, recruiting for the United States service, to take the Indians with his men to the rendezvous at Zanesville. From thence they were ordered to be sent with his recruits to the head-quarters of General Harrison, at Seneca, at which place they were discharged.

Another incident occurred in Lieutenant Shane's journey to head-quarters, which illustrates the deep-rooted prejudices entertained by many at that time against the Indians. The lieutenant with his company stopped a night at Newark. The three Indians were guarded as prisoners, and that duty devolved by turns on the recruits. A physician, who lived in Newark, and kept a small drug shop, informed the officer that two of his men had applied to him for poison. On his questioning them closely what use they were to make of it, they partly confessed that it was intended for the Indians. It was at night when they applied for it, and they were dressed in fatigue frocks. In the morning the lieutenant had his men paraded, and called the doctor to point out those who had meditated such a base act; but the doctor, either unwilling to expose himself to the enmity of the men, or unable to discern them, the whole company being then dressed in their regimentals, the affair was passed over with some severe remarks by the commanding officer on the unsoldier-like conduct of those who could be guilty of such a dastardly crime of poisoning.

A singular legal anecdote is related as having occurred at New Philadelphia at an early day.

The court was held on this occasion in a log tavern, and an adjoining log stable was used as a jail, the stalls answering as cells for the prisoners. Judge T. was on the bench, and in the exercise of his judicial functions severely reprimanded two young lawyers who had got into a personal dispute. A huge, herculean backwoodsman, attired in a red flannel shirt, stood among the auditors in the apartment which served the double purpose of court and bar-room. He was much pleased at the judge's lecture—having himself been practising at *another bar*—and hallooed out to his worship—who happened to be cross-eyed—in the midst of his harangue, "give it to 'em, old gimlet eyes!" "Who is that?" demanded the judge. He of the flannel shirt, proud of being thus noticed, stepped out from among the rest, and drawing himself up to his full height, vociferated "*it's this 'ere old hoss!*" The judge, who to this day never failed of a pungent repartee when occasion required, called out in a peculiarly dry nasal tone, "sheriff! take that *old hoss*, put him in *the stable*, and see that he is *not stolen* before morning."

Dover.

Dover, 3 miles NW. of New Philadelphia, was laid out in the fall of 1807, by Slingluff and Deardorff, and was an inconsiderable village until the Ohio canal went into operation. It is now, through the enterprize of its citizens and the facilities furnished by the canal, one of the most thriving villages upon it, by which it is distant from

View in Zoar.

[On the right is shown the hotel; on the left, the store—beyond, up the street, is a building of considerable elegance, the residence of Mr. Bimeler. Among the carefully cultivated shrubbery in the gardens adjoining, are cedar trees of some twenty feet in height, trimmed to almost perfect cylinders.]

Cleveland 93 miles. Its situation is fine, being upon a slight elevation on the west bank of the Tuscarawas, in the midst of a beautiful and fertile country. The view was taken on the line of the canal: Deardorff's mill and the bridge over the canal are seen on the right; in the centre of the view appears the spire of the Baptist church, and on the extreme left, Welty and Hayden's flouring mill. The town is sometimes incorrectly called Canal Dover, that being the name of the post-office It contains 1 Presbyterian, 1 Lutheran, 1 Moravian, 1 Baptist, and 1 Methodist church; 6 mercantile stores, 1 woollen factory, 2 furnaces, 1 saw and 2 flouring mills, 3 tanneries, 2 forwarding houses, and had in 1840, 598 inhabitants, since which it is estimated to have doubled its population.

Eleven miles N. of the county seat, and eight from Dover, is the settlement of a German community, a sketch of whom we annex from one of our own communications to a public print.

In the spring of 1817, about two hundred Germans from Wirtemberg embarked upon the ocean. Of lowly origin, of the sect called Separatists, they were about to seek a home in the New World to enjoy the religious freedom denied in their fatherland. In August they arrived in Philadelphia, poor in purse, ignorant of the world, but rich in a more exalted treasure. On their voyage across the Atlantic, one young man gained their veneration and affections by his superior intelligence, simple manners and kindness to the sick. Originally a weaver, then a teacher in Germany, and now entrusting his fortunes with those of like faith, Joseph M. Bimeler found himself, on reaching our shores, the acknowledged one whose sympathies were to soften and whose judgment was to guide them through the trials and vicissitudes yet to come. Acting by general consent as agent, he purchased for them on credit 5,500 acres in the county of Tuscarawas, to which the colonists removed the December and January following. They fell to work in separate families, erecting bark huts and log shanties, and providing for their immediate wants.

Strangers in a strange land, girt around by a wilderness enshrouded in winter's stern and dreary forms, ere spring had burst upon them with its gladdening smile, the cup of privation and suffering was held to their lips and they were made to drink to the dregs. But although poor and humble, they were not entirely friendless. A distant stranger, by chance hearing of the distress of these poor German emigrants, sent provisions for their relief—an incident related by some of them at the present day with tears of gratitude.

For about eighteen months they toiled in separate families, but unable thus to sustain themselves in this then new country, the idea was suggested to combine and conquer by the mighty enginery of associated effort. A constitution was adopted, formed on purely republican and democratic principles, under which they have lived to the present time. By it they hold all their property in common. Their principal officers are an agent and three trustees, upon whom devolve the management of the temporal affairs of the community. Their offices are elective, females voting as well as males. The trustees serve three years, one vacating his post annually and a new election held.

For years the colony struggled against the current, but their economy, industry and integrity enabled them to overcome every obstacle and eventually to obtain wealth. Their numbers have slightly diminished since their arrival, in consequence of a loss of fifty persons in the summer of 1832, by cholera and kindred diseases, and poverty in the early years of their settlement, which prevented the contracting of new matrimonial alliances.

Their property is now valued at near half a million. It consists of nine thousand acres of land in one body, one oil, one saw and two flouring mills, two furnaces, one woollen factory, the stock of their domain and money invested in stocks. Their village, named Zoar, situated about half a mile east of the Tuscarawas, has not a very prepossessing appearance.

Every thing is for use—little for show. The dwellings, twenty-five in number, are substantial and of comfortable proportions; many of them log, and nearly all unpainted. The barns are of huge dimensions, and with the rest are grouped without order, rearing their brown sides and red tiled roofs above the foliage of the fruit-trees, partially enveloping them. Turning from the village, the eye is refreshed by the verdure of the meadows that stretch away on either hand, where not even a stick or a chip is to be seen to mar the neatness and beauty of the green sward.

The sound of the horn at day-break calls them to their labors. They mostly work in groups, in a plodding but systematic manner that accomplishes much. Their tools are usually coarse, among which is the German sythe, short and unwieldy as a bush-hook, sickles without teeth, and hoes clumsy and heavy as the mattock of the southern slave. The females join in the labors of the field, hoe, reap, pitch hay, and even clean and wheel out in barrows the offal of the stables. Their costume and language are that of Germany. They are seen about the village going to the field with implements of labor across their shoulders, their faces shaded by immense circular rimmed hats of straw—or with their hair combed straight back from their foreheads and tied under a coarse blue cap of cotton, toting upon their heads baskets of apples or tubs of milk.

Systematic division of labor is a prominent feature in their domestic economy, although here far from reaching its attainable perfection. Their clothing is washed together, and one bakery supplies them with bread. A general nursery shelters all the children over three years of age. There these little pocket editions of humanity are well cared for by kind dames, in the sere and yellow leaf.

The selfishness so prominent in the competitive avocations of society, is here kept from its *odious* development by the interest each strikingly manifests in the general welfare, as only thus can their own be promoted. The closest economy is shown in all their operations—for as the good old man Kreutzner, the Boniface of the community, once observed in broken English, when starting on a bee line for a decaying apple cast by a heedless stranger into the street—"*saving make rich!*" Besides acting as host in the neat village inn, this man, Kreutzner, is the veterinary Æsculapius of this society, carrying out the universal economy still farther by practicing on the homœopathic principles! Astonishing are the results of his skill on his quarto-limbed patients, who, from rolling and snorting under acute pains of the abdominal viscera, are, by the melting on the lips of their tongues of a few pills of an infinitesimal size, lifted into a comfortable state of physical exaltation.

With all the peculiarities of their religious faith and practice we are unacquainted; but, like most sects denominated Christian, there is sufficient in their creed, if followed, to make their lives here upright, and to justify the hope of a glorious future. *Separatists* is a term applied to them, because they separated from the Lutheran and other denominations. They have no prayers, baptisms nor sacraments, and, like Jews, eschew pork. Their log church is often filled winter evenings, and twice on the Sabbath. The morning service consists of music, instrumental and vocal, in which a piano is used, together with the reading and explanation of the scriptures by one of their number. The afternoon exercises differ from it in the substitution of catechising from a German work for biblical instruction.

They owe much of their prosperity to Bimeler, now an old man, and justly regarded as the patriarch of the community. He is their adviser in all temporal things, their physician to heal their bodily infirmities, and their spiritual guide to point to a purer world. Although but as one of them, his superior education and excellent moral qualities have given him a commanding influence, and gained their love and reverence. He returns the affection of the people, with whom he has toiled until near a generation has passed away, with his whole soul. He has few thoughts for his fatherland, and no desire to return thither to visit the home of his youth. The green hills of this beautiful valley enclose the dearest objects of his earthly affections and earthly hopes.

The community are strict utilitarians, and there is but little mental development among them. Instruction is given in winter to the children in German and English. They are a very simple-minded, artless people, unacquainted with the outer world, and the great questions, moral and political, which agitate it. Of scarcely equaled morality, never has a member been convicted of going counter to the judicial regulations of the land. Thus they pass through their pilgrimage with but apparently few of the ills that fall to the common lot, presenting a reality delightful to behold, with contentment resting upon their countenances and hearts in which is enthroned peace.

The following is a list of villages in the county, with their distances and directions from New Philadelphia, and their population in 1840, some of which are thriving places, and have since much increased: Bolivar, at the junction of the Sandy and Beaver with the Ohio canal, 11 N., 253; Lockport, on the Ohio canal, 2 SW., 191; New Cumberland, 10 NE., 138; Port Washington, on the Ohio canal, 18 SW., 116; Shanesville, 12 W., 226, and Sandyville, 12 NE., on the Sandy and Beaver canal, 243. Eastport, Lawrenceville, Rogersville, Strasburg, Westchester, Gnadenhutten, Trenton and Uhrichsville are also small places: the last of which is a thriving town, on Stillwater creek, by which large quantities of produce are shipped to the Ohio canal, only a few miles distant.

UNION.

Union was formed April 1st, 1820, from Delaware, Franklin, Madison and Logan, together with a part of old Indian territory. The surface is generally level, and most of the soil clayey. The southwestern part is prairie land, and the north and eastern woodland of great fertility when cleared. In the eastern part are valuable limestone quarries. The principal products are corn, grass, wheat, oats, potatoes, butter and cheese. The following is a list of its townships in 1840, with their population.

Allen,	714	Jackson,	352	Paris,	1151
Claiborne,	497	Leesburgh,	720	Union,	894
Darby,	736	Liberty,	922	Washington,	154
Dover,	457	Mill Creek,	524	York,	439
Jerome,	868				

The population of Union, in 1830, was 3,192, and in 1840, 8443, or 19 inhabitants to the square mile.

The first white men who ever made a settlement within the county were James Ewing and his brother Joshua. They purchased land and settled on Darby Creek, in what is now Jerome Township, in the year 1798. The next year came Samuel Mitchell, David Mitchell, Samuel Mitchell, jr., Samuel Kirkpatrick, and Samuel McCullough; and in 1800, George Reed, Samuel Reed, Robert Snodgrass, and Paul Houston.

James Ewing's farm was the site of an ancient and noted Mingo town, which was deserted at the time the Mingo towns, in what is now Logan county, were destroyed by Gen. Logan of Kentucky, in 1786. When Mr. Ewing took possession of it, the houses were still remaining, and, among others, the remains of a blacksmith's shop, with coal, cinders, iron-dross, &c. Jonathan Alder, formerly a prisoner among the Indians, says the shop was carried on by a renegade white man named Butler, who lived among the Mingoes. Extensive fields had formerly been cultivated in the immediate vicinity of the town.

The county was erected through the exertions of Col. James Curry, who was then a member of the state legislature. He resided within the present boundaries of the county from the year 1811 until his death, which took place in the year 1834. He served as an officer in the Virginia continental line, during the chief part of the revolutionary war. He was taken prisoner when the American army surrendered at Charleston, S. C. In early youth he was with the Virginia forces at Point Pleasant, at the mouth of the Kenhawa, and took part in the battle with the Indians at that place. His account of that battle differed, in one respect, from some of the accounts of it which we have read. His recollection was perfectly distinct, that when the alarm was given in the camp, upon the approach of the Indians in the morning, a limited number of men from each company were called for, and sent out with the expectation that they would have a fine frolic in the pursuit of what they supposed to be a mere scouting party of Indians. After the party thus detached had been gone a few minutes, a few scattering reports of rifles began to be heard. Momently, however, the firing became more rapid, until it became apparent that the Indians were in force. The whole available force of the whites then left the camp. During the forenoon, Mr. C. received a wound from a rifle ball which passed directly through the elbow of his right arm, which disabled him for the remainder of the day.

During his residence in Ohio he was extensively known, and had many warm friends among the leading men of the state. He was one of the electors by whom the vote of the state was given to James Monroe for president of the United States. The last of many public trusts which he held was that of associate judge for this county.*

Central view in Marysville.

Marysville, the county seat, so named from a daughter of the original proprietor, is 30 miles NW. of Columbus, on Mill Creek, a tributary of the Scioto. It contains 1 Presbyterian and 1 Methodist church, an academy, 1 newspaper printing office, 3 mercantile stores, and had in 1843, 360 inhabitants; it is now estimated to contain about 600.

Milford, 5 miles SW. of Marysville on Big Darby, is a flourishing village, having 1 Presbyterian and 1 Methodist church, 3 mercantile stores, and about 400 inhabitants. The following is a list of places in the county with their population in 1840:—Essex 34, Fairsburgh 20, Liberty 44, Richwood 99, Washington 10, and York 49.

* The preceding historical items respecting this county were communicated by a resident.

VAN WERT.

Van Wert was formed April 1st, 1820, from old Indian territory. It was named from Isaac Van Wart, one of the three captors of Maj. Andre in the revolutionary war, who resided near Tarrytown, New York, at the time of his death, in 1828, aged 68 years. The surface is level, and the top soil loam, and the sub-soil blue marl and very deep, and what is remarkable, of such tenacity that water will not sink through it. Hence, in wet seasons, the crops are poor from the water standing on the soil. When the country is cleared and drained, this difficulty will be obviated. The soil is very rich, and the surface covered with a great variety of timber. The principal product is Indian corn. The following is a list of the townships in 1840, with their population.

Harrison,	168	Pleasant,	192	Washington,	47
Hoaglin,	40	Ridge,	211	Willshire,	434
Jennings,	88	Tully,	99	York,	181
Liberty,	117				

The population of Van Wert in 1840, was 1577, or about 4 persons to the square mile.

Van Wert received its present boundaries and name in the spring of 1820, two years after the lands of the northwestern part of Ohio were purchased from the Indians, by the treaty of St. Mary's. With most of the 14 counties formed by the same act, it was almost an entire wilderness, the surveyors' marks upon the township lines being, with a few exceptions, the only traces of civilization in the whole region.

The ridge upon which stand the towns of Van Wert and Section Ten, is a subject of curiosity to strangers. It is of great utility to the people of this county and the others, (Putnam, Hancock, Wyandot to Seneca,) through which it passes, being at all seasons the best natural road in this part of Ohio. It is composed entirely of sand and gravel, and has an average width of about half a mile. Its highest point is generally near the south side, from which it gradually slopes to the north. The timber is such as is usually found upon the river bottoms, and although upon it are as large trees as elsewhere, yet in their character they form a striking contrast with the forest on either side.

At a depth of about 16 feet through sand and gravel, pure cold water is found, while through the clayey soil in the country adjacent, it is often necessary to dig from 20 to 40 feet. The ridge passes out at the northwest corner of the county, and is temporarily lost in the high sandy plain near Fort Wayne. Crossing the Maumee, it can be distinctly traced, running in a northeasterly direction; when, although frequently eccentric and devious in its course, it runs nearly parallel with the river, being distant from it from 1 to 10 miles: it is again lost in the sandy plains nearly north of Napoleon. Has not this ridge been the boundary of a *great bay of Lake Erie!* when its waters were, perhaps, 180 feet higher than now? The sand, gravel, round smooth stones and shells, all bear evidence of having been deposited by water, and the summit of the ridge is every where at the same level, or relative altitude.

Van Wert, the county seat, is 136 miles NW. of Columbus, and was founded in 1837, by James Watson Riley, Esq. It is handsomely situated on a natural ridge, elevated about 20 feet above the general surface of the country, on a fork of the Little Auglaize. It contains 2 stores, 1 grist and 2 saw mills, and about 200 inhabitants

The site of the town of Van Wert, has evidently been an Indian town, or a place for winter quarters; the timber standing when first visited by the writer, and probably by white men, in 1825, was all small and evidently of a growth of less than 50 years, and several wooden houses, covered with bark, were in pretty good repair when the town was laid out in 1837; numerous graves, on a commanding bluff upon the bank of the creek, as well as the deep worn trails upon the ridge, up and down the creek, and in various other directions, bear witness that this deeply sequestered, yet pleasant spot, unknown to the whites in all the wars, from St. Clair's defeat to the close of the late war, and in fact, until after the treaty of St. Mary's, was cherished by the Indians as a peaceful and quiet home, where they could in security leave their women and children, when they sallied out upon the war path, or hunting excursions.

At the time of laying out the town plat, an old Indian of the Pottawatomie tribe, was encamped near, and told the writer that he had with his family spent forty winters there, and had expected there to leave his bones; but, added he, the game will soon disappear after your chain has passed over the ground; in a few days I shall take my leave, and, added he, while tears almost choked his utterance, I shall never return again to this place, and the haunts of the deer, the bear and the raccoon, will soon be broken up, and brick houses take the place of my wigwam!! This Indian had been a brave, said "he owned a farm on the river Raisin, in Michigan, which he bought from the government." He had a red haired French woman, of near his own age, a prisoner taken from Montreal in infancy, for his wife; but every winter he returned to his native haunts.

Soon after the first settlement of Van Wert, a spring of clear pure well water was found, which had been carefully hidden years before by the Indians, with a piece of bark about 6 feet square. This bark had been peeled from a black walnut, flattened out, the earth scraped away from around the spring for about 16 inches in depth, the bark laid flat over all, and then the whole carefully covered with earth, so that no trace of the spring could be seen. After removing the bark, the spring again overflowed and resumed its old channel to the creek.

Capt. James Riley was the first white man who settled in Van Wert county; he moved his family into the forest, on the St. Mary's river, in January, 1821, and began clearing up a farm and the erection of mills. In 1822, he laid out a town on the west bank of the river, opposite his mills, and named it *Willshire*, in honor of his benefactor who redeemed him from African slavery. His sufferings during his shipwreck on the coast of Africa, and subsequent captivity among the Arabs, have been detailed in a volume by himself, with which the public are already familiar. In 1823, he was elected as a single representative to the state legislature, from the territory which now, comprises the counties of Preble, Miami, Darke, Shelby, Mercer, Allen, Van Wert, Putnam, Paulding, Defiance, Williams, Henry, Wood and Lucas, fourteen counties, which now, with a largely increased ratio of votes, send eight representatives and four senators. During that session, which is justly pointed to as pre-eminent in usefulness, to that of any one previous or subsequent, he bore a conspicuous part, and assisted in maturing the four great measures of the session, viz: the act for improving the state by navigable canals; the revenue act, in which the first attempt to establish an *ad valorem* system of taxation, was made; the act providing a sinking fund, and an act for the encouragement of common schools; the last named, and so much of the first as relates to the Miami canal, were originated by him, and called his measures.

Capt. Riley lived at Willshire 7 years, but his health and constitution had been destroyed by his sufferings in Africa, and in the spring of 1828, he was carried to Fort Wayne for medical aid; after lingering on the verge of death for several months, he was taken on a bed to New York, and in 1830, had so far recovered as to resume his nautical life. In 1831, he made a voyage to Mogadore, to visit his benefactor, Mr. Willshire, established a trade there, and subsequently made nine voyages to that country, during one of which he sent his vessel home in charge of another, and travelled through Spain, to Montpelier in France, for the benefit of surgical aid. The winter of 1839–40, he spent at Mogadore and the city of Morocco, which latter town he visited in company with Mr. Willshire, and, in consequence of this visit, the Emperor granted him a license to trade with the people of his seaports, during life, upon highly favorable conditions, never before granted to any christian merchant. On the 10th of March, 1840, he left New York in his brig, the Wm. Tell, for St. Thomas, in the West Indies, died when three days out, and was consigned to the ocean. The vessel returned to Mogadore for the cargo provided by him, and was wrecked and lost while at anchor in the harbor; all on board, save one, perishing.*

Willshire, founded in 1822, by Capt. James Riley, is in the sw. corner of the county, on the St. Mary's river, and contains 1 church,

* The sketch of the county is from a correspondent.

2 stores, 2 grist and 1 saw mill, and about 100 inhabitants. Section Ten is on the Miami Extension canal, and has a good canal water power, as well as being the best accessible point on the canal from the county towns of Van Wert, Putnam and Allen. It was laid out in 1845, by O. H. Bliss and B. F. Hollister, and has about 300 inhabitants.

WARREN.

Warren was formed from Hamilton, May 1st, 1803, and named from Gen. Joseph Warren, who fell at the battle of Bunker's Hill. The surface is level or undulating, and the soil very fertile, producing annually over a million of bushels of corn. Considerable water power is furnished by its streams. The principal crops are corn, oats and wheat. The following is a list of its townships in 1840, with their population.

Clear Creek,	2821	Hamilton,	1718	Union,	1617
Deerfield,	1875	Salem,	2955	Washington,	1306
Franklin,	2455	Turtle Creek,	4951	Wayne,	3392

The population of Warren in 1820 was 17,838, in 1830, 21,474, in 1840, 23,073, or 57 inhabitants to the square mile.

In the latter part of September, 1795, about one month after the treaty of Greenville, Mr. Bedell from New Jersey, made the first settlement in the county. Previous to this, Mill Creek, eleven miles from Cincinnati, was the frontier settlement in the Miami valley. He erected a block house as a defence against Indians about a mile south of Union village, at a place since known as *Bedell's station.* Shortly after, a settlement was commenced at Deerfield by Gen. David Sutton, Capt. Nathan Kelly and others. In the course of two or three years many other settlements were made, principally by people from New Jersey.

Among the early settlers was Capt. Robert Benham. He lived in a double cabin about a mile below Lebanon, on what is now known as the Fearney farm, where he died a few years previous to the late war. He was one of a party of seventy men who were attacked by Indians near the Ohio, opposite Cincinnati, in the war of the revolution, the circumstances of which here follow from a published source.

In the autumn of 1779, a number of keel boats were ascending the Ohio under the command of Maj. Rodgers, and had advanced as far as the mouth of Licking without accident. Here, however, they observed a few Indians, standing upon the southern extremity of a sandbar, while a canoe, rowed by three others, was in the act of putting off from the Kentucky shore, as if for the purpose of taking them aboard. Rodgers immediately ordered the boats to be made fast on the Kentucky shore, while the crew, to the number of seventy men, well armed, cautiously advanced in such a manner as to encircle the spot where the enemy had been seen to land. Only five or six Indians had been seen, and no one dreamed of encountering more than fifteen or twenty enemies. When Rodgers, however, had, as he supposed, completely surrounded the enemy, and was preparing to rush upon them, from several quarters at once, he was thunderstruck at beholding several hundred savages suddenly spring up in front, rear, and upon both flanks! They instantly poured in a close discharge of rifles, and then throwing down their guns, fell upon the survivors with the tomahawk! The panic was complete, and the slaughter prodigious. Maj Rodgers, together with forty-five others of his men, were quickly destroyed. The survivors made an effort to regain their boats, but the five men who had been left in charge of them, had immediately put off from shore in the hindmost boat, and the enemy had already gained possession of the others. Disappointed in the attempt, they turned furiously upon the enemy, and aided by the approach of darkness, forced their way through their lines, and with the loss of several severely wounded, at length affected their escape to Harrodsburgh.

Among the wounded was Captain Robert Benham. Shortly after breaking through the enemy's line he was shot through both hips, and the bones being shattered, he fell to the ground. Fortunately, a large tree had lately fallen near the spot where he lay, and with great pain, he dragged himself into the top, and lay concealed among the branches. The Indians eager in pursuit of the others, passed him without notice, and by midnight all was quiet. On the following day, the Indians returned to the battle-ground, in order to strip the dead and take care of the boats. Benham, although in danger of famishing, permitted them to pass without making known his condition, very correctly supposing that his crippled legs would only induce them to tomahawk him upon the spot in order to avoid the trouble of carrying him to their town. He lay close, therefore, until the evening of the second day, when perceiving a raccoon descending a tree, near him, he shot it, hoping to devise some means of reaching it, when he could kindle a fire and make a meal. Scarcely had his gun cracked, however, when he heard a human cry, apparently not more than fifty yards off. Supposing it to be an Indian, he hastily reloaded his gun, and remained silent, expecting the approach of an enemy. Presently the same voice was heard again, but much nearer. Still Benham made no reply, but cocked his gun and sat ready to fire as soon as an object appeared. A third halloo was quickly heard, followed by an exclamation of impatience and distress, which convinced Benham that the unknown must be a Kentuckian. As soon, therefore, as he heard the expression, " whoever you are—for God's sake answer me!" he replied with readiness, and the parties were soon together. Benham, as we have already observed, was shot through both legs! the man who now appeared, had escaped from the same battle, *with both arms broken!* Thus each was enabled to supply what the other wanted. Benham having the perfect use of his arms, could load his gun and kill game with great readiness, while his friend having the use of his legs, could kick the game to the spot where Benham sat, who was thus enabled to cook it. When no wood was near them, his companion would rake up brush with his feet, and gradually roll it within reach of Benham's hands, who constantly fed his companion, and dressed *his* wounds, as well as his own—tearing up both of their shirts for that purpose. They found some difficulty in procuring water at first, but Benham at length took his own hat, and placing the rim between the teeth of his companion, directed him to wade into the Licking, up to his neck, and dip the hat into the water (by sinking his own head.) The man who could walk, was thus enabled to bring water, by means of his teeth, which Benham could afterwards dispose of as was necessary.

In a few days they had killed all the squirrels and birds within reach, and the man with the broken arms was sent out to drive game within gunshot of the spot to which Benham was confined. Fortunately, wild turkeys were abundant in those woods, and his companion would walk around and drive them towards Benham, who seldom failed to kill two or three of each flock. In this manner they supported themselves for several weeks, until their wounds had healed, so as to enable them to travel. They then shifted their quarters, and put up a small shed at the mouth of Licking, where they encamped until late in November, anxiously expecting the arrival of some boat, which should convey them to the falls of Ohio.

On the 27th of November, they observed a flat boat moving leisurely down the river. Benham hoisted his hat upon a stick and hallooed loudly for help. The crew, however, supposing them to be Indians—at least suspecting them of an intention to decoy them ashore, paid no attention to their signals of distress, but instantly put over to the opposite side of the river, and manning every oar, endeavored to pass them as rapidly as possible. Benham beheld them pass him with a sensation bordering on despair, for the place was much frequented by Indians, and the approach of winter threatened them with destruction, unless speedily relieved. At length, after the boat had passed him nearly half a mile, he saw a canoe put off from its stern, and cautiously approached the Kentucky shore, evidently reconnoitering them with great suspicion. He called loudly upon them for assistance, mentioned his name, and made known his condition. After a long parley, and many evi dences of reluctance on the part of the crew, the canoe at length touched the shore, and Benham and his friend were taken on board. Their appearance excited much suspicion. They were almost entirely naked, and their faces were garnished with six weeks' growth of beard. The one was barely able to hobble upon crutches, and the other could manage to feed himself with one of his hands. They were taken to Louisville, where their clothes (which had been carried off in the boat which deserted them) were restored to them, and after a few weeks confinement, both were perfectly restored.

Benham afterwards served in the northwest throughout the whole of the Indian war—accompanied the expeditions of Harmar and Wilkinson—shared in the disaster of St. Clair and afterwards in the triumph of Wayne.

Broadway, Lebanon.

Lebanon, the county seat, is 28 miles NE. of Cincinnati, 80 SW. of Columbus, and 22 S. of Dayton, in a beautiful and fertile country. Turnpikes connect it with Cincinnati, Dayton, and Columbus. It is also connected with Middletown, 19 miles distant, by the Warren county canal, which, commencing here, unites there with the Miami canal.

This vicinity was first settled in the spring of 1796, by Henry Taylor, who built a mill one mile west, on Turtle Creek. Shortly after, Ichabod Corwin, John Osbourn, Jacob Vorhees, Samuel Shaw, Daniel Bonte, and a Mr. Manning, settled near him. Lebanon was laid out in the fall of 1803, by Ichabod Corwin, Ephraim Hathaway, and Silas Hurin. Then one house was on its site, a two story log dwelling, built in 1797, by Ichabod Corwin, which stood on Broadway, opposite the present residence of Mr. Edwin A. Wilds. When the town was laid out, this was occupied as a tavern by Ephraim Hathaway, under the sign of *a black horse*, and continued a place of "entertainment" for travellers until about 1810. A store was also opened in this building in the summer of 1803, by John Huston. Justice as well as food and clothing, was for a time dispensed there, —the act forming the county, making this the place for holding courts, which it continued to be for about three years, when the first court house, now used as a town hall, was built. Among the early settlers of Lebanon, are recollected the names of Wm. Ferguson, Daniel F. Reeder, John Adams, Joshua Hollingsworth, John Prill, Peter Yauger, Samuel M'Crea, David Corwin, Richard Cunningham, Wm. R. Goodwin, and Judge Joshua Collet, the first lawyer in the county. In 1806 the Western Star, then a Jeffersonian paper, and now continued, was established by Judge John M'Lean. Lebanon is the present residence of Hon. Thomas Corwin. In 1810 the town was incorporated.

The Little Miami railroad runs four miles east of Lebanon, to which it is contemplated to construct a branch. The Warren county canal is supplied by a reservoir of 30 or 40 acres N. of the town. Lebanon is regularly laid out in squares, and compactly built. It contains 1 Presbyterian, 1 Cumberland Presbyterian, 2 Baptist, 1 Episcopal Methodist, and 1 Prot. do. church, 2 printing offices, 9 dry goods and 6 grocery stores, 1 grist and 2 saw mills, 1 woollen manufactory, a classical academy for both sexes, and had in 1840, 1,327 inhabitants.

The late Judge FRANCIS DUNLAVY, who died at Lebanon, in 1839, was born in Virginia, in 1761. When ten years of age his father's family removed to western Pennsylvania. At the early age of 14 years he served in a campaign against the Indians, and continued mostly in this service until the close of the revolution. He assisted in building Fort M'Intosh, about the year 1777, and was afterwards in the disastrous defeat of Crawford, from whence, with two others, he made his way alone through the woods without provisions, to Pittsburgh. In '87 he removed to Kentucky, in '91 to Columbia, and in '97 to this neighborhood. By great perseverance he acquired a good education, mainly without instructors, and part of the time taught school and surveyed land until the year 1800. He was returned a member of the convention from Hamilton county which formed the state constitution. He was also a member of the first legislature in 1803, at the first organization of the judiciary was appointed presiding judge of the first circuit. This place he held 14 years, and though his circuit embraced 10 counties, he never missed a court, frequently swimming his horse over the Miamies rather than fail being present. On leaving the bench he practiced at the bar 15 years, and then retired to his books and study. He was a strong-minded philanthropic man, of great powers of memory, and a most useful member of society.

The Hon. Jeremiah Morrow resides in the southern part of the county. He was a member of the convention which formed the state constitution, a representative in congress at various times, a member the United States' senate from 1813 to 1319, and governor of Ohio from 1822 to 1826. His highness the Duke of Saxe Weimar, who was in this country in 1825, gives in his travels a pleasant description of the then chief magistrate of the state.

The dwelling of the governor consists of a plain frame house, situated on a little elevation not far from the shore of the Little Miami, and is entirely surrounded by fields. The business of the state calls him once a month to Columbus, the seat of government, and the remainder of his time he passes at his country seat, occupied with farming, a faithful copy of an ancient Cincinnatus; he was engaged at our arrival in cutting a wagon pole, but he immediately stopped his work to give us a hearty welcome. He appeared to be about fifty years of age; is not tall, but thin and strong, and has an expressive physiognomy, with dark and animated eyes. He is a native of Pennsylvania, and was one of the first settlers in the state of Ohio. He offered us a night's lodging at his house, which invitation we accepted very thankfully. When seated round the chimney fire in the evening, he related to us a great many of the dangers and difficulties the first settlers had to contend with........ We spent our evening with the governor and his lady. Their children are settled, and they have with them only a couple of grandchildren. When we took our seats at supper, the governor made a prayer. There was a bible and several religious books lying on the table. After breakfasting with our hospitable host, we took our leave.

Union village, 4 miles W. of Lebanon, is a settlement of Shakers, or as they call themselves, "the United Society of Believers." They came here about the year 1805, and now number near 400 souls. The village extends about a mile on one street. The houses and shops are very large, many of them brick, and all in a high degree neat and substantial. They are noted for the cleanliness and strict propriety of conduct characteristic of the sect elsewhere, and take no part in politics or military affairs, keeping themselves completely aloof from the world, only so far as is necessary to dispose of their garden seeds and other products of agriculture and articles of mechanical skill. They own here about 3000 acres of land, and hold all their property in common.

Shakers Dancing.

The community are divided into five families, each family having an eating-room and kitchen. A traveller thus describes their ceremonies at the table.

Two long tables were covered on each side of the room, behind the tables were benches, and in the midst of the room was a cupboard. At a signal given with a horn, the brothers entered the door to the right, and the sisters the one to the left, marching two and two to the table. The sisters in waiting, to the number of six, came at the same time from the kitchen, and ranged themselves in one file opposite the table of the sisters; after which, they all fell on their knees, making a silent prayer, then arose, took hold of the benches behind them, sat down and took their meal in the greatest silence. I was told this manner was observed at all their daily meals. They eat bread, butter and cakes, and drank tea. Each member found his cup filled before him—the serving sisters filling them when required. One of the sisters was standing at the cupboard to pour out the tea—the meal was very short, the whole society rose at once, the benches were put back, they fell again on their knees, rose again, and wheeling to the right, left the room with a quick step. I remarked among the females some very pretty faces, but they were all, without exception, of a pale and sickly hue. They were disfigured by their ugly costume, which consists of a white starched bonnet. The men likewise had bad complexions.

Franklin is 10 miles NW. of Lebanon, on the Dayton and Cincinnati turnpike, with the Miami canal running east of it, and the Miami river bounding it on the west. It was laid out in 1795, a few months after the treaty of Greenville, within Symmes' purchase, by its proprietors, two young men from New Jersey, Daniel C. Cooper and Wm. C. Schenck, father of the Hon. Robt. Schenck. The first cabin was built by them, on or near lot 21 Front street. In the spring of '96, six or eight cabins stood on the town plot. A church, common for all denominations, on the site of the Baptist church, was the first erected; it was built about the year 1808.

View in Franklin.

The town is on a level plot, and regularly laid out. The view shows on the right the Methodist church, next to it, merchants' block, beyond the Baptist church, and on the extreme left, the spire of the Presbyterian church. Franklin contains 3 churches, a high school, 4 dry goods and 2 grocery stores, 2 forwarding and commission houses, and had in 1840, 770 inhabitants.

Waynesville is 9 miles NE. of Lebanon, on the Cincinnati and Columbus turnpike. This place was laid out in 1802, by Samuel Highway, for himself and others. This vicinity was first settled in 1796, by Mr. Highway, Dr. E. Baine and others. Its first settlers were Friends, who now comprise a large part of its population. About a quarter of a mile east of the village runs the Little Miami railroad. From near this road the town, which lies principally upon a side hill, shows to great advantage. Within a few years past, Waynesville has taken a start, and is now a thriving business town, containing 2 Friends' meeting-house, 1 Methodist church, 4 mercantile stores, 2 flouring and 2 saw mills, 1 woollen and 1 last factory, and had in 1840, 427 inhabitants, since which it has nearly doubled in population.

About 6 miles east of Lebanon, on the Little Miami river, is a very extensive ancient fortification, called *Fort Ancient.* The extreme length of these works, in a direct line, is nearly a mile, although, following their angles—retreating and salient—they reach probably a distance of six miles. The drawing and description annexed are from the article of Caleb Atwater, Esq., in the Archæologia Americana.

The fortification stands on a plain, nearly horizontal, about 236 feet above the level of the river, between two branches with very steep and deep banks. The openings in the walls are the gateways. The plain extends eastward along the state road, nearly level, about half a mile. The fortification on all sides, except on the east and west where the road runs, is surrounded with precipices nearly in the shape of the wall. The wall on the inside varies in its height, according to the shape of the ground on the outside, being generally from eight to ten feet; but on the plain, it is about nineteen and a half feet high inside and out, on a base of four and a half poles. In a few places it appears to be washed away in gutters, made by water collecting on the inside.

At about twenty poles east from the gate, through which the state road runs, are two mounds, about ten feet eight inches high, the road running between them nearly equidistant from each. From these mounds are gutters running nearly north and south, that appear to be artificial, and made to communicate with the branches on each side. North-east from the mounds, on the plain, are two roads, *B*, each about one pole wide, elevated

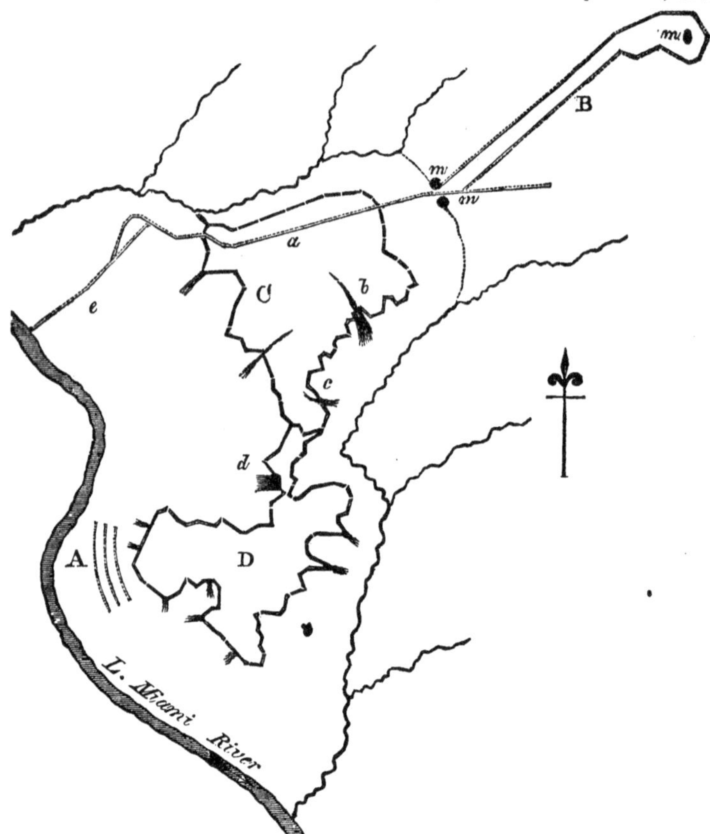

Fort Ancient.

about three feet, and which run nearly parallel, about one-fourth of a mile, and then form an irregular semicircle round a small mound. Near the southwest end of the fortification are three circular roads, *A*, between thirty and forty poles in length, cut out of the precipice between the wall and the river. The wall is made of earth.

Many conjectures have been made as to the design of the authors in erecting a work with no less than 58 gateways. Several of these openings have evidently been occasioned by the water, which had been collected on the inside until it overflowed the walls and wore itself a passage. In several other places the walls might never have been completed.

The three parallel roads, *A*, dug, at a great expense of labor, into the rocks and rocky soil adjacent, and parallel to the Little Miami river, appear to have been designed for persons to stand on, who wished to annoy those who were passing up and down the river

The Indians, as I have been informed, made this use of these roads in their wars with each other and with the whites. Whether these works *all* belong to the same era and the same people, I cannot say, though the general opinion is that they do. On the whole, I have ventured to class them among "Ancient Fortifications," to which they appear to have higher claims than almost any other, for reasons too apparent to require a recital.

The two parallel lines, *B*, are two roads very similar to modern turnpikes, and are made to suit the nature of the soil and make of the ground. If the roads were for foot races, the mounds were the goals from whence the pedestrians started, or around which they ran. The area which these parallel walls enclose, smoothed by art, might have been the place where games were celebrated. We cannot say that these works were designed for such purposes; but we can say, that similar works were thus used among the early inhabitants of Greece and Rome.

Harveysburg, so named from George Harvey, who laid it out about 30 years since, is a flourishing town, 13 miles NE. of Lebanon, and contains 2 Friends' meeting-houses, 1 United Brethren and 1 Methodist church, 1 classical academy, 5 dry goods stores, and about 500 inhabitants. Springboro', 9 N. of Lebanon, has 1 Friends' meeting-house and 1 Universalist church, 4 stores, 2 grist mills, and about 90 dwellings. Palmyra, 8 SW. of Lebanon, on the Cincinnati turnpike, has 1 Methodist and 1 Universalist church, 4 stores, and about 70 dwellings. Deerfield, Roachester, Butlersville, Morrow, Ridgeville and Yankeetown, are villages, the largest of which may contain 350 inhabitants.

WASHINGTON.

WASHINGTON was formed July 27th, 1788, by proclamation of Gov. St. Clair, being the first county formed within the limits of Ohio. Its original boundaries were as follows: "Beginning on the bank of the Ohio river, where the western boundary line of Pennsylvania crosses it, and running with that line to Lake Erie; thence along the southern shore of said lake to the mouth of Cuyahoga river: thence up the said river to the portage between it and the Tuscarawas branch of the Muskingum; thence down that branch to the forks, at the crossing place above Fort Laurens; thence with a line to be drawn westerly to the portage, on that branch of the Big Miami, on which the fort stood that was taken by the French in 1752, until it meets the road from the lower Shawnese town to Sandusky; thence south to the Scioto river, and thence with that river to the mouth, and thence up the Ohio river to the place of beginning." The surface is generally hilly and broken, excepting the broad strips of alluvial land on the Ohio and Muskingum. In the middle and western part are extensive tracts of fertile land. The uplands near the large streams are commonly broken, but well adapted to pasturage. The principal products are corn, wheat, oats, potatoes, dairy products, fruit and wool. The following is a list of its townships in 1840, with their population.

Adams,	791	Independence,	335	Roxbury,	1225
Aurelius,	886	Jolly,	582	Salem,	881
Barlow,	880	Ludlow,	539	Union,	888
Belpre,	1296	Lawrence,	571	Warren,	931
Decatur,	439	Liberty,	515	Waterford,	1166
Fearington,	1019	Marietta,	2689	Watertown,	1128
Grandview,	514	Newport,	1678	Wesley,	991

The population of Washington in 1820, was 10,425; in 1830, 11,731, and in 1840, 20,694, or 31 inhabitants to a square mile.

This county was the first settled in Ohio, and under the auspices of the New England Ohio company. Its early settlers were from New England, the descendants of whom constitute the larger share of its present population.

Fort Harmar.

In the autumn of 1785, a detachment of United States troops, under the command of Maj. John Doughty, commenced the erection, and the next year completed Fort Harmar, on the right bank of the Muskingum, at its junction with the Ohio. It was named in honor of Col. Josiah Harmar, to whose regiment Maj. Doughty was attached. It was the first military post erected by Americans within the limits of Ohio, excepting Fort Laurens, built in 1778. (See p. 485.) The outlines of the fort formed a regular pentagon, embracing within the area about three-quarters of an acre. Its walls were formed of large horizontal timbers, and the bastions of large upright timbers, of about 14 feet in height, fastened to each other by strips of timber tree-nailed into each picket. In its rear, Maj. Doughty laid out fine gardens. It continued to be occupied by United States troops until September, 1790, when they were ordered to Cincinnati. A company under Capt. Haskell continued to make the fort their head-quarters during the Indian war, sending out occasionally small detachments to assist the colonists at Marietta, Belpre and

Waterford, in guarding their garrisons against the Indians. The barracks and houses not needed for the accommodation of the troops, were occupied by the inhabitants living at Marietta, on the opposite side of the Muskingum.

In the autumn of 1787, the directors of the Ohio company organized in New England, preparatory to a settlement. Upon the 23d of November, they made arrangements for a party of 47 men to set forward under the superintendence of Gen. Rufus Putnam; and not long after, in the course of the winter, they started on their toilsome journey. Some of these, as well as most of those who followed them to the colony, had served in the war of the revolution, either as officers or soldiers, being men who had spent the prime of their lives in the struggle for liberty.

"During the winter of 1787–8, these men were pressing on over the Alleghanies by the old Indian path which had been opened into Braddock's road, and which has since been followed by the national turnpike from Cumberland westward. Through the dreary winter days they trudged on, and by April were all gathered on the Yohiogany, where boats had been built, and started for the Muskingum. On the 7th of April they landed at the spot chosen, and became the founders of Ohio, unless we regard as such the Moravian missionaries.

"As St. Clair, who had been appointed governor the preceding October, had not yet arrived, it became necessary to erect a temporary government for their internal security; for which purpose a set of laws was passed, and published by being nailed to a tree in the village, and Return Jonathan Meigs was appointed to administer them. It is a strong evidence of the good habits of the people of the colony, that during three months, but one difference occurred, and that was compromised. Indeed, a better set of men altogether, could scarce have been selected for the purpose, than Putnam's little band. Washington might well say, 'no colony in America was ever settled under such favorable auspices as that which was first commenced at the Muskingum. Information, property and strength, will be its characteristics. I know many of the settlers personally, and there never were men better calculated to promote the welfare of such a community.'

"On the 2d of July, a meeting of the directors and agents was held on the banks of the Muskingum, for the purpose of naming the new-born city and its public squares. As the settlement had been merely 'The Muskingum,' the name Marietta was now formally given to it, in honor of Marie Antoniette.

"On the 4th of July, an oration was delivered by James M. Varnum, who, with S. H. Parsons and John Armstrong, had been appointed to the judicial bench of the territory, on the 16th of October, 1787. Five days later, the governor arrived and the colony began to assume form. The ordinance of 1787, provided two district grades of government for the northwest territory, under the first of which the whole power was in the hands of the governor and three judges, and this form was at once organized upon the governor's arrival. The first law, which was 'for regulating and establishing the militia,' was published upon the 25th of July; and the next day, appeared the governor's proclamation, erecting all the country that had been ceded by the Indians east of the Scioto river into the county of Washington.

"From that time forward, notwithstanding the doubt yet existing as to the Indians, all at Marietta went on prosperously and pleasantly. On the 2d of September, the first court was held, with becoming ceremonies,"* which was the first civil court ever convened in the territory northwest of the Ohio.

"The procession was formed at the Point, (where most of the settlers resided,) in the following order:—1st, The high sheriff, with his drawn sword; 2d, the citizens; 3d, the officers of the garrison at Fort Harmar; 4th, the members of the bar; 5th, the supreme judges; 6th, the governor and clergyman; 7th, the newly appointed judges of the court of common pleas, Generals Rufus Putnam and Benj. Tupper.

"They marched up a path that had been cut and cleared through the forest to Campus Martius Hall, (stockade,) where the whole counter-marched, and the judges, (Putnam and Tupper,) took their seats. The clergyman, Rev. Dr. Cutler, then invoked the divine blessing. The sheriff, Col. Ebenezer Sproat, (one of nature's nobles,) proclaimed with his solemn 'O yes,' that a court is opened for the administration of even-handed justice to the poor and the rich, to the guilty and the innocent, without respect of persons; none to be punished without a trial by their peers, and then in pursuance of the laws and evidence in the case.' Although this scene was exhibited thus early in the settlement of the state, few ever equalled it in the dignity and exalted character of its principal participators. Many of them belong to the history of our country, in the darkest as well as most splendid periods of the revolutionary war. To witness this spectacle, a large body of Indians was collected, from the most powerful tribes then occupying the almost entire west. They had assembled for the purpose of making a treaty. Whether any of them entered the hall of justice, or what were their impressions, we are not told."†

"The progress of the settlement, [says a letter from the Muskingum,] is sufficiently rapid for the first year. We are continually erecting houses, but arrivals are faster than we can possibly provide convenient covering. Our first ball was opened about the middle of December, at which were fifteen ladies, as well accomplished in the manners of polite circles as any I have ever seen in the old states. I mention this to show the progress of society in this new world; where, I believe, we shall vie with, if not excel, the old states, in every accomplishment necessary to render life agreeable and happy."

Soon after the landing, preparations were made to build the stockaded fort, Campus Martius, to which allusion has already been made; and although it was begun in the course of that year, it was not entirely completed with palisades and outworks, or bastions, until the winter of 1791.

The walls formed a regular parallelogram, the sides of which were 180 feet each. At each corner was erected a strong block-house, surmounted by a tower and sentry box. These houses were 20 feet square below and 24 feet above, and projected 6 feet beyond the curtains, or main walls of the fort. The intermediate curtains were built up with dwelling houses, made of wood, whip-sawed into timbers four inches thick, and of the requisite width and length. These were laid up similar to the structure of log houses, with the ends nicely dove-tailed or fitted together so as to make a neat finish. The whole were two

* Annals of the West. † Dr. S. P. Hildreth, in the American Pioneer.

stories high, and covered with good shingle roofs. Convenient chimneys were erected of bricks, for cooking and warming the rooms. A number of the dwelling houses were built and owned by private individuals, who had families. In the west and south fronts were

Campus Martius in 1791.

strong gateways; and over that, in the centre of the front looking to the Muskingum river, was a belfry. The chamber underneath was occupied by the Hon. Winthrop Sargent, as an office, he being secretary to the governor of the N. W. Territory, General St. Clair, and performing the duties of governor in his absence. This room projected over the gateway, like a block-house, and was intended for the protection of the gate beneath in time of an assault. At the outer corner of each block-house was erected a bastion, standing on four stout timbers. The floor of the bastion was a little above the lower story of the block-house. They were square, and built up with thick planks to the height of a man's head, so that when he looked over he stepped on a narrow platform, or "banquet," running round the sides of the bulwark. Port-holes were made for musketry, as well as for artillery, a single piece of which was mounted in the southwest and northeast bastions. In these the sentries were regularly posted every night, as more convenient of access than the towers; a door leading into them from the upper story of the block-houses. The lower room of the southwest block-house was occupied for a guard-house. Running from corner to corner of the block-houses was a row of palisades, sloping outwards, and resting on stout rails. Twenty feet in advance of these was a row of very strong and large pickets, set upright in the earth. Gateways through these admitted the inmates of the garrison. A few feet beyond the outer palisades was placed a row of abattis, made from the tops and branches of trees, sharpened and pointing outwards, so that it would have been very difficult for an enemy to have penetrated even within their outworks. The dwelling houses occupied a space from 15 to 30 feet each, and were sufficient for the accommodation of forty or fifty families, and did actually contain from 200 to 300 persons, men, women and children, during the Indian war.

Before the Indians commenced hostilities, the block-houses were occupied as follows:—the southwest one by the family of Gov. St. Clair; the northwest one for public worship and holding of courts. The southeast block-house was occupied by private families; and the northeast as an office for the accommodation of the directors of the company. The area within the walls was 144 feet square, and afforded a fine parade-ground. In the centre was a well, 80 feet in depth, for the supply of water to the inhabitants in case of a siege. A large sun-dial stood for many years in the square, placed on a handsome post, and gave note of the march of time. It is still preserved as a relic of the old garrison.

After the war commenced, a regular military corps was organized, and a guard constantly kept night and day. The whole establishment formed a very strong work, and reflected great credit on the head that planned it. It was in a manner impregnable to the attacks of Indians, and none but a regular army with cannon could have reduced it. It is true, that the heights across the Muskingum commanded and looked down upon the defences of the fort; but there was no enemy in a condition to take possession of this advantage.

The garrison stood on the verge of that beautiful plain overlooking the Muskingum, on which are seated those celebrated remains of antiquity; and erected probably for a similar purpose, the defence of the inhabitants. The ground descends into shallow ravines on the north and south sides; on the west is an abrupt descent to the river bottoms, or alluvions; and the east passed out on to the level plain. On this the ground was cleared of trees beyond the reach of rifle shots, so as to afford no shelter to a hidden foe. Extensive fields of corn were growing in the midst of the standing girdled trees beyond. The front wall of the garrison was about 150 yards from the Muskingum river. The appearance of the fort from without was grand and imposing; at a little distance resembling one of the military palaces or castles of the feudal ages. Between the outer palisades and the river were laid out neat gardens for the use of Gov. St. Clair and his secretary, with the officers of the company.

Opposite the fort, on the shore of the river, was built a substantial timber wharf, at which was moored a fine cedar barge for twelve rowers, built by Capt. Jonathan Devoll, for Gen. Putnam; a number of pirogues, and the light canoes of the country; and last, not least, "the May-Flower," or "Adventure Galley," in which the first detachment of colonists were transported from the shores of the Yohiogany to the banks of the Muskingum. In these, especially the canoes, during the war, most of the communications were carried on between the settlements of the company and the more remote towns above on the Ohio river. Travelling by land was very hazardous to any but the rangers, or spies. There were no roads nor bridges across the creeks, and for many years after the war had ceased, the travelling was nearly all done by canoes on the rivers.*

The names of the early settlers who came the first season to Marietta, as far as recollected, were as follows:

Of the *agents*, were Gen. Putnam, Winthrop Sargeant, secretary of the territory, Judges Parsons and Varnum of the settlers, Capt. Dana, Capt. Jonathan Devol, Joseph Barker, Col. Battelle, Major Tyler, Dr. True, Capt. William Gray, Capt. Lunt, the Bridges, Ebenezer and Thomas Cory, Andrew M'Clure, Wm. Mason, Thomas Lord, Wm. Gridley, Gilbert Devol, Moody, Russels, Deavens, Oakes, Wright, Clough, Green, Shipman, Dorrance, the Maxons, Wells, &c. The first boat of families arrived on the 19th of August, in the same season, consisting of Gen. Tuppers, Col. Ichabod Nye, Col. Cushings, Major Coburn's, and Major Goodale's.

In the spring of 1789, settlements were pushed out to Belpre, Waterford, and Duck Creek, where they began to clear and plant the land, build houses and stockades. Among the first settlers at Waterford, were Benjamin Convers, Gilbert Devol, sen., Phineas Coburn, Wm. Gray, Col. Robert Oliver, Major Hatfield White, Andrew Story, Samuel Cushing, John Dodge, Allen and Gideon Devol, George, William, and David Wilson, Joshua Sprague, with his sons William and Jonathan, Capt. D. Davis, Phineas Coburn, Andrew Webster, Eben Ayres, Dr. Farley, David Brown, A. Kelly, James and Daniel Convers.

At Belpre, (the French for "beautiful meadow") were three stockades, the upper, lower, and middle; the last of which was called "farmer's castle," which stood on the banks of the Ohio, nearly, if not quite, opposite the beautiful island, since known as "Blannerhassets," the scene of "Burr's conspiracy." Among the persons at the upper, were Capt. Dana, Capt. Stone, Col. Bent, Wm. Browning, Judge Foster, John Rowse, Mr. Keppel, Israel Stone. At farmer's castle, were Col. Cushing, Major Haskel, Aaron Waldo Putnam, Col. Fisher, Mr. Sparhawk, and it is believed George and Israel Putnam, jr. At the lower, were Major Goodale, Col. Rice, Esq. Pierce, Judge Israel Loring, Deacon Miles, Major Bradford, and Mr. Goodenow. In the summer of 1789, Col. Ichabod Nye and some others built a block-house at Newberry, below Belprie. Mr. Nye sold his lot there to Aaron N. Clough, who, with Stephen Guthrie, Jos. Leavins, Joel Oakes, Eleazer Curtis, Mr. Denham, J. Littleton, and a Mr. Brown, were located at that place during the subsequent Indian war.

Every exertion possible for men in these circumstances, was made to secure food and prepare for future difficulties. Col. Oliver, Major Hatfield White, and John Dodge, of the Waterford settlement, began mills on Wolf Creek, about three miles from the fort, and got them running; and these, the first mills in Ohio, were never destroyed during the subsequent Indian war, though the proprietors removed their families to the fort at Marietta. Col. E. Sproat and Enoch Shephard, began mills on Duck Creek, three miles from Marietta, from the completion of which they were driven by the Indian war. Thomas Stanley began mills higher up, near the Duck Creek settlement; these were likewise unfinished.

* The engravings of Fort Harmar and Campus Martius, together with the accompanying descriptions, are from the communications of Dr. S. P. Hildreth, in the Am. Pioneer.

The Ohio company built a large horse mill near Campus Martius, and soon after, a floating mill. *

During the Indian war, which soon succeeded the first settlements, the inhabitants suffered much for the necessaries of life. Although some of the settlers were killed, and others carried into captivity, yet the massacre at Big Bottom, (see p. 377,) was the most alarming event. The escape of the settlers from greater suffering from this source, was owing to the strong fortifications erected, and the admirable judgment and foresight they displayed in taking precautions against danger. Among the incidents connected with the troubles with the Indians, to which we have barely space to allude, was the taking prisoner at Waterford, of Daniel Convers, (then a lad of 16, now of Zanesville,) who was carried to Detroit, the murder of Warth while at work near Fort Harmar: the taking prisoner of Major Goodale, of Belpre, who was, it is supposed, murdered; the death of Capt. Rogers, who was out with Mr. Henderson, as a spy, and was killed near the Muskingum, about a mile from Marietta; the death of a Mr. Waterman, near Waterford, and the narrow escape of Return J. Meigs, into Fort Harmar, by his fleetness of foot, while pursued by the enemy. On the other hand retaliation was in a measure inflicted upon the Indians, and among those most active in this duty was Hamilton Carr, a man eminently distinguished as an Indian hunter and spy. During the war a stockade was erected near the mouth of Olive Green Creek, above Waterford, which became the frontier garrison, and had in it about seven or eight men and boys able to bear arms. Just before Wayne's victory, Aug. 4th, 1794, they lost one man, a Mr. Abel Sherman, who went into the woods incautiously, and was killed by the Indians. A tomb-stone with a scalped head rudely carved upon it, marks the spot where he lies.

Among the inmates of this garrison was Geo. Ewing, esq., father of the Hon. Thomas Ewing. His fortune and history were similar to that of many of the revolutionary officers who emigrated to the west at that early day. He inherited a handsome patrimony and sold it, investing the proceeds in bonds and mortgages, and entered the continental army as a subaltern officer in 1775, he being then but little over 21 years of age. He continued to serve, with a few short intermissions, during the war. When the bonds fell due, they were paid in continental money, which, proving worthless, reduced him to poverty. In 1785, he migrated to the west, and remained on the Virginia side of the Ohio until 1792, when he crossed over and settled at Olive Green.

From the communication of one of the early settlers at Olive Green, we annex some facts respecting their privations and the discovery of a salt well.

The inhabitants had among them but few of what we consider the necessaries and conveniences of life. Brittle wares, such as earthen and glass, were wholly unknown, and but little of the manufactories of steel and iron, both of which were exceedingly dear. Iron and salt were procured in exchange for ginseng and peltry, and carried on pack horses from Ft. Cumberland or Chambersburg. It was no uncommon thing for the garrison to be wholly without salt for months, subsisting upon fresh meat, milk and vegetables, and bread made of corn pounded in a mortar—they did not yet indulge in the luxury of the hand-mill.

There had been an opinon, founded upon the information of the Indians, that there were

* From the "Reminiscences of the First Settlement of Ohio," by Horace Nye, published in the Western Recorder.

salt springs in the neighborhood, but the spot was carefully concealed. Shortly after Wayne's victory, in 1794, and after the inhabitants had left the garrison and gone to their farms, a white man, who had been long a prisoner with the Indians, was released and returned to the settlements. He stopped at Olive Green, and there gave an account of the salt springs, and directions for finding them. A party was immediately formed, (of whom George Ewing, jr., then a lad of 17, was one,) who, after an absence of 7 or 8 days, returned, to the great joy of the inhabitants, with about a gallon of salt, which they had made in their camp kettle. This was, as I think, in August, 1795. A supply, though a very small one, was made there that season for the use of the frontier settlement.

Whether this salt spring was earlier known to the whites I am unable to say. It may have been so to spies and explorers, and perhaps to the early missionaries; but this was the first discovery which was made available to the people.

Marietta College.

Marietta, the county seat, and the oldest town in Ohio, is on the left bank of the Muskingum, at its confluence with the Ohio, 104 miles SE. of Columbus. It is built principally upon a level plot of ground, in the midst of most beautiful scenery. Many of the dwellings are constructed with great neatness, and embellished with handsome door-yards and highly cultivated gardens. Its inhabitants are mostly of New England descent, and there are few places in our country that can compare with this in point of morality and intelligence—but few of its size that have so many cultivated and literary men. Marietta contains 1 Presbyterian, 1 Episcopal, 1 Baptist, 1 Methodist, 1 German do., 1 Universalist and 1 Catholic church; a male and female academy, in excellent repute; a college, 2 public libraries, 1 bank, 1 or 2 printing offices, a variety of mechanical and manufac turing establishments, about 20 mercantile stores, and in 1840, had a population of 1814.

Ship building, which was carried on very extensively at an early day, and then for a season abandoned, has again been commenced, and is now actively prosecuted. From the year 1800 to 1807, the business was very thriving. Com. Abm. Whipple, a veteran of the revolution, conducted the one first built, the St. Clair, to the ocean.

At that time Marietta was made "a port of clearance," from which vessels could receive regular papers for a foreign country. "This circumstance was the cause of a curious incident, which took place in the year 1806 or 1807. A ship, built at Marietta, cleared from that port with a cargo of pork, flour, &c., for New Orleans. From thence she sailed to England with a load of cotton, and being chartered to take a cargo to St. Petersburg, the Americans being at that time carriers for half the world, reached that port in safety. Her papers being examined by a naval officer, and dating from the port of Marietta, Ohio, she was seized, upon the plea of their being a forgery, as no such port was known in the civilized world. With considerable difficulty the captain procured a map of the United States, and pointing with his finger to the mouth of the Mississippi, traced the course of that stream to the mouth of the Ohio; from thence he led the astonished and admiring naval officer along the devious track of the latter river to the port of Marietta, at the mouth of the Muskingum, from whence he had taken his departure. This explanation was entirely satisfactory, and the American was dismissed with every token of regard and respect."

Marietta College was chartered in 1835. It was mainly established with a view to meet demands in the west for competent teachers and ministers of the gospel. The institution ranks high among others of the kind, and its officers of instruction are such as to merit the confidence of the enlightened patrons of thorough education. A new college edifice has lately been reared, and from the indications given, the prospects of the institution for a generous patronage are highly auspicious. The catalogue for 1846–7, gives the whole number of students at 177, of whom 60 were undergraduates, and 117 in the preparatory academy. The officers are Henry Smith, M. A., president; John Kendrick, M. A., J. Ward Andrews, M. A., and Hiram Bingham, M. A., professors; Samuel Maxwell, M. A., principal of the academy, and Geo. A. Rosseter, M. A., tutor.

Among the early settlers of Marietta were many who merit extended sketches; we have, however, but space for brief notices of a few of the more prominent.

Rufus Putnam was born April 8th, 1738, O. S., at Sutton, Massachusetts. At the age of 15, he was apprenticed to a millwright, with whom he served four years, and then enlisted as a common soldier in the French and Indian war. He served faithfully three years, was engaged in several actions, and was at the time the army disbanded, in 1761, serving as ensign, to which office his good conduct had promoted him. After this, he resumed the business of millwright, at which he continued seven or eight years, employing his leisure in studying mathematics and surveying.

He was among the first to take up arms in the revolutionary contest, and as an evidence of the estimation in which he was held, was appointed lieut. colonel. He was afterwards appointed, by congress, military engineer. He served throughout the war with honor, and was often consulted and held in high estimation by Washington. On the 8th of January, 1783, he was honored with the commission of brigadier general, having some time previously served as colonel. He was appointed by the Ohio company superintendent of all business relating to their contemplated settlement; and in April, 1788, commenced the first settlement at Marietta. In 1789, he was appointed by Washington a judge of the supreme court of the territory. On the 5th of May, 1792, he was appointed brigadier general in the army of the United States, destined to act against the Indians; but resigned the next year, in consequence of ill health. In October, 1796, he was appointed surveyor general of the United States, in which office he continued until 1803. He was a member, from this county, of the convention which formed the state constitution. From this time his advanced age led him to decline all business of a public nature, and he sought the quiet of private life. He died at Marietta, May 1st, 1824, at the age of 86.

General Putnam was a man of strong, good sense, modest, benevolent, and scrupulous to fulfill the duties which he owed to God and man. In person he was tall, of commanding appearance, and possessed a frame eminently fitted for the hardships and trials of war. His mind, though not brilliant, was solid, penetrating and comprehensive, seldom erring in conclusions.

Return Jonathan Meigs was born at Middletown, Ct., in 1765, graduated at Yale, studied law and was admitted to the bar in his native town. He was among the first settlers of Marietta. In the winter of 1802–3, he was elected chief justice of the supreme court of the state. The next year he resigned this office, having received from Jefferson the appointment of commandant of the United States' troops and militia in the upper district of Louisiana, and shortly after was appointed one of the judges of the territory of Louisiana. In April, 1807, he was commissioned a judge of Michigan territory; resigned the commission in October, and becoming a candidate for governor of Ohio, was elected, in a spirited canvass, over his competitor, General Massie; but not having the constitutional qualification of the four years' residence in the state, prior to the election, his election was contested and decided against him. In the session of 1807–8, he was appointed senator in congress, which office he afterwards resigned, and was elected governor of Ohio in 1810. In the war with Great Britain, while holding the gubernatorial office, he acted with great promptness and energy. In March, 1814, having been appointed post-master general of the United States, he resigned that office, and continued in his new vocation until 1823, during which he managed its arduous duties to the satisfaction of Presidents Madison and Monroe. He died at Marietta, March 29th, 1825. In person he was tall and finely formed, with a high retreating forehead, black eyes, and aquiline and prominent nose. His features indicated his character, and were remarkably striking, expressive of mildness, intelligence, promptness and stability of purpose. His moral character was free from reproach, and he was benevolent, unambitious, dignified, but easy of access.

Rev. Daniel Story, the earliest protestant preacher of the gospel in the territory northwest of the Ohio, except the Moravian missionaries,* was a native of Boston, and graduated at Dartmouth in 1780. The directors and agents of the Ohio company having passed a resolution in 1788, for the support of the gospel and the teaching of youth, Rev. Manasseh Cutler, one of the company's directors, in the course of that year engaged Mr. Story, then preaching at Worcester, to go to the west as a chaplain to the new settlement at Marietta. In the spring of 1789, he commenced his ministerial labors as an evangelist, visiting the settlements in rotation. During the Indian war from 1791 to 1795, he preached, during most of the time, in the northwest block-house of Campus Martius. The Ohio company at the same time raised a sum of money for the education of youth, and employed teachers. These testimonials sufficiently prove that the company felt for the spiritual, as well as the temporal affairs of the colonists.

When the war was over, Mr. Story preached at the different settlements; but as there were no roads, he made these pastoral visits by water, in a log canoe, propelled by stout arms and willing hearts. In 1796, he established a Congregational church, composed of persons residing at Marietta, Belprie, Waterford and Vienna, in Virginia. Mr. Story died December 30th, 1804, at the age of 49 years. He was a remarkable man, and peculiarly fitted for the station he held.†

Herman Blannerhasset, whose connection with the ill-fated project of Aaron Burr has given his name a wide-spread notoriety, was a resident of Marietta as early as 1796. About the year 1798, he commenced his improvements on the beautiful island since known by his name, embosomed on the Ohio, near the lower end of this county. He afterwards resided upon it for a number of years, surrounded with all that made life dear, when the tempter entered this Eden and forever blighted his earthly prospects. After years of

---

* Rev. Manasseh Cutler, agent of the Ohio company, although not employed as a clergyman, in 1788, prior to Mr. Story's emigration, had voluntarily delivered several sermons at Marietta.

† The preceding biographical sketches are abridged from those elsewhere published, and written by Dr. S. P. Hildreth.

wandering, he finally died in 1822, on the island of Guernsey. His beautiful and accomplished wife subsequently returned to this country, and preferred claims against the United States, but without success. She died in New York, in 1842. The island will ever remain a memento of the fate of this unfortunate family, around whose melancholy fortunes the genius of Wirt has weaved a tribute of eloquence alike imperishable.

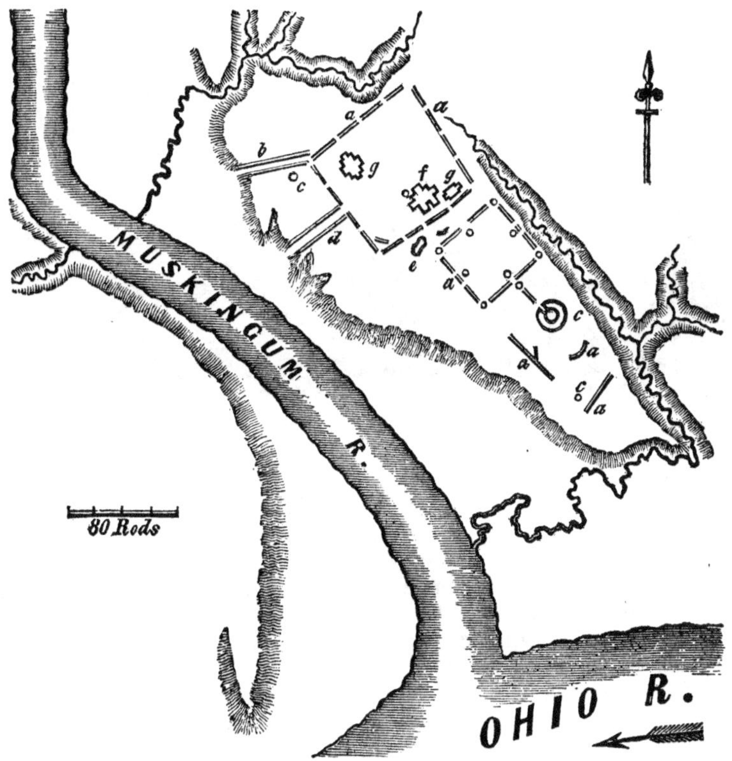

Ancient Works, Marietta.

At Marietta are some ancient works, which, although not more remarkable than others in the state, and not as extensive as some, are more generally known, from having been so frequently described and alluded to by travellers. The description which follows is from Harris's Tour, and the engraved plan from the Archæologia Americana.

"The situation of these works is on an elevated plain, above the present bank of the Muskingum, on the east side, and about half a mile from its junction with the Ohio. They consist of walls and mounds of earth, in direct lines, and in square and circular forms.

"The largest square fort, by some called the town, contains 40 acres, encompassed by a wall of earth from 6 to 10 feet high, and from 25 to 36 feet in breadth at the base. On each side are three openings, at equal distances, resembling 12 gateways. The entrances at the middle are the largest, particularly on the side next to the Muskingum. From this outlet is a covert way, formed of two parallel walls of earth, 231 feet distant from each other, measuring

Mound at Marietta.

from centre to centre. The walls at the most elevated part, on the inside, are 21 feet in height, and 42 in breadth at the base; but on the outside average only five feet in height. This forms a passage of about 360 feet in length, leading by a gradual descent to the low grounds, where, at the time of its construction, it probably reached the river. Its walls commence at 60 feet from the ramparts of the fort, and increase in elevation as the way descends towards the river; and the bottom is crowned in the centre, in the manner of a well-founded turnpike road.

"Within the walls of the fort, at the northwest corner, is an oblong elevated square, 188 feet long, 132 broad, and 9 feet high; level on the summit, and nearly perpendicular at the sides. At the centre of each of the sides, the earth is projected, forming gradual ascents to the top, equally regular, and about 6 feet in width. Near the south wall is another elevated square, 150 feet by 120, and 8 feet high, similar to the other, excepting that instead of an ascent to go up on the side next the wall, there is a hollow way 10 feet wide, leading 20 feet towards the centre, and then rising with a gradual slope to the top. At the southeast corner is a third elevated square, 108 by 54 feet, with ascents at the ends, but not so high nor perfect as the two others. A little to the southwest of the centre of the fort is a circular mound, about 30 feet in diameter and 5 feet high, near which are four small excavations at equal distances, and opposite each other. At the southwest corner of the fort is a semi-circular parapet, crowned with a mound, which guards the opening in the wall. Towards the southeast is a smaller fort, containing 20 acres, with a gateway in the centre of each side and at each corner. These gateways are defended by circular mounds.

"On the outside of the smaller fort is a mound, [shown in the engraving,] in form of a sugar-loaf, of a magnitude and height which strike the beholder with astonishment. Its base is a regular circle, 115 feet in diameter; its perpendicular altitude is 30 feet. It is sur rounded by a ditch 4 feet deep and 15 feet wide, and defended by a parapet 4 feet high, through which is a gateway towards the fort, 20 feet in width."

Harmar, from the Virginia shore of the Ohio.

Harmar is very pleasantly situated on the south bank of the Muskingum, opposite Marietta. It contains 1 Methodist church, a male and female academy, 5 mercantile stores, 1 steam mill, 1 extensive foundery, a large hotel, (shown on the left of the view,) and had in in 1840, 692 inhabitants. Steamboat building has been extensively carried on here. It will probably become a manufacturing town, a grant having lately been given by the state to use the waters of the Muskingum at the dam.

The following are the names of small villages in this county, with their population in 1840. Beverly 317, Plymouth 141, Watertown 126, and Lowell 92. The last named has since much increased. It is on the Muskingum, 10 miles above Marietta, where a high dam across the river furnishes much water power, and will probably at some future day make this an important seat of manufactures.

WAYNE.

Wayne was established by proclamation of Gov. St. Clair, Aug. 15th, 1796, and was the third county formed in the N. W. Territory. Its original limits were very extensive, and were thus defined in the act creating it. "Beginning at the mouth of the Cuyahoga river, upon Lake Erie, and with the said river to the Portage, between it and the Tuscarawas branch of the Muskingum; thence down the said branch to the forks at the carrying place above Fort Laurens; thence by a west line to the east boundary of Hamilton county, (which is a due north line from the lower Shawnese town upon the Scioto river,) thence by a line west-northerly to the southern part of the Portage, between the Miamis of the Ohio and the St. Mary's river; thence by a line also west-northerly to the southwestern part of the Portage, between the Wabash and the Miamis of Lake Erie, where Fort Wayne now stands; thence by a line west-northerly to the southern part of Lake Michigan; thence along the western shores of the same to the northwest part thereof; (including the lands upon the streams emptying into the said lake;) thence by a due north line to the territorial boundary in Lake Superior, and with the said boundary through Lakes Huron, Sinclair and Erie to the mouth of Cuyahoga river, the place of beginning." These limits embrace what is now a part of Ohio, Indiana, Illinois, Wisconsin, and all of Michigan, and the towns of Ohio City, Chicago, Sault St. Mary's, Mackinaw, etc. The surface of the county is mostly rolling, but interspersed with numerous glades of level land; the prevailing soil is a deep clayey loam, capable of the highest fertility. Coal of an excellent quality abounds in the northeastern part, and excellent quarries of limestone in the south: it is one of the best counties for wheat in Ohio. The principal productions are wheat, oats, corn, grass, potatoes, sheep and swine. The following is a list of its townships in 1840, with their population.

Baughman,	1741	Franklin,	1504	Perry,	2100
Canaan,	1826	Green,	1751	Plain,	2134
Chester,	1985	Jackson,	1645	Salt Creek,	2223
Chippewa,	1787	Lake,	1145	Sugar Creek,	2223
Clinton,	873	Milton,	1352	Wayne,	1841
Congress,	2008	Mohecan,	2046	Wooster,	3119
East Union,	1864	Paint,	1610		

The population of Wayne, in 1820, was 11,933; in 1830, 23,327; and in 1840, 36,015, or 68 inhabitants to a square mile. In February, 1846, the principal part of the townships of Jackson, Lake, Mohecan and Perry were taken from Wayne to form a part of the new county of Ashland.

This county was named from Gen. ANTHONY WAYNE. He was born in Chester county, Pa., January 1st, 1745. After leaving school he became a surveyor, and paid some attention to philosophy and engineering, by which he obtained the friendship of Dr. Franklin, who became his patron. He entered the army of the revolution in 1775, and was made brigadier general in 1777. He was in the army through the war, and particularly distinguished himself in the battles of Brandywine, Germantown and Monmouth. His attack upon Stony Point, in July, 1779, an almost inaccessible height, defended by 600 men and a strong battery of artillery, was the most brilliant exploit of the war. At midnight, he led his troops with unloaded muskets, flints out, and fixed bayonets, and without firing a single gun, carried the fort by storm and took 543 prisoners. He was struck, in the attack, by a musket ball in the head, which was momentarily supposed to be a mortal wound; he [illegible]led to his aids to carry him forward and let him die in the fort. The crowning acts of his life were his victory over the Indians on the Maumee, and the treaty of Greenville in 1795. His life of peril and glory was terminated in 1796, in a cabin at Presque Isle, (now Erie, Pa.,) then in the wilderness. His remains were there deposited, at his own request, under the flag-staff of the fort, on the margin of Lake Erie; and were removed in 1809, by his son, to Radnor church-yard, Delaware county, Pa. Wayne was one of the best generals of the revolution. He was irresistible in leading a charge, and a man of great impetuosity of character, bordering on rashness; but he conducted his last campaign with great caution and skill.

Killbuck's creek, in this county, was named from Killbuck, a Delaware chief. His village, called Killbuck's town, was on the road from Wooster to Millersburg, on the east side of the creek, about 10 miles south of Wooster. It is laid down on maps published as early as 1764. When the country was first settled, Killbuck was a very old man. There were several chiefs by this name.

Central View in Wooster.

An Indian settlement stood just south of Wooster, on the site of the Baptist burying-ground. It was named Beaver-hat, from an Indian chief of that name, who resided there with a few others. His Indian name was *Paupelenan*, and his camp or residence was called by him *Apple chauquecake*, *i. e*, "Apple Orchard." The Indian trail from Pittsburgh to Lower Sandusky, passed just north of Beaver Hat.

Wooster, the county seat, named from Gen. David Wooster, an officer of the revolution, is 93 miles northeast of Columbus, and 52 southerly from Cleveland, on the stage road between the two places. It is situated near the junction of Apple with Killbuck creek, on a gradual slope of ground, elevated about 50 feet above the latter, and is surrounded by a beautiful undulating country. To the south, from the more elevated parts of the town, is seen the beautiful valley of the Killbuck, stretching away for many miles, until the prospect is hid by the highlands in the county of Holmes, 12 or 14 miles distant. Wooster is compactly and well built, and is a place of much business. The view was taken near Archer's store, and shows a part of the public square, with the west side of Market street: the county buildings are shown on the left, and the spire of the Baptist church in the distance. The town contains 1 Presbyterian, 1 Methodist, 1 German Lutheran, 1 German Reformed, 1 Seceder, 1 Disciples, 1 Lutheran, 1 Baptist church, a female seminary in good repute, 4 grocery, 10 dry goods, 2 hardware, 2 book and 3 drug stores, 1 bank, and had in 1840, 1913 inhabitants, and now is estimated to contain 2700. Carriage making is extensively carried on.

This county lies within what was once called "the New Purchase," a very extensive tract, lying south of the Reserve, east of the Tuscarawas, north of the Greenville treaty line, and extending as far west as the western line of the Reserve. The land office for this tract was at Canton, Col. Thomas Gibson, register, and Col. John Sloan, now of Wooster, receiver. The first lands were sold in this district at Canton, in 1808, when was purchased the sites of Mansfield, Richland county, Wooster, and a few scattering tracts in the purchase.

Wooster was laid out in the fall of 1808, by the proprietors, John Beaver, William Henry and Joseph H. Larwill, on a site 337 feet above Lake Erie. The first house built in the county was a log structure now standing on Liberty street, in Wooster, immediately west of the residence of William Larwill. It was raised about the time the town was laid out, and was first occupied by William Larwill and Abraham Miller, a young man. The next spring the father of the latter moved in from Stark county, with his family—the first that settled in the town—and opened it as a house of entertainment. About the same time, James Morgan, from Virginia, settled with his family on Killbuck, just north of the old Indian town. In 1810, the yellow brick building on the north side of Liberty street, adjoining the public square, was erected by John Beaver, being the first brick edifice erected in the county. In the fall of 1808, a road was cut from what is now Massilon, to Wooster, which was, it is said, the first road made in the county. The first state road running through the county, from Canton to Wooster, was laid out in 1810, by the commissioners.

When Wooster was settled, there were no white inhabitants between it and the lake; on the west, none short of the Maumee, Fort Wayne and Vincennes; on the south, none until within a few miles of Coshocton, and those on the Tuscarawas were the nearest on the east. Wooster was made the seat of justice for the county, May 30th, 1811. Previously, the whole county was comprised in Killbuck township, which had, by the census of 1810, but 320 inhabitants. Wooster was not the first county seat. The spot chosen by the first commissioners was on an eminence now known as Madison hill, about 1¼ miles southeast of the town, on land then owned by Bezaleel Wells & Co., which place they called Madison. But a single cabin was afterwards built there. The selection displeased the people of the county, which resulted in the legislature appointing new commissioners, who located it at Wooster.

The first mill was erected in the county in 1809, by Joseph Stibbs, of Canton, on Apple creek, about a mile east of Wooster. Some time after, Stibbs sent a man by the name of Michael Switzer, who opened for him, in a small building attached to the mill, a store, consisting of a small stock of goods suitable for the settlers and Indians.

One morning a singular incident occurred. In the store was William Smith, Hugh Moore, Jesse Richards, J. H. Larwill and five or six Indians. Switzer was in the act of weighing out some powder from an eighteen pound keg, while the Indians were quietly smoking their pipes filled with a mixture of tobacco, sumach leaves and kinnickinnick, or yellow willow bark, when a puff of wind coming in at the window, blew a spark from one of their pipes into the powder. A terrific explosion ensued. The roof of the building was blown into four parts, and carried some distance—the sides fell out, the joists came to the floor—and the floor and chimney alone were left of the structure. Switzer died in a few minutes—Smith was blown through the partition into the mill, and badly injured. Richards and the Indians were also hurt, and all somewhat burned. Larwill, who happened to be standing against the chimney, escaped with very little harm, except having, like the rest, his face well blackened, and being knocked down by the shock.

The Indians, fearful that they might be accused of doing it intentionally, some days after called a council of citizens for an investigation, which was held on the bottom, on Christmas run, west of the town.

In the war of 1812, a block-house was erected in Wooster, on the site of Col. John Sloan's residence. It was built by Captain George Stidger, of Canton, and was intended more particularly for a company he had here and other troops who might be passing through the country.

The following is a list of small villages in the county, with their distances and directions from Wooster, the largest of which may contain 350 inhabitants. Congress 11, and New Pittsburg 9 NW.; Jefferson 4, and Reedsburg, 8 W.; Blachneyville, 8 NSW.; Millbrook, 6 SW.; Moreland, 6 S.; Edinburgh 6, and Mt. Eaton, 14 SE.; Moscow 10, and Dalton, 13 E.; Smithville 6, Bristol 13, Chippewa 15, and Doyleston, 17 NE.

WILLIAMS.

WILLIAMS was formed from old Indian territory, April 1st, 1820, and organized in April, 1824. It was named from David Williams, a native of Tarrytown, N. Y., and one of the three captors of Maj. Andre, in the war of the revolution. The surface is slightly rolling or level. In the west are oak openings with a light sandy soil. In the north is a rich black soil. The principal crops are corn, potatoes, oats and wheat. The following is a list of its townships in 1840, with their population.

Brady,	351	Florence,	119	Springfield,	359
Bridewater,	110	Hicksville,	67	St. Joseph,	191
Centre,	339	Jefferson,	363	Superior,	166
Defiance,	944	Milford,	175	Tiffin,	222
Delaware,	201	Mill Creek,	110	Washington,	98
Farmer,	281	Pulaski,	279		

The population of Williams in 1830, was 1039, and in 1840, 4464, or 6 inhabitants to the square mile. This county was much reduced in 1845, by the formation of Defiance, to which the townships of Defiance, Delaware, Farmer, Hicksville, Milford, Tiffin and Washington, now belong.

This county is now settling fast. The population are principally from Ohio, New England, New York, Pennsylvania and Germany. Previous to 1835, there were but few families within its present limits.

Bryan, the county seat, is 173 miles NW. of Columbus and 18 from Defiance. It was laid out in 1840, and named from Hon. John A. Bryan, formerly auditor of the state, and later charge de affairs to Peru. It is a small village, containing perhaps 40 or 50 dwellings.

WOOD.

Wood was formed from old Indian territory, April 1st, 1820, and named from the brave and chivalrous Col. Wood, a distinguished officer of engineers in the war of 1812. The surface is level, and covered by the black swamp, the soil of which is a rich, black loam, and very fertile, and peculiarly well adapted to grazing. The population are mainly of New England descent, with some Germans The principal crops are corn, hay, potatoes, oats and wheat. The following is a list of the townships in 1840, with their population.

Bloom,	437	Liberty,	215	Perrysburg,	1041
Centre,	97	Middleton,	193	Plain,	272
Freedom,	238	Milton and Weston,	539	Portage,	199
Henry,	213	Montgomery,	609	Troy,	383
Jackson,	26	Perry,	559	Washington,	244

The population of Wood in 1830, was 1096, and in 1840, 5458, or 10 inhabitants to the square mile.

This county lies within the Maumee valley, a country as yet new and thinly settled, but destined to be one of the most highly cultivated and densely populated in the west. We annex a sketch of its early history, in a communication from Hezekiah L. Hosmer, Esq., of Perrysburg.

The military expeditions against the Indian tribes in the west, commenced under the colonial governments about the middle of the last century, were finally terminated on this river, by the decisive victory of Gen. Wayne, in 1794. Previous to that event, no portion of the west was more beloved by the Indians than the valleys of the Maumee and its tributaries. In the daily journal of Wayne's campaign, kept by George Will, under date of August 6th, 1794, when the army was encamped 56 miles in advance of Fort Recovery, the writer says: "We are within 6 miles of the Auglaize river, and I expect to eat green corn to-morrow." On the 8th of the same month, after the arrival of the army at the Camp Grand Auglaize, (the site of Fort Defiance,) he continues: "We have marched 4 or 5 miles in corn-fields down the Auglaize, and there is not less than 1000 acres of corn around the town." This journal, kept from that time until the return of the army to Fort Greenville, is full of descriptions of the immense corn-fields, large vegetable patches, and old apple trees, found along the banks of the Maumee, from its mouth to Fort Wayne. It discloses the astonishing fact, that for a period of eight days while building Fort Defiance, the army obtained their bread and vegetables from the corn-fields and potatoe patches surrounding the fort. In their march from Fort Defiance to the foot of the rapids, the army passed through a number of Indian towns, composed of huts, constructed of bark and skins—which afforded evidence that the people who had once inhabited them were composed, not only of Indians, but of Canadian French and renegade Englishmen.

What the condition of the valley was for some years after Wayne's campaign, may be gathered from the following extracts from one of Judge Burnet's letters, published by the Ohio Historical society. After assigning some reasons for the downfall of the Indians, he says: "My yearly trips to Detroit, from 1796 to 1802, made it necessary to pass through some of their towns, and convenient to visit many of them. Of course, I had frequent opportunities of seeing thousands of them, in their villages and at their hunting camps, and of forming a personal acquaintance with some of their distinguished chiefs. I have eat and slept in their towns, and partaken of their hospitality, which had no limit but that of their contracted means. In journeying more recently through the state, in discharging my judicial duties, I sometimes passed over the ground, on which I had seen towns filled with happy families of that devoted race, without perceiving the smallest trace of what had once been there. All their ancient settlements, on the route to Fort Defiance, and from thence to the foot of the rapids, had been broken up and deserted. The battle-ground of Gen. Wayne, which I had often seen in the rude state, in which it was when the decisive action of 1794 was fought, was so altered and changed that I could not recognize it, and not an indication remained of the very extensive Indian settlements which I had formerly seen there. It seemed almost impossible that in so short a period, such an astonishing change could have taken place." These extracts prove, that even after the battle of Presque Isle, although crushed and humbled, the Indian refused to be divorced from the favorite home and numerous graves of his race. A chain of causes which followed this battle, finally wrested from him the last foothold of his soil. These may be said to have commenced with the treaty of Greenville, made on the 3d of August, 1795, with the Wyandots, Ottawas, and other tribes, located in this region. By this treaty, among various other cessions of territory, a tract of land 12 miles square at the foot of the rapids, and one of 6 miles square at the mouth of the river, were given to the United States. This treaty was followed by the establishment of the boundaries of the county of Wayne, which included a part of the states of Ohio, Indiana, and the whole of Michigan.

Notwithstanding this actual declaration of ownership by the government, few only of the whites of the country, were willing to penetrate and reside in this yet unforsaken abode of the Indian. Col. John Anderson was the first white trader of any notoriety on the Maumee. He settled at Fort Miami as early as 1800. Peter Manor, a Frenchman, was here previous to that time, and was adopted by the chief Fontogany, by the name of *Sawendebans*, or "the Yellow Hair!" Manor, however, did not come here to reside until 1808. Indeed, I can not learn the names of any of the settlers prior to 1810, except the two above mentioned. We may mention among those who came during the year 1810, Maj. Amos Spafford, Andrew Race, Thomas Leaming, Halsey W. Leaming, James Carlin, Wm. Carter, George Blalock, James Slason, Samuel H. Ewing, Jesse Skinner, David Hull, Thomas Dick, Wm. Peters, Ambrose Hickox, Richard Gifford. All these individuals were settled within a circumference of 10 miles, embracing the ampitheatre at the foot of the rapids, as early as 1810. Maj. Amos Spafford came here to perform the duties of collector of the port of Miami. He was also appointed deputy post-master. A copy of his return to the government as collector, for the first quarter of his service, ending on the 30th June, 1810, shows the aggregate amount of exports to have been $5640,85. This was, for skins and furs, $5610,85, and for 20 gallons of bear's oil, $30.

When war broke out in 1812, there were 67 families residing at the foot of the rapids. Manor—or Minard, the Frenchman above alluded to—states that the first intimation that the settlers had of Hull's surrender at Detroit, manifested itself by the appearance of a party of British and Indians at the foot of the rapids, a few days after it took place. The Indians plundered the settlers on both sides of the river, and departed for Detroit in canoes. Three of their number remained, with the intention of going into the interior of the state. One of these was a Delaware chief by the name of Sac-a-manc. Manor won his confidence, under the pretence of friendship for the British, and was by him informed, that in a few days a grand assemblage of all the northwestern tribes was contemplated at Fort Malden, and that in about two days after that assemblage, a large number of British and Indians would be at the foot of the rapids, on their march to relieve Fort Wayne, then under investment by the American army, as was supposed. He also informed him, that when they came again, they would massacre all the Yankees found in the valley. Sac-a-manc left for the interior of the state, after remaining a day at the foot of the rapids. The day after his departure, Minard called upon Maj. Spafford, and warned him of the hostile intentions of the Indians, as he had received them from Sac-a-manc. The major placed no confidence in them, and expressed a determination to remain, until our army from the interior should reach this frontier. A few days after this conversation, a man by the name of Gordon was seen approaching the residence of Maj. Spafford in great haste. This individual had been reared among the Indians; but had previous to this time received some favors of a trifling character from Maj. Spafford. The major met him in his corn-field, and was informed that a party of about 50 Pottawatomies on their way to Malden had taken this route, and in less than two hours would be at the foot of the rapids. He also urged the major to make good his escape immediately. Most of the families at the foot of the rapids had left the valley after receiving intelligence of Hull's surrender. The major assembled those that were left on the bank of the river, where they put in tolerable sailing condition an old barge, in which some officers had descended the river from Fort Wayne, the previous year. They had barely time to get such of their effects as were portable on board, and row down into the bend below the town, before they heard the shouts of the Indians above. Finding no Americans here, the Indians passed on to Malden. The major and his companions sailed in their crazy vessel down the lake, to the Quaker settlement at Milan, on Huron river, where they remained until the close of the war. Sac-a-manc, on his return from the interior of the state, a few days after the event, showed Manor the scalps of three persons that he had killed during his absence, on Owl creek, near Mount Vernon. At the time mentioned by him, a detachment of the British army, under command of Colonel Elliott, accompanied by about 500 Indians, came to the foot of the rapids. They were anxious to obtain guides. Manor feigned lameness and ignorance of the country, above the head of the rapids, a distance of 18 miles up the river. By this means, he escaped being pressed into their service above that point. He accompanied them that far with his cart and poney, and was then permitted to return. On his return he met Col. Elliott, the commander of the detachment, at the foot of Presque Isle Hill, who stopped him, and after learning the services he had performed, permitted him, with a curse, to go on. A mile below him, he met a party of about 40 Pottawotamies, who also desired to know where he was going. Manor escaped being compelled to return, by telling them he was returning to the foot of the rapids, after forage for the army. The British and Indians pursued their march up the river, until they saw the American flag waving over Winchester's encampment at Defiance, when they returned in double quick time to Canada. On their return, they burned the dwellings, stole the horses and destroyed the corn-fields of the settlers at the foot of the rapids.

Manor, soon after his arrival at the foot of the rapids, went down the river to the British fleet, then lying at the mouth of Swan creek, under command of Capt. Mills. Here he reported himself, told what he had done for the army, and desired leave to go to his family at the mouth of the river. Capt. Mills, having no evidence of his loyalty beyond his own word, put him under hatches as a prisoner of war. Through the aid of his friend, Beaugrand, Minard was released in a few days, joined his family, and was afterwards a scout for our army during the remainder of the war. He is now living at the head of the rapids, on a reservation of land granted him by the government, at the request of his Indian father, Ton-tog-sa-ny.

After peace was declared, most of the settlers that had lived here previous to the war, returned to their old possessions. They were partly indemnified by government for their losses. Many of them lived in the block-houses on Fort Meigs, and one or two of the citizens of our town were born in one of them. The settlement of the valley was at first slow, but the foot of the rapids and vicinity was settled long before any of the rest. In 1816, government sent an agent to lay out a town, at the point best calculated for commercial purposes. That agent sounded the river from its mouth, and fixed upon Perrysburg. The town was laid out that year, and named after Com. Perry, by Hon. Josiah Meigs, then comptroller of the treasury. This county was then embraced in the county limits of Logan county—Bellefontaine, being the county seat. When the limits of Wood county were first determined, there was a great struggle between these three towns at the foot rapids—Orleans, Maumee and Perrysburg, for the county seat. The decision in favor of Perrysburg was the cause of the abandonment of the little town of Orleans, which soon after fell into decay.

The last remnant of the powerful Ottawa tribe of Indians removed from this valley west of the Mississippi in 1838. They numbered some interesting men among them. There was Nawash, Ockquenoxy, Charloe, Ottoca, Petonquet, men of eloquence, remembered by many of our citizens. Their burying-grounds and village-sites, are scattered along both banks of the river, from its mouth to Fort Defiance.

This part of the Maumee valley has been noted for military operations. Wayne's victory over the Indians, (see page 318,) Aug. 20th 1794, was gained within its borders. It was also the theatre of some important operations in the war of 1812.

About the middle of June, 1812, the army of Hull left Urbana, and passed through the present counties of Logan, Hardin, Hancock and Wood, into Michigan. They cut a road through the forest, and erected Forts M'Arthur and Findlay on the route, and arrived at the Maumee on the 30th of June, which they crossed at or near the foot of the rapids. Hull surrendered at Detroit on the 16th of the August following.

In the same summer, Gen. Edward W. Tupper, of Gallia county, raised about 1000 men for six months' duty, mainly from Gallia, Lawrence and Jackson counties, who, under the orders of Gen. Winchester, marched from Urbana north by the route of Hull, and reached the foot of the Maumee rapids. The Indians appearing in force on the opposite bank, Tupper endeavored to cross the river with his troops in the night; but the rapidity of the current, and the feeble, half-starved condition of his men and horses were such, that the attempt failed. The enemy soon after collected a superior force, and attacked Tupper in his camp, but were driven off with considerable loss. They returned to Detroit, and the Americans marched back to Fort M'Arthur.

On the 10th of January, 1813, Gen. Winchester, whose troops had been stationed at Forts Wayne and Defiance, arrived at the rapids, having marched from the latter along the north bank of the Maumee. There they encamped until the 17th, when Winchester resumed his march north, and was defeated with great loss on the 22d, on the River Raisin, near the site of Monroe, Michigan.

On receiving information of Winchester's defeat, Gen. Harrison sent Dr. M'Keehan from Portage river with medicines and money to Malden, for the relief of the wounded and the prisoners. He was accompanied by a Frenchman and a militia man, and was furnished with a letter from Harrison, addressed to any British officer whom he might meet, describing his errand. The night after they left, they halted at the Maumee rapids to take a few hours sleep, in a vacant cabin upon the north bank of the river, about 50 rods north of the present bridge. The cariole in which they travelled was left at the door, with a flag of truce set up in it. They were discovered in the night by a party of Indians, accompanied, it is said, by a British officer; one of the men was killed, and the others taken to Malden, where the doctor was thrown into prison by Proctor and loaded with irons.

After the defeat of Winchester, Gen. Harrison, about the 1st of Feb., established his advanced post at the foot of the rapids. He ordered Capt. Wood, of the engineer corps, to fortify the position, as it was his intention to make this point his grand depot. The fort erected was afterwards named Meigs, in honor of Governor Meigs.

Harrison ordered all the troops in the rear to join him immediately. He was in hopes, by the middle of February, to advance upon Malden, and strike a blow that should, in some measure, retrieve the misfortunes that had befallen the American arms in this quarter.

On the 9th of February, intelligence was brought of the encampment of about 600 Indians, about 20 miles down, near the Bay shore. Harrison had with him at this time about 2000 men at the post. The same night, or that following, 600 men left the fort under Harrison, and marched down the river on the ice about 20 miles, when they discovered some fires on the north side of the river, which proved to have been that of the Indians who had fled the day before. Here the detachment, which had been joined by 500 men more from the post, waited a few minutes, without having time to warm themselves, it being intensely cold, when the object of the expedition was made known. This was to march after the Indians; and all those unable by fatigue to continue, were ordered to follow the next day. On resuming the line of march, the army had proceeded only about two miles when their only cannon, with the horses attached, broke through the ice. This was about two hours before morning, and the moon unfortunately was nearly down. In endeavoring to extricate the horses, Lieut. Joseph H. Larwill, who had charge of the piece, with two of his men, broke through the ice and narrowly escaped drowning. The army thereupon halted, and a company ordered to assist in recovering the cannon, which was not accomplished until daybreak. Some of the men gave out from being wet, cold and fatigued; but the lieut., with the remainder, proceeded with the cannon after the main army, which they overtook shortly after sunrise, on an island near the mouth of the bay. The spies were then arriving with the intelligence that the Indians had left the river Raisin for Malden. Upon this the troops, having exhausted their provisions, returned, arriving at Fort Meigs just as the evening gun had been fired, having performed a march of 45 miles on the ice in less than 24 hours.*

A few days after this, about 250 men volunteered to go on an enterprize of the most desperate nature. On Friday, the 26th, the volunteer corps destined for this duty were addressed on parade by Gen. Harrison, who informed them, that when they had got a sufficient distance from the fort, they were to be informed of the errand they were upon, and that all who then wished could return, but not afterwards. He represented the undertaking as in a high degree one of peril and privation; but he promised that those who deported themselves in a gallant and soldierlike manner should be rewarded, and their names forwarded to the general government.

The corps took up their line of march and concentrated at what is now Lower Sandusky, where was then a block-house, on the site of Fort Stephenson, at that time garrisoned by two companies of militia.

The force which was under the command of Capt. Langham, consisted of 68 regulars, 120 Virginia and Pennsylvania militia, 32 men under Lieut. Madiss, and 22 Indians, making, with their officers, 242 men; besides these, were 24 drivers of sleds and several pilots.

On the morning of the 2d of March, they left the block-house, with six days' provisions, and had proceeded about half a mile when Capt. Langham ordered a halt. He addressed the soldiers and informed them of the object of the expedition, which was to move down to Lake Erie and cross over the ice to Malden, and, in the darkness of night, to destroy with combustibles the British fleet and the public stores on the bank of the river. This being done, the men were to retreat in their sleighs to the point of the Maumee bay, when their retreat was to be covered by a large force under Harrison. At this time, independent of the garrison at Malden, in that vicinity was a large body of Indians, and it required a combination of circumstances to render the enterprize successful. Capt. Langham gave liberty for all who judged it to be too hazardous, to withdraw. About 20 of the militia and 6 or 7 of the Indians availed themselves of the liberty. The rest moved down the river in sleighs, and took the land on the west side of the bay, passing through and across the peninsula, and crossed at the bay of Portage river, and soon came in view of the lake and its embosoming islands. Some of the men walking out on the ice of the lake, were alarmed by what was judged to be a body of men moving towards them. It was subsequently discovered to be the rays of the sun, reflecting on ice thrown up in ridges.

The party encamped near the lake, and being without any tents, were thoroughly wet by the snow and rain. After the guards were stationed, and all had retired to rest, the report of a musket was heard, and every man sprang to his post, ready for action. It proved to have been a false alarm—an accidental discharge through the carelessness of one of the men. Capt. Langham was almost determined to have the soldier shot for his carelessness, as it now had become particularly necessary for the utmost precaution; but motives of humanity prevailed, and he was suffered to go unpunished.

On the next morning, March 3d, they proceeded on the ice to Middle Bass island, some 17 miles from their encampment. Just before they left the lake shore, an ensign and 13 of the militia, one of the Indian chiefs and several of the Indians, deserted them. During their progress to the island, the weather was stormy, wind blowing and snowing, and in places it was quite slippery. They arrived at the northwest side of the island early in the afternoon, when the weather moderated.

In the course of the afternoon, sled tracks were discovered on the ice, going in the direction of Malden. These were presumed to have been made by two Frenchmen, who left Sandusky the day before the corps of Langham. They had then stated they were going to the river Huron, which was in an opposite direction: the officers now felt assured they were inimical to their designs, and were on their way to give the British notice of their intentions. Moreover, to the north of the island on which they were, the ice was weak, and the lake appeared to be broken up to the north.

---

* MSS. journal of Joseph H. Larwill.

It being the intended route to go by the western Sister island, to elude the spies of the enemy, the guides gave it as their opinion that it was totally impossible to go to Malden; that the river Detroit and the lake from the middle Sister were doubtless broken up, and that there was a possibility of getting as far north as the middle Sister; but as the distance from that to Detroit river, 18 miles, had to be performed after night, they could not attempt going, being fully satisfied that they could not arrive at the point of destination, and as the weather was and had been soft, that, should a southerly wind blow up, the lake would inevitably break up, and they might be caught on it or one of the islands. They then affirmed they had gone as far as they thought it either safe or prudent, and would not take the responsibility on them any farther. Capt. Langham called the guides and officers together. He stated that he had been instructed to go no farther than the guides thought safe, asked the opinion of the officers, who unanimously decided that it was improper to proceed, and that they should return.

The weather having slighly improved, although still unfavorable, a second council was called of the officers and guides, but with the same result. The captain then called the men and gave the opinion of their superiors, and presented the importance of the expedition to the government should they succeed; on the other hand, he represented that they might be lost on the lake by the breaking up of the ice, without rendering any service to their country, who would thus be deprived of the choice troops of the army. The soldiers, on thus being called for their opinion, expressed themselves as ready to go wherever their officers would lead; at the same time, said they should abide by the decision of their superiors, whose judgment was better than their own.

The party returned by the way of Presque Isle, at which point they met Gen. Harrison with a body of troops. From thence they proceeded to Fort Meigs in safety. In the course of their journey back, they found the lake open near the western Sister island.*

On the 9th of March, the day being very fine, several of the men went down as far as the old British fort. Some of them discovered a party of Indians, and gave the alarm. The latter fired at them, and one man, while running, was shot through the left skirt of his coat. Luckily a hymn-book which he carried there received the ball, which was buried in its leaves. The men escaped safely into the fort; but Lieut. Walker, who was out hunting wild fowl, was killed. His body was found the next day and brought into the fort, where his grave is to be seen at the present day.

Harrison had determined, if possible, to regain Detroit, and in a measure atone for the disasters of the war in this quarter; but the weather had proved unfavorable for the transportation to Fort Meigs of a sufficient body of troops for such an object. His force there was diminished, soon after his arrival, by the expiration of the term of service of a part of those at the rapids, and nothing more was left for him but to remain on the defensive. Satisfied that, in his weakened condition, the enemy would make a descent from Malden upon the fort as soon as the ice broke up in the lake, he left in March for the interior, to hasten on all the troops he could raise to its defence. On the 12th of April he returned at the head of a detachment of troops, and applied himself with great assiduity to completing the defences.

About this time a Canadian Frenchman, with about a dozen of his own countrymen, all volunteers, had a desperate boat fight with an equal number of Indians in the river, near the north side of the large island below the fort, and defeated them. The whites were all either killed or wounded, except the captain and two of his men. As they were returning to the fort, they saw a solitary Indian, the sole survivor of his party, rise up in one of their two canoes and paddle to the shore.

[*Explanations.*—*a*, grand battery, commanded by Capt. Daniel Cushing; *b*, mortar battery; *e*, *i*, *o*, minor batteries; *g*, battery commanded at the 2d siege by Col. (now Gen.) Gaines; *c*, magazines. The black squares on the lines of the fort represent the position of the block-houses. The dotted lines show the traverses, or walls of earth, thrown up. The longest, the grand traverse, had a base of 20 feet, was 12 in height, and about 900 in length. The traverses running lengthwise of the fort, were raised as a protection against the batteries on the opposite side of the river, and those running

* The foregoing narrative of this enterprize is from the MSS. journal of Joseph H. Larwill, who was a lieutenant in the party.

crosswise, were to defend them from the British batteries on this side. The British batteries on the north side of the river, were named as follows: *a*, queen's; *b*, sailors; *d*, king's, and *c*, mortar. The fort

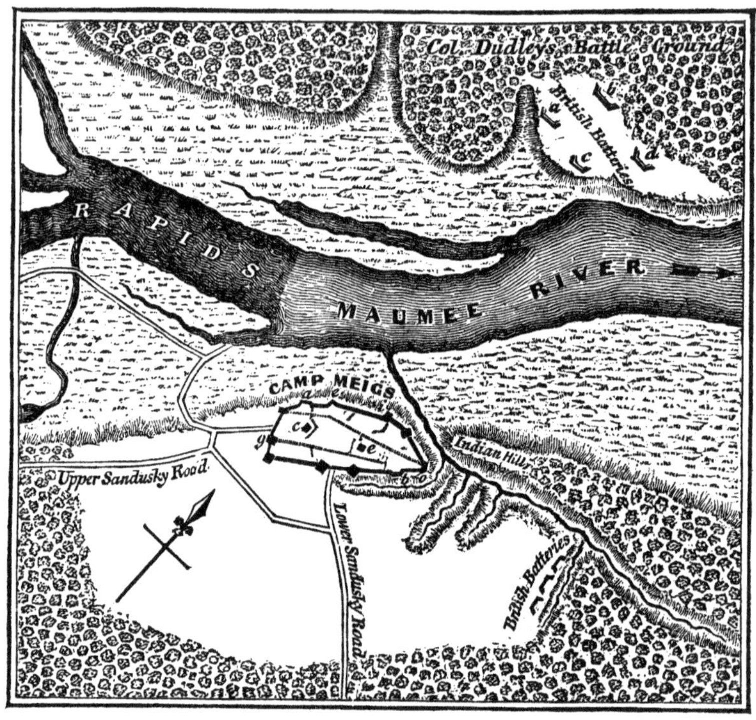

*Fort Meigs and its Environs.**

stood upon high ground, on the margin of a bank, elevated about 60 feet above the Maumee. The surface is nearly level, and is covered by a green sward. The outline of the fort is now well defined, and the grand traverse yet rises six or eight feet from the surrounding ground. The work originally covered about 10 acres, but was reduced in area between the two sieges, to accommodate a smaller number of troops. Just above, a large number of sunken graves indicate the locality of the soldiers' burying-ground. The graves of Lieut. Walker and Lieut. M'Cullough—the last of whom was shot while conversing with General Harrison—are within the fort. The first is surmounted by a small stone, with an inscription—the last is enclosed by a fence. (See page 328.) To understand the position of Fort Meigs, with reference to the British fort and surrounding country, see map on page 319.]

* From the survey of Lieut. Joseph H. Larwill, made between the two sieges, July 19th, 1813.

"On the breaking up of the ice in Lake Erie, General Proctor, with all his disposable force, consisting of regulars and Canadian militia from Malden, and a large body of Indians under their celebrated chief, Tecumseh, amounting in the whole to two thousand men, laid siege to Fort Meigs. To encourage the Indians, he had promised them an easy conquest, and assured them that General Harrison should be delivered up to Tecumseh. On the 26th of April, the British columns appeared on the opposite bank of the river, and established their principal batteries on a commanding eminence opposite the fort. On the 27th, the Indians crossed the river, and established themselves in the rear of the American lines. The garrison, not having completed their wells, had no water except what they obtained from the river, under a constant firing of the enemy. On the first, second, and third of May, their batteries kept up an incessant shower of balls and shells upon the fort. On the night of the third, the British erected a gun and mortar battery on the left bank of the river, within two hundred and fifty yards of the American lines. The Indians climbed the trees in the neighborhood of the fort, and poured in a galling fire upon the garrison. In this situation General Harrison received a summons from Proctor for a surrender of the garrison, greatly magnifying his means of annoyance; this was answered by a prompt refusal, assuring the British general that if he obtained possession of the fort, it would not be by capitulation.* Apprehensive of such an attack, General Harrison had made the governors of Kentucky and Ohio minutely acquainted with his situation, and stated to them the necessity of reinforcements for the relief of Fort Meigs. His requisitions had been zealously anticipated, and General Clay was at this moment descending the Miami with twelve hundred Kentuckians for his relief.

"At twelve o'clock in the night of the fourth, an officer† arrived from General Clay, with the welcome intelligence of his approach, stating that he was just above the rapids, and could reach him in two hours, and requesting his orders. Harrison determined on a general sally, and directed Clay to land eight hundred men on the right bank, take possession of the British batteries, spike their cannon, immediately return to their boats, and cross over to the American fort. The remainder of Clay's force were ordered to land on the left bank, and fight their way to the fort, while sorties were to be made from the garrison in aid of these operations Captain Hamilton was directed to proceed up the river in a periauger, land a subaltern on the left bank, who should be a pilot to conduct Gen. Clay to the fort; and then cross over and station his periauger at the place designated for the other division to land. General Clay, having received these orders, descended the river in order of battle in solid columns, each officer taking position according to his rank. Col. Dudley, being

---

*"The conversation which took place between General Harrison and Major Chambers, of the British army, was, as nearly as can be recollected, as follows:—

"*Major Chambers.*—General Proctor has directed me to demand the surrender of this post. He wishes to spare the effusion of blood.

"*General Harrison.*—The demand under present circumstances, is a most extraordinary one. As General Proctor did not send me a summons to surrender on his first arrival, I had supposed that he believed me determined to do my duty. His present message indicates an opinion of me that I am at a loss to account for.

"*Major Chambers.*—General Proctor could never think of saying anything to wound your feelings, sir. The character of General Harrison, as an officer, is well known. Gen. Proctor's force is very respectable, and there is with him a larger body of Indians than has ever before been embodied.

"*General Harrison.*—I believe I have a very correct idea of General Proctor's force; it is not such as to create the least apprehension for the result of the contest, whatever shape he may be pleased hereafter to give to it. Assure the general, however, that he will never have this post *surrendered* to him upon any terms. Should it fall into his hands, it will be in a manner calculated to do him more honor, and to give him larger claims upon the gratitude of his government, than any capitulation could possibly do."

† This messenger was Capt. William Oliver, now of Cincinnati, then a young man, noted for his heroic bravery, He had previously been sent from the fort at a time when it was surrounded by Indians, through the wilderness, with instructions to General Clay. His return to the fort was extremely dangerous. Capt. Leslie Coombs, now of Lexington, Ky., had been sent by Col. Dudley to communicate with Harrison. He approached the fort, and when within about a mile, was attacked by the Indians, and after a gallant resistance was foiled in his object and obliged to retreat with the loss of nearly all of his companions. Oliver managed to get into the fort through the cover of the darkness of the night, by which he eluded the vigilance of Tecumseh and his Indians, who were very watchful and had closely invested it.—H. H.

the eldest in command, led the van, and was ordered to take the men in the twelve front boats, and execute General Harrison's orders on the right bank. He effected his landing at the place designated, without difficulty. General Clay kept close along the left bank until he came opposite the place of Col. Dudley's landing, but not finding the subaltern there, he attempted to cross over and join Col. Dudley; this was prevented by the violence of the current on the rapids, and he again attempted to land on the left bank, and effected it with only fifty men amid a brisk fire from the enemy on shore, and made his way to the fort, receiving their fire until within the protection of its guns. The other boats under the command of Col. Boswell, were driven further down the current, and landed on the right to join Col. Dudley. Here they were ordered to re-embark, land on the left bank, and proceed to the fort. In the mean time two sorties were made from the garrison, one on the left, in aid of Col. Boswell, by which the Canadian militia and Indians were defeated, and he enabled to reach the fort in safety, and one on the right against the British batteries, which was also successful."*

"Col. Dudley, with his detachment of eight hundred Kentucky militia, completely succeeded in driving the British from their batteries, and spiking the cannon. Having accomplished this object, his orders were peremptory to return immediately to his boats and cross over to the fort; but the blind confidence which generally attends militia when successful, proved their ruin. Although repeatedly ordered by Col. Dudley, and warned of their danger, and called upon from the fort to leave the ground; and although there was abundant time for that purpose, before the British reinforcements arrived; yet they commenced a pursuit of the Indians, and suffered themselves to be drawn into an ambuscade by some feint skirmishing, while the British troops and large bodies of Indians were brought up, and intercepted their return to the river.† Elated with their first success, they considered

---

*"The troops in this attack on the British battery were commanded by Col. John Miller, of the 19th United States regiment, and consisted of about 250 of the 17th and 19th Regiments, 100 twelve-month volunteers, and Capt. Seebre's company of Kentucky militia. They were drawn up in a ravine under the east curtain of the fort, out of reach of the enemy's fire; but to approach the batteries it was necessary, after having ascended from the ravine, to pass a plain of 200 yards in width, in the woods beyond, which were the batteries protected by a company of grenadiers, and another of light infantry, upwards of 200 strong. These troops were flanked on the right by two or three companies of Canadian militia, and on the left by a large body of Indians under Tecumseh. After passing along the ranks and encouraging the men to do their duty, the general placed himself upon the battery of the right rear angle, to witness the contest. The troops advanced with loaded, but trailed arms. They had scarcely reached the summit of the hill, when they received the fire of the British infantry. It did them little harm; but the Indians being placed in position, and taking sight or aim, did great execution. They had not advanced more than fifty yards on the plain before it became necessary to halt and close the ranks. This was done with as much order by word of command from the officers as if they had been on parade. The charge was then made, and the enemy fled with so much precipitation that although many were killed none were taken. The general, from his position on the battery, seeing the direction that a part of them had taken, dispatched Major Todd with the reserve of about fifty regulars, who quickly returned with two officers and forty-three non-commissioned officers and privates. In this action the volunteers and militia suffered less than the regulars, because from their position the latter were much sooner unmasked by the hill, and received the first fire of all the enemy. It was impossible that troops could have behaved better than they did upon this sortie."

† After Dudley had spiked the batteries which had but few defenders, some of his men loitered about the banks and filled the air with cheers. Harrison, and a group of officers who were anxiously watching them from the grand battery (*a*,) with a presentiment of the horrible fate that awaited them, earnestly beckoned them to return. Supposing they were returning their cheers, they reiterated their shouts of triumph. Harrison seeing this, exclaimed in tones of anguish, "*they are lost! they are lost!*—can I never get men to obey my orders?" He then offered a reward of a thousand dollars to any man who would cross the river and apprize Col. Dudley of his danger. This was undertaken by an officer. Upon arriving at the beach he attempted to launch a large perogue which was drawn up there, but before this could be effected, and he with the assistance of some men could reach the middle of the river, the enemy had already arrived in force from below.

This defeat of Dudley was occasioned by the impetuous valor of his men. In one of the general orders after the 5th of May, Harrison takes occasion to warn his men against that rash bravery which he says "is characteristic of the Kentucky troops, and if persisted in is as fatal in its results as cowardice."

the victory as already gained, and pursued the enemy nearly two miles into the woods and swamps, where they were suddenly caught in a defile and surrounded by double their numbers. Finding themselves in this situation, consternation prevailed; their line became broken and disordered, and huddled together in unresisting crowds, they were obliged to surrender to the mercy of the savages. Fortunately for these unhappy victims of their own rashness, General Tecumseh commanded at this ambuscade and had imbibed since his appointment more humane feelings than his brother Proctor. After the surrender and all resistance had ceased, the Indians, finding five hundred prisoners at their mercy, began the work of massacre with the most savage delight. Tecumseh sternly forbade it, and buried his tomahawk in the head of one of his chiefs who refused obedience. This order accompanied with this decisive manner of enforcing it, put an end to the massacre. Of eight hundred men only one hundred and fifty escaped. The residue were slain or made prisoners. Colonel Dudley was severely wounded in the action, and afterwards tomahawked and scalped.

"Proctor, seeing no prospect of taking the fort, and finding his Indians fast leaving him, raised the siege on the 9th of May, and returned with precipitation to Malden. Tecumseh and a considerable portion of the Indians remained in service; but large numbers left it in disgust, and were ready to join the Americans. On the left bank, in the several sorties of the 5th of May, and during the siege, the American loss was eighty-one killed and one hundred and eighty-nine wounded."

When the enemy raised the siege, they gave a parting salute, which killed 10 or 12, and wounded double that number. "However," says one who was present, "we were glad enough to see them off on any terms. The next morning found us something more tranquil; we could leave the ditches, and walk about with something more of an air of freedom than we had done for the last 14 days; and here I wish I could present to the reader a picture of the condition we found ourselves in, when the withdrawal of the enemy gave us time to look at each other's outward appearance. The scarcity of water had put the washing of our hands and faces, much less our linen, out of the question. Many had scarcely any clothing left, and that which they wore was so begrimmed and torn by our residence in the ditch and other means, that we presented the appearance of so many scarecrows."

The British force under Proctor, during the siege, amounted, as nearly as could be ascertained, to 3200 men, of whom 600 were British regulars, 800 Canadian militia, and 1800 Indians. Those under Harrison, including the troops who arrived on the morning of the 5th, under Gen. Clay, were about 1200. The number of his men fit for duty, was, perhaps, less than 1100.

We give below an extract from an article on the siege of Fort Meigs, by Rev. A. M. Lorraine, originally published in the Ladies' Repository, for March, 1845.

One afternoon, as numbers were gathered together on the "parade," two strangers, finely mounted, appeared on the western bank of the river, and seemed to be taking a very calm and deliberate survey of our works. It was a strange thing to see travellers in that wild country, and we commonly held such to be enemies, until they proved themselves to be friends. So one of our batteries was cleared forthwith, and the gentlemen were saluted with a shot that tore up the earth about them, and put them to a hasty flight. If that ball had struck its mark, much bloodshed might have been prevented; for we learned subsequently that our illustrious visitors were Proctor and Tecumseh. The garrison was immediately employed in cutting deep traverses through the fort, taking down the tents and preparing for a siege. The work accomplished in a few hours, under the excitement of the occasion, was prodigious. The grand traverse being completed, each mess was ordered to excavate, under the embankment, suitable lodgings, as substitutes for our tents. Those rooms were shot proof and bomb proof, except in the event of a shell falling in the traverse and at the mouth of a cave.

The above works were scarcely completed before it was discovered that the enemy, under cover of night, had constructed batteries on a commanding hill north of the river. There their artillery men were posted; but the principal part of their army occupied the old English fort below. Their Indian allies appeared to have a roving commission, for they beset us on every side. The cannonading commenced in good earnest on both sides. It was, however, more constant on the British side, because they had a more extensive mark to batter. We had nothing to fire at but their batteries, but they were coolly and deliberately attended to; and it was believed that more than one of their guns were dismounted during the siege. One of our militia men took his station on the embankment, and gratuitously forewarned us of every shot. In this he became so skillful, that he could, in almost every case, predict the destination of the ball. As soon as the smoke issued from the muzzle of the gun, he would cry out "shot," or "bomb," as the case might be. Sometimes he would exclaim, "block-house No. 1," or "look out, main battery;" "now for the meat-house;" "good-by, if you will pass." In spite of all the expostulations of his friends, he maintained his post. One day there came a shot that seemed to defy all his calculations. He stood silent—motionless—perplexed. In the same instant he was swept into eternity. Poor man! he should have considered, that when there was no obliquity in the issue of the smoke, either to the right or left, above or below, the fatal messenger would travel in the direct line of his vision. He reminded me of the peasant, in the siege of Jerusalem, who cried out, "woe to the city! woe to the temple! woe to myself!" On the most active day of the investment, there were as many as five hundred cannon balls and bombs* thrown at our fort. Meantime, the Indians, climbing up into the trees, fired incessantly upon us. Such was their distance, that many of their balls barely reached us, and fell harmless to the ground. Occasionally they inflicted dangerous and even fatal wounds. The number killed in the fort was small, considering the profusion of powder and ball expended on us. About eighty were slain, many wounded, and several had to suffer the amputation of limbs. The most dangerous duty which we performed within the precincts of the fort, was in covering the magazine. Previous to this, the powder had been deposited in wagons, and these stationed in the traverse. Here there was no security against bombs; it was therefore thought to be prudent to remove the powder into a small block-house, and cover it with earth. The enemy, judging our designs from our movements, now directed all their shot to this point. Many of their balls were red-hot. Wherever they struck, they raised a cloud of smoke, and made a frightful hissing. An officer, passing our quarters, said, "boys, who will volunteer to cover the magazine?" Fool-like, away several of us went. As soon as we reached the spot, there came a ball and took off one man's head. The spades and dirt flew faster than any of us had before witnessed. In the midst of our job, a bomb-shell fell on the roof, and lodging on one of the braces it spun round for a moment. Every soldier fell prostrate on his face, and with breathless horror awaited the vast explosion which

---

* A large number of cannon balls were thrown into the fort, from the batteries on the opposite side of the river. Being short of a supply, Harrison offered a gill of whiskey for every cannon ball delivered to the magazine keeper, Mr. Thomas L. Hawkins, now residing at Lower Sandusky. Over 1000 gills of whiskey were thus earned by the soldiers.

For safety against bombs, each man had a hole dug under ground in rear of the grand traverse, which, being covered over with plank, and earth on top, fully protected them. When the cry *bomb* was heard, the soldiers either threw themselves upon the ground, or ran to the holes for safety. A bomb is most destructive when it bursts in the air, but it rarely explodes in that way: it usually falls with so much force as to penetrate the earth, and when it explodes, flies upwards and in an angular direction, in consequence of the pressure of the earth beneath and at its sides; consequently, a person lying on the ground is comparatively safe.

A heavy rain at last filled up the holes, rendering them uninhabitable, and the men were obliged to temporarily sleep in their tents. Then every once in a while, the startling cry, "BOMB!" aroused them from their slumbers. Rushing from their tents, they watched the course of the fiery messenger of death, as it winged its way through the midnight sky, and if it fell near, fall flat upon the ground; otherwise, return to their tents, only to be aroused again and again by the startling cry. So harrassing was this, so accustomed had the men become to the danger, and so overpowering the desire for sleep, that many of the soldiers remained in their tents locked in the embrace of sleep, determined, as one said, not to be disturbed in their slumbers "if ten thousand bombs burst all around them."—*H. H.*

we expected would crown all our earthly sufferings. Only one of all the gang presumed to reason on the case. He silently argued that, as the shell had not bursted as quick as usual, there might be something wrong in its arrangement. If it bursted where it was, and the magazine exploded, there could be no escape: it was death any how; so he sprung to his feet, seized a boat-hook, and pulling the hissing missile to the ground, and jerking the smoking match from its socket, discovered that the shell was filled with inflammable matter, which, if once ignited, would have wrapped the whole building in a sheet of flame. This circumstance added wings to our shovels; and we were right glad when the officer said, "that will do: go to your lines."

The following particulars of the defeat of Col. Dudley were published in a public print many years since by Joseph R. Underwood, who was present on the occasion, in the capacity of lieutenant in a volunteer company of Kentuckians, commanded by Captain John C. Morrison.

After a fatiguing march of more than a month, Gen. Clay's brigade found itself, on the night of the 4th of May, on board of open boats, lashed to the left bank of Miami of the Lakes, near the head of the rapids, and within hearing of the cannon at Fort Meigs, which was then besieged by the British and Indians. Very early on the morning of the 5th, we set off, and soon began to pass the rapids. We were hailed by a man from the right bank, who proved to be Captain Hamilton, of the Ohio troops, with orders from Gen. Harrison, then commanding at the fort. He was taken to the boat of General Clay's, and from that to Col. Dudley's, this last being in advance of the whole line. Captain Morrison's company occupied the boat in which the colonel descended. It being a damp, unpleasant morning, I was lying in the stern, wrapped in my blanket, not having entirely recovered from a severe attack of the measles. I learned that we were to land on the left bank, storm the British batteries erected for the purpose of annoying the fort; but what further orders were given, I did not ascertain. Hearing that we were certainly to fight, I began to look upon all surrounding objects as things which to me might soon disappear forever, and my mind reverted to my friends at home, to bid them a final farewell. These reflections produced a calm melancholy, but nothing like trepidation or alarm. My reveries were dissipated by the landing of the boat, about a mile or two above the point of attack. Shortly before we landed, we were fired upon by some Indians from the right bank of the river, and I understood that Captain Clarke was wounded in the head. The fire was returned from our boats, and the Indians fled, as if to give intelligence of our approach. Captain Price and Lieutenant Sanders, of the regular army, landed with us and partook in the engagement, having under command a few regular soldiers, but I think not a full company. The whole number of troops that landed, amounted probably to 700 men. We were formed on the shore in three parallel lines, and ordered to march for the battery at right angles with the river; and so far as I understood the plan of attack, one line was to form the line of battle in the rear of the battery, parallel with the river; the other two lines to form one above and one below the battery, at right angles to the river. The lines thus formed were ordered to advance, and did so, making as little noise as possible—the object being to surprise the enemy at their battery. Before we reached the battery, however, we were discovered by some straggling Indians, who fired upon us and then retreated. Our men pleased at seeing them run, and perceiving that we were discovered, no longer deemed silence necessary, and raised a tremendous shout. This was the first intimation that the enemy received of our approach, and it so alarmed them that they abandoned the battery without making any resistance. In effectuating the plan of attack, Captain J. C. Morrison's company were thrown upon the river, above the battery. While passing through a thicket of hazel, toward the river, in forming the line of battle, I saw Colonel Dudley for the last time. He was greatly excited; he railed at me for not keeping my men better dressed. I replied, that he must perceive from the situation of the ground, and the obstacles that we had to encounter, that it was impossible. When we came within a small distance from the river, we halted. The enemy at this place had gotten in the rear of our line, formed parallel with the river, and were firing upon our troops. Capt. J. C. Morrison's company did not long remain in this situation. Having nothing to do, and being without orders, we determined to march our company out and join the combatants. We did so accordingly. In passing out, we fell on the left of the whole regiment, and were soon engaged in a severe conflict. The Indians endeavored to flank and surround us. We drove them between one and two miles, directly back from the river. They hid behind trees and logs, and poured upon us, as we advanced, a most destructive fire. We were from time to time ordered to charge. The orders were passed along the lines, our field officers being on foot. . . . . . Shortly after this, Capt. J. C. Morrison was shot through the temples. The ball passing behind the eyes and cutting the optic nerve, deprived him of his sight. . . . . Having made the best arrangement for the safety of my much esteemed captain that circumstances allowed, I took charge of the company and continued the battle. We made several charges afterwards, and drove the enemy a considerable distance. . . . . At length orders were passed along the line directing us to fall back and keep up a retreating fire. As soon as this movement was made, the Indians were greatly encouraged, and advanced upon us with the most horrid yells. Once or twice the officers succeeded in producing a temporary halt and a fire on the Indians; but the soldiers of the different companies soon became mixed—confusion ensued—and a general rout took place. The retreating army made its way towards the batteries, where I supposed we should be able to form and repel the pursuing Indians. They were now so close in the rear, as to frequently shoot down those who were before me. About this time I received a ball in my back, which yet remains in my body. It struck me with a stunning, deadening force, and I fell on my hands and knees. I rose and threw my waistcoat open to see whether it had passed through me; finding it had not, I ran on, and had not proceeded more than a hundred or two yards before I was made a prisoner. In emerging from the woods into an open piece of ground, near the battery we had taken, and before I knew what had happened, a soldier seized my sword and said to me, "Sir! you are my prisoner!" I looked before me and saw, with astonishment, the ground covered with muskets. The soldier, observing my astonishment, said: "your army has surrendered," and received my sword. He ordered me to go forward and join the prisoners. I did so. The first man I met whom I recognized, was Daniel Smith, of our company. With eyes full of tears, he exclaimed: "Good Lord, lieutenant, what does all this mean." I told him we were prisoners of war. . . .

On our march to the garrison, the Indians began to strip us of our valuable clothing and other articles. One took my hat, another my hunting shirt, and a third my waistcoat, so that I was soon left with nothing but my shirt and pantaloons. I saved my watch by concealing the chain, and it proved of great service to me afterwards. Having read, when a boy, Smith's narrative of his residence among the Indians, my idea of their character was that they treated those best who appeared the most fearless. Under this impression, as we marched down to the old garrison, I looked at those whom we met with all the sternness of countenance I could command. I soon caught the eye of a stout warrior painted red. He gazed at me with as much sternness as I did at him, until I came within striking distance, when he gave me a severe blow over the nose and cheek bone with his wiping stick. I abandoned the notion acquired from Smith, and went on afterwards with as little display of hauteur and defiance as possible.

On our approach to the old garrison, the Indians formed a line to the left of the road, there being a perpendicular bank to the right, on the margin of which the road passed. I perceived that the prisoners were running the gauntlet, and that the Indians were whipping, shooting and tomahawking the men as they ran by their line. When I reached the starting place, I dashed off as fast as I was able, and ran near the muzzles of their guns, knowing that they would have to shoot me while I was immediately in front, or let me pass, for to have turned their guns up or down the lines to shoot me, would have endangered themselves, as there was a curve in their line. In this way I passed without injury, except some strokes over the shoulders with their gun-sticks. As I entered the ditch around the garrison, the man before me was shot and fell, and I fell over him. The passage for a while was stopped by those who fell over the dead man and myself. How many lives were lost at this place I cannot tell—probably between 20 and 40. The brave Captain Lewis was among the number. When we got within the walls, we were ordered to sit down. I lay in the lap of Mr. Gilpin, a soldier of Captain Henry's company, from Woodford. A new scene commenced. An Indian, painted black, mounted the dilapidated wall, and shot one of the prisoners next to him. He re-loaded and shot a second, the ball passing through him into the hip of another, who afterwards died, I was informed, at Cleveland, of the wound. The savage then laid down his gun and drew his tomahawk, with which he killed two others. When he drew his tomahawk and jumped down among the men, they endeavored to escape from him by leaping over the heads of each other, and thereby to place others between themselves and danger. Thus they were heaped upon one another, and as I did not rise, they trampled upon me so that I could see nothing that was going on. The confusion and uproar of this moment cannot be adequately described. There was an excitement among the Indians, and a fierceness in their conversation, which betokened on the part of some a strong disposition to massacre the whole of us. The British officers and soldiers seemed to interpose to prevent the further effusion of blood. Their expression was—"*Oh, nichee, wah!*" meaning, "oh! brother, quit!" After the Indian who had occasioned this horrible scene, had scalped and stripped his victims, he left us, and a comparative calm ensued. The prisoners resumed their seats on the ground. While thus situated, a tall, stout Indian walked into the midst of us, drew a long butcher knife from his belt and commenced whetting it. As he did so, he looked around among the prisoners, apparently selecting one for the gratification of his vengeance. I viewed his conduct, and thought it probable that he was to give the signal for a general massacre. But after exciting our fears sufficiently for his satisfaction, he gave a contemptuous grunt and went out from among us.

About this time, but whether before or after I do not distinctly recollect, Col. Elliott and Tecumseh, the celebrated Indian chief, rode into the garrison. When Elliott came to where Thomas Moore, of Clarke county, stood, the latter addressed him, and inquired "if it was compatible with the honor of a civilized nation, such as the British claimed to be, to suffer defenceless prisoners to be murdered by savages?" Elliott desired to know who he was. Moore replied that he was nothing but a private in Captain Morrison's company—and the conversation ended. . . . Elliott was an old man—his hair might have been termed, with more propriety, white than gray, and to my view he had more of the savage in his countenance than Tecumseh. This celebrated chief was a noble, dignified personage. He wore an elegant broadsword, and was dressed in the Indian costume. His face was finely proportioned, his nose inclined to the aquiline, and his eye displayed none of that savage and ferocious triumph common to the other Indians on that occasion. He seemed to regard us with unmoved composure, and I thought a beam of mercy shone in his countenance, tempering the spirit of vengeance inherent in his race against the American people. I saw him only on horseback. . . .

Shortly after the massacre in the old garrison, I was the subject of a generous act. A soldier with whom I had no acquaintance, feeling compassion for my situation, stripped off my clothes, muddy and bleeding, offered me his hunting shirt, which the Indians had not taken from him. At first I declined receiving it, but he pressed it upon me with an earnestness that indicated great magnanimity. I inquired his name and residence. He said that his name was James Boston, that he lived in Clarke county, and belonged to Capt. Clarke's company. I have never since seen him, and regret that I should never be able to recall his features if I were to see him.

Upon the arrival of Elliott and Tecumseh, we were directed to stand up and form in lines, I think four deep, in order to be counted. After we were thus arranged, a scene transpired scarcely less affecting than that which I have before attempted faintly to describe. The Indians began to select the young men whom they intended to take with them to their towns. Numbers were carried off. I saw Corporal Smith, of our company, bidding farewell to his friends, and pointing to the Indian with whom he was to go. I never heard of his return. The young men, learning their danger, endeavored to avoid it by crowding into the centre, where they could not be so readily reached. I was told that a quizzical youth, of diminutive size, near the outside, seeing what was going on, threw himself upon his hands and knees, and rushed through the legs of his comrades, exclaiming, "*Root, little hog, or die.*" Such is the impulse of self-preservation, and such the levity with which men inured to danger will regard it. Owing to my wound, I could not scuffle, and was thrust to the outside. An Indian came up to me and gave me a piece of meat. I took this for proof that he intended carrying me off with him. Thinking it the best policy to act with confidence, I made a sign to him to give me his butcher knife—which he did. I divided the meat with those who stood near me, reserving a small piece for myself—more as a show of politeness to the savage, than to gratify any appetite I had for it. After I had eaten it and returned the knife, he turned and left me. When it was near night, we were taken in open boats about nine miles down the river, to the British shipping. On the day after, we were visited by the Indians in their bark canoes, in order to make a display of their scalps. These they strung on a pole, perhaps two inches in diameter, and about eight feet high. The pole was set up perpendicularly in the bow of their canoes, and near the top the scalps were fastened. On some poles I saw four or five. Each scalp was drawn closely over a hoop about four inches in diameter; and the flesh sides, I thought, were painted red. Thus their canoes were decorated with a flag-staff of a most appropriate character, bearing human scalps, the horrid ensigns of savage warfare. We remained six days on board the vessel—those of us, I mean, who were sick and wounded. The whole of us were discharged on parole. The officers signed an instrument in writing, pledging their honors not to serve against the king of Great Britain and his allies during the war, unless regularly exchanged. It was inquired whether the Indians were included in the term "allies." The only answer was, "that his majesty's allies were known." The wounded and sick were taken in a vessel commanded by Captain Stewart, at the mouth, I think, of Vermillion river, and there put on shore. I afterwards saw Captain Stewart, a prisoner of war at Frankfort, Kentucky, together with a midshipman, who played Yankee Doodle on a flute, by way of derision, when *we* were first taken on board *his* vessel. Such is the fortune of war. They were captured by Commodore Perry, in the battle of Lake Erie. I visited Captain Stewart to requite his kindness to me when, like him, I was a prisoner.

The following is a British account of the siege of Fort Meigs, from the London New Monthly Magazine for December, 1826, written by an officer in their army.

Far from being discouraged by the discomfiture of their armies under Generals Hull and Winchester, the Americans dispatched a third and more formidable one under one of their most experienced commanders, General Harrison, who, on reaching Fort Meigs, shortly subsequent to the affair at Frenchtown, directed his attention to the erection of works, which in some measure rendered his position impregnable. Determined, if possible, to thwart the movements of the enemy, and give the finishing stroke to his movements in that quarter, General Proctor (lately promoted) ordered an expedition to be in readiness to move for the Miami. Accordingly, towards the close of April, a detachment of the 41st, some militia and 1500 Indians, accompanied by a train of battering artillery, and attended by two gun-boats, proceeded up that river and established themselves on the left bank, at the distance of a mile, and selected the site for our batteries. The season was unusually wet, yet in defiance of every obstacle, they were erected in the same night, in front of the American fortress, and the guns transported along the road in which the axle-trees of the carriages were frequently buried in mud. Among other battering pieces were two twenty-four pounders, in the transportation of which 200 men, with several oxen, were employed from 9 o'clock at night, until daylight in the morning. At length, every precaution having been made, a gun fired from one of the boats was the signal for their opening, and early on the morning of the 1st of May, a heavy fire was commenced, and continued for four days without intermission, during which period every one of the enemies' batteries were silenced and dismantled. The fire of the twenty-four pound battery was principally directed against the powder magazine, which the besieged were busily occupied in covering and protecting from our hot shot. It was impossible to have artillery better served: every shot that was fired sank into the roof of the magazine, scattering the earth to a considerable distance, and burying many of the workmen in its bed, from which we could distinctly see their survivors dragging forth the bodies of their slaughtered companions. Meanwhile the flank companies of the 41st, with a few Indians, had been dispatched to the opposite shore, within a few hundred yards of the enemy's works, and had constructed a battery, from which a galling cross-fire was sustained. Dismayed at the success of our exertions, Gen. Harrison, before our arrival, already apprised of the approach of a reinforcement of 1500 men, then descending the Miami, under General Clay, contrived to dispatch a courier on the evening of the 4th, with an order to that officer to land immediately and possess himself of our batteries on the left bank, while he (General Harrison) sallied forth to carry those on the right. Accordingly, at 3 o'clock on the morning of the 5th, General Clay* pushed forward the whole of his force, and meeting with no opposition at the batteries, which were entirely unsupported, proceeded to spike the guns, in conformity with his instructions; but elated with his success, and disobeying the positive orders of his chief, which was to retire the instant the object was effected, continued to occupy the position. In the meantime, the flying artillery-men had given the alarm, and three companies of the 41st, several of militia, and a body of Indians, the latter under the command of their celebrated chieftain, Tecumseh, were ordered to immediately move and re-possess themselves of the works. The rain, which had commenced falling in the morning, continued to fall with violence, and the road, as has already been described, was knee deep in mud; yet the men advanced to the assault with the utmost alacrity and determination. The enemy, on our approach, had sheltered themselves behind the batteries, affording them every facility of defence. Yet they were driven at the point of the bayonet from each in succession, until eventually not a man was left in the plain. Flying to the woods, the murderous fire of the Indians drove them back upon their pursuers, so that they had no possibility of escape. A vast number were killed, and independently of the prisoners taken by the Indians, 450, with their second in command, fell into our hands. Every man of the detachment, on this oc-

* This is an error, as the reader will perceive.

casion, acquitted himself to the entire satisfaction of his superiors. Among the most conspicuous for gallantry, was Major Chambers, of the 41st, acting deputy quarter-general to the division. Supported by merely four or five followers, this meritorious officer advanced under a shower of bullets from the enemy, and carried one of the batteries, sword in hand. A private of the same regiment being opposed, in an isolated condition, to three Americans, contrived to disarm them and render them his prisoners. On joining his company at the close of the affair, he excited much mirth among his comrades, in consequence of the singular manner in which he appeared, sweating beneath the weight of arms he had secured as trophies of victory, and driving his captives before him with an indifference and carelessness which contrasted admirably with the occasion. Of the whole of the division under General Clay, scarce 200 men effected their escape. Among the fugitives was that officer himself. The sortie made by General Harrison, at the head of the principal part of the garrison, had a different result. The detachment supporting the battery already described, were driven from their position, and two officers, Lieutenants M'Intyre and Hailes, and thirty men were made prisoners. Meanwhile it had been discovered that the guns on the left bank, owing to some error on the part of the enemy, had been spiked with the ramrods of the muskets, instead of the usual instruments: they were speedily rendered serviceable, and the fire from the batteries renewed. At this moment a white flag was observed waving on the ramparts of the fort, and the courage and perseverance of the troops appeared about to be crowned with the surrender of a fortress, the siege of which had cost them so much toil and privation. Such, however, was far from being the intention of General Harrison. Availing himself of the cessation of hostilities which necessarily ensued, he caused the officers and men just captured to be sent across the river for the purpose of being exchanged; but this was only a feint for the accomplishment of a more important object.

Drawing up his whole force, cavalry and infantry, on the plain beneath the fortress, he caused such of the boats of General Clay's division as were laden with ammunition, in which the garrison stood in much need, to be dropped under the works, and the stores immediately disembarked. All this took place in the period occupied for the exchange of prisoners. The remaining boats, containing the private baggage and stores of the division, fell into the hands of the Indians still engaged in the pursuit of the fugitives, and the plunder they acquired was immense. General Harrison having secured his stores, and received the officers and men exchanged for his captives, withdrew into the garrison, and the bombardment was recommenced.

The victory obtained at the Miami, was such as to reflect credit on every branch of the service; but the satisfaction arising from the conviction, was deeply embittered by an act of cruelty, which, as the writer of an impartial memoir, it becomes my painful duty to record. In the heat of the action, a strong corps of the enemy, which had thrown down their arms and surrendered prisoners of war, were immediately dispatched under an escort of 50 men, for the purpose of being embarked in the gun-boats, where it was presumed they would be safe from the attacks of the Indians. This measure, although dictated by the purest humanity, and apparently offering the most probable means of security, proved of fatal import to several of the prisoners. On reaching our encampment, then entirely deserted by the troops, they were met by a band of cowardly and treacherous Indians, who had borne no share in the action, yet who now, guided by the savage instinct of their nature, approached the column, and selecting their victims, commenced the work of blood. In vain did the harrassed and indignant escort endeavor to save them from the fury of their destroyers. The phrenzy of these wretches knew no bounds, and an old and excellent soldier named Russell, of the 41st, was shot through the heart, while endeavoring to wrest a victim from the grasp of his murderer. Forty of these unhappy men had already fallen beneath the steel of the infuriated party, when Tecumseh, apprised of what was doing, rode up at full speed, and raising his tomahawk, threatened to destroy the first man who refused to desist. Even on those lawless people, to whom the language of coercion had hitherto been unknown, the threats and tone of the exasperated chieftain, produced an instantaneons effect, and they retired at once humiliated and confounded.*

---

* Drake, in his life of Tecumseh, in quoting a letter from Wm. G. Ewing to John H. James, Esq., of Urbana, gives full particulars of Tecumseh's interference on this occasion, which we here copy.

"While this blood-thirsty carnage was raging, a thundering voice was heard in the rear, in the Indian tongue, when, turning round, he saw Tecumseh coming with all the rapidity his horse could carry him, until he drew near to where two Indians had an American, and were in the act of killing him. He sprang from his horse, caught one by the throat and

The survivors of this melancholy catastrophe were immediately conveyed on board the gun-boats, moored in the river, and every precaution having been taken to prevent a renewal of the scene, the escorting party proceeded to the interment of the victims, to whom the rites of sepulture were afforded, even before those of our own men, who had fallen in the action. Col. Dudley, second in command of Gen. Clay's division, was among the number of the slain.

On the evening of the second day after this event, I accompanied Maj. Muir, of the 41st, in a ramble throughout the encampment of the Indians, distant some few hundred yards from our own. The spectacle there offered to our view, was at once of the most ludicrous and revolting nature. In various directions were lying the trunks and boxes taken in the boats of the American division, and the plunderers were busily occupied in displaying their riches, carefully examining each article, and attempting to divine its use. Several were decked out in the uniforms of the officers; and although embarrassed in the last degree in their movements, and dragging with difficulty the heavy military boots with which their legs were for the first time covered, strutted forth much to the admiration of their less fortunate comrades. Some were habited in plain clothes; others had their bodies clad with clean white shirts, contrasting in no ordinary manner, with the swarthiness of their skins; all wore some articles of decoration, and their tents were ornamented with saddles, bridles, rifles, daggers, swords and pistols, many of which were handsomely mounted and of curious workmanship. Such was the ridiculous part of the picture; but mingled with these, and in various directions, were to be seen the scalps of the slain drying in the sun, stained on the fleshy side with vermillion dyes, and dangling in air, as they hung suspended from the poles to which they were attached, together with hoops of various sizes, on which were stretched portions of human skin, taken from various parts of the human body, principally the hand and foot, and yet covered with the nails of those parts; while scattered along the ground were visible the members from which they had been separated, and serving as nutriment to the wolf-dogs by which the savages were accompanied.

As we continued to advance into the heart of the encampment, a scene of a more disgusting nature arrested our attention. Stopping at the entrance of a tent occupied by the Minoumini tribe, we observed them seated around a large fire, over which was suspended a kettle containing their meal. Each warrior had a piece of string hanging over the edge of the vessel, and to this was suspended a food, which, it will be presumed we heard not without loathing, consisted of a part of an American; any expression of our feelings, as we declined the invitation they gave us to join in their repast, would have been resented by the Indians without much ceremony. We had, therefore, the prudence to excuse ourselves under the plea that we had already taken our food, and we hastened to remove from a sight so revolting to humanity.

Since the affair of the 5th, the enemy continued to keep themselves shut up within their works, and the bombardment, although carried on with vigor, had effected no practicable breach. From the account given by the officers captured during the sortie, it appears that, with a perseverance and toil peculiar to themselves, the Americans had constructed subterranean passages to protect them from the annoyance of our shells, which sinking into the clay, softened by the incessant rains that had fallen, instead of exploding were speedily extinguished. Impatient of longer privations, and anxious to return to their families and occupations, numbers of the militia withdrew themselves in small bodies, and under cover of the night; while the majority of Indians, enriched by plunder and languishing under the tediousness of a mode of warfare so different from their own, with less ceremony and caution, left us to prosecute the siege as we could.

Tecumseh at the head of his own tribe, (the Shawnees,) and a few others, amounting in all to about 400 warriors, continued to remain. The troops also were worn down with constant fatigue; for here, as in every other expedition against the enemy, few even of the officers had tents to shield them from the weather. A few pieces of bark torn from

---

the other by the breast, and threw them to the ground; drawing his tomahawk and scalping knife, he ran in between the Americans and Indians, brandishing them with the fury of a mad man, and daring any one of the hundreds that surrounded him, to attempt to murder another American. They all appeared confounded, and immediately desisted. His mind appeared rent with passion, and he exclaimed almost with tears in his eyes, "Oh! what will become of my Indians." He then demanded in an authoritative tone, where Proctor was; but casting his eye upon him at a small distance, sternly inquired why he had not put a stop to the inhuman massacre. "Sir," said Proctor, "your Indians cannot be commanded." "Begone!" retorted Tecumseh, with the greatest disdain, "you are unfit to command; go and put on *petticoats*."

the trees, and covering the skeleton of a hut, was their only habitation, and they were merely separated from the damp earth on which they lay, by a few scattered leaves, on which was generally spread a blanket by the men, and a cloak by the officers. Hence, frequently arose dysentery, ague, and the various ills to which an army encamped on a wet and unhealthy ground, is inevitably subject; and fortunate was he who possessed the skin of a bear or buffalo, on which he could repose his wearied limbs, after a period of suffering and privation, which those who have never served in the wilds of America, can with difficulty comprehend. Such was the position of the contending parties towards the middle of May, when Gen. Proctor, despairing to effect the reduction of the fort, caused preparations to be made for the raising the siege. Accordingly the gun-boats ascended the river, and anchored under the batteries, the guns of which were conveyed on board under a heavy fire from the enemy. The whole being secured, the expedition returned to Amherstburg, the Americans remained tranquil within their works, and suffered us to depart unmolested.

Gen. Harrison having repaired the fort from the damage occasioned by the siege, left for the interior of the state, to organize new levies, and entrusted the command to Gen. Green Clay. The enemy returned to Malden, where the Canadian militia were disbanded. Shortly after commenced the *second siege* of Fort Meigs.

On the 20th of July, the boats of the enemy were discovered ascending the Miami to Fort Meigs, and the following morning, a party of ten men were surprised by the Indians, and only three escaped death or capture. The force which the enemy had now before the post, was 5000 men under Proctor and Tecumseh, and the number of Indians was greater than any ever before assembled on any occasion during the war, while the defenders of the fort amounted to but a few hundred.

The night of their arrival, Gen. Green Clay dispatched Capt. M'Cune, of the Ohio militia, to Gen. Harrison, at Lower Sandusky, to notify him of the presence of the enemy. Capt. M'Cune was ordered to return, and inform Gen. Clay to be particularly cautious against surprise, and that every effort would be made to relieve the fort.

It was Gen. Harrison's intention, should the enemy lay regular siege to the fort, to select 400 men, and by an unfrequented route reach there in the night, and at any hazard break through the lines of the enemy.

Capt. M'Cune was sent out a second time with the intelligence to Harrison, that about 800 Indians had been seen from the fort, passing up the Miami, designing, it was supposed, to attack Fort Winchester at Defiance. The general, however, believed that it was a ruse of the enemy, to cover their design upon Upper Sandusky, Lower Sandusky, or Cleveland, and accordingly kept out a reconoitering party to watch.

On the afternoon of the 25th, Capt. M'Cune was ordered by Harrison to return to the fort, and inform Gen. Clay of his situation and intentions. He arrived near the fort about daybreak on the following morning, having lost his way in the night, accompanied by James Doolan, a French Canadian. They were just upon the point of leaving the forest and entering upon the cleared ground around the fort, when they were intercepted by a party of Indians. They immediately took to the high bank with their horses, and retreated at full gallop up the river for several miles, pursued by the Indians, also mounted, until they came to a deep ravine, putting up from the river in a southerly direction, when they turned upon the river bottom and continued a short distance, until they found their further progress in that direction stopped by an impassable swamp. The Indians foreseeing their dilemma, from their knowledge of the country, and expecting they would naturally follow up the ravine, galloped thither to head them off. M'Cune guessed their intention, and he and his companion turned back upon their own track for the fort, gaining, by this manœuvre, several hundred yards upon their pursuers. The Indians gave a yell of chagrin, and followed at their utmost speed. Just as they neared the fort, M'Cune dashed into a thicket across his course, on the opposite side of which other Indians had huddled, awaiting their prey. When this body of Indians had thought them all but in their possession, again was the presence of mind of M'Cune signally displayed. He wheeled his horse, followed by Doolan, made his way out of the thicket by the passage he had entered, and galloped around into the open space between them and the river, where the pursuers were checked by the fire from the block-house at the western angle of the fort. In a few minutes after their arrival, their horses dropped from fatigue. The Indians probably had orders to take them alive as they had not fired until just as they entered the fort; but in the chase, M'Cune had great difficulty in persuading Doolan to reserve his fire until the last extremity, and they therefore brought in their pieces loaded.

The opportune arrival of M'Cune no doubt saved the fort, as the intelligence he brought was the means of preserving them from an ingeniously devised stratagem of Tecumseh, which was put into execution that day, and which we here relate.

Towards evening, the British infantry were secreted in the ravine below the fort, and the cavalry in the woods above, while the Indians were stationed in the forest, on the Sandusky road, not far from the fort. About an hour before dark, they commenced a sham battle among themselves, to deceive the Americans into the belief that a battle was going on between them and a re-inforcement for the fort, in the hopes of enticing the garrison to the aid of their comrades. It was managed with so much skill, that the garrison instantly flew to arms, impressed by the Indian yells, intermingled with the roar of musketry, that a severe battle was being fought. The officers even of the highest grades were of that opinion, and some of them insisted on being suffered to march out to the rescue. Gen. Clay, although unable to account for the firing, could not believe that the general had so soon altered his intention, as expressed to Capt. M'Cune, not to send or come with any troops to Fort Meigs, until there should appear further necessity for it. This intelligence in a great measure satisfied the officers, but not the men, who were extremely indignant at being prevented from going to share the dangers of their commander-in-chief and brother soldiers, and perhaps had it not been for the interposition of a shower of rain, which soon put an end to the battle, the general might have been persuaded to march out, when a terrible massacre of the troops would have ensued.

The enemy remained around the fort but one day after this, and on the 28th, embarked with their stores and proceeded down the lake, and a few days after met with a severe repulse, in their attempt to storm Fort Stephenson.

We are informed by a volunteer aid of Gen. Clay, who was in the fort at the second siege, that preparations were made to fire the magazine, in case the enemy succeeded in an attempt to storm the fort, and thus involve all, friend and foe, in one common fate. This terrible alternative was deemed better, than to perish under the tomahawks and scalping knives of the savages.

The soldiers of the northwestern army, while at Fort Meigs, and elsewhere on duty, frequently beguiled their time by singing patriotic songs. A verse from one of them, sufficiently indicates their general character.

> Freemen, no longer bear such slaughter,
> Avenge your country's cruel woe,
> Arouse and save your wives and daughters,
> Arouse, and expel the faithless foe.
> CHORUS—Scalps are bought at stated prices,
> Malden pays the price in gold.

Perrysburg, the county seat, named from Com. Perry, is 123 miles NW. of Columbus, on the Maumee river, just below Fort Meigs. It was laid out in 1816, at the head of navigation on the river. It contains 1 Presbyterian, 1 Methodist and 1 Universalist church, 2 newspaper printing offices, 8 mercantile stores, and had by the census of 1840, 1041 inhabitants. The building of steamers and sail vessels has been carried on here to a considerable extent. A canal for hydraulic purposes has been constructed here. It commences in the rapids of the Maumee, 5 miles above, and has 18 feet fall, affording power sufficient to carry 40 runs of stone.

A correspondent, residing in Perrysburg, has communicated to us a sketch of the speculations which attracted so much attention to the Maumee valley, some years since.

The notable era of speculation, embracing the years 1834, 5, 6, and part of '37, first attracted public attention to the Maumee valley, as a commercial mart. From the mouth of the river to the foot of the rapids, the country swarmed with adventurers. Those that did not regard any of the settlements (for neither of the beautiful villages of Toledo, Maumee or Perrysburg, were more than settlements at that time) as the points designated by nature and legislation for the great emporium, purchased tracts of land lying between and below these towns, and laid out cities. It would amuse one to take the recorded maps of some of these embryo cities, with the designated squares, parks and public buildings, and walk over the desolate sites of the cities themselves. Manhattan, at the mouth of the river; Oregon, 5 miles above; Austerlitz, 6 miles, and Marengo, 9 miles, were joint contenders with the villages that have grown up, for the great prize. They all had their particular advantages. Manhattan based her claim upon the location at the exact debouchure of the river. Oregon, in addition to all the advantages claimed by the other towns, added the facilities of the location for engaging in the *pork* business, and her leading proprietor, in a placard posted up publicly in 1836, professed his belief, that these particular advantages were greater even, than those enjoyed by the city of Cincinnati. Marengo based her claims upon the fact, that her location was at the foot of the rock bar, and therefore at the virtual head of navigation. The result of all this was, that hundreds of young men, from the east and south, flocked to this valley during the years above named, with the hope of speedily amassing a fortune; and of this number it is not too much to say, that full three-quarters, having no means at the commencement and depending upon some bold stroke for success, left the valley before the close of the year 1837, hopelessly involved. All these towns, some eleven, if I recollect rightly, in number, still form a part of the primeval forests of the Maumee, most of them, after ruining their proprietors, have been vacated, and the sounding names by which they were known, are a by-word, a reproach, or the butt-end of the coarse jokes of the more recent and fortunate adventurers in the valley.

Perrysburg, from Maumee City,

Gilead, at the head of the Maumee rapids, 18 miles above Perrysburg, has about 150 inhabitants. There is much water power at that point. Otsego, Bowling Green and Portageville, are also small places in the county. The last, 18 miles south of the county seat, marks the site of one of Hull's encampments, when on his march to Detroit.

WYANDOT.

WYANDOT was formed from Crawford, Marion, Hardin and Hancock, February 3d, 1845. The surface is level and the soil fertile. About one-third of it is prairie land, being covered by the Sandusky plains. These plains are chiefly bounded by the Sandusky, the Little Scioto and the *Tyemochte*, which last signifies in the Wyandot language, "around the plains." This tract in its natural state is covered with a rank wild grass several feet in height, and in some parts are interspersed beautiful groves of timber. The following is a list of the townships in Wyandot:

Antrim,	Marseilles,	Ridge,
Crane,	Mifflin,	Salem,
Crawford,	Pitt,	Sycamore,
Eden,	Richland,	Tyemochte,
Jackson,		

Wyandot having been so recently formed, it's population is unknown; it is, however, thinly settled, but is rapidly populating.

This county was, from an early day, a favorite residence of the Wyandot Indians; it is noted for being the scene of Crawford's defeat in June 1782, and his subsequent death by the most cruel tortures.

Crawford's Battle Ground.

The view representing Crawford's Battle Ground was taken on the road to Tiffin 3 miles north of Upper Sandusky, and 1 west of the Sandusky river. The action, it is said, began some distance north of the cabin shown, in the high grass of the prairie in which the Indians were concealed. The parties afterwards were engaged in the grove or island of timber represented in the view, called at this day "*Battle Island*," in which the principal action was fought. Many of the trees now bear the marks of the bullets, or rather the scars on their trunks made by the hatchets of the Indians in getting them out after the action. The large oak on the right of the view has these relics of that unfortunate engagement. A part of the whites slain were buried in a small swamp about 30 rods south of the spot from whence the drawing was taken. It is not shown in the view as the scene is represented to the eye as if looking in a northern direction.

The annexed history of Crawford's campaign we take from Doddridge's Notes:

Crawford's campaign, in one point of view at least, is to be considered as a second Moravian campaign, as one of its objects was that of finishing the work of murder and plunder with the christian Indians at their new establishment on the Sandusky. The next object was that of destroying the Wyandot towns on the same river. It was the resolution of all those concerned in this expedition not to spare the life of any Indians that might fall into their hands, whether friends or foes. It will be seen in the sequel that the result of this campaign was widely different from that of the Moravian campaign the preceding March.

It should seem that the long continuance of the Indian war had debased a considerable portion of our population to the savage state of our nature, Having lost so many relatives by the Indians and witnessed their horrid murders and other depredations on so extensive a scale, they became subjects of that indiscriminating thirst for revenge which is such a prominent feature in the savage character, and having had a taste of blood and plunder without risk or loss on their part, they resolved to go on and kill every Indian they could find, whether friend or foe.

Preparations for this campaign commenced soon after the return of the Moravian campaign in the month of March, and as it was intended to make what was called at that time "a dash," that is an enterprize conducted with secresy and dispatch, the men were all mounted on the best horses they could procure. They furnished themselves with all their outfits except some ammunition, which was furnished by the Lieutenant Colonel of Washington county, [Pennsylvania.]

On the 25th of May, 1782, 480 men mustered at the old Mingo towns, on the western side of the Ohio river. They were all volunteers from the immediate neighborhood of the Ohio, with the exception of one company from Ten Mile in Washington county. Here an election was held for the office of commander-in-chief for the expedition. The candidates were Col. Williamson and Col. Crawford; the latter was the successful candidate. When notified of his appointment it is said that he accepted it with apparent reluctance.

The army marched along "Williamson's trail" as it was then called, until they arrived at the upper Moravian town, in the fields belonging to which there was still plenty of corn on the stalks, with which their horses were plentifully fed during the night of their encampment there.

Shortly after the army halted at this place, two Indians were discovered by three men, who had walked some distance out of the camp. Three shots were fired at one of them, but without hurting him. As soon as the news of the discovery of Indians had reached the camp, more than one half of the men rushed out, without command, and in the most tumultuous manner, to see what happened. From that time, Col. Crawford felt a presentiment of the defeat which followed.

The truth is, that notwithstanding the secrecy and dispatch of the enterprize, the Indians were beforehand with our people. They saw the rendezvous on the Mingo bottom, knew their number and destination. They visited every encampment immediately on their leaving it, and saw from the writing on the trees and scraps of paper that "no quarter was to be given to any Indian, whether man, woman or child."

Nothing material happened during their march until the sixth of June, when their guides conducted them to the site of the Moravian villages, on one of the upper branches of the Sandusky river; but here, instead of meeting with Indians and plunder, they met with nothing but vestiges of desolation. The place was covered with high grass, and the remains of a few huts alone, announced that the place had been the residence of the people whom they intended to destroy, but who had moved off to Scioto some time before.

In this dilemma what was to be done? The officers held a council, in which it was determined to march one day longer in the direction of Upper Sandusky, and if they should not reach the town in the course of the day, to make a retreat with all speed.

The march was commenced the next morning through the plains of Sandusky, and continued until about two o'clock, when the advance guard was attacked and driven in by the

Indians, who were discovered in large numbers, in the high grass, with which the place was covered. The Indian army was at that moment about entering a piece of woods, almost entirely surrounded by plains; but in this they were disappointed by a rapid movement of our men. The battle then commenced by a heavy fire from both sides. From a partial possession of the woods which they had gained at the onset of the battle, the Indians were soon dislodged. They then attempted to gain a small skirt of wood on our right flank, but were prevented from doing so by the vigilance and bravery of Maj. Leet, who commanded the right wing of the army at that time. The firing was incessant and heavy until dark, when it ceased. Both armies lay on their arms during the night. Both adopted the policy of kindling large fires along the line of battle, and then retiring some distance in the rear of them, to prevent being surprised by a night attack. During the conflict of the afternoon, three of our men were killed and several wounded.

In the morning our army occupied the battle ground of the preceding day. The Indians made no attack during the day, until late in the evening, but were seen in large bodies traversing the plains in various directions. Some of them appeared to be employed in carrying off their dead and wounded.

In the morning of this day a council of the officers was held, in which a retreat was resolved on, as the only means of saving their army. The Indians appeared to increase in number every hour. During the sitting of this council, Col. Williamson proposed taking one hundred and fifty volunteers, and marching directly to Upper Sandusky. This proposition the commander-in-chief prudently rejected, saying, "I have no doubt but that you would reach the town, but you would find nothing there but empty wigwams, and having taken off so many of our best men, you would leave the rest to be destroyed by the host of Indians with which we are now surrounded, and on your return they would attack and destroy you. They care nothing about defending their towns; they are worth nothing. Their squaws, children and property, have been removed from them long since. Our lives and baggage are what they want, and if they can get us divided they will soon have them. We must stay together and do the best we can."

During this day preparations were made for a retreat by burying the dead, burning fires over their graves to prevent discovery, and preparing means for carrying off the wounded. The retreat was to commence in the course of the night. The Indians, however, became apprized of the intended retreat, and about sundown attacked the army with great force and fury, in every direction, excepting that of Sandusky.

When the line of march was formed by the commander-in-chief, and the retreat commenced, our guides prudently took the direction of Sandusky, which afforded the only opening in the Indian lines and the only chance of concealment. After marching about a mile in this direction, the army wheeled about to the left, and by a circuitous route gained the trail by which they came, before day. They continued their march the whole of the next day, with a trifling annoyance from the Indians, who fired a few distant shots at the rear guard, which slightly wounded two or three men. At night they built fires, took their suppers, secured the horses and resigned themselves to repose, without placing a single sentinel or vidette for safety. In this careless situation, they might have been surprised and cut off by the Indians, who, however, gave them no disturbance during the night, nor afterwards during the whole of their retreat. The number of those composing the main body in the retreat was supposed to be about three hundred.

Most unfortunately, when a retreat was resolved on, a difference of opinion prevailed concerning the best mode of effecting it. The greater number thought best to keep in a body and retreat as fast as possible, while a considerable number thought it safest to break off in small parties and make their way home in different directions, avoiding the route by which they came. Accordingly many attempted to do so, calculating that the whole body of the Indians would follow the main army; in this they were entirely mistaken. The Indians paid but little attention to the main body of the army, but pursued the small parties with such activity that but very few of those who composed them made their escape.

The only successful party who were detached from the main army was that of about forty men under the command of a Captain Williamson, who, pretty late in the night of the retreat, broke through the Indian lines under a severe fire, and with some loss, and overtook the main army on the morning of the second day of the retreat.

For several days after the retreat of our army, the Indians were spread over the whole country, from Sandusky to the Muskingum, in pursuit of the straggling parties, most of whom were killed on the spot. They even pursued them almost to the banks of the Ohio. A man of the name of Mills was killed, two miles to the eastward of the site of St. Clairsville, in the direction of Wheeling from that place. The number killed in this way must have been very great, the precise amount, however, was never fairly ascertained.

At the commencement of the retreat Col. Crawford placed himself at the head of the army and continued there until they had gone about a quarter of a mile, when missing his son, John Crawford, his son-in-law, Major Harrison, and his nephews, Major Rose and William Crawford, he halted and called for them as the line passed, but without finding them. After the army had passed him, he was unable to overtake it, owing to the weariness of his horse. Falling in company with Doctor Knight and two others, they travelled all the night, first north, and then to the east, to avoid the pursuit of the Indians. They directed their courses during the night by the north star.

On the next day, they fell in with Captain John Biggs and Lieutenant Ashley, the latter of whom was severely wounded. There were two others in company with Biggs and Ashley. They encamped together the succeeding night. On the next day, while on their march, they were attacked by a party of Indians, who made Col. Crawford and Doctor Knight prisoners. The other four made their escape, but Captain Biggs and Lieutenant Ashley were killed the next day.

Colonel Crawford and Doctor Knight were immediately taken to an Indian encampment at a short distance from the place where they were captured. Here they found nine fellow prisoners and seventeen Indians. On the next day they were marched to the old Wyandot town, and on the next morning were paraded, to set off, as they were told, to go to the new town. But alas! a very different destination awaited these captives! Nine of the prisoners were marched off some distance before the colonel and the doctor, who were conducted by Pipe and Wingenund, two Delaware chiefs. Four of the prisoners were tomahawked and scalped on the way, at different places.

Preparations had been made for the execution of Colonel Crawford, by setting a post about fifteen feet high in the ground, and making a large fire of hickory poles about six yards from it. About half a mile from the place of execution the remaining five of the nine prisoners were tomahawked and scalped by a number of squaws and boys. Colonel Crawford's son and son-in-law were executed at the Shawnese town. * * *

Dr. Knight was doomed to be burned at a town about forty miles distant from Sandusky, and committed to the care of a young Indian to be taken there. The first day they travelled about twenty-five miles, and encamped for the night. In the morning the gnats being very troublesome, the doctor requested the Indian to untie him that he might help him to make a fire to keep them off. With this request the Indian complied. While the Indian was on his knees and elbows, blowing the fire, the doctor caught up a piece of a tent pole which had been burned in two, about eighteen inches long, with which he struck the Indian on his head with all his might, so as to knock him forward into the fire. The stick, however, broke, so that the Indian, although severely hurt, was not killed, but immediately sprang up; on this the doctor caught up the Indian's gun to shoot him, but drew back the cock with so much violence that he broke the main spring. The Indian ran off with an hideous yelling. Doctor Knight then made the best of his way home, which he reached in twenty-one days, almost famished to death. The gun being of no use, after carrying it a day or two, he left it behind. On his journey he subsisted on roots, a few young birds and berries. * * * * * * *

Thus ended this disastrous campaign. It was the last one which took place in this section of the country during the revolutionary contest of the Americans with the mother country. It was undertaken with the very worst of views, those of plunder and murder; it was conducted without sufficient means to encounter, with any prospect of success, the large force of Indians opposed to ours in the plains of Sandusky. It was conducted without that subordination and discipline so requisite to insure success in any hazardous enterprize, and it ended in a total discomfiture. Never did an enterprize more completely fail of attaining its object. Never, on any occasion, had the ferocious savages more ample revenge for the murder of their pacific friends, than that which they obtained on this occasion.

Should it be asked what considerations led so great a number of people into this desperate enterprize? Why with so small a force and such slender means they pushed on so far as the plains of Sandusky?

The answer is, that many believed that the Moravian Indians, taking no part in the war, and having given offence to the warriors on several occasions, their belligerent friends would not take up arms in their behalf. In this conjecture they were sadly mistaken. They did defend them with all the force at their command, and no wonder, for notwithstanding their christian and pacific principles, the warriors still regarded the Moravians as their relations, whom it was their duty to defend.

We have omitted to copy from the preceding the account of the burning of Col. Crawford, for the purpose of giving the details more fully. "The spot where Crawford suffered," says Col. John Johnston, "was a few miles west of Upper Sandusky, on the old trace leading to the Big Spring, Wyandot town. It was on the right hand of the trace going west, on a low bottom on the east bank of the Tyemochte creek. The Delawares burnt Crawford in satisfaction for the massacre of their people at the Moravian towns on the Muskingum." It was at a Delaware town which extended along the Tyemochte. The precise spot is now owned by the heirs of Daniel Hodge, and is a beautiful green with some fine oak trees in its vicinity.

The following is from Heckewelder, and describes an interview which Crawford had with the Indian chief, Wingenund, just previous to his death. Some doubts have been expressed of its truth as the historian Heckewelder has often been accused of being fond of *romancing*, but Col. Johnston, (good authority here,) expresses the opinion that "it is doubtless in the main correct."

Wingenund, an Indian chief, had an interview with Col. Crawford just before his execution. He had been known to Crawford some time before, and had been on terms of friendship with him, and kindly entertained by him at his own house, and therefore felt much attached to the colonel. Wingenund had retired to his cabin, that he might not see the sentence executed; but Crawford sent for him, with the faint hope that he would intercede for and save him. Wingenund accordingly soon appeared in presence of Crawford, who was naked and bound to a stake. Wingenund commenced the conversation with much embarrassment and agitation, as follows:

Wingenund—"Are you not Col. Crawford?"

Crawford—"I am."

Wingenund, somewhat agitated, ejaculates, "So!—yes!—indeed!"

Crawford—"Do you not recollect the friendship that always existed between us, and that we were always glad to see each other?"

Wingenund—"Yes! I remember all this, and that we have often drank together, and that you have been kind to me."

Crawford—"Then I hope the same friendship still continues."

Wingenund—"It would, of course, were you where you ought to be, and not here."

Crawford—"And why not here? I hope you would not desert a friend in time of need. Now is the time for you to exert yourself in my behalf, as I should do for you were you in my place."

Wingenund—"Colonel Crawford! you have placed yourself in a situation which puts it out of my power, and that of others of your friends, to do any thing for you."

Crawford—"How so, Captain Wingenund?"

Wingenund—"By joining yourself to that execrable man, Williamson, and his party—the man, who, but the other day, murdered such a number of Moravian Indians, knowing them to be friends; knowing that he ran no risk in murdering a people who would not fight, and whose only business was praying."

Crawford—"But I assure you, Wingenund, that had I been with him at the time, this would not have happened. Not I alone, but all your friends, and all good men, whoever they are, reprobate acts of this kind."

Wingenund—"That may be; yet these friends, these good men, did not prevent him from going out again to kill the remainder of these inoffensive, yet foolish Moravian Indians. I say foolish, because they believed the whites in preference to us. We had often told them they would be one day so treated by those people, who called themselves their friends! We told them there was no faith to be placed in what the white man said; that their fair promises were only intended to allure us, that they might the more easily kill us, as they had done many Indians before these Moravians."

Crawford—"I am sorry to hear you speak thus; as to Williamson's going out again, when it was known he was determined on it, I went out with him to prevent his committing fresh murders."

Wingenund—"This the Indians would not believe, were even I to tell them so."

Crawford—"Why would they not believe?"

Wingenund—" Because it would have been out of your power to have prevented his doing what he pleased."

Crawford—" Out of my power! Have any Moravian Indians been killed or hurt since we came out?"

Wingenund—" None; but you first went to their town, and finding it deserted, you turned on the path towards us. If you had been in search of warriors only, you would not have gone thither. Our spies watched you closely. They saw you while you were embodying yourselves on the other side of the Ohio. They saw you cross the river—they saw where you encamped for the night—they saw you turn off from the path to the deserted Moravian town—they knew you were going out of your way—your steps were constantly watched, and you were suffered quietly to proceed until you reached the spot where you were attacked."

Crawford felt that, with this sentence, ended his last ray of hope, and now asked, with emotion, " what do they intend to do with me?"

Wingenund—" I tell you with grief. As Williamson, with his whole cowardly host, ran off in the night at the whistling of our warriors' balls, being satisfied that now he had no Moravians to deal with, but men who could fight, and with such he did not wish to have anything to do—I say, as they have escaped and taken you, they will take revenge on you in his stead."

Crawford—And is there no possibility of preventing this? Can you devise no way of getting me off? You shall, my friend, be well rewarded if you are instrumental in saving my life."

Wingenund—" Had Williamson been taken with you, I and some friends, by making use of what you have told me, might perhaps have succeeded in saving you; but as the matter now stands, no man would dare to interfere in your behalf. The king of England himself, were he to come on to this spot, with all his wealth and treasure, could not effect this purpose. The blood of the innocent Moravians, more than half of them women and children, cruelly and wantonly murdered, calls loudly for revenge. The relatives of the slain, who are among us, cry out and stand ready for revenge. The nation to which they belonged will have revenge. The Shawanese, our grandchildren, have asked for your fellow-prisoner; on him they will take revenge. All the nations connected with us cry out, revenge! revenge! The Moravians whom you went to destroy, having fled, instead of avenging their brethren, the offence is become national, and the nation itself is bound to take revenge!"

Crawford—" My fate is then fixed, and I must prepare to meet death in its worst form."

Wingenund—" I am sorry for it, but cannot do anything for you. Had you attended to the Indian principle, that as good and evil cannot dwell together in the same heart, so a good man ought not to go into evil company, you would not be in this lamentable situation. You see now, when it is too late, after Williamson has deserted you, what a bad man he must be. Nothing now remains for you but to meet your fate like a brave man. Farewell, Col. Crawford!—they are coming. I will retire to a solitary spot."

The savages then fell upon Crawford. Wingenund, it is said, retired, shedding tears, and ever after, when the circumstance was alluded to, was sensibly affected.

The account of the burning of Colonel Crawford is related in the words of Dr. Knight, his companion, and an eye-witness of this tragic scene.

When we went to the fire, the colonel was stripped naked, ordered to sit down by the fire, and then they beat him with sticks and their fists. Presently after I was treated in the same manner. They then tied a rope to the foot of a post about fifteen feet high, bound the colonel's hands behind his back and fastened the rope to the ligature between his wrists. The rope was long enough for him to sit down or walk round the post once or twice, and return the same way. The colonel then called to Girty, and asked if they intended to burn him? Girty answered, yes. The colonel said he would take it all patiently. Upon this, Captain Pipe, a Delaware chief, made a speech to the Indians, viz., about thirty or forty men, sixty or seventy squaws and boys.

When the speech was finished, they all yelled a hideous and hearty assent to what had been said. The Indian men then took up their guns and shot powder into the colonel's body, from his feet as far up as his neck. I think that not less than seventy loads were discharged upon his naked body. They then crowded about him, and to the best of my observation, cut off his ears; when the throng had dispersed a little, I saw the blood running from both sides of his head in consequence thereof.

The fire was about six or seven yards from the post to which the colonel was tied; it was made of small hickory poles, burnt quite through in the middle, each end of the poles remaining about six feet in length. Three or four Indians by turns would take up, individually, one of these burning pieces of wood, and apply it to his naked body, already burnt black with the powder. These tormentors presented themselves on every side of him with the burning faggots and poles. Some of the squaws took broad boards, upon which they would carry a quantity of burning coals and hot embers, and throw on him, so that in a short time he had nothing but coals of fire and hot ashes to walk upon.

In the midst of these extreme tortures he called to Simon Girty, and begged of him to shoot him; but Girty making no answer, he called to him again. Girty then, by way of derision, told the colonel he had no gun, at the same time turning about to an Iudian who was behind him, laughed heartily, and by all his gestures seemed delighted at the horrid scene.

Girty then came up to me and bade me prepare for death. He said, however, I was not to die at that place, but to be burnt at the Shawanese towns. He swore by G—d I need not expect to escape death, but should suffer it in all its extremities.......

Colonel Crawford, at this period of his sufferings, besought the Almighty to have mercy on his soul, spoke very low, and bore his torments with the most manly fortitude. He continued in all the extremities of pain for an hour and three quarters or two hours longer, as near as I can judge, when at last, being almost exhausted, he lay down on his belly; they then scalped him, and repeatedly threw the scalp in my face, telling me, "that was my great captain." An old squaw (whose appearance every way answered the ideas people entertain of the devil) got a board, took a parcel of coals and ashes and laid them on his back and head, after he had been scalped; he then raised himself upon his feet and began to walk round the post; they next put a burning stick to him, as usual, but he seemed more insensible of pain than before.

The Indian fellow who had me in charge, now took me away to Captain Pipe's house, about three-quarters of a mile from the place of the colonel's execution. I was bound all night, and thus prevented from seeing the last of the horrid spectacle. Next morning, being June 12th, the Indian untied me, painted me black, and we set off for the Shawanese town, which he told me was somewhat less than forty miles distant from that place. We soon came to the spot where the colonel had been burnt, as it was partly in our way; I saw his bones lying among the remains of the fire, almost burnt to ashes; I suppose, after he was dead, they laid his body on the fire. The Indian told me that was my big captain, and gave the scalp halloo.

The following extract from an article in the American Pioneer, by Joseph M'Cutchen, Esq., contains some items respecting the death of Crawford, and Girty's interference in his behalf, never before published. He derived them from the Wyandot Indians, who resided, a few years since, in this county, some of whom were quite intelligent.

As I have it, the story respecting the battle is, that if Crawford had rushed on when he first came among the Indians, they would have given way and made but little or no fight; but they had a talk with him three days previous to the fight, and asked him to give them three days to collect in their chiefs and head men of the different tribes, and they would then make a treaty of peace with him. The three days were therefore given; and during that time all their forces gathered together that could be raised as fighting men, and the next morning Crawford was attacked, some two or three miles north of the island where the main battle was fought. The Indians then gave back in a south direction, until they got into an island of timber which suited their purpose, which was in a large plain, now well known as Sandusky plains. There the battle continued until night. The Indians then ceased firing; and, it is said, immediately afterwards a man came near to the army with a white flag. Colonel Crawford sent an officer to him. The man said he wanted to talk with Colonel Crawford, and that he did not want Crawford to come nearer to him than twenty steps, as he (Girty) wanted to converse with Crawford, and might be of vast benefit to him. Crawford accordingly went out as requested. Girty then said, "Col. Crawford, do you know me?" The answer was, "I seem to have some recollection of your voice, but your Indian dress deprives me of knowing you as an acquaintance." The answer was then, "My name is Simon Girty;" and after some more conversation between them, they knew each other well. Girty said, "Crawford, my object in calling you here is to say to you, that the Indians have ceased firing until to-morrow morning, when they intend to commence the fight; and as they are three times as strong as you are, they will be able to cut you all off. To-night the Indians will surround your army, and when that arrangement is fully made, you will hear some guns fire all around the ring. But there is a large swamp or very wet piece of ground on the east side of you, where there will be a vacancy; that gap you can learn by the firing, and in the night you had better march your men through and make your escape in an east direction."

Crawford accordingly in the night drew up his men and told them his intention. The men generally assenting, he then commenced his march east; but the men soon got into confusion and lost their course. Consequently, the next day they were almost to a man cut off, and, as history tells us, Crawford taken prisoner. He was taken by a Delaware; consequently the Delawares claimed the right, agreeably to their rules, of disposing of the prisoner. There was a council held, and the decision was to burn him. He was taken to the main Delaware town, on a considerable creek, called Tymochtee, about eight miles from the mouth. Girty then supposed he could make a speculation by saving Crawford's life. He made a proposition to Capt. Pipe, the head chief of the Delawares, offering three hundred and fifty dollars for Crawford. The chief received it as a great insult, and promptly said to Girty, "Sir, do think I am a *squaw?*" *If* you say one word more on the subject, I will make a stake for you, and burn you along with the white chief." Girty, knowing the Indian character, retired and said no more on the subject. But, in the meantime, Girty had sent runners to the Mohican creek and to Lower Sandusky, where there were some white traders, to come immediately and purchase Crawford—knowing that he could make a great speculation in case he could save Crawford's life. The traders came on, but too late. When they arrived, Crawford was tied to a stake, blacked, his ears cut off and part burnt—too much so to live had he been let loose. He asked Girty to get a gun and shoot him; but Girty, knowing the rebuke he got the day before, dared not say one word.

Notwithstanding the above, the cruelty of Girty to Crawford at the stake, is established by other sources than that of Dr. Knight. Col. Johnston informs us, that he has been told by Indians present on the occasion, that Girty was among the foremost in inflicting tortures upon their victim. This, however, does not materially conflict with the above, when we regard the motives of Girty in his behalf as having been mercenary.

By the treaty concluded at the foot of the Maumee rapids, Sept. 29th, 1817, Hon. Lewis Cass and Hon. Duncan M'Arthur, commissioners on the part of the United States, there was granted to the Wyandot tribe a reservation of twelve miles square in this county, the centre of which was Fort Ferree, at Upper Sandusky, and also a tract of one mile square on the Cranberry Swamp, on Broken Sword creek. At the same time was granted to the Delawares a tract of three miles square, adjoining the other, on the south. Their principal chief was Capt. Pipe, son of the chief so officious in the burning of Crawford.

The Delawares ceded their reservation to the United States in 1829. The Wyandots ceded theirs by a treaty made at Upper Sandusky, March, 17th, 1842, they being the only Indians remaining in the state. The commissioner on the part of the United States was Col. John Johnston, who had then the honor of making the last Indian treaty in Ohio—a state, *every foot of whose soil has been fairly purchased by treaties* from its original possessors. The Wyandots left for the far west in July, 1843, and numbered at that time about 700 souls.

The Wyandots were the bravest of the Indian tribes, and had among their chiefs some men of high moral character.

With all other tribes but the Wyandots, flight in battle, when meeting with unexpected resistance or obstacle, brought with it no disgrace.....With them, it was otherwise. Their youth were taught to consider anything that had the appearance of an acknowledgment of the superiority of the enemy as disgraceful. In the battle of the Miami rapids, of thirteen chiefs of that tribe who were present, one only survived, and he badly wounded. Some time before this action, Gen. Wayne sent for Capt. Wells, (see p. 323,) and requested him to go to Sandusky and take a prisoner, for the purpose of obtaining information. Wells—who had been bred with the Indians, and was perfectly acquainted with their character—answered that he could take a prisoner, but not from Sandusky, because Wyandots would not be taken alive.*

We annex a brief sketch of the Wyandot, or *Huron* tribe, as they were anciently called, in a letter from the Rev. Joseph Badger (see page 482) to John Frazier, Esq., of Cincinnati, dated Plain, Wood county, Aug. 25th, 1845.

Having been a resident missionary with the Wyandot Indians before the late war, and obtained the confidence of their chiefs in a familiar conversation with them ; and having a good interpreter, I requested them to give me a history of their ancestors as far back as they could. They began by giving a particular account of the country formerly owned by their ancestors. It was the north side of the river St. Lawrence, down to Coon lake, and from thence up the Utiwas. Their name for it was Cu,none,tot,tia. This name I heard applied to them, but knew not what it meant. The Senecas owned the opposite side of the river and the island on which Montreal now stands. They were both large tribes, consisting of many thousands. They were blood relations, and I found at this time they claimed each other as cousins.

A war originated between the two tribes in this way. A man of the Wyandots wanted a certain woman for his wife ; but she objected, and said he was no warrior : he had never taken any scalps. To accomplish his object, he raised a small war party, and in their scout, fell upon a party of Seneca hunters, killed and scalped a number of them. This procedure began a war between the nations, that lasted more than a century, which they supposed was fully a hundred winters before the French came to Quebec. They owned they were the first instigators in the war, and were generally beaten in the contest. Both tribes were greatly wasted in the war. They often made peace ; but the first opportunity the Senecas could get an advantage against them, they would destroy all they could, men, women and children. The Wyandots, finding they were in danger of being exterminated, concluded to leave their country, and go far to the west. With their canoes, the whole nation made their escape to the upper lakes, and settled in the vicinity of Green Bay, in several villages, but, after a few years, the Senecas made up a war-party and followed them to their new settlements, fell on one of their villages, killed a number and returned. Through this long period, they had no instruments of war but bows, arrows, and the war club.

Soon after this, the French came to Quebec, and began trading with Indians, and supplied them with fire-arms and utensils of various kinds. The Senecas having got supplied with guns, and learned the use of them, made out a second war-party against the Wyandots—came upon them in the night, fired into their huts and scared them exceedingly : they thought at first it was thunder and lightning. They did not succeed so well as they intended. After a few years, they made out a third party, and fell upon one of the Wyandot villages and took them nearly all ; but it so happened at this time, that nearly all the young men had gone to war with the Fox tribe, living on the Mississippi.

Those few that escaped the massacre by the Senecas, agreed to give up and go back with them and become one people, but requested of the Senecas to have two days to collect what they had and make ready their canoes, and join them on the morning of the third day at a certain point, where they had gone to wait for them and hold a great dance through the night. The Wyandots sent directly to the other two villages which the Senecas had not disturbed, and got all their old men and women, and such as could fight, to consult on what measures to take. They came to the resolution to equip themselves in the best manner they could, and go down in perfect stillness so near the enemy as to hear them. They found them engaged in a dance, and feasting on two Wyandot men they had killed and roasted, as they said, for their beef; and as they danced, they shouted their victory and told how good their Wyandot beef was. They continued their dance until the latter part of the night, and being pretty tired, they all laid down and soon fell into a sound sleep. A little before day, the Wyandot party fell on them and cut them all off; not one

* Discourse of General Wm. H. Harrison, in the Collections of the Historical Society of Ohio.

was left to carry back the tidings. This ended the war for a great number of years. Soon after this, the Wyandots got guns from the French traders and began to grow formidable. The Indians, who owned the country where they had resided for a long time, proposed to them to go back to their own country. They agreed to return, and having proposed themselves as a war-party, they returned—came down to where Detroit now stands, and agreed to settle in two villages, one at the place above mentioned, and the other where the British fort, Malden, now stands.

But previously to making any settlement, they sent out in canoes the best war-party they could make, to go down the lake some distance to see if there was an enemy on that side of the water. They went down to Long Point, landed, and sent three men across to see if they could make any discovery. They found a party of Senecas bending their course around the Point, and returned with the intelligence to their party. The head chief ordered his men in each canoe to strike fire, and offer some of their tobacco to the Great Spirit, and prepare for action. The chief had his son, a small boy, with him: he covered the boy in the bottom of his canoe. He determined to fight his enemy on the water. They put out into the open lake: the Senecas came on. Both parties took the best advantage they could, and fought with a determination to conquer or sink in the lake. At length the Wyandots saw the last man fall in the Seneca party; but they had lost a great proportion of their own men, and were so wounded and cut to pieces that they could take no advantage of the victory but only to gain the shore as soon as possible, and leave the enemy's canoes to float or sink among the waves. Thus ended the long war between the two tribes from that day to this.

Col. John Johnston relates, in his "Recollections," an interesting account of an Indian council, held at Upper Sandusky in 1818, on the occasion of the death of TARHE, or "the Crane," a celebrated chief of the Wyandots.

Twenty-eight years ago, on the death of the great chief of the Wyandots, I was invited to attend a general council of all the tribes of Ohio, the Delawares of Indiana, and the Senecas of New York, at Upper Sandusky. I found, on arriving at the place, a very large attendance. Among the chiefs was the noted leader and orator, Red Jacket, from Buffalo. The first business done was the speaker of the nation delivering an oration on the character of the deceased chief. Then followed what might be called a monody, or ceremony, of mourning and lamentation. Thus seats were arranged from end to end of a large council-house, about six feet apart. The head men and the aged took their seats facing each other, stooping down their heads almost touching. In that position they remained for several hours. Deep, heavy and long continued groans would commence at one end of the row of mourners, and so pass round until all had responded, and these repeated at intervals of a few minutes. The Indians were all washed, and had no paint or decorations of any kind upon their persons, their countenances and general deportment denoting the deepest mourning. I had never witnessed any thing of the kind before, and was told this ceromony was not performed but on the decease of some great man. After the period of mourning and lamentation was over, the Indians proceeded to business. There were present the Wyandots, Shawanese, Delawares, Senecas, Ottawas and Mohawks. The business was entirely confined to their own affairs, and the main topic related to their lands and the claims of the respective tribes. It was evident, in the course of the discussion, that the presence of myself and people (there were some white men with me) was not acceptable to some of the parties, and allusions were made so direct to myself that I was constrained to notice them, by saying that I came there as the guest of the Wyandots by their special invitation; that as the agent of the United States, I had a right to be there or any where else in the Indian country; and that if any insult was offered to myself or my people, it would be resented and punished. Red Jacket was the principal speaker, and was intemperate and personal in his remarks. Accusations, pro and con, were made by the different parties, accusing each other of being foremost in selling lands to the United States. The Shawanese were particularly marked out as more guilty than any other; that they were the last coming into the Ohio country, and although they had no right but by permission of the other tribes, they were always the foremost in selling lands. This brought the Shawanese out, who retorted through their head chief, the Black Hoof, on the Senecas and Wyandots with pointed severity. The discussion was long continued, calling out some of the ablest speakers, and was distinguished for ability, cutting sarcasm and research—going far back into the history of the natives, their wars, alliances, negotiations, migrations, &c. I had attended many councils, treaties and gatherings of the Indians, but never in my life did I witness such an outpouring of native oratory and eloquence, of severe rebuke, taunting national and personal reproaches. The council broke up late, in great confusion, and in the worst possible feeling. A circumstance occurred towards the close, which more than anything else exhibited the bad feeling prevailing. In handing round the wampum belt, the emblem of amity, peace and good will, when presented to one of the chiefs, he would not touch it with his fingers, but passed it on a stick to the person next him. A greater indignity, agreeable to Indian etiquette, could not be offered. The next day appeared to be one of unusual anxiety and despondency among the Indians. They could be seen in groups everywhere near the council-house in deep consultation. They had acted foolishly—were sorry; but the difficulty was, who would first present the olive branch. The council convened late and was very full; silence prevailed for a long time; at last the aged chief of the Shawanese, the Black Hoof, rose—a man of great influence, and a celebrated orator. He told the assembly they had acted like children, and not men, on yesterday; that him and his people were sorry for the words that had been spoken, and which had done so much harm; that he came into the council by the unanimous desire of his people present, to recall those foolish words, and did there take them back—handing strings of wampum, which passed round and was received by all with the greatest satisfaction. Several of the principal chiefs delivered speeches to the same effect, handing round wampum in turn, and in this manner the whole difficulty of the preceding day was settled, and to all appearance forgotten. The Indians are very courteous and civil to each other, and it is a rare thing to see their assemblies disturbed by unwise or ill-timed remarks. I never witnessed it except on the occasion here alluded to; and it is more than probable that the presence of myself and other white men contributed towards the unpleasant occurrence. I could not help but admire the genuine philosophy and good sense displayed by men whom we call savages in the transaction of their public business; and how much we might profit in the halls of our legislatures by occasionally taking for our example the proceedings of the great Indian council at Sandusky.

Upper Sandusky, the county seat, is on the west bank of the Sandusky, 63 miles north of Columbus. It was laid out in 1843, and now contains 1 Methodist church, 6 mercantile stores, 1 newspaper printing office and about 500 inhabitants. In the war of 1812, Gen. Harrison built here Fort Feree, which stood about 50 rods NE. of the court house, on a bluff. It was a square stockade of about 2 acres in area, with block-houses at the corners, one of which is now standing. One mile north of this, near the river, Gov. Meigs encamped, in August, 1813, with several thousand of the Ohio militia, then on their way to the relief of Fort Meigs. The place was called "the Grand Encampment." Receiving here the news of the raising of the siege of Fort Meigs, and the repulse of the British at Fort Stephenson, they prosecuted their march no farther, and were soon after dismissed.

Crane Town, 4 miles NE. of the court house, was the Indian town of Upper Sandusky. After the death of Tarhe, the Crane, in 1818, the Indians transferred their council-house to the present Upper Sandusky, gave it this name, and called the other Crane Town. Their old council-house stood about 1½ miles N. of Crane Town. It was built principally of bark, and was about 100 feet long and 15 wide. Their last council-house, at the present Upper Sandusky, is yet standing near the river bank. It is a small frame structure, resembling an ordinary dwelling.

The Methodists sustained a mission among the Wyandots for many years. Previous to the establishment of the Methodists, a portion of the tribe had been for a long while under the religious instruction of the Catholics. The first Protestant who preached among them at Upper Sandusky was John Stewart, a mulatto, a member of the Methodist denomination, who came here of his own accord in 1816, and gained much influence over them. His efforts in their behalf paved the way for a regularly established mission a few years after, when the Rev. James B. Finley—at present chaplain of the Ohio penitentiary—formed a church and established a school here. This was the first Indian mission formed by the Methodists in the Mississippi valley.

Wyandot Mission Church, at Upper Sandusky.

The mission church building was erected of blue limestone about the year 1824, from government funds, Rev. Mr. Finley having permission from Hon. John C. Calhoun, then secretary of war, to apply $1333 to this object. The church stands upon the outskirts of the town, in a small enclosure, surrounded by woods. Connected with the mission was a school-house, and a farm of one mile square.

The following inscriptions are copied from monuments in the grave-yard, attached to the mission church.

BETWEEN-THE-LOGS,* died December, 1826, aged 50 years.

REV. JOHN STEWART, first missionary to the Wyandots; died December 17th, 1833, aged 37 years.

SUM-MUN-DE-WAT, murdered December 4th, 1845, aged 46 years. Buried in Wood county, Ohio.

The remains of Sum-mun-de-wat were subsequently re-interred here. He was, at the time of his death, on a hunting excursion with his family in Hancock county. In the evening, three white men with axes entered their camp, and were hospitably entertained by their host. After having finished their suppers, the Indian, agreeable to his custom, kneeled and prayed in his own language, and then laid

* He was among the first converts under the labors of John Stewart, and afterward became the most celebrated preacher among the Wyandots.

down with his wife to sleep. In the night, these miscreants wh had been so kindly treated, rose on them in their sleep, and murdered Sum-mun-de-wat and his wife with their axes, in the most brutal manner. They then robbed the camp and made off, but were apprehended and allowed to break jail. In speaking of this case, Col. Johnston says, that in a period of 53 years, since he first came to the west, he never knew of but one instance in which a white man was tried, convicted and executed for the murder of an Indian. This exception was brought about by his own agency in the prosecution, sustained by the promptness of John C. Calhoun, then secretary of war, who manifested an interest in this affair, not often shown on similar occasions in the officers of our government.

Sum-mun-de-wat is frequently mentioned in the Rev. Mr. Finley's interesting history of the Wyandot mission, published by the Methodist book concern at Cincinnati. The following anecdote which he relates of this excellent chief, shows the simple and expressive language in which the christian Wyandots related their religious feelings.

"Sum-mun-de-wat amused me after he came home, by relating a circumstance that transpired one cold evening, just before sun-down. 'I met,' said he, 'on a small path, not far from my camp, a man who ask me if I could talk English.' I said, 'Little.' He ask me, 'How far is it to a house?' I answer, 'I dont know—may be 10 miles—may be 8 miles.' 'Is there a path leading to it?' 'No—by and by dis go out, (pointing to the path they were on,) den all woods. You go home me—sleep—me go show you to-morrow.' Then he come my camp—so take horse—tie—give him some corn and brush—then my wife give him supper. He ask where I come. I say, 'Sandusky.' He say, 'You know Finley?' 'Yes,' I say, 'he is my brother—my father.' Then he say, 'He is *my* brother.' Then I feel something in my heart burn. I say, 'You preacher?' He say, 'Yes;' and I shook hands and say, 'My brother!' Then we try talk. Then I say, 'You sing and pray.' So he did. Then he say to me, 'Sing and pray.' So I did; and I so much cry I cant pray. No go sleep—I cant—I wake—my heart full. All night I pray and praise God, for his send me preacher to sleep my camp. Next morning soon come, and he want to go. Then I go show him through the woods, until come to big road. Then he took me by hand and say, 'Farewell, brother; by and by we meet up in heaven.' Then me cry, and my brother cry. We part—I go hunt. All day I cry, and no see deer jump up and run away. Then I go and pray by some log. My heart so full of joy, that I cannot walk much. I say, 'I cannot hunt.' Sometimes I sing—then I stop and clap my hands, and look up to God, my heavenly Father. Then the love come so fast in my heart, I can hardly stand. So I went home, and said, 'This is my happiest day.'"

The history of the mission relates an anecdote of Rohn-yen-ness another of the christian Indians. It seems that after the conflict of Poe (see page 106) with the Indians, the Wyandots determined on revenge.

Poe then lived on the west side of the Ohio river, at the mouth of Little Yellow creek They chose Rohn-yen-ness as a proper person to murder him, and then make his escape. He went to Poe's house, and was met with great friendship. Poe not having any suspicion of his design, the best in his house was furnished him. When the time to retire to sleep came, he made a pallet on the floor for his Indian guest to sleep. He and his wife went to bed in the same room. Rohn-yen-ness said they both soon fell asleep. There being no person about the house but some children, this afforded him a fair opportunity to have executed his purpose; but the kindness they had both shown him worked in his mind. He asked himself how he could get up and kill even an enemy, that had taken him in, and treated him so well—so much like a brother? The more he thought about it, the worse he felt; but still, on the other hand, he was sent by his nation to avenge the death of two of its most valiant warriors; and their ghosts would not be appeased until the blood of Poe was shed. There, he said, he lay in this conflict of mind until about midnight. The duty he owed to his nation, and the spirits of his departed friends, aroused him. He seized his knife and tomahawk, and crept to the bedside of his sleeping host. Again the kindness he had received from Poe stared him in the face; and he said, it is mean, it is unworthy the character of an Indian warrior to kill even an enemy, who has so kindly treated him. He went back to his pallet, and slept until morning.

His kind host loaded him with blessings, and told him that they were once enemies, but now they had buried the hatchet and were brothers, and hoped they would always be so. Rohn-yen-ness, overwhelmed with a sense of the generous treatment he had received from his once powerful enemy, but now his kind friend, left him to join his party.

He said the more he reflected on what he had done, and the course he had pursued, the more he was convinced that he had done right. This once revengeful savage warrior, was overcome by the kindness of an evening, and all his plans frustrated.

This man became one of the most pious and devoted of the Indian converts. Although a chief, he was as humble as a child. He used his steady influence against the traders and their fire-water.

On the bank of the river, half a mile above Upper Sandusky, is a huge sycamore, which measures around, a yard from its base, 37 feet, and at its base over 40 feet. On the Tyemochte, about 6 miles west, formerly and perhaps now stands, another sycamore, hollow within, and of such generous proportions, that Mr. Wm. Brown, a surveyor, now residing in Marion, with 4 others, several years since, slept comfortably in it one cool autumnal night, and had plenty of room.

It was to this county that the celebrated Simon Kenton was brought captive, when taken by the Indians. We have two anecdotes to introduce respecting him, communicated orally by Major James Galloway of Xenia, who was with him on the occasion. The first illustrates the strength of affection which existed among the early frontiersmen, and the last their vivid recollection of localities.

In January, 1827, I was passing from Lower Sandusky, through the Wyandot reservation, in company with Simon Kenton. We stopped at Chaffee's store, on the Tyemochte, and were sitting at the fire, when in stepped an old man dressed in a hunting shirt, who, after laying his rifle in a corner, commenced trading. Hearing my companion's voice, he stepped up to him and inquired, "are you Simon Kenton?" he replied in the affirmative. "I am Joseph Lake," rejoined he. Upon this, Kenton sprang up as if by electricity, and they both, by a simultaneous impulse, clasped each other around the neck, and shed tears of joy. They had been old companions in fighting the Indians, and had not met for 30 years. The scene was deeply affecting to the bystanders. After being an hour or two together, recalling old times, they embraced and parted in tears, never again expecting to meet.

While travelling through the Sandusky plains, Kenton recognized at the distance of half a mile, the identical grove in which he had run the gauntlet, in the war of the revolution, *forty-nine* years before. A further examination tested the truth of his recollection, for there was the very race-path still existing, in which he had ran. It was near a road leading from Upper Sandusky to Bellefontaine, 8 or 10 miles from the former. I expressed my surprise at his remembering it. "Ah!" replied he, "I had a good many reasons laid on my back to recollect it."

Little Sandusky, on the Sandusky river, in the south part of the county; Cary, on the line of the Mad river railroad, in the western part; M'Cutchensville, on or near its north line, and Marseilles, in the southwest part, on the Bellefontaine road, are small but thriving villages, containing each about 200 inhabitants. Oregon, Mexico, Tyemochte, Crawfordsville, Bowshersville and Wyandot are smaller places.

ADDENDA,

HISTORICAL, DESCRIPTIVE AND STATISTICAL.

This addenda consists in part of articles received too late for insertion in the body of the work, as well as of those that could not well be introduced there.

OHIO.

OHIO,* the northeastern of the western states, is bounded north by Michigan and Lake Erie; east by Pennsylvania and Virginia; south by the Ohio river, which separates it from Virginia and Kentucky; and west by Indiana. It is between 38° 30′ and 42° N. lat., and between 80° 35′ and 84° 47′ W. lon., and between 3° 31′ and 7° 41′ W. lon. from W. It is 210 miles long from north to south, and 200 miles broad from east to west; containing 40,000 square miles, or 25,600,000 acres. The population in 1790, was 3,000; in 1800, 45,365; in 1810, 230,760; in 1820, 581,434; in 1830, 937,637; in 1840, 1,519,467; being the third in population in the United States. Of these, 775,360 were white males; 726,762 do. females; 8,740 were free colored males; 8,603 do. females. Employed in agriculture, 272,579: in commerce, 9,201; in manufactures and trades, 66,265; in mining, 704; navigating the ocean, 212; do. rivers, canals and lakes, 3,323, learned professions, 5,663.

The number of counties in which it is divided, was, in 1830, 73; in 1840, 79, and in 1847, 83. Columbus, on the Scioto, just below the confluence of the Whetstone, is the seat of government; but Cincinnati is the largest and most commercial city.

The interior of the state, and the country bordering on Lake Erie, are generally level, and in some places marshy. From one-quarter to one-third of the state, comprehending the eastern and southeastern part, bordering on the Ohio river, is generally hilly and broken. The interval lands on the Ohio, and several of its tributaries, have great fertility. On both sides of the Scioto, and of the Great and Little Miami, are the most extensive bodies of rich and level land in the state. On the head waters of the Muskingum and Scioto, and between the Scioto and the two Miami rivers, are extensive prairies, some of them low and marshy, producing a great quantity of coarse grass, from 2 to 5 feet high; other parts of the prairies are elevated and dry, with a very fertile soil, though they are sometimes called barrens. The height of land which divides the waters which fall into the Ohio from those which fall into Lake Erie, is the most marshy of any in the state; while the land on the margins of the rivers is generally dry. Among the forest trees are black walnut, oak of various species, hickory, maple of several kinds, beech, birch, poplar, sycamore, ash of several kinds, pawpaw, buckeye, cherry and white-wood, which is extensively used as a substitute for pine. Wheat may be regarded as the staple production of the state, but Indian corn and other grains are produced in great abundance. Although Ohio has already become so populous, it is surprising to the traveller to observe what an amount of forest is yet unsubdued.

The summers are warm and pretty regular, but subject, at times, to severe drought. The winters are generally mild, but much less so in the northern than in the southern part of the state. Near Lake Erie, the winters are probably as severe as in the same latitude on the Atlantic. In the country for 50 miles south of Lake Erie, there are generally a number of weeks of good sleiging in the winter; but in the southern part of the state, the snow is too small in quantity, or of too short continuance, to produce good sleighing for any considerable time. In the neighborhood of Cincinnati, green peas are produced in plenty by the 20th of May. In parts of the state, near marshes and stagnant waters, fevers

* The above concise geographical and statistical description of Ohio, is principally abridged from Sherman & Smith's Gazetteer of the United States.

and agues and billious and other fevers are prevalent. With this exception, the climate is healthy.

Salt springs have been found on Yellow creek, in Jefferson county; on the waters of Killbuck, in Wayne county; on Muskingum river, near Zanesville; and at various other places. Bituminous coal is found in great quantities in the eastern part of the state, and iron ore in various places.

The Ohio river, which gives name to the state, washes its entire southern border. This river is 908 miles long, from Pittsburgh to its mouth, by its various windings, though it is only 614 in a straight line. Its current is gentle, with no falls excepting at Louisville, Ky., where there is a descent of 22½ feet in two miles, but this has been obviated by a canal. For about half the year it is navigable for steamboats of a large class, through its whole course. The Muskingum, the largest river which flows entirely in the state, is formed by the junction of the Tuscarawas and Walholding rivers, and enters the Ohio at Mariëtta. It is navigable for boats 100 miles. The Scioto, the second river in magnitude flowing entirely within the state, is about 200 miles long, and enters the Ohio at Portsmouth. Its largest branch is the Whetstone or Olentangy, which joins it immediately above Columbus. It is navigable for boats 130 miles. The Great Miami is a rapid river in the western part of the state, 100 miles long, and enters the Ohio in the southwest corner of the state. The Little Miami has a course of 70 miles, and enters the Ohio 7 miles above Cincinnati. The Maumee is 100 miles long, rises in Indiana, runs through the northwest part of this state, and enters Lake Erie at Maumee bay. It is navigable for steamboats to Perrysburg, 18 miles from the lake, and above the rapids is boatable for a considerable distance. The Sandusky rises in the northern part of the state, and, after a course of about 80 miles, it enters Sandusky bay, and thence into Lake Erie. The Cuyahoga rises in the north part of the state, and, after a curved course of 60 miles, enters Lake Erie at Cleveland. It has a number of falls, which furnish valuable mill seats. Besides these, Huron, Vermilion, Black, Grand and Ashtabula rivers fall into Lake Erie.

Lake Erie borders this state for about 150 miles, and has several harbors, among which the largest are made by Maumee and Sandusky bays. Besides these are the harbors of Huron, Cleveland, Fairport and Ashtabula.

Among the principal literary institutions, is the University of Ohio, at Athens; the Miami University, at Oxford; the Franklin College, at New Athens; the Western Reserve College, at Hudson; Kenyon College, at Gambier, (Episcopal;) Granville College, at Granville, (Baptist;) Marietta College, at Marietta; the Oberlin Collegiate Institute, at Oberlin; Cincinnati and Woodward Colleges, at Cincinnati. Willoughby University, at Willoughby, is a medical institution, with a college charter. Lane Theological Seminary, at Cincinnati, was founded in 1829. There are also theological departments in Kenyon, Western Reserve and Granville Colleges, and in the Oberlin Institute; a Lutheran theological school at Columbus; two medical and one law school at Cincinnati. At all these institutions there were, in 1840, 1,717 students. Since 1840, other literary and scientific institutions have been established; among which is the Medical College, at Cleveland; Wittemberg College, at Springfield, and the Ohio Wesleyan University, at Delaware. There were in the state 73 academies, with 4,310 students; 5,186 common and primary schools, with 218,609 scholars. There were 35,394 white persons, over 20 years of age, who could neither read nor write.

This state has a number of important works of internal improvement. The Ohio canal extends from Cleveland, on Lake Erie, 307 miles, to Portsmouth, on the Ohio. It has a navigable feeder of 14 miles to Zanesville; one of 10 miles to Columbus; and one of 9 miles to Lancaster; one to Athens of fifty miles; the Walholding branch of 23 miles; the Eastport branch of 4 miles, and the Dresden of 2 miles. This great work was begun in 1825, and was finished in 1832, at a cost of $5,000,000. The Miami canal extends from Cincinnati, 178 miles, to Defiance, where it meets the Wabash and Erie canal. The cost was $3,750,000. The whole distance to Lake Erie is 265 miles. The Warren canal, a branch of the above, extends from Middletown, 20 miles, to Lebanon. The Sandy and Beaver canal is to extend from the Ohio canal, at Bolivar, 76 miles, to Ohio river, at the mouth of Little Beaver creek. Cost estimated at $1,500,000. The Mahoning canal extends from the Ohio canal, at Akron, 88 miles, 8 of which are in Pennsylvania, to Beaver river, at a cost of $764,372. Milan canal extends 3 miles, to Milan, to which steamboats now ascend. The Mad River and Little Miami railroads form a continuous line from Cincinnati to Sandusky City. A railroad is partly constructed from the latter place, through Mansfield, Mount Vernon, to Columbus, and various routes are projected for railroads in different parts of the state.

The governor is elected by the people for two years. The senators are chosen biennially, and are apportioned according to the number of white male inhabitants over 21 years of age. The number can never be less than one-third, nor more than half of the number of the representatives. The representatives are apportioned among the counties according to the number of inhabitants over 21; and there can never be more than 72, nor less than 36.

The judges of the supreme and other courts are elected by the joint ballot of the legislature, for the term of seven years.

The right of suffrage is enjoyed by all white male inhabitants, over 21 years of age, who have resided in the state one year next preceding the election, and who have paid or been assessed with a state or county tax.

The first permanent English settlement in Ohio, was made April 7th, 1788, at Marietta; and the first judicial court was held there in September of the same year, under an act of congress passed in 1786. The next settlement was that of Symmes' purchase, 6 miles below Cincinnati, in 1789. The next was made by French emigrants, at Gallipolis, in 1791. The next was made on Lake Erie, at Cleveland and Conneaut, in 1796, by emigrants from New England. In 1799 the first territorial legislature met at Cincinnati, and organized the government. Early in 1800, Connecticut relinquished her jurisdiction over the Western Reserve, and received a title to the land, which she sold to constitute her great school fund. In 1802, Ohio formed her state constitution, and was admitted to the union.

PUBLIC LANDS.*

In most of the states and territories lying west of the Alleghany mountains, the United States, collectively, as a nation, owned, or did own, the soil of the country, after the extinguishment of the aboriginal Indian title. This vast national domain comprises several hundreds of millions of acres; which is a beautiful fund, upon which the general government can draw for centuries, to supply, at a low price, all its citizens with a freehold estate.

When Ohio was admitted into the federal union as an independent state, one of the terms of admission was, that the fee-simple to all the lands within its limits, excepting those previously granted or sold, should vest in the United States. Different portions of them have, at diverse periods, been granted or sold to various individuals, companies, and bodies politic.

The following are the names by which the principal bodies of the lands are designated, on account of these different forms of transfer; viz:

1. Congress Lands.
2. U. S. Military.
3. Virginia Military.
4. Western Reserve.
5. Fire Lands.
6. Ohio Co's. Purchase.
7. Donation Tract.
8. Symmes' Purchase
9. Refugee Tract.
10. French Grant.
11. Dohrman's do.
12. Zane's do.
13. Canal Lands.
14. Turnpike do.
15. Maumee Road Lands.
16. School do.
17. College do.
18. Ministerial do.
19. Moravian do.
20. Salt Sections.

Congress Lands are so called, because they are sold to purchasers by the immediate officers of the general government, conformably to such laws as are, or may be, from time to time, enacted by congress. They are all regularly surveyed into townships of six miles square each, under authority, and at the expense of the national government.

All Congress lands, excepting Marietta and a part of Steubenville district, are numbered as follows:

6	5	4	3	2	1
7	8	9	10	11	12
18	17	16	15	14	13
19	20	21	22	23	24
30	29	28	27	26	25
31	32	33	34	35	36

VII ranges, Ohio company's purchase, and Symmes' purchase, are numbered as here exhibited:

36	30	24	18	12	6
35	29	23	17	11	5
34	28	22	16	10	4
33	27	21	15	9	3
32	26	20	14	8	2
31	25	19	13	7	1

---

* This article is abridged from the Ohio Gazetteer.

The townships are again subdivided into sections of one mile square, each containing 640 acres, by lines running parallel with the township and range lines. The sections are numbered in two different modes, as exhibited in the preceding figures or diagrams.

In addition to the foregoing division, the sections are again subdivided into four equal parts, called the Northeast quarter section, Southeast quarter section, &c. And again, by a law of congress, which went into effect in July, 1820, these quarter sections are also divided by a north and south line, into two equal parts, called the east half quarter section, No. and west half quarter section, No. which contain eighty acres each. The minimum price has been reduced by the same law, from $2.00 to $1.25 per acre, cash down.

In establishing the township and sectional corners, a post is first planted at the point of intersection; then on the tree nearest the post, and standing within the section intended to be designated, is numbered with the marking iron, the range, township and number of the section, thus:

R 21 T 4 S 30†	R 20 T 4 †S 31
R 21† T 3 S 1	†R 20 T 3 S 6

The quarter corners are marked 1-4 south, merely.

Section No. 16, of every township, is perpetually reserved for the use of schools, and leased or sold out, for the benefit of schools, under the state government. All the others may be taken up either in sections, fractions, halves, quarters, or half quarters.

For the purpose of selling out these lands, they are divided into eight several land districts, called after the names of the towns in which the land offices are kept, viz: Wooster, Steubenville, Zanesville, Marietta, Chillicothe, etc., etc.

The *seven* ranges of townships are a portion of the Congress lands, so called, being the first ranges of public lands ever surveyed by the general government, west of the Ohio river. They are bounded on the north by a line drawn due west from the Pennsylvania state line, where it crosses the Ohio river, to the United States Military lands, 42 miles; thence south to the Ohio river, at the southeast corner of Marietta township, thence up the river to the place of beginning.

Connecticut Western Reserve, often times called New Connecticut, is situated in the northeast quarter of the state, between Lake Erie on the north, Pennsylvania east, the parallel of the 41st degree of north latitude south, and Sandusky and Seneca counties on the west. It extends 120 miles from east to west, and upon an average 50 from north to south: although, upon the Pennsylvania line, it is 68 miles broad, from north to south. The area is about 3,800,000 acres. It is surveyed into townships of five miles square each. A body of half a million acres is, however, stricken off from the west end of the tract, as a donation, by the state of Connecticut, to certain sufferers by fire, in the revolutionary war.

The manner by which Connecticut became possessed of the land in question, was the following: King Charles II, of England, pursuing the example of his brother kings, of granting distant and foreign regions to his subjects, granted to the then colony of Connecticut, in 1662, a charter right to all lands included within certain specific bounds. But as the geographical knowledge of Europeans concerning America, was then very limited and confused, patents for lands often interfered with each other, and many of them, even by their express terms, extended to the Pacific ocean, or South sea, as it was then called. Among the rest, that for Connecticut embraced all lands contained between the 41st and 42d parallels of north latitude, and from Providence plantations on the east, to the Pacific ocean west, with the exception of New York and Pennsylvania colonies; and, indeed, pretensions to these were not finally relinquished without considerable altercation. And after the United States became an independent nation, these interfering claims occasioned much collision of sentiment between them and the state of Connecticut, which was finally compromised, by the United States relinquishing all their claims upon, and guaranteeing to Connecticut the exclusive right of soil to the 3,800,000 acres now described. The United States, however, by the terms of compromise, reserved to themselves the right of jurisdiction. They then united this tract to the territory, now state of Ohio.

Fire Lands, a tract of country so called, of about 781 square miles, or 500,000 acres, in the western part of New Connecticut. The name originated from the circumstance of the state of Connecticut having granted these lands in 1792, as a donation to certain sufferers by fire, occasioned by the English during our revolutionary war, particularly at New London, Fairfield and Norwalk. These lands include the five westernmost ranges of the Western Reserve townships. Lake Erie and Sandusky bay project so far southerly, as to leave but the space of six tiers and some fractions of townships between them and the 41st parallel of latitude, or a tract of about 30 by 27 miles in extent.

3	2
4	1

This tract is surveyed into townships of about five miles square each; and these townships are then subdivided into four quarters; and these quarter townships are numbered as in the accompanying figure, the top being considered north. And for individual convenience, these are again subdivided, by private surveys, into lots of from fifty to five hundred acres each, to suit individual purchasers.

United States Military Lands are so called from the circumstance of their having been appropriated, by an act of congress of the 1st of June, 1796, to satisfy certain claims of the officers and soldiers of the revolutionary war. The tract of country embracing these lands is bounded as follows: beginning at the northwest corner of the original VII ranges of townships, thence south 50 miles, thence west to the Scioto river, thence up said river to the Greenville treaty line, thence northeasterly with said line to old Fort Laurens, on the Tuscarawas river, thence due east to the place of beginning; including a tract of about 4000 square miles, or 2,560,000 acres of land. It is, of course, bounded north by the Greenville treaty line, east by the "VII ranges of townships," south by the Congress and Refugee lands, and west by the Scioto river.

These lands are surveyed into townships of five miles square. These townships were then again, originally, surveyed into quarter townships of two and a half miles square, containing 4000 acres each:—and subsequently, some of these quarter townships were subdivided into forty lots of 100 acres each, for the accommodation of those soldiers holding warrants for only 100 acres each. And again, after the time originally assigned for the location of these warrants had expired, certain quarter townships which had not then been located, were divided into sections of one mile square each, and sold by the general government, like the main body of Congress lands.

2	1
3	4

The quarter townships are numbered as exhibited in the accompanying figure, the top being considered north. The place of each township is ascertained by numbers and ranges, the same as Congress lands; the ranges being numbered from east to west, and the numbers from south to north.

Virginia Military Lands are a body of land lying between the Scioto and Little Miami rivers, and bounded upon the Ohio river on the south. The state of Virginia, from the indefinite and vague terms of expression in its original colonial charter of territory from James I., king of England, in the year 1609, claimed all the continent west of the Ohio river, and of the north and south breadth of Virginia. But finally, among several other compromises of conflicting claims which were made, subsequently to the attainment of our national independence, Virginia agreed to relinquish all her claims to lands northwest of the Ohio river, in favor of the general government, upon condition of the lands, now described, being guaranteed to her. The state of Virginia then appropriated this body of land to satisfy the claims of her state troops employed in the continental line, during the revolutionary war.

This district is not surveyed into townships or any regular form: but any individual holding a Virginia military land warrant may locate it, wherever he chooses, within the district, and in such shape as he pleases, wherever the land shall not previously have been located. In consequence of this deficiency of regular original surveys, and the irregularities with which the several locations have been made; and the consequent interference and encroachment of some locations upon others, more than double the litigation has probably arisen between the holders of adverse titles, in this district, than there has in any other part of the state, of equal extent.

Ohio Company's purchase is a body of land containing about 1,500,000 acres; including, however, the donation tract, school lands, &c., lying along the Ohio river; and including Meigs, nearly all of Athens, and a considerable part of Washington and Gallia counties. This tract was purchased of the general government in the year 1787, by Manasseh Cutler and Winthrop Sargeant, from the neighborhood of Salem, in Massachusetts, agents for the "Ohio company," so called, which had then been formed in Massachusetts, for the purpose of a settlement in the Ohio country. Only 964,285 acres were ultimately paid for, and of course patented. This body of land was then apportioned out into 817 shares, of 1173 acres each, and a town lot of one-third of an acre to each share. These shares were made up to each proprietor in tracts, one of 640 acres, one of 262, one of 160, one of 100, one of 8, and another of 3 acres, besides the before mentioned town lot.

Besides every section 16, set apart, as elsewhere, for the support of schools, every section

29 is appropriated for the support of religious institutions. In addition to which were also granted two six miles square townships, for the use of a college.

But unfortunately for the Ohio company, owing to their want of topographical knowledge of the country, the body of land selected by them, with some partial exceptions, is the most hilly and sterile of any tract of similar extent in the state.

Donation tract is a body of 100,000 acres, set off in the northern limits of the Ohio company's tract, and granted to them by congress, provided they should obtain one actual settler upon each hundred acres thereof, within five years from the date of the grant; and that so much of the 100,000 acres aforesaid, as should not thus be taken up, shall revert to the general government.

This tract may, in some respects, be considered a part of the Ohio company's purchase. It is situated in the northern limits of Washington county. It lies in an oblong shape, extending nearly 17 miles from east to west, and about 7½ from north to south.

Symmes' purchase, a tract of 311,682 acres of land, in the southwestern quarter of the state, between the Great and Little Miami rivers. It borders on the Ohio river a distance of 27 miles, and extends so far back from the latter between the two Miamis, as to include the quantity of land just mentioned. It was patented to John Cleves Symmes, in 1794, for 67 cents per acre. Every 16th section, or square mile, in each township, was reserved by congress for the use of schools, and sections 29 for the support of religious institutions, beside 15 acres around Fort Washington, in Cincinnati. This tract of country is now one of the most valuable in the state.

Refugee tract, a body of 100,000 acres of land granted by congress to certain individuals who left the British provinces during the revolutionary war, and espoused the cause of freedom. It is a narrow strip of country, 4½ miles broad from north to south, and extending eastwardly from the Scioto river 48 miles. It has the United States' XX ranges of military or army lands north, and XXII ranges of congress lands south. In the western borders of this tract is situated the town of Columbus.

French grant, a tract of 24,000 acres of land, bordering upon the Ohio river, in the southeastern quarter of Scioto county. It was granted by congress, in March, 1795, to a number of French families, who lost their lands at Gallipolis, by invalid titles. Twelve hundred acres, additional, were afterwards granted, adjoining the above mentioned tract at its lower end, toward the mouth of Little Scioto river.

Dohrman's grant is one six mile square township, of 23,040 acres, granted to Arnold Henry Dohrman, formerly a wealthy Portuguese merchant in Lisbon, for and in consideration of his having, during the revolutionary war, given shelter and aid to the American cruisers and vessels of war. It is located in the southeastern part of Tuscarawas county.

Moravian lands are three several tracts of 4000 acres each, originally granted by the old continental congress, July, 1787, and confirmed, by the act of congress of 1st June, 1796, to the Moravian brethren at Bethlehem, in Pennsylvania, in trust and for the use of the christianized Indians living thereon. They are laid out in nearly square forms, on the Muskingum river, in what is now Tuscarawas county. They are called by the names of the Shoenbrun, Gnadenhutten and Salem tracts.

Zane's tracts are three several tracts of one mile square each—one on the Muskingum, which includes the town of Zanesville—one at the cross of the Hocking river, on which the town of Lancaster is laid out—and the third, on the left bank of the Scioto river, opposite Chillicothe. They were granted by congress to one Ebenezer Zane, in May, 1796, on condition that he should open a road through them, from Wheeling, in Virginia, to Maysville, in Kentucky.

There are also three other tracts, of one mile square each, granted to Isaac Zane, in the year 1802, in consideration of his having been taken prisoner by the Indians, when a boy, during the revolutionary war, and living with them most of his life; and having, during that time, performed many acts of kindness and beneficence toward the American people. These tracts are situated in Champain county, on King's creek, from three to five miles northwest from Urbana.

The Maumee land roads, are a body of lands, averaging 2 miles wide, lying along 1 mile on each side of the road from the Maumee river at Perrysburg, to the western limits of the Western Reserve; a distance of about 46 miles; and comprising nearly 60,000 acres. They were originally granted by the Indian owners, at the treaty of Brownstown in 1808, to enable the United States to make a road on the line just mentioned. The general government never moved in the business, until February, 1823, when congress passed an act, making over the aforesaid lands to the state of Ohio; provided she would, within 4 years thereafter, make and keep in repair, a good road throughout the aforesaid route of 46 miles. This road the state government has already made; and obtained possession, and sold most of the land.

Turnpike lands, are forty-nine sections, amounting to 31,360 acres, situated along the western side of the Columbus and Sandusky turnpike, in the eastern parts of Seneca, Crawford and Marion counties. They were originally granted by an act of congress, on the 3d of March, 1827, and more specifically by a supplementary act, the year following. The considerations for which these lands were granted, were that the mail stages and all troops and property of the United States, which should ever be moved and transported along this road, shall pass free from toll.

The Ohio canal lands, are lands granted by congress to the state of Ohio to aid in constructing her extensive canals. These lands comprise over 1 million of acres, a large proportion of which is now (1847) in market.

School Lands. By compact between the United States and the state of Ohio, when the latter was admitted into the Union, it was stipulated, for and in consideration that the state of Ohio should never tax the congress lands; until after they should have been sold 5 years; and in consideration that the public lands would thereby more readily sell, that the one thirty-sixth part of all the territory included within the limits of the state, should be set apart, for the support of common schools therein. And, for the purpose of getting at lands, which should, in point of quality of soil be on an average with the whole land in the country; they decreed that it should be selected, by lot, in small tracts each, to wit: that it should consist of section number 16, let that section be good or bad, in every township of congress lands; also in the Ohio company, and in Symmes' purchases; all of which townships are composed of 36 sections each; and for the United States' military lands, and Connecticut Reserve; a number of quarter townships, 2½ miles square each, (being the smallest public surveys therein, then made,) should be selected by the secretary of the treasury, in different places throughout the United States' military tract; equivalent in quantity, to the one thirty-sixth part of those two tracts respectively. And for the Virginia military tract, congress enacted that a quantity of land equal to the one thirty-sixth part of the estimated quantity of land contained therein, should be selected by lot, in what was then called the "New Purchase," in quarter township tracts of 3 miles square each. Most of these selections were accordingly made: but, in some instances by the carelessness of the officers conducting the sales, or from some other cause, a few sections 16 have been sold; in which case, congress, when applied to, have generally granted other lands in lieu thereof; as for instance, no section 16 was reserved in Montgomery township, in which Columbus is situated; and congress, afterwards granted therefor, section 21, in the township cornering thereon to the southeast.

College townships, are three 6 miles square townships, granted by congress; two of them to the Ohio company, for the use of a college to be established within their purchase, and one for the use of the inhabitants of Symmes' purchase.

Ministerial Lands. In both the Ohio company and in Symmes' purchase, every section 29, (equal to one thirty-sixth part of every township,) is reserved, as a permanent fund for the support of a settled minister. As the purchasers of these two tracts came from parts of the union where it was customary and deemed necessary to have a regular settled clergyman in every town, they therefore stipulated in their original purchase, that a permanent fund, in land, should thus be set apart for this purchase. In no other part of the state, other than in these two purchases, are any lands set apart for this object.

Salt Sections. Near the centre of what is now Jackson county, congress originally reserved from sale, thirty-six sections, or one six mile square township, around and including what was called the Scioto salt licks; also one quarter of a 5 mile square township in what is now Delaware county; in all, forty-two and a quarter sections, or 27,040 acres. By an act of congress of the 28th of December, 1824, the legislature of Ohio was authorized to sell these lands, and to apply the proceeds thereof to such literary purposes, as said legislature may think proper; but to no other purpose whatever.

OFFICERS OF THE TERRITORIAL GOVERNMENT,

APPOINTED IN 1788, UNDER THE ORDINANCE OF CONGRESS

Arthur St. Clair, Governor.

Samuel H. Parsons, James M. Varnum, John Cleves Symmes, Judges.

Winthrop Sargeant, Secretary. William H. Harrison was subsequently appointed secretary of the territory; he was afterwards elected delegate to congress.

GOVERNORS OF THE STATE,

AFTER THE ADOPTION OF THE CONSTITUTION.

Edward Tiffin, elected and sworn, 3d March,	1803
Thomas Kirker,* (acting governor part of the year,)	1808
Samuel Huntington, elected and sworn in,	1808
Return J. Meigs, do. do.	1810
Othniel Looker,* (acting governor part of the year,)	1814
Thomas Worthington, elected,	1814
Ethan Allen Brown, do.	1818
Allen Trimble,* (acting governor part of the year,)	1822
Jeremiah Morrow, elected,	1822
Allen Trimble, do.	1826
Duncan McArthur, do.	1830
Robert Lucas, do.	1832
Joseph Vance, do.	1836
Wilson Shannon, do.	1838
Thomas Corwin, do.	1840
Wilson Shannon, do.	1842
Thos. W. Bartley,* (acting governor,)	1843
Mordecai Bartley, elected,	1844
William Bebb, do.	1846

MEMBERS OF THE CONVENTION,

WHO FORMED THE STATE CONSTITUTION, ADOPTED IN CONVENTION AT CHILLICOTHE, NOVEMBER 29TH, 1803.

EDWARD TIFFIN, President and representative from the county of Ross.

Adams County.—Joseph Darlinton, Israel Donalson and Thomas Kirker.

Belmont County.—James Caldwell and Elijah Woods.

Clermont County.—Philip Gatch and James Sargent.

Fairfield County.—Henry Abrams and Emanuel Carpenter.

Hamilton County.—John W. Browne, Charles Willing Byrd, Francis Dunlavy, William Goforth, John Kitchel, Jeremiah Morrow, John Paul, John Riley, John Smith and John Wilson.

Jefferson County.—Rudolph Bair, George Humphrey, John Milligan, Nathan Updegraff and Bezaleel Wells.

Ross County.—Michael Baldwin, James Grubb, Nathaniel Massie and T. Worthington.

Trumbull County.—David Abbott and Samuel Huntington.

Washington County.—Ephraim Cutler, Benjamin Ives Gillman, John M'Intire and Rufus Putnam.

Thomas Scott, secretary of the convention.

The following embraces the names of all the members of the U. S. Senate and House of Representatives, who have from time to time been elected, and have represented Ohio in the National Congress.

SENATORS OF CONGRESS.

	In. Out.		In. Out.
William Allen,	1837–49	Thomas Morris,	1833–39
Ethan A. Brown,	1822–25	Jeremiah Morrow,	1813–19
Jacob Burnet,	1828–31	Benjamin Ruggles,	1815–33
Alexander Campbell,	1809–13	John Smith,	1803–08
Thomas Corwin,	1845–51	Benjamin Tappan,	1839–45
Thomas Ewing,	1831–37	Edward Tiffin,	1807–09
S. Griswold,	1809–09	William A. Trimble,	1819–22
William H. Harrison,	1825–28	Thomas Worthington,	1803–07; 1810–14
Joseph Kerr,	1814–15		
Return J. Meigs,	1808–10		

* Those marked with a star, were presidents of the senate, who were, by the constitution, governors for short periods only.

REPRESENTATIVES IN CONGRESS.

John Alexander,	1813–17
J. Alexander, jr.,	1837–39
William Allen,	1833–35
John W. Allen,	1837–41
S. J. Andrews,	1841–43
Levi Barber,	1817–19 1821–23
Mordecai Bartley,	1823–31
Reasin Beall,	1813–15
Philemon Beecher,	1817–21 1823–29
James M. Bell,	1833–35
William K. Bond,	1835–41
J. Brinckerhoff,	1843–47
Henry Brush,	1819–21
James Caldwell,	1813–17
John W. Campbell,	1817–27
David Chambers,	1821–23
John Chaney,	1833–39
David Clendenin,	1815–17
Charles G. Coffin,	1838–39
Eleutheros Cooke,	1831–33
Thomas Corwin,	1831–40
Benjamin S. Cowen,	1841–43
Joseph H. Crane,	1829–37
William Creighton,	1813–17 1827–33
John D. Cummings,	–47
Frais A. Cunningham,	–47
John Davenport,	1827–29
Ezra Dean,	1841–45
Columbus Delano,	–47
William Doane,	1839–43
Alexander Duncan,	1837–41 –45
James J. Faran,	–47
Paul Fearing,	1801–03
James Findlay,	1825–33
Elias Florence,	–45
George Fries,	–47
James W. Gazley,	1823–25
Joshua R. Giddings,	1839–47
Patrick G. Goode,	1837–43
John M. Goodenow,	1829–31
Thomas L. Hamer,	1833–39
Alexander Harper,	1837–47
William H. Harrison,	1799–1800 1816–1819
John Hastings,	1839–43
Samuel Herrick,	1817–21
Peter Hitchcock,	1817–19
Elias Howell,	1835–37
William H. Hunter,	1837–39
William W. Irvin,	1829–33
David Jennings,	1825–26
P. B. Johnson,	–45
Benjamin Jones,	1833–37
William Kennon,	1829–33 1835–37
James Kilbourne,	1813–17
Daniel Kilgore,	1835–39
Humphrey H. Leavitt,	1831–34
D. P. Leadbetter,	1837–41
A. Loomis,	1837–38
Robert T. Lytle,	1833–35
Samson Mason,	1835–43
Joshua Mathiot,	1841–43
James Matthews,	1841–45
Duncan M'Arthur,	1823–25
W. C. M'Causlen,	–45
J. J. M'Dowell,	1843–47
John M'Lean,	1813–16
William M'Lene,	1823–29
Jeremiah M'Lene,	1833–37
William M'Millan,	1800–01
William Medill,	1839–43
Robert Mitchell,	1833–35
Calvary Morris,	1837–43
Joseph Morris,	1843–47
Jeremiah Morrow,	1803–13 1841–43
Francis Muhlenberg,	1828–
Isaac Parish,	1839–41 –47
John Patterson,	1823–25
William Patterson,	1833–38
E. D. Potter,	–45
Augustus L. Perril,	–47
N. G. Pendleton,	1841–43
Joseph Ridgeway,	1837–43
Thomas R. Ross,	1819–25
Joseph M. Root,	–47
William Russell,	1827–33 1841–43
William Sawyer,	1843–47
R. C. Schenck,	1843–47
Thomas Shannon,	1826–27
Matthias Shepler,	1837–39
James Shields,	1829–31
John Sloane,	1819–29
Jonathan Sloane,	1833–37
David Spangler,	1833–37
William Stanberry,	1827–33
D. A. Starkweather,	1839–41 1845–47
Samuel Stokeley,	1841–43
Bellamy Storer,	1835–37
Henry Swearingen,	1839–41
George Sweeney,	1839–43
Henry St. John,	1843–47
Jonathan Taylor,	1839–41
John Thompson,	1825–27 1829–37
Joseph Vance,	1821–35 1843–47
J. J. Vanmeter,	–45
Samuel F. Vinton,	1823–37 1843–47
Taylor Webster,	1833–39
D. R. Tilden,	1843–47
Allen G. Sherman	–47
John B. Weller,	1839–45
Elisha Whittlesey,	1823–39
William Wilson,	1823–27
John Woods,	1825–29
John C. Wright,	1823–29

CLARK COUNTY.*

There are three old men now living in this county, viz., John Humphries, David Lowry and Griffith Foos, from whom we have gathered the following particulars respecting the early history of Springfield, and also some incidents connected with the first settlements made in the vicinity. Messrs. Humphries, Lowry and Foos, are all men of great respectability, and are well known to all the early settlers of this region of Ohio.

John Humphries is now 83 years of age, David Lowry about 77, and Griffith Foos about 75.

John Humphries came to what is now Clark county with General Simon Kenton, in 1799; with them emigrated six families from Kentucky, and made the first settlement in the neighborhood of what is now Springfield, north of the ground on which was afterwards located the town. At this time, he is the only survivor of those of his companions and associates who were at the time heads of families. Mr. Humphries speaks of a fort which was erected on Mad river, two miles from the site of Springfield; this fort contained within its pickets 14 cabins, and was erected for the purpose of common security against the Indians.

David Lowry came into Ohio in the spring of 1795. He built the first flat boat, to use his own language, "that ever navigated the Great Miami river from Dayton down, which was in the year 1800." He took the same boat to New Orleans, laden with pickled pork, 500 venison hams, and bacon. Lowry, with one Jonathan Donnell, made the second settlement within what is now the limits of Clark county; Demint's was the third settlement. The first corn crop raised in the neighborhood of Springfield was in 1796. Two men, whose names were Krebs and Brown, cultivated the crop. Lowry hunted for the party while they were engaged in tending the crop; the ground occupied was about 3 miles west of the site of Springfield. He raised a crop of corn the ensuing year, and also accompanied the party that surveyed and laid out the first road from Dayton to Springfield. He and Jonathan Donnell killed, in one season, in their settlement, 17 bears, and in the course of his life, he states he has killed 1000 deer; and that he once shot a she bear and 2 cubs in less than three minutes.

Griffith Foos, with several other persons, came into what is now Springfield, in the month of March, 1801. They were in search of a healthy region, having become wearied with the sickly condition of the Scioto valley. The laying off what is now called the old town of Springfield, was commenced March 17th, 1801. Mr. Foos commenced the first public house ever kept in the place: it was a log house, situated on the lot directly opposite to the National hotel, now kept by William Werden. He opened his house in June, 1801,

* Communicated by a resident of Springfield.

and continued it without intermission until the 10th of May, 1814. He states that he and his party were 4½ days getting from Franklinton, on the Scioto, to Springfield, a distance of forty-two miles. In crossing Big Darby, they were obliged to carry all their goods on horseback, and then to drag their wagon across with ropes, while some of the party swam by the side of the wagon to prevent it from upsetting. In 1807, in consequence of the alarm which the neighborhood felt on account of the Indians, Mr. Foos' house was turned into a fort. This was the first building erected in the place. Saml. Simonton erected the first frame house in the county in 1807. Wm. Ross built the first brick house, which is still standing on the SE. corner of South and Market streets.

These early settlers represent the county at that day as being very beautiful. North of the site of Springfield, for 14 miles, upon the land which is now thick with woods, there could not, from 1801 to 1809, have been found a sufficiency of poles to have made hoops for a meat cart. The forest consisted of large trees, with no undergrowth, and the ground was finely sodded.

Mr. Griffith Foos speaks of an old hunter by the name of James Smith, from Kentucky, who was at his house in 1810, who stated that he was in this neighborhood fifty years previously with the Indians, and that up the prairie, NE. of the town of Springfield, they started some buffalo and elk.

The first house of worship built in Springfield was in 1811: one man gave the ground—Foos gave a handsome young horse ($10) towards hewing the logs and preparing the shingles. It was a place of worship free to all denominations, and was built right south of a public house which stands directly west of Mill run, on the south side of the national road.

The early settlers were unequalled for their kindness, honesty and hospitality. Mr. Foos says, that, at his raising, there were present 40 men before breakfast, and from a distance of from 7 to 10 miles; and Lowry says, that at Isaac Zane's raising, there were persons from 40 miles distance.

DEFIANCE COUNTY.

The annexed description of the settlement at the junction of the Auglaize with the Maumee about the year 1792, is from the narrative of O. M. Spencer:

On this high ground, (since the site of Fort Defiance, erected by General Wayne, in 1794,) extending from the Maumee a quarter of a mile up the Auglaize, about two hundred yards in width, was an open space, on the west and south of which were oak woods, with hazel undergrowth. Within this opening, a few hundred yards above the point, on the steep high bank of the Auglaize, were five or six cabins and log houses, inhabited principally by Indian traders. The most northerly, a large hewed log house, divided below into three apartments, was occupied as a warehouse, store, and dwelling, by George Ironside, the most wealthy and influential of the traders on the point. Next to his were the houses of Pirault, (Pero,) a French baker, and M'Kenzie, a Scot, who, in addition to merchandizing, followed the occupation of a silversmith, exchanging with the Indians his brooches, ear-drops, and other silver ornaments, at an enormous profit, for skins and furs. Still farther up were several other families of French and English; and two American prisoners, Henry Ball, a soldier taken at St. Clair's defeat, and his wife, Polly Meadows, captured at the same time, were allowed to live here, and by labor to pay their masters the price of their ransom; he by boating to the rapids of the Maumee, and she by washing and sewing. Fronting the house of Ironside, and about fifty yards from the bank, was a small stockade, enclosing two hewed log houses, one of which was occupied by James Girty, (brother of Simon,) the other, occasionally, by M'Kee and Elliot, British Indian agents, living at Detroit.

From this station I had a fine view of the large village more than a mile south, on the east side of the Auglaize, of Blue Jacket's town, and of the Maumee river for several miles below, and of the extensive prairie covered with corn, directly opposite, and forming together a very handsome landscape.

DELAWARE COUNTY.

The following article respecting Delaware County, was communicated for this work by Dr. H. C. Mann, of Delaware:

Delaware, the county seat, was laid out in 1808, by Col. Moses Byxbe, and Hon. Henry Baldwin, of Pittsburgh, who had purchased a large tract of land for that purpose. They sold the lots at private sale at the uniform price of $30, the purchaser taking his choice. Joseph Barber put up the first cabin in the fall of 1807. It stood close to the Spring, and was made of poles, Indian fashion, fifteen feet square, in which he kept tavern. The principal settlers were Messrs. Byxbe, Wm. Little, Dr. Lamb, Solomon Smith, Elder Jacob Drake, (Baptist preacher,) Thomas Butler, and Ira Carpenter. In the spring of 1808, Moses Byxbe built the first frame house on William street, lot 70, and the first brick house was erected the ensuing fall, by Elder Drake, on Winter street, where Thomas Pettibone's mansion now stands; being unable to get but one mason, *his wife* laid all the brick of the inside walls. The court house was built in 1815, the year in which the town was incorporated. The Methodists commenced the first meeting house in 1823, now the school house, but it was not finished for several years. The old churches of the 1st Presbyterians and the Episcopalians were built in 1825, upon the sites on which the present beautiful edifices were erected in 1845. The 2d Presbyterian church was erected in 1844, the new Methodist church in 1846, and the Lutheran church in 1835.

The town now contains 4 taverns, one, the Hinton House, being among the largest in Ohio, having over 100 rooms, 8 dry goods stores, 3 drug stores, 1 shoe store, 1 confectionary and variety store, and 2 small groceries; 2 Divisions of the Sons of Temperance, 1 Odd Fellows Lodge, 1 Masonic Society, 2 printing offices, from which issue weekly the "Olentangy Gazette," (Whig,) by Abel Thomson, and the "Loco Foco," (Dem.,) by George F. Stayman. The latter commenced in 1845, the former in 1821, by Hon. E. Griswold, then called the "Delaware Patron and Franklin Chronicle." The first paper in town was published in 1818, by Rev. J. Drake and Jos. S. Hughs. Delaware also contains 2 saw mills, 1 flouring mill, 1 oil mill, and the woollen factory of Messrs. Howard & Sharp, carrying on quite an extensive business; 8 lawyers, 7 physicians, a full quota of mechanics, 275 dwellings, and about 2000 inhabitants, including South Delaware, which properly belongs to it, though not included in the corporation. The Delaware Bank, with a capital of $100,000, is a branch of the State Bank. A bank was opened in 1812, but failing to get a charter the next winter, it wound up, redeeming all its notes; and during the same year, a swindling concern, called the "Scioto Exporting Co." was started by a posse of counterfeiters, who drew in some others, but it was destroyed by the citizens before they could get a large amount of paper afloat.

Ohio Wesleyan University was chartered in 1842, and the preparatory department opened the following year, and the college regularly organized in the fall of 1845. The present faculty consists of Rev. Edward Thomson, M. D., president and professor of moral science and belleslettres; Rev. Frederick Merrick, A. M., prof. natural science; Rev. Herman M. Johnson, A. M., prof. ancient languages and literature; Rev. L. D. M'Cabe, prof. mathematics; William G. Williams, A. B., principal of preparatory department, and E. C. Merrick, A. B., assistant. The college library consists of over 1000 volumes, obtained by donations, and is constantly increasing. Connected with it is a cabinet gallery of paintings, in which are several splendid specimens of artistical skill. The laboratory will this year be supplied with ample chemical and philosophical apparatus. There are two literary societies connected with the institution, each of which has a hall with suitable furniture, and a small library. The tuition is $30 in the college, and $20 in the preparatory department.

Endowment.—This university received nothing from government, but originated in the liberality of the citizens of Delaware, embracing all denominations, who donated the building and ten acres of land, valued at $10,000. Five acres adjoining, including the President's house, at $5,000—a farm near Marion, at $10,000—other lands at $2,000, and notes $45,000, all obtained by subscription, making a total amount of $72,000. These scholarship notes were obtained in various parts of the state, each one hundred dollars entitling the debtor to five years tuition, the interest payable annually. Last year the receipts were, interest on notes, $2,500, rent of farm, $300, tuition, $1,000; total, $3,800. Expenses for professors' salaries, $3,350. A new and elegant chapel of limestone is now erecting, and will be finished in 1848. Its cost is to be defrayed from the proceeds of a small 8vo. volume of original sermons, 45 in number, by the elder Methodist ministers. It has just issued from the press, (June, 1847,) and the first edition of 5000 vols. sold in six weeks. This manifestation of spirit, connected with the fact that the first annual catalogue exhibits an array of 162 pupils, warrants the conclusion that the institution is destined to flourish remarkably. It must be so, as this is the only college in the state under the control of the Methodists, who in the same bounds number 150,000 communicants, just being properly awakened in the important cause of education.

History.—The first settlement in the county was made May 1st, 1801, on the east bank of the Olentangy, five miles below Delaware, by Nathan Carpenter and Avery Powers, from Chemango county, N. Y. Carpenter brought his family with him, and built the first cabin near where the farm house now stands. Powers' family came out towards fall, but he had been out the year before to explore the country and select the location. In April, 1802, Thomas Celler, with Josiah McKinney, from Franklin county, Pa., moved in and settled two miles lower down, and in the fall of 1803, Henry Perry, from Wales, commenced a clearing and put up a cabin in Radnor, three-fourths of a mile south of Delhi. In the spring of 1804, Aaron, John, and Ebenezer Welch, (brothers,) and Capt. Leonard Monroe, from Chenango, N. Y., settled in Carpenter's neighborhood, and the next fall Col. Byxbe and his company, from Berkshire, Mass., settled on Alum creek, and named their township Berkshire. The settlement at Norton, by William Drake, and Nathaniel Wyatt; Lewis settlement, in Berlin, and the one at Westfield, followed soon after. In 1804, Carpenter built the first mill in the county, where the factory of Gun, Jones, & Co. now stands. It was a saw mill, with a small pair of stones attached, made of boulders, or "nigger heads," as they are commonly called. It could only grind a few bushels a day, but still it was a great advantage to the settlers. When the county was organized, in 1808, the following officers were elected, viz.: Avery Powers, John Welch and Ezekiel Brown, commissioners. Rev. Jacob Drake, treasurer, Dr. Reuben Lamb, recorder, and Azariah Root, surveyor. The officers of court were Judge Belt, of Chillicothe, president, Josiah M'Kinney, Thomas Brown and Moses Byxbe, associate judges; Ralph Osborn, prosecuting attorney, Solomon Smith, sheriff, and Moses Byxbe, jr., clerk. The first session was held in a little cabin that stood north of the sulphur spring. The grand jury sat under a cherry tree, and the petit jury in a cluster of bushes on another part of the lot, with their constables at a considerable distance to keep off intruders.

Block-houses.—This being a border county, during the last war, danger was apprehended from the Indians, and a block-house was built in 1812, at Norton, and another, still standing on Alum creek, 7 miles E. from Delaware; and the present dwelling of L. H. Cowles, Esq., NE. corner of Main and William streets, was converted into a temporary stockade. During the war this county furnished a company of cavalry, that served several short campaigns as volunteers, under Capt. Elias Murray, and several entire companies of infantry were called out from here at different times by Gov. Meigs, but the county never was invaded.

Drake's Defeat.—After Hull's surrender, Capt. Wm. Drake formed a company of Rangers in the northern part of the county to protect the frontier from marauding bands of Indians who then had nothing to restrain them; and when Lower Sandusky was threatened with attack, this company, with great alacrity obeyed the call to march to its defence. They encamped the first night a few miles beyond the outskirts of the settlement. In those days the captain was a great wag, and naturally very fond of sport, and being withal desirous of testing the courage of his men, after they had all got asleep he slipped into the bushes at some distance, and discharging his gun, rushed towards the camp yelling Indians! Indians! with all his might. The sentinels, supposing the alarm to proceed from one of their number, joined in the cry and ran to quarters; the men sprang to their feet in complete confusion, and the courageous attempted to form on the ground designated the night before in case of attack; but the first lieutenant, thinking there was more safety in depending upon *legs* than *arms*, took to his heels and dashed into the woods. Seeing the consternation and impending disgrace of his company, the captain quickly proclaimed the hoax and ordered a halt, but the lieutenant's frightened imagination converted every sound into Indian yells and the sanguinary war-whoop, and the louder the captain shouted, the faster he ran, till the sounds sank away in the distance, and he supposed the captain and his adherents had succumbed to the tomahawk and the scalping-knife. Supposing he had been asleep a few minutes only, he took the moon for his guide and flew for home, but having had time to gain the western horizon she led him in the wrong direction, and after breaking down sapplings and running through brush some ten miles through the woods, he reached Radnor settlement just at daybreak, bare-headed and with his garments flowing in a thousand streams. The people, roused hurriedly from their slumber, and horrified with his report that the whole company was massacred but him who alone had escaped, began a general and rapid flight. Each conveyed the tidings to his neighbor, and just after sunrise they came rushing through Delaware, mostly on horseback, many in wagons, and some on foot, presenting all those grotesque appearances that frontier settlers naturally would, supposing the Indians close in their rear. Many anecdotes are told, amusing now to us who cannot realize their feelings, that exhibit the varied hues of courage and trepidation characterizing different persons, and also show that there is no difference between real and supposed danger, and yet those actuated by the latter seldom receive the sympathies of their fellows. One family, named Penry, drove so fast that they bounced a little boy, two or three years old, out of the wagon, near Delaware, and did not miss him till they had gone five or six miles on their way to Worthington, and then upon consultation concluded it was too late to recover him amid such imminent danger, and so yielded him up as a painful sacrifice! But the little fellow found protection from others, and is now living in the western part of the county. One woman, in the confusion of hurrying off, forgot her babe till after starting, and ran back to get it, but being peculiarly absent minded she caught up a stick of wood from the chimney corner, and hastened off, leaving her child again quietly sleeping in the cradle! A large portion of the people fled to Worthington, and Franklinton, and some kept on to Chillicothe. In Delaware, the men who could be spared from conveying away their families, or who had none, rallied for defence, and sent scouts to Norton to reconnoitre, where they found the people quietly engaged in their ordinary avocations, having received a message from the captain; but it was too late to save the other settlements from a precipitate flight. Upon the whole it was quite an injury to the county, as a large amount of produce was lost from the intrusion of cattle and the want of hands to harvest it; many of the people being slow in returning and some never did. Capt. Drake, with his company, marched on to Sandusky, to execute the duty assigned him, without knowing the effect produced in his rear. He has since been associate judge, and filled several other offices in the county, and is still living, respected by his neighbors, and characterized by hospitality and good humor, and his strong penchant for anecdote and fun.

Early Customs.—I learn from the old pioneers that during the early period of the county the people were in a condition of complete social equality; no aristocratic distinctions were thought of in society, and the first line of demarkation drawn was to separate the very bad from the general mass. Their parties were for raisings and log rollings, and the labor being finished, their sports usually were shooting and gymnastic exercises with the men, and convivial amusements among the women; no punctilious formality, nor ignoble aping the fashions of licentious Paris, marred their assemblies, but all were happy and enjoyed themselved in seeing others so. The rich and the poor dressed alike; the men generally wearing hunting shirts and buckskin pants, and the women attired in coarse fabrics produced by their own hands; such was their common and holiday dress; and if a fair damsel wished a superb dress for her bridal day, her highest aspiration was to obtain a common American cotton check. The latter, which now sells for a shilling a yard, then cost one dollar, and five yards was deemed an ample pattern; silks, satins, and fancy goods, that now inflate our vanity and deplete our purses, were not then even dreamed of. The cabins were furnished in the same style of simplicity; the bedstead was home-made, and often consisted of forked sticks driven into the ground with cross poles to support the clapboards or the cord. One pot, kettle, and frying-pan, were the only articles considered indispensable, though some included the tea-kettle; a few plates and dishes upon a shelf in one corner, was as satisfactory as is now a cupboard full of china, and their food relished well from a puncheon table. Some of the wealthiest families had a few split bottom chairs, but as a general thing, stools and benches answered the place of lounges and sofas, and at first the green sward or smoothly leveled earth served the double purpose of floor and carpet. Whisky toddy was considered luxury enough for any party—the woods furnished abundance of venison, and corn pone supplied the place of every variety of pastry. Flour could not for some time be obtained nearer than Chillicothe or Zanesville; goods were very high, and none but the most common kinds were brought here, and had to be packed on horses or mules from Detroit, or wagoned from Philadelphia to Pittsburgh, thence down the Ohio river in flat boats to the mouth of the Scioto, and then packed, or hauled up. The freight was enormous, costing often $4,00 per ton. Tea retailed at from two to three dollars a pound, coffee 75 cents, salt $5 to $6 per bushel, (50 lbs.) The coarsest calicoes were $1 per yard, whisky from $1 to $2 per gallon, and as much of the latter was sold as of all other articles, for several years after Delaware was laid out; but it must be remembered that this then was the border town, and had considerable trade with the Indians. It was the common practice to set a bottle on each end of the counter, for customers to help themselves gratuitously to enable them to purchase advantageously! Many people suffered hardships and endured privations that now would seem insupportable. In the fall of 1803, Henry Perry, after getting up his cabin near Delhi, left his two sons and returned to Philadelphia for the remainder of his family, but finding his wife sick, and afterwards being sick himself, could not get back till the next June. These two little boys, Levi and [illegible], only eleven and nine years old, remained there alone, eight months, fifteen miles from any white family, and surrounded by Indians, with no food but the rabbits they could catch in hollow logs; the remains of one deer that the wolves killed near them, and a little corn meal that they occasionally obtained of Thomas Cellar, by following down the "Indian trace." The winter was a severe one, and their cabin was open, having neither daubing, fire-place, nor chimney; they had no gun, and were wholly unaccustomed to forest life, being fresh from Wales, and yet these little fellows not only struggled through but actually made a considerable clearing! Jacob Foust, at an early day, when his wife was sick and could obtain nothing to eat that she relished, procured a bushel of wheat, and throwing it upon his shoulders, carried it to Zanesville to get it ground, a distance of more than 75 miles, by the tortuous path he had to traverse, and then shouldering his flour retraced his steps home, fording the streams and camping out nights.

Biography.—Colonel *Moses Byxbe* was for several years the most prominent man in the county, being the owner of some 8000 acres of valuable land in Berkshire and Berlin, and joint owner with Judge Baldwin of about thirty thousand acres more, the sale of which he had the entire control. These were military lands, which he sold on credit, at prices varying from two and a half to ten dollars an acre. He possessed a complete knowledge of human nature, and was an energetic and prompt business man. Upon the organization of the county he was elected one of the associate judges, and continued to hold the office till 1822. He was afflicted with partial insanity before he died, which occurred in 1827, at the age of 67.

Solomon Smith, Esq., was born in New Salem, N. H., and came here with Col. Byxbe in 1804. He was the first sheriff in the county, and was the first justice of the peace in the township, which office he held, by repeated elections, more than twenty years. He was also the first post-master, and continued many years in that capacity. The responsible offices of county treasurer and county auditor he also filled for many years, and discharged the duties of all these stations with an accuracy seldom excelled, and a fidelity never questioned. In him was exhibited an instance of a constant office-holder and an honest man, and for a long time he possessed more personal popularity than any other man in the county. He died of congestive fever, at Sandusky City, on his return from New York, July 10th, 1845, in his 58th year, and his remains were brought here for interment.

Hon. *Ezekiel Brown* was born in Orange county, N. Y., in 1760, and moved to Northumberland county, Pa., when about ten years old. In 1776, he volunteered and marched to join Washington's army, which he reached just after the battle of Trenton. He participated in four different engagements, and in '78, joined a company of rangers, called out against the Indians. On the 24th of May, when out scouting with two others, they came across a party of fifteen Indians watching a house, and were themselves discovered at the same moment. The Indians fired and killed one man, and Brown and his comrade instantly returned the fire, wounding an Indian, and then fled. The other escaped, but he was not fleet enough, and was captured. They were Delawares and Cayugas, and first took him to Chemung, an Indian town on Tioga river, where he had to run the gauntlet, being badly beaten, and received a severe wound on his head from a tomahawk, but he succeeded in reaching the council-house without being knocked down. After a few days, they resumed their march to the north, and met Colonel Butler with a large body of British, tories and Indians, on their way to attack Wyoming, and he was compelled to run the gauntlet again to gratify the savages. This time he did not get through, being felled by a war-club and awfully mangled. He recovered, and proceeded on to the main town of the Cayugas, where Scipio, N. Y., now stands, and having again passed the gauntlet ordeal successfully, he was adopted by a family, in the place of a son killed at Fort Stanwix. Afterwards he was taken to Canada, and kept to the close of the war in '83, when he received a passport from the British general, M'Clure, and returned, after an absence of five years, to his friends in Pennsylvania. In 1800, he moved to Ohio, and in 1808, he settled near Sunbury, and was immediately elected one of the first county commissioners. Afterwards he was elected associate judge, and served in several minor offices, and died about five years ago, leaving the reputation of an upright man.

Captain *John Minter*, from Kentucky, one of the early settlers in Radnor, and brother-in-law of Col. Crawford, who was burnt by the Indians, was, in his younger days, a great hunter, and became famous for a terrible bear fight, in which he came very near losing his life. When hunting alone one day, he came across a very large bear and fired at him. The bear fell, and re-loading his gun, Minter advanced, supposing him dead, and touched his nose with the muzzle of the gun, when he instantly reared upon his hind legs to seize him. Minter fired again, which increased his rage, only inflicting a flesh wound, and then threw his hatchet at him; and as the bear sprang forward to grasp him, he struck him with the rifle on the head with all his might, producing no other effect than shivering the gun to pieces. Too late then to escape, he drew his big knife from its sheath and made a plunge at his heart, but old Bruen, by a stroke of his paw, whirled the knife into the air, and enfolding its weaponless owner with his huge arms, both rolled to the ground. A fearful struggle then ensued between the combatants: one ruled by unvarying instinct, and the other guided by the dictates of reason. The former depended wholly upon hugging his adversary to death, while the latter aimed at presenting his body in such positions as would best enable him to withstand the vice-like squeeze till he could loosen the grasp. He was about six feet in height, possessing large bones and well developed muscles, and being properly proportioned, was very athletic. The woods were open and clear of underbrush, and in their struggles they rolled in every direction. Several times he thought the severity of the hug would finish him; but by choking the bear, he would compel him to release his hold to knock off his hands, when he would recover his breath and gain a better position. After maintaining the contest in this way several hours, they, happily for him, rolled back near where his knife lay, which inspired him with buoyant hope, but he had to make many ineffectual efforts before he could tumble the bear within reach of it. Having finally recovered it, he stabbed him at every chance till he at last bled to death, only relaxing his hold when life became extinct. He attempted to get up, but was too much exhausted, and crawling to a log, against which he leaned, his heart sickened as he contemplated the scene. Not a rag was left on him, and over his back, arms and legs his flesh was lacerated to the bones by the claws of the bear. By crawling and walking he reached home after night, with no other covering than a gore of blood from head to foot. His friends, who went out next morning to survey the ground and bring in the trophy, said the surface was torn up by them over a space of at least half an acre. After several weeks he recovered, but he carried with him the cicatrices and welts, some of which were more than a quarter of an inch thick, till he died, which occurred about 15 years ago. He never desired another bear hug, but gave up hunting, and turning his attention to agriculture, left his children a comfortable patrimony and a good name.

Rev. *Joseph S. Hughes*, from Washington, Pa., came to Delaware in 1810, and organized the first Presbyterian church here, and also those in Liberty and Radnor. For a short time, he was chaplain in the army, and was with Hull when he surrendered, at which time he returned. The societies being unable to pay much salary, he sought his support mainly from other sources, serving several years as clerk of the court, and afterwards in the capacity of editor. He possessed a liberal education, superadded to oratorical powers of a superior order by nature. As an orator he is described as being graceful, mellifluous, persuasive and convincing, and he has left the reputation among many of the old settlers of being the most effective speaker that they have ever heard. In the social circle, too, he excelled, but unfortunately he had an indomitable penchant for festivity and sport. Many anecdotes are related detracting from his clerical character, and when dwelt upon, we must not forget to associate the habits and customs of the times in which they occurred. For instance, it is said that one time, on the occasion of a wedding at Capt. Minter's, after the ceremonies had been solemnized and the luxuries duly honored, he started off about dusk to go to a place some five miles through the woods, but after dark returned somewhat scratched by the bushes, and reported having been lost, and concluded to stay till morning. According to the general custom on such occasions, all the young folks in the settlement had assembled for a frolick, and they charged him with having returned to participate with them, and as he was a good musician, and their "knight of the bow" had disappointed them, they insisted upon his playing the fiddle for them to dance, which he did all night, with an occasional intermission for refreshment or to romp! Some of the old citizens say also that he was a good hand at pitching quoits, and as it was common to choose sides and pitch for the "grog," he seldom even then backed out! For these and other charges he was arraigned before the presbytery, where, declining all assistance, and relying on his own ingenuity and eloquence, he made a successful defence. He continued to preach as "stated supply" till he was suddenly cut off by an epidemic fever in the fall of 1823, and was interred in the old burying ground, but no tombstone points out the place where his mouldering remains lie. He was succeeded in 1824 by Rev. Henry Vandeman, the first installed pastor, and who has retained his charge ever since, a fact that is mentioned, because in the west preachers seldom retain a pastoral charge so long, and in this presbytery there is no similar instance, excepting that of Dr. Hodge, of Columbus.

ANTIQUITIES.—The remains of ancient fortifications are found in three places in the county, the most remarkable of which is in the lower part of Liberty, about eleven miles below Delaware, on the east bank of the Olentangy.

INDIAN VILLAGES.—There were formerly two villages belonging to the Delawares, mostly within the limits of the present town of Delaware. One occupied the ground around the east end of William street, and the other was at the west end, extending from near the saw-mill to the hill side. Upon the ground now occupied by the town, they cultivated a corn-field of about four hundred acres. The Mingoes had a small village half a mile above town, on "horse shoe bottom," where they also raised corn.

Many of the old pioneers entertained towards the Indians an inveterate hatred, and did not consider it really criminal even to murder them. One time, after the last war, a dead Indian was seen floating down the Scioto on two logs, lashed together, having his gun and all his accoutrements with him. He had been shot, and the people believed the murderer was George Shanon, who had been in service considerably during the war, and one time when out, not far from Lower Sandusky, with a small company, fell in with a party of warriors and had to retreat. He lingered behind till he got a shot, and killed one. As soon as he fired, several Indians sprang forward to catch him alive, but being swift on foot, he could easily keep ahead, when he suddenly came to an open field, across which he had to run or be cut off. The Indians gained the first side just as he was leaping the fence on the other and fired at him, one ball entering his hip. He staunched the blood by stuffing the hole with a portion of his shirt, that they might not track him, and crawled into the brush; but they gave up the chase, thinking they had not hit him, and being convinced of his superior fleetness. Shanon got into camp and was conveyed home, but he was always lame afterwards, and fostered an unrelenting desire for vengeance towards the whole race, not excepting the innocent and harmless. As late as 1820, two Indians were murdered on Fulton's creek. A party came down there to hunt, as was customary with them every fall, and Henry Swartz ordered them off. They replied, "no! the land belongs to the white man—the game to the Indian," and insisted that they were friends and ought not to be disturbed. A few days after, two of their number were missing, and they hunted the entire country over without finding them, and at last found evidence of human bones where there had been a fire, and immediately charged Swartz with killing and burning them. They threatened vengeance on him, and for several years after he had to be constantly on his guard to prevent being waylaid. It was never legally investigated, but the neighbors all believed that Swartz, aided probably by Ned Williams, murdered and disposed of them in the manner the Indians suspected, and at one time talked of driving them out of the settlement. They were considered bad men, and never prospered afterwards.

Norton, 10 miles N. of the county seat; Waldo, 12 do.; Woodbury, 12 NE.; Westfield, 12 NNE.; Edin, 6 E.; Sunbury, 12 E.; Lockwin, 16 SSE.; Galena, 12 SE.; Stratford, 3 E.; Williamsville, 10 S.; Belle Point, 7 SW.; Milleville, 6 W.; Delhi, 8 NW., and Middletown, 13 miles NW., are all villages in the county of less than 200 inhabitants, but several of them handsome and thriving.

SIGNIFICATION AND ORIGIN OF THE NAME OHIO.

The Shawanoese called the Ohio river, *Kis,ke,pi,la Sepe*, i. e., Eagle river. The Wyandots were in the country generations before the Shawanoese, and consequently their name of the river is the primitive one, and should stand in preference to all others. Ohio may be called an improvement on the expression, *O,he,zuh*, and was no doubt adopted by the early French voyagers in their boat songs, and is substantially the same word as used by the Wyandots: the meaning applied by the French, fair and beautiful, "*la belle rivere*," being precisely the same as that meant by the Indians—great, grand and fair to look upon.*

GALLIA COUNTY.

The annexed article respecting the Scioto company and its connection with the Ohio company, has been communicated to us by the venerable Ephraim Cutler, of Washington county. Judge Cutler is the son of Rev. Dr. Manasseh Cutler, who was the agent for the New England Ohio company, in making the contract with congress for their lands. His opportunities for accurate information upon this subject, renders his testimony of great historical value.

The Scioto land company has been the subject of considerable mystery, and the cause of much misrepresentation. I am not precisely informed concerning its origin. It was probably started during the negociation of Dr. Cutler with the old congress, in 1787, for the Ohio company purchase. Dr. Cutler arrived in New York, July 5th, and carried on his negociations for a week; he was then absent another week on a visit to Philadelphia, where the convention that formed our federal constitution was sitting. On his return to New York, the project for the Scioto company was broached to him by Col. William Duer, as appears by the following extract from the Dr.'s journal. "Colonel Duer came to me with proposals from a

* Col. John Johnston.

number of the principal characters in the city, *to extend our contract, and take in another company.*"*

The arrangements of Dr. Cutler with the government, *made room* for *another company.* But this other association was entirely distinct from the Ohio company. Yet it has been represented that the Ohio company was concerned in the alledged wrongs towards the French emigrants of 1790, who were induced to come over in expectation of beneficial acquisitions of land in this quarter, by the agency of Joel Barlow. But this imputation is entirely groundless. What were the actual regulations and doings of the Scioto company previous to or connected with that agency, I have never learned. Dr. Cutler contracted for a million and half acres for the Ohio company. In connection with his negociation, the "board of treasury" were empowered to sell all west of the 7th range, up to the northwest corner of T. X, to the Scioto, and south to the Ohio. This would have included Zanesville and Columbus. It was estimated at five million acres—much below the actual amount.

The arrangements and objects of the Ohio company and the Scioto company are believed to have been very different. The aim of the Ohio company was, actual settlement by shareholders. The lands obtained were ultimately to be allotted in shares, of which no one was to hold more than five shares.

The object of the Scioto company seems to have been, solely and simply, land speculation; to purchase of congress—nominally, at two-thirds of a dollar per acre—paying mostly in continental paper money, at that time passing at enormous discount—so that, in fact, the actual cost, per acre, might not be more than eight or ten cents, then to sell at prices which would yield them enormous profits.

That any dishonest intention was entertained by Colonel Duer, or the other associates of the Scioto company, I have no belief. Dr. Cutler speaks of the association as comprising "some of the first characters in America." Their object, no doubt, was to make large profits by the purchase and sale of public lands.

It is understood that Joel Barlow was by them authorized to offer lands in France, and to invite French emigrants; but of his authority or instructions, we have no specific information. In this matter, the Ohio company had as little concern as in the South Sea bubble.

But the splendid project of the Scioto company was blighted. Probably they expected to purchase public securities, to pay for their purchase of congress, at the excessively low rates of 1787. But the adoption of the federal constitution, and the successful establishment of the federal government, under Washington and his compatriots, raised the credit of those securities and blasted the hopes of speculation. Meantime, the French emigrants were *coming.*

---

* The reader will find in the article "Ohio," in the North American Review for Oct., 1841, all that transpired between Dr. Cutler and Colonel Duer, at the time he made the purchase for the Ohio company, extracted from the private journal of the former.

The Scioto company purchase was not effected, and where should these emigrants go?

Certain persons, who styled themselves "trustees to the proprietors of the Scioto lands," applied to Gen. Rufus Putnam and Dr. Manasseh Cutler, two of the directors of the Ohio company, for the purchase of certain interests in this company. The persons who thus styled themselves "trustees," were William Duer, Royal Flint, and Andrew Cragie. They bargained with General Putnam and Dr. Cutler for 148 "forfeited shares" in the Ohio company. The 8, 3, and 160 acre lots, and the town lots, had been already allotted and drawn. The undrawn portions—equal to 100, 262 and 640 acres to each share, were to be located in a body, in the southwest corner of the purchase, viz.:

Townships	1, 2, 3,	in range	14.
"	1, 2, 3, 4, 5,	"	15.
"	1, 2, 3,	"	16.
"	1, 2, 3, 4,	"	17.

And so much of south of T. 4—R. 16,
and T. 5—R. 17,

as would make up in all 196,544 acres, in this compact body.

This contract was ratified by the Ohio company. The lands for the French settlement of Gallipolis, (which is in the 14th range,) were located and occupied, I suppose, in consequence of this arrangement. General Putnam, as agent for Duer & Co., provided, at some $2,000 expense, for the accommodations of the French emigrants there, and by the failure of Duer & Co., had to lose most or all of it.

The Scioto company not only failed in securing the large purchase contemplated, but did not succeed in obtaining the interest for which they stipulated in the lands of the Ohio company. They did not pay, and the contract with Putnam and Cutler became a nullity. All that was required by the contract was, that the Scioto company associates should pay as much proportionably, as the Ohio company were to pay congress, and relinquish to the Ohio company the preemption right, which the Scioto company was understood to have in reference to lands lying north of the Ohio company's location. All was failure on the part of the Scioto company. The French emigrants were planted at Gallipolis, and General Putnam was left to pay some $2,000 expended in behalf of the Scioto company.

It is rather surprising that any complaint should have been made against the Ohio company for *selling* the lands in and about Gallipolis to the French, for $1.25 per acre. It was, in truth, an act of favor and courtesy, in deference to the misfortunes of the French. The Ohio company was under no obligation to them. They had no agency in inviting or deceiving them. How much blame there was in the case, and to whom it belonged, we are not now able to decide. Barlow was poetic—but we know not that he was intentionally false. Most probably the emigrants were greatly beguiled by their own vivid imaginations. We may well enough suppose there was more poetry than truth in the whole concern.

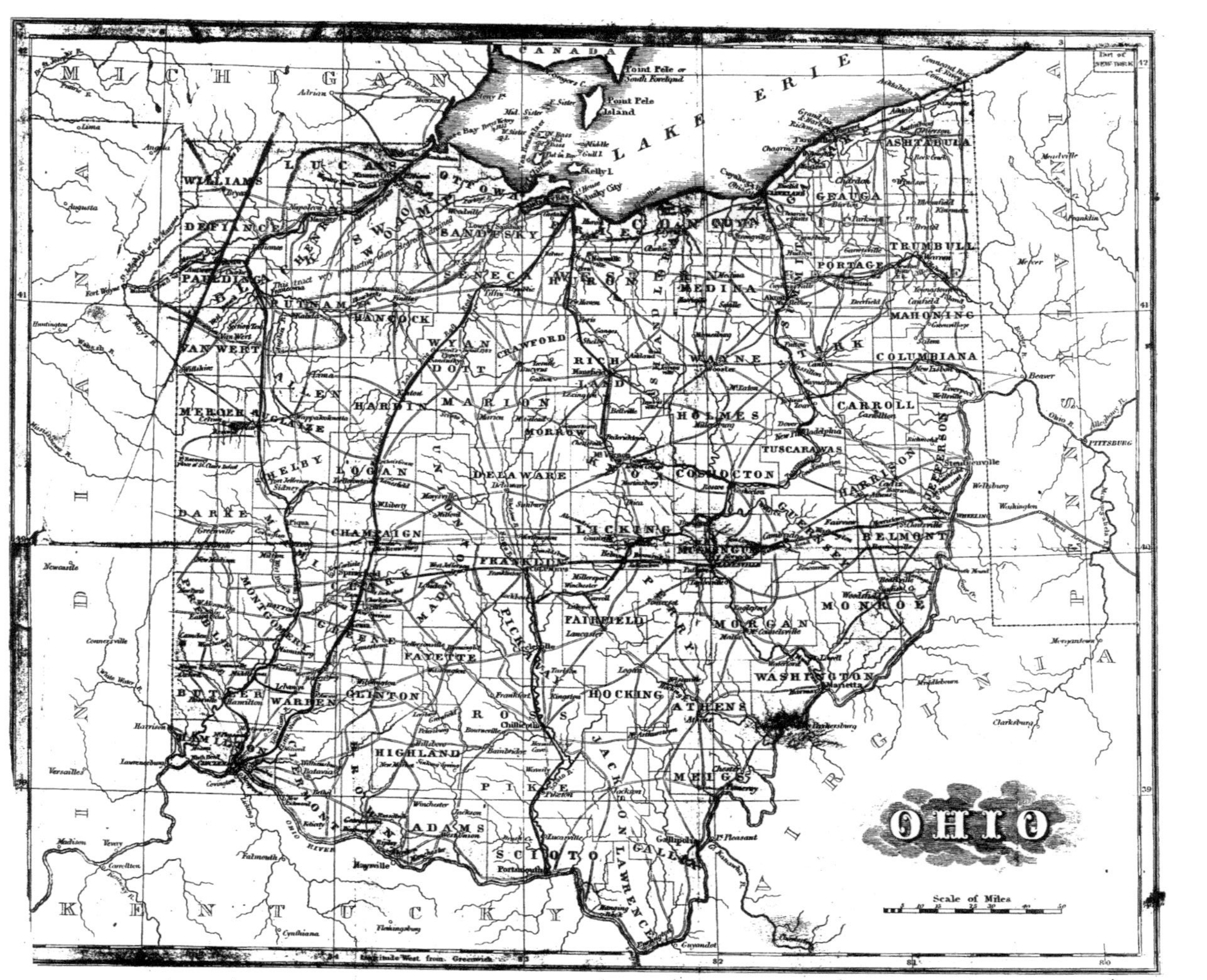
OHIO
Scale of Miles
LAKE ERIE
CANADA
MICHIGAN
INDIANA
KENTUCKY
VIRGINIA
PENNSYLVANIA
WILLIAMS
LUCAS
OTTOWA
DEFIANCE
HENRY
WOOD
SANDUSKY
HURON
LORAIN
CUYAHOGA
GEAUGA
ASHTABULA
TRUMBULL
PORTAGE
MEDINA
SENECA
PAULDING
PUTNAM
HANCOCK
MAHONING
VAN WERT
WYANDOTT
CRAWFORD
RICHLAND
WAYNE
STARK
COLUMBIANA
ALLEN
HARDIN
MARION
HOLMES
CARROLL
MERCER
AUGLAIZE
MORROW
TUSCARAWAS
SHELBY
LOGAN
UNION
DELAWARE
KNOX
COSHOCTON
HARRISON
JEFFERSON
DARKE
MIAMI
CHAMPAIGN
LICKING
MUSKINGUM
GUERNSEY
BELMONT
FRANKLIN
CLARK
MADISON
PERRY
MONTGOMERY
PREBLE
GREENE
FAIRFIELD
MORGAN
MONROE
FAYETTE
PICKAWAY
WASHINGTON
BUTLER
WARREN
CLINTON
ROSS
HOCKING
ATHENS
HAMILTON
HIGHLAND
VINTON
JACKSON
MEIGS
CLERMONT
BROWN
PIKE
ADAMS
SCIOTO
GALLIA
LAWRENCE
OHIO RIVER
PITTSBURG
WHEELING
Steubenville
Parkersburg
Marietta
Portsmouth
Maysville
Covington
Point Pele Island
Point Pele or South Foreland
Kelly I.
Longitude West from Greenwich

OUTLINE SKETCH OF THE GEOLOGY OF OHIO.

COMMUNICATED FOR THIS WORK BY CHARLES WHITTLESEY, OF THE LATE GEOLOGICAL CORPS OF OHIO.

In the state of Ohio, no primitive rocks are found in place. Her rocks are all sedimentary and stratified, and as they are nearly horizontal, the strata that appear at the surface are few. Her geology is, therefore, very simple and easily understood, especially when we compare it with that of Pennsylvania and New York, where a much greater variety of formations is seen. The lowest visible rock in Ohio is the "blue limestone" of Cincinnati, which is also the lowest in a physical, as well as in a geological sense.

The bed of the Ohio river, near Cincinnati, is 133 feet below the level of Lake Erie, and is the most depressed portion of the state of Ohio, being only 431 feet above tide water. Here the blue limestone is seen, with its beds of "dun" and "blue" marl. The strata dip in all directions from the south-western angle of the state, which occupies a crown, or geological summit, rather than a synclinal axis.

Any one would be convinced of this by travelling from thence in any direction and observing the rocks. If he should go up the Ohio river, he would perceive that the surface of the blue limestone descends, and finally passes beneath its channel at a distance of less than 100 miles. In the same way, on descending the river, he would discover the hills about Madison, in —— county, capped by a different rock, the "cliff limestone," which overlies the "blue," and arriving at the falls of the Ohio, at Louisville, the "cliff," continually sinking, reaches the bed of the river and causes the falls. Go up the Great Miami to D[illegible] and th[illegible] makes its appearance, although the descent in this directio[illegible]ght. [illegible]t of the disappearance of the blue is here owing to the rise of the country. In the same way, if one passes up the valley of the Licking or the Kentucky rivers, the overlying cliff settles down into the level of the blue, and apparently occupies its place in the horizon.

We have no means of ascertaining the thickness of the blue limestone, for we have not penetrated through it to the rocks beneath; yet it is estimated at more than 1000 feet, 600 to 700 of which are visible.

If we group the rocks of Ohio according to their lithological characters, there are *five distinct divisi*[illegible] that any person will discover on examination. The difference in ap[illegible]hardness, color and composition is so marked that no more natu[illegible]sion could be made.

1st.	*Limestone*, [illegible]e thickness in Adams county, according to Dr. Locke, ...	772 feet.
2d.	*Black shale*, thickness at the same place, . . .	251 "
3d.	*Fine grained sandstone*, thickness, . . .	343 "
4th.	*Conglomerate*, "	200 "
5th.	Coal series, " estimated, . .	2000 "
	Thickness in Ohio, ...	**3566 "**

This is dividing the rocks, not according to strict geological rules, but according to external characters.

A person travelling from the west line of Adams county eastward, to the Little Scioto, in Scioto county, would pass over the outcropping edges of all these rocks, and would see all the formations of Ohio.

They here plunge in the direction south 80½° east, and sink to the eastward at the rate of 37 4-10 feet per mile ;* consequently, the cliff limestone, the upper member of the great limestone deposit, which, at West Union, Adams county, is 600 feet above the river at Cincinnati, at Brush Creek, 6 miles east, is found only about 350 feet above the same level.

And the fine grained sandstone which caps the hills east of Brush Creek, and west of the Scioto, as we approach the Little Scioto, sinks to the base of the hills and appears beneath the conglomerate. This inclines continually to the river surface, and plunges beneath the coal.

In other parts of the state, as will be seen hereafter, although the same rocks prevail, and always in the same order, their thickness, mass and dip will be different. There is no place where they can all be seen in so short a space as in Adams and Scioto counties, and here Dr. Locke made his section in 1838.

As we proceed along the outcrop of these strata, by which is meant the irregular line of junction between the faces of the strata, we find that, in a level country, it coincides with a horizontal line separating one rock from another ; and following the union of these rocks—for instance, the black shale and the fine grained sand stone—to the northward, we shall observe a *change* in the *direction* of the line of bearing, and also of the dip or plunge.

Rockville, Waverly, Chillicothe, Reynoldsburg, Mansfield and Newburg, are towns in or near the western edge of the "fine grained sandstone," or at its "outcrop," forming a continuous, but crooked line from the Ohio river to Lake Erie. By the attached map of the state, the fine grained sandstone will be seen to occupy an irregular belt about 10 miles wide, embracing those places. Next, westerly, is a strip of the black shale accompanying the fine grained sandstone, somewhat broader, and bounded by it on the east. On the west of the whole, and covering about one-third of th[illegible]te, in t[illegible]st and north-west, is the cliff or buff-colored limestone.

In the southwest corner, is the blue limesto[illegible]ccupying [illegible]ircular space from West Union, by way of Dayton, to the state line.

On the east of the line of towns above given, is the conglomerate, bending around from Cuyahoga falls to Benton, in Geauga county, and then eastward into Pennsylvania. Adjacent to this line of outcrop, are the coal bearing rocks, occupying the east and southeastern part of Ohio, within a line from Sharon, on the Pennsylvania line to Ravenna, Akron, Wooster, Dover, Brownsville, on the National road, Logan and Hanging Rock. If we examine any of these rocks over large tracts of country, a[illegible]s 10, 40, or 100 miles apart, we soon discover that the line of out[illegible] in direction, and with it the line of greatest dip or plunge, which is a[illegible]t *angles* to the line of bearing.

Thus, from Rockville to Chillicothe, the course is north, about 10° east, and corresponds very nearly with the line of outcrop of the fine grained sandstone for that distance. The dip at Rockville is given at s. 80½° east, almost a right angle, and the rate of dip 37 feet per mile. At the other end of

---

* 2d vol. Ohio Geo. Report, page 238.

the line, at Chillicothe, the general dip, rejecting fractions, is south 70° east, 30 feet to the mile, the line of bearing thus makes a curve to the *eastward*, and the line of dip a corresponding change to the *southward*. This is the universal law; consequently, when we course around the edge of the coal basin to the northward, and the line of bearing changes to an almost *easterly* direction, the dip is nearly *south*. It would be thus, if we should make the

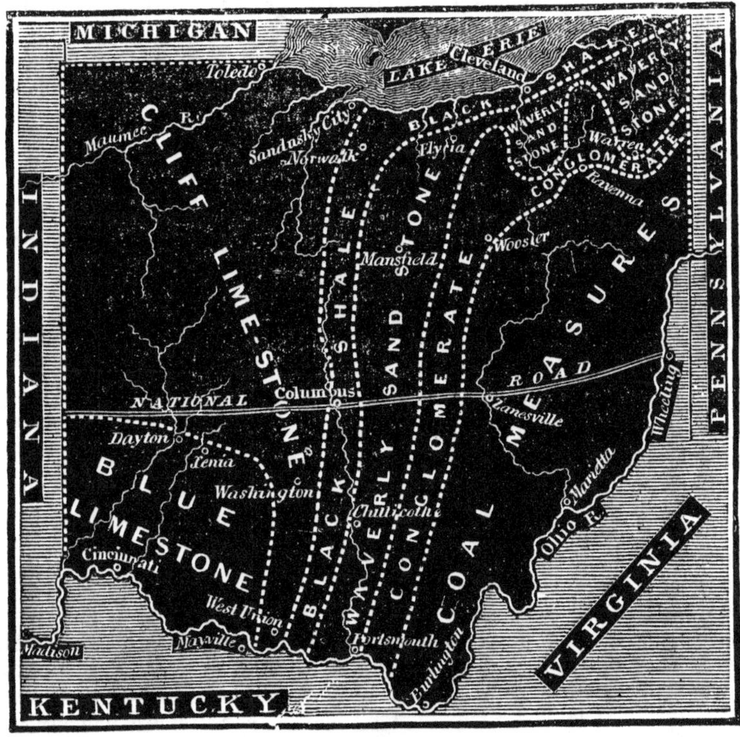

Outline Map of the Geological Formations of Ohio.

entire circuit of the great Alleghany coal field. Pursuing its northern boundary through Meadville, in Pennsylvania, we should soon turn southward, and, arriving at the Portage summit railroad, should observe the lowest bed of coal there at the door of the station-house, on the summit of the Alleghanies, 2500 feet above the ocean, it would be found plunging rapidly to the *westward*. Following down the Alleghanies to the southwest, through Pennsylvania, Virginia and Tennessee, to the southern termination of this great coal bason, the rocks and the coal strata are found to dip more and more to the northward, and finally, at the flexure of the course, when we turn back to the north, the dip changes from north to northeast. Continuing on northward, on the west side of the coal field, through Tennessee, across the Cumberland and Kentucky rivers to the Ohio, we come to the starting point, the dip being northeasterly, easterly, and finally south of east.

These lines of dip point to a common centre, or depression in the strata, at the foot of the western slope of the Alleghanies, in Virginia.

In farther illustration of the geological map, it should be said that the scale is too small to give the exact outlines of the formations, even if they were exactly known. In the northeastern part, I have attempted to show the limits of the strata, but without success, owing to the limited scale of the map. For instance, much of the county of Medina is represented as being a conglomerate rock at the surface; but the streams, particularly the south branch of Rocky river, cut through the conglomerate and reach the fine grained sandstone beneath. It is the same with Rocky, Cuyahoga, Chagrin and Grand rivers, and Ashtabula and Conneaut creeks. The shale and this sandstone, therefore, extend in narrow bays up the valleys of these streams and their branches. Between the fine grained sandstone and the conglomerate, is a mass of coarse grained sandstone, without pebbles, which furnishes the grindstones of Lake Erie, extending from the Vermillion river, through Lorain county and Cuyahoga, into Lake county; but where it terminates I do not know. At Newburg, Warrensville and Chagrin falls, the section of this intermediate mass is as follows—beginning at the top of the fine grained sandstone:

1st. Black shale, with thin layers of sandstone, . . . 10 feet.
2d. Red shale, very soft, ... 30 "
3d. Grindstone grit, ... 40 "
4th. Shale, ash color, and layers of sandstone to lower face of conglomerate, ... 81 "

In Lorain county, the coarse sandstone grit appears almost to displace the fine grained sandstone and red shale—thickening downwards at Elyria to the black shale. Farther examination is necessary to classify these intermediate strata.

The projecting ridges of highland between the Black and Cuyahoga rivers, the Cuyahoga and the Grand and Mahoning rivers, are composed of conglomerate, as the surface rock, its most northerly point being an outlier, called the little mountain, within 5 or 6 miles of the lake at Kirtland, and elevated 600 feet above it.

The grindstone grit, red shale and ash-colored shale vary much in thickness, and at the south of Elyria, owing to the drift, it cannot, without farther examination, be decided where they cease, and where the fine grained sandstone rock may be first seen. In the valley of the Cuyahoga, they are seen distinctly at Brandywine Mills, and at the Peninsula in Boston; and between Peninsula and Old Portage, appear to run out and to be lost in the shaly portions of the fine grained sandstone.

So with the narrow belt of fine grained sandstone overlying the shale, or black slate formations, and skirting the highlands that overlook the lake, it is not easy to determine the line of division between the two formations, particularly in the valleys of Grand river and the Mahoning.

Returning to the consideration of dip, a few instances more may be given, to show the surprising regularity of the sedimentary rocks of Ohio, and also the change in direction which has just been noticed.

Take the town of Chillicothe, in Ross county, the village of Newburg, in Cuyahoga county, and a point in the west line of Crawford county, all situated at the surface of the "black shale"—these three points form a triangular plane of stratification, of which we know mathematically the relative elevations and the distances. By a trigonometrical calculation, we deduce the "line of bearing" and the "dip" of this rock, or the plane of its superior face. The result is as follows: course of dip S. 59½° east; bearing N. 30½° east.

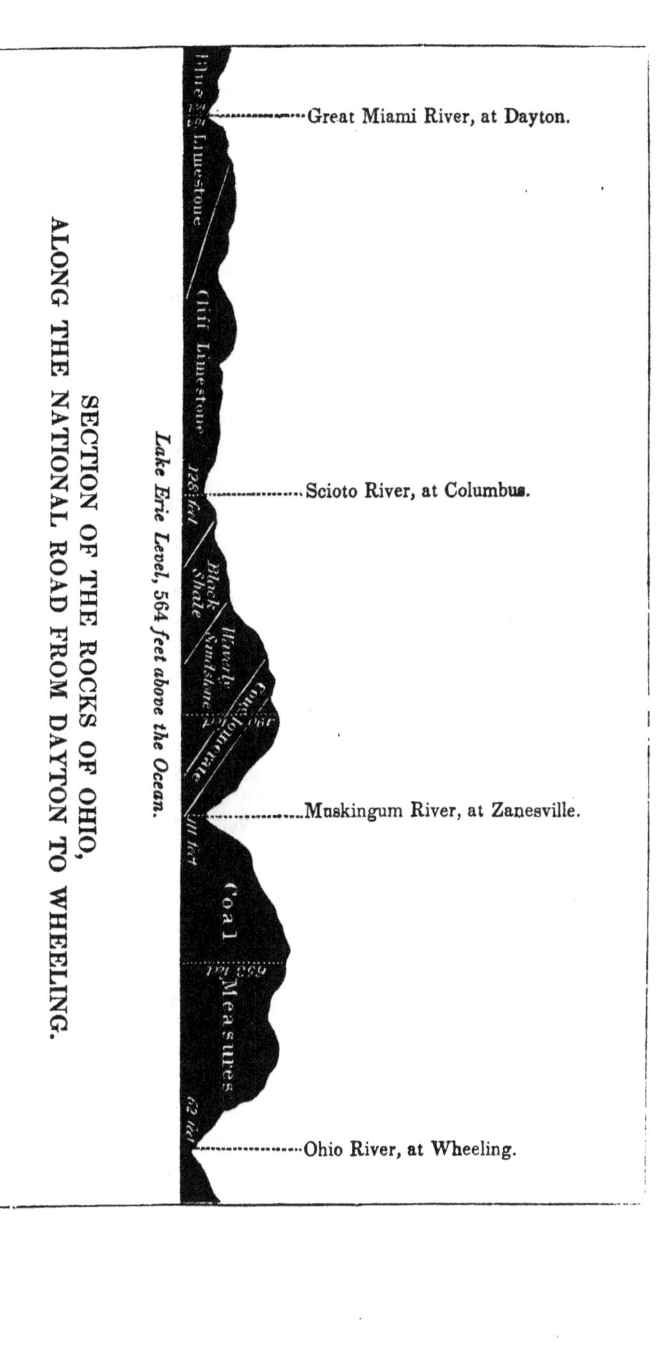

SECTION OF THE ROCKS OF OHIO,
ALONG THE NATIONAL ROAD FROM DAYTON TO WHEELING.

Taking three points in the lowest bed of coal, Tallmadge, Youngstown and Sharon, we obtain for the bearing, N. 77½° east; dip, S. 12½° E.; amount, 20 6-10 feet per mile. These results, therefore, are not surmises and speculations, but physical facts, arrived at by measurement.

A "geological section" is an imaginary vertical cut, made through the rocks on a line of dip or greatest inclination; and since this line, in Ohio as elsewhere, is constantly changing, the section made at any place does not represent the bearing or plunge of the rocks at others, but only their order of superposition.

A general section is here given, extending from Dayton to Columbus, Zanesville and Wheeling, taken from the geological reports of Ohio. It shows all the general formations of Ohio, but on a scale so diminutive, that the subordinate members, or subdivisions of the formations do not appear. This would require a plan many feet long.

To comprehend this section fully, it is necessary to imagine the cut made along the line indicated, and one half of the mass removed, so that the observer has a view of the edges of the strata.

On a scale so limited, it is necessary to reject a very important member of the geological column, the "drift," "superficial materials," or "diluvial deposits," as it is variously named: a coating of earth, gravel, clay, stones and boulders, that overspread the whole country, hiding the rocks from view. This will, however, be touched upon in its place.

The relation between the horizontal and vertical distances must, of course, be disregarded in the scale here adopted; for if it was obscured, the elevations would be comparatively nothing, and little could be shown. The consequence of this disproportion is, to make the angles of dip appear much *greater* than they really are, bnt this cannot be avoided.

The horizontal line represents the level of the lake, and the irregular line above it, the surface of the earth, the elevations of which are in figures at a few points. As a survey has been made along the National road, this can be done with great accuracy.

The order of strata is here seen to be the same as given above. Near the west line of the state, or the section, the dip is slight. It is probably greater in a northerly direction. It is not very rapid between Dayton and Columbus, but increases materially between Columbus and Zanesville, in crossing the rocks between the limestone and the coal.

Dr. Locke gives the dip, at Montgomery and Miami counties, at N. 14° east, 6 feet per mile. At Columbus, I found it to be, S. 81° 52′ east, 22 feet 73 hundredths per mile.

The thickness of these formations is very variable at different points. The "fine grained sandstone," at Newburg, is not to exceed 80 feet in thickness, at Reynoldsburg and Jacktown about 500 feet, at Waverly 250 to 300 feet, and at Brush creek, Adams county, 343 feet. The "black shale" is more uniform, being at Brush creek 251, Alum creek 250 to 300, in Crawford county about 250. At Newburg, and alone the lake shore, its thickness is unknown.

The conglomerate is more irregular. In Jackson county, by estimate, 200 feet; in Licking county 100; Cuyahoga falls 100 to 120; Burton, Geauga county, 300.

The great limestone formation is divided into several numbers. At Cincinnati, at the bed of the river, there is—

1st. A blue limestone and slaty marlite.

2d. Dun colored marl and layers of lime rock, . .	250 feet.
3d. Blue marl and layers of blue limestone, . . .	160 "
4th. Marl and bands of limestone, with immense numbers of shells to surface.	

In Adams county, the detailed section is thus—

1st. Blue limestone and marl,	
2d. Blue marl, ...	25 feet.
3d. Flinty limestone, ...	51 "
4ih. Blue marl, ...	100 "
5th. Cliff limestone, ...	89 "

The coal measures of Ohio, like those of England and Pennsylvania, are composed of alternate beds of coarse grained sandstone, clay shales, layers of iron stone, their beds of limestone, and of numerous strata of coal. If the geological explorations of the state had been prosecuted, there is little doubt but the number of coal beds, or strata, lying one above the other, would have been shown to be as numerous as 40 or 45, and that there are 15 or 20 of them thick enough to be worked.

Here, as usual, the coal region is also an iron region. From Jacktown, on the western edge of our coal field, to Concord, in Muskingum county, in Mr. Foster's section, (2d Geol. Reports, p. 72,) a distance of about 42 miles, there are shown eight beds, or separate strata, of coal, and seven beds of limestone.

In my section, (2d Report, p. 57,) from Freedom, in Portage county, to Poland, in Trumbull county, about 35 miles, there are five distinct strata—three of them in places capable of being wrought. Among them are distributed three beds of limestone and many beds of iron ore.

Dr. Hildreth made a section of the hills at Dillon's furnace, Muskingum county, from the bed of the Licking or Pataskala river upward, 206 feet. In this vertical distance, there were four beds of iron ore, two of coal, and one of limestone.

But by far the greatest mass of coal and iron measures is composed of sandstone and shale. The beds of coal and iron are comparatively thin; the beds of sandstone from 10 to 20, and 80 feet thick; of shale, 5 to 50 feet thick. A bed of coal is considered workable, if the roof and drainage are good, when the thickness is *three feet*. If it is four feet, it is considered a good mine, and very few of them average five feet. Occasionally it increases to six, and, in one or two cases, to ten and eleven feet, for short distances; but for such extreme thickness the mine is certain to suffer, in consequence of its irregularity. The cases where a bed of the ordinary "heft" of four feet falls below that standard, are much more numerous than where there is a greater thickness.

In Lawrence and Scioto counties, in the distance of 30 miles, across the edge of the strata may be seen eight principal beds of ore, and new ones are being discovered. There are also four beds of coal and three of limestone.

The ore varies in thickness from 4 inches to 12, thickening up, in some places, to 2 feet; but this is an irregularity.

There are 17 furnaces, on the Ohio side, supplied with ore, flux and fuel to drive the engines, from the strata represented in the section. A large portion of the ore is taken from beds of a few inches in thickness, the rule being to strip a *foot* of earth for an *inch* of ore.

Sometimes beds of 2 or 3 inches are worked a few feet into the hill; but, in general, the valuable beds are from 4 to 6, 7 and 10 inches in thickness.

The calcareous ore, resting upon the second bed of limestone from the bottom of the section, being very rich, is sometimes obtained by drifting, but far the greatest part of it is procured by "stripping." The hills, or, more properly, the valleys of this region are so numerous, that the strata crop out, continually showing their edges to the miner along the slopes. Here he can follow the stratum into the earth till it becomes too deep, and then work along the side hill at the same level. The immense length of the line of outcrop for each bed, in a country completely intersected by hills and valleys, can easily be imagined. If, instead of being uneven and hilly, it had been flat, the strata remaining as near horizontal as they now are, it will be readily seen that none but such as are thick enough to "drift" would be worthy of attention.

Among the iron beds, there are but two or three that would, at present, pay for working by drifting. The ores are not all of them fit for use, in the present state of metallurgy, on account of silicious impurities that render them hard to melt; but the exceeding value of this region is caused by the general goodness of the ores in relation to ease of reduction.

There are many parts of the United States where richer ores may be found, and in thicker beds, but probably none where iron may be produced with as little fuel as on the Ohio river. They range from 30 to 40 per cent. of iron, and are so happily tempered with calcareous and aluminous matter, that they require a small amount of flux. But where a flux is needed, it is found everywhere in the limestone beds which nature has interspersed with the other mineral strata.

The abundance of these materials will appear from an examination of the section.

The iron interest of Ohio has materially improved since 1837. At that time, it was thought to be a good yield if a furnace produced 3½ to 4 tons per day. This was with the old-fashioned cold blast. In 1829, an improvement was introduced at the Clyde works, Scotland, by Mr. Robert Neilson, of Glasgow, which consists principally in using a blast of *hot*, instead of *cold*, air. Mr. Dunlop, of the Clyde works, and Mr. Dixon, of the Calder iron works, improved upon Mr. Neilson, by raising the temperature of the blast from 300 to 600 degrees, Fahrenheit. This improvement did not reach Ohio until 1841–2, although it was recommended by Dr. Hildreth in his Geological Report of 1836. The result is, an increase of product of nearly one-half, raising the daily yield from 3½ to 5, 6, and even 7½ tons per day, diminishing the consumption of charcoal, per ton, from 250 bushels to 160 or 180.

In April, 1844, Mr. Gliddon, the master and owner of the "Franklin Furnace Junior," Lawrence county, Ohio, gave me the yields of his furnace during a blast of 8 months, 1 day and 4 hours, commencing May 8th, 1843, at 1845½ tons of 2268 pounds, or 7 tons 65 hundredths per day. Charcoal per ton, before the hot blast, 210 bushels; for this blast, 161 bushels. Stone coal per ton, for engine and hot blast, 18 bushels and 9-10ths of a bushel. cost of ore per ton of iron, $3.17; the amount of ore, 2 tons 54-100ths.

The saving in charcoal of 49 bushels, at $1.75 the hundred bushels, is 85½ cents per ton. But the great item is in the labor, the same hands turning out about 40 per cent. more iron.

There is scarcely a doubt but the cost of iron may be still more reduced by the use of *mineral coal*, in whole or in part, in the place of charcoal; an experiment now going on in the counties of Summit and Mahoning with apparent success.

When these expectations shall be realized, it will be seen by a due consideration of the extent of the mineral region of Ohio, its richness in all the materials of value in the manufacture of iron, that this state will soon turn out immense quantities of that metal.

By the census of 1840, she had 72 furnaces, which produced 35,236 tons of pig metal the year previous. She had 19 forges, that made 7,466 tons of bar iron in the same time.

In this notice of the Ohio strata, I have not spoken of them by the scientific divisions and names, because their place and nomenclature in the system is not yet well settled among geologists.

The geological survey of the state was abandoned by the legislature when it was about one-third completed, and upon the work done no *final* report was made or required. The survey was dropped by the sudden withdrawal of the funds, the corps never having been formally disbanded.

Two annual reports were made, but not anticipating the abandonment of the survey, they contained only such facts as appeared to be of present practical value, reserving the theoretical and purely scientific matter for a future and final report.

Since that time, the splendid reports on the New York survey have been made, and as those geologists had a great range of observation, from the coal down to the primitive rocks, their classification has become, for the present, the standard for the United States.

In Ohio, many formations, well developed in New York, are *wanting*, leaving gaps in the series. Mr. Hall, of the New York survey, in his extended geological map of the western states, makes the blue limestone of Cincinnati equivalent to the Trenton and Birdseye group of New York members of the lower Silurian system, within two formations of the bottom of the sedimentary rocks. These are the "Potsdam sand stone," which rests on the primitive, and the "calciferous sand rock," lying between the Potsdam and the Trenton limestone.

In New York, next above the Trenton, is—1st, "Utica slate;" 2d, "Shawangunk grits;" 3d, "Hudson river group;" 4th, "Medina sandstone;" 5th, "Clinton group"—*all wanting* in Ohio.

Next above these rocks, in New York, is the "Niagara limestone," represented in Ohio, according to Mr. Hall, by the lower part of the cliff limestone, the upper part being here the geological equivalent of the "Helderberg limestone" of New York.

Between the Helderberg and the Niagara is found the "Onondaga salt group," of which only uncertain traces are found in Ohio. Our "black shale," which rests on the cliff limestone, represents the "Hamilton group" of New York, and the New York geologists discover in our fine grained, or "Waverly sand stone" the "Portage and Chemung group" of southern New York, which there plunges south and beneath the coal series, as it does here. Our conglomerate, underlying the coal, does not reach New York, but follows the edge of the coal field, as I have above described it, around through Pennsylvania, Virginia, Tennessee and Kentucky, back to Ohio.

The coincidence and equivalency of our rocks with those of New York cannot, in all respects, be regarded as settled. The fossils of the Ohio rocks, the great guide in classifying formations, have not been fully discovered or studied. The division of the fine grained sandstone into two members, equivalent to the Portage and Gardeau rocks, did not occur to the Ohio geologists, but may, notwithstanding, be a good division. There will, probably, be occasion to

74

divide the blue limestone into more members than are given above, when its multitude of fossils are completely understood.

An attempt was made at the meeting of the "Association of American Geologists and Naturalists," at Washington, May, 1844, by Professor H. D. Rogers, to adopt a system of names for the several formations, that should answer for the whole United States. Hitherto, the geologists of each state, following the example of those of England, have given to their strata the name of a locality or region, by which the same rock, when it crosses a state line, takes another name or designation. To make the science easy to learners and readers, and to give simplicity to the system among its professors, a nomenclature that shall be uniform in the United States, and even over the world, is indispensable.

The coal series of Ohio present no striking difference from the coal fields of other states and kingdoms, except in the presence of the "buhr stratum." All coal-bearing strata present alternate beds of iron ore, sand stone, shales, limestone and coal in their beds, and consequently changing frequently as we ascend or descend in the series.

In the 1st Geological Report of Ohio, p. 28, Dr. Hildreth notices the "calcareo siliceous," or "buhr stone rock," of the coal series of Ohio, which resembles very closely the French buhr," used in this country for mill stones, and imported from France. On Raccoon's creek, and at other places in the south, near the Ohio river, this rock is wrought into mill stones to a considerable extent; but millers, as yet, prefer the foreign buhr, at a considerably higher price.

In this brief view of the outlines of the geology of Ohio, I shall omit to notice the fossils, because upon this subject geologists are, as yet, only partially instructed.

The most numerous and striking are the trees, plants and stems of the coal-bearing rocks, the shells and corals and crustacea of the limestone, and the timber, leaves and dirt-buds of the "drift," or "diluvium." The latter is the general term for the earthy covering that conceals the rocks, varying in thickness from nothing to 200 feet.

It is sometimes called the "superficial deposits," having been brought on by some force, after the deposition and induration of the rocky beds.

There are many theories respecting the manner in which this immense mass of clays, sand and gravel was brought on, the discussion of which would occupy much space.

The "boulders," or lost rocks, that lie scattered over this state in most of its parts, and of the northern half of the United States, are objects of great curiosity, because they have evidently been transported a great distance. They are fragments of primitive rocks, granite, gneiss and Hornblende rock, which do not exist in place in Ohio, nor within about 400 miles in any direction.

As we go northward to the mountain ranges that skirt Lake Superior, we find the nearest rocks that answer to the specimens found here; and from this and other reasons, it is conclusively shown that they *are from the north.* In almost every quarry where the superficial earth has been stripped off, especially on the summits of hills, we find scratches, grooves and furrows, that are in a northerly and southerly direction, varying from N. 15° to N. 40° west. There is an evident connexion between the boulders and these diluvial furrows, and also with the drift or diluvium itself. It is supposed by some geologists that the drift and the boulders were brought on by the action of glaciers of ice moving down from the north, in remote ages, when the northern hemisphere was, as the Alps are now, bound up in continual winter.

By others, that the waters of the Northern Ocean once stood several thousand feet higher than at present, and that by means of heavy currents in those ancient seas, the drift and boulders were brought on.

Others join the two theories, and suppose an elevated state of the waters and a great degree of cold, but not continual, as in the Alps, and currents of water acting in a double capacity as transporters of sand, clay and gravel, and of huge icebergs, that enclosed and brought along the rocks we now see.

By this supposition, a greater number of the phenomena of the drift can be explained than by the aqueous or the glacial alone. It is called the "aqueo-glacial" theory. The glacial explains how the scratches and furrows may have been formed, but by this the sands, clay and gravel should be mixed and in confusion, whereas we find them stratified; and more, we observe in Ohio and the west, that the boulders are *not mixed* with the superficial mass, but lie *upon* it, being spread over the surface.

By the aqueous doctrine, it does not seem probable that a force could be acquired sufficient to tear off and transport huge rocks many hundred miles; and if it could, should they not be mingled with the mass, and not rest upon it?

Icebergs are now seen floating in the ocean of many square miles in extent, and 2000 feet thick.

If the ocean or lake waters were elevated, so as to cover the highest land in Ohio, which is near the sources of Mad river, about 900 feet above the lake, or 1450 above the ocean, one of those largest icebergs would not float in the basin of Lake Erie. In Massachusetts, the same grooves, boulders and scratches which are seen here, are met with much *higher than any land in Ohio*, at 2400, 2600 and at 3200 feet above the level of the sea.

These facts show conclusively, either that the waters were higher, or the highlands lower than at present. If masses of ice existed then as now, and drifted southward, they would be likely to embrace fragments of the northern rocks, and in passing across our ranges of hills, would wear away the most exposed points, leaving scratches and furrows on the rocks.

The superficial deposits of Ohio are arranged into *four* geological formations, and, in the order of age, are as follows:

1st, The "ancient drift," resting upon the rocks of the state.

2d, The Lake Erie marl and sand deposits.

3d, The drift occupying the valleys of large streams, such as the Great Miami, the Ohio and Scioto.

4th, The "boulders," or, as it may be called, the "boulder stratum."

In these, we do not take into account the "alluvium," or earthy deposit, now going on, not as the result of an universal geological change, but by the action of floods, rains, bogs, vegetable decay, concretion, etc.

The "ancient drift," or drift formation, No. 1, of Ohio, has not, as I know, furnished any shells from which it can be determined whether it was of "*marine*" or salt water origin, or a "lacustrine" or fresh water deposit. It is distinctly stratified in the following order.

1*st*. At the bottom, *blue clay*, or "hard pan," with gravel stones, of both primitive and sedimentary rocks, and contains carbonate of lime. These gravel stones are not, in general, as much worn as in the superior strata, and are scratched and striated—thickness sometimes 150 feet.

2*d*. The *yellow clay*, or "hard pan," of the well-diggers, with gravel stones similar to the "blue hard pan"—the stratum in general not as thick.

3*d*. Sand and gravel less perfectly stratified, and embracing more pebbles of the sedimentary rocks, such as limestone, sand stone, iron ore, coal and shale—the pebble more polished and rounded.

No. 1 of these divisions includes great numbers of logs, trees, leaves, sticks, and what the well-diggers call "grape vines." All these members occupy the surface at different places; but, in general, it is made up of Nos. 3 and 4. *Drift formation* No. 2, or the "Lake Erie deposits," are not satisfactorily *proved* to be newer than No. 1; yet the preponderance of evidence and all analogy are in favor of placing it above the "hard pans" in geological order. It is, however, often lower in natural level, occupying the basin of Lake Erie.

The section is as follows:

1st. From the lake level upwards, fine blue marly sand, 45 to 60 feet.

Its depth below the surface of the water is unknown—probably 50 to 100 feet, making a thickness of 95 to 160 feet.

2d. Coarse grey water-washed sand, . . . 10 to 20 feet.

3d. Coarse sand and gravel, not well stratified, to surface, 20 to 50 "

The lake ridges from Erie to Norwalk belong to this stratum.

Stratum No. 1 of this formation is easily dissolved by the action of water, and it is upon this, being at the water level, that the principal encroachment of the lake is effected. It may be traced along the shore around the western half of the lake in Ohio, Michigan and Canada, everywhere undergoing loss by the perpetual movement of the waves, and sliding into the lake in heavy masses. It contains carbonate of lime, magnesia, alumina, iron, sulphur, silex, and a few decayed plants, sticks and leaves. There are also pebbles of primitive rocks, but they are not numerous. Its upper surface is almost horizontal, for the difference between the south shore at Cleveland and the north shore at Port Burwell, in Canada, does not exceed 15 feet. It is heavy and compact, so as to be impervious to water, causing numberless springs to flow out at its upper edges. In contact with water, it becomes quicksand, and is easily washed away. The coarse sandy stratum, No. 2, resting upon it, is porous, and suffers the water to settle through it readily. It is the same with No. 3, on the surface stratum or soil, occupying a long, narrow belt along the south shore, and also the broad and level region of southeastern Michigan and the western portion of "Canada West," between Lakes Erie and Huron.

The ridges of sand and sandy materials that are so common over all this space, appear to have been formed *beneath the surface* of the ancient waters, and were formerly parallel with the ancient shore.

They are seen at various levels above the lake, from 30 to 140 and 200 feet, but of greater length and regularity, is 90 to 120 feet. They were probably formed when the waters were at various heights, and by the same process that sand bars are now formed in the lakes and the ocean. Beneath the surface on the coast of the United States, opposite the states of New-Jersey, Delaware, Maryland, Virginia and North and South Carolina. In Lake Erie, also, such ridges are known to form, having a general direction parallel with the shore. Should the water recede rapidly, or the bed of the ocean rise suddenly, they would be left in form and extent like our lake ridges. Similar ridges or terraces surround Lake Ontario. At Toronto, on the northern shore, Mr. Roy has given the elevation of several of them, referred to the lake level as follows. The base of the 1st, or nearest ridge to the lake, 108 feet; 2d, 208 feet; 3d, 288 feet, and the highest near the summit, between Lakes Ontario and Simcoe, was found to be 680 feet, or 448 feet above Lake Erie. In Canada, those of the northern shore of Lake Ontario extend across the level region between Lake Erie and Lake Huron, forming there ridges that belong to Lake Erie. Examination will no doubt show, hereafter, higher ridges on the south shore of Lake Erie than those above given.

Formation No. 3 of the drift of Ohio, being that which is found in the valleys of large rivers and lowlands, but of greater extent and thickness than the alluvium, does not, so far as I know, possess within itself subdivisions of strata like formations Nos. 1 and 2. Its pebbles are numerous, and generally form rocks of a sedimentary kind. Pebbles of primitive rocks may be occasionally seen, but seldom. In the valleys of the Scioto and the two Miamies, rivers flowing in or near the limestone formation, the gravel is principally of limestone, well water worn and rounded.

The "Hickory Plains" at the forks of the White Water and Great Miami, and also between Kilgores mill and New Richmond, in Ross county, and in Pickaway county, are examples of this modification of the drift. It is probably the result of heavy diluvial currents, that exerted themselves irregularly during the *subsidence of the waters*, and acting in the direction of the great valleys.

The *fourth* and superior member of the drift, and the last action of the drift period, is the *boulder itself*. I call it a formation, because it appears to be due to a separate geological epoch, occurring after the three formations above noticed were in place. It may be called a *stratum*, for it covers a greater surface than any rocky stratum, and is disposed in regular order over all other deposits except the alluvial. At the best, it is not mingled with the subordinate beds, however it may be at Canada East and New England. It is the result of some force different from that which brought on the sands and clay. The boulders themselves must have been deposited in a short space of time, or they would have been found embedded in the drift. The waters must have retired soon after they were brought on, or the sediment would soon have covered them. They were probably dropped from masses of floating ice as the waters receded. But, in this sketch, it would be out of place to discuss the theories of the presence of the drift and the boulders.

In laying down the outlines of the grindstone grit, it should be observed, that, on the west, the junction between it and the fine grained sand stone is covered with drift, and, therefore, its limits are conjectural.

The grit and its shales appear to be in the form of a wedge between the conglomerate and the fine grained sand stone, which, as we go from the lake, diminishes in thickness, and is displaced by the Waverly thickening up.

This accounts for the appearance of the Waverly in the east fork of Rocky river, at Old Portage, and at Warren, Trumbull county, where its surface is higher than at the lake. Along an east and west line through these places, the surface of the Waverly, or fine grained sand stone, has been elevated by an upward increase of thickness.

VOCABULARIES OF THE SHAWANOESE AND WYANDOTT LANGUAGES, ETC

[THE following article was communicated for this work by the venerable Col. John Johnston, of Upper Piqua, Ohio, who, for about half a century, has been an agent of the United States over the Indians of the west. See page 363.]

The Wyandotts had resided on the soil of Ohio long before the French or English visited the country. Forty-six years ago, I took a census of them, when they numbered 2300 souls. In 1841 and 2, I was, as the commissioner of the United States, negotiating with them a treaty of cession and emigration, when it was found, by actual and accurate count, that, in a little less than 50 years, they had been reduced to the number of 800; none had emigrated—all that was left were the subjects of my negotiation. I had been their agent a great part of my life; and after being separated from them for 11 years by the power of the Executive, it fell to my lot, under the appointment of my honored and lamented friend and chief, President Harrison, to sign and seal the compact with their chiefs for their final removal from their cherished homes and graves of their ancestors, to which, of all their race, I had ever known they were the most tenderly attached, to the country southwest of Missouri.

The Shawnoese came into Ohio not long anterior to Braddock's campaign of 1754. They occupied the country contiguous to the Wyandotts, on the Scioto, Mad river, the Great Miami, and the upper waters of the Maumee of the lake, being in the light of tenants at will under the Wyandotts. They were their devoted friends and allies in all their wars with the white people—these two tribes having been the last of the natives who have left us, for there is not an Indian now in Ohio, nor an acre owned by one of their race within its limits.

I have thought that a specimen of the respective languages of these tribes might form a proper item in the history of a state so lately owned and occupied by the primitive inhabitants. The vocabulary, as far as it goes, is accurate, and may be relied upon. The reader will at once observe the great dissimilarity in the two languages, not one word in the whole being common to both. In all their large councils, composed of both tribes, interpreters were as necessary between the parties as it was between the Indians and the United States' officers. Not so with the Shawanoese, Delawares, Miamies, Putawatimies, Chippeways, Ottawas, Wee,as, Kickapoos and Piankeshawas—all of whom had many words in common, and clearly establishing a common origin. Almost all the tribes I have known, had tradition that that their forefathers, at some remote period, came from the west; and this would seem to strengthen the commonly received opinion of Asiatic descent. Many of the Indian customs, even at this day, are strictly Jewish: instance the purification of their women, the year of Jubilee, the purchase of wives, &c.

All the Indians have some sort of religion, and allege that it was given to their forefathers, and that it would be offensive to the Great Spirit to throw it away and take up with any other. They all believe that after this life is ended, they will exist in another state of being; but most of their sacrifices and petitions to their Maker are done with a view to the procuring of temporal benefits, and not for the health of the immortal part.

Death has no terrors to an Indian: he meets it like a stoic. The fate of the soul does not appear to give him the smallest uneasiness. I have seen many die, and some in full confidence of a happy immortality; such were not taught of the Christian missionaries. In innumerable instances I have confided my life and property to Indians, and never, in time of peace, was my confidence misplaced. I was, on one occasion, upwards of a week, in a time of high waters, alone, in the month of March, with a Delaware Indian in the woods, whom I ascertained afterwards to be a notorious murderer and robber; and having every thing about my person to tempt a man of his kind—a good horse, equipments, arms, clothing, &c.—and yet no one could be more provident, kind and tender over me than he was. When the chiefs heard that I had taken this otherwise bad man for a guide, they were alarmed until informed of my safety. I have had large sums of public money, and public dispatches of the greatest importance, conveyed by the Indians, without in any case suffering loss.

VOCABULARY OF THE SHAWANOESE.

One—Negate.
Two—Neshwa.
Three—Nithese.
Four—Newe.
Five—Nialinwe.
Six—Negotewathe.
Seven—Neshwathe.
Eight—Sashekswa.
Nine—Chakatswa.
Ten—Metathwe.
Eleven—Metath,we, Kit,en,e,gate.
Twelve—Metathwe, Kiteneshwa.
Thirteen—Metathwe, Kitenithwa.
Fourteen—Metathwe, Kitenewa.
Fifteen—Metathwe, Kitenealinwe.
Sixteen—Metathwe, Kitenegotewathe.
Seventeen—Metathwe, Kiteneshwathe.
Eighteen—Metathwe, Kitensashekswa.
Nineteen—Metathwe, Kitenchakatswe.
Twenty—Neesh,wa,tee,tuck,e.
Thirty—Nithwabetucke,
Forty—Newabetucke.
Fifty—Nialinwabetucke.
Sixty—Negotewashe.
Seventy—Neshwashe.
Eighty—Swashe.
Ninety—Chaka.
One hundred—Te,pa,wa.
Two hundred—Neshwatepawa.
Three hundred—Nithwatepawa.
Four hundred—Newe-tepawa.
Five hundred—Nialinwe-tepawa.
Six hundred—Negotewathe-tepawa.
Seven hundred—Neshwethe-tepawa.
Eight hundred—Sashekswa-tepawa.
Nine hundred—Chakatswe-tepawa.
One thousand—Metathwe-tepawa.
Two thousand—Neshina,metathwe,tepawa.
Three thousand—Nethina,metathwe,tepawa
Four thousand—Newena,metahwe tepawa.
Five thousand—Nealinwa metathwe tepawa.
Old man—Pashetotha
Young man—Meaneleneh.

Chief—Okema.
Dog—Weshe.
Horse—Meshewa.
Cow—Methothe.
Sheep—Meketha.
Hog—Kosko.
Cat—Posetha.
Turkey—Pelewa.
Deer—Peshikthe.
Raccoon—Ethepate.
Bear—Mugwa.
Otter—Kitate.
Mink—Chaquiwashe.
Wild cat—Peshewa.
Panther—Meshepeshe.
Buffalo—Methoto.
Elk—Wabete.
Fox—Wawakotchethe.
Musk rat—Oshasqua.
Beaver—Amaghqua.
Swan—Wabethe.
Goose—Neeake.
Duck—Sheshepuk.
Fish—Amatha.
Tobacco—Siamo.
Canoe—Olagashe.
Big vessel or ship—Misheologashe.
Paddle—Shumaghtee.
Saddle—Appapewee.
Bridle—Shaketonebetcheka.
Man—Elene.
Woman—Equiwa.
Boy—Skillewaythetha.
Girl—Squithetha.
Child—Apetotha.
My wife—Neewa.
Your wife—Keewa.
My husband—Wysheana.
Your husband—Washetche.
My father—Notha.
Your father—Kotha.
My mother—Neegah
Grandmother—Cocumtha

My sister—Neeshematha.
My bother—Neethetha.
My daughter—Neetanetha.
Great chief—Kitchokema.
Soldier—Shemagana.
Great soldier, as Gen. Wayne, } Kitcho, great, and Shemagana, soldier.
Hired man, or servant—Alolagatha.
Englishman—by the Ottawas, Sagona.
" by Putawatimies and Chippeways, the same.
" by the Shawanoese, Englishmanake.
Frenchman—Tota.
American—Shemanose, or big knives, first applied to the Virginians.
The lake—Kitchecame.
The sun—Kesathwa.
" by the Putawatimies, Chippeways and Ottawas, Keesas.
The moon—Tepeth,ka,kesath,wa.
The stars—Alagwa.
The sky—Men,quat,we.
Clouds—Pasquawke.
The rainbow—Quaghcunnega.
Thunder—Unemake.
Lightning—Papapanawe.
Rain—Gimewane.
Snow—Conee.
Wind—Wishekuanwe.
Water—Nip,pe.
" by the Putawatimies, Ottawas and Chippeways, Na,bish.
Fire—Scoate.
Cold—We,pe.
" Putawatimie, Sin,e,a.
Warm—Aquettata.
Ice—M'Quama.
The earth—Ake.
The trees, or the woods—Me,te,quegh,ke.
The hills—Mavueghke.
Bottom ground—Alwamake.
Prairie—Tawaskota.
Friend—Ne,can,a.
" in Delaware, N'tschee.
" in Putawatimie, Ottawa and Chippeway, Nitche.
River—Sepe.
Pond—Miskeque.
Wet ground, or swamp—Miskekope.
Good land—Wesheasiske.
Small stream—The,bo,with,e.
Poor land—Mel,che,a,sis,ke.
House—Wig,wa.
Council house, or great house—Takatchemaka wigwa.
The great God, or good spirit—Mishemenetoc.
The bad spirit, or the devil—Watchemenetoc.
Dead—Nep,wa.
Alive—Lenawawe

Sick—Aghqueloge.
Well—Weshelashamama.
Corn—Da,me.
" by the Putawatimies, M'tame.
Wheat—Cawasque.
Beans—Miscoochethake.
Potatoes—Meash,e,tha,ke.
" by the Putawatimies, Peng,acs.
Turneps—Openeake.
Pumpkins—Wabegs.
Mellons—Usketomake.
Onions—Shekagosheke.
Apples—Me,she,me,na,ke.
Nuts—Pacanee.
Nut—Pacan.
Gun—Metequa.
Axe—Te,ca,ca.
Tomahawk—Cheketecaca.
Knife—Manese.
" by the Putawatimies, Comong.
Powder—Macate.
Flints—Shakeka.
Trap—Naquaga.
Hat—Petacowa.
Shirt—Peleneca.
Blanket—Aquewa.
" by the Putawatimies, Wapyan, or wabscat, wapyan, i. e. white blanket.
Handkerchief—Pethewa.
Pair of leggings—Me,tetawawa.
Eggs—Wa,wa,le.
Freshmeat—Weothe.
" by the Putawatimies, We,as.
Salt—Nepepimme.
" by the Putawatimies, Su,ta,gin.
Bread—Ta,quan,e.
" Putawatimies, Quasp,kin—a Shawanoese would say, Meet,a,lasqwa.
I have got no bread—Ta,qu,ana.
Kettle—A,coh,qua.
Sugar—Me,las,sa.
Tea—Shis,ke,wapo.
Medicine—Cho,beka.
I am very sick—Olame,ne,taghque,lo,ge.
I am very well—Ne,wes,he,la,shama,mo.
A fine day—Wash,he,kee,she,ke.
A cloudy day—Mes,quet,wee.
My friend—Ne,can,a.
My enemy—Matche,le,ne,tha,tha.
The Great Spirit is the friend of the Indians—Ne,we,can,e,te,pa, we,sphe,ma,mi,too.
Let us always do good—We,sha,cat,we,lo, ke,we,la,wapa.
Bell—To,ta,gin.
Plenty—Ma,la,ke,
Cut,e,we,ka,sa, or Blackfoot, the head chief of the Shawanoese, died at Wapoghkonetta in 1831, aged about 105 years.
She,me,ne,too, or the Snake, another aged chief, emigrated with the nation west.
Fort, or garrison—Wa,kargin.

SPECIMEN OF THE WYANDOTT, OR HURON LANGUAGE.

One—Scat.
Two—Tin,dee
Three—Shaight.
Four—An,daght.
Five—Wee,ish.
Six—Wa,shaw.
Seven—Soo,ta,re.
Eight—Ace,tarai.
Nine—Ain,tru.
Ten—Augh,sagh.
Twenty—ten,deit,a,waugh,sa.
Thirty—Shaigh,ka,waugh,sa.
Forty—An,dagh,ka,waugh,sa.
Fifty—Wee,ish,awaugh,sa.
Sixty—Waw,shaw,wagh,sa,
Seventy—Soo,ta,re,waugh,sa.
Eighty—Au,tarai,waugh,sa.
Ninety—Ain,tru,waugh,sa.
One hundred—Scu,te,main,gar,we.
The great God, or good spirit—Ta,main,-de,zue.
Good—Ye,waugh,ste.
Bad—Waugh,she.
Devil, or bad spirit—Deghshee,re,noh.
Heaven—Ya,roh,nia.
Hell—Degh,shunt.
Sun—Ya,an,des,hra.
Moon—Waugh,sunt,ya,an,des,hra.
Stars—Tegh,she.
Sky—Cagh,ro,ni,ate.
Clouds—Oght,se,rah.
Wind—Iru,quas.
It rains—Ina,un,du,se.
Thunder—Heno.
Lightning—Tim,mendi,quas.
Earth—Umait,sagh.
Deer—Ough,scan,oto.
Bear—Anu,e.
Raccoon—Ha,in,te,roh.
Fox—Th,na,in,ton,to.
Beaver—Soo,taie.
Mink—So,hoh,main,dia.
Turkey—Daigh,ton,tah.
Squirrel—Ogh,ta,eh.
Otter—Ta,wen,deh.
Dog—Yun,ye,nah.
Cow—Kin,ton,squa,ront.
Horse—Ugh,shut,te, or man carrier.
Goose—Yah,hounk.
Duck—Yu,in,geh.
Man—Air,ga,hon.
Woman—Utch,ke.
Girl—Ya,weet,sen,tho.
Boy—Oma,int,sent,e,hah.
Child—Che,ah,ha.
Old man—Ha,o,tong.
Old woman—Ut,sindag,sa.
My wife—Azut,tun,oh,oh.
Corn—Nay,hah.
Beans—Yah,re,sah.
Potatoes—Da,ween,dah.
Mellons, or pumpkins—O,nugh,sa.
Grass—E,ru,ta.
Weeds—Ha,en,tan.
Trees—Ye,aron,ta.
Wood—O,tagh,ta.
House—Ye,anogh,sha.
Gun—Who,ra,min,ta.
Powder—T'egh,sta.
Lead—Ye,at,ara.
Flints—Ta,wegh,ske,ra.
Knife—We,ne,ash,ra.
Axe—Otto,ya,ye.
Blanket—Deengh,tat,sea.
Kettle—Ya,yan,e,tith.
Rum—We,at,se,wie.
River—Ye,an,da,wa.
Bread—Da,ta,rah.
Dollar—Sogh,ques,tut.
Shirt—Ca,tu,reesh.
Leggins—Ya,ree.
Bell—Te,ques,ti,egh,tas,ta.
Saddle—Quagh.she,ta.
Bridle—Cong,shu,ree.
Fire—Sees,ta.
Flour—Ta,ish,rah.
Hog—Quis,quesh.
Big house—Ye,a,nogh,shu,wan,a.
Corn field—Ya,yan,quagh,ke.
Musk rat—Se,he,ash,i,ya,hah.
Cat—Dush,rat.
Wild cat—Skaink,qua,hagh.
Mole—Ca,in,dia,he,nugh,qua.
Snake—To,en,gen,seek.
Frog—Sun,day,wa,shu,ka.
Americans—Sa,ray,u,migh, or big knives.
Englishman—Qu,han,stro,no.
Frenchman—Tu,hugh,car,o,no.
My Brother—Ha,en,ye,ha.
My sister—A,en,ya,ha.
Father—Ha,yes,ta.
Mother—Ane,heh.
Sick—Shat,wu,ra.
Well—Su,we,regh,he.
Cold—Ture,a.
Warm—Ote,re,a,ute.
Snow—De,neh,ta.
Ice—Deesh,ra.
Water—Sa,un,dus,tee,the, the origin of Sandusky, the bay, river and county of that name.
Friend—Ne,at,a,rugh.
Enemy—Ne,mat,re,zue.
War—Tre,zue.
Peace—Scan,o,nie.
Are you married—Scan,dai,ye.
I am not married yet—Augh,sogh,a,sante,-te,sandai,ge.
Come here—Owa,he.
Go away—Sa cati,arin,ga.
You trouble me—Ska,in,gen,tagh,qua.
I am afraid—I,agh,ka,ron,se.
I love you—Yu,now,moi,e.
I hate you—Yung,squa,his.

I go to war—A,yagh,kee.
I love peace—Eno,moigh,an,dogh,sken,onie.
I love all men—Away,tee,ken,omie.
I have conquered my enemy—O,negh,e,ke,-wishe,noo.
I don't like white men—Icar,tri,zue,egh,har,-taken,ome,enu,mah.
Indians—I,om,when.
Negro—Ahon,e,see.
Prisoner—Yan,dah,squa.
He is a thief—Run,neh,squa,hoon.
Good man—Room,wae,ta,wagh,stee.
Fish—Ye,ent,so.
Plums—At,su,meghst.
Apples—Sow,se,wat.
Fruit—Ya,heeghk.
Sugar—Se,ke,ta. Honey—the same.
Bees—Un,dagh,quont.
Salt—Anu,magh,ke,he,one, or the white people's sugar.
Moccasin—Aragh,shee.
How do you do—Tu,ough,qua,no,u.
I am sorry—I,ye,et,sa,tigh.
I am hungry—Yat,o,regh, shas,ta.
You will be filled—E,sagh,ta,hah.
I am dying—E,hye,ha,honz.
God forgive me—Ho,ma,yen,de,zuti,et,te,-rang.
Auglaize river—Qus,quas,run,dee, or the falling timber on the river.
Blanchard's fork of the Auglaize—Quegh,-tu,wa, or claws in the water.
Sandusky—Sa,un,dus,tee, or water within water-pools.
Muskingum—Da,righ,quay, a town or place of residence.
Cayuhoga—Ya,sha,hia, or the place at the wing.
Miami of the lake—Cagh,a,ren.du,te, or standing rock at the head of the rapids of this river. There is in the middle of the stream a large elevated rock, which, at a distance, very much resembles a house. The place was named by the French Roche de Boef, and hence the standing rock river.
The sea of salt water—Yung,ta,rez,ue.
The lakes—Yung,ta,rah.
Detroit—Yon,do,tia, or great town.
Defiance, now the county seat of Defiance county, at the junction of the Auglaize and Miami of the lake—Tu,enda,wie, or the junction of two rivers. After defeating the Indians in 1794, Gen. Wayne, on his return, built Fort Defiance, thereby proclaiming defiance to the enemy.
Chillicothe town—Tat,a,ra,ra, or leaning bank. Chillicothe is Shawanoese, and is the name of one of their tribes.
Cincinnati—Tu,ent,a,hah,e,wagh,ta, a landing place, where the road leaves the river.
Ohio river—O,he,zuh,ye,an,da,wa, or something great.
Mississippi—Yan,da,we,zue, or great the river.

NAMES OF RIVERS BY THE SHAWANOESE—SPOKEN SHA,WA,NO.

Ohio, i. e. Eagle river.—See page 574.

Ken,a,wa—meaning having whirlpools, or swallowing up. Some have it that an evil spirit lived in the water, which drew substances to the bottom of the river.

Sci,o,to was named by the Wyandotts, who formerly resided upon it. A large town was at Columbus, having their cornfields on the bottom grounds opposite that city. The Wyandotts pronounce the word *Sci,on,to*, signification unknown.

Great Miamie—Shi,me,a,mee,sepe, or Big Miamie.

Little Miamie—Che,ke,me,a,mee,sepe, or Little Miamie.

Mus,king,um is a Delaware word, and means a town on the river side. The Shawanoes call it Wa,ka,ta,mo,sepe, which has the same signification.

Hock,hock,ing is Delaware, and means a bottle. The Shawanoese have it Wea,tha,-kagh,qua,sepe—Bottle river.

Auglaize river—Cow,the,na,ke,sepe, or falling timber river.

Saint Mary's river—Ca,ko,the,ke,sepe, or kettle river—cako,the,ke, a kettle.

Miamie of the lake—Ot,ta,wa,sepe, or Ottawa river. The Ottawas had several towns on this river as late as 1811, and down to within 10 years. They occupied the country about the lake shore, Maumee bay and the rapids above Perrysburgh.

Blanchard's fork of the Auglaize—Sha,po,qua,te, sepe, or Tailor's river. See p. 237.

Sandusky river—called by the Shawanoese Po,ta,ke,sepe, a rapid river.

Detroit strait, or river—Ke,ca,me,ge, the narrow passage, or strait.

Kentucky is a Shawanoese word, and signifies at the head of a river.

Licking river, which enters the Ohio opposite the city of Cincinnati—the Shawanoese have it, Ne,pe,pim,me,sepe, from Ne,pe,pim,me, salt, and sepe, river, i. e. salt river.

Mad river—by the Shawanoese, Athe,ne,sepe,athe,ne, a flat or smooth stone, and sepe, river, i. e. a flat or smooth stone river.

INDEX TO CITIES AND PRINCIPAL VILLAGES.

GENERAL INDEX.

CENSUS OF OHIO FOR 1850.

ANNEXED is given the Census of the various Counties and Townships of Ohio for the year 1850. The populations of the towns are also given where-ever the returns were made by the Assistant Marshals. The Towns are distinguished from the Townships by *italics*, and immediately follow the name of the townships in which they are situated.

The total population of Ohio, in 1840, was 1,519,467 and in 1850, 1,980,-960 of which 23,495 were returned as colored.

ADAMS COUNTY. 18,943.

Green, 1,520; Monroe, 1,191; Sprigg, 3,190; Liberty, 1,498; Tiffin, 1,523; *West Union*, 462; Winchester, 1,693; Wayne, 1,682; Jefferson, 1,543; Scott, 1,270; Franklin, 1,962; Meigs, 1,438.

ALLEN COUNTY. 12,116.

Lima, 757; Monroe, 924; Richland, 990; Spencer, 336; Amanda, 588; Shawnee, 756; Sugar Creek, 756; German, 1,008; Perry, 923; Auglaize, 1,344; Bath, 1,512; Jackson, 1, 176; Marion, 672; *Section Ten*, 374.

ASHLAND COUNTY. 23,826.

Jackson, 1,533; Ruggles, 1,085; Sullivan, 1,101; Troy, 849; Orange, 1,826; Vermillion, 2,459; Montgomery, 1,928; *Ashland*, 1,264; Mohican, 1,775; Milton, 1,432; Clear Creek, 1,205; Perry, 1,789; Greene, 1,904; Mifflin, 891; Lake, 883; Hanover, 1,902.

ASHTABULA COUNTY. 28,767.

Jefferson, 625; *Jefferson*, 439; Austinburg, 1,285; Harpersfield, 1,279; Trumbull, 805; Lenox, 731; Morgan, 888; Hartsgrove, 650; Rome, 744; Orwell, 825; Windsor, 1,033; Dorset, 236; New Lime, 628; Colebrook, 688; Cherry Valley, 839; Ashtabula, 1,356; *Ashtabula*, 821; Conneaut, 1,877; *Conneaut*, 817; Monroe, 1,587; Sheffield, 845; Kingsville, 1,494; Plymouth, 753; Saybrook, 1,374; Denmark, 241; Pierpont, 999; Richmond, 706; Andover, 963; Williamsfield, 982; Wayne, 899; Geneva, 1,358.

ATHENS COUNTY. 18,217.

Lee, 961; Waterloo, 1,016; Trimble, 924; York, 1,391; Athens, 1,463; *Athens*, 898; Canaan, 1,142; Alexander, 1,735; Troy, 1,421; Carthage, 1,087; Rome, 1,309; Bern, 819; Ames, 1,482; Dover, 1,233; Lodi, 1,336.

AUGLAIZE COUNTY. 11,341.

Goshen, 336; Wayne, 672; Union, 1,008; Clay, 840; Pusheta, 1,008; Duchouquet, 905; *Wapakoneta*, 504; Logan, 336; German, 1,470; *Minster*, 428; *New Bremen*, 344; Saint Mary's, 693; *St. Mary's*, 874; Washington, 688; Noble, 309; Salem, 400; *Kossuth*, 76; Moulton, 450.

BELMONT COUNTY. 34,599.

Richland, 4,366; Flushing, 1,811; Pease, 3,517; Pultney, 2,250; Smith, 1,797; Washington, 1,534; Mead, 1,634; Warren, 1,914; *Barnesville*, 820; Somerset, 2104; *Somerton*, 192; Goshen, 1,862; *Belmont*, 155; Union, 1,873; *Morristown*, 455; Wheeling, 1,217; *Shepardstown*, 90; *Uniontown*, 194; Colerain, 1,321; *Farmington*, 45; York, 1,312; Wayne, 1918; Kirkwood, 2,208.

BROWN COUNTY. 27,334.

Union, 2,424; *Levana*, 174; *Ripley*, 1,780; Byrd, 2,085; *Russelville*, 386; *Decatur*, 171; Huntington, 1,877; *Aberdeen*, 807; Lewis, 1,998; *Fecsburg*, 186; *Higginsport*, 536; Jackson, 1,150; *Carlisle*, 112; Pleasant, 1,457; *Georgetown*, 617; Perry, 2,465; *Fayetteville*, 318; Scott, 930; *New Hope*, 106; Clark, 1,282; *Hamersville*, 131; *Brownsville*, 38; Pike, 1,022; Green, 632; *Benton*, 37; Eagle, 1,134; *Fincastle*, 145; Washington, 987; *Sardinia*, 198; Franklin, 1,107; *Arnheim*, 61; Sterling 981.

BUTLER COUNTY. 30,794.

Fairfield, 2771; *Hamilton*, 3,207; Union, 2,173; Liberty, 1,501; Madison, 2,242; Wayne, 1,502; St. Clair, 2,602; Hanover, 1,493; Reily, 1,716; Milford, 2,068; Oxford, 2,007; *Oxford*, 1,134; Morgan, 1,706; Ross, 1,648; Lemon, 1,722; *Middletown*, 1,092; *Monroe*, 210.

CARROL COUNTY. 17,685.

Center, 1,189; Union, 805; Monroe, 1,117; Orange, 1,577; Perry, 1,277; Loudon, 840; Lee, 1,220; Washington, 1,020; Harrison, 1,268; Augusta, 1297; East, 987; Fox, 1,452; Brown, 2,099; Rose, 1,537.

CHAMPAIGN COUNTY. 19,743.

Goshen, 1,260; *Mechanicsburg*, 682; Rush, 893; *Lewisburg*, 302; *Woodstock*, 205; Union, 1,646; Salem, 1,635; Mad River, 1,868; Urbana, 1,394; *Urbana*, 2,020; Jackson, 1,735; Johnson, 1,573; Adams, 1,123; Concord, 1,110; Harrison, 968; Wayne, 1,429.

CLARK COUNTY. 22,174.

Green, 1,275; Madriver, 1,493; *Enon*, 294; Bethel, 1,748; *Donnelsville*, 196; *New Carlisle*, 634; *Midway*, 69; Pike, 1,317; *Northampton*, 147; Madison, 947; *Selma*, 47; *South Charleston*, 414; German, 1,912; Harmony, 1,804; Springfield, 2,206; *Springfield*, 5,108; Morefield, 1,214; Pleasant, 1,349.

CLERMONT COUNTY. 30,449.

Batavia, 2,789; Williamsburg, 1,885; Tate, 2,901; Franklin, 3,061; Ohio, 4,474; Union, 1,800; Monroe, 1,897; Washington, 2,540; Jackson, 1,241; Goshen, 1,937; Miami, 2,690, Stone Lick, 1,840; Wayne, 1,394.

CLINTON COUNTY. 18,837.

Richland, 1,975; Union, 2,320; *Wilmington*, 1,238; Wayne, 1,435; Adams, 869; Vernon, 1,468; Marion, 995; Jefferson, 810; Clark, 1,653; Washington, 1,216; Chester, 1,600; Liberty, 1,232; Green, 2,025.

COLUMBIANA COUNTY. 33,601.

Unity, 2,095; Fairfield, 2,385; Salem, 1,960; Perry, 2,371; Knox, 2,155; Butler, 1,692; Center, 2,818; Hanover, 2,859; West, 2,110; Liverpool, 729; *Liverpool*, 835; Washington, 963; *Salineville*, 237; Yellow Creek, 853; *Wellsville*, 1,549; Middleton, 1,436; *Clarkson*, 91; Elk Run, 1,559; St. Clair, 1,115; *Calcutta*, 147; *Fredericktown*, 99; Franklin, 1,164; Wayne, 974; Madison, 1,405.

COSHOCTON COUNTY. 25,671.

Perry, 1,340; Washington, 996; Pike, 1,079; New Castle, 1,227; Bedford, 1,221; Tiverton, 842; Virginia, 1,227; Linton, 1,375; *Jacobsport*, 219; Adams, 1,419; White Eye, 1,132; Mill Creek, 872; La Fayette, 1,040; Oxford, 1,113; Tuscarawas, 741; *Coshocton*, 850; Bethlehem, 822; Franklin, 966; Keene, 1,079; Crawford, 1,552; Monroe, 760; Jefferson, 929; Jackson, 2,037; Clark, 833.

CRAWFORD COUNTY. 18,177.

Lykens, 1,185; Holmes, 1,239; Auburn, 951; Vernon, 1,276; Jackson, 1,711; Polk, 1,318; Sandusky, 822; Liberty, 1,782; Bucyrus, 2,315; Cranberry, 1,042; Chatfield, 1,351; Texas, 544; Todd, 578; Dallas, 406; Whetstone, 1,657.

CUYAHOGA COUNTY. 48,105.

Cleveland City, 17,041; East Cleveland, 2,343; Newburg, 1,542; Mayfield, 1,117; Warrensville, 1,409; Orange, 1,063: Euclid, 1,447: Solon, 1,033: Chagrin Falls, 1,250: Bedford, 1,854: Independence, 1,485: Brecksville, 1,116: Royalton, 1,253: Strongsville, 1,199: Middleburg, 1,490: Olmstead, 1,216: Dover, 1,102: Rockport, 1,441: Brooklyn, 6,375: Parma, 1,320.

DARKE COUNTY. 20,277.

Butler, 1,446: Twin, 1,400: Monroe, 918; Washington, 1,250: Greenville, 2,372: *Greenville*, 1,044: German, 1,502: Harrison, 1,705: Adams, 1,416: Neave, 888: Wayne, 1,162: Franklin, 551: Mississenawa, 378: Patterson, 319: Wabash, 309: Allen, 290: Jackson, 566: York, 499: Richland, 798: Brown, 684: Van Buren, 780.

DEFIANCE COUNTY. 6,966.

Defiance, 391: *Defiance*, 890: Highland, 365: Richland, 702: Adams, 432: Noble, 389: *Brunersburg*, 169: Tiffin, 544: *Evansport*, 165: Delaware, 445: Washington, 428: Farmer, 894: Milford, 645: Hicksville, 507.

DELAWARE COUNTY. 21,814.

Radnor, 1,204: Thompson, 732: Marlborough, 587: Berkshire, 1,555: Genoa, 1,369: Harlem, 1,182: Trenton, 1,238: Delaware, 1,247: *Delaware*, 2,075: Liberty, 1,051: Orange, 1,150: Berlin, 1,151: Concord, 1,369: Scioto, 1,126: Troy, 976: Oxford, 828: Brown, 1,176: Porter, 1,037: Kingston, 761.

ERIE COUNTY. 18,578.

Perkins, 1,217: Milan, 2,697: Sandusky City, 5,088: Margaretta, 1,537: Huron, 1,397: Kelley's Island, 186: Oxford, 984: Groton, 884: Berlin, 1,582: Vermillion, 1,513: Florence, 1,491.

FAIRFIELD COUNTY. 30,257.

Auburn, 626: Madison, 1,164: Bern, 2,656: Violent, 2,060: *Pickerington*, 180: *Canal Winchester*, 274: Liberty, 2,209: *Baltimore*, 492: *Basil*, 200: Walnut, 1,795: *Millersport*, 126: New Salem, 210: Bloom, 1,904: *Lithopolis*, 386: Amanda, 1,536: *Royalton*, 252: Greenfield, 2,113: Hocking, 1,846: Richland, 1,777: Pleasant, 2,011: *Lancaster*, 3,483: *Oakland*, 133: Clear Creek, 1,606: Rush Creek, 1,218.

FAYETTE COUNTY. 12,736.

Madison, 864: Marion, 842: Paint, 1,253: Jefferson, 1,872: Union, 1,821: *Washington*, 569: Wayne, 1,253: Perry, 1,088: Green, 951: *Buena Vista*, 107: Concord, 836: *Staunton*, 87: Jasper, 1,193.

FULTON COUNTY. 7,780.

Chesterfield, 538: Dover, 381: Royalton, 570: Amboy, 460: Pike, 485: Fulton, 625: Swan Creek, 621: York, 784: Clinton, 708: Franklin, 720: Gorham, 906: German, 982.

FRANKLIN COUNTY. 42,880.

Columbus City, 17,867: Montgomery, 1,326: Truro, 1,589: *Reynoldsburg*, 564: Franklin, 1,852: Sharon, 1,008: *Worthington*, 501: Blendon, 1,303: Plain, 1,393: *New Albany*, 168: Perry, 1,169: Clinton, 1,186: Washington, 996: *Dublin*, 274: Norwich, 1,053: Brown, 681: Prairie, 1,043: Jackson, 1,550: Pleasant, 968: *Harrisburg*, 103: Hamilton, 1,485: Madison, 1,997: *Groveport*, 483: Mifflin, 1,095: Jefferson, 1,236.

GALLIA COUNTY. 17,064.

Ohio, 504: Guyan, 560: Huntington, 1,308: Morgan, 1,128: Raccoon, 1,474: Springfield, 1,230: Cheshire, 1,410: Gallipolis, 420: *Gallipolis*, 1,686: Addison, 924: Green, 1,276: Perry, 1,208: Greenfield, 952: Walnut, 905: Clay, 949: Harrison, 1,008.

GEAUGA COUNTY. 17,823.

Chardon, 1,622: Hampden, 919: Munson, 1,194: Newbury, 1,253: Burton, 1,064: Claridon, 1,006: Middlefield, 918: Thompson, 1,211: Troy, 1,163: Auburn, 1,182: Chester, 1,103: Bainbridge, 1,013: Huntsburg, 1,007: Russell, 1,083: Parkman, 1,383: Montville, 702.

GREENE COUNTY. 21,947.

Sugar Creek, 3,082: Xenia, 7,156: Beaver Creek, 2,063: Bath, 2,079: Miami, 1,613 *Clifton*, 252: Ross, 1,367: Silver Creek, 2,565: Cæsar Creek, 1,870.

GUERNSEY COUNTY. 30,472.

Adams, 865; Madison, 1,524; Wheeling, 1,159; Liberty, 1,004; Jefferson, 857; Monroe, 1,086; Washington, 972; Londonderry, 1,551; Knox, 755; Westland, 1,126; Beaver, 1,785; *Williamsburg*, 207; Millwood, 1,409; *Millwood*, 216; Oxford, 1,496; *Fairview*, 444; *Middletown*, 267; Wills, 1,326; *Washington*, 757; *Elizabethtown*, 136; Richland, 981; *Senecaville*, 457, Seneca, 1,291; *Mt. Ephraim*, 121; Buffalo, 834; *Point Pleasant*, 105; *Hartford*, 113; Jackson, 1,191; Center 1,067; Cambridge, 1,448; *Cambridge*, 1,041; Spencer, 1,418; *Cumberland*, 431; Wright, 978; *New Gottengen*, 54.

HAMILTON COUNTY. 156,850.

Cincinnati City, 115,438; Fulton, 3,223; Spencer, 1,656; Columbia, 2,416; Anderson, 3,050; Mill Creek, 6,287; Storrs, 1,675; Green, 3,948; Delhi, 1,942; Sycamore, 3,731; Symmes, 1,115; Colerain, 3,125; Miami, 1,557; Whitewater, 1,567; Crosby, 1,548; *Harrison*, 940; Springfield, 3,632.

HANCOCK COUNTY, 16,774.

Findlay, 774: *Findlay*, 1,258: Allen, 870: Washington, 1,222: Cass, 621: Big Lick, 2,008: Amanda, 1,162: Marion, 904: Orange, 724: Van Buren, 536: Union, 1,150: Portage, 614: Blanchard, 1,051: Pleasant, 522: Liberty, 874: Delaware, 1,035: Jackson, 830: Eagle, 950: Madison, 667.

HARDIN COUNTY. 8,251.

Pleasant, 1,059: *Kenton*, 1,065: Dudley, 529: Hale, 428: Taylor Creek, 531: Goshen, 590: Blanchard, 252: Buck, 462: Jackson, 530: Washington, 391: Liberty, 422: McDonald, 582, Marion, 368: *Huntersville*, 84: Cessna, 303: Roundhead, 520: *Roundhead*, 135.

HARRISON COUNTY. 20,160.

Morefield, 1,022: *Morefield*, 44; Freeport, 1,221: Cadiz, 1,309: *Cadiz*, 1,144: Nottingham, 1,236: Franklin, 911: *Deersfield*, 289: *Franklin*, 150: Washington, 1,255: Short Creek, 1,490: *Harrisville*, 300: *Georgetown*, 160: Archer, 876: German, 1,361: Rumley, 1,088: North, 1,121: Monroe, 1,152: Stock, 888: Athens, 1,085: *New Athens*, 331: Green, 1,527.

HENRY COUNTY. 3,432.

Napoleon, 566; Flat Rock, 406; Washington, 531; Ridgeville, 148; Freedom, 83; Pleasant, 338; Marion, 77; Harrison, 515; Richfield, 136; Damascus, 233; Liberty, 399.

HOCKING COUNTY. 14,119.

Benton, 933; Ward, 823; Marion, 1,746; Falls, 1,772; *Logan*, 798; Good Hope, 635; Laurel, 1,126; Perry, 1,217; Salt Creek, 1,094; Washington, 1,640; Starr, 1,045; Green, 1,290.

HIGHLAND COUNTY. 25,781.

Liberty, 2,683; *Hillsborough*, 1,392; Fairfield, 3,174; Madison, 1,163; *Greenfield*, 1,011; Paint, 2,678; Union, 1,408; Newmarket, 1,528; Concord, 1,501; Jackson, 1,449; Dodson, 1,217; Hamer, 942; Marshall, 1,187; Brushcreek, 1,515; Salem, 813; Clay, 1,108; White Oak, 1,012.

HOLMES COUNTY. 20,458.

Hardy, 2,424; Kilbuck, 1,245; Monroe, 966; Prairie, 1,451; Mechanic, 1,647; Berlin, 1,452; Walnut Creek, 1,077; German, 1,517; Salt Creek, 1,699; Richland, 1,349; Knox, 1,215; Washington, 1,468; Ripley, 1,330; Paint, 1,618.

HURON COUNTY. 26,203.

New London, 1,329; Clarksfield, 1,454; Wakeman, 704; Townsend, 1,333; Hartland, 1,024; Greenwich, 1,050; Fitchville, 1,178; Norwalk, 1,718; *Norwalk*, 1441; Ridgefield, 1,944; Richmond, 609; Lyme, 1,859; Norwich, 1,021; Sherman, 1,134; Peru, 1,632; Bronson, 1,219; Fairfield, 1,594; New Haven, 1,398; Greenfield, 1,332; Ripley, 1,230.

JACKSON COUNTY. 12,724.

Bloomfield, 1,403; Madison, 1,515; Jefferson, 1,036; *Jackson*, 480; Lick, 1,021; Franklin, 1,295; Milton, 1,477; Washington, 756; Hamilton, 664; Scioto, 1,347; Jackson, 714; Liberty, 1,017.

JEFFERSON COUNTY. 20,133.

Mt. Pleasant, 1,848; Wells, 1,822; Springfield, 1,300; Brush Creek, 1,120; Ross, 1,144; Saline, 1,088; Knox, 1,902; Island Creek, 1,981; Steubenville, 1,084; *Steubenville*, 6,140; Cross Creek, 1,912; Salem, 2,191; Wayne, 1,801; Smithfield, 1,882, Warren, 1,918.

KNOX COUNTY. 28,870.

Clinton, 802; *Mount Vernon*, 3,710; Pleasant, 909; College, 522; Monroe, 1,323; Howard, 1,002: Pike, 1,720; Miller, 1,063; Morgan, 823; Clay, 960; *Martinsburg*, 280; Jackson, 1,078; Butler, 762; Harrison, 751; *Millwood*, 240; Union, 952; Brown, 1,535; Jefferson, 1,485; Middleburg, 1,091; Berlin, 1,158; Morris, 1,027; Liberty, 1,322; Milford, 1,350; Hillier, 1,141; Wayne, 1,152; *Fredericktown*, 712.

LAKE COUNTY. 14,655.

Leroy, 1,128; Mentor, 1,571; Concord, 1,031; Willoughby, 2,081; Kirtland, 1,598; Painesville, *Painesville*, 3,128; Madison, 2,987; Perry, 1,131.

LAWRENCE COUNTY, 15,247.

Union, 1,318; Fayette, 1,112; Perry, 924; Upper, 2,494; Rome, 1,134; Windsor, 1,001; Mason, 1,132; Aid, 884; Lawrence, 534; Elizabeth, 2,529; Decatur, 2,052; Washington, 646; Symmes, 487.

LICKING COUNTY. 38,845.

St. Albans, 1,422: *Alexandria*, 349: Monroe, 1,030: *Johnstown*, 357: Jersey, 1,230: Hartford, 1,426: Bennington, 1,169: *Appleton*, 42: McKean, 1,378: Harrison, 1,447: Lima, 973: Etna, 1,307: Newark, 1,228: *Newark*, 3,778: *Lockport*, 42: Granville, 1,345: *Granville*, 771: Madison, 1,025: Licking, 1,115: *Jacktown*, 256: Bowling Green, 870: *Linville*, 188: *Brownsville*, 480: Union, 1,631: *Luray*, 88: *Hebron*, 649: Newton, 1,364: Burlington, 1,389: Washington, 941: *Utica*, 420: Eden, 1,013: Mary Ann, 1,000: Fallsbery, 1,206: Perry, 1,254: Hanover, 1,187: Liberty, 1,190: Franklin, 1,057: Hopewell, 1,226.

LOGAN COUNTY. 19,168.

Lake, 1,774: Rush Creek, 1,458: Zane, 1,090: McArthur, 1,376: Richland, 1,170: Harrison, 984: Perry, 1,405: Jefferson, 2,043: Monroe, 1,438: Bokes Creek, 583: Liberty, 1,263: Union, 804: Bloomfield, 671: Stokes, 489: Pleasant, 805: Washington, 667: Miami, 775: *Quincy*, 373.

LORAIN COUNTY. 26,091.

Ridgeville, 1,212: Columbia, 1,236: Eaton, 1,111: Carlisle, 1,512: Avon, 1,782: LaGrange, 1,402: Grafton, 947: Penfield, 672: Elyria, 1,176: *Elyria*, 1,482: Wellington, 1,556: Sheffield, 908: Black River, 659: Amherst, 1,400: Brownhelm, 1,082: Henrietta, 1,042: Huntington, 1,173: Rochester, 896: Brighton, 669: Camden, 1,025: Russia, 2,061: Pittsfield, 1,088.

LUCAS COUNTY. 12,381.

Waynesfield, 2,371: Port Lawrence, 149: *Toledo*, 3,859: Manhattan, 541: Oregon, 449: Washington, 1,161: Sylvania, 751: Springfield, 782: Waterville, 958: Providence, 467: Richfield, 399: Wing, 261: Spencer, 273.

MADISON COUNTY. 10,012.

Fairfield, 623: Pleasant, 1,066: *Mt. Sterling*, 115: Range, 988: Stokes, 590: Deer Creek, 436: *La Fayette*, 147: Jefferson, 634: *West Jefferson*, 436: Canaan, 565: *Amity*, 120; Darby, 383: *Pleasant Valley*, 168: Monroe, 403: Pike, 381: *Rose Dale*, 42: Somerford, 616; *Somerford*, 139: Union, 1,647: *London*, 513.

MAHONING COUNTY. 23,733.

Smith, 1,544: Green, 1,774: Canfield, 1,463: Jackson, 1,140: Milton, 1,123: Berlin, 1,376: Ellsworth, 953: Goshen, 1,721: Coitsville, 982: Boardman, 1,026: Beaver, 2,144: Springfield, 2,385: Poland, 2,126: Youngstown, 2,802: Austintown, 1,174.

MARION COUNTY. 12,554.

Marion, 980: *Marion*, 1,307: Scott, 717: Claridon, 1,342: Richland, 1,229: Pleasant,

1,198: Grand Prairie, 474: Tully, 736: Big Island, 600: Montgomery, 643: Grand, 336: Salt Rock, 347: Waldo, 1,008: Prospect, 848: Green Camp, 383: Bowling Green, 406.

MEDINA COUNTY. 21,433.

Wadsworth, 1,622: Chatham, 1,165: La Fayette, 1,332: Homer, 1,102: Harrisville, 1,477: Westfield, 1,122: Medina, 1002: *Medina*, 1008: Sharon, 1,519: Granger, 1,313: Hinckley, 1,416: Brunswick, 1,417: Liverpool, 2,164: York, 1,228: Spencer, 1,336; Litchfield, 1,332: Guilford, 1,800: Montville, 1,078.

MEIGS COUNTY. 17,960.

Salisbury, 2,909: *Pomeroy*, 1,637: Olive, 924: Lebanon, 1,008: Letart, 966: Sutton, 1,596: Salem, 1,418: Scipio, 1,406: Bedford, 908: Chester, 1,410: *Chester*, 190: Orange, 946: Columbia, 897: Rutland, 1,745.

MERCER COUNTY. 7,712.

Marion, 1,428: Jefferson, 504: Hopewell, 294: Center, 504: Granville, 546: Butler, 210: Franklin, 378: Union, 756: Dublin, 883: Liberty, 208: Black Creek, 504: Washington, 420: Gibson, 504: Recovery, 573.

MIAMI COUNTY. 24,957.

Spring Creek, 1,273: *Rossville*, 113: *Huntersville*, 227: Washington, 982: *Piqua*, 3,280: Newberry, 1,690: *Covington*, 451: *Clayton*, 76: Brown, 1,379: Elizabeth, 1,433: Staunton, 1,453: Lost Creek, 1,455: Bethel, 1,656: Concord, 1,448: *Troy*, 1,956: Monroe, 2,014: Union, 2,255: *Milton*, 369: Newton, 1,447.

MONROE COUNTY. 28,367.

Switzerland, 1,215: Sunsbury, 1,532: Stock, 1,107: *Carlisle*, 116: Enoch, 1,438: Elk, 956: Bethel, 1,028: Malaga, 1,561: *Malaga*, 138: *Miltonsburg*, 145: Seneca, 1,841: *Calais*, 96: *Summerfield*, 153: Union, 1,930: Ohio, 1,443: *Bearsville*, 103: *Sardis*, 118: Perry, 1,460: *Antioch*, 107: Salem, 1,311: *Clarington*, 341: Wayne, 1,177: Washington, 944: Adams, 1,182: Center, 2,551: *Woodsfield*, 395: Franklin, 1,590: Greene, 1,226: Jackson, 1,163.

MONTGOMERY COUNTY. 38,217.

Dayton City, 10,976: Washington, 1,826: Miami, 3,456: Van Buren, 1,401: Mad River, 1,464: Wayne, 1,090: Butler, 1,974: Harrison, 2,059: German, 2,789: Jackson, 2,012: Randolph, 1,883: Jefferson, 1,808: Madison, 1,668: Clay, 1,905: Perry, 1,906.

MORGAN COUNTY. 28,593.

Malta, 1,302: *Malta*, 530: Penn, 1,370: Marion, 1,764: Windsor, 1,593: Union, 1,795: Deerfield, 1,325: Morgan, 650: *McConnelsville*, 1,660: Olive, 2,015: Jackson, 1,249: Center, 1,439: Meigsville, 1,512: Bristol, 1,725: Homer, 1,590: York, 1,207: Bloom, 1,346: Noble, 1,702: Manchester, 1,337: Brookfield, 1482.

MORROW COUNTY. 20,240.

Washington, 1,137: Canaan, 1,223: Cardington, 1,358: Bloomfield, 1,443: Troy, 640: Perry, 1,150: Chester, 1,620: Congress, 1,651: Franklin, 1,456: Gilead, 1,680: South Bloomfield, 1,395: Westfield, 1,414: Lincoln, 891: Harmony, 1,041: Bennington, 1,265: Peru, 876.

MUSKINGUM COUNTY. 45,053.

Jackson, 1,232: Licking, 1,434: Rich Hill, 1,495: Meigs, 1,680: Springfield, 1,302: *Putnam*, 1,674: Harrison, 1,534: Brush Creek, 1,392: Clay, 653: Blue Rock, 1,476: Newton, 2,356: *Uniontown*, 340: Perry, 1,038: Washington, 1,380: Salt Creek, 1,215: Wayne, 1,244: *Duncan's Falls*, 196: Highland, 956: Union, 902: *Norwich*, 324: *New Concord*, 334: Adams, 998: Falls, 2,124: Hopewell, 2,378: Jefferson, 1,377: *Dresden*, 1,445: Madison, 1,047: Monroe, 978: Muskingum, 1,509: Salem, 111: *Zanesville*, 7,929.

OTTAWA COUNTY. 3,310.

Clay, 293: Benton, 54: Harris, 407: Salem, 187: Erie, 292: Carroll, 403: Portage, 377: *Port Clinton*, 249: Bay, 359: Danbury, 503: Van Rensselear, 186.

PAULDING COUNTY. 1,766.

Jackson, 58: Benton, 61: Harrison, 62: Washington, 155: Brown, 368: Auglaize, 304: Crane, 287: Carryall, 471.

PERRY COUNTY. 20,774.

Monroe, 1,429: Saltlick, 1,747: Bearfield, 1,710: Monday Creek, 1,124: Reading, 2,744: *Somerset*, 1,240: Madison, 991: Hopewell, 1,386: Thorn, 1,890: Clayton, 1,554: Harrison, 1,073: Jackson, 1,740: Pike, 2,146.

PICKAWAY COUNTY. 21,110

Circleville, 431: *Circleville*, 3,411: Salt Creek, 1,332: *Fulton*, 514: Pickaway, 1,425: Walnut, 1,840: Madison, 885: Harrison, 1,176: Scioto, 1,347: Darby, 1,166: Monroe, 1640: Jackson, 1,041: Wayne, 644: Deer Creek, 1,354: Perry, 1,120: Muhlenburg, 585: Washington, 1,199.

PIKE COUNTY. 10,955.

Marion, 900: Union, 564: Beaver, 520: Seal, 1,521: *Piketon*, 690: Jackson, 1,351: *Sharon*, 114: Pee Pee, 643: *Waverly*, 678: Newton, 386: *Jasper*, 75: Camp Creek, 390: Sunfish, 371: Pebble, 914: Benton, 639: Perry, 519: *Cynthiana*, 134: Mifflin, 546.

PORTAGE COUNTY. 24,387.

Brimfield, 1,015: Suffield, 1,275: Randolph, 1,730: Paris, 1,019: Windham, 813: Franklin, 1,750: *Ravenna*, 2,239: Streetsborough, 1,108: Aurora, 823: Shalersville, 1,190: Mantua, 1,139: Hiram, 1,106: Nelson, 1,383: Rootstown, 1,308: Charlestown, 809: Freedom, 996; Atwater, 1,119; Deerfield, 1,371; Palmyra, 1,093; Edinburg, 1,101.

PREBLE COUNTY. 21,748.

Washington, 1,758; *Eaton*, 1,302; Jasper, 908; Somers, 2,085; Lanier, 1,694; Gratis, 2,117; Dixon, 1,192; Israel, 1,641; Monroe, 1,344; Harrison, 2,094; Twin, 1,950; Jackson, 1,405; Jefferson, 2,258.

PUTNAM COUNTY. 7,221.

Van Buren, 172; Blanchard, 1,395; Riley, 849; Pleasant, 714; Ottawa, 1,166; Liberty, 322; Greensburg, 634; Union, 515; Sugar Creek, 550; Jennings, 557; Perry, 262; Monterey, 85.

RICHLAND COUNTY. 30,877.

Sharon, 1,949; Springfield, 2,100; Jackson, 1092; Sandusky, 617; Jefferson, 2,564; Perry, 923; Troy, 1,542; Washington, 1,914; Bloomingrove, 1,430; Plymouth, 1,664; Butler, 1,139; Weller, 1,290; Cass, 1,430; Mifflin, 1,104; Franklin, 1,257; Worthington, 2,006; Monroe, 1,720; Madison, 1,579; *Mansfield*, 3,557.

ROSS COUNTY. 32,084.

Scioto, 1,596; *Chillicothe*, 7,098; Union, 2,666; Deerfield, 1,315; Concord, 2,672; Buckskin, 2,104; Greene, 1,995; Colerain, 1,408; Harrison, 878; Springfield, 1,162; Liberty, 1,126; Jefferson, 845; Franklin, 642; Huntington, 1,659; Twin, 2,239; Paxton, 1,556; Paint, 1,123.

SANDUSKY COUNTY. 14,529.

Sandusky, 1,138; *Fremont*, 1,492; Riley, 682; Green Creek, 1,288; Ballville, 1,556; York, 1,811; Townsend, 969; Rice, 483; Washington, 1,499; Madison, 557; Woodville, 1,069; Jackson, 1,092; Scott, 793.

SCIOTO COUNTY. 18,729.

Wayne, 219; *Portsmouth*, 4,011; Harrison, 1,102; Bloom, 1,648; Porter, 1,674; Green, 2,545; Clay, 872; Jefferson, 840; Madison, 1,367; Vernon, 1,105; Washington, 706; Morgan, 280; Union, 705; Brush Creek, 652; Nile, 1,003.

SENECA COUNTY. 27,105.

Reed, 1,494; Venice, 1,830; Thompson, 1,668; Adams, 1,416; Bloom, 1,743; Clinton, 1,668; *Tiffin*, 2,728; Jackson, 996; Pleasant, 1,592; Big Spring, 1,932; Eden, 1,584; Hopewell, 1,288; Louden, 1,781; Liberty, 1,400; Scipio, 2,323; Seneca, 1,662.

SHELBY COUNTY. 13,956.

Loramie, 1,049; Orange, 922; McLean, 775; Dinsmore, 701; Washington, 1,261; Turtle Creek, 792; Perry, 899; Clinton, 762; *Sidney*, 1,302; Franklin, 788; Van Buren, 629; Green, 1,078; Cynthean, 797; Salem, 1,496; Jackson, 705.

STARK COUNTY. 39,888.

Plain, 2,211; Lake, 1,732; *Greentown*, 251; *Union*, 245; Washington, 2,066; Lexington, 1,996; Marlborough, 2,133; Paris, 2,740; Osnaburg, 2,227; Nimishillin, 2,587; Canton, 1,722; *Canton*, 2,604: Lawrence, 2,292: Tuscarawas, 2,041: Pike, 1447: Sandy, 1,273: Sugar Creek, 1,743: Jackson, 1,512: Perry and *Massillon*, 4,668: Bethlehem, 2,398.

SUMMIT COUNTY. 27,481.

Richfield, 1,262: Bath, 1,400: Copley, 1,541: Northampton, 1,147: Boston, 1,180: Northfield, 1,474: Twinsburg, 1,281: Portage, 1,160: *Akron*, 3,266: Hudson, 1,457: Stow, 1,702: Talmadge, 2,456: Coventry, 1,300: Springfield, 1,907: Norton, 1,346: Franklin, 1,674: Green, 1,928.

TRUMBULL COUNTY. 30,540.

Hartford, 1,258: Fowler, 1,089: Vienna, 1,007: Bazetta, 1,302: Howland, 919: Warren, 2,957: Braceville, 956: Champion, 1,070: Southington, 1,013: Farmington, 1,283: Mesopotamia, 959: Bloomfield, 789: Bristol, 1,124: Kinsman, 1,005: Vernon, 828: Gustavus, 1,226: Johnson, 1,099: Mecca, 872: Greene, 959: Newton, 1,678: Lordstown, 1,379: Weathersfield, 1,717: Liberty, 1,328: Hubbard, 1,272: Brookfield, 1,451.

mn

TUSCARAWAS COUNTY. 31,732.

Goshen, 1,482: *N. Philadelphia*, 1,415: *Lockport*, 178: Fairfield, 874: Oxford, 959: *New Comerstown*, 476: Salem, 1,584: *Port Washington*, 269: Mill, 934: *Uricksville*, 577: Union, 944: Warren, 937: *New Cumberland*, 203: Sandy, 1,005: *Sandyville*, 223: Lawrence, 917: *Bolivar*, 302: *Zoar*, 249: Sugar Creek, 1,018: *Shanesville*, 382: Wayne, 2,233: *Strausburg*, 109: York, 1,304: Auburn, 1,246: Bucks, 1,326: Jefferson, 1,058: Warwick, 1,195: Dover, 3,252: Rush, 1,332: Clay, 1,261: Perry, 1,396: Washington, 1,092.

UNION COUNTY. 12,205.

Jackson, 436; Claibourn, 919; Leesburg, 701; York, 831; Paris, 982; *Marysville*, 605; Dover, 700; Liberty, 1,258; Taylor, 400; Washington, 333; Union, 994; *Millford Center*, 211; Allen, 979; Darby 881; Jerome, 1,249; Mill Creek, 726.

VANWERT COUNTY. 4,793.

Washington, 355; *Section Ten*, 402; Willshire, 906; *Willshire*, 147; Pleasant, 349; *Vanwert*, 270; Hoaglin, 125; Union, 84; Tully, 242; Harrison, 513; Liberty, 424; York, 375; Ridge, 400; Jennings, 201.

VINTON COUNTY. 9,353.

Elk, 1,221; *McArthurstown*, 424; Brown, 648; Clinton, 886; Vinton, 460; Richland, 1,193; Harrison, 580; Wilksville, 1,037; Eagle, 476; Jackson, 835; Swan, 1,154; North Brown, 439.

WARREN COUNTY. 25,560.

Union, 1,712; Turtle Creek, 3,342; *Lebanon*, 2,088; Deerfield, 1,863; Hamilton, 2,068; Salem, 3,525; Washington, 1,566; Clear Creek, 2,770; Franklin, 2,542; Wayne, 4081.

WASHINGTON COUNTY. 29,512.

Lawrence, 814; Newport, 1,427; Grandview, 1,154; Independence, 728; Adams, 1,293; Union, 1,165; Jolly, 1,014; Ludlow, 1,051; Waterford, 1,693; Aurelius, 1,251; Barlow, 1,062; Salem, 1,246; Liberty, 1,224; Belpre, 1,623; Fearing, 1,254; Decatur, 807; Warren, 1,462; Westley, 1,561; Watertown, 1,374; Roxbury, 1,098; Marietta, 1,069; *Marietta*, 3,133; *Harmar*, 1,006.

WAYNE COUNTY. 33,045.

Greene, 2,059; East Union, 1,940; Wooster, 1,283; *Wooster*, 2,797; Wayne, 2,079; Congress, 2,341; Chester, 2,335; Plain, 2,375; Canaan, 1,923; Clinton, 1,121; Franklin, 1,450; Paint, 1,627; Sugar Creek, 2,321; Salt Creek, 1,670; Chippewa, 2,637; Milton, 1,360; Baughman, 1,727.

WILLIAMS COUNTY. 8,018.

Center, 882; St. Joseph, 589; Pulaski, 760; Springfield, 782; Brady, 1,128; Jefferson, 1,016; Mill Creek, 408; Madison, 225; Superior, 723; Bridgewater, 493; Northwest, 343; Florence, 669.

WOOD COUNTY. 9,165.

Webster, 237; Weston, 546; Middleton, 331; Washington, 504; Plain, 592; Center, 357; Portage, 405; Bloom, 659; Milton, 244; Henry, 321; Jackson, 74; Liberty, 237; Perrysburg, 581; *Perrysburg*, 1,199; Freedom, 454; Troy, 559; Lake, 152; Montgomery, 924; Perry, 889.

WYANDOT COUNTY. 11,169.

Marseilles, 539; Crane, 761; *Up. Sandusky*, 783; Mifflin, 570; Salem, 738; Eden, 643; Antrim, 756; Pitt, 886; Richland, 599; Ridge, 501; Sycamore, 880; Tymochtee, 1,817; Crawford, 1,301; Jackson, 395.

NEW COUNTIES.

AUGLAIZE COUNTY was created February 14th, 1848, from Allen and Mercer Counties. St. Mary's (see page 353), and Wapakoneta (see page 29), are the principal villages, and the first named the county seat. For its townships, and their population in 1850, see page 600.

MORROW COUNTY was formed February 24th, 1848, from Richland, Knox, Delaware, and Marion Counties. Mt. Gilead (see page 344), is the county seat. See page 605, for a list of its townships and their population.

FULTON COUNTY was formed February 28th, 1850, from Lucas, Henry and Williams Counties. A list of its townships, and their population, are given on page 602.

VINTON COUNTY was formed March 23d, 1850, from Gallia, Athens, Hocking, Ross, and Jackson Counties. Its townships, and their populations for 1850, are given on page 607. M'Arthurstown is the county seat.

NOBLE COUNTY was formed from Guernsey, Monroe, Washington, and Morgan Counties, in March, 1851.

www.ingramcontent.com/pod-product-compliance
Lightning Source LLC
LaVergne TN
LVHW021058110826
845150LV00001B/109

* 9 7 8 1 4 2 5 5 6 6 2 0 3 *